*U.S. Aerial Armament in World War II Vol. 1*

# U.S. Aerial Armament in World War II

## The Ultimate Look:

## Vol. 1: Guns, Ammunition, and Turrets

William Wolf

**Schiffer Military History**
Atglen, PA

Book Design by Ian Robertson.


Library of Congress Control Number: 2009925581



Printed in China.
ISBN: 978-0-7643-3235-7

We are interested in hearing from authors with book ideas on related topics.

Published by Schiffer Publishing Ltd.
4880 Lower Valley Road
Atglen, PA 19310
Phone: (610) 593-1777
FAX: (610) 593-2002
E-mail: Info@schifferbooks.com.
Visit our web site at: www.schifferbooks.com
Please write for a free catalog.
This book may be purchased from the publisher.
Please include $5.00 postage.
Try your bookstore first.

In Europe, Schiffer books are distributed by:
Bushwood Books
6 Marksbury Avenue
Kew Gardens
Surrey TW9 4JF, England
Phone: 44 (0) 20 8392-8585
FAX: 44 (0) 20 8392-9876
E-mail: Info@bushwoodbooks.co.uk.
Visit our website at: www.bushwoodbooks.co.uk
Free postage in the UK. Europe: air mail at cost.
Try your bookstore first.

# Contents

# Preface

While researching and writing my "Ultimate Look" series of bomber books, including the B-29, B-32, B-18, and B-25, I realized two things. One, that there was no definitive book available regarding American World War II aerial armament and ordnance. Two, I had a large source of technical manuals, microfilm, books, and magazines in my library on the various aspects of the subject on which I had to spend hours and hours digging out material for these books. Since I had been scheduled to write a history of the Fifth Fighter Command in WWII next I asked Bob Biondi, my Schiffer editor, if I could do a book on U.S. aircraft armament and ordnance first, as I now had a large amount of material collected. It was not long into my gathering of further data that I realized that the subject would have to be divided into three books: this book on Guns, Ammunition, and Turrets; Volume 2 on Bombs, Bombsights, and Bombing; and Volume 3 on Air-Dropped, Air-Launched, and Secret Weapons. I hope this first volume will serve as an easy reference and definitive work on the subject for WWII aviation enthusiasts.

# Acknowledgments

My lifelong hobby has been WWII aerial combat, and over the past 35 years I have collected over 16,000 books and magazines, along with hundreds of reels of microfilm on the subject. I probably have nearly every book written on WWII aviation and complete collections of every aviation magazine published since 1939. Also included in my collection are hundreds of aviation unit histories; intelligence reports; pilot, crew, flight, and training manuals; and technical, structural, and maintenance manuals for aircraft ordnance, armament, engines, and equipment. My microfilm collection includes vintage intelligence reports; hundreds of USAF, USN, and USMC group and squadron histories and After Combat Reports; complete Japanese Monograph series; and complete U.S. Strategic Bombing Surveys, as well as complete USAF Historical Studies. Over the years I have been fortunate to meet many fighter aces, other pilots, and fellow aviation buffs that have shared stories, material, and photographs with me (I have over 5,000 photos of fighter aces alone). I have made numerous multi-day expeditions to various military libraries, museums, and photo depositories with my copy machine and camera, accumulating literally reams of information and 1,000s of photographs.

Over the past decade I have completed eight books on WWII aviation that included many hundreds of photos and drawings, many in color. Most of the photos gathered for this volume and the others were from the WWII era and before, and over the years were not well cared for and showed their age. As described above, almost all were copies, or copies of copies made before the Digital/Photoshop Age by a standard film 35mm camera on a copystand; many hundreds at a time over several days while visiting various facilities. At one time I had a photo darkroom where I developed 1,000s of rare photos from microfilm negatives that were not of the best quality. Many photos were copied from printed dot-type photos from contemporary World War II publications. Reproductions of the many technical drawings were made by my non-digital drum copy machine 20 years ago or more from yellowed manuals that originally were poorly printed on poor quality wartime paper. So I apologize in advance for the quality of some photos and drawings in this book (despite being photoshopped), but I feel marginal photos are better than no photos in describing topics in this book.

The author wishes that every person who contributed photos and materials to my collection over the past 35 years could be specifically mentioned. Over the years the origin of some of the 1,000s of photos I have been lent to copy or have copied and collected have become obscured. Most are from military and government sources, but many are from private individuals, so I also apologize if some of the photos are miscredited.

And last but not least, for the ninth time thanks go to my persevering wife, Nancy, who allows me to spend many hours researching and writing, and patiently (mostly) waits while I browse bookstores and visit air museums in search of new material and photos. Also, I thank her because her car sits out in the hot Arizona sun as my WWII library luxuriates in the remodeled, air-conditioned three-car garage.

# Part One

## Aircraft Machine Gun

# 1

# The Browning .30 and .50 Caliber Infantry Machine Guns

**Section 1: Browning Model 1895 .30 Caliber Infantry Machine Gun**
John Moses Browning was born in Ogden, UT, on 21 (or 23) January 1855 of Mormon parents. His father Jonathon was a gunsmith, and John entered the family business with little formal education, where he served as an apprentice for ten years at the time the cartridge firearm was replacing the percussion lock firearm. He applied for his first gun patent on the 1878 Single Shot Rifle that he sold to Winchester Arms; an association that lasted for many years. John and his brother Matthew formed the J.M. & M.S. Browning Company, in which John served as the gun specialist and Mathew as the marketing and patent specialist. In 1886, John developed and Matthew patented the repeating rifle that was sold to Winchester on a royalty basis as the milestone Winchester Model 86 lever-action rifle. The Browning brothers designed and sold guns not only to Winchester, but also to Colt, Remington, and others to establish their reputation as America's premier gun designers. While working on gun ballistics John Browning observed that the escaping gases from the muzzle were perfectly timed to be used to operate the gun's mechanisms and as a source for sustained fire. On 22 November 1890, Matthew sent a letter to Colt Patent Fire Arms of Hartford, CT, saying they had developed a "new automatic machine gun… that could be made as cheaply as a common sporting rifle." The letter went on to describe the 40 pound gun, including the mount, as being entirely automatic and able to shoot standard government .45 caliber cartridges at 360 rounds per minute.

In 1893 the U.S. Navy Department was conducting machine gun trials that included the Maxim, the improved 16mm Gatling gun, and the French Darne gun, and also added the Colt Browning gun to the competition. The Colt Browning entry was concluded to be the best choice, and an order was let for 50 guns under the stipulation that Colt could promise perfect operation with rimless cartridges and a maximum uninterrupted rate of fire of 400 rounds per minute (rpm). The gas operation of the Colt gun was very uncomplicated, as its construction and mechanism consisted of less than 100 parts. The cartridges were fed from a canvas belt, and the recoil and vibration were so minimal that the gun could be fired from the shoulder. Although the gun had few shortcomings, a major problem occurred during prolonged firing, as it became so hot that a round could detonate, or "cook off," in the chamber and demolish the breech mechanism.

The gun was officially designated as the Colt Browning, Model 1895, but was given the soubriquet "potato digger" by sailors due to the action of the gas actuating arm that moved in an arc beneath the muzzle. The Model 1895 was introduced into Navy service as the Mark I firing the 6mm (.236 inch) cartridge. It was used with great success in the Spanish-American

**John Browning** (Author's Collection)

**John Browning** poses with his Colt Browning, Model 1895 which was nicknamed by the Navy as the "potato digger" due to the action of the gas actuating arm that moved in an arc beneath the muzzle. (Author's Collection)

War in 1898, which stimulated the Army's interest in the gun. However, the Army used the .30-.40 caliber cartridges, and an Army-Navy Board convened and standardized rifle caliber ammunition to the Army 30-40 standard. The Navy rechambered its guns to .30-.40 and designated it as the Mark I Modification 1. When the .30-.40 caliber cartridge was discontinued in favor of the Springfield .30 the Navy again rechambered its Brownings, but kept the Mark I Modification 1 designation. The gun was further modified in 1902 and 1904, and sold in large quantities to European and Latin American countries. While the Navy eagerly adopted the Model 1895, the Army continued its loyalty to the carriage-mounted Gatling guns until the First World War broke out, when it became apparent that the Gatling was too cumbersome and not suitable for modern warfare.

By 1900 nearly three quarters of all repeating, lever, and pump action sporting arms on the market sprung from John Browning's genius and were manufactured by Winchester. However, the Winchester/Browning association would come to an end in 1902 when Winchester President T.G. Bennett refused to pay Browning a royalty on his new automatic shotgun. Previously Winchester had paid outright for Browning's gun patents, but Browning was so confident that this revolutionary auto-loading shotgun would become an instant sales success that he demanded a royalty payment instead. Bennett refused and was wrong, as Browning took his shotgun to the Belgium company Fabrique Nationale of Herstal, and there would not be another successful automatic shotgun for 54 years.

**Section 2: Browning Model 1917 .30 Caliber Infantry Machine Gun**

In his investigations of gun mechanisms John Browning determined that the short recoil was the most efficient and practical mechanism for attaining a high rate of fire, and in 1901 he was granted a patent for a short recoil, water-cooled machine gun that integrated the basic Browning automatic gun principles. But the peacetime American government withheld funding for the gun, and Browning concentrated his business on the civilian sporting market.

In 1917, when America entered the war, the Army had only 1,100—mostly obsolete—machine guns in inventory, including only 158 Model 1895 Brownings. Only then did the government ask American manufacturers to submit designs for a domestically manufactured machine gun to equip American Expeditionary Forces who would be on their way to fight in Europe. In May 1917, a new design based on a neglected 1901 Browning patent, was tested at the Springfield Arsenal, where the gun fired 20,000 rounds without a malfunction. In 1917 the U.S. Government offered Browning $750,000 for the rights to his automatic firearms, and the patriotic Browning agreed, knowing that if he were paid the standard royalty for the use of his design he would have received almost $13 million. The Model 1917 Colt Browning was a water-cooled recoil-operated .30 caliber gun that was characterized by its breech that locked to the barrel with a locking piece that moved up and down as each round was fired. The bolt and barrel recoiled together until the bullet left the barrel. The bolt then unlocked, and was moved abruptly to the rear by an accelerating lever until it was stopped by a cylindrical buffer at the rear of the gun. The return spring then forced the bolt forward to fire the next round.

The new Browning machine gun was delivered in the heavy, water-cooled version and the automatic rifle, to become famous as the Browning Automatic Rifle, or the B.A.R. The Browning Model 1917 was quickly approved as the Army's standard infantry machine gun and automatic rifle, and the two became the basis for Colt Browning machine guns for the next six decades. Once the Model 1917 was adopted it received high manufacturing priority and 43,750 were produced: 31,150 by Westinghouse, 12,000 by Remington, and only 600 by Colt. However, very few saw action in France during the war, as over 23,000 were returned to their manufacturers due to a design defect. Browning engineers had made poor choice for the metals used for the gun's fabrication, and during high rates of fire the lower portion of the receiver separated after a few rounds and the gun became inoperative. This defect was not remedied until after the Armistice was signed. An air-cooled adaptation of the .30 caliber Model 1917 was designed for aircraft use and designated as the Model 1918. This gun would become the standard .30 caliber (.303 in Britain) aircraft machine gun.

**John Browning** in another posed photo with his new water-cooled recoil-operated .30 caliber Model 1917 Colt Browning machine gun that was characterized by its breech that locked to the barrel with a locking piece that moved up and down as each round was fired. (Author's Collection)

The Browning Machine Gun Caliber .50, basic M2 was produced in seven versions and would become the standard American aircraft weapon into the Korean War. (U.S. Army)

**Section 3: Browning .50 Caliber M-2 Infantry Machine Gun**

The Browning .30 caliber machine gun had been in action for only a short time when the military realized that a heavier caliber gun was required to counter the armored vehicles and aircraft that were beginning to appear on the battlefield. The British and French had increased the caliber of their guns from .303 and 6mm (.236 caliber) to .50 caliber and more. In 1917, Gen. John Pershing issued directives to American arms manufacturers to develop designs for a new heavy caliber automatic gun. John Browning had been working on a .50 caliber version of his .30 caliber gun, preserving its ease of construction and basic operating qualities. Meanwhile, the Winchester Repeating Arms collaborated with Browning to develop a cartridge for the new .50 caliber gun. However, the constraints of time caused Winchester to upscale its .30/06 case by adding a rim on it to convert it to the .50 caliber standard. When Pershing received the cartridge specification in mid-July 1918, he rejected it, asking for a rimless redesign that culminated in the successful new 5.5 inch cartridge with a 707 grain bullet. Six .50 caliber prototype guns were ready by mid-September 1918 for endurance tests that would identify and eliminate any design flaws inherent in any new weapon. The gun was thoroughly tested and accepted as the Browning Machine Gun Caliber .50, basic M2. The M2 was produced in seven versions: an Army and Navy anti-aircraft water-cooled model, two heavy barreled infantry service models, and fixed, flexible, turret aircraft guns. The water-cooled .50 caliber machine gun was too heavy for infantry use, while the air-cooled gun experienced barrel heating problems and gave way to the lighter .30 caliber gun.

# 2

# American Aircraft Machine Guns of World War I

**Section 1: Lewis Gun .303/.30 Caliber Aircraft Machine Gun**

The Lewis Automatic Light Machine Gun, simply known as the Lewis Gun, was invented by U.S. Army Colonel Isaac Newton Lewis of the Coast Artillery. The 1884 West Point graduate was a brilliant designer and engineer who used the basic features of the 1910 machine gun design of Samuel McClean, who had sold patents of his automatic rifle to the Automatic Arms Company of Buffalo, NY. When Automatic Arms found the McClean gun to be impractical for use and difficult to produce it asked Lewis to re-engineer the gun, keeping the crucial gas piston feed from the barrel and the spiral spring that activated the rotating bolt mechanism. Notably, Lewis added a circular top-feeding magazine and a tubular finned air cooling jacket. The gun weighed only 28 pounds, which was considerably lighter than its competitors: Vickers at 63 pounds, Colt at 93 pounds, and the Maxim gun, which weighed in at a hefty 153 pounds. The company stated that its rate of fire was 500 to 600 rpm at a muzzle velocity of 2,450 fps, which compared favorably with its rivals. However, when compared to the continuous 250 round enclosed belts of the heavier Vickers machine guns the Lewis gunner required great speed and dexterity in changing the 47 round (97 later in aircraft models) magazines when reloading the Lewis Gun in order to maintain this stated rate of fire. The magazine feed mechanism was more reliable than the belt feeds, which often had jamming problems. Since the Lewis Gun was made up of only 62 parts it was easy to manufacture, and six could be produced in the same time as one of the Vickers Guns.

In early June 1912 Col. Lewis, a flamboyant promoter, set up a demonstration at the Army Aviation School at College Park, MD, during which a machine gun was fired from an aircraft for the first time. School Commandant Capt. Charles De Forest Chandler and pilot Lt. Thomas De Witt Milling took off, with Chandler having a Lewis gun strapped to his leg. When the aircraft approached the field at 600 feet and 50 mph Chandler opened fire on a 9x45 foot piece of cheese cloth, and then the two came around for a second firing run. After they landed it was found that all but five of the 47 rounds had hit the target. The 21 September 1912 issue of *Literary Digest* entitled "Our Future Flying Batteries" enthusiastically stated:

> "At a height of a quarter of a mile or greater and moving at a speed of 50 miles per hour it will be possible with this gun to pour in the most destructive fire on the deck and fire control masts of battleships and upon the unprotected personnel of land defenses without endangering the aeroplane or its crew-it being practically impossible to attack successfully the rapidly moving aeroplane from below. The

**Colonel Isaac Newton Lewis** (Author's Collection)

gun also opens a new field of attack and defense in that it will be used as an offensive weapon against other aeroplanes similarly armed."

Even with this sterling report, the Army considered the demonstration as a stunt and continued its apathetic attitude towards military aviation. The U.S. Army Ordnance Board also tested the gun, but never published the results and made no decision about its future.

Note: On 20 August 1910, Lt. Jacob E. Fickel fired the first shots from an aircraft when he boarded a Signal Corps Curtiss biplane piloted by C.F. Willard at Sheepshead Bay Race Track near New York City. In four passes he scored two hits on a 3x3 foot target with a .30-06 caliber Springfield M1903 rifle. Fickel repeated his demonstration in Boston a month later, using an Army semi-automatic pistol.

Col. Lewis became so disgruntled with Army's handling of his gun that he resigned his 30 year commission and sailed to Europe, where he hoped to peddle his (and the Automatic Arms Co.) gun to more amenable governments and arms manufacturers. Lewis' first stop was Belgium in 1913, where he demonstrated his gun, which was so well-received by their Army that the Belgian government built a new factory, the Armes Automatiques Lewis, in Liege. Importantly and uncharacteristically, the Belgium Lewis gun version was to use .303 caliber ammunition that matched the standard British caliber. At the time, the British also required a light machine gun and, learning of the Belgium Lewis Gun that used .303 caliber ammunition, the British Small Arms Co. (BSA) of Birmingham was granted a production license in 1914. By mid-1914 both European factories were at maximum production on the infantry Lewis Gun version, with the gun being nicknamed the "Belgium Rattlesnake" by the Germans when they first encountered it on the battlefield. Soon the Savage Arms Co. of Utica, NY, was contracted to manufacture the American-invented Lewis Gun for the British under license!

The Mark II Lewis Gun was preferred to the more common and established Vickers Gun for mounting in early war aircraft for use by gunners and observers, or as an additional machine gun. It was lightweight and used much less ammunition than the Vickers Gun, as it was to be fired in short bursts, which was ideal for air combat. However, because it used an open bolt firing cycle it could not be synchronized for firing through the propeller as could the Vickers Gun. For aircraft use a 97 round magazine replaced the 47 round magazines (but made the gun too heavy for infantry use). The aircraft type magazine had an increased depth of its pan and needed to be carefully stored, as its underside was open and exposed to outside contaminants. When used as an aerial gun, the Lewis Gun's jacket fins, which cooled the infantry gun by air flowing over them, were removed as the outside air flowing over the gun in the air provided sufficient cooling. With the cooling jacket removed the gun only weighed 20 pounds. The aerial Lewis Gun's recoil was reduced by the addition of a gas check.

In early June 1912 Col. Lewis set up a demonstration at the Army Aviation School at College Park, MD during which School Commandant Capt. **Charles De Forest Chandler** (with pilot Lt. **Thomas De Witt Milling**) fired a machine gun from an aircraft for the first time in history. (Author's Collection)

Lt. **Jacob E. Fickel** fired the first shots from an aircraft when he boarded a Signal Corps Curtiss biplane piloted by **C.F. Willard** on 20 August 1910. (Author's Collection)

After his gun was rejected by America, Lewis continued to modify the gun in an effort to develop a light infantry assault rifle. He returned to America in June 1916 and again offered the variations of the gun to the Secretary of War Newton Baker, but his offer was rejected (ignored?). Later in 1916 the patriotic Lewis returned $17,500 to the U.S. Treasury Department for the royalties he earned on 353 guns that were diverted from the Savage British contract to the U.S. Army for deployment during the Mexican border war. Finally, in late 1915 the War Department ordered 40,000 aircraft guns for $2.25 million, but declined to order the gun for trench warfare, as the Ordnance Department was committed to John Browning and his new Model 1917 machine gun that was under developmental testing. At the time Savage Arms was continuing its contract to the British government and running at full capacity at 1,800 infantry guns of .303 caliber per month.

The Lewis Machine Gun was easily identified by its circular 97 round magazine that replaced the 47 round magazines but made the gun too heavy for infantry use. (USAAF)

Because it used an open bolt firing cycle the Lewis gun could not be synchronized for firing through the propeller and was used by aircraft gunners and observers. (USAAF)

After America entered the war in 1917, it was found that its military had only 1,100 mostly outdated machine guns in its arsenal, and that the new Browning .30 caliber Model 1917 would not be available until late 1918 due to defects. Col. Lewis realized that America would be unable to supply the 75,000 light and heavy machine guns required to equip its million man army and fledgling air service, and urged the War Department to adopt his gun. The Savage Arms British contract was to be completed by mid-April 1917, and Savage President A.E. Borie offered his two factories for the production of the American Lewis Gun. However, the American gun needed to be rechambered to the American .30 caliber standard from .303 caliber and would have to undergo testing by the Bureau of Ordnance. To further confuse matters, the Bureau of Ordnance asked Borie to also manufacture the new Browning machine gun. Borie refused, not wanting to manufacture two different guns, and also knowing the Browning was mostly a "paper gun" that was having problems, and that accepting a contract would be fraught with production delays. Once the Ordnance Department tests were completed very successfully in early May 18,400 Lewis infantry guns were ordered on paper. When the American production of the gun continued to lag, Lewis again became so exasperated that in early December he wrote a letter accusing Secretary Baker of acting on "misinformation" that caused him and his gun a "serious injustice." Lewis outlined the success of his gun, stating that the over 70,000 guns in use showed that it was "no longer a new and untried weapon. It has met every military requirement under the grueling test of more than three years of daily service on the battlefields of Europe." Lewis then altruistically offered to return royalty payments on past ($2.5 million) and on any future Lewis Gun orders, and also to reduce payments to Automatic Arms Co. by 43%, which was his stake in the company (Lewis was a rich man from his European royalties). The letter caused Col. Lewis and A.E. Borie to be summoned before the Senate Military Affairs Committee to testify as to why the Lewis gun was not yet in the American arsenal. In his testimony Lewis repeated his opinions on the Secretary of War and Ordnance Department's prejudice against his gun, and of his efforts to convince and entice them with his offers to return royalties. Savage Arms President Borie stated that the Ordnance Department was at fault, "as it was not run on a business-like basis," and its failure to grant Savage Arms large enough orders to keep both of its factories running at the capacity afforded by the British contracts. The first order for the Lewis aircraft gun was made soon after the hearing, and from the time of the first deliveries in February 1918 and until the Armistice on 11 November 1918 a total of 32,957 were delivered; averaging 3,500 per month with a high monthly delivery of 6,000 in October, the last month of the war. However, the new Marlin Aircraft Machine Gun Model 1917 became the primary *synchronized* American automatic aerial machine gun of World War I.

**Section 2: Marlin-Rockwell .30 Caliber Aircraft Machine Gun**

In 1914 Colt modified its 1895 "Potato Digger" into the Colt Automatic Gun, Model 1914, by replacing its thick heavy barrel with a lighter finned barrel. This was a simple major modification, but the other changes were minor, with the problematic Potato Digger apparatus remaining unchanged. Once World War I broke out Colt was deluged with orders for its machine gun and agreed to license its production to the Marlin Arms Corporation of New Haven, CT. Marlin had been in the firearms industry since 1870 when founder J.M. Marlin began producing pistols and revolvers under Ballard patents. In 1880 Marlin introduced a repeating lever action rifle that has become the company's trademark weapon from that time onward.

The Marlin-Rockwell Corporation wished to simplify the Model 1914 Browning and chose Swedish-born **Carl Swebilius** (upper left) to do the redesign which would become America's standard synchronized aerial machine gun of World War I. (Author's Collection)

In 1915 the Marlin Arms Corporation was purchased by a J.P. Morgan-backed syndicate which was the exclusive purchasing agent for armament and war materiel for the British. Marlin was reorganized with eminent industrialist Albert Rockwell as its President for the purpose of mass producing machine guns. To produce its machine gun Marlin was to pay Colt a royalty of $100 per gun ($55 to Colt and $45 to Browning) for the first 5,000 guns, and then $75 per gun ($33.75 to Browning) until the royalty payment reached $1,500,000. At this payment point Marlin could manufacture and sell as many guns as possible without further royalty payments. Marlin could also sell spare parts and accessories for a 10% royalty payment. After producing the Browning Model 1914 machine gun for infantry use for over a year; in 1916 Albert Rockwell reorganized Marlin Arms into the Marlin-Rockwell Corporation. Rockwell wished to simplify the Model 1914 Browning, and chose Swedish-born Carl Swebilius to do the redesign. After starting as a barrel driller at the age of 16, Swebilius rose to head the company's experimental department, becoming one of America's eminent firearm designers; receiving over 60 patents during his lifetime. Swebilius began his redesign by replacing the Browning swinging gas lever (potato digger) with a straight-line gas-actuated piston. The design was submitted to the Navy in February 1917, and after successful testing at the end of April the Navy ordered 1,605 guns designated as the Mark V.

Once the potato digger action had been eliminated Swebilius' next step was to convert the gun into an aerial gun, essentially by making the barrel thinner. The new gun, the Marlin Aircraft Machine Gun, Model 1917 (7-MG Aeroplane Gun was the official Air Service designation), became the primary synchronized American automatic aerial machine gun of World War I. In 1917 38,000 aircraft guns were ordered, and by May 1918 22,400 had been produced. That month production was stopped for a month for retooling to make the changes required for firing through-the-propeller gun synchronization, making trigger and feed mechanism modifications, and increasing the gun's rate of fire.

On 1 January 1918 the Signal Corps requested the design of a new firing mechanism that could fire either singly or automatically when used with four-bladed propellers, and with the new and improved Nelson mechanical synchronizing gear. The capability to be adapted to fire single shots or fully automatic was to permit much better synchronization than using only full automatic. Both Marlin-Rockwell and the Signal Corps began work on the new mechanism.

On 8 January 1918, Marlin submitted its design for a new firing mechanism to the Signal Corps, whose own design was also ready for competitive testing. Marlin-Rockwell's design had the hydraulic and mechanical trigger motors attached to the front of the lock container, which was redesigned, and the hammer substantially lightened to increase the rate of fire. Tests were conducted at the end of January and showed the Marlin-Rockwell design to be suitable, while the Signal Corps design was summarily rejected due to its parts breaking easily. The revised Marlin-Rockwell aircraft machine gun was the first gas-operated machine gun to be successfully synchronized for firing through the propeller, and a contract for 15,000 motors and modified firing mechanisms was placed with the company.

In the Marlin-Rockwell design the cartridges were fed into the gun through an opening in the left side of the plate by a standard Colt belt. The feed mechanism was modified to allow the reliable use of the metallic disintegrating belt link. Marlin machine guns could use either a fabric or a disintegrating metal link belt that could hold 250 or 500 rounds. During the war metallic links were normally used in aircraft because of the problem of disposing of the fabric belt's loose end after firing. The belts were usually carried on a drum or in a feed box attached to the bottom of the gun.

The decreased gas pressure of the 1918 model reduced the number of breakages and stoppages caused by recoil. The Marlin's wide range of gas adjustments made it very reliable, and it would fire under the most extreme conditions. The gun was equipped with a 60-watt, 12-volt electric heater that was riveted to the inside of the bottom plate of the gun and was supplied by the generator.

In air combat an increased rate of fire was important, as a target was in view for only a short time, and barrel overheating was not a problem, as only short bursts of fire could be made. The gun's rate of fire was increased by lightening the bolt by a pound and using stronger driving springs, which increased the power of the recoil spring. The redesigned gun weighed 23.5 pounds. Also, a booster attachment to the muzzle increased the rate of fire from 900 to 1,200 rounds per minute at a range of 2,500 yards.

The alteration and redesign of so many components caused them to no longer be interchangeable with similar parts of the older guns, so to distinguish the new gun from the old it was designated as the Marlin Aircraft Machine Gun, Model 1918 (8-MG Air Service designation). On 17 September 1918 an order for 5,000 of the redesigned guns was placed with Marlin-Rockwell, to be followed by an order for an additional 10,000 on 17 December. Production on the order was to begin in early October 1918 once the initial order for the 38,000 1917 Marlin guns had been completed. On 1 October 1918 another order for 5,000 additional aircraft guns was let to Remington Arms, but that company was already over-extended, and the contract was transferred to New England Westinghouse. Many technical flaws became evident during later endurance tests and the gun was found

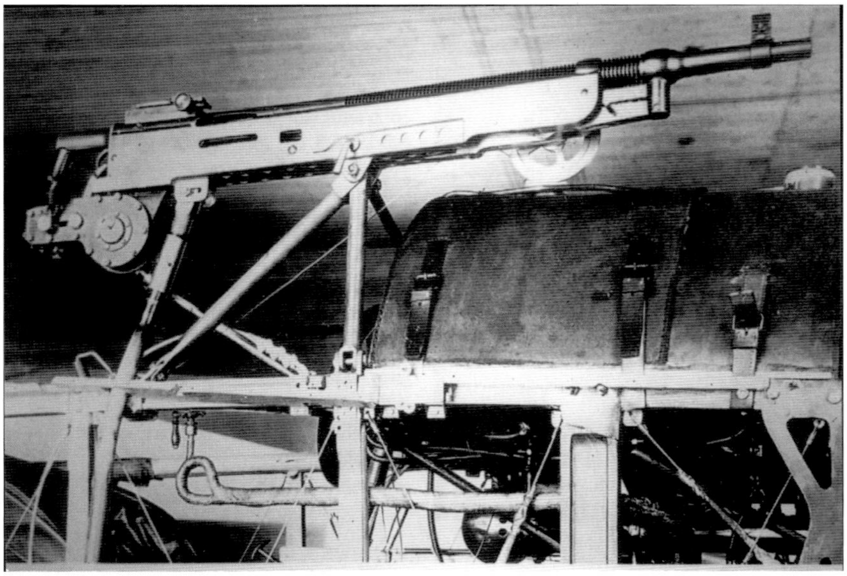

Nearly 39,000 Marlin Machine Guns were produced for American aerial use during World War I. After the Armistice the Marlin 1918 models remained in service and were eventually replaced by the .30 caliber Browning Model 1918M1 aircraft machine gun which did not see combat during World War I due manufacturing problems. (USAAF)

unsuitable for mounting on aircraft. The Model 1918M1 was developed to correct the problems inherent in the Model 1918, but the gun never was used in combat. The first shipment of 2,000 was sent to France on 11 October 1918—only a month before the Armistice—and was not received in time for use at the front. The development of the Marlin as a flexible gun was also undertaken with promising success, but the war ended before it could be fully developed. When the war ended these Model 1918 contracts were terminated after Westinghouse produced 1,679 guns and Marlin 3,399 for a total of 5,078 guns (of the 20,000 contracted).

**Marlin Production Totals**

| **Model** | **Total** |
|---|---|
| Model 1917 (U.S. Navy Mark V) | 1,605 |
| Model 1917 (7-MG) | 38,000* |
| Model 1918 (8-MG) | 5,078 |
| Total | 44,683** |

*2,648 of this total were converted for tank use
**2,816 additional Model 1917s were produced as Army training guns

Although the Marlin gun initially was considered a stop gap measure, it was continually improved, and was deemed to be "quite satisfactory" in quality, reliability, and synchronization with both the Nelson and CC apparatus, but not the equal of the British Lewis and Vickers machine guns. After the war ended the Model 1918 guns were withdrawn from service and shipped to the Springfield Arsenal for "remodeling" and redevelopment into a modified new design to be designated as the Model 1919 Aircraft Gun. Neither gun was put into production at the time, and the Marlin Model 1918 remained as America's first line aircraft machine gun.

After the war, in late March 1920, the War Department convened periodic meetings of the Aircraft Armament Board, which was to consider the development of aircraft machine guns and aircraft cannon. After making many interim recommendations the Board's final report in 1925 recommended "that the Marlin machine gun, model of 1918, be continued in service, but with no further steps to improve the development. It is further believed that this gun is a satisfactory air service weapon, although its limitations are acknowledged." The Board concluded:

"In the event that a more satisfactory type of gun passes successful tests and is accepted by the Air Service as a satisfactory machine gun for their use, upon completion of the redesign and tests now in progress it is recommended that these Marlin models of 1918 be withdrawn from service and held in reserve for emergency use only."

# 3

# Inter-War American Aircraft Machine Guns

**Section 1: American Automatic Gun Designations 1925-1950**
Automatic weapons for the U.S. Armed Forces were procured, with minor exceptions, by two agencies: the Ordnance Corps of the Army, and the Bureau of Ordnance of the Navy. When a project was activated to develop a new gun or to modify a standard gun, a distinctive designation was assigned to identify it.

The Army method prior to 1925 was to assign a designation of model and year to each design (i.e. Model 1918). After that, the model was abbreviated with a capital M and consecutive numbers were assigned (i.e. Model 1918M1). Guns in the developmental stage were given numbers with a capital T prefixed. To indicate changes in the development stages, the capital letter E could be suffixed to the T number followed by an Arabic numeral. Experimental changes to standard or M-numbered items were also indicated by suffixed E numbers. Standard, or M-numbered items with approved changes, or standardized alterations, were identified by suffixed A numbers.

When a Navy ordnance gun was approved for testing, it was assigned a Mark number. The gun kept this Mark number whether finally approved for service use or rejected. Modifications to the original Mark design were dealt with similarly. To fully identify an automatic gun the caliber had to be mentioned, followed by the correct letter and number designations. In some cases it was necessary to name the gun or mechanism, for example: Gun, Machine, Caliber .50 M2 or 20mm Machine Gun Mechanism Mk 2 Mod O. This type of complete identification was needed since T numbers, M numbers, and Mark and Mod numbers began with No. 1 for each of the various types of ordnance and for other military equipment.

The prefix "AN" was used extensively during World War II, and when joined to a model number, it sometimes caused the mistaken idea that there was a physical difference between a gun so marked and one that carried only the model number. In the designation Gun, Machine, Caliber .50, AN–M2, and Gun, Machine, Caliber .50 M2, the AN signifies that the weapon was adopted by *both* the Army and the Navy, and there was no difference between the two guns and the basic design.

From 1926 to 1950 there were four different lists from which T numbers were assigned to automatic aircraft guns.

**Gun, Machine**

| T-Number | | Bore |
|---|---|---|
| T1 | T65 | .30 Cal. |
| T1 | T60 | .50 Cal. |
| T1 | T66 | .60 Cal. |
| T54 | T56 | 20mm |

**Gun, Automatic**

| T-Number | | Bore |
|---|---|---|
| T1 | T129 | 20mm |
| T120 | T121 | 30mm |

**Gun, 37mm**

| T-Number | | Bore |
|---|---|---|
| T1 | T49 | 37mm |

**Gun, Cal. 90 (23mm)**

| T-Number | | Bore |
|---|---|---|
| T1 | T4 | .90 Cal. |

Note: All numbers between the low and the high were not necessarily assigned to machine or automatic guns, as some were proof, sub-caliber, or other types.

**Section 2: American Machine Gun Manufacturers on Armistice Day**

**Colt Patent Fire Arms Mfg. Co.**
M1914 Colt Machine Gun (gas operated)
M1915 Vickers Machine Gun
M1917 Browning Machine Gun (water-cooled)
M1918 Browning Machine Rifle

**Martin-Rockwell Corp.**
M1917 Marlin Machine Gun (Colt licensed M1914)
M1918 Marlin Aircraft Machine Gun
M1918 Browning Aircraft Machine Gun (air-cooled)
M1918 Browning Machine Rifle

In 1924 Colt decided on a redesign of its M1918M1 which had been previously modified to facilitate its manufacture, This new gun was designated as the M1919 of which only 1,031 were produced. (USAAF)

A M1919 M1 mounted on Scarff ring on a Keystone B4A bomber. (USAAF)

**New England Westinghouse**
M1917 Browning Machine Gun (water cooled)
M1918 Browning Aircraft Machine Gun (air-cooled)
M1919 Browning Tank Machine Gun (air-cooled)

**Remington Arms Co.**
M1917 Browning Machine Gun (water-cooled)

**Savage Arms Corp.**
Lewis Ground and Aircraft Machine Guns

**Winchester Repeating Arms Co.**
M1918 Browning Machine Rifle

**Section 3: Browning .30 Caliber Aircraft Machine Gun**

The .30 caliber Browning Model 1918M1 aircraft machine gun did not see combat during World War I due to manufacturing problems. The metals chosen for its construction were not adequate, as the high rate of fire caused the lower portion of the receiver to expand making the gun inoperative after only a few bursts of fire. The Browning aircraft machine gun was evolved from the slow-firing, water-cooled infantry model with its parts decreased in size and lightened. However, this gun could not stand up to the demand for the increased rate of fire when the Army switched from M1906 ball ammunition that fired at 850 to 1,000 rpm to the more powerful M1 .30 caliber ammunition that fired at 1,050 to 1,250 rpm. The new, heavier cartridge placed additional stress on the gun and also caused feeding problems. The basic problems were corrected, but the gun proved to be difficult to manufacture, and only 500 were completed by the end of the war; the first guns weren't delivered until just after the Armistice.

After the war the need for a revised U.S. aircraft machine gun diminished, and its development proceeded at a much more unhurried pace, with an aircraft machine gun that would serve for many years in the future being the new objective. Many changes were suggested; some of which were involved and costly. A major renovation or an entirely new design were the possible solutions, and the Aircraft Armament Board was formed in 1920 to study American aircraft armament and make any recommendations on changes that would be necessary to meet future requirements. When the Board first met on 29 March 1920 it outlined numerous changes in the Browning machine gun, and also deliberated on the possible qualities of larger caliber aircraft guns that were sure to be required in the future. The Board met numerous times over the next five years and made its final report in 1925.

The Aircraft Armament Board included in its 1925 final report an extensive section on the redesign of the Browning .30 caliber aircraft machine gun and specifications and suggestions for the development of future .50 caliber guns. Among the suggestions were the alteration of the existing defective .30 caliber guns to operable condition and the redevelopment and the modification, addition, and elimination of various parts for a new gun.

Between 1921 and 1923, Capt. Walter Gorton, an ordnance officer stationed at the Springfield Arsenal, Springfield, MA, worked to improve the Browning designs, and developed the Model 1921 Fixed and Model 1922 Flexible .30 Caliber Aircraft guns. The first two Model 1921 prototypes were tested at the Springfield Arsenal, after which they were modified and then retested at Aberdeen Proving Ground and McCook Field, where further improvements were suggested and implemented. The gun was standardized to be used in the flexible or fixed configuration by the use of different mounts. The Model 1921 weighed 20 pounds and the rate of fire was set at 1,000 rpm. The gun included left and right hand feeds and a flash hider. The Model 1922 Flexible also had right and left hand feeds, but its parts were not interchangeable with the Model 1921 or the Model 1918 guns. The Model 1922 was successfully tested on 3 July 1922. Neither gun was placed into production, as there was no government funding and Colt was working on a more promising redesign of the M1918M1.

Meanwhile, in 1924 Colt had decided on a redesign of the M1918M1, which had been previously modified to facilitate manufacture. This new gun was designated as the M1919, of which only 1,031 were produced. The recommended redesign was no problem, as John Browning had brilliantly designed the original .30 caliber aircraft machine gun with every part calculated to be reduced in its size and weight so that its ground version weighed 50% more. Because it was adequately cooled in the air by the rushing slipstream the barrel could be made thin and light through the use of a special cooling jacket that was drilled with a number of holes or slots. The number of holes in the military version was 56 in four rows or 27 slots in six rows. One of the major shortcomings of the gun was that it could not be fed from the right side, which made installation on aircraft difficult, especially in side-by-side gun installations. Colt began manufacture of the gun under three different government contracts, beginning with 350 guns on 23 December 1923; 375 on 15 April 1926; and 200 on 18 April 1927. Meanwhile, in 1926 Colt began development of an entirely new .30

caliber machine gun design which was originally designated as the T2 and later as the M2.

**Browning .30 Caliber Aircraft Machine Gun M2**

At the end of World War I there were six U.S. machine gun manufacturers: Colt, Marlin-Rockwell, New England Westinghouse, Remington, Savage, and Winchester. After the war Westinghouse, which had no experience, left the fire arms business and Winchester, Remington, Savage, and Marlin went back to their previous sporting arms business. This left Colt and their close ties to John Browning as America's only machine gun manufacturer.

Between 1925 and 1928 Colt engineers worked diligently to develop the T1, and in 1927 two prototypes were ready for testing. The T1 prototype weighed 18.44 pounds, was 38.5 inches long, and fired at 1,350 rpm. In a Report of 21 March 1929 the Ordnance Department found the gun to be unsatisfactory and in need of improvement, but noted that Colt had solved the problem of fully interchangeable dual, right or left, feed mechanisms. During that year Colt narrowed the receiver and internal working parts, which decreased the gun's weight, but also increased its rate of fire, as the gun's recoil mechanism was much lighter. The design of the gun was fixed on 21 March 1929 as the T2, and it was recommended that the gun be standardized as the M2. On 12 March 1931 the gun was standardized as the M2 for use on all types of aircraft in either fixed or flexible mounts. The M2 was also known as the MG40 and later as the AN-M2. The commercial version of the M2 was first offered in 1930 as the Model 1930, and then in 1931 as the Model 1931. In 1932 the gun was redesignated as the MG40-2 (the -2 distinguished it from the heavy barreled Model MG38-40-1). Once the heavier MG38-40-1 was no longer desired by purchasers the popular MG40-2 was simply referred to as the MG40.

In the lean inter-war years licensing the gun overseas kept Browning viable as a military gun manufacturer. In Britain, Vickers and BSA produced 468,000 Browning .30s and spares for another 100,000 under license. John Browning worked with the Belgian military and developed the FN series of guns: the FN30 infantry gun and the FN 38 and 39 aircraft guns.

**.30 Caliber Aircraft Machine Gun M2**
**Colt Deliveries to the U.S. Government**

| | |
|---|---|
| **Before 1935** | **3,121** |
| **1935** | **1,554** |
| **1936** | **3,882** |
| **1937** | **870** |
| **1938** | **427** |
| **1939** | **1,786** |
| **1940** | **1,574** |
| **1941** | **14,200** |
| **1942** | **15,414** |
| **1943** | **4,210** |
| **TOTAL** | **47,029** |

**.30 Caliber Aircraft Machine Gun M2 (as .303)**
**Colt Direct Sales to the Royal Air Force**

| | |
|---|---|
| **1935** | **75** |
| **1936** | **0** |
| **1937** | **575** |
| **1938** | **1,000** |
| **1939** | **0** |
| **1940** | **1,426** |
| **1941** | **8,864** |
| **1942** | **20** |
| **TOTAL** | **11,960** |

**.30 Caliber Aircraft Machine Gun M2 (as 7.5mm)**
**Colt Direct Sales to the French Air Attaché**

| | |
|---|---|
| **1939** | **400** |
| **1940** | **1,000** |
| **TOTAL** | **1,400** |

**.30 Caliber Aircraft Machine Gun M2 (as .303)**
**Colt Direct Sales to the Netherlands East Indies**

| | |
|---|---|
| **1940** | **549 fixed** |
| | **40 flexible** |
| **1941** | **1,174 fixed** |
| | **353 flexible** |
| **1942** | **414 fixed** |
| **TOTAL** | **2,530** |

**Commercial Sales**

Colt sold 4,091 aircraft guns to commercial buyers who were U.S. aircraft manufacturers, who mounted them in the aircraft they were selling to buyers from foreign air forces such as China (699), Turkey (573), Netherlands East Indies (424), Iraq (75), Iran (60), Canada (60), Belgium (55), and several South American air forces, such as Columbia (144), Bolivia (68), Brazil (14), and Venezuela (6).

**Colt Royalties**

Initial royalties paid by Colt to John Browning were $6 per gun, but by 1943 this figure had decreased to $5 per gun. However, under the British contract Browning's royalties were more beginning at $8.75 for the first 1,000 guns and then dropping $0.25 per each 1,000 guns thereafter, ending at $7.50 for guns 5,000 to 13,000. This royalty schedule remained in effect until 31 January 1942 when the British were manufacturing all the .30 caliber guns they required.

**John Browning: The Legacy**

Browning died suddenly at 71 in Liege, Belgium, on 26 November 1926, while overseeing the manufacture of his guns there. During his lifetime John Browning had 128 patents involving more than 80 individual firearms. Upon his death Browning's son, Val, who had 38 firearms patents of his own, assumed the company's presidency, serving until 1963 when his son, John Val, took over for 14 years until the company was acquired by Fabrique Nationale of Belgium in 1977. In 1988 Browning's North American Division acquired a 37% interest in Winchester, which continues to make high quality sporting guns. Today the Browning family has no ownership in the North American Browning Division, which only makes products concerned with hunting and fishing.

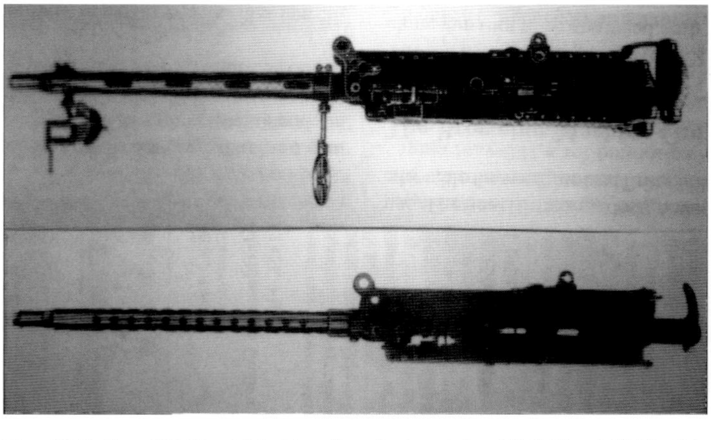

The .30 Caliber M2 Fixed Machine Gun (top) and the .30 Caliber M2 Flexible Machine Gun (bottom). (USAAF)

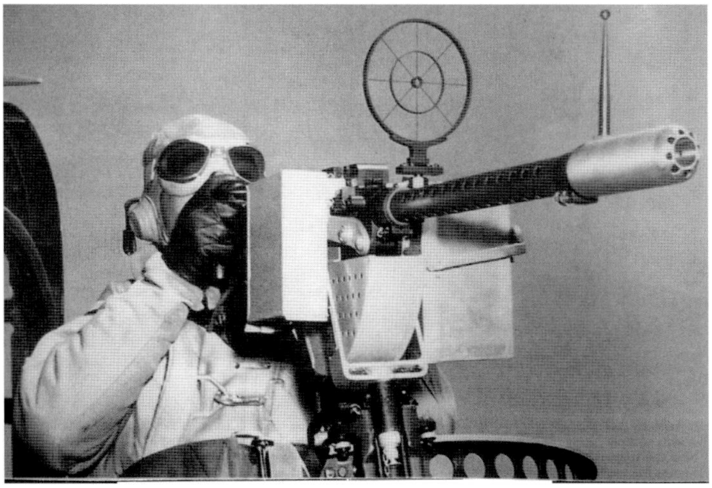

U.S. Navy flexible .30 caliber AN M2 machine gun mounted on a Scarff-type ring. The ammunition was fed from the box on the gunner's left while the spent cartridges fell into the left box and the links into the semi-circular drum under the gun. (USN)

**Describing the Browning .30 Caliber M2**

Colt tried to maintain the outstanding basic Browning design while further simplifying its manufacture. The .30 Caliber Aircraft Machine Gun M2 was completed at a time when a peacetime America lost interest in the military and withheld funding for machine gun projects. By the time of Pearl Harbor the .30, known as the BAMG (Browning Automatic Machine Gun), was America's first line machine gun in both single and twin flexible mounts, and as fixed wing or nose guns. The fixed M2 weighed 21.5 pounds, while the flexible M2 gun weighed 23 pounds, with the recoiling parts weighing 6.56 pounds and barrel weighing 3.81 pounds in both versions. Both types were 39.7 inches long with 23.9 inch barrels with four grooves and a 1:10 twist.

**The .30 Caliber M2 Fixed**

The belt-fed, recoil-operated, air-cooled .30 caliber M2 Fixed Machine Gun was recognized as a fixed gun by its operating slide group and the absence of requirements for manual operation. It was mounted rigidly to the aircraft by a trunnion bolt in the front and rear mounting post. The gun was fired by a trigger motor unit in synchronized installations and by an electric trigger control when installed outside of the propeller arc. The trigger motor, or trigger control, could be installed on either side of the gun. The early fixed guns experienced problems that were solved by the Springfield Arsenal in 1930. The E3 trigger motors malfunctioned due to their mounting on receiver plates that were too thin. The trigger locking cams also needed to be redesigned. The operating slide had to be installed on the side opposite to that on which the trigger motor was installed. Identical mounting provisions were present on both sides of the gun, and no additional parts were needed to change the operating slide group from one side of the gun to the other. The gun could be fed from the left or right hand side and could be changed to either feed by reversing a few components. All components of the fixed gun could be used in the flexible gun except those of the operating slide group.

The fixed gun, when firing rapid semi-automatic bullets through the propeller, used a synchronizing system comprised of a synchronizer impulse generator that was part of the aircraft's engine; a trigger motor connected to the gun; and an electrically-controlled solenoid. The impulse generator and trigger motor were connected by a flexible tube and wire assembly. The trigger motor was timed to the propeller revolutions so that the bullets would pass between the spinning propeller blades. The semi-automatic synchronized fire slowed the gun's rate of fire significantly. (Synchronizing gear will be discussed in detail in Part Seven/Chapter 2)

**The .30 Caliber M2 Flexible**

The basic structure of the M2 flexible gun was identical to the fixed gun, and all flexible gun components were common and completely interchangeable. The flexible gun was installed inside the aircraft's fuselage on a mount that allowed a gunner to move and aim the gun using sights. The mounts were supplied by the Army, and were usually installed as part of the fuselage during manufacture. A retracting slide group assembly mounted on the side of the gun was used instead of the operating slide group used in fixed assemblies. This retracting slide group was usually installed on the right hand side of the gun, but could be changed to the left hand side without additional parts. This slide group allowed the retraction of the bolt by hand for loading, unloading, and clearing the gun. The flexible gun had dual spade hand grips, a manual trigger and safety, and an internal trigger bar which were not found on the fixed gun. Magazines and ejected link belts were used to feed the gun.

**Use in World War II**

Early in the war the .30 caliber machine gun was used on a flexible mount in situations where the .50 caliber gun was too unwieldy. Soon after America entered combat it was found that the .30 caliber machine gun was inadequate against fast, armored German aircraft and armored vehicles that were appearing on the battlefields. The .30 caliber aircraft gun was

In the inter-war years the .30 caliber gun was thought to be adequate for combat on such fighters as the **Seversky P-35** but soon after America entered combat it was found that the .30 caliber machine gun was inadequate against fast, armored German aircraft and armored vehicles that were appearing on the battlefields. (USAAF)

The American .30 caliber aircraft gun was discontinued except for its installation on several Navy aircraft such as this **Douglas SBD-5 Dauntless** which were of use against the more lightly armored Japanese in the Pacific. (USN)

discontinued except for its installation on several Navy aircraft for use against the more lightly armored Japanese in the Pacific. The .30 caliber aircraft machine gun served an important function throughout the war in its employment as the standard equipment for training range practice because of its smaller rounds.

**.30 Caliber Training Machine Guns**

Machine Gun Trainers, M.22 Caliber, M3/M4/M5

The M2 Browning was also used in training in the .22 caliber models fitted with the same .22 subchamber that was installed in the ground version. In this configuration fitted with a special adapter for metallic belt feeding it was designated as the M5. The M3 (1917 and 1917A1) and M4 (1919A4) had adapters to use fabric belts.

Machine Gun Trainers, Caliber .30, T9 and T10

The standard M2 .30 caliber aircraft machine gun could be modified into a T9 and later a T10 training machine gun by a supplied kit that allowed the firing of a frangible bullet at an armored target aircraft in air-to-air firing. The kit consisted of a barrel that was threaded at the muzzle to accept the booster piston; a modified barrel jacket; and locking devices. There was a short round stop attached under the cover to help eliminate stoppages caused by short rounds which occurred when frangible bullets fractured during feeding into the gun. The T10 Trainer introduced in 1945 used a much smaller and simplified booster that added the power the frangible bullet needed to operate the mechanism. (See Part Three: Ammunition, Chapter 2, Frangible Bullet T-44 and Part Eight: Gunnery Training, Chapter 2, Pinball Training)

**The Browning .30 and .50 Caliber Machine Gun Compared**

The operation and care of the two guns was similar, and the only differences "which must be known to use, clean, and adjust the gun" were specified on just a single page in the Gunner's Information Manual.

**Differences in Performance and Construction**

| Gun | .50 Caliber | .30 Caliber |
|---|---|---|
| Weight (pounds) | 62 | 21.25 |
| Length Overall (inches) | 57.09 | 39.72 |
| Barrel Length (inches) | 36 | 23.9 |
| Barrel Weight (pounds) | 9.75 | 3.75 |
| Rate of Fire (rounds per minute) | 750-850 | 1,330 |
| Muzzle Velocity (feet per second) | 2,900 | 2,715 |
| Chamber Pressure (psi) | 50,000 to 52,000 | 48,000 to 50,000 |
| Maximum Range (yards) | 7,200 | 3,400 |
| Lands and Grooves (number) | 8/8 | 4/4 |
| Feed | Right | Right or Left |

**Section 3: Browning .50 Caliber Aircraft Machine Gun**

Near the end of the First World War the Germans installed heavily armored sections to their aircraft that rendered rifle caliber aerial machine guns obsolete. America was one of the nations that realized that larger caliber guns were the wave of the future when President Theodore Roosevelt's son Quentin found that his .30 caliber bullets were ineffective when they bounced off a heavily armored German Gotha bomber that then killed him with its return fire. Soon after Quentin Roosevelt's death Gen. John J. Pershing sent the Army Ordnance department minimum specifications for a new larger caliber aircraft machine gun and large caliber cartridge. Pershing's specifications asked for a gun with a minimum muzzle velocity of 2,750 fps and a cartridge with a caliber of at least .50 inch.

**M 1918**

The first cartridge developed by Winchester was an upscaled .30 rimmed round, and in firing tests in summer 1918 did not meet Ordnance Department specifications. A rimless round was designed, and a sample cartridge was sent to Colt and John Browning. Using the sample round and data supplied by Winchester, Browning designed his upscaled version of his .30 caliber machine gun designated as the Model 1918 Browning .50 Caliber Machine Gun. In September 1918 Winchester was contracted to build six air-cooled .50 caliber aircraft guns. Components from water-cooled guns were sent by Colt to Winchester, whose engineers subsequently developed parts for an air-cooled aircraft machine gun from them.

The Model 1918 was built in two versions: the water-cooled ground version built by Colt and the air-cooled version built by Winchester. Colt completed its gun on 15 August 1918 and successfully tested it on 10 October. Winchester did not complete its gun until 12 November 1918 after development was stalled when the trigger motor was not completed. First tests with a 707 grain cartridge produced a muzzle velocity of 2,370 fps, but Winchester's new .50 caliber round did not meet minimum muzzle velocity specifications. The Winchester installed a new 30.5 inch barrel gun and improved the balance of the round's powder charge to rectify the situation. Tests for both guns were successful, and the Ordnance Department ordered 5,000 of each gun, but with the aircraft gun given priority. The Armistice in November caused the cutback in military appropriations, and further commercial development of the gun was discontinued by Colt and Winchester, and the gun, cartridges, and drawings were given to the government.

**M 1921**

On 2 September 1919 Colt was awarded a contract to develop a production model of the water-cooled .50 caliber machine gun. This contract was revised to include an air-cooled .50 caliber aircraft, tank, and anti-aircraft gun using a new, more powerful .50 caliber cartridge that was under development. Fred Moore, General Works Manager at Colt, refined the 1918 model as the Browning Model 1921 air-cooled aircraft machine gun. On 15 June 1923 the gun was standardized as the air-cooled Model 1921 flexible and fixed aircraft models. The Model 1921 heavy, water-cooled infantry version was not standardized until 7 April 1925, but only as an anti-aircraft version, as the gun was much too heavy for use as an infantry weapon. While many of the parts on the aircraft gun were interchangeable, the critical and most costly parts were not, particularly the receiver. This condition persisted until the early 1930s. Between 1921 and 1937 these guns were used experimentally in aircraft installations and as anti-aircraft guns, and several basic shortcomings were revealed: both guns fed only from the left, which made side-by-side mounting in an aircraft difficult; the .50 ammunition had relatively low velocity of 2,700 fps, which was approximately the same as .30 caliber ammunition; the guns fired at a low 500-600 rpm; and the lightweight barrels quickly overheated. Between 1927 and 1930 the Army and Navy conducted studies and comparative tests on various applications of the .50 caliber gun, but prior to 1933 no requirements were published for an improved gun. Between 1927 and 1932 the Ordnance Department was very under-funded; so much so that not one machine gun was manufactured in the U.S. in 1928!

**M2**

During this time each of the services required a specialized machine gun to meet its needs, with the Army Air Corps needing a light, rapidly firing gun with alternate side feeding. By spring 1933 the Colt Company modified the two .50 caliber Model 1921 guns into a M1921 M2 air-cooled aircraft gun, a M1921 M2 heavy barreled gun, and a M1921 M2 water-cooled model. These three guns used the same basic receiver and internal parts that included major innovations originated by Colt's Dr. Samuel Green, and other parts developed by the company for their commercial guns. Green's work made way for the manufacture of one excellent receiver that could be quickly adapted for use in seven different types of guns: ground and turret heavy barrel (i.e. air-cooled) guns; fixed, flexible, and turret aircraft guns; and Army and Navy anti-aircraft water-cooled guns. The simplified design of these guns made manufacture, maintenance, and training easier because of their basic similarity.

The M1921 aircraft gun was developed from the anti-aircraft version, which only fed from the left side of the receiver and caused feeding problems in side-by-side installations in aircraft. The experimental Model 1922 and Model 1923 could be fed from either side, and the Model 1923 was standardized as the M2 aircraft gun on 5 October 1933. The last M1921s were declared obsolete in March 1943.

The guns were primarily tested at Aberdeen, Franklin Arsenal, and Wright Field by the Army, and by the Navy at the Dahlgren Naval Proving Ground. The successful tests sparked new interest in the guns, but at the time the Army lacked funds for further development; however, it was able to interest the Navy in continuing the project. Adm. E.B. Larimer, Chief of the Navy Bureau of Aeronautics (BuAER), authorized $150,000 for development and the purchase of the improved gun. During this time Colt instituted a policy of preparing basic drawings and then establishing tolerances that would regulate manufacture and quality control. This policy was so successful that during World War II, eight different manufacturers were able to mass produce guns and parts that were interchangeable. These eight companies producing the M2 were: Colt Patent Arms Co., Savage Corp., Buffalo Arms Corp., Frigidaire, AC Spark Plug, Brown-Lipe-Chappin, General Motors/Saginaw Division, and Kelsey Hayes Wheel Co.

The M2 would become trouble-free, and arguably the most effective heavy aircraft machine gun of World War II. The only problem with the M2 was its short barrel life caused by the ammunition used that was not designed with a copper driving band, and the exceedingly hard armor-piercing rounds quickly damaged the barrel's rifling. This situation would never become a problem, as U.S. barrel production was always sufficient for operational demands.

Meanwhile, in 1933, the USAAC requested that a .30 caliber version of the M2 be developed as the .50 caliber version proved to be too heavy and unmanageable for use in contemporary biplanes. Two models were produced: the M9/40 pilot's gun and the M9/40/2 observer's free mounted gun. The British conducted competitive trials pitting the Colt M9/40 and M9/40/2 against the Vickers, Hotchkiss, Darne, and Madsen machine guns. The .30 Colt guns were selected and service trials were conducted, during which the cordite-filled cartridges used by the British caused serious problems. The cordite-filled rounds proved to be very sensitive compared to the nitro cellulose charged rounds used by most nations. The service trials also revealed feed mechanism problems were caused by the use of cordite propellant, and the solution to these problems required extensive modifications of the gun. The British modified the M9/40 to fire cordite ammunition; this gun was a very different gun from the original, and was to become one of the best rifle caliber aerial machine guns of the war. The American M9/40, firing cellulose-filled cartridges, experienced no significant problems in its development or in service. Belgian FN also produced successful versions of the Browning in several different calibers.

When the British considered transitioning to heavier guns for turret installation they considered the Browning .50 machine gun because of the heavy weight of the twin 20mm cannon installation. A number of turret designs using the .50 Browning were produced, but only the Rose Brothers turret was used in operations in only a few Lancasters.

On 18 June 1937 a conference was held at the Aberdeen Proving Ground during which a group of Air Force personnel, headed by Air Corp's Chief, Gen. H.H. Arnold, requested that the Ordnance Division increase the rate of fire of the .50 caliber aircraft machine gun, which was currently 600 rpm for a 750 grain projectile fired at a velocity of 2,500 fps. Following the Aberdeen Conference, the Springfield Arsenal and Colt Company undertook the development of higher cyclic rate .50 caliber machine guns. Subsequent improvement in .50 caliber ammunition resulted in the adoption in 1937 of an improved propellant with an increased velocity to 2,700 fps, but the cyclic rate was not significantly improved. Work was done to increase muzzle velocity and reduce muzzle flash and smoke by increasing the 36 inch barrel length by nine inches, which was too long for aircraft installation, and the 36 inch barrel was retained on the aircraft version. Work continued during 1938 and 1939 at the Springfield Arsenal and Colt with no progress made in increasing the cyclic rate for the aircraft gun. In 1939 the M2 aircraft machine gun was rated at 600 rpm on a fixed test mount, but when it was installed on an aircraft mount the rate decreased to 500 rpm due to the mount's resiliency and the heavy load of the ammunition belt (30.25 pounds per 100 rounds) on the gun's feed mechanism. The rate of fire in later guns increased by Colt engineers to 750-850 rpm by using lighter bolts, lighter barrels, and using double driving springs and a muzzle booster. Nonetheless, the AAC wanted a 1,000 rpm rate in order to take full advantage of the .50 caliber round. Colt and the Springfield Arsenal collaborated on the development of a high-speed .50 caliber gun in the T21 and T22 series, which will be discussed later.

# 4

## Browning .50 and .30 Caliber Aircraft Machine Gun Production

In 1939 the Rock Island Arsenal production line was the only machine gun production line operating in the U.S., and it was only capable of producing 25 .30 caliber machine guns per day. In March 1941 the War Plans Division of the Headquarters Services of Supply announced a set of machine gun requirements which were to be immediately implemented by the Small Arms Division into a two year program based upon a six day, 120 hour work week. But once war came it became evident that a further expansion of the machine gun industry was required. In February 1942 the War Munitions Program established what quantity of each type of gun was needed. The .30 caliber production was reset at 100,400 against the previous 1942 requirement of 80,850, while the .50 caliber production was reset at 185,000 against the 1942 requirement of 115,000 guns.

The .30 caliber machine gun was comprised of 189 individual parts, of which 187 were steel, requiring machining from rough forgings, bar stock, flat steel, and tubing involving over 1,800 individual processes. For instance, the breech bolt parts required 304 individual machining operations. Over 8,000 drawings were required, and thousands of specialized tools had to be designed and manufactured before one component could be manufactured. To bring the Brownings into mass production required a gigantean effort involving the purchase of land for new factories in addition to expanding and modernizing the older existing factories. Studies were done to establish the design and organization for efficient new factories. To expedite production older machine tools and equipment were refurbished while new, improved, and specialized machinery was designed and manufactured. There also was a shortage of skilled labor, and new personnel had to be hired and trained. Contractors, subcontractors, and suppliers of materials, supplies, and equipment had to be found and contracted.

The Colt Patent Fire Arms Company was the only active inter-war machine gun producer in America, and began to work urgently with the Ordnance Department in developing production methods to mass produce Browning weapons in its facilities. Meanwhile, the Small Arms Division contacted two additional sources of Browning licensed production: Savage Arms and General Motors. Savage Arms of Utica, NY, which had produced the Lewis gun during World War I, was a leading manufacturer of quality sporting guns, and in 1939 was subcontracted to build the famous Thompson submachine gun. The 1940-41 Munitions Program authorized Savage to build a machine gun plant in Illion, NY, with a capacity to produce 25,000 .50 caliber and 10,000 Browning .30 caliber Brownings. On 6 September 1940 the Ordnance Department negotiated a contract with Savage to produce 2,200 .50s and 1,100 .30s per month. Colt was to provide Savage (and GM) with pertinent manufacturing data and drawings, along with tools, dies, jigs, and gauges.

The expansion of existing facilities was important to the increased Browning machine gun production, and the Under-Secretary of War, the War Production Board, and the War Site Board approved a number of expansion projects. In January 1942 Buffalo Arms was granted approval to expand its facilities to produce 5,100 Model 1919 A-4 .30 caliber machine guns per month. On 18 February 1942 the General Motors Saginaw Steering Gear Division was granted funds to produce 19,000 Model 1919 A-4 .30 caliber machine guns per month, while on 25 February 1942 the GM Brown-Lipe-Chapin Division was to be expanded to produce 3,000 Model 1917 A-1 .30 caliber machine guns per month. The GM Frigidaire Division was authorized to expand to produce 7,250 .50 caliber M2s and 1,950 water-cooled .50s. Additional expansion was to be carried out by the GM AC Spark Plug Division and the Wheel Company.

In early 1942 the Air Force decided to use the .50 caliber machine exclusively for combat and demote the .30 gun for training, and to maintain the minimal requirements of aircraft in production using the .30 machine gun. On 2 July 1942 the Small Arms Division presented another revised aircraft machine gun program, which greatly decreased the .30 machine requirement and increased the .50 gun requirement from 29,000 per month in June to 44,000 per month. This could be realized by redirecting the production of other types of guns and expanding .50 production by granting additional procurement of manufacturing equipment. On 25 August 1942 Buffalo Arms was to convert part of its .30 caliber production to 3,000 .50 M2s per month, but continued its .30 M2 production at 5,000 per month. Brown-Lipe-Chapin and Savage Arms were also changed over from .30 to .50 guns. By October 1942 the .50 M2 aircraft gun requirements were further increased and the .30 M2 aircraft gun decreased, resulting in factory conversions. Colt was to convert its 1,400 per month production of water-cooled guns to the heavy barrel, air-cooled guns. Kelsey-Hayes and High Standard were also to convert their water-cooled guns to air-cooled guns. By the end of 1942, the production of water-cooled guns was regarded as sufficient to meet requirements after Frigidaire discontinued its manufacture of the water-cooled gun, leaving Colt as the only company manufacturing it. At the end of 1942 Frigidaire, High Standard, and AC Spark Plug were producing the M2 heavy barrel guns. By February and March 1943, .30 caliber aircraft M2 gun production was concluded at Buffalo Arms, Colt, and Brown-Lipe-Chapin. However, in July 1943, when an emergency requirement for the .30 caliber M2 occurred, Buffalo Arms was positioned to resume production of the weapon while Colt and Brown-Lipe-Chapin were not.

By March 1943 it was decided that only one machine gun type was to be manufactured in each factory:

| Gun Type | Manufacturer |
|---|---|
| .30 M1917A1 | Rock Island Arsenal |
| .30 M1919A4 | Buffalo Arms (until July 1943) |
| .30 M1919A4 | Saginaw Steering Gear (GM) |
| .30 M1919A6 | Saginaw Steering Gear (GM) |
| .50 | Buffalo Arms |
| .50 | Colt Patent Fire Arms |
| .50 | High Standard |
| .50 | Savage Arms |
| .50 | Kelsey-Hayes |
| .50 | Brown-Lipe-Chapin (GM) |
| .50 | Frigidaire (GM) |
| .50 | AC Spark Plug (GM) |

During 1944, requirements for the .50 caliber aircraft gun again increased, as U.S. aircraft production had increased exponentially, and 583,596 guns were projected for the year, but 515,220 were actually manufactured with 45,000 guns per month produced. Once U.S. aircraft production decreased the monthly .50 caliber gun production decreased to 30,000 per month, with Buffalo Arms ceasing all Browning production.

**Machine Gun Industry Integration Committee**

During the war the Machine Gun Industry Integration Committee was established, which included representatives of the 11 machine gun manufacturers. The Integration Committee would meet periodically with the Small Arms Division of the Ordnance Department to exchange information and ideas on improving machine gun design and manufacture. During its tenure Integration Committee improved the design, material use, and manufacture of nearly all of the 270 parts of the .50 caliber and 189 parts of the .30 caliber machine guns.

**General Motors**

In April 1938 insightful General Motors presented an engineering study on the feasibility of manufacturing Browning machine guns to the War Department, which was impressed by the company's ability to mass produce precise interchangeable small parts. It would not be until 29 May 1940 that the War Department placed the first order with an auto manufacturer, which was an "educational" order for 500 .30 caliber guns. On 13 September 1940 the War Department issued ORD-474 for the immediate production of 71,225 Browning machine guns, which was the first of several large orders made during the war. Under this first contract the following GM divisions were to produce these quantities:

| GM Division | MG Type | # Produced |
|---|---|---|
| Frigidaire | .50 M2 AC | 19,998 |
| AC Spark Plug | .50 M2 AC | 14,741 |
| AC Spark Plug | .50 M2 HB | 7,385 |
| Brown-Lipe-Chapin | .30 M2 AC | 9,097 |
| Saginaw Steering | .30 M1919A4 | 20,004 |

When negotiating contracts, the original prices were based on data provided by existing gun costs, and consideration was given to the higher start up costs of producing the initial small production quantities. There were provisions for price re-determination during production, as costs were expected to decrease, which they did from 84% to 75%. The four GM divisions met with the Small Arms Division of the Ordnance Department to discuss changes which when initiated improved quality, quantity, reduced costs, and accelerated production.

Once these contracts were negotiated GM began the process of refurbishing old buildings for the production of machine guns and building new ones, and then equipping them with the machinery necessary for production. GM was able to obtain several hundred old machines used in World War I machine gun production from the Springfield Arsenal, which were updated, and were particularly useful in training and developing new techniques and processes. GM purchased over 8,000 new machines valued at $28.8 million. GM instituted the use of punch press and multiple spindle drilling procedures; replacing milling and drilling, which resulted in increased production and lower costs. Conveyor and mechanical handling equipment aided mass production. The number of alloyed steels was reduced from 28 grades to 12. GM hired thousands of new employees to augment its work force, and then began training 15,000 employees in machine gun production. GM immediately began to search for the hundreds of subcontractors and suppliers of materials and equipment that were urgently needed. GM field representatives were trained as liaisons to the Army to aid in training. GM would eventually print 2.25 million manuals, booklets, and charts that were circulated for training and maintenance.

**Saginaw Steering Gear Division GM**

Saginaw Steering Gear was formed in April 1906 to manufacture automobile parts, and would develop into one of the world's largest manufacturers of steering gears and components for automobiles, trucks, and buses. During the war Saginaw was the foremost producer of the M1919A4 .30 caliber machine gun. The company's Saginaw Malleable Iron Division developed malleable iron castings called "ArmaSteel" made of pig iron and scrap steel, which replaced alloyed steel that was in short supply. ArmaSteel was strong and wear resistant, could be easily and quickly cut, and reduced the number of machining operations.

The company manufactured the M1919A4, M1919A5, and 1919A6 from 1941 to 1945.

| 1941 | 1942 | 1943 | 1944 | 1945 | Total |
|---|---|---|---|---|---|
| 14,239 | 139,985 | 109,929 | 73,460 | 30,240 | 367,853 |

The company had seven major contracts for 367,853 guns totaling $53,207,000. The average cost of first shipment of guns was $213.88 and was decreased to a final cost of $54.72.

**AC Spark Plug Division GM**

In peacetime the Flint, MI, company was a major producer of automotive spark plugs, oil filters, fuel pumps, air cleaners, and instruments.

The company manufactured the Browning .50 caliber M2 aircraft machine gun.

| 1941 | 1942 | 1943 | 1944 | 1945 | Total |
|---|---|---|---|---|---|
| 2,758 | 19,212 | 4,028 | 0 | 0 | 26,098 |

The company manufactured the Browning .50 caliber M2 HB fixed, flexible, and turret type aircraft machine gun.

| 1941 | 1942 | 1943 | 1944 | 1945 | Total |
|---|---|---|---|---|---|
| 825 | 37,437 | 98,945 | 108,000 | 52,822 | 295,029 |

The company had six major contracts for 295,029 guns totaling $95,860,000.

**Brown-Lipe-Chapin Division GM**
Brown-Lipe-Chapin of Syracuse, NY, was a subsidiary of General Motor's Guide Lamp Division, and in the prewar manufactured head lights, tail lights, bumper guards, and zinc die castings for GM automobiles.

The company manufactured the Browning .30 caliber M2 aircraft gun.

| 1941 | 1942 | 1943 | 1944 | 1945 | Total |
|---|---|---|---|---|---|
| 982 | 24,262 | 8,007 | 62,168 | 0 | 95,419 |

The company had four contracts for 95,419 .30 caliber M2s totaling $22,684,000.

The company manufactured the Browning .50 caliber M2 aircraft gun.

| 1941 | 1942 | 1943 | 1944 | 1945 | Total |
|---|---|---|---|---|---|
| 0 | 0 | 33,213 | 62,168 | 24,408 | 119,789 |

The company had four contracts for 119,789 guns totaling $143,089,000.

**Frigidaire Division GM**
This GM division located in Dayton, OH, was a major prewar producer of household appliances, such as electric ranges, refrigerators, freezers, water heaters, and air conditioners. Frigidaire was known for its high quality guns, and was a leader in developing engineering and production methods. The company produced 16,977 .50 caliber M2 water-cooled machine guns in 1943 for $4,653,000, but its major production was of the .50 caliber M2 aircraft gun.

| 1941 | 1942 | 1943 | 1944 | 1945 | Total |
|---|---|---|---|---|---|
| 4,205 | 47,397 | 118,515 | 130,816 | 44,890 | 345,823 |

The company had eight contracts for 345,823 guns totaling $66,734,000.

**Buffalo Arms**
In 16 November 1940 the Houde Engineering Corporation of Buffalo, an automobile parts maker, was contracted by the British Purchasing Commission to manufacture 9,000 M1919A4 .30 caliber machine guns and 9,000 .30 caliber aircraft machine guns based on the Colt MG 40, which was essentially the Browning M2. The guns were to be manufactured to British specifications, and Houde was to be able to increase production capacity to another 4,500 units. Colt was engaged to provide technical assistance in the manufacture. Houde Engineering became the Buffalo Arms Corporation and began its new factory in January 1941, but the facility was taken over in March by the Defense Plant Corporation once Lend-Lease was enacted; however, the plant was operated by Buffalo Arms.

By mid-1942 the GM Saginaw Plant was producing enough .30 caliber Brownings, and Buffalo Arms reduced its .30 caliber production and increased its .50 caliber production. There was a shortage of labor in the Buffalo area, as there were a number of other defense contractors vying for personnel (e.g. Bell Aircraft), and much of Buffalo Arms work was subcontracted, as 153 of the 189 .30 caliber machine gun parts and 150 of the 230 .50 caliber parts were sent out. There were criticisms from combat theaters of machine guns manufactured by companies other than Colt, especially Buffalo Arms, but an inquiry showed that the problem was not due to the inexperience of the gun manufacturers, but due to the aircraft builder's inexperience in installing the guns in their aircraft. As a remedy, the Ordnance Department contracted Colt to place armament technicians in aircraft plants to supervise gun installation. Complaints against Buffalo Arms guns continued in 1944, as their quality control did not follow Ordnance Department guidelines, and Ordnance Department inspectors were placed in the plant and the problems subsided. Nonetheless, the company was one of the highest cost gun producers, and in January 1945 its contract was terminated, but the factory was free to continue to produce other small arms parts. The company manufactured both the .30 and .50 caliber aircraft guns.

Browning .30 caliber M2 Aircraft Machine Gun

| 1941 | 1942 | 1943 | 1944 | 1945 | Total |
|---|---|---|---|---|---|
| 3,129 | 55,134 | 12,057 | 24,980 | 0 | 95,300 |

Browning .30 caliber M1919 Aircraft Machine Gun

| 1941 | 1942 | 1943 | 1944 | 1945 | Total |
|---|---|---|---|---|---|
| 0 | 18,000 | 21,300 | 0 | 0 | 38,300 |

Three Browning .30 contracts for 113,600 guns totaled $22,358,000.

Browning .50 caliber M2 Aircraft Machine Gun

| 1941 | 1942 | 1943 | 1944 | 1945 | Total |
|---|---|---|---|---|---|
| 0 | 0 | 38,100 | 45,250 | 3,000 | 86,350 |

Three Browning .50 contracts for 86,350 guns totaled $43,113,000.

**Kelsey-Hayes Wheel Co.**
The Kelsey Wheel Company merged with the Hayes Wheel Company in 1927, and became one of the largest automotive wheel companies in America. In October 1940 Kelsey-Hayes manufactured .50 caliber machine guns under contract from the British, but after Lend-Lease became effective the U.S. government assumed the British contracts. The company built the .50 caliber M2 aircraft gun.

| 1941 | 1942 | 1943 | 1944 | 1945 | Total |
|---|---|---|---|---|---|
| 2,494 | 35,855 | 45,432 | 10,759 | 14,000 | 108,540 |

The company had 12 contracts for 108,540 guns totaling $103,990,000.

**High Standard Manufacturing Corp.**
The High Standard Corporation of New Haven, CT, was founded in 1926 as a manufacturer of tools for the northeastern firearms manufacturers, but began to manufacture guns in 1932 under prominent firearms designer Carl Swebilius. The company was a quality machine gun manufacturer, and initially developed the high-speed machine gun project, which was completed by Frigidaire using many of High Standards innovations to develop the M3. The company manufactured 9,386 M2 water-cooled fixed and flexible Browning machine guns in 1942 and 1943.

Browning .50 caliber M2 Aircraft Basic

| 1941 | 1942 | 1943 | 1944 | 1945 | Total |
|---|---|---|---|---|---|
| 13,375 | 46,182 | 90,082 | 109,877 | 47,200 | 306,716 |

Browning .50 caliber M2 Fixed and Flexible

| 1941 | 1942 | 1943 | 1944 | 1945 | Total |
|---|---|---|---|---|---|
| 0 | 11,440 | 7,280 | 0 | 0 | 18,720 |

During the war High Standard received seven .50 caliber machine gun contracts totaling $58,510,000. (Note: High Standard currently manufactures a line of high quality .22 caliber target pistols.)

**Savage Arms Corporation**

Savage Arms of Utica, NY, was a dependable supplier of the Browning machine gun, and manufactured nearly all of the components of its guns.

Browning .30 caliber M2 Aircraft

| 1941 | 1942 | 1943 | 1944 | 1945 | Total |
|---|---|---|---|---|---|
| 0 | 14,800 | 0 | 0 | 0 | 14,800 |

Browning .50 caliber M2 Aircraft

| 1941 | 1942 | 1943 | 1944 | 1945 | Total |
|---|---|---|---|---|---|
| 4,568 | 48,840 | 101,492 | 103,950 | 36,511 | 295,361 |

The company received four machine gun contracts during the war totaling $67,067,000. The initial contract for $27,648,000 was let for the .30 caliber M2 aircraft machine gun, and was to run from September 1940 to September 1944, but as the need for the .30 caliber aircraft gun subsided the contract included the increased manufacture of the .50 M2 aircraft gun. In August 1944 another .30 contract was let for $2,401,000.

**Colt Patent Fire Arms Company**

Browning .30 caliber M2 Aircraft

| 1940 | 1941 | 1942 | 1943 | 1944 | 1945 | Total |
|---|---|---|---|---|---|---|
| 3,633 | 7,606 | 22,602 | 4,200 | 0 | 0 | 38,041 |

Colt received three .30 caliber contracts totaling $6,521,000.

Browning .50 caliber M2 Aircraft

| 1940 | 1941 | 1942 | 1943 | 1944 | 1945 | Total |
|---|---|---|---|---|---|---|
| 3,359 | 11,487 | 38,616 | 46,324 | 52,500 | 16,940 | 169,226 |

Browning .50 caliber Fixed and Flexible

| 1940 | 1941 | 1942 | 1943 | 1944 | 1945 | Total |
|---|---|---|---|---|---|---|
| 972 | 5,969 | 14,835 | 28,169 | 3,450 | 0 | 47,426 |

Colt received eight .50 caliber contracts totaling $166,116,000, which also included 53,047 Browning .50 water-cooled fixed and flexible machine guns.

Final inspection of the .30 caliber machine gun at the General Motors Saginaw plant, which was one of five GM Divisions that manufactured both .30 and .50 Browning guns. (USAAF)

**Rock Island Arsenal**

The Rock Island Arsenal was a government facility that was established on the Mississippi River near Moline, IL, in 1862, and manufactured and remanufactured .30 caliber Browning machine guns during the war, along with manufacturing tools, gauges, and a multitude of spare parts. The Arsenal also pursued research and development projects, and helped civilian commercial manufacturers set up and produce machine guns.

Browning .30 M19179A1

| 1941 | 1942 | 1943 | 1944 | 1945 | Total |
|---|---|---|---|---|---|
| 0 | 12,068 | 30,724 | 0 | 11,065 | 53,857 |

Browning .30 M1919A4 and M1919A5

| 1941 | 1942 | 1943 | 1944 | 1945 | Total |
|---|---|---|---|---|---|
| 0 | 1,716 | 27,988 | 3,114 | 0 | 31,818 |

Browning .30 M1917 converted to M1917A1

| 1941 | 1942 | 1943 | 1944 | 1945 | Total |
|---|---|---|---|---|---|
| 5,406 | 559 | 0 | 0 | 0 | 5,965 |

**Rebuilders**

Machine gun refurbishment and overhaul, along with implementing modifications, was a large part of Rock Island's responsibilities. The rebuilders checked and gauged all parts for serviceability, and any upgraded and redesigned parts were to be installed. All rebuilt guns were to be fitted with a new barrel. The average cost to rebuild a .30 caliber Browning machine gun was $13.51 less parts, while the cost for a .50 caliber gun was $44.00 less parts. Rock Island's main rebuild was to convert M1917 guns to the M1917A1 configuration:

Browning .30 M1917 converted to M1917A1

| 1941 | 1942 | 1943 | 1944 | 1945 | Total |
|---|---|---|---|---|---|
| 5,406 | 559 | 0 | 0 | 0 | 5,965 |

The majority of the rebuilding was done by government facilities, but some commercial manufacturers were contracted to rebuild machine guns. In addition to Rock Island, the other government rebuilders (with initials) were:

| | |
|---|---|
| Augusta Arsenal, GA | AA |
| Benicia Arsenal, CA | BA |
| Mt. Rainier Ordnance Depot, WA | MR |
| Raritan Arsenal, NJ | RA |
| Red River Arsenal, TX | RRA |
| Rock Island Arsenal, IL | RIA |
| Springfield Arsenal, MA | SA |

All Browning Machine guns rebuilt in the U.S. were to be stamped on the receiver with the initials of the rebuilding facility. If the same facility rebuilt the same gun it was not required to do an additional stamping, but if a different facility rebuilt the gun for a second time it was to stamp its mark under the mark of the first rebuilder. The markings for the primary rebuilders are listed above.

**U.S. Machine Gun Production in World War II**
**(Total Production July 1939 through June 1945)**

| **.30 Caliber** | **1939** | **1940** | **1941** | **1942** | **1943** | **1944** | **1945** | **Total** |
|---|---|---|---|---|---|---|---|---|
| Aircraft Fixed | 759 | 2230 | 8261 | 59883 | 8007 | ---- | ---- | 79140 |
| Aircraft Flexible | 60 | 1403 | 3419 | 29959 | ---- | 5950 | ---- | 40791 |
| Aircraft w/Fixed backplate | ---- | ---- | 37 | 26956 | 16257 | 19030 | 1522 | 63802 |
| 1919A4/A5 Fixed | ---- | ---- | 1670 | 42986 | 5964 | ---- | ---- | 49750 |
| 1919A4 Flexible | ---- | ---- | 14282 | 1438877 | 127379 | 73460 | 16320 | 375331 |
| 1919A4 Mod. | ---- | 2283 | 12338 | 1792 | ---- | ---- | ---- | 16423 |
| 1919A6 | ---- | ---- | ---- | ---- | ---- | 23329 | 10000 | 33329 |
| **TOTAL by YEAR** | **849** | **5916** | **40010** | **304563** | 157607 | 121769 | 27842 | 658556 |
| .50 Caliber | 1939 | 1940 | 1941 | 1942 | 1943 | 1944 | 1945 | Total |
| Aircraft Basic | 1667 | 3359 | 40933 | 236102 | 477229 | 515220 | 97732 | 1372242 |
| Hard Barrel Fixed | ---- | ---- | 1 | 1161 | 689 | ---- | ---- | 1851 |
| Hard Barrel Flexible | 812 | 972 | 2448 | 70639 | 107277 | 120664 | 18702 | 321514 |
| Turret | ---- | ---- | ---- | 415 | 26291 | 37677 | 11298 | 75681 |
| Water Cooled Fixed | 200 | 528 | 2422 | 8724 | 1200 | ---- | ---- | 13074 |
| Water Cooled Flexible | ---- | 96 | 3547 | 6111 | 26969 | 3450 | ---- | 40173 |
| **TOTAL by YEAR** | **2679** | **4955** | **49351** | **323152** | 639655 | 677011 | 127732 | 1824535 |

(National Archives)

# 5

# The Browning .50 Caliber Aircraft Machine Gun in World War II

**Section 1: Development**

Late in September 1939, Gen. Arnold issued a statement describing the ideal characteristics of an improved .50 caliber machine gun:

1) Cyclic rate: Maximum consistent with other design requirements, not less than 1,000 rpm (a major consideration).
2) Time of flight: 0.7 second to 600 yards.
3) Effectiveness: Penetration of 3/4 inch armor plate at 600 yards with armor-piercing bullets.
4) Overall length of gun: 68 inches maximum.
5) Weight: Minimum possible consistent with performance.
6) Type of fire: Full automatic.
7) Feed: Right and left hand.
8) Cooling: Air-cooled, maximum efficiency possible with aerodynamic barrel jacket for distance of at least 20 inches aft of muzzle.
9) Control: Hand trigger and trigger motor.
10) Sight: No provision.
11) Trunnion reactions: Lowest possible consistent with performance.
12) Mounting: Suitable for fixed or flexible use.

**T21**

By the end of 1939, the Springfield Arsenal had collected data leading to the adoption of a lighter (by approximately 9.5 pounds) gun with a shorter barrel and double driving springs, which would increase the rate of fire of the standard M2 aircraft gun. In January 1940, using this data, Springfield produced a high cyclic rate gun that was ready for testing at Aberdeen. The gun fired a smaller 710 grain projectile which further increased the muzzle velocity to 2,810 fps at an anticipated higher rate of 997 rpm. However, the gun was unsatisfactory, because of excessive breakages and malfunctions, but Springfield continued to work.

A second high-speed gun was developed through a collaboration of Colt and the Springfield Arsenal. It was tested at Aberdeen Proving Ground in May 1940, but the results were once more unsatisfactory with excessive breakages and malfunctions. The gun was further improved, and a third test, in November 1940 at Aberdeen, revealed the same faults. The Colt gun underwent further redesign, designated as the T21, and was tested a fourth time at Aberdeen in September 1942. The results continued to be unsatisfactory, and Colt discontinued its high-speed gun program. Despite its failure, the importance of the T21 project was the establishment of a standard of performance for an acceptable high-speed gun: one breakage, and five malfunctions were to be permitted in 5,000 rounds of firing at 1,200 rounds per minute.

**T22**

During the early fall of 1942 the High Standard Manufacturing Co. designed a high cyclic rate .50 caliber machine gun in two models designated as the T22. The company submitted these guns to Aberdeen for testing on 10 August 1942, and one gun was fired on that date. The test gun fired 556 rounds at a cyclic rate of 1,066 rounds per minute. The test results were unsatisfactory, with five stubbed rounds and two failures to feed occurring. Even though the performance of the T22 was inadequate, it was considered to have sufficient potential to justify further development. A research and development contract was tendered to High Standard on 16 September 1942 for two additional T22 guns and the modification of the two failed guns. High Standard sent the new guns and the reworked original two guns to Aberdeen, where they underwent only limited firing tests. Afterward, one gun was shipped to Wright Field and two to Eglin Field for further, more extensive testing during October 1942. These tests revealed several structural weaknesses, but further development was again recommended. In November 1942, another research and development contract for six additional T22 guns was let. The fifth gun was first fired on 21 November 1942 at Aberdeen, and the results were poor, so the gun was returned to High Standard for modifications. The remaining T22 guns on order were delivered to Aberdeen and tested 11 December 1942, again with unsatisfactory results.

**T22E1**

The T22E1 was a version of the T22 tested in February 1943 and failed due to a broken sear after firing only 111 rounds.

**T22E2**

The T22E2 was tested in March 1943 firing 3,700 rounds at a cyclic rate of 1,219 rounds per minute, but incurring a very unacceptable 43 malfunctions and seven breakages.

**T22E3**

There are no records available on this model.

**T22E4**

The T22E4 was tested in August 1943 firing 5,000 rounds at a cyclic rate of 1,108 rpm with an improved but unacceptable 36 malfunctions and 2 breakages.

**T22E5**

Two T22E4 guns were built, but when fired at Aberdeen their rate of fire was less than the desired 1,000 rpm.

**T22E6**

In the development of this gun an effort was made to hold changes from the standard 1942 Browning M2 gun to a minimum. The introduction of the T22E6 seemed to advance the development of the high-speed gun even though the initial tests on 13 December 1943 were disappointing, as cracks occurred in the new lighter bolts supplied with the guns. New bolts were remade and the guns were retested two weeks later. The results again showed a high number of malfunctions and breakages, but these guns were considered greatly improved over previous models. Ten T22E6 guns were ordered from High Standard on 25 January 1944, and the order was later increased to 25 in order to supply 10 guns requested by the Navy Bureau of Ordnance for testing at the Naval Proving Ground Dahlgren, and five more guns to the AAF at Aberdeen Proving Ground.

Aberdeen received its T-22E6s on 17 March 1944, and each was given check firings of 200 rounds and subsequently were sent elsewhere for evaluation: five to Wright Field and two to Dahlgren. Tests of the remaining T22E6 guns were continued at Aberdeen with the guns fired under the various conditions to be expected in service. The Wright Field report of their tests recommended further development of the gun to bring about changes which were stated to be essential before the gun could be used in aircraft installations. The 26 August 1944 Naval Proving Ground report on their tests of their T22E6 guns recommended further development and non-acceptance of the T22E6 gun for service use in its existing form. Many of the defects revealed during testing were inherent in the mechanism of the T22E6 gun, and the Ordnance Department decided that further development would not produce a satisfactory weapon. Even though further development of the T22E6 gun was not continued, certain innovations of the weapon were incorporated in the T36 (M2A1) and T25E3 (M3) guns.

**T25**

Continuing the search for an acceptable high-speed machine gun, the Ordnance Department placed a contract with General Motors Frigidaire Division on 4 August 1943 for the development of the T25 series of .50 caliber guns. In the development of the T25 the Ordnance Department placed no restrictions on the number of changes from the M2 gun, except the basic mechanism of the M2 gun was to be used. Frigidaire was instructed to correct specific known mechanical limitations of the M2 gun, and the company was permitted to proceed by making all other necessary changes to provide reliable gun functioning at 1,200 rpm. There was no requirement for interchangeability of the components of the two guns. Among the components redesigned by Frigidaire were the back plate buffer, barrel buffer, and receiver. It was not until 10 March 1944 that the first T25 gun was submitted to Aberdeen for testing. During the first test the gun performed adequately for the first 2,000 rounds, but from that point on, excessive breakage and malfunctions occurred, and at 3,100 rounds the test was discontinued because of the breakage of the back plate buffer.

**T25E1**

After the T25 was discontinued work was immediately started on a second gun, the T25E1, which was tested at Aberdeen 10 May 1944. Testing showed that this gun was completely unsatisfactory, as there were nine breakages and three malfunctions occurring in only 770 fired rounds, and the test was stopped. Although the gun's performance was unsatisfactory, it had specific desirable characteristics to be incorporated in future models.

**T25E2**

To determine the causes of the unsatisfactory functioning of the E1, the T25E2 gun was assembled by substituting the bolt, top cover, and recoil booster of the T22E6 gun for corresponding components of the T25E1 gun. The T25E2 was fired at Aberdeen in June 1944, and the E2 continued to function unsatisfactorily; the test was stopped after 1,800 rounds were fired. The gun was carefully examined, and the conclusions indicated that the nested helical springs in the back plate buffer were breaking and causing extreme impact forces on the gun's components.

**T25E3 (M3)**

The first T25E3 gun was tested at Aberdeen 1 July 1944 with greatly improved results over that of the T25E1 and E2, with the cyclic rate average increased to 1,250 rpm. Eight malfunctions occurred, but for the first time in the T-series development, it was possible to determine the specific cause of each malfunction. A projecting corner on the bolt was responsible for "shorting" rounds in the feedway, thus causing failures to feed. The remainder of the malfunctions was caused by fatigue of the sear spring.

To permit more comprehensive tests of the T25E3 gun, 12 additional guns were immediately ordered and were completed in October 1944. Two guns remained at Frigidaire to be used in further development, while the remainder was delivered to Aberdeen. For a positive check on the performance of the initial T25E3 gun no changes were made in these new guns from the T25E3 gun already tested. During October 1944, three T25E3 guns were tested in the standard 5,000 round endurance test at Aberdeen. Thirteen out of the fifteen malfunctions were failures to feed, or lightly struck primers that were traced to the premature release of the firing pin by the sear. The problem was solved by new sears. Further tests were more promising, and the Ordnance Committee procured 1,100 T25E3 guns: 100 to establish the final engineering design, and 1,000 to be procured by Industrial Service to enable the development of production facilities, and the majority to provide guns for extended service tests. On 14 December 1944 the Ordnance Committee procured an additional 1,000 T25E3 guns to be used by the Navy for evaluation. Following the above authorization, a Research and Development contract was placed with Frigidaire on 6 December 1944 for 100 T25E3 guns. The first gun was delivered 6 January 1945, and the hundredth gun was delivered 12 February 1945.

Acceptance tests were conducted during January and February 1945, while flight tests were flown in March at Wright Field. After the tests were satisfactorily completed, and to expedite procurement of the T25E3, the AAF requested the gun be standardized in April 1945. The Ordnance Committee acted immediately to standardize the T25E3 gun as Gun, Machine, Caliber .50, M3 Aircraft, Basic, and also reclassified the Caliber .50 Aircraft Machine Gun M2 as Limited Standard. Large scale procurement of M3 guns was begun, and by the end of September 1945 approximately 2,400 guns had been manufactured, but too late to see combat.

**T26**

The T26 was a separate modification of the Browning M2 gun produced and tested at Aberdeen. It included a short-round device submitted by the AAF, the cover assembly of the T22E5, and the extractor assembly and back plate assembly taken from the T22 series. A muzzle booster with a .65 inch hole was used, as well as a pneumatic buffer and a modified sideplate switch.

**T27**

In parallel with the development of the T22E6 gun, High Standard Manufacturing provided a kit of parts which could be used to convert the standard M2 gun to a high-speed weapon. The first two forms of this gun, designated the T27, were submitted to Aberdeen for testing on 1 January 1944. The tests of both guns were discontinued before the completion of the regular 5,000-round test due to malfunctions and breakages. During the next 14 months 18 guns of the T27 series were tested at Aberdeen, but the results of these tests revealed greater than normal malfunctions and breakages, and actual danger to personnel and equipment.

**T27E1**

In testing two E1 guns blew up, and the tests were discontinued about February 1945.

**T27E2**

It seems that the T27E2 did not continue beyond the blueprint stage.

**T27E3**

The T27E3 was tested in March 1944 and suffered numerous malfunctions.

**T27E4**

When tested in April 1944 the E4 fired at a high rate of 1,330 rpm, but suffered numerous breakages and malfunctions.

**T27E5**

When tested in June 1944 the E5 experienced excessive malfunctions, and the tests were concluded after the only gun blew up.

**T27 E6**

The T27E6 was tested early in 1945, and successfully fired 5,000 rounds at a rate of over 1,000 rpm with only one breakage of a major part, but one of the four guns tested had 11 malfunctions.

**T27E7**

In March 1945 the last T27 of the series was overdeveloped to E7, which tested successfully, completing the 5,000 round test without exceeding the number of acceptable malfunctions, but suffered excessive breakage of minor parts. While the testing results improved, the gun's performance remained unsatisfactory, and in March 1945 it was decided that no further consideration would be given this weapon.

**T28**

In April 1944, contracts were placed at the Springfield Arsenal for the development of a 1,200 rpm and a 1,500 rpm caliber .50 aircraft machine gun. Some progress was made in the design of the 1,200 rpm gun, designated the T28, and two guns were made and tested. However, at the time of completion of these guns the early standardization of the M3 (T26E3) gun was anticipated, and it was decided to discontinue this project.

**T34**

After the failure of the T28 it was decided to concentrate available personnel at Springfield on the development of the 1,500 rpm gun, which was designated T34. The T34 was to have an entirely new mechanism, operating on a principle suitable for very high-speed firing. Preliminary drawings of this gun were received in August 1945, and after careful study the Springfield Arsenal was requested to supply additional drawings and information to make possible an appraisal of the potentialities of the new mechanism.

**T36**

During the continual development of a high-speed caliber .50 machine gun, a number of important improvements were made which were applicable to the standard M2. In September 1944, it was decided to immediately integrate these test-proven features into the M2 gun. The improved gun, designated as the T36, was designed to accomplish limited but important objectives, compared to the M2 gun. Among these objectives were the reduction of continuing malfunctions; an increase in the cyclic rate of fire by approximately 100 rpm; and to increase belt lift capacity to 30 pounds minimum. Changes in the M2 gun were kept to a minimum to achieve of these objectives.

Four T36 machine guns were given endurance tests of 5,000 rounds each during September 1944 at Aberdeen. These guns were fired from the nose of a P-38 under strictly controlled conditions representative of the actual aircraft installation. Additional T36 guns were submitted to the AAF and the Navy Bureau of Ordnance for evaluation. On 12 October 1944, the Ordnance Committee authorized the procurement of 31,336 T36 guns. This procurement was discontinued after approximately 8,000 guns had been produced because of the unexpected progress made in the development of the T25E3 high-speed gun, which led to its standardization as the M3 earlier than had been thought possible. Following the standardization of the M3 gun, the T36 gun was reclassified as Limited Standard, and redesignated as Gun, Machine, Browning, Caliber .50, Machine, Aircraft, Basic. There was no further procurement of the T36.

**T38**

In June 1945, Ordnance Committee authorized Frigidaire to further develop the M3 with a requirement for a 1,500 rpm caliber .50 machine gun, designated T38. Subsequent to this authorization in July 1945, a contract was placed with the Frigidaire division to provide for a continuation of the development of the M3 (T25E6) gun in an effort to increase its cyclic rate to 1,500 rpm. Limited firing tests were conducted on this gun at cyclic rata of 1,450 to 1,500 rpm, but the development did not progress sufficiently to permit an evaluation of the gun before the war ended.

## Section 2: Summary of the Browning M1/M2/M3 Series

### Gun, Machine, Caliber .50 M1

The experimental Browning T2 caliber .50 machine gun was standardized for cavalry and infantry without modification as the MI. This model never went into production.

### Gun, Machine, Caliber .50 M2

Further development of the Browning system produced the M2 series, which was standardized in 1933. The three principal versions were water-cooled, aircraft, and heavy barrel. The three guns utilized the same basic receivers. The water-cooled gun was for antiaircraft use; the heavy-barrel gun was intended for use by and against armored vehicles, and the aircraft gun with its 36 inch air-cooled barrel was for use in aircraft. Later, several other varieties were standardized, all of which used the same basic receiver. An important characteristic of the M2 series is the ability to convert from one type to another.

**Gun, Machine, Caliber .50 M2A1**

In 1944, the procurement of 31,336 of the T36 guns was authorized. This procurement was discontinued after approximately 8,000 guns had been produced because of the unexpected progress made in the development of the T25E3 high-speed gun, which led to its standardization as the M3 earlier than had been thought possible. Following the standardization of the M3 gun, the T36 gun was reclassified as limited standard, and redesignated Gun, Machine, Browning, Caliber .50, M2A1, Aircraft, Basic.

**Gun, Machine, Caliber .50 M2E1**

The records do not indicate the M history of the M2E1.

**Gun, Machine, Caliber .50 M3**

In 1945 the caliber .50 Browning T25E3 was standardized as the M3. There were slight variations in guns of early and later manufacture. The M3 gun was based upon the caliber .50 aircraft machine gun M2 and had essentially the same exterior dimensions, except for the increased diameter of the back plate buffer and the length added by the recoil booster. It fired at a cyclic rate of approximately 1,200 rpm with standard ammunition and links. Nearly all parts of the M3 gun differed in detail from those of the M2, having been improved in design and metallurgy.

# 6

# The Browning .50 Caliber M2 Aircraft Machine Gun

## Section 1: General Background

The .50 caliber machine gun was designed by Browning after World War I to fire powerful high velocity ammunition at a high muzzle velocity, giving it a long effective range, good armor penetration, and outstanding accuracy. However, these qualities came at the cost of a mediocre rate of fire, heavy barrel wear, and a relatively heavy installation weight. Nonetheless, the Browning 50 caliber machine gun was extremely reliable, and its standardization allowed the production of over 1.8 million of the many different versions for all U.S. military forces both on the ground and in the air during World War II.

The U.S. avoided the use of a mixture of different guns on a single aircraft, as was seen on some *Luftwaffe* fighter aircraft that were armed with two, or even three different aircraft guns. Mixing gun types resulted in the concomitant ammunition, servicing, and sighting and different trajectory problems. The U.S. did not continue to develop the Browning's excellent short-recoil mechanism into larger caliber guns as did the Japanese, who used the Browning mechanism as the basis for its development of cannon caliber guns, such as their Army Ho-103 and Ho-5.

Larger caliber guns were not required by the U.S. during World War II, as the .50 caliber machine gun continued to be found satisfactory against smaller targets, such as fighters and medium bombers, which were the nucleus of the dwindling Axis air forces. Instead of larger guns the U.S. concentrated on increasing the muzzle velocity and rate of fire of the .50 caliber gun; installing them in large enough numbers, six or eight. Most American fighters were large enough and powerful enough to accommodate the installation of this many guns, and some American prototypes carried as many as ten guns. (The heavy aircraft machine gun versus the aircraft cannon controversy will be discussed at length later.)

During 1940 the M2 was modified to increase its rate of fire from 600 rpm to 750-850 rpm by using a lighter barrel and double recoil springs. In this form the gun's designation remained the M2. Despite this increase in the rate of fire the M2 continued to be only ordinary when compared to the average rate for heavy machine guns, which varied from 700 to 1,050 rpm (contemporary 20mm cannons had rates of fire between 400 and 850 rpm). The M3, which entered service during the last months of the war, had a rate of fire of 1,200 rpm.

## Section 2: The M2 Description

### General

The .50 caliber Browning aircraft machine gun weighed 64.5 pounds and was 57 inches long (barrel 36 inches). Its rate of automatic fire averaged 700 to 800 rounds per minute (12-15 rounds per second) depending on attachments, such as a flash suppresser or muzzle booster. Its muzzle velocity was 2,700 to 2,850 feet per second (1,900mph). Its extreme range (extent of forward travel) was 20,000 to 21,500 feet, and its effective range (bullet able to penetrate airframe or engine to cause damage) was 3,400 to 3,500 feet. All of these performance figures varied in the field due to internal (e.g. age and condition of the mechanism and barrel, the age and type of the ammunition, and type of feed) and external (e.g. temperature, air density) conditions.

The Browning was an automatic, recoil operated, air-cooled, belt fed machine gun. It was an automatic weapon, as after the first cartridge was loaded and the gun was cocked (an operation called charging), it continued firing as long as the trigger was held down. A semi-automatic weapon, such as the .45 caliber pistol, fired only one shot each time the trigger was

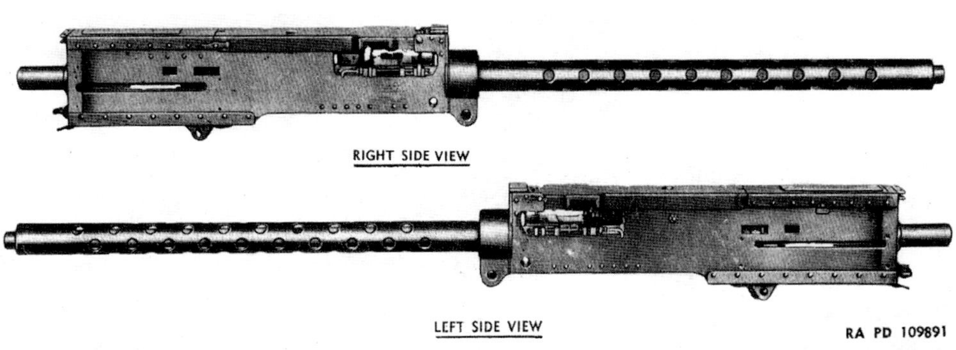


BROWNING MACHINE GUN, CAL. .50, AN-M2, AIRCRAFT, BASIC

# MACHINE GUN CALIBER .50, M2, AIRCRAFT BASIC

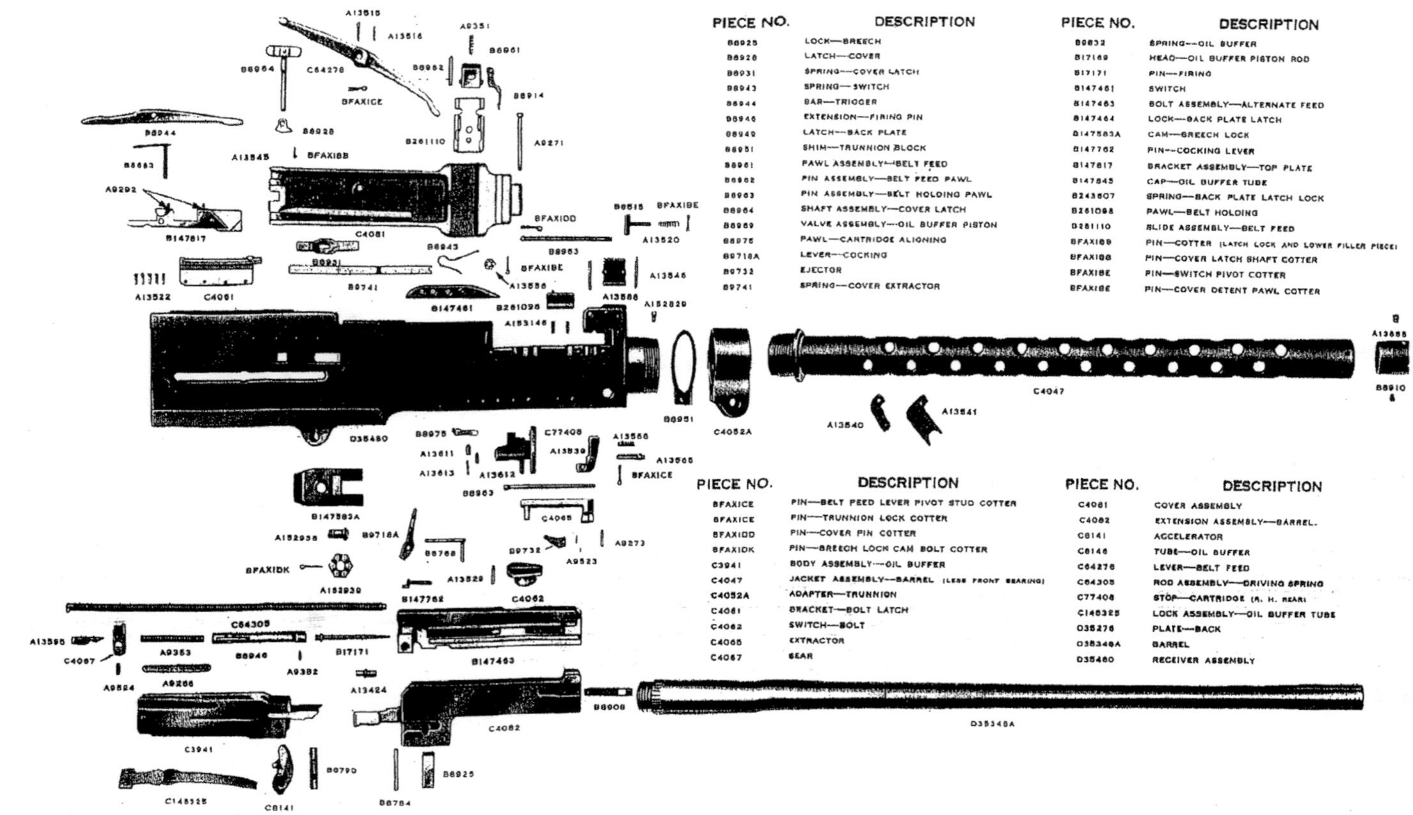

| PIECE NO. | DESCRIPTION |
|---|---|
| B8925 | LOCK—BREECH |
| B8928 | LATCH—COVER |
| B8931 | SPRING—COVER LATCH |
| B8943 | SPRING—SWITCH |
| B8944 | BAR—TRIGGER |
| B8946 | EXTENSION—FIRING PIN |
| B8949 | LATCH—BACK PLATE |
| B8951 | SHIM—TRUNNION BLOCK |
| B8961 | PAWL ASSEMBLY—BELT FEED |
| B8962 | PIN ASSEMBLY—BELT FEED PAWL |
| B8963 | PIN ASSEMBLY—BELT HOLDING PAWL |
| B8964 | SHAFT ASSEMBLY—COVER LATCH |
| B8969 | VALVE ASSEMBLY—OIL BUFFER PISTON |
| B8975 | PAWL—CARTRIDGE ALIGNING |
| B9718A | LEVER—COCKING |
| B9732 | EJECTOR |
| B9741 | SPRING—COVER EXTRACTOR |
| B9832 | SPRING—OIL BUFFER |
| B17169 | HEAD—OIL BUFFER PISTON ROD |
| B17171 | PIN—FIRING |
| B147461 | SWITCH |
| B147463 | BOLT ASSEMBLY—ALTERNATE FEED |
| B147464 | LOCK—BACK PLATE LATCH |
| B147583A | CAM—BREECH LOCK |
| B147762 | PIN—COCKING LEVER |
| B147817 | BRACKET ASSEMBLY—TOP PLATE |
| B147845 | CAP—OIL BUFFER TUBE |
| B243607 | SPRING—BACK PLATE LATCH LOCK |
| B261098 | PAWL—BELT HOLDING |
| B261110 | SLIDE ASSEMBLY—BELT FEED |
| BFAXIBB | PIN—COTTER (LATCH LOCK AND LOWER FILLER PIECE) |
| BFAXIBG | PIN—COVER LATCH SHAFT COTTER |
| BFAXIBE | PIN—SWITCH PIVOT COTTER |
| BFAXIBE | PIN—COVER DETENT PAWL COTTER |

| PIECE NO. | DESCRIPTION |
|---|---|
| BFAXICE | PIN—BELT FEED LEVER PIVOT STUD COTTER |
| BFAXICE | PIN—TRUNNION LOCK COTTER |
| BFAXIDD | PIN—COVER PIN COTTER |
| BFAXIDK | PIN—BREECH LOCK CAM BOLT COTTER |
| C3941 | BODY ASSEMBLY—OIL BUFFER |
| C4047 | JACKET ASSEMBLY—BARREL (LESS FRONT BEARING) |
| C4052A | ADAPTER—TRUNNION |
| C4061 | BRACKET—BOLT LATCH |
| C4062 | SWITCH—BOLT |
| C4065 | EXTRACTOR |
| C4067 | SEAR |
| C4081 | COVER ASSEMBLY |
| C4082 | EXTENSION ASSEMBLY—BARREL. |
| C8141 | ACCELERATOR |
| C8146 | TUBE—OIL BUFFER |
| C64276 | LEVER—BELT FEED |
| C64305 | ROD ASSEMBLY—DRIVING SPRING |
| C77408 | STOP—CARTRIDGE (R. H. REAR) |
| C146325 | LOCK ASSEMBLY—OIL BUFFER TUBE |
| D35276 | PLATE—BACK |
| D35346A | BARREL |
| D35460 | RECEIVER ASSEMBLY |

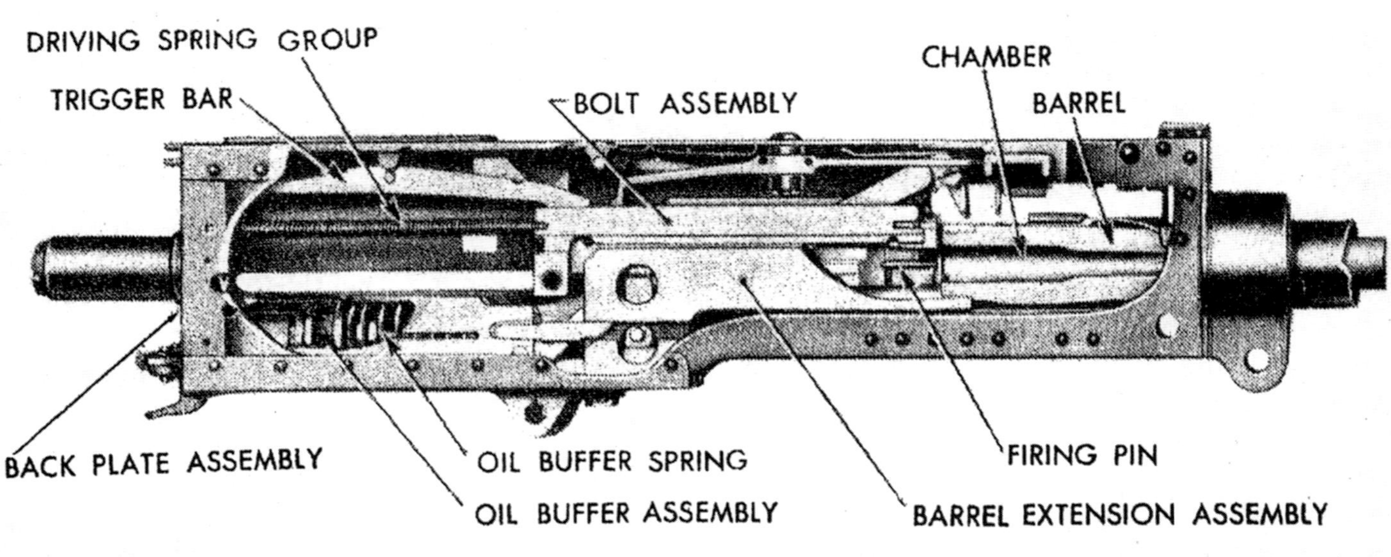


RA PD 109909

*Figure 43. Receiver section of gun—cutaway view.*

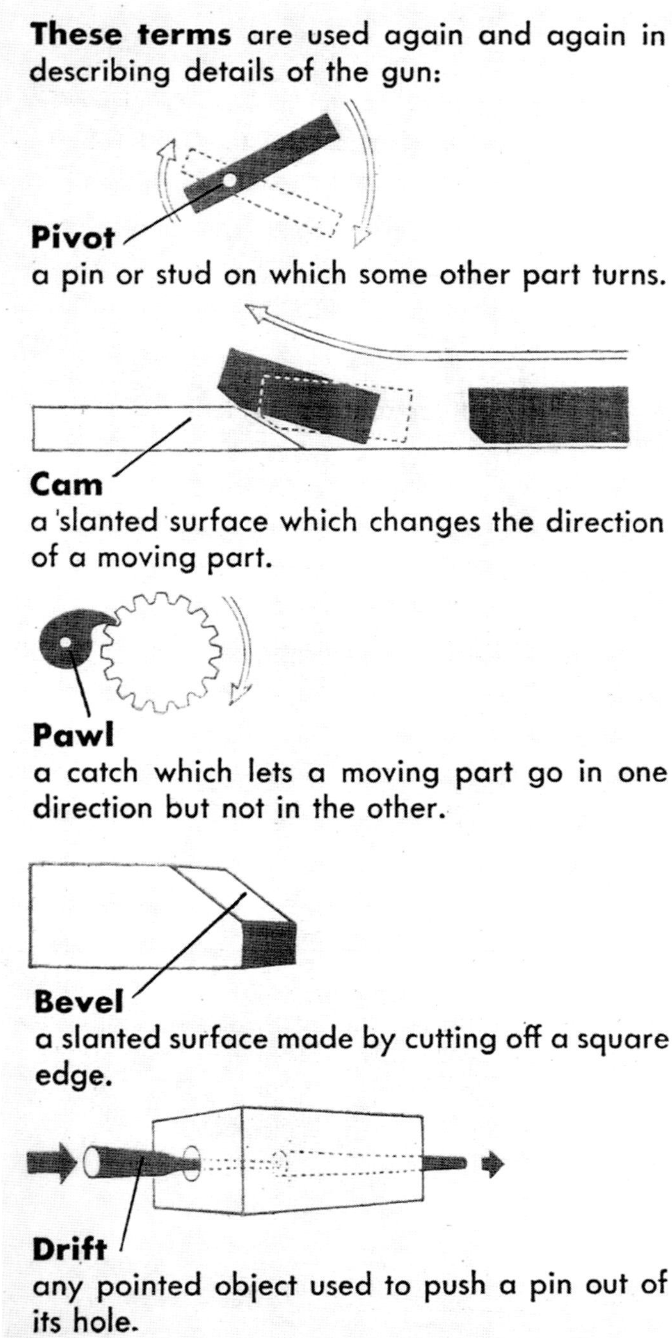


BASIC TERMS

squeezed. The BMG was air-cooled, with air circulating through holes in the barrel jacket keeping the barrel from heating up too quickly. Compared to firing on the ground, this method was effective because the air at high altitudes was very cold and the gun protruded into the cold slipstream. On the ground, air-cooled guns heated up more rapidly, and long bursts could not be fired without damaging the barrel, so machine guns designed for ground use were water-cooled, or had a heavy barrel that could tolerate more heat. The aerial .50 caliber machine gun was mounted as a flexible or fixed gun. As a free or flexible gun, the gunner could swing it from side to side or up and down to fire in any direction. In the fixed configuration the guns were immovable, with the whole plane needing to be turned to aim the guns.

**Manufacturer and Serial Numbers** (USAAF)

Though the .50 caliber bullet lacked the punch of a 20mm or 75mm cannon shell, the concentrated firepower from six or eight machine guns had a devastating effect. There were four basic types of .50 caliber ammunition: armor piercing (distinguished by a painted black tip), tracer (red tip), incendiary (blue), and armor piercing incendiary (silver). The bullet weighed about 1.6 ounces and was about 5.5 inches long (.50 caliber ammunition will be discussed in detail later).

**Identification: Serial Numbers and Manufacturer**

The serial number, manufacturer, and patent numbers were stamped on the right side (looking from the rear) of the receiver:

No.123456 GVT. INSPT.
Browning Machine Gun
US CAL. .50 Model 19XX
MAN'FD BY AC SPARK PLUG DIV.
GENERAL MOTORS CORP.
FLINT, MICH. USA
PATENT NOS.111111-1, 222222-2, 333333-3

The serial number was also stamped on the receiver top plate.

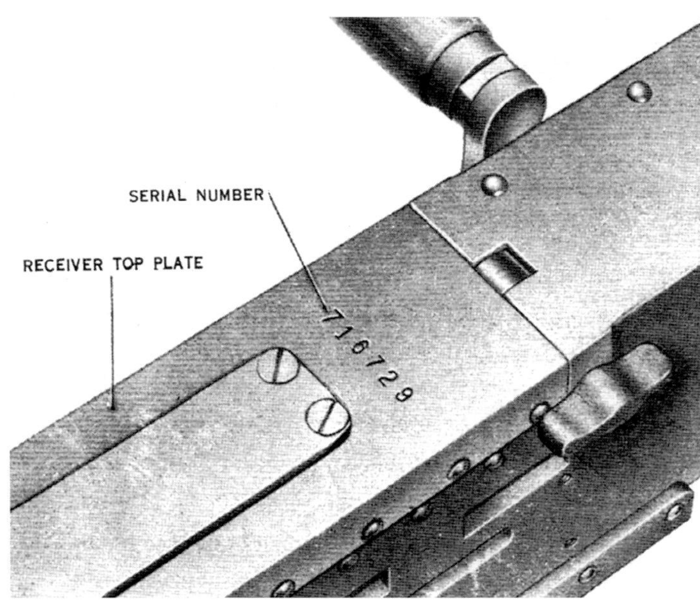


**Serial Number on Receiver** (USAAF)

**Definitions and Terms**

Along the inside of the barrel (the bore) were twisting cut out spaces called grooves, while the wide ridges between the grooves were called the lands. The lands and grooves could vary in number, depth, shape, direction of twist (right or left), and twist rate (turns per unit barrel length). The grooves and lands together were called the rifling, which caused the bullet to spin in flight, improving its stability much like a football during a forward pass. Without rifling the bullet would travel like a wobbly football pass, and the gun would lose most of its accuracy along with range. In general rifling is a constant rate of twist (spiral) down the barrel; usually measured by the length of travel required to produce a single spin.

The caliber of a gun was the distance across the inside of the barrel, measured from land to land. The Browning machine gun was a caliber .50 because the barrel was 50/100ths of an inch wide, or half an inch. The bullet or projectile was just minutely wider than 1/2 inch in order to create a tight seal that prevented any propelling gases from escaping when the gun was fired, and also the added width pressed the bullet into the grooves.

The cartridges, called rounds, were hooked together with metal links to form a long ammunition belt which allowed them to be fed consecutively into the gun. While it was being fired the cartridge was held in an enlarged

## THE SEVEN GROUPS

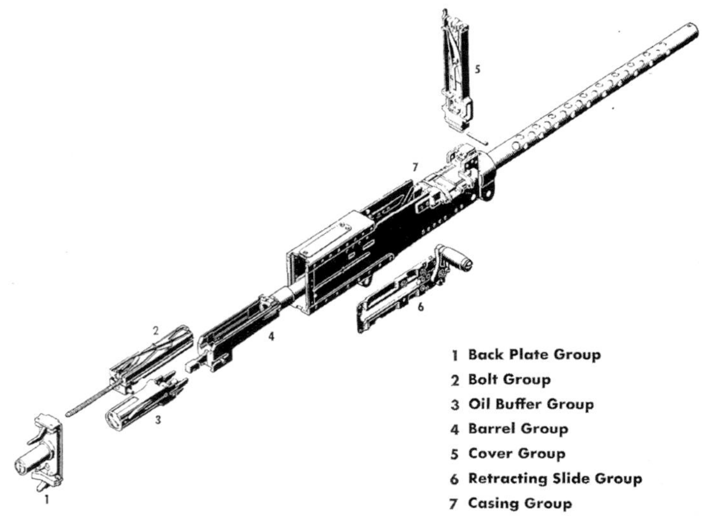

1 Back Plate Group
2 Bolt Group
3 Oil Buffer Group
4 Barrel Group
5 Cover Group
6 Retracting Slide Group
7 Casing Group

## BACKPLATE GROUP

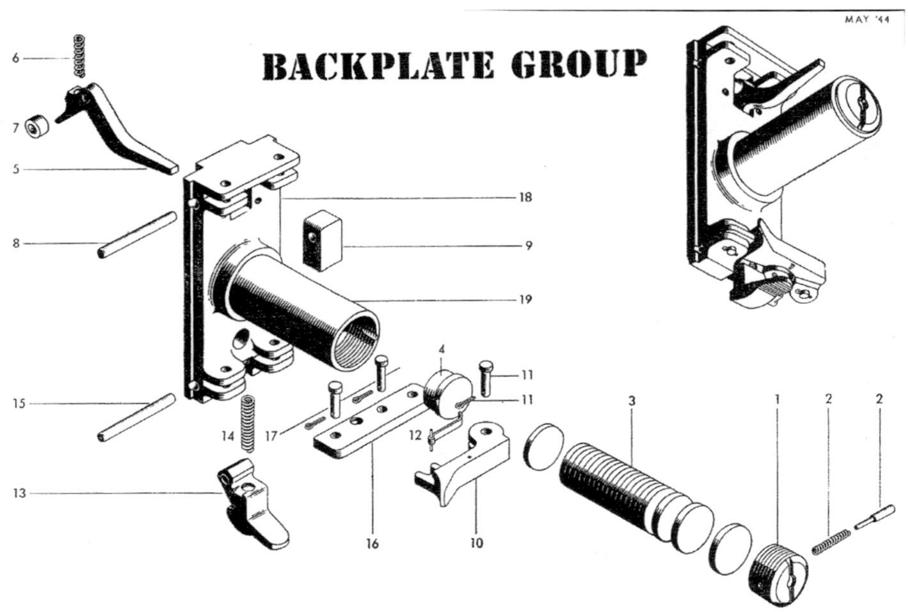


| | Nomenclature | Function |
|---|---|---|
| 1 | BUFFER ADJUSTING SCREW | Adjusts the pressure on the buffer disks. |
| 2 | BUFFER ADJUSTING SCREW PLUNGER AND PLUNGER SPRING | Prevent the buffer adjusting screw from turning freely. |
| 3 | BUFFER DISKS | Absorb the shock of the bolt's recoil. |
| 4 | BUFFER PLATE | Passes the shock of the bolt's recoil on to the buffer disks and prevents battering of the back plate. |
| 5 | TRIGGER | Raises the rear end of the trigger bar, making the front end press down on the sear to release the firing pin and fire the gun. |
| 6 | TRIGGER SPRING | Returns the trigger to position. |
| 7 | SPACER | Keeps the trigger the proper distance from the side. |
| 8 | TRIGGER PIN | Holds the trigger and provides a pivot for it. |
| 9 | BACK PLATE FILLER PIECE | Fills the trigger hole when the trigger is not installed. |
| 10 | LATCH LOCK | Locks the latch. |
| 11 | LATCH LOCK PIN AND COTTER PIN | The pin holds the latch lock and provides a pivot for it; the cotter pin keeps the latch lock pin in place. |
| 12 | LATCH LOCK SPRING AND PIN | The spring, which is held in the latch lock by its pin, pushes against the latch lock to hold it in place. |
| 13 | LATCH | Holds the back plate down. |
| 14 | LATCH SPRING | Pushes against the latch to keep it locked. |
| 15 | LATCH PIN | Holds the latch and provides a pivot for it. |
| 16 | LOWER FILLER PIECE | Provides a mounting for the latch lock. |
| 17 | LOWER FILLER PIECE PINS (TWO) AND COTTER PINS (TWO) | Hold the lower filler piece in position. |
| 18 | BACK PLATE | Encloses the back end of the receiver, and keeps the oil buffer group from moving back. |
| 19 | BUFFER TUBE | Houses the buffer adjusting screw, buffer disks, and buffer plate. |

opening called the chamber at the rear of the barrel. The cartridge case was basically a metal shell with an extracting groove near its base that allowed parts inside the gun to pull the case out of the ammunition belt and then pull it out of the chamber after it had been fired. Inside the case were the primer and the propelling charge. The primer was a small charge of high explosive which would detonate when the gun's firing pin struck it, in turn detonating the propelling charge, which burned out instantaneously and propelled the bullet out the muzzle.

The gases created by the propelling charge created an enormous chamber pressure of 50,000 pounds per square inch inside the cartridge case, about 10,000 pounds of which propelled the bullet forward; some of this force was absorbed by the barrel, and another 10,000 pounds produced a backward kick called the recoil, which ejected the cartridge case and drove some of the gun parts as far back as they could move. After the recoil, these parts rebounded against springs and buffers that started them forward again in the counter recoil. After each shot the empty cartridge case was pushed out of the gun, while the used links were ejected out to one side.

## BOLT GROUP

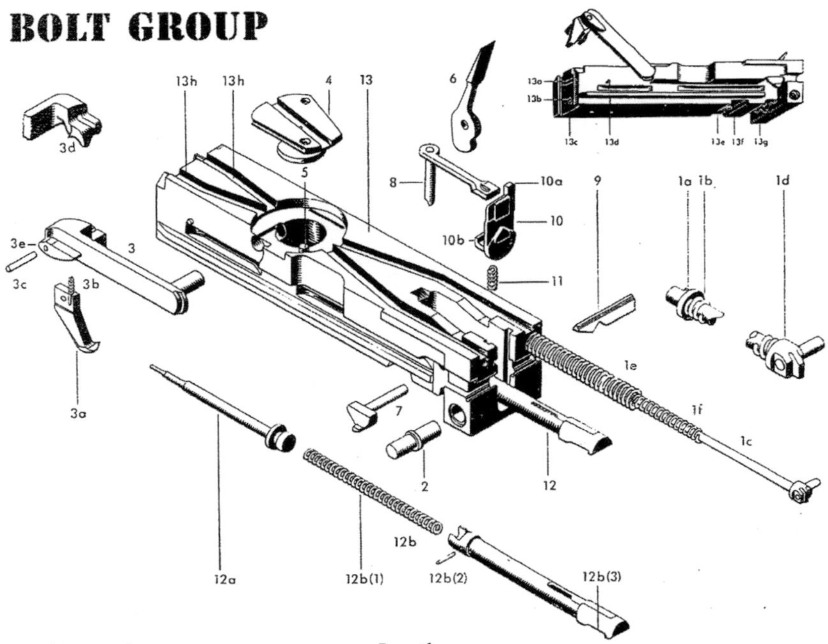


| Nomenclature | Function |
|---|---|
| 1 DRIVING SPRING ROD ASSEMBLY | Smooths out the action of the bolt in automatic fire and helps push it forward on counter recoil; returns the bolt to battery position in hand charging. |
| a DRIVING SPRING ROD COLLAR STOP PIN | |
| b DRIVING SPRING ROD COLLAR | |
| c DRIVING SPRING ROD | |
| d DRIVING SPRING ROD HEAD AND RETAINING PIN | |
| e OUTER DRIVING SPRING | |
| f INNER DRIVING SPRING | |
| 2 BOLT STUD | Connects the bolt to the retracting slide group. |
| 3 EXTRACTOR ASSEMBLY | Pulls the new round from the ammunition belt and helps feed it into the chamber; ejects the last empty case in the ammunition belt. |
| a EJECTOR | Helps support the new round for extraction from the belt and feeding into the chamber; ejects the last spent case in a belt. |
| b EJECTOR SPRING | Holds the ejector against the round. |
| c EJECTOR PIN | Holds the ejector in place and provides a pivot for it. |
| d EXTRACTOR HOOK | Extracts the new round from the belt by hooking into the extracting groove. |
| e EXTRACTOR LUG | Rides under the extractor switch and over the extractor cam to guide the extractor assembly on counter recoil. |
| 4 BOLT SWITCH | Provides a clear track along either the right or left cam groove, depending on the direction of feed. |
| 5 BOLT SWITCH STUD | Keeps the bolt switch from turning. |
| 6 COCKING LEVER | Cocks the firing mechanism; keeps the gun from firing too soon. |
| 7 COCKING LEVER PIN | Holds the cocking lever in place and provides a pivot for it. |
| 8 SEAR STOP ASSEMBLY | The sear stop holds the sear in place. Its pin provides a compression point for the firing pin spring. |
| 9 SEAR SLIDE | Pushes the sear down to release the firing pin when the gun is fired from the side. |
| 10 SEAR | Holds the firing pin back until the trigger is pressed. |
| a SEAR TIP | Rides under the trigger bar to cam down the sear in automatic fire. |
| b SEAR NOTCH | Hooks into the notch on the firing pin extension to hold the firing pin back until the trigger is pressed. |
| 11 SEAR SPRING | Pushes the sear up into place after each round is fired. |
| 12 FIRING PIN ASSEMBLY | |
| a FIRING PIN | Fires the round by hitting the primer. |
| b FIRING PIN EXTENSION ASSEMBLY | |
| (1) FIRING PIN SPRING | Forces the pin forward when the trigger is pressed. |
| (2) FIRING PIN SPRING STOP PIN | Holds the firing pin back until the trigger is pressed. |
| (3) FIRING PIN EXTENSION NOTCH | Hooks onto the sear notch to hold the firing pin back until the trigger is pressed. |
| 13 BOLT BODY | Houses the parts of the bolt group. Its two cam grooves make it possible for ammunition to be fed into either side of the gun. |
| a T-SLOT | Extracts the spent case from the chamber and helps support the new round entering the chamber. |
| b RECOIL PLATE | Provides a shield of harder metal to receive the recoil of the primer. |
| c FIRING PIN PORT | Provides a hole which enables the firing pin to hit the primer. |
| d EXTRACTOR STOP PIN | Stops the downward motion of the extractor assembly. |
| e BREECH LOCK RECESS | Provides a space for the breech lock to enter the bolt to lock it to the barrel extension. |
| f MIDDLE PROJECTION | Turns the accelerator to the rear in hand charging. |
| g LOWER PROJECTION | Works with the accelerator to speed up the bolt on recoil and slow it down on counter recoil. |
| h CAM GROOVES | Guide the belt feed lever (of the cover group) as its lug rides in the grooves. |

**Gun Groups**

When the gun fired, about 150 working parts were set in motion; parts recoiling and counter recoiling, locking and unlocking, compressing and expanding, pivoting, sliding, pushing, pulling, and opening and closing. These parts can be categorized into seven main groups. These groups are presented in the order that they were usually removed from the gun during stripping.

The **back plate group**, at the rear of the receiver, absorbed the force of the bolt's recoil. In flexible mountings a spade grip, trigger, and safety were added.

The **bolt group** was the most dynamic part of the seven groups; shuttling from the battery position to the rear of the gun and back again about 14 times a second, drawing live rounds from the ammunition belt, loading them into the chamber, striking them with the firing pin, pulling the empty cases from the chamber, and ejecting them out the bottom of the gun.

The **oil buffer group** was the brake that stopped the recoiling barrel group. Its main part was a sealed cylinder filled with oil. When the barrel and barrel extension recoiled they drove a piston into the cylinder, forcing the oil through two slots in the side of the piston head. The impact of the barrel and barrel extension was so powerful that all the oil was forced through the slots in a small fraction of a second.

The **barrel group** included the barrel and the barrel extension that screwed onto it. This group also recoiled, but not nearly as far as the bolt group. The barrel was sometimes called the "tube" in early war maintenance manuals.

The **cover group**, which enclosed part of the top of the receiver, was the main mechanism for feeding the ammunition belt into the gun.

The **retracting slide group**, which could be mounted on either side of the receiver, was used to charge the gun for the first shot.

## OIL BUFFER GROUP

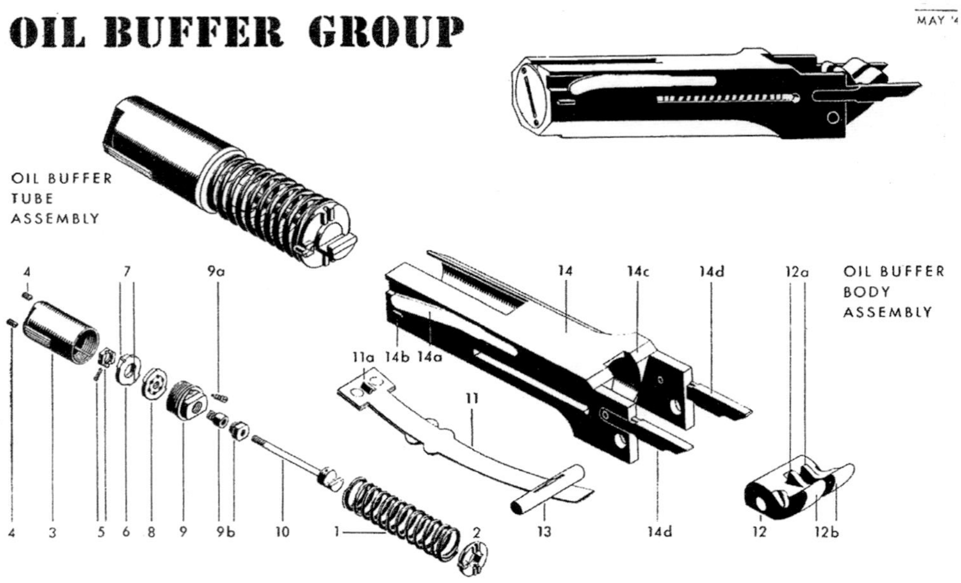


| | Nomenclature | Function |
|---|---|---|
| | **Oil Buffer Tube Assembly** | |
| 1 | OIL BUFFER SPRING | Helps absorb the recoil of the barrel group and push it forward on counter recoil. |
| 2 | OIL BUFFER SPRING GUIDE AND SPRING GUIDE KEY | The spring guide, which is prevented from turning by the spring guide key, holds the oil buffer spring in place. |
| 3 | OIL BUFFER TUBE | Houses the oil buffer parts. |
| 4 | FILLER SCREWS (TWO) | Provide openings for filling the oil buffer tube. |
| 5 | PISTON HEAD NUT AND PIN | Hold the head and valve on the piston rod. |
| 6 | PISTON VALVE | Closes and opens the holes in the piston rod head. |
| 7 | VALVE KEYS (TWO) | Keeps the valve from turning. |
| 8 | PISTON ROD HEAD | Pushes into the oil to absorb the recoil of the barrel group. |
| 9 | TUBE CAP | Closes the front of the oil buffer tube. |
| | a RELIEF VALVE ASSEMBLY | Lets the oil escape if the pressure gets too great. |
| | b PACKING GLAND ASSEMBLY | Prevents oil leakage around the piston rod. |
| 10 | PISTON ROD AND HOOK | Connect the barrel extension shank with the piston rod head. |
| | **Oil Buffer Body Assembly** | |
| 11 | OIL BUFFER TUBE LOCK<br>a PROTRUSION | The front end keeps the accelerator tips from bouncing up. The protrusion keeps the oil buffer tube from turning freely. |
| 12 | ACCELERATOR<br>a ACCELERATOR LOCKING LUGS<br>b ACCELERATOR TIPS | Serves as an energy transmitter, a locking device, and a timing device. Its functions are explained fully in the discussion of cycle of operations (page G-52). |
| 13 | ACCELERATOR PIN | Holds the accelerator and provides a pivot for it. |
| 14 | OIL BUFFER BODY | Houses all parts of the oil buffer group. |
| | a OIL BUFFER BODY SPRING LOCK | Holds the oil buffer group in place when the back plate is off. |
| | b OIL BUFFER BODY GUIDES (TWO) | Fit into slots in the receiver to help hold the oil buffer group in its place. |
| | c SHOULDERS | Prevent the tips of the accelerator from turning too far down. |
| | d BREECH LOCK DEPRESSORS (TWO) | Forces the breech lock down by camming down the breech lock pin. |

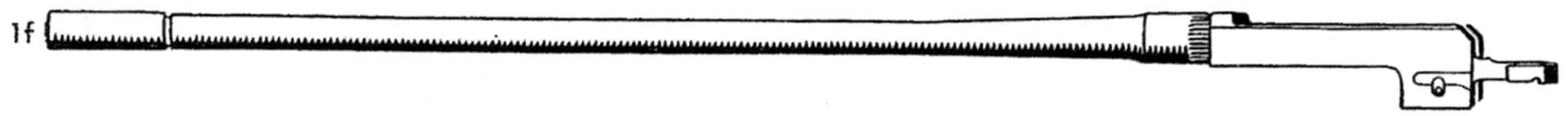


# BARREL GROUP

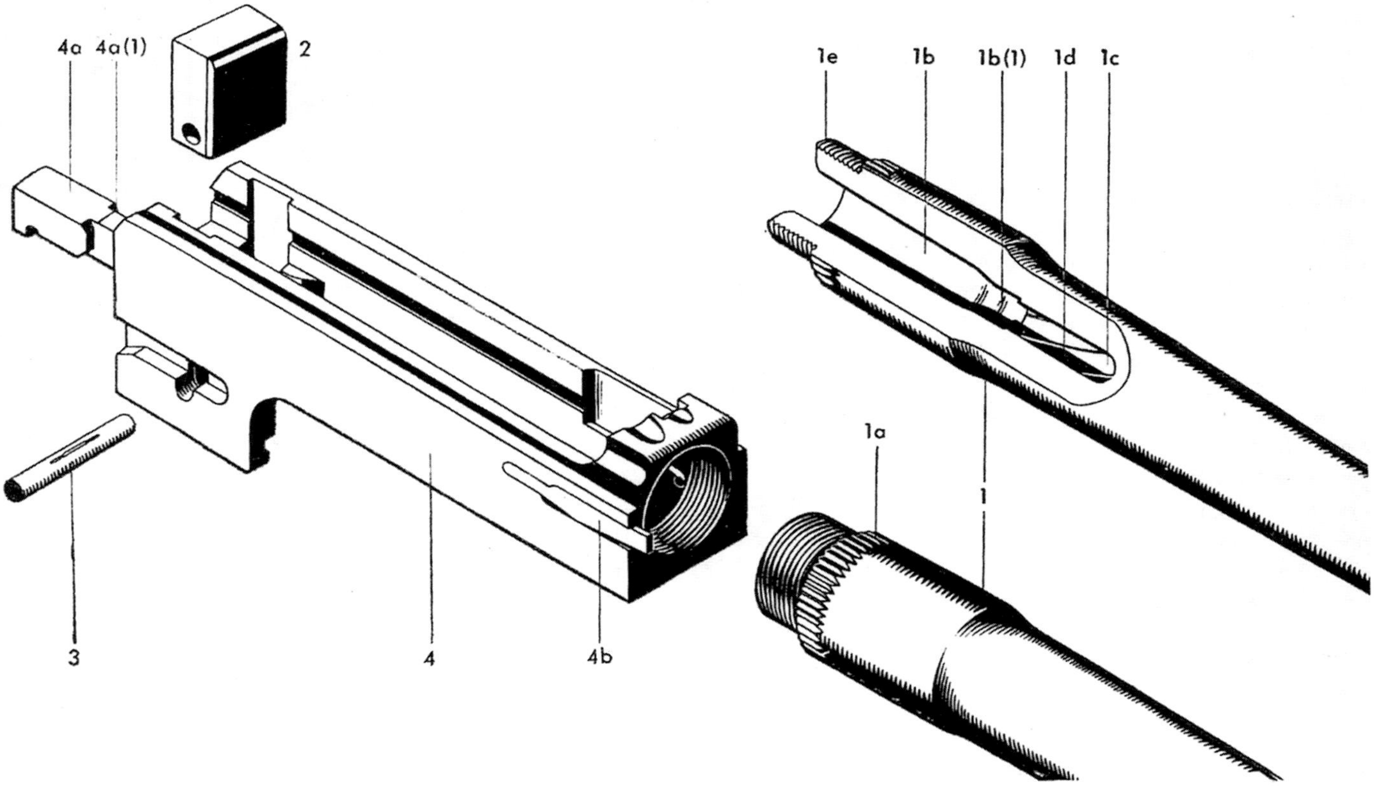


| Nomenclature | Function |
|---|---|
| 1 BARREL | Gives the bullet direction and spin. |
| a BARREL LOCKING NOTCHES | Fit against the barrel locking spring to keep the barrel from turning freely. |
| b CHAMBER | Houses the round while it is being fired. |
| (1) SHOULDERS OF CHAMBER | Support the front end of the cartridge case. |
| c LANDS (EIGHT) } RIFLING<br>d GROOVES (EIGHT) } | Give the projectile its spin. |
| e BREECH END OF BARREL | |
| f MUZZLE END OF BARREL | |
| 2 BREECH LOCK | Locks the bolt to the barrel extension. |
| 3 BREECH LOCK PIN | Holds the breech lock in the barrel extension; hits the depressors on the oil buffer body to force the breech lock down during recoil. |
| 4 BARREL EXTENSION | Serves as a connection between the bolt, barrel, oil buffer, and receiver. |
| a BARREL EXTENSION SHANK AND HOOK | Connect the barrel extension to the oil buffer tube assembly. |
| (1) SHANK SHOULDERS | Provide a surface for the accelerator to lock the barrel extension to the oil buffer body. |
| b BARREL LOCKING SPRING | Fits into the barrel locking notches to keep the barrel from turning freely. |

# COVER GROUP

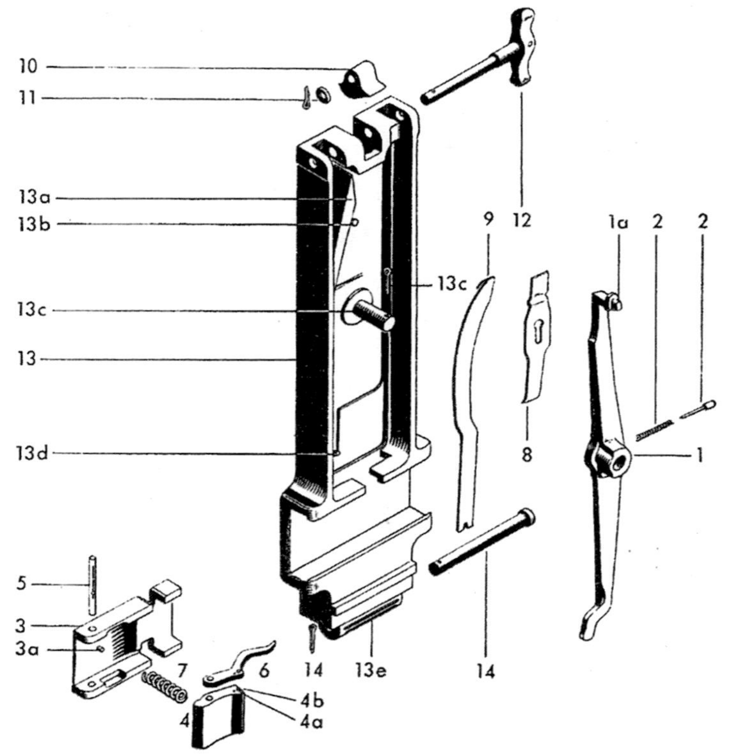


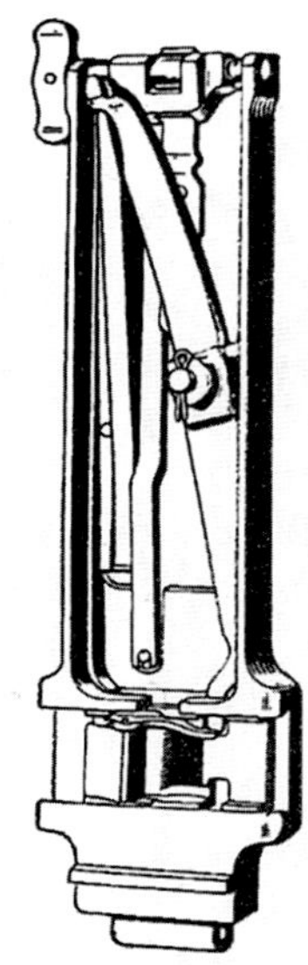

| Nomenclature | Function |
|---|---|
| 1 BELT FEED LEVER | Pivots from side to side to operate the feeding mechanism. |
| a BELT FEED LEVER LUG | Rides in the bolt's cam grooves to move the lever from side to side. |
| 2 BELT FEED LEVER PLUNGER AND PLUNGER SPRING | Hold the belt feed lever in position when the cover is raised. |
| 3 BELT FEED SLIDE | Moves from side to side to feed the ammunition belt into the gun. |
| a BELT FEED PAWL SPRING STUD | Helps hold the pawl spring in place. |
| 4 BELT FEED PAWL | Pushes the new round into the feedway. |
| a PAWL ARM LOCATING PIN<br>b PAWL ARM PIN | Hold the pawl arm in place. |
| 5 BELT FEED PAWL PIN | Holds the belt feed pawl and provides a pivot for it. |
| 6 BELT FEED PAWL ARM | Prevents double feeding. |
| 7 BELT FEED PAWL SPRING | Pushes the belt feed pawl down behind the new round. |
| 8 COVER LATCH SPRING | Presses against the cover latch to keep it locked. |
| 9 COVER EXTRACTOR SPRING | Holds the extractor assembly down while it is pulling a new round from the belt; cushions the shock when the extractor assembly is cammed up at the end of the counter recoil stroke. |
| 10 COVER LATCH | Holds the cover down. |
| 11 COTTER PIN AND WASHER | Hold the cover latch shaft in the cover. |
| 12 COVER LATCH SHAFT AND LEVER | The shaft holds the cover latch. The lever serves as a handle to turn the shaft and unlock the latch. |
| 13 COVER | Houses the parts of the cover group. |
| a COVER EXTRACTOR CAM | Cams down the extractor assembly on recoil. |
| b COVER LATCH SPRING STUD | Holds the cover latch spring in place. |
| c BELT FEED LEVER PIVOT STUD AND COTTER PIN | The stud serves as a pivot for the belt feed lever. The cotter pin holds the lever on the stud when the cover is closed. |
| d COVER EXTRACTOR SPRING STUD | Helps hold the cover extractor spring in place. |
| e DETENTS | Grooves that work with the detent pawl (on the receiver) to hold the cover in any one of three positions when it is raised. |
| 14 COVER PIN AND COTTER PIN | Fasten the cover to the receiver. |

42
'44

# RETRACTING SLIDE GROUP

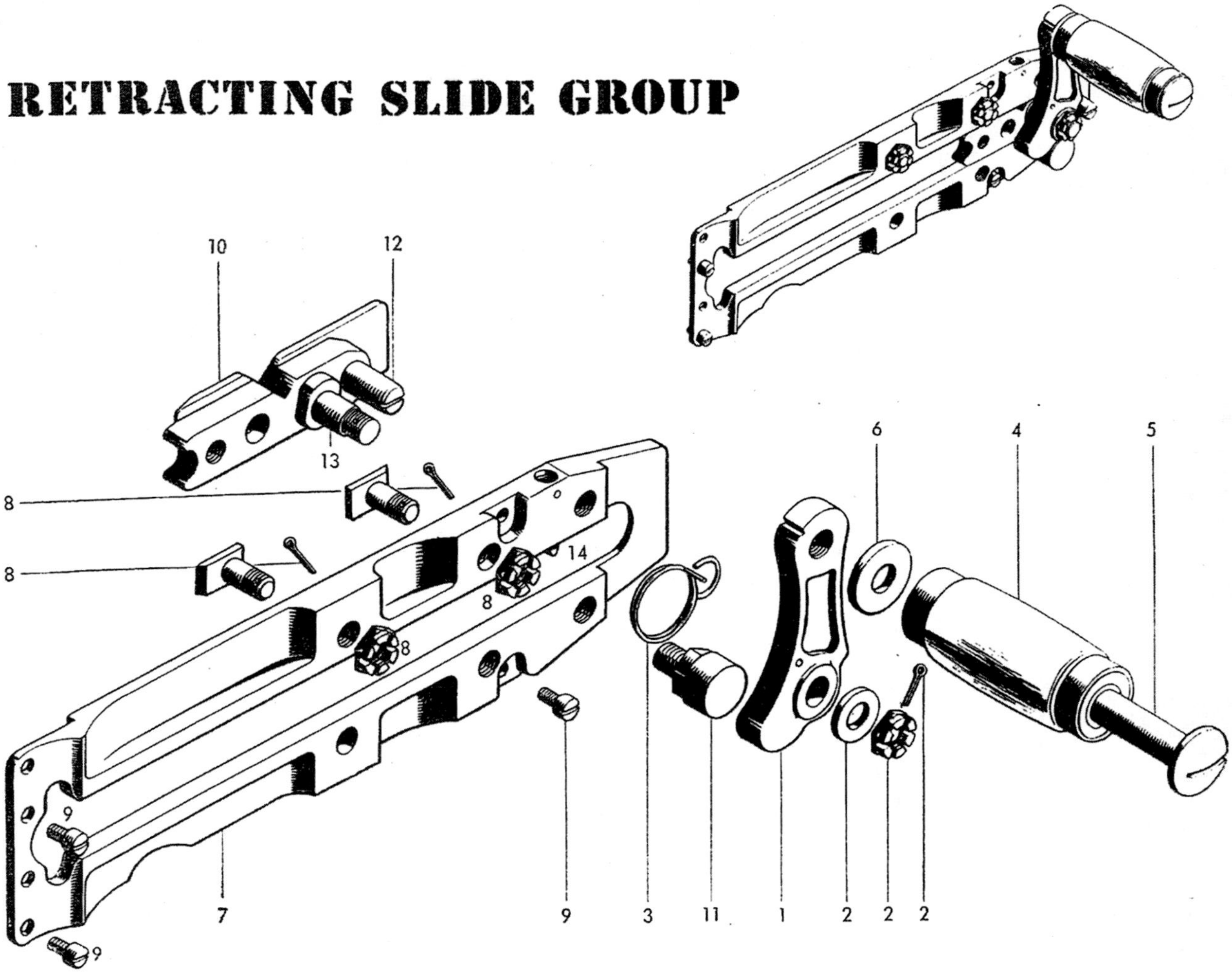


| Nomenclature | Function |
|---|---|
| 1 LEVER | Pulls back the retracting slide in hand charging. |
| 2 LEVER STUD NUT, WASHER, AND COTTER PIN | Hold the lever on the lever stud. |
| 3 LEVER SPRING | Keeps the lever forward when not in use. |
| 4 GRIP OR CHARGING HANDLE | Is pulled back to hand charge the gun. |
| 5 GRIP BOLT | Fastens the grip to the lever. |
| 6 GRIP WASHER | Prevents binding between grip and lever. |
| 7 BRACKET | Holds the retracting slide and provides a slot in which the slide moves back and forth. |
| 8 BRACKET BOLTS, NUTS, AND COTTER PINS (TWO OF EACH) | Help fasten the bracket to the receiver. |
| 9 BRACKET SCREWS (THREE) | Help fasten the bracket to the receiver. |
| 10 RETRACTING SLIDE | Works against the bolt stud to move the bolt back in hand charging. |
| 11 LEVERAGE STUD | Supports the bottom end of the lever, making it easier to pull back. |
| 12 LEVER STOP | Stops the forward movement of the lever. |
| 13 LEVER STUD | Fastens the retracting slide lever to the slide and provides a pivot for the lever. |
| 14 PLUNGER AND PLUNGER SPRING | Keep the retracting slide forward when not in use. |

The **casing group** enclosed all the parts of the gun. It included the receiver, which was a rectangular steel box that contained the working mechanism and the barrel jacket that supported and protected the barrel.

**Barrel Manufacture**

The metal for barrel manufacture was a high quality steel that had no voids, hard or soft spots, no carbide crystals, nodules, or other imbedded impurities. The steel needed to have strength, durability, and be easily cut and shaped. The steel was produced in long bars or rods—usually12 to 20 feet long—and sent to the barrel manufacturer for processing.

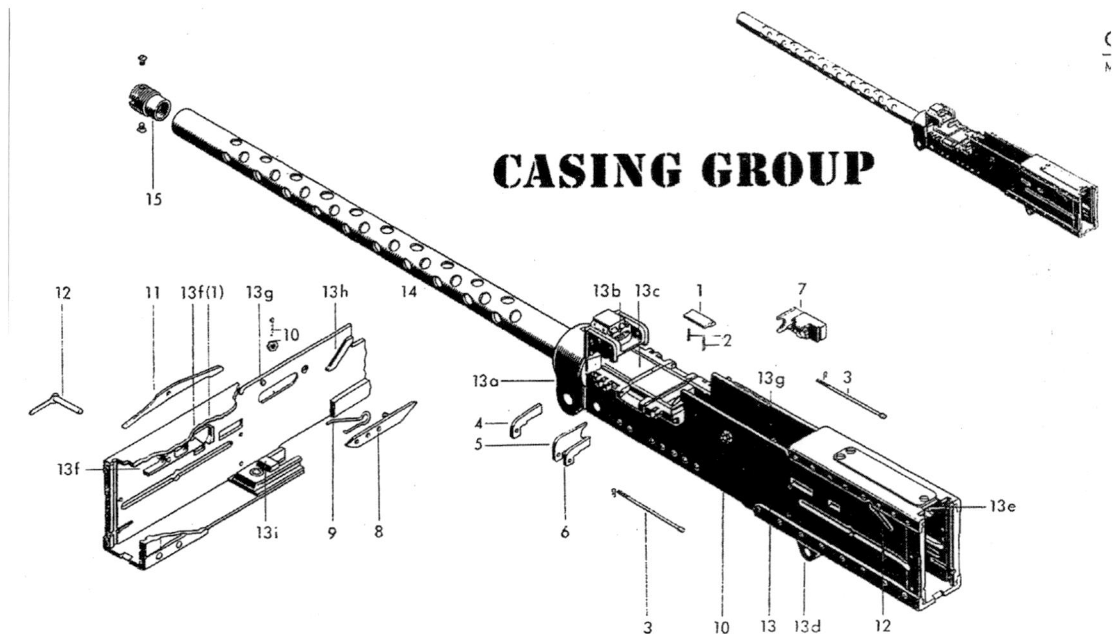


| Nomenclature | Function |
|---|---|
| 1 BELT HOLDING PAWL | Holds the ammunition belt in the feedway. |
| 2 BELT HOLDING PAWL SPRINGS (two) | Force the belt holding pawl up behind the next round. |
| 3 BELT HOLDING PAWL PINS (two) | Hold the belt holding pawl and the cartridge stops. |
| 4 FRONT CARTRIDGE STOP | Holds the front of the cartridge in the correct position. |
| 5 LINK STRIPPER | Strips the links off the cartridge case. |
| 6 REAR CARTRIDGE STOP | Holds the rear of the cartridge in the correct position. |
| 7 RIGHT-HAND REAR CARTRIDGE STOP ASSEMBLY | Serves as a combination rear cartridge stop, link stripper, and short round eliminator when the gun feeds from the left. |
| 8 EXTRACTOR SWITCH AND SWITCH PIVOT | The switch cams the extractor assembly down at the beginning of counter recoil to aline the new round with the chamber. |
| 9 EXTRACTOR SWITCH SPRING | Returns the switch to its original position. |
| 10 EXTRACTOR SWITCH PIVOT NUT AND COTTER PIN | Fasten the extractor switch to the receiver. |
| 11 TRIGGER BAR | Pushes down the sear when the trigger is pressed. |
| 12 TRIGGER BAR PIN | Holds the trigger bar and provides a pivot for it. |
| 13 RECEIVER | Houses the working parts of the gun. |
| a TRUNNION ADAPTER | Serves as a front mounting for the gun. |
| b DETENT PAWL | Holds the cover up by pushing into the detents in the cover. |
| c TRUNNION BLOCK | Provides a bearing for the breech end of the barrel; forms the bottom of the feedway; serves as a spacer for the sideplates. |
| d REAR MOUNTING HOLES | Serve as the rear mounting for the gun. |
| e REAR TRIGGER BAR STOP | Keeps the rear end of the trigger bar from going so high that the front end rides the top of the bolt. |
| f TOP PLATE BRACKET | Holds the trigger bar. |
| (1) FRONT AND REAR COCKING LEVER CAMS (OR "V-SLOT") | Cam the cocking lever backward and forward. |
| g BOLT STOP | Provides a means of locking the bolt to the rear. |
| h EXTRACTOR CAM | Cams the extractor assembly up on the last part of counter recoil. |
| i BREECH LOCK CAM | Cams the breech lock up on counter recoil; prevents forward movement of the oil buffer body; holds the barrel extension down. |
| 14 BARREL JACKET | Houses the barrel and holds the front barrel bearing. Its holes insure uniform cooling of the barrel. |
| 15 FRONT BARREL BEARING | Supports the front end of the barrel and prevents whip. In firing, the barrel slides through this bearing and the trunnion block. |

Barrel bore drilling at the Rock Island Arsenal. (Smithsonian)

The most difficult procedure in barrel manufacture was drilling the long, straight continuous hole through very hard steel rod. The prospective barrel was placed in a support that was spun at high rpms (2,000-6,000). A stationary tungsten carbide drill bit was carefully and very accurately mounted on a rod, and was moved into the spinning barrel rod at about an inch per minute. The drill bit had a cutting edge on only one side, so that cutting oil could be forced at high pressure (1,000 to 1,600 psi) into the newly drilled hole (bore) to cool, lubricate, and flush the area. The oil passed the opposite side of the drill bit's single cutting edge and flowed back to flush the chips ("swarf") back out the hole being drilled. Once the hole had been drilled it was not as smooth as required, and its final bore dimension (caliber) needed to be attained. The hollowed barrel was kept stationary while a hollow reamer mounted on a long hollow shaft rotated at about 500 rpms. The barrel was moved into the spinning reamer, which entered the bore, and cutting oil was pumped at 200 psi to cool, lubricate, and flush.

**Rifling**

The most important procedure in barrel manufacture was rifling, which was the placement of spiraled grooves inside the length of the bore of the barrel. The .30 caliber barrel consisted of four grooves .004 inches deep and 0.171 inches wide bored from a spiral of one turn in 10 inches. The .50 caliber barrel consisted of eight grooves spiraling one turn in 15 inches.

The most important procedure in barrel manufacture was rifling which was the placement of spiraled grooves inside the length of the bore of the barrel using a hook-shaped cutting tool which was placed into a head and drawn inside the bore at a specified rate of twist to slowly cut one groove at a time. (Smithsonian)

In the late 1930s the "Hook Tool" or "Cut Rifling" method was used, in which the hook-shaped cutting tool was placed into a head and drawn inside the bore at a specified rate of twist to slowly cut one groove at a time. The barrel was indexed at the end of each insertion to measure the depth of the rifling grooves and then reinserted until the desired depth of the groves was reached. Once the proper depth was reached the barrel was rotated (indexed) to the position of the next groove. The procedure took about 20 minutes for each barrel and required a skilled laborer. This method was used to manufacture the famous two groove Springfield rifle barrel and was used until the late 1930s.

The Hook Tool method was too slow, turning out only 50 to 75 rifled barrels per day in the hands of a skilled operator. In late 1938 William Baumbeck, Chief Superintendent of the Rock Island Arsenal, and the Illinois Tool Works began a study on developing a long toothed broach that was inserted into a barrel that was held in a special mount. Three broaches were used: a roughing broach, a finishing broach each with 18 teeth, and a barrel burnishing broach. The broaches held in a special fixture were inserted inside the bore and turned while being bathed in cutting oil. The broach had the advantage of being able to cut multiple grooves during a single pass. The broach was pulled through the bore at a slow, constant feed, and turned as it was inserted to give the required twist rate. The first barrels were test-rifled in September 1940 at Rock Island on 1,000 .30 caliber machine gun barrels. Of the first 824 completed barrels only 16 were rejected, and the average number produced per hour was 25 (vs. three by the Hook Tool Method) by a quickly-trained operator. In May 1942 the Hook Tool Method was discontinued entirely, and by January 1943 the hourly average for the broached tool method was 35 barrels; the life of the broaches was increased to 2,500 passes. The cost per barrel was \$0.20 vs. \$0.27 for the Hook Tool, which was a substantial savings, when considering that Rock Island produced 715,000 barrels during the war.

During the war the fast and economical "Button" rifling method was developed and is the most common rifling method in use today. The carbide football-shaped button was extremely hard and had a highly polished negative of the rifling pattern on its surface. During the rifling procedure the bore first had to be lubricated, and the button attached to a rod was pulled through the bore; the raised rifling pattern on its surface impressed itself onto the softer surface inside the barrel, creating grooves in a cold forming process. There were two buttons: the simple button and the combination button. The simple button was fast (a minute per barrel) and very inexpensive, and was used first, but left burrs at the edge of the lands which had to be removed in another procedure. A combination button was developed that consisted of a rifling and finishing button that pressed in the lands and smoothed their edges in one pass. Since the passing of the oversized button through a smaller hole caused great stress in the barrel, it was necessary to stress relieve the barrels after the rifling procedure. Stress relieving consisted of baking the barrels at 600°C with a slow, controlled cool down process requiring 12 to 24 hours depending on the type of steel.

**Barrel Jacket**

The barrel jacket was perforated to allow cooling, and was stationary to prevent anything from impeding or rubbing against the barrel, which moved during firing. It was locked in place by screwing the front barrel bearing into the rear of the jacket and tightening a small set screw, then screwing this unit into the receiver and then tightening a small set screw.

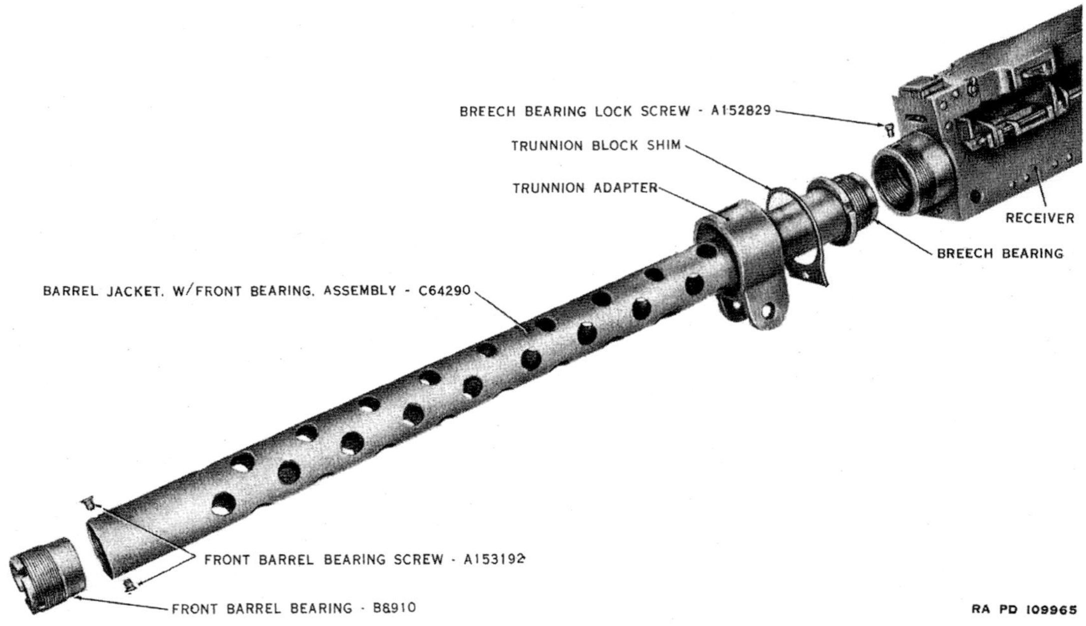


**Barrel Jacket Group**

Attaching the jacket to the receiver at the Frigidaire factory (Smithsonian)

**Barrel Liners and Plating**

Barrel wear, called "erosion," continued to be a serious problem throughout the war, and gunners and fighter pilots were directed to fire short bursts, leaving intervals to allow for cooling. From initial cold firing 75 rounds could be fired without barrel damage, but then the firing bursts were to be restricted to 25 rounds, so the rifling in the barrel would not be worn out. There were several causes of barrel erosion: softening of the bore surface by the heat absorbed by the gases produced by the rapidly burning gunpowder of the cartridge; the chemical reaction on the steel barrel caused by the powder gases; and the expansion of the barrel caused by temperature and pressure.

In 1942 the Ordnance Department engaged several companies and universities to investigate solutions to the barrel erosion problem. Among the methods to decrease barrel wear were: cooling the barrel; use of a heavier barrel to dissipate heat; and improving the materials used in the manufacture of the barrels.

Cooling the barrel seemed to be the obvious answer, but the standard water-cooling jacket used on ground machine guns was not suitable for aircraft use. Purdue University investigated an injection system in 1942 that injected a liquid coolant directly into the gun's barrel between successive rounds. Although the method doubled barrel life it was too complicated for practical use. Heavier barrels were another obvious answer, but reduced the rate of fire of the gun and increased its weight, both of which were unacceptable for aircraft use, especially since barrel wear was only reduced a small amount.

At the time there were no steel alloys that had erosion-resistant qualities, so barrel liners and barrel plating were considered. In February 1942 the Crane Company of Chicago and the Geophysics Laboratory at Carnegie Institute investigated a liner that needed to retain its hardness at high temperatures and be erosion-resistant and ductile. They developed an alloy liner named Stellite No.21, which was an alloy of cobalt, chromium, and molybdenum. The liner attached to the breech end of the barrel, which reduced barrel wear, and when combined with chromium plating reduced barrel wear even more. Stellite No.21 had a very low melting point, and as long as double-based powder wasn't used the liner was excellent.

However, installing the Stellite liner in the barrel was a problem, and in June 1942 the Crane Company began work on producing a nine inch liner. The length of the liner was set due to the casting process to fabricate liner and the shortage of cobalt. It would not be until 1944 that a serviceable liner was perfected, but in the meantime the solution was to simply produce more steel replacement barrels, which was well within U.S. industrial capacity. The liner had twice the life of the standard steel barrel, and 2,000 Stellite barrels were built for field testing in the B-29. The tests were very successful and large contracts were let, and by September 1945 over 200,000 liners had been produced. The Stellite liners were manufactured by the Hayes Stellite Co. of Kokomo, IN, for $7.50 per liner, and when the liners were removed they were sent to the Springfield Arsenal for refurbishment and reuse.

Chromium plating of the barrel proved to be effective when the surface of the bore under the plating had been first hardened by nitriding. The cost of nitriding and chrome plating was $17.49, and was contracted to American Hammered Piston Ring of Baltimore, Crane of Chicago, Doehler-Jarvis of Grand Rapids, and Guide Lamp of Anderson, IN.

On 20 January 1945 Headquarters, Army Ground Forces, observing the success of the .50 caliber Stellite-lined barrels requested that the process be used for .30 caliber barrels. The National Defense Research Committee was able to develop the Stellite-lined barrel for the .30 caliber Browning without conducting service tests due to the success of the .50 caliber barrels. On 26 July 1945, the Ordnance Committee approved production for Stellite liners. Chromium plating and chromium lined barrels were also developed, but did not see much use in World War II; they were, however, commonly used in the Korean War.

**Safety Wiring**

Safety wiring was used to keep nuts and screws from loosening. The wire was placed around the nut in a direction that a pull on the wire would tighten the nut. The wire was placed through a hole in the nut and brought around the side of the nut, and the two ends of the wire were twisted together. The twisted wire was then pulled around the nut in a direction that tightened the nut. The two ends of the wire were twisted together, cut off, and tucked out of the way.

**Spade Grip**

The spade grip assembly attached to the rear of the receiver back plate and consisted of two vertical handle grips, trigger, and trigger safety. The inverted U-shaped trigger was located in the back plate immediately over the safety. When the trigger was depressed by both or either thumbs (if the safety was in the FIRE position), the trigger bar was actuated releasing the firing mechanism, firing a round of ammunition. When the trigger was released a spring automatically returned to the inoperative position. The trigger safety was attached to the rear of the back plate under the trigger and was slid laterally; moving it to the right exposed a letter "S" for Safety.

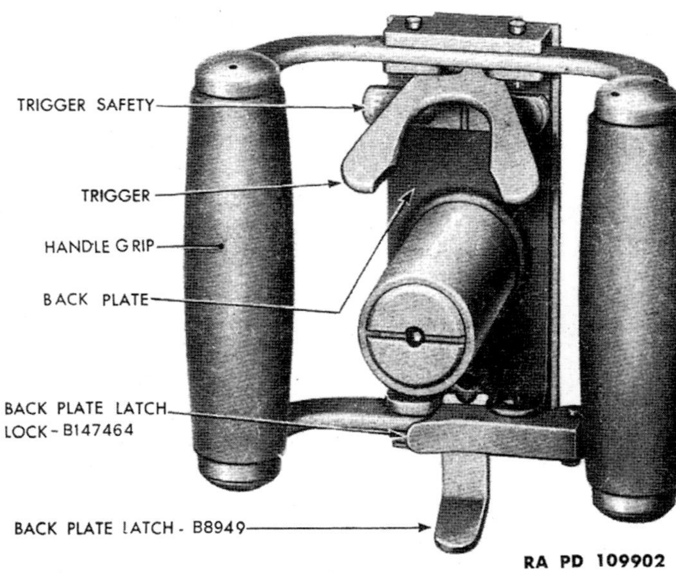


**SPADE GRIP** (USAAF)

**Gun Heaters**

During high altitude bombing missions temperatures could reach minus 50° F, and an electric heating unit was provided which could be clamped over the gun cover to prevent the parts from freezing together. There were two types of heaters: one with the side plate extending down the left side of the gun and the other with the side plate extending down the right side. The part that extended down was to be placed opposite the charging handle. The heater was installed by first turning its two clamps straight up. The gun cover was raised, and the heater unit was slid down as far as possible. The top clamp was turned down and back until it snapped into a catch, and then the lower clamp was turned up and back into the catch. The heater was turned ON when the unit was plugged into the bomber's electrical system, but was not to be left plugged in when not connected to the gun.

**SAFETY WIRING** (USAAF)

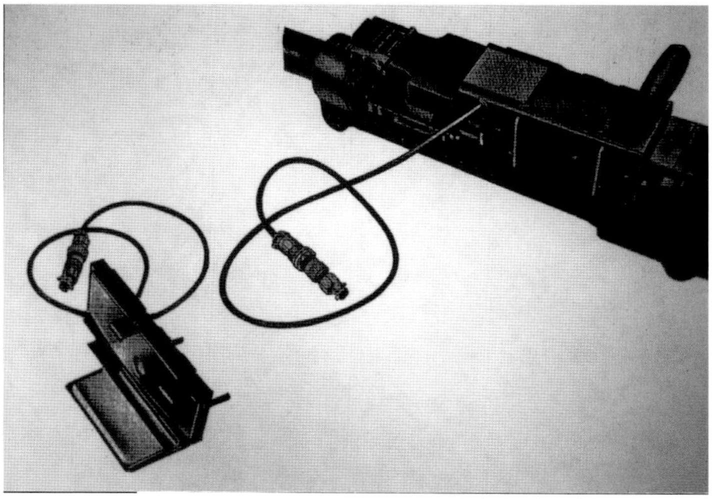

**GUN HEATER** (USAAF)

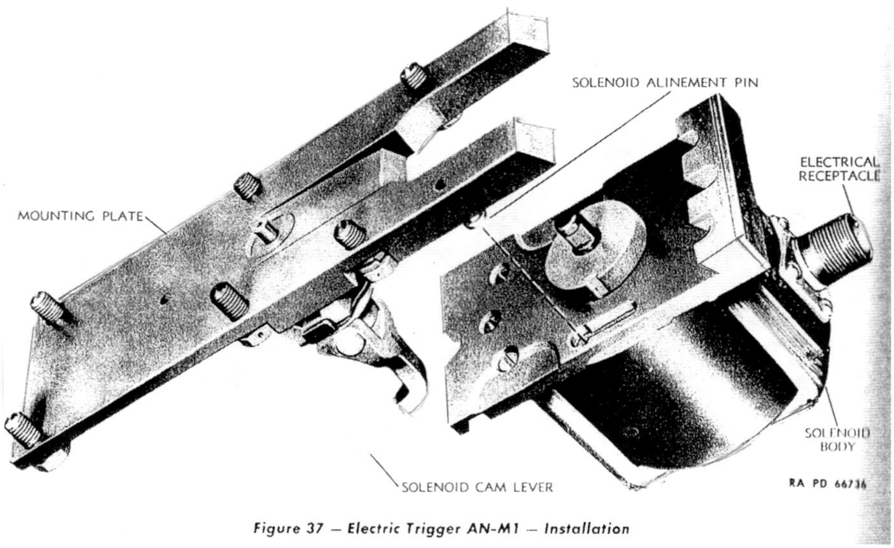


**ELECTRIC TRIGGER** (USAAF)

**Electric Trigger**
The electric trigger AN-M1 was a remote control mechanism designed to fire machine guns and cannon in aircraft equipped with 24-volt electrical systems. Prior to its standardization it was designated by the AAF as the G17 Solenoid and by the Navy as the Electric Trigger Control Mk I. The electric trigger was attached to the receiver plate, and was comprised of the mounting plate assembly and solenoid body.

**Section 3: Loading the Ammunition**
**Left hand or Right hand Ammunition Feed**
In order to change the gun from right hand to left hand feed, or vice-versa, parts of the bolt, cover, and receiver group parts had to be repositioned as seen in the accompanying drawing. TM9-225, the .50 caliber technical manual, described four procedures for the bolt group, six for the cover group, and four for the receiver group, which had to be followed and then "carefully inspected to determine that all parts have been properly assembled."

**Bomber**
In a bomber ammunition was carried in steel or wooden containers that were usually mounted above or to the side of the gun position. The ammunition was loaded into the container with the single end of the links going in first so that the double end went into the gun. Armorers placed the rounds into the container in even layers while checking for defective cartridges as they were placed. The container was mounted in the bomber with its roller toward the gun. The methods of mounting the containers varied in different aircraft and different combat theaters; either sitting on the floor or fastened onto a rack with clamps, pins, or straps.

The ammunition belt fed out of the top of the container over a roller and through a flexible feed chute attached to the gun. The feed chute was attached to the container, open side up, by pushing its two hooks into the slats in the sides of the container and pulling them under the pin that held the roller. Sometimes pins or clamps were used to fasten the chute. The feed chute adapter on the gun was mounted on the same side as the belt holding pawl. The belt holding pawl pin, which was straddled with the projections of the feed chute adapter, was removed, and then was replaced once the belt was inserted to hold the belt. The feed chute was attached to the adapter by squeezing the two handles on the bottom of the flexible feed

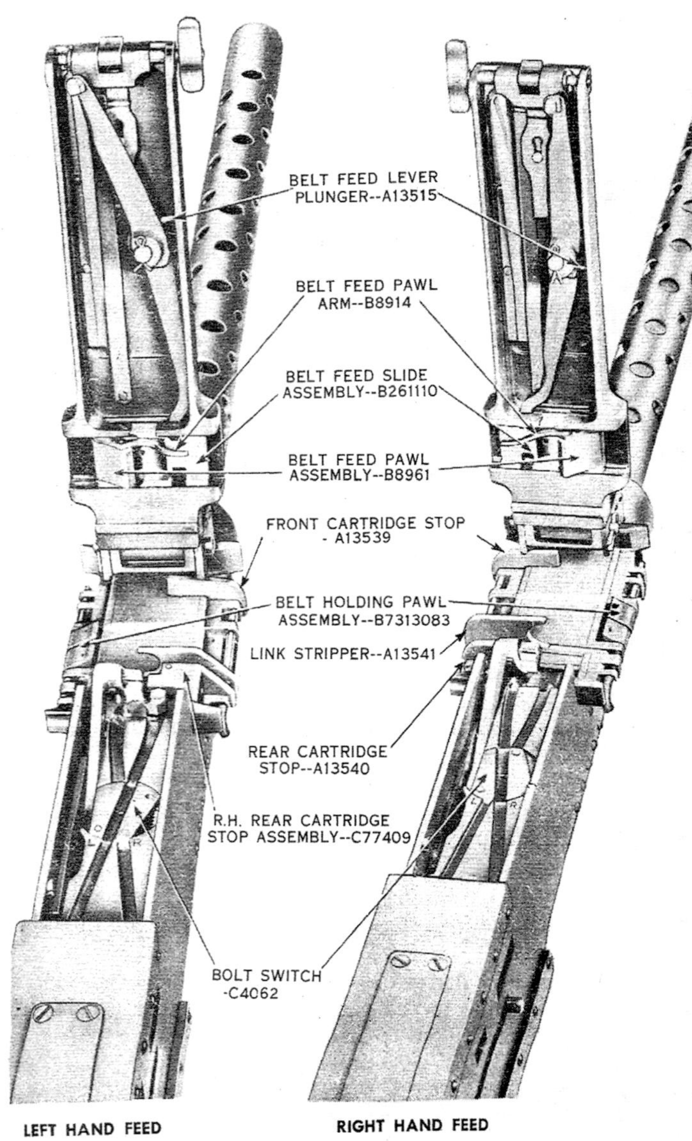


**LEFT** and **RIGHT HAND AMMUNITION FEED** (USAAF)

chute, which opened a slot in the front of the chute. The slot was pushed down over the T-shaped wings of the adapter and the handles were then released. The ends of the ammunition belt were fed over the roller and into the top of the chute, pulled down into the gun, and the end of the belt was ready to be loaded into the feedway.

**Fighter**

When loading ammunition into a fighter wing there were three or four longitudinally partitioned ammunition bays located outboard of the guns parallel to the leading edge of the wing. Large hinged ammunition access covers covered these ammunition bays. The ammunition was removed from its storage container and loaded into the guns. Rigid feed chutes and rollers aided in feeding the linked ammunition from the bays, with the ends of the ammunition belt fed over the roller and into the top of the chute, then pulled down into the gun, and the end of the belt was loaded into the feedway.

**Loading Ammunition Belts into the Gun**

Before takeoff the ammunition needed to be inspected for proper loading in the belt, and to determine if the belt and ammunition box were in proper alignment and secured. The cover was closed before the first round was loaded into the feedway, and was to remain closed as long as ammunition was being fed. The double loop was fed through the feed opening until the first cartridge was beyond the belt feeding pawl. The bolt was then fully retracted and allowed to move forward freely. The first cartridge was then placed in the belt into a position in the feedway, where it could be gripped by the extractor. The bolt was then pulled completely open to the rear and released. This action positioned a cartridge in the chamber and the extractor gripped the next cartridge in the belt. The gun was then fully loaded, cocked, and ready to fire once the sear was depressed.

**Section 4: Operation of the .50 Caliber M2 Machine Gun**

The operation of the M2 was divided into manual and mechanical procedures. Manual operation was defined as that operation performed by the gunner, while mechanical operation was that automatically performed by the gun when it was fired.

**Manual Operation**

Loading

Loading included two separate operations: first entering the loaded belt properly into the gun's belt opening, and secondly operating the gun mechanism until it was closed with the cartridge in the chamber and another cartridge in the feedway gripped by the extractor for extraction during the next recoil. The first operation could be performed with the cover either opened or closed. Either way the double end of the loop was to enter through the feed opening until the first cartridge was beyond the belt holding pawl with the cover closed. The bolt was to be pulled completely to the rear by the retracting slide on a flexible gun and by the operating slide on a fixed gun, and then released. The second operation consisted of pulling the bolt completely to the rear and then allowing it to spring forward. This operation had to start with the action completely closed and the extractor gripping the cartridge in the feedway.

Unloading

To be certain that the gun was unloaded it was necessary to lift the cover, remove the belt, and retract the bolt to be able to make a visual inspection of the feedway, T-slot, and chamber. Then the bolt was released, the cover lowered, and the trigger or sear mechanism was pressed to relieve the tension on the firing pin spring.

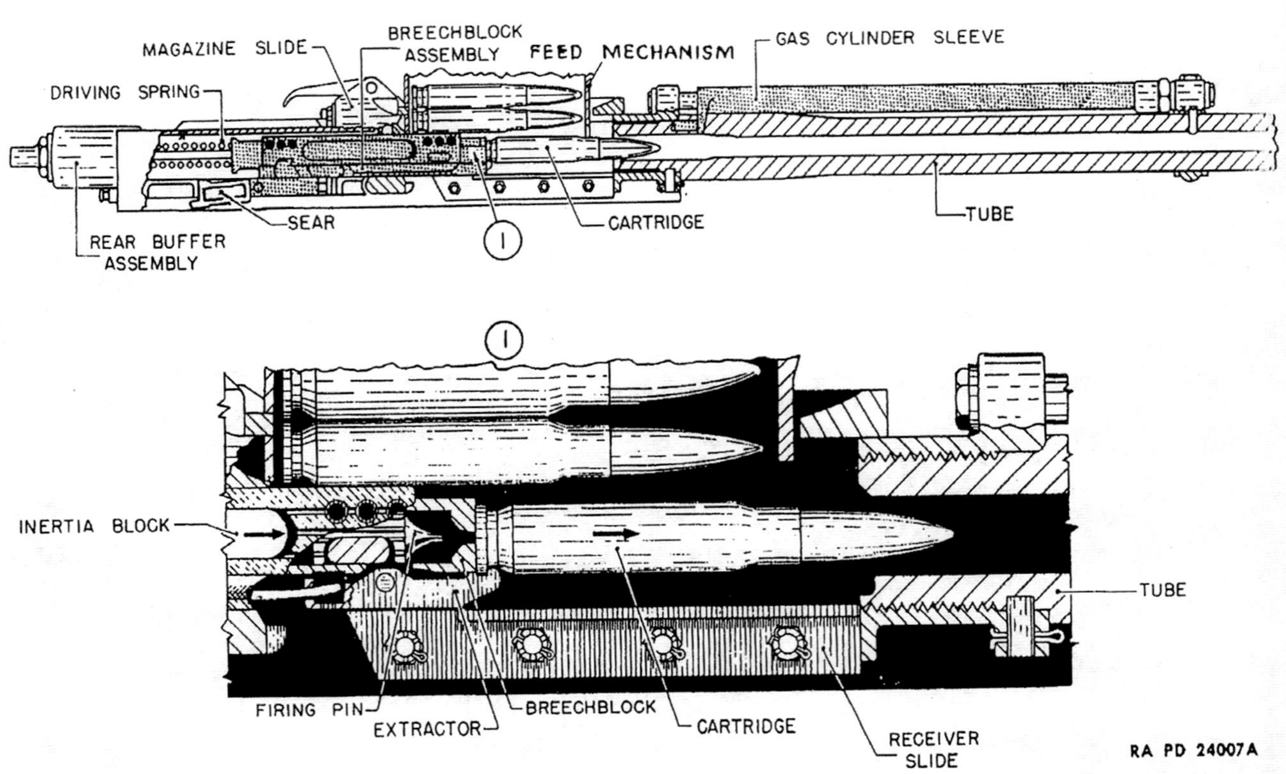


**Figure 20 — Gun Mechanism During Ramming**

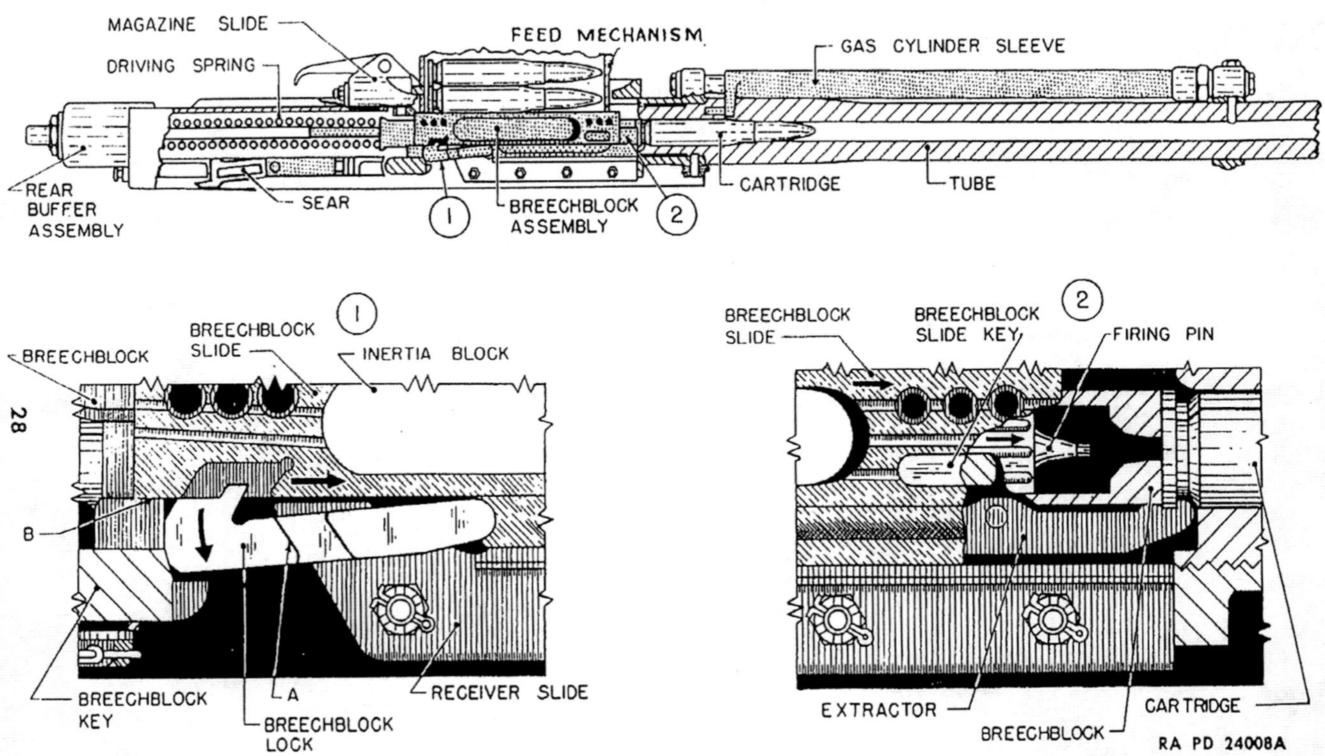


**Figure 21 — Gun Mechanism Ready to Fire**

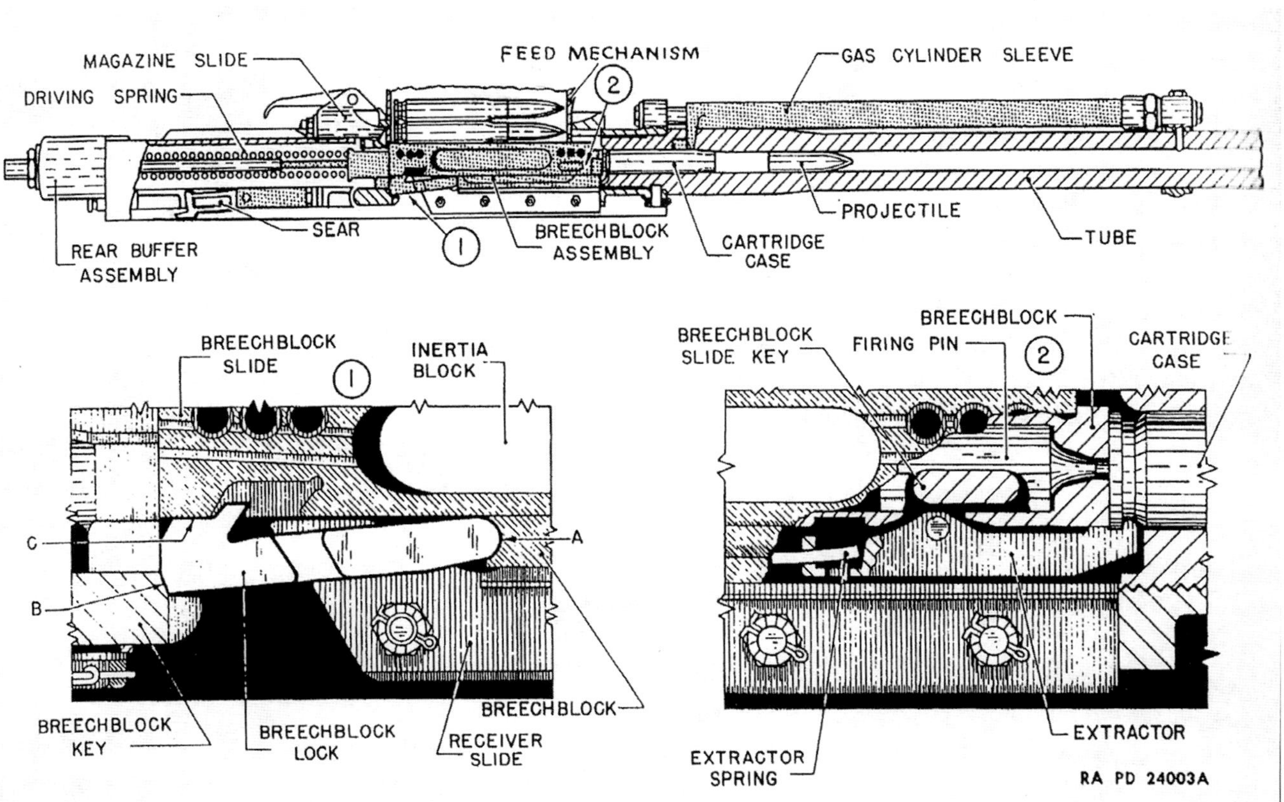


Figure 16 – Gun Mechanism Shortly After Firing

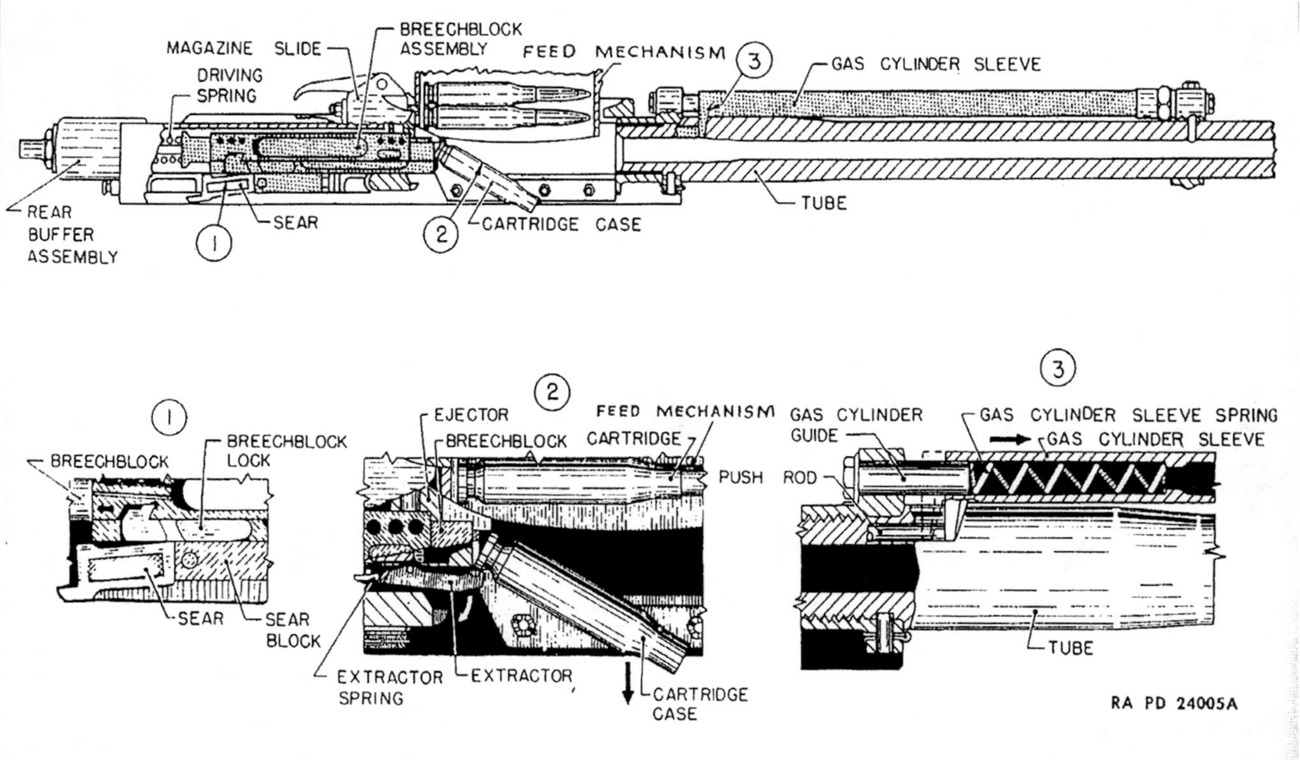


Figure 18 – Gun Mechanism – Cartridge Being Ejected

**Section 4: Mechanical Operation**

Back plate Trigger Action on the First Shot (Flexible Gun)

When the rear end of the trigger, which was pivoted in the center, was pressed down, its forward end pushed up the rear end of the trigger bar, which was pivoted in the center and acted as a lever that caused the front end to press down upon the top of the sear, forcing it down and releasing the sear notch from the shoulder of the firing pin. The firing pin spring forced the firing pin forward to fire the cartridge.

Synchronizing Mechanism Action in Firing (Fixed Gun)

The stroke of the trigger motor slide forced the sear slide inward, which then forced the sear downward to release the sear notch from the shoulder of the firing pin. The firing spring forced the firing pin forward to fire the cartridges.

Remote Control Action in Firing (Fixed Gun)

A stroke of the solenoid plunger forced the sear slide inward and the sear downward, releasing the sear notch from the shoulder of the firing pin. The firing pin spring forced the firing pin forward to fire the cartridge.

Backward Movement of the Recoil Mechanism

The explosion of the cartridge forced the barrel to the rear, carrying the barrel extension with it along with the bolt, which was locked to the barrel extension by the breech lock. When the barrel recoiled about 3/4 inch, the breech lock pin struck the cam surfaces of the breech lock depressors. This unlocked the bolt from the barrel extension and allowed the bolt to continue to the rear. As the barrel extension moved to the rear it struck the accelerator and turned it backward.

Backward Movement of the Accelerator

When the accelerator turned backward, it struck the bottom projection on the bolt and accelerated it to the rear. The shoulders on the barrel extension shank engaged behind the claws of the accelerator, locking the barrel and barrel extension in their rearmost position to the buffer body.

Backward Movement of the Bolt

As the bolt moved backward the driving spring was compressed. The cartridge, gripped by the extractor, was taken from the belt by the bolt, while an empty case from the chamber was gripped in the T-slot. The cam lug on the extractor rode along the top of the switch until it was near the end of the backward movement of the belt. Then the extractor was forced downward by the action of the cover extractor cam until its cam lug was below the switch.

Action of the Oil Buffer

The oil buffer spring was compressed when the barrel and barrel extension moved backward simultaneously. This spring compression was caused by the action of the oil buffer piston that was linked directly with the barrel extension by a hook on the shank projecting from the rear of the barrel extension and the hook on the forward end of the oil buffer piston rod. The oil buffer piston rod head and oil buffer piston valve were driven rearward in the oil buffer tube, forcing the oil through the restricted openings in both the piston rod head and valve. This action supplemented the action of the oil buffer spring by bringing the heavy recoiling parts to rest without shock or strain on the gun, which could damage it. On the counter-recoil, or forward movement, of the barrel and barrel extension, the oil in front of the piston rod head forced back the piston valve, uncovering the throttling ports and permitting the oil to pass readily from the forward to the rear side of the piston rod head and valve, which allowed the rapid return of the components to the firing position.

First Action of Feeding

As the bolt moved backward, the stud on the belt feed lever riding in its cam groove in the top of the bolt moved the feed belt pawl laterally into position behind the next cartridge. The ammunition belt was prevented from falling out of the gun by the belt holding pawl.

Cocking Action

As the belt moved backward, the upper end of the cocking lever was forced forward by the top plate bracket attached to the top plate, which brought the lower end to the rear. When the lower end of the cocking lever moved to the rear it moved the firing pin with it, withdrawing the firing pin from the face of the bolt and compressing the firing pin spring against the sear stop pin. The shoulder of the firing pin engaged in the sear notch under the pressure of the sear spring.

Action of the Driving Spring

When the rear of the bolt struck the horizontal buffer plate, its remaining force was absorbed in the fiber buffer plate discs. When the rear end of the bolt struck the lower vertical buffer plate, its remaining force was absorbed in the fiber buffer discs and the friction of the lower buffer and upper buffer. The driving spring that had been compressed by the backward action of the bolt then forced the bolt forward.

Forward Movement of the Bolt

When the bolt started forward, the cam lug on the extractor, located under the switch, rotated the extractor downward. This action caused the extractor to force the cartridge down the T-slot in line with the chamber. The ejector knocked the empty case from the T-slot and held the cartridge in line with the chamber. Without the action of the ejector the empty case could have fallen out. The upper end of the cocking lever was forced backward and the lower end moved forward away from the rear of the firing pin.

Release of the Recoiling Parts

The lug on the lower rear end of the bolt struck the accelerator and rotated it forward. This action unlocked the barrel extension from the oil buffer body. The barrel extension remained connected to the oil buffer piston rod. When the accelerator was tripped, the barrel extension and barrel moved forward assisted by the oil buffer spring. Part of the forward force of the bolt acted through the accelerator to push the barrel extension forward.

Loading and Locking Action

The extractor rose as its cam lug moved along the top of the extractor cam and the ejector moved outward, leaving the cartridge in the chamber engaged by the T-slot. The extractor gripped the first round in the belt, ready to extract it, and was firmly held down by the cover extracting spring. The breech lock was forced upward by the breech lock cam and locked the breech just before the recoiling mechanism reached the firing position. The breech lock engaged a recess cut in the bottom of the bolt and locked it firmly to the barrel extension and against the rear of the barrel.

Second Action of Feeding

As the bolt moved forward, the stud on the end of the belt feed lever riding in its cam groove in the top of the bolt feed pawl moved in a lateral direction. The belt feed pawl carried the first cartridge against the cartridge stops, ready to be gripped by the extractor. The next cartridge was carried over the belt holding pawl, which moved up behind it and held it in position to be engaged by the belt feed pawl on its return movement.

Trigger Action in Automatic Fire

If the hand trigger was held down, the sear was disengaged just before the bolt had reached its forward position, releasing the firing pin. The gun thus fired automatically, repeating the previous operations. The release of the firing pin actually occurred when the recoil mechanism was 1/8 inch from the forward position, but after the breech was locked.

**Gun Operation Under Unusual Conditions**

Cold and High Altitude

Cold and high altitude occurred together, and it was necessary that all moving parts of the gun be kept absolutely free of moisture. Excess oil on the working parts, especially on the firing mechanism and small spring-operated parts, could congeal and cause sluggish action or malfunction. If the guns were left mounted in the aircraft in cold climates they were to be covered to prevent frosting. Guns that were removed and taken inside from the cold were to be allowed to reach room temperature before cleaning. The general rule was that lubrication was to be limited to moving parts and contacting surfaces, and was to be applied as lightly as possible.

Hot Climates

In hot climates dust settled on oiled surfaces, and the guns were to be inspected and the dust removed, and the guns be lightly relubricated. However, the thin film of oil on the gun could be quickly dispersed in the heat. The guns were to be covered to protect them from the dust. Perspiration on the hands contained acid which contributed to rusting. In humid climates the gun had to be inspected for rust, particularly the unexposed surfaces.

(USN)

Dusty or Sandy Climates

In areas where dust and sand were common the guns were to be kept covered at all times; inside or outside the aircraft. Dust and sand that got into the mechanism and barrel could adhere to lubricated surfaces and form a gummy paste that could cause abrasive wear and malfunction. In this climate it was particularly important that the lubricant be lightly applied only to moving parts and contacting surfaces

Salt Air

Guns mounted in aircraft based near the sea were prone to rusting, as salt had a tendency to destroy the rust-preventative qualities of oil. In this environment guns were to be inspected more frequently and lubricated normally.

**Section 5: Cleaning the .50 Caliber Machine Gun**

Without exception all gunners, bombardier/gunners, and navigator/gunners were responsible for cleaning their guns no later than the evening of the day they were last fired. When the guns were fired, the pores in the metal opened and expanded, and with this expansion some moisture was absorbed. After the guns were cleaned and stored the metal pores contracted, forcing this small amount of moisture to the surface and rust began to form. Once rust began to form one cleaning could not prevent further rusting, and the guns had to be cleaned every day for at least seven days, and left with a thin coating of oil after each cleaning.

During cleaning all working parts of the gun were disassembled and cleaned thoroughly with gasoline, which was immediately wiped dry. The parts were then wiped with a rag moistened with Spec. No. AXS 777 oil. A clean patch saturated with bore cleaner was fit into the slot at the end of the cleaning rod and pushed through the barrel several times; this process was repeated two or three times until the patch no longer collected grime. If the barrel still did not seem to be clean, a cleaning brush was inserted into the barrel. Another clean dry patch was used to remove any remaining bore cleaner before the thin application of AXS 777 lubricating oil. It was recommended to oil the parts by wiping them with a lightly oiled rag, as too much oil in the low temperatures of high altitudes could congeal and cause malfunctions. AXS 777 lubricating oil was not considered a suitable preservative and rust inhibiter, and was to be applied every 48 hours. While cleaning the gun the oil buffer was to be filled with Recoil Oil Spec. No. 2-36D, and it was to be checked again before reassembly to be sure that it had not leaked and was completely full. On damp and rainy days, the moisture on the receivers, barrel jackets, and barrel jacket bearings was to be wiped clean to prevent gun freezing at altitude.

**Section 6: Bell Machine Gun Adapters**

General

The Bell Machine Gun Adapter was developed by Bell Aircraft engineers in collaboration armament specialists from the AAF and Navy Bureau of Ordnance. It was a portable, lightweight cradle consisting of two steel tubes and a hydraulic absorption unit that could be quickly attached to a hand-held .50 caliber machine gun by two bolts. It added less than an inch to the overall dimension of the .50 caliber gun and only three pounds to its weight. The normal recoil forces of the .50 caliber Browning were so great that the adapter required a recoil damper to insure accuracy. When the adapter was attached to the gun mount by a yoke, the gun could be swung up and down and side-to-side. The entire gun(s) recoiled a short distance inside the adapter against a cushion of springs and fluid or compressed air, which acted as shock absorbers. This device kept the gun steadier and increased the life of the gun and mount by tempering the recoil shock.

Mark 6 Series

This adapter was designed to hold a single .50 caliber Browning machine gun. The frame assembly had two built-in hydraulic shock absorbers that functioned similarly to the gun's oil buffer units. Only the pistons and rear mounting slides recoiled with the gun, while the bearer bars and back guard did not. There was a bracket provided to mount the Mark 9 and Mark 9 Model 1 gunsight. The yoke for the adapter was provided by the aircraft manufacturer so that the angles of fire could be determined for each installation.

Mark 10 Series

The Mark 10 adapter was intended for a single .50 caliber hand-held machine gun, and was a side firing mount equipped with a spring and hydraulic shock absorbing device. The gun recoiled inside the mount, which necessitated the design of a sliding trigger in the housing plate assembly and special speed tongues on the magazine holder. The adapter had chest and shoulder pads to give maximum control and leverage. When the gun was trained the gunner moved with the adapter, so the tendency for the gunner's eye to move away from the sight was reduced to a minimum.

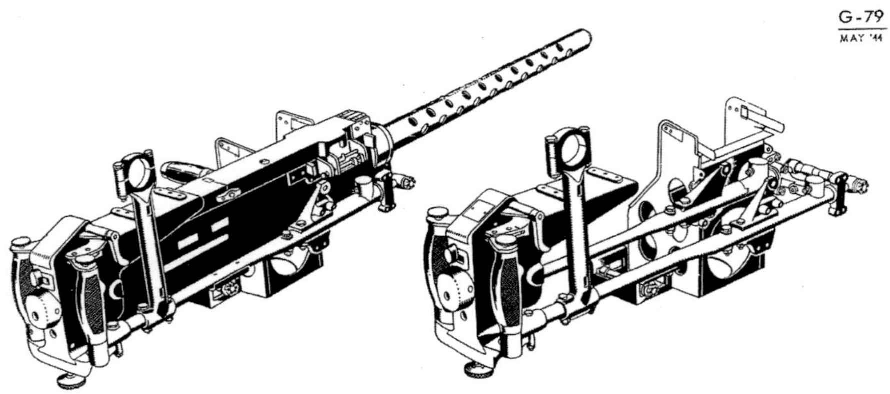


**GUN MOUNT ADAPTER**

**MARK 6 MOD 3**

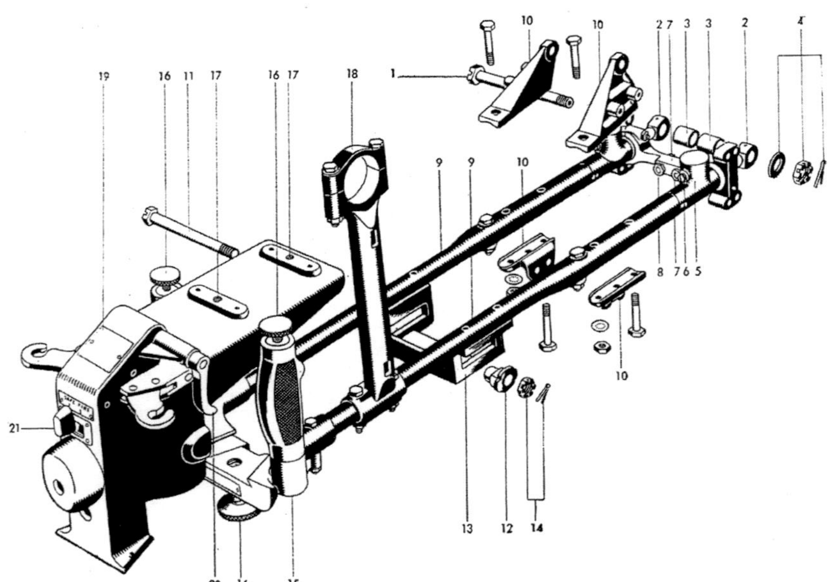

**Parts of the Mark 6 Mod 3**

1 FRONT MOUNTING BOLT
2 PISTON RODS AND EYELETS
3 SPACERS
4 WASHER, NUT AND COTTER PIN
5 HYDRAULIC SHOCK ABSORBER UNITS
6 FILLER PLUGS
7 FRONT FRAME SEPARATORS
8 FRONT FRAME SEPARATOR BOLTS
9 BEARER BARS
10 YOKE FITTINGS
11 REAR MOUNTING BOLT
12 REAR MOUNTING SLIDES
13 REAR MOUNTING BRACKET
14 NUT AND COTTER PIN
15 SPADE GRIPS
16 KNURLED SCREWS
17 SIGHT MOUNTING HOLES
18 SIGHT MOUNTING BRACKET
19 BACK GUARD ASSEMBLY
20 TRIGGER
21 SAFETY
22 TRIGGER BAR
23 TRIGGER BAR SPACER AND SPRING

All Mark 10 adapters (Models 1, 2, and 3) were essentially identical, and with a few exceptions their parts could be interchanged. The different models accommodated gunners standing on either the left or right side of the gun: the Mark 10 and Model 2 adapter were designed for the right hand side, and the Model 1 and 3 for the left hand side of the adapter. The Mark 10 and Model 1 were provided with telescopic sight brackets, while the Models 2 and 3 were provided with brackets for the MK 9 or MK 9 Model 1 reflector sight.

Mark 11 Series

The Mark 11 was designed for twin .30 caliber flexible machine guns via pneumatic shock absorbers. During firing the piston rods and rear mounting slides recoiled with the gun, while the bearer bars and back guard remained stationary. The continuous feed unit on the outboard side of each gun insured the straight feeding of the ammunition belt into the gun feedway at all angles of fire. The left gun was fed from the port side and the right from the starboard side. There was a push button on the top of each adapter

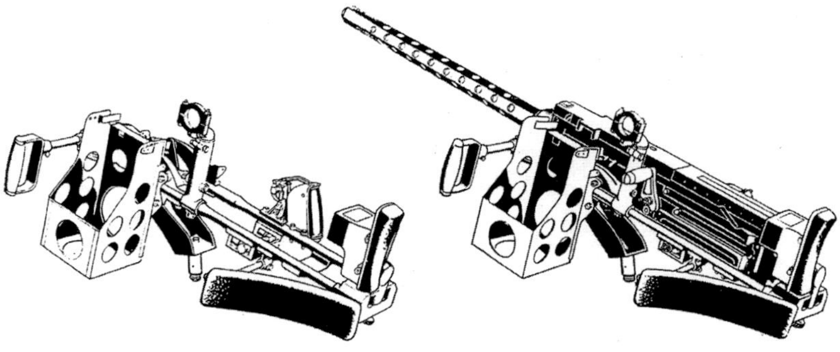

**GUN MOUNT ADAPTER**

**MARK 10 MOD 3**

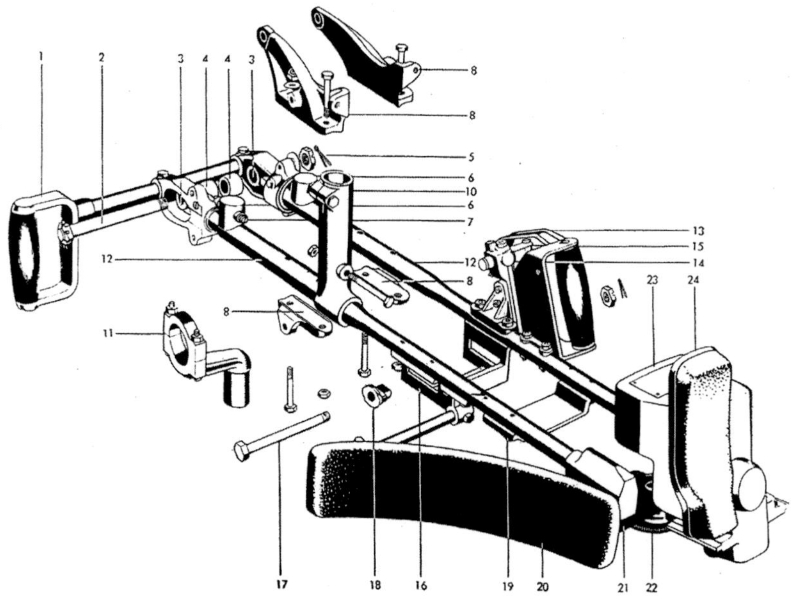


**Parts of the Mark 10 Mod 3**

1 FRONT HAND GRIP
2 FRONT MOUNTING BOLT
3 PISTON RODS AND EYELETS
4 SPACERS
5 WASHER, NUT AND COTTER PIN
6 HYDRAULIC SHOCK ABSORBER UNITS
7 FILLER PLUGS
8 YOKE FITTINGS
9 YOKE
10 SIGHT MOUNTING BRACKET POST
11 SIGHT MOUNTING BRACKET
12 BEARER BARS
13 REAR HAND GRIP ASSEMBLY
14 TRIGGER ASSEMBLY
15 TRIGGER
16 REAR MOUNTING BRACKET
17 REAR MOUNTING BOLT
18 REAR MOUNTING SLIDES
19 BEARER BAR SEPARATOR
20 CHEST PAD
21 BACK GUARD SUPPORT
22 KNURLED SET SCREW
23 BACK GUARD
24 SHOULDER PAD

hand grip, with the left grip button operating the gunner's microphone and the right grip button operating the gun camera that was installed on the left gun. There were left and right link deflectors that caused the ejected links into a centrally located link ejection chute. There was no provision for spent cartridge cases. The Mark 11 had three models, with the Model 3 having an improved bracket for mounting the MK 9 or MK 9 Model 1 reflector sight. The Model 3 absorbed the recoil by a pneumatic shock absorber.

Mark 12 Series
The Mark 12 was similar to the Mark 11 twin .30 gun mount adapter, but its continuous feed unit provided more clearance in cramped areas.

**Parts of the Mark 11 Mod 3**

1 FRONT SUPPORT
2 FRONT MOUNTING BOLT
3 PNEUMATIC SHOCK ABSORBER UNITS
4 PISTON RODS
5 BEARER BARS
6 REAR MOUNTING SLIDE
7 REAR MOUNTING BOLT
8 LINK EJECTION CHUTE
9 LINK DEFLECTORS
10 ARMOR PLATE BRACKET
11 REFLECTOR SIGHT BRACKET
12 REFLECTOR SIGHT SUPPORT ADJUSTMENT ASSEMBLY
13 BACK GUARD SUPPORT
18 FORE POST
19 FORE POST BRACKET ASSEMBLY
20 RINGSIGHT
21 RINGSIGHT BRACKET ASSEMBLY
22 CONTINUOUS FEED UNIT
23 CONTINUOUS FEED UNIT GUIDE
24 CONTINUOUS FEED UNIT MOUNTING STUD
25 CHUTE AND ROLLER UNIT
26 ECCENTRIC BOLT
27 AMMUNITION ROLLER SHAFT
28 AMMUNITION ROLLER
29 CONTINUOUS FEED PAWL
30 CONTINUOUS FEED PAWL PIN

# 7

# .60 Caliber Machine Gun

After America entered the war the Army Ordnance Department realized that an aircraft machine gun would be needed with a caliber larger than the standard Browning .50 and began the development of a .60 caliber gun.

**Modifying the 20mm Hispano to .60 Caliber Standards**

Bendix 15mm Machine Gun

The first attempt to meet the specifications for the .60 caliber aircraft machine gun was to modify a 20mm Hispano-Suiza automatic cannon, and the Eclipse Machine Division of the Bendix Aviation Corp. was contracted to do the adaptation using 15mm rounds. The new gun was 100.625 inches long with a 67.5 pound barrel and weighed 115 pounds (the barrel weight was 47.8 pounds). The rate of fire was 600-700 rpm at a muzzle velocity of 3,000 fps. The system of operation was gas unlocking and blowback actuating. The new gun's receiver was identical, and parts of the gun were interchangeable with the 20mm M1. The principal difference was in the barrel, which was chambered for the 20mm case, and was bored and rifled for the 15mm bullet and fixed in relation to the mount. The entire gun was rigidly mounted, and the Hispano muzzle brake and recoil mechanism were eliminated. A Burgess feeder which was operated by the recoil of the gun was tried first, but was unsuccessful. The pilot model was equipped for a 47 round spring wound magazine mounted rigidly on the gun. This magazine was similar in appearance to the 60 round drum, which was standard on the 20mm M1 gun.

The pilot gun fired more than 800 of the 15mm rounds, but further testing was discontinued after it became apparent that the muzzle velocity obtainable from the 15mm cartridges used was approximately 150 to 200 fps less than could be achieved with the .60 caliber cartridge case. A modification of the 20mm Hispano-Suiza cannon would be required using 20mm rounds.

TI8 Hispano-Suiza Conversion

A second modification of the 20mm Hispano-Suiza M1 cannon was made by rechambering the barrel for caliber .60 cartridges and boring and rifling for the caliber .60 bullet. Corresponding changes were made in the bolt and extractor. This gun, officially designated as the Caliber .60, T18, fired a small number of rounds (not more than 50) automatically before a radical redesign of the Hispano-Suiza cannon appeared to be necessary if the gun was to meet aircraft requirements. Work on this model was discontinued.

T18E1

After the T18 project was terminated further study of .60 caliber mechanisms was conducted by developing a new design and a modification of the 20mm Hispano-Suiza M2; designated as the T18E1 because of the previous work on the T18. In August 1944, work was reopened to determine whether a .60 caliber machine gun could be produced from the 20mm M2 gun by replacing or modifying a small number of parts. Since there were several thousand unused 20mm guns available it was important that the conversion be successful.

Work was begun by the Autoyre Co. of Oakville, CT, in August 1944, to determine whether a caliber .60 cannon could be quickly and easily developed from the M2. The specifications called for a gun with a rapidly detachable barrel, a new feeding mechanism, a front sear that could be synchronized, and a recoil adapter. An extension was fastened to the forward end of the receiver to provide for the quickly removable barrel. The existing gas-operated method of unlocking the bolt was retained. The

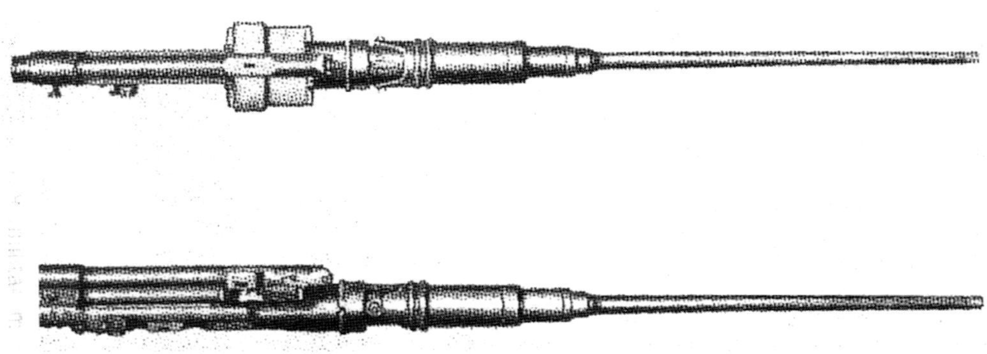

**1-6-7-1 GUN, MACHINE, CALIBER .60, T17E5** (USAAF)

feed mechanism was operated by an additional gas piston and cylinder mounted above the unlocking cylinder, and a new link was also developed to facilitate the design of the feed mechanism. This upper piston was arranged so that gas pressure would compress the feed springs, which would then expand and feed the belt as rapidly as the timing of the gun permitted. The cartridge was forced from the bottom of the feed link and was not pushed through it. The.60 caliber cartridge was larger in diameter than the 20mm cartridge and, accordingly, the height of the bolt was increased so that the extracted case would not be pushed off by the following round.

Tests at Aberdeen Proving Ground showed that the gun functioned reasonably well, but had ejection ad feeding problems. Difficulty was encountered with ejection, which required a complete redesign of the ejector assembly, but it was the link used with the new ejector that proved to be one of the major sources of the trouble. The feeding difficulties were traced to the slowness of the feed and the faulty design of the feedway opening.

The development program and final tests were transferred to the Springfield Arsenal because of the heavy workload at Aberdeen. During testing Springfield found more problems, and concluded that an extensive modification would have to be made on the M2, which contravened the original purpose of an easy conversion. The amount of work required to change or replace existing parts to only produce a conversion were not justified, and the T-18 project was discontinued.

**Modifying of the German MG151/20 to .60 Caliber Standards**

T17

In September 1942, the Ordnance Department initiated a scheme to convert the excellent German Mauser MG 151/20 to a .60 caliber machine gun under the designation Caliber .60 Machine Gun T17. The MG 151/20 was a 20mm short-recoil-operated, air-cooled, belt-fed German weapon that had been captured from a downed *Luftwaffe* bomber during the Battle of Britain and sent to the United States for study and development. In October 1942 Colt undertook this conversion, and found it necessary to rechamber the barrel, lengthen the receiver, feedway, bolt, cam tube, and cover, and also to make several other minor design changes, including new links provided by the Autoyre Co. The initial requirement for the T17 gun called for a quickly detachable and replaceable barrel, and Springfield Arsenal made the first barrels integrating the barrel design from the MG 151/20. Further developmental work on the gun barrel was done by the Springfield Arsenal and Frankford Arsenal.

The first test firing of the gun was at the Colt factory on 23 November 1942, where Colt found that the recoil was very strong and that cartridge extraction occurred too early, as evidenced by expanded cases. It was assumed that the gun's rate of fire would be much above the preferred rate, so a recoil brake could be added to the muzzle, but this change reduced the rate of fire more than expected. The gun was then sent to the Aberdeen Proving Ground, where it fired approximately 350 rounds that determined that the rate of fire was approximately 700 rpm at a muzzle velocity of 3,000 fps. Unlocking and extraction occurred too early, and it was revealed that minor modifications were necessary to strengthen certain portions of the bolt and to provide for later unlocking in extraction.

T17E1

In January 1943 the Frigidaire division of General Motors, Dayton, OH, was contracted to provide ten pilot models of the T17E1. The model was to be basically the same as the T17, except that the rate of fire was to be increased to 800 rpm and the high trunnion reactions were to be lowered by incorporating a recoil adapter in the design developed by the Edgewater Steel Co. Links for the gun were developed by the Autoyre Co. Complete drawings of the T17E1 gun were prepared by Frigidaire, and an engineering study was made to redesign the weapon for cheaper mass production.

The pilot model T17E1 was delivered to Aberdeen Proving Ground for testing on 2 May 1943. Tests indicated that the bolt was either made of incorrect materials or had been overhardened, as the locking lugs and a section of the bolt face were broken after only a few rounds had been fired. New components were made, but after firing 70 rounds in late May 1943, an explosion occurred that ruptured the cartridge case and destroyed all of the operating parts of the gun, necessitating the T17E1's termination.

T17E2

Frigidaire was then asked to prepare two additional T17E2 models which would use strengthened components and a barrel with a thicker walled chamber, as the chamber had expanded during tests of earlier models. SAE 1060 steel had been used in the T17E1 wherever possible, but in the T17E2 this policy was abandoned and SAE 4640 steel was substituted. Fabrication of these models involved the use of sheet metal stampings and hydrogen brazing. In May 1943 the General Electric Co. of Bridgeport, CT, accepted a contract to develop an electric charger for the T17E2 gun, as it seemed that the best prospect for the successful development of this gun would be by using a charger integral with the gun. Two T17E2 machine guns were delivered to Aberdeen Proving Ground for testing on 25 August 1943. The first gun was equipped with manual charging, firing equipment, and recoil adapters, and fired 557 rounds before ejection difficulties developed. After modification of the ejector the gun functioned reasonably satisfactorily, with a rate of fire of 600 rpm. The second gun was provided with the General Electric electrical charging and firing solenoids, but fired only 143 rounds before malfunctioning. A combination gun was built from parts of guns Nos. 1 and 2 and fired 397 rounds at 658 rpm at a maximum muzzle velocity of 3,696 fps. Numerous malfunctions were encountered which indicated that considerable further development work was needed.

T17E3

To continue development of the T17 series seven T17E3 guns with both mechanical and electrical ignition were ordered from Frigidaire during September 1943. The electrical ignition mechanism was duplicated from the captured *Luftwaffe* MG 151/20 cannon, while a bolt with the sear forward was developed, as it was expected that this arrangement together with the electric ignition would permit synchronization of the gun with either electric or percussion primed ammunition. On 16 November 1943 Frigidaire was requested to develop four auxiliary gun chargers to be used as a standby in case of the failure of the electric charger.

On 15 December 1943 the Navy became very interested in the project, and the Frigidaire order was increased to ten guns. Soon the Navy ordered the delivery of 2,500 caliber .60 aircraft machine guns in 1944, along with auxiliaries and spare parts. The Navy order initiated the limited procurement of the T17E3 in mid-December 1943; even though preliminary service tests of the Frigidaire gun had not been performed. This procurement was to be started immediately by the Rock Island Arsenal, and this rush order would require large expenditures to put the changes in the design of the components into production. However, a major portion of the tooling for the gun would ultimately be usable, and would save valuable time in getting completed guns into combat.

The T17E3 was 92 inches long and weighed 135 pounds, including the recoil mounting adapter, the electrical charger and solenoid, and the feed mechanism. The rate of fire was 600 rpm at a muzzle velocity of 3,500 fps. On 23 December 1943 the AAF asked the Ordnance Committee to increase the original Rock Island procurement to 5,025 guns, with 25 guns of this procurement allotted to the Ordnance Corps for experimental purposes. Two T17E3 test guns manufactured by Frigidaire were delivered to Aberdeen Proving Ground on 29 December 1943. The breech ring on one gun broke after a few hundred rounds, severely damaging the gun. The other gun successfully fired several thousand rounds, but it fired erratically, with frequent and long hesitations, and a 25 round burst was considered good.

During January 1944 the Battelle Memorial Institute, Columbus, OH, was awarded a research grant to make recommendations on heat treatment and other metallurgical operations of the .60 machine gun. Using Battelle's recommendations Frigidaire engineers worked during February and March 1944, and were able to decrease the weight of the bolt to five pounds, to increase the diameter of the bolthead roller trunnions, and to remove the link stripper from the feedway. In April and May in 1944 this gun was tested, and fired 100 rounds at a uniform cyclic rate (estimated to be approximately 600 rpm) without a stoppage. Malfunctions were reduced to 1% and breakages to 0.3%.

On 13 March 1944 regular weekly conferences were initiated by the United States Army's Small Arms Development Division, Research and Development Service to integrate all information on the progress of the Frigidaire development of the T17E3 project. In these meetings, all changes in the gun design were discussed and transmitted to the Industrial Service, which in turn sent the information to the Rock Island Arsenal. By June 1944 the Industrial Service furnished the Rock Island Arsenal with complete drawings for the T17E3, and all accessories developed up to that time except the bore-cooling device. At the time tooling at Rock Island Arsenal was approximately 80% completed; aided by the modification of components and assemblies and the simplification of the design, which facilitated set up and future manufacture. For firing demonstrations Rock Island Arsenal had completely assembled three T17E3 machine guns from parts made at the Arsenal and by its subcontractors. These guns suffered feeding malfunctions after only 100 rounds, and further firing tests disclosed that the guns fired erratically with a cyclic rate of approximately 600 rpm. Frequent bolthead and breech ring breakages were encountered. Rock Island Arsenal breech rings failed at an average of 1,000 rounds each, while Frigidaire breech rings were failing at an average of 5,000 rounds. Difficult cartridge extraction was encountered with frequent breakages of extractors. As a result of this performance manufacturing operations were reduced.

Meanwhile, Army Ordnance invited Navy, Rock Island, Industrial Service, and Army Ordnance representatives to Aberdeen Proving Ground on 15 August 1944 to witness a firing demonstration of the most recently developed Frigidaire gun. A 1,000 test rounds were fired with one malfunction and no breakages. A few days later a firing test was conducted at the Frigidaire factory, and 2,138 rounds were fired without a malfunction. A development study was initiated to facilitate the integration of recent Frigidaire developments into the Rock Island production line, which was still months from ready.

T17E4

The E4 developed by Sanford Engineering Co. was similar to the T17E3 with a modification of the mechanism to use ammunition belted in a new link.

T17E5

The gun standardized as the caliber .60 T17E5 aircraft machine gun was a recoil-operated, air-cooled, belt-fed weapon developed by the GE Frigidaire Division. The gun was 91.7 inches long with a 60 inch barrel, and it weighed 127 pounds with the charger (the barrel weighed 30.25 pounds). It fired at a rate of 700-750 rpm at a muzzle velocity of 3,400-3,500 fps. When fired at a muzzle velocity of 3,500 fps, the projectile had a range of 5,520 yards. It fired a T77 Cartridge that weighed 0.607 pounds (including one link), while the projectile weight was 1,150 grains (Note: There are 437.5 grains per ounce). The belt was of the metallic link disintegrating type for either left or right hand feeding. Firing was by means of a solenoid, but a manual release for the sear was also provided. The T17E5 was provided with a shock absorbing adaptor that also served as a front mounting. The gun was charged by an electric charger mounted in the cover and fired from an open bolt. The gun was composed of several groups of parts: barrel, cover group, bolt group, feedway and ejector group, receiver and barrel support group, and adaptor group.

T19

The T19 designation was assigned to an experimental design to be developed by the High Standard Manufacturing Co. This design can not be traced beyond drawing board phase.

T31

On 1 July 1944 the Gazda Engineering Co., RI, was contracted to develop a gun similar to the 20mm Oerlikon machine gun, but was to include an "inertia locking flywheel," a continuous belt feed, and a rate of fire in excess of 1,000 rpm and be capable of fire interruption (fired from a closed bolt). By November 1944 manufacture of the gun parts had begun, and on 16 January 1945, receipt of the last assembly drawings of the gun parts was accepted; but a complete set of detail drawings on all parts was never received. The gun was a composite which used a modified 20mm Oerlikon bolt buffer, a modified 20mm Oerlikon receiver, the T17E3 feed box and feed system, and a quick release barrel similar to the MG 151 (German), and the gun was charged by a 20mm (T2) Bendix hydraulic charger. In June 1945 Gazda fired 40 rounds from the gun before the rack which connected the drive springs to the bolt broke. At the end of September 1945, this gun was fired again in the presence of a representative of the Office, Chief of Ordnance, and after a few rounds a number of other parts broke and the project was discontinued.

T39

The T39 .60 caliber machine gun only differed from the T17E3 in its special bolt and bolthead that was interchangeable with the percussion bolt, and also in its contact switch wired to an external power source to fire electrically primed ammunition. The first electrical bolt was a copy of the German MG 151/20, and provided outstanding ignition time and was unusually free from "contact bounce." However, the contactors that passed through the bolt and bolthead cam fractured regularly, and as this design was intricate it required a major modification of the bolt, bolthead and bolthead cam, and receiver. Frigidaire redesigned this bolthead, reducing the number of contactors required, and also reduced the number of modifications required to convert T17 guns to T39 guns.

To expedite the T39 program the Frankford Arsenal Laboratory independently redesigned the T17E3, and although their E3 required less modification of the T17 parts, it failed because of excessive breakage of parts. Arrow Engineering Co. of Chicago was engaged to redesign the El. This redesign was called the E4, and had an improved firing pin and contact mechanism in the bolt and a knife blade switch between the bolt and the receiver. The timing of the bolt was the same as in the E2. Quality Hardware Corp. was then engaged to develop the E5. The timing of this firing pin was brought about by the movement of the bolt body in relation to the bolthead, and was independent of the bolt switch. This design also incorporated a chatterproof contact in the bolt. Test data on the E5 bolt assembly was submitted and eventually accepted.

An assortment of other experimental electrical unit designs was tested, and efforts were made to modify T17E3 guns, along with T39 weapons using electrical units produced by the Alpha Engineering & Machine Works. Fifty of these guns were furnished to Rock Island Arsenal for testing. Results of the tests were unsatisfactory, and further development of electrical firing units for this gun was limited due to the changeover to the successful T17E5 mechanism. Of the tests that were conducted at the

Aberdeen Proving Grounds to obtain data for possible use in future gun development, the designs tested did not prove to be satisfactory; however, sonic features in their switch and contact designs did appear desirable. The Naval Gun Factory at Washington, DC, also built two types of boltheads of the T39 type.

**Postwar Development**

At the end of World War II, the .60 caliber machine gun was considered very promising, with manufacturing problems mostly overcome and with production drawings stabilized. With a continued delivery of uniform production parts performance of the gun became predictable, the malfunctions were localized, and their number and occurrence were reduced. But with the war winding down the .60 caliber machine gun project was no longer a priority; however, work continued in the immediate post-war on the successful T17E3, and several other promising .60 caliber projects begun during the late war.

In March 1946, the average malfunction rate was one per thousand rounds. More than 309 T17E3 guns had been manufactured, and more than 950,000 rounds of ammunition of various types had been fired by them. Tests were continued to determine the life of the various components and to reduce the malfunctions. The components requiring early replacement after a 1,000 rounds were the firing pin and the drive spring. Because the major components of the gun appeared to be serviceable for much more than 5,000 rounds, work was started to establish a 10,000 round life for the gun by replacing a few parts at 5,000 rounds and by continuing the replacement table beyond that point. Ground tests in several aircraft and Eglin Field Air Force Proving Ground tests were completed, and the Ordnance Department certified that it believed the gun to be operational. Consideration was also being given to use of the gun as an antiaircraft weapon in armored vehicles.

The T39 variation of the T17E3 was continued in the post-war. In 1946 a P-38L (#44-23601) had three .60 machine guns installed experimentally at Elgin AFB, but tests were not successful, as the guns showed structural deficiencies, and the shell links failed whenever the aircraft underwent positive or negative acceleration.

In 1947 the demand for a short aircraft gun led to a radical redesign of the T17 type gun to produce a version known as the T51. The buffer, receiver, bolt, and barrel were shortened to the minimum possible overall length of 52 inches.

# Part Two
## Aircraft Cannon

An aircraft cannon is defined as a gun of 20mm (.79 caliber) and above. But cannon over 37mm (1.46 caliber) never found wide use as aircraft weapons, although through the years there were many attempts to employ them, both for air-to-air and air-to-ground combat. The cannon was deemed to be a desirable aircraft weapon due to its promise of scoring the single-shot destruction of a large bomber, a tank, or a small vessel. But this promise was offset by the cannon's disadvantages of excessive weight, limited ammunition supply, and a low rate of fire that produced considerable recoil.

# 1

# 20mm Aircraft Cannon

**Background**
The rifle caliber machine gun was the primary aerial gun of the First World War and for the inter-war years. During this time there was an effort to develop aerial guns of 20mm or more, but these weapons would not reach their culmination until the next World War.

**Ehrhard Gun**
During World War I, the German War Ministry set specifications for an airborne machine cannon of not more than 37mm, 154 pounds, and was to be able to fire ten rounds in rapid succession. There were two automatic 20mm guns under development at the time, the Becker and the Ehrhardt guns. The 20mm Ehrhardt FlzK (*Fllugzeugkannon*, or aircraft cannon) was developed by Rheinmetall. The gun weighed 79 pounds and fired a 20x70FB shell at 250 to 300 rpm. The gun was only produced in small quantities and did not see combat. However, its development was continued after the war by Solothurn, a Swiss subsidiary established by Rheinmetall in order to develop armaments away from the restrictions imposed on Germany by the post-war armament treaties.

**Becker Gun**
In 1913, Dr. Reinhold Becker developed and patented the simple Advanced Primer Ignition (API) blowback system, in which the round was detonated before it was fully chambered while the bolt continued to move forward. The initial rearwards movement of the cartridge case was slowed by stopping the forward movement of the bolt before it could push the cartridge backwards again (e.g. the recoil reversed the forward momentum of the bolt and then pushed it backwards). This delay gave the cartridge enough time for the projectile to leave the barrel. Because the the primer was fired before the cartridge was fully chambered the system was given the name Advanced Primer Ignition. Since the API system distributed the recoil energy over a long period of the firing cycle, a lighter and simpler mounting could be used. The Becker gun weighed only 66 pounds, plus 11 pounds for the 15 round ammunition box, and had a rate of fire of 300 rounds per minute. The gun had spade grips with two triggers; the right trigger for firing single rounds and the left for fully automatic fire. Since the Becker gun used the API system it could only be fired from an open bolt, and could not be used with synchronized fire through the propeller.

In 1915 Becker received assistance from the Spandau Arsenal in the development of his gun, and in 1917 he received an order to build guns for the German Air Service, while Spandau and MAN-Nurnberg were awarded contracts from the German army to supply the gun for an anti-tank role. During the war there were a large number of projects invovling the Becker gun, including its mounting in a few bombers and naval airships, where it saw limited operational service. It never saw service mounted in fighter aircraft.

In 1919 Becker sold his patent to the Swiss armament company SEMAG (Seebach Machinenbau Aktien Gesellschaft), which continued to market the gun while developing a more powerful version that fired the 20x100RB round. In 1924 SEMAG sold the rights to the Becker gun to another Swiss company, Werkzeug Maschinenfabrik Oerlikon, that was located in the Zurich suburb of Oerlikon. This company modified the gun into the F, L, and S series of the basic Becker design, but these guns found only a small market.

**Oerlikon**
By 1930, the Oerlikon F series gun had basically remained the same as the Model 1918 Becker gun and Fritz Herlach, who later became instrumental in the Rheinmetall-Borsig armament organization, completely redesigned the gun specifically for installation in an aircraft wing as the FF. The name FF was derived from the German *flugelfest*, meaning "wing-mounted, fixed." The 53 pound gun fired the 20x70RB cartridge of the Becker gun and had a muzzle velocity of 1,980 fps and a cyclic rate of 520 rpm via a belt feed designed to allow the ammunition to be carried in flat boxes in the wings. In 1933 the FF was introduced into service but was unsatisfactory, and a

**BECKER 20mm CANNON** (AFHRC)

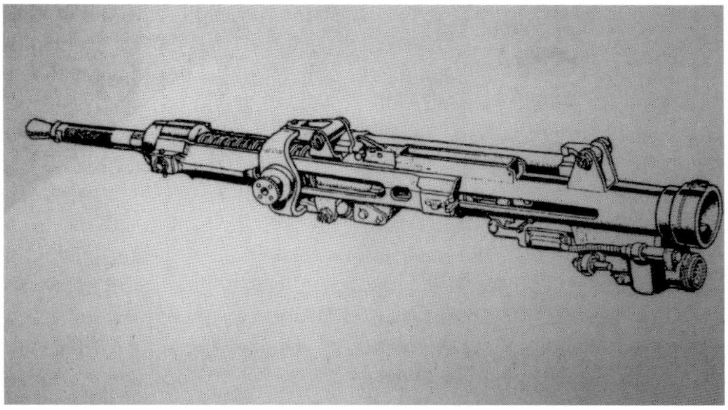

**OERLIKON 20mm CANNON** (AFHRC)

revised model appeared in 1935 that was a great improvement over the F, L, and S models weighing less and having higher rates of fire. The revised FF chambered a 20x72RB cartridge carrying a heavier projectile. The standard ammunition feed was a 60 round drum with a 15 round box, and a 45 round drum was available for flexibly-mounted guns.

The FF was one of the first 20mm guns to be compact and light enough to be placed into the wing of an aircraft, and served as the inspiration for many World War II 20mm cannon, including the French, British, and U.S. Hispano-Suiza HS 404, the German MG FF, and the Japanese Type 99 cannon.

Oerlikon arms sales increased dramatically in the mid-1930s with the European rush to rearmament. A modified version of the FF using a longer and slightly more powerful 20x80RB cartridge was manufactured by the German Ikaria Werke Berlin, which called it the MG FF. In 1940 the *Luftwaffe* put the *Minengeschoss* (mine shell) HE shell into service. The M-*Geschoss* weighed significantly less, and its reduced recoil necessitated a rebalancing of the gun's bolt weight and return spring strength. The *Minengeschoss* round was manufacured from pressed instead of milled brass. This round had much thinner walls and therefore carried more explosive. The revised gun using the mine shell was designated the MG-FFM, and the remaining MG-FFs were modified to the MG-FFM standard, but continued to be called MF-FFs. These guns were fed by 60 round drums during World War II, although late in the war 30 and 90 round drums were introduced. The resulting MG FFM became a standard *Luftwaffe* weapon, but beginning in late 1940 they were replaced by the innovavtive and excellent Mauser MG 151/20 cannons, which were based on the earlier Oerlikon FF S.

The French decided to use the larger FF S version, as they were interested in an engine mounting with the gun firing through the propeller hub. This Oerlikon gun was modified by the French Hispano-Suiza company under license as the HS 7, with the minor variant HS 9 having differences in the mountings. The 136 pound Oerlikon FF S used the same 20x80RB cartridge, but could only fire at 280 rpm, and was seen as being too heavy and too slow-firing. Oerlikon redeveloped the gun over the years to produce the Oerlikon FF S, which weighed only 86 pounds, and fired a more powerful 20x110RB round at 2,740 fps at 470 rpm.

In 1939, Oerlikon licensed the FF and FF L to the Imperial Japanese Navy which produced it as the Type 99-1 (1941) and Type 99-2 (1942). The low muzzle velocity of the FF continued to be of concern, so Oerlikon continued its development that led to the 66 pound FF L that fired a 20x101 round at 2,475 fps. The Oerlikon FF L was mechanically similar to the FF, but used a larger 20x100RB cartridge to obtain a higher muzzle velocity. Japan manufactured a modified version of the FF L called the Type 99-2 that used a 20x101RB cartridge.

**Hispano-Suiza**

In 1898 Spanish artillery captain Emilio de la Cuadra founded the La Cuadra Electric Automobile Company in Barcelona. While visiting Paris, de la Cuadra met Swiss engineer Marc Birkigt and hired him to work in Spain, where he developed the company's first gasoline-powered automobiles. In 1902 the company was sold and became Fabrica Hispano Suiza de Automoviles (Spanish-Swiss Automobile Factory) and began building luxury cars. By the first decade of the century France was providing Hispano-Suiza a larger market for their cars than Spain, and in 1911 a new factory, Hispano France, was established in the Paris suburb of Levallois-Perret which then moved to larger facilities at Bois-Colombes in 1914, where it took the name Hispano-Suiza.

During World War I Marc Birkigt directed the company's new aircraft engine division, where he pursued an innovative technique in developing aircraft engines. Instead of machining separate steel cylinders and then bolting them to a crankcase, he used cast aluminum blocks into which thin steel liners were screwed, making the engine lighter, stiffer, and easier to manufacture. This engine was a V-8, and was the first of what are today known as "cast block" engines. The engine featured overhead cams, propeller reduction gearing, and a number of other features that didn't appear on most other engines until the late 1920s. Another major design element which would be a feature of all future Hispano-Suiza military engines was the use of a hollow propeller drive shaft that allowed a gun to be placed so that it could be fired through the propeller spinner, thereby avoiding the need for a synchronizer gear.

After World War I Hispano-Suiza returned to automobile engine design, and in 1919 introduced the H6 engine, which was comparable to the Rolls Royce engines, and through the 1920s and into the 1930s the company built a series of luxury cars. In 1923 the French arm of Hispano-Suiza was incorporated as Societé Française Hispano-Suiza, with the Spanish parent company holding 71% of the shares, and from that point the French company became more independent.

In 1936, with another war threatening, the French government directed Hispano-Suiza to discontinue automobile production, and to return solely to the production of aircraft engines. The company introduced a new series of water-cooled V-12 engines, and the Hispano-Suiza 12Y would power nearly all French aircraft. However, Hispano was unable to meet the demand for these engines, and when war came in 1940 many French fighters sat on the ground without engines.

In the late 1930s Mark Birkigt designed a new and much improved version of the FF S with a revised action, much faster rate of fire, and somewhat higher muzzle veocity. The result was the Type 404, or HS 404, which arguably was the best aircraft cannon of its time. The 404 was widely used on pre-war French designs, notably in installations firing through the drive shaft of the Hispano-Suiza 12Y engine, a system known as a "moteur canon."

In Britain the Air Staff embraced the HS 404, but at the time the country's two major armanent manufacturers were committed to the production of the Browning .303 and the Vicker's VGO gun. The Air Staff asked Hispano to build and equip a factory at Grantham to manufacture the gun in Britain. Once the war began, a number of shadow factories were established to increase the production of 20mm guns. The Hispano cannon were installed into the slim wing of a few Spitfires, and the operational results were very good when the gun was operable, which was sporadic. The unreliable gun was withdrawn from service for modifications, and the resulting MK II was an excellent weapon, and in 1941 was accepted by the Royal Air Force and Fleet Air Arm. The large, strong wings of the Hawker Hurricane could easily carry four MK IIs to replace its eight Browning .303 machine guns. The Bristol Beaufighter carried four Hispanos in the lower fuselage and six wing-mounted .303s. However, due to technical difficul-

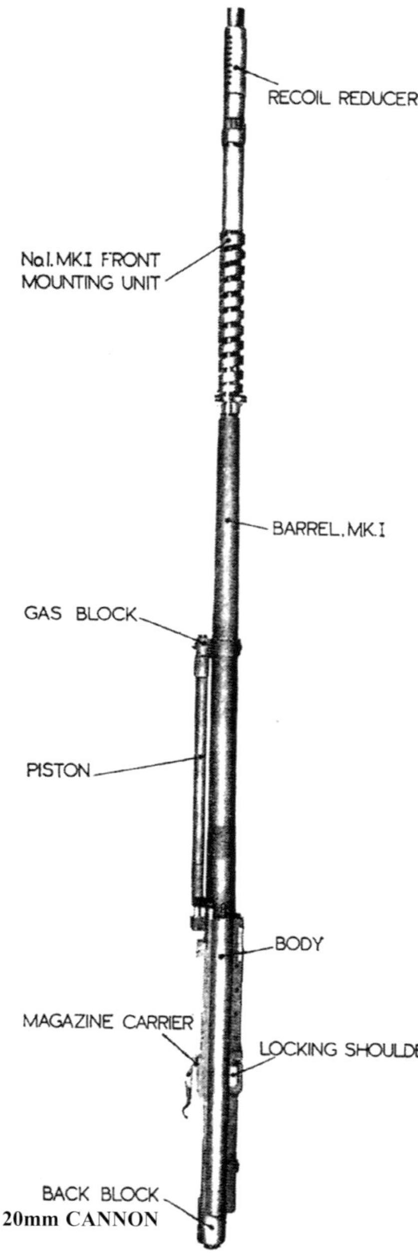


**HISPANO-SUIZA MkI 20mm CANNON**
(AFHRC)

ties, most Spitfires were able to mount only two cannons accompanied by four .303 caliber machine guns or two .50 caliber machine guns. The Hispano's initial rate of fire was 700 rpm, but had to be slowed to 600 rpm to improve reliability, and although this rate of fire was relatively low, the more powerful 20x110 cartridge compensated for this inadequacy.

**American Development of the Hispano-Suiza**

As early as 14 December 1939 the U.S. received 33 Hispano-Suiza 20mm cannon from France for preliminary installation and trials (20 went to the Navy and 13 to the AAC). The U.S. War Department approved a large cannon and ammunition manfacturing program in 1941, and the HS 404 was licensed for use in America as the M1. Both the USAAC and USN planned to transition to the 20mm cannon from the Browning .50 caliber machine gun as soon as sufficient numbers were manufactired. However, when the license-manufactured guns were delivered they were found to be very unreliable and experienced a large number of misfires due to the round being "lightly struck" by the firing pin.

During 1941 and 1942 British factories were falling behind in their manufacture of Mk I Hispano cannons, and the Air Ministry decided to purchase them from American manufacturers. In the negotiations it was decided that the guns were not to be purchased, but to be issued as Lend-Lease, and being so the guns were to be the standard American guns and not manufactured as per British drawings, which were measured in the metric system. The British realized that the American M1 guns, parts, and ammunition would not be interchangeable with their Mk I, and they sent drawings, test reports, and other relevant information to Washington in hopes that the Americans would implement them to produce an improved M1. The Americans utilized the British metric plans, but the important suggested modifications of shortening the chamber and using a triple wire return spring were not implemented.

The British Inspection Department conducted comparative tests in early 1942 and found the American-produced M1 Hispanos had significant problems with lightly struck caps and misfeeds that occurred four to five times more frequently than in their British-built counterparts. The Inspection Department knew the source for the lightly struck cap was the shortened American chamber but found no cause for the misfeeds, as the American guns were well made. After thousands of the American-made Hispanos arrived in England they were judged as unsuitable for operational use by the Director of Equipment

In April 1942 an example and drawings of the British Mk II were sent to the U.S. for study and tests. The British strongly recommended that American and British ordnance representatives meet to discuss methods of expediting the standardization of the cannon. A comparison of the British MK II to the American M1 (MK I) revealed that the necessary changes were relatively minor and would lead to standardization as the AN-M2. However, the British version had slightly different chamber dimensions, being 1/16 inch shorter. The British insisted that their chamber was better because it was shorter and would solve the lightly struck misfire problem, since the cannon was fired inertially and depended on the shoulder of the chamber to offer resistance and to position the cartridge.

Another problem occurred when the American Ordnance Department insisted that all rounds needed to be lubricated before they were to be inserted into the magazine. The shells were lubricated by dipping a cloth in a special lubricating preservative which was wrung out before application. Each cartridge case was then wiped with the cloth to coat it with a light film of oil. However, among U.S. ordnance engineers there were two "oiling" factions; one that adamantly believed that the AN-M2 could never be accepted into the U.S. arsenal as long as the cartridges had to be lubricated, while the other faction maintained that oiling was important only as long as it improved the gun's performance. The 1941 RAF Hispano MK I and MK II Handbook, 1641E, strictly prohibited the oiling or waxing of ammunition. No agreement could be reached, and throughout the war U.S. AN-M2 guns used oiled ammunition.

Tests were conducted at the Proving Grounds at Eglin Field, Aberdeen, Wright Field, and Kenvil to determine the superiority of the British chamber design. Despite results favoring the British MK II chamber, Army Ordnance engineers remained unconvinced, and in early April 1942 additional tests were conducted. The official conclusions were "that the manufacture of the American 20mm automatic M1 and AN-M2 be continued in the United States without modification to the chamber….and that no chamber with the small cone moved 1/16 inch to the rear (as was done in the British chamber) be considered for manufacture in the United States." The 20mm cannons to be manufactured in the U.S. for the British were not to be manufactured with British chamber size until both the M1 and AN-M2 were throughly tested in England.

The chamber size issue was not raised again until the 20mm ammunition manufacturers found numerous light striking misfires when testing their cartridges for reliability. Ammunition company investigation of the misfires showed that the light strikes on the primer were due to an error in the gun and not a result of defective ammunition. Further testing was scheduled in June 1942 at Aberdeen using 90 M1 and AN-M2 guns selected from the different manufacturers using all types of ammunition, both from accepted and rejected lots. After examining the early test results the engineers concluded that two modifications needed to be made to rectify the light striking malfunction. Not surprisingly, they recommended that the chamber be shortened 1/16 inch to the British length. They also recommended that the extractor ring be replaced with a solid plug that would position the rounds with the extractor. The tests continued until the end of January 1943, when engineers from Aberdeen presented their final report to representatives of the Ammunition Branch, the Industrial Division, Artillery Branch, Technical Division, and the Field Service. Four modifications were recommended and accepted. The chamber was to be shortened one millimeter, or about 1/32 inch; the extractor spring was to be a cantilever type; the standard firing pin was to be shaved 1/16 inch from the rear of the key slot to give "float"; and the breechblock slide springs were to be strengthened.

By late 1942 the USAAF had 40 million rounds of 20mm ammunition in storage, but the 56,410 guns that had been manufactured needed to be modified so it could be fired dependably. External changes, such as modifying the firing pin and extractor spring, were relatively easy, but the shortening of the barrel chamber would cost as much in both time and money as it would to remake a new barrel. The modification of the chamber would also take a number of installed cannons out of action. Nonetheless, the Industrial Division immediately authorized the modifications, but differences remained between the British MK II and the American AN-M2.

Once the modified guns arrived in Britain from the American manufacturers the Army Ordnance Department began wide-ranging competitive trails against the British MK II. Two guns each were shipped from International Harvester, Oldsmobile, and Bendix for the trials in July and August 1943, with representatives from the Army Ordnance Department and the British Air Mission observing 2,000 round firing tests. The British MK IIs were mounted in the left wing of a RAF Hurricane fighter, and two AN-M2s each from Oldsmobile and International Harvestor were mounted in the right wing. A number of combat maneuvers were simulated, such as dives, turns, and G-loading. There was one stoppage in the Oldsmobile gun, but the IH gun completed the tests with a cracked breechblock. Each British MK II had a sear failure, and one suffered a cracked breechblock after firing 1,400 rounds. The Bendix guns were fired in ground tests against the MK IIs and had a "creditable showing." The British Ministry of Aircraft even went so far as to pronounce the "American guns as good as British guns and are acceptable for service use," but this was obviuosly untrue, as the American-built 20mm AN-M2 remained unsatisfactory throughout the war.

Despite the dubiously good results of the tests the British abandoned the American-made Hispano versions, as they had increased their domestic production to the point where U.S. cannons were no longer needed. The British upgraded their cannnon to the Hispano Mk V which had a shorter barrel, weighed less, and had a higher rate of fire, although at the expense of a somewhat lower muzzle velocity.

Throughout the war, the U.S. Navy had desired to transition away from the .50 caliber machine gun to the cannon, but this conversion never occurred. As late as December 1945 the Army's Chief of Ordnance was still trying to complete additional changes to the design to allow the AN-M2 to enter USAAF service. Late in the war the British and the Americans independently improved their 20mm cannons as the Mk V and AN-M3 respectively by shortening and lightening it while increasing its rate of fire

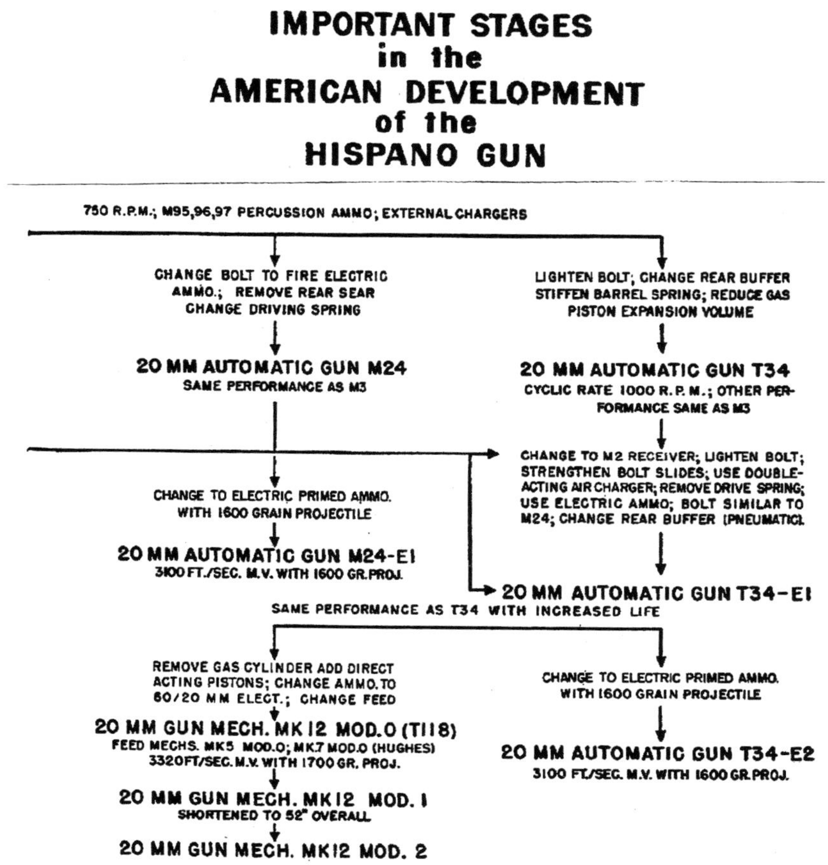


in the American development of the Hispano-Suiza Gun.

to 750 rpm, but reliability problems continued to plague the design. The English Molins Company developed a Hispano capable of firing 1,000 rpm, but it was not adopted, as acceptance would have interfered with current domestic 20mm production. After the war the USAF finally standardized a version of the M3 cannon as the M24, which was similar except for the use of electrically primed ammunition.

**20mm Guns with T and M Numbers**

**T1**

The Hispano-Suiza Type 404 was tested in the United States beginning in 1938 and was officially designated the Gun, Automatic, 20mm Tl.

**T9**

The T9 was a standard Hispano M2 gun with a modified chamber.

**T10**

The T10 was a standard Hispano M2 gun with a different modification to the chamber.

**T12**

The T12 was a standard Hispano M2 guns with another chamber design.

**T14**

The T14 was a standard Hispano M2 gun except for the chamber and the origin of the rifling was 1mm short.

**T15**

The T15 was a standard Hispano M2 gun with chamber modified to the design used on the British Mark II gun.

**T16**

The T16 was developed by the United Shoe Machinery Corp. and had the same ballistics as the M1 and M2. This project was canceled in August 1944.

**T18**

The T18 gun was a Hispano M2 which used a mechanical unlocking means actuated by the recoil of the gun instead of the gas cylinder. The mechanical unlock was supplied with two cams, the slopes of which were 40° and 30°, respectively. Preliminary tests showed that such a device could be practical, but after thorough testing at Aberdeen Proving Ground on a flexible mount it was decided in July 1944 to cancel this development, since the unlocking mechanism lowered the gun's rate of fire.

**T19**

The Draper Corp. of Hopesdale, MA, a textile loom manufacturer, developed this gun, which was lighter and more compact than any previous 20mm gun. The T19 used gas to operate the integral feed mechanism, and the receiver body was a modified M2 inverted with a double key arrangement. A key plate strengthened the receiver which had been weakened by the removal of the charging cylinder. The buffer had both inner and outer preloaded concentric springs, which provided a yielding instead of a solid stop in ease of occasional excess force of the blown back. The tube had an additional gas port for the gas-operated feed so located that it came in the next rifling groove ahead of the regular port.

**T20**

The T20 was developed by Colt, which utilized a gas-operated feed from a Hispano 20mm gun to overcome the difficulties encountered in recoil-operated feed mechanisms. One pilot model of the T20 was produced and proved successful in test at the Colt firing range. The feed mechanism was gas-operated and fed the bolt by a reciprocating pawl similar to that on the caliber .50 machine gun.

**T21**

There are no records concerning the history of the T21.

**T22**

The Ordnance Corps contracted Colt to develop a gun based on the German MG151 but was to use a different locking system. The standard 20mm round was loaded for a higher velocity.

**T23**

The T23 was developed by Colt using a Hispano gun unlocked by recoil instead of gas pressure. In adapting the mechanical unlock unit Colt made the following modifications to the M gun: the gas port was plugged and the gas cylinder bracket removed; the gas tube attachment lug was modified at the rear by cutting a slot in it; and the push rod holes were increased in depth and two new push rods were used. The action of the mechanical unlock mechanism was simple. On firing a round, the gun recoiled, turning the actuating levers so that the ball end of both levers made contact with and moved the two push rods. The push rods then acted upon the breech lock slides. From this point on, action on unlocking the bolt was the same as in the standard gas-operated gun.

**T24**

T24 was a Colt redesign of the T22 using a larger cartridge case.

**T24E1**

This gun was a modification of the T24 having 0.006 chrome plate in the bore.

**T24E2**

This gun was a modification of the T24 having a 0.010 chrome plate in the bore.

**T25**

The United Shoe Machinery Corp. modified a conventional M2 bolt with a searing arrangement that would prevent the firing pin from striking the primer when the bolt slides had reached the battery position. When the gun fired, the sear was actuated by means of a solenoid, releasing the firing pin, which was carried into the primer by action of a separate firing pin spring. As the round was fired and the bolt unlocked by the conventional method of the Hispano-Suiza type guns, the firing pin was cocked by the slides and held on sear position until the bolt was again returned to battery and the sear released as described above. However, in December 1944 T25 development was considered completed because of the advanced state of the T31 and its pending acceptance in the AAF.

**T26**

The T26 was developed by Oldsmobile to determine to what extent the standard 20mm automatic guns M1 and M2 could be reduced in weight without negatively affecting the life of their parts or without increasing the hazards of breakage or malfunction during firing. During August 1943, it was decided to modify several M1s and M2s to the following requirements: a reduction in weight of approximately 25 pounds; a decrease in barrel length of 15 inches; and being capable of using a nonadjustable ring-spring adapter and of firing with the bolt closed and locked. These changes were not to reduce the muzzle velocity not more than 4,800 fpm and maintain a cyclic rate of about 750 rpm. The T26 with the T14 feed mechanism weighed about 110 pounds, approximately the weight of the German MG 151/20 provided with the same accessories. The T26 gun was not capable of synchronization.

**T27**

The T27 was a M2 cannon redesigned by Oldsmobile for firing with the bolt closed and locked. The mechanism of the T27 was similar to that of the T25 gun, and consideration was given to its application to the M2 gun. The T27 was completed and tested along with the T26 gun. The T27 gun was also incapable of synchronized fire, and the near-future requirement by the AAF for a new design of a 20mm gun was that it could provide synchronous fire through the propeller arc, using both electric and percussion primed ammunition. This non-synchronization as well as the selection of the T31 gun by the USN and AAF caused the cancellation of the development of the T27 and T26 guns in August 1944.

**T28**

The T28 was a M2 gun redesigned by Watervliet Arsenal for firing from the battery position.

**T29**

This gun was the same as the T28 except for electric firing. Watervliet Arsenal developed both the 20mm automatic gun T28, capable of mechanical synchronization, and the 20mm automatic gun T29, capable of electrical synchronization. Both guns fired with the bolt forward in a closed and locked position.

**T30**

Except for having a six inch shorter barrel there are no records of the T30.

**T31**

The Watervliet pilot model incorporated the features of the T28 and T29 guns, and was completed with firing achieved by changing the design of the bolt and then incorporating the desirable features of the T26 gun. The new rear-seared, automatic blowback and gas-operated cannon was designated as the 20mm automatic gun T31. The basic difference between the 20mm AN-M2 and the 20mm T31 was that the latter was a lightweight, high-speed gun having the recoil system and cradle built into the gun, whereas the AN-M2 guns used the Edgewater adapter mount, which was a part of the airplane to which the gun was attached. The basic concept of the T31 cradle and recoil system came from Oldsmobile and design and development of the weapon was also by Oldsmobile, which would produce it in quantity. The T31 gun complete with feeder, cradle, recoil system, and solenoid weighed 116 pounds, while the AN-M2 basic gun without mounts or solenoid weighed 115 pounds. The T31 gun had an overall length of 77.75 inches, while the AN-M2 was 92.8 inches overall. The rate of fire of the T31 was approximately 720 rpm, while that of the AN-M2 gun was about 100 rpm less. The T31 would become the M3, which would be the first reliable American 20mm cannon and was adopted by the Navy in the post-war as the M24.

**T31E1**

This designation was assigned to the forward seared mechanical percussion bolt design.

**T31E2**

This designation was assigned to the forward seared electric ignition design which was standardized as the M24 series.

**T32**

The feed mechanism of this gun was to be operated by the same gas piston used to unlock and accelerate the bolt. The operation of this gas piston was as follows: high-pressure gases flowed through the gas orifice when the projectile uncovered the orifice on its forward travel through the bore of the gun. The high-pressure gases passed through the valve, completely filling the chamber. As the projectile moved down the barrel the pressure receded and, since there was a larger piston area on the forward end of the piston than on the rear end, the high-pressure gases in the chamber moved the piston to the rear, thus closing the valve. With the valve closed, the pressure in the chamber continued to move the piston to the rear until the end of the piston uncovered the orifice so that the gas in the chamber could exhaust through the barrel. The bolt returned the piston to the right upon its return to the in-battery position, and the cycle was repeated when the new round was fired. The bolt was locked in-battery by a sliding block that moved upward as the bolt assembly entered the in-battery position. The gas piston cams the sliding block down and accelerated the bolt rearward. The stroke of the piston also operated a helical spline on the feed mechanism, keeping the sprocket wound. There were no drive springs in the gun, and the guns charged by firing a .30 caliber blank cartridge. There were two rails in the receiver of the gun that had two cam paths: one for guiding the round into the chamber and one for ejecting the extracted cartridge case. The gun was designed for electrically fired ammunition. The bolt assembly telescoped the bolt buffer, allowing a shorter receiver design. There was no change in the barrel design to allow for the increased heating due to the higher cyclic rate; however, placing the gas operating piston near the cartridge chamber of the barrel added more metal at the "hot spot," giving a better holdover for the heat.

**T33**

The T33 design was to be capable of firing the new special high-velocity 3,500 fps ammunition; was to have an integral crossfeed capable of lifting a 100 pound load of ammunition; was to have a right or left feed by interchangeable components; was to be able to fire at 750 rpm; and was to have a 5,000 pound maximum trunnion load. Design work was started late in 1944 and was nearly completed by June 1945, at which time the contract was terminated at Oldsmobile and turned over to Armour Research Foundation, Chicago, for completion, but Armour would only complete a wooden mockup before the end of the war, which caused the contract to be terminated.

**T33E1**

The T33E1 was a modification of the T33 which included 0.006 chrome plating in bore.

**T33E2**

The T33E1 was a modification of the T33 which included 0.010 chrome plating in bore.

**T33E3**

The T33E3 was produced in two types based on the German Rheinmetall 20mm gun. The Model A used pivot locks in the barrel extension and was chambered for the large T7 cartridge. Only one gun was built and tested. The Model B, designed by Armour Research Foundation and built by the Naval Gun Factory, incorporated a new bolt and rotary locks, a rammer actuated by bolt recoil, a gas-operated feeder utilizing feed pawls instead of sprocket, and design features which greatly simplified manufacture, assembly, and servicing.

**T34**

The T34 was developed by Oldsmobile and based on the 20mm M3 gun with modifications to increase the cyclic rate of fire to 1,000 rpm. The gun's modifications were: the installation of a new type breechblock buffer, stronger recoil spring, lighter recoiling parts, and the installation of a higher pressure gas operating system. As originally designed, the T34 was chambered for the large T5 case, but in April 1945 it was converted to standard ammunition to fulfill a Navy requirement for high cyclic rate shipboard defense cannon for use against Japanese suicide planes. By V-J Day, when the project was suspended temporarily, 12 T34 guns, which Oldsmobile alleged to have a parts life of 1,500 rounds, had been delivered. Tests revealed numerous deficiencies, chiefly short-lived parts such as driving spring, firing pins, gas piston rings, receiver, slicks, and slide key, and the T34 project continued under a low priority..

**T34E1**

T34T1 was the electric-fired version of the T34 gun, but development did not begin until March 1948.

**20mm Machine Gun Mechanism with Mark and Mod Numbers**

**Mk 1**

No Mk I was assigned to United States equipment. British Oerlikon Mk I.

**Mk 2 Mod 0**

Manufactured from drawings prepared for production of the British Mark II Oerlikon,

**Mk 2 Mod 1**

Refinement of the Mk 2 Mod 0.

**Mk 3**

No Mk 3 was assigned to United States equipment. British Mk III.

**Mk 4 Mod 0**

Same as Mk 2, except for tolerances with limited interchangeability with the Mk 2. Manufactured by Oerlikon from drawings prepared by NOP Centerline.

**Mk 4 Mod 1**

Differed from Mk 4 Mod 0 in having new breech casing rear cap and shortened trigger. Manufactured by Oerlikon for use on mounts Mk 20, Mk 21, and Mk 24.

**Mk 4 Mod 2**

The Mk 4 Mod 2 was modified from the Mod 0 as follows: the breech bar cam was attached to the right breech bar, a special trigger was added for use with Solenoid Mk 29, and the solenoid Mk 29 replaced the trigger cover plate. The Mod 2 used a back cover without handgrips to permit the use of a right hand recoil operated belt feed.

**Mk 4 Mod 3**

The Mk 4 Mod 3 was changed from the Mod 0 the same as the Mod 2, except it used a back cover without handgrips; that permitted the use of left hand recoil operated belt feed.

**Mk 4 Mod 4**

The Mod 4 differed from Mod 0 in that trigger, breech bar securing bolt retaining pins, hand grip, and magazine catch lever were redesigned or modified to suit the Mk 15 mount.

**M 4 Mod 5**

Eliminated double-loading machining for stop oil on Mk 4 Mod 0.

**Mk. 4 Mod 6**

Eliminated machining for double-loading stop on Mk 4 Mod 1.

**MK 5**

No Mk 5 assigned to United States equipment. British Oerlikon.

**Mk 6**

Experimental Oerlikon design by Pontiac. Similar to Mk 4.

**Mk 7**

No Mk 7aissigned to United States equipment. Reserved for British gun.

**Mk 8 Mod 0**

The Mk 8 Mod 0 was the 20mm T31 (M3) adapted to Mark 25 mount by Emerson Electric Co., St. Louis. This gun was designed to use the Hispano as a shipboard antiaircraft defense against suicide planes.

**Mk 8 Mod 1**

The Mk 8 Mod 1 was the 20mm T31 (M3) adapted to Mark 22 mount for shipboard antiaircraft use.

**20mm Aircraft Gun M1 and 20mm Automatic Aircraft Gun AN-M2 General Description**

The 20mm Automatic Gun was a combination blowback and gas-operated aircraft weapon designed to be mounted as a fixed gun in the wing or fuselage, but also could be mounted to fire through the propeller hub or as a flexible turret gun. It could not be synchronized to fire between propeller blades. The gun was air-cooled and had a cyclic rate of fire of 600 to 700 rpm; fed by a drum-type magazine using a disintegrating belt.

The name and serial number of the gun and the name of the manufacturer were stamped on the top of the receiver just to the rear of the magazine slide. The serial number of the barrel (called a "tube" in the 20mm Technical Manual TM9-227), the name of the gun, and the name of the barrel manufacturer were stamped on the gun just ahead of the gas cylinder bracket. The serial number of the gun and the barrel were usually different, but the number on the receiver was the actual serial number of the gun.

**Gun Type Designation**

The gun type designations were based on the type of adapter, sear actuating mechanism, and charger used with the basic M1 or AN-M2 Gun (also called the M2). The Types A, B, C, and D models were used by the USAAF, while the E model was used by the USN, and the F and G models were used by the British.

Type A: Consisted of the basic M1 or AN-M2 Gun with an AN-M1 adapter, an AN-M1 electric trigger, and a M2 manual charger.

Type B: Consisted of the basic M1 or AN-M2 Gun with a M6 adapter, an AN-M1 electric trigger, and a M2 manual charger.

Type C: Consisted of the basic M1 or AN-M2 Gun with a M7 adapter (with thread protector), an AN-M1 electric trigger, and a M1 manual charger.

Type D: Consisted of the basic M1 or AN-M2 Gun with a M7 adapter (with M1 muzzle brake), an AN-M1 electric trigger, and a M2 manual charger.

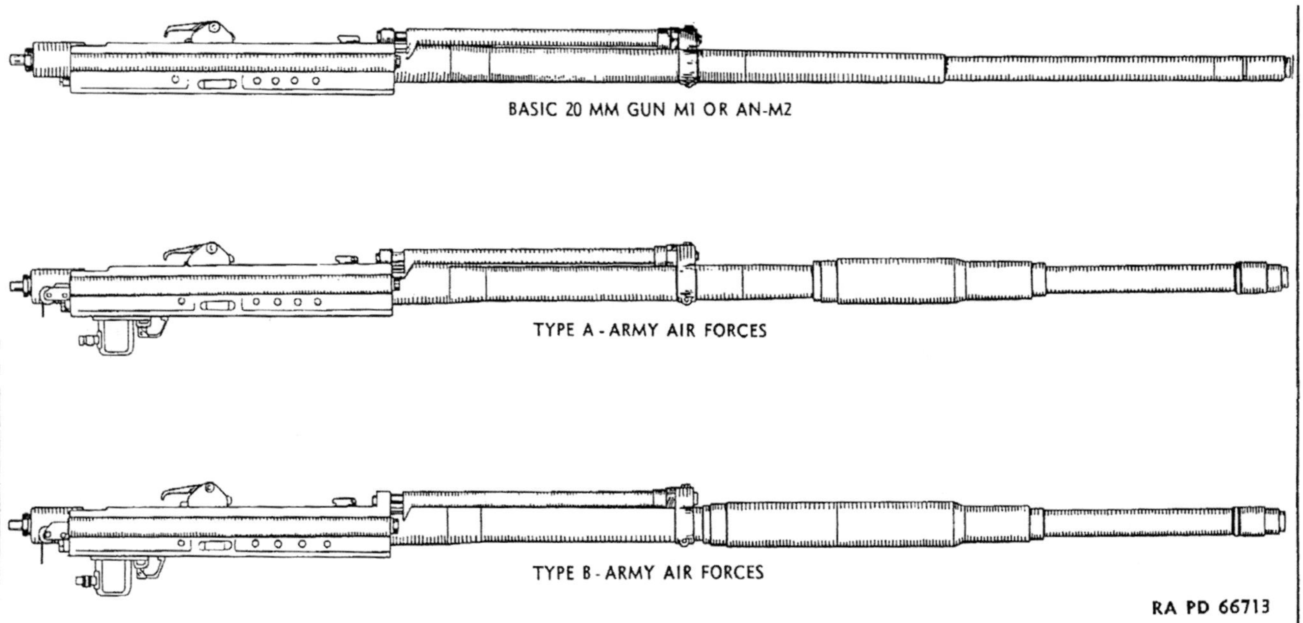


GUN TYPE DESIGNATION CHART

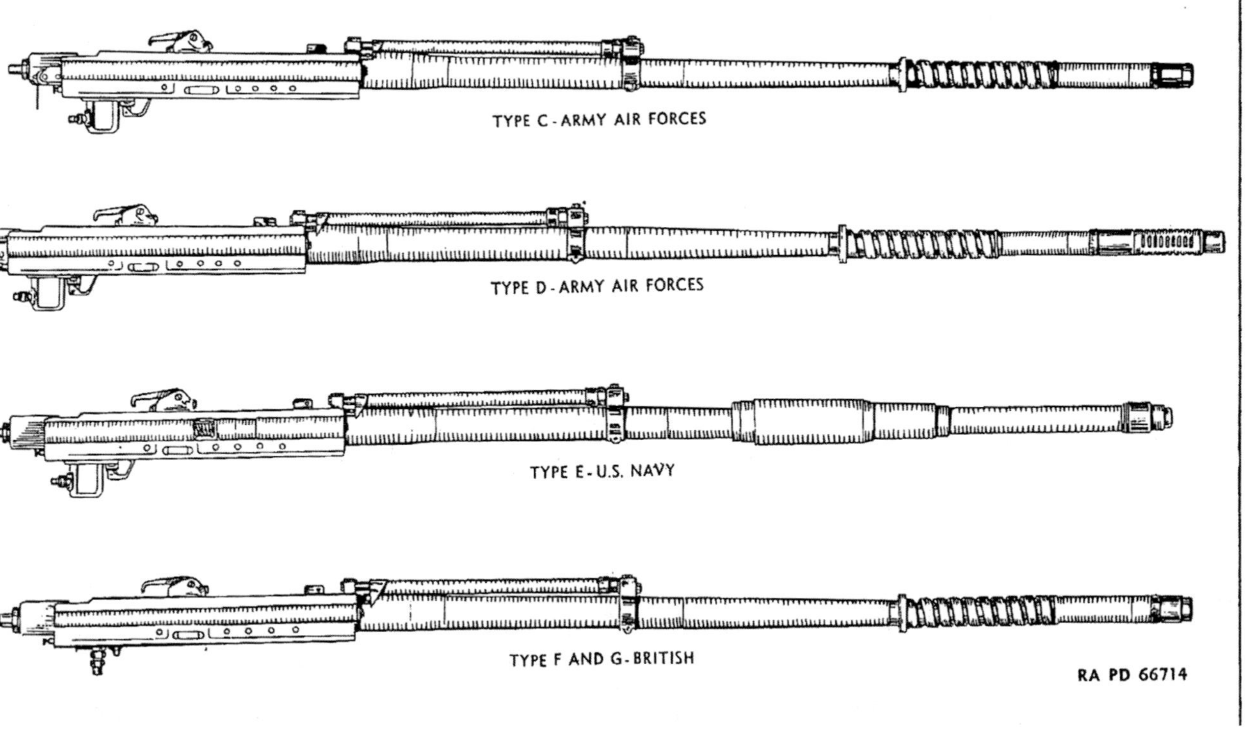


**U.S. HISPANO GUN TYPE DESIGNATIONS**

Type E: Consisted of the basic AN-M2 Gun (only) with an AN-M1 adapter, an AN-M1 electric trigger, and a M1 hydraulic charger.

Type F: Consisted of the basic M1 Gun with the M-7 adapter (with thread protector), and a M1 sear mechanism.

Type G: Consisted of the basic AN-M1 Gun with a M7 adapter (with thread protector), and a M1 sear mechanism.

The differences between the M1 and AN-M2 were in manufacture only, and did not affect the use or care of the gun, but served to identify the different models. The two guns were identical in the construction of the barrel and the working parts, with the only difference being found in the dimensions and shapes of some of the parts of the receiver which served to identify them (the AN-M2 receiver was .2 inch longer). Each receiver slide on the AN-M2 had a projection that fit into a slot in the side of the receiver and the receiver slide bolts were locked by cotter pins. The M1 receiver slide had no flanges and were riveted instead of bolted to the receiver.

**Basic Data**

| | |
|---|---|
| Weight of basic M1 or M2.gun | 102 pounds |
| Overall length of the basic gun | 93.7 inches |
| Weight of barrel | 47.5 pounds |
| Length of barrel | 67.5 inches |
| Weight of 20mm adapter | 11.3 pounds |
| Weight of electric trigger | 0.5 pounds |
| Weight of 20mm feed mechanism | 2.6 pounds |
| Weight of 20mm M6 adapter | 14 pounds |
| Weight of 20mm M7 adapter (thread protector) | 7.5 pounds |
| Weight of 20mm M7 (muzzle break) | 10.7 pounds |
| Weight of M1 muzzle brake | 4.6 pounds |
| Weight of sear mechanism M1 | 1.3 pounds |
| Weight of manual charger M2 | 1.5 pounds |
| Muzzle Velocity (He-I or ball ammunition) | 2,850 fps |
| Muzzle Velocity (AP ammunition) | 2,950 fps |
| Rate of Fire | 600-700 rpm |
| Rifling | |
| Number of grooves | 9 |
| Depth of grooves | 0.015 inches |
| Width of lands | 0.068 inches |
| Twist, uniform, right hand slope | 7° |
| Length | 63.03 inches |
| Bore of barrel | |
| Across rifling lands | 0.797 inches |
| Across rifling grooves | 0.817 inches. |
| Chamber pressure (max.) | 42,000 psi |
| Travel of projectile in barrel | 63.69 inches. |
| Method of Feed | Magazine (spring-loaded) |
| Magazine Capacity | 60 rounds |
| Magazine Weight (Empty) | 22 pounds, 3 ounces |
| Magazine Weight (Full 60 shells) | 56 pounds |
| Weight of one complete 20mm round | 9 ounces |

**Basic Gun Assemblies**

Barrel (Tube)

The M1 barrel was bored and rifled to accommodate the projectile's driving band. The rear of the bore was increased in diameter to form a chamber which was coned to conform to the contour of the brass cartridge case. Externally the barrel was reduced in diameter from the breech towards the muzzle. It was threaded at the breech end for attachment of the recoil reducer or muzzle thread protector. The barrel screwed into the body and was secured by a retainer. The barrel of the M2 differed from the M1 only in external dimensions. The barrel carried the shell from the magazine out of the muzzle and accommodated the front mounting apparatus.

Gas Cylinder and Sleeve Group

The function of this group was to aid in unlocking the breechblock. It consisted of a piston as part of a sleeve extension that terminated in a yoke that engaged two push rods projecting through the front of the receiver.

Receiver Assembly

The receiver assembly housed most of the gun's working parts and consisted of the receiver body and the receiver plate, which was riveted to the rear underside. At the front end, the body was threaded internally to receive the barrel; a vertical hole was drilled from the under side to accommodate the barrel locking pin. A lug on top of the body was threaded internally to receive the gas cylinder sleeve guide. Longitudinal holes were drilled through the front of the body on each side below the lug to house the push rods that pushed the breechblocks slides to the rear. The front underside of the body was open to permit the ejection of empty cartridge cases. At its rear, the under side of the receiver was partially closed by the receiver plate that housed the sear block group and accommodated the firing mechanism. The rear of the body had dovetail grooves for attaching the rear buffer assembly. Two guideways on top of the receiver body accommodated the magazine slide group.

Magazine Slide Group

The magazine slide group mounted the ejector and provided a means for securing a feed mechanism to the gun.

Breechblock Assembly

The breechblock assembly consisted of the bolt assembly, two breechblock slides with springs and guide for the springs, a breechblock slide key, inertia blocks, firing pin, breechblock lock, and extractor, extractor spring, and breechblock slide key. This whole group was housed in the receiver. Its function was to carry the round from the mouth of the feed mechanism into the chamber, fire the round, extract and eject the empty case, and support it until it was deflected out of the receiver by the ejector. The breechblock was machined from a solid piece of steel with the rear bored from the rear to accommodate the firing pin and return spring. The top edges of the breechblock were cut away to clear the edges of the ejector, while the front face was recessed to accommodate the base of the cartridge case.

Breechblock Locking Key

The breechblock locking key passed through the transverse slots in the sides of the receiver.

Sear Block Group

The sear block group consisted of the sear and sear block together with the sear buffer springs, plungers, and blocks. The sear assembly was housed in the bottom plate and was retained by the pressure of the sear buffer springs. The sear was operated by the shaft of a firing mechanism, and its function was to retain the breechblocks in the retracted position by engaging the recess in the bottom of the breechblock lock. The sear buffer blocks, one of steel and the other of fiber, provided a front abutment for the sear buffer springs and plungers. The function of the sear buffer springs was to absorb the shock when the sear and breechblock engaged.

Rear Buffer Assembly

The rear buffer assembly was joined to the receiver body by a dovetail connection and a lock plunger that engaged a slot in the receiver plate and prevented the vertical sliding of the rear buffer. The function of the rear buffer was to cushion the shock of the recoiling breechblock assembly, stop the recoil, and start the breechblock assembly on its forward movement. This action and the action of the driving spring accelerated the breechblock assembly rapidly on the start of its forward movement and maintained the firing speed.

Driving Spring Group

The driving spring group consisted of the driving spring, guide, and plunger. The function of the driving spring was to drive the breechblock group forward to fire the first round and to assist in firing all rounds. It also retarded the rearward motion of the bolt.

**The Operation of the 20mm Gun Through a Firing Cycle**

In the blowback system there was no positive lock between the bolt and the barrel. The weight of the bolt and force of its recoil spring acted to keep the breech closed. The expanding gases from the fired round overcame this inertia and "blew back" the breech. The breech had to be kept sealed with the cartridge case until the round left the barrel and gas pressures decreased. The weight of the bolt and spring pressure ensured this would occur. The blow back system was only practical for weapons using relatively low pressure rounds.

At the instant of firing, the projectile was propelled down the barrel by the expanding gases. After striking the cartridge primer the firing pin was in the forward position, while the breechblock was held in its forward position by the action of the breechblock lock. The lock engaged the breechblock and pressed against the surface of the breechblock key. The breechblock slide engaged the lock, preventing it from being forced upward too soon.

As the projectile moved forward, it passed the gas port and a portion of the expanding gases entered the gas port. The gases passed through the gas cylinder vent plug, entered the gas cylinder, and exerted pressure on the gas cylinder sleeve. The yoke on the aft end of the gas cylinder sleeve engaged the push rods and pushed them rearward. The push rods then contacted the breechblock slides, which were connected by the breechblock slide key and also engaged the slot in the bottom of the firing pin. As the breechblock slides were forced rearward by the push rods, the key carried the firing pin rearward. When the lock was moved to a horizontal position the breechblock was forced to the rear by direct blowback.

When the breechblock assembly was moved to the rear, the empty cartridge case that had been forcing the bolt back by the blowback action was contracted on the upper edge by the two prongs of the ejector, forcing the cartridge case to pivot about and force the forward end of the extractor downward. The cartridge case left the lip of the extractor and moved through the opening in the bottom of the receiver, completing the ejection of the empty cartridge case. When the cartridge case released itself from the extractor, the extractor returned to its normal position by the action of the extractor spring. Concurrently, the gas cylinder sleeve had been returned to the forward position. The gas cylinder spring sleeve, which had been compressed during the rearward movement of the sleeve, expanded when the gas pressure dropped and forced the sleeve and piston forward.

When the breechblock was far enough to the rear and able to clear the feed mechanism, a new round was forced downward into the mouth of the feed mechanism by a spring in the mechanism that maintained pressure on the new rounds. In recoiling, the breechblock compressed the driving spring. As the breechblock approached the end of its rearward movement, it collided with the rear buffer and compressed the buffer spring, which absorbed the remaining force of recoil and caused the breechblock to stop. As the breechblock stopped, the inertia blocks continued to move rearwards in their slots in the breechblock slides until they reached the end of the slots. Meanwhile, the breechblock started forward again and the inertia blocks remained in a rearward position with respect to the breechblock slides during the forward motion of the breechblock. At this time the sear was held in a downward position during automatic fire, allowing the breechblock to move through its cycle without being caught and held to the rear.

The rear buffer spring and the driving spring expanded, forcing the breechblock forward. During this motion the breechblock engaged the new cartridge, which had been positioned in the mouth of the feed mechanism. As the cartridge was forced forward, it dropped into a recess in the bolt where it was gripped by the lip on the extractor as it entered the chamber.

As the breechblock reached the end of its forward motion, it seated against the end of the barrel which closed the chamber. The momentum of the slides and the action of the slide springs caused the sliders to continue to move forward, releasing the breechblock lock. At the same time, the cams of the lock were engaged by the cam surfaces on the receiver slides which, together with the action of the breechblock slide cams on the level of the lock, cammed the lock downward. The lock seated against the breechblock key and was locked in its downward position by the lower surface of the slides which moved over the end of the lock. When the slides reached the end of their forward motion, the inertia blocks continued to move forward for a short distance, counteracting any tendency that the slides could have to rebound. As the breechblock slides continued to move forward, they carried the firing pin with them on the breechblock slide key. The firing pin was free to move on the breechblock slide key and continued forward on the force of its inertia. Thus, the firing pin struck the primer of the cartridge even though the breechblock slides could have rebounded somewhat. As the firing pin struck the primer of the cartridge, it fired it and began the cycle over again.

To stop the gun from firing, the firing mechanism was released and the sear was forced upward. As the breechblock moved rearward it forced the sear down. As the breechblock moved forward, the sear rose again and entered a recess in the underside of the breechblock lock, which engaged the lock and stopped the forward motion of the breechblock assembly. The shock of stopping was absorbed by the sear buffer springs and plungers in the sear block.

**Adapters**

The adapter was a self-contained tubular unit that slipped over the barrel of the gun. The adapter basically consisted of a ring spring assembled under compression in series with a coil spring. The adapter was designed to reduce the effective recoil and counter-recoil forces of the gun on its supporting structure and accurately control the amount of recoil travel within definite limits (0.833 inch to 1.167 inches). It provided a front mounting assembly for the gun, and also permitted the gun to recoil the required distance to operate the AN-M1 feed mechanism or any other feed mechanism that obtained its power from the recoil movement of the gun.

**Electric Trigger**

The electric trigger AN-M1 was a remote control mechanism designed to fire 20mm guns in aircraft equipped with 24-volt electrical systems.

**Chargers**

Hydraulic Charger M1

This charger was installed on U.S. Navy 20mm Aircraft Guns AN-M2 to provide charging or safetying by remote control. The charger consisted of a spring guide assembly, a piston spring, and a cylinder and piston assembly; all of which were assembled inside the cylinder charger housing on the right hand side of the gun.

*Figure 59 – 60-round Magazine – Front View*

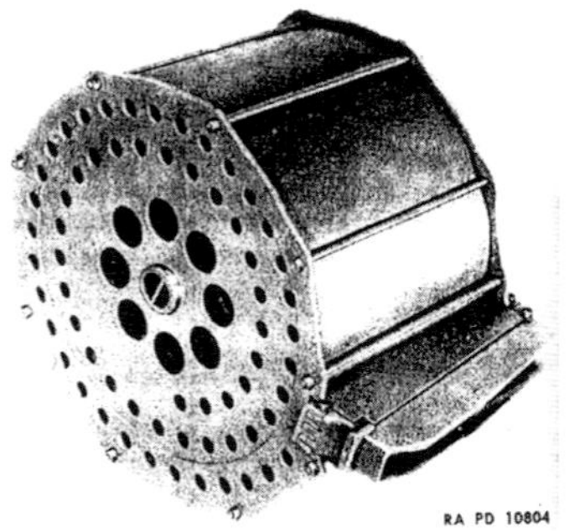

*Figure 60 – 60-round Magazine – Rear View*

**60 ROUND 20mm MAGAZINE** (USAAF)

Manual Charger M2
This charger, previously designated as the B6 charger by the AAF, consisted of a flanged charger slide for engaging and retracting the breechblock, a slide spring for returning the slide to its forward position, and a spring guide that closed the rear end of the charger housing. The slide was actuated by manually pulling the slide cable.

**Feed Mechanisms**
The AN-M1 Feed Mechanism used the recoil energy of the gun to feed rounds into the gun. The rounds were connected on a belt with links, and the function of the feed mechanism was to draw the belt into the gun, separate the rounds from the links, and feed the rounds, one at a time, into the breech. There were two distinct mechanisms: one for right hand feeding and the other for left hand feeding.

All rounds were to be lubricated just before they were to be inserted in the magazine of belts. Lubrication was performed by dipping a cloth in a special oil lubricating preservative and then wringing it out and wiping the cartridge case in a light film of oil. During the "oiling" the armorer was to take extreme precaution to avoid getting oil on the primer or the joint where the case was crimped to the projectile.

**Magazines**
The 20mm magazine was designed to hold 60 rounds of ammunition and consisted of the front and rear plates with the rods, outer casing; mouth and throat plate; spring and spring casing with front plate disk and tensioning tube; and feed arm axis tube with feed arm bracket, feed arm plate, link, axis bush, and platform tube.

**U.S. 20mm Cannon Development Based on the German MG151/20**
**T22**
In December 1943, Colt Patent Fire Arms received the requirements for their development of an experimental 20mm gun based on the operating principles of a captured German Mauser MG151/20, but was to utilize the movement of the bolt to operate the feed mechanism. The gun, designated as the 20mm Automatic Gun T22, was to fire existing 20mm ammunition used by the M2 gun; the feed mechanism was to be of the disintegrating link-belt type and be capable of taking different lengths of shell. The gun was be of the self-locking blowback type with a cyclic rate of fire of 575 to 650 rpm; the round had to be controlled at all times in the gun and was to be fed from either right or left side without the addition of extra parts; and the belt pull was to be at least the permitted limit of 75 pounds. The T22 was to have the following desirable items in common with the MG-151/20: mechanical unlocking, location and type of adapter, quickly removable barrel with interrupted concentric rings, and the reciprocating bolt on the axis of the weapon. Unlike the MG151/20, the T22 did not use a rotating bolthead for unlocking and had much simpler lines than either the MG151/20 or the American 20mm AN-M2.

The air-cooled T22 was 78 inches long and weighed 112 pounds, and was of the short recoil operated type, with the mechanical unlocking of the breech delayed until the residual pressure in the bore dropped to a safe point for unlocking. While the AN-M2 and T31 guns were a combination blowback and gas-operated type, the T22 could be seared on the right in the rear, or open bolt position, and on the left or right in the forward, or closed bolt position. A set of trunnions on the adapter housing connected the gun to its mounting, and two additional trunnions were carried on the receiver body for firing from fixed trunnions if needed. The gun fired standard 20mm Hispano-Suiza ammunition at a rate of fire of 575-650 rpm with a muzzle velocity of 2,800 fps. In testing the T22 was unable to penetrate more than 1.125 inch of armor, which was below the 1.5 inches specified. By the end of 1944, the T22 continued to fall short of requirements in testing and a new development program was initiated to produce a cannon capable of fulfilling these requirements with a higher muzzle velocity than guns under production or development. Increased muzzle velocity would result in a decrease in time of flight and would increase armor penetration. On 9 August 1945, just as the atomic bombs were being dropped on Japan, the T22 program was canceled while experimental work continued on the T24, which was designed and operated on the same principles as the T22.

**T24**
The T24 was 100 inches long and weighed 141.375 pounds with the barrel, but without the eight pound adaptor. It had a rate of fire of 700-750 rpm with a muzzle velocity of 3,500 fps. The T24 had right hand or left hand feed without extra parts, a forward sear, a bolt holding back sear, a mechanical feed for link belt, and a quickly detachable 63 inch barrel. The weapon could be operated by an electric trigger or solenoid from the right or left hand side, as was required, and was capable of synchronized fire. Since the T24 gun was of the short-recoil operated type, the unlocking of the breech was delayed until the residual pressure in the barrel dropped to a degree where it was safe for unlocking. The basic structure of the gun consisted of a receiver, built up by riveting, which was composed of the following main parts: receiver body, two side plates, and a back plate. The T24 was designed to use the new 20mm, 3,500 fps T5E1 round that had a much larger case than the standard round, so the T24 chamber was larger and the receiver 2.5 inches greater in diameter than the T22; otherwise, the firing mechanisms of the two guns were identical. Between 14 February 1945 and 24 August 1945, 40 tests were conducted using the T24 at the Colt factory or the Aberdeen Proving Ground. After the late August tests it seems that testing stopped with the end of the war, as there are no records of further work on the T24.

**Johnson 20mm Cannon**
In early 1942 the Navy Bureau of Ordnance commenced a 20mm aircraft cannon program to either replace or supplement the existing troubled Hispano-Suiza cannon, which was slated to be the standard Navy cannon. In July Dr. Henry Allen, director of the Franklin Institute, Philadelphia, and Vice Chairman of the National Defense Research Committee (NDRC), discussed the problem of the belt-feed system with Melvin Johnson, the president of Johnson Automatics, Inc. of Boston. Johnson had graduated with a BS from Harvard in 1931 and a law degree in 1934, but had shown an aptitude for sporting rifles and ordnance and accepted a Second Lieutenant commission in the ROTC program. In the mid- to late 1930s he worked on developing an automatic infantry rifle and light machine gun for his Johnson Automatics Company. However, the Johnson Automatic Rifle did

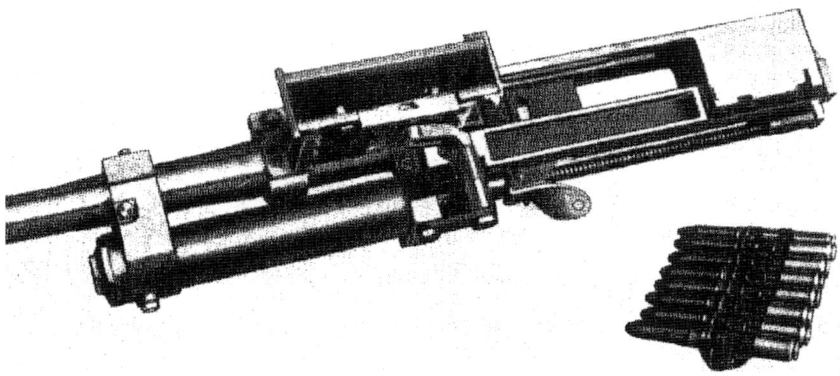

**JOHNSON 20MM CANNON** (AFHRC)

not show any marked advantages over the M1 Garand to which the Army was committed and this Johnson project was terminated.

In August 1942, Johnson and C.B. Gardiner visited the Navy Proving Grounds at Dahlgren, VA, where they observed the operation and testing of the Hispano-Suiza cannon. Afterward, Johnson wrote a letter to the NDRC and the Bureau of Ordnance recommending the development of a completely new aircraft cannon designed for belt feed. The Bureau of Ordnance granted a developmental contract to Johnson Automatics that stipulated explicit service specifications for the new gun. In mid-1942, the requirements for cyclic rate of fire were not especially high, but soon these requirements became higher and were combined with the requirement for a right hand and left hand self-feeding gun mechanism and a removable barrel. A major requirement, intended to overcome a drawback of the Hispano-Suiza system, was a self-feeding gun mechanism which did not require external forces to actuate the belt so in order to pull its own belt, this gun was constructed with a reciprocating breechblock. A key problem Johnson encountered was that the Navy initially specified the use of 20mm Oerlikon ammunition, which he felt was unsuitable for the required performance of the contract. Ultimately 20mm Hispano-Suiza ammunition was substituted even though this ammunition was never intended for use in a gas-operated, belt-fed system, especially one in which a cartridge was to be pulled to the rear out of a closed loop belt.

In less than 18 months, Johnson had a firing model ready which was followed by three other models:

First Model: This model was originally planned for Oerlikon ammunition, and later was adapted for Hispano-Suiza ammunition intended to fire at 600-900 rpm at a muzzle velocity of 2,750 fps. The 97 inch long, 115 pound gun was designed for installation in the wing, fuselage, or turret. Firing tests were conducted between mid-January to mid-April 1943 when work on this model was discontinued in favor of the next models.

Second and Third Models: These models were designed as belt-fed automatic, gas-operated air-cooled cannon. The second model appeared on paper in the beginning of December 1943, but was replaced by the third model in February 1944 before the former was built. This third air-cooled Johnson gun was 90 inches long (not including the muzzle brake) with a 67.5 inch barrel and weighed 120 pounds (44 pound barrel). The gun was gas-actuated, sliding wedge, gas unlocking, blowback with a right or left feed. It had a rate of fire of 500-900 rpm at a muzzle velocity of 2,800 fps.

Fourth Model: The fourth Johnson gun incorporated the basic mechanism of the earlier guns but at a greatly reduced weight, and had a potential 1,000 rpm rate of fire. Work on this model was started during the summer of 1945, but had only progressed to the drawing board stage by VJ-Day when the contract was terminated.

**U.S. Army Air Force 20mm Cannon Installations**

**Curtiss P-36 Hawk**

A P-36F (s/n 38-172) had been under testing at Eglin in December 1939 to investigate the installation of two 23mm Madsen cannon mounted in underwing gondolas. The Madsens were removed, as they greatly decreased the aircraft's performance, and in February 1940 two of the 13 Hispano cannon allocated to the ACC in December 1939 were installed in 38-172. Initial tests conducted at the Curtiss Buffalo plant were successful, and on 15 August 1940 the fighter was sent to Eglin for further testing at the proving grounds. The P-36 was the first contemporary American fighter to carry the 20mm cannon.

**Lockheed P-38 Lightning**

The definitive P-38 armament configuration featured four .50 caliber machine guns with 500 rpg and a Hispano 20mm cannon with 150 rounds replacing the unreliable Oldsmobile 37mm gun mounted on the YP-38 and P-38D production version (there was no P-38B or C). While the machine guns had been arranged symmetrically in the nose in earlier variants, they were staggered above the 20mm cannon on the P-38E and later versions, with the .50 muzzles protruding from the nose in the relative lengths of roughly 1:4:6:2. This was done to ensure a straight ammunition belt feed into the weapons, as the earlier arrangement led to jamming. The rate of fire was about 650 rpm for the 20x110mm cannon round (130 grain shell) at a muzzle velocity of about 2,887 fps and an effective range of approximately 1,200 yards. Continuous fire was 15 seconds with an ammo belt composition of 2 AP, 2 tracer, and 2 HE. There was a separate thumb-operated cannon trigger located on the front of the wheel/yoke and a .50 caliber gun trigger located on the forward side of the wheel (however, this arrangement could vary). P-38E (#42-12866) was used as a test-bed for the proposed XP-49 armament to be armed with two 20mm cannon and four .50 caliber guns.

P-36F (s/n 38-172) mounting 20mm cannon in underwing pods. (USAAF)

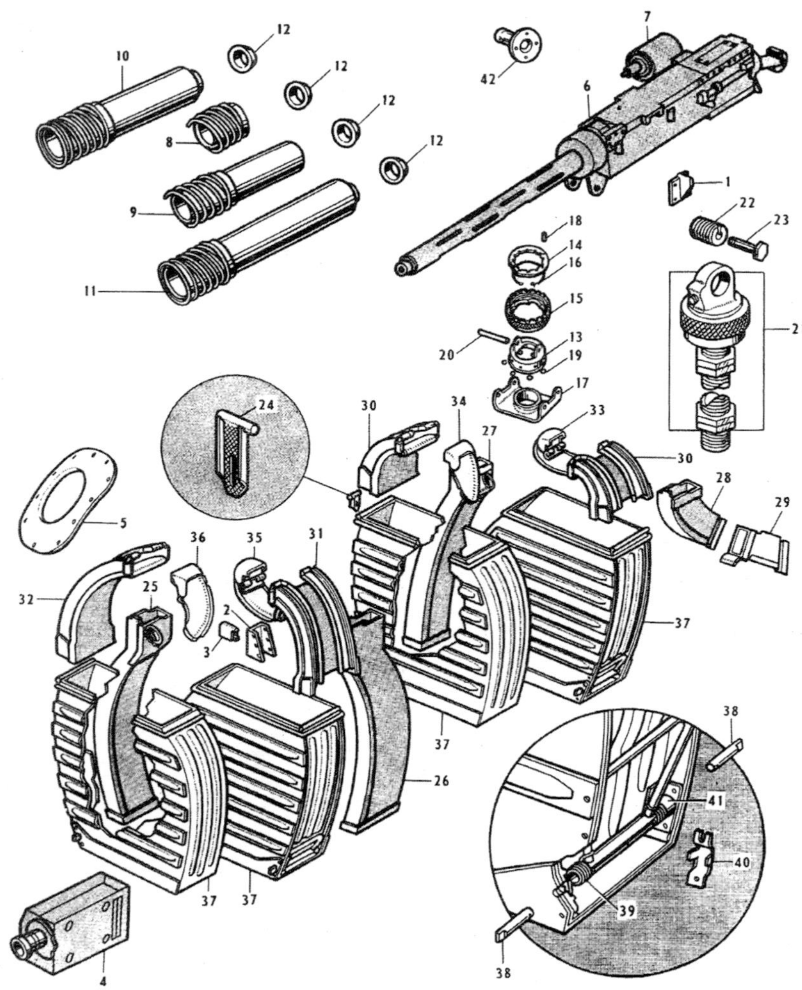


**P-38 20mm Hispano Installation** (USAAF)

Good photo of 20mm cannon (lower center) and .50 caliber machine gun installation in the P-38 nose compartment. (USAAF)

Standard P-38 nose armament with four .50 caliber Browning Machine Guns placed in a semi-circle above a single 20mm cannon. (USAAF)

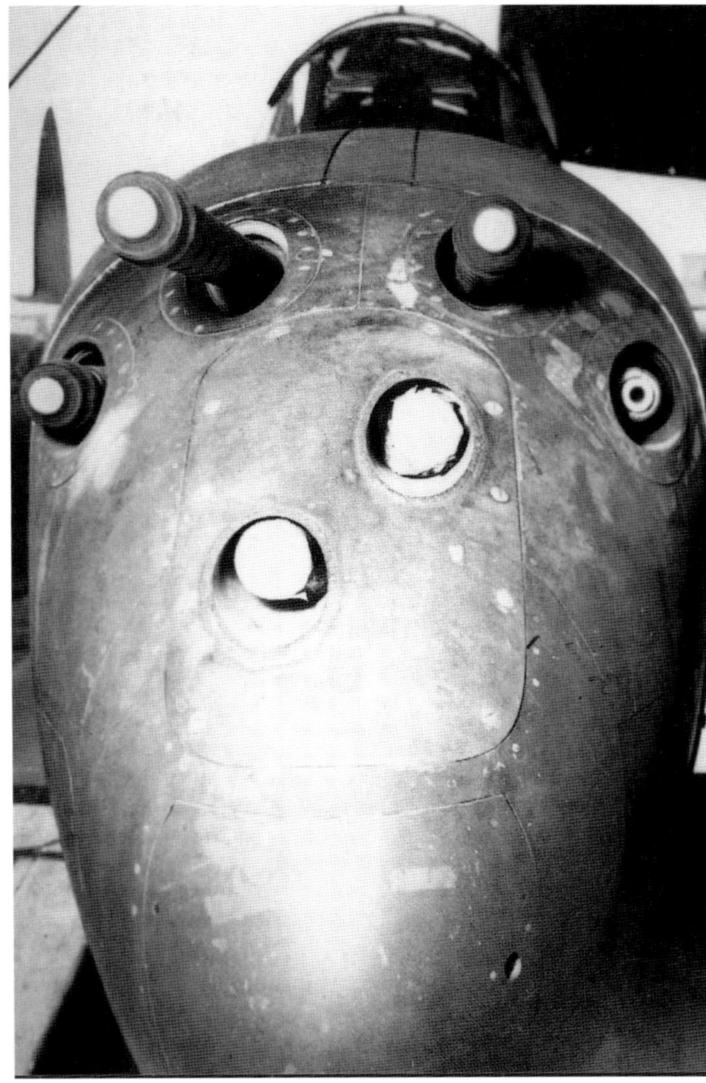

P-38E (#42-12866) was used as a test-bed for the proposed XP-49 armament to be armed with two 20mm cannon and four .50 caliber guns. (USAAF)

**Bell P-400 (P-39) Airacobra**

The British elected to install the Hispano 20mm cannon in place of the 37mm cannon in the P-39C export version, which the British dubbed the Airacobra I. When America entered the war 179 of these fighters were diverted from the RAF and over 100 were sent to Australia as the redesignated P-400 mounting the 20mm cannon firing 60 rounds through the propeller spinner. Additional armament was two synchronized .50s installed in the cowling and a pair of .30s in each wing. The Hispano was intensely disliked by American pilots over Guadalcanal because of its constant jamming problems, low rate of fire, and dissimilar trajectory to the machine guns.

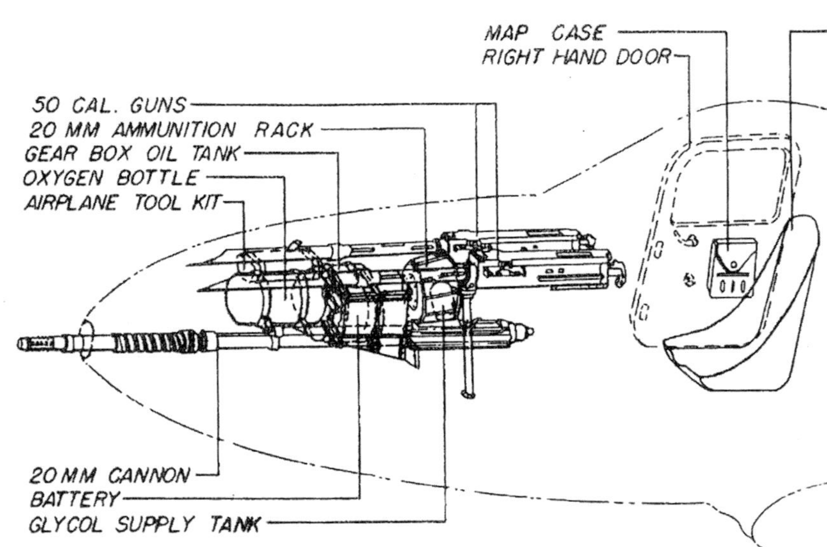


P-39D Nose Armament (USAAF)

A **Bell P-400 Airacobra** of the 13th Fighter Command firing its 20mm cannon while flying over Guadalcanal from a cover painting by Steve Ferguson from my book the *13th Fighter Command in World War II: Air Combat over Gaudalcanal and the Solomons.* (Author/ Ferguson)

**A-20 with four 20mm cannon in the nose compartment.** (USAAF)

**Douglas A-20 Havoc/P-70 Nighthawk**

The A-20G was ordered as a medium attack bomber on 1 June 1942 and delivered in February 1943 equipped with a solid nose that was introduced to increase the forward fire power for strafing missions. The nose contained four 20mm M2 cannon with 60 rpg in the forward nose section with the barrels protruding a long distance outside the nose, complimented by two .50 caliber machine guns with 350 rpg mounted in the lower rear part of the nose. The M2 cannon had a low rate of fire and encountered jamming problems, and after 250 G-models were produced the four cannon were replaced by four nose mounted .50s in the G-5-DO production block.

After considering the successful British Havoc, the AAC modified the A-20 into 59 P-70 jury-rigged night fighters equipped with the British A1 Mk IV radar unit, carrying four 20mm cannon fed by 60 rpg in a ventral tray located in the bomb bay.

**20mm ventral tray installation.** (USAAF)

**Boeing B-17 Flying Fortress 20mm Cannon**

The armament of the first B-17 models was found to be inadequate, and an early B-17C (40-2046) was sent to Eglin Field from Wright Field on 16 May 1942 for evaluation. The bomber was equipped with an experimental Sperry remote fire control system and two 20mm cannon mounted in the nose. The 20mm cannon were tested for their ability to ward off head-on enemy fighter attacks. The Eglin report stated that:

"(the B-17 was) restricted to maneuvers that could be performed within a three-airplane formation. On this basis it was impossible to hold an attacking airplane within the sights of the cannon long enough to fire effectively. The B-17 could not be effectively maneuvered against an airplane attacking from the front. It is recommended that flexible guns or a .50 caliber turret be installed on the B-17 as protection against a nose attacks."

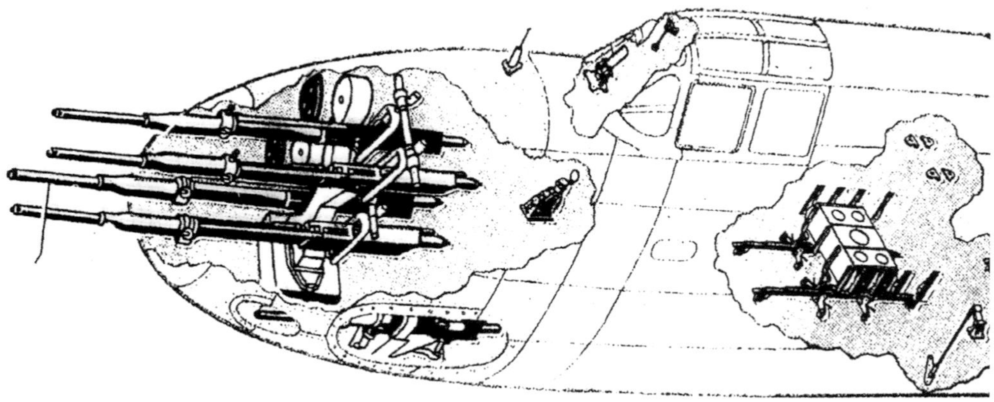

**20mm NOSE INSTALLATION** (USAAF)

A 20mm installation in the nose compartment of a 385th Bomb Group B-17 with the ammunition drum on top and a bracing cable on the right side. (USAAF)

As a solution .50 caliber Cheek guns were installed, but were found to be inadequate, and no answer was found until the Bendix A-16 Chin turret was installed on the B-17G. However, various Groups in the 8th Air Force experimented with in-the-field 20mm nose mountings. In August 1943 the 385th Bomb Group installed a single 20mm gun in the nose of a B-17F (42-5897). Although the gun was securely mounted, its weight and excessive recoil made it difficult for the gunner to control.

In the spring of 1944, the 97BG jury-rigged a 20mm cannon in the tails of five of its B-17Gs to replace the twin .50s. The intention of the installation was to discourage *Luftwaffe* fighters that lobbed rockets from outside the range of the B-17's normal .50 Brownings. For this reason the bombers carrying these guns flew at the rear of their formations. The guns were used operationally, but were found to have limited fields of fire, which nonetheless did have a psychological effect on the approaching German fighter pilot, who became intimidated when he saw 20mm shells being lobbed at his aircraft.

20mm installation in the tail of a B-29. (USAAF)

**Boeing B-29 Superfortress 20mm Cannon**

As part of the January 1940 AAC "Superbomber" specifications the Lockheed XB-30, a proposed (and never built) bomber version of the company's Constellation airliner, mounted two .50 caliber machine guns and a 20mm cannon in the tail. As part of these specifications, in March 1940 a 20mm cannon was mounted in the tail turret of the Boeing Model 345, which was a B-29 Superfortress superbomber precursor. The B-29's defensive armament was built around the General Electric Central Fire Control System, which included five sighting stations and associated equipment directing two upper and two lower remote turrets, each mounting two .50 caliber machine guns, with the tail turret being the only manned gun station. The tail turrets of early B-29s mounted a 20mm cannon and twin .50 caliber machine guns supplied with 1,000 rpg carried in a pair of large boxes located forward of the horizontal stabilizer, and tracks carried the ammunition aft to the tail gunner. The 20mm cannon carried 110 to 125 rounds and could be fired separately of or along with the machine guns. However, the cannon had a different trajectory than the machine guns and only fired 7 to 11 rounds per minute, and concurrent firing of the three guns was not effective, as the computer only calculated for the .50 caliber machine guns. It was recommended that the 20mm be fired only when the attacker was at close range (not more than 600 yards), when the bullet drop of the machine guns and cannon were similar. Characteristically, the 20mm cannon had feed mechanism problems and were later deleted in some models. The tail turret and guns were equipped with cut off switches and mechanical stops that limited its vertical and horizontal movement to 30° in all directions.

**Consolidated Vultee XP-81**

The projected single-seat, long-range escort XP-81 was scheduled to carry six wing-mounted 20mm cannon but never progressed beyond the unarmed prototype stage.

**U.S. Navy 20mm Cannon Installations**

The U.S. Navy would be the primary user of the 20mm cannon during the war, mounting over 90% of these guns in U.S. service. On 11 March 1943, the first 20mm gun mounted by the Navy was installed by the Bureau of Aeronautics Aircraft Armament Unit (AAU) at it test facility at Norfolk, VA. Navy BuAer, already realizing the importance of a larger caliber gun, officially accepted the gun for naval aircraft use the following day. The Curtiss-Wright Aeronautical Corp. of Columbus, OH, shipped the wing of a SB2C for a mock up installation of a cannon for proof firing. The AAU continued testing this mock up cannon installation until August 1943, when the 20mm guns were installed in SB2C scout dive bombers coming off the assembly line (SB1C serial #200 was the first). The first SB2C entered

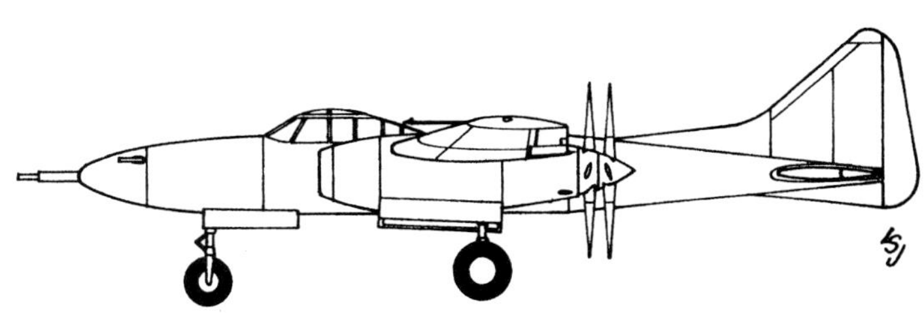

**XP-81** (Jones via Merriam)

service on 11 November 1943 and first saw action in March 1944, where the gun suffered chronic problems. Extensive reports were sent back listing the causes of malfunctions (feeder failure, faulty ammunition, and inadequate maintenance), but did not place direct blame on the flawed gun.

After the Navy began to install the 20mm cannon, a series of malfunctions occurred that could not be easily corrected in the midst of peak production without shutting down the line for retooling. Again, the most serious problem was the larger chamber size. The Navy found an interim remedy to the oversized chamber problem by coating the cartridge case with a heavy lubricant that functioned as "fluid fit," allowing the cartridge to slip back at the beginning of pressure build up and filling the extra space between the breech lock and breech lock key. This "temporary" solution remained in effect throughout the war. When the Chief of the Bureau of Ordnance evaluated the 20mm M2 and its M3 successor on 26 December 1945, he issued a report entitled the "Reactivation of Certain 20mm Automatic Gun Development Projects and 20mm Ammunition Projects." Among the findings outlined in the report were:

**F4U-1C 20mm**

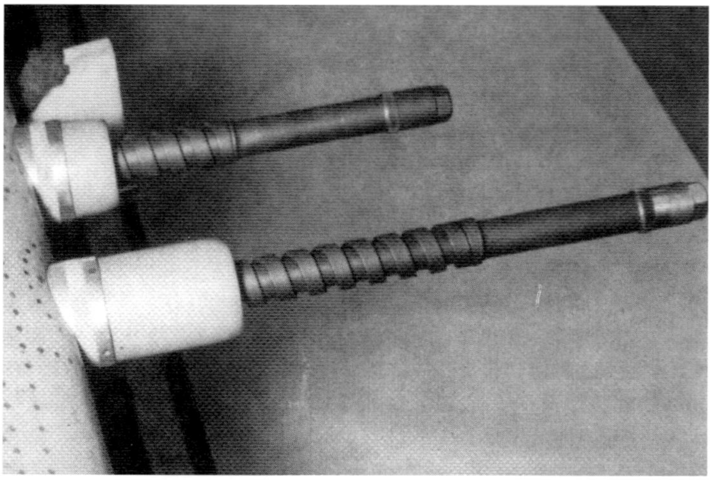

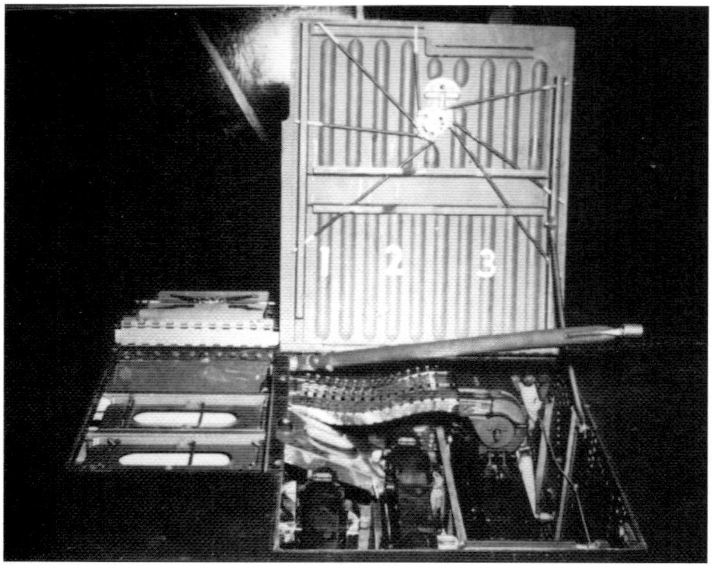


(all USMC)

"There is a firm requirement on the part of the Navy Department for the use of 20mm automatic guns in practically all Navy combat aircraft currently in design and currently designated combat operational aircraft."

The Chief felt that although the 20mm guns had "certain objections and defects;" these could be overcome to make the "continued development of this type weapon highly desirable." Among the correctable "objections and defects" were:

1) The profile of the gun was too large and cumbersome for proper placement in VF-type (i.e. Navy fighter aircraft) wings.
2) The cyclic rate of fire was too low.
3) The total weight of the gun and its associated equipment should be greatly decreased.
4) The accrued tolerances (e.g. to artillery standards) were too great "to give uniformly efficient operation in these guns."
5) The need for lubricating the ammunition prior to use was deemed undesirable and was to be eliminated.
6) The ballistics were to be improved, and an electrically primed round was to be developed.
7) And finally, the ammunition should be manufactured to fit the chamber of the gun in which it would be fired and "not fit two of these weapons; namely the American and British 20mm automatic guns."

Despite these objections, which the Navy felt could be rectified, the bottom line was that the Navy saw the advantage of the 20mm cannon.

The Navy records for 20mm AN-M2 cannon installation are sketchy, but their records credit over 5,800 aircraft having 11,600 20mm guns installed with the SB2C and -W as the main recipients along with a very small number of F4U-1Cs. Although the U.S. produced a total of 135,000 20mm cannon, most were never mounted in an aircraft.

**Brewster F2A Buffalo**

Brewster attempted to upgrade the Buffalo's firepower by investigating the use of 20mm cannon in place of the wing .50s. The project was abandoned when further development of the controversial and inadequate fighter was cancelled.

**Chance-Vought F4U-1C Corsair**

Most models of the F4U carried six .50s, but the 200 F4U-1Cs were armed with four 20mm cannon that proved to be very unreliable. The F4U-1C carried only 924 20mm rounds for four cannon compared to the 2,400 rounds for six .50 caliber guns. Although the 20mm cannon were much more powerful than the .50 caliber machine guns, most pilots favored the extra ammunition and longer duration of fire. Nonetheless, the Navy continued its search for increased firepower, and in the last months of the war the Navy ordered the F4U-4 and requested that four 20mm M2 be installed on this version. Before any deliveries were made the more reliable, lighter, and faster-firing M3 cannon were available, and would be installed on the post-war F4U-4C model.

### Grumman F6F Hellcat

The first XF6F-1 prototype (02981) was the test bed for the XF6F-4, and was armed with four wing-mounted 20mm cannon, replacing the six .50 caliber machine guns. The XF6F-1 was first flown in early October 1942 but never was accepted for production. A mixed armament of two .50 machine guns and two 20mm cannon first was tested on a late model F6F-3 and was later installed on F6F-5N night-fighters.

**XF6F-4** (USN)

**F6F-5N** (USN)

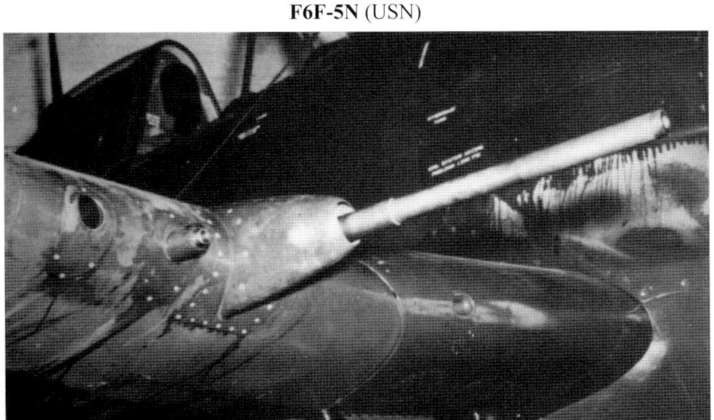

**F6F-5N** (USN)

### Curtiss SB2C Helldiver

The SB2C-1C mounted two 20mm cannon instead of the four .50 caliber machine guns of the previous -1 model. The 20mm barrel passed through the outer section of the wheel well, with the muzzle protruding through the underside of the wing leading edge, rather than being installed directly through it. The guns were fed by two 100 round ammunition boxes mounted just inboard each cannon. There was a redesigned underwing access panel with a single slot through which cartridges were ejected and a second smaller slot through which links were ejected.

**SB2C 20mm**

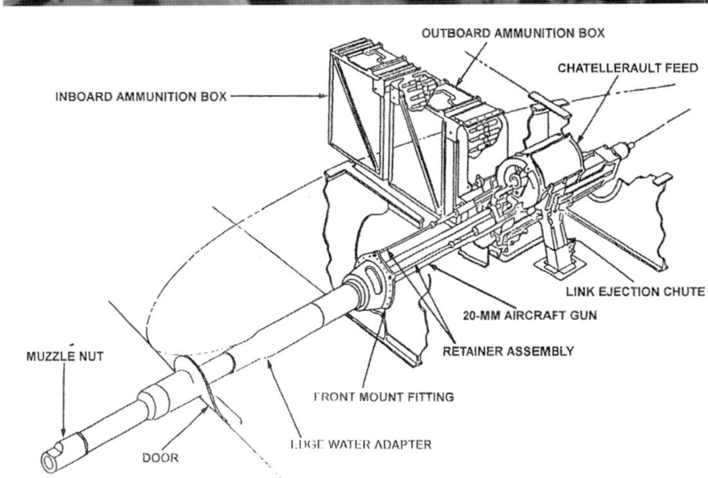


(all USN)

**ERCO 220 Turret** (USN)

**Curtiss XF14C**
The Navy ordered three prototypes of the XF14C as a new carrier fighter powered by a piston and jet engine and armed with four wing-mounted 20mm cannons. The XF14 was the last fighter Curtiss built for the Navy and testing continued until late 1946 when the program was cancelled as pure jet carrier fighters came on line.

**Douglas BTD Destroyer**
Douglas developed the BTD, ordered as the XSB2D-1, in June 1941 to replace its SBD Dauntless dive bomber. The design was to feature an internal weapons bay and two 20mm cannon in the wings.

**ERCO X220TH-1 Turret**
The ERCO X220TH-1 (Model 6081) waist turret was an experimental model turret contracted by the U.S. Navy in June 1945 to be equipped with 20mm cannon. It was intended to replace PB4Y-2 side turrets equipped with 50 caliber machine guns.

**ERCO Dorsal Ball Turret**
The Navy ordered this ERCO turret in quantity, and began a project to build a twin 20mm turret with a self-contained gasoline power drive and pressurized cabin for the PBB-1 Sea Ranger. The AAF and the Materiel Division were unable to use the ERCO design because it was too heavy and was powered with a Vickers drive unit, which was already in short supply. This proposal died when the Sea Ranger project was cancelled.

**Post-war Development**
In the post-war the Navy embarked on an immediate and continuing improvement of 20mm guns and ammunition, while the Army worked on a long-range program of developing the optimal aircraft gun of an undetermined caliber.

# 2

# 23mm (.90 Caliber) Aircraft Cannon

**USAAC .90 Caliber Automatic Aircraft Cannon**

During the 1930s the interest in developing larger caliber aircraft guns emerged in Europe, and the Army Ordnance Department undertook the development of a .90 caliber gun (.90 inches equals 22.86mm). The T1 was the first .90 caliber model and was quite unwieldy, weighing 205 pounds including its 50 pound, flat drum feed. The air-cooled gun used the slow long-recoil system with the extra recoil absorbed by a standard spring-oil-type hydraulic system. The maximum rate of fire was a very slow 150 rounds per minute and could be adjusted by a valve inside a buffer that controlled oil flow. The feed magazine weighed 80 pounds, was located on top of the receiver, and was very slow and complicated. The fused projectile was considered to be effective firing at a good 2,850 fps, but the low rate of fire and feeding mechanism were inferior to existing guns and the project was cancelled.

The T1 was soon followed by the T2 air-cooled, magazine-fed model that utilized the straight blow back system that was the only energy used in the gun's operation. The T2 closely resembled the Oerlikon from which it was copied but not duplicated, as it assumed much larger proportions. The 97 inch T2 weighed 240.5 pounds, excluding the feeder. The gun was mounted on an aircraft by four trunnions attached 90° apart at the forward end of the receiver. Cartridges were initially fed to the gun by a drum magazine containing 48 rounds positioned on top of the receiver by a spring-loaded bracket. The rounds had to be waxed before use, which was usually an inherent drawback of the straight blowback system. Later a flat feeder operating from the recoil of the gun was developed but also proved to be inadequate. Each cartridge was removed from the feed by the bolt in its forward movement while the next round was positioned by a clip and spring contained in the mouth of the feed. The magazine could be set to feed two to 48 rounds by a large gear located at the rear of the magazine bracket. The gun had a low rate of fire at 400 to 450 rpm and was too heavy for aircraft use, so the T2 project was abandoned. A T3 was developed, but was essentially the same as the T2 and it too was cancelled.

**23mm Madsen Automatic Aircraft Cannon**

In 1902 the Dansk Rekylriffel Syndikat of Copenhagen, Denmark, developed an 8mm automatic firing mechanism for a machine gun named the Madsen, after the Danish Minister of War, who initially supported the gun for adoption. Over the years the Madsen mechanism was modified for use with nearly all rifle sized cartridges. In 1926, the company upscaled the machine gun mechanism for a high-quality 23mm aircraft cannon that was air-cooled, short-recoil operated, and magazine-fed with a 180 rpm rate of fire. The cannon was almost identical to the company's 20mm anti-aircraft gun and was characterized by its breech block, which pivoted at its rear end, giving it three different positions for firing, ejection, and chambering. It could be used for both flexible and wing mounting, but not for engine installation due to the excessive vibration from automatic fire.

The 23mm Madsen had a major advantage over other contemporary cannons, as it was belt fed rather than drum fed. Cannon ammunition drums were large and required space for their installation, and the number of shells carried was limited, usually to 60. The Madsen's disintegrating link belt required much less space and could carry 100 rounds for the same amount of weight as a 60 round drum. Nonetheless, the Madsen cannon was still too large to be installed in an aircraft wing not specifically designed for cannon installation and needed to be placed in an underwing gondola (pod), which seriously decreased aircraft performance. Also, the metal links tended to rust or corrode due to moisture or condensation in the magazines. In the field the links were boiled in oil until Madsen could supply chrome-plated links. The rimmed ammunition was specifically designed for use in the air and on the ground as an anti-tank weapon. The muzzle velocity of the 23mm cartridge was not as high as the 20mm cartridge, but could be filled with more explosive than the 20mm cartridge, which with its higher velocity had more penetrating power. A hydraulic buffer cylinder was installed on the cannon to help absorb the larger recoil caused by the larger cartridge.

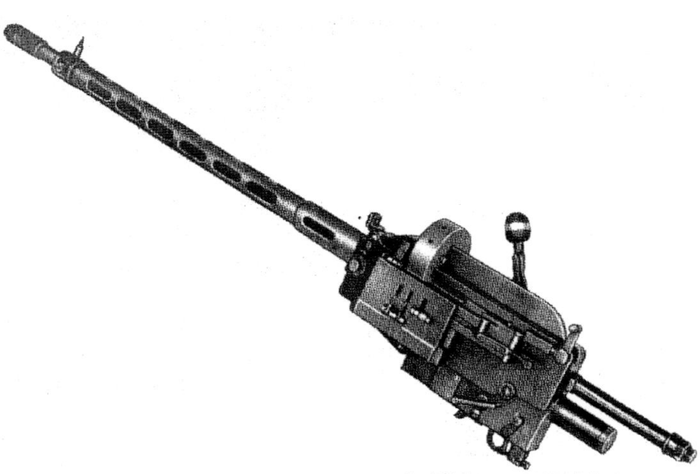

Figure 23-1. 23-mm Madsen Automatic Aircraft Cannon.

(USAAF)

The **Curtiss XP-36F** had one Madsen cannon with 100 rpg placed in a detachable gondola under each wing outboard of the landing gear. (USAAF)

Development of the cannon proceeded very slowly, and interest in the gun was lacking until the revival of aircraft cannon in the mid-1930s. During the 1936 Paris Exposition the company, now known as the Dansk Industri Syndikat, exhibited a Fokker G-1 equipped with two belt-fed Madsen cannon with 100 metal-linked rounds installed in each wing. Several countries, including the United States, expressed interest in the gun, and on 18 May 1937 a contract for four guns, 5,000 rounds of ammunition, and accessories was purchased for $28,611. The guns arrived in New York in November and were sent to Wright Field and the Dahlgren, VA, Naval Proving Ground for study and testing, where the gun was found to have a low rate of fire and was unreliable, particularly its feed mechanism.

| **Madsen 23mm Cannon** | |
|---|---|
| Weight (pounds) | 118.8 |
| Overall Length (inches) | 78.4 |
| Barrel Length (inches) | 47 |
| Rate of Fire (rpm) | 400 |
| Muzzle Velocity (fps) | 2395 |
| Length of Recoil (inches) | 3.9 |
| Weight of Round (ounces) | 11.9 |
| Weight of Projectile (ounces) | 6 |
| Practical Range (yards) | 1,000 |

**Installation of the 23mm Cannon in American Aircraft**

Two of the 23mm Madsens that the Army purchased from Denmark were installed in the Curtiss XP-36F (s/n 38-172, the 172nd P-36A). One Madsen cannon with 100 rpg was placed in a detachable gondola (pod) under each wing outboard the landing gear. In tests at Eglin in December 1939 the guns performed well, but the wing pod increased the fighter's weight and drag and decreased its top speed, so that this aircraft's development was terminated after one model. These two Madsens were replaced by French Hispano 20mm cannon purchased in December 1939, and this aircraft underwent tests using that armament.

The Madsen cannon were used in combat by an American aircraft. A Hawk-75Q and CW-21 were sent in crates to the Chinese in February 1939 as demonstration aircraft. These aircraft were assembled and flown by Curtiss factory representatives Robert Fausel (the CW-21) and George Weigle (the H-75Q) for five months in comparative trials against other aircraft flown by the Chinese. At the time the Chinese were at war with the Japanese, and on 4 May an "American" pilot flying the CW-21 engaged what was described as a "Japanese-Italian Fiat Br.20," firing at it from long-range without result. The next day Weigle flew the Hawk to Chungking, where he encountered a large Japanese air raid. Gen. Claire Chennault states in his memoir *Way of a Fighter* that the Japanese "met unexpected opposition from what, I believe, were the first aircraft to use cannon in combat," shooting down four bombers before he turned back. However, on the 5th Weigle tried to return to Chungking but crashed into a hillside and was killed. When Fausel recovered Weigle's body he found that the Madsens had not been fired (via Gerry Beauchamp: *Curtiss Hawk 75*).

With the renewed interest in aircraft cannon the U.S. had considered the Madsen for several developing aircraft. An armament proposal for the original P-38 included six .50 caliber machine guns and a 23mm cannon, but the preproduction YP-38s were fitted with a 37mm M4 cannon instead, along with two .50s, and .two .30s.

The Grumman prototype XF5F-1 Skyrocket designed for the Navy was to mount four 23mm Madsen guns in its short nose but no armament was ever installed. The Bell Model 5 Airabonita, also designed for the Navy, was to all intents and purposes a tail-dragging P-39 Airacobra. One of its proposed armament configurations was a 23mm Madsen (or a .50 caliber machine gun) firing through the propeller hub and two .30 machines mounted in the nose.

The Madsen had been tested extensively in France in 1937 against the 20mm Hispano-Suiza and Oerlikon and was found to have reliability and stamina problems. With its poor performance in testing, America's interest in the 23mm Madsen cannon abated and the 37mm cannon, particularly the ballyhooed American Armament Corporation 37mm cannon, became the favored large caliber aircraft gun.

# 3

# 37mm Cannon

## History

Throughout the history of air combat designers tried to adapt large caliber cannon of 37mm and more for aircraft use for both air-to-air combat and more so for air-to-ground use. However, the inherent disadvantages of the large gun—significant weight, limited ammunition supply, low rate of fire, poor accuracy due to low muzzle velocity, and extreme recoil—have, even to this day, been the major drawbacks to their development and use.

The 1868 Declaration of St. Petersburg banned any projectile weighing less than 400 grams (14 ounces) which was explosive or contained incendiary materiel. At that time 400 gram projectiles were 37mm in caliber, and this ban was abided by until 1918 and the First World War, after which explosive, incendiary, and tracer bullets were used in projectiles as small as rifle caliber.

Trials to mount large caliber aircraft cannon appear to have originated in France in 1910, when Gabriel Voisin mounted a 37mm 1885 naval-type Hotchkiss gun in one of his biplanes. During World War I there was substantial interest in mounting a large caliber gun in aircraft but resulting in few viable installations. Several hundred French Breguet 5 and Voisin 4 single-engine pusher-type aircraft were equipped with the 37mm Hotchkiss guns, but being manually loaded their rate of fire was very low, and thus ineffective for air-to-air combat, although they were used as ground attack aircraft.

After World War I, a Committee of International Jurists met at The Hague in 1922 to draft a policy for the conduct of air warfare. Basically they allowed the use of explosive, incendiary, or tracer projectiles by and against aircraft, and although the draft was not officially ratified, major nations readily agreed to its position. Nonetheless, in the inter-war years the Soviet Union was the only major power to actively pursue the use of 37mm and larger guns for air-to-ground and air-to-air use. America, like most war-weary post-war nations, sporadically and unenthusiastically investigated the development of the 37mm cannon in the inter-war years.

In 1920, there is a brief mention of early aerial cannon experimentation by the USAAC engineering department at McCook Field, which adapted the Boeing-built GA-1 bomber to carry a 37mm cannon of an unknown manufacturer. In May 1920, the Ordnance Aircraft Armament Subcommittee directed the development of a 37mm fully automatic aircraft cannon of the semi-flexible, full-flexible, and motorized type. The existing Baldwin 37mm automatic cannon was selected to be modified, but the project was discontinued in July 1923 in favor of modifying the Browning machine gun to fire existing stocks of 37mm ammunition by using its principles of the operation. During 1923 the Watervliet Arsenal also designed a 37mm cannon that was to have a muzzle velocity of 2,000 feet per second using the Browning machine gun design principles. After the drawings were submitted the project was cancelled as the gun was too heavy and its recoil too excessive, and also because there were no funds available to build a pilot model. However, in 1924 funds were provided to build one Watervliet gun that was to be tested by the Ordnance Department.

Meanwhile, low-level investigation continued primarily to adapt French 37mm guns, attempting to improve their muzzle velocity, rate of fire, and reliability. The results of these tests were acquired by the Colt Patent Firearms Company, which had engaged John Browning to further develop the French guns, even though aircraft structures at the time were not strong enough to mount such large weapons. In September 1924 Colt completed two automatic 37mm cannons designed by Browning: one with a muzzle velocity of 2,000 fps and the other with 1,350 fps. The Ordnance Department decided to test the two Colt guns and the Watervliet gun, but the Watervliet gun had reliability problems and was withdrawn from the tests by the Arsenal. The two Colt guns were extensively tested at the Aberdeen Proving Grounds, but the Ordnance Department concluded that no more work would continue on the 37mm cannon, ostensibly due to the excessive recoil, but more probably due to budgetary considerations and isolationist attitudes in America post-war.

In the mid-1930s, when aircraft design evolved to all-metal construction, it became possible to mount heavier and far more effective armament ranging from the .50 caliber machine gun and theoretically to the 75mm cannon, and further work on the 37mm gun was resumed. The Vickers-Armstrong Company in England made a significantly improved 37mm gun which was combat-tested and proven in the Spanish Civil War. Work was restarted on the 37mm aerial gun in America in December 1935 when the Chief of Ordnance ordered tests to determine the effects of high explosive 37mm, 25mm, 20mm, and .50 caliber projectiles on aircraft structures. From these tests standards for the development of 20mm and 37mm aircraft cannon were formulated.

## Baldwin 37mm Aircraft Cannon

Just after World War I the U.S. Army contacted prominent American ordnance engineer A.S. Baldwin to adapt the French Puteaux aircraft cannon for installation on American aircraft as a flexible mount or as a motor cannon firing through a propeller hub. Baldwin collaborated with the Poole Engineering and Machine Co. of Baltimore, and with his assistant, a Mr. Metz, was contracted to start work on the first automatic aircraft cannon subsidized by the Ordnance Department.

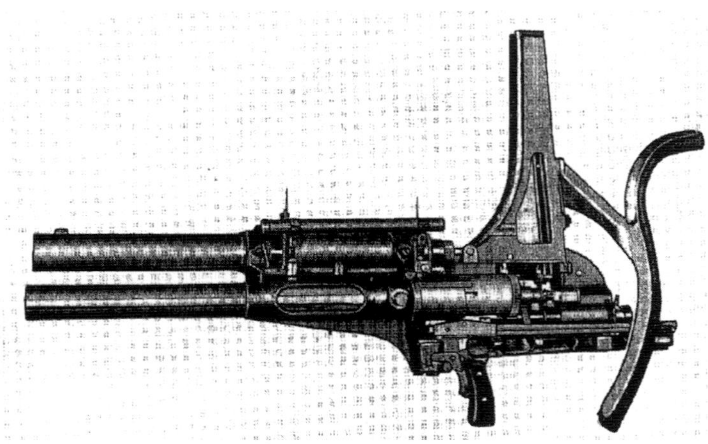

The **Baldwin 37mm cannon** was a completely unsatisfactory design that led John Browning to investigate a new 37mm design. (AFHRC)

The Baldwin cannon was a slightly refined version of the French Puteaux cannon, which itself was a copy of the British Vickers cannon. The cannon weighed 140 pounds with the magazine empty and utilized the long recoil system. It fired a one pound projectile at a rate of 120 rpm with a velocity of 1,350 fps. The recoil cylinder, like that of the Puteaux, was located on top of the barrel. The trigger mechanism was a pistol-grip type located beneath and slightly to the right of the bottom of the receiver. The barrel had four longitudinal ribs cut on it: two of them engaged slideways in the receiver and acted as a track to guide the barrel during the long stroke back and forth. The feed system, which the Ordnance Department considered "the poorest design to be found on any automatic weapon," was simply two pieces of heavy metal crimped to form a T-slot to hold the rims of eight cartridges as they dropped into position for chambering by the bolt. To aim the gun, the gunner rested his shoulder against a curved shoulder piece which was well offset in order to miss being struck by the charging handle that returned with the bolt. For air firing a heavy canvas bag was fastened under the receiver to catch the spent cartridge cases.

On 4 September 1919 the first trial was held at McCook Field, Dayton, OH, with the gun mounted in an aircraft for ground testing to evaluate its mechanism and the effect of the recoil on the aircraft structure. Tests found the recoil had no effect on the aircraft structure, but the gun's performance was completely unsatisfactory, particularly the feed mechanism, which chronically malfunctioned.

Further tests of the Baldwin cannon were conducted periodically with little or no improvement shown, as the feed mechanism continued to cause the majority of the malfunctions. Baldwin requested that the Ordnance Department allow him to prepare a new design, but he was ordered to rework this design into a functioning gun. Soon Army Ordnance became so anxious over Baldwin's lack of success that they hired John Browning and Fred Moore of rival Colt Patent Firearms to examine the gun and make any suggestions that would improve its performance. On 29 November 1920 Browning and Moore visited the Aircraft Armament Division in Washington, DC, to inspect the gun. After several minutes Browning candidly asked, "Where do they put the bait? This thing surely is some kind of a rat trap as it can't possibly be an automatic gun." Time would prove Browning's observation right. The Navy also fired the weapon at its proving grounds with the usual negative results, and on 22 November 1921 the Army Ordnance Department officially discontinued developmental and experimental work on the Baldwin aircraft cannon.

The Baldwin cannon had shown no design originality, especially from an ordnance engineer with Baldwin's abilities, and the result was an ungainly weapon prone to chronic critical feeding problems. The only accomplishment of the Baldwin cannon was to interest John Browning in developing a workable 37mm cannon.

On 1 March 1921 Baldwin left Poole Engineering, and in fall 1922 he contacted the Army Ordnance Procurement Board with drawings for an automatic cannon operated by compressed air. On 26 October 1922, after thorough scrutiny by the Chief of Ordnance, Baldwin's new project was rejected as "This office does not look with favor upon the utilization of compressed air for the operation of automatic cannon ....It is not believed that pneumatically operated cannon would be practicable for aerial use."

**American Armaments Company 37mm Cannon**

With the revival of interest in aircraft cannon, the American Armament Co. of New York City developed a 37mm automatic aircraft cannon in 1933, and Company Director J.J. Miranda and B.P. Joyce, its chief engineer, spent many days abroad promoting their new cannon. This air-cooled, clip-fed cannon, which operated by its long recoil, had a rate of full automatic fire of 60 rpm at an extremely low muzzle velocity of 1,200 fps. American Armament chose the 37mm projectile because it could carry a greater amount of high explosive than the 20mm projectile. To make their cannon adaptable to the various types and sizes of military aircraft the American Armaments cannon was developed in two models: the shorter (30 inch) 37mm cannon was designated as the Type M (Movable), while the larger cannon (60 to 75 inches) was the Type F (Fixed). The Type M was usually mounted in the aircraft nose or in a turret, and was capable of 360° traverse and 15° depression and 60° elevation. The Type M cannon was mounted on a ring around the edge of the turret and was traversed manually or by power gearing. In both types the mechanisms and the size of their projectiles were to be identical; the main difference was in the gun weight and the muzzle velocity. Despite the company's claim that their cannon was entirely new it was actually a adaptation for air use of the Puteaux cannon previously developed in both the United States (by Baldwin) and Europe (by Poland, Finland, and Spain, among others).

Poland was the first nation to show an interest in the cannon, but was put off by its low muzzle velocity. Its contract with the American Armament Co. stipulated that the muzzle velocity was to be increased significantly and the ballistics improved. The concerned Poles went so far as to post a bond equal to the cost of manufacture and demonstration of the weapon which would be assigned to the company if the tests were successful. Competitive trials held in Poland pitted the American Armaments cannon against the

One of the many American Armaments Company's publicity drawings extolling the virtues of its 37mm cannon. (AFHRC)

antiquated Vickers COW gun. The Vickers cannon not only consistently outperformed the American gun, but the tests showed that American Armament had not increased its muzzle velocity at all and the Poles ordered the return of the bond. American Armaments next convinced Italy to try their weapon, but soon that nation discovered that they too had been boondoggled and terminated their association with the company.

American Armament was very successful in its public relations work in the United States, as it convinced virtually every popular aviation magazine and ordnance publication to feature its gun in extravagant articles illustrated with artists' concepts of large bombers armed with numerous cannon firing from fixed wing positions and powered turrets. Both the American public and politicians were convinced that their air force had an automatic cannon that was the best in the world.

To fire the American Armament cannon, the chambering of the first round required two men. This operation was very awkward, as the breech had to be opened with a special tool that moved the pinion on the breech operating shaft. After the cartridge was chambered it was fired by a striker hitting the firing pin with a sharp blow. The barrel and its extension then recoiled at distance greater than the overall length of the loaded round. At this time the breech was unlocked by the camming down of the barrel and breech lock. The lock moved toward the battery position while the extractor attached to the carrier remained seared to the rear. When the barrel assembly was a half inch from the battery position the sear holding the carrier was released and this assembly began to move home. The feed system, which held a clip of five cartridges, consisted of a recoil-operated cage which rotated to feed the rounds through an opening in the loading tray. The carrier picked up the positioned cartridge and snapped over the rim as it was chambered. The final forward movement of the carrier cammed up the breech lock and the gun would be ready to repeat the cycle.

The operation of the gun required a gunner who was very coordinated and ambidextrous in both hand and foot. The gunner sat on a rotating seat facing the gun with his eye at the sight at all times. With his left hand he operated the elevating handwheel and with his right hand he traversed the gun by a wheel. He fired the gun with his left foot while his right foot operated the breech pedal that locked the gun in traverse, thus releasing his right hand to feed clips of ammunition to the magazine.

The sight was a "right angle sight," with the eyepiece located on the left trunnion of the gun so it would remain fixed with respect to the gunner's eye in any position of the gun. The sight had a wide angle of vision and a magnification of two. The sight reticule was scribed with a series of cross hairs so that the gunner could set the gun range and relative speed of the airplane and the target.

The fully automatic gun used five round clips, and the firing mechanism could be set on SAFE, SINGLE SHOT, or FULL AUTOMATIC. Day and night tracers were supplied to aid sighting. The gun was designed so that the last round could not be fired until a new magazine of five rounds was inserted or unless the gunner intentionally fired it. This feature prevented a delay in firing, as before firing the gun the first round had to be fed manually.

The Type F (Fixed) cannon differed from the Type M (movable) only in size and weight, and originally it was assumed that this would relegate it to fixed placement, but when larger aircraft appeared it was considered suitable to be mounted in power operated turrets. The muzzle velocity of the Type F depended on the length of the barrel: the 60 inch barrel gave a muzzle velocity of 2,000 fps, while the 75 inch barrel yielded a muzzle velocity of 2,700 fps. The recoil would also depend on the length of the barrel.

**Comparison of American Armament Corp. Cannons**

| Specification | Type M | Type F |
|---|---|---|
| Length | 30 inches | 75 inches |
| Muzzle Velocity | 1,250 fps | 2,700 fps |
| Weight of Projectile | 1.1 lbs. | 1.1 lbs. |
| Weight of Complete Round | 1.4 lbs. | 1.72 lbs. |
| Length of Recoil | 10 inches | 15 inches |
| Recoil Pull | 1,000 lbs. | 1,700 lbs. |
| Recoil Mechanism | Hydraulic Spring System | |
| Weight of Gun | 135 lbs. | 360 lbs. |
| Rate of Fire | 125 rpm | 90 rpm |
| Weight of 5 Round Clip | 8.2 lbs. | 8.2 lbs. |
| Elevation | 15 to 60° | 15 to 60° |
| Traverse | 360° | 360° |

### Colt Fire Arms Manufacturing Company Browning 37mm Aircraft Cannon

After John Browning inspected and rejected the Baldwin cannon in late November 1920, the gun was sent to the Colt factory for further analysis, and again the gun was deemed unusable. Colt President S.M. Stone generously offered to undertake a new cannon design at any fee specified by the Government that was acceptable to both Colt and John Browning. The Air Corps wrote specifications for the new cannon and Browning built a prototype in his experimental shop in Ogden, UT. The gun fired a one pound projectile at a somewhat higher rate of 150 rpm but at a velocity of only 1,400 fps. Colt quickly built two more models that successfully fired a heavier projectile at a much higher velocity. However, in the mid-1920s an anti-military apathy developed and the Browning gun projects were suspended, and America's foremost arms manufacturer had to turn to manufacturing home electrical appliances and plastic products to remain solvent.

In 1929 the English Armstrong-Whitworth Company obtained rights from Colt to produce the 37mm Browning mechanism along with rights to the mechanism of a 20mm cannon. Just as production of these two Colt models had gotten well under way, Armstrong-Whitworth was taken over by the Vickers Arms Co., Ltd., and the manufacture of the Browning mechanisms was moved to the Vickers Erith factory where a few of the 20mm and the 37mm were commercially produced. Most of these guns were sold to Spain, which designated them as the Colt 20mm and 37mm Automatic Guns. Great Britain was also experiencing public reaction against any weapon development, and without government support the Vickers factory was forced to stop production after this limited sale to Spain.

### 37mm Gun Automatic M1/T9 Aircraft Gun

In May 1920, the Ordnance Subcommittee on Aircraft Armament undertook the development of 37mm fully automatic aircraft cannon of the semi-flexible, full-flexible, and engine-mounted type. The existing Baldwin 37mm automatic cannon was selected to be modified, and the design studies continued through 1921 and 1922 until July 1923, when the Subcommittee recommended that the project be discontinued in favor of designing a new 37mm gun using the operating principals of the Browning machine gun. The Subcommittee delineated the project as "modifying a Browning gun, as might be considered necessary, in order to function with types of 37mm ammunition in existence."

At the end of October 1923 Capt. Thomas Jervey of the Watervliet Arsenal, under the supervision of the Artillery Division, Ordnance Department, designed a 37mm gun using the principles of the Browning machine gun. The completion of detailed production drawings of the Watervliet 37mm gun were approved in November 1923, but soon afterwards the Ordnance Department recommended that the further design of the Browning type 37mm gun be discontinued and the project was cancelled, as the gun was considered too heavy, the recoil too excessive, and besides, there were no funds to build a prototype. However, in April 1924 the Ordnance Committee approved funds to build one Watervliet gun based on the previously submitted detailed drawings. The gun was to have a muzzle velocity of 2,000 fps and operate on the machine gun principal using the ammunition under development by Colt. The heavy 304 pound Watervliet cannon met the muzzle velocity requirement of 2,000 fps and was proof fired in February 1924, with the tests continuing until August 1925.

In September 1924, John Browning of Colt Fire Arms independently completed two 37mm Automatic Guns: M1, and an aircraft gun with a 2,000 fps muzzle velocity and a 37mm automatic anti-aircraft gun with a muzzle velocity of 3,000 fps. The Ordnance Department tested their reliability, rate of fire, accuracy, trunnion reaction, and general function. By May 1925 they obtained the guns for testing at the Aberdeen Proving Ground and the Ordnance Department recommended "that no further work be done by the Ordnance Department on 37mm guns for the Air Service until the results of the contemplated tests (on the Watervliet guns) are known." Then a month later the Watervliet Arsenal recommended that no further tests or development be done on their gun as "in view of the fact that there are two 37mm guns (the Browning 37mms) in possession of the Ordnance Department that functioned more reliably." The Ordnance Department then concluded that no more work would be continued on any 37mm cannon ostensibly due to the excessive recoil and stoppages, and also due to the vibration of its gun mount. However, the reason was more probably due to the austere budgetary considerations and isolationist attitudes in America in post-war. The guns were discontinued in 1927.

It would not be until December 1935 that there was any renewed interest in the development of an American 37mm cannon. The Adjutant General stated in a letter:

"It is desired that the Chief of the Air Corps, in collaboration with the Chief of Ordnance, draw up a program of investigation and tests with the objective in view of developing the military characteristics of a weapon designed primarily for the destruction of airplane materiel."

Tests were conducted to determine the effect of HE instantaneous fused projectiles of 37mm, 23mm, 20mm, and .50 caliber guns on aircraft structures supplied by the Air Corps. During 1936 these tests were completed at Aberdeen, and the Air Corps Technical Committee formulated the military characteristics of three types of aircraft cannon which were submitted to the Chief of Ordnance for approval. The characteristics of the type from which the 37mm cannon were developed were:

1) The minimum caliber was 20mm, while the maximum was the largest caliber that permitted automatic fire.
2) The minimum muzzle velocity was to be 2,000 feet per second.
3) The maximum cyclic rate was to be that which would insure reliable functioning.
4) The type of fire was fully automatic.
5) Left and right hand feed was desirable.
6) The minimum number of rounds was to be ten.
7) The projectile was to be high explosive, impact fused.
8) The maximum weight of the gun was to be 200 pounds.
9) The maximum recoil (trunnion) was to be 4,000 pounds.
9) Maximum possible stability.
10) The mounting was to be flexible power operated.

However, early in 1938 studies showed a renewed desirability and feasibility of a 37mm aircraft gun, and the 37mm Browning M1 design abandoned in 1927 was resurrected and a new mount developed. The Browning 37mm 2,000 fps gun entered comparative tests with other cannon and was found to be a suitable aircraft weapon with some revision of the charging and link ammunition feed mechanisms. The 1939 Army appropriation bill allowed for funds for the procurement of 37mm aircraft guns and the Ordnance Committee adopted the Browning 2,000 fps gun as a "Limited Procurement Type" on 23 June 1938 under the designation "37mm Automatic Gun, T9."

By September 1938, six 37mm T9 Guns were in the process of being manufactured by Colt, while the aircraft in which they were to be mounted were scheduled to be delivered by October. An additional 39 T9 guns were to be purchased from Colt during the fiscal year 1 July 1939. Of these 39 guns, 26 were to be mounted in 13 Bell FM-1 fighter aircraft wile the remaining 13 guns were to be placed in 13 AAC fighters.

Tests of the T9 at Aberdeen showed that the gun would not fire in the inverted and depressed positions. A T9 gun was returned to Colt for correction, and was modified and returned to Aberdeen in mid-September for further firing tests. The T9 functioned in every position except in elevations above 70°, but this was not considered to be a serious problem, as opportunities to fire above 70° were infrequent, except when mounted as a turret mounted flexible gun.

In the fall of 1939, with the scheduled delivery of aircraft to be fitted with the T9 approaching, it was imperative that there were no further delays to interfere with completion of the 39 guns on the production line. On 31 October 1939 the Ordnance Committee ordered these 39 guns to be accepted after several minor modifications were made. Until January 1940 the T9 was subjected to extensive ground firing tests, and one was mounted in an aircraft and fired both on the ground and in the air. On 28 December 1939 the Ordnance Committee standardized the 37mm Automatic Gun, T9, Limited Procurement Type to the Gun, Automatic, 37mm, M4. On 15 February 1940 the M4 was officially approved.

**Summary of the M1**

Gun, Automatic, 37mm M1

The M1 was a 3,000 fps antiaircraft gun and 2,000 fps aircraft gun designed by Browning. The guns were tested at Aberdeen Proving Ground on 23 June 1925 and were standardized, despite some relatively minor problems discussed previously that contributed to their being destandardized in 1927.

Gun, Automatic, 37mm M1E1

In 1937 the M1 guns were modified and improved and redesignated M1 E1.

Gun, Automatic, 37mm M1A1

In October 1938 the gun was standardized as the M1A1, but without a water jacket. In addition to improvements in the functioning of the mechanism there was another change in the gun: the velocity was dropped from the hoped-for-but-not obtained 3,000 fps to the more realistic 2,800 fps. This reduction also cut down barrel erosion.

Gun, Automatic, 37mm M1A2

The accuracy of the M1 had always been unsatisfactory, and investigation showed that the projectile was unstable in flight. In 1939 an increase was made in the twist of the rifling from 1 turn in 35 to 1 in 30 calibers. The modified gun was designated the M1A2. A year later, a final change was made in the characteristic of the gun; the muzzle velocity was reduced again, to 2,600 fps.

Gun, Automatic, 37mm M1A2E1
The 37mm gun M1A2 was tested at high altitude to determine whether it would be satisfactory as an aircraft gun. As the results of the tests were favorable, in May 1942 the AAC initiated a project to mount the M1A2 in the nose of the A-20, requesting that an endless articulated belt magazine be furnished with the gun. Designed for this installation, the 37mm endless belt magazine T9 was similar to the M6 magazine on the 37mm gun M4 installed in the Bell P-39, except that the thrust of the loaded belt on the short turns was moved on wheels instead of on the magazine trackway. To accommodate the magazine M9, the M1A2 gun was modified with a loading handle and a lock frame comprising a carrier lifter cam. It was subsequently discovered, from extensive firing tests in a "bathtub" installation projecting below the bomb bay, that the blast from the two guns was so severe that the lower part of the fuselage was damaged, particularly in the area around the front landing wheel doors. Since this condition could only be overcome by extensive reinforcement of the aircraft structure, it was decided to use the T20E1 gun and not the M1A2E1. As the T20E1 gun used a disintegrating link belt type feed, the requirement for the T9 magazine no longer existed. Therefore, although the 37mm endless belt magazine T9 functioned satisfactorily, its development was cancelled in October 1943.

**The 37mm Gun Automatic M4 Aircraft Gun**
**Description**

**M4 Specifications**

| | |
|---|---|
| Caliber | 37mm (1,457 inches) |
| Weight of Gun (w/o magazine) | 213 pounds |
| Weight of 30 round Magazine | 33.5 pounds |
| Weight of 30 round Magazine (loaded) | 93.4 pounds |
| Weight of 15 round Magazine | 12.5 pounds |
| Weight of 15 round Magazine (loaded) | 41.5 pounds |
| Weight of Barrel | 55 pounds |
| Overall Length of Gun | 89 inches |
| Length of Barrel | 65 inches |
| Muzzle Velocity | 2,000 feet per second |
| Cyclic Rate of Fire | 125-150 rounds per minute |
| Length of Bore | 65 inches (44.6 calibers) |
| Chamber Volume | 6.96 cubic inches |
| Ammunition | |
| Projectile Weight | 1.93 and 1.34 pounds |
| Weight of Charge | 1.25 grains |
| Maximum Powder Pressure | 25,000 pounds per square inch |
| Weight of 20 rounds in Packing Box | 61 pounds |
| Dimension of 20 Round Packing Box | 15 1/8 x11 11/16 x 13 7/32 inches |

The 37mm automatic gun M4 used the energy of the recoil to load, fire, and eject projectiles automatically. It consisted of two discrete elements, recoiling and non-recoiling. The recoiling element consisted of the barrel (called the tube in TM 9-240), barrel extension, recuperator piston rod, lock frame, and lock frame driving spring assemblies. The non-recoiling element consisted of the trunnion block assembly, feed box assembly, and recuperator cylinder.

Feed Mechanism
As standardized, the M4 was supplied with two feed mechanisms: a five round feeder clip and 15 round magazine. The five round clip was for use

**37mm Gun M4** (USAAF)

when the gun was flexibly mounted and operated by a gunner, while the 15 round magazine was supplied for use in an installation without a gunner, such as the P-39, where space limitations in the nose dictated the 15 round magazines. To load the 50 round magazine the feed door was removed from the magazine and the lock frame was retracted. One round of ammunition was pressed into the spring clip closest to the right side of the feed box. It was important that the grooves in the rotating band of this and every other projectile engaged the mating projection of the spring clip. The loading handle was pulled back, moving the belt one clip and filling the next clip, which emerged from the feed box. The clips were continued to be filled with the belt moving until all 30 rounds had been inserted as indicated by resistance to further movement of the belt.

When the .30 caliber machine guns were removed from the Airacobra, there was space available for additional 37mm ammunition. In October 1940, due to this space increase, Wright Field requested that an endless belt type feed for the M4 be developed and delegated Colt to study the ammunition supply modification. The company determined that the endless belt feed was feasible for the P-39, and on 24 October 1940 the Ordnance Committee authorized a belt feed that was to be similar to the articulated link belt used in the 15 round magazines. The belt was to be flexible and to have the maximum length possible to supply the maximum number of rounds for the P-39. The mock up was to be tested at Aberdeen and a P-39 was to be sent to Hartford, CT for installation and testing. By March 1941, the extensive ground tests at Aberdeen and the aerial P-39 tests proved the endless belt feed mechanism was ready for production by Colt. The endless belt magazine consisted of an elliptical channel shaped to fit the inner contour of the P-39 nose cowling. The channel locked the gun receiver at the position of the regular feeding tray and guided the endless belt composed of conventionally designed ammunition clips joined together. With the successful testing of the endless feed belt both on the ground and in the air the feeding device was standardized as the "Belt, Endless, 37mm, M6, for 37mm Automatic Gun. M4" on 17 April 1941, but the nomenclature was changed in November to "Magazine, Endless Belt, 37mm, M6" which was more descriptive of the type.

Function of the Gun Elements During the Firing Cycle
When the firing button was pushed by the gunner it caused the solenoid on the top cover at the rear of the trunnion block to pull the trigger, which then pulled the trigger bar, rotating the top of the trigger lever to the rear. At the same time the breechblock, in the battery position, elevated the front end of the trigger trip and depressed the rear. The trigger connector, which was pivoted at the center of the trigger lever, was forced to the rear. The elevation of the breechblock and the pulling of the trigger caused the trigger connector to press the sear rearward. The sear rotated out of engagement with the hammer, which was driven forward by its spring until

it struck the firing pin. The firing pin struck the primer and the propelling charge was ignited.

When the cartridge fired, the gun recoiling elements were all driven as a unit rapidly backward for 9.625 inches, after which the counter-recoil of the barrel and the barrel extension was started by the recuperator. The lock frame and the driving spring rods continued to move rearward until the lock frame struck the buffer and was caught and held by the carrier dog. Most of the energy of the recoil was absorbed by the recuperator.

At about one half of the recoil distance, the forward part of the operating lever was rotated by cams from its engagement in a slot in the breechblock. This action forced the breechblock downward until it stopped on the breechblock stop. This opened the breechblock so that when the lock frame and the barrel extension separated the extractor drew the cartridge case out of the chamber. As the barrel extension moved forward, the rear of the ejector was cammed upward by the ejector operator stud on the lock frame. The forward end of the ejector was forced downward, hitting the empty case and forcing it out the open underside of the trunnion block.

As the barrel extension moved forward, a stud on its right side rotated the feed lever forward. Rotation of the feed lever was transferred to movement of the feed slide through the feed lever swivel, feed lever crank, and the feed supply lever. The feed slide moved toward the right of the feed box (looking forward), carrying with it the feeder clip and allowing the next round to be fired. As the new round neared the center of the feed box it was cammed downward by the stripper cam on the feed box frame. At the same time it struck the carrier catch and pushed it to the right to release the carrier. The carrier snapped down, hitting the round to help force it downward, and simultaneously disengaged the carrier dog from the lock frame. The released lock frame was driven forward by its driving springs, and as it moved its forward end forced the cartridge into the chamber. The spring actuated extractor mounted on the lock frame slipped around the base of the cartridge and engaged it for the next cartridge extraction. The operating lever moved forward with the lock frame and engaged the breechblock, forcing it upward into the closed position. The gun was again ready when the trigger was pulled.

Inspection and Cleaning

The guns were to be inspected every 24 hours, and if the gun action seemed to be dry or dirt was present the gun was to be removed, and the barrel and breechblock cleaned, relubricated, and reassembled and then manually checked. Aircraft lubricants had to be free flowing due to the extremely low temperatures at high altitudes. Grease, dried oil, and gum had to be carefully removed and the gun relubricated with Oil, Lubricating, for Aircraft Instruments and Machine Guns, U.S. Army Specification No. 2-27, before the gun was reassembled.

**Colt M4 Procurement, Requirements, and Production**

Procurement

On 27 August 1940, to expedite M1A2 anti-aircraft gun manufacture, Colt was authorized $3,754,775 (not including a fixed fee) for machinery, equipment, tools, dies, gauges, etc. to turn out 200 guns per month. Then, on 19 December 1941 the contract was changed so that $3,097,393 of the previous total was to be used for the manufacture of the M1A2 anti-aircraft guns at a rate of 150 per month. The remaining $657,392 was to be expended for the manufacture of the aircraft M4 gun at a rate of 400 per month. An additional $95,000 was allotted to increase the production of the M1A2 and M4 guns to 500 guns each per month and to begin the production of the M9 aircraft gun. On 10 June 1943, $600,000 more was authorized (($4,452,775 total) to maintain a rate of 500 M4 guns per month and increase the rate of M9 guns per month to 450. On 16 October 1944, $550,000 was supplemented to add 300 M4E3 guns (later standardized as the M10).

Requirements

By 10 June 1941 the total requirement for 1940 and 1941 was 2,188 guns, with a more sizeable quantity to be expected for the 1942 requirement. Additional requirements were included in the Army Supply Program during the last half of 1941 and early 1942, so that by 5 May 1942, the Army Supply Program requested 14,906 guns to be delivered before 1 January 1943. On 21 October 1942 there was a reduction in the Army Supply Program to 12,564 guns, of which 390 had been produced prior to 1 January 1942, 3,654 were required during 1942, and the remaining 8,520 during 1943. On 5 December 1942 the 1943 requirement was further reduced by 814 guns, making the total authorized requirement 11,760 guns. On 1 March 1943 the requirement was again reduced by 518 guns, reducing the balance to 11,232. Before 1 January 1943, 6,521 guns had been delivered, and 4,711 were to be manufactured in 1943. On 6 April 1943, 5,430 guns were authorized for production for the first half of 1944, increasing the total authorization to 16,521 guns. However, on 13 August 1943 the 1944 requirement was deleted entirely and the 1943 requirement was reduced by 3,142 to 1,569, making the total authorization 8,090 guns (then for some unknown reason 11 guns were added to the 1943 requirement). By the time the last reduction had been requested, more guns than required had been produced and production was not stopped immediately, as this stoppage would have wasted too much materiel on hand.

Production

Before the first order for M4 guns had been made, 45 guns were ordered for experimental purposes. On 11 December 1939, three weeks before the gun was standardized, the Army Supply Program authorized 159 guns to be installed in the P-39 fighter, and the Springfield Ordnance District negotiated a contract with Colt Fire Arms. It was not until 17 September 1940 that an additional procurement for 909 guns was allocated to the Springfield District, who again contracted Colt. Colt began shipping its first M4s in March 1941 and was producing 50 per month by July; 390 by January 1942; and 500 per month by July 1942, a rate which was maintained until January 1943 when the Army reduced the quantity to 350 per month. The 350 per month rate was maintained from January to June 1943 after a total of 8,667 had been manufactured: 390 in 1941, 5,167 in 1942, and 3,110 in 1943, when production ended at the end of November. The Colt factory had never been equipped to machine 37mm forgings, so finished and proofed barrels were supplied as Government Furnished Equipment (GFE) throughout production. The average price per M4 unit (adjusting for the GFE barrel) was $1,785 at the beginning of production and later was reduced to $1,655 per gun.

**Oldsmobile Division M4 Procurement, Requirements, and Production**

Because of its expertise in design and engineering, the Oldsmobile Division of General Motors, Lansing, MI, was contracted as a 37mm M4 gun supplier in January 1942 when an order for 1,500 M4 guns was placed. Within weeks another contract for 4,695 guns was negotiated, bringing the total to 6,195 guns. In early January 1942, only a few days after the original 1,500 37mm M4 gun production order was placed, $3,887,914 was granted for machinery, equipment, tools, dies, etc. At the end of March 1942, $1,815,000 was allocated for machinery, equipment, tools, dies, etc., for the production of 37mm M1A2 guns. Approximately $1,240,000 of that amount was spent when the contracts for the M1A2 guns were cancelled after only a few guns were manufactured. An additional $3,957,914 (for a total of $5,200,000) was subsequently awarded to Oldsmobile for M4 and later M9 and M10 production.

The first M4 guns were manufactured by Oldsmobile in August 1942, and by October a monthly rate of 250 guns was achieved. By 1 January

1943, 964 M4s had been delivered at a rate of 500 guns per month in May. The reduction of 37mm guns in the Army Supply Program during the summer of 1943 caused the Army to cancel Oldsmobile's M4 contracts and the last guns were produced in August 1944 after a total of 2,779 guns had been produced: 964 in the last five months of 1942 and 1,815 in 1943, when production was terminated in July. At the beginning of production the cost per unit was $2,758, almost a $1,000 more than Colt's initial costs. However, by the end of production this unit price was reduced to $1,678, only $23 more than Colt's average unit cost.

On 1 August 1943, the Army Supply Program reduced its requirements for the M4 aircraft gun, and it became necessary to eliminate either Colt or Oldsmobile as a supplier. Although Oldsmobile did an exceptional job in converting its automobile production to guns, the Army Supply Program decided to eliminate the auto company in favor of Colt, which was the low cost producer, but also was a major designer and supplier of automatic weapons. After the war Oldsmobile would return to the automobile business while Colt would remain in the armaments business.

**Summary of the M4 Models**

Gun Automatic, 37mm M4

The modifications made on the T9 model to produce the M4 resulted in a number of important improvements. The back plate of the M4 was reinforced and the buffer on the back plate assembly was changed; the recuperator bushing ports of the recuperator cylinder were enlarged to increase the rate of fire; a stronger carrier catch spring enabled the carrier catch to return faster to its normal position; the trigger extension mechanism on the T9 lock frame was placed on the extension tube of the M4; and helical springs on the buffer of the M4 replaced the Belleville springs of the T9.

Gun, Automatic, 37mm M4E1

In 1941 the Army Air Corps, in order to increase the armament of certain aircraft, established requirements for aircraft with wing-mounted 37mm automatic guns fed from the fuselage. This requirement made it necessary to develop a gun with right hand feed to pair with the left hand feed of the M4. To supply this need the M4 gun was modified to feed from the right and was designated 37mm automatic gun M4E1.

Gun, Automatic, 37mm M4E2

The M4E2 gun had a modified feedbox and tube extension; the left side plate was slotted to receive the feed assembly lever when the gun was fed from the right side. The M4E2 gun was changed from a right hand to left hand feed by shifting the following parts of the feedbox mechanisms. The feed slide lever was taken from the right bracket, turned upside down, and placed in the left bracket; the feed crank was rotated 180° so that the opposite feed crank stud engaged the slot in the feed slide lever; the feed slide was taken from the right side of the feedbox frame, turned around, and inserted in the left side of the feedbox frame; and the stops in the pawl assembly were turned upside down and interchanged. The complete assembly was shifted to the left.

Gun Automatic, 37mm M4E3

The M4E3 was simply the M4 modified for use with a disintegrating link belt feed mechanism to feed from the left side. The method of feeding was the same as that of the standard feedbox, except in the shape of the parts and in the operation of the stop and holding pawls. Attached to the forward end of the recuperator was a cylindrical expansion chamber, closed at the top, into which the oil could flow as it expanded. The development of the M4E3 was given a low priority to permit earlier development of the high velocity 37mm automatic gun with a disintegrating link belt feed mechanism. As soon as this latter development was completed and the gun standardized as 37mm automatic gun M9, the development of the M4E3 was assigned higher priority because of the increasing difficulty in providing endless belt feed mechanisms for the M4 gun.

Gun, Automatic, 37mm M4E4

This gun was similar to the M4E3 except that it incorporated a right hand feed.

**37mm Gun Automatic M9 Aircraft Gun Development**

**T19**

At the request of the AAF, the Ordnance Department commenced a project to modify the 37mm M4 for installation in the Bell P-63 Kingcobra fighter aircraft to attack mechanized ground forces. Until April 1942 the military requirements for this gun had not been established for lack of data, so the Ordnance Department established a set of requirements for the gun designated as the 37mm Automatic Gun, T19. Among the requirements were:

1) The Maximum weight of gun, barrel, and feeding device was not to exceed 400 pounds.
2) The number of rounds carried in the belt or magazine was not to be less than 15.
3) The gun was to be capable of firing both the 1.92 pound AP projectile at 2,900 fps and the 1.34 pound HE projectile at 2,600 fps. As a second choice the gun was to be able to fire the 1.66 pound AP shell at 3,100 fps and the 1.34 pound HE shell at 2,600 fps.
4) The rate of fire was to be the highest possible, 100 to 120 rpm.
5) The charging and firing of the gun was to be by remote control and be fed by a disintegrating belt, or secondly by a magazine feed mechanism.
6) The gun was to be able to fire at elevations from +35° to -70°, and either mounted in the normal position or on its right or left sides.
7) The gun was to operate at temperatures as low as -52° F.

**T20**

Soon after the start of the T19 program, Oldsmobile began studies for the redesign of the 37mm Anti-aircraft Gun, M1A2 for aircraft installation. The changes in the M1A2 gun included a disintegrating link belt feed mechanism which would facilitate the firing of the 1.92 pound AP, the 1.66 pound HE, and 1.34 pound HE projectiles and make a stronger gun. The Subcommittee on Aircraft Armament authorized the development of the M1A2 project, and Oldsmobile was to produce two prototypes for testing at Aberdeen by 1 August 1942. The prototypes were redesignated as the 37mm Gun, T20.

After testing, the T20s were shipped to Wright Field for AAF service testing to determine if the gun met requirements for 37mm high velocity gun. At Wright the various questions were to be investigated:

1) Was there a requirement for the 37mm gun in the P-39 and could it be installed in that fighter?
2) Could the gun be installed easily in an aircraft or did it require modifications?
3) Did the gun perform satisfactorily under flight conditions, including dives, turns, acceleration, etc.?
4) Was the belt pull, flexibility, and link strength satisfactory for aircraft use?
5) Did the gun need mounting trunnions or slides (as in the M1A2, 37mm anti-aircraft gun)?

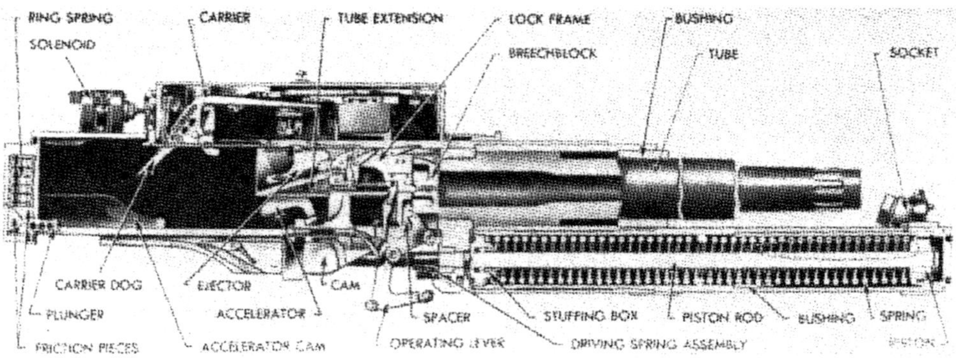


**37mm Gun M9 (T20E1)** (USAAF)

The T20 was substantially the 37mm Gun, M1A2, modified to incorporate a disintegrating link belt feed, and a change in barrel and external recoil mechanism dimensions to allow the installation of the gun in the P-39. The tests showed it was advantageous to eliminate the special barrel and recoil mechanism in order to install it in the P-39 and to use the barrel of the M1A2 gun. With this modification the T20 was redesignated as 37mm Gun, T20E1. Further testing at Aberdeen and Eglin Field demonstrated that a few minor modifications were required and the gun met almost all its requirements. During the tests the recoil trunnion reaction was 13,000 pounds, not 10,000; and while the gun functioned mounted on its side, its installation in the aircraft was limited to 45° rotation from its normal position. The gun fired all types of 37mm ammunition, and the barrel life was 600 rounds of AP fired at 2,900 fps.

**M9 (T20E1)**

Procurement, Requirements, and Production

On 24 December 1942 the 37mm M9 (T20E1) was adopted and standardized, and a procurement order for 7,000 guns and accessories, spare parts, and 1,000 ammunition links per gun to be delivered in the 1943 requirement was authorized and approved on 21 January 1943. Of these guns 4,100 were to be delivered as a left hand feed and 2,900 as right hand feed. Of the 7,000 guns, 3,400 were allotted to the Springfield Ordnance District (Colt) and 3,600 to the Detroit Ordnance District (Oldsmobile). Both companies were already engaged in the manufacture of the 37mm Anti-aircraft Gun, M1A2, and 37mm Aircraft Gun M4. On 1 March 1943, 523 additional left handed M9 guns were added by the Army Supply Program for manufacture in 1944, for a total of 7,523 guns. Then, on 1 August 1943, the requirement was decreased by 4,949 guns to 2,051, decreasing the 1944 total to 7,242 guns. In 1944, the first Army Supply Program change again reduced the number of guns to 3,930 after 1,782 had been manufactured prior to 1 January 1944. The 2,168 guns authorized were to be discontinued at the earliest possible time without wasting materiel on hand.

Colt already was authorized $3,754,775 for machinery, equipment, tools, dies, etc. to produce the M1A2 and M4, and on 5 February 1943 was granted an additional $95,000 for the concurrent (with the M1A2 and M4) production of the M9 at 450 per month. The first 52 M9s were shipped by Colt in September 1943, and by 1 January 1944 754 M9s were produced. The Army Supply Program reduction in early 1944 eliminated Colt as a M9 producer at the end of February 1944 after 243 M9s had been produced. The unit cost of the 1,000 M9s manufactured by Colt was $2,340 (including the cost of the GFE barrels).

Oldsmobile had developed the M9 from the M1A2 Anti-aircraft Gun, and in addition to the $5,197,914 allotted for the manufacture of the M4 and M1A2 guns, Oldsmobile was granted an additional $39,900 for the M9 gun. The first 50 M9 Oldsmobile guns were completed in June 1943 and 1,010 guns were shipped in 1943 (none in August and December). During the first five months of 1944 1,920 guns were produced with a maximum monthly rate of 650 during the first two months. The average initial cost of the M9 was $3,690, while the last gun produced cost $2,958. Oldsmobile's M9s cost more than Colt's because Oldsmobile subcontracted more parts. The reduction of M9 requirements in February 1944 led to the elimination of Oldsmobile as a M9 producer in May 1944 after the company had completed 1,920 in that year and 2,930 total.

In March and April 1943 the Navy took delivery of 420 each month and then accepted only five for the last quarter of 1943. In 1944, a total of 179 (78 in August) were accepted when the contract was terminated in August with a total of 1,024 guns. The AAF did not accept its first M9 until October 1943 when 179 were accepted in the last quarter. From January through August 1944, the AAF accepted 1,016 M9s for a total of 1,196 guns.

Description

The M9 had clean lines despite being very heavy at 405 pounds, but the weight was necessary to handle the high velocity (3,050 fps) rounds of ammunition. The M9 operated on the long recoil principle, and was designed primarily for aircraft use. Because it could not be successfully synchronized it was mounted to fire either through the propeller hub or outside of the propeller arc. The gun was triggered by remote control via an electric solenoid. Ammunition feeding could be to either the left or right hand, but necessitated the changing of the box; the parts inside operated the mechanism in either direction. The cartridges were fed into the left or right side of the box and the empty links were ejected through a slot on the opposite side. The empty cartridge cases were ejected through a longitudinal opening between the bottom of the receiver and the side plates. The mechanism depended upon the unusually long recoil movement (greater than the overall length of the loaded round) for its operational power. Both recoil and counter recoil forces were controlled by a hydro-spring buffing mechanism. The vertical sliding-wedge breech lock was the most uncomplicated type yet designed for an automatic gun, as it not only insured position locking, but also the control of the critical measurement of head space. An air charger made it possible to load the first round readily for firing either by hand or by remote control if the gun was not easily accessible to the gunner. The cartridges were linked between the shoulders of the rounds halfway up the projectile. The links, however, were lifted by a stripper, leaving the cartridge free to be positioned.

Operation

To operate the engine-mounted Browning 37mm for firing through the propeller hub the pilot first pushed the charger button in to actuate the loader for jacking the mechanism to the rear. A round was stripped from the belt and was chambered as the mechanism moved forward. The gun was then cocked, loaded, and locked, ready to fire. When the trigger was pulled it closed the firing switch circuit by the use of an electric solenoid.

When the cartridge was fired and the projectile driven down the bore, an equal force was applied in the opposite direction against the face of the breechblock. Thus the barrel, the barrel extrusion, the breechblock, and the lock frame, which were all securely locked together, moved rearward during 10.75 inches of recoil, at which point the operating lever guide pin, following its front cams, caused the pin to rotate to bring the breechblock downward. This movement also threw the lower end of the cocking lever forward. The hammer spring was compressed and the latching hook was forced back on its sear to cock the hammer. The rearward movement was controlled by the recuperator, which was a cylinder with a spring-loaded piston and oil. The fluid behind the piston was forced through slots to the front side as the piston moved rearward. The opening decreased in area as it approached the end of its stroke, thus providing a positive buffing action. The lock-frame assembly was not affected by the retarding action of the recuperator since it was unlocked from the barrel extension. Consequently, when the barrel and its extension were near the end of their rearward travel, the lock frame separated from these parts and continued to recoil, speeded up by the accelerator. This part was actuated by a cam mounted on the rear of the side plate. The accelerator rode upwards on an inclined surface of a cam while its lower part pushed backwards against a lug on the lock frame body. This suddenly-applied mechanical advantage gave the recoil of the frame added impetus. The rear of the lock frame then struck the buffer plunger, compressing the ring spring and forcing the two friction pieces upward and outward against the inside of the back-plate housing. Then the remaining force of recoil was transmitted to the back-plate assembly. The frame rebounded from the buffer plunger because of the action of the ring springs. After traveling in counter recoil a short distance a carrier dog engaged its notch in the frame holding the piece stationary while the barrel and its extension continued on in counter recoil movement. Initial extraction of the empty cartridge case occurred at the instant the lock frame separated from the barrel extension. Engagement of the rim of the case by the extractor claw fully loosened the round at this time. When the frame was held to the rear and the barrel and its chamber moved forward on counter recoil the empty case was completely withdrawn from the chamber. At this point an ejector was pivoted downward by a cam on the upper flange of the left side plate. The protruding rear end of the ejector deflected the empty case downward between the side plates clear of the operating parts. The compressed driving spring furnished the energy to speed the lock frame towards battery. During recoil the feed lever operating stud on the side of the barrel extension contacted the lower end of the lever, pivoting it rearward. The stud passed under the end of this piece and then snapped back into position, so that during counter recoil the operating stud pushed its lower end forward. This actuated the feed crank, which in turn moved the feed slide containing a cartridge over one space. The feed slide return lever, plunger, and spring then forced the slide toward the inlet side of the feedway to engage the next round. The new round had been indexed, and the cartridge then released the carrier latch from the carrier-lock frame. The barrel and extension had already reached full battery and the lock frame, ramming the round ahead of it, started chambering it. During this final movement the operating lever following the upper cam grooves pushed the breechblock up to lock and support the base of the cartridge during the act of firing. The gun, being cocked, loaded, and locked, would continue the cycle of operation as long as the electric trigger was actuated and ammunition remained in the belt.

**Use in Combat**

While the Browning M9 was used to a very limited degree by the USAAF during World War II, it was, especially in the early war, the primary offensive aerial cannon of the Soviets, as thousands were furnished to Russia on the Bell Airacobra fighter. Its installation permitted firing through the hollow propeller hub, thus eliminating the need for synchronization. The Russians found that the high-velocity armor-piercing projectile was particularly good when fired on enemy tanks in close infantry ground support. During developmental work, these 37mm automatic cannon were mounted in the wings of American planes. However, as there was no urgent need for these large cannon it only saw use at experimental stations and proving grounds.

**M9 Summary**

Gun Automatic, 37mm M9

After tests of the T20E1 gun at Aberdeen Proving Ground and at Eglin Field, recommendations resulted in minor modifications in improving the functioning of the gun for use in aircraft. It was approved in January 1943 for standardization as a 37mm gun M9. The 37mm automatic gun M9 was basically the same as the MIA2 in general appearance and functioning. The chief differences in the appearance of the two guns were in the shape of the recuperator expansion tube socket and the position of the recuperator expansion tube. The M9 gun socket was built with a filler screw and bracket on each side, while the gun socket of the M1A2 gun had a single filler screw and bracket on the right side only. In the M9 gun the expansion tube was placed to the rear of the socket and extended upward at an angle. In the M1A2 gun the expansion tube was in front of the socket and parallel with the gun tube. Unlike that of the M1A2 gun, the M9 gun tube had splines machined at its muzzle end. The flats machined at approximately the middle of the M1 A2 gun tube for application of the tube wrench were not incorporated in the M9 gun tube. The cartridge tray for the MIA2 gun feedbox was not used with the M9 gun, as the M9 gun used an inlet feed chute and a link ejection chute attached to the feedbox by eyebolts and wing nuts. The lower end of the operating lever on the M9 gun had a round hole to admit a charging pin, while the M1A2 gun's operating lever had a triangular hole to permit the use of a priming rod. A sighting slot was incorporated in the trunnion block of the M9 gun, near the tube lock depressor, but the M1A2 gun had no such slot.

Gun, Automatic, 37mm M9E1

In November 1943 the Army Air Corps requested the Ordnance Department to modify a 37mm M9 gun so that it could be installed in its Bell P-63 Kingcobra fighter. The following January a project was authorized for this purpose with the designation 37mm automatic gun M9E1. The requirements outlined by the Army Air Corps called for reduction of the tube diameter and modifications of related parts to allow removal of the gun through the propeller hub. Weight added at the tapered section in front of the bearing allowed a reduced section near the muzzle for freedom of movement in boresighting.

Gun, Automatic, 37mm M9A1

Firing tests of M9E1 models conducted at Aberdeen indicated that the operation of the gun was completely satisfactory. An HE shell was detonated in one M9E1 barrel to determine the characteristics of the barrel and materiel. Results of this test were also completely satisfactory and indicated that the barrel was sufficiently strong to withstand any firing that would be encountered in service. In September 1944 the M9E1 gun was standardized as 37mm automatic gun AN–M9Al.

Gun, Automatic, 37mm M9A1El

This gun was a project to utilize M9 barrels to supplement production of M9A1 guns.

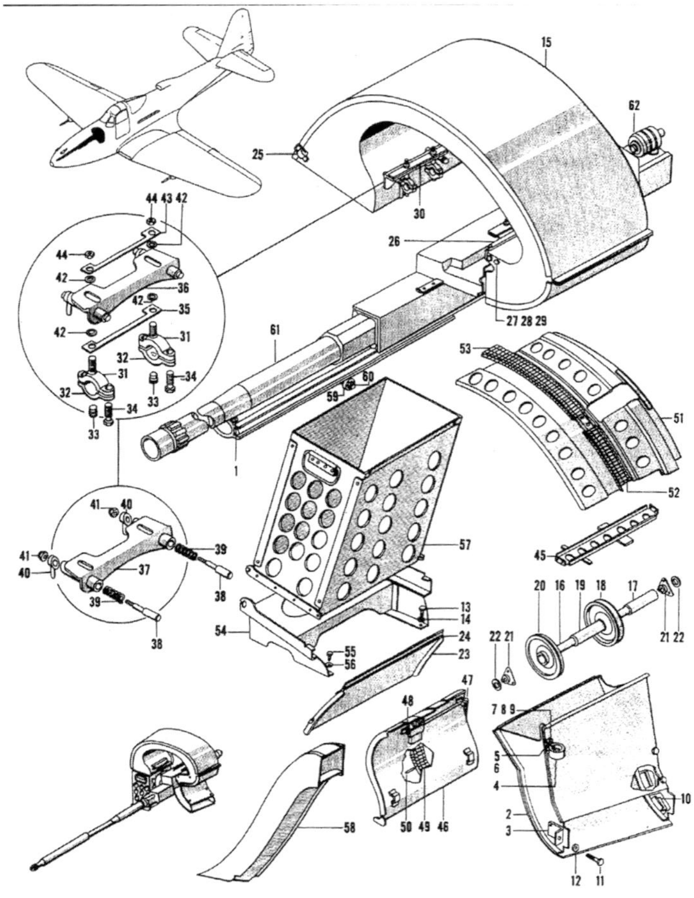

**37mm Gun M10** (USAAF)

### 37mm Gun Automatic M10/M4E3 Aircraft Gun

In early 1942, the Ordnance Department studied methods of adapting a disintegrating link belt feed to the 37mm M4 cannon and found this could be accomplished with minor modifications. The Subcommittee on Aircraft Armament authorized these modifications on 4 June 1941, and four prototypes were ordered for testing at Aberdeen and for use by the AAC. On 3 November 1942, the Ordnance Officer at Wright Field requested ten 37mm M4E3 guns be manufactured for test and installation, and on 14 January 1943 requested the increase of the four M4 prototypes to ten.

Before the development of the M4E3 was started, a program to study magazine feed from left or right had been progressing. But once the M4E3 project was started its link feed mechanism developed by Oldsmobile was considered more advantageous and the magazine feed project was discontinued in March 1943. By July 1943, the development of the M4E3 was in the pilot testing stage at Aberdeen. The tests ended in July 1943 with 4,000 rounds fired through the left hand feed and 2,700 rounds from the right with the results showing some problems with the left hand feed. The weight lifting capacity of the left hand feed was 25 pounds with an eight round belt, but modifications increased this to 75 pounds, in addition to the eight round belt. Feeding failures occurred with left hand feeding firing bursts of 20 rounds. Jams also occurred in the link ejection chute. These problems were minor and would not be encountered if the gun were mounted in its normal position. At the same time, the right hand feed M4E4 was being tested and encountered similar problems as the M4E3.

The Oldsmobile Division—the designers of the gun—studied the modifications that were suggested by Aberdeen and would incorporate them into future guns. By July 1943 aerial firing tests of the M4E3 gun had not started, as the Air Force had not made a P-39 available. Despite this, the AAF directed that this gun be installed in the 201st production model of the Bell P-63 Kingcobra. The M4E3 had proved to fire 25 to 30 rpm faster than the M4 gun, and because of the disintegrating link belt it could carry 28 additional rounds for a total of 58 rounds. The installation of ten M4E3 guns was scheduled to begin on 10 October 1943, with 125 guns scheduled in November and 450 in December. This schedule could not be met, as by July the gun was not standardized for procurement because of minor modifications to the feed box and because no service test had been conducted since an aircraft had not arrived for air firing of the modified guns. By 13 August 1943 the scheduled production for 1943 was 1,187 guns, and for 1944 it was 7,808 (total 8,995 guns), while two more changes in September and October 1943 reduced the total to 8,273 guns (300 in 1943 and 7,973 in 1944). All this scheduling could not change the fact that the production of the standardized gun could not begin until March 1944, as the materiel needed to be procured and production setup. In order to meet the preliminary requirements of the M4E3 gun and to assure uninterrupted production, an order for 2,500 guns to be produced immediately was approved on 1 October 1943. Since both Colt and Oldsmobile were producing 37mm guns allocations for procurement were made as follows: 1,500 to the Detroit Ordnance District (Oldsmobile) and 1,000 to the Springfield Ordnance District (Colt). Oldsmobile was awarded an additional $39,900 (over the $5,197,914 total for manufacture of the M1A2 and M4) for M10 production, and Colt was awarded an additional $550,000 (over the $5,000,000) for M10 production.

It was not until February 1944 that all modifications to the M4E3 recommended by Aberdeen and the AAF were completed at Watervliet Arsenal. Since the gun was to be the standard armament for the P-63, on 13 April 1944 the 37mm Gun, M4E3 was redesignated as the Gun, Automatic, 37mm, M10. On 1 February 1944 the program was reduced to 5,835 guns, with 150 to be produced before 1 January 1944. On 25 May 1944 the Army Supply Program authorized an additional 3,302 guns for the first half of 1945 (9,137). Then, on 28 June 1944, the requirement for 1944 was reduced by 1,935 to 3,750 and the first half of 1945 requirement was reduced by 2,045 guns to 1,259 guns, reducing the grand total to 5,119 guns scheduled.

In December 1943 Oldsmobile produced 150 pilot models, and a maximum monthly production of 425 guns was reached in April 1944. After its order for 1,500 M10s was completed in May 1944 the Army Supply Program eliminated Oldsmobile as a M10 producer while Colt continued production. Colt produced 20 M10s in March 1944, reaching a maximum monthly production total of 300 in June 1944, and completed its order for 1,000 M10s by 1 September 1944. After the completion of the 1,000 continued M10 production reached 1,950 more in 1944 and completed 200 per month through August 1945, adding 26 more in September when the contract was cancelled (for some reason five were manufactured in January 1946). The Colt cost per gun was $1,625 less the barrel, which was furnished by the government, while the final cost of the Oldsmobile M10 was $2,060. A total of 5,081 M10s were produced (3,581 by Colt and 1,500 by Oldsmobile).

#### Summary of the M10

Gun, Automatic, 37mm M10

The Army Air Corps, which was kept fully informed of the progress of Ordnance development of the 37mm automatic guns M4E3 and M4E4, at this juncture directed that the M4E4 be placed in the P-63. This action was taken because the M4E4 fired 25 to 30 shots faster and had double the ammunition capacity of the M4. However, the M4E3 and M4E4 were not yet ready for standardization, since minor modifications to the feedbox were necessary and the gun had not been service tested. It was expected that the

### Comparative Data: 37-mm Automatic Guns, M4, M9, and M10

| Characteristic | M4 | M9 | M10 |
|---|---|---|---|
| Gun length, overall . . . inches | 89.5 | 104 | 89.57. |
| Gun weight, without mount and accessories . . . pounds | 213 | 405 | 231. |
| Rate of fire (average) . . . rounds/minute | 140 to 150 | 140 | 150 to 165. |
| Muzzle velocity (HE shell) . . . feet/second | 2,000 | 2,600 | 2,000. |
| Muzzle velocity (AP shell) . . . do | 1,825 | 2,800 to 3,050 | 1,825. |
| Weight of projectile (HE) . . . pounds | 1.34 | 1.34 | 1.34. |
| Weight of projectile (AP) . . . do | 1.66 | 1.92 or 1.66 | 1.66. |
| System of operation | Long recoil | Long recoil | Long recoil. |
| Type of recoil operation | Automatic | Automatic | Automatic. |
| Length of recoil . . . inches | 9⅝ | 10¾ | 9¾. |
| Recuperator oil capacity . . . ounces | 42 | 72 | 42. |
| System of locking | Vertical rising wedge | Vertical sliding wedge | Vertical rising wedge. |
| System of feeding | Recoil actuated | Recoil actuated | Recoil actuated. |
| Method of headspace | Not adjustable | Factory set | Not adjustable. |
| Location of feed opening | Top of receiver either right or left hand. | Top of receiver either right or left hand. | Top of receiver either right or left hand. |
| Location of ejection opening | Bottom of receiver | Bottom of receiver | Bottom of receiver. |
| Method of charging | Hydraulic, air or manual | Hydraulic, air or manual | Hydraulic. |
| Method of cooling | Air | Air | Air. |
| Barrel length . . . inches | 65 | 78 | 65. |
| Barrel weight . . . pounds | 55 | 120 | 57.5. |
| Rate control | None | None | None. |
| Barrel removal | Can be removed readily | Can be removed readily but not designed for field replacement. | Can be removed easily. |
| Bore: | | | |
| Number of grooves | 12 | 12 | 12. |
| Groove depth . . . inches | 0.020 | 0.020 | 0.020. |
| Groove width . . . do | 0.2314 | 0.2314 | 0.2314. |
| Pitch | 1.48 turns in 65 inches | 1.56 turns in 78 inches | 1.48 turns in 65 inches. |
| Direction of twist | Right hand | Right hand | Right hand. |
| Form of twist | Constant | Constant | Constant. |
| Width of lands . . . inches | 0.150 | 0.150 | 0.150. |
| Number of turns rifling in tube, approximately. | 1.48 | 1.56 | 1.48. |

first 400 guns would differ from the standard gun in minor details; therefore, they would require modification at a later date. It was also expected that by December 1943, when the first 400 guns would be completed, all modifications would have been approved and standard drawings would be available according to which the remaining guns of the initial procurement could he produced. Consequently, in August 1943, the procurement of the M4E3 gun was increased to 2,500. By March 1944, all ground tests and aerial tests of the modified gun had been satisfactorily performed, and the M4E3 and M4E4 were standardized as the 37mm automatic gun M10, with separate stock numbers issued for right and left side feed.

**Use of the 37mm Cannon**

In the late 1930s there were six different cannons under consideration by the AAF and Army Ordnance: 20mm Hispano-Suiza (France), 20mm Oerlikon (Swiss), 37mm (Colt), 23mm Madsen (Danish), 90 caliber (Colt), and 90 caliber (Watervliet). When the war in Europe broke out President Roosevelt issued orders to greatly increase America's aircraft production, but this armament indecision was to have significant consequences.

In January 1940 the AAC found it had only 45 37mm cannons available, and 26 of these were assigned to the British for evaluation. In his Estimated Monthly Delivery Schedule of 5 January 1940 Col. Carl Spaatz projected that 110 cannon would be required in 1940 and another 101 in the first half of 1941. Over the next 18 months the XB-19 program was to receive one 37mm cannon; the YFM-1 program was to receive 13 cannons; and the YP-38 (13) and P-38 (66) were scheduled to receive 79 cannons, while the P-39 (13) and P-39C (80) were to install 93 cannons. During the entire year of 1941 only three 37mm cannons were delivered by December, so that by January 1941 there was a deficit of 65 cannons to be delivered. There was a ten month hiatus with no cannons delivered as Colt retooled and improved its production. The shortage was alleviated when the P-38 program substituted its need for the 37mm cannons by installing 20mm Hispano cannon and the British evaluation shipment was cancelled. Once

**Douglas B-19** (USAAF)

B-19 dorsal turret which contained a combined .30 inch machine gun and 37mm cannon. (USAAF)

production was restarted supply could not meet demand and the Chief of Ordnance transferred engineers from the nearby Springfield Arsenal to help Colt meet quotas, which they eventually accomplished.

When the first P-39Cs were ready in early 1941 production delays in the Curtiss electric propellers and the 37mm cannons slowed the delivery of completed P-39 airframes, and many completed P-39s waited without armament; on 7 December 1941 only five fighter groups were equipped with combat-ready P-39s.

**U.S. Aircraft Equipped with 37mm Cannon**

Douglas XB-19

The XB-19 was the largest American aircraft built until the appearance of the B-36 Peacemaker in 1946. The heavily-armed bomber bristled with six .30 caliber and five .50 caliber machine guns and two 37mm cannons, which were combined with one .30 inch machine gun in each of the nose and forward dorsal turrets.

Bell FM-1 Airacuda

At the time of the Airacuda's conception the AAC standard armament was the .30 caliber machine gun to be provisionally replaced by the .50 gun later. Bell Aircraft Company founder Larry Bell insisted that designer Robert Woods include a cannon in his design as per AAC multi-place fighter specifications. The AAC favored the Oerlikon 20mm cannon, but Bell added a Sperry automatic fire control system (a modified ground anti-aircraft system) and a Sperry gyro-stabilized auto-pilot that were integrated with an optical sight. This Sperry system favored a 37mm Colt Browning cannon which Bell had preferred from the start. This fire control system was required to quickly work out the 37mm cannon's ballistic (trajectory) and tracking (high closing speeds) problems. The 37mm guns were linked to the sight by using electrically actuated servo-motor valves that controlled a hydraulic pressure system that moved the guns in azimuth and elevation.

The YFM-1 was powered by two pusher V-1710 engines mounted in nacelles that contained a glazed gunner's compartment forward. Each nacelle was equipped with a Colt Browning 37mm automatic cannon and a parallel .30 caliber machine gun operated by electrical motors. It was locally controlled by a gunner through an electrical hand control box containing the trigger, or from an electric fire control box located at the navigator's station located behind the pilot in the fuselage. A distributing switch in each nacelle was responsible for the selection of control. Each cannon was restricted to only a 25° effective cone of fire by limit switches. The gun was fed by 11 ammunition boxes containing two clips of five rounds located in the gunner's station of each nacelle. (The YFM-1 is described in detail in Part Ten/Section 1/Chapter 1)

**Bell P-39 Airacobra and P-63 Kingcobra**

The Bell design called for a 25mm cannon, but an updated French Hotchkiss was the only contemporary 25mm cannon, and it was secret and not available for export. The Madsen 23mm cannon was then contemplated,

**Bell XFM-1** (USAAF)

A 37mm cannon and .30 caliber machine gun installation in the front of the XFM-1's pusher-type engine nacelle. (USAAF)

**Bell P-39 Airacobra** (USAAF)

but its low rate of fire and erratic feeding mechanism led to its rejection. The only option was the installation of the 37mm T9 long-recoil cannon which had been previously installed in the Bell FM-1 Airacuda. The weapon had a low rate of fire and low velocity, and Bell considered it an interim solution that would remain operational throughout the war in the P-39 and P-63. The British elected to install the Hispano 20mm cannon in place of the 37mm cannon in the P-39C export version which the British dubbed the Airacobra I. The armament of the 1940 P-39 was to be the heaviest carried by an American production fighter to that time, replacing the standard two rifle caliber machine guns that armed pursuit aircraft. The YP-39 service test aircraft was fitted with a 37mm cannon which was to become the heavy armament configuration of the production P-39C through Q models.

The initial P-63A-1 through A-8 production block had the M4 37mm (30 rpg) cannon installed. Later P-63s were mainly delivered to the Soviet Union under Lend-Lease, and the final P-63-10 block was delivered with the M4 being replaced by the M10 supplied by 58 rounds. The spent cartridges were ejected into a container and emptied on the ground. The barrel was covered by a cylindrical tube fitted with a notched connector that served as a receptacle for a starter crank of an auxiliary starter mounted on a truck. This method of starting the Allison engine was effective in the cold conditions found on the Eastern Front.

The cannon was loaded by pulling the loading handle located in the upper left hand side of the front panel. It was charged by pulling the charging handle located in the upper right hand side of the front panel. The cannon

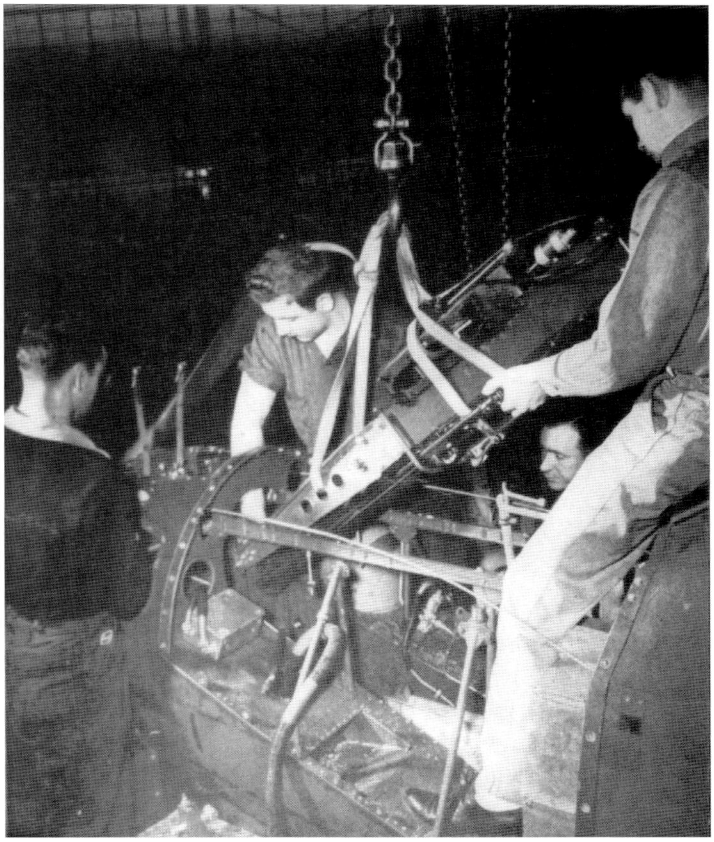

Installation of a 37mm cannon in the nose of a P-39. No synchronization gear was needed as the gun fired through the propeller hub. Since the engine of the Airacobra was placed behind the cockpit there was plenty of room for armament. (USAAF)

was fired by placing the cannon switch on the left hand side of the instrument panel to ON and squeezing the trigger located on the forward side of the control column. The pilot was to limit the bursts to five rounds and needed to be aware of the maximum of 15 rounds available when firing.

The only American fighter to be armed with the powerful 37mm M9 cannon (not to be confused with the T9, which was the forerunner of the less powerful M4) was the only P-63D-1 built whose M9 was supplied with a 48 round magazine.

37mm cannon with a 15 round magazine is complimented by two .50 and two .30 cowling mounted machine guns. (USAAF)

**Bell P-63 Kingcobra** (USAAF)

**Lockheed YP-38** (USAAF)

**Douglas A-26 Invader** (USAAF)

**Douglas XA-20F Havoc**
After use in its experimental XA-20F remote-controlled turret program (see Part Five/Chapter 2) Douglas sent this airframe to be modified at Wright Field to mount a fixed forward-firing 37mm cannon in the nose. There is no information available about this program.

**Lockheed YP-38 Lightning**
Modifications were made to the cowling of the XP-38 to accommodate the more powerful Allison engine of the 13 YP-38s, and although not all YPs were armed several housed two .50s (200 rpg), two .30s (500 rpg), and a single 37mm Oldsmobile cannon (15 rpg) that was licensed from Madsen of Denmark. The ammunition was stored in vertical magazines that were accessed by two hinged doors. The 37mm cannon was allocated for the P-39 and experimental models of the A-26 and was replaced by 20 cannon.

**Martin XB-26E Marauder**
In 1943, the AAF contracted Martin to build an experimental ground attack and a bomber version of their earlier XB-26E, which was a greatly reduced in weight version of their B-26C/D. The strafer version was a B-26B-40 (42-43319) fitted with a revised nose containing a fixed forward-firing 37mm cannon and two .50 caliber machine guns, along with a twin-tube under the fuselage rocket launcher. Tests were successful, but the B-26E (the unofficial designation) never went into production. An alternate nose version of the B-26B was contemplated to carry four 37mm nose cannons with two more 37mm cannon carried under the bomb bay.

**Douglas A-26 Invader**
The A-26 was designed to replace the B-25, B-26, and A-20. The prototypes were armed with assorted nose gun arrays including two 37mm cannon, a 75mm cannon and two .50 caliber machines, one 37mm cannon and four .50s, a 75mm and a 37mm cannon, and six .50 Brownings.

**Consolidated P4Y Corregidor**
The Consolidated P4Y Corregidor patrol bomber was to be armed with a 37mm cannon in its bow position but the program was cancelled.

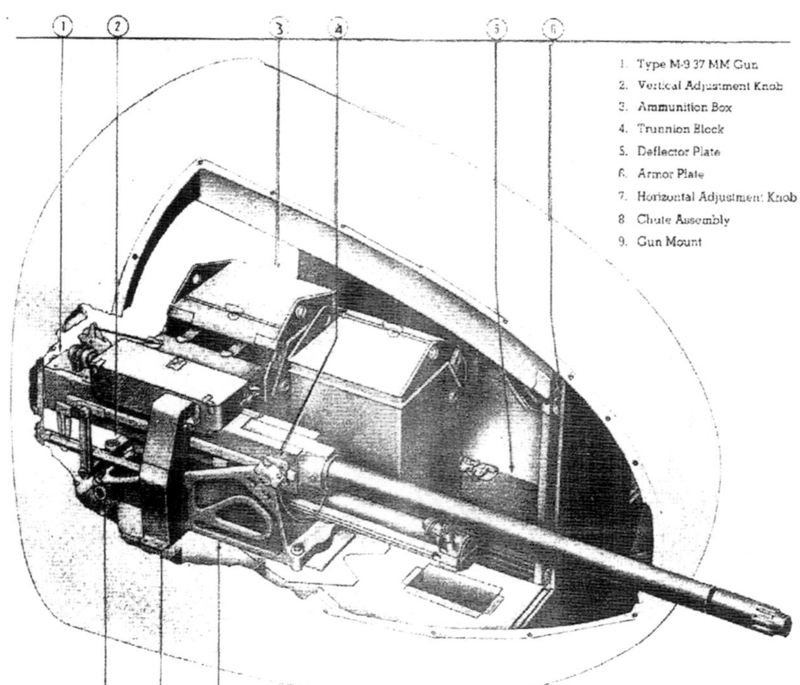


Drawing of an all-purpose metal nose of an experimental A-26 armament installation containing two 37mm cannons (the right-hand installation is shown). (USAAF)

# 4

# 75mm Aircraft Cannon

## U.S. Development and Testing

The background of mounting large caliber guns in aircraft has previously been discussed in the 37mm section. When metal airframes appeared in the 1930s much heavier weapons became more practical, and Browning's work was taken up by the U.S. Ordnance Department. Encouraging results led to a proposal to include 37mm and 75mm cannon in the armament options for a number of new attack aircraft.

In 1932 America decided that the .50 caliber machine gun was to be its air forces' standard aircraft gun and no funds were to be expended on aircraft weapons over that size. To reiterate, interest was renewed in larger caliber aircraft guns in December 1935 when the Adjutant General's Office ordered the Chief of the Air Corps and Chief of Ordnance to conduct tests at the Aberdeen Proving Grounds to determine the effect of high explosive instantaneous fused projectiles of 75mm, 37mm, 25mm, 20mm, and .50 inch on aircraft structures.

The results were forwarded to the Air Corps Technical Committee that studied and formulated the characteristics of the various aircraft cannon which were, in turn, forwarded to the Chief of Ordnance for approval. The maximum caliber was determined not to exceed 75mm with a muzzle velocity of 1,500 to 2,000 feet per second and with a recoil of 4,000 to 8,000 pounds on a fixed or semi-flexible mounting. The semi-automatic high explosive, time or impact fused, projectile was to have its cartridge case ejected automatically. In early 1936, rather than developing a domestic aircraft cannon, the U.S. investigated the possibility of purchasing cannon manufactured by foreign countries, but negotiations were hindered either by bureaucracy or unreasonable prices and conditions of sale. Since there was no urgency in the cannon issue it was not until March 1938 that it was established that there was a demand for an aircraft cannon, and since foreign purchase was not viable it was determined that various American designed cannon should be developed. The Ordnance Committee recommended that a 75mm semi-automatic cannon that could fire a HE shell at 1,500 to 2,000 feet per second be developed along with the mount, fire controller, and fuse setter. The size and weight of the cannon predetermined a fuselage mounting in a twin-engine aircraft.

In a meeting on 1 November 1938 at Wright Field the Air Corps and the Ordnance Committee ordered that an existing Model 1897 75mm cannon and its control system was to equip the first B-18 available for static tests at Wright. The DB-1 (B-18) prototype was fitted with a fixed forward firing 75mm cannon with a shortened muzzle in the forward bomb bay. After static tests this aircraft was to be shipped to Aberdeen Proving Ground for

In November 1938 the Air Corps and Ordnance Committee installed a Model 1897 75mm cannon and its control system into a B-18 for static tests at Wright Field. (USAAF)

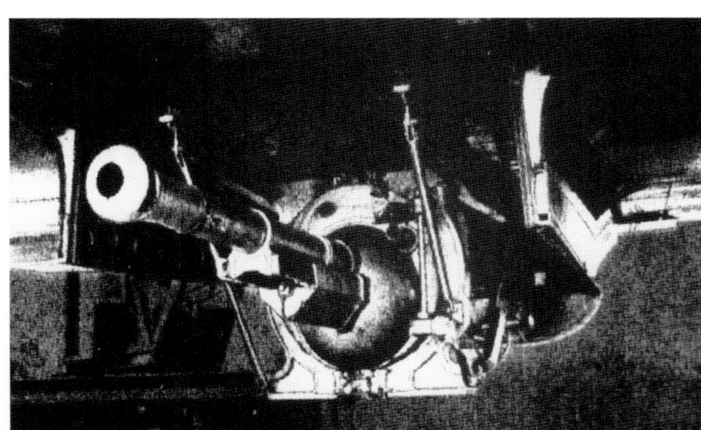

**Model 1897 75mm Cannon** (USAAF)

further testing. However, the aircraft was also being used for radio tests at Wright and would not be available to Aberdeen until April or May 1939.

On 30 April 1940, the Plans Division of the USAAC projected it would require about a year to create a new and lighter weight type of gun if manual loading were utilized and longer if automatic loading were required. Approval using the B-18 was requested to determine:

1) Trajectory effect from a heavy aerial mounted gun
2) Viability of an airborne stereoscopic rangefinder
3) Accuracy on towed targets at ranges of from 2,000 to 3,500 yards
4) If a military requirement existed for a combat airplane based on such a weapon system

Col. G.M. Barnes directed Captain Horace Quinn of the Army Ordnance Department to continue the testing program as Chief of the Aircraft Armament Development Section. With a flyable B-18 still unavailable Quinn installed a test 75mm cannon and fire control system in the fuselage of a scrapped Douglas B-18 for static ground testing. A major concern at the time was to determine if existing airframe structures could endure the stress of the heavy blast and recoil of such a large caliber gun, which the static testing positively verified, as the fuselage and mounting suffered no adverse effects. This simple improvised experimental installation also provided data on the final military mounting of a newly designed 75mm cannon, its fire control system, and the type of aircraft that could carry it.

Ultimately Quinn acquired a flyable production model B-18 at Langley Field, VA, and transferred it to Aberdeen for flight testing. A standard field Model 1897 75mm cannon with limited elevation and traverse; a shortened muzzle; and its telescopic sight and range finder was mounted in the B-18's bomb bay. The simple improvised experimental installation was to provide data on the accuracy and effectiveness on hitting a target and also to determine the final military mounting of a newly designed 75mm cannon and its fire control system. The basic stereo-telescopic sight proved to be an accurate range finder, and it was possible to fire accurately against towed aerial targets and ground targets. The average error at 3,000 yards was 50 feet and at 1,500 yards it was 35 feet. The B-18 tests proved convincingly that mounting a 75mm cannon in an aircraft was practical from both an engineering and tactical standpoint, but that the development of a new 75mm cannon and fire control system was necessary, rather than improve the existing antiquated cannon and fire control system.

Captain Quinn's flight tests produced a lighter weight 75mm aerial cannon with increased clout than the original French piece. Five different gun mounts were tested, and the result was a lighter and more effective mount that anchored the cannon to the airframe. The improved M4 recoil mechanism was married to the new gun, and the new arrangement proved that the 75mm cannon were adaptable to production combat twin-engine aircraft. These successful early tests stimulated continued but cautious AAC interest, and the improved cannon was demonstrated at Eglin Field in 1940 under the direction of Col. Barnes in order to interest private companies to play a role in its further development. Meanwhile, Victor Lucht, an Ordnance department engineer, developed a recoil mechanism which led to precise operation of the assembled cannon and recoil mechanism.

The joint Air Corps and Ordnance Committees recommended that development of the cannon/fire control system be started immediately. The Air Corps was to initiate the design and manufacture of an aircraft to mount the cannon when facilities became available but not later than the fiscal year 1942. The performance characteristics of the carrying aircraft were determined to be 394 mph maximum and 364 mph cruising (at 25,000 feet), a range of 1,080 miles, and an endurance of three hours. Two types of noses were projected; one to mount a manually operated 75mm gun and the other to mount a semi-automatic 75mm gun. The gun with mount and recoil dampener was to weigh 1,340 pounds and fire a 19.7 pound shell at 1,850 feet per second. With these new requirements the outdated B-18 would pass further 75mm cannon testing to other aircraft. During its development the appearance of the 75mm gun and its mounts varied due to the space limitations and design characteristic of the intended aircraft. Up to the end of 1944, the 75mm cannon had been proposed for or placed in the A-20, XA-38, XP-58, P-71, XA-26B, and B-25H airplanes, while during the same period the M5 gun was also installed in the M24 light tank.

**Early 75mm Aircraft Guns**

The first 75mm aircraft cannon, standardized as the 75mm gun M4, with aircraft gun mount M6, was essentially an adaptation of the 75mm gun M3 designed for tanks. Subsequent research and development resulted in lighter guns known as the 75mm gun M5, with aircraft gun mount M9, and the 75mm gun M10, with aircraft gun mount M10. These installations weighed about 500 pounds less than the M4 gun with the M6 mount. This weight reduction was the result of using high-strength steel alloy and concentric recoil mechanisms. This weight reduction allowed the installation of additional forward-firing.50 caliber machine guns.

In October 1940 approval was given for the Ordnance Corps, in cooperation with the Air Corps, to proceed with the design and manufacture of a combat unit consisting of a 75mm gun, an aircraft mount, a stereoscopic rangefinder, and a fire control system, as well as an airplane designed and built to carry this combat unit. The Ordnance Corps was to design and manufacture the gun, mount, and fire control system immediately, while the Air Corps was to start the design and manufacture of the airplane when facilities became available, but not later than fiscal year 1942.

In December 1942, the Engineering Division of the Air Force Materiel Center ordered that two M4 37mm cannons be adapted to a bomb bay installation on the B-25. Previously in mid-1942, during extensive tests using a similar 37mm installation on a Douglas A-20 Havoc, it had been demonstrated that the blast effect from a high velocity 37mm round was so damaging to the fuselage that the A-20 project was abandoned, as the practicality of reinforcing the fuselage was prohibitive. Concurrent with these efforts, another 37mm gun installation was place in the Martin Model 187 Baltimore, but the success or failure of this installation is unknown. Despite the A-20 failure, the Engineering Division of the Materiel Center considered the B-25 fuselage to be the strongest and most well built of any current American bomber, and on that opinion authorized further tests.

NAA engineers realized that the success of the 37mm project depended completely on the blast effects on the aircraft structure as would be determined during preliminary tests. North American prepared a brief proposal which advocated the installation of two 37mm M4 cannon in a deep "bathtub-type" fairing. B-25C (41-12800) was transferred to North American on 12 February 1943 for use as a test aircraft for the project. Ground testing had determined that a distance of 16 inches under the fuselage was the maximum aerodynamic distance from the fuselage to mount the 37mm guns. The fairing was designed in three sections into the bathtub housing consisting of a forward section attached to the fuselage structure and a center section of two doors hinged from the longerons. The aft section, containing a parafrag bay, was secured to the aft fuselage structure and blended into the bottom turret. The 37mm cannons were a module subassembly and provided with quick release pins for easy installation and removal with a standard bomb hoist. The B-25 tests, like the A-20 tests, also established that structural damage from the blast of the 37mm cannon was so severe that major structural changes to the airframe would have to be made before the concept could be made to work. The project also was abandoned before any further conversions could be carried out.

After this failure the Engineering Division of the Air Force Materiel Center recommended that any future 37mm installations in the B-25 be made in the navigator crawl tunnel. A crawl tunnel installation was subsequently completed on a B-25 at the Kansas City Division, but the 37mm gun was not adaptable to that location, as it was necessary to load the ammunition through a port in the flight deck just behind the pilot. This location proved to be inefficient, since it provided minimum space for the gunner and the stowage of ammunition.

Plans were made to mount the 75mm gun M2 in the nose of an XP-71 plane, with a bulkhead separating the gun and the crew. Although this type of plane was to be primarily a high altitude fighter, requirements had also materialized for a plane with a large cannon whose primary mission was to destroy ground targets. Consequently, it was planned to mount the 75mm Gun M3 in the XA-26B plane then under development.

75mm Cannon Designations April 1942

The designation of the various 75mm cannon and mounts is very confusing. The designations as of April 1942 were:

1) For use in hand loaded, fixed gun installations:
    - T13>75mm Gun
    - T21>75mm Concentric Recoil System
    - T13>75mm Aircraft Gun Mount
2) For use with 75mm Feed Mechanism:
    - T9>75mm Gun
    - T26>75mm Concentric Recoil System
    - T15>75mm Aircraft Gun Mount

Note: As improvements and modifications were made on the guns, recoil systems, and mounts the designations changed with E subtypes. For example, the T13 gun was modified into the T13E1; the T13, T14, and T15 mounts into the T13E1, T14E1, and T15E1 mounts; and the T21, T26, and T27 concentric recoil systems into the T21E1, T26E1, and T27E1 concentric recoil systems (concentric recoil system, the T21 that was being developed for use in light tanks was to be used, saving 500 pounds in weight). A new mount to replace the T13 was designated as the 75mm Airplane Mount, T13E1 that, in turn, would be replaced by the M6 mount to facilitate manufacture and not delay installation with the 75mm gun on the B-26B and B-25G..

**M2/M3**

The 75mm guns M2 and M3 were derived from the 75mm gun T6. The Ordnance Corps originally planned to use the T6 low-velocity antiaircraft gun as armament for the medium tank. Later it was found that the T6 gun would have to be modified to make it suitable for use in tanks, and the modified design was designated 75mm gun T7. The firing mechanism of the T7 gun used a trigger on for the use of a solenoid, instead of the lanyard type of trigger actuation as used on the T6 gun. Its recoil mechanism was rotated 90° about the barrel. With the addition of an operating handle for initial opening of the breech, the T7 gun was standardized in April 1941 and designated 75mm gun M2 as part of the armament of medium tank M3.

Improvements in tank design required mounting the 75mm gun in the turret rather than in the right sponson mount. When a gyrostabilizer was installed the gun became out of balance because of breech preponderance; however, this difficulty was overcome by lengthening the barrel from 28.47 calibers to 37.5 calibers. This modified T3E1 gun was standardized as 75mm gun M3 in June 1941.

The M3 gun required two mounts: 75mm aircraft gun mount T3 without a muzzle cover, and 75mm aircraft gun mount T3E1 with an automatic muzzle cover. The muzzle cover was designed to prevent flarebacks caused by the action of the air blast through the open gun tube, which might carry powder gas and unconsumed particles of burning powder rearward into

The petal-shaped muzzle cover was to aid in the loading of the gun by reducing the force caused by the air blast through the barrel while the airplane was in flight. (USAAF)

the airplane. In addition, the muzzle cover was to aid in the loading of the gun by reducing the force caused by the air blast through the tube while the airplane was in flight.

In June 1942, at a meeting of representatives of the Air Corps and the Ordnance Corps in California, it was decided to replace the 75mm M3 gun in the production XA-26B medium bomber with the 75mm T9 gun. Pending development of the T9 gun, however, production was authorized for 750 mounts using the M3 gun. The T3E1 mount was modified to facilitate manufacture after relocating trunnions in such a way that the T9 gun could be installed without further change in the production airplane. In August 1942 this mount was standardized as 75mm airplane gun mount M6. To fit the M6 mount, the M3 tube had a seat machined on it to accommodate the muzzle cover spline ring. Standardization of this modified M3 gun as 75mm gun M4 took place at the same time that the M6 mount was standardized.

**M4**

In the fall and winter of 1942, the M4 gun on the M6 mount underwent firing tests using M72 and M61 projectiles against an M4 tank hull. Firing tests were also conducted with a towed target representing a submarine with the deck awash. In March 1943, trunnion reactions were measured and extensive tests of the muzzle cover were made under conditions simulating a plane at rest on the ground. By April 1943 slight modifications had been made to the muzzle cover, and the gun and mount were in production. Tests conducted at Eglin in May 1943 showed that the petals of the muzzle cover would not stay closed; accordingly, the Air Force abandoned the muzzle cover as a requirement.

The 75mm gun M4 was a single-shot, hand loaded, flat-trajectory weapon with an automatically operated vertical sliding wedge type of breechblock. A breech ring anchored two recoil mechanisms. The breech

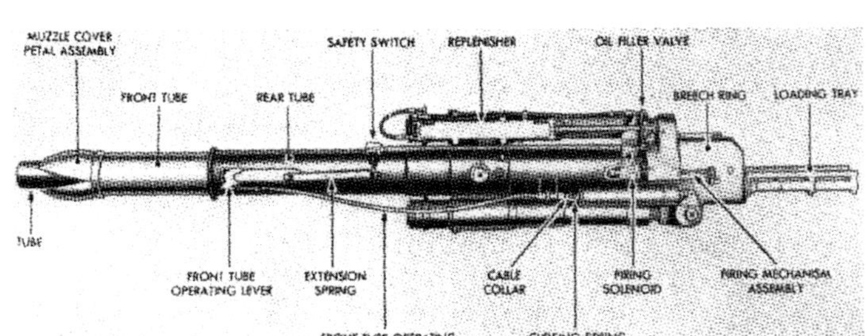


Figure 5–4. Ordnance Corps 75-mm Gun M4 on Mount M6. Left side view.

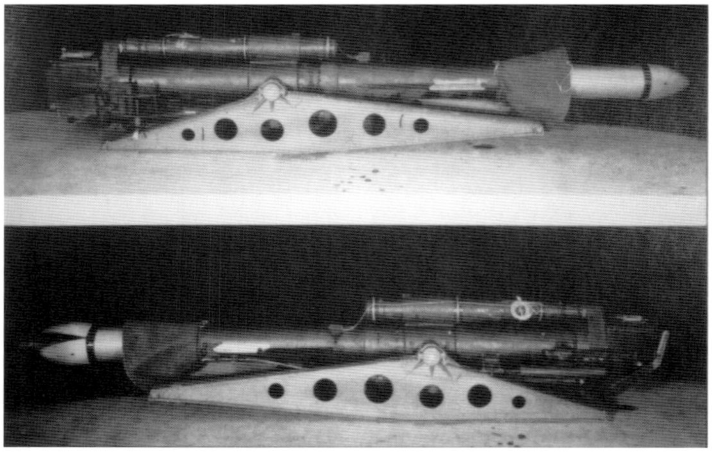

**75mm Gun M4** (USAAF)

mechanism was composed of a breech block percussion type mechanism, right- and left hand extractors, breech operating shaft, breech and breech-block operating cranks, and a chain terminal crank connected to the breech closing mechanism. The 75mm airplane gun mount M6 consisted of a cradle in which the tube assembly was supported longitudinally in a large central boring. Bored sections of the cradle above and below the tube boring and parallel to the tube carried two recoil cylinders. A replenisher mechanism was mounted on the left side of the upper section of the cradle; an electrical firing circuit was on the left rear side of the central section of the cradle, and a cam ejector mechanism was on the right rear side of the cradle.

The muzzle cover mechanism consisted of a rear tube, front tube, and muzzle cover petals, which opened automatically when a round was inserted in the chamber and then closed on the counter recoil of the gun, A safety switch, connected to the electrical firing device, prevented firing of the gun when the muzzle was closed.

**M5**

Initiated in May 1942, the 75mm gun T9, which was designed as a lightweight 75mm gun for aircraft use, had the same ballistic characteristics as those of the 75mm M4. Two pilot models were constructed: one had a closed and the other an open breech ring, In December 1942 these pilot models were redesignated as 75mm guns T9 and T13 respectively. The T9 gun was intended for use with mechanical loading devices and the T13 gun with hand loading installations. In November 1942 limited procurement was approved for 100 T9 guns, with 75mm feed mechanisms T13 anti 75mm aircraft gun mounts T15, all for installation in experimental aircraft.

In March 1943, during a preliminary test of the 75mm feed mechanism T13 with the 75mm gun T9, a power failure of considerable magnitude developed making it necessary to balance the breech ring so that the center of gravity of the recoiling parts lay on the centerline of the bore. Because of the similarity between the breech rings of the T13 and T9 guns this was also necessary for the T13 gun.

These balanced guns were designated 75mm guns T9E1 and T13El. Extensive tests were conducted at Aberdeen Proving Ground with production 75mm guns T13E1, including extended firing at excess pressure, cold room firing, and detonation tests. Examination of tubes at Watervliet Arsenal showed that satisfactory tubes could be obtained only when the tube was heat treated after boring during the manufacturing process.

The prototype B-25H airplane with 75mm gun T13E1 and 75mm airplane gun mount T13E2 was subjected to service tests at Eglin Field. Following this test, standardization of the equipment as 75mm gun M5, 75mm aircraft gun mount M9, and firing lock M15 was authorized in March 1944.

The M9 aircraft gun mount consisted of a cradle which formed the outer cylinder of the concentric recoil mechanism. Two trunnions located on the cradle provided for mounting the gun, recoil mechanism, and cradle in the airplane. The cradle supported the replenisher and the recoil guide. The counter recoil spring was located ahead of the cradle and was enclosed by the rear tube. A front cover was snapped in place on the front end of the rear tube. A hinged guide was provided on the rear right side of the cradle to guide the gun during recoil and counter recoil. During inactive periods the guide could be swung across the rear face of the breech ring to conserve space.

The M15 firing lock was operated by a motor driven firing actuator controlled by a cannon selector switch and firing button, which were aircraft equipment mounted in the pilot's compartment.

In May 1944 the Joint Aircraft Committee adopted the above with the nomenclature of 75mm gun AN-M5, 75mm aircraft gun mount AN-M9, and firing lock AN-M15 as standard for use by the Army, Navy, and the British. The 75mm gun AN-M5 was mounted as a fixed installation in the nose of the plane. The vertical sliding wedge-type breech mechanism of the AN-M5 gun was opened manually for the first round and closed by the action of the projectile, tripping the extractors and allowing the breech to close under pressure of the housing spring. During counter recoil, the breech mechanism was opened automatically by action of the breech operating crank as it struck the breech operating cam on the mount. A collar on the forward end of the gun tube retained the counter recoil spring.

The 75mm gun M5 used the standard 75mm gun rifling with a twist of 1 turn in 25.58 calibers. The stability factor of 75mm HE shell M48 was 1.373 when fired on the ground; when fired from an airplane in flight (because of the increase in linear velocity with no increase in rotational velocity) the stability factor was reduced and reached a value of 1.000 for a true air speed of 228 miles per hour at sea level. At higher speeds the stability factor was even less. This condition of instability precluded the application of adequate fire control and substantially reduced the effectiveness of the round.

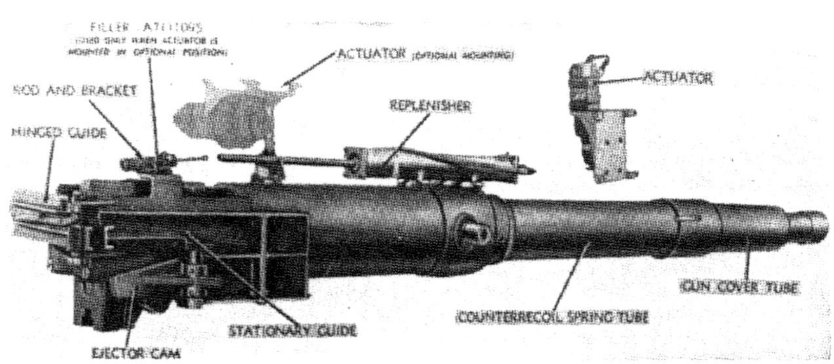


Figure 5–2. Ordnance Corps 75-mm Gun M5.

To improve the stability of 75mm HE shells M48 for aircraft firing, it was necessary to provide a gun with increased twist. Accordingly, two 75mm guns M4 were made with a twist of rifling of 1 turn in 22 calibers. With this increased twist, the stability factor for ground firing of 75mm shell M48 was raised to1.857, with a corresponding increase for aerial firing. Extended firing tests were conducted with one of these guns at Aberdeen Proving Ground, and the second gun was sent to Eglin Field for aerial firing. The results of Eglin Field tests were in agreement with the increased stability factor and indicated satisfactory stability with HE shell M48 when fired from a gun with a twist of 1 turn in 22 calibers. Two other barrels with a rifling twist of 1 turn in 22 calibers were built and tested at Aberdeen Proving Ground. One of these guns had the standard 75mm gun form of rifling and the other, a modified 75mm howitzer form of rifling (28 lands and grooves 0.30 inch. deep with a fillet radius of (.003 inch).

One gun of each type was fired approximately 1,000 rounds at maximum rated pressure and ambient outdoor temperature, followed by 200 rounds at 115% maximum rated pressure and -50°F. Series of shell M48 and projectile APC M61 inert were fired for recovery and examination of the rotating bands at intervals of 500 rounds. In addition, spin measurements were taken with a M48 shell fired from the standard gun contour of rifling to obtain comparative results of firing from a new gun and from one which had been fired approximately 1,800 rounds. The results of these tests indicated that there was no appreciable loss of spin in a gun which had been fired 1,800 rounds. Accordingly, it was approved in July 1944 that the twist of rifling of 75mm gun tubes for aircraft use be increased to 1 turn in 22 calibers, retaining the standard form of rifling for 75mm guns. These guns were then designated 75mm gun M5A1 and 75mm gun T9E2, and the 75mm gun M5 for aircraft use was reduced to limited standard. In November 1944 the Joint Aircraft Committee considered further development of the M5A1 gun. It was pointed out that although the AN-M5 gun was satisfactory for firing from aircraft, such as the B-25, at speeds up to 230 to 250 mph it was unsatisfactory on the A-26 and in other aircraft having maximum speeds above 250mph. Consequently, the M5A1 gun was standardized as 75mm gun AN-M5A1, and the AN-M5 gun reduced to substitute standard, with the understanding that the AN-M5 would not be procured for airplanes having speeds above 250mph.

By the end of 1944, extensive research work had produced 75mm guns of increased firepower than those the field artillery had used in World War I. Many differences were evident: the original field artillery weapon weighed 1,015 pounds, but the modern aircraft gun of the same bore weighed only 406 pounds. The M5 was three calibers longer than the French model. The hydropneumatic recoil system used by the French permitted a recoil of 46 inches, while the airplane gun hydrospring concentric recoil system limited the recoil to 21 to 23 inches.

The trend of 75mm development was marked by a reduction in weight and increase in firepower. Increased firepower was attained through the development of an automatic feed mechanism and a fuse setter-rammer. On 1 July 1944, for the first time, a 75mm gun was fired automatically in bursts of three rounds from an airplane in flight. Aircrews were released for other purposes than gun loading because power operation made possible use of the gun in aircraft where space was inadequate for manual operation. A cyclic rate of three rounds per minute and ammunition capacity of 20 rounds was achieved.

**M10**

75mm Gun T9E2

In July 1944 75mm gun T9E2 with 75mm feed mechanism T13 and 75mm gun mount T15E2 were installed in the Beech XA-38 Grizzly and ground fired at Tulsa, OK. This test was basically a proof test of the aircraft structure. Concurrently, the gun unit was fired from the XA-38 in flight at Great Bend, KS, and during testing the mechanism performed satisfactorily. The 75mm gun T9E2 differed slightly from the 75mm gun M5A1, but was used with the T15E2 mount and T13 feed mechanism. It was not interchangeable with the 75mm gun M5A1 and M9 mount. The breech rings were manufactured from the same castings and were identical, except that provision was made on top of the breech ring of the T9E2 gun for mounting the feeder mechanism which initiated the operation of the feed mechanism. The T15E2 mount differed from the M9 only in the location of the trunnion and a provision for bases and pads for mounting the feed mechanism. Standardization of the T9E2 gun as the 75mm gun M10, the feed mechanism T13 as the M4, and the T15E2 mount as the mount M10 were approved in October 1944.

75mm Gun T9E3

In August 1944 a development program was authorized to reduce the installation weight of the combination T9E2 gun, T13 feed mechanism, and the T15E2 mount in the XA-38. The new gun was designated as the 75mm gun T9E3 and was to be provided with new bearing surfaces to guide it in recoil, to mount the piston of the recoil mechanism directly on the tube, and to have the standard 75mm gun rifling with a uniform right hand twist of 1 turn in 22 calibers. The T9E3 ballistic characteristics were to be identical with the T9E2. A new mount designated as the 75mm airplane gun mount T15E4 was to be used with this new gun.

This mount, unlike its predecessors, which were of the hydrospring concentric recoil type, embodied a hydropneumatic concentric recoil mechanism. Modifications to the T13 feed mechanism were carried on with the designation 75mm feed mechanism T13E1. Tests of the gun, mount, and feed mechanism arrangement revealed that excess impact load was caused by rapid ejection. A new ejector cam for the T13E4 mount was consequently required to slow down the ejection. Before the completion of this cam design, but not before the weapon had been successfully modified to fire fully automatic, the Aberdeen Proving Ground was ordered to stop further testing, as rockets were proved successful.

Until the T9 was ready on 18 August 1942, the Air Corps ordered 1,500 M4 guns (at $1,451 per unit) to be manufactured by the Watervliet Arsenal, and 1,500 M6 mounts (at $1,188 per unit) by the Rock Island Arsenal were ordered for 1942 and 1943, but none were delivered in 1942. In 1943, 1,293 guns were produced and 890 in 1944 for a total of 2,183, of which 750 were the M4 gun/M6 mounts and the balance of 1,433 were T9 guns/T13E1 mounts. The completed guns were sent from Watervliet to Rock Island to be joined with the mounts.

**75mm Cannon Aircraft Installations**

Curtiss XP-71 Proposed 75mm Cannon Installation

The long-range (3,000 miles) Curtiss XP-71 was proposed in November 1941 as an advanced heavy two-man in tandem escort fighter having a pressurized cockpit. It was to be powered by two wing-mounted 3,450 hp Pratt & Whitney R-4360 Wasp Major engines driving 13.5 foot pusher contra-rotating propellers. The armament was to be two 37mm (60 rpg) and one 75mm cannon (20 rpg) mounted in the nose. Two prototypes were ordered but were cancelled on the drawing board on 26 August 1943, as planners doubted the feasibility of such a large (62 feet long /82 foot wingspan) and heavy (40,000 pounds gross) fighter.

Lockheed P-38G Proposed 75mm Cannon Installation

As part of the concern that the AAF did not have an efficient ground attack fighter-bomber Wright Field undertook preliminary design for a proposed derivative of the P-38G with a T-9 75mm cannon augmented by twin .50 caliber machine guns with 300 rpg. The design revised and enlarged the entire central nacelle into one with a nose section that was acutely angled from the top rearward to accommodate the cannon's barrel, which extended aft under the pilot's seat. A second seat was added to the elongated cockpit behind the pilot to house the cannoneer and the ammunition. Since the cannon was so large the P-38's nosewheel configuration had to be modified so that the gear had to turn 45° to fit flat into its wheel bay. The heavy weight of the cannon would have precluded its installation on the lightweight P-38 and the proposal never got beyond the provisional design stage.

Grumman TB2F Proposed 75mm Cannon Installation

The proposed TB2F was a very large twin-engined torpedo bomber that was equipped in the mock up stage with a dorsal turret with twin .50s, a retractable ventral ball-type turret with two .50s, four .50s in the wing roots, two .50s on the port side of the nose, and a 75mm in the starboard side of the nose. As projected the TB2F was much too large even for the Midway class carriers and was cancelled.

Beech XA-38 Grizzly 75mm Cannon Installation

In March 1942 Beech Aircraft Company began design work on a ground attack bomber (the Beech Model 28) to replace the Douglas A-20 Havoc. In December 1942, the AAC awarded Beech a contract to build two prototypes designated the XA-38 "Destroyer" by Beech; however, the name was changed to the AAF's choice "Grizzly" once manufacture began. The twin tail bomber was powered by twin Wright by R-3350 radial engines that also powered the B-29 Superfortress. The Beech bomber was heavily armed with a 20 round semi-automatic feed T15E1 75mm cannon protruding from its streamlined nose, and sighted by a Type N-6 reflector sight. In addition, the Grizzly mounted two nose .50 caliber machine guns and two remotely controlled .50s each in the ventral and dorsal turrets that were sighted by a periscopic system through a Plexiglas observer's position located in the rear fuselage. Development lagged, and the first flight did not take place until 7 May 1944. Once in the air, the XA-38's flight test results were initially unsatisfactory due to engine problems, slowing development through 1944 and into 1945. The semi-automatic 75mm gun assembly was too heavy at 1,800 pounds, and it was concluded that better results could be achieved with a manually loaded gun. Also, the firing of the cannon filled the cockpit with combustion gases. The two auxiliary nose .50 caliber machine guns were not a heavy enough addition to the cannon on a firing run and the remotely sighted turrets had chronic sighting problems. However, by mid-1945 most of the Grizzly's engine and armament problems were solved. The aircraft had a maximum speed of 376 mph (cruise at 344 mph) and was heavily armed, but the few Wright 3350 engines that could be released from the B-29 program were allotted to the Douglas BT2D-1 and Martin BTM Mauler programs, and the two prototypes were the only Grizzlies built. Both were scrapped after the war.

Douglas XA-26 75mm Cannon Installation

In late 1940 Wright Field wished to replace the Douglas A-20 Havoc attack bomber with an attack bomber that was to include the 75mm cannon that was also proposed for the B-25. In April 1942 Douglas, under the direction of the renowned Ed Heinemann, began developmental work for the production of a 75mm equipped twin-engine destroyer aircraft using the third Douglas XA-prototype which was designated XA-26B. The aircraft was equipped with a 75mm cannon that initially was a M3 tank gun on a fixed T3 mount that needed to be manually loaded from inside the aircraft. On 2 June 1942, representatives of the Offices of the Chief of the Air Corps and Ordnance met at the Douglas El Segundo, CA, plant and decided that the M3 tank gun would be replaced by the new lightweight 75mm T9 gun then under development. In the summer of 1942 the Army ordered 500 B-26Bs with the 75mm cannon nose section and 200 with the six .50 caliber machine gun nose section. An alternate nose version was contemplated to carry four 37mm nose cannons with two more 37mm cannon carried under the bomb bay. By the end of 1942 the AAF ordered Douglas to concentrate on the 75mm cannon nose. A consequence of the trials was the development of an automatic muzzle cover that opened with the closing of the breechblock and closed on the gun's recoil, preventing firing residue gases from entering the aircraft. Meanwhile, Douglas continued working on the development of an all-purpose nose that could accommodate a variety of weapons that included 37mm cannon and .50 caliber machine guns. Tests with the 37mm cannon were unsuccessful, and in mid-March 1943 the AAF, continuing to be enamored with the 75mm, let a second production order for 500 A-26Bs equipped with the 75mm cannon. Meanwhile, the A-26 ran into serious developmental problems, particularly with its wing, and with the developmental problems in the B-29 program Hap Arnold made a choice and gave priority to the heavy bomber program. Meanwhile, the 75mm cannon mounted in the B-25 got indifferent reviews in combat and the 75 mm cannon in the A-26 was deleted.

**Douglas XA-26 Invader** (USAAF)

**Beech XA-38 Grizzly** (USAAF)

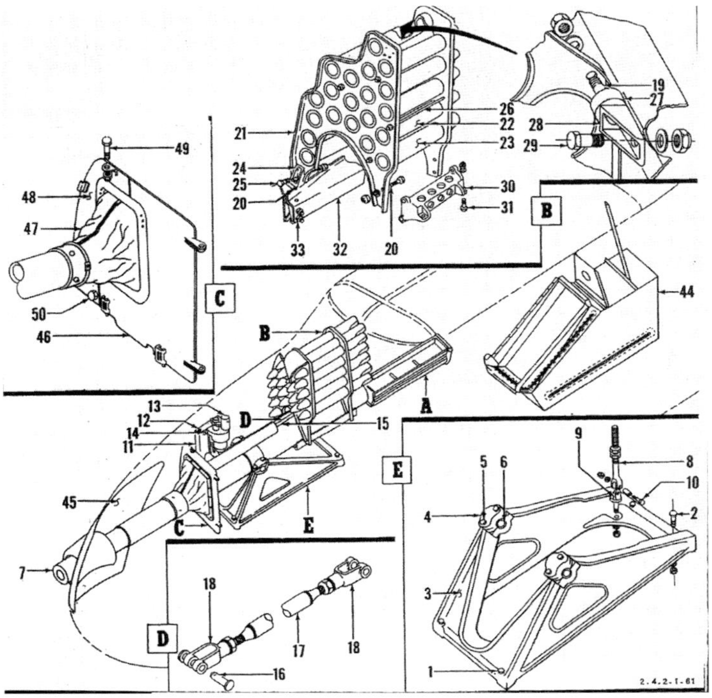

A-26 75mm Gun Installation (USAAF)

### B-25 75mm Cannon Testing

The AAC was looking to develop a ground attack bomber to replace the Douglas A-20, but the estimated development time to bring this concept to fruition would have been at least a year (i.e. the Beech XB-38), but the AAC needed an immediate remedy and that was the B-25. So even before its future role of strafer had been delineated, the B-25 was found to be capable of being easily adapted into a long-range attack bomber that was both heavily armed and able to carry a useful bomb load.

After the AAC decided to equip the B-25 with the 75mm cannon the drawings and data from previous trials were sent to Edgar Schmued, Head of North American's Confidential Design Group, who was instrumental in the development of the renowned P-51 Mustang. Since time was of the essence, Schmued gave George Wing only three days to develop a preliminary layout of the B-25 cannon installation. Wing's layout proposed that the bomb bay would be the best location for the large gun, with its long barrel extending through the bombardier's crawl tunnel and out the nose. After further deliberation, it was found that if placed in the bomb bay the gun and the chain feed loading mechanism would have occupied too much space and significantly decreased the bomb load. The next option was to place it in the navigator's compartment and crawl tunnel, but to do so the chain feed apparatus was abandoned in favor of the smaller, more efficient, and less

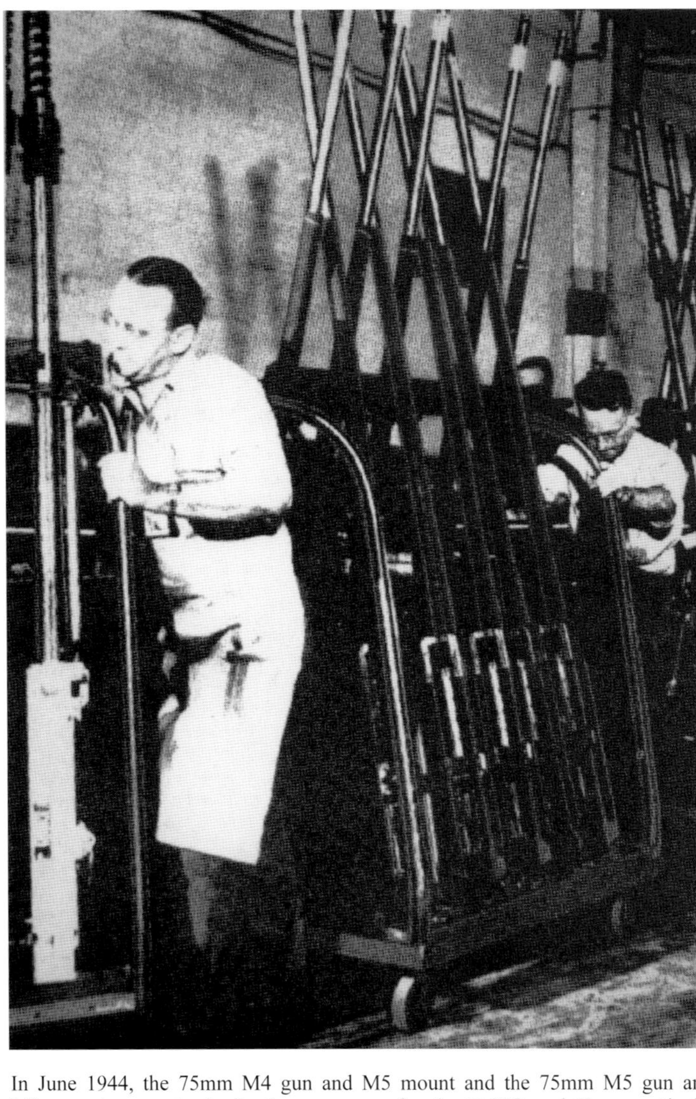

In June 1944, the 75mm M4 gun and M5 mount and the 75mm M5 gun and M9 mount were standardized as weapons for the B-25G and H, respectively. (USAAF)

### 75mm Cannon Standardization for the B-25G & H

In late March 1943, the AAF requested the standardization of the lightweight 75mm gun so that the guns and mounts would be available for installation in the B-26 and B-25 with an order for 1,267 guns and mounts contemplated. By October 1943, sufficient tests had been conducted at Aberdeen that the AAF ordered standardization of the Oldsmobile-built T13E1 75mm Gun, T21E2 recoil system, and T13E2 mount. On 29 January 1944 this standardization was approved as the M5 (former T13E1) 75mm gun and M9 (former T13E2) 75mm mount. In June 1944, the 75mm M4 gun and M5 mount and the 75mm M5 gun and M9 mount were standardized as weapons for the B-25G and H, respectively. The unit cost of the M4 gun was $933 and the M6 mount was $1,188. The T13E1 cannon weighed less than the M4, but also was appreciably different in its basic design and appearance. The breech mechanism design was more cylindrical and markedly more uncomplicated. The recoil cylinder was concentric, with the rear barrel section and the oil compensator and associated oil lines remaining on the top of the gun. To prevent the barrel from rotating on its axis, a large stop was mounted on the right rear of the gun and extended well aft of the breech. After firing a spent shell case was ejected from the recoiling cannon against a shell deflector that sent the case down a chute and overboard. After an ejected casing hit another aircraft the spent casings were collected and stowed inside. On 25 June 1943 a modification to the 75mm mount and recoil mechanisms was made by removing the counter recoil spring from inside the recoil cylinder and placing it forward of the cylinder mounted around the gun tube. This modification reduced the overall length of the recoil mechanism and reduced the weight.

The M5 standardized gun had rifling with a twist of one turn in 25.58 calibers, which when fired from an airplane caused an instability that did not permit the use of adequate fire control and greatly reduced the effectiveness of the round. To correct the problem an extra twist of rifling to one turn in 22 calibers were added to the barrel, and tests at both Aberdeen and Eglin concurred that the M5 was greatly improved, and on 5 July 1944, the new gun, redesignated the M5A1, was approved as standard costly hand loading system used on all production B-25G and H models. Wing's final proposal was submitted to the AAC for approval, and a M4 75mm aircraft cannon was provided to the NAA Armament Engineering Group for production design and flight testing.

In Wing's design the cannon and its recoil mechanism would require 14 feet with the crawl tunnel to the nose accommodating the barrel, while the navigator's compartment, located immediately behind the flight deck, provided adequate space for the breech, recoil stroke, and a working area for the cannoneer (loader) and an ammunition rack. When the gun was placed in this location the muzzle and its firing blast were unacceptably aft of the front of the aircraft (i.e. inside the aircraft). The obvious resolution was either a shorter nose or much longer and heavier barrel. The "simple" solution, entailing 380 new drawings and 13,000 engineering man hours, but requiring no major airframe changes or cannon redesign, was to fabricate a new solid nose section that was 26 inches shorter than the original glass "bombardier" nose. But even with this change the cannon muzzle remained slightly aft of the forward contour of the new nose. The solid nose section also allowed the fitting of two .50 caliber machine guns which were projected to be used to range in the cannon while providing some forward firepower once the 21 round cannon ammunition supply had been expended.

When firing the 75mm cannon the nose was subjected to a powerful muzzle blast on the nose, and the consequences needed to be studied to determine if any structural reinforcement for the airframe were needed. For testing, NAA engineers equipped a complete forward fuselage with a cannon and trucked it from Mines Field to a secluded area in the sand dunes near the Pacific Ocean adjacent to the field. Non-explosive rounds using increasingly powerful propellant charges were fired into the dunes, and the nose structure was then progressively strengthened until it was able to withstand the prolonged firing of rounds loaded to 115% of normal charges.

For the initial flight tests a B-25C-1 (41-13296) was modified as XB-25G and fitted with the 75mm cannon and two other .50 caliber nose guns and the twin .50s in the dorsal turret. The XB-25G was flown by company test pilot Ed Virgin and test engineer Paul Brewer, usually accompanied by other flight test and armament engineers. The first two test flights occurred on 22 October 1942 and investigated the procedure and function of cannon loading and firing using dummy rounds. The second test investigated the effect of the new heavy nose on flight characteristics, which found stalls to be normal, and diving to 340 mph uncovered no problems. The next day the first inflight firing tests were conducted over the Pacific Ocean by Ed Virgin, Paul Brewer, and Col. Horace Quinn, who had been instrumental in conducting the first 75mm cannon trials with the B-18 back in 1938. To determine the effect of firing, the 75mm cannon was fired using rounds loaded to 50% and 75% of full propellant charge. Firing was found to cause a sharp bang, but Virgin reported that it was no worse than expected. These partially filled rounds at times caused an impressive fire ball to ignite ahead of the aircraft when the round was fired. This phenomenon was due to the incomplete combustion of the propellant within the barrel, with the unburned powder igniting into a fire ball outside the aircraft. The fire ball was usually followed by a forceful, secondary shock, which did not occur with full propellant charges. Further tests using full charge live rounds caused no problems and the initial testing phase was concluded. It was feared that the firing of the cannon would damage the ear drums, but the sound was a thud lasting only a fraction of a second, and ultimately the relentless loud drone of the B-25's R-2600 engines caused more than one B-25 crewman some lifetime hearing loss.

For testing, NAA engineers equipped a complete forward fuselage of a B-25 with a cannon and tested it in a secluded area in the sand dunes near the Pacific Ocean. (NAA via Rice)

To convert the XB-25G into an attack bomber, it was flown to Kansas City on 31 October for the installation of bomb control equipment and then returned to California for further testing. After ten hours flight time it was flown to Eglin Field, FL, on 22 November for continued testing by the Air Force. After successful testing, NAA received AAF contract AC 27390 for 400 cannon-equipped B-25G-5 and-10s (without ventral turrets) that were delivered to the Army between May and August 1943, with a small number remaining at the AAF School of Applied Tactics at Orlando, Florida. The B-25 modification center in Kansas City modified five B-25Cs (42-32384 through 32388) and 58 B-25B-25C-20s and -25s with a solid nose with two .50s and the 75mm cannon designated as the B-25G (some were modified by the Republic Modification Center at Evansville, IN).

Tests showed that the cannon had weakening effects on the airframe, particularly around the wing leading edge close-in at the wing root and also along the cannon (port) side of the fuselage, where rivets would loosen and pop and constantly have to be replaced. The B-25 with the 1,300 pound cannon installed was chronically nose heavy with all this weight forward of the aircraft's center of gravity, which caused the pilot to use a large amount of nose up trim to keep the aircraft flying straight and level. Mechanics reported a lot of wear and tear on the nosewheels, dampers, and the hydraulic shocks from the forward weight of the cannon. The heavy recoil of the gun caused it to be jolted out of alignment, requiring constant maintenance and boresighting.

Although the cannon carrying B-25G was not as successful in combat as anticipated NAA received an order for an additional 1,000 B-25H attack strafers that carried the lighter weight 75mm cannon, four nose guns (vs. two), two waist guns, two.50s in the dorsal turret (which was moved forward to the navigator's compartment), twin .50s in the tail, and the pair of .50 blister packs located on either side of the fuselage. Up to the end of the Second World War, the 75mm cannon of the B-25G was the second largest gun fitted to any aircraft, exceeded in size only by the 105mm cannon experimentally equipped on the Italian Piaggio P.108A. In the postwar the B-25's 75mm was exceeded by the 105-mm howitzer carried by the Lockheed AC-130 Spectre gunship, which is described later..

**Description of the 75mm Cannon and Accessories**

Cannon Assembly

The B-25 cannon assembly consisted of the 75mm M4 cannon and its M6 recoil mount, and later the 75mm T9 cannon and its Type T-13E1 recoil mount. The cannon muzzle projected forward through the blast tube in the lower nose section. The early model M4 cannon were originally fitted with a protective muzzle cover consisting of metal "petals" that sprang open before use. These covers would not always open properly even after a stronger spring was installed and they were canceled in later versions. The breech extended aft to the left forward side of the cannoneer's compartment. The cannon mount assembly was bolted to the floor in the tunnel beneath the left side of the pilot's compartment. The recoil mount consisted of a concentric recoil mechanism, an oil replenishing cylinder and an indicator tube, the trunnions, and the actuator assembly that controlled the firing of the cannon. An ammunition loading tray was attached to the cannon breech ring. A vertical leveling clevis mounted at the end of the gun provided boresighting adjustments. The opening through which the cannon protruded was covered by an armored panel. A dust and gas seal was secured to the cannon barrel and attached to the armored panel. For loading the cannon, the cannoneer was provided with a folding seat, a cannon recoil foot guard, a leg strap, and a wooden loading ram.

The cannon and ammunition weighed a very substantial 1,296 pounds. The recoil length was 21 inches with a powder pressure of 38,000 pounds per square inch. A Type N-9 gun and bombsight and Type A-3 gun and bombsight head were mounted on the instrument glare shield immediately in front of the pilot. The pilot fired the cannon by pressing the trigger under the left hand side of the control wheel, while the machine guns were fired by pressing the trigger under the right hand side of the control wheel. The 75mm projectile was 26 inches long and three inches in diameter and weighed 20 pounds, equivalent to 78 .50 caliber bullets, of which 15 pounds was

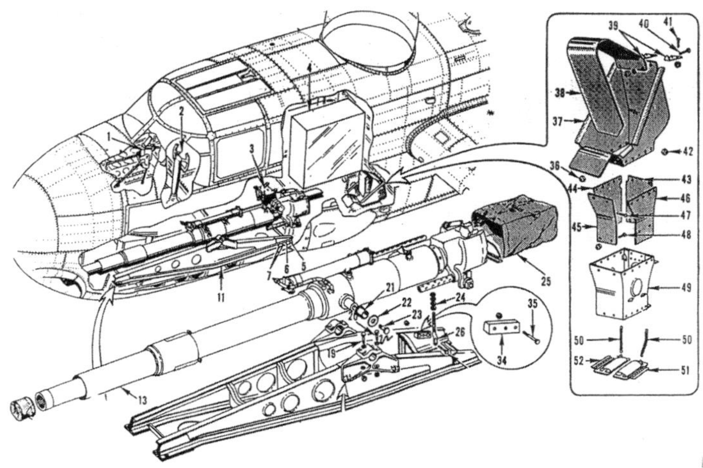

**75mm Gun Installation B-25G** (USAAF)

75mm cannon installation on a contemporary restored B-25H, *Barbie III*. (Author/*Barbie III*)

Interior view of the *Barbie III* 75mm cannon installation. (Author/*Barbie III*)

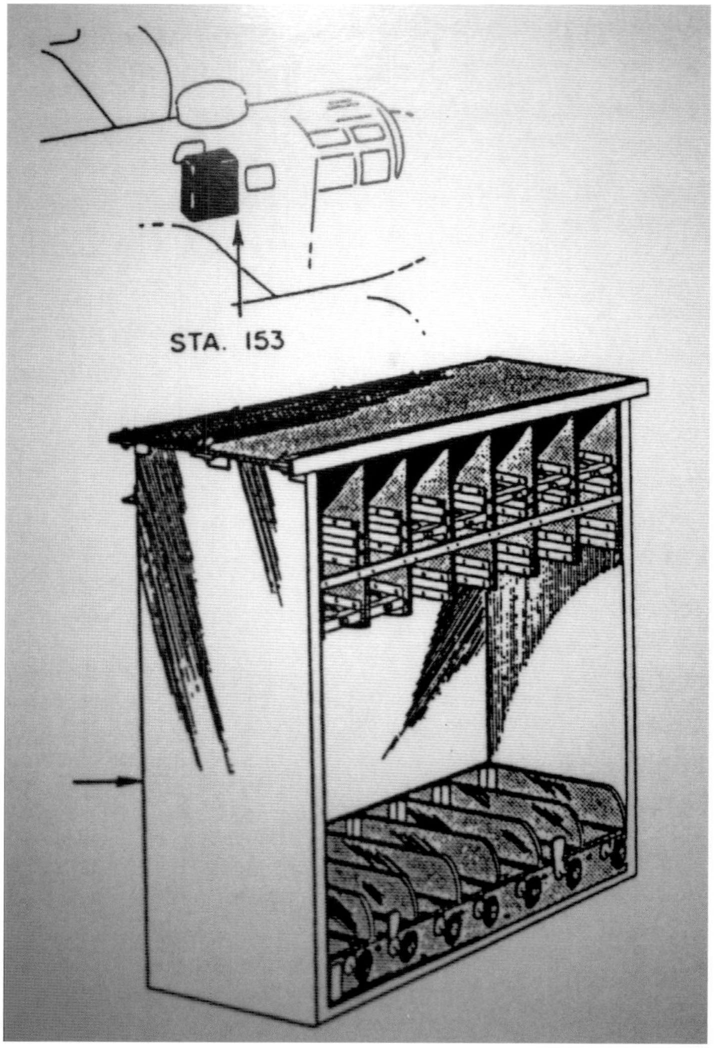


Armor-plated 21 round ammunition rack located in the navigator's compartment. (USAAF)

the projectile, which contained 1.5 pounds of TNT. After firing the spent shell case was ejected from the recoiling cannon against a shell deflector that sent the case down a chute and overboard.

Cannon Ammunition Stowage Rack

The cannon ammunition stowage rack was installed on the navigator's shelf directly above the cannon breech. The ammunition rack was a box fabricated from armor plate containing an upper rack and a lower rack, which together provided for seven vertical stowage sections, with each section stowing three rounds for a total of 21 rounds. A retainer in the upper rack held the noses of the rounds and a selective lock in the lower rack secured their bases. The retainers could be inserted into three positions to accommodate the different lengths of the armor-piercing, high explosive, and smoke shells.

**Cannon Operation**

Operation of the Cannon by the Cannoneer

Preparation

Most of the B-25 cannoneer/navigators were former bombardier/navigators, and probably were the only commissioned cannon loaders in the history of the U.S. Army. Once the cannoneer entered the aircraft he unsnapped the leather strap that held the metal seat, which folded flat against the right wall of the compartment, clear of the front entrance hatch. Once the seat was unfolded and lowered, he latched the cannon recoil guard located on the front entrance hatch inner door and lowered the ammunition loading tray to the loading position. Once in the air the cannoneer had to sit in his small compartment without outside reference, bouncing on his small uncomfortable folding seat that was mounted on the rear of the cannon, his legs straddling the cannon breech. As a safety precaution the cannoneer fastened the leg strap to keep his leg away from the recoil mechanism in the bouncing aircraft and made certain that the breech was always closed when the cannon was not in use.

The cannoneer stowed the 75mm shells in the rack by placing the lower rack locks in the open position by pulling out the knobs and letting them snap back. He then placed the upper rack retainers in their desired positions. The rounds were stowed into their respective stowage sections by engaging the noses with the retainers and locking the rounds in each section by pulling out the knob and letting it snap back.

Often there were problems with dented cannon shell cases, and cannoneers made it SOP on the way to the target to take each shell out of the

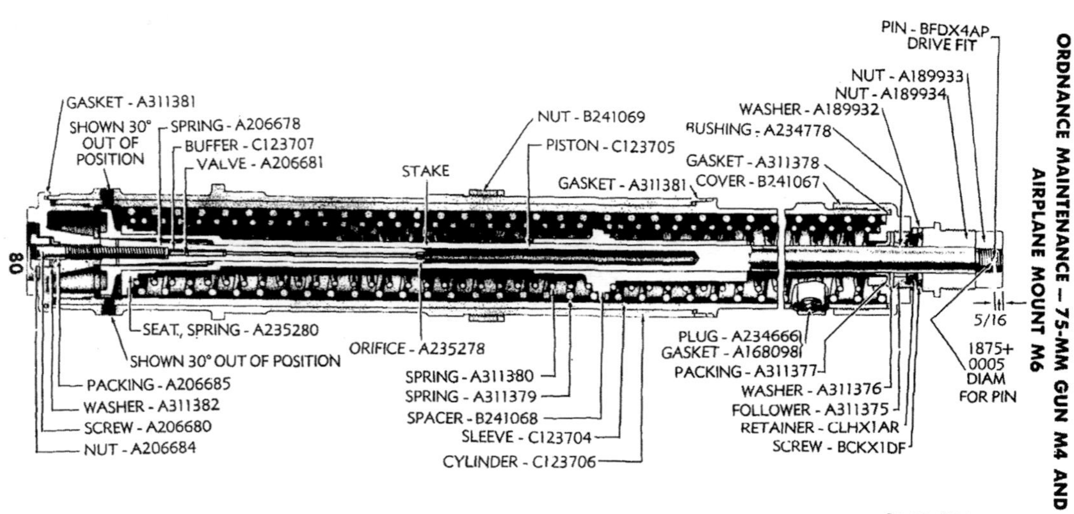


**Figure 85 — Diagram of Recoil Cylinder**

(USAAF)

rack, put it into the cannon block, and close the breech to make sure it would go in and eject properly, and then he placed each acceptable shell back in the rack while any casing that did not load easily or eject properly was set aside. It is interesting to note that once the 75mm cannon reached combat over New Guinea it was classified as a secret weapon, and the cannoneers were not allowed to eject spent shells from the aircraft for the Japanese to capture. However, after a few firing runs these casings would accumulate and roll around on the already cramped compartment floor.

### In Combat

It was a difficult job for the cannoneer to remove a cannon shell from the wall rack and insert it into the breech while in the jinking B-25 flying on deck. The cannoneer opened the breech with the cocking wrench that was strapped to the panel at the right side of the compartment. He fitted the wrench to the spline shaft at the left side of the cannon breech ring and pushed it down, after which he removed the wrench and stowed it. He released the ammunition lower rack lock for each section by pulling out the lock knob with a quick snap. A round was removed from the rack and placed on the loading tray, during which time the pilot used a stopwatch to determine the actual range which the cannoneer preset into each shell to explode at a predetermined range (in seconds) or on contact.

Once the range was set, the round was pushed forward into the chamber with the wooden loading ram and the breech closed and automatically armed the shell. When the shell was ready to be fired the cannoneer reached up and tapped the pilot on the back and then leaned back to wait for the pilot to fire while clinging to a small handle on the wall.

General Motors Oldsmobile Division magazine advertisement "Fire-Power is our Business" for its 75mm cannon. (Author/GM)

After firing the counter recoil stroke lowered the breech block and cocked the gun, the expended shell case was ejected, and the breech block was locked open (in the lower position) and ready for the loading of the next round.

If a shell misfired, or if the cannon or firing circuit became inoperative, or if the round was defective, the cannoneer was to wait five minutes before removing the live round or to work on the cannon to determine the cause of the malfunction. He had to be careful to keep to one side of the cannon until the round was removed. After waiting, he opened the breech with the cocking wrench, removed the round from the chamber, and jettisoned it through the ejection chute. Never, under any circumstances, was the cannoneer to use his hands to release the extractors to close the breechblock. He was to use an empty cartridge case or the wooden loading ram.

After considerable practice and dexterity a skilled cannoneer could load at most four rounds of the 21 supplied during a single long run on the target. The 75mm cannon's low muzzle velocity of 1,930 feet per second required a high trajectory that without a satisfactory sighting mechanism made the gun inaccurate. A long, low-level, direct run without evasive action on the target left the attacker vulnerable to enemy AA fire and usually precluded firing more than two rounds.

## Operation of the Cannon by the Pilot

### Preparation

After takeoff the pilot would charge the nose guns manually while the cannoneer would manually charge the blister guns and cannon. To keep the nose guns at operating temperature after takeoff, the pilot pulled out the NOSE GUN HEAT control knob that was located above the pilot's CABIN AIR control. To sight the cannon, nose guns, and blister guns, he set the gunsight reflector at 0°. If the reflector was set for bombing or the gunsight was malfunctioning he would use the ring and bead sight as a backup. The pilot turned the gunsight rheostat ON. To ready the cannon and fixed guns for firing, he turned the cannon and gun safety switches to FIRE.

### In Combat

The original cannon gunsight was the standard ring and bead with no means of mechanically adjusting for range. After the B-25s reached combat sighting was by either an electric N-3 to 6 series sight (see previous discussion) or a modified A-1 radar sight. Using the N-series sights the pilot opened fire at 2,000 yards and had fired two more rounds over the next 1,000 yards before beginning effective machine fire from the fixed guns. The N-series sight was equipped with a range adjustment knob that the cannoneer used to dial in the estimated range (range estimation was emphasized during training). The cannons were bore sighted at 1,000 yards and were fired at altitudes starting from 1,000 feet and descending to 500 feet at the end of the attack. With his line of sight on the target, as seen through the gunsight, the pilot preset the gunsight for the desired range by rotating an adjusting knob (See N-3B/N-3C Gunsight Part Four Chapter 2). He would squeeze the firing button when he estimated that he had reached the preset range to the target. For a second shot he would quickly reset the sight for a shorter range and repeat the firing procedure. In practice it was found that the pilot was more accurate at the closer, but more vulnerable, ranges.

### AN/APG-13 Radar Sighting

Using the radar sight firing was commenced at 5,000 yards, and as many as four or five rounds could be fired before the pilot began to fire the fixed machine guns. The number of rounds fired by either sight was subject to the loading skill of the cannoneer and then on the condition and maintenance of the gun (especially boresighting), as well as the speed and straight course of the aircraft during the attack. (For a complete discussion of the AN/APG-13 "Falcon" Radar Sight Firing see Part Four/Chapter 4 Radar)

**The 75mm Cannon in Combat**

Enemy land targets available for air attack in the Pacific were sporadic, and usually were hidden from the air by the jungle, particularly troops, gun emplacements, vehicles, etc. The cannon could have been very effective against tanks or armored vehicles and columns of trucks, which the Japanese did not use on their small island bastions. On those rare occasions when units could deploy their B-25Gs in line abreast formation and open a barrage of fire with as many shells as possible leaving the barrels in the shortest time, the effect on the target was devastating.

Bridges were difficult targets for air attack with any type of ordnance, but a cannon attack was more effective and accurate than a bombing attack. Bridges were usually narrow and short, between 25 and 50 feet long, which was not a very large target during a bombing run from more than a mile away at a height of 50 to 70 feet. However, the heavily armed B-25G or H could get off two or three cannon rounds and then strafe the usually flimsy jungle bridges, and when over the target drop 250 pound anti-personnel bombs with 15 second delay fuses.

The 75mm cannon was very effective against shipping, as the barrage tactics could be devastating with several B-25s following one another in tandem from seven miles out. The lead aircraft fired two ranging shots and the other bombers followed, firing their cannons as quickly as they could and then, when in range, raked the target with their four nose and two dorsal turret machine guns until they were over the enemy ship, when they would drop bombs.

To determine the suitability of the 75mm cannon in an anti-submarine role tests were scheduled for the 23rd Anti-submarine Squadron. The USAAF Squadron was temporarily designated as a special test unit and assigned to the Navy in the Caribbean, and in late August 1943 was assigned 16 B-25Gs to test the 75mm cannon. Because the AAF Anti-submarine Command (AAFAC) was being withdrawn from U-Boat patrols at the time the tests were never concluded. It was found that the 75mm shells were quite capable of penetrating the hull of a submarine, and at least one B-25 crew later claimed to have sunk a Japanese sub using cannon fire, but the claim was not officially confirmed.

# 5

# 105mm Cannon

In August 1943, after the 75mm cannon was approved and under development, the Chief of Ordnance requested that one 90mm, one 105mm, and one added 155mm cannon and their suitable mounts be developed and delivered to the AAF as air-to-ground aircraft weapons. Of these guns the 90mm cannon, firing a 23.4 pound shell, was thought to be most effective against heavily armored vehicles and surface shipping. Because of its high velocity, the fixed 90mm gun, either manually or mechanically loaded, was considered for air-to-ground or air-to-air use at ranges normally used by attack aircraft. However, it appears that the 90mm gun was not developed for aircraft use, as it was given a high priority for its use as America's primary anti-aircraft gun, especially when controlled by SCR-584 radar against V-1 Buzz Bombs over England. The 155mm concept was quickly discarded as much too unwieldy for aircraft installation.

The reliable **105mm Field Howitzer M2A1** was the basis for the aircraft version of the 105mm cannon. (U.S. Army)

The 105mm howitzer was considered the most viable candidate for a large caliber air-to-ground aircraft gun, as 105mm high explosive ammunition was readily available and an armor piercing round could be quickly developed. The installation of the 105mm T7 Gun with a T17 Mount was to include power controlled elevation, power feed mechanism, and fire control equipment. In approving the development of a 105mm cannon and mount HQ, AAF, requested that the gun be compact, lightweight, and have a "low trunnion reaction" (low recoil). The AAF had authorized one 105mm gun and mount, but Ordnance Department test requirements and installation studies showed that four additional units and two mock ups were required. It was decided that the howitzer barrel and breech ring were to be identical in each, but that the four mounts, Models #1 through #4, should differ in the materials used in certain components. The recoil spring sleeves, recoil spring seat rings, and front and rear bearings were to be fabricated from different combinations of steel, aluminum, textolite, and bronze. The mock up units were to be used for installation studies and the four pilot model guns and mounts for firing tests.

On 4 November 1943 an informal conference was held; it was attended by the Chief of Ordnance, the Chief of the Technical Division, Ordnance Department, and Hap Arnold to discuss the development of the 105mm aircraft cannon. It was determined that the unit should have the same general characteristics as the 105mm Field Howitzer, M2A1:

| | |
|---|---|
| Weight | 1,300 pounds |
| Length of Bore | 30 calibers (approx.) |
| Chamber Capacity | 153 cubic inches |
| Muzzle Velocity | 1,600 feet per second |
| Length of recoil | 36 inches (approx.) |
| Type of Recoil Mechanism | Hydrospring concentric |
| M1 (HE) Round Weight | 42 pound round/33 pound projectile/4.8 pound TNT<br>5 zones of propelling charge weighing 3.66 pounds |
| Dimensions | 31 inches total/14.6 inch case |

(The 105mm Field Howitzer M2A1 was the most important and most produced piece of U.S. field artillery in World War II with 8,536 units manufactured.)

On 6 January 1944 the AAF requirement was changed from one to three units. On 26 January the Chief of Ordnance, War Department requested that one 105mm aircraft howitzer and mount be shipped to the Navy's Dahlgren, VA, Proving Ground for testing. On 30 March 1944 the Committee on Aircraft Armament designated the aircraft howitzer as the 105mm Howitzer, T12 and the four mounts as Mount, T12 (Model #1); Mount T12E1 (Model #2); Mount T12E2 (Mount #3); and T12E3 (Mount #4). Past experience in the development of the 75mm aircraft cannon had shown that additional units would be needed for testing. For the development of the 105mm Aircraft Howitzer T12 and the four mounts the procurement of four units with suitable mounts and two wooden mockups was approved.

In early May 1944 the AAF Air Office, Ordnance requested 12 howitzers and mounts, but on 17 May 1944 initial production orders were issued to the Watervliet Arsenal, NY, for 25 guns and to the Rock Island Arsenal, IL, for 25 mounts. This order was increased to 30 units on 7 July to both Arsenals. To expedite the procurement and manufacture of these units the 105mm T12 and Mounts T12 were classified as "Limited Procurement" items on 15 June 1944. The Watervliet Arsenal had considerable experience in designing large caliber guns and it was not necessary to furnish it with additional funds for machinery or equipment for their manufacture. Watervliet prepared manufacturing drawings for the 105mm, T12 under the direction of the Chief of Ordnance. Four howitzers were completed and tested at Aberdeen. Rock Island Arsenal also had an extensive background in designing recoil mechanisms and mounts, and it also required no additional funding to manufacture the mounts. Watervliet estimated that an initial average gun cost would be $3,000 per unit, while Rock Island estimated the cost of its mount to be $1,750.

During testing at Aberdeen Proving Ground three blast tubes of different diameters (six, eight, and nine inches) were installed to reduce muzzle flash. Night tests comparing the three blast tubes and a gun with no blast tube demonstrated that the gun without a blast tube showed almost no flash, while the nine inch tube had a flash 25 feet long and eight inches in diameter and the six and eight inch tubes showed a flash nine inches in diameter and 35 feet long. Further Tests showed that the barrel length should be increased by 48 inches from 124 inches (30 calibers) to 172 inches (42 calibers) to reduce flash and also increased muzzle velocity by 50 feet per second. The additional 48 inches added only 72 pounds, while the nine inch blast tube added 110 pounds. In additional to the increase in barrel length, several minor modifications to the gun and mounts were made. The AAF, Ordnance Committee requested 30 units: 25 for aircraft installation, one for installation studies and test firing from aircraft, and four for extended ground firing and future development. On 12 August 1944 the modified guns were approved as "Gun, 105mm, T7 and Mount, Gun, Aircraft; the 105mm T17 and the 105mm Howitzer, T12 with Mounts T12, T12E1, T12E2,, and T12E3 were to be discontinued.

Only seven guns were manufactured by Watervliet Arsenal before 1 January 1945 and 12 more during the first three months of 1945, four more in April, and the balance of seven of the 30 authorized in May. The Rock Island Arsenal only produced two T17 mounts before 1 January 1945 and three more during the first quarter. After 15 May 1945 the production of the T17 mounts was suspended pending changes in design. As the war was winding down the requirement for the 105mm aircraft cannon diminished and the project was cancelled. There is no record of the 105mm cannon being installed in an American aircraft in World War II, although it was proposed for installation on the A-26 using Falcon radar with a 12,000 yard sweep (Falcon radar was used in the CBI on B-25s mounting a 75mm cannon).

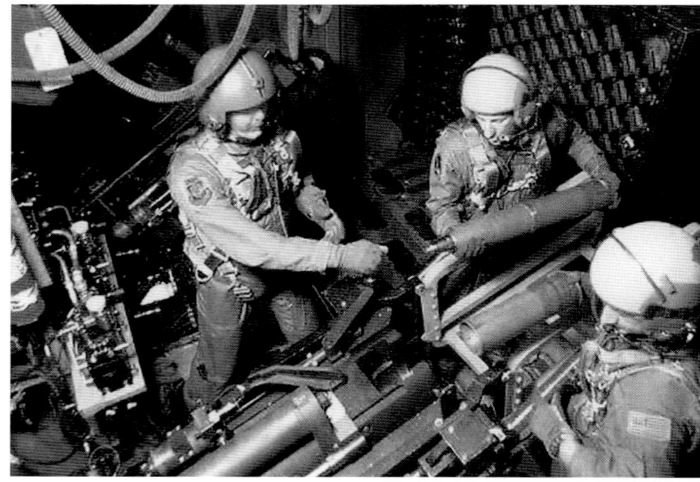

The Lockheed-Boeing AC-130H Spectre and AC-130U Spooky gunships of the 1980s and 1990s carried a M102 105mm cannon fired from the left rear door. (USAAF)

Other 105mm Aircraft Cannon Installations

The Lockheed-Boeing AC-130H *Spectre* and AC-130U *Spooky* gunships of the 1980s and 1990s carried a M102 105mm cannon fired from the left rear door. The 3,000 pound M102 was derived from the Army field artillery M1A1 howitzer and was supplied with 100 rounds fired at six to ten rounds per minute by a firing crew of four. During the Vietnam War the *Spectre* gunships destroyed more than 10,000 trucks and conducted hundreds of close air support missions. AC-130s suppressed enemy air defense systems and attacked ground forces in Grenada during Operation *Urgent Fury*. During *Operation Desert Storm*, AC-130s provided close air support and air base defense for ground forces.

The Italian Piaggio P.108A was a four engine anti-shipping bomber that was armed with a 102mm naval cannon that was the largest gun carried by an aircraft in World War II. The 3,300 pound gun was installed in the centerline of the lower nose section at a slight downward angle. A magazine contained 50 rounds weighing 44 pounds each firing a 25.25 pound projectile at 2,500 feet per second. It was reported that about 200 rounds were test fired at altitudes ranging from 5,000 to 15,000 feet. The gun had no undesirable effects on handling, except to further slow the already underpowered bomber. Due to the problems in developing a new sight only one P-108A was fitted with the cannon before the Italian Armistice on 3 September 1943.

# 6

# Cannon vs. Machine Gun Controversy

**The Aircraft Machine Gun vs. the Aircraft Cannon**

The difference between a machine gun and cannon was that the machine gun fired a solid slug, while the cannon fired rounds called shells that could be solid, but were often hollow and filled with explosive or incendiary material. The solid machine gun round did its damage through kinetic energy that was the function of projectile weight times its velocity squared. The .50 caliber slug weighed about 1.6 ounces, while the 20mm projectile weighed 4.6 ounces and the 37mm projectile weighed 17.6 ounces. The machine gun had a somewhat higher muzzle velocity (the speed at which the projectile leaves the barrel). Thus, the machine gun round's kinetic energy was greater, as its higher muzzle velocity was squared. It also had a higher rate of fire than the cannon that meant it could fire more rounds per minute, or more correctly, per second, to do damage. The muzzle velocity affected the round's kinetic energy and the flight time to the target. The shorter the time to the target gave the target less time to maneuver. Guns with higher muzzle velocities were more likely to hit a target, could be fired at longer ranges, and caused more damage.

Aircraft cannon were a more deadly weapon due to their heavier explosive shells that, depending on their design, would explode on contact, or penetrate and then explode, or set a fire. A solid machine gun slug would penetrate the skin of the target and then depend on its kinetic energy to cause damage. However, a cannon weighed much more than a machine gun, as a 37mm cannon weighed 135 pounds and a 20mm cannon weighed 118 pounds vs. a .50 caliber machine gun that weighed 52 pounds and a .30 caliber machine gun that weighed 24 pounds. Therefore, only considering gun weight and not rate of fire, two machine guns could fire twice as many rounds per second than one cannon. Cannons inherently fired shells at a lower rate per minute (i.e. 20mm at 700-800 rpm/37mm at 150 rpm) than machine guns fired their bullets (i.e. .50 caliber at 800 rpm/.30 caliber at 1,300 rpm). Also, cannon shells weighed more and were larger than machine gun rounds, so a cannon-equipped aircraft could carry far fewer rounds than a machine gun-equipped aircraft. The P-39 equipped with a 37mm gun could carry 30 rounds per gun; the 20mm cannon carried by the P-38 were supplied with 150 rpg; the eight .50 caliber machine guns of the P-47 or the six of the P-51 carried between 400-450 rpg; and the .30 caliber machine guns of the P-39 carried 1,000 rpg, while the B-25 carried only 21 75mm cannon rounds. Fewer cannon shells meant a shorter firing time at a lower rate of fire. The 30 rounds of 37mm shells fired by a P-39 had duration of fire of 11.8 seconds, while its four .30 caliber machines with 1,000 rpg fired for 67 seconds per gun. The P-38's 20mm cannon fired 150 rounds at 11.2 rounds per second in 13.4 seconds. The .50 caliber machine gun fired 12 rounds per second for a duration of 35 seconds (425 rounds). A skilled cannoneer in a B-25 could fire from two to four shells during a firing run but, of course, the Mitchell's four fixed nose guns and dorsal turret twin .50s would then open up once they were in range. A cannon shell caused more damage per hit, but there were less potential hits when compared to the higher rate of fire and more rounds found in machine gun equipped fighters. Many British and *Luftwaffe* fighters carried a combination of machine guns and cannon, with the machine guns being used to find range and attain hits and the cannon to deliver the lethal blow. The RAF replaced its light Browning .303 caliber machine guns with the Hispano-Suiza 20mm cannon, as one 20mm shell did much more damage than four .303 hits, which were ineffective against the armor plate and self-sealing fuel tanks of contemporary combat aircraft. The 20mm cannon with its explosive shell would leave a large hole upon impact. The American combat aircraft .30 caliber machine gun was replaced with the .50 caliber. Both projectiles left small, clean entrance holes in a metal fuselage surface, but after they hit they would be deflected and begin to tumble end over end. The larger .50 caliber bullet would cause a substantially larger exit, or secondary hole than the .30 caliber bullet.

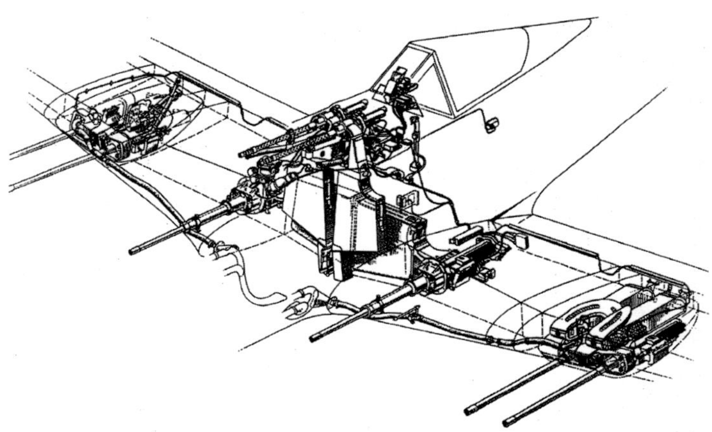

This very heavily-armed FW190 typifies the *Luftwaffe's* dependence on multiple machine guns and cannon of different calibers: 2 MG17 (900 rpg), 2 MG151/20 (250 rpg)m and 2x2 MG 151/20 in underwing pods (150 rpg). (Author)

| GUN/AMMO (lbs) | Gun Weight (lbs) | Muzzle Velocity (ft/sec) | Rounds per Gun (lbs/sec) | Projectile Weight | Rate of Fire (rps) | Duration of Fire (sec) | Weight of Fire |
|---|---|---|---|---|---|---|---|
| Browning .30 cal. Machine Gun | 24 | 2,600 | 1,000 | 0.025 | 15.0 | 66.5 | 0.40 |
| Browning .50 cal. Machine Gun | 52 | 2,800 | 425 | 0.100 | 10.2 | 19.6 | 0.90 |
| Hispano-Suiza 20mm Cannon | 118 | 2,800 | 150 | 0.290 | 11.2 | 13.4 | 3.20 |
| M4 37mm Cannon | 135 | 1,800 | 30 | 1.100 | 1.5 | 11.8 | 1.65 |

**Brief Chronology of Aircraft Armament in World War II**

At the start of the war there was a broad choice of armament available to the combatants, including light machine guns, heavy machine guns, and cannon. But as the air war evolved most of the major combatants had settled on either heavy machine guns or cannon with a collective predilection for belt fed guns of all calibers. The light machine gun, firing light rifle caliber rounds, became less important as aircraft protective armament and self-sealing fuel tanks became a necessity for combat aircraft. This settling on armament types occurred as armament designers in Germany and Japan were faced with destroying the armadas of Allied heavy bombers devastating their nation's war-making infrastructure. Meanwhile, the Allies did not have to contend with enemy heavy bombers and concentrated on protecting their own bombers from enemy fighters. The Americans found that fighters with six or eight .50 caliber heavy machine guns were adequate for destroying German and Japanese fighter aircraft, while the British discontinued the .303 rifle caliber machine guns for the 20mm Hispano cannon (though often mixed with .303s).

In the final year of the war there was a general realization (except for the Americans) that the 20mm cannon was to be the standard fighter armament. Cannon were reliable belt fed weapons with a high muzzle velocity and fired at an acceptable rate of fire that insured an increased hit probability and destructive power. These factors offset their heavy installed weight and disproportionate recoil that precluded the use of more than two in a fighter. Consequently, these cannon were often mixed with machine guns that had different ballistic characteristics, different ammunition, and maintenance requirements. Cannon of larger caliber were installed by the Germans and Japanese to confront Allied heavy bombers. The 30mm German MK 108 and the Japanese HO-155 were employed, but proved to be very heavy with a low velocity, and reduced the carrying aircraft's performance to a point that it was too vulnerable against enemy fighters.

**Aircraft Guns and Cannon of World War II**
**Weight of Fire (lbs./sec.)**

| GUN | USA | UK | Germ | USSR | IJA | IJN |
|---|---|---|---|---|---|---|
| **LMG** | 0.42 | 0.46 | 0.40 | 0.79 | 0.35 | 0.42 |
| **HMG** | 1.34 | 1.34 | 1.15 | 1.85 | 1.26 | 1.52 |
| **20mm** | 2.87 | 2.87 | 2.82 | 2.82 | 3.09 | 2.31 |
| **30mm** | ----- | ----- | ----- | 6.88 | 5.18 | 5.78 |

LMG= Light Machine Gun HMG=Heavy Machine Gun
IJA= Japanese Army IJN=Japanese Navy

Light Machine Guns (LMG)

Light machine guns, often referred to as rifle caliber machine guns, varied in caliber from 0.295 inches (7.5mm) to 0.315 inches (8mm). The LMG was the standard gun used in World War I fighter aircraft, but had demonstrated a lack of destructive capacity. The LMGs that were more reliable and had higher rates of fire were in use in early World War II, but were withdrawn from operations by 1943, as they were ineffective against enemy aircraft with armor plate protection and self-sealing fuel tanks. However, since there was no other alternative the .Browning .303 remained in RAF service in Bomber Command bomber turrets.

Heavy Machine Guns (HMG)

Heavy caliber machine guns, sometimes called medium caliber machine guns, were generally thought of as .50 caliber, but ranged from 0.43 inches (11mm) to 0.59 inches (15mm). The heavy caliber projectile could weigh more than four times more than a rifle caliber machine gun projectile. The HMG fired at high muzzle velocities, giving them very good ballistic characteristics, but the HMGs had a much lower rate of fire than LMGs. Despite the increase in aircraft armor protection during the war the .50 caliber continued to be successful against the more common enemy fighters and light bombers. HMG projectiles were usually a mixture of incendiary and AP rounds.

Light Aircraft Cannon

Generally the definition of a light aircraft cannon was a gun of 20mm because the 20mm projectile was considered the smallest workable caliber in which explosive projectiles could be used, although smaller caliber explosive projectiles were produced but were ineffective. Incendiary and AP rounds were also available for cannon. Fuses were always required for high explosive rounds and the sensitivity of the fuse was significant. A fuse that was too sensitive (firing too fast) would be ineffective, as it would explode when hitting the outer skin of an aircraft, while a fuse that was not sensitive enough (firing too slow) meant the projectile could pass through the target before it would explode.

Heavy Aircraft Cannon

Heavy aircraft cannon were usually considered those of 37mm and above and were used for bomber interception and ground attack. The anti-bomber cannons fired projectiles with a large quantity of high explosive and had a lower muzzle velocity, which gave them a lower recoil and thus less weight (less recoil meant lighter mounts). The ground attack cannon had a relatively high muzzle velocity for better armor penetration using AP projectiles against shipping and armor.

**Axis-Allied Armament Development During World War II**

In September 1939, when the European war broke out the standard armament of aircraft of the combatants were rifle caliber light machine guns, and by 1945 the standard, except for the American air forces, was the 20mm cannon and larger. Since the fighters of the American Air Forces (the USAAF, USN, and USMC) were arguably the decisive factor in winning World War II in the air, were the Americans correct in continuing the use of the Browning .50 caliber machine gun while the rest of the combatants transitioned to cannon caliber guns?

Eight .303 caliber Browning Machine Guns mounted in the wing of a Hawker Hurricane IIa. Despite their number the small caliber guns were considered too light and were replaced by four 20mm cannon in the IIc. (AFHRC)

British Aerial Armament Development

In 1939, the RAF Hurricanes and Spitfires were notable for their heavy battery of eight wing-mounted .303 Browning machine guns that delivered twice as much firepower as any contemporary fighter. The Hawker Hurricane IIA carried eight .303 guns in its wings and the IIb carried 12! But once in combat this would-be aerial arsenal proved to be less effective than anticipated. The eight reliable guns fired 160 rounds per second, but they were originally harmonized to converge at 400 yards, which caused the bullet strikes on the target to be more spread out on the target than at shorter ranges. As armor plate and self-sealing fuel tanks became more widespread in 1940, it was necessary to concentrate fire at much closer ranges. The .303 bullets were too small to contain sufficient HE or incendiary material to cause great damage in case of a direct hit, and also lacked penetrating power with most of the bullets being deflected or tumbled when first hitting the fuselage skin or structure.

As early as World War I the British suspected that the .303 LMG was ineffective as an aircraft gun, and this realization became evident as aircraft became faster and stronger. The Browning .50 caliber HMG was contemplated by the British, but was rejected since its projectile was considered not destructive enough, and the search turned to the excellent new French Hispano-Suiza HS 404 20mm cannon. The HS 404 was selected, and the Westland Whirlwind fighter was designed to carry these cannon. Problems arose in setting up factories to produce the HS 404 and very few were available for the Battle of Britain. Attempts were made to fit it into the slim, flexible wing of the Spitfire. To accommodate the large drum magazines of the HS 404, which was designed to be carried along the engine or in the fuselage, the cannon was turned on its side in the wing, which resulted in significant malfunctions. During the war constant modifications were made to accommodate the cannon for wing mounting, but it was much more reliable in fuselage mountings in the twin engine Mosquito, Beaufighter, and Whirlwind. The HS 404 was superior to the German MG-FF as it had a higher rate of fire (60 rounds per minute faster), and had a larger shell that produced a much higher muzzle velocity which increased the hit probability and projectile penetration. The RAF never adopted the German Minengeschoss shell expertise, so its shells only carried half the HE/I explosive capacity, but the heavier shell could penetrate aircraft structure better and cause more damage. The 60 round drum was

The Hawker IId was equipped with two Vickers 40mm Type S cannons carried in underwing pods as well as two Browning .303 caliber machine guns. (AFHRC)

20mm Hispano-Suiza HS 404 cannon barrel being installed in a Hawker Hurricane. (AFHRC)

**20mm Ikaria Werke Berlin MG-FF** (AFHRC)

**13mm Rheinmetall-Borsig HMG 131** (AFHRC)

replaced by belt feed, but the Hispano was twice the weight and length of the MG-FF (See Part Two: Cannon/Chapter 1: 20mm).

The Hawker Mk IID was equipped with two Vickers 40mm Type S cannons carried in underwing pods as well as two Browning .303 caliber machine guns. These cannons were initially developed in the 1930s as defensive armament for British bombers. Later the gun was adapted as an aerial anti-tank and ground attack weapon firing armor piercing rounds for anti-tank missions or high explosive rounds for other ground attack assignments. The Vickers 40mm cannon weighed 295 pounds firing a 2.5 pound shell from its 15 round magazine at 100 rpm. An 1,800 pound 57mm cannon was developed and installed in a Mosquito FB XVIII to fire a seven pound shell from a 25 round magazine at 75 rpm.

*Luftwaffe* Aerial Armament Development

In the early 1930s the *Luftwaffe*, influenced by the French use of engine-mounted cannon, issued a specification for a fighter mounting two rifle caliber machine guns or a solitary 20mm cannon. The cannon selected was the large Rheinmetall-Borsig MG C/30L gun which was a powerful, high velocity, slow-firing cannon mounted to fire through the propeller hub, but proved to be unacceptable for aerial combat; it was of use in a ground attack role.

While looking to develop a purpose-designed German aircraft cannon the *Luftwaffe* then took a different tact by choosing the small, low-velocity, Swiss-designed Oerlikon 20mm FF cannon, which it modified and put into production by the Ikaria Werke Berlin as the MG-FF. Twin MG-FFs were slated to be installed around the engine of the Me-109E, but problems resulted in their installation of one in each wing; augmented by two engine-mounted 7.92mm MF 17 LMGs synchronized to fire through the propeller arc. In 1939, many Me-109s were armed with four LMGs. The MG-FF weighed more than twice as much as a 7.92 MG 17 and fired only half as fast at 540 rounds per minute. The MG-FF's muzzle velocity was less, which produced a different trajectory and time-to-target. The cannon was fed by a 60 round drum that limited the cannon to only seven seconds of firing time. The projectiles weighed 12 times as much as a .303 round, and when it hit its target the HE filler caused severe blast damage and sent HE shell fragments throughout the target.

In May 1940 the Me-109E was equipped with a modified MG-FFM adapted to fire the new Minengeschoss (mine shell) ammunition, which was constructed with very thin walls, and the lighter shells allowed a higher muzzle velocity. The shell contained double the amount of HE and/or incendiary. While the AP or solid shot needed to hit a relatively small, critical area to be effective, the HE projectile could cause significant damage no matter where it hit the target.

The *Luftwaffe* and Rheinmetall-Borsig continued to design cannon during the war. Since the size and weight of cannon limited their number to one or two the MG 131 was developed as a 13mm HMG to replace the

**20mm Mauser MG151/20** (AFHRC)

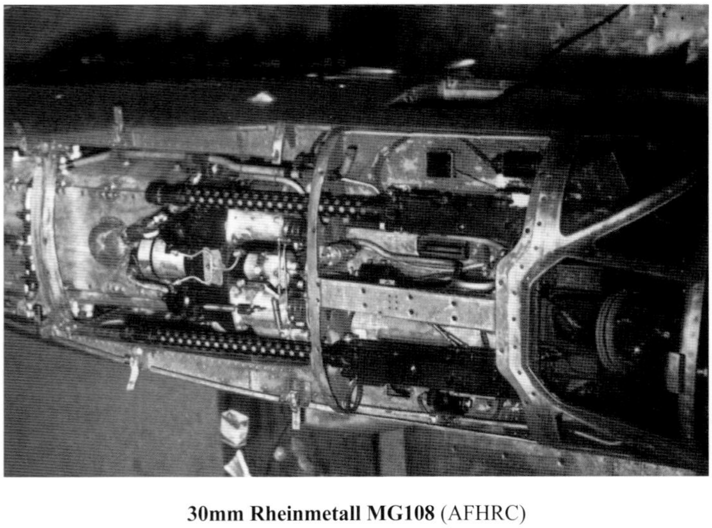

**30mm Rheinmetall MG108** (AFHRC)

**30mm Rheinmetall MG101** (AFHRC)

7.92mm LMG that had augmented German cannon installations. The MG 131, while light and small, was the least powerful operational HMG of the war.

With a purpose-designed cannon not realized in 1941, the MG-FFM was replaced by the Mauser MG 151. The original MG 151 cartridge was a high velocity 15mm round that was replaced by the 20mm rounds used in the MG-FFM. These 20mm rounds sacrificed muzzle velocity for the greater penetration and explosive effect of the larger shell. The MG 151/20 fell in between the MG-FFM and the HS 404 in size, weight, and muzzle velocity but had a higher rate of fire at 720 rounds per minute. The 151/20 became the standard *Luftwaffe* gun between 1942-1944. U.S. ordnance experts felt the MG 151/20 design was excellent and later copied it as the .60 caliber T17, but only 300 were produced.

The Rheinmetall MG 103 and MG 108 were both 30mm, but the MK 103 was a very large, high velocity, slow firing cannon that was used in bomb bay or wing pod installations, while the MG 108 was half the size and weight, firing a much smaller, low velocity shell at a respectable rate of 600 rounds per minute. Using the 30mm M-Geschoss HEI shells, which contained four times the HEI as the 20mm version, the MK 108 needed only three or four hits on a B-17 to destroy it, as compared to 20 hits with a 20mm M-Geschoss HEI shells.

The *Luftwaffe* had a number of innovative cannon designs in development at the end of the war. The 30mm MG 101 was a huge 9.67 foot/396 pound upscaled version of a 20mm anti-tank gun and was installed in the under fuselage bomb racks of the Hs 129. The Me 410A-1/U4 Hornet was a purpose-built bomber destroyer that had its nose armament removed and replaced by a single 50mm BK 5 cannon in the bomb bay. This gun was adapted from a German Army PAK 38 anti-tank gun. The BK 5 cannon weighed 1,190 pounds and was 12.4 feet long and fired 21 rounds from a cylindrical magazine at a rate of 50 rounds per minute. The 50mm BK cannon was also mounted in the Me-262 jet fighter. The 55mm Mk 112 was in development for installation in the Do 335 but was terminated by the end of the war. The 55mm Mk 114 was under development for the Me 262 but proved to be too heavy, and development was stopped in late 1944. The very effective 75mm Pak 40 anti-tank gun was considered for aircraft use as the BK 75, but was found to have inadequate rate of fire and excessive recoil and muzzle blast and was terminated. The MG 213 was a revolver-type cannon that could be converted to fire either 20mm or 30mm rounds at 1,200 rpm but was captured by the Allies, and became the basis for American post-war revolver cannon development. At the end of the war the 30mm SG 117 was introduced containing a drum of seven barrels which could be fired in rapid, shotgun-like succession. Soon the SG 118 cannon, which had three sets of seven barrel drums, was under development. The G-104 was projected to fire a 1,400 pound, 365mm projectile from a 33 foot recoilless rifle tube suspended under the fuselage of a Ju 288

As typified by this **Yak-9** nearly all Soviet fighters had fuselage-mounted armament fired through the spinner because their slender wooden wings were not strong enough to support machine guns or cannon. (AFHRC)

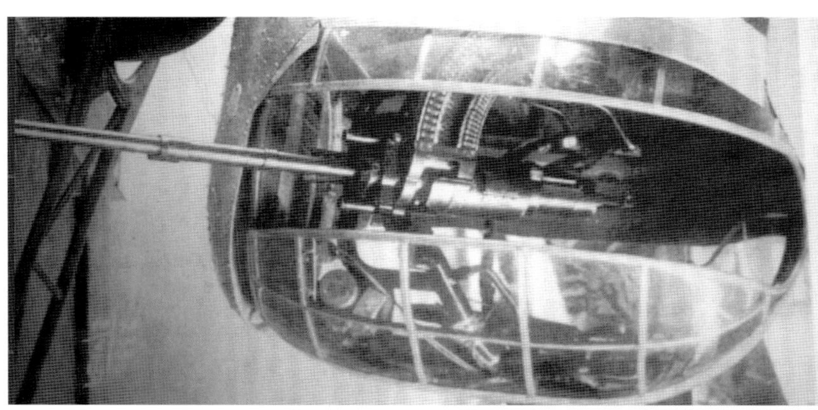

The .50 caliber (12.7mm) Universal Berezin (UB) and the 20mm ShVAK cannon (shown) were considered excellent guns of their caliber, but their installation in the nose limited their ammunition capacity. (AFHRC)

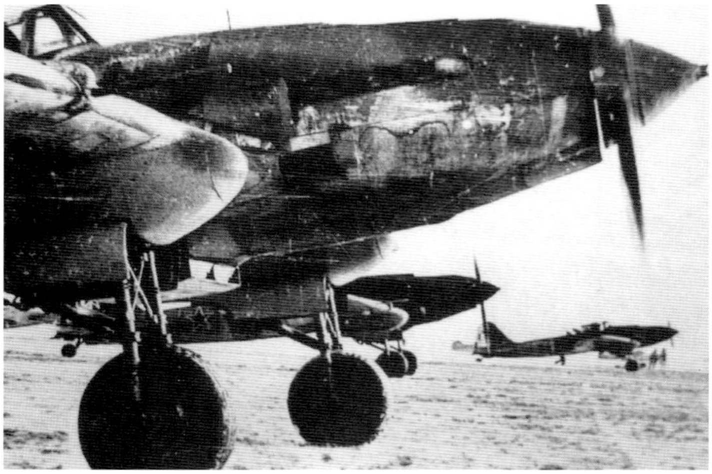

The **Il-2 Sturmovik** ground attack aircraft of which a record for military aircraft with 36,163 being built was armed with one defensive 12.7mm Berezin in the rear cockpit; one 7.62mm ShKAS and one 20mm ShVAK cannon in each wing (which were sometimes substituted with two 23mm or 37mm cannon in later models). (AFHRC)

bomber. The consequence of this multitude of guns and ammunition was the manufacturing, logistical, and maintenance problems involved.

Soviet Aerial Armament Development

When the Soviets entered the war in June 1941 they had the .30 caliber LMG, the .50 caliber (12.7mm) Universal Berezin (UB), and the 20mm ShVAK cannon in service. Nearly all Soviet fighters had fuselage-mounted and/or through the spinner armament because their slender wooden wings were not strong enough to support machine guns or cannon. Although the Soviet Air Force possessed some of the finest aircraft guns of the war their fighters were generally under-gunned. The MiG-1/2/3s were armed with one 12.7mm Berezin UB and two 7.62mm ShKAS. The LaGG-3/LA-5 and Yak-1/7/9s were armed with one 12.7mm Berezin UB and one 20mm ShVAK—both excellent guns, but the two were supplied by only 350 rounds. Eventually the late model La-5/7s, the MiG-200 series, and Yak-9s were equipped with two and sometimes three 20mm ShVAK cannons. The renowned Il-2 Sturmovik ground attack aircraft, which achieved a record for military aircraft with 36,163 built, was armed with one defensive 12.7mm Berezin in the rear cockpit, and one 7.62mm ShKAS and one 20mm ShVAK cannon in each wing (sometimes substituted with two 23mm or 37mm cannon in later models).

The ShKAS had a high muzzle velocity and rate of fire and, although it was considered to be the best of the best rifle caliber aerial machine guns of the war, the Russians realized that heavy machine guns and cannon caliber guns were preferable and abandoned the ShKAS. The Berezin UB was also arguably the best HMG of the war, having similar performance to the Browning .50 caliber, but it had a significantly higher rate of fire. The UBK was installed in aircraft wings while the UBS was for cowling installation, which was the usual Soviet fighter installation. The ShVAK was a modified and enlarged ShKAS and was considered an excellent cannon, comparable to the MG 151/20 due to its powerful punch, small size, and high rate of fire. The ShVAK was the standard Soviet fighter armament throughout the war. However, by 1945 it was being replaced by the much lighter (at 53 pounds), high performance Berezin B-20, which was also considered among the best cannon of the war. Russia also developed the 23mm VYa-23 and the 37mm NS-37 but their weight, recoil, and low rate of fire relegated them to limited use.

Japanese Aerial Armament Development

Of all the combatants, the Japanese used more different guns, using more different types of ammunition, than any other nation. This was SOP for the Japanese military, which was plagued by inter-service Army-Navy rivalry and lack of collaboration throughout the war, with each branch independently producing virtually identical weapons using non-compatible ammunition. The Japanese aircraft weapons generally were copies of foreign models.

The Japanese Army Air Force (JAAF) Type 89 fixed 7.7mm LMG for use with synchronized and wing gun use in fighter aircraft were copied from the British Vickers machine gun. There also was an unrelated Type 89 flexible 7.7mm LMG. The Type 100 (Type-1) was a copy of a Czech LMG design, while the Type 98 was based on the *Luftwaffe* 7.92mm MG 15 used as a flexible rear mount. The Japanese Navy Air Force (JNAF) copied the Lewis gun for its 7.7mm Type 92 LMG, while the Type 97 was an improved Vickers, and its Type 1 was derived from the German MG 15.

Both the JAAF and JNAF copied the Browning .50 caliber machine gun as its standard HMG. The JAAF HO-103 (Type 1) weighed less and had a higher rate of fire, but fired a smaller Vickers round (12.7x81mm vs. 12.7x99mm). The JNAF Type 3 also copied the Browning but at 13.2mm instead of 12.7mm, and used the larger Hotchkiss 99mm cartridge. The Navy also used the Type 2 HMG that was a version of the German MG 131 also at 13.2mm.

The Japanese use of cannon caliber weapons also was a muddle of non-conformity. Early in the war, the Army used the 20mm Type 94 copy of the already obsolete Oerlikon L as a flexible gun. The heavy Type 97 anti-tank gun had a low rate of fire and was utilized as the magazine-fed Ho-1 for a flexible installation in bomber turrets; the drum-fed Ho-3 was an improvement. In August 1943, a Japanese submarine delivered 800 MG 151/20 from Germany to be installed in the Ki-61 fighter. The Army 20mm Ho-5 was a spin-off of the Browning M1921 .50 caliber machine gun and was considered the best Japanese gun to equip a fighter in the war. It was lightweight and was belt fed rather than drum fed, so it had a high rate of fire. Toward the end of the war the Japanese experienced a shortage of high strength alloys and the barrel pressures, and hence the muzzle velocities, had to be reduced about 15%. The Ho-155 was an upscaled and modified version of the 20mm Ho-5. The Ho-203 was a widely-used 37mm cannon, while the limited-use Ho-204 was the largest adaptation the Browning M1921 to be used in World War II. The Ho-301 was a limited production 40mm cannon that was unusual in that it used caseless ammunition but had an effective

Japanese aircraft weapons generally were copies of foreign models. The renowned Zero was armed with two light 7.7mm (.303 caliber) Type 97 (an improved Vickers) machine guns in the engine cowling and two 20mm Type 99 (based on the Oerlikon FF) in the wings. (AFHRC)

Both the JAAF and JNAF copied the Browning .50 caliber machine gun as its standard heavy machine gun with the JAAF's Ho-103 (Type 1) weighing less and having a higher rate of fire. (AFHRC)

range of only 500 feet. The Ho-401 and Ho-402 were upscaled versions of the 37mm Ho-203. The experimental JNAF 75mm Type 88 cannon was a copy of the pre-war Vickers Anti-Aircraft gun but saw no service.

The Navy cannon were the Type 99-1 that was based on the Oerlikon FF F and the Type 99-2 based on the Oerlikon FF L. Both types were manufactured in different models, with the later models converting from 60 round drum feed to belt feed. The Type 99-1 equipped the early AM Zero, but its poor rate of fire and low muzzle velocity caused it to be replaced by the Type 99-2. The 99-2 had a much higher muzzle velocity due to its larger cartridge case, but its rate of fire was also lower (the later model 5 had an increased rate of fire but was too late for operations). The Model 52b Zero mounted one 20mm cannon in each wing, while the Model 52c was equipped with a 20mm (inboard) and 13mm machine (outboard) in each wing. Both mounted a 13mm cowling machine gun, while the Model 52 cowling gun were 7.7mm machine guns. The JNAF upscaled the Oerlikon FF to a 30mm round as the Type 2 and near the end of the war developed their superior 30mm cannon as the Type 5.

American Aerial Armament Cannon Development

When American entered the war in 1941, its aerial arsenal was committed to the Colt Browning .50 caliber and .30 caliber machine guns. The M2, by contemporary standards, was somewhat heavy and had an average rate of fire, but its muzzle velocity was high, which gave it very good ballistic characteristics. The gun was easy to manufacture and very reliable. Efforts were made to diversify to heavier weapons, and the 20mm Hispano-Suiza HS 404 cannon was selected and produced in large numbers. The Browning M4 and American Armaments Co. 37mm cannon were produced and equipped the Bell P-39s and P-63s that were mostly sent to Russia as Lend-Lease aircraft. A 75mm cannon was developed and saw operational use in the B-25, mainly in the anti-shipping role. The F4U-1C was armed with four 20mm Hispano cannon fed by 230 rounds each (924 total) and four .50 caliber fed by 390 rounds each (2,350 total).

**Heavy Machine Guns vs. Cannon**

Among the heavy machine guns the Russian Berezin UB was considered the best of that category. When compared to the Browning M2 it was lighter (55 pounds versus 64 pounds), and fired rounds of equal power at 1,050 rounds per minute versus 780 rounds per minute at similar muzzle velocities (860/880). Among other heavy machine guns the M2 fared better since it fired a more powerful round that gave it an advantage in range and penetration, but had a slightly lower rate of fire than both the German MG 131 and both the Japanese Army Ho-3 and Navy Type 3 Browning copies. The most powerful HMG was the 15mm German MG 151, but it was heavier at 93 pounds and had a slower rate of fire. All factors considered, the M2 ranked behind the Berezin UB and could only be considered average when compared to the others.

Empirically comparing the M2 to 20mm cannon is difficult due to the great differences in size, weight, and performance among the cannon types, and then to compare the effectiveness of the various types of ammunition. The MG-FFM and Type 99-1 weighed less than the M2 but were significantly inferior in terms of rate of fire and muzzle velocity. The Japanese Ho-5 and Type 99-2, the Soviet ShVAK, and the *Luftwaffe* MG-15 1/2 were all somewhat heavier with lower muzzle velocities, but generally, these three cannon were more powerful and effective than the M2. The British/American HS 404 was much heavier than the M2 with a much lower rate of fire until the British Mk V appeared at the end of the war. The late war Soviet B-20 weighed less than the M2 and had the same rate of fire and approximated its muzzle velocity, but its efficiency and power were much greater than the M2 values and was clearly the best 20mm cannon of the war.

The comparison of the .50 caliber M2 and the various cannon types does not take ammunition into consideration. In this category, .50 caliber ammunition causes the M2 to be inferior. The 20mm shells were two or three times heavier than .50 caliber bullets and their HEI content appreciably increased their effectiveness. HE ammunition was available for .50 caliber bullets, but the amount was so small the American Air Forces did not fire them in combat. The initial belt loading for the M2 was a mixture of AP and incendiary bullets with some tracers. In 1944 the M8 AP, which was based on the Soviet B32 AP round used in the Berezin guns, was introduced and predominated. Tests demonstrated the 20mm shell with 10% of its weight comprised of HE or Incendiary was approximately twice as destructive as a plain steel projectile of a similar size and weight. This was a figure that the M2 could not begin to match, as even the superior M8 .50 caliber API bullets introduced at the end of the war contained only one tenth the incendiary as the 20mm SAPI. The U.S. Navy pitted the .50 caliber M2 against the 20mm Hispano and found that the 20mm was three times more effective than the M2. This meant that the standard RAF armament of four 20mm cannon was twice as destructive as a six gun P-51 Mustang and one and a half times that of an eight gun P-47 Thunderbolt. Note that four HS 404s weighed 528 pounds while six Brownings weighed 384 pounds and eight weighed 512 pounds. The Hispano had a similar muzzle velocity, but the M2 did have superior ballistics that gave it better range and hit probability. However, this factor was not significant at normal combat ranges. The 20mm projectiles were heavier and less aerodynamic, but this also was not significant at normal combat ranges.

Probably more telling than the statistical supremacy of the 20mm cannon over the M2 .50 caliber machine gun was the choice of weapon by the combatants. The *Luftwaffe* chose the 20mm model of the MG 151 over the 12.7mm in spite of its poorer ballistics. Both the JAAF and JNAF copied and made use of the Browning .50 caliber machine gun as its standard HMG. Both services made increasing use of cannon during the war with the Army Ho-5, a cannon spin-off of the Browning .50, considered the best Japanese fighter aircraft gun. The Berezin UB .50 caliber was the best HMG of the war, yet the Soviets turned to the heavier 20mm ShVAK that had a lower muzzle velocity and rate of fire. Both the Germans and the Japanese were forced to equip with larger caliber, more destructive cannon in order to cope with the heavy Allied bombers ravaging their nations.

Conversely, there were reasons that America did not utilize 20 mm weapons that were being mass produced. The foremost reason was that the M2 was satisfactory in its combat role. In both the ETO and the Pacific the principal targets were fighter aircraft and then light or medium bombers. If the Axis had heavy, well-armored bombers in inventory, the deficiencies of the .50 Browning would have been exposed and the Americans would have been forced to turn to equipping their interceptors with 20mm cannon. During the war production of the American 20mm Hispano reached over 56,0000 guns, but the gun encountered critical manufacturing problems that kept it from attaining a standard of reliability.

**The Bottom Line**

**Comparison of the Major Aircraft Guns of WWII**

| GUN TYPE | Cartridge Caliber (mm) | Gun Wt. (lbs) | Bullet Wt. (lbs) | Muzzle Velocity (ft/sec) | Rate of Fire (rps) | Wt. of Fire (lbs/sec) | Effect |
|---|---|---|---|---|---|---|---|
| **.30** | 7.7x56 | 22.0 | 0.024 | 2,460 | 20 | 0.48 | 20 |
| **MG 131** | 13x64 | 37.5 | 0.075 | 2,460 | 15 | 1.13 | 48 |
| **Ho-103** | 12.7x81 | 50.7 | 0.073 | 2,526 | 15 | 1.10 | 45 |
| **.50 M2** | 12.7x99 | 63.9 | 0.095 | 2,920 | 13 | 1.24 | 60 |
| **12.7 Berezin** | 12.7x108 | 55.1 | 0.106 | 2,756 | 17 | 1.80 | 97 |
| **MG 151** | 15x96 | 92.6 | 0.126 | 3,150 | 12 | 1.21 | 94 |
| **Type 99-1** | 20x72 | 52.9 | 0.282 | 2,625 | 8 | 2.26 | 108 |
| **MG-FFM** | 20x80 | 61.7 | 0.203 | 2,297 | 9 | 1.83 | 126 |
| **MG 151/20** | 20x82 | 92.6 | 0.203 | 2,625 | 12 | 2.44 | 192 |
| **Ho-5** | 20x94 | 81.6 | 0.174 | 2,395 | 14 | 2.44 | 154 |
| **ShVAK** | 20x99 | 92.6 | 0.209 | 2,592 | 13 | 2.72 | 143 |
| **Type 99-2** | 20x101 | 77.2 | 0.282 | 2,461 | 8 | 2.26 | 120 |
| **HS 404** | 20x110 | 110.2 | 0.287 | 2,822 | 10 | 2.87 | 200 |
| **HS V** | 20x110 | 92.6 | 0.287 | 2,723 | 12.5 | 3.59 | 250 |
| **MK 108** | 30x90 | 132.3 | 0.728 | 1,657 | 10 | 7.28 | 580 |
| **MK103** | 30x184 | 310.9 | 0.728 | 2,922 | 7 | 5.10 | 693 |
| **37mm M4** | 37x145 | 211.6 | 1.340 | 2,001 | 2.5 | 3.35 | 160 |

Destructive Effect is an approximate rating of an aircraft gun's firepower conceived by Anthony Williams. It is calculated by multiplying the projectile weight, muzzle velocity, rate of fire, and a multiplier for the average percentage of incendiary or high explosive materiel contained in the projectile (e.g. 5% content multiplier is x 1.5; 10% is x2; and 15% is x2.5; etc.)

Criterion

The prototypical gun would fire the greatest number of the largest projectiles at the highest muzzle velocity in the shortest period of time. The aircraft that mounted the gun had to fly as fast and high and far as feasible, and have a maximum amount of space available for the ammunition to feed it. However, a gun firing a large projectile has a low muzzle velocity and a gun with a high rate of fire has a reduced duration of fire.

In order to determine the efficiency of an aircraft gun and the armament of individual aircraft three basic qualities of a gun must be evaluated:

Rate of Fire (rounds per second or minute)
Weight of the projectile (in pounds)
Muzzle velocity of the projectile (in feet per second)

These factors could determine operational suitability. For structural penetration muzzle velocity and projectile weight were required. For accuracy and a flat trajectory a high muzzle velocity was required. To score a high number of hits on a target a high rate of fire was needed.

The most cited measurement of firepower has been weight of fire (pounds of projectile per minute), probably because of its ease of calculation: number of projectiles fired per minute times the weight of the type of projectile fired.

The ideal gun supposition does not take into consideration the matter of special guns for special purposes, both offensively and defensively. For a dogfighter the rate of fire was crucial because of the necessity of snapping off the greatest number of shots in the very short periods of time of each combat contact. A high rate of fire insured scoring of the greatest number of hits and delivering an adequate weight of fire to cause the greatest amount of damage to the relatively lightly-built enemy fighter. The best gun for air-to-air combat was the smallest gun with the highest rate of fire and projectile power to adequately damage the target to destruction. For a bomber interceptor fighter the gun had to fire a heavy, powerful projectile as quickly as possible to inflict as much damage possible with each of the fewer hits to the heavily-built and well-protected bomber.

The bomber's guns were defensive and had to be long-range to hold off the enemy fighters, and these guns had to form an all encompassing field of concentrated fire without having any blind spots

Armament designers were faced with the problem of determining the best possible combination of weight of fire delivered in a specified time against the density of a pattern of projectiles. Only small bullets fired by machine guns with a high rate of fire could deliver the desired dense pattern of bullets that had the possibility of scoring a large number of hits. The larger weight of fire delivered by cannon firing heavy shells at a low rate of fire could not achieve the same dense pattern. The rate of fire, or cyclic rate, was the number of rounds fired per minute, and combined with the muzzle velocity to affect the density pattern. In a dogfight the best pilots could keep their point of aim within a four or five foot circle while the journeyman pilot did well to maintain a 20 foot circle. During firing, the point of impact of the bullets on the target within the circle would occur several times. So if the bullets were arriving at closer intervals with a higher rate of fire, then the probability of scoring a hit was increased dramatically. The average pilot using six or eight machine guns firing at a high cyclic rate could "hose away" at the target while the same pilot firing a low number of cannon shells had to be a proficient marksman and close in to the target to get a zero deflection shot. Upgrading from LMG and HMG to 20mm cannon was optimal for attacking bombers. However, in the violent maneuvering of a dogfight, the cannon's low muzzle velocity made wide-angle deflection shooting very difficult, particularly at longer ranges.

Even though the 20mm cannon was statistically and objectively the better weapon, the almost exclusive American use of the .50 caliber M2 was justified. The M2 was satisfactory for its purpose and was the only satisfactory aircraft gun being manufactured in the country. When America entered the war the M2 was proven, and manufacturers were contracted and in quantity production for easy supply. The Axis, especially the Japanese, with their plethora of aerial armament and ammunition, encountered critical logistical problems in their deployment. The M2's destructive deficiency was countered by the size and engine power of the fighters carrying them. The horsepower of American fighters allowed them to be equipped with six to eight Brownings with quantity overcoming destructive quality.

Of America's major fighter aircraft only the P-38 was armed with a cannon-caliber gun, but its pilots preferred using its four nose-mounted .50 caliber machine guns over the 20mm cannon in combat. It was the P-47 Thunderbolt with eight .50 caliber machine guns, and the P-51 Mustangs, F6F Hellcats, and F4U Corsairs that mounted six .50s that led to the success of the American Air Forces during World War II. The bottom line in the machine gun vs. cannon controversy is that American air forces using the Browning .50 caliber M2 machine gun won the war in the air.

**USN and USAF Post-War Aircraft Armament**

USN

As pointed out earlier, the U.S. Navy was the principal user of the 20mm cannon during the war, mounting over 90% of these guns in U.S. service. Although the Navy found limited combat use of these cannon during the war, the effectiveness of the British and German 20mm guns led the Navy to continue their use in the post-war. The Navy's first jet fighters (the FH Phantom, F2H Banshee, and F9F Panther) mounted four lighter, shorter, and faster firing (850 rpm) M3 versions of the wartime Hispano MkV gun. The USN continued its use of the 20mm cannon (the upgraded Colt Mk12 firing a lighter projectile with a larger explosive charge) on its supersonic swept-wing fighters into the time when guided missiles were thought to be the wave of the future and would make the aircraft gun obsolete. The Mach 2 Vought F8U Crusader came into service still mounting four 20mm Mk12 cannons with 144 rpg, but also carried four AIM-9 Sidewinder air-to-air missiles on cheek rails in the lower fuselage. Since the F8 was intended for close combat the McDonnell F-4 Phantom II was designed, like other interceptors of the day, without cannon armament, but carried various combinations of the AIM-9A Sidewinder, AIM-4 Falcon, or AIM-7 Sparrow to be radar controlled by the Weapons Systems Officer (WSO). The weight, bulk, and vulnerability of the electronics required for their use made it attractive to save weight by leaving the guns out. However, the all-missile fighter had shown some critical deficiencies in early air combat over Vietnam, as the Sparrow, Falcon, and Sidewinder air-to-air missiles did not function to expectations. They were expensive, unreliable, and vulnerable to countermeasures, and one six-barrel General Electric 20 mm M61 Vulcan Gatling cannon carrying 639 rounds was installed. The major problem in equipping the Phantom with an internal cannon was in locating a space to install it. The longer pointed nose of the F-4C reconnaissance version was fitted with an AN/APG-30 radar set, and an external pod that could carry a single six-barrel 20-mm General Electric M61 rotary cannon was mounted under the nose. The M61 was the first rotary cannon demonstrating high reliability with a very high rate of fire, and by firing through several barrels their wear was decreased. The M61 had a belt feed, but this could tolerate the strain of firing rates higher than 4,000 rpm. The M61A and most U.S. rotary cannon used a beltless feed mechanism in which the rounds were transported on a conveyer belt system and empty cartridge cases were transported back into the drum.

USAF

In the post-war the standard armament of USAF fighters continued to be six Browning .50 M3 machine guns that fired faster than the M2 version used in WWII. Combat experience in Korea demonstrated that this armament was woefully inadequate, as the Russian-built North Korean MiG-15s often sustained numerous hits from the .50s and escaped across the sanctuary of the Yalu River. It was only the superior training of the American pilot using better gunsights while flying the somewhat better North American F-84 Sabre that gave the American pilots the advantage. The Air Force did equip the Northrop F-89 Scorpion all-weather night fighters (with six guns) and F-86K fighter-bombers (with four guns) with the 20mm M24, a version of the Hispano M3 of the U.S. Navy modified to fire electrically primed ammunition. Later the Pontiac M39 20mm revolver cannon was installed on the F-86H Sabre, F-100 Super Sabre, and Northrop F-5 fighters. During the Korean campaign 30mm cannon were contemplated but rejected, as guided missiles were thought to soon make the cannon outmoded, and two F-89C prototypes were the only American fighters that would ever mount 30mm cannon. The Air Force adopted the Navy's F-4 Phantom II and introduced the Convair F-106 Delta Dart without cannon, but like the Navy, the Air Forces' combat experience in Vietnam also caused it to install the 20mm Vulcan M61 in their fighters.

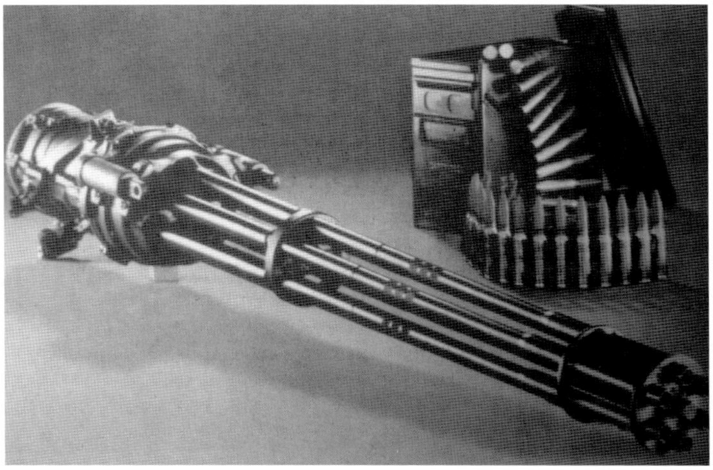

The six-barrel **General Electric 20mm M61 Vulcan Gatling Cannon** carrying 639 rounds was used in Vietnam. (USAF)

# Part Three

## Ammunition

# 1

# Introduction

Aircraft ammunition may be generally classified as small arms ammunition for light (rifle caliber) and heavy machine guns and the shells used in the smaller caliber cannon. The light or rifle caliber machine guns generally are of between 6.5mm (.26 inches) to 8mm (.32 inches) caliber; the heavy machine guns are of between 12.7 (.50 inches) to 15mm (.59 inches) caliber; while automatic cannons are of 20mm (.79 inches) or more. American aircraft guns generally utilized standard ground gun ammunition, unlike the *Luftwaffe*, whose ammunition and guns were specifically designed for aircraft use.

Even though aerial guns and ammunition were based on ground weapons, ammunition ordnance engineers needed to incorporate a number of special characteristics into them, with target vulnerability being the determining factor. Among the engineer's goals was to reach a high muzzle velocity to achieve both accuracy and reduction of the trajectory curve, and to get the bullets and shells on the target in the shortest possible time. They needed to keep the individual bullets and shells to a minimum weight so that the aircraft could carry the maximum load of ammunition.

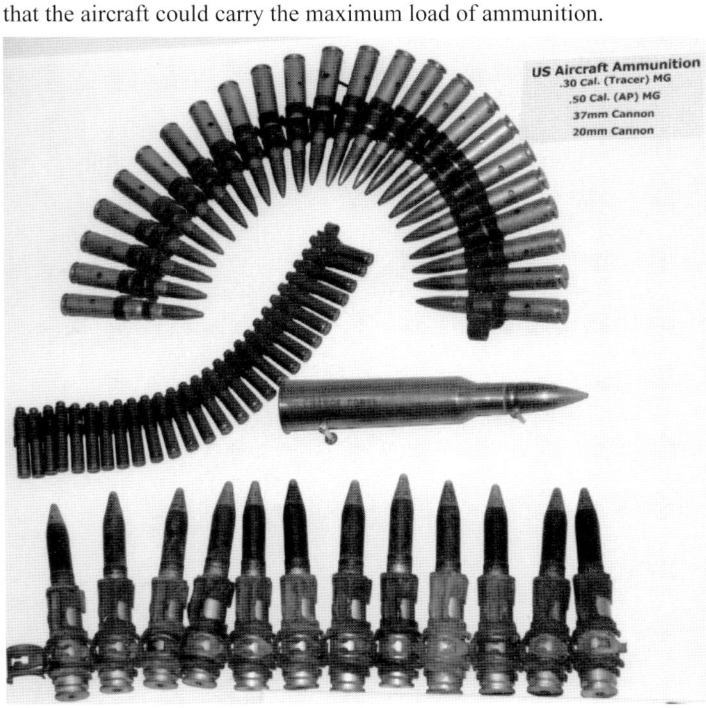


Author's collection of ammunition: .50 caliber (top), .30 caliber (middle left), 37mm (middle right), and 20mm (bottom).

Before embarking on a comprehensive description of the various types of aircraft ammunition, it would be beneficial to understand the fundamentals of ammunition composition and include a few definitions.

**Cartridge**
A round of ammunition consisting of a projectile (that may be a bullet, shell, or shot); a propellant to push the projectile from the gun; a primer to ignite the propellant; and a cartridge case that holds everything together.

Cartridges are typically described by their caliber (spelled "calibre" in the UK), which is the approximate diameter of the projectile. Caliber measurements are given in inches in the U.S. and UK or millimeters in Europe and Japan. The .50 caliber cartridge bullet measures about .50 inches in diameter, or 12.7mm. Caliber is approximately the same size as the projectile diameter because two different measurements are used: the diameter of the projectile or the diameter of the bore, which is the inside diameter of the gun barrel. Gun barrels are usually rifled, which are spiral grooves cut into the bore that cause the projectile to spin, significantly improving the accuracy of the fired projectile. In order to hold the projectile firmly in the barrel, the projectile diameter was therefore somewhere between the diameter of the bore and that of the rifling.

**Cartridge Case**
During storage, feeding, and firing, the cartridge case served as a strong waterproof container for cartridge components, both primer and propellant. The function of the cartridge case was called obturation, the expansion and sealing of the chamber against the escape of gases to the rear when the cartridge was fired. The explosive composition inside the primer was detonated by the impact of the percussion firing pin or upon closure of an electrical circuit. The detonation of the primer ignited the propellant grains, and the cartridge case acted as an insulator between the propellant powder and the hot walls of the chamber of a rapid-firing gun. The high pressure of the generated combustion gases forced the projectile or bullet out of the cartridge case and out of the barrel of the weapon at high velocity.

Cartridge cases normally had straight walls or were bottle-shaped ("bottleneck"). As a rule handguns had straight walled cases and rifles, machine guns, and cannons were of the bottleneck type. Despite its weight and cost, brass was the most commonly used cartridge case material as it expanded instantly to form a seal without splitting open. Brass is a metal alloy composed of approximately 70% copper and 30% zinc and is non-magnetic. A magnet could be used to separate brass cases from steel cases, which were often coated with copper or lacquer to prevent rust. Steel was

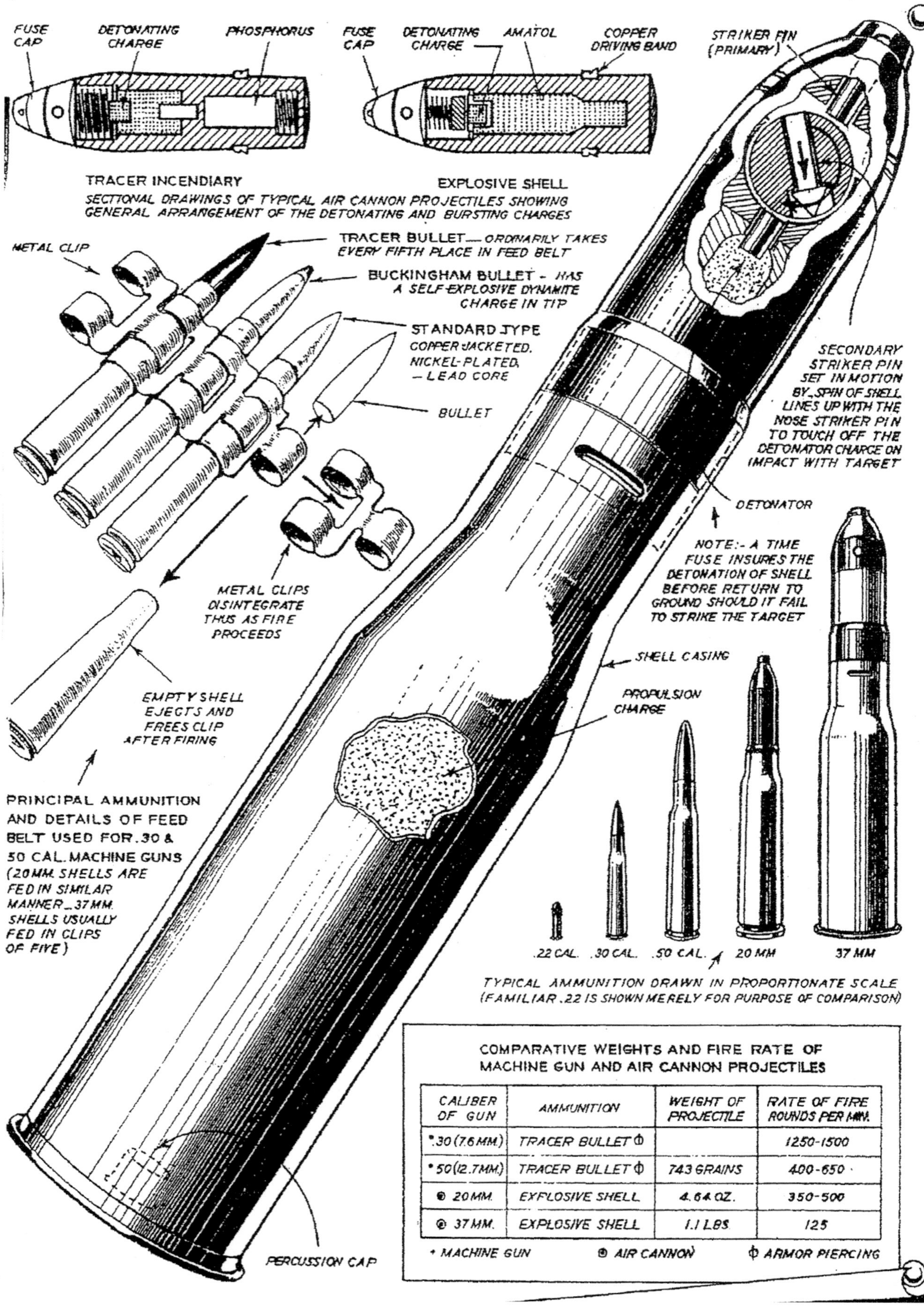


COMPARATIVE WEIGHTS AND FIRE RATE OF MACHINE GUN AND AIR CANNON PROJECTILES

| CALIBER OF GUN | AMMUNITION | WEIGHT OF PROJECTILE | RATE OF FIRE ROUNDS PER MIN. |
|---|---|---|---|
| •.30 (7.6MM) | TRACER BULLET Φ | | 1250-1500 |
| •.50 (12.7MM) | TRACER BULLET Φ | 743 GRAINS | 400-650 |
| ⊗ 20MM. | EXPLOSIVE SHELL | 4.64 OZ. | 350-500 |
| ⊗ 37MM. | EXPLOSIVE SHELL | 1.1 LBS | 125 |

• MACHINE GUN ⊗ AIR CANNON Φ ARMOR PIERCING

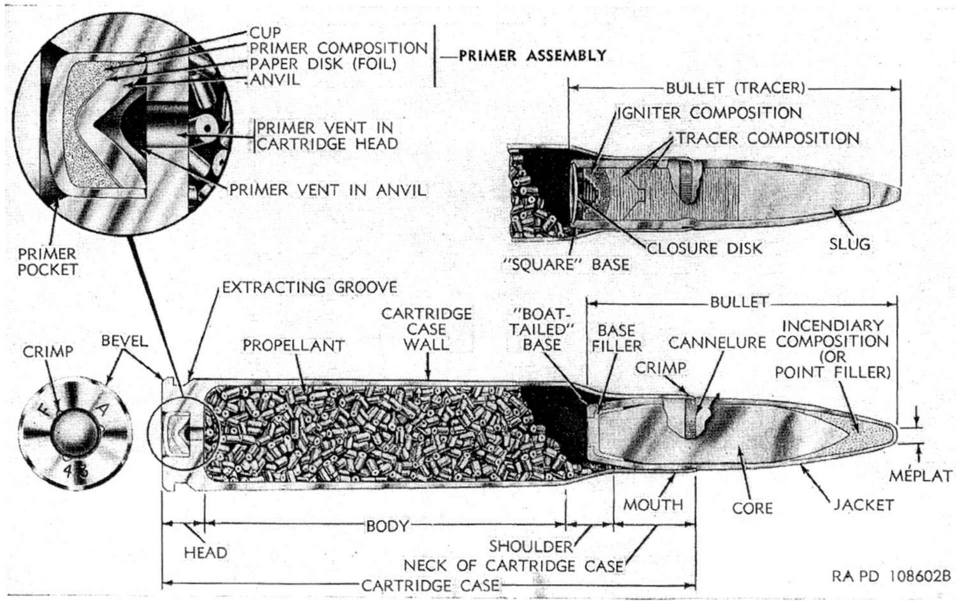


*Figure 3. Cartridge terminology.*

**CARTRIDGE TERMINOLOGY** (USAAF)

used in cannon-size shells because of its extra strength and was somewhat lighter and cheaper. The dummy round was made of drawn steel, and steel cartridge cases were developed for .45 caliber and .30 caliber ammunition for pistol and carbine use in early 1943.

Cases were manufactured by a series of stamping and drawing procedures from a brass disc called a "blank." A thick disk was stamped from a sheet of brass and then forced into a cup shape and gradually, by several draws, extended to more than the desired length. The mouth of this cup, which contained any impurities, was cut off and discarded, leaving the base with its extraction rim or groove and primer chamber. The primer anvil and fire holes around it were formed and the cartridge case neck was formed ("necked down") to the proper length. Between most of the manufacturing stages it was necessary to heat treat the cartridge cases to a specified temperature and allow them to cool at a controlled rate (as brass had a tendency to work-harden and become brittle).

The cases of military rounds usually had thicker walls than commercial cases, and cases with thicker walls required somewhat less powder to realize the same pressure and velocity as cases with thinner walls and with the same powder charge; thick-walled cases generated greater pressures than thin-walled cases.

To make the cartridge waterproof and to keep the propellant dry, the primer was sealed in the primer seat and the bullet was sealed in the neck of the cartridge case by a thin film of lacquer or varnish at the time of manufacture. An extruder groove, turned in the head of the cartridge case, provided a means of removing the case from the chamber.

The basic components of a cartridge case are the head, rim, and neck, with the head at the base and the neck at the opposite end. Usually cartridge cases have an identifying headstamp around the primer pocket than gives information about the cartridge. Military cartridges had the year of manufacture (e.g. stamped as 1944 or 44), caliber, and the manufacturer's letters, which were frequently coded to conceal the identity of the manufacturing plant.

Cartridge case design had several basic requirements: it had to locate the projectile in the exact position in the firing chamber; it had to be easy to extract after firing; and it had to operate satisfactorily in automatic weapons. Accurate positioning in the firing chamber was critical to the proper ignition of the primer. It was also important to the ballistics of the gun, since the projectile had to be in the same place relative to the conical section leading to the rifling to maintain constant pressure characteristics. The distance between the face of the bolt and the part of the chamber that positions the cartridge was called the "headspace." The first method of positioning the cartridge correctly was by placing a rim around the head of the case. The rim remained outside the chamber or in a recess so that it was flush with the breech face. The rim also provided something for the extractor to catch onto so that the fired case could be extracted from the chamber. Rimmed cases loaded into belts on automatic weapons had to be withdrawn backwards from the belt before being pushed forwards into the chamber.

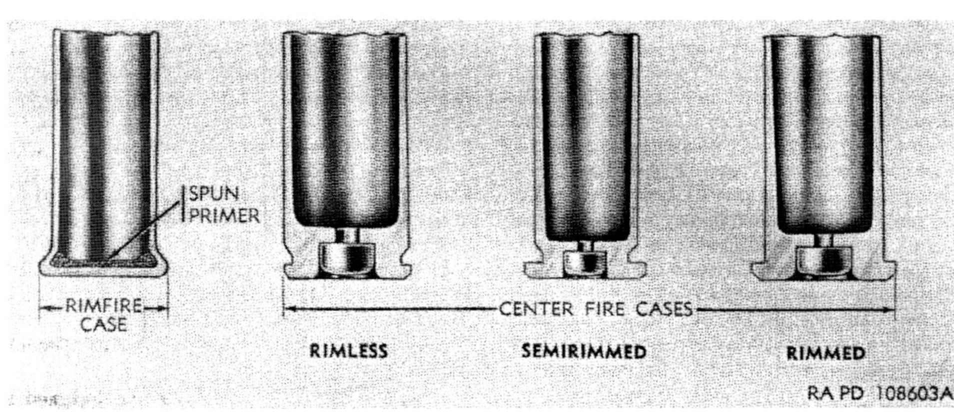


**TYPES of CARTRIDGE CASES** (USAAF)

Identifying a Cartridge

Type of round (20x95R for example):

The first number 20 denotes the caliber of the barrel (in mms). For rifled barrels this was the smallest internal diameter, with the diameter of the projectile being slightly larger. The second number is the length of the cartridge case (in mms) with Alphabetical suffixes, such as R for Rimmed, SR for Semi-Rimmed, RB for reBated Rims (sometimes called RR), and B for Belted cartridge cases. Variations in the size and shape of the cartridge generally depended on the use and operation of the specific gun. Most guns could fire several types of ammunition and they were often mixed. Machine gun ammunition could be armor piercing, tracer, or incendiary, or a combination, while cannons could also use high explosive shells.

**Ammunition Propellants**

Explosives are a basic part of ammunition, and for military purposes were divided into two basic groups: propellants and high explosives. The fundamental difference between the two was the speed at which they exploded, with propellants exploding at a relatively slower rate than high explosives, which exploded almost instantaneously. Propellants were explosives that were primarily used for propelling the projectile from the gun, while high explosives were used principally as a filler or a bursting charge for explosive components such as projectiles, bombs, grenades, and as initiators. The main requirement of a propellant was that it should explode rapidly, generating a large mass of gas to propel the bullet without damaging the weapon.

Black powder (or gunpowder) was the first propellant developed and used, and would remain the only one until the end of the 19th century, when smokeless powder was introduced. During World War II .50 caliber ammunition contained only single base nitrocellulose propellant charges. Depending on the desired characteristics, each type of propellant could be of flake, tubular, spherical, or modified spherical shape. Propellant charges for each type of cartridge could be varied slightly in daily production to compensate for slight differences in burning characteristics and residual moisture content. Granulations of the propellant and weights of the cartridge charges were instituted to meet specification requirements for velocity and pressure for each type of cartridge. The single-based propellant contained 98% nitrocellulose and was normally extruded in a tubular shape with a single perforation. Other chemical agents were added to minimize smoke and flash, to maintain desired performance throughout long periods of storage under extreme conditions of temperature and moisture, and to permit the loading of uniform charges in the cartridge.

An explosive train was a series of explosions beginning with a small amount of sensitive explosive and terminating with a large amount of comparatively insensitive explosive. Generally, there were two explosive trains: the propelling charge explosive train and the bursting charge explosive train. The propelling charge explosive train consisted of primer, igniter or igniting charge, and propelling charge. The small flame from the sensitive explosive of the primer was transmitted and intensified by the igniter so that the large quantity of the relatively insensitive explosive of the propelling charge burned with enough force to propel the projectile. The components in the propelling charge train were an electric or percussion primer and a propelling charge. The firing pin ignited the primer by impact or electrical impulse, and the detonation flame passed through the vent that led to the propellant chamber and ignited the propelling charge; the expansion of the resultant gases forced the bullet or projectile out through the barrel of the weapon.

Smokeless Propellant Powders

During World War II all explosives used as propellants had a nitrocellulose base and were commonly known as "smokeless powders." Black powder as a propellant had been completely superceded by smokeless powder. Smokeless nitrocellulose powder in the perforated grain form was used in U.S. small and large caliber weapon ammunition. The single perforated grain was used in small caliber weapons, smaller caliber cannons, and some howitzers. Powders with seven grains were used in larger caliber weapons.

During manufacturing varying organic or inorganic substances were added to give the powder improved qualities for special purposes. Smokeless powder was neither entirely smokeless nor a powder. It was manufactured in the form of flakes, strips, pellets, or perforated cylindrical grains. The cylindrical grains were fabricated in varying lengths and diameters. Web size, the average thickness of the powder between the perforations, was the critical dimension. The color of the grains varied from light amber to deep brown or black. Unconfined smokeless powder burned much like cellulose with little ash or smoke, but when confined its rate of burning increased with temperature and pressure. Smokeless powder had to be protected against moisture, high temperature, and changes in temperature, and was always packed in airtight containers. Moisture absorbing or hygroscopic materials were added and were used in propellants for most guns and cannon.

Other Powders

Pyro Powder

Pyro powder, or pyrocellulose, was a straight nitrocellulose powder that was the standard powder in service for many years before the war. It had the disadvantage of producing a muzzle flash upon firing, absorbed moisture, (hygroscopic) and had a relatively low explosive potential.

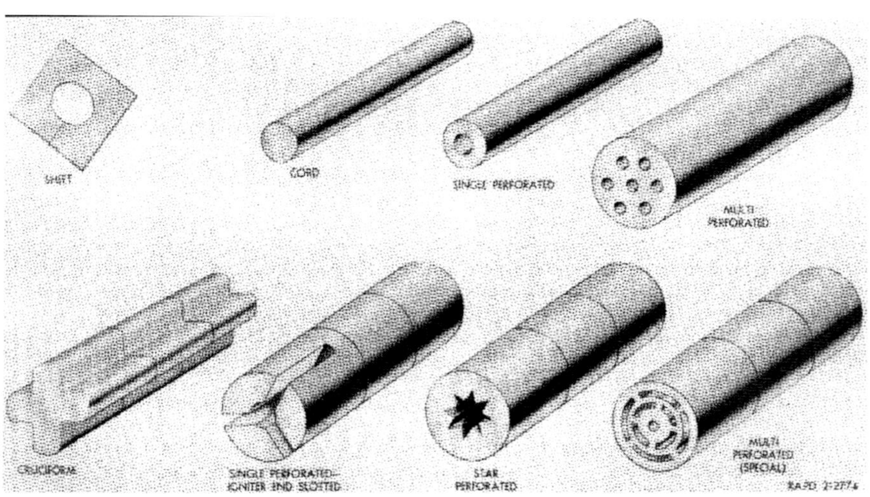


**SHAPES and FORMS of PROPELLANT GRAINS** (USAAF)

Double-Based Powders
Double-Based powders contained both nitrocellulose and nitroglycerine (to increase explosive potential), and also small amounts of inorganic salts to reduce flash and increase ignition.

FNH and FN Powders
Flashless-nonhygroscopic (FNH) powders were mixtures of nitrocellulose and other substances which cooled combustion and thus reduced flash. It contained hygroscopic substances to reduce hygroscopicity. FNH powder could be flashless in one gun but not completely flashless in another. When FNH powder was selected to be used in weapons in which flash occurred it was designated NH powder. Guncotton, a nitrocellulose of high nitration, was used in the manufacture of FNH powders.

EC Smokeless Powder
EC Smokeless Powder, or EC Blank Fire, was manufactured from nitrocellulose with inorganic nitrates and was colored orange or pink. It was very hygroscopic and sensitive to friction, shock, and heat, and had to be stored and handled carefully, as it burned rapidly in the open and exploded readily when confined. Its main use was in fragmentation grenades, but it was also used in .30 and .50 caliber blank cartridges.

**Primer (Cap)**
The primer, also called the cap, consisted of zinc or copper, or a composition of both, that was malleable and deformed easily when struck by the firing pin. Beneath the cap there was a primer composition pellet of sensitive explosive, a paper disk, and a brass anvil. The explosive was sealed in place by a layer of varnish that also waterproofed the explosive. The primer was held in place by the "upsetting" of the case metal around the cap to lock it in place, which caused a small portion of the case metal to overlap the cap and hold it in place. The joint between the case and the cap was called the "annulus," and was sealed with a waterproof varnish that was colored to indicate the type of bullet which was loaded in the case. When the firing pin struck the primer cap and compressed the primer composition between the cap and the anvil the composition exploded. Holes or vents in the anvil allowed flame to pass through the primer vent in the cartridge case and ignited the propellant.

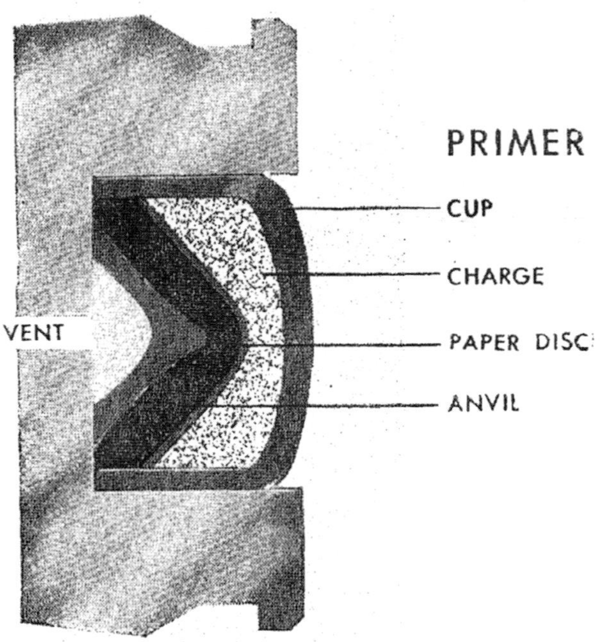


**PRIMER** (USAAF)

Early primer composition was based on fulminate of mercury, potassium chlorate, and antimony sulfide; with the first sensitive to the blow and the other two to increase the heat and flame of the explosion. This composition had its disadvantages, as the mercuric salts from the explosion attacked the brass in the cartridge case, making it unsuitable for reloading, while the potassium salts were deposited on the bore of the gun. When gunpowder was the propellant this did not matter, as the washing necessary to remove the powder fouling also removed the salts. When smokeless powder was introduced the military continued to use the fulminate mixture because they did not reload and insisted on ample washing of the rifle bore, and considered the reliability and power of the fulminate mixture more valuable.

**Projectiles/Bullets**
Bullets for service use had a metal core or slug that was covered with a gliding metal or a gliding metal clad steel jacket. Tracer bullets had a lead alloy core or slug, while other bullets had steel cores. Ball, incendiary had a soft core steel core and were not intended for armor penetration. All armor-piercing bullets had hardened steel alloy cores with a point filler of antimony lead between the jacket and core. Ball M33 bullets had point filler of inert material, such as sodium carbonate, monohydrate. Incendiary composition was the point filler for armor-piercing-incendiary, armor-piercing-incendiary-tracer, and incendiary bullets. Armor-piercing-incendiary-tracer and tracer bullets had a base filler of igniter and tracer composition in the base of the core. Armor-piercing-incendiary bullets had a base filler of lead. Bullets had a cylindrical or conically tapered base. The cylindrical base was called "square" and the conically tapered base was called "boat-tailed." A cannelure (an annular knurled groove) was rolled or cut into the jacket to provide a recess into which the cartridge case was crimped. A second cannelure or knurl could be present on some bullet types, such as the incendiary bullet, as a method of identification during manufacture.

**Ammunition Classification and Types**
Classification
Ammunition was classified as to use: service, practice, or drill:

1) Service ammunition was that "used for effect" (e.g. combat).
2) Practice ammunition was provided for training and could contain a small quantity of low-explosive filler to act as a spotting charge or the filler could be inert.
3) Drill ammunition was always inert and was used in training for loading, handling, and servicing the weapon.

Types
The basic types of ammunition included Ball, Armor-Piercing (AP), Armor-Piecing Incendiary (API), Armor-Piercing-Incendiary-Tracer (APIT), Incendiary (I), Tracer (T), and Dummy. High Explosive (HE) was available for cannon caliber guns. Short ranges were the rule in aerial warfare, and thus the quantity of propellant in the shells was smaller than in a similar caliber ammunition used in ground guns, where the range needed to be three or four times longer. Additionally, by reducing the amount of propellant it allowed more explosive to be carried in the shell. At shorter ranges armor plate could be more easily penetrated by direct hits and the unprotected areas of an aircraft could suffer serious damage. The *Luftwaffe* combined these four basic components into many combinations. For example, their 13mm, which was comparable to the .50 caliber had such combinations as HET, HEIT, and APT. In the last year of the war the USAAF generally replaced all its .50 caliber ammunition with API and its 20mm with HEI, both of which proved superior.

**Types of Ammunition**

| Type | Use | Color of Tip | How It Works |
|---|---|---|---|
| **Ball** | Against personnel and light material targets | Unpainted; plain metal | The outer jacket point contains a lead and antimony filler that covers the tip of the underlying steel core. When the projectile hits a target, the soft outer jacket and filler smears, giving the steel core a grip. The core then penetrates the surface instead of being turned aside. |
| **Armor-Piercing** | Against armored aircraft and vehicles, concrete shelters, and other bullet-resisting targets | Black | The projectile is the same as the ball cartridge, except that the core is made of very hard tungsten-chrome steel to give it greater penetrating power. |
| **Armor-Piercing Incendiary** | Used to set fire to armor-plated inflammable targets. | Aluminum or Medium Blue | Similar to the armor-piercing projectile, except that there is incendiary compound behind the steel core. |
| **Armor-Piercing Incendiary-Tracer** | Used to set fire to armor-plated inflammable targets | Red | Similar to the API except it contained a tracer materiel |
| **Incendiary** | Used to set fire to explosive or very inflammable targets | Light blue | In front of the jacket is an incendiary composition that is sealed by plugs of an alloy that easily melts. As the bullet goes through the barrel, the heat melts the plugs and the incendiary composition is set on fire as it meets the air. |
| **Tracer** | For observing fire, it makes a streak of light easily seen at night and usually is visible in daylight | Red | Inside the outer metal jacket is a slug of lead and antimony. Behind it is a pocket of tracer composition that is set afire by the propelling charge as the projectile leaves the cartridge case. |
| **Dummy** | Training | Unpainted (hole in side of case) | Has no priming or propelling charge. |

These types of ammunition will be described in detail in the .30 caliber, .50 caliber, 20mm, and 37mm configurations.

**Ammunition Feeds**

Box

Ultimately, ammunition had to be stored in the aircraft and then be fed into a gun. The method of supplying cartridges to the breech was a fundamental and critical design consideration. The most uncomplicated method was the box magazine, in which a strong spring located at the end of the box containing the cartridges forced the cartridges into the gun mechanism. The box could be mounted to the side or bottom of the gun, but a top-mounting was favored on larger guns since gravity could facilitate feeding. The disadvantage with the box feed mechanism was that it was restricted to a limited number of cartridges; otherwise, the feed boxes would become too long and unwieldy.

Drum

The drum (sometimes called a "pan") contained rounds arranged in a circle, pointing inwards, that were fed into the gun by a circular spring. Some drums contained more than one layer of rounds. These drums were propelled by a spring or rotated by the gun as it fired. In the drum magazine, the rounds were parallel to each other in a coil array and were moved by a spring that was wound tight when the drum was loaded. Drums often had unwieldy shapes for installation and were commonly used with machine guns on flexible mounts on which the gun could move freely.

Belt

Generally, the drum and box fed magazines had a limited capacity of rounds with a maximum of 100. The belt was a better alternative, as a larger number of rounds could be linked to a belt that could be stored in a box or tray with a practical shape. The belt was pulled through the mechanism by the

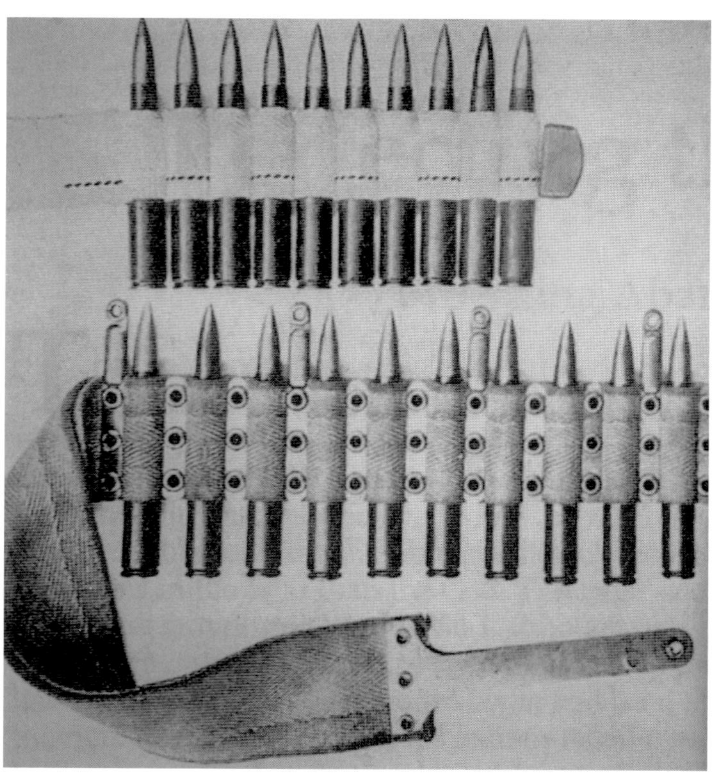

**Marlin Fabric Belt** (USAAF)

action of the gun as it fired; each cartridge was pushed or pulled out of the belt and into the chamber. Early belts were fabric, but by the beginning of the war metal disintegrating-link belts were standard. However, for a short period during 1943 some fabric belts were issued for U.S. .50 caliber machine guns due to a production shortage of disintegrating links. The disintegrating type belt, after the removal of the round, broke into links that could be collected or dumped overboard. The belt could be as long as the feeding mechanism could pull. However, the belt feed mechanism was more complicated than that of a drum, especially for the heavier cannon rounds. For this reason most cannon had drums. During the Second World War there was an ongoing controversy over the different types of projectiles that were to be used in a belt. There was no one answer, and different air forces preferred different combinations depending on the type of gun employed and the mission.

**Fabric Belts and Metal Links**

Fabric Belts

The .30 caliber machine gun was designed to be fed by a fabric belt, and infantry .30 caliber machine guns used a fabric belt until the end of World War II when metallic links were introduced for infantry use. However, metallic links were previously reserved for aircraft use, as expended fabric belts could not be used in fixed aircraft gun positions and were not easily disposed of from an aircraft in flight from flexible gun positions.

Russell Manufacturing, Middletown, CT, which patented the fabric belt in 1916, was the primary supplier of U.S. .30 caliber fabric belts. In 1936 Russell was awarded another patent for an improved 250 round fabric belt, and after Pearl Harbor granted the government a license to use their belt without a royalty. By 1942 there were six other manufacturers producing the belt for ground use, and by mid-1944 28 million belts had been issued with over half by Russell.

In 1942 there was temporary steel shortage in the U.S., and the Ordnance Department had to adopt a 100 round .50 caliber fabric belt designated as the Belt, Ammunition, Caliber .50 M7. Russell had previously manufactured .50 caliber fabric belts under a foreign contract and was able to begin belt production at once. Bedsides Russell two other companies also manufactured the aircraft belt: International Braid of Providence and Oehrle Brothers of Philadelphia. Colt Patent Fire Arms and Heintz Manufacturing Co. of Philadelphia produced hand-belting machines to load .50 caliber cartridges into the fabric belts. A total of 15.9 million belts were manufactured at a cost of 68 cents each.

Metal Link Belts

Metallic link belts appeared to be a simple design, but their manufacture required precision to guarantee dependable functioning under a number of harsh circumstances that could cause dangerous stoppages. Strict quality control and inspections were critical, and the entire belt depended on the quality of an individual link.

Flexible metallic link belts were comprised of a strip of steel formed with two loops on one side and one loop on the other. The steel strip was blanked and formed, heat treated, and then rustproofed. A cartridge was inserted through the two loops and the single loop of another link, which formed a continuous belt of any length.

Figure 9. Ammunition Belt Links

(USAAF)

Flexibility and ease and cost of manufacture were always a priority for linked belts with Fedders Manufacturing Co. of Buffalo manufacturing 536 million. (AFHRC)

The Rock Island Arsenal was the only manufacturer of the standard M1 metallic machine gun links in the inter-war years. In 1940 Rock Island let contracts to the Fort Pitt Bedding Co. of Pittsburgh and three other companies to manufacture .50 caliber links for aircraft use, and the next year General Aviation Equipment Co. and the Jackes Evans Co. were contracted to produce .30 caliber links that were originally used in the Marlin 1917 machine gun. For 1942 the estimated demand for both .30 and .50 caliber links rose to 18 billion pieces! To meet the demand the Metallic Link Integration Committee was convened and the 1943 link requirement was met, and the actual demand for links diminished to 13 billion links.

The .30 and .50 Caliber M2 Link

In 1940 the Armaments Laboratory at Wright Field conducted studies on the standard M1 links and the new experimental M2 links. The new M2 was determined to be superior in belt flexibility to the M1 in view of the higher cyclic rates of new model machine guns. The .30 and .50 caliber M2 links were standardized on 16 January 1941 by the Ordnance Department for immediate production. Once the requirement for .30 caliber machine guns in powered turrets moved to placing .50 caliber guns, the Chief of Ordnance ruled that there was no longer a priority for further development of the .30 caliber M2 link.

Flexibility and ease and cost of manufacture were always a priority for linked belts. The Springfield Arsenal worked on several experimental modifications of ammunition links made from plastic and aluminum. The plastic links were found to be unable to endure climatic and temperature extremes at high altitudes, while the aluminum links were not flexible and elastic enough, and their further development was abandoned.

Chuting was a series of interlocking links whose interiors fit the shape of the cartridges and which were joined to form two narrow stainless steel tracks at the end of each cartridge. A fully extended chute contained 14 links per foot that could be compressed. It could be bent to a 12 inch radius and twisted 90° around 12 inches of its extended length without fouling the ammunition.

The major producers of .50 caliber links were:

Fedders Manufacturing Co., Buffalo: 536 million links manufactured
Edward Katzinger Co., Chicago: 326 million
Westclox Division of General Time, Peru, IL: 320 million
Crown Cork & Seal, Baltimore: 240 million
Western Newell Manufacturing, Freeport, IL: 230 million
Wilson Jones Co. Lincolnshire, IL: 200 million
National Stamping, Detroit: 200 million

The average cost per 1,000 .50 caliber links ranged between $9.75 and $11.15.

Metallic Link Bags
Canvas bags were used to collect expended links on aircraft and anti-aircraft machine guns. Western Tent and Awning of Lincoln, NE, was the largest bag supplier, charging $1.19 per bag.

**Linking, Delinking, and Cartridge Repositioning Devices**
.50 Caliber Ammunition Link Loading Machine
The .50 caliber M2 link loading machine was used for rapid loading of ammunition into metallic links. The machine was mounted by screws through holes in its base to a suitable stand for loading. The links were placed in a specified position adjacent to each other on a flat loading bed. The cartridges were placed in a series of parallel grooves in the loading bed with their points facing the U-shaped stops. The loading handle was pushed forward to a stop, which loaded the cartridges to the correct depth in the links. The following devices were used to extract or link rounds of a .50 caliber link belt:

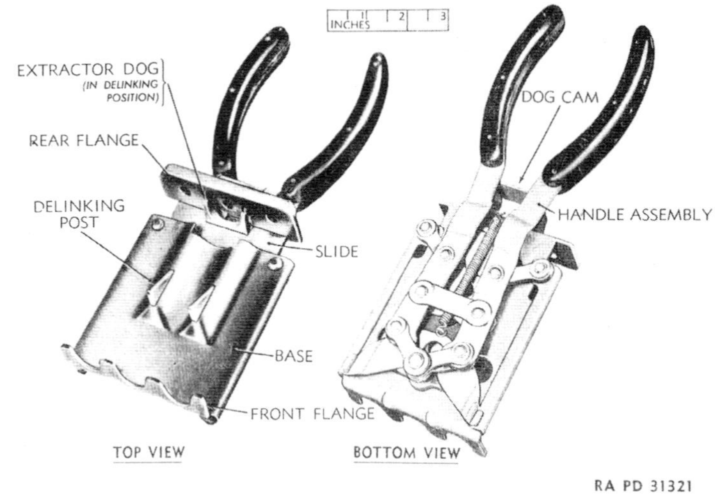

*Figure 29. Hand linker-delinker, cal..50, M12.*

**HAND LINKER-DELINKER, .50 caliber, M12** (USAAF)

Hand Linker/Delinker, Caliber .50 M12
The hand linker/delinker was used to break, assemble, and align belts of .50 caliber ammunition at any position in the belt. It could extract a defective round quickly and then relink a new round in metallic link belts. This tool could insert or extract a single cartridge and could align three cartridges. The linker/delinker worked on the compound leverage principal and consisted of a base, slide, and handle assembly. Major suppliers were F.B. Schuster and White Sewing Machine, which sold the M12 for $1.85 per unit.

Manual Link/Delinking Machine, Caliber .50, M7
The M7 could manually insert .50 caliber cartridges into .50 caliber links to form a linked belt, or it could remove .50 cartridges from a linked belt. The M7 consisted of a base, handle, slide, and delinker, and could be conveniently attached to a bench or ammo box. The linking procedure began with the delinking bar up and by pushing the loading handle forward, which loaded the rounds to the correct depth in the links. For delinking, the delinking bar was down and the loading handle was pushed forward until the delinker caught the notch on the rim of the cartridge case. The loading handle was then pulled back, removing the cartridges from the links. This device could link or delink ten rounds at a time. Among the suppliers were Bridgeport Hardware, Coburn Trolley Track, McCord Radiator, F.B. Schuster, Serv-Well Burner, and Silent Glow Oil Burner which produced the M7 for an average cost of $7.65.

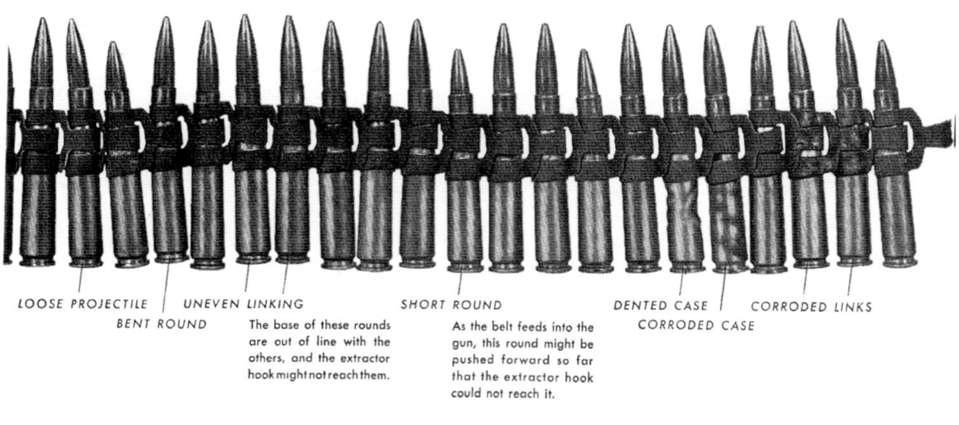


**METAL BELT PROBLEMS** (USAAF)

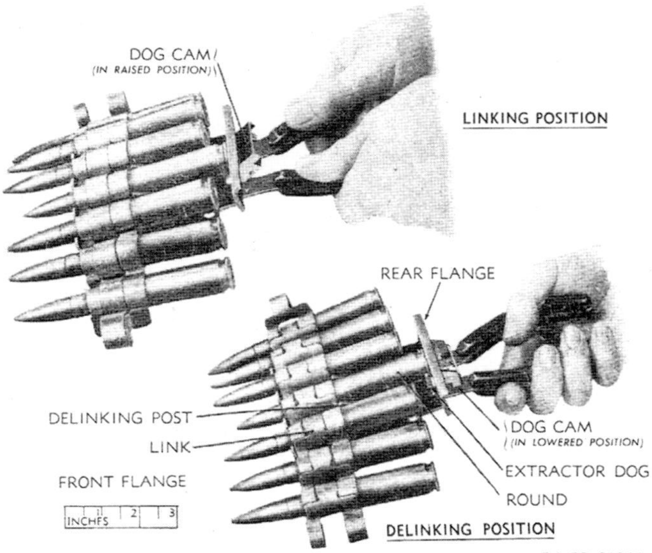


*Figure 30. Linking and delinking cartridges.*

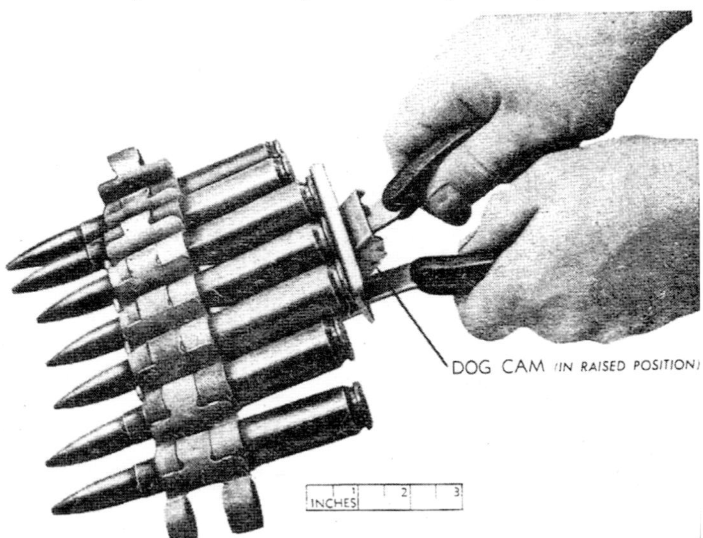


*Figure 31. Aligning cartridges.*

(USAAF)

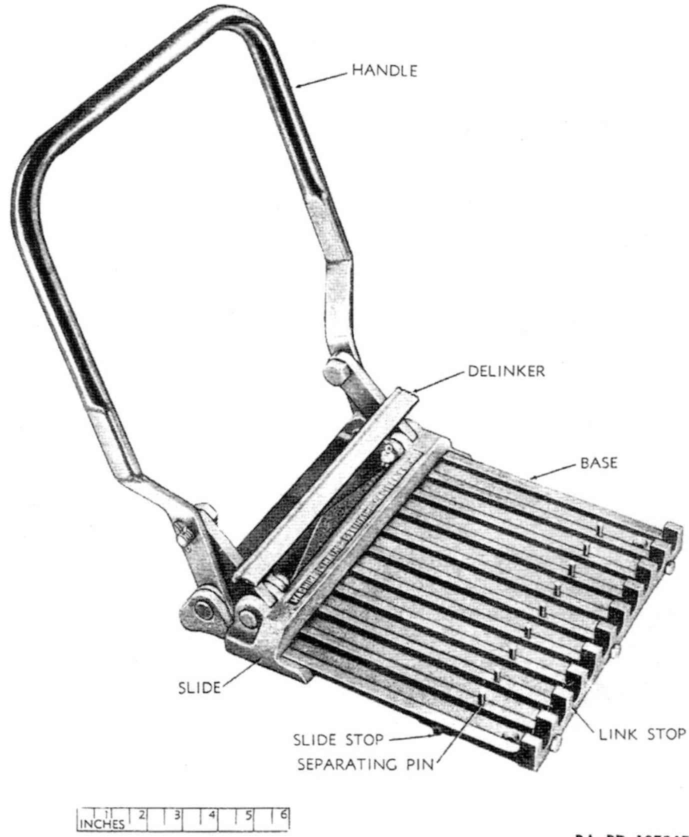


**LINK-DELINKING MACHINE, .50 caliber, M7** (USAAF)

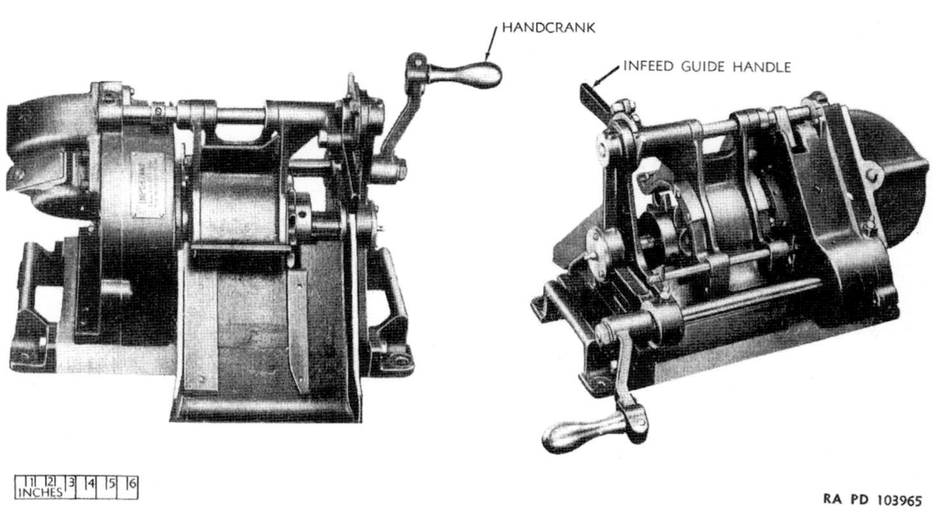


*Figure 41. Repositioning machine, cal..50, M15.*

**REPOSITIONING MACHINE, .50 caliber, M15**
(USAAF)

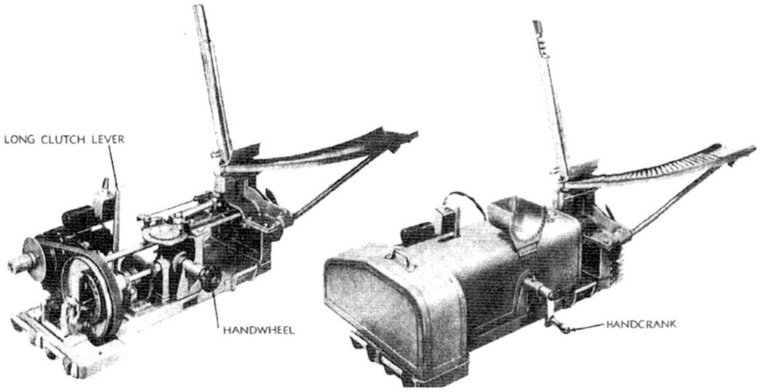


**POWERED LINKING MACHINE, .50 caliber, M5** (USAAF)

Repositioning Machine, .50 Caliber, M15
The M15 was a small, portable, hand-operated machine for repositioning cartridges that were misaligned or loose in the link belts due to the shifting of links or improper depth of cartridge insertion in the links.

Powered Linking Machine, Caliber .50 M5 and
Delinking Attachment M7
The 312 pound M5 provided an electric power-operated (110-volt) machine for linking .50 caliber ammunition to form a metallic link belt at much greater speed than by using the M7 manually operated linker. The M7 delinking attachment could be easily attached to delink cartridges. A hand crank was supplied in the event of an electrical failure. The normal operating speed of the M5/M7 was 135 to 150 rpm. The machine was manufactured by Package Machinery of Springfield, MA, for $1071.

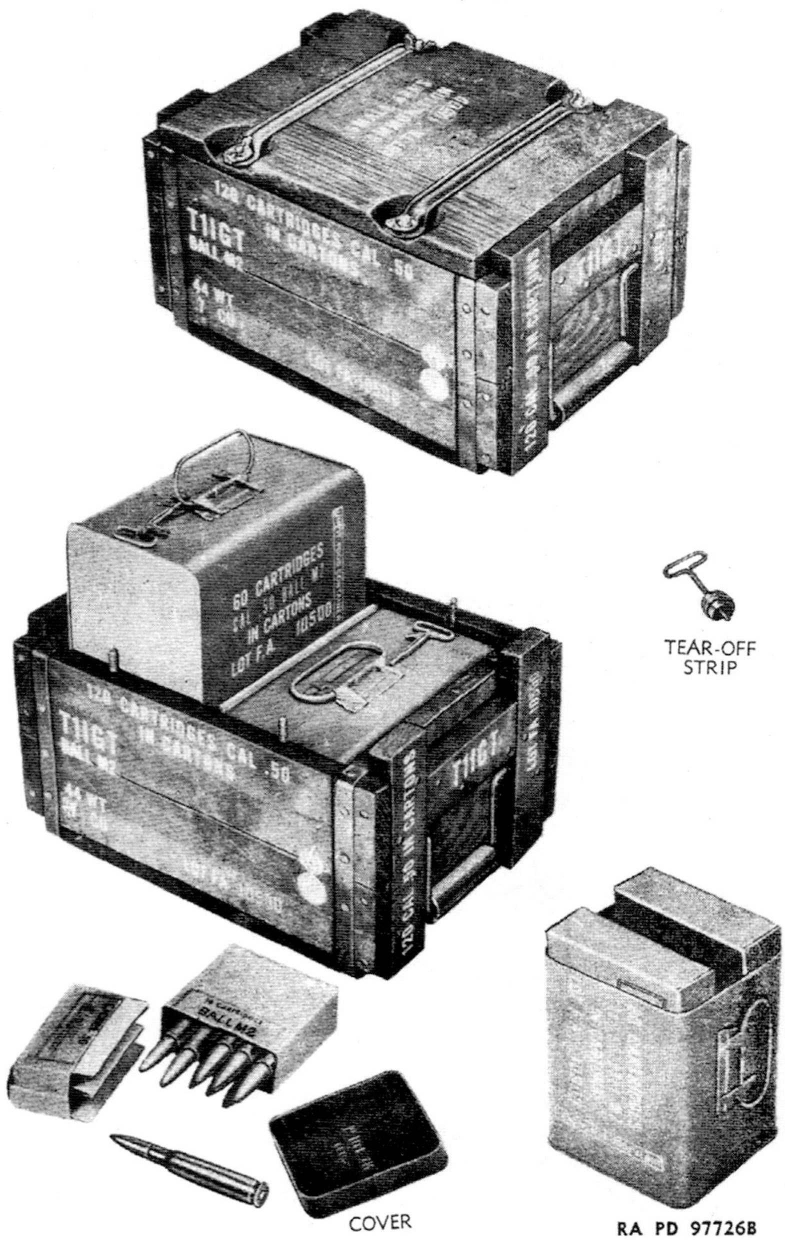


*Figure 127. M12 box containing cal..50 cartridges in cartons in M10 metal cans.*

**M12 BOX/M10 METAL CANS** (USAAF)

Ruptured Case Extractor Tool, .50 Caliber
This tool was designed to remove ruptured cartridge cases from the barrel chamber by using the leverage of the gun's cocking handle. The extractor tool was a single piece of steel with its rear end machined to fit into the T-slot of the bolt, while the front end was machined and divided to provide spring-type extracting shoulders. The tool was inserted into the bolt T-slot in the same manner as inserting a cartridge, and the bolt was then released and driven forward by the gun's driving spring. The extracting shoulders were driven into the ruptured case and expanded to seize the case. The bolt was then cocked to the rear, which pulled the tool and ruptured case out with it. Suppliers of the tool were Daniels Machine and Die, Johnson Lawn Mower, and Teller and Cooper, which manufactured the item for $3.46.

**Packing**
Methods for packing, handling, storing, and transporting .30 and .50 caliber ammunition were found in the USAAF Supply Manual. With a few exceptions .30 and .50 caliber ammunition was issued in metal containers and packed for shipment in wooden boxes designed to withstand all conditions. The metal containers had hinged covers sealed by a rubber gasket. These containers were referred to as "groovers," as the empty containers were often used as makeshift latrines, which left grooves on the user's bottom. The larger 20mm and 37mm ammunition was packed differently and are described individually.

In 1944, to protect ammunition in the moist tropics of the Pacific Theater, Chrysler (Evansville) and the American Can Company worked on developing a large hermetically sealed can that opened with a key like a can of Spam. Two million sealed cans were used by the infantry where moisture was more of a problem than for arming aircraft guns at an airfield where the metal boxes could be opened under cover.

**Loading Ammunition into Boxes for Gun Use**
To facilitate loading ammunition into an ammunition box one box cover plate hinge pin was removed, allowing the cover plate on the lower front side of the box to swing open. The ammunition belt was loaded into the box in a standard fold-in pattern, starting with the single loop end, with cartridges pointing inboard as viewed through the cover plate opening. After loading the cover plate was closed and the pin was replaced.

**Loading Ammunition into a Bomber**
There were two methods used to load ammunition boxes through the bomb bay. With the first method the armorer or gunner lifted each box straight up, using brute strength, supporting the container on one knee and lifting. If a bomb hoist hook was available it was attached over the lugs on the upper sides of the box. The rope clutch was inserted into the split tube on the box with its bail or grip stop ring in position between the rope and the box. The rope clutch allowed the rope to pass through it in the downward direction only, facilitating hoisting and installing the box. The ammo box was hoisted into position with the bar over the upper support hook. The draw latch was secured on the underside and the hoist rope assembly was removed. Once raised, there was a bar on the top edge of the box that was to hook on the inside of a large ring casting over the gunner's head and hung down on either side of the center columns. At the bottom of each box was a bar that fit into a bracket on the controller housing and was held there by a latch pin. The pin was pushed all the way in and turned a quarter turn to lock it. Once inside the aircraft the boxes were placed on the floor and moved to the gun position on grooved ammunition rollers. The boxes were either placed on the floor or hung on mounting hooks located on the fuselage wall. The ammunition box was lifted so that its mounting bars and latches attached over the fuselage wall mounting hooks.

# 2

# Ballistics

**Ballistic Categories**
Ballistics can be divided into three categories:

1) Internal Ballistics: What occurs inside the gun from the time the cartridge is fired to the time the projectile leaves the muzzle.
2) External Ballistics: Relates to the flight of the projectile from muzzle to target
3) Terminal Ballistics: Explains what happens when the target is hit.

1) Internal Ballistics
When the primer ignites the propellant gas is produced, which rapidly forms a great pressure that pushes the projectile out of the cartridge case and up the barrel. As described previously, the characteristics of the propellant powder causes it to generate the maximum pressures nearly immediately to push the projectile up the barrel. This is the reason that the gun's structure was thickest in this area. As the projectile accelerates up the barrel there is more space behind it and the pressures decrease but remain substantial as the projectile leaves the barrel. Once the projectile leaves the barrel there is a rapid expansion of the gases in the open air, causing the distinctive "bang" of a fired gun. This final expansion, along with the projectile leaving the grip of the barrel, results in the final thrust to the projectile so that its maximum velocity occurs just beyond the muzzle.

Muzzle Energy
Muzzle energy is the measure of the striking power of the bullet when it leaves the muzzle of the gun. It is calculated by squaring the muzzle velocity and multiplying it by the weight of the bullet and then applying a factor to convert it to the units of measure. In the U.S. muzzle energy is measured in foot pounds (muzzle velocity in feet per second; bullet weight in grains; and dividing their product by a factor of 450,420, which compensated not only for the different units of measure but also for gravity). In Europe the Joule is the unit of measure for muzzle energy.

Recoil
The force of the recoil is created by the momentum of the projectile and the escaping gas. Projectile momentum is calculated by multiplying the projectile weight by the muzzle velocity, while the measurement of escaping gases is much more difficult to calculate because it is contingent on the burning characteristics of the propellant and the length of the barrel. The recoil "experienced" or recoil "blow" is different from the recoil force, as it depends on the weapon and its mounting and acts in accordance with Newton's law of equal and opposite reactions; the rearward momentum of the gun equals the forward momentum of the projectile plus the expanding gases. When firing the same ammunition a heavier weapon will recoil more slowly, giving it a smooth push back as compared to the sharper "kick" of a lighter weapon. The recoil momentum of both is the same, but was delivered in a different way: the lighter weapon recoils more quickly but at a higher energy and is perceived to "kick harder." For this reason heavier military guns are fitted to a mounting which doesn't reduce the recoil force but reduces the greatest recoil blow by spreading out the recoil force over a longer time, thereby placing less strain on the mounting and allowing a lighter mounting to be used. The Edgewater mounting used with aircraft heavy machine guns and cannons substantially reduced peak recoil. Self-loading guns, being either recoil or gas-operated, reduced the recoil effect since some of the energy was used to drive the loading mechanism.

The "long recoil" automatic gun mechanism had a greater recoil damping effect, as the barrel recoiled a large distance between firing and resulted in a slow-firing gun, such as the 37mm and 75mm cannons. There is a widespread misconception that the 75mm M4 cannon used in the B-25G and H models had a significant effect on the Mitchell's airspeed when fired, and claims were made by some crews that the aircraft was even brought to a very fleeting mid-air stop! This fallacy is exposed when comparing the speeds and weights of the 21 pound 75mm shell traveling at 1,500 to 2,000 fps and the 25,000 pound bomber traveling at 290 fps (200mph).

2) External Ballistics
Only two factors determine the external ballistics of the projectile: the muzzle velocity and the ballistic coefficient.

Muzzle Velocity
Muzzle velocity is the speed of a projectile with respect to the muzzle at the instant the projectile leaves the weapon measured in feet per second or meters per second. Muzzle velocities range from 1,100 fps for pistols to 6,000 fps for tank guns, which is the upper limit that can be realized with chemical propellants.

In conventional guns using gunpowder, muzzle velocity is determined by the quality (burn speed and expansion) and quantity of the propellant, the mass of the projectile, and the length of the barrel. A slower burning propellant requires a longer barrel to burn completely, but can conversely use a heavier projectile. A faster burning propellant may accelerate a lighter projectile to higher speeds if the same amount of propellant is used. In a gun, the pressure resulting from the process is a limiting factor.

A balance between propellant quality and quantity, projectile mass, and barrel length must be found if both safety and optimal performance is to be accomplished.

The time of flight of a projectile to the target was to be as short as possible, as it not only gave the target less time to maneuver and escape but offered a flatter trajectory that reduced sighting errors. Combat studies demonstrated that by reducing the flight time to a target by one third the probability of scoring a hit was increased by four times. The velocity of a projectile is greatest at the muzzle and then decreases steadily due to air resistance. Generally, lighter projectiles lose velocity more rapidly than heavier ones. While a lighter projectile will move faster, it will not carry more kinetic energy (the work needed to accelerate a body of a given mass from rest to its current velocity), and if physically smaller, must carry a smaller internal explosive charge if it is to deliver kinetic energy equivalent to a heavier round. Because the propellant charge is mostly burned before the projectile has moved very far down the barrel, adding length to the barrel will not indefinitely increase the muzzle velocity. A projectile has an upper limit for muzzle velocity, and to maximize muzzle velocity a high ballistic coefficient is needed.

Ballistic Coefficient

The ballistic coefficient (BC) of a body is a measure of its ability to overcome air resistance in flight. Ballistic coefficient is significant because it determines the rate at which the projectile decelerates, and in combination with the muzzle velocity determines the maximum range (at any given gun elevation) and the time of flight to any distance. There are two factors that determine ballistic coefficient: the sectional density and form factor. The sectional density is the ratio between caliber and projectile weight, while form factor measures the aerodynamic efficiency of the projectile's shape. BC is a function of mass, diameter, and drag coefficient (the drag force on any object, which is approximately proportional to the square of its velocity through the air).

Ballistic coefficient is calculated by multiplying the sectional density ratio (SDR), which is the measurement of the weight and length of a projectile, in comparison with its caliber times the aerodynamic efficiency of the projectile. The higher the SDR the better would a projectile retain its velocity (with aerodynamic shapes equal): .30 caliber = 0.245, .50 caliber = 0.397, and 20mm = 0.462. Ballistic coefficient is measured in units of pounds per square inch or kilograms per square meter. BC is inversely proportional to the deceleration, and a high number indicates a low deceleration. These calculations established that the ballistic coefficient of large caliber guns was generally better than smaller caliber guns. However, heavy machine gun bullets were steel cored and heavy for their caliber, while cannon shells were hollow and filled with light chemical materiel.

Trajectory

The time of flight then determines the amount that the projectile dropped, which was a constant amount determined by gravity. This curved path of the projectile produced by muzzle velocity, the ballistic coefficient, and gravity drop is the trajectory of the projectile. Therefore, in firing at long-ranges a short time of flight is advantageous, as it maximizes the probability of a hit by flattening the trajectory. Also, the projectile strikes the target at a greater muzzle velocity and has a greater effect. The advantages of greater muzzle velocity in decreasing projectile flight time are obvious as are the disadvantages: the need for more propellant, a heavier gun (and mounting), a longer barrel, greater recoil, and a lower rate of fire for automatic weapons.

Rifling

The stability of the projectile is an essential characteristic of external ballistics. If bullet or cannon shell were fired from a smooth barrel it would begin to tumble and miss the target. Early smooth bore muskets fired round ball bullets so tumbling was not a problem, but ball shot tended to drift because they were not perfectly symmetrical. For more accuracy at longer ranges the answer was rifling, which was cutting grooves into the inside of the barrel that caused the long, pointed bullet to spin rapidly and offset any asymmetries.

The first projectiles used in rifled barrels had studs to fit the rifling grooves but these projectiles loaded too slowly. The next step was to design a polygonal section barrel with bullets shaped to fit. This led to the Minie-type bullet that had a hollow base designed to expand under the pressure of firing and cling onto the rifling. The ultimate solution was bullets with copper-nickel metal jackets that were slightly larger in diameter than the bore of the gun. Cannon shells were usually made of steel, which was too hard, and a copper driving band was added near the base of the projectile. This band was larger in diameter than the shell and was gripped by the rifling.

On firing the bullet was squeezed into the rifling grooves, leaving the characteristic angled identifying grooves engraved on the bullet made famous by CSI TV programs. Spin is the rotational motion of a bullet imparted by the rifling of the barrel during its passage up the barrel. Spin is necessary in order to stabilize the bullet in flight and keep it traveling point first. The amount of spin depends almost completely on its length in relation to its caliber (See Part One/Chapter 6/Section 2: Caliber, Lands, Rifling).

3) Terminal Ballistics

It proved difficult to compare armor piercing capabilities of various cartridges due to the firing distances, striking angle, the quality or composition of the armor itself, and the definition of "penetration." The U.S. definition of penetration specified that 50% of the rounds fired had to pass through the target, while other nations set a higher percentage or did not require the round to completely penetrate. AP testing was generally performed in ground tests firing at stationary ground targets and the results from the air tests could vary. Air tests fired at moving targets varied if the target was moving toward or away from the fired projectiles. The speed of the firing aircraft had to be added to the muzzle velocity of the gun (e.g. 300 mph added 435 fps to the muzzle velocity). When an AP projectile passed first through the thin aluminum fuselage skin of an enemy aircraft it could go into yaw, which was the deflection of the projectile tip from its straight line flight. The deflected projectile then would not strike the armor point-on, which reduced its armor penetrating capacity. It was found that the maximum damage was caused when an AP projectile had only enough power to penetrate the armor, and those AP projectiles striking at higher velocities would punch less damaging smaller holes through the armor.

A .30 caliber bullet was determined to be only one quarter as destructive as a .50 caliber bullet, but a 30mm shell was tested as four more times as destructive as the .50 caliber bullet.

Coefficients of Destruction for Projectile Classes
(Compared to .50 caliber bullets)

.30/.303/7.92mm Value= 0.25
.50/13mm Value=1
15mm Value=1.5
20mm Value=2
30mm Value=4

**Range**

Range was not too important when the aircraft fired only one gun mounted near the gunsight. However, range was critically important when two to eight guns were contained in the wings and were a relatively long distance from the sight base. Wing-mounted guns were harmonized so that all the bullets met at a predetermined point in order to provide a concentration of fire, which was the purpose for multiple armament. Therefore, the range at which the guns were harmonized to meet was the best range to fire. In combat the fighter pilot had to fire at the correct harmonized range because at ranges of more than 300 yards bullets begin to lose their penetrating power and bullet drop becomes a factor. Another factor was the vibration of the firing guns, which caused the bullets to scatter and increased as the range increased. Therefore, shooting at excessive ranges created:

1) A loss in the penetrating power of bullets.
2) An increase in gravity drop, which the pilot had to allow for.
3) A very scattered bullet pattern, which meant that the pilot had to fire a much longer burst to have the same effect as firing at short ranges.
4) Errors in deflection allowances. Correct deflection allowance also depended on correct range estimation.

Effective Range

The maximum effective range of a gun was often not determined by the type of gun but external factors, such as the training and proficiency of the pilot or gunner, the stability of the fighter aircraft or turret as gun platform, the quality of the sights, and most importantly, the character of the target.

Armament characteristics that influenced effective range are the rate of fire, the number of guns, the hitting power of those guns, and the external ballistics. A higher rate of fire increases the pattern density and the probability of scoring a hit at long-range. When the Hispano cannon rate of fire was increased from 750 to 1,000 rpm its effective range was increased by 15%. Less powerful guns needed to have concentrated fire to increase their striking power to have an effect.

Loss of Penetrating Power

When a bullet was fired from the fixed guns of a fighter flying at 400 mph it had a very high velocity on the order of 3,000 feet per second (2,000 mph). This initial velocity was lost very quickly due to air resistance, with half being lost when the bullet had traveled about 600 yards. This meant a significant decrease in hitting power at long ranges with the bullets unable to penetrate the thinnest armor plating.

Gravity Drop

Gravity draws a dropped object toward the earth at 32 feet per second, per second, causing fired bullets to travel in a slight curve that depends on the muzzle velocity. No allowance for gravity drop was required when firing at ranges up to 250 yards. Because most guns were mounted below the line of sight, they had to be canted upward if they were to meet at the point of harmonization. Harmonization allowed for sizeable bullet drop when the fighter was level about its horizontal axis, but when banking his aircraft the pilot had to bear in mind to aim up and not ease the stick back to raise the nose, as this pulled the nose around the horizon and not up at all. Firing at ranges of more than 300 yards was not recommended.

As the range of the bullet increased so did the gravity drop. A bullet took more than twice as long to travel 600 yards as it did to travel the first 300 yards because it was decelerating at an increasing rate. This meant that the pull of gravity had more than twice as long to act over 600 yards than over 300 yards, and thus the gravity drop at 600 yards was more than four times that at 300 yards because the gravity has an acceleration of 32 feet per second, per second. The sight and guns were not harmonized to allow for gravity drop at 600 yards, so if the pilot opened fire at 600 yards he had to make an additional allowance for this greater gravity drop by an amount which, at best, he could only guess.

Bullet Pattern and Density

When the wing guns were harmonized they were positioned to give a predetermined pattern at a definite range (usually 250 to 300 yards). This pattern was calculated to give the best possibility of effective shooting from point-blank range up to some optimum range outside of which the chance of success quickly declined. With any type of gun the bullet pattern spread out as the range increased. This meant that the area of the pattern produced at 400 yards was four times larger than that produced at 200 yards, but the pattern area enclosed practically every bullet fired. In terms of bullet density, the pattern at 400 yards contained only one quarter of the number of bullets per square foot contained in the pattern at 200 yards. If a fighter fired 200 rounds, this burst yielded a bullet density of approximately 12 bullets per square foot at 200 yards, but at 400 yards the density was decreased to three bullets per square foot.

Due to the slight inaccuracies inherent in the gun, the slight movement in the gun mounting, and the vibration of the aircraft, the bullets fired would approximately cover a circular area of approximately 20 feet in diameter at 400 yards. During harmonization of the guns the speeding up of the guns to obtain additional coverage was not recommended, as that would cause the loss of too much concentration and the fire would be ineffective.

Deflection Allowances

When the pilot fired at a target maneuvering at an angle from his line of flight, he had to turn his aircraft continually so that he could hold the target at the correct deflection and sighting while he fired his guns. If the pilot did not hold his aim the first bullet hit the front of the target, but by the time the second bullet covered the distance to the target the target would have moved on its course 12.5 feet, which equaled 7.5 feet behind the first, and the third round 7.5 feet behind the second, etc. Thus, the faster the speed of the target the less was the concentration of fire if the pilot did not turn with the target and keep his sights trained.

# 3

# Identifying Ammunition

### Standard Nomenclature Lists (SNL)

Ammunition was completely identified by painting, marking (including the lot number), and accompanying data cards and tags. Standard Nomenclature Lists identified items by a specific name and were mandatory. Standard Nomenclature consisted of an item name or abbreviation, a colon, and additional item identification established in accordance to Federal Item Identification Guides for Supply Cataloging. For aircraft gun ammunition (other than blank or dummy ammunition) the item name consisted of the word "cartridge" followed by its caliber, weight, or size. Additional item identification consisted of the type of projectile, model number, and any other description necessary to completely identify the item, such as "steel case" if the cartridge case was steel, fuse nomenclature if the cartridge was fused, and "linked" if the cartridges were packed in cartridge links.

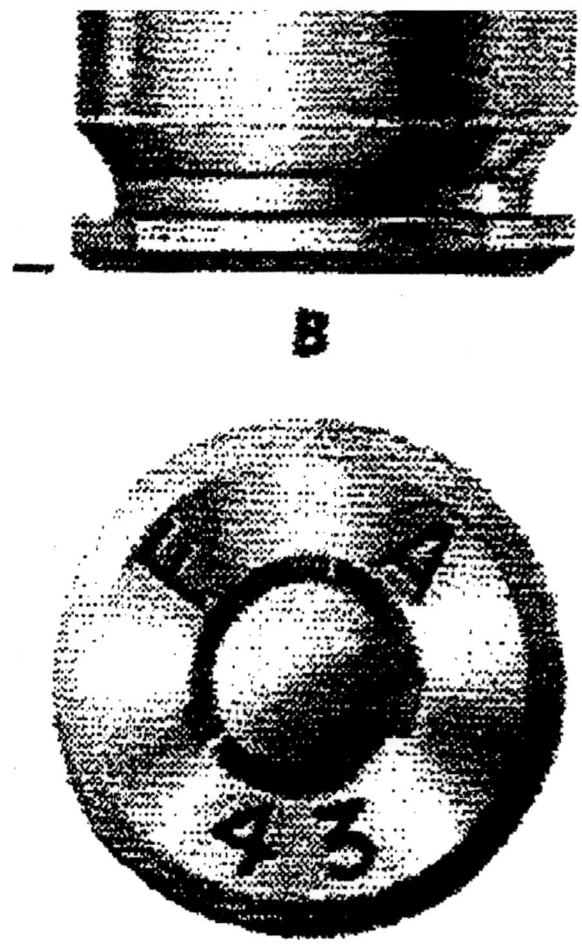


This **headstamp** shows that this .50 caliber cartridge was manufactured at the Franklin Arsenal in 1943. (USAAF)

### Identification

The type, caliber, model, and ammunition lot number, including the symbol of the manufacturer, were necessary for complete identification of .50 caliber ammunition. The following helped in identifying ammunition:

1) The physical appearance of the cartridge and the color of the painted bullet tip.
2) The stamping on the base of the cartridge case. Because of the small size this marking was a stamping of the manufacturer's initials (headstamp) and year of manufacture on the base of the cartridge case (See below).
3) The markings on the outside of the original packing boxes and cartons.
4) The 6.5 x 15 inch identification card sealed inside the metal liner on top of the ammunition in each box.

**Headstamps**

| Ordnance Plant | Headstamp |
|---|---|
| Allegheny | KS |
| Denver | DEN |
| Des Moines | DM |
| Eau Claire | EW* |
| Evansville | EC |
| Evansville (Sunbeam) | ECS |
| Frankfort Arsenal | FA |
| Kings Mill | PC |
| Lake City | LM |
| Milwaukee | M |
| Remington Arms | RA |
| St. Louis | SL |
| Twin City | TW |
| Utah | UT or U |
| Western Cartridge | WCC |
| Winchester Repeating Arms | WRA |

* The head stamp EC was used for the first several production lots, but was soon changed to EW to avoid confusion with Evansville EC

Caliber .30 ball ammunition was also manufactured for the Ordnance Department in Canada. Ammunition produced at the Defence Industries Ltd., Verdun, Quebec Works was identified by the Head Stamp VC, and that produced by the Dominion Arsenal, Quebec, was stamped DAQ.

**Model Number**

To distinguish a particular design, a model designation was assigned when the model was classified as an adopted type. The model designation was an important part of Standard Nomenclature and was part of the marking on the item. Prior to World War I, the year that the design was adopted was preceded by an "M" and used as the model designation (M1919, for example). From World War I to 1 July 1925 a "Mark" number (abbreviated "Mk") was assigned and followed by a Roman numeral (e.g. Mk II). The first model was Mk I, while subsequent modifications had an added Roman numeral (e.g. Mk I, Mk II, etc.). From July 1925, model designation included an "M" followed by Arabic numerals with modifications denoted by the letters A, B, C, etc. followed by the appropriate Arabic numeral. Thus, M2A1 indicated the first modification of an item that was originally designated as M2. Items standardized for use by both the Army and Navy were designated as AN proceeding the model designation; for example, AN-N2A1.

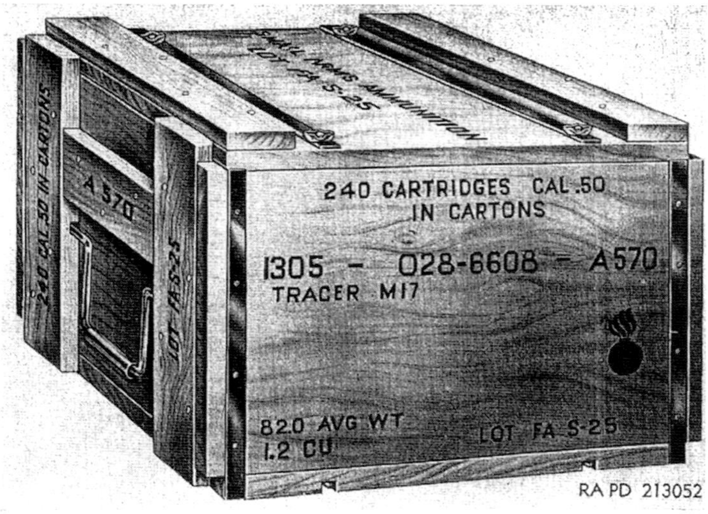


*Figure 1. Caliber .50 ammunition packing box M23.*

This **M23 packing box** contains 240 .50 caliber M17 tracer cartridges in cartons with a Lot # FA S-2S. (USAAF)

**Lot Number**

When ammunition was manufactured a lot number, which was to be an essential part of its identification, was assigned following relevant specifications. The lot number was stamped or marked on every piece of ammunition, on all packing containers, and on all accompanying data cards and tags. It was required for all records, including reports on condition, functioning, and accidents in which the ammunition was involved. To provide for the most uniform functioning all the components of any one lot were manufactured under as identical conditions as possible. All rounds in any one lot were to be comprised of projectiles, primers, and propellant, all of one lot number. Cartridges for which the lot number was lost were placed in grade 3 unserviceable ammunition, which would not be issued or fired.

**Ammunition Data Card**

The 5x8 inch ammunition data card contained the pertinent information about an item and its components and was placed in each packing box, and when required, assembling and firing instructions were to be included on the release side of the card.

**Painting and Marking**

Generally, aircraft cartridge cases were not painted, but the packing boxes were painted brown with marking in yellow with a distinctive color band as follows:

| | |
|---|---|
| Ball | Red |
| Armor-Piercing | Blue on Yellow |
| Ball and Tracer | 3 Stripe Band: Yellow, Red, Green |
| Tracer | Green on Yellow |
| Blank | Blue |
| Dummy | Green |

The marking stenciled on the packing containers included all information necessary for complete identification.

**Bullet and Cannon Shell Markings**

The projectile tips of bullets were usually painted to identify its type:

| Bullet | Tip Color |
|---|---|
| Ball | None (copper-nickel jackets without any paint.) |
| AP | Black Tip |
| API (M8) | Silver Tip |
| API (M49) | Silver Tip or Light blue ring on rear |
| Tracer (M1 & M21) | Red Tip |
| Tracer (M10) | Orange Tip |
| Tracer (M17) | Maroon Tip |
| APIT (M20) | Red + Silver ring on rear |
| Incendiary (M1) | Light Blue |
| Incendiary (M23) | Blue Tip + Light Blue ring on rear |
| Spotter/Tracer | Yellow + Red |
| Dummy | None (three holes drilled in cartridge case) |
| High Pressure Test | None (Tinned cartridge case) |

20mm Hispano cannon projectiles were painted and then marked in White or Black:

| Cannon Shells (20mm) | Projectile Color | Color of Marking |
|---|---|---|
| Ball | Black | White |
| AP | Black | White |
| APT | Black | White |
| API | Black with Light Blue nose | Black |
| Incendiary | Grey with Light Blue Nose | Black |
| HE | White or Yellow | Black |
| HEI | Half OD, Half Red | Black |
| HET | Grey or Dark Blue | Black |

**Ammunition Grade**

Ammunition was manufactured to exacting specifications and was thoroughly inspected and tested before acceptance. As a result of this testing the ammunition was allocated a grade. Ammunition in storage was periodically retested to check if it needed to be regraded.

Ammunition for 20mm aircraft cannon was not graded. Ammunition for the .50 caliber gun was graded either as Grade AC (Aircraft) or Grade MG (Machine Gun) because of the varying characteristics of the several different types of .50 caliber guns and the location of the gunner relative to the gun. Grade AC ammunition lots indicated minimum or no probabilities of misfires or other malfunctions which may cause stoppages in remote weapons, such as aircraft and anti-aircraft guns. All other ammunition lots were graded as MG, and within allowable specification limits were intended for use on ground machine guns under the immediate, direct control of a gunner.

**Priority of Issue**

Ammunition was to be used in a certain order: limited standard, substitute standard, and standard. Ammunition with the longest or the most unfavorable storage conditions were to be used first. For lots of equal age the smallest lot was to be used first.

**Checking Ammunition**

The ammunition belts were to be laid out on a clean, dry floor in long rows and examined carefully. If a clean, dry area was not available the ammunition was to be checked by loading it, double-end first, into a box and then loading into a can, single-end first, watching for defective rounds as the belt was pulled into the can.

# 4

# U.S. Ammunition Manufacturers

**Introduction**

In the inter-war years the minimal needs of the American military services were met by the Frankford Arsenal, located in Philadelphia. Frankford had originally opened in 1816 and was the center of American small arms ammunition design and development until it closed in 1977. During World War II Frankford played a principal part in U.S. industrial mobilization, providing oversight and expertise while supervising the operation of the new ordnance plants. Frankford's realm during the war was small arms research and development, and its productivity was limited to manufacturing the initial production lots of ammunition of all calibers and types of experimental and service ammunition.

Once war seemed inevitable the U.S. government looked to build ordnance plants with certain requirements in mind. The plants were to be located inland away from the threat of enemy attack and away from large population centers that would be endangered by an explosion, but with access to a large available labor pool that did not have to be skilled. In obtaining the land the federal government was heavily lobbied by local business and political leaders who aided in the condemnation of public property and supplying infrastructure. Even though local companies and workforce were given preference, housing shortages inevitably occurred during the plant construction phase when skilled and semi-skilled construction workers from outside areas were necessarily hired and also imported from within by the primary contractors. Housing was supplied only to top military and construction personnel, and trailer parks developed and local renters prospered from the ordinary worker. The completed plants were autonomous communities with infrastructure in place: roads and railways, sewer and water systems, hospitals and fire departments, and maintenance and strict security. Once the plants were completed and operating most of the plant workers were hired from a 50 mile radius, but still many came from further away. Contractors realized that these plants would be phased out after the war and did not care to invest in housing, which was a continuing problem throughout the war..

**Ordnance Plants**

| **Plant** | **PlantOperator** |
|---|---|
| **Government Owned Ordnance Plants (GOCO)** | |
| Alleghany MD | Kelly Springfield (1942-43) |
| Denver CO | Remington Arms (1941-44) |
| Des Moines IA | US Rubber (1941-45) |
| Evansville, IN | Chrysler (1942-44) |
| *Evansville, IN | Sunbeam Refrigerator (1943-44) |
| Frankfort Arsenal, PA | US Government (1816-1977) |
| **Kings Mill, OH | Remington (1942-44) |
| Lake City, MO | Remington (1941-44) & Olin (1945) |
| Lowell, MA | Remington (1942-43) |
| Milwaukee, WI | US Rubber (1942-43) |
| St. Louis, MO (as US Cartridge) | Olin (1941-45) |
| Twin Cities, MN | Federal Cartridge (1941-45) |
| Utah, UT | Remington (1941-43) |

**Commercially Owned Plants**

| | |
|---|---|
| Federal Cartridge, MN | (1941-45) |
| Peters Cartridge, OH | (1941-45) |
| Remington Arms, CT | (1941-45) |
| Sparklet Devices, OH | (1941-45) |
| Stant Manufacturing Co, IN | (1941-45) |
| Union Metallic Cartridge Co, CT | (1941-45) |
| Winchester Cartridge Co, CT | (1941-45) |
| Winchester Repeating Arms, CT | (1941-45) |

First draw in cartridge manufacture. (AFHRC)

Trimming raw cartridge cases. (AFHRC)

Cartridge case anti-corrosion bath. (AFHRC)

Inspection of finished .30 caliber cartridge cases. (AFHRC)

**Canadian Plants Under U.S. Conract**

Dominion Arsenal, Quebec (1944-45)

Defence Industries, Quebec (as Verdun Ordnance Works (1944-45)

* Manufactured cases that were loaded by the Evansville Chrysler Plant with the ESC headstamp.

** This plant was operated by Remington Arms under the Peters Cartridge Co. name and was supported by the commercial facilities owned by Peters.

**Ammunition Manufacture**

Cartridge and Projectile Manufacture

To produce the multi-millions of bullets and shells used in the global war required mass production assembly line techniques utilizing literally miles of motorized belts, and conveyors were employed from initial machining of the cartridge cases to the remote explosive-filling areas to final inspection and storage. Various functions previously done by hand were mechanized or combined, such as hand-feeding to water-proofing and gauging machines. Bullets and shells previously hand-carried to various factory and Ordnance Department inspection stations were carried by conveyors as part of the assembly line. Packing of the finished cartridges was done quickly and efficiently by specialized machines. The typical cartridge was made up of seven basic parts, but went through 48 processing operations and 300 to 350 inspections in its manufacture. Total rejections were less than 0.1% of production.

Explosive Handling and Loading

Millions of pounds of powder and high explosive were safely handled during the war, and in 1944 the explosives industry ranked second in safety only to the women's garment industry. The powder was tested repeatedly by the mills that manufactured it, and then again by the ammunition manufacturers upon receiving it. The ammunition manufacturer divided this tested explosive into six packages that were stored under constant temperature (120°F) and humidity (75-85%). After a week it was retested and compared to the powder from the other packages to determine if the divergence fell within set limits. To test uniformity, samples were taken from six packages and blended and then comparatively test fired with cartridges loaded from each of the six packages. The ballistics department tested the powder once more before it was loaded.

The buildings where explosives were processed and loaded were spaced in accordance to Ordnance Department specifications and were located several miles from the main factory, and even further from residential areas. The building's walls were thick, while the construction of the roofs was flimsy so that in case of an explosion most of the force would be directed upward. Heavy concrete or earth deflectors were located around storage warehouses so that there would be no domino effect in case of an explosion. All employees in danger areas wore special non-conductive shoes that automatically dissipated electrical charges into copper wires embedded in the cement floors. Of course smoking, matches, and lighters were not allowed. In handling and processing explosives the temperature and humidity were closely monitored and the cleaning of the machinery was given a high priority. Lightning was an uncontrollable threat, and the Department of Commerce set up many specialized weather stations around the country's ammunition plants. When a thunder storm approached the explosive mixing houses were closed, explosive loading was stopped, and the area cleared and cleaned as quickly as possible. Explosive mixtures were transported from the mixing houses to the loading houses in low-slung wooden carts with non-conducting metal frames and rubber tires. The cart's dead man's brake prevented it from moving accidentally, and its low center of gravity made it very difficult to overturn. The explosives were carried in the cart in rubber cups that were cooled and kept moist with ice. Once outside the loading houses the cups were taken from the cart and placed in a compartment with an outer and inner door leading to the inside. Once the cartridges were loaded and the primers were inserted conveyors took the finished cartridges to the storage areas. Thousands of finished rounds were fired daily from fixed gun mounts to check velocity, pressure, and accuracy after loading.

# 5

# .30 Caliber Ammunition

The M1903 .30 caliber round was developed for the U.S. Model 1903 Springfield service rifle and replaced the rimmed 30-40 Krag round as the standard U.S. .30 caliber military round. The 30'03 ("thirty ought three") was a 220 grain round nosed bullet with a muzzle velocity of 2,300 fps. Due to European cartridge developments at the time it was replaced by a lighter 150 grain round fired at an increased muzzle velocity of 2,700 fps that was designated as the Cartridge, Ball, Caliber .30, M1906, or the famous thirty ought six (30'06). This round was slightly shortened and had a copper-nickel jacket that was silver in color. In 1925 the U.S. Army converted to the heavier boat-tailed 172 grain projectile with a copper-colored metal gilded metal jacket (gilded metal is a 95% copper and 5% zinc alloy that was similar to brass). This cartridge was designated as the Cartridge, Ball, Caliber .30 M1 and was manufactured until October 1941, when the remaining stocks were set aside for aircraft use.

In 1940 the 150 grain M2 ball cartridge was adopted mainly to accommodate the M1 Garand semi-automatic rifle and was the standard .30 caliber round of World War II. However, the heavier, more powerful M1 cartridge was superior for machine gun use, as it provided a longer range (5,000 vs. 3,500 yards). The Ordnance Department did not wish to manufacture and issue two different types of .30 caliber service ammunition

Prior to America's entry into the war 138 million rounds (25%) of U.S. .30 caliber ammunition was sent to England, so after Pearl Harbor there was a shortage of .30 caliber ammunition in the U.S. The Ordnance Department stepped up production exponentially by manufacturing .30 caliber ammunition in 12 ordnance plants, but it was not until 1943 that the supply problem was overcome, which soon became a surplus. Pre-World War II ammunition stocks were 65% ball, 20% armor-piercing, and 15 % tracer. Once the ammunition supply problem was solved and combat studies analyzed, the ratio was changed to 80% armor-piercing and 20% tracer. By 1944 only four of the 12 plants manufacturing .30 caliber ammunition were still operating, but with the increased ammunition expenditures at D-Day and the Battle of the Bulge, along with losses due to poor storage in late 1944, the Ordnance Department increased production by 100%. A staggering 25 billion rounds of .30 caliber was manufactured in the U.S. at the 12 government owned and contractor operated ordnance plants.

**.30 Caliber Ammunition Types**

Cartridge, Ball, Caliber .30 M2

As described previously, the standard U.S. .30 caliber round was the Cartridge, Ball, Caliber .30 M2, intended for use against enemy personnel and light unarmored targets. There were 1.69 billion rounds of ball ammunition manufactured at a cost of $45 per 1,000 rounds.

Cartridge, Armor-Piercing, Caliber .30 M2

The Armor-Piercing .30M2 cartridge was identified by its black tip. The projectile's core was hardened steel instead of the lead of the M2 ball. The projectile weighed 166 grains and fired at a muzzle velocity of 2,715 fps. There were 929 million rounds of M2 incendiary ammunition manufactured at $51 per 1,000 rounds.

Cartridge, Tracer, Caliber .30 M1

The M1 tracer round was identified by its red tip. The 150 grain projectile fired at 2,700 fps and the 17 grain tracer compound burned a bright red for approximately 1,000 yards. There were 463 million rounds of M1 tracer ammunition manufactured at $55 per 1,000 rounds, and 24.6 million rounds of M2 tracer ammunition manufactured at the same cost per 1,000 rounds.

Cartridge, Incendiary, Caliber .30 M1

Originally, the .30 caliber incendiary M1 was mainly used in the .30 caliber aircraft gun, and once the .30 was replaced by the .50 for aircraft armament the manufacture of .30 caliber incendiary ammunition was ceased in November 1943. The .30 caliber incendiary cartridge was identified by its light blue tip. The projectile was not boat-tailed so it could contain incendiary material that would ignite on contact with the target. The projectile

.30 Caliber Tracer Cartridge Case (Author's Collection)

weighed 140 grains and had a muzzle velocity of 3,050 fps. There were 249 million rounds of M1 incendiary ammunition manufactured at $77.50 per 1,000 rounds.

Cartridge, Armor-Piercing Incendiary, Caliber .30 M14

Combat showed that the incendiary round was effective against enemy aircraft only if direct hits were made on their fuel tanks, and the M14 was developed for aircraft use. The M14 round was identified by its silver tip. The projectile weight was 151 grains and had a muzzle velocity of 2,780 fps.

Frangible Bullet T44

In early 1942, while at Harlingen, TX, gunnery training base, Maj. Cameron Fairchild suggested a requirement for a harmless disintegrating bullet that was to be used in flexible gunnery training to be fired at a real fighter under virtual combat conditions. Fairchild advanced his idea to Drs. Paul Gross and Marcus Hobbs at Duke University who experimented with .22 caliber rifle bullets. The first frangible bullets used tempered glass, and then the two professors settled on a Bakelite (an early plastic composed of phenolic resin) and powdered lead composition that crumbled easily upon impact. In July 1942 Fairchild advanced his frangible bullet proposal to the National Defense Research Committee (NDRC) and the Army's Ordnance Department which rejected the idea, saying that any frangible bullet would not have the same ballistic characteristics as actual ammunition and could not be fired from standard machine guns. Nonetheless, the NDRC granted limited funding and the development of the idea was delegated to the Duke contingent for continued development in conjunction with the Bakelite Corporation, while Princeton University was to conduct firing tests. By April 1944 the Bakelite/lead-filled bullets were refined for production and DuPont had developed the proper propellant powder. The round designated as the T44 was identified by its green tip followed by a white band to distinguish it from other more high-powered and potentially devastating .30 caliber rounds. It was fired by a slightly modified .30 caliber machine gun firing 800 rounds per minute at a very low muzzle velocity of 1,360 feet per second. Special sights were developed to compensate for the differences between the .50 caliber machine gun fired in combat and the .30 caliber machine gun that fired the frangible bullet. During the heavy training schedule it was found that the frangible bullet tips would fracture, causing the guns to jam. These "short rounds" continued to cause problems throughout the program. The powder used did not burn cleanly and caused accumulated carbon deposits and more jamming problems. An improved T-74 cartridge using a more effective powder which provided more consistent muzzle velocities and left fewer carbon deposits was being developed at the end of the war (See Part Seven/Chapter 2: Pinball for a description of the RP-63 pinball target aircraft and pinball training.).

Cartridge, Dummy, Caliber .30 M2

Dummy cartridges were manufactured and issued for training personnel for simulated firing, loading practice, and bench test firing. The M1906 dummy round, which had longitudinal identifying grooves, was replaced in 1944 by the M2, which had two identifying holes drilled in its brass (or steel) case.

.30 Caliber Primers

All the .30 caliber ammunition manufactured during World War II had corrosive primers because these primers remained stable under all types of climatic conditions and had a long storage life. During the decade 1931 to 1941, the Ordnance Department was unsuccessful in developing a satisfactory non-corrosive primer which had been used in commercial sporting rounds for a number of years. It would not be until the early 1950s that non-corrosive primers were adopted as standard.

# 6

# .50 Caliber Ammunition

**Background**

In spring 1918 the AEF General Staff sought a large caliber projectile of 670 grains with a minimum muzzle velocity of 2,700 fps. Originally, the British had investigated the German 13mm (.50 caliber) anti-tank cartridge, but American Expeditionary Force Commander Gen. John Pershing thought their study to be inadequate; however, its data merited assigning the Winchester Repeating Arms Co. to assume the American development of the .50 caliber cartridge for a machine gun to be developed by the Colt Fire Arms Co. under the direction of John Browning.

The first cartridge developed by Winchester was an upscaled .30 rimmed round, and in firing tests in summer 1918 it did not meet Ordnance Department specifications. A rimless round was then designed and a sample cartridge was sent to Colt. Using this sample round John Browning designed an upscaled version of his .30 caliber machine gun designated as the Model 1918 Browning. In September 1918 the new gun and cartridge were to be refined under John Browning, and Winchester was contracted to build six air-cooled .50 caliber aircraft guns from components developed and built by Colt (See Part One/Chapter 3/Section 3).

Once the 1918 Browning machine gun was contracted it was found that the Winchester round lacked power, and Winchester began to develop a cartridge with more penetrating power. On 10 December 1918 the Ordnance Department reassigned all future manufacture of the new round to the Frankfort Arsenal in Philadelphia, but ammunition standards were to be established by Winchester. Winchester then continued to supply the military with the original underpowered .50 caliber ammunition through 1919.

When the Model 1921 Browning was officially accepted the Frankfort Arsenal was assigned to improve on the Winchester round. Frankfort increased the chamber pressure and velocity, and in 1923 introduced the Cartridge, Caliber .50 M1923, which had a 800 grain steel core and was a tapered base (boat-tail) projectile with a 2,580 fps muzzle velocity.

Due to lack of Congressional appropriations no further work was done on developing the .50 round until the early 1930s when the Cartridge, Caliber .50 M1 was introduced in 1931. The M1 was a 750 grain steel core gilded metal projectile with a muzzle velocity of 2,660 fps. Tests showed that the M1 could penetrate 5/8 inch armor plate at 500 yards.

As war approached .50 caliber ammunition R&D increased, and the Cartridge Caliber .50 M2 was accepted in 1941. The cartridge fired a 711.5 grain projectile at a muzzle velocity of 2,800 fps and was so reliable and accurate that it was used throughout World War II, and remains in U.S. service to date. During World War II all American service cartridges used corrosive primer mixtures, and it wasn't until 1949 that the conversion

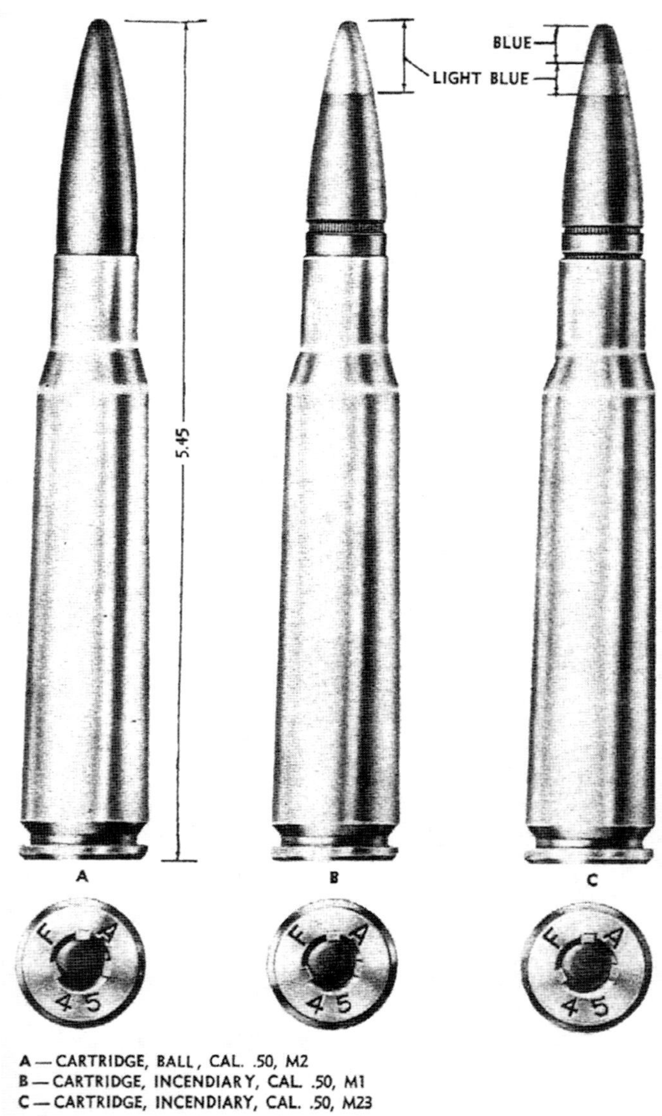


**.50 Caliber BALL and INCENDIARY (I)** (USAAF)

to non-corrosive primers was initiated and would not be completed until 1954.

**U.S. .50 Caliber Ammunition**
**Ball**

Early .50 caliber ammunition, like the actual "ball" used in old muzzle-loading rifles, had a bullet that lacked the special characteristics of material or construction which distinguished newer types (e.g. Armor-Piercing), and was continued to be designated as "ball" even though it was pointed. This early "ball" cartridge was the oldest service type cartridge and was replaced for combat use by other types, but the term was carried over to describe a type of ammunition used mainly for training purposes. The only air combat use of this "ball" ammunition in World War II was for emergency use at Pearl Harbor and in the Philippines in 1941 and 1942.

Cartridge, Ball, .50 Caliber M2

The M2 ball cartridge was introduced in 1941 and was the standard ball round used by infantry machine guns in World War II.

Cartridge

Ball cartridges were assembled with bullets that had lead or mild steel cores. The cartridge was 5.35 inches long and did not have any identifying markings, except being unpainted natural metal.

Bullet

The bullet consisted of three parts: metal or metal-clad jacket, a soft steel core, and an inert point filler. The 711.5 grain projectile was fired at a muzzle velocity of 2,810 fps. The bullet was 2.31 inches long and had a boat-tailed base. The outer jacket point contained a lead and antimony filler

| Authorized rounds and components | Average muzzle velocity (ft. per sec.) (36-in. bbl.) | Time of flight to 1,000 yards (sec.) | Elevation (deg.) | Maximum range (yd.) | Weight of rounds (lb.) |
|---|---|---|---|---|---|
| CARTRIDGE, armor-piercing, cal..50, M2. | 2,840 | 1.38 | 35 | 7,275 | 0.26 |
| CARTRIDGE, armor-piercing-incendiary, cal..50, M8. | 2,950 | 1.40 | 30 | 6,375 | 0.25 |
| CARTRIDGE, armor-piercing-incendiary-cal..50, T49. | 3,450 | ? | 30 | 5,500 | 0.23 |
| CARTRIDGE, armor-piercing-incendiary-tracer, cal..50, M20[1]. | 2,950 | 1.40 | 30 | 6,375 | 0.24 |
| CARTRIDGE, ball, cal..50, M2. | 2,840 | 1.38 | 35 | 7,275 | 0.26 |
| CARTRIDGE, incendiary, cal..50, M1. | 2,990 | 1.362 | 35 | 5,960 | 0.24 |
| CARTRIDGE, incendiary, cal..50, M23. | 3,450 | ? | 30 | 5,500 | 0.23 |
| CARTRIDGE, tracer, cal..50, M1[2, 3]. | 2,730 | 1.366 | 30 | 5,470 | 0.25 |
| M1 alternative[2, 3]..... | 2,900 | 1.366 (?) | 35 | 5,350 | 0.25 |
| CARTRIDGE, tracer, cal..50, M10[4]. | 2,900 | ? | 35 | 5,350 | 0.25 |
| CARTRIDGE, tracer, cal..50, M17[5]. | 2,900 | ? | 35 | 5,350 | 0.25 |
| CARTRIDGE, tracer, headlight, cal..50, M21[6]. | 2,730 | ? | 30 | 5,470 | 0.25 |
| M21 alternative[6]........ | 2,900 | ? | 35 | 5,350 | 0.25 |
| CARTRIDGE, blank, cal..50, M1 (T40). | ......... | ......... | ......... | ......... | ......... |
| CARTRIDGE, dummy, cal..50, M2. | ......... | ......... | ......... | ......... | ......... |
| LINK, metallic belt, cal..50, M1. | ......... | ......... | ......... | ......... | ......... |
| LINK, metallic belt, cal..50, M2. | ......... | ......... | ......... | ......... | ......... |
| LINK, metallic belt, cal..50, T31E2. | ......... | ......... | ......... | ......... | ......... |

1. Dim trace to 300 yards and bright trace to 1,750 yards.
2. Trace to 1,800 yards.
3. Limited to use in ground machine guns in continental United States and for training purposes only.
4. Dim trace to 150 yards and bright to 1,900 yards.
5. Trace to 2,450 yards.
6. Brilliant trace to 550 yards, visible from the target.

that covered the tip of the underlying steel core. When the projectile hit a target the soft outer jacket and filler smeared, giving the steel core a grip, and the core then penetrated the surface instead of being turned aside.

There were 105 million rounds of M2 ball ammunition manufactured at $97.50 per 1,000 rounds.

**Incendiary (I)**

Incendiary rounds were first developed during World War I when the bullet was filled with phosphorous and was ignited by the actual firing of the round. Generally, incendiary rounds were limited to use by aircraft armament to set the fuel tanks of targets on fire.

The common construction of an incendiary round was a jacketed bullet with the front half of the core removed and the space filled with white phosphorous that had the property of igniting spontaneously when coming in contact with the air. When the bullet was crushed on impact on a hard target the phosphorous was freed and immediately ignited. Phosphorous ammunition was dangerous and invariably leaked, causing many disastrous ammunition dump fires. During World War II, the incendiary composition was changed to barium nitrate and powdered aluminum and magnesium, and relied on the impact on the target to split the bullet and friction to ignite the mixture.

Cartridge, Incendiary, Caliber. 50 M1

Cartridge

This cartridge was 5.45 inches long and was identified by the light blue tip and by the second, knurled cannelure rolled into the bullet jacket.

Bullet

The bullet consisted of a metal jacket, a hollow, cylindrical steel body, a lead-antimony base slug, and a core and point filler of incendiary composition. The bullet was 2.09 inches long and had a square cylindrical base.

Cartridge, Incendiary, Caliber. 50 M23 (T48)

The M20 API was very effective against piston-powered aircraft because of their highly inflammable gasoline. However, when the German jets appeared their aviation kerosene was found to have a much higher flash point than gasoline and was much more difficult to set on fire. The Des Moines Ordnance plant developed the T48 cartridge with a projectile containing an incendiary compound specifically designed for igniting jet fuel. The T48 was so successful that it was soon standardized as the M23.

Cartridge

The cartridge was 5.45 inches long and was identified by the medium blue bullet tip with a light blue annulus to the rear.

Bullet

The 511 grain M23 bullet was similar in external appearance to the M1 Incendiary and consisted of a metal jacket, a clad steel container, a lead-antimony base slug, and an incendiary materiel which was greater than the amount in the M1. The bullet was 2.29 inches long and had a square cylindrical base. It was fired with a muzzle velocity of 3,400 fps.

De Wilde Incendiary Round

When the British found that they were going to use American Lend-Lease aircraft mounting the Browning .50 caliber machine gun they decided to replace the inferior American incendiary ammunition with the redesigned de Wilde incendiary round designated by the British as the .5 inch Incendiary B Mark IIZ. The de Wilde incendiary bullet had been developed in secret at Woolwich Arsenal at the start of the Battle of Britain by Maj. C. Aubrey Dixon and was an entirely new design. It was called "de Wilde" ammunition by the British as a subterfuge to make the Germans think it was based on the work of a Belgian based in Switzerland named de Wilde and not a new design.

**Armor-Piercing (AP)**

The AP bullet was first patented by Georg Roth of Vienna in 1903, but only came into use during World War I when snipers used it to penetrate the small steel shields that were being used as firing loopholes in trenches. Later tanks became the targets for AP bullets, but by World War II tanks had become more heavily armored and the AP bullet found a use in aerial combat.

The AP round was designed to penetrate light steel armor. It was formed of a hard steel core surrounded by a lead sleeve with both contained in the standard jacket. This type of design permitted the core to have the optimum point for piercing while the bullet had the optimum shape for accurate flight. The purpose of the lead sleeve was to add mass to the bullet so that it would sustain its velocity, and partly to provide a yielding substance beneath the jacket that would yield when the rifling engraved the jacket material. If there were no lead sleeve the engraving would impress directly on the steel core and would be ineffectual. The soft sleeve reduced the chance that the round would ricochet off the armor protecting the target. On impact the lead sleeve and jacket were stopped while the piercing core continued through the target, and the collapsed lead acted as a support to hold the bullet in alignment during the penetration.

Cartridge, Armor-Piercing, Caliber .50 M2

The U.S. Army Specification for the M2 AP round was developed by the Frankfort Arsenal and was approved as standard by the Ordnance Committed on 31 August 1939.

Cartridge

This cartridge was designed for use against aircraft armor, armored vehicles, concrete pillboxes, and "similar bullet-resisting targets." It was 5.45 inches long and was identified by a black bullet tip.

Bullet

The bullet consisted of three parts: metal jacket, a hardened core of tungsten-chrome or manganese molybdenum steel, and a point filler of antimony-lead alloy. The length was 2.31 inches overall with a 9° taper beginning 0.386 inches from the base. The projectile was fired at 2,930 fps and could penetrate a one inch armor plate at 200 yards.

If large quantities of AP ammunition were fired in moderately long bursts the barrel soon wore out; sometimes as quickly as during one active sortie. The .50 bullet was an enlarged version of the rifle caliber bullets, and with this type of projectile the body of the bullet was forced into the grooves of the rifling to provide the necessary spin. It was easy to achieve this spin when using a relatively soft lead bullet with its thin nickel-copper casing. When using AP rounds their hardened steel core and thin case did not "give" when engaging the rifling. Thus, the AP bullet did not give as good a gas seal as the lead bullet and some hot, high pressure gas escaped past the AP bullet and abraded the barrel. The solution was to redesign the AP bullet by adding a copper driving band similar to that on the 20mm shell. But implementing this remedy would have caused the shutting down and the re-tooling of the AP bullet production lines, so the easy answer to the problem was to manufacture more barrels.

There were 329 million rounds of AP ammunition manufactured at $108.50 per 1,000 rounds.

**Armor-Piercing Incendiary (API)**
API ammunition was used to set fire to armor-protected inflammable targets and replaced the Armor-Piercing M2 and the Incendiary M1. It was similar to the armor-piercing projectile, except that there was incendiary compound behind the steel core.

Cartridge, Armor-Piercing Incendiary, Caliber. 50 M8
By early 1943, combat reports revealed that an API round was needed. The M8 had been used previously for anti-aircraft gun .50 caliber ammunition. The M8 round was effective when manufactured in small quantities, but when mass-produced it lost muzzle velocity; in due course the manufacturing problems were solved and the use of the round increased.

Cartridge
The cartridge was 5.45 inches long and was identified by its aluminum-colored bullet tip.

Bullet
The bullet consisted of the same three parts as the standard M2 AP bullet, but the point filler was replaced by an incendiary composition and also contained a lead alloy base filler seal. The bullet was 2.31 inches long, weighed 662 grains, and was fired at a muzzle velocity of 2,910 fps. The round was linked with four M8s to one tracer round.

Cartridge, Armor-Piercing Incendiary, Caliber. 50 M20
In 1943 the M8 round was modified into the experimental T28 API round by adding additional incendiary and a new tracer compound. In June 1944 the T28 was officially adopted as the M20 API, which was very successful in combat, requiring only a few hits to set an enemy aircraft on fire (especially the highly inflammable Japanese aircraft). The M8 API round has been considered the best .50 caliber round of the war.

Cartridge
The cartridge was 5.45 inches long and was identified red bullet tip and aluminum annulus in the rear.

Bullet
The projectile weighed 619 grains with a muzzle velocity of 2,910 fps. The visible trace started at about 100 yards and continued to at least 1,600 yards. The M8 bullet was able to completely penetrate 7/8 inch armor plate at 100 yards.

Cartridge, Armor-Piercing Incendiary, Caliber .50 T-49
The T-49 was a higher velocity experimental API than the M8 that was developed in 1945.

Cartridge
The cartridge had the same dimensions, but was identified by the medium blue bullet tip with an aluminum color annulus at the rear.

Bullet
The 501 grain bullet consisted of the same three parts as the M2 AP and M8 with a point that was replaced by an incendiary composition. The bullet was shorter at 1.935 inches and had a square base. It fired at a muzzle velocity in excess of 3,430 fps, which was found to cause severe barrel erosion, and the T49 project was subsequently discontinued.

There were 70.3 million rounds of API ammunition manufactured at $114 per 1,000 rounds.

**Tracer**
A tracer is a bullet that leaves a visible mark or "trace" while in flight so that the gunner can observe the path and striking point of the bullets and make any necessary adjustments, but the high visibility of the tracer warns the target. Tracer rounds had a slightly different trajectory from regular rounds, especially in .30 caliber form. The ballistic problem with the tracer was that just after leaving the gun's muzzle the regular round and the tracer would have the same speed and trajectory, but as the tracer bullet traveled the tracer composition was burned away and the weight and balance of the bullet changed, so the tracer bullet would have a different trajectory. The use of the tracer as a sighting device is discussed in detail in Chapter Four: Gunsights.

The 8AF reported the following disadvantages of tracers. Tracer-firing gunners tended to ignore their sights and use the tracers as a (poor) sighting aid, as the tracer offered serious optical illusions. Each tracer round linked in a belt meant the loss of an effective destructive round, as the tracer had no armor-piercing effect and negligible incendiary properties. However, the tracer did have the effect of warning other gunners in the bomber and in surrounding bombers in the formation of an impending attack, as gunners tended to become less alert after hours in the cold and on oxygen. Also, interrogated *Luftwaffe* fighter pilots confirmed that the tracer did have a

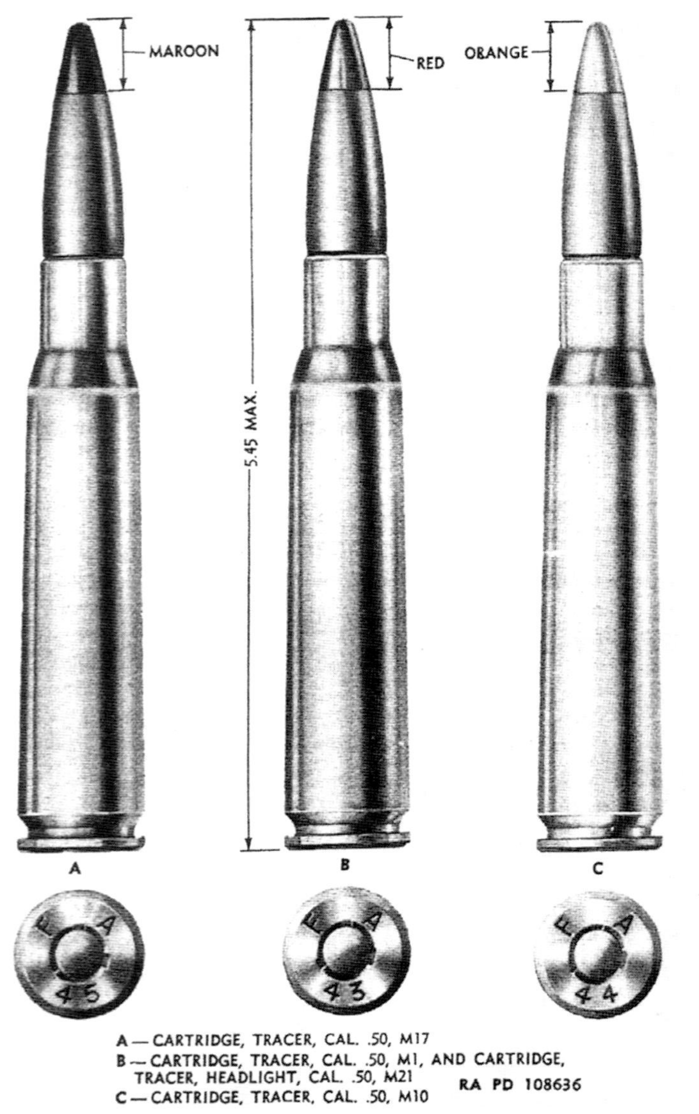


**.50 Caliber ARMOR-PIERCING (AP)** (USAAF)

definite deterrent effect on their attack, especially after the introduction of the more brilliant "headlight" tracer in 1944. U.S. fighter pilots did not like to use tracers, as they would warn the enemy of the initiation of an attack. In early war fighter aircraft some units placed a single strip of five tracers 50 rounds from the end of each belt as a warning of low ammunition, but this practice was discontinued, as it also warned the enemy that his adversary was low on ammunition.

Tracer rounds resembled ball rounds, but had the rear portion of the bullet core removed and the space filled with a chemical, or the chemical pressed directly into the bullet or loaded into a copper tube that was inserted into the bullet. Inside the outer metal jacket was a slug of lead and antimony. The pocket of tracer composition was set afire by the propelling charge as the projectile left the cartridge case. It is commonly believed that tracers were filled with phosphorous, but tracer mixtures were based on barium nitrate and powdered magnesium with strontium nitrate added to give the red color. The mixture burned during the bullet's flight, releasing red sparks that because of the persistence of human vision appeared as a continuous line of red. The brightness of the trace could be varied to match the conditions to which it was to be employed. The M21 "headlight" tracer left a particularly brilliant trace.

There were numerous types of tracer cartridges used during World War II.

Cartridge, Tracer, Caliber .50 M1

The M1 tracer was adopted in 1931 and replaced in 1944 by the M17 tracer.

Cartridge

The tracer was used for firing observation, and the bright red trace began at 250 feet from the gun and continued for approximately 1,600 to 1,800 yards. The cartridge was 5.45 inches long and was identified by its red tip.

Bullet

The projectile weighed 676 grains and fired at a muzzle velocity of 2,700 fps. The bullet consisted of three parts: a gilded steel metal jacket or copper-washed metal-clad jacket, an antimony-lead slug that filled the forward end of the jacket, and tracer and igniter compositions that filled the remainder. Unlike the bullets for AP and Ball cartridges, the tracer bullet was cylindrical to the base, which was open to allow the propelling charge to ignite the tracer materiel. The overall length of the bullet was 2.40 inches.

Cartridge, Tracer, Caliber .50 M2

The M2 was adopted in 1942 and used only until 1943. The M2 was similar to the M1 apart from a steel core was used. The tip of the round was painted white.

Cartridge, Tracer, Caliber .50 M10

The M10 was adopted in 1943 and was used to lessen the initial blinding effect of the M1 and M2 tracer during observation during firing.

Cartridge

This less bright cartridge served the same purpose as the Tracer M1. The cartridge was 5.45 inches long and was identified by the orange bullet tip.

Bullet

The appearance and external ballistics of the M10 was the same as for the Tracer M1 or M2 with a steel-clad jacket. The M10 either had a 150 yard delay or a dim trace for the first 225 yards of flight, followed by a bright trace for the next 1,600 to 1,900 yards. The round was for day or night use. The projectile weighed 643 grains and fired with a muzzle velocity of 2,860fps.

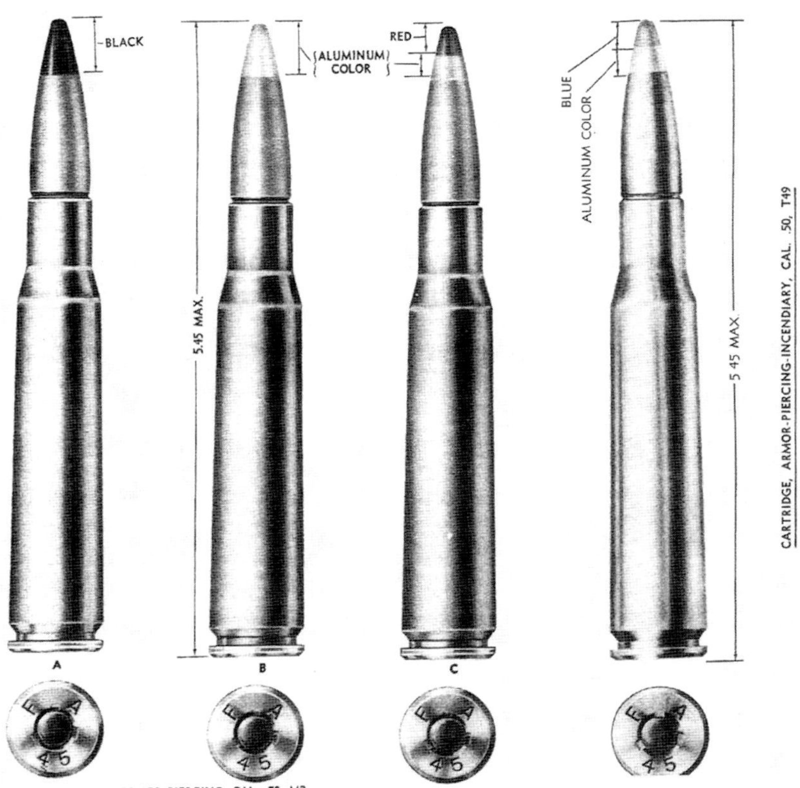


A — CARTRIDGE, ARMOR-PIERCING, CAL. .50, M2
B — CARTRIDGE, ARMOR-PIERCING-INCENDIARY, CAL. .50, M8
C — CARTRIDGE, ARMOR-PIERCING-INCENDIARY-TRACER, CAL. .50, M20

**.50 Caliber TRACER (T)** (USAAF)

Cartridge, Tracer, Caliber .50 M17
The M17 replaced the Tracer M1/M2 as a specially requested brighter tracer round for daylight use. The M17 was replaced by the M20 for aircraft use in March 1945.

Cartridge
The cartridge was 5.45 inches long and was identified by its brown bullet tip.

Bullet
The appearance and external ballistics of the M17 were the same as the M1/M2 with a metal-clad steel jacket, except that the M17 had a bright trace beginning at about 250 yards to about 2,450 yards of flight. The projectile weighed 643 grains with a muzzle velocity of 2,860 fps.

Cartridge, Tracer, Caliber .50 M21 "Headlight"
The M21 was adopted in 1945 principally for aircraft use.

Cartridge
The cartridge measured 5.45 inches long and was identified by its red bullet tip.

Bullet
The description and exterior ballistics of the M21 were the same as the Tracer M1/M2, except it had an incendiary compound mixed with the tracer compound. The projectile weighed 699 grains with a muzzle velocity of 2,840 fps. The trace of the M21 when viewed from the front was about three times brighter than the M1/M2 Tracer due to its igniter materiel rather than its tracer composition. The M21 had a very bright trace to about 550 yards and had some incendiary effect at 150 to 330 yards that became negligible after 600 yards. To minimize the disadvantages and maximize the advantages of tracers the 8AF used headlight tracers only in the nose and tail positions of their bombers, where pointblank shots predominated and where optical illusion was maximized. The linkage was one tracer to four AP rounds repeated in these positions and straight AP in all other gun positions.

There were 135.9 million rounds of tracer ammunition manufactured at $120.50 per 1,000 rounds.

**Cartridge, Dummy, Caliber .50 M1 and M2**
The dummy M1 and M2 was used for training personnel in loading and unloading machine guns and ammunition belts, or to bench test gun ejection and extraction mechanisms. The cartridge was 5.45 inches long and was identified by having no primer, and by the three holes drilled at equal distances around the middle of the case, which was either brass or steel.

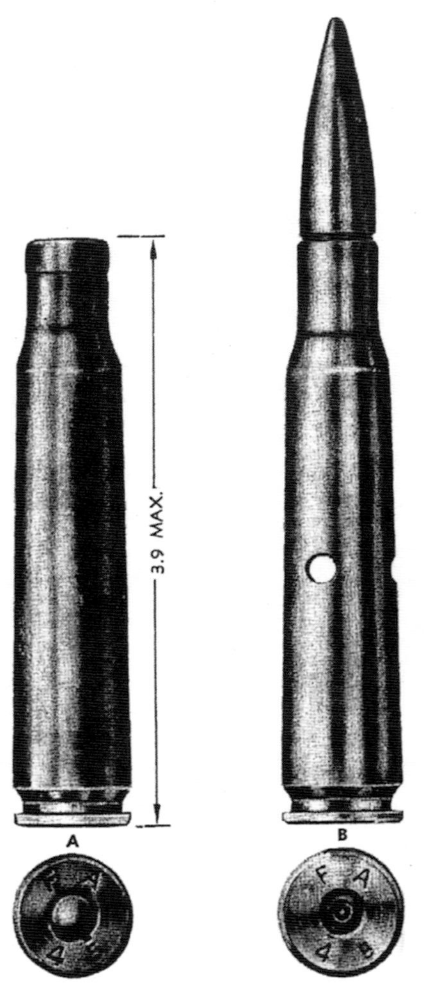


A — CARTRIDGE, BLANK, CAL. .50, M1 (T40)
B — CARTRIDGE, DUMMY, CAL. .50, M2

**.50 Caliber BLANK and DUMMY** (USAAF)

The bullet was metal or metal-clad steel jacket and measured 2.40 inches long and a square cylindrical base.

**Cartridge, Blank, Caliber .50 M2**

The blank M2 was used for training with special blank-firing devices attached to the gun. The cartridge had no bullet and measured 3.91 inches long, and was identified by a shallow annular groove located approximately 1/4 inch from the mouth, which serves as a seat for the wad, which was a disk punched out of 1/16 inch strawboard sheet, lacquered on both sides before insertion into the mouth of the case. After loading a heavy coat of lacquer was painted on the wad and the mouth was crimped.

**High Explosive**

During the war work was done to develop a high explosive .50 caliber round but did not meet with success because of the small size of the projectile prevented the insertion of explosive material.

**.50 Caliber Ammunition**

| Cartridge Type | Weight of Round (lbs) | Avg. Muzzle Velocity ( fps) | Time of Flight* (sec) | Maximum Range (yards) |
|---|---|---|---|---|
| Ball M1 | 0.26 | 2,840 | 1.38 | 7,275 |
| AP M2 | 0.26 | 2,840 | 1.38 | 7,275 |
| AP M8 | 0.25 | 2,950 | 1.40 | 6,375 |
| API T49 | 0.23 | 3,450 | 1.10 | 5,500 |
| API-T M20 | 0.24 | 2,960 | 1.40 | 6,375 |
| I M1 | 0.24 | 2,990 | 1.36 | 5,960 |
| I M23 | 0.23 | 3,450 | 1.10 | 5,500 |
| T M1 | 0.25 | 2,730 | 1.37 | 5,470 |
| T M10 | 0.25 | 2,900 | 1.37 | 5,350 |
| T M17 | 0.25 | 2,900 | 1.37 | 5,350 |
| T M21 | 0.25 | 2,730 | 1.36 | 5,470 |

* To 1,000 yards

The trajectories of the .50 caliber service bullet, except the incendiary M23 and API T49 cartridges, matched at 1,000 yards. The time of flight did not differ by more than 1/10 second under specified conditions. The bullets of M23 and API T49 cartridges were lighter than other service bullets, weighing about 500 grains, and had a muzzle velocity of 3,450 fps and had matched ballistics.

**Quantities and Cost of .50 Caliber Ammunition Types in World War II**

| Type | Quantity (million) | Cost (per 1,000 rounds) |
|---|---|---|
| Ball M2 | 105.00 | $97.50 |
| AP M2 | 328.90 | $108.50 |
| API M8 | 70.31 | $114.00 |
| Tracer M1 | 135.88 | $120.50 |

# 7

# .60 Caliber Ammunition

On 11 January 1939, the Ordnance Committee established a requirement for the development of an anti-tank rifle to fire a bullet which would penetrate a minimum of 1.25 inches of armor plate at normal impact at a range of 500 yards. The Committee used information from abroad and data from tests against light armor at the Aberdeen Proving Ground to determine the expected performances of various gun calibers from .30 to .80 caliber. The Committee established that a .60 caliber cartridge with the following characteristics was the lightest that could be expected to meet the armor penetration requirements that were formally established by the Ordnance Committee on 7 February 1939:

| | |
|---|---|
| Caliber | 0.60 inches |
| Weight of Bullet | 1,200 grains |
| Muzzle Velocity | 3,420 feet per second |
| Striking Velocity at 500 Yards | 2,850 feet per second |

As originally conceived, the .60 caliber cartridge case represented, with minor dimensional differences, an expansion of the 0.276 caliber cartridge case developed during 1925-1929. Frankford Arsenal and Aberdeen Proving Ground were requested to make a study of a complete round with the above characteristics and recommend a design.

Winchester was granted a contract to develop the .60 caliber round that would meet the requirements, and to manufacture Mann-type barrels for testing the rounds. In testing the performance of the Winchester ammunition was unacceptable, as the flight of the bullet was very erratic and failed to penetrate 1.25 inch armor plate at 100 yards. It was inaccurate as close as 50 feet due to the barrel rifling being engraved unevenly. On completion of the Winchester contract in September 1940, the project was assigned to the Frankford Arsenal Ordnance Laboratory.

On 22 May 1941, the Ordnance Committee approved the development of a caliber .60 aircraft machine gun, and in October 1942 the AAF reaffirmed its interest in the development of the .60 caliber aircraft machine gun and requested three test models. On 27 October 1942, a conference was held at Frankfort Arsenal to begin the development and manufacture of armor-piercing and tracer ammunition for the .60 caliber tank rifle and aircraft machine gun.

On 22 May 1943, the requirement for the .60 caliber anti-tank rifle was terminated by the Ordnance Committee because of the relative ineffectiveness of such ammunition against the new types of heavier armored enemy vehicles. However, the development of .60 caliber ammunition for the aircraft machine gun continued, and by 2 December 1943 ball, armor-piercing, incendiary, and armor-piercing-tracer ammunition had been developed.

In the initial development of .60 caliber aerial ammunition, primary consideration was given to the armor-piercing cartridge. A duplicate round, with a mild steel core in place of a hardened steel core, was considered for training purposes. In the course of development work on the armor-piercing bullet, it seemed advisable to develop base-capped bullets with the bare steel cores. Mild steel cores were used for tests to determine bullet stability.

The imminent production of ammunition on a relatively large scale in December 1943, as well as attempts to increase barrel life by increasing the depth of rifling, led to the development and testing of a number of modifications of the original .60 caliber cartridge case.

The T1/T1E1/T1E2/T1E3 series and T2/T2E1/T2E2/T2E3 series were modified types of .60 caliber cases that had adapted rifling groove at .606 inch (E1), thick necks at .03 inch (E2), or an E1 with a thicker neck at .35 inch (E3). The T2E4 case had a rifling groove diameter of 0.604 inch and a thick neck of .30 inch, and was adapted to the .604 inch rifling groove diameter. As a result of successful firing at Aberdeen Proving Ground, Frankfort Arsenal, and the St. Louis Ordnance Plant, the T2E4 cartridge case was adopted for mass production. All production ammunition was assembled with this case.

# 8

## 20mm Ammunition

20mm ammunition was issued as fused complete rounds of fixed ammunition. "Fixed" refers to a propelling charge that was not adjustable and to a round that was fed into the gun as a unit. The propellant charge was assembled loosely in the cartridge case that was rigidly crimped to the projectile. The ammunition was classified as high explosive, high explosive incendiary, armor piercing-tracer, and ball with the Standard Nomenclature completely identifying each round.

**High Explosive (HE)**

HE rounds were manufactured by boring out the core of the solid projectile and filling it with high explosive. TNT was the type of high explosive generally used in HE shells during World War I, but often TNT was mixed with ammonium nitrate to produce Amatol, which was as effective and less expensive, but was susceptible to contamination by moisture. In the inter-war years new and more powerful explosives were developed including RDX (**R**esearch **D**epartment e**X**plosive), Pentolite, Tetryl (Composition Exploding CE), and Torpex (a mixture of RDX, TNT, and aluminum).

**20mm Cartridge HE-I MK I with Fuse PD 253**

The HE-I shells were conventional thick-walled types with less HE capacity, but with much more kinetic energy, generating larger and heavier fragments that carried further and impacted deeper than those produced by the *Luftwaffe* M-geschoss shell. This round was for use against light skinned targets, functioning with both explosive and incendiary effect. After the shell penetrated the target the high explosive filler was detonated, the shell was shattered into fragments, and the incendiary composition ignited. The round consisted of a primer and a propelling charge contained in a brass cartridge case that was crimped rigidly to the projectile and a "superquick" fuse. The 0.29 pound projectile contained 0.03 pounds of high explosive and incendiary fillers. The round was 7.19 inches long and weighed 0.57 pounds. The propelling charge weighed 0.07 pounds, consisting of loose flashless nonhygroscopic (FNH) smokeless powder contained in a cartridge case.

**20mm Cartridge AP-T M75**

This fuseless round consisted of a primer and a propelling charge contained in a brass cartridge case that was crimped rigidly to the projectile. The projectile was a solid steel shot and contained a red tracer composition in its base. The round was 7.22 inches long and weighed 0.64 pounds, of which the projectile weighed 0.37 pounds. The propelling charge weighed 0.07 pounds and consisted of loose flashless nonhygroscopic (FNH) smokeless powder contained in a cartridge case. This round was for use against armored targets.

**20mm Cartridge Ball**

The ball round consisted of a primer and a propelling charge that was contained in a brass cartridge case crimped rigidly to the projectile. The

**20mm Linked Cartridges** (Author's Collection)

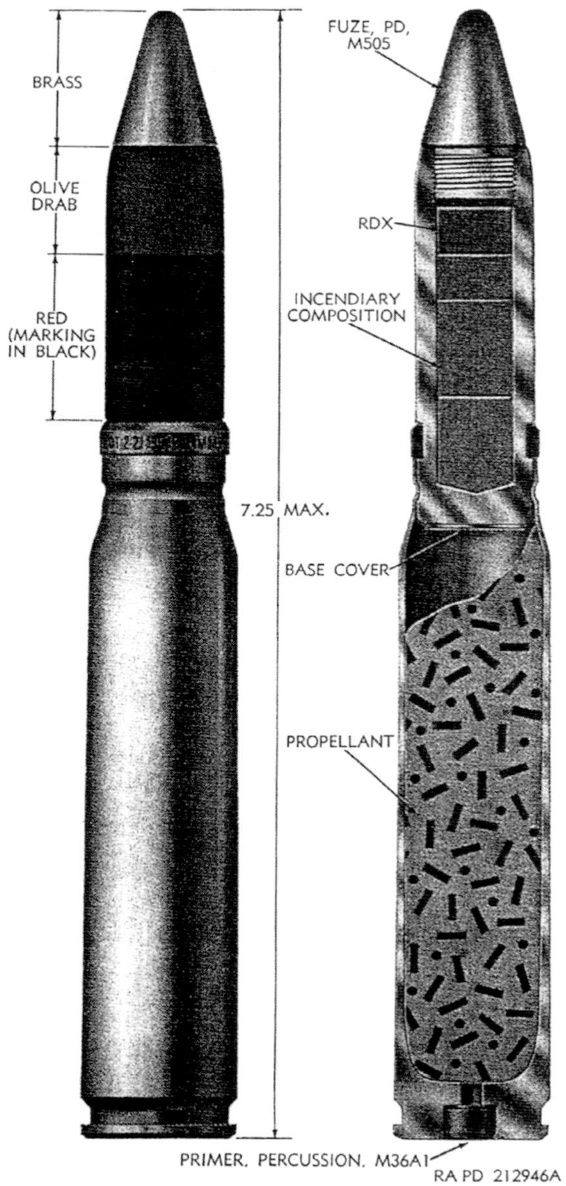


*Figure 7. Cartridge, 20 millimeter: HEI, M58 (T241), w/fuze, PD, M505.*

**20mm HEI, M58** (USAAF)

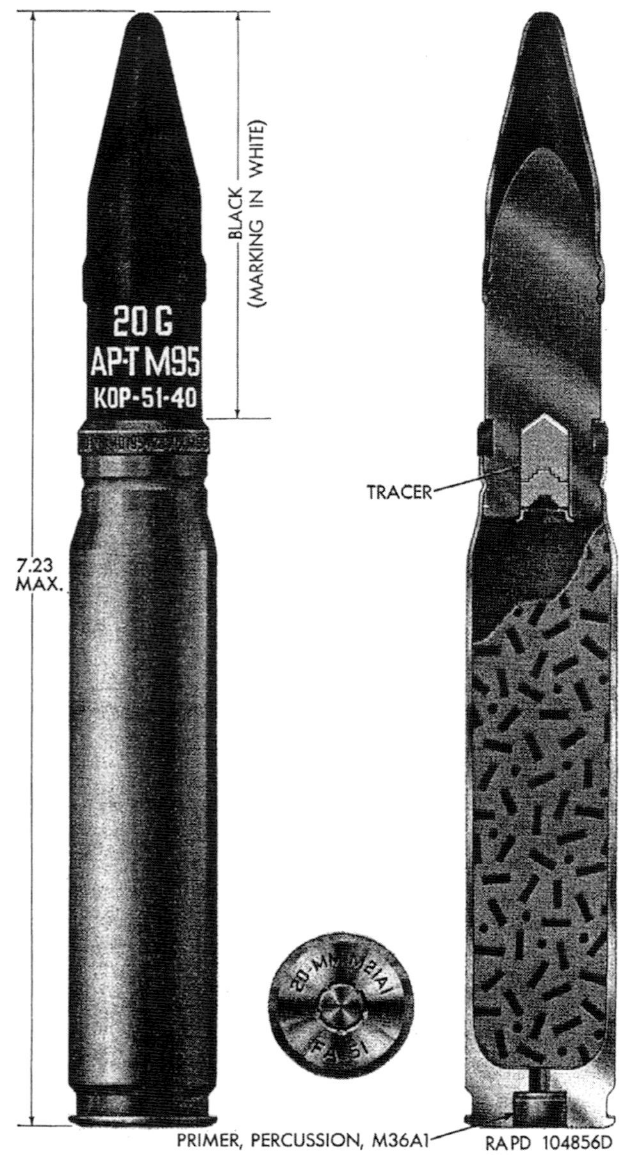


*Figure 6. Cartridge, 20 millimeter: AP-T, M95.*

**20mm AP-T, M96** (USAAF)

projectile contained no explosive and had no fuse, and was similar in shape and ballistic properties to the point-fused HE-I round. The round was 7.23 inches long and weighed 0.57 pounds, of which the projectile comprised 0.29 pounds. The propelling charge weighed 0.07 pounds and consisted of loose flashless nonhygroscopic (FNH) smokeless powder contained in a cartridge case. This complete round was used against personnel and light materiel targets and for practice.

**20mm High Capacity Cases T5 and 77**

Toward the end of the war, as enemy aircraft and vehicle armor increased in thickness, the Ordnance Department designed a new case for 20mm projectiles to improve armor penetration by aircraft guns by increasing muzzle velocity. Preliminary testing revealed that a high muzzle velocity of 3,500 fps could be attained using a barrel 78 inches long. When using the standard 20mm armor-piercing projectile, one inch face-hardened armor was penetrated at 200 yards. The T5 case was not extensively used.

**20mm Fuses**

A fuse is a mechanical device used in a projectile to explode at a desired time and circumstance. A fuse designed to function upon impact with a target was classified as an impact type, while a fuse designed to function upon immediate impact with a light materiel target was classified as a superquick fuse. The Fuse P.D 253 MK I or MK II was an instantaneous percussion fuse of the impact type, for penetration of light armor and the

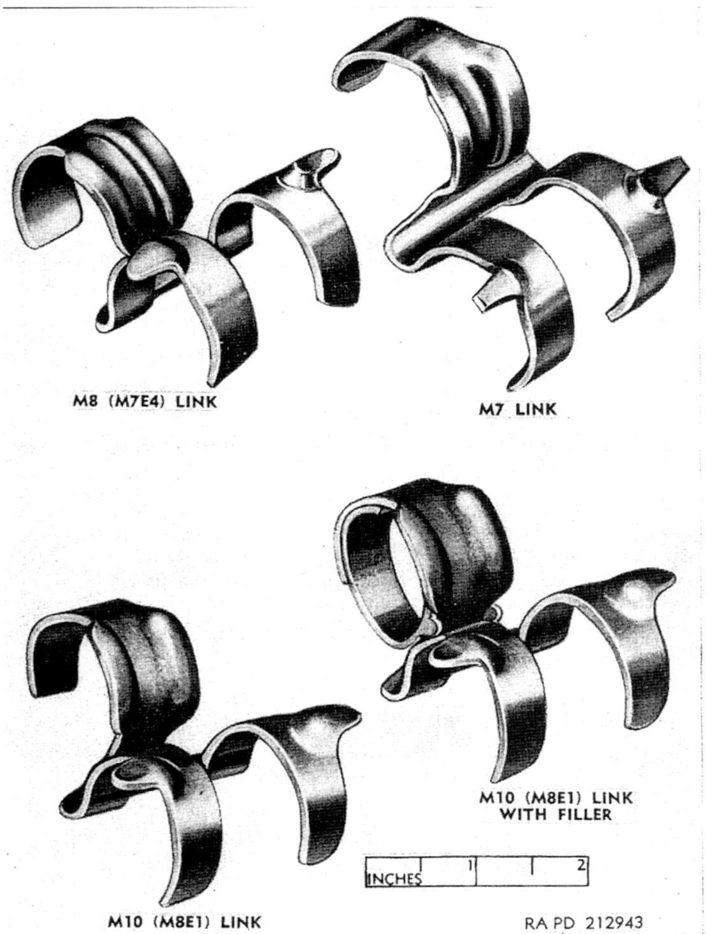


*Figure 5. Cartridge links and cartridge link filler for ammunition for 20-mm gun M3.*

**Cartridge Links and Cartridge Link Filler** (USAAF)

heavier armor of aircraft. They were used with 20mm HE-I aircraft ammunition and were issued assembled to the HE-I projectile of the fixed complete round of Cartridge HE-I MK I.

**Self-Destruct Systems**

Since aerial combat could often take place over friendly territory self-destruct systems were incorporated in rounds before they could cause collateral damage. They could vary from simple chemical systems that took a preset time to burn or complicated mechanical fuses. Nearly all cannon shells were designed so that an explosive charge inside the projectile would explode in flight after its tracer component had completed its burning—about seven to ten seconds. This elapsed time could be preset during manufacture and the timed ammunition could be chosen as dictated by tactical requirements.

**20mm Identification**

Mark or Model

At the time ammunition was adopted as type, a model designation was assigned. This model designation became a fundamental part of the standard nomenclature of the ammunition and was included in its marking. The model designation consisted of the letter M followed by an Arabic numeral, and modifications were indicated by adding the letter A and the appropriate Arabic numeral. M1A1 indicated the first modification for which the original model designation was M1. An exception was found in some models of 20mm ammunition that were designated as "Mark" (abbreviated MK) followed by a Roman numeral. The unusual nomenclature of some rounds was due to the names originating from British, U.S. Navy, or U.S. Army Ordnance.

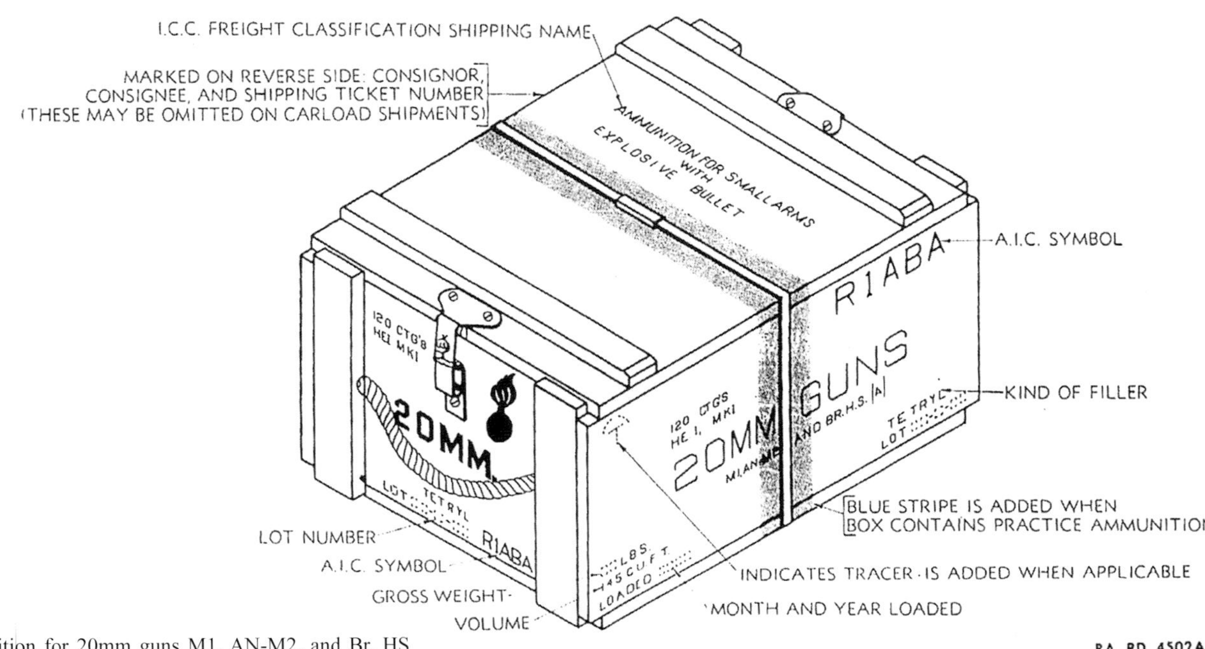


Packing box for ammunition for 20mm guns M1, AN-M2, and Br. HS (USAAF)

Lot Number
When ammunition was manufactured an ammunition lot number, which became a basic part of marking, was assigned conforming to applicable specifications. The lot number was stamped or marked on every complete round and on all packing containers. It was required for recording the condition, functioning, and any accidents in which the ammunition was involved. For uniform functioning all rounds of one lot the projectiles, fuses, primers, and propellant powder comprising those rounds were to be from one lot.

Painting
Projectiles were painted to prevent rust, but also to provide a quick method of identification as to type.

20mm Painting

| | |
|---|---|
| High Explosive Incendiary | Yellow ogive, red body; black marking |
| Armor-Piercing | Black; marking in white |
| Ball (inert) | Black; marking in white |

Marking
The following was marked or stamped on the components of each 20mm round:

A) Projectile
Stenciled
HEI: Type of filler
AP: Caliber and type of weapon firing; Model of projectile; and "WITH TRACER."

Ammunition lot number and loader's initials.

Stamped in Metal
HEI and Practice (On body): Manufacturer's initials or symbol; Lot number of empty projectile; Month and year of manufacture.
AP (On base end): Manufacturer's initials or symbol; Lot number of empty projectile; Month and year of manufacture; Caliber and designation of shot.
Designation and caliber of case; Manufacturer's initial or symbol; Year of manufacture (in full).

B) Fuse (Stamped in metal)
Model and designation of the fuse.
Loader's lot number.
Year of loading.

**Packing**
Complete 20mm rounds were packed to withstand conditions usually found in the field. 20mm ammunition was packed in cartons (ten rounds per carton) which were enclosed in metal-lined wooden boxes. Twelve cartons (120 rounds) were sealed in metal-lined packing boxes. 120 HE-I rounds (0.57 pounds per round) weighed 94.8 pounds, while 120 AP rounds (0.64 pounds per round) weighed 103 pounds. The packing box dimensions were 18.7x13.2x10.3 inches totaling 1.48 cubic inches. Since explosives were harmfully affected by moisture and high temperatures care had to be taken to protect ammunition. Fused HE ammunition was particularly sensitive to excessive shock, very high temperatures, and direct sunlight. Care was to be taken not to break the moisture-resistant seal until the round was to be used. Protection or safety devices were not to be removed from fuses until just before use.

**Oiling Rounds**
Although the use of oil or grease on ammunition was normally prohibited, its use on 20mm cartridges was necessary to prevent jamming in American-made Hispano cannon. A cloth was immersed in Oil, Lubricant, Preservative, Special and then wrung out, and was to be used to wipe the body of each cartridge case before inserting the round into the magazine or belt. If Oil, Lubricant, Preservative, Special was not available then Oil, Lubricant, Preservative, Light was to be used. "Extreme" care was to be taken not to get oil on the primer or joint at the mouth of the cartridge case. Only one day's supply of ammunition was to be lubricated at a time. Rounds oiled for firing and not fired that same day were to be wiped dry to prevent the accumulation of dust and grit, and to prevent the seepage of oil around the primer and mouth of the cartridge case. When used again these rounds were to be re-oiled before use.

# 9

# 37mm Ammunition

37mm ammunition was issued in fixed complete rounds that were fed into the gun as a unit. The cartridge case was rigidly crimped to the impact-type fused projectile. The ammunition was either high explosive, armor-piercing, or practice. The HE contained high explosive filler, while the practice type contained no filler, but all types could use tracers. The tracer in the HE projectile was shell-destroying because if the projectile did not hit the target the trace material would burn through and destroy the projectile.

**37mm Identification**

37mm ammunition and its components were completely identified by painting, marking, and accompanying data card. Model designation consisted of the letter M followed by an Arabic numeral. Modifications were indicated by the letter A and the suitable Arabic numeral. M55A1 was the first modification of the M55 practice shell. All shells were painted to prevent rust, and the 37mm color schemes were yellow for HE and blue for the practice rounds.

The following information was stenciled on the projectile:

1) Caliber and type of cannon in which it was to be fired.
2) Model of projectile.
3) Lot number of loaded projectile.

Because the lot number of a loaded projectile was not usually required after the complete round was assembled it was stenciled below the rotating band, where it was covered by the neck of the cartridge case.

The following was stenciled in black on the base of the cartridge case:

1) Caliber and cannon in which it was to be fired.
2) Powder lot number.
3) Muzzle velocity in fps.
4) Ammunition lot number and loader's initials.

**37mm Ammunition Types**

The 37mm ammunition types were: M54 HE shell; M56 HE with PD (point detonating) fuse; M80 AP shot; M55A1 practice shell; and M50 practice shell with dummy fuse. The 37mm M4 cannon used the same ammunition M54 HE and M55A1 Practice shells as the M1A2 anti-aircraft gun, but different cartridge cases were necessary due to the larger chamber of the M4 aircraft gun. The overall length of the M51 and M74 AP shells used in the M3A1, M5A1, and M6 tank and anti-tank guns were too large for use in the aircraft gun.

M54 HE Standard Shell

The complete round weighed 1.99 pounds and the projectile weighed 1.34 pounds. The 0.16 pound M2 powder charge was a Hercules NG formula of single perforated grains with a 0.03 inch web to give the projectile a 2,000 fps muzzle velocity. The M54 shell used a M56 point detonating fuse. The M54 also carried a shell-destroying tracer fuse that had a burning time of three seconds that set off an igniting relay charge of 1.68 grains of Grade A-5 Army Black Powder that ignited a relay pellet to detonate the charge and destroyed the projectile before it impacted the ground.

The bursting tetryl charge weighed 0.10 pound, and the alternate Composition A charge weighed 0.105 pounds. The tetryl loading consisted of a 200 grain tetryl pellet pressed into the cavity. The Composition A bursting charge was similarly loaded as the tetryl charge, except that the relay pellet with the Composition A weighed 36 grains versus 23 grains for the pellet used in the tetryl load.

M80 AP Shot

The weight of the completed round was 2.31 pounds and the weight of the AP shot was 1.66 pounds. The round had a length of 9.75 inches and a diameter of 1.77 inches. The propelling charge weighed 0.15 pound of M2 Hercules NG powder with a single-perforated grain and 0.03 inch web. The shot was a monoblock projectile with a tracer element that burned for three seconds and had no fuse or bursting charge.

37mm shell from author's collection.

M55A1 Practice Standard Shell
The M55A1 was a high explosive shell that was slightly modified for use in practice. The complete round weighed 1.99 pounds and the fired shell weighed 1.34 pounds. The 0.16 pound M2 powder charge was Hercules NG of single perforated grains with a 0.03 inch web and yielded a muzzle velocity of 2,000 feet per second. It contained a red tracer and dummy fuses (either M50, M501, M50B2, or M50B3). The M50 was a plastic composition, while the other three fuses were made from low carbon steel machined to have the same weight and shape as the M56 point-detonating fuse used with the M54 Standard projectile.

**Packing**
Twenty rounds weighing 61 pounds were packed in a sealed metal-lined wooden packing box that measured 15.1x11.7x13.2 inches. Complete rounds and ammunition components were to be packed to withstand conditions that were ordinarily encountered in the field. Since explosives were harmfully affected by moisture and high temperatures care was to be taken to protect ammunition. Fused HE ammunition was particularly sensitive to excessive shock, very high temperatures, and direct sunlight. Care was to be taken not to break the moisture-resistant seal until the round was to be used. Protection or safety devices were not to be removed from fuses until just before use.

**American Armament Corporation 37mm Cannon Ammunition**
American Armament Corporation (AAC) developed an effective type of ammunition for its pre-war 37mm cannon. The projectiles were loaded with cast TNT and carried a very sensitive and quick-action nose fuse. The fuses were so sensitive that even fabric-covered sections of a target's empennage would ignite them. The explosive train acted so quickly that even though the projectile was traveling at high velocity the shell moved only an extremely short distance during the explosive train and a large hole was made in the target. Cast TNT was chosen to obtain the maximum amount of explosive into the available space and to produce the maximum explosive effect. The American Armament Corporation developed a safety "bore safe" or "detonator safe" device that held the mercury fulminate detonator so it could not explode during handling or while in the bore. Once the projectile passed the muzzle the safety device was moved into the firing position.

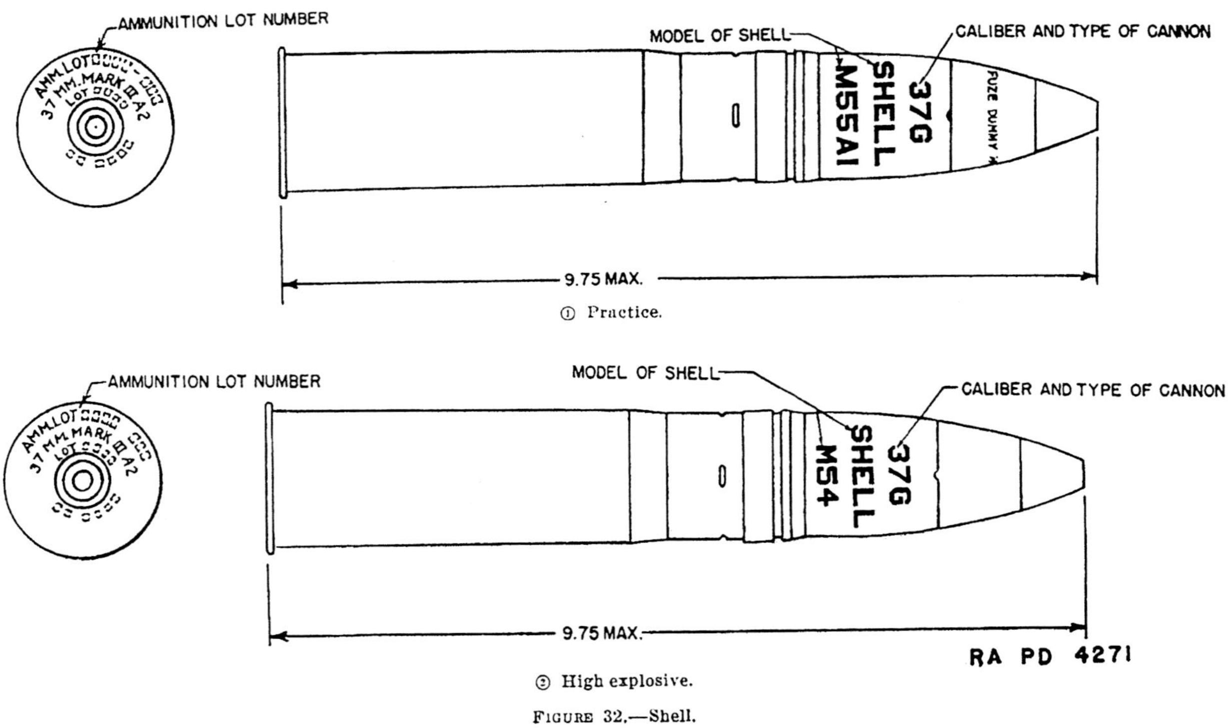


**37mm Shell M55A1 and M54** (USAAF)

# 10

## 75mm Ammunition

The 75mm M48 HE projectile was 26 inches long and three inches in diameter and weighed 20 pounds (equivalent to 78 .50 caliber bullets), of which 15 pounds was the projectile that contained 1.5 pounds of TNT and a propellant weight of .92 pounds. Armor-piercing and smoke shells were the other types of 75mm shells.

Bottom left: Comparison of a 75mm shell and a belt of .50 caliber machine gun bullets (one 75mm shell was equivalent to 78 .50 caliber bullets). (Author/Barbie III) Bottom right: North American Aviation publicity photo of pretty girl worker holding 75mm cannon shell in front of the company's B-25 G. (Author/NAA)

# 11

# Ammunition Expended in World War II

**USAAF Ammunition Expenditure by Theater in World War II**
**(In 1000s of Rounds)**

**.30 Caliber Ammunition Expenditure**

| Theater | 1942 | 1943 | 1944 | 1945 | Total |
|---|---|---|---|---|---|
| ETO | 53 | 616 | 23 | 58 | 750 |
| MTO | 8 | 247 | 730 | 27 | 1,012 |
| PTO | 3 | 46 | 282 | 42 | 373 |
| FEAF | 326 | 2,345 | 2,116 | 5 | 4,792 |
| CBI | 4 | 157 | 37 | ---- | 198 |
| Alaska | 28 | 132 | ---- | ---- | 160 |
| 20AF | ---- | ---- | ---- | ---- | ---- |
| Total | 422 | 3,443 | 3.188 | 132 | 7185 |

**.50 Caliber Ammunition Expenditure**

| Theater | 1942 | 1943 | 1944 | 1945 | Total |
|---|---|---|---|---|---|
| ETO | 1,660 | 27,964 | 104,444 | 61,351 | 195,419 |
| MTO | 1,439 | 17,652 | 50,699 | 19,777 | 89,507 |
| PTO | 38 | 647 | 5,727 | 4,552 | 10,964 |
| FEAF | 982 | 11,186 | 39,481 | 52,183 | 103,832 |
| CBI | 170 | 3,305 | 17,917 | 14,527 | 35,919 |
| Alaska | 248 | 1,117 | 107 | 251 | 1,723 |
| 20AF | ---- | ----- | 2.036 | 9,332 | 11,368 |
| Total | 4,537 | 61,871 | 220,411 | 161,913 | 448,732 |

**20mm Ammunition Expenditure**

| Theater | 1942 | 1943 | 1944 | 1945 | Total |
|---|---|---|---|---|---|
| ETO | 3 | 20 | 802 | 267 | 1,092 |
| MTO | 13 | 230 | 432 | 144 | 819 |
| PTO | ---- | ---- | 8 | 26 | 34 |
| FEAF | 13 | 133 | 344 | 725 | 1,215 |
| CBI | ---- | 7 | 71 | 191 | 269 |
| Alaska | 7 | 47 | ---- | ---- | 54 |
| 20AF | ---- | ---- | 25 | 7 | 32 |
| Total | 36 | 437 | 1,682 | 1,360 | 3,515 |

**37mm Ammunition Expenditure**

| Theater | 1942 | 1943 | 1944 | 1945 | Total |
|---|---|---|---|---|---|
| ETO | ---- | ---- | ---- | ---- | ---- |
| MTO | ---- | 6 | 7 | ---- | 13 |
| PTO | ---- | 1 | 1 | ---- | 2 |
| FEAF | ---- | 16 | 90 | ---- | 106 |
| CBI | ---- | ---- | ---- | ---- | 0 |
| Alaska | 1 | 1 | ---- | ---- | 2 |
| 20AF | ---- | ---- | ---- | ---- | ---- |
| Total | 1 | 24 | 98 | ---- | 123 |

**75mm Ammunition Expenditure**

| Theater | 1942 | 1943 | 1944 | 1945 | Total |
|---|---|---|---|---|---|
| ETO | ---- | ---- | ---- | ---- | ---- |
| MTO | ---- | 2 | 2 | ---- | 4 |
| PTO | ---- | ---- | ---- | 6 | 6 |
| FEAF | ---- | 12 | 4 | ---- | 16 |
| CBI | ---- | ---- | 3 | 2 | 5 |
| Alaska | ---- | ---- | ---- | ---- | ---- |
| 20AF | ---- | ---- | ---- | ---- | ---- |
| Total | 0 | 14 | 9 | 8 | 31 |

**Ammunition Expended by the USAAF by Theater and Aircraft Type**

**Ammunition Expended in the ETO**
**(Machine Gun & Cannon in 1,000s of Rounds)**
**(August 1942 to August 1945)**

| Total | | 1942 | 1943 | 1944 | 1945 | Total |
|---|---|---|---|---|---|---|
| Machine Gun: | .30 cal. | 53 | 616 | 23 | 58 | 750 |
| | .50 cal. | 1,660 | 27,964 | 104,444 | 61,351 | 195,419 |
| Cannon: | 20mm | 3 | 20 | 802 | 267 | 1,092 |
| Heavy Bombers | | | | | | |
| Machine Gun: | .30 cal. | 53 | 598 | 2 | ---- | 653 |
| | .50 cal. | 1,660 | 26,101 | 40,123 | 9,003 | 76,887 |
| Medium & Light Bombers | | | | | | |
| Machine Gun: | 50 cal. | ---- | 598 | 4,595 | 1,631 | 6,824 |
| Fighters | | | | | | |
| Machine Guns: | .30 cal. | ---- | 18 | 21 | 58 | 97 |
| | .50 cal. | ---- | 1,265 | 59,726 | 50,717 | 111,708 |
| Cannon: | 20mm | 3 | 20 | 802 | 267 | 1,052 |

**Ammunition Expended in the MTO**
**(Machine Gun & Cannon in 1,000s of Rounds)**
**(August 1942 to May 1945)**

| Total | | 1942 | 1943 | 1944 | 1945 | Total |
|---|---|---|---|---|---|---|
| Machine Gun: | .30 cal. | 8 | 247 | 730 | 27 | 1,012 |
| | .50 cal. | 1,439 | 17,652 | 50,699 | 19,717 | 89,507 |
| Cannon: | 20mm | 13 | 230 | 432 | 144 | 819 |
| | 37mm | ---- | 6 | 7 | ---- | 13 |
| | 75mm | ---- | 2 | 2 | ---- | 4 |
| Heavy Bombers | | | | | | |
| Machine Guns: | .30 cal. | 4 | 13 | ---- | ---- | 17 |
| | .50 cal. | 943 | 7,659 | 24,130 | 4,947 | 37,679 |
| Medium & Light Bombers | | | | | | |
| Machine Guns: | .30 cal. | 4 | 99 | 48 | 14 | 165 |
| | .50 cal. | 92 | 2,702 | 2,751 | 1,075 | 6,620 |
| Cannon: | 75mm | ---- | 1 | 2 | ---- | 3 |
| Fighters | | | | | | |
| Machine Guns: | .30 cal. | ---- | 135 | 682 | 13 | 830 |
| | .50.cal. | 404 | 7,291 | 23,818 | 13,695 | 45,208 |
| Cannon: | 20mm | 13 | 230 | 428 | 144 | 815 |
| | 37mm | ---- | 6 | 7 | ---- | 13 |
| | 75mm | ---- | 1 | ---- | ---- | 1 |

**Ammunition Expended in the PTO**
**(Machine Gun & Cannon in 1,000s of Rounds)**
**(August 1942 to May 1945)**

| Total | | 1942 | 1943 | 1944 | 1945 | Total |
|---|---|---|---|---|---|---|
| Machine Guns: | .30 cal. | 3 | 46 | 282 | 42 | 373 |
| | .50 cal. | 38 | 647 | 5,727 | 4,552 | 10,964 |
| Cannon: | 20mm | ---- | ---- | 8 | 26 | 34 |
| | 37mm | ---- | 1 | 1 | ---- | 2 |
| | 75mm | ---- | ---- | ---- | 6 | 6 |
| Heavy Bombers | | | | | | |
| Machine Guns: | .30 cal. | 3 | 37 | 221 | 41 | 302 |
| | .50 cal. | 28 | 594 | 2,204 | 1,188 | 4,015 |
| Medium & Light Bombers | | | | | | |
| Machine Guns: | .50 cal. | 3 | 25 | 997 | 494 | 1,519 |
| Cannon: | 75mm | ---- | ---- | ---- | 6 | 6 |
| Fighters | | | | | | |
| Machine Guns: | .30 cal. | ---- | 9 | 61 | 1 | 71 |
| | .50 cal. | 6 | 28 | 2,526 | 2,870 | 5,430 |
| Cannon: | 20mm | ---- | ---- | 8 | 26 | 34 |
| | 37mm | ---- | 1 | 1 | ---- | 2 |

**Ammunition Expended by the FEAF**
**(Machine Gun & Cannon in 1,000s of Rounds)**
**(1942 to August 1945)**

| Total | | 1942 | 1943 | 1944 | 1945 | Total |
|---|---|---|---|---|---|---|
| Machine Guns: | .30 cal. | 326 | 2,345 | 2,116 | 5 | 4,792 |
| | .50 cal. | 982 | 11,186 | 39,481 | 52,183 | 103,832 |
| Cannon: | 20mm | 13 | 133 | 344 | 725 | 1,215 |
| | 37mm | ---- | 16 | 90 | ---- | 106 |
| | 75mm | ---- | 12 | 4 | ---- | 16 |
| Heavy Bombers | | | | | | |
| Machine Guns: | .30 cal. | 35 | 245 | 117 | 4 | 401 |
| | .50 cal. | 133 | 1,977 | 4,413 | 2,637 | 9,160 |
| Cannon: | 20mm | ---- | 1 | ---- | ---- | 1 |
| Medium & Light Bombers | | | | | | |
| Machine Guns: | .30 cal. | 122 | 1,634 | 1,193 | 1 | 2,950 |
| | .50 cal. | 221 | 6,756 | 24,393 | 30,662 | 62,032 |
| Cannon: | 20mm | ---- | 4 | 1 | ---- | 5 |
| | 75mm | ---- | 12 | 4 | ---- | 16 |
| Fighters | | | | | | |
| Machine Guns: | .30 cal. | 169 | 466 | 806 | ---- | 1,441 |
| | .50 cal. | 628 | 2,453 | 10,675 | 18,884 | 32,640 |
| Cannons: | 20mm | 13 | 128 | 343 | 725 | 1,209 |
| | 37mm | ---- | 16 | 90 | ---- | 106 |

**Ammunition Expended in the CBI**
**(Machine Gun & Cannon in 1,000s of Rounds)**
**(February 1942 to August 1945)**

| Total | | 1942 | 1943 | 1944 | 1945 | Total |
|---|---|---|---|---|---|---|
| Machine Guns: | .30 cal. | 4 | 157 | 37 | ---- | 198 |
| | .50 cal. | 170 | 3,305 | 17,917 | 14,527 | 35,919 |
| Cannon: | 20mm | ---- | 7 | 71 | 191 | 269 |
| | 75mm | ---- | ---- | 3 | 2 | 5 |
| Heavy Bombers | | | | | | |
| Machine Guns: | .30 cal. | 4 | 101 | ---- | ---- | 105 |
| | .50 cal. | 51 | 950 | 625 | 578 | 2,214 |
| Medium & Light Bombers | | | | | | |
| Machine Guns: | .30 cal. | ---- | 56 | 35 | ---- | 91 |
| | .50 cal. | 5 | 290 | 2,270 | 2,824 | 5,389 |
| Cannon: | 75mm | ---- | ---- | 3 | 2 | 5 |
| Fighters | | | | | | |
| Machine Guns: | .30 cal. | ---- | ---- | 2 | ---- | 2 |
| | .50 cal. | 114 | 2,065 | 15,012 | 11,125 | 28,316 |
| Cannon: | 20mm | ---- | 7 | 71 | 191 | 269 |

**Ammunition Expended in Alaska**
**(Machine Gun & Cannon in 1,000s of Rounds)**
**(March 1942 to August 1945)**

| Total | | 1942 | 1943 | 1944 | 1945 | Total |
|---|---|---|---|---|---|---|
| Machine Guns: | .30 cal. | 28 | 132 | ---- | ---- | 160 |
| | .50 cal. | 248 | 1,117 | 107 | 251 | 1,723 |
| Cannon: | 20mm | 7 | 47 | ---- | ---- | 54 |
| | 37mm | 1 | 1 | ---- | ---- | 2 |
| Heavy Bombers | | | | | | |
| Machine Guns: | .30 cal. | 17 | 29 | ---- | ---- | 46 |
| | .50 cal. | 156 | 250 | 27 | 98 | 531 |
| Medium & Light Bombers | | | | | | |
| Machine guns: | .30 cal. | 2 | 19 | ---- | ---- | 21 |
| | .50 cal. | 14 | 135 | 80 | 153 | 382 |
| Fighters | | | | | | |
| Machine Guns: | .30 cal. | 9 | 84 | ---- | ---- | 93 |
| | .50 cal. | 78 | 732 | ---- | ---- | 810 |
| Cannon: | 20mm | 7 | 47 | ---- | ---- | 54 |
| | 37mm | 1 | 1 | ---- | --- | 2 |

**Ammunition Expended by the 20th Air Force (Machine Gun & Cannon in 1,000s of Rounds) (June 1944 to August 1945)**

| Total | | 1944 | 1945 | Total |
|---|---|---|---|---|
| Machine Guns: | .50 cal. | 2,036 | 9,332 | 11,368 |
| Cannon: | 20mm | 25 | 7 | 32 |
| Very Heavy Bombers | | | | |
| XX Bomber Command | | | | |
| Machine Guns: | .50 cal. | 1,155 | 237 | 1,392 |
| Cannon: | 20mm | 13 | ---- | 13 |
| XXI Bomber Command | | | | |
| Machine Guns: | .50 cal. | 881 | 6,680 | 7,561 |
| Cannon: | 20mm | 2 | ---- | 2 |
| Fighters | | | | |
| Machine Guns: | .50 cal. | ---- | 2,415 | 2,415 |
| Cannon: | 20mm | 2 | ---- | 2 |

Note: All AAF charts adapted from USAAF, AAF Statistical Digest, Office of Statistical Control, December 1945.

**Section 2: USN**

**U.S. Navy Ammunition Expended in World War II Land & Shipping Targets By Aircraft Type, Carrier & Land-Based Sorties**

| | Aircraft Land Targets | | Shipping Targets | |
|---|---|---|---|---|
| **Type** | **Sorties** | **Ammo** | **Sorties** | **Ammo** |
| **Carrier-Based** | 111,918 | 42,529 | 25,966 | 7,665 |
| F6F | 45,637 | 25,895 | 11,415 | 5,257 |
| F4U, FG | 6,919 | 4,075 | 1,074 | 571 |
| FM | 10,890 | 6,376 | 1,023 | 611 |
| F4F | 461 | * | 102 | * |
| SB2C, SBW | 14,310 | 1,722 | 4,823 | 514 |
| SBD | 4,246 | 410* | 1,656 | 93* |
| TBF, TBM | 29,448 | 4,051 | 5,731 | 619 |
| TBD | 27 | * | 142 | * |
| **Land-Based** | 111,228 | 27,512 | 10,055 | 4,791 |
| F4U, FG | 43,151 | 14,600 | 3,428 | 944 |
| F6F | 2,647 | 638 | 281 | 85 |
| U/i VF | 51 | 0 | 0 | 0 |
| SBD | 41,981 | 6,581* | 1,909 | 123* |
| SB2C, SBW | 2,099 | 332 | 96 | 22 |
| SB2U | 2 | * | 17 | * |
| TBF, TBM | 8,995 | 1,087* | 846 | 43* |
| PB4Y | 1,280 | 898 | 1,775 | 2,910 |
| PV | 2,060 | 733 | 372 | 178 |
| PBJ | 7,919 | 2,471 | 210 | 28 |
| PBY | 690 | 75* | 581 | 175* |
| PBM | 95 | 54 | 329 | 268 |
| PB2Y | 66 | 12 | 46 | 15 |
| U/I VB | 26 | 0 | 14 | 0 |
| **TOTAL** | 223,166 | 70,041 | 36,021 | 12,456 |

Adapted from U.S. Navy, *Naval Aviation Combat Statistics: World War II*, Office of Naval Intelligence, Wash., DC, 17 June 1945.

Note: Ammunition expended is in 1,000s of rounds.

* Does not cover the period prior to August 1943 for carrier-based aircraft and prior to October 1943 for land-based aircraft, as ammunition expenditures were not listed in Action Reports prior to these dates. The USN estimated that an additional two to three million rounds were expended in strafing but not reported, of which approximately 80% was by land-based aircraft and approximately 80% against land-based targets. This lack of data for these prior periods (before August and October 1943) was estimated to effect the figures with asterisks (*) by 5% or more. For other aircraft types the ammunition expenditure was estimated to be 95% or more accurate.

All types of fighters expended 70% of all ammunition. Most ammunition was expended against non-airborne targets, and the amount of ammunition expended against enemy aircraft is not available. Only 14,308 of all USN aircraft sorties (5%) involved air combat and many only briefly. The USN estimated that not over 20% of all ammunition expenditures (17.5 million rounds) were used in air combat with a minimum of 70 million rounds expended on other targets.

**USN Ammunition Expenditures in 1945 By Aircraft Type: Carrier, Land-Based, and Patrol**

| Aircraft Type | Rounds of Ammunition Expended .30-.50 | 20mm |
|---|---|---|
| **Carrier-Based** | | |
| F6F | 14,450 | 0 |
| F4U | 4,963 | 141 |
| FM | 4,616 | 0 |
| SB2C | 326 | 474 |
| TBM | 2,489 | 0 |
| Total | 26,844 | 615 |
| Land-Based | | |
| F4U | 6,653 | 297 |
| F6F | 192 | 0 |
| FM | 31 | 0 |
| SBD | 2,940 | 0 |
| SB2C | 164 | 225 |
| TBM | 299 | 0 |
| Total | 10,248 | 522 |
| Patrol | | |
| PB4Y | 3,299 | 7 |
| PBJ | 1,672 | 0 |
| PV | 409 | 0 |
| PBM | 332 | 0 |
| PB2Y | 19 | 0 |
| PBY | 9 | 0 |
| Total | 5,740 | 7 |
| Grand Totals | 42,832 | 1,144 |

Adapted from U.S. Navy, *Naval Aviation Combat Statistics: World War II*, Office of Naval Intelligence, Wash., DC, 17 June 1945.

Note: Ammunition expended in 1000s of rounds.

# Part Four

## Gunsights, Gun Cameras, and Radar

# 1

# Introduction and Early Development

**Section 1: The Gunner as a Sight**

The gunner's eyes acting as a gunsight were nearly perfect whether the gunner was sitting in a bomber turret traveling at 200 mph tracking an incoming enemy fighter attacking at 350 mph or was a fighter pilot flying at 350 mph with an opponent approaching head-on at the same speed. Despite these high speeds, the human eye was able to follow the attacking aircraft and was able to register an abrupt change of more than 1/32 of a second. However, the human physical reflex in which the eye sent impulses to the muscles had an average lag time of 0.44 second. During this brief time the target could have moved 50 to 70 yards. Improved gunner selection narrowed the field down to applicants with superior reflexes, but even a trigger finger only a tenth second too late would put the burst of fire off target. Human mental processes were not fast enough to instantly calculate a sighting problem involving airspeeds of hundreds of feet per second while also considering such complicating factors as windage, drift, trajectory, and range. Therefore, throughout the years the quest of armament designers was to develop the ultimate gunsight. In 1943 the search culminated with the computing gunsight that computed the complex and constantly changing sighting problems at any instant. The gunner sighted the target, but the computer aimed the guns at a point where the target would be when the guns fired.

**Section 2: Early Gunsight Development**

The guns of the first military aircraft were identical to those used by the infantry with the standard adjustable V backsight and a blade foresight. This gunnery system was very successful when fixed on a tripod for use on the ground, but for use in the air, with the aircraft maneuvering in three dimensions at high speeds, the gunner found he had little time to take aim with the gun vibrating on its mount. The basic requirements for an aerial gunsight were that it be large enough, with unobstructed viewing, and be quick and easy to use. Because air combat ranges were generally shorter than for ground weapons intricate range adjustments were not required.

Early gunners encountered three key problems in aerial gunnery. The first was to find a method of determining the range of the target; the second was the effect of his aircraft's forward speed; and the last was the difficultly of deflection shooting, leading the target so that it flew into the gunner's bullets. Since not every gunner could be a natural marksman like World War I super aces von Richtofen, Bishop, Fronck, and Rickenbacker, gunsight designers labored to furnish the average pilot with a sighting system that would take the guesswork out of aiming.

**Gate Sight**

The first purpose-built aerial gunsight for fixed guns was the Gate Sight, which was introduced by the Germans in 1915 and was standard until 1916. It was made up of a basic aiming mark at one end and a gate-type frame at the other that could be adjusted in width to correspond with the expected wingspan of the enemy aircraft at a predetermined firing distance, usually 200 yards. The gunner only had to line up the front and rear sights and keep the target within the gate until the target's wings filled it. The Germans placed the gate at the front of the gun and used the gun's standard rear sight, while the British used the gate frame as the rear sight. Though the sight had no problems when the gunner attacked from directly behind the target aiming directly at it, the disadvantage of the Gate Sight was that if the attack was at an angle to the enemy aircraft, the pilot had no method of determining where to aim ahead of the target in order to hit it (deflection shooting).

**Ring and Bead Sight**

The Iron Ring Sight consisted of a metal ring located near the gunner's face that had a smaller central inner ring held in place by radial wires. The bead was the front sight mounted on a pylon-supported small bead sight located near the muzzle and was used by the gunner to line up the gun. The inner ring of the rear sight was slightly larger than the bead of the foresight, and the pilot aligned the inner ring of the rear sight with the bead of the foresight onto the target. For deflection shooting an outer ring was added to correspond to a target speed of 200mph. This sighting system had the advantage of having the ring and bead placed several inches above the barrel, which provided the gunner with an increased field of vision. An improved Ring and Bead sighting system persisted well into World War II and is discussed in detail later.

**Norman Vane Sight**

In 1917, the newly developed semi-automatic Norman Vane Sight was introduced for use on free-mounted guns in multi-place aircraft. It was an improvement on the ring and bead sight, as it made allowances for the speed of the gunner's aircraft and aided him in deflection shooting. The Vane Sight consisted of a number of small horizontal and vertical vanes designed so that their axis was always parallel with the line of flight, and they were mounted on a rotating column that allowed vertical and lateral movement. The vanes were supported by an arm that pivoted on the column, and this arm extended to an adjustable bead sight that could be set to any

The semi-automatic **Norman Vane Sight** appeared in was introduced for use on free-mounted guns in multi-place aircraft. It was an improvement on the ring and bead sight as it made allowances for the speed of the gunner's aircraft and aided him in deflection shooting. (AFHRC)

speed by a spring catch. The rear sight was the standard fixed ring, but the front sight was placed near the muzzle protruding out into the slipstream so it could pivot horizontally like a weather vane. The aiming mark was located at the same end of the pivoting arm as the vane. In this position the wind forced the vane towards the rear of the plane while simultaneously moving the aiming mark in the same direction. The gunner had to swing the gun forward to align the sight on the target, which automatically aimed the gun far enough ahead of the target to hit it. The vane sight also automatically compensated for the angle of fire and the speed of the aircraft. At higher speeds the spring-loaded vane was forced further to one side, while at shallower aiming angles the wind had less effect. The vane sights were developed into more complex designs and were used until World War II, when the maximum aircraft speeds exceeded the maximum 200 mph speed setting of the sight.

**Aldis 1.8 inch Sights**

In their quest to develop a satisfactory gunsight aerial gunsight designers turned to ground weapon optical sights using telescopes with cross-hairs, but found that these had fields of vision that were too narrow and that the aircraft engine vibration distorted viewing. In 1916 the British Aldis Brothers Company developed a zero magnification telescope that measured 31.5 inches long and two inches in diameter. The zero magnification solved the field of view and vibration problems.

Inside the telescope were a series of 1.8 inch diameter lenses (hence the name) with no magnification. The sighting marker was two concentric circles engraved on a plain glass screen that were seen in the field of view when looking through the tube. The outer circle corresponded to a target speed of 200 mph and was used for deflection shooting much the way it was when using the ring and bead sight. The inner circle was much smaller and only defined the center of the tube. The Aldis sight had the advantage of having the sighting elements and target in simultaneous focus so that the pilot's head did not have to be placed exactly in the center of the sight, because the engraved markings remained on the target even if viewed at a slight angle. The best results were obtained when the gunner's eye was five inches from the end of scope, giving a 20° field of vision.

Because the air war was escalating in 1916 the sight was pushed into production and sent to elite frontline units which became enamored with the Aldis Sight, and by 1917 it had become the standard British aerial gunsight for the next 20 years until the demise of the slow biplane. The French Air Force adopted the sight in 1918 manufactured by the Chrétien Company, and the German Oigee Company produced a limited number of telescopic sights before the war ended.

**Section 3: The Tracer as a Sighting Device**

When tracer ammunition was developed in early World War I it was thought to be a panacea in gunsighting, as the gunner could follow the target with the trajectory of the burning tracers. But in practice, although it appeared that the tracer bullets were hitting the target, they were actually missing it by a large distance. At the time aircraft speeds were slow enough to allow the use of an alternative system of sighting, and the use of the tracer as a sighting device was abandoned until 1940 when a new technique for its use was developed.

In early World War II British Bomber Command rear turret gunners found that when they were attacked by German fighters flying a Pursuit Curve (an attack when the fighter's guns were always bearing on the bomber) they had problems in allowing for deflection. The rear turret gunner, seated at the far end of the bomber, had no fixed reference from which to judge if the target was moving across his line of fire or approaching with no divergence to the right or left. The Gunnery Research Office (GRO) of the Aeroplane and Armament Experimental Establishment (A&AEE) of the Royal Air Force at Boscombe Down investigated the problem, and on 17 April 1940 distributed a confidential report to gunnery instructors at Bomber Command entitled "The Use of Tracer as an Aid to Air Sighting." The report believed that the use of tracers could solve the range and deflection direction problem. At the time the G4 round (day tracer bright) and G5 round (night tracer dim) were in use, both having a 600 yard burning range. Range could be determined by comparing the location of the target to the end of the tracer path. The position of the tracers in the reflector gunsight sighting ring was used to determine the angle of deflection for straight on and pursuit curve attacks. The amount of deflection required was set forth in the "Zone System of Sighting Allowance," a set of rules which the gunners found to be too complicated to remember in combat especially when being attacked by a fighter that was visible for only a few seconds. Instead, the gunners went back to the old standby; aiming in front of the target and firing.

In the U.S. it was also believed that the increased aircraft speeds during World War II made tracer use for sighting practicable, provided it was used in conjunction with other sighting systems. In June 1942 the AAF Flying Training Command was convinced that a student tracer training course was essential, but once instituted instructors found that student-gunners using tracers tended to depend on them and ignored their gunsights. In mid-1943 AAF HQ issued a directive that not more than 10% of the ammunition used by gunnery students should be loaded with tracer rounds, and then it should only be fired during the final phases of training after students became proficient with their gunsights.

In fall 1943, tests were conducted at Kingman Army Air Field to determine the shortcomings of tracer sighting. One of the tests involved a maneuvering AT-23 towing a target at high-speed and a B-17 firing on it with tracers. The test report stated:

"In every case the individual whose tracers appeared to be piercing the target and who might be considered to have high scores received no hits on the target, and in every case the individuals whose tracer appeared not to pierce the target were in all cases the individuals who received hits on the target."

Used correctly tracers facilitated the visual checking of the harmonization of guns and sights, and indicated whether there was proper lead in deflection shooting. The *Gunner's Information File* emphasized that the gunner should "never use it as the sole means of sighting. When you use it, it should be used in connection with your ring sight and your regular sighting method." Tracer bullets did not curve more than any other bullet, but when they were fired from a moving gun they appeared to "cut back," much like a stream of water from a swinging garden hose. The gunner did not realize that he saw the tracer's light, not the bullet, and that the light did not give the same effect of distance as a bullet. The scientific explanation was that a light half the size of another equal light was not twice as far away; and when it was twice as far away, it was only a quarter the size of the other.

# 2

# Types of Gunsights

**Section 1: Iron Ring Sight or Ring and Bead Gunsight**
The Iron Ring Sight was a metal ring or set of rings at the rear of the gun and a metal post and bead at the front of the gun. The gun was sighted by looking through the rings along the bead at the top of the post, aiming at the target.

Ring and Bead Sights on Flexible Gus
There were two types of Flexible Gun Iron Sights: the Sight Base and the Fixed Base. The B-11, B-13, and B-15 Sight Base Iron Sights had their 35 mil angles made at the gunner's eye level by keeping it at a definite distance behind the rings. Each of these sights had a definite sight base. The distance between the rings and post did not matter. The Fixed Base Iron Sights had their 35 mil angles made at the post by maintaining a definite angle between the post and rings; the angles were built into the sight by means of a fixed base. The distance between the rings and post did not matter.

Position Firing rules held true for both types of sights: "Place the dot between the attacking fighter and the tail of your bomber, along the fighter's apparent line of motion." However, there was one important difference. When the gunner made a deflection shot with the B-11, B-13, and B-15 Sight Bases he needed to keep the bead in the center of the ring and place the ring center between the target and the tail of the bomber. But when aiming a Fixed Base Sight the gunner did not keep the bead in the center of the ring and did not keep the ring center between the target and the target and the bomber's tail. Instead, the gunner was to hold his bead on the target and keep both the bead and target lined up with the appropriate ring on the side toward the bomber's tail. Many flexibly mounted guns continued using the ring and bead sight throughout the war.

Ring and Bead Sights on Fixed Guns
When attacking the enemy, the pilot aimed along the fore and aft axis of his fighter (e.g. along the line of flight). When approaching the enemy from directly behind (zero deflection) the pilot simply lined up the bead and ring on the target and fired. With the same alignment, from his eye toward the target, a rudimentary deflection angle could be derived if the gunner

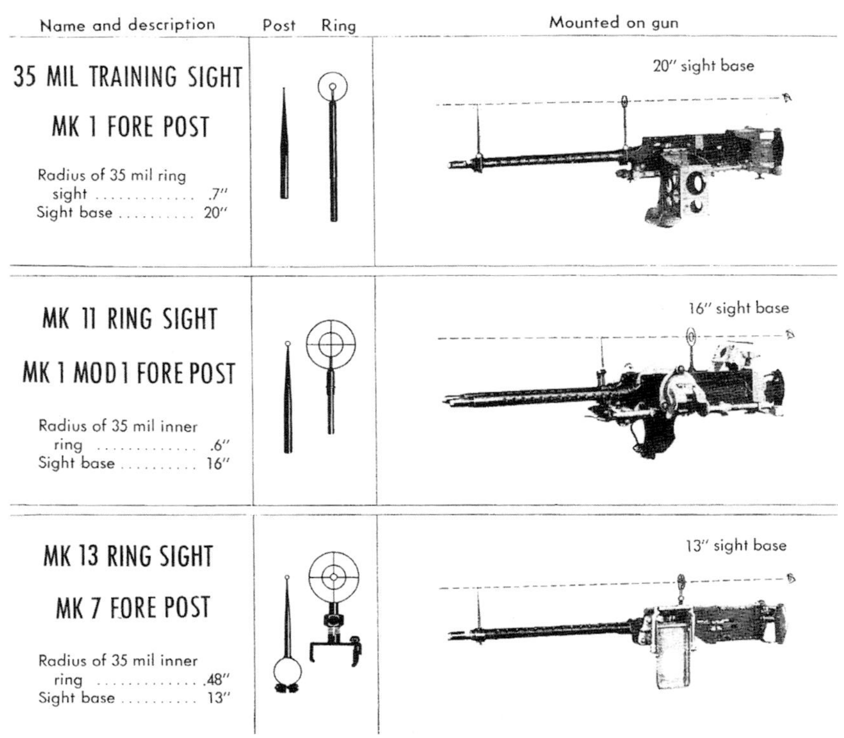


**Iron Ring Sight or Ring and Bead Gunsight** (USAAF)

placed the bead on the outside ring away from the direction that the target was traveling. The size of the outer ring was irrelevant, but veteran pilots favored a ring designed for target speed of 100 miles per hour, called the "100 mile per hour ring." When approaching a target that was flying on a course 90° different from his course, the pilot using a 100 mph ring sight centralized his eye and the bead in the inner ring. The pilot maneuvered his fighter to place the target on the outer ring of the sight while flying directly at the center bead. By maintaining this aim the pilot should have hit the target. The angle of deflection is the angle between the line of the pilot's eye and the outer ring to target and the line through the inner ring and the bead (which is the path of the bullets). So when the pilot fired at a target moving other than directly toward or away from him, he had to allow for an angle of deflection (lead the target).

The size of the outer ring could be calculated using the following data:

1) The distance between the pilot's eye to the ring sight, in feet.
2) The average speed of the bullet, in feet per second.
3) The speed of the target in feet per second.

The distance from the eye in feet divided by the bullet speed in feet per second times the speed of target in feet per second equaled the size of the outer ring in feet.

Advantages of the Ring and Bead Sight
The ring and bead sight had the advantage of being sturdy, and remained in working condition unless it was bent, broken, or rusted. Its only maintenance was occasionally oiling it to prevent rust so that the adjustment and mounting screws worked easily. The reflector sight was much superior to the ring and bead sight and replaced it, but the ring and bead sight was retained in case of failure of the reflector sight.

Disadvantages of the Ring and Bead Sight
When using the ring and bead sight, because the size of the outer ring had been calculated according to the distance the pilot's eye was from the ring sight, it was essential that the pilot place his eye at this exact distance; otherwise the basic allowance given by the outer ring would vary. If the pilot's eye was only 1/8 inch laterally out of line it would cause an error of 20 feet at 400 yards. The reflector sight, as long as there was an image visible on the windshield, automatically compensated for the position of the pilot's head.

When using the ring and bead sight the eye, like a camera, had to be in focus to see an object clearly; consequently, if the distant target was in focus then the closer sights had to be out of focus and were not seen distinctly. The reflector sight provided the pilot with the dot and ring's image superimposed on the target. When using the ring and bead sight pilots never seemed to take sufficient lead, as a full allowance of deflection had to be made for any angles from 90° to 60°.

**Section 2: Optical Sight**

**U.S. "N" Series of Optical Sights**

In 1931 the German Oigee company developed an optical sight, designated as the ENI (Electrische Nivellier Instrument, or Electrical Leveling Instrument). At the time Germany was prohibited from producing armaments, and this gunsight was designated as a "leveling" instrument by Oigee. Lt.Col. Jacob West, the U.S. Air Attaché to Germany, secured an example of the ENI sight and forwarded it to the Wright Field Armament Laboratory for evaluation.

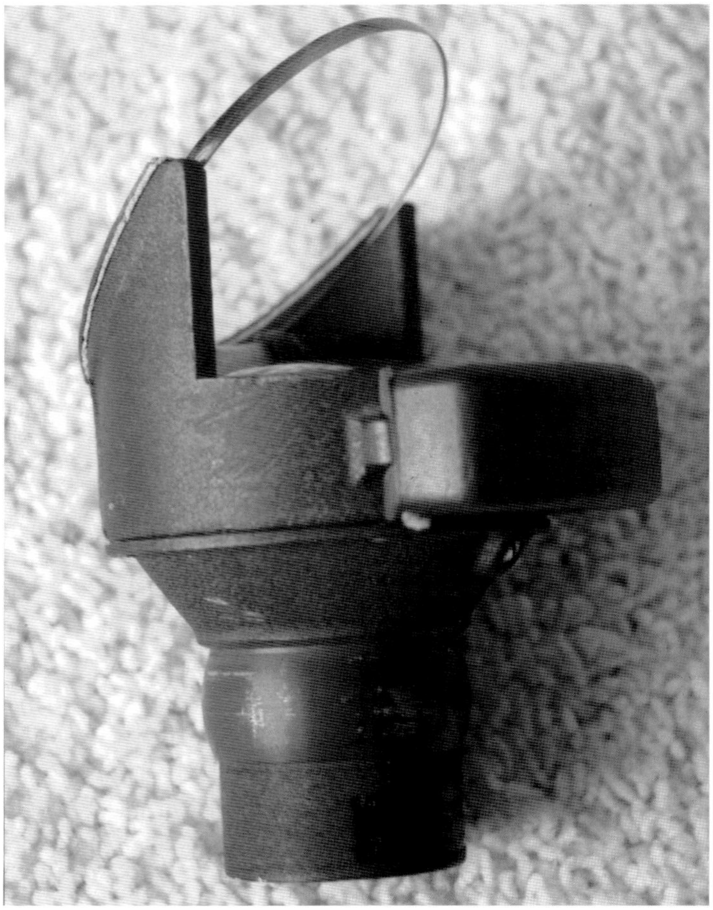

**N2B** (Author's Collection)

**N-2/2A/2B/2C Optical Gunsight**

Ernest Baldridge redesigned the Oigee ENI into the American version, which had an L-shaped housing in which a central cross graticule was surrounded by eight small arrows to assist sighting. A graticule was a cross hair aiming mark projected through the focal plane of a collimating lens and reflected to a glass screen. The first prototype, the N2, was tested using the Curtiss XP6H (P-6E fighter) by the 8th Pursuit Group in January 1933. These tests were successful and led to the modified N2 design in 1936 that was accepted for use in USAAC fighter aircraft as the N-2A/B/C series in the P-35, P-39, and early P-38s and P-40s.

**N-3B/N-3C Optical Gunsight**

The N-3B/N-3C Optical Gunsight was typically used by B-25 bomber pilots and P-47 fighter pilots as both a gunsight and bombsight. The N-3B/C was mounted on the left side of the cockpit in front of the pilot for sighting guns and bombs. The sight was equipped with an A-1 combination gunsight and bombsight head with a variable reflector. The sight could be adjusted from a gunsight position which was parallel to the aircraft's flight path to a bombing position that was from 1° to 15° below the flight path. A calibrated adjustment knob on the sight provided several stops that could be preset for various bombing angles. These stops also kept the reflector in the adjusted position.

The N-3B/N-3C Optical Gunsight housing contained a lamp, a circle-and-dot reticle, a flat mirror, and a two component lens assembly. The N-3 Manual stated the following:

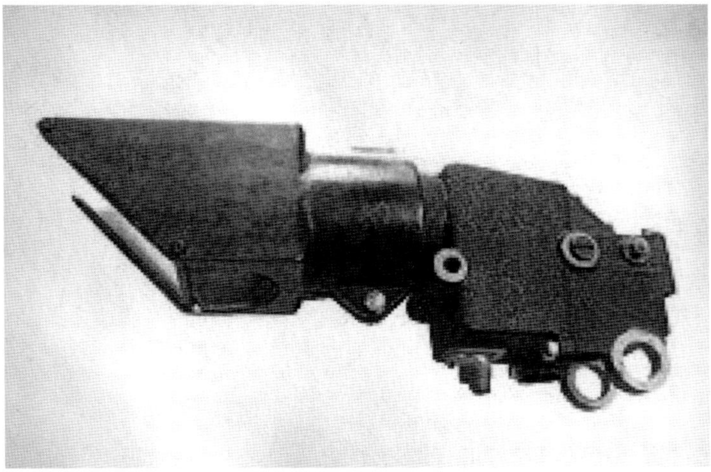

**N-3A Optical Gunsight** (USAAF)

**N-6A Optical Gunsight** (USAAF)

"When the gunsight rheostat is turned on, light passes through the transparent reticle pattern which is on opaque glass; to the mirror and is reflected upward through the lens onto the reflector. As viewed through the reflector, the reticle image appears superimposed on the target. As the reflector rotates forward when being adjusted for bombing, the line of sight of the reticle image lowers with respect to the flight path of the airplane."

A rheostat was provided for turning the lamp on and regulating the light intensity of the reticle image on the reflector. A spare gunsight lamp was stowed on the instrument panel to the right of the sight. Should the electrical gunsight become inoperative, an auxiliary ring and bead sight was mounted on the instrument panel shield to the right of the sight with the corresponding bead sight attached to the fuselage forward of the windshield.

**N-3B Optical Gunsight** (USAAF)

**N-6/N-6A Optical Gunsight**

The N-6 and N-8 series of optical gunsights were typically used by turret gunners until the introduction of the K-series of computing sights. The compact single ring N-6 and N-6A were sister optical gunsights that used one ring instead of the three rings found on the later N-8s. The N-6 and N-6A sights were installed on a fixed mount between the guns, forward of the gunner's face.

N-6 Pre-flight Check

The sight glass was checked for cleanliness and for tightness by turning the adjusting knob. The rheostat was tested and the toggle switch was flipped ON to check both bulb filaments. The ring and dot were checked for sharpness and clarity, and if they appeared blurry then the base Armament Unit was to be informed. The sight was to be centered on some target and the gunner was to move his head from side to side to check if the rings and dot stayed on the target. If they moved away, the gunner was to inform the Armament Unit.

Operating the N-6

The N-6 was an open-type sight that moved with the turret in azimuth and was connected to the gun elevation shaft so that the sight (gunner's field of view) was always pointed in the direction in which the guns were aimed and moved up and down with the guns. The sight had an illuminated reticle with a rheostat located above the gunner's left hand in the controller casting on the N-6 and on the extension light bracket below the left control handle on the N-6A. The rheostat turned the gunsight light ON and controlled the light intensity that could be varied to meet the operating conditions of bright sunlight or night flying. Two concentric circles were projected on the sight glass, and the center of the field of view was marked by the center of these two circles and was the point on which the guns were trained. The two circles were used in the same way as the ring sight and dot on a flexible machine gun installation. The rad was always 35 mils, no matter the position of the gunner's head. A toggle switch on the housing operated the sight bulb. At its center position the switch was OFF and in either of the other two positions, pushed away or pulled toward the gunner, it turned ON one of the two duplicate filaments inside the bulb in case of burnout. Two spare lamps were stowed in the controller housing between the control handles. If strong sunlight or a bright cloud bank was encountered a polarized green glass sunscreen (not found on the N-8) attached to the forward side of the reflector could be swung down. Before the sun screen was rotated the adjusting knob was to be pulled out so as not to break the sun screen glass. A ring and bead sight was provided as a back up in case of total sight failure.

Care of the N-6
The care of the N-6 was very easy, and the gunner's main duty was to be sure that the sight was operating before each mission and if any repairs were required, the Armament Unit was summoned to make them. All exposed glass was to be kept free of fingerprints, grease, and dirt using a clean piece of chamois or soft tissue paper and liquid lens cleaner. Oil was never to be used on any part of the sight. The bulb was to be replaced if one filament burned out or after every third mission, and a spare was to be carried by the gunner or navigator on each mission. To change the bulb, the bottom of the sight housing was removed by pressing the two buttons on the sides.

**N-8/N-8A Optical Gunsights**
Generally, the N-8/N-8A was almost identical in operation, care, and preflight checks to the N-6/N-6A. The N-8/N-8A Gunsight was a three-ring optical sight with a simple arrangement of mirrors with a single light bulb located inside a small metal housing. Its construction was similar to the N-6, and the rad also was always 35 mils no matter the where the gunner held his head.

Operating the N-8 Sight
The N-8 was used by sighting the target through a glass screen on which the light bulb cast the dot, with the three rings showing the gunner where to aim. The dot showed the gunner exactly where the guns were pointed. The three rings made it easy to determine any deflection up to three rads by simply placing the target on the appropriate ring. The mirror arrangement allowed the sight to operate under all situations. As with the N-6, each rad was equal to a 35 mil angle no matter where the gunner held his head as he looked into the sight.

**Howard Grubb** developed the superlative Grubb astronomical telescopes and is generally credited with perfecting the periscope and reflector gunsight. (AFHRC)

**USAAF Optical Gunsights**

| Sight | Use | Aircraft Use |
|---|---|---|
| **C-4** | Fighter | A-12, P-26 |
| **Type 3** | Fighter | P-38J, P-51D, P-61B |
| **N-1** | Fighter | XP-6H (P-6E) |
| **N-2** | Gunner | B-25. B-26 |
| | Training | T-6 |
| **N-2A** | Fighter | P-35A, P-40D, P-40N |
| **N-2B** | Fighter | P-35A, P-38, P-39C |
| **N-2C** | Fighter | P-39 |
| **N-3A** | Fighter | P-38, P-39K/L, P-40, P-47B/D, P-51A/B, P-61 |
| | Gunner | B-17. B-24, B-25, B-26 |
| **N-3B** | Fighter | P-38F/J, P-39, P-47D, P-51B/C |
| | Training | T-6 (and SNJ) |
| | Gunner | B-25G/J |
| **N-3C** | Fighter | P-38, P-39K/L, P-40, P-51 |
| | Training | T-6 |
| | Gunner | B-25J, B-26 |
| **N-6** | Fighter | P-61 |
| | Gunner | B-17G (dorsal & nose) |
| **N-6A** | Fighter | P-61 |
| | Gunner | B-24, B-25, B-26 |
| **N-8** | Gunner | B-17, B-25, B-26 (tail) |
| **N-8A** | Gunner | B-17, B-25 |
| **N-9** | Fighter | P-51D/K, P-47, P-63 |
| | Gunner | B-17 |

**Section 3: Development of Fighter Aircraft Fixed Gun Reflector Sights**
**Grubb Reflector Sight**
The reflector gunsight was the most successful aerial gunsight of all time, remaining in service from its standardization and introduction by the RAF in 1937 until today. The reflector sight was invented by celebrated Scottish optical instrument designer Sir Howard Grubb, who joined his father, Thomas, in developing the superlative Grubb astronomical telescopes, and is generally credited with perfecting the periscope. Grubb filed for British patent No.12,108: "Improvements in sighting devices for guns," three years before the Wright Brothers' first flight in 1903. In 1901, the Royal Dublin Society published Grubb's paper, "A new collimating telescopic gunsight for large and small ordnance." Grubb's gunsight design was so thorough that throughout the years no significant improvement was made to the original basic design.

The reflector sight consisted of an upright tubular housing containing a light in its base that was aimed through an opaque glass plate containing engraved "aiming marks" known as a "reticule." The image of the graticule (cross hair aiming mark) was projected through the focal plane of a collimating lens and reflected to a glass screen mounted at 45° at the gunner's eye level. This sight gave an aiming mark, usually a ring with a center dot on the reflector screen, giving the gunner a clear view of the target with the graticule pattern superimposed on it. The advantage of the reflector sight was that the pilot or gunner only had to operate the aircraft or gun so the graticule lined up with the target. The collimating lens allowed that no matter what distance the gunner's head was positioned from the sight, up, down, sideways, the graticule always moved with it.

However, when Grubb tried to sell his sight there was no interest until 1914 when World War I broke out. The Vickers Company then enlisted Grubb as a consultant and established a design and production team to develop a reflector sight for use as a military aerial gunsight. The first prototype was completed in 1915 and a patent was applied for, but

**Oigee Reflector Sight**

for unknown reasons Vickers elected not to produce the sight and it was never used on an aircraft.

**Oigee Reflector Sight**

In 1918, the Optiche Anstall Oigee Company of Berlin reworked the Grubb patent to develop two aircraft reflector sights. One version could be used by day and night, while a smaller version was for night use only. A small electric bulb was used as a light source and the reflector was an elliptical glass screen. The sight could be harmonized with the gun by a screw and clamp. In 1918 several of the larger sights were mounted on Fokker Dr.1 aircraft of *Jasta* 12 for operational trials while others were tested on Albatros D.Va aircraft, but there are no records of any operational use. In 1920 Benjamin Foulois, American Military Attaché to Germany, was given a demonstration of the sight and was impressed enough to send one to the U.S. Army Engineering Division at McCook Field, but McCook engineers showed no interest in the Oigee sight.

**Barr and Stroud Reflector Gunsight Background**

After the Grubb sight was abandoned by Vickers no further work was done on developing reflector sights in England until 1926, when the optical firm of Barr and Stroud Ltd. of Glasgow submitted a design for a pilot's gunsight.

In 1888 Dr. Archibald Barr, an engineering professor, and Dr. William Stroud, a physics professor, both at Yorkshire College, collaborated in designing an infantry rangefinder that was ultimately unsuccessful but led to the formation of Barr and Stroud Patents Ltd. in 1895. While continuing the development of patents for optical rangefinders for army and naval use, Stroud maintained his distinguished teaching career until 1909 and Barr until 1913. That year the two professors formed Barr and Stroud Ltd., and would develop their small company into a worldwide leader and supplier of military optical equipment. The Barr & Stroud field rangefinder was a standard rangefinder for most European armies before and during World War I, and B&S naval rangefinders were accepted by the Royal Navy and remained in service on board all British warships until the introduction of radar during World War II. For many years bird watchers and naturalists considered Barr and Stroud binoculars the "Rolls Royce" of binoculars.

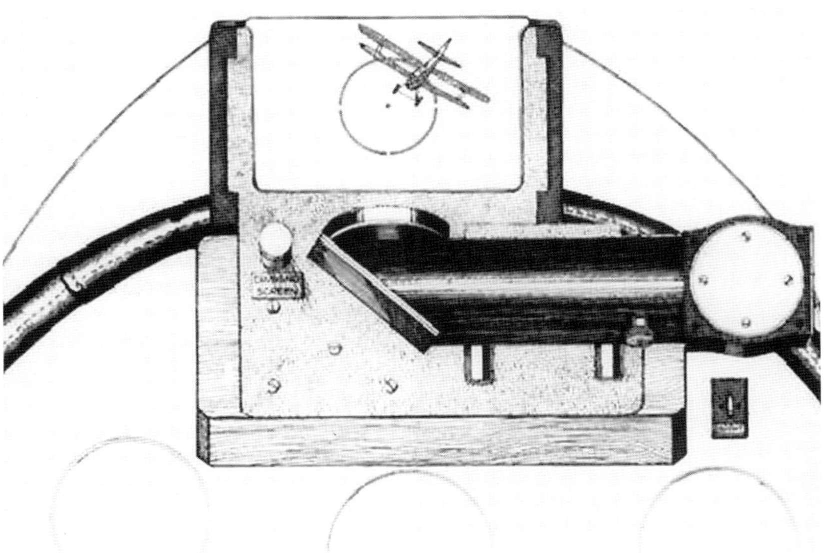

**Barr & Stroud GD1 Aerial Reflector Gunsight** (AFHRC)

**Barr & Stroud GD-2B Aerial Reflector Gunsight** (AFHRC)

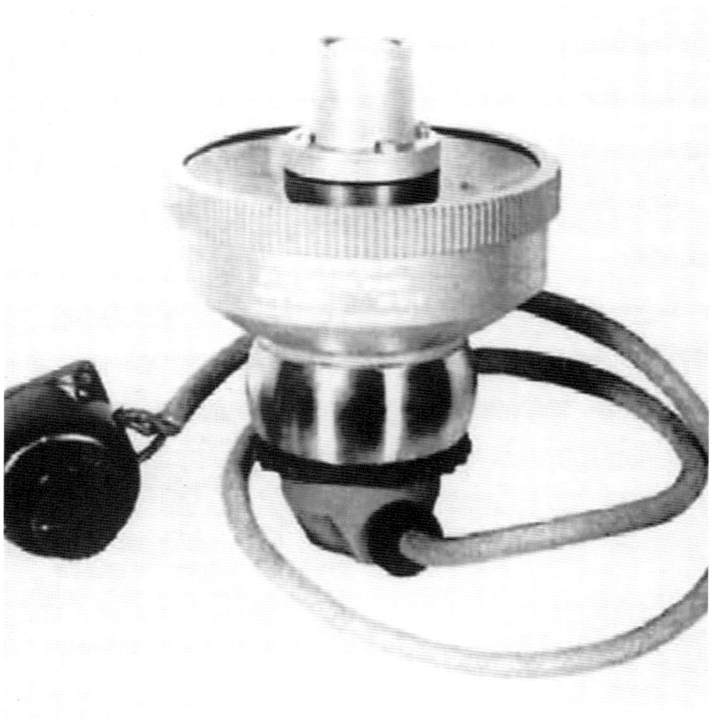

**Barr & Stroud GD5 Aerial Reflector Gunsight** (AFHRC)

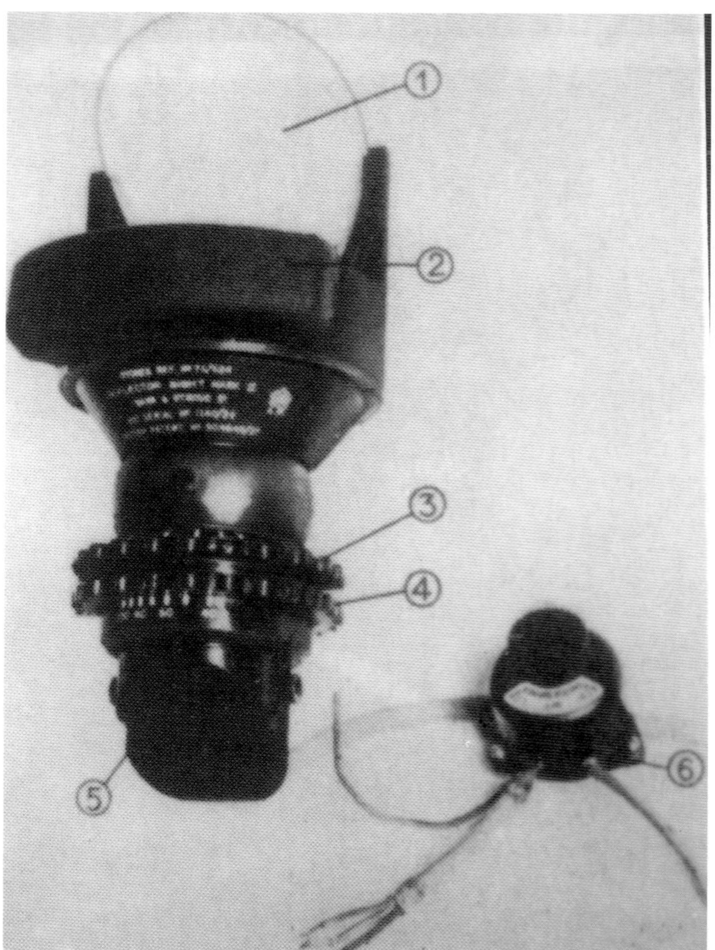


**Barr & Stroud GM2/MKII Aerial Reflector Gunsight** (AFHRC)

The B&S prototype GD1 aerial gunsight was tested on an Avro 504 and initially was found to be unsuitable. The sight was completely redesigned as the GD2A and accepted and produced in 1927 in limited quantities as the GD2B/1927, proving to be excellent in quality and function. During the inter-war years all work on gunsights was considered top secret and there is not much information available on the subject. At the time there was a worldwide economic depression and anti-military sentiment, and thus there were no orders for the B&S sights.

GD5-GD12

In 1935, the company introduced the GD5 gunsight designed specifically for the new Hawker Demon fighter. During testing the Demon pilot made a bumpy landing and hit his face on the protruding sight, experiencing the first of many bloody noses suffered in the years to come by fighter pilots from hitting their gunsights. The GD5 proved to be unsuitable, as the windscreen projection system caused problems with double imaging and the sight was difficult to manufacture. Instead, the Demon fighters were equipped with the Aldis and ring and bead sights. The GD5 underwent a number of modifications for use in the new Hawker PV3 Fury (the last Hawker biplane) as the GD12 but no orders for were received. Barr and Stroud's revolutionary GM 1 reflector sights were under development and were considered the gunsights of the future, and would render the GD12 obsolete.

**Barr and Stroud Fixed Fighter Aircraft Reflector Gunsights**

GM1

In 1935 B&S undertook the development of a new prototype sight designated as the Type GM 1, which had an integral reflector that would be more adaptable for sequential production. In using the innovative sight the pilot first set the span dial to the known wingspan of his prospective target, then the range dial to the maximum range required for accurate fire. When the target coincided with the area in the reflector it was within range and the gunner would fire.

GM2/MkII

The GM2 prototype and components were tested at Farnborough, and then air firing tests were conducted at Martlesham in a Bristol Bulldog. The results of the trials instigated several modifications, and the modified sight was designated the Type GM2 and patented in 1937 when it was accepted as the standard fixed gunsight of the RAF. The first sights of an initial order of 1,600 equipped several Gloster Gladiator squadrons in 1938. Orders increased for installation on the new Spitfire and Hurricane fighters ordered after Chamberlain's Munich debacle later that year. With a European war looming, Barr and Stroud informed the Air Staff that it would be unable to furnish enough GM2 sights. Ironically, there was no other optical company in the UK that was technologically able to produce the GM2 and a contract was let to the C.P. Goertz Austrian Optical Company of Vienna to produce the sight. The future enemy company produced 700 before war broke out in September 1939 when Goertz fell into Nazi hands.

The GM2 was the standard sight used by RAF Fighter Command during the Battle of Britain and into 1941, when it was modified because the circular sighting screen was found to have minor optical flaws and was replaced by a four inch square reflector screen. Also, since combat reports revealed that the sun screen was rarely used it was deleted. The modified sight was Service designated as the Reflector Sight Mark II Pilot's Sight. The GM2 Mark II remained in production at Barr and Stroud throughout the war, and in 1941 the Salford Electrical Instrument Company of Weybridge was licensed to meet increased production demands for the GM2 Mark II. By the end of the war more than 84,000 GM2 gunsights had been manufactured.

In 1942, the U.S. Navy adopted the GM2 as the Illuminated Sight Mark 8. The U.S. version was not equipped with the stadiametric ranging device with its graticule being a ring and center dot. The British-made version found extensive use in equipping USAAF fighter squadrons and remained in service until the introduction of the gyro sight in 1944.

GM2 Operation

The GM2 would become the most important gunsight of early World War II and was the first reflector sight to use adjustable Stadiometric ranging, which solved the longstanding gunsight problem of determining range.

Stadiametric Range Finding, or the Stadia Method, was a technique of measuring distances with a telescopic instrument. The term Stadia was derived from the Greek meaning a unit of length. Stadiametric Ranging had been in use since the 1850s when the stadia apparatus was used to measure range for artillery pieces. Besides its principal use for military gunsights, Stadiametric Range Finding was also used extensively in surveying instruments and in some expensive binoculars. Today it has been replaced by infrared, microwave, and laser range finding methods.

The Stadia Method was based on the principle that in similar triangles the corresponding sides were proportional (i.e. for a right triangle with a given angle, the ratio of adjacent side length to opposite side length was constant). By using a reticle with marks of a known angular spacing, the principle of similar triangles could be used to either find the distance to targets of known size, or to find the size of targets at a known distance.

Combat studies showed that a pilot or gunner would often start to fire as soon as the target came into view in the sight. The GM2 sight specified precisely when the target was at an effective predetermined range, and also correctly compensated for bullet drop. In its early artillery use the stadia consisted of a glass or brass plate perforated with an elongated triangular hole. To determine barrel elevation the artillery range man held the plate at arm's length and compared the height of the distant infantry or cavalry soldier targets with graduated markings in hundreds of yards engraved along the top of the triangular hole. The GM2 used an adjustable opening in the horizontal aiming line; the complete graticule consisted of a bright orange circle that had horizontal and perpendicular lines overlaid. When adjusting the GM2 the pilot set the target's range and the type of target aircraft by turning two knurled knobs located at the base of the housing, causing the horizontal bar of the bright orange circle to have an opening in the center. In combat the pilot closed on the target until its wingspan fit into the opening and then aimed at a predetermined distance above it to allow for bullet drop. This procedure was straightforward during a tail attack, in which the target was flying straight and level. If the target was turning or flying across the line of sight then a deflection angle had to be predicted.

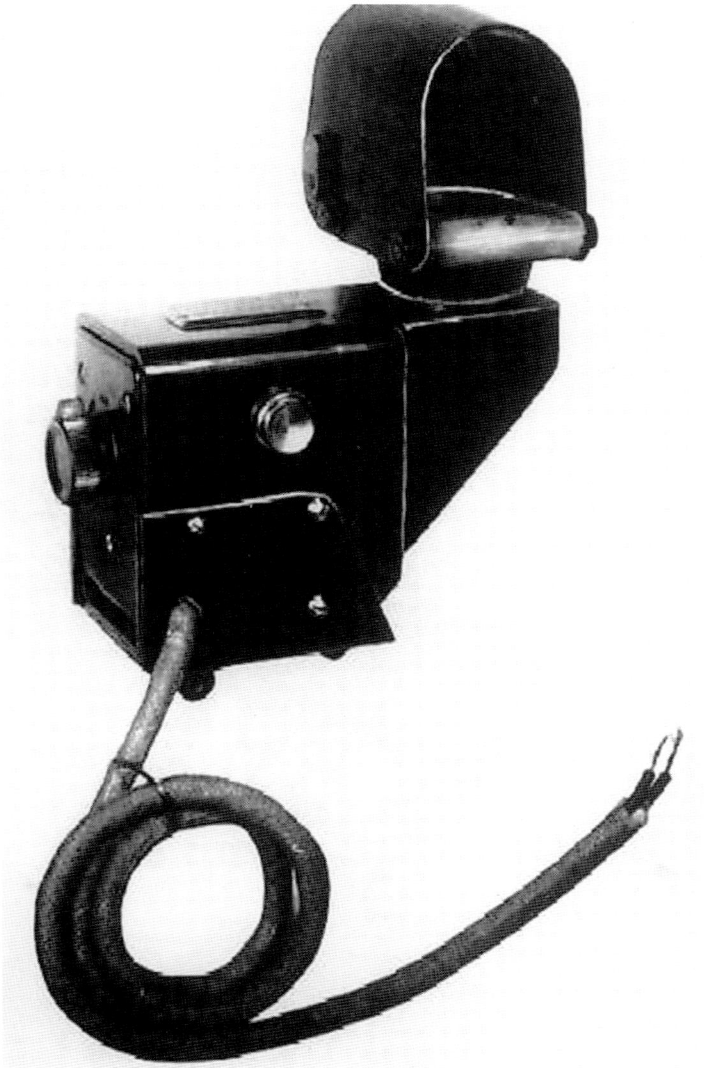

**Barr & Stroud J1 Aerial Reflector Gunsight** (AFHRC)

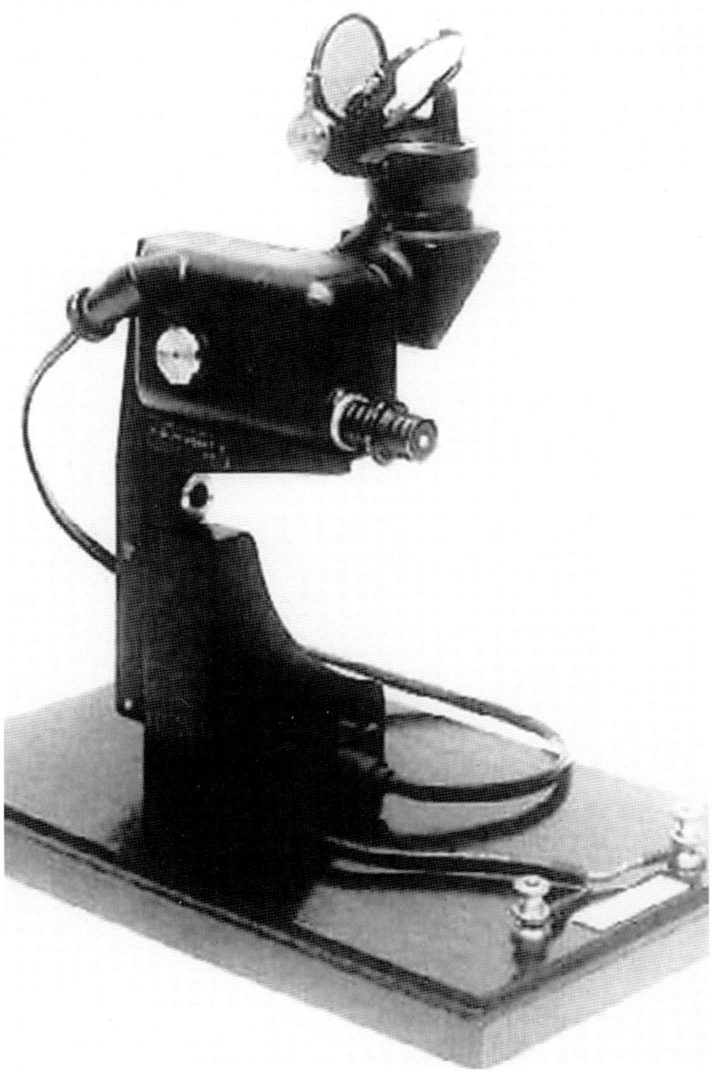

**Barr & Stroud GH6 Aerial Reflector Gunsight** (AFHRC)

The range finding ability of the GM2 was ideal for attacking slow moving bombers, but was found to be lacking when pursuing nimble fighter aircraft. The three inch circular reflector screen of the GM2 was much larger than the GD 5 and was fitted with a large rubber pad in front of the lens housing to protect the pilot's face. A sun screen, controlled by a knurled knob, pivoted and swung out from the base. The sighting unit was powered by 12-volt DC current and its light source was a dual filament bulb. The pilot controlled the light via a three position switch, OFF, NIGHT, and DAY, mounted on the instrument panel under the sight housing. The DAY position switched on the 18-watt filament to generate a clear, bright graticule, while the NIGHT position switched on the 6-watt filament to generate a very dim graticule that was sufficient for night viewing.

**Section 4: Development of Turret and Free Gunsights**
**Barr and Stroud Turret and Free Reflector Gunsight**

J1

Barr and Stroud developed the Type J1 gunsight for turrets and free guns in 1926. The J1 was mounted on an elevated bracket on the mid-barrel of a Lewis gun and consisted of a circular reflector screen mounted over a cone-shaped lens housing with a rear sun screen which could be raised. The J1 tested to be accurate, and only a few improvements were recommended, but nonetheless it was decided to develop a new design.

GH6

The sight designated as the GH6 consisted of a rectangular lamp housing offset from the center line of the gun. A bulb projected a ring graticule from the side of the housing onto a prism, which aimed the image through a system of lenses onto a small circular reflector screen that was equipped with a swinging smoked-glass sun screen located behind it. The GH6 was accepted for testing, but during night trials in 1934 the light from searchlights caused a "dazzle" on the reflector screens, causing it to be discontinued for the next series of Barr and Stroud developments.

GJ3

In the mid-1930s, as bomber speeds increased gunners were exposed to and immobilized by the aircraft's powerful slipstream. Initially windscreens were installed to protect the gunners, followed by rotating glazed domes or copulas; and then by enclosed, powered turrets equipped with guns that were distant from the gunner's line of sight. The position of the guns necessitated a sight remote from but linked to the gun movement. Barr & Stroud developed the GJ3 that eventually would be produced in the greatest numbers of any British sight. The GJ3 consisted of a detachable lamp unit and an upright sight head, with the glass reflector screen mounted to a housing over the lens tube. The optics and electrical units of the prototype GJ3 sight were tested and found satisfactory at Farnborough, while air firing trials were successfully completed at Martlesham Heath with a few minor improvements recommended. B&S was given an initial production order with the sight given the service title of the Mark III Free Gun Reflector Sight.

Mk III Turret Sight

When Mk III turret sight production began the Barr and Stroud lens-making factory was at capacity, as the Mk III and Mk II pilot's sights required many high-quality lenses and the subcontractors were unable to meet the demand. B&S then decided to produce a version of the Mk III using stadiametric ranging, but gunners found it to be difficult to operate with the heavy flying gloves required at high altitudes, and lenses for the original Mk III were procured. The Mk III series was one of the most successful reflector sights ever developed, as nearly every turret in RAF Bomber Command was equipped with it. The Mk III was accepted by the U.S. Air Force and U.S. Navy as the Mark 9 and produced in America by the Woolensak Optical Co. of Rochester, NY.

**Section 5: American Reflector Gunsights**
**Mark 9**

The Mark 9, developed from the Barr & Stroud Mk III, was a two ring reflector sight in a simple arrangement of a single electric light bulb inside a small housing, a reticle, lens, and reflector plate.

Pre-flight Check

The gunner checked the reflector plate for cleanliness and the rings and pipper for sharpness and clarity. The knurled thumb screw switch was tested to be sure that both filaments of the light bulb were functioning and that the dimmer worked correctly. The gunner checked that the spare bulb was available.

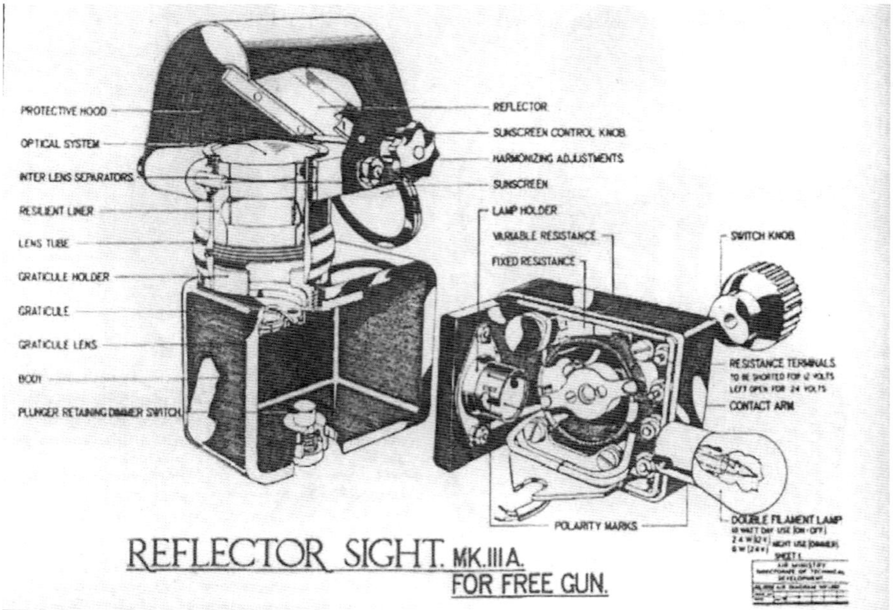


**Barr & Stroud MKIII Aerial Reflector Gunsight** (AFHRC)

**American Mark 9 Reflector Gunsights** (AFHRC)

Operating the Mark 9

Located on the side of the sight case was a knurled thumb screw switch that could be turned to "OFF," "DAY," and "NIGHT" to allow varying degrees of light. A 21-6 candlepower double filament, double contact, type S8, 24-28-volt frosted inside lamp bulb was used inside the sight. The lamp bulb had a white line on one side of its base, while the lamp socket in the sight had a white line on its side. The lamp bulb had to be placed in the lamp socket so that the mark on the base of the lamp bulb lined up with the white line on the lamp socket in the sight or the lamp would not light or could burn out.

The sight was operated by looking at the target through a glass plate on which the light bulb projected a dot called a "pipper," and two rings that showed the gunner where to aim. The gunner placed the pipper between the attacking aircraft and the tail of his bomber along the fighter's line of apparent motion (Position Firing). To apply any deflection of up to two rads, the gunner simply placed the fighter in the appropriate place as per the Position Firing diagram. To apply deflection greater than two rads, the gunner imagined additional rings outside the "real" two rings and at the same distance apart as the 35 mil and 70 mil rings. He then placed the attacker with reference to the appropriate imaginary ring as per Position Firing diagrams. In using reflector sights there was no problem in lining up the bead and pip as the optical system made it unnecessary to maintain a set sight base. Each rad was always equal to a 35 mil angle, even if the gunner moved his head as he looked into the sight. When firing into the sun there was a sun filter located in front of the hooded section that could be positioned in or out of the line of sight by a scalloped thumb wheel.

**Mark 9 Mod 1 Sight**

The Mark 9 Mod 1 Sight was identical to the Mark 9, except that it operated on a 12-volt system versus the 24 to 28-volt system used by the Mark 9. The sight used a 21-6 candle power, double filament double contact, type S8, 12-volt lamp that was frosted inside.

**Section 6: Development of Computing Gunsights**

**Gyroscopic Lead Computing Sight**

The use of a gyro to facilitate deflection shooting was advocated as early as 1917 by RCF Wing Commander L.J. Wackett and Maj. Melville Jones, but it was not until 1936 that mathematics professor Dr. L.B.C. Cunningham of the RAF Education Branch developed the mathematics that could solve the problem of air-to-air deflection shooting. Cunningham stated that a gyroscope could "offset the line of sight from the gun line, through an angle determined by the rate of turn of the sight line." Dr Cunningham's premise depended on a gyroscope's ability to resist any rotation of its axis. If a gyro was fastened on a rod on which a ring and bead sight was mounted, any effort to follow a crossing target depended on the target's crossing speed. A gyro sight would have to present the gunner with a sight line held back by the gyro, while the line of flight and guns would be in front of this sight line; if the gunner kept to the sight line indicated by the gyro, his guns would automatically point correctly in direct relation to the rate of turn. At the time Cunningham's groundbreaking insight was overlooked by the RAF because the revolutionary Barr & Stroud GM Reflector GM2 gunsight was near completion.

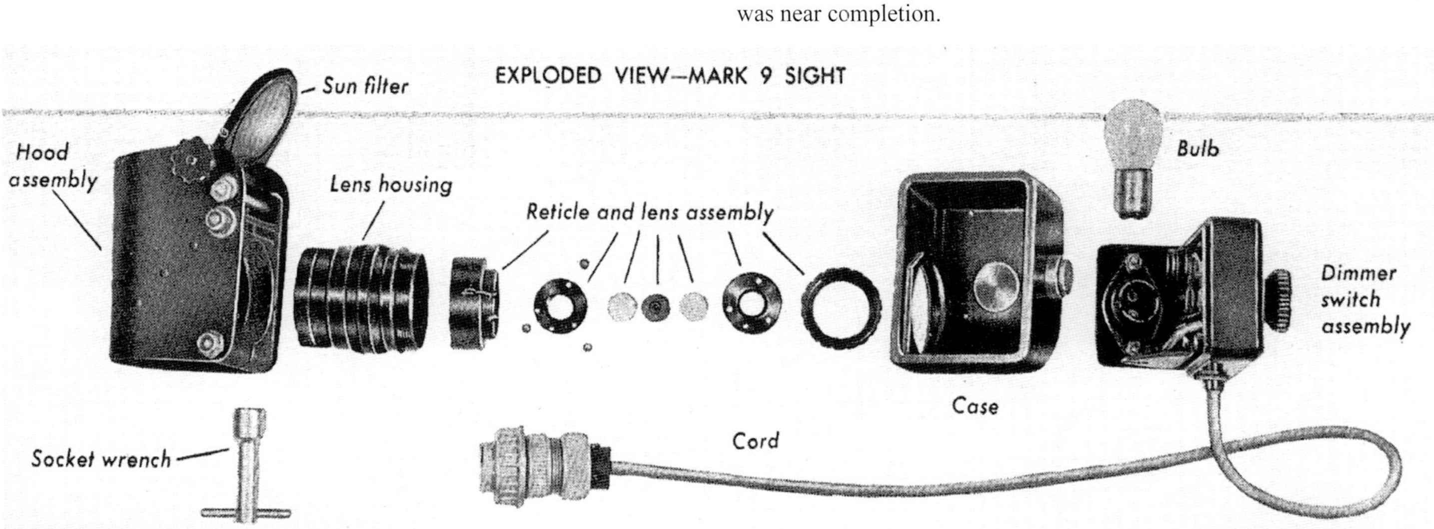


(USAAF)

In 1938, the Air Staff scheduled wide-ranging tactical exercises at Northolt to evaluate all facets of air combat and tactics in anticipation of an approaching war. During the exercises the new G45 gun camera was installed in several fighters that also were fitted with the new GM2 gunsight. The films of simulated combat maneuvers were analyzed by armament specialists from the Royal Aircraft Establishment at Farnborough, who found that very few pilots were proficient in deflection shooting. The renowned Dr. Henry Tizard, the head of the Committee for the Scientific Survey of Air Defense, received the report and forwarded it to the Air Staff, which became concerned about the deficiencies of the GM2. The Air Ministry appointed the Director of the Royal Aircraft Establishment (RAE) at Farnborough to explore an "airborne predictor gunsight" for use in fighter aircraft and bomber gun turrets. The project was top secret, high priority, and given carte blanche.

Farnborough used Dr. Cunningham's overlooked mathematical premises as a starting point for his development of the new sight. While Cunningham was proven correct, Farnborough's primary problem with the sensitive gyros was to design a sturdy unit that could function in the stress of combat. In October 1939, two similar experimental gyro sights were ready to be installed at Boscombe Down: one in the normal position in a Hurricane fighter and the other in the retractable ventral Frazer Nash 25 turret of a Wellington bomber. By the summer of 1940 the test results were encouraging, in that the rudimentary sights could predict the lead angle correctly. The RAE Director reported to the Air Staff that a potentially operational sight designated as the Mk I GGS (Gyro Gunsight) was ready for testing and was assigned the code name "Type 6 Mechanism." He also pointed out that it was obvious that extensive redesign would be required.

**Mk I Gyro Gunsight**

In mid-1940, the RAE Director announced that the operational gyro-controlled sight, designated as the Mk I, was ready for trials. The Mk I gyro was connected to a shaft by a universal joint and driven by an electric motor. A saucer-shaped dome that revolved under the influence of four electro-magnets was attached to the shaft. The ball-shaped end of the shaft was moved by a complicated linkage mechanism that controlled the moving graticule. When the gyro was spinning any axial movement was resisted, so that when the sight was turned to follow a target, the gyro caused the moving graticule to lag behind the direction in which the guns were pointing. The amount of lag depended on the rate of turn. The angle of deflection was also influenced by range, altitude, and bullet drop, and the gunner pre-set these parameters by pointers on the control box which provided current to the electro-magnets. The magnets acted on the dome and this movement, along with that exerted by the gyro, provided the exact angle of deflection.

Once the Mk I design was completed, the Air Staff ordered Ferranti and Elliott Bros. (London) Ltd. to organize production even before the sight was tested. In September 1940, when the head of the RAF Gunnery Research Unit learned that the Mk I was going into production before testing, he contacted the Air Staff to point out the inherent problems of placing untried, off the drawing board equipment into production. Nonetheless, Ferranti and Elliott was instructed to continue its pre-production preparations. In early 1941, Farnborough had finished the first Mk I prototypes and installed them in a Spitfire and in the turret of a Boulton-Paul Defiant for preliminary trials, which were successful. The Air Staff then ordered Ferranti and Elliott to begin limited production, and soon the first Mk Is were fitted in Spitfires and Hurricanes of Fighter Command operational squadrons. In order that the new sights wouldn't fall into German hands they were only to be used against *Luftwaffe* raids over south England during July and August 1941. Meanwhile, the Air Staff decided to continue only limited production until final operational tests were completed. In September 1941 Sir Sholto Douglas, the Chief of Fighter Command, reported to the Air Staff that the Mk I was "far from satisfactory" because the sight was too sensitive, and its small eyepiece limited the pilot's vision and presented a danger to the pilot's face in case of a crash landing. The Mk I was installed into Bomber Command Wellington rear turrets, and while the gunners showed improved marksmanship, there were complaints about the illumination of the graticule for night operations, the above mentioned restrictions of the small eyepiece, and the unevenness of the moving graticule. After receiving these reports the Air Staff decided to postpone full production of the Mk I, with limited production to continue to supply enough sights only for training and practice.

**Mk II Gyro Gunsight**

The staff at Farnborough included some of the finest British scientists, including (recently Knighted) Sir Melville Jones (the WW-I gyro gunsight advocate), A.A. Hale, B. Sykes, and Grp.Capt. Ford, who were aided by the Ferranti Company's expertise in the manufacture of the gyro and electrical components. The Farnborough group did not modify the Mk I as much as to develop a virtually new design that included many unique technological developments. In the new design the altitude and airspeed calibrating unit of the original Mk I had been found to be excellent and was continued without modification. The basic solution to the Mk I's problems was remarkably simple; a mirror was attached to the end of the gyro column and reflected the illuminated graticule of a reflector sight upwards onto the reflector plate of the sight. When the gyro turned the illuminated graticule moved to the correct position to allow for deflection.

The Farnborough Mk II design also added a ranging capability. The moving graticule consisted of a ring of six diamonds that were adjustable in diameter to correspond with the wingspan of the target aircraft. Prior to firing the type of enemy aircraft was dialed into the sight, which allowed it to calculate the range by utilizing the same stadiometric principle as the GM2 horizontal opening.

The reflector screen of the new sight was a large 4.7 x 2.4 inch glass plate on which the gunner viewed two separate illuminated graticules. The left graticule was fixed and was normally switched off, but could be used as an ordinary reflector sight if the gyros failed. The primary use of the fixed graticule was to harmonize the sight and guns. The right graticule, consisting of the six diamonds, was the moving graticule and was controlled by the gyro. The diameter of the six diamonds was adjusted by foot pedals in the turret variety of the sight and by a twist grip on the pilot's joystick in the fighter type. Both types could be dimmed for night action or used individually by switching either one off.

The initial prototype sights produced by Farnborough were tested by the Armament Research Unit in July 1943, and it soon became evident that the problems of the Mk I had been remedied, so the Air Staff let a production contract to Ferranti for a purpose-built factory in Edinburgh to manufacture both the turret and fighter versions of the sight that were to be designated as the Gyro Gunsight GGS Mk IIC (turret) and the Mk IID (fighter). The first production Ferranti Mk II sights were ready by the end of 1943 and were lauded by both new and veteran pilots and gunners. The sight was licensed for manufacture in America as the K-14 (USAAF) and MK 18 (U.S. Navy).

**Section 7: American Computing Gunsights**

**Position Firing vs. Computing Sighting**

At the time the British were having problems with their Mk 1 gyro gunsight and were embarking on designing the Mk II, Sperry issued an early bulletin (August 1942) on their estimate of the future operational use of the computing gunsight. The bulletin stated that computing gunsights would function best at longer ranges, while the auxiliary ring and bead sight was to be used at close ranges because the computer could not rapidly track the relative angles and ranges to the target in order to compute the required lead azimuth and elevation angles.

The concept of Position Firing had a profound influence on flexible gunnery from 1943 onward. Position Firing was based upon the course or pursuit curve which an enemy aircraft had to fly in order to attack a bomber, and upon the gunner firing on the attacking aircraft when it was in a position to make an attack. This established gunnery principle contrasted to those of computing sights and ballistics, and provoked questions and caused differences of opinion among American armament experts. A major question was to determine the distance to begin firing: before the enemy was close enough to attack or when it was near enough to have more certain damaging effect? Armament tests showed that allowing the attacker to get in close and then to begin firing at 600 yards was the most effective method, although there were those who continued to insist that firing at 1,200 yards was better.

Once the computing gunsight was available the value of Position Firing was debated among high ranking AAF officers. During a Tampa Flexible Gunnery Training Conference in April 1944, Brig.Gen. U.G. Ent, Commanding General of the Second Air Force, stated that three key factors were interfering with the standardization and simplification of flexible gunnery training. The first issue was the controversy over methods of sighting flexible guns and the ranges at which they were effective. The second was the controversy about the effectiveness of computing sights then in use, while the third was the controversy over tow-target practice versus blank ammunition fired simultaneously with the gun camera (For a complete explanation of Position Firing see Part Nine/Chapter 6: Bomber Turret Air-to-Air Tactics.).

**USAAF Computing Gunsights**

| Sight | Use | Aircraft Use |
|---|---|---|
| K-3 | Gunner | B-17 |
| K-4 | Gunner | B-17, B-24 |
| K-7 | Gunner | N/A |
| K-8 | Gunner | B-26? |
| K-9 | Gunner | B-24 |
| K-10 | Gunner | B-17 (tail), B-24 (nose), B-25J (tail) |
| K-11 | Gunner | B-24 (nose), B-32 (nose) |
| K-13 | Gunner | B-17G (waist), B-24 (waist) |
| K-14 | Fighter | P-51D, P-47D |
| K-14A | Fighter | P-51D |
| K-14B | Fighter | P-47D, P-51D |
| K-14C | Fighter | P-51D |
| K-15 | Gunner | B-17 |
| K-15A | Gunner | B-24 |
| K-17 | Gunner | B-17, B-24 |
| A/C/D/F | Gunner | B-29 (optical unit of sighting station) |

**Sperry K-3/K-4**

The Sperry K-3 sight was mounted in the company's dorsal turret. It was used by sighting through a glass screen mounted in an optic head, similar to looking into an optical sight. Three lines called reticles were visible on the K-3's glass screen: one was horizontal and two vertical. These reticles were used instead of the ring to line up the target.

The Sperry K-4 was an upside down adaptation of the K-3 that was designed especially for the company's ball turret. Instead of being mounted

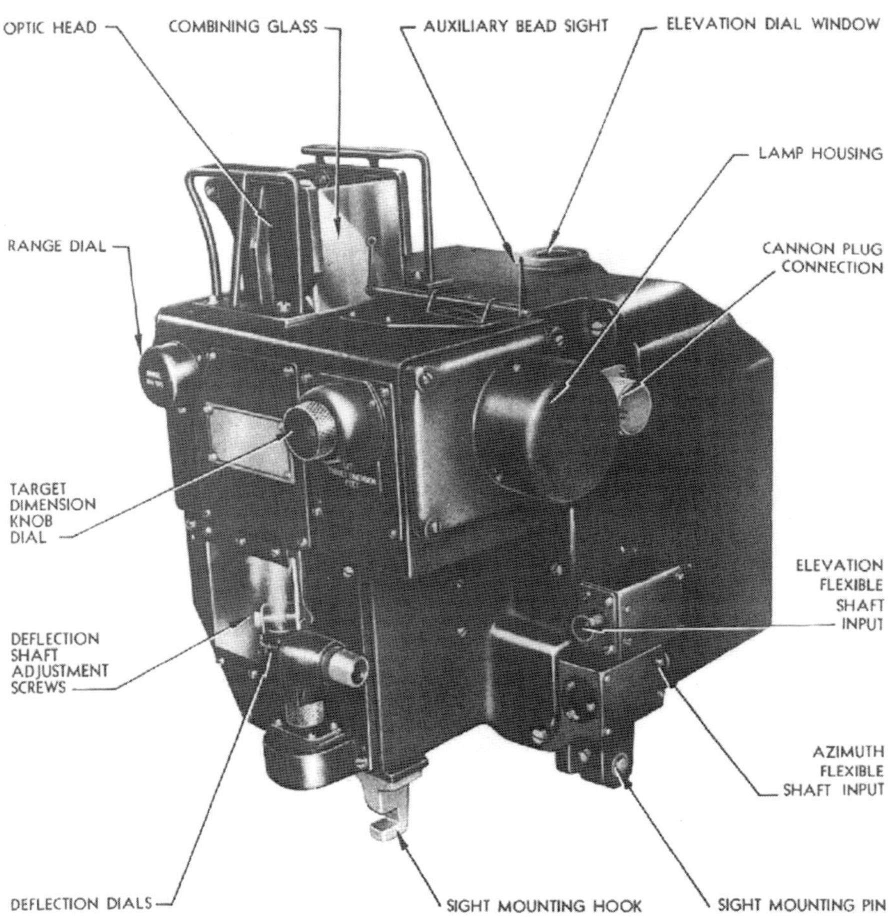


**Figure 788—Sperry Caliber .50 Computing Sight Model K-4**

upright, it was hung down from the turret's sight cradle, reversing the position of the dials. The range control was a pedal operated by the gunner's left foot. In all other respects the K-4 was exactly like the K-3.

Pre-Flight Check
Before takeoff, the gunner turned the sight switch ON/OFF and checked to be sure that the reticles would light and the rheostat worked. The reticle lamp switch was flipped both ways, and if one of its two filaments did not work, the bulb was to be replaced. The guns were to be tracked to the left, right, up, and down. The gunner was to be sure that the reticles moved closer together and farther apart as the range control was turned. The reticles were supposed to drag somewhat, moving across the optic head in the opposite direction.

K-3/4 Sight Computer
Connected with the K-3/4 sight's optic head was a basic computer that calculated deflections and directed the guns to the correct angle. In order to make its computations the computer required three specific pieces of information about the target:

1) The target wing span, which was furnished by setting the target dimension dial located on the sight housing.
2) The range of the target was provided by adjusting the range control to keep the vertical reticles framing the target. The range control was a knob or motorcycle-type handgrip located on the turret control handles.
3) The apparent motion of the target was supplied by tracking the target so that the vertical reticle was always across the center of the target.

Once this information was provided the K-3/4 computer made its computations, which could increase the sight's effective range to 1,000 yards.

Operating the K-3/4
The sight switch located on the front panel of the sight housing was turned ON, which would light the reticles and start the computer. The proper reticle brightness was adjusted by the rheostat located on the sight housing. The filter was adjusted for proper contrast. As soon as the gunner spotted an enemy fighter he needed to identify it to determine its wingspan in order to set the target dimension dial. The gunner tracked the target by moving his guns to keep the horizontal reticle across the center of the target. By turning the range control, the reticles could be moved closer or further apart. He continued moving the range control until the vertical reticles framed the width of the target's wingtips. In order for the computer to make the proper computations of range the reticles had to be kept on the wingtips of the target. If the target banked the gunner was to keep an imaginary circle through its wingtips framed by the vertical reticles. If the top or bottom of the target was seen instead of the nose, then the gunner was to frame an imaginary circle with the reticles through the wingtips. Targets approaching from the side would seem to be a particular problem, as the wingspan could not be seen. However, this was not the case, as wingspan and length on most aircraft were nearly equal. Ranging would be accurate if the fuselage was framed or an imaginary circle was drawn through the ends of the fuselage. It was helpful for the gunner to be proficient in aircraft recognition, because if it were known that the wingspan of the target were significantly longer than the fuselage then the reticles could be kept at a corresponding distance from the ends of the fuselage. The target dimension indicator dial registered wingspans only up to 60 feet. For the very few enemy aircraft that had wingspans exceeding this, the gunner was to set the dial to half the target wingspan and then frame only the center half of the target. The target was within the range of the guns as soon as its wingtips reached the

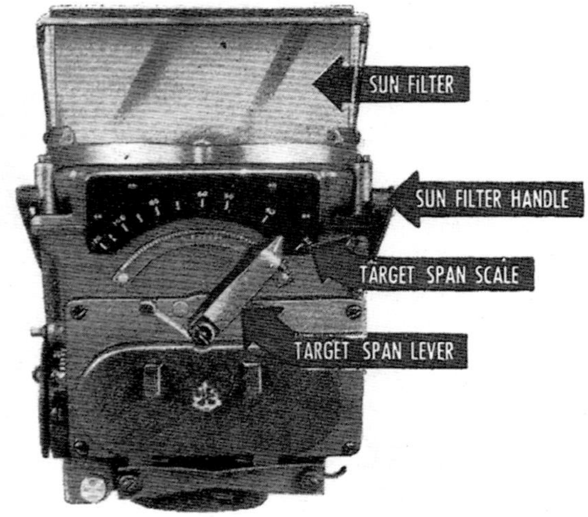


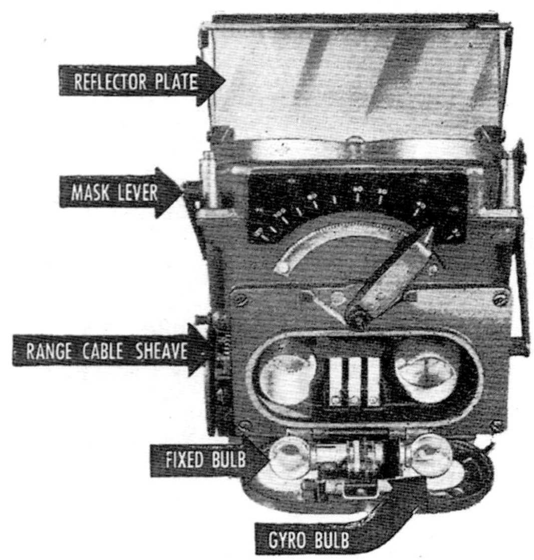

**The Mark 18 (USN), K-14 (USAAF), and MK II (RAF) Computing**

vertical reticles, which could only be set close enough together for 1,000 yards. The gunner was to track the target as smoothly as possible, as the sight was only effective when it was given a clear, smooth depiction of the target's apparent movement. In fighter aircraft using the K-3/4s the pilot had to be well-trained to cage and uncage the gyros when taking part in violent aerobatics so as not to damage the gunsight. When the gyros were caged the K-3/4 sighting system acted as a simple reflector gunsight.

Care of the K-3/4

The optic head of the K-3/4 was very fragile, and care was to be taken not to bump or jar it. It was never to be touched except to clean the reflector glass, dust shield, and sun filter. No adjustment or lubrication of the sight was to be done by the gunner. The turret was not to be operated unless the sight switch was ON or the computer could be damaged. The sight switch was not to be turned ON before the turret's main power switch had been turned ON.

### The Sperry K-9

The Sperry K-9 was installed in Martin dorsal turrets. Like the K-4, its range control was operated by a pedal by the left foot. The computer, instead of being directly connected to the sighting unit, was mounted in the turret separately and was connected to the optic head with flexible shafts and booster motors. In all other respects, the K-9 was exactly like the K-3 sight.

**Gunsight** (USAAF)

### The Mark 18 (USN), K-14 (USAAF), and MK II (RAF)

#### Introduction

The Mark 18/K-14 was the licensed U.S. version of the successful British MK II, which was an electrically operated computing, reflector-type sight designed for use in power turrets and fighter aircraft. The Mark 18/K-14 contained two sights: both the "ordinary" fixed electrical sight and gyro-actuated optical systems. The later "A" version of this sight differed only in that the latter had range lines on the fixed reticle that were used for aiming rockets.

The fixed optical system projected a cross hair on the reflector glass, surrounded by a 70 mil ring that could be removed by pulling down the masking lever on the left side of the sight. The gyro system projected a variable diameter circle of six diamond-shaped pips surrounding a central dot. The fixed sight could be used alone, but ordinarily the cross hair was used (when the ring was deleted) to show the amount of lead the gyro sight was allocating.

When using the gyro system the gunner entered the proper settings on the control units, enabling him to then range and track the target as the sight automatically computed the point of aim, no matter the situation. The sight had two optical systems and two reticles. When the gunner looked at the two reticles through the reflector plate they appeared to be projected into space. The left reticle, called the fixed reticle, was viewed with the left eye and resembled the inner ring of the Mark 9 reflector sight. The reticle on the right side of the reflector plate, viewed with the right eye, was called the gyro, or movable reticle. This reticle consisted of a center "pipper" that was surrounded by six diamond-shaped "pips" arranged in a circle.

### Components of the Mark 18/K-14 Gunsight

#### Reticles

Gyro Reticle

The circle formed by the six diamond-shaped pips of the gyro reticle could be made to spread out or close in. When the turret was operated the gyro reticle (the center pipper and six diamonds) moved around the reflector plate. The gyro reticle automatically computed the correct deflection if the gunner framed, or "spanned," in an imaginary circle drawn so that it cut the inside points of the six diamond pips of the gyro reticle and also formed the center of the imaginary circle.

Fixed Reticle

The fixed reticle was essentially the same as the inner ring of the Mark 9 reflector sight. The only difference was that the center of the fixed reticle was a cross instead of a round pipper as in the Mark 9. The fixed cross indicated the direction the guns were pointing. The fixed reticle was used for aligning the two reticle systems for boresighting, for maintenance and gunner checks, and as a standby sight in case of malfunction of the gyro reticle. Sighting with the fixed reticle was the same as with the Mark 9 sight, except it had only a one rad ring, whereas the Mark 9 had a one and two rad ring,

**Sighting Head**

The sighting head was the sight. It contained the reflector plate through which the gunner viewed the fixed and gyro reticles.

Sighting Head Components

The *sun filter control* was a lever on the right hand side of the sighting head. On bright sunny days the sun filter was raised by lifting the handle.

The *fixed reticle mask lever handle* was located on the left side of the sighting head. The handle, when depressed, blanked out the ring of the fixed reticle and left only the center cross showing.

The *range cable sheave* was located below the fixed reticle mask lever. It mechanically connected to the movable reticle and controlled the movement of the six diamond pips, and was numbered in feet from 600 to 2,400.

The *target span scale* was located on the sighting head directly in front of the gunner. It was numbered from 30 to 120, which represented the size of the target in feet. The target span lever was moved side-to-side to correspond to the known dimensions of the target.

A *double-latched door* that opened downward was located just under the target span scale and lever. Both latches were depressed to open the door. Inside the doors were two lamp bulbs that provided light for the two reticles.

The *silica gel cell* was located on the front of the sighting head on the side farthest away from the gunner. It was a small plastic container filled with a blue gel type material that dried out the air entering the sighting head and prevented the sight from fogging.

The *gyro pot* was a large cup located to the side of the silica gel cell that housed the gyro and electromagnets of the computing mechanism.

The *gyro motor housing* was the small cup located under the silica gel cell and housed the electric motor that turned the gyro.

Two small *adjusting screws* were located on the sighting head next to the gyro motor housing. One screw could not be turned unless the silica gel cell was removed. These two screws adjusted the fixed mirror within the sighting head so that the fixed reticle could be aligned with the gyro reticle. The adjusting screw under the silica gel cell provided the horizontal adjustment, while the other provided vertical adjustment.

The *azimuth boresighting ring* was located on the bottom of the sighting head. This ring was equipped with four notches that allowed the movement of the sighting head. The sighting head could be moved to the left or right by loosening the mounting bracket bolt projecting from the bottom of the sighting head the number of notches necessary to harmonize to the guns.

An *anti-vibration mount* was provided under the sighting head near the mounting bracket to absorb shock.

**Selector-Dimmer**

The selector-dimmer consisted of a four-point switching device and a rheostat. It was usually mounted near the gunner's left hand within easy reach. The selector-dimmer unit enabled the gunner to turn on either the fixed or gyro reticle, or both at the same time.

A pointer located on the face of the unit could be turned to the following positions:

FIXED: Only the fixed reticle was visible through the reflector plate. This switch was used for boresighting, maintenance and gunner's checks, and when the fixed reticle was used as a standby light.
FIXED & GYRO: Both the fixed and gyro reticles were visible through the reflector plate. This switch position was used for daytime firing, for alignment of the two reticle systems, and for gunner checks.
GYRO DAY: Only the gyro reticle was visible. This switch was optional for daytime firing.
GYRO NIGHT: Only the gyro reticle was visible. This switch position was used for night firing because combat ranges at night are necessarily short.

On the outer circumference of the selector-dimmer unit was a knurled ring (dimmer) that operated the rheostat controlling the brightness of the reticles. The dimmer was turned counterclockwise for increased brightness and clockwise for dimming the reticles.

**Altitude and Airspeed Unit**

This unit was mounted so that its numbers were visible and control pointers were easily reached. The top half of this unit was the airspeed section and was numbered from 0 to 250 mph. The indicated airspeed (IAS) of the gunner's aircraft was entered ("set in") by moving the pointer to the correct number. The lower half of the unit was the altitude section and was numbered in thousands of feet from 0 to 40. The altitude was set in by moving the pointer to the correct figure.

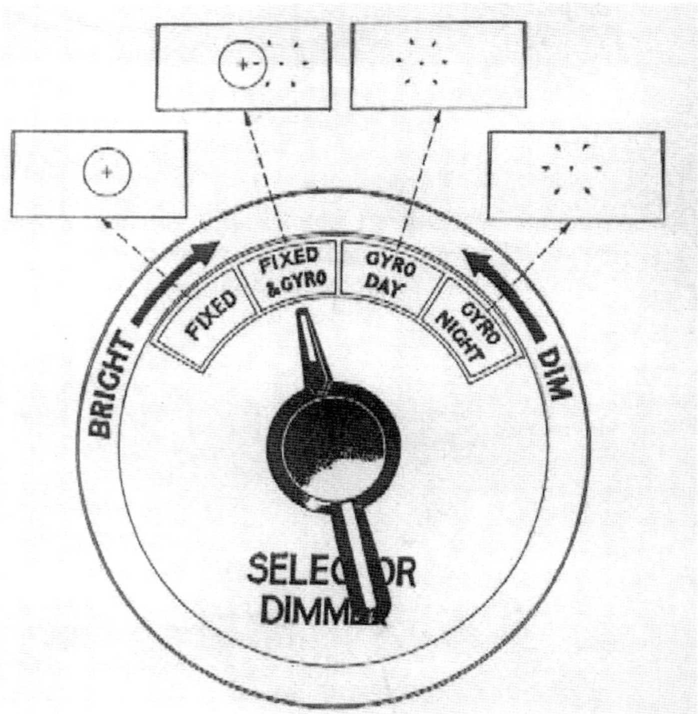


**Selector-Dimmer** (USAAF)

**Gunner's Pre-flight Check**

1) The gunner checked that all glass surfaces were clean and tested the operation of the sun filter and the fixed reticle mask lever. The range cable sheave was checked so it would not rotate when the sighting head was moved back and forth on its sliders, or when the guns were elevated or depressed.

2) The color of the silica gel cell was to be blue when it was dry, but lost its blue color and turned pinkish white as it absorbed moisture. If it were not blue it was to be replaced. The moist gel could be dried out by removing it from the cell and heating it in a metal container over a low flame until it return to its original blue color.

3) The light bulbs were to be inspected and replaced if the glass was blackened or after every five hours of sight operation. The bulb reflector receptacles were also to be cleaned.

4) The sheaves and range cables between the sighting head and the foot pedals were inspected for smooth, unimpeded operation. The fully depressed position of the left and right foot pedal stops were to correspond to 2,400 and 600 feet respectively on the range unit sheave. The over-ride springs were not to "give" before the pedals reached their stops. The 1,250 foot marking on the rage unit sheave was to correspond to 1,250 feet on the range cable sheave on the sighting head.

5) The selector-dimmer unit pointer was turned to each of its four positions. The dimmer ring was to rotate from dim to bright. The airspeed and altitude unit pointers were to turn easily and cover their scales.

6) All electric cables to the junction box and to the various units were to be checked for secure, correct connection.

7) Pipper Check: If there was no external power source, the turret was to be operated manually, and not on the aircraft batteries. If no distant target were available then an optical gauge was to be used. The checking procedure was easier to understand if the gunner remembered that the fixed cross was boresighted to the guns; therefore, the allowance between the fixed cross and the gyro pipper exhibited the angle between the sight axis and gun bore. In making a pipper check a series of inspections were made on the Selector-Dimmer Unit (on FIXED, FIXED & GYRO, GYRO DAY, and GYRO NIGHT settings), the Range Unit, Altitude and Airspeed Unit, Azimuth Unit, and Elevation Unit.

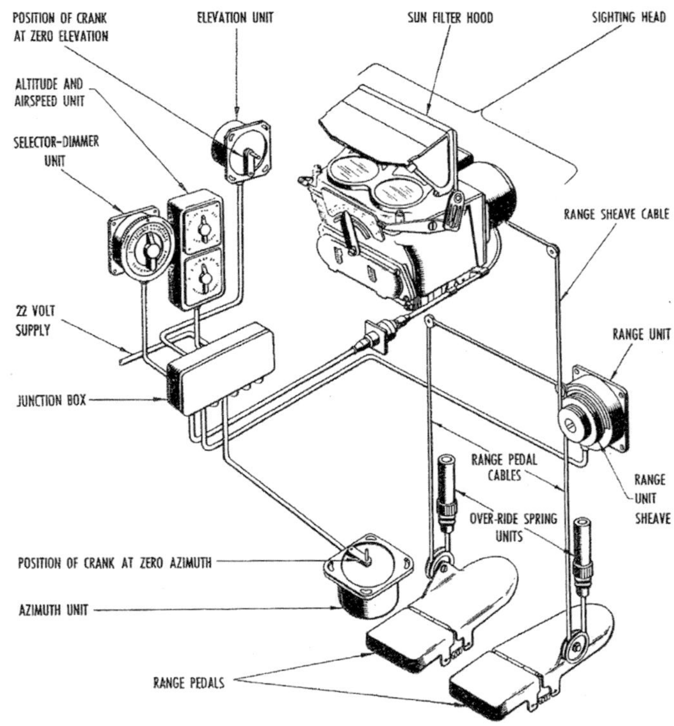


**Gun Assembly for the MK 18 Turret Gunsight** (USAAF)

**Boresighting**

Boresighting the Mark 18 established a parallel relationship between the center of the fixed cross of the fixed reticle and the bore axes of the guns.

**Operating the Mark 18 Sight For Daytime Firing**

***Preparation***

The Main Power Switch and the Sight Power Switch were turned ON. Before the engines were started, the Selector-Dimmer was turned to the FIXED & GYRO position, and then the knurled dimmer ring was turned until the reticle reached the desired brightness. When the selector was turned to FIXED only the ring and cross were to be reflected. When turned to FIXED & GYRO the ring, cross, and diamonds and dots were to be reflected. And

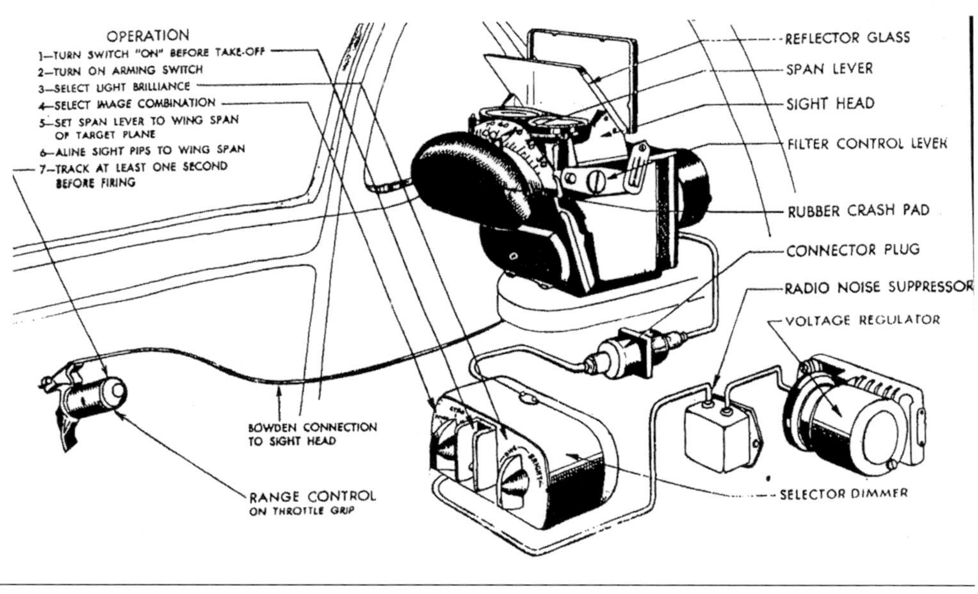


**Gun Assembly for the MK 18 Fighter Gunsight** (USAAF)

when the selector was turned to GYRO only the diamonds and dots were to be reflected. In all selections the diamonds and dots were to be clear and sharp with the dimmer control checked for control of brightness. The gun switch was set to GUNSIGHT and CAMERA. The battery was turned ON, or an outside power source was used to start the gyro. When the sight was equipped on fighter aircraft, to avoid damage to the gyro it was to be running during every takeoff and landing and was only to be turned OFF in case of failure. When used in turrets the gyro was to be run up to speed for several seconds and to prevent unnecessary wear, the sight was to be switched ON only when the enemy was encountered. Once the gyros ran up to speed, the gunner set the altitude and airspeed of his aircraft on the Altitude and Airspeed Unit. However, during an attack, when the enemy fighter pilot was taking evasive action, this setting was suspended. The range adjusting pedals or twist grip was checked for the 2,400 to 600 foot settings. Once in flight the gunner checked the lamps by opening the lamp compartment and feeling the bulbs (a cold bulb indicated that the bulb had not been burning). Also, once in flight the sun shades were adjusted or raised if necessary. When installed on a fighter aircraft, the gyros of a gunsight that was ON would affect the magnetic compass. To make compass adjustments a separate compass correction card was mounted on the instrument panel for the pilot's reference and use.

***Wingspan Setting***

The wingspan scale reading from 30 to 120 feet was located on the front of the sight. Before takeoff, the gunner was to set the wingspan for the enemy aircraft likely to be encountered on the mission. But if different types of fighters were attacking, the gunner had to change the settings when tracking each, so it was imperative that the gunner was current and knowledgeable in enemy aircraft recognition. However, if the gunner was poor or unsure of identifying aircraft the rule of thumb for wingspan settings was single-engine aircraft at 25 feet, twin-engine aircraft at 60 feet, and four engine aircraft at 110 feet.

***Ranging***

Turret-Mounted Sight

After the gunner set the correct wingspan for the attacking enemy fighter he had to range and track it accurately if the sight was to compute the deflection. On turret-mounted sights the gunner ranged the enemy by using two foot pedals attached to cables in the turret. By pushing the right pedal down, the "aiming" or "ranging" circle (or an imaginary circle drawn through the inside points of the six diamond pips of the gyro reticle) got larger. The six diamonds would move further away from the center pipper, thus making the aiming circle larger. This was minimum range. If the gunner depressed the left pedal to its limit, the diamonds moved closer toward the center pipper and the aiming circle became smaller. This was maximum range. The gunner was to be sure to frame the enemy aircraft within the aiming circle to get hits and not within the six-sided figure framed by joining the pips with straight lines.

If the enemy approached within 600 feet, the ranging circle would not get any larger and the gunner had to hold the right pedal all the way down and keep the pipper on the target. Sometimes it was not possible for the gunner to span on a full square view of the target's wingspan. If he had a full square view of the fuselage, instead of the wingspan, he was to still set the wingspan on the target span scale. However, to span properly the gunner was to keep the pipper on the enemy aircraft's cockpit and one edge of the aiming circle on the target's tail. This procedure succeeded because enemy fighters were approximately one half as long from cockpit to tail as from wingtip to wingtip. When the position of the target did not present a full square view of either his wings or fuselage the gunner was to set the wingspan, as usual, and then was to span on whatever target dimension appeared largest. In other cases the target could appear wider than long or longer than wide, or as a mass in the sky. When ranging on any of these target situations, the gunner was to keep the ranging circle somewhat larger than necessary to touch the longest dimension of the target that was apparent to the gunner, which was approximately 1/10$^{th}$ the diameter of the ranging circle on either side of him. As soon as the angle of the enemy attack changed so that the gunner could see the full wingspan or full fuselage he was to use the wingspan and fuselage ranging procedure.

Fighter-Mounted Sight

On fighter-mounted sights a twist grip was located on the throttle and attached to the sight by cable and pulleys that connected with the range pulley, which contained a dial calibrated from 2,400 to 600 feet. When the twist grip was full counter-clockwise the indicator read 2,400 feet, and as the grip was moved clockwise the indicator showed the range to be shortening.

***Tracking***

Turret-Mounted Sight

As the attacking enemy fighter closed the gunner had to "track" it by keeping it framed within the ranging circle. It was frequently necessary for the gunner to "slew," or rapidly move the turret, initially to acquire the target. The gunner was to always keep the right pedal fully depressed regardless of the range of the target. If this was not done the gyro reticles could "tumble" (drift entirely off the reflector plate), and the sight would momentarily be out of action. When slewing, the gunner had to pick up the target with the fixed reticle and swing ahead of it along its line of apparent motion. The fixed reticle showed the gunner where his guns were pointing. To help the gyro reticle catch up, the gunner had to reverse the direction of slewing along the target's path and then depress the left pedal to frame the target with the gyro reticle. The target was to be tracked smoothly and deliberately or the sight would not compute properly. Once the target was spanned the gunner had to track it for a short distance before opening fire to allow the computer to calculate deflection.

Fighter-Mounted Sight

When an enemy encounter was likely the pilot was to keep the twist grip on 600 feet and place it in that setting when shifting from one target to another. The grip was to be left in this position until the dot was on or near the target, at which time the pilot was to twist the grip to obtain the proper framing of the target. This practice lessened the chance for over-ranging, prevented over-correction, and gave the pilot the opportunity to fire more quickly. Once acquiring the target and while maneuvering, the fighter pilot had to keep the dot on the enemy and use the twist grip to adjust the reticle of diamonds so that the inner points surrounded the target.

**Night Firing**

After turning the Main Power Switch and Sight Power Switch ON the Selector-Dimmer was to be turned to GYRO NIGHT. The knurled ring (dimmer) of the unit was turned until the gyro reticle to the desired brightness (medium). No setting was required for the altitude and airspeed unit or the target span scale and their pointers could be left in any position. Ranging was not necessary, and nothing had to be done with the foot pedals or twist grip. The sight was set at a fixed range of 450 feet, as the range for firing at night rarely exceeded that distance.

**Firing with the Fixed Reticle in Case of Malfunction**

If the gyro reticle malfunctioned, the fixed reticle was to be used as a standby sight. To use the fixed reticle (had a 35 mil radius of one rad), the dimmer was turned to adjust the brightness of the reticle, and then the fixed reticle was used similarly to using the Mark 9 sight.

**K-13 Computing Gunsight**

**Automatic Gun Laying and Tracking (AGLT) Radar Gunsight** (AFHRC)

**Section 8: Radar Gunsight**

Automatic Gun Laying and Tracking (AGLT) Radar Gunsight

The RAF was the only combatant to make use of a radar gunsight during the war when it introduced the AGLT sets in the FN50 tail turrets of 90 Lancaster bombers in 1944 under the codename "Village Inn." The set was developed by Dr. Philip Dee, who had developed 10cm radar and was able to find and track and fire on a target in total darkness with the computer calculating the target's range, lead angle to the target, and bullet drop.

# 3

# Gun Cameras

The gun camera, officially titled the Gunsight Aiming Point Camera (GSAP), was manufactured by the Fairchild Camera and Instrument Company of Jamaica, NY, and the Morse Instrument Company of Hudson, OH. The Type AN-N-4 and AN-N-6, Type AN-6N, and KB-3 16mm motion film gun camera body consisted of a shutter, motor, drive mechanism, a reset film footage indicator, and a Type A-6 film magazine containing 50 feet of film.

Before takeoff a fresh film magazine was inserted into the camera by releasing the camera magazine access cover by pressing the knobs forward and pulling the cover open. The magazine was inserted with the film opening toward the lens and its footage indicator toward the side of the camera that was mounted toward the turret or guns. The magazine latch was pulled up as far as possible and then the access cover was closed. The footage indicator knob on the camera body was pushed in until the dial read "50," which was the number of feet of film available in a fresh magazine. After the camera had been used, the dial showed how many feet had been exposed during the mission.

The AN-N-6 camera had a built-in overrun mechanism, while the AN-N-4 had a separate overrun mechanism. The amount of overrun control could be set for the amount of time the camera would run after triggers were released. This time was usually determined by the combat theater or by special mission instructions. The plain lens consisted of an f/3.5 telephoto lens, a sunshade, and a No.12 minus blue interchangeable glass filter. The bore sight adapter focused the camera on the bullet convergence point. The electrically operated drive mechanism could be set for 16, 32, or 64 frames per second. The diaphragm stops were marked "B" (bright), "H" (hazy), and "D" (dull) to allow for various light conditions. Before takeoff the diaphragm ring on the camera was preset for one of three types of lighting conditions (weather) expected on the mission. However, in practice lighting conditions varied and the camera was unable to adjust, and would often provide unclear footage that was either over or under exposed.

Two types of camera mounts were used in fighter aircraft: the early North American Aviation type and the later Type C-1 mount. On early fighter aircraft the opening on the leading edge of the wing for the gun

**Gunsight Aiming Point Camera (GSAP) Type AN-N-4 and AN-N-6** (Author's Collection)

camera was covered by glass. On later fighters the opening was sealed by a spring-loaded metal plate that was actuated by a cable attached to the landing gear. The cable opened the plate when the gear was raised and closed the plate when the gear was lowered, which protected the camera from damage from debris during takeoff and landing. Cameras used in turret guns were mounted directly on the gun or on a turret structure near the gun.

The camera switch on the control box was turned ON to activate the gun camera system. The guns and camera were controlled by a three-way toggle switch (GUNS, CAMERA, and SIGHT). When the trigger(s) was pressed the guns fired and the cameras operated if the toggle was in the GUN position. The CAMERA and SIGHT positions on the toggle took motion pictures when the trigger was pressed but did not fire the guns. The camera was sighted by a boresighting adapter slightly below the gunsight line so that the camera remained on the target for a longer period after the pullout from the gunnery run. The camera could be set to stop operating as soon as the trigger was released, but it was usually set to continue to operate for three seconds after firing to show the fate of the intended target. With this extended running time there would not be enough film available before all the ammunition was fired. So as not to waste film the gunner would turn off the camera switch when he test-fired the gun. When the gun switch was ON self-contained automatic heaters kept the camera mechanism warm.

The lens and filter were to be kept clean. Dust was to be removed with a camel hair brush and the lens and filter with lens tissue or a clean dry lint free cloth. A puff of breath could be used to moisten the lens or filter but never water, cleaning fluid, or alcohol.

The utilization of gun cameras greatly aided in authenticating victory claims. Each unit did its own evaluation of combat film and would forward conclusive film to higher echelons for confirmation. After the processing of the film the sequence of evaluation was to submit a written Encounter Report to wing headquarters describing the encounter, including the angle, distance, and duration of the gunfire, and describe observable hits.

# 4

## Gun Laying and Intercept Radar

**Background and Early Development**

James Maxwell's theoretical work in the early 1870s and Heinrich Hertz' experiments in the 1880s established the properties of radio waves, but it was not until the fall of 1922 that Drs. Hoyt Taylor and Leo Young of the U.S. Naval Aircraft Radio Laboratory were conducting communication experiments when they noticed reflections of high frequency radio waves bouncing off buildings and then off a ship in the Potomac River as they passed between a transmitter and a portable receiver located on the opposite shore. Their work led to the formation of the U.S. Naval Research Laboratory (NRL) Anacosta and active research into **R**adio **D**irection **F**inding (RDF) and **Ra**dio **D**etection **a**nd **R**anging (Radar). On 24 June 1930 Dr. Lawrence Hyland, working under Hoyt Taylor at the NRL, was credited with the first detection (albeit accidental) of an aircraft by "radio echo equipment." These early systems were found to have limited ranges and had poor target location ability, and RDF work progressed slowly through lack of government interest and funding.

In the mid-1930s Americans were testing pulse radars for measuring distances by having a transmitter receive its own signals that were bounced off an airplane in flight. The first successful reflected signals were received on 28 April 1936. The Army Signal Corps worked to develop ground-based SCR-268 pulse radars, but again work proceeded very slowly through lack of funds, and also there was very little flow and exchange of information. Large amounts of electrical power were required to generate the radio waves (in wavelengths of one to three meters), and the size of the antennas required them to be fixed in a stationary position, which excluded their use in aircraft. Aircraft flying through the directional radio beam created a temporary blip on a cathode ray scope that disappeared once the aircraft had passed through the beam, as a sweeping band of a rotating radar beam was not yet developed. It was not until October 1940 that a jury-rigged SCR-268 was placed in a B-18 bomber and successfully located an ore boat on Lake Erie (for a detailed look at this experiment see my book *The Douglas B-18 Bolo: The Ultimate Look from Drawing Board to U-Boat Hunter*, Schiffer, PA, 2006).

In mid-1939, with a European war looming President Roosevelt formed the National Advisory Committee for Aeronautics (NACA) as a center for the collection of civilian and military aeronautical data. On 27 June 1940 FDR established the National Defense Research Committee (NDRC) under MIT's Dr. Vannevar Bush, with Dr. Karl Compton as the head of Division D physics, which included the study of microwaves, the foundation of radar.

In the meantime, in January 1935 Britain, seeing the future threat of aerial attack, engaged Henry Tizard to form the Committee for the Scientific Survey of Air Defense, which led Dr. Robert Watson-Watt of the National Physical Laboratory and Hugh Dowding of the RAF to construct the celebrated "Chain Home" belt of fixed, long-wave warning radar stations that were able to detect incoming aircraft at over 100 miles. Like U.S. radars, British radar required massive towers and enormous electrical power consumption. This elementary warning radar furnished the Ground Control Interception (GCI) radar controller with the range, altitude, and bearing data to vector a night fighter by radio to within several miles of a target. To complete the interception of the enemy another method of detection had to be employed, and the search for Air Intercept (AI) radar was on.

By August 1937 a handmade, experimental AI model small enough to fit into an aircraft was ready. Work on this AI set continued slowly, and the Mark I Airborne Interception Radar entered combat in September 1939, installed in the Bristol Blenheims of 25 Squadron searching the North Sea for mine-laying German seaplanes at night. The AI Mark I set had limited range and experienced serious interference on its radar scope from ground returns. Succeeding versions (the AI Mark II and III) were not an improvement. The Mark IV airborne radar, which used 1.5 meter long waves, was installed in Beaufighters and Douglas Bostons, and was tested against *Luftwaffe* night raiders. Unfortunately, ground returns produced clutter on the Mark IV radar scope that obscured any target flying under the radar

**Drs. Hoyt Taylor** (shown) and **Leo Young** were influential in forming the U.S. Naval Research Laboratory and active in researching Radar and RDF. (Author)

beam aimed at the ground. When other radar returns were received they were indistinct and required a very skilled, intuitive, and lucky operator to make correct readings for successful interceptions. Even so, British night fighter Mark IV radar operators gained their first victory in November 1940 and claimed a remarkable 102 victories out of 200 airborne radar contacts during the Night Blitz that occurred from March to June 1941.

Notwithstanding this success, the Mark IV's limitations were evident, and work continued to develop AI radar based on centimetric or microwave radar (wavelengths below 10 centimeters). Low microwave frequencies could produce more focused beams with greater resolution, and at the end of the decade there was no source that was powerful enough to generate short waves. The British Admiralty established a committee to study radar operating at ten centimeter microwaves. A team at Oxford's Clarendon Laboratory was assigned to develop a microwave receiver, and another team at the University of Birmingham was to develop the microwave transmitter. To test their designs microwaves had to be generated for the circuits to detect. At the time there were two methods to generate microwaves: the magnetron developed in 1935 by Hans Hollmann in Berlin and the new American invention, the klystron, developed by brothers Russell and Sigurd Varian at Stanford in August 1937. Ironically, during World War II the Germans ignored Hollmann's magnetron and relied mainly on the low-powered klystron technology for their radar system microwave generation, while the Allies used the far more powerful but frequency-drifting technology of the cavity magnetron for microwave generation (note: the most well-known use of the cavity magnetron is in the microwave oven).

In 1940, Drs. John Randall and Henry Boot of the University of Birmingham produced a working prototype combining the features of Hollmann's cavity magnetron and adding liquid cooling and a stronger cavity. The result was the initial breakthrough in centimetric radar, the 3,000 Mc (10cm) "magnetron oscillator" or "Cavity Magnetron." The two scientists made their first microwave transmission on 21 February 1940, which had a maximum power output three times that of any other device, but the device's frequency could not be accurately controlled. Randall and Boot continued to work on controlling the magnetron's frequency by sampling the output signal and then synchronizing their receiver to whatever frequency was actually being generated (where precise frequency control is required the klystron was used). The Cavity Magnetron was supplied to Cambridge's Cavendish Laboratory, headed by Dr. Philip Dee, whose team built a 9.1 centimeter radar system which was referred to as ten centimeter for expediency. In March 1941 Dee's group installed a 10 cm experimental set known as "AIS," referring to its S-band operation, in a Blenheim. During tests of the AIS, Dee's team rediscovered that radar reflections could reveal different types of terrain which eventually led to the development of H2S ground targeting radar in April 1942.

Though the Americans had made great progress in many areas of radar, they lacked the magnetron breakthrough necessary to power microwave airborne radar. In September 1940, more than a year before the United States entered the war, the British Tizard Mission shared its radar achievements with the U.S. National Defense Research Committee (NDRC) in what has been described as "an unselfish display of good faith." However, France had just fallen and Britain lacked the funds to develop the magnetron on a large scale, so Churchill agreed that Sir Henry Tizard should offer the magnetron to the Americans in exchange for their financial and industrial help. The NDRC established Division 14 in October 1940 to produce a U.S. 10 centimeter radar based on the British magnetron under the direction of the newly established Radiation Laboratory at the Massachusetts Institute of Technology (MIT) in Boston.

**SCR-540 (British Mark IV)**

The U.S. commitment of resources to the 10 centimeter radar project soon surpassed the small British development program. By March 1941 MIT microwave airborne radar was flying in an Air Corps B-18 bomber and was detecting aircraft at slant ranges up to eight miles. At first, wartime demands forced the Western Electric Company to produce the SCR-540 as a 1.5 meter long wave radar set (equivalent to the British Mark IV). The SCR-540 had two Type A indicators: one for azimuth and the other for elevation. There were two external antennas: the azimuth receiving antennas on each side of the fuselage and the elevation receiving antenna on the outboard of a wing. The maximum beacon range was 100 miles, while the maximum search range was 3.25 to 3.75 miles with an accuracy of +/-10%. No targets could be detected at ranges greater than the aircraft's altitude. Azimuth was 70° forward on either side of the line of flight, while elevation was +/-20° from forward of the line of flight. The SCR-540 unit consisted of seven components weighing about 225 pounds, the largest (13" x 6" x 26") weighing 32 pounds. One operator and one maintenance man were required. The set was installed in the P-70, Beaufighters, and A-20s.

**SCR-520 (British Mark VIII)**

The SCR-520 was a 10 centimeter microwave set powered by 100 kilowatts supplied by Randall and Boot's magnetron. A spinner connected to a transmitter and a receiver was placed in the nose. The SCR-520 scan was a "spiral" scan, since the dish was rotated about its axis and gradually deflected sideways, configuring a spiral in the sky to an angle of 45°. The deflection was then slowly returned to the zero position and then the procedure was repeated. The maximum range was three, ten, and 100 miles (effective range was four miles on the P-38M, five miles on the P-70, and seven miles on the PBY). The SCR-520 used a single tube with a circular

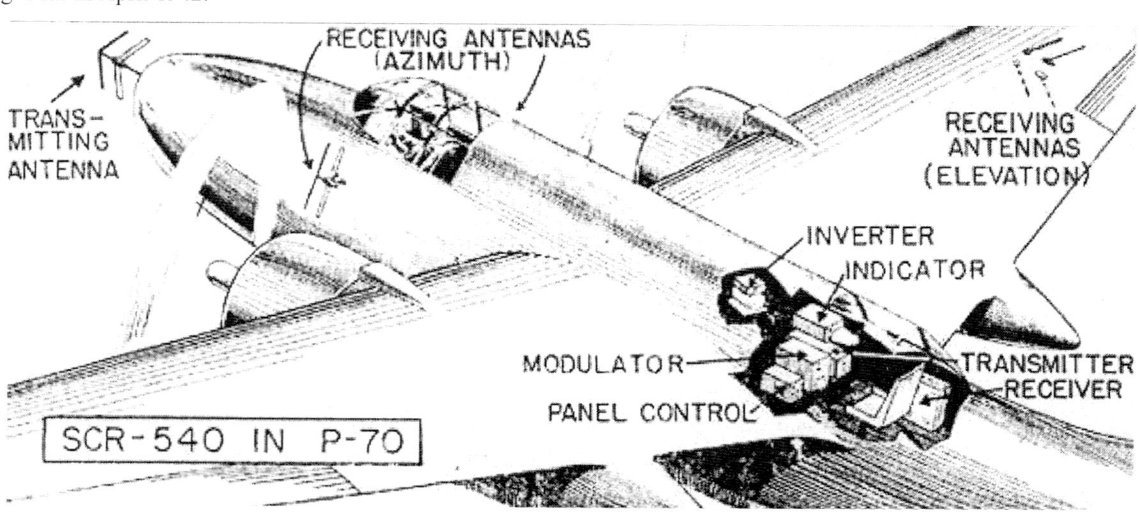

**SCR-540 Transmitting Antenna (USAAF)**

**SCR-540 Elevation Receiving Antenna (USAAF)**

**SCR-540 Azimuth Receiving Antenna** (USAAF)

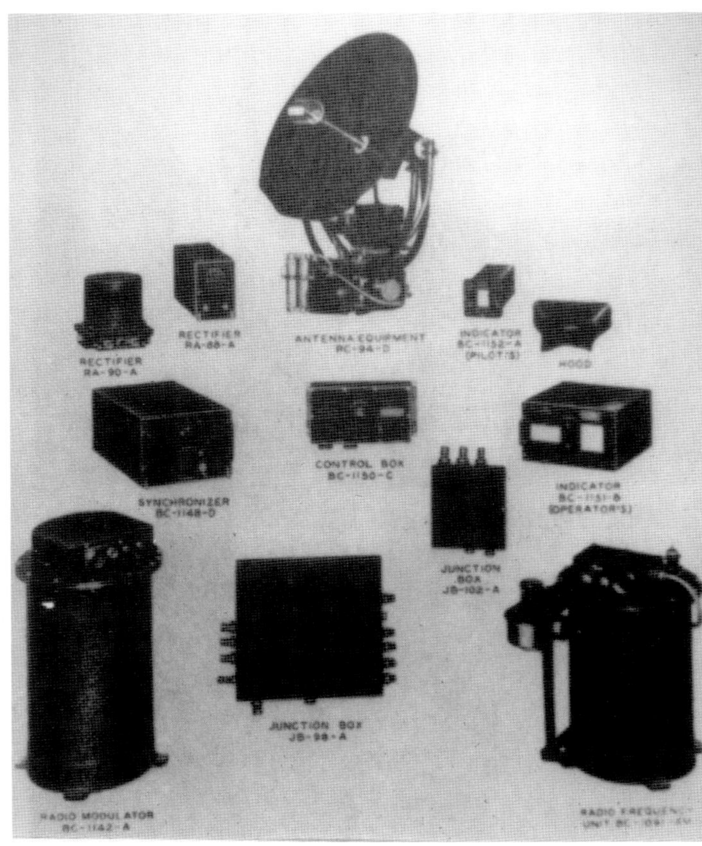


**Components of the 520A radar set.** (USAAF)

display. The target range was measured from the center of the tube with the target appearing as a segment of a circle; its angular position defined the azimuth and elevation, and the length of the segment showed how much the target was off axis. As the target approached the axis of the aircraft, the segment gradually extended to a full circle. The azimuth limit was 180° forward (+/-3% accuracy), and elevation limits were -10° to +65° (+/-2% accuracy). The set was comprised of six major components weighing 850 pounds, with the largest (28" x 29" x 40") weighing 180 pounds. One operator and one maintenance man were required. In England the serious U-boat threat in the North Atlantic diverted most initial production of the airborne radar from aerial night fighting to antisubmarine operations using ASV (Air-to-Surface-Vessel) radar.

**SCR-520A, SCR-720 (AN/APG-1), and SCR-720A (AN/APG-2)**

Development

The next American AI radar, designed and developed by the NDRC's MIT Radiation Laboratory, was designated the AI-10. The set was innovative and entirely different from the British SCR-520 (AI MKVIII), especially in the design of the scanner. The aerial was fastened inside the scanner dish, and the entire assembly was counterbalanced and mounted on ball and roller bearings so that it could spin continuously at 350 rpm about a vertical axis. A typical production set had a 30 inch scanner and produced a peak power of 100 kW.

In February 1941 the Army Air Corps ordered 15 production AI-10 sets to be installed in the prototypes of America's new purpose-designed night fighter, the twin-engine Northrop XP-61. One of these sets was sent to Bell Labs for modifications in order to facilitate production by Western Electric, which was Bell Telephone's production company. The modified set was designated the SCR-520A. Meanwhile, in June 1941 an AI-10 was installed for the Royal Canadian Air Force in a Boeing 247 transport and was flown to the UK for tests and evaluation against the British AI Mk VIII radar. The tests were completed in September 1941 and the RAF ordered ten sets for installation on Beaufighters, but these AI sets were converted to ASV-10 sets for anti-submarine searches, which were more important due to the concerted *Kriegsmarine* U-Boat attacks at the time.

SCR-720 radar set being tested at the Westinghouse factory. (USAAF)

During the evaluation of the AI-10 set it was found that the British AI Mk VIII had a more sensitive receiver, but the American SCR-520A set had a higher pulse rate and greater peak Radio Frequency (RF) power. The best features of these two sets were merged and became the more advanced anti-jam radar designated SCR-720 (British AI Mk X). In 1943, the SCR-720 set was at last ready to enter production and was installed in the USAAF P-61 and the RAF Mosquito. SCR-520A production was then cancelled at the 108th set. Later, the SCR-720A and -720B sets were developed concurrently with the A configurations produced for American use and the B to British standards. Later improved C and D versions were developed for American and British use respectively.

Description and Operation

Although very complicated in configuration and use, the SCR-720 was considered the best night fighter radar used in World War II. The microwave energy from the magnetron tube was sent to a transmitter/receiver aerial

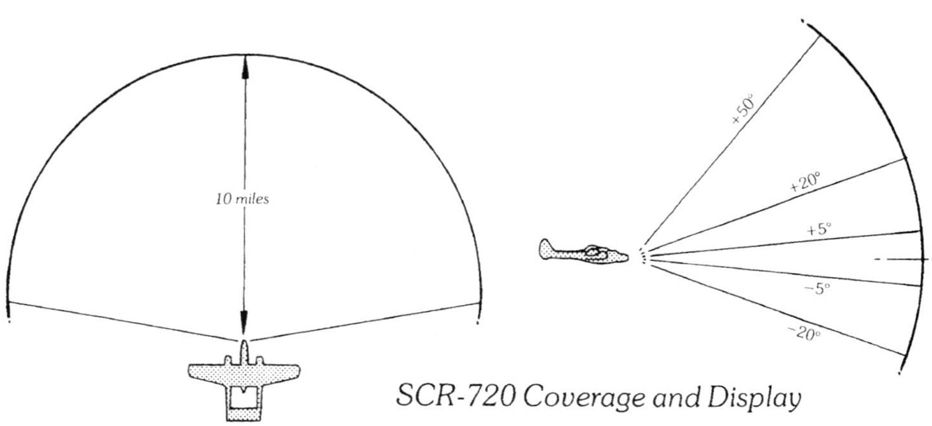


SCR-720 Coverage and Display

The SCR-720's transmitter aerial and reflector dish rotated through 360° in the horizontal plane, although radar pulses were only transmitted when the assembly was pointing forwards. This arrangement meant that its maximum range of about 10 miles was achieved on the forward beams, as well as straight ahead. This offered a significant improvement in performance over the British centimetric radars. The scanner could also be adjusted to 'nod' between various limits in elevation, so that for example when operating at low level, ground returns could be reduced to the minimum by selecting a lower limit of −5°.

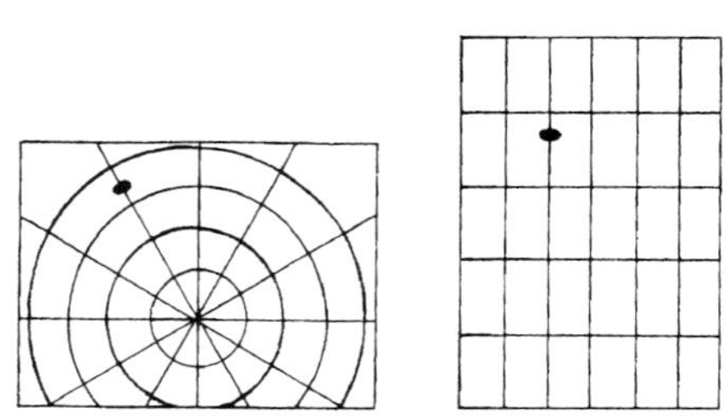

Elevation Display    Plan View Display

which was mounted in a frame facing a parabolic reflector. An electric motor in the SCR-720 spun the parabolic dish continually at 360 rpm about its vertical axis while a second motor slowly tilted the whole assembly between selected elevation limits up and down, which effectively traced out a coil in the sky. The rear half of the scanner (about 210°) was covered, as its field of scan was blocked by the structure of the aircraft. The beam was a cone of energy rather than the balls or bursts of energy of German and previous British radars.

The beam width was 10° with a vertical rotational speed of 360 rpm (100 rpm for the beacon range). There were 12 scan lines up and 12 down, giving a full scan time of four seconds. The scanner transmitted as it swept through a 75° left to 75° right arc ahead of the aircraft with the beam remaining constant, so that the Direction Finding (DF) accuracy and range remained constant at about 5° and ten miles.

The amount of vertical scanning or tilt could be selected by the operator and had five switched ranges. The maximum scan was +40° to -20° down to -5° to +10° up (when homing onto a beacon a fixed -5° was used). During the search mode, the gimbal frame carrying the scanner moved up and down with the operator selecting the vertical arc—typically between 50° above the horizon to 20° below—but this could be reset on the ground to different limits. Once a blip was seen the arc could be adjusted to narrower limits, so that by repainting the blip more often it could be seen better even in the presence of jamming. The range could also be selected from two miles, five miles, ten miles, and up to 100 miles for use with a homing beacon. Besides its detection, ranging, and interception of enemy aircraft the SCR-720 could also function as a beacon or homing device, a navigational aid, and an IFF (Identification Friend or Foe) device.

The SCR-720 had two display tubes: the left scope (the "C" scope) displayed the target as a spot on a map-like picture called PPI (Plan Position Indicator) in the sky ahead of the fighter on an azimuth/elevation grid. The right display tube, the "B" scope, also had an azimuth calibration on the horizontal axis, but the vertical axis showed the range of the target. A range marker line, adjustable by the operator, could be moved up and down the trace to select a particular target. The control used to adjust the marker was calibrated in range, giving a more accurate reading from that obtained from the graticule markings. Only when this marker line overlaid the target did the target appear on the left hand "C" scope.

**AN/APG-13 Radar Controlled "Falcon" Cannon Gunsight Radar**

The B-25H was equipped with the 75mm cannon sighted by an optical N-6 series gunsight that had a range of 5,000 yards, which would allow the aircraft to keep out of the 2,000 yard range of Japanese light 25mm AA guns. However, due to its low muzzle velocity the accuracy of the cannon was poor at long ranges, and the Mitchell pilots made their attacks at shorter, more accurate ranges that also left them more exposed to AA fire. The solution was the AN/APG-13A Falcon radar set developed by General Electric, which operated on the S-band and would provide continuous range data to the gunsight that would enable it to make the essential large elevation corrections to allow for the large gravity drop of the 15 pound projectile. The radar equipment operated by the navigator made precise aiming much easier, as it identified the target from much longer ranges (6,000 yards) and enabled the exact range to a target to be determined at all times during an attacking run.

**Components**

The entire AN/APG-13A weighed approximately 105 pounds and was composed of four major components:

Endfire Antenna

The endfire antenna, the most obvious component, was mounted on the upper nose of the aircraft on the axis of the 75mm cannon. It provided a sweep of 28 degrees of azimuth and elevation.

Indicator

The indicator was a radar scope that was operated by the copilot. Once the pilot had identified his target, the copilot would acquire it on the indicator at about 6,000 yards. As the attack on the target continued, the copilot turned a crank on the side of the indicator unit keeping the range step on the radar scope lined up with the left hand side of the target echo. A cam would turn which would change the angle of the pilot's optical reflector sight, providing continual range corrections to the gun sight and eliminating the need for the pilot to estimate ranges and manually adjust the optical reflector sight.

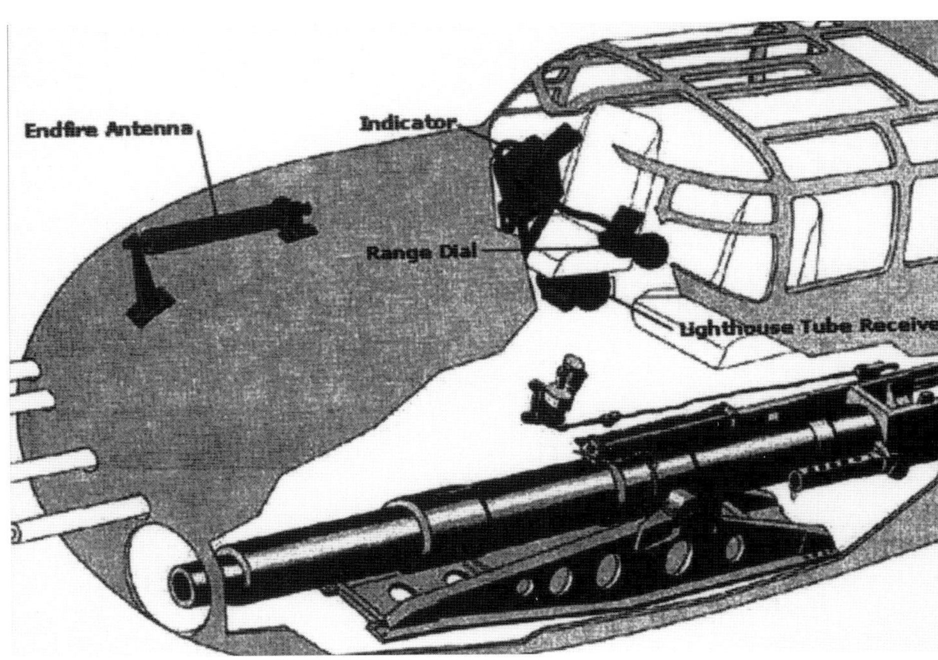


**General Electric AN/APG-13A Falcon radar** set was used by the B-25H equipped with the 75mm cannon and sighted by an optical N-6 series gunsight. (USAAF)

Range Dial
The range dial was located near the gun sight and operated by the same action that adjusted the optical reflector sight. The range dial provided the pilot with the range to the target, enabling him to determine when to commence firing and when to break off the attack in order to remain outside the range of light AA fire.

Lighthouse Tube Receiver
The lighthouse tube receiver was located under the copilot's seat and received the radar signal from the endfire antenna and fed the signal to the indicator.

**Operation**
When using the AN/APG-13A radar set the pilot and radar operator sat side-by-side, with the pilot acquiring a target visually in his reflector sight. The radar operator would then begin tracking the target on the 6,000 yard radar sweep of the "M" scope screen and maintain the range step in line with the left hand side of the target echo by turning a dial on the left hand side of the radar indicator unit. The indicator unit would automatically turn a cam that moved the elevation angle of the pilot's reflector sight, and the range data was sent to the range dial located near the gunsight. The so-called "Super-elevation" compensation for the trajectory drop of the projectile was provided to the optical sight. The pilot kept the target sited in the crosshairs in the reflector sight while dialing in the windage, and then could either open or break off firing using the provided ranges. When using the radar sight cannon firing was commenced at 5,000 yards, and as many as four or five rounds could be fired before the pilot began to fire the fixed nose machine guns at closer ranges. The number of cannon rounds fired using the AN/APG-13A and N-6 sight was subject to the loading skill of the cannoneer, and also on the condition and maintenance of the gun (especially boresighting), as well as the speed and straight course of the aircraft during the attack. The Falcon was ineffective against land-based targets, as it was not able to discriminate targets from the surrounding terrain. The heavy recoil of the large 75mm gun caused it to be jolted out of alignment, requiring constant maintenance and boresighting.

**Testing**
Five examples of preproduction AN/APG-13A radar ranging equipment installed in B-25Hs numbered 43-4584, -4071, -4924, -4989, and -4601 were made available to the AAF Testing Board. Tests were conducted against a destroyer silhouette from ranges of 5,000 to 2,000 yards with 56% success and 35% from the extreme but safer 5,000 to 4,000 yard range. Later tests on the AN/APG-13 conducted at Boca Raton, FL, used three inexperienced pilots on attack runs between 4,800 and 2,000 yards. The pilots fired 117 shells, firing four to five on each run, and scored an outstanding 104 hits and only 13 misses. Project Director Lt.Col. John Mullen reported: "Any pilot with a minimum of training can be expected to fire an almost perfect score. The operation of the radar is quite simple and should require little training. The test results were amazing. Each time the cannon was fired while the target was in the sights a direct hit was registered." Capt. R.S. Bowditch, one of the test pilots, stated: "After firing 46 rounds on my first aerial gunnery, I consider my score remarkable. Use of the sight involved no skill or experience and after firing a few rounds even the most inexperienced pilot should have no difficulty getting a high percentage." The operation of the radar set proved to be relatively easy, and the navigators of the B-25s could be taught to operate them, removing the need for an extra radar operator crewman.

In June 1944, 16 B-25Hs under Lt.Col. Neil Newman tested the production version AN/APG-13A radar in combat for the 5AF. Since there were few suitable enemy shipping targets available, the tests consisted of 19 training and practice flights against small offshore rocks and islands. Radar electrical and mechanical malfunction caused three mission failures, while radar operator inexperience accounted for two more failures. Two anti-shipping missions did not find shipping and were directed toward strafing land-based targets, for which the AN/APG-13A was useless. Only one mission actually attacked an enemy transport vessel, but the pilot did not fly at the airspeed required for radar/gunsight computation and all the shells fell short. Later AN/APG-13A sets allowed the pilot to set the speed that was to be maintained throughout the attack run.

Also in June 1944, the 14AF tested three B-25Hs against Japanese Yangtze River shipping that was delivering supplies for the Japanese invasion of central China. Three test missions under the command of Maj. P.J. Riemar were flown against gunboats using P-38s to provide top cover against any Japanese fighters. On the first mission the three B-25s fired 42 rounds, scoring a number of hits but no sinkings. On the second mission against Changsha River shipping a cargo ship, a fuel vessel, and several small motor cargo boats were sunk by 12 hits and many "probable" hits of the 61 rounds fired. On the third mission two B-25s conducted an hour sweep of the Yangzte, destroying one large steamer and four river boats.

**AN/APG-15 A and B Fire Control Radar**
As the Japanese fighter defenses waned and it was determined that their only effective mode of attack was from the rear only the tail guns on the B-29s were retained, and the bomber was stripped of its upper and lower turrets and side sighting blisters. The armament revisions in the field did not change the bomber's designation, but the 311 Eagle (ANAPQ-7) radar-equipped B-29s modified at Bell-Marietta were redesignated as the B-29B. These bombers were equipped with the new AN/APG-15B radar fire control system that located and fired on an incoming enemy aircraft.

The 12cm (2.5GHz) AN/APG-15 was designed to detect enemy aircraft and give accurate range information to the gunner in the tail turret who controlled the .50 caliber machine guns. This radar program began in February 1943 for use in the B-17 and B-24 in the ETO as the AN/APG-5, but by the summer of 1944 it was given priority in the B-29 program, first as the AN/APG-14. The AN/APG-15 was a lightweight basic short-range radar unit designed by General Electric and was mounted in the tail turret; it had a range of about 2,000 yards. In tests the APG-15 was two and a half times more accurate as manual ranging and scored three to four times the number of hits. It was to be used in the Eagle-equipped Bomb Wings, as their bombers were to be stripped of all armament except a tail gunner and

The 12cm **AN/APG-15** was designed to detect enemy aircraft and give accurate range information to the gunner in the tail turret who controlled the .50cal machine guns. (USAAF)

two scanners. Ground personnel, lacking training, had problems maintaining the APG-15 in the field due to its complexity. The gunners also had insufficient training in its use, but it was its design that caused the major problems: it had no IFF capabilities, making it unable to distinguish friend or foe; and its search-lock on ability was insufficient.

**A Summary of AN/APG S-Band Intercept and Gun Laying Radar**

**AN/APG-1:** (SCR-720) S-Band Intercept Radar; used in P-61.
**AN/APG-2:** (SCR-720A) S-Band Intercept and Gun Laying Radar; used in P-61B.
**AN/APG-3:** General Electric Tail Gun Laying Radar; used in B-29 and B-36B.
**AN/APG-5:** S-Band Gun Laying/Range-Finding Radar; used in B-17 and B-24.
**AN/APG-8:** S-Band Turret Fire Control Radar; used in B-29B.
**AN/APG-13:** General Electric S -Band Nose Gun Laying Radar (*Falcon*); used with the 75mm nose gun of B-25H.
**AN/APG-14:** S-Band Gun Sight Radar; used in B-29.
**AN/APG-15:** S-Band Tail Fire Control Radar; used in B-29B and PB4Y.
**AN/APG-16:** Experimental 3cm version designed for B-32s
Note: S-Band radar ranges from 2 GHz to 4 GHz = 9.6cm to 19cm

**USAAF Art and Science of Night Fighter Radar Interception**

There were two basic types of radar interception: free-lancing and Ground Control Intercept (GCI). Free-lancing required considerable luck, as the coverage of the AI radar installed in the fighter was too limited. GCI proved to be the most satisfactory method, since the fighter was directed to a target by a ground station equipped with powerful radar. Once directed by GCI to the vicinity of the target the fighter's AI radar could detect the target and completed the intercept.

The land-based CGI Station was the basic control component of the night fighter. It was managed by a fighter director and was able to operate as an independent radar detection and control station. "Bogeys" (unidentified night intruders) were detected on the GCI radar screen, and once detected the IFF (Identification, Friend or Foe) homing signal was verified. If there was no verifying reply the Bogey was determined to be an enemy whose speed, altitude, and direction were radioed by VHF (Very High Frequency voice channel) to orbiting fighters on Bat CAP (Bat = radar Combat Air Patrol).

Bat CAP was usually scheduled for two hours, with enough overlap to insure that two defending fighters were always at altitude. GCI vectored (directed) the circling fighter to an area as close as possible to the enemy radar contact. The fighter pilot flew toward the enemy and, using his airborne radar set, could usually pick it up at two miles. The three inch diameter indicator scope was mounted at the center of the instrument panel. A parabolic sweep line, looking like a beaded necklace, moved vertically up and down the phosphorescent screen every two seconds. If the target were in range, its echo would appear as two small dots about 3/16th of an inch apart horizontally. A target "ghost" was left behind on the screen as the sweep line passed. The target's distance was designated by the vertical position of the dots on the scope. When the enemy was first contacted its double dot was located at the top of the screen, and as the night fighter closed the dot moved toward the bottom of the screen. Since the scanner was a transmitter and receiver there was a limit on how close the target could be approached. This limit occurred because the detecting echo would come back while the radar was continuing to transmit. This cut off of the echoes would generally occur at 300 yards. On the scope, a target on the left of the line of flight would show up as a pair of dots to the screen's left. If the enemy were above its attacker, the right dot would be above the left dot. Thus, both altitude and bearing were simultaneously represented on one screen.

In making an interception, the pilot would first try to bring the dots to the vertical center of the screen and then, by adjusting his altitude, he would bring the dots side-by-side. The dots would move to the scope's

Radar operator's station in the P-61. (USAAF)

**Northrop P-61 Black Widow** mounting a SCR-720 radar set. (USAAF)

An **AN/APS-6 radar unit** in an external radome was installed underneath the nose of the P-38M. (USAAF)

bottom as overtaking speed was increased. The final approach was vital in order that a visual contact could be made while not becoming the target of a rear gunner. The approach speed had to be carefully regulated so as not to overshoot the slower bomber target. Throttling back quickly to avoid overshooting would cause the engine exhausts to flare past their dampening extensions, threatening detection by the enemy. Pilots usually wore goggles with red lenses an hour before takeoff as night vision, which is not affected by red light, took about three quarters of an hour to peak. All cockpit lighting, except the radar screen, was red, and usually kept on low gain. Once closing on the enemy to a point where he was able to go off his onboard radar the pilot began to look outside his cockpit. The search technique was not to look directly at the point the target should be at but at a point 15 to 20° away because the periphery of the eye's retina is more acute and could pick up the dim silhouette more easily. The pilot also had to consider the relative brightness of the night when making a visual contact. The general rule was for the pilot to make the target a silhouette and not allow his night fighter to be silhouetted. The pilot could utilize starlight or moonlight to search for targets above and hide in the darkness below, unless, of course, there were bright clouds below. Or he could use the ambient light of the horizon, especially near dawn or dusk, while hiding in the approaching or retreating daylight. So, depending on lighting conditions, the enemy's silhouette or undampened exhausts could be seen at 100 to 1,000 yards. In the ETO, Air Force night fighter pilots were required to positively identify the bogey visually under all circumstances. Once visual contact was made and confirmed to be an enemy the night fighter closed to get into firing position, usually astern, with the clock position depending on lighting conditions and the enemy's defensive armament. Short bursts were fired, not only to conserve ammunition, but also to assess the damage inflicted and to maintain night vision in the glare of the muzzle flashes.

(For a description of AAF night fighters: P-70, P-61, and P-38M see Part Ten/Chapter 3/Section 3)

**Navy and Marine Corps Fighter AI Radar**

In late 1940 the Navy was working with the Radiation Laboratory on large shipboard radars, intended not only for air and surface warning, but also for GCI direction for fighters. At the same time airborne American microwave Air-to-Surface (ASV) anti-submarine radar had priority, but development of AI radar that would fit a single-seat carrier-based fighter was initiated. The physical requirements for AI radar were that it was to be small and lightweight enough to fit into a single-engine fighter. It needed to be uncomplicated so that it could be operated by the pilot, who also had to simultaneously fly the fighter and listen to GCI control—all at night. It was to be difficult to jam, to be used with IFF apparatus, and could also be used to detect surface vessels and fixed targets.

**SCR-537**

By August 1941 the Radiation Laboratory had assembled components for the SCR-537 (AI-3) for testing, and by December Sperry received a contract for development and production under Radiation Laboratory supervision. Meanwhile, on 2 November 1941 the Radiation Laboratory proposed a complete installation to the Navy, and six days later the Navy asked the Chance Vought Company to study the conversion of their XF4U-2 Corsair into a night fighter. On 28 January 1942 the Navy mock-up review board accepted the Chance Vought proposal for the XF4U-2 with the radar unit contained in the fuselage behind the pilot's seat and with a waveguide installed along the right wing to a scanner located in a fairing near the tip. A spiral scan with a 120° cone at 15 scans per minute was used for search. A 10° conical scan was required for a blind firing in which accurate aiming was needed. The single cathode ray tube (CRT) display in front of the pilot showed a Type G presentation with "wings" growing on the target blip in inverse proportion to the range.

The Navy began SCR-537 radar flight trials in April 1942 using a JRB Twin Beech utility transport with the scanner placed in the nose. Initial pointing error problems occurred due to sea return, humidity, and altitude, where performance decreased above 20,000 feet. Work continued, and soon the pointing error had been decreased to acceptable limits. In June the set

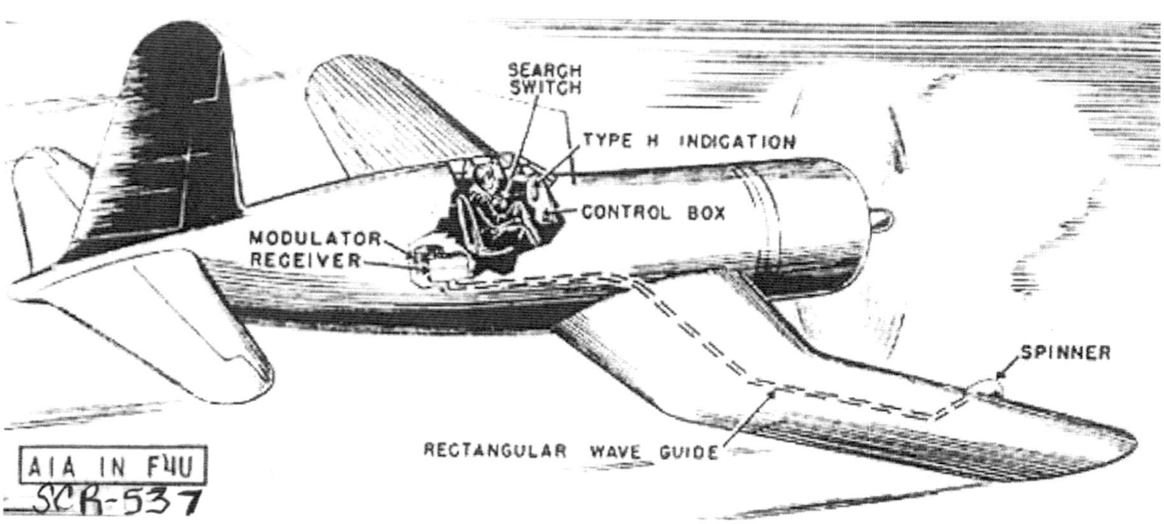


The **Vought XF4U-2 Corsair** was fitted with the radar unit contained in the fuselage behind the pilot's seat and with a waveguide installed along the right wing to a scanner located in a fairing near the tip. (USAAF)

was sent to Marine Corps Air Station Quonset Point, RI, for testing and training. A second set was installed in an F4U which was delivered as an operable night fighter in October 1942. However, the heavy conventional daylight combat demand for the F4U-1 caused Chance Vought to cancel the F4U-2 night fighter program. By late 1942 the first Sperry set, designated the AIA, was in production for the Grumman F6F Hellcat. A total of 604 AIAs were delivered and installed in F6F-3E and -5N Hellcats, and as the Al XI VA in British NF Fireflies and TF Sea Mosquitoes. In 1943 this radar was given the new Army/Navy designation of AN/APS-4 and tested in a Beechcraft JRB.

**AN/APS-4**

The AN/APS-4 radar (British designation is AI Mk XV) was a lightweight 150 pound airborne search and interception set manufactured by Western Electric and used primarily by carrier based aircraft: F4U-4E, F6F-3E/5E, SB2C-5, SBF-4E (Canadian Helldiver), TBF-3, TBM-3S, and XBT2C-1. It was X-Band Intercept radar, which was part of the microwave frequency range from 7 to 12.5 GHz. All major components were contained in a single pressurized housing similar to a Mk 41 depth bomb and attached in the same manner as an ordinary bomb. Its multiple uses were for locating and homing on ships and coastal targets; for locating enemy aircraft and making interception approaches; and for navigating. Reliable maximum ranges were 15 miles on surfaced submarines (broadside), 30 miles on 4,000-8,000 ton ship, 75 miles on well-defined coastline, and 5 miles on aircraft, which could be tracked to 300 feet. Range accuracy was ±-5%. The set covered ±75° in bearing with a bearing of accuracy ±3°. The set covered -30° to +10° in elevation when searching and ±30° when intercepting with an elevation accuracy of ±3°. The total primary power required was provided by a combination AC-DC primary generator (10 amps. 27.5 V DC and 1000 watts, 115 V, 800-2400 cycles AC) or from primary 68 amps. 27.5 V DC generator, requiring the use of a motor-alternator. The AN/APS-5 Intercept Radar was a development of AN/APS-4 and was used in the F4U-4N.

The AAF modified two P-38J-20s (44-23544 and 44-23549) in Australia in autumn 1944 for use as single-seat night fighters with AN/APS-4 radar in a pod under the starboard wing. The modifications were tested in New Guinea and the Philippines. P-38J-5 (42-67104) was tested at Wright Field and Orlando as a two-place night fighter with a radar operator sitting on a jump seat just aft of the pilot. The AN/APS-4 radar was initially mounted under the fuselage in a pod just aft of the nosewheel. The pod was easily damaged by stones thrown up by the nosewheel during take-offs and

**AN/APS-6 radar pod** installed on the starboard wing. (USN)

landings and was repositioned under the starboard wing, but that resulted in interference from the adjacent engine nacelle.

**AN/APS-6**

The AN/APS-6 Intercept Radar was a development of U.S. Navy AIA radar manufactured by Sperry and used by the Navy in the F6F-3N/5N, F4U-4N/5N, and F7F-4N, and by the AAF in the P-38M. Altogether a total of 5,260 AN/APS-6 sets were delivered, 2,161 sets by August 1, 1945, at a unit price of $10,936.

In January 1943 work began on an improved radar set using the new Daimo Victor scanner, Stromberg Mk II modulator, and the Westinghouse pressurized RF (Radio Frequency) head, which deleted the need for the long waveguide from fuselage to wing pod. This radar was completed by October 1943 and ready for flight testing in an SNB-1 (Beech Kansan). In April 1944, Westinghouse began to deliver production sets designated the APS-6. The APS-6A had been delivered a few months earlier, but because of difficulties with its new RF head, the new receiver was changed to the Philco APS-4 type. Before production APS-6 sets were cleared for installation many modifications were needed, including changing the polarization of the aerial feed through 90° to improve beacon reception. Although sea clutter continued to be a major problem, this miniaturized set generally functioned proficiently in combat maneuvers and even at heights above

**Grumman F6F-5N Hellcat** carrying the lightweight AN/APS-6 airborne search and interception set manufactured by Western Electric. (USN)

**AN/APS-6 S-Scope** installed in the pilot's instrument panel. (USN)

**AN/APS-6 radar scanner** located inside the wing pod. (USN)

30,000 feet. It was able to paint coastlines on the scope at 40 miles, and its dependable search range was seldom less than five miles, while its minimum range was only 360 feet. The scope was mounted in the middle of the instrument panel and accommodations were made in cockpit lighting; the panel was painted flat black for night flying. Extended flame dampers were added to the exhaust stubs.

The 3cm set had an average power output of 40 watts with the dipole radiating the transmitted impulse and receiving the return echo. The dipole was mounted on an 18 inch scanner dish enclosed in a nacelle faired into the starboard wing, three feet from the tip. The pods caused no vibrations in the cockpit and the fighter's stability and maneuverability were unchanged, though in a sideslip the pod falsely increased the airspeed reading. When installed on the leading edge of the starboard wing of the F4U-2 the entire installation weighed 242 pounds. To compensate for this increased weight the removal of the outboard machine gun in the wing with the scanner pod was required and the opening covered. The scanner pod reduced the aircraft's speed by only two mph. When installed on the F6F-3 there was no effect on its armament or speed.

The scanner searched in a cone whose apex was the scanner and whose axis was dead ahead. The scanner rotated at no less than 1,200 rpm in sweeping through a 60° forward spiral scan in bearing and elevation out to three miles, completing a search every second. A three dimensional picture was projected onto the scope. Azimuth was read from the target's position to the left or right of the scope's center line, which was an extension of the fighter's longitudinal axis. Range was read from its position on the vertical scale that was graduated from three miles at the top to zero at the bottom. Relative altitude was read from the semaphore indicator which was a pair of dots: the left one (the reference dot) indicated the fighter, while the right one was the target indicator. If the right dot was above the reference dot, the target was flying above the night fighter at the same angle as the angle between the two dots and at the same distance shown on the scope's vertical scale. As the night fighter closed the altitude differential, the imaginary line that joined the two dots became more nearly horizontal. As the range closed the dots moved down the vertical scale toward the aero range. When the range indicated a half mile or less the pilot moved the set from Stage A (ranges between three and one half mile) to Stage B, or gunsight range (less than a half mile). The transmitted impulse moved in a circular path at an angle of rotation of 7° instead of 60°, and the echo's strength (i.e. the target's range) was indicated by the length of the target's wings, which got larger on both sides of the scope's vertical line. If the night fighter pilot remained astern of the target the wings continued to be equally spaced on each side of the line. When the pilot closed on the target the wings were a point on the scope that indicated it was 250 yards ahead, which was the firing range of the guns.

**USN/USMC Art and Science of Night Fighter Radar Interception**

Navy night fighting technique was greatly aided by British VHF radio and IFF identification equipment while the Radiation Laboratory developed the excellent GCI radar for fleet carrier use and installed the nine ton prototype

**F4U-5N** of VF(N)-101 off the carrier Enterprise equipped with AN/APS-6 radar. (USN)

in the new *Lexington* (CV-16). This radar, designated Search Microwave (SM), had a large dish (12 feet high x 6 feet wide) that scanned conically to give the azimuth, elevation, altitude, speed, and range of multiple targets so that a Fighter Director Officer (FDO) could direct fighters to an interception. The SM had a reliable detection range of 35 miles on a medium bomber 500 feet above optical horizon. General Electric, Syracuse, NY, manufactured the SM radars with the first ready in August 1943. However, the 3cm AI radar deployment was delayed due to a number of operational use problems, including close GCI control of a day fighter used at night and the use of day fighters in conjunction with radar-directed searchlights at night. The only night fighting method that was used operationally was to operate as a two- to four-aircraft team, with from one to three fighters co-operating with a larger "sensor" aircraft fitted with radar. The common sensor aircraft was either the Grumman TBF Avenger with ASV* or the Douglas SBD Dauntless with Westinghouse ASB**. The team would remain in tight formation, preferably without showing any lights, while the large surveillance radars of the fleet scanned from horizon to horizon. Once an approaching enemy force was detected, the GCI controller would vector the team towards it until the team's airborne radar, used in the air-to-air search mode, had made a good contact. The radar operator, observing his scope, would then guide the formation until the enemy aircraft were close enough to be seen visually to be intercepted. In the Pacific, before the introduction of IFF into the Navy or Marine Corps, night fighter pilots were required to make positive visual ID before firing on a possible "friendly." But after IFF introduction in mid-1944, pilots of AI-equipped fighters were authorized to fire upon unseen and/or visually unidentified aircraft. After combat the scattered team aircraft returned to the carrier individually. Night landings were made easier by GCI, which vectored the Bat CAP aircraft back to base. Nonetheless, a night landing was always a scary situation whether it was on a landing strip, or especially on the narrow 70 foot wide deck of a moving escort carrier. This team system, while seeming to be unwieldy, was quite successful, and was continued for many years using an even more complicated system of the hunter/killer team type used in anti-submarine warfare.

*Air-to-Surface-Vessel (ASV) radar was a microwave set that was developed in parallel with AI radars that could be carried by patrol aircraft to hunt for ships and submarines at night or in bad weather. ASV radars were able to differentiate ships from the clutter returned from the surface of the water.

**Air-to-Surface-Bombing (ASB) radar was the first operational U.S. airborne radar to be widely used for bombing, detection of ships and surfaced submarines, and airborne intercept. ASB was the first radar to be used, and was almost universally in carrier-based aircraft. Referred to as the "Workhorse of Naval Aviation," ASB radar was successful in attacking and destroying Japanese shipping and Japanese aircraft. (For a description of USN night fighters see Part Ten/Chapter 2)

# Part Five

## Remote Sighting and Central Fire Control

# 1

# Sperry Remote Sighting and Central Fire Control

**Background and Development**

XFM-1

In August 1936 a special committee from Wright Field was selected to examine a proposal from the Sperry Gyroscope Company of New York for a twin 37mm cannon fire control system for use in the as yet to be developed Bell Aircraft Company XFM-1 Airacuda. The Committee reported: "According to the present state of development of the art, it appears that an exact theoretical solution of fire control with a free gun and a free target is improbable." The committee remarked on the following limitations in the Sperry proposal: "The mounts and gear drives were drawings only and not yet perfected in detail; the system presupposed an accurate external range finder to apply a range rate input; the technical problems of synchronizing the hydraulic valves to coordinate the movement of two remote guns were not perfected in detail; and, moreover, there is some doubt as to the advisability of installing flexible forward guns in a 300 mph airplane of the XFM-1 fighter type."

After evaluating this report the Materiel Division felt strongly that it was too "conservative," and stipulated that the "very purpose of purchasing such an installation as that considered in the Sperry proposal was to seek experience in an unexplored field through experimental expenditure." Gen. Arnold backed the Materiel Division, which after collecting 11 endorsements was able to have the project approved by the Secretary of War for procurement during the 1937 fiscal period, at an estimated cost of $93,000.

The Sperry fire control unit for the XFM-1 consisted of a computing unit and a telescopic sight arranged to lay twin 37mm cannons by a joystick-controlled hydraulic drive powered by Vickers units. The system was unique, as the sight followed the guns instead of the opposite, which was conventional in gun control systems. The XFM-1 computer unit contained ball carriage speed controls that added and subtracted differentials, and precision-cut, three-dimensional ballistic cams. In the future all these elements would contribute to the success of their K-series gunsights. Sperry depended entirely upon the Ordnance Department for the basic ballistic information that went into its computer cams. The earlier Sperry and Douglas 37mm projects were seriously impaired by the fact that as late as 1937 Ordnance had inadequate ballistic data on the 37mm cannon.

In June 1938 a conference of Bell, Sperry, and Wright Field representatives examined the power-drive problem and considered the possibility of converting the project to an all-electric system, which was "in line with the general trend toward the use of electric systems throughout the airplane." It was Sperry's opinion that the all-electric system would also be the next stage in the evolution of fire control equipment. The original XFM-1 computer was based upon the assumption that the relative positions of the gun control system and attacker would change only a small amount, which would suit a computer capable of only small angular rates of prediction and hydraulic-driven turrets capable of lower angular rates. With the change from the hydraulic to electric system, Sperry expected to realize higher angular rates of 3° per second. This prediction rate was set as an objective, in Sperry's terms, as "the minimum that should be attempted if we are to keep pace with the rapid development that must take place in the art." The goal was raised to 6° per second in the specifications of the AAC contract signed 9 December 1938 for 13 of the Sperry fire controls at $27,400 after the experimental model had been tested in a B-18. However, the XFM-1 project developed slowly, and by January 1939 Wright Field was looking for simpler and more compact power drive units.

Meanwhile, the XFM-1 fire control units went into limited and late production. A test of the equipment in a XFM-1 at Bell's Buffalo plant prompted Bell to issue this terse opinion: "satisfactory for the purpose intended." The XFM-1 fire control project continued on at Wright Field long after it had become superseded, although as late as 1942 some consideration was given to renovate the project for use in the tail cannon installation in the B-24. The importance of this unsuccessful project lay in the experience gained by both Sperry and Wright Field in fire control systems.

**.30 Caliber Central Fire Control Project**

As discussed previously, the XFM-1 Airacuda 37mm project was an immediate priority in 1936, delaying the .30 caliber fire control project until

In August 1936 the **Bell XFM-1 Airacuda** was selected by the Sperry Gyroscope Company for a twin 37mm cannon fire control system. (USAAF)

the Sperry proposal of March 1939, which embraced a computing sight for use in connection with hand-held flexible .30 caliber machine guns. The Sperry proposal specified a reflex or collimator sight unit to be mounted above the machine gun spade grips, where it could be provided azimuth and elevation rates by flexible shafts and data on relative lateral velocity, slant range, and indicated airspeed by manual input dials.

Concurrent with this computing sight project, Sperry drew up tentative specifications for a "means for laying one or two indirectly controlled caliber .30 flexible machine guns from a central (remote) station, including flexible cables up to eight feet long for transmitting sighting station rates to a power-operated gun mount by means of Maxson torque converters." In June 1939 Sperry's research engineers were preparing a comprehensive treatise that was to outline every phase of the fire control problem. Since the study would cost a significant $150,000, Sperry executives were anxious to sign a contract from Wright Field for a fire control system to offset the outlay. Although the Armament Laboratory was prepared to let a contract in 1939, it had to wait for 1940 fiscal year funding before it could make any large disbursements. In order to get started, a $24,000 Authority for Purchase was prepared for a .30 caliber computing sight and an $8,000 disbursement was authorized for starting work on a central station fire control (CFC) system for .30 caliber machine guns.

The central station fire control project was an extension of the work done on the original Sperry .30 caliber flexible gunsights, which had revealed the need for a combined system incorporating the sight, computer, and remote control power-driven gun mount. While preparing data for the .30 caliber sight project the Materiel Division was forced to conclude, "Consideration of fire control in its broader phases cannot be longer delayed." The Division realized it had very little information concerning bombardment aircraft defense, particularly on the methods of pursuit aircraft attack on bombers. However, it was the "SECRET" status imposed on the information that was available that caused the delays. For example, the Materiel Division withheld its information file on aircraft designs, machine gun dimensions and performance, and pursuit attack until Sperry actually signed a contract. Once the information was available Sperry engineers of its Aircraft Armament Department prepared "A Treatise on Defensive Armament for Bombardment Type Airplanes" which covered the fire power problem, evaluating a wide range of factors, including volume of fire, dispersion, encounter duration, weight limitations, size limitations, personnel requirements, ease of maintenance, reliability, and cost. Sperry's experience with the XFM-1 Bell fighter project materially aided their work on this Treatise. The Sperry Treatise concluded that a fire control system should contain a minimum of two sighting stations and computers, with each consisting of a combination of dorsal and ventral periscopes with a 36° scanning cone. Sperry preferred a stadiametric range finder after the stereoscopic and coincidence range finder systems were found unsatisfactory in experimental testing.

Sperry selected the internal self-contained hydraulic drive unit after extensively testing the electric and external hydraulic drive systems. This system was found "best suited for conducting the excessive torque loads in certain positions, wide temperature and pressure variations dependent upon altitude changes, and difficulties incident to unbalanced torque loadings arising with one gun firing."

Sperry offered to build an experimental, remote, retractable turret mounting twin .50 caliber machine guns and a computing sight for $116,325, or for $79,835 each in quantity orders. Sperry intended to build the computer and drive-control combination, but considered the turrets to be "integral parts of the airplane structure and therefore appropriately part of the airplane manufacturer's contract." Rapid design changes created problems between the Materiel Division and Sperry, as no system or program reached completion in its projected form. In order to deal with these changes Sperry designed all components for interchangeable use as nearly as possible. The proposed CFC system was to utilize the hydraulic controls perfected for the .30 caliber turret, while the computing sight was also designed for hand-held gun use. Sperry wanted all units to be "salvageable, with each unit sufficiently flexible to be adaptable to a combination of problems."

During the early 1940s Sperry and the Materiel Division continued to search for a solution to the bombardment aircraft armament problem. Attempts to place a computing sight into a locally controlled turret caused the turret to become overcrowded with apparatus and placed the gunner off center. Sperry then proposed a sighting station remote from the guns. In order to orient the sight with the guns, the turret would be linked mechanically by flexible shafts or electrically by control circuits. Sperry was not concerned which connection would be approved, as it was anxious to develop its CFC system from locally controlled turret components to a standard design that would be insurance against the failure of any single component.

**Sperry Remote Turrets**

In May 1940 Boeing had anticipated that it would equip the B-17C with a twin .50 dorsal retractable turret linked to a remote sighting station containing a computer, and a similar ventral remote using a non-compensating Keuffel and Esser driftmeter sight within the structure of the turret itself. After an Air Corps Board rejected the idea of using a modified driftmeter ventral sight, Boeing warned the Materiel Division that delays involved in replacing the sight "will kill the whole turret program for all B-17C airplanes." As a result Boeing was unwilling to plan the B-17C armament on any basis of "mythical anticipated development." So Boeing decided to arm the B-17C with two waist handheld .50 caliber machine guns mounting computing sights, the dorsal remote guns, and the ventral guns using a modified driftmeter sight. The Air Corps decided that Sperry was to provide the sight, computers, flexible shafts, power units, and controls, while Boeing was to build the turret dome or enclosure, the ring gear mounting, gun mounts, and gear trains. However, while the AAC consigned turret construction (and cost) to Boeing, the company preferred to be provided with ready-built turret units as Government Furnished Equipment (GFE)

As the B-17C armament project neared completion engineering problems and delays developed. The Sperry system operated on 24-volts DC, while the B-17C was powered by a 12-volt DC system thus necessitating temporary power packs to test the system, but this makeshift installation produced unreliable test results. For tow target testing the Materiel Division was unable to obtain the faster B-23 to replace the B-18 as a target tow plane. The discrepancy between the relative speeds of a B-18 or even a B-23 and a modern fighter attacking along a pursuit curve are obviously large, and was one of the many problems plaguing the Sperry project.

By July 1940 the delayed Sperry fire control system was threatening to jeopardize B-17 production and had to be abandoned for a more immediate solution to the armament problem. A meeting was called between representatives of the Armament Branch and Sperry, where it was decided that Sperry would build a locally controlled dorsal turret mounting twin .50 caliber guns each carrying 400 rounds of ammunition, and the turret was to be provided with a compensating sight once available. The new equipment confirmed Sperry's "salvageable principle," as the new equipment was constructed almost entirely from components planned for the other more complex Sperry systems.

In the meantime, the Armament Branch had been conducting extensive trials to determine the best type of turret installation. Ventral turrets, in particular, were a quandary due to the problem of sighting below the fuselage. In August 1940 a Work Authorization Sheet was prepared "to cover all work in connection with the development of a retractable type flexible gun turret for installation is the floor of a bombardment type airplane." In September this work order was modified "to cover extension of the investigation to include consideration of a spherical, non-retractable turret." The Materiel Division found this spherical ventral turret, to be commonly referred to as a ball turret, to be so good that rough drawings were sent to Sperry to develop. Production was authorized for installation on the B-17E instead of the originally planned remote system. In December 1940, as the ball turrets were still in the pre-production stage, the Materiel Division and Sperry signed a contract for 540 dorsal local turrets for $7,185 each ($3,879,900 total) and 113 ventral remote turrets at $11,275 each ($1,274,075 total). The ventral remote units were to equip B-17s until the 113th aircraft, when it was expected that the ball turrets would be in production.

Since Boeing had strongly objected to supplying the turret as a part of the aircraft the AAC decided to supply turrets as Government Furnished Equipment. Sperry was unable to perform the heavy casting and machine work for the 540 dorsal turrets and contracted Steel Products Engineering Company of Springfield, OH, as a subcontractor to complete the dorsal turret. The Briggs Manufacturing Company of Detroit was subcontracted for the actual assembly and heavy tooling work on the Sperry ventral turret.

From the drawing board to combat the Sperry ventral remote turret was plagued with the typical disadvantages of a remote turret: mechanical complexity; the stationary gunner had orientation problems with his distant guns; the unavoidable fouling of the scanning head; and the restricted cone of vision. As early as November 1941, the Materiel Division had doubts about the ventral remote turret:

"Preliminary information indicates that while it is difficult to pick up a target initially, as soon as it is picked up, it can be held easily in the sight and hits can be scored. After firing 2,000 rounds at a target on the ground, the outfit at Salt Lake says that the turret is no good. It is the belief of the Armament Section that after thorough training in firing at air targets this turret will be far better than present rumors indicate and no one is justified at the present time in saying that it is useless."

The cost of the turret was $11,275 with the controls adding $1,855, while the complicated sighting station and computer cost $4,569. Basically the remote turret consisted of an autosyn 115-volt AC control operating from an inverter. Movement of the control handle transmitted signals through an autosyn system to a remote amplifier. The amplifier produced impulses of sufficient magnitude to turn an inertial motor which was linked to the booster tilting a standard Vickers unit. The autosyn position control circuit was so delicate and required such critical adjustment that the services of a highly trained engineer were necessary to keep it functioning. By the fall of 1941 these turrets had become so complex for the average armorer that Sperry had to organize a special course to train maintenance men in the ventral turret's intricacies.

**Sperry CFC Heavy Bomber System**
**Background**

The R-40-B study contracts of November 1939 called for a very long-range bomber to operate at very high altitudes and over long distances. The turret gunners in the proposed bomber would have to suffer the cold at high altitudes and use oxygen for long periods. All early turret designs from the first enclosed turret mounted in the B-10 in 1934 to the huge contemporary XB-19 bomber with its hydraulically assisted turrets experienced the same problems. Besides operator discomfort, installation was complicated and difficult, the turrets were heavy and cumbersome, control was uneven, and visibility was limited. The Air Materiel Command promoted better turret and gunnery systems, particularly a system with remote turrets controlled by central fire control. The remotely controlled turret was particularly desirable, as its low profile reduced drag and it could be used to advantage in pressurized aircraft. Also, by using a remote gunnery system the crew would not have to use oxygen and be exposed to high altitude cold for long periods, as the engineers designed pressurized air-conditioned crew cabins. This meant the gunners were comfortably stationed inside the cabins at sighting stations with the turrets and guns located outside.

Under the R-40-B specifications both the B-29 and B-32 were scheduled to be equipped with pressurized crew cabins, and much time and expense was invested in its development jointly by Boeing (as the company had previous pressurization experience with its B-307 Stratoliner) and the Air Materiel Command engineers. On 20 March 1940 Sperry Gyroscope, General Electric, Bendix, and Westinghouse were requested to submit remote turret proposals by an Armament Laboratory Circular of March 1940. The first proposal concerning such a system was submitted by Sperry on 28 March 1940. The proposal covered one fire control system consisting of two computers, three sets of gun controls, and a central switchboard. The Sperry computer unit utilized the company's experience gained in designing the computer for the XFM-1. Gun turrets, the auxiliary power plant, and permanent wiring were considered integral parts of airplane structure and were not included in the proposal. Although Sperry's delivery date was three months behind Bendix, it did have a slightly lower unit cost, as Sperry quoted a price of $137,245 that was to be only the manufacturing cost, exclusive of development and preliminary design costs. In the competition Sperry scored 1,000 points and finished much ahead of the GE system with 790 points, while the Bendix system trailed with 645 points. The Armament Laboratory directed Sperry to develop its proposal in detail, preparing estimates on materials, facilities, and priorities. Boeing (B-29), Consolidated (B-32), and North American (B-28) were to be in contact with Sperry regarding the CFC system, and suggested that Sperry apprise GE and Bendix with its CFC progress "in order to maintain an adequate point of departure for future proposals." A contract to build a prototype system was authorized by Purchase #160333, dated 1 April 1940. Six more systems were contracted for on 2 June 1941. Meanwhile, Bendix concentrated on developing both hydraulic and electric turrets for manned and unmanned use (This March 1940 Circular is discussed later in more detail from the GE prospective.).

**Sperry CFC Development**

Sperry Gyroscope was founded in 1910 by Elmer Sperry in Brooklyn, NY, and during the First World War he and his son Lawrence collaborated with the Navy to develop the first aircraft stabilizer, gyro-stabilized bomb sights, and automatic fire control systems. In 1918 Lawrence organized his own company, which often competed with his father's company until the younger Sperry died in an aircraft accident over the English Channel in 1924. During the 1920s Elmer Sperry relinquished the daily operation of Sperry Gyroscope to professional managers and independently and unsuccessfully concentrated on the development of the diesel engine until the end of his life in 1930. However, during this decade Sperry Gyroscope became known as a military think tank renowned for its scientists and engineers, who developed numerous aircraft and marine instruments. In 1929 the Sperry Gyroscope was incorporated, and in 1933 the Sperry Corporation was incorporated as a holding company for many other smaller businesses, including Sperry Gyroscope, Ford Instrument Company, and Intercontinental Aviation Inc. During the 1930s and 1940s Sperry collaborated with MIT and Stanford to develop the microwave technology that led to the development of radar. During World War II the company grew exponentially and moved to larger facilities at Lake Success, Long Island, NY, to develop computer controlled and stabilized bombsights, mobile airborne radar, automated takeoff and landing systems, automatic pilots, and computing aircraft and anti-aircraft fire control systems. The Varian brothers, Russell and Sigurd, who had

**Dr. Herbert Grosch** was instrumental in developing the optical system for the Sperry CFC and would later become a computer scientist with IBM. (Author)

invented the klystron tube that had led to the success of World War II radar, headed the brilliant Sperry scientific team. Soon Edward Ginzton and W.W. Hanson and a contingent of Stanford University researchers would join Sperry to make the company's Research and Development facilities among the best in the world. Dr. Herbert Grosch was hired to join the Sperry Garden City Lab as a fire control scientist. Grosch would have a long and illustrious career, becoming one of the first computer scientists at the IBM Watson Laboratory and creating Grosch's Law, which described the relationship between computer processing speed and cost. Grosch was assigned to design a double-ended aircraft periscope that was to be used on the top-secret pressurized B-29 and B-32 and the projected B-28 bombers. Grosch's job was to be the intermediary between Kodak's Hawkeye Works Division and its renowned optical expert, Rudolf Kingslake, and the Sperry/Garden City computer team that knew nothing about optics.

In his autobiography, *Computer, Bit Slices From a Life*, Grosch describes his work on the Sperry system in 1943:

"....I was entering a new world of optical complexity. Of course, the K&E (Keuffel & Esser) Navy rangefinders were fantastic, but those designs had been frozen since Pearl Harbor. My Sperry project was in the design stage or at least in design revision after prototyping. It was a double-ended aircraft periscope, to stick out of the top and bottom of the secret new B-29 bomber, mid-fuselage. There were small plastic domes through which the optics looked at attacking aircraft. When a gunner tracked a plane across the zero elevation 'equator,' a prism flipped the eyepiece field from upper to lower periscope, or vice versa. The junction case also contained an analog computer featuring three dimensional cams, rate gyros, and a hundred pounds of ancillary gear. Outputs from the system were to control remote machine gun turrets on the top and bottom of the plane, and at the tail. But that was some years in the future, in fact so was the B-29, which was still under design and test at Boeing Seattle. And it too had competition in 1943. The telescope and all its complex optics had been designed, and would be built by the Hawkeye Works of Eastman Kodak, in Rochester. Sperry Gyroscope furnished the central box and the entire gun turret complex, with much hydraulics from Vickers, another division of Sperry Corporation. My major job was to keep track of Kodak progress, check proposed design improvements, approve the optical tests at Hawkeye, and generally represent Garden City (Sperry HQ) crew in a completely novel arena. They knew fire control, radar (the Varian brothers were big guns on the staff), and hydraulics. As far as lenses and prisms were concerned, well, they knew they were made of glass. Usually! It was fascinating. There were all kinds of new ideas. The plastic domes on the ends of the periscopes introduced a systemic error in elevation; should we put a mechanical correction cam in the computer or make the inner and outer surfaces of the domes non-concentric? Would new eyepiece designs (like the ones in today's most expensive binoculars and actually a copy of a Zeiss patent) really improve gunner performance-wider field, yes, but more distortion?"

**The XFM-1 and the Sperry CFC**

See Part Two/Chapter 3: 37mm Aircraft Cannon

**The North American XB-28 and the Sperry CFC**

In the original concept Sperry was to build their Remote System for the projected B-28 bomber. In February 1940 the North American XB-28 (NA-63) design was contracted as a high altitude medium bomber to complement the company's B-25. When the prototype rolled out in March 1942 it bore little resemblance to the Mitchell, except for the twin-engines and tricycle landing gear. It had a cylindrical fuselage ending in a large empennage topped by a single vertical tail. The cabin was pressurized by exhaust-driven engine blowers. The gunners sat directly behind the cockpit, aiming and controlling their dorsal and ventral turrets and tail turret with the Sperry remote periscopic sights linked to mechanical computers. The sights protruded above and below the fuselage on either side of the fuselage centerline. The gunners could operate either dorsal or ventral turrets depending on the master control panel settings. The tail turret was controlled from the right hand computer console. All turrets were equipped

**North American XB-28** (Author)

with twin .50 caliber machine guns. The design was not pursued beyond the prototype stage, as combat experience demonstrated that the B-25 had developed its low altitude bombing techniques to such a high degree that there was no need for a pressurized medium bomber to operate at high altitudes to bomb the same targets.

**Sperry CFC Contracts, Tests, and Problems**

Sperry now had contracts for seven systems, and in addition was manufacturing turrets, gunsights, autopilots, and bombsights for several types of airplane. Soon Sperry found that it was going to be unable to meet all their delivery schedules on the various projects. The Air Materiel Division desired to maintain two sources of supply for fire control systems as an insurance to have at least one succeed. It was decided, therefore, to have General Electric manufacture its own system, but it was to be used with the Sperry computer and to have Briggs Body Company, Detroit, manufacture the Sperry-designed turrets. Briggs was given two contracts for turrets: 107 turret sets for B-29s and 360 sets for B-32s.

Even with the CFC delivery restructuring it became evident that remote control systems would not be ready in time to meet early deliveries of B-29s. There was a faction in the AAC that opted for building the first B-29s and B-32s without pressurized cabins and adding manned gun positions similar to the B-17. On 27 December 1941, General B.F. Meyers of the Materiel Division informed the Technical Executive at Wright Field that provisions were to be made to supply at least the first 100 B-29s with locally controlled, manned turrets. Fire control systems were to be installed as soon as they were accepted as satisfactory and production was sufficient to meet deliveries.

An initial report from Elgin Field Proving Grounds, where the Sperry XB-20 type CFC system was being tested on the B-17C (as YB-29s were unavailable), revealed problems, such as inadequate cooling air for the computer, no provisions for keeping the optical tubes dry, and the probable inefficiency of the drive control and gun charger at low temperatures. The major difficulty, however, was with the periscope sighting system, which had a limited field of view that made locating targets difficult. The entire CFC system was found not to be effective at ranges over 500 yards if the bomber was required to maneuver while firing its guns. Sperry insisted that these difficulties could be remedied and that its system was basically sound.

In December 1941, the Air Staff sent Col. Kenneth Wolfe and Colonels Leonard Harman and Roger Williams to Boeing in Seattle with orders to abandon the remote sighting system and install conventional turrets. After protracted discussions Boeing executives, backed by their engineering department, convinced Wolfe et al that the General Electric electronic remote armament system was the solution to the remote turret dilemma (The GE CFC aspect of the Wolfe visit is further discussed in the GE segment.). Back at Wright Field, the Experimental Engineering Section determined that the GE system was a viable substitute for the Sperry system. Small quantities of the B-29s were chosen to be equipped with the General Electric system instead of the Sperry system, and direct GE sighting was to be used in place of the Sperry periscopic sight. The EES also considered making a similar CFC change in the B-32 project. When it was found that substantial problems were being encountered in adapting the Sperry computer for use with the General Electric system in the XB-28 project, the Experimental Engineering Section recommended that the Sperry facilities be converted to the manufacture of the entire General Electric system.

At a conference held at Wright Field in April 1942, it was decided that while the first three experimental B-29s were to be equipped with the Sperry system, the production models would carry General Electric equipment. On 16 May 1942 an early B-17C (#40-2046) was sent to Eglin Field from Wright Field for evaluation. The bomber was equipped with an experimental Sperry remote fire control system and two 20mm cannons mounted in the nose (see Part Two/Chapter 1/20mm Cannon). The Sperry unit was tested for its potential for use in the unavailable B-29 and was compared to the experimental General Electric unit that had been installed in a B-24C. The results of the Central Fire Control comparison showed the Sperry system to be more accurate while the GE system was more reliable, but neither could be used in the B-17 or B-24, as they were not "sufficiently stable firing platforms for accurate operation of a central fire control system."

The 100 Sperry systems already under contract were to be procured as "insurance" as standby or alternate equipment. B-32s were to continue to use the Sperry system, with the provision to change to direct (GE) sighting if that proved advantageous on B-29s. At the time no CFC plans were made for the XB-28s, pending a decision as to whether this type of aircraft was even to be produced. So both the retractable turret and the Sperry periscope concept were virtually set aside, and the decision was made to use the General Electric Central Station Fire Control System that was now considered to be the only viable solution on all aircraft that were to use the CFC system. Despite the decision to use the untried GE system, Sperry and Grosch continued to develop the Sperry Central Station Computer System as a back up to the GE unit, as much time and expense had already been invested in its development.

**Description of the Sperry System**

The Sperry system placed the gunner and the P-4 electromechanical analog computer with its periscope sight inside the pressurized fuselage and the turrets outside, where they could be made smaller and retractable, resulting in a cleaner, more aerodynamic aircraft. The remote turret aiming system consisted of upper or lower sighting periscopes mounted on the P-4 computer base and turret selector panels. Sperry supplied the Central Control Computer Station and the entire gun turret works with the turret hydraulics being built by its Vickers division. The computer was enclosed in a 29.75L x 12H x 20W inch black cast aluminum case. The analog computer was made up of three-dimensional cams, rate gyros, and ancillary equipment. The two periscopes were built by the Hawkeye Works of Eastman Kodak in Rochester, NY. One periscope was approximately 29 inches long and the other 38.75 inches, and both were 5 inches in diameter and weighed 100 and 125 pounds, respectively. The periscopes were located in small plastic domes at the top and bottom mid-fuselage of the bomber. Each double-ended periscope had rotating heads that permitted the sweep of a 30° cone of vision, covering both the upper and lower hemispheres with respect to the airplane. The two different periscope lengths allowed the P-4 computer to be located in either single or dual configuration at different fuselage locations with the shorter used in the upper position. The selector

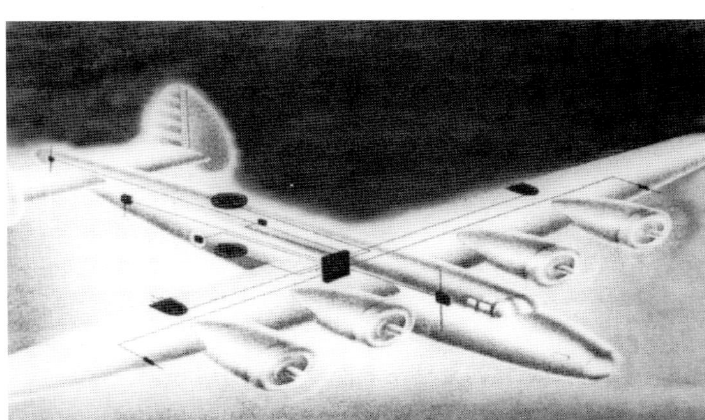

Fig.5. Sperry concept for the Central Station Computer System.

(CAM via Hahn)

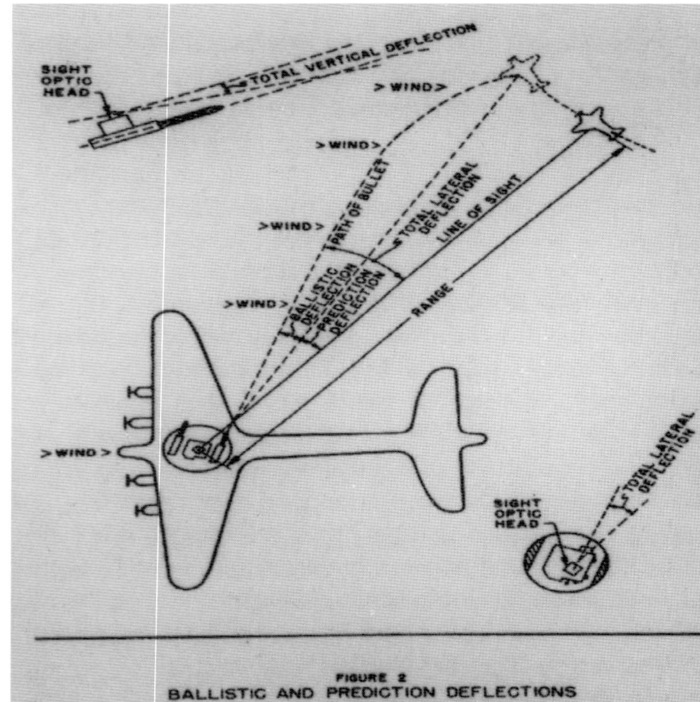


Fig.8. Geometry of air-to-air gunfire control problem.

(CAM via Hahn)

Only known Sperry computer and periscope in existence is displayed at the Cradle of Aviation Museum. (CAM via Hahn)

panels allowed the gun turrets to be switched among linked computers in case a turret or computer was inoperative.

### Operation of the Sperry CFC System

The gunner sighted the target through the periscope and tracked it with the power-operated computer that automatically, through the gun controls, rotated the turrets and elevated the guns. The periscope aiming system allowed one central controller to direct as many as five turrets containing twin .50 caliber machine guns or 20mm cannons from a console in the forward compartment near the navigator's station. Besides being able to transfer control to other gunners who were in better firing positions, the central controller, on signals from spotters, was also able to switch from any turrets that were damaged or inoperable. Another scanner positioned in the waist controlled the upper and lower turrets through a second periscope. With only two periscopes there was a lack of orientation on the target and additional sighting stations had to be added. Two waist gunners scanned through ring and bead spotting sights in two fuselage blisters, and the bombardier had one in the nose compartment. Once these additional spotters had the target in their sights the controller was able to take over at his station and track the target. If the target was seen broadside the determination of the

Fig 9. Periscope with case removed

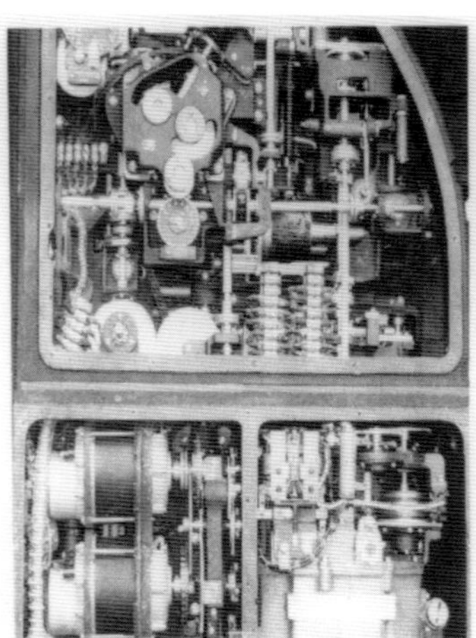

Fig 10. P-4 with left panel removed

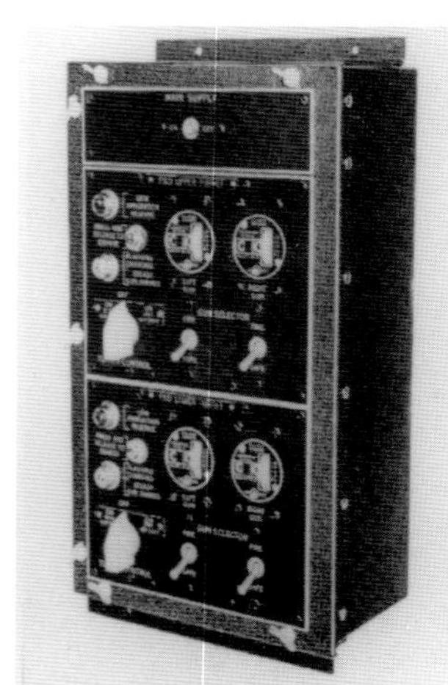

Fig 4a. Forward turret control panel

Fig 4b. Rear turret control panel

(CAM via Hahn)

wingspan was reasonably easy, but the target approaching from any other angle would require the gunner to mentally calculate the trigonometry of the viewing angle in order to enter the wingspan into the computer. This auxiliary spotting system involved a precise and well-practiced vocal communications system via the bomber's interphone system. If the target was transferred the controller had to continue to align it in the lighted reticle of his sight, reconfirm the identity of the target, and use his memory of the specific recognition data of the target aircraft to enter the wingspan into the computer (on the upper right hand side of the computer). The computer calculated corrections for altitude, speed, temperature, ballistics, deflection, and parallax to determine azimuth and elevation lead angles (range to the target was displayed on a dial on the left computer panel) to the selected gun turret needed to fire at an attacking aircraft. The analog computer could only direct one gun turret at a time to a selected target.

The controller continued to track the enemy by constantly keeping its wingtips centered in the sight by adjusting a dial or by using a foot pedal. The foot pedal was connected to a rate gyro mounted on the base of the computer that measured the rate of change that when multiplied by the range determined the speed of the target along its flight path. The ballistics (drag coefficient) of the bullets of the guns was known and their trajectories were computed. A dial (on the upper left of the computer) was set by the controller to the indicated airspeed and the computer calculated true airspeed based on altitude. The computer could then calculate the gun turret lead angle at which the bullets and target would converge, and then set the gun turret in both azimuth and elevation to aim at that point. When the controller tracked a target across the zero-elevation midline (above or below horizontal) of the sight, a prism rotated the eyepiece field from the upper to lower periscope (or vice versa) and flip-flopped the target in the sight, which made smooth tracking difficult.

**B-29s and B-32s in Sperry CFC Testing**

During testing a XB-29 equipped with the Sperry system was sent to Eglin, FL, for firing tests under Kenneth Eidnes, a gunner in the 509th Bomb Group who was the Director of B-29 armament tests. The program was headed by Col. Paul Tibbetts, who would later fly the *Enola Gay* on its atomic bomb mission over Hiroshima. There is a question concerning which XB-29 was used in the Sperry system testing. In the Eglin Armament tests it was probably the first XB-29 prototype that was used, as it was originally fitted with the Sperry system. However, in December 1942 XB-29 #1 developed so many engine problems in testing that it was detached from the testing program and would not fly for another seven months. After XB-29 #2 was destroyed in the Eddie Allen crash in February 1943 XB-29 #3 was the only XB-29 available, and this aircraft was used as Boeing's Flight Test Ship and continued flying until 1947.

Col. Tibbetts and Robert Caron flew the XB-29 from Seattle to Eglin. This aircraft was equipped with the Sperry system and was to be compared to the GE system. For the Remote Control Gunnery tests Sperry sent a technical representative to Eglin. In his book *Fire of a Thousand Suns*, gunner George "Bob" Caron describes his encounter with the Sperry system and the Sperry representative:

"Tibbetts assigned Caron the task of evaluating the performance of the General Electric firing systems of the YB-29 which he knew as intimately as a surgeon knows gall bladders against the Sperry remote-controlled hydraulic system of the XB-29-of which he knew nothing. In fact, few people did, other than the Sperry technical representative....On their first meeting, the representative was waiting for Caron at the flight line, manual in hand."

The Sperry system equipped the XB-32 #2 and #3 prototypes, but in January 1943 the system was removed from the third XB-32 prototype and experimental turrets were installed and tested. The second XB-32 continued as a test aircraft throughout the war, but it is not known if the Sperry periscopic sighting system was removed; test flight engineers William Chana and R.T. LeVine cannot remember the defensive armament of the XB-32s or find any mention of firing tests or armament equipment in that aircraft in their logbooks. The Pilot's Handbook for the XB-32 shows that the projected defensive armament consisted of three P-4 periscope gunsight computers, upper and lower turrets, rear mounted twin .50 caliber machine guns, a 20 mm cannon in each wing (mounted outboard of the outboard engines), and nose mounted .50 caliber machine guns. In early November 1943, the AAF decided that all future B-32s were to be equipped with conventional manned turrets armed with dual .50 machine guns in the nose, dorsal, ventral, and tail positions. Once it was decided to use the conventional turret system on the B-32 there weren't any aircraft available to develop and test the new B-32 turret arrangement. A Ford-built B-24J-20-FO (44-48802) was quickly modified for testing to carry the Sperry designed/Briggs built nose, tail, and ball turrets that were to be used on the B-32.

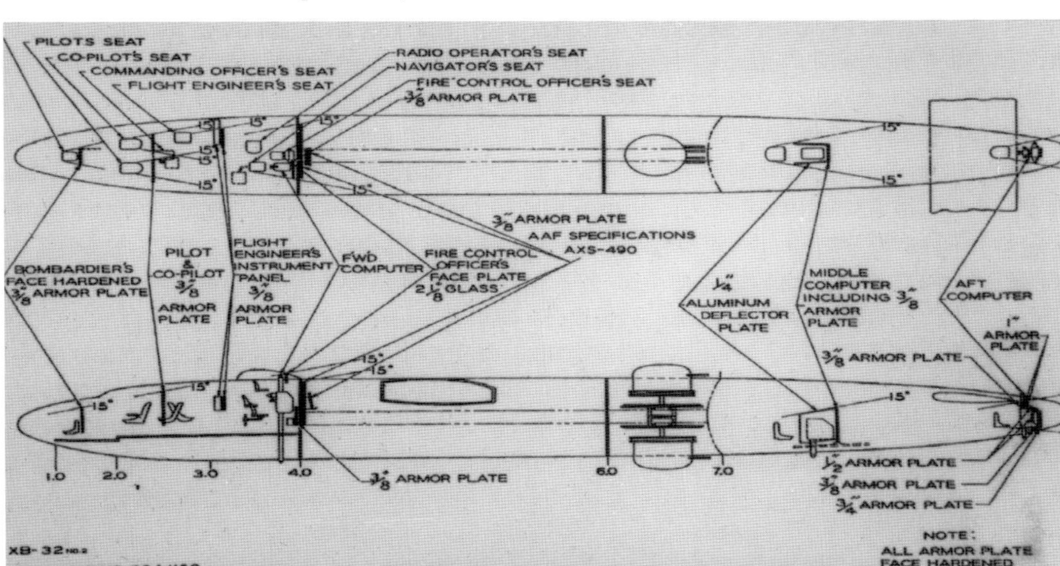


Fig.6. XB-32 with Sperry Station Computer System defensive armament.

(Sperry via CAM/Hahn)

**Sperry CFC Testing Problems**

Periscope

The Sperry periscope was found to have several disadvantages. The principal drawback was its small field of vision, as the eyepieces did not give a wide enough field without creating distortion. The plastic domes at the ends of the periscopes caused a systemic error in elevation calculation. The inner and outer surfaces of the dome were not concentric and confused the computer. To compensate for only two periscopes and the lack of orientation on the target spotters were added. These spotters were to inform the controller of targets, but that entailed developing an involved vocal communications system via the bomber's interphone. Other Sperry optical system problems occurred in the cold temperatures of high operating altitudes, causing the optical prisms to be heated. Overall the Sperry periscopic sighting system was complicated to operate and it had an inherent inability to compute "real-time" positioning data for directing the turrets at close ranges.

Computer

The second problem was that Sperry had adapted the electromechanical analog computer for CFC use. Originally it had been developed in conjunction with their Ford Instrument Division for use in naval gun directors and AA fire control systems. The analog computer had no memory and could track only one target at a time. If there were more than one target within the controller's field then he could only choose one. Also, having no memory the computer had problems tracking nearby targets, as it was unable to sustain calculations because of the rapidly changing relative ranges and angles to the target to compute the required lead azimuth and elevation angles. Only years later would high-speed digital computers with memory be developed. The Sperry analog computer design was much larger and more cumbersome than the small optical gunsight computer (K-series) and a small electromechanical bombsight computer the company was developing at the time. This computer had chronic malfunctions that were impossible to remedy in the air and sometimes had to be sent from Eglin back to the Sperry factory on Long Island for repair. The computer system also had problems functioning at low temperatures

Turret System

Testing determined the turret system to be unacceptable, as the nose and tail positions had inadequate firepower and there was a blind spot forward of the wing tips. There also was a rear blind spot since the tail turret was controlled by the waist spotter periscope and an attack from directly behind the tail could not be seen from the waist periscope.

**Testing Report of 30 December 1942**

Testing led to a report that was submitted by the Proving Ground Command at Eglin Field on 30 December 1942, and which threw an unfavorable light on both the GE and Sperry remote systems. They found that neither was tactically suitable for defense of the B-29 and B-32 airplanes, and again recommended that provisions be made immediately to install locally controlled turrets in both airplanes. The disadvantages of the central station system were listed as follows:

1) Complexity of system and consequent maintenance problems;
2) Possibility of shutting down the entire system by a few hits;
3) Inability to defend against simultaneous attacks;
4) Inability to service guns quickly;
5) Inability to operate guns manually in case of electrical failure;
6) Limited scanning in Sperry system;
7) Unsatisfactory computer in General Electric system; and
8) Inherent inaccuracy in both systems due to parallax.

Only two advantages were found, namely:
1) Less total weight, and
2) Greater ease of aircraft pressurization.

A month later, another Eglin report found the system "vulnerable" and "not functionally reliable," as it had many chronic maintenance problems that were impossible to correct during flight. The report again concluded that the only benefit of the system was that it made pressurization easier and weighed much less than a conventional turret system, but the report held out hope that the system's problems would eventually be solved. Meanwhile, Sperry saw that its periscopic remote sighting system program was going nowhere and pulled Grosch from the project, transferring him to the vital computerized K14/MK18 gunsight project. The K14 allowed turret gunners in the B-24 and B-17 and, ironically, on any reconfigured B-32s to automatically lead attacking enemy fighters.

**The Sperry CFC Program Continues**

Shortly thereafter it was decided that locally controlled conventional turrets would be used in B-32s, and that the bomber would not be pressurized. Sperry and Briggs were notified on 13 February 1943 that their contracts for B-32 systems were cancelled (360 fire control systems from Sperry and 360 sets of turrets from Briggs). This left Sperry and Briggs tooled for full production, but only with contracts for B-29 systems that consisted of only 100 Sperry units and 100 sets of Briggs turrets. There were no requirements for the B-29 systems except for "insurance" purposes. Production Engineering Section, Wright Field, asked that Materiel Command, Washington, make a decision on the matter, so that either installation could be planned or contracts be cancelled.

The B-29 Sperry contracts were not cancelled; they were, in fact, augmented. Sperry held that the impending B-29 cancellations, along with the B-32 cancellations, would result in the loss of sources for materials and of subcontractors who would go elsewhere, and it would be impossible to pick up production again in case there was a sudden demand for their system. Sperry suggested that their B-32 CFC contract be changed to permit their systems under that contract to be transferred as additional systems for the B-29 program. Maj.Gen. O.P. Echols, who had insisted upon the original purchase of 100 sets of Sperry Central Station Fire Control Systems for the B-29 as an insurance against a possible failure of the General Electric Systems, and who thought that the Sperry system might prove to be superior to the General Electric system, then recommended that Sperry's suggestion concerning CFC transfer from the B-32 contract be adopted.

Accordingly, cancellations of Sperry and Briggs contracts for B-32 equipment were rescinded (22 February 1943) and the contracts were converted to provide for equivalent quantities for the B-29 series, making a total of 460 sets for B-29s. The converted systems were to be equipped with the auxiliary target locating sights recently developed by Sperry. These converted sights would be provided for in a Change Order contract AC-25456, dated 31 August 1943, at a cost of $1,332,850. It was pointed out by Aeronautical Equipment Branch, Wright Field, that all Sperry systems were to be stored until such time as aircraft were allocated for installation of the equipment.

On 20 May 1943 Production Division, Wright Field, asked Materiel Division, Washington, if such an allocation was going to be made; and if not, they recommended that the contract with Briggs for turrets also be cancelled. The value of the Sperry computers would not be jeopardized, since they could be used with General Electric turrets and Briggs facilities would be released for the manufacture of manned conventional turrets, which were needed as the air war escalated. Materiel Command informed the Production Division by authority of the Commanding General, AAF,

Hap Arnold, that no allocation of the Sperry system was to be made at that time, but that Sperry computers and sights would continue to be made for use with General Electric turrets. Briggs production of remotely controlled turrets, however, was to be slowed to conform to General Motor's production of B-29 bombers.

In the meantime, tests of the Sperry system were proceeding at Eglin Proving Ground and trial flights indicated that the system was entirely unsuitable for operational employment. The opinion of Wright Field, as expressed by Brig.Gen. C.E. Branshaw, was that the Sperry system was "coming in about third in this race, the winner being the General Electric system and second place going to the locally operated turret installation." General Branshaw recommended, in the event it was decided to use some armament installation other than the General Electric system, that locally controlled turrets be used. He continued by stating that, in the interest of economy, and because the General Electric system was sufficiently developed, that the Sperry equipment would no longer be required as "insurance," and that the Sperry and Briggs contracts be cancelled.

The Materiel Division did not agree that the contracts should be cancelled, as they considered it essential that the relative merits of the three systems be determined by actual air trials before a decision was made. Of course, Sperry protested that adequate trials had not been made, and asked that a decision regarding cancellation be withheld for at least three months. General Electric, confident in its system and wanting to end the CFC debate for good, was insistent that Wright Field not only follow through with test of Sperry equipment at Marietta, GA, but that they participate in tests at Eglin Field to the extent that complete comparative reports could be made. Thus, the Sperry system was given a reprieve.

**The Sperry CFC Program is Cancelled**

Conclusive comparative reports were never made since the continuing B-29 CFC test program was far behind schedule, largely due to difficulties with the YB-29 aircraft, which were frequently grounded because of various engine troubles. On 13 December 1943, the Production Engineering Section reported that tests on General Electric equipment were just beginning and that results would not be forthcoming until the middle of March 1944, while it was expected that the Sperry tests would be completed during February 1944. Meanwhile, a conference was called to immediately analyze the B-29 armament program and to determine a course of action concerning it. Once the Sperry results were known, it was decided to initiate immediate action to cancel Sperry fire control equipment for use in the B-29s and to proceed with a plan for installing the more promising GE remotely controlled turrets. The two outstanding Sperry contracts, AC-25456 and AC-26160, for 460 sets of the Sperry system were cancelled as of 23 February 1944. (Thanks to Mort Han and the Cradle of Aviation Museum (CAM), Garden City, LI, NY, for much of the information on the Sperry CFC System. The CAM has a P-4 computer and periscope on display.)

# 2

# General Electric CFC Systems

### B-18 GE Remote Tail Gun

In July 1938 the Materiel Division at Wright Field was exploring ideas for the "obvious necessity" of remote control guns located in pressurized cabins and tail positions. The Division requested that General Electric Company's Schenectady plant investigate the development of electric variable-speed drive systems, hoping to utilize this large prosperous, diversified company's outstanding research and design facilities. At the time the metadyne and pliodyne drive systems seemed to have the most potential, as each was a variation of the shorted-armature, controlled-field drive units that were used extensively with heavy industrial equipment that required constant speed under varying torque loads. General Electric had previous experience working on Navy contracts using various electric drives with gun controls. In November 1938 representatives of the Navy, the Materiel Division, and GE met in Schenectady to reach a decision on the drive system to be used in the B-18 tail gun installation. The Bowman pliodyne system, a multiple contact control devised for Navy searchlights, was rejected, but the metadyne system originally designed for Navy five inch shipboard gun controls was selected. The GE engineers asked the Materiel Division to forward all available information that would facilitate the preparation of their initial proposal. Although General Electric had promised to present a proposal in two weeks, difficulties arose as the company was not completely familiar with the problems of aircraft design, and it was not until 3 March 1939 that their final proposal and detailed specifications were ready.

GE offered to sell its remote tail gun system, which included a number of innovative features, including a compensating sight, to the Materiel Division for $25,000. The single .30 caliber gun was controlled through a 40° cone of fire by the new and improved amplidyne drive system, which was a modification of the earlier metadyne system. The unit had a 30° per second maximum speed within a 75-watt to 350-watt range of power consumption. The compensating sight was able to correct for ballistics and parallax, but range, air speed, and relative target speed were entered as constants. The gunner was stationed in the dorsal B-18 turret and sighted through either one of a pair of standard collimator, illuminated reticle, and parallax-reducing sights that were designed to give a relatively unobstructed line of vision past the empennage. The original specifications called for turret rotation via a bicycle pedal type system, but this was never perfected. The remote .30 caliber gun was charged by a system of cables and pulleys and carried only 185 rounds in its magazine. Eight months later, in November 1939, the experimental tail gun was finally ready for firing tests at Aberdeen Proving Grounds.

### Materiel Division's February 1940 CFC Circular Letter

As mentioned previously, as early as November 1938 a memo from the Armament Laboratory to the Assistant Secretary of War called attention to the introduction of pressurized cabins that would necessitate a "central control position from which various machine guns and cannon can be remotely controlled." It was not until January 1940 that representatives of the Armament Laboratory and several turret manufacturers interested in fire control projects investigated the CFC question comprehensively. On 2 February the Chief of the Materiel Division's Experimental Engineering Section sent a circular letter to Bendix, General Electric, Sperry, and Westinghouse delineating provisional requirements for a complete CFC system.

The circular letter contemplated the installation of seven .50 caliber guns, a provision for scanning throughout the entire sphere, a computing sight, a cut out or interrupter device to protect the critical structures of the plane from gunfire, and all the other equipment which had been perfected for use in local turrets, such as hydraulic charging, reflex sighting, etc. The system was to mount twin .50 caliber guns in dorsal and ventral turrets, each with 360° azimuth and 90° elevation, a single .50 in the tail with a 30° cone of fire, and single rear-firing .50 gun in each engine nacelle with 40° cones of fire. The proposed system was to incorporate a twin periscopic mechanism positioned so that the gunner could easily look up momentarily from the station to pick up an approaching target by eyesight. The computing sight was to compensate for ranges up to 1,000 yards and airspeeds of 325 mph as well as for parallax. However, no stipulation was made for stabilization, although it required the inclusion of a range finder to obtain continuous range input without affecting tracking ability. Because weight and balance was vital, manufacturers presenting design proposals were instructed to reduce weight wherever possible. In addition, the specifications required that existing aircraft electrical systems provide 12-volt DC current in limited amounts only, and auxiliary power plants were to be compulsory. Finally, the circular letter required that all submitted proposals be of a design suitable for interchangeable use in more than one type of aircraft as initially, the Armament Laboratory assumed that its proposals for a fire control system would be for installation on the A-20, but later the B-26 was another option.

The CFC concept was so new and unexplored that the Armament Laboratory had difficulty describing the exact composition of the equipment it required in its proposal. This ambiguity made it difficult for the manufacturers to analyze the proposal and its problems and then to be able to give a reasonable quote on a complete CFC system. The Armament Laboratory assumed that the turret and aircraft designers of the manufacturing companies would have ideas regarding CFC weights and dimensions, mounts, sights, and retracting mechanisms. But when an Armament Laboratory representative visited several interested manufacturers, the Laboratory found that the manufacturers were generally uninformed about the subject and bewildered about what their responsibilities would involve. In order to facilitate coordination between turret and aircraft manufacturers, on 9 February 1940 the Materiel Division sent telegrams to Boeing, Consolidated, Douglas, Lockheed, and Martin, authorizing these companies to directly negotiate with turret designers on problems of space, weight, and balance.

The Armament Laboratory recommended that turret manufacturers be allowed two to four weeks to prepare schematics along with weight and power estimates to meet a future specific circular proposal. These preliminary studies would then give the Laboratory a comparative basis for deciding whether or not to continue the project. The manufacturers wanted payment for their preliminary proposals, as they often involved comprehensive engineering studies which some manufacturers might be unwilling to assume unless a method of payment could be set up to reimburse the studies that were rejected. No solution was reached at the time, but it was a question that would need to be addressed once America entered the war.

Majors Frank Carroll and Grandison Gardner met with the heads of the Armament Laboratory and the Experimental Engineering Section in late February 1940 to reach "a definition of terms and a delineation of responsibilities" for CFC fire control equipment. The various types of sighting stations and gun positions were standardized and preliminary armament specifications were delineated for the B-17 B-24, A-20, B-25, and A-26. A minimum requirement of at least two sighting stations was established for heavy bombardment aircraft, and current CFC requirements were correlated with the Equipment Laboratory.

**Materiel Division's March 1940 CFC Circular Letter**

Toward the end of March 1940 another circular letter was prepared by the Materiel Division's Armament Laboratory and sent to the four major turret manufacturers: Bendix, GE, Sperry, and Westinghouse. The Armament Laboratory, drawing from its previous experience, carefully drafted a clear and concise circular, especially pertaining to general design requirements. The circular specified that manufacturers submit their proposals in only 11 days, on 1 April. The manufacturers were to include a quotation on five fire control systems, together with complete drawings, and a statement relating to future delivery schedules. The general requirements for a complete system for a four-engine heavy bomber included prerequisites for installation in a pressurized cabin, twin .50 turrets throughout the bomber, and twin .50s with a 20mm cannon in the tail. Not less than ten .50 caliber machine guns and a cannon were to be distributed in at least five emplacements controlled from two or three sighting stations; all-around defense with a crew of six or seven; reliability at speeds up to 450 mph and at 40,000 foot ceiling with deliveries to begin in one year.

A few days before the competition deadline, Sperry and GE telephoned Wright Field to confirm that they were submitting formal proposals. Bendix submitted its proposal on 1 April, but Westinghouse was eliminated, as it was unable to prepare a proposal in time. Westinghouse finally presented its belated proposal on 9 April, but the Armament Laboratory considered it "very clumsy and unduly complicated."

The three design proposals were similar enough for the Armaments Lab to form a basis for comparison:

| Company | Delivery | Unit Cost | Cost of 5 | System |
|---|---|---|---|---|
| **Bendix** | 12 months | $84,000 | $420,000 | 2 stations/6 guns |
| **Sperry** | 15 months | $83,790 | $418,950 | 2 stations/6 guns |
| **GE** | 18-20 months | $90,000 | $450,000 | 3 stations/6 guns |

Because all these bids were prepared on short notice none came close to meeting the minimum Armament Laboratory requirements. The Armaments Laboratory felt that they did, however, "provide an accurate index of the evolution in fire control equipment to that time, since they all represented the projects under development by the several competitors" and were evaluated as to merit.

Reiterating the Armament Laboratory's analysis, the Sperry proposal won the competition with a figure of merit of 1,000 points, GE was second with 790 points, and Bendix was last with 645 points. Both GE and Bendix trailed by a wide margin, as they were severely penalized because, unlike Sperry, neither company submitted more than a rudimentary drawing of the vital computer unit. The Sperry computer unit utilized the company's experience gained in designing the computer for the XFM-1. Bendix solved the computer's critical range-finding problem by adding another operator to the aircraft's crew who would continuously input range or approximations of a fixed range. Sperry engaged Keuffel & Esser for its optical units; GE planned to purchase its optics from Bausch & Lomb, who were already inundated with other contracts; while Bendix was going to use in-house optical units built by relatively inexperienced personnel. The Armament Laboratory directed Sperry to develop its proposal in detail, preparing estimates on materials, facilities, and priorities. The Armament Laboratory suggested that aircraft manufacturers and GE and Bendix were to be kept in the loop by Sperry regarding the progress on its CFC system to facilitate any future developments.

The experimental contracts that were granted to GE, Sperry, and Bendix from 1936 through 1939 were beginning to achieve results. At the end of April 1940 both GE and Sperry guaranteed 90 day delivery of local turrets without compensating sights, with peak production expected in September or October of 1940. To eliminate the necessity of different sight and gun installations for each type of aircraft, these contractors were trying to standardize them. However, fire control equipment development beyond the local turret stage faltered due to the lack of range finders and the Materiel Division's inadequate production capacity of sight optics. On 9 April the Materiel Division contacted instrument and optical companies American Optical, Kollmorgan Optical, Rochester University, Simpson Optical, Spenser Lens, and Wollensak Optical for "a brief statement of your interest as well as an account of your resources in personnel and manufacturing facilities."

**The CFC System Loses Favor**

In March 1940 ACC officers familiar with CFC fire control expressed a "very definite impression that while its development was promising, it would be several years before the system could be made ready for combat use." Whatever promise the CFC held for the future, the conventional locally controlled turret had reached quantity production and, for at least the next two years, America's foremost armament concern was to concentrate on the problems involved in perfecting local turrets for existing aircraft rather than on the development of remote and CFC systems. Development would continue on the CFC systems with the GE system favored, but the CFC project was not a priority. It was not until January 1942 that the GE system was chosen over the Sperry system, and not until May 1944 that a B-29 would take a GE CFC system into combat.

**GE Central-station Fire Control System**

The Materiel Division was very anxious to have research work continue at Schenectady, where GE project engineers conceived two very promising Central-station Fire Control systems. One system involved a completely synchronous control of all guns (nacelle, tail, and dorsal and ventral turrets) from a single sighting station equipped with a computer unit. The other system involved a combination control plan in which one sighting station and computer would control all aft-firing guns (the nacelle and tail positions), while another station and computer would control the dorsal and ventral turrets. Neither of these two systems was simple or trouble free, but GE favored the latter system, which called for only ten amplidynes and ten drive motors and offered the increased reliability of two gunners rather than one.

Wright Field and GE representatives met in Schenectady in February 1940. The conference proved so successful that notes taken by the Armament Laboratory at the meeting indicated a "clearing of the fog and getting new ideas that the personnel involved favored frequent repetition of the process." The proposals reached at the meeting were drafted and forwarded to the Armament Laboratory and recommended that "a careful analysis of the GE proposals be made so we can give them a decision in order that they will not be too far amiss from the other competitors." Initially, GE had pictured three installations similar to the remotely controlled B-18 tail gun for use on the A-20 nacelle-tail combination. Preliminary engineering findings had indicated a critical weight and balance problem that could make it impossible to utilize the existing equipment with .50 caliber guns. The Materiel Division was frustrated in testing these assumptions in an experimental installation when it was unable to obtain an A-20.

In March 1940 GE prepared specifications for a complete fire control system involving two computers and two sighting stations with the dorsal turret, ventral turret, and tail gun positions so set up that it was possible for either station to take control of the tail gun drive. The ventral station was periscopic, but the dorsal station was mounted in a direct sighting observation dome. The GE CFC installation utilized control with a selsyn AC rectifier and an electron tube impulse-amplifier circuit operating in conjunction with an amplidyne drive.

General Electric proposed a cost of $95,000, exclusive of optics, for a complete fire control system to be delivered one year after the date of contract (March 1942). The Materiel Division declined this offer and GE made another during the following month in which the whole system, also less optics, was priced at $75,000. Both Bausch & Lomb and Keuffel & Esser were willing to quote prices on the optical units under development for the fire control system. Both companies were in peak production, already overburdened with Ordnance and Navy contracts, and neither were eager to undertake a lengthy experimental program. In addition, the CFC optical system was still in the design stage and its cost could not be accurately quoted.

The development of the GE fire control system's optics both with regard to cost and design development undoubtedly delayed the program. A GE proposal for CPC sets, complete in production quantities, was priced at a single set for $25,000 and 13 successive sets at $10,000 each, or:

| | | | |
|---|---|---|---|
| 1 plane | $11,500 dorsal turret | $13,500 | ventral turret |
| 10 planes | $4,300 dorsal turret | $5,700 | ventral turret |
| 20 planes | $2,900 dorsal turret | $3,100 | ventral turret |
| 50 planes | $2,400 dorsal turret | $2,600 | ventral turret |

These prices were tied to a production schedule: one turret in 90 days, two turrets in 120 days, five turrets per week in 16 weeks, and 10 turrets per week in 20 weeks. This proposal included only the drive and control sets and not the internal ring gear, which proved to be a most difficult tooling process and delayed the planned production and delivery schedule, and significantly delayed the entire course of CFC development

**GE Ventral Turrets**

The increasing probability of an extended delay in the development of GE fire control equipment led the Materiel Division to consider either a series of interim measures or a simplified fire control system. In May 1940, both the B-24 and the B-17 were inadequately armed, and again the Division considered it more practical "to plan local turrets in predictable quantities for immediate production than to put too much faith in fire control systems of uncertain status."

A General Electric proposal presented a dorsal local turret for the B-17C that resembled the Martin B-26 type at a cost of $55,000, less the cost of optical components. This turret mounted twin .50s and utilized the amplidyne speed control, thumb switch slewing speed control, sprocket-type ammunition boosters, provided for manual retraction, and utilized a compensating sight. Typical of that stage of turret development was that the design specified a 60° per second maximum azimuth rotation speed but failed to establish any minimum.

The Materiel Division, in its urgent need to develop ventral hemispheric fire coverage for heavy bombers, engaged GE to undertake several projects. A "shallow type bottom turret" designed for the Douglas B-23 was converted for use as a power turret by using an amplidyne azimuth drive system. However, the limitations of this installation were immediately obvious and the unit proved inadequate, so GE initiated other projects.

A new $50,000 GE proposal for an improved ventral gun design consisted of a spherical turret with an amplidyne speed control system and utilized a simple N2-A reflector sight without any compensating features. This turret proposal was immediately followed by a similar one for a ventral turret to include amplidyne speed control in azimuth and selsyn position control in elevation. None of these GE spherical ventral turrets went beyond the design stage, partly because other manufacturers delivered more practical units and also because General Electric's focus was on the more complex fire control systems. In June 1940 the Materiel Division negotiated a contract with GE to include one tail and nacelle gun fire control system for the A-20 at $50,000 and one combination dorsal and ventral turret fire control system for the B-24C at $95,000.

**Douglas A-20 Havoc Remote Fire Control System**

In June 1940 the Materiel Division let the $50,000 contract to General Electric to develop a remote fire control system for a tail and two rear-firing nacelle positions for the Douglas A-20. When weight and balance considerations deleted the tail gun new specifications stipulated dorsal and ventral turrets with a double-ended periscopic sight used in conjunction with rear-firing guns in each nacelle. Additional weight and balance

This Douglas A-20A which was redesignated as the XB-20B as part of the A-20B contract for testing purposes. (USAAF)

problems occurred while incorporating this system in all three positions on an A-20A, which was redesignated as the XB-20B as part of the A-20B contract for testing purposes.

The reconfigured GE system introduced low profile dorsal and ventral turrets and an improved computer but developed slowly. Even as late as the end of August 1940, when the XB-20B fire control system was at the point where major design changes could not be made, GE had requested the advice of Douglas designers concerning such critical elements as the mounting ring bearing system, the location of the elevation drive gear sector, and the type of ammunition feed to be employed. Even though the A-20 program had received a high priority, it was evident that the GE system would not be ready for installation on the initial production A-20As or on the A-26, which was beginning development with the GE remote fire control system as standard. To save the GE remote project, the Materiel Division let another contract for $60,000 in December 1940.

Tests at Aberdeen Proving Ground in February 1941 graded the GE installation as only "satisfactory," but the next month Wright Field's Contract Section notified Douglas that the turrets were ready to install in the A-20, though at the time Havoc production exceeded GE turret development. In order that the remote turrets could be installed directly on the bomber without drawings Douglas sent an A-20 to the GE factory to test the installation. Meanwhile, conventional manned .30 machine gun positions were to be retained on the A-20A combat bomber until the GE system was ready and under production. The AAC made an A-20A available to Douglas and GE as a test platform for the GE system and remote turrets that even then was considered a possibility to eventually equip the A-26 and perhaps forthcoming A-20 models. This A-20A (39-725), the last A-20A, was transferred from the Douglas production line to the company's El Segundo modification center and was redesignated the XA-20F. (Note: The next to last A-20A serial was actually 39-797, but the original 39-725 airframe was sent earlier to the Navy as the only BD-1, and Douglas built this second replacement 39-725 at the end of A-20A production.)

By July 1941, before the XA-20F was sent to Eglin Field, FL, for armament tests, modifications were finished and flight testing was completed. However, the armament specifications remained in limbo. By the end of August 1941 these specifications had been revised again to exclude the nacelle guns completely. Flight tests in September 1941 established that the GE dorsal turret was "very reliable," while a report from the Air Corps Proving Ground stated: "All pilots and gunners are enthusiastically pleased with the operation of the General Electric (dorsal) turret in the A-20A airplane." However, the ventral turret was found to be deficient. As with

The AAC made an A-20A (39-725) available to Douglas and GE as test platform for the GE system and remote turrets which was redesignated as the XA-20F. (USAAF)

all new turrets, particularly those with remote sighting, the GE ventral unit had a number of faults: the scanning area was too limited; gunners found it difficult to keep oriented with the guns without a revolving seat or target locator; and the sight exhibited excessive vibration that was coupled with a quality of reflecting an operational movement in the control lever during pull-outs. These operating problems were of little consequence because the ventral turret for the A-20 was not ready to be shipped to Wright Field for tests until January 1942. Thus, the A-20 ventral turret project became the A-26 ventral turret project. After armament testing was concluded the XA-20F was transferred to Wright Field in December 1941 for more testing. The basic remote firing system installed in this aircraft was the same as the one installed in the XA-26 in spring 1942. (Note: A-20A 39-725 continued as a test bed for three more years, including modification to its nose to test the 37mm T-20-E-1 cannon, before it was scrapped in late 1945.)

The A-20 fire control system consisted of a pair of twin .50 guns mounted in dorsal and ventral turrets controlled from a remote sighting station. Using a Douglas concept, Bausch & Lomb developed a double-ended periscope with single eyepiece sighting which significantly permitted the use of one controller instead of two; an important factor in a twin-engine bomber. The drive system was the standard GE amplidyne with selsyn control of the turrets, which used the AC electric power derived from a dynamotor that converted DC to AC power. The drive was to reach an azimuth speed of 60° per second and a 40° per second elevation speed with an allowable mechanical or gear train creep of seven mils. The system was to be equipped with mechanically operated spring limit stops rather than electric limit switches, but the sighting station was designed to switch off the drive when it reached the limits of the predetermined zone of fire. The A-20 turret incorporated a number of ingenious features, including a continuous feed ammunition system in which a fabric belt lifted shells to the machine gun, and when the triggers closed the firing circuit, an additional circuit energized a drive which wound the empty bolt on reels that served as a booster system.

GE considered the delivery of the A-20 Remote system as conditional upon an early order for a production prototype, but the Materiel Division was reluctant to allocate funds assigned for experimental development to the design of a prototype. The Experimental Engineering Section wanted development and the Production Engineering Section wanted production, while GE wanted a contract to offset engineering costs. Also, the Materiel Division wanted GE to assume total accountability for all aspects of turret production so that the company would be responsible for any problems that could arise with components obtained from subcontractors.

**GE CFC Systems for the XA-26, XP-61, XB-28, and XB-33**

While working on the A-20 remote turret project, General Electric signed a contract in June 1941 to build fire control systems for the Martin XA-26 and the Northrop XP-61. This system was to be similar to that used with the initial A-20 double turret arrangement, or to the single four-gun dorsal turret eventually installed on the P-61. GE production had become extremely complex due to two Catch 22 factors. The GE systems were designed primarily for aircraft that were not in production, and because these designs were for complete systems rather than individual turrets, GE production plans had to be contingent upon aircraft production. During the summer of 1941, GE was contacted about designing systems for the North American XB-28 and Martin XB-33, whose futures were uncertain. GE was already committed to the undeveloped XA-26 and XP-61 aircraft and was reluctant about accepting projects which did not guarantee large production orders. In June GE had a manufacturing capacity of 330 turret units per month, but was reluctant to expand any further, as all GE fire control projects were previously essentially limited to experimental contracts. However, by August the awarding of production contracts seemed much more likely, and GE considered a plan to make use of Emerson floor space to expand GE output.

By December 1941 Emerson was negotiating with GE to secure manufacturing rights for the amplidyne drive on a license and royalty basis, and the Materiel Division was promoting GE for a $12,000,000 machine tool financing plan. The following chart shows the limited extent of GE production in January 1942:

| A/C | Units on Contract | Additional Required | Delivered to Date |
|---|---|---|---|
| **P-61** | 215 | 360 | 0 |
| **A-26** | 503 | 0 | 0 |
| **B-28** | 2 | 600 | 0 |
| **B-33** | 402 | 0 | 0 |

These figures indicate the narrow range of GE production up through January 1942, especially in view of the fact that neither the B-28 nor B-33 existed beyond the experimental stage; but in May an exceptionally large contract for more than $98,000,000 was negotiated with GE for 3,924 units involving the four production airplanes mentioned above. While the development of these systems continued over the next several years, this contract represented the high point of GE turret design and anticipated production.

Sperry had used most of 1941 and into 1942 for organizing its remote firing system production, and GE did not arrive at the production phase until the middle of 1942, mainly due to delays in the completion of anticipated aircraft models. Several of the other turret manufacturers did not take so long to begin production, or at least the developmental stage of their projects overlapped early production.

**Northrop P-61 Black Widow Remote Fire Control System**

The P-61 remote turret program was delayed by GE, which was having difficulties in filling higher priority orders for B-29 remote turrets. Only 37 of the 45 P-61A-1s produced were equipped with the dorsal turret. However, when these 37 turrets were installed, even though they were streamlined, they encountered buffeting problems when they were either elevated or rotated in azimuth while in flight. The dorsal turret was further streamlined, but the air flow around it activated a buffeting when it was moved right to left, causing 364 of the 663 P-61As and Bs to be delivered without this turret, which was faired over. Various remedies were tried to cure the buffeting problem which were all basically hat-like coverings attached to the top of the turret, and all were unsuccessful until the P-61B-15 production block; the improved GE A-4 turret was reintroduced, and the improved GE A-7 was introduced on Block -20s. There were seven -25s built which were test beds for the Western Electric APG-1 Gun Laying Radar/GE Remote controlled dorsal turret.

When the dorsal remote turret was equipped on the Black Widow its four .50s were supplied with 560 rpg. It had a full 360° movement in azimuth and 90° in elevation, covering the full hemispheric field of fire above the aircraft. The movement of the turret was controlled from two sighting stations, with the forward gunner having full control of the turret at all times unless that control was transferred to the radio operator-gunner in the rear compartment. The pilot was able to control the guns only if the forward gunner moved the guns directly forward and locked the turret. The forward gunner's seat could be rotated into a locked 0° or 180° position by a lever on the left side of the seat. The sight could be adjusted to the individual gunner's eye level by a locking wheel near the top of the support column and the distance from his eyes by a collar and set screw on the elevation arm. The turret control box was mounted below the right

**Northrop P-61 CFC Gallery**

**Northrop P-61 Black Widow** (USAAF)

**Dorsal Remote Turret** (USAAF)

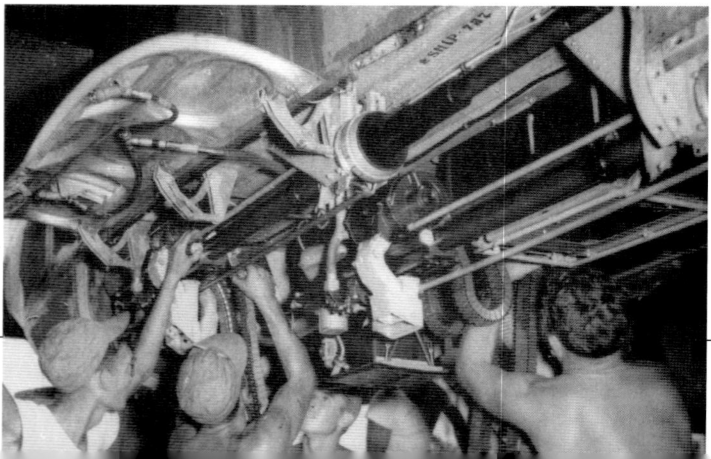
**Ventral 20mm Cannon Installation** (USAAF)

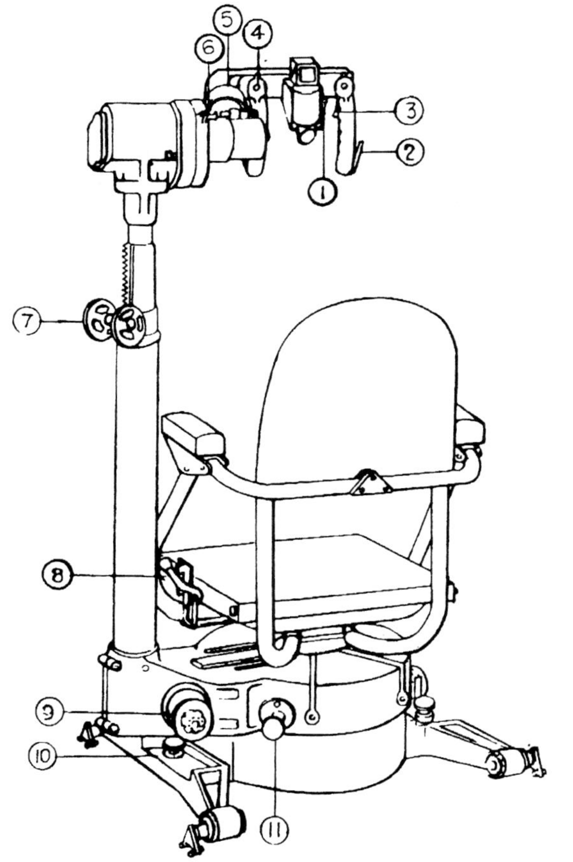


1 SIGHT LAMP SWITCH
2 GRIP
3 FIRING TRIGGER
4 INTER-PHONE SWITCH
5 HUB ASSEMBLY
6 ELEVATION GEAR
7 WHEEL ASSEMBLY
8 SEAT CONTROL LEVER
9 RHEOSTAT
10 SIGHT LOCKING KNOB
11 STOWAGE LOCK

**Gunner's Position** (USAAF)

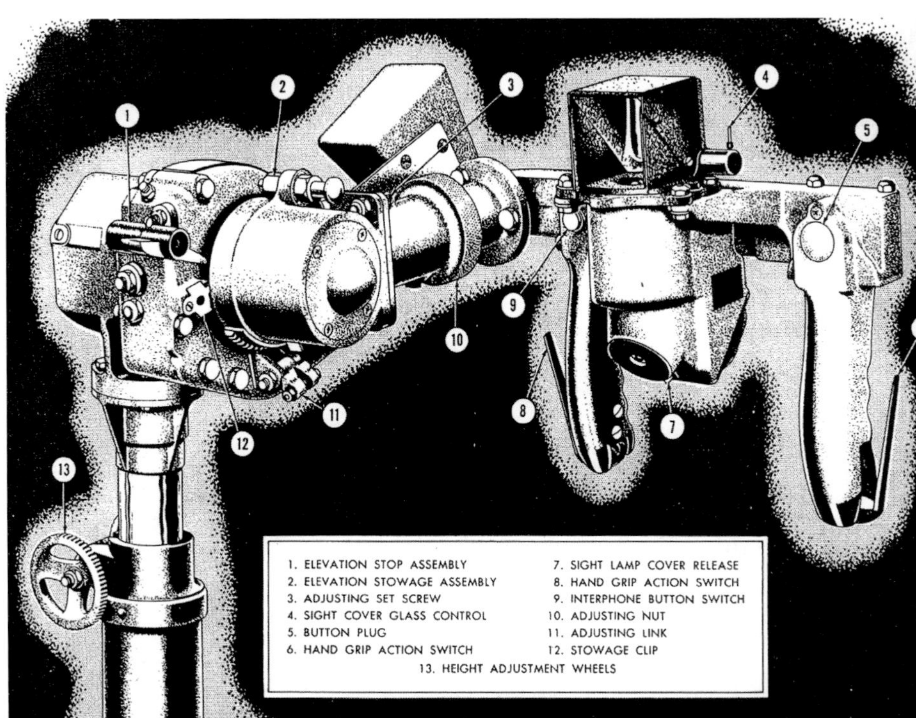


**Sighting Station Controls** (USAAF)

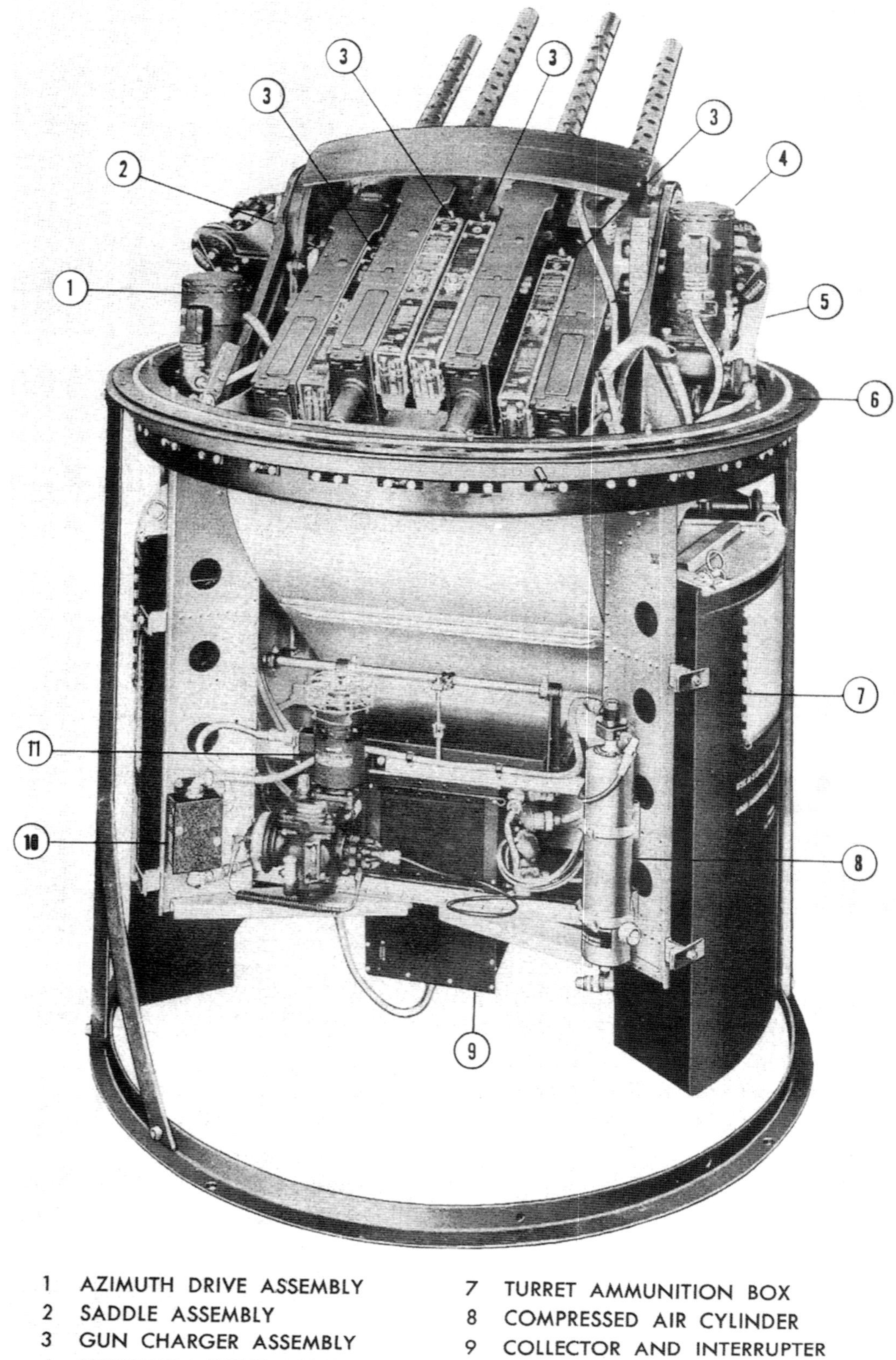


| | | | |
|---|---|---|---|
| 1 | AZIMUTH DRIVE ASSEMBLY | 7 | TURRET AMMUNITION BOX |
| 2 | SADDLE ASSEMBLY | 8 | COMPRESSED AIR CYLINDER |
| 3 | GUN CHARGER ASSEMBLY | 9 | COLLECTOR AND INTERRUPTER ASSEMBLY |
| 4 | ELEVATION DRIVE ASSEMBLY | 10 | JUNCTION BOX |
| 5 | AMMUNITION BOOSTER | 11 | COMPRESSOR |
| 6 | RING ASSEMBLY | | |

**P-61 Dorsal Turret** (USAAF)

**North American XB-28** (USAAF)

rail in the gunner's compartment. It contained circuit breakers; a switch that controlled the amplidyne, dynamotor, and air compressor; and GUNS switch that provided a way of disconnecting the firing circuits. The turret operating power supply switches located on a panel to the right of the forward gunner were to be switched ON. Then the dynamotor switch was turned ON and 30 seconds later the amplidyne switch was turned ON to activate the azimuth and elevation generators, after which the safety switch was turned ON. The sighting station firing controls were mounted on the two grips attached to the sighting arm. Each grip contained a palm action switch and a trigger switch. The trigger switch was mounted on the side of the grip away from the gunner and all four .50s were fired by the trigger on either sighting station. The palm action switches were mounted on the outboard side of the grips. They were depressed by palm pressure, and pressure on either or both provided complete control over the turret. Movement of the sighting station control left or right rotated the turret in azimuth and elevation of the sighting arm elevated the turret guns.

**North American XB-28 Remote Fire Control System**

An important parallel project to the GE A-20 remote fire control system was the Sperry installation designed for North American's proposed twin-engine (P&W R-2800s) XB-28 pressurized high altitude bomber. The XB-28 measured 56.4 feet long and 22.9 feet high with a wing span of 72.6 feet and featured tricycle landing gear. The initial North American plan called for a single .30 caliber hand-held nose gun and a similar gun in the tail, but as early as October 1939 the Armament Laboratory had insisted that .50 caliber guns be used in those positions also. In February 1940 the XB-28 contract called for a fire control system of twin .50s in three positions: dorsal and ventral turrets, and a tail installation. In April 1940 the Materiel Division had selected Sperry to manufacture the XB-28 fire control system, because Sperry fire control developments were more advanced than any others. Later, as Sperry facilities were overburdened, the Materiel Division requested that GE assume the XB-28 remote fire control project. The Materiel Division preferred the Sperry sight and computer unit to that designed by General Electric and decided to have GE build the turrets to include Sperry sighting and computer units (which promised potential problems).

The original XB-28 turrets had to be designed and built by North American the GE turrets were not ready, but General Electric would design and build the remote turrets in the subsequent XB-28A. Both company's turrets were low silhouette and very clean and aerodynamic. The remote turrets were operated by the primary gunner and the radio operator/gunner from the pressurized crew compartment. There was no nose turret, as it was thought that the aircraft's high speed would make head on attacks unlikely. The twin .50 tail turret was remotely controlled from the crew compartment and driven by azimuth and elevation motors. It could be serviced by a low, narrow crawlway.

Each gunner was provided with an 18 inch diameter, 180° hemisphere fish-eye scanning lens whose port was cut into each side of the upper fuselage forward of the leading edge of the wing. Together the two fish eyes were to provide 360° coverage to enable the gunners to visually find and identify targets and determine the direction of their attack. In fact, gunners were only able identify targets flying within the center 60° cone of these fish eyes. Outside this optical range targets were too small and distorted, and the gunner was able only to determine what direction the target was moving and he had to wait until it closed to periscope range to make an ID. Production B-28s were scheduled to have a 20 inch scanning lens mounted in the entry hatch for downward gunner viewing and another 15 inch lens in the floor of the bombardier's nose compartment.

The original installation specifications had Sperry develop the computers and control systems and North American build the gun mounts and actual turret structure. The Sperry periscope was found to have several major disadvantages as discussed earlier, and the incorporation of the Sperry sight and computer unit into the GE system caused serious problems, which should have been anticipated. When GE assumed the XB-28A fire control project it was decided that the entire unit would be built by GE, but the XB-28A program self-cancelled on 4 August 1943 when the prototype crashed into the Pacific Ocean on a test flight.

**Martin XB-33 Remote Fire Control System**

In late 1940, when the AAC was continuing to solicit high altitude twin-engine medium bomber designs, the Martin Company presented its Model 190, to be designated the XB-33, as a possible twin-engine replacement for its B-26 Marauder. The design featured a pressurized fuselage and resembled Martin's recently developed PBM Mariner Navy Patrol bomber. It was slated to use two 1,800hp Wright P-3350 engines and was to measure 71 feet long, 22.5 feet high, and to have a 100 foot wingspan. The continued evolution of the design caused a great increase in weight that precluded Martin from achieving the performance specifications required by the AAC. Martin set aside the XB-33 program and expanded it to a four-engine program, the XB-33A.

At the time Martin was in competition with Boeing and Consolidated for a Long-Range heavy bomber design and felt its Model 190 showed promise. Martin was awarded a contract (AC-18645) to begin construction

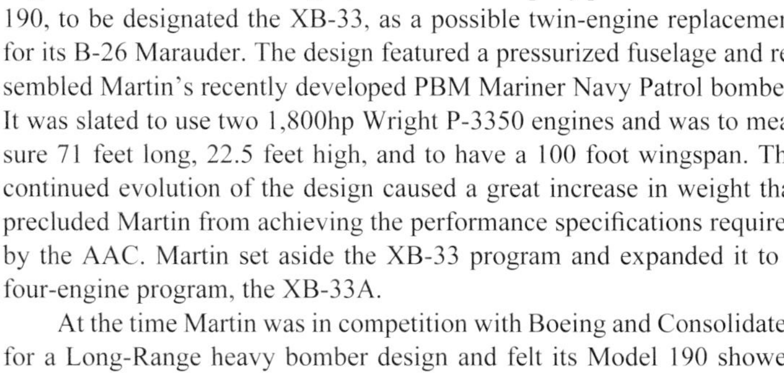

**Martin XB-33** (Jones via Merriam)

of two prototype XB-33A airframes. On paper the "Super Marauder" was to have a 79.8 foot long by 24 foot high fuselage and 134 foot wingspan. It was to be powered by four 1,800hp Wright R-2600-15 Cyclones with two-stage GE CMC-3 turbosuperchargers that were to give the bomber a top speed of 345 mph at 39,000 feet (cruise at 242 mph) over a range of 2,000 miles. The empty weight was 65,000 pounds (gross 98,000 pounds) with a bomb capacity of 10,130 pounds. The fuselage was to house a remote firing system that operated power turrets of twin .50cal machine guns in the nose, forward belly, upper rear, and tail, with 3,000 rounds of ammunition feeding the eight .50cal machine guns. The AAF ordered two prototypes, but the proposed performance specs were so promising that on 17 January 1942 the AAC ordered 402 XB-33As before the prototypes were built! The bombers were to be produced at the Martin Omaha factory when it was available after B-26 production phased out in April 1943. However, the B-33 project was cancelled on 25 November 1942 when the Omaha plant was assigned to manufacture the B-29. But by this time the course of the war and the need for a third Long-Range heavy bomber to join the B-29 and the B-32 was redundant, and the two unfinished prototypes were dismantled.

**Boeing B-29 Superfortress CFC System**
**Development**

The problem in designing the armament system for the B-29 and its B-32 backup was to furnish adequate protection against enemy fighter attack, but also not to over-arm the bomber, producing a deleterious weight and space problem that would diminish the bomber's performance. Because the B-29 was to operate at very high altitudes and over long distances engineers had designed pressurized crew cabins, which meant the gunners were to be stationed inside the cabins at sighting stations (blisters) controlling small aerodynamic powered turrets via a computerized gunsight.

The remote control turret system had many advantages over the contemporary manned armament systems found on the unpressurized B-17 and B-24, whose gunners needed to use oxygen masks and were exposed to freezing cold and to the noise and vibration of the firing guns. Since the remote turrets were unmanned they could be smaller, creating less drag which meant a concomitant increase in aircraft performance. The turrets and gunners could each be placed in positions to afford the optimal protection against enemy fighter attacks, and also permitted the isolated placement of vital armament electronic operating equipment in protected areas that also allowed easier servicing access and expedited improved weight distribution and pressurization of the cabins.

When the Sperry fire control system was being tested at Eglin Field it presented so many problems that Sperry was unable to meet its promised delivery schedules for the high-priority B-29 program. In December 1941, the Air Staff sent Col. Kenneth Wolfe, head of the Wright Field Armament Section, along with Colonels Leonard Harman and Roger Williams of Wright Field to Seattle with orders to abandon the remote sighting system and install conventional manned turrets to get the B-29 project moving forward. (This meeting has previously been described from the Sperry viewpoint.) The trio met with Boeing's Ed Wells and N.D. Showalter, who were adamant against installing conventional turrets, as these turrets would reduce the B-29's aerodynamic integrity and the bomber would not meet the performance specifications that the AAC had set. The Superfortress was so aerodynamically clean that lowering the landing gear caused as much drag as the rest of the aircraft! Over that weekend Boeing engineers built wind tunnel mockups and Wells and Showalter were able to demonstrate their position on not using conventional turrets to Wolfe, who agreed, but asked Boeing to use retractable turrets similar to the Sperry ball turrets used on the B-17. Boeing engineers countered Wolfe's request by replying that the gunners could not be sustained in the freezing environment of these turrets, and that there was not enough room in the B-29 for them. Fortunately Roger Williams, Wolfe's aide, had learned that General Electric was developing an electronic remote armament system and recommended it be investigated for use in the B-29.

**Testing**

Like the Sperry system, the early GE system also suffered from a limited scanning area through its periscope, and the gun controller had problems with orientation without a revolving seat or target locator that moved in conjunction with the turrets. The scanning limitation was solved by Bausch & Lomb, which developed a small double-ended reflector gunsight with a single eyepiece sighting station. In the General Electric sighting system the gun controller could rotate the sighting station in any direction during scanning. When the gunsighting station was engaged its every motion was replicated by the turret(s). Central to the GE system were the selsyn generators on the sighting station that moved the selsyn control transformers on the turret. Each selsyn brought together the action of the turret and its guns. Each turret had two selsyn transformers controlling azimuth and two controlling elevation. The basis of the GE system was an optical reflector gunsight computer located at four sighting stations in the fuselage that would calculate lead azimuth and elevation angles which were electrically transmitted to position non-retractable hydraulic turrets. The GE system eliminated the periscopes and the retractable turrets. (For a detailed description of the GE remote systems see my book: *The Boeing B-29 Superfortress: The Ultimate Look from Drawing Board to Combat*, Schiffer, PA, 2005.)

Unfortunately, when the GE system was tested at Eglin Air Proving Ground it was found to be unsatisfactory to defend either the B-29 or B-32 due to its vulnerability, complexity, and inherent inaccuracy. It had many chronic maintenance problems that were impossible to correct during flight. However, the system did have the major advantage of making pressurization easier, and it weighed much less than a conventional turret system. Despite the optimism surrounding the GE remote system, in May 1944, only days before the B-29 was to go into combat, the final Eglin report concluded that the GE system was unsuited for unescorted missions where the airplane could be subjected to focused fighter attacks. A month later, another Eglin report found the system "vulnerable" and "not functionally reliable," but also held out hope that its problems would be solved. In tests it was found that the GE system could not fire accurately on concentrated frontal attacks that were favored by aggressive *Luftwaffe* fighters and were the most prevalent Japanese attack mode on American bombers at the time. A possible answer was to add more forward firing guns by placing a new four-gun upper turret or a four-gun nose installation. Gen. Grandison Gardner of the Eglin Proving Ground suggested that the 20mm/twin .50 machine gun tail turret configurations be adapted to be mounted in the B-29 nose, but design proposals had to eliminate the bombardier's station to install the new turret and the project was dropped. The only logical solution was to add two additional .50 machine guns to the twin guns in the existing dorsal forward turret position with contour followers and increased ammunition. The standard GE four-gun P-61 Black Widow turret was modified by Emerson Electric and installed in both turret positions. Tests determined that the four-gun installation in the forward turret was preferred to the two-gun type, but the installation added nearly a half-ton in weight and decreased the bomber's range by 188 miles (but the top speed by only three mph). However, doubling the firepower did not necessarily double the new turret's effectiveness, as it had a larger bullet dispersion and scored nearly half the hits per gun as the two gun turret (5% vs. 9%), or only 1% more hits for the turret's four guns.

**General Description**

The defensive armament of the B-29 was the General Electric Model 2CFR55B1 Central Station Fire Control System. The heart of the GE CFC system was the five sighting stations, computers, and the human factor; the gunners. The CFC system connected to two dorsal and two ventral turrets, each mounting two .50 caliber machine guns which were augmented by a conventional tail turret mounting two .50 caliber machine guns and a 20mm cannon.

The B-29 *Standard Procedures for Gunners* stated that the gunner in the B-29 system had to know "only two tricks." The first was to track accurately and smoothly with the sight, and the other was "learning to work as a team with the other gunners so that you can transfer back and forth to get the maximum fire power." All sighting stations functioned similarly, but there were minor differences in the control boxes.

**B-29 Sighting Stations**

Designing a Sighting Station

The primary consideration in designing a sighting station was to devise and locate its components in such a manner as to keep the blister size to a minimum to reduce drag as much as possible. In designing the sight, its size was of primary importance, and parts of its design were compromised from the ideal to meet this requirement. The sighting domes became chronically frosted at high altitudes and various remedies were tried from fans, heaters, and pressure ducts that blew heated air over them, but none of these fixes were truly successful and the problem continued throughout the war, and was only alleviated when the XX Bomber Command began bombing at much lower altitudes.

Pedestal Sighting Station Parts

Azimuth Assembly

The azimuth assembly formed the base of the sight and had two selsyn (self-synchronized) generators that were rotated by means of precise gearing. The selsyns transmitted an electrical signal matching the exact azimuth position of the line of sight. The azimuth assembly contained part of the auxiliary equipment of the sight, such as a rheostat for controlling reticle brightness, a switch for deleting the computer from the system, and a stow pin for locking the sight into azimuth.

Elevation Unit

The elevation unit also had two selsyn generators that rotated as the sight was moved in elevation and transmitted an electrical signal matching the exact elevation position of the line of sight. The gunner controlled the position of the line of sight by manipulating handwheels on this unit. The gunner lightly rested the thumbs of each hand on a trigger, and a slight

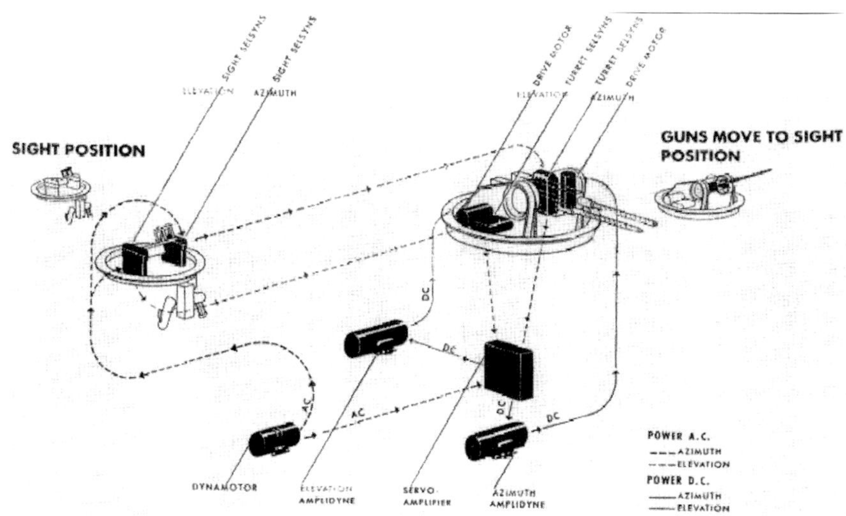


**Dynamics of CFC Sighting** (USAAF)

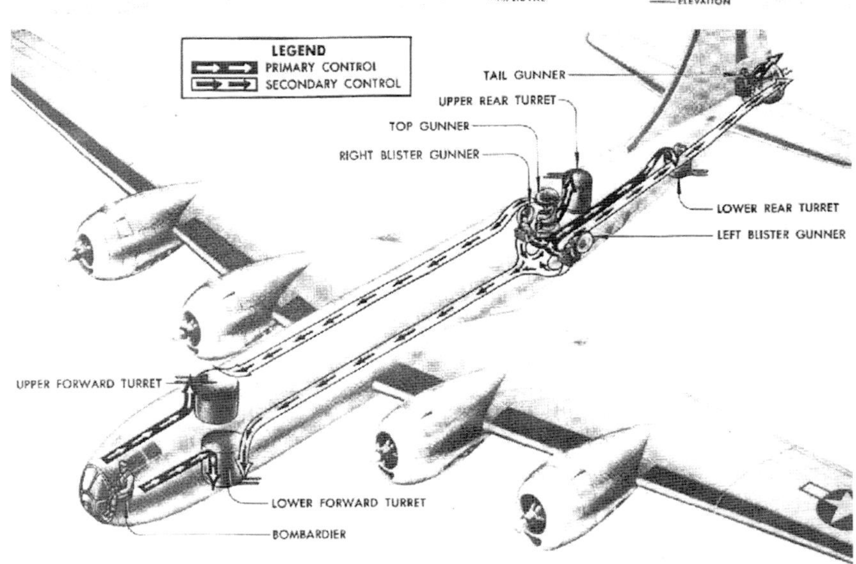


*Figure 4-392. Primary and Secondary Gun Control Diagram*

pressure on either one would fire the guns. The action switch located under the palm of his left hand had to be depressed to complete the circuit between the sighting action and the remote turret. If the gunner removed his hand from the left handwheel the switch was in the open position, and his gunsight could no longer control his primary or secondary turret. The turrets under his control were transferred automatically to one of the other sighting stations. Superimposed on the right handwheel was a smaller wheel with which the gunner made more accurate range adjustments.

Retiflector Sight

The sights on the CFC system were retiflector sights that were connected with a rudimentary computer mounted away from the sighting station. The sights and the computer calculated deflections for any attacking fighter. The navigator supplied part of the information the computer required via the interphone. The navigator's information included indicated air speed, pressure, altitude, and outside temperature, which allowed the computer to calculate the bomber's true air speed and the air density, all of which affected the speed of the bullet to the target. The remainder of the information was supplied by the gunner, who set the enemy fighter's wingspan by turning a target size knob; tracked the attacker to give the computer its motion; and framed the target by turning a range wheel or grip that supplied the data to the computer to calculate the distance to the target.

There were two kinds of retiflector sights used on the B-29 that were identical except for minor details. In the top sighting station, the sight was mounted on a ring and operated by two grip-type handles, and all other stations had sights mounted on pedestals and operated with two handwheels. There were five retiflector sights strategically located in the bomber that controlled the turrets through five electro-mechanical computers. The General Electric/Bell & Howell sights were provided at these stations: bombardier station, upper gunsighting station, left hand sighting station, right hand sighting station, and tail gunner station. This reflector type sight was mounted on a short pedestal and contained selsyn motors and rate gyros that operated in two planes. The selsyns connected the sight with the turret, and the rate gyros provided the computers with the target's speed and direction of movement. Pairs of course (1:1 ratio) and fine ratio (31:1) selsyns controlled the movement of the turrets in azimuth and elevation. Selsyn signals were corrected by single parallax (at the tail gunner and bombardier stations) or double parallax (in all rear cabin stations) computers and were amplified by servo amplifiers. This sight allowed the gunner to visually aim it and also to provide an electrical signal that relayed the distance to the target. Range was obtained by utilizing the principle that, within some limits, the apparent size of an object was dependent on the distance to the object and on its physical size. In using the sight the gunner needed to know or estimate the wingspan of the target before it began to attack. When the gunner looked into the 45° inclined, clear glass plate of the sight he saw the image of a circle of orange dots surrounding a center "pipper" that was reflected onto the screen from a concave spherical mirror. The projected image was focused to infinity and allowed the gunner to sight through the glass with both eyes. The movement of the range control handle changed the size (diameter) of the circle of dots so that a range (distance) to the target was simultaneously furnished to the computer so it could make corrections. On the front of the sight cover was a wingspan setting dial that the gunner used to select the target's wingspan. The dial also illuminated a figure on top of the sighting screen that provided a visual manifestation of the selected wingspan. To use the sight the gunner aimed the center "pipper" directly at the target and adjusted the size of the circle of orange dots so that the target's wingspan just filled its diameter. As the target neared, the gunner slowly turned the range control handle to keep the target constantly encompassed by the circle of dots. Micro-switch triggers mounted on the sight cover, one under each hand, fired the guns. The sights had a flip down sunshade and a metal ring-and-post sight for use in case of electronics failure.

**Computer Location** (USAAF)

Computers

Computer Production

The GE Type 2CH-Type computer design was divided into 17 components and was placed into limited production without the usual development and testing. Of course there were initial problems, but considering the advanced design of such an intricate piece of equipment, there were only a relative few modifications required and General Electric sent out the components to its divisions and subcontractors for mass production. GE licensed computer production to the Singer's Elizabethport works in September 1943, and Singer reached a production rate of 250 per week by the end of 1944 and over 500 per week by July 1945, by which time the factory had manufactured 20,794 computers.

Computer Location in the B-29

The five electro-mechanical computers of the Superfortress were housed in armored compartments under the cabin floors. They were of two types that allowed for single and double parallax angles. The double parallax computers controlling the upper sighting station and the blister sighting station were located in the center of the airplane and beneath the floor just aft of the upper rear turret. The double parallax computer for the right blister was located forward of the double parallax computer for the left blister. The tail sighting station single parallax computer was located beneath the floor and just aft of the upper rear turret. The navigator's barometric altitude and indicated air speed and temperature computer was located at his station.

Computer Types

The GE 2CH-Type computer was designed to allow the gunner to sight directly on his target and cause the gun bore axes of the turret or turrets that he was controlling to be changed from a position parallel to the line of sight to a position that would cause the projectiles to hit the target. One computer was used to remotely control each of the five sighting stations.

**The GE Type 2CH-Type Computer** (USAAF)

The single-parallax 2CH1C1 computer was used to control the tail turret sighting station that controlled one turret and the nose sighting station that controlled two turrets with approximately the same azimuth parallax base-length. The 2CH1D1 double parallax computer was used to control the dorsal sighting station and both blister sighting stations, which controlled two or more turrets whose parallax base-length was sufficiently different to require two different parallax connections.

Computer Connections

Each computer made three connections: ballistics, lead, and parallax. The ballistics connection compensated for windage and gravity that would cause the projectile to deviate from a straight course. The lead connection compensated for the distance the target traveled from the time the projectile left the gun until it was to hit the target. The parallax connection compensated for the distance along the longitudinal axis of the aircraft between the turret and the sight controlling the turret.

Connecting the Computer to the System

The three connections formed a single connection which was introduced into the system by differential selsyn generators that were electrically connected between the selsyn generators on the sighting stations and the selsyn control transformers on the turret. The 2CH1C1 single parallax computer had four differential selsyn generators while the 2CH1D1 double parallax computer had eight. When the rotors of the differential selsyn generators were rotated by an amount determined by the computer and supplied by the three connections they altered the signals from the selsyn generators on the sighting station so that the turret guns would be changed by the amount of the total correction from a position parallel to the line of sight.

Computer Input Calculations

To calculate the ballistics corrections the computer required:

Azimuth and elevation gun position
True air speed and density altitude (a function of altitude and temperature)
Range (distance) of the target from the gunner's sight.

To calculate lead corrections the computer required:

Relative velocity of the target in relation to the line of sight.
Range of the target from the gunner's sight.
Density altitude
Ballistics as it affected the projectile's flight time.

To calculate parallax corrections the computer required:

Azimuth and elevation gun position.
Range of the target from the gunner's sight.

The Computer obtained the necessary inputs from:

1) The azimuth and elevation gun positions were obtained from the selsyn system.
2) The range of the target was supplied by each gunner to his computer by the range potentiometer in his sight. The potentiometer varied when the gunner adjusted the range handwheel or grip to keep the reticle spanning the target.
3) The true airspeed was obtained from the navigator's handset unit which computed true air speed from the indicated air speed set in by the navigator. Density altitude was also obtained from the navigator's handset determined by the barometric altitude and temperature which were set by the navigator.
4) Relative velocity of the target in relation to the gunner's aircraft was sent to the computer by two gyroscopes in the sighting system.

The computer calculated and automatically corrected for:

Lead: Calculated the distance the target aircraft traveled during the time the bullet was to be in flight. (Much like the lead a hunter must allow for to hit a flying duck).

Parallax: Calculated the distance between the sighting mechanism and the gun barrel.

Windage: Calculated the effect of the speed of the aircraft through the air on the bullet as it traveled to the target.

Bullet Drop: Calculated the pull of gravity on the trajectory of the bullet traveling toward the target.

If there was damage or malfunction of the computer system the gunner could operate the turret through his sight independent of automatic computing. The gunner would have to lead the target with the sight so that the guns that were following the exact direction of the sight would also lead the target.

How the Computer Converted Electrical Inputs into Mechanical Inputs

The computer was basically a mechanical rather than an electrical calculator. Before the electrical inputs could be utilized by the calculating mechanism, it was necessary that they were converted into mechanical inputs by two types of follow-up systems: the selsyn type and the potentiometer type. The selsyn type follow up system was very similar to the type used in positioning the turret guns from a sighting station. It was used to provide the computer with azimuth and elevation gun positions. The potentiometer was the device that was the heart of the electric turret, as it regulated electro-motive force (EMF) known as voltage. The potentiometer acted as a rheostat dividing voltage, and was similar to a volume control rheostat that increased the volume when the knob was turned up.

Gunsights and the Computer

The gunsights, which were placed at known distance from the turrets which they operated (the nose and tail), were controlled through single parallax computers, while gunsights that were operated at varying distances from their turrets (switching between the top and side gunners) were controlled by the double parallax computers. The computers had to calculate parallax, ballistics, and deflection angles. The parallax angle resulted from the guns and sight being located a distance apart, and a preset correction was programmed into the computer. The ballistics angle was a combination of gravity drop and bullet trail, which were characteristics of bullets in flight. The deflection angle compensated for the distance traveled by the target during the flight of the bullets. To calculate the ballistics and deflection angles, the gunsight provided the computer with the necessary data: the target's speed, range, and direction. The navigator provided additional data, such as altitude (barometric), outside temperature, and IAS (indicated air speed) via interphone. Once the data was imputed, the computer calculated the sighting data and formulated a correction that was transmitted to the system between the gunsight and the turret via differential selsyns that adjusted the tracking of the guns in regard to the line of sight. The sighting was continually point blank (e.g. directly at the target), and if the gunner tracked the target smoothly through his sight and adjusted the range correctly as the target drew near, the computers made the other calculations needed for accurate aerial gunnery.

Computer Warning Lights

The computer warning light located at the left side of the sight's optic head was designed to prevent gunner errors when using the computer, such as forgetting to turn IN the computer standby switch or accidentally turning it to STANDBY while using the sight.

Warning Light in the Top Sighting Station

The computer automatically cut out when the sight was raised 80° or more, causing the warning light to flash ON, and as soon as the gun was lowered the warning light went out. If this happened the gunner was to track another target or turn around in a half circle and try to track the target from the other side.

Warning Light in the Side Stations

The computer cut out when the guns were lowered to 80° or more and the warning light went ON, and the gunner was to cease tracking the current target. There was no warning light in the tail position as the standby switch was locked to the IN position.

**Gunners and the Central Fire Control System**

The Central Fire Control System removed the guesswork out of "point of aim," but required practice to achieve skill in tracking, firing, and ranging to give the system enough accurate data to obtain a higher percentage of hits. Each gunner was personally responsible for his guns and turrets, but turret specialists repaired turrets and station ordnance personnel did gun repair.

In the B-29 CFC system, the top gunner, called the Central Fire Control Gunner (CFCG), was the key man in the system. He sat in an elevated swivel-type chair that was sometimes known as the "Barber's Chair" that was located under a clear plastic sighting dome located slightly forward of the dorsal aft turret and in front of the rear tunnel entrance. The base of the chair contained slip rings to transmit electrical current from the power source to the sight. The sight could be moved 60° on the horizontal without swiveling the stool but further traverse of the sight without a corresponding rotation of the stool would break the electrical circuit. The CFCG controlled the master gunnery panel that assigned turrets to each remote gunner, but had primary control of the upper rear turret and secondary control of the dorsal forward turret. There were many combinations of turret control in this system and the five gun positions were sited to cover every angle of attack with immediate concentrated firepower. In this system individual gunners (except the tail gunner) had primary control of a specified turret and secondary control of others. A gunner with control of a turret could hand over its control to gunners with secondary control. A system of signals was developed between gunners to allow quick hand off of turret control.

The two waist gunners divided the primary control of the ventral rear turret and secondary control of the ventral forward turret. The waist gunners, one on the port and one on the starboard, sat facing aft and had a 180° horizontal traverse and a converging angle of vision below the airplane. These sighting blisters were installed in the side of the fuselage, opposite each other, in the rear pressurized section. Stenciled somewhere around the outside of the blister were the words, "Cut thru Glass for Emergency Rescue." In this system the gunner who had in his direct vision the incoming enemy aircraft could not only fire his primary turret but could also "borrow" a second turret to increase his firepower.

The bombardier remained in his regular station in the nose where he had the largest range of vision, and thus had primary control of both the dorsal and ventral forward turrets and could use them singly or together (The function and duties of the CFC gunners are discussed in depth later.).

**Guns and Turrets**

The five turrets were electrically controlled and operated. The guns were mounted within the turret assemblies so that they could move up and down in a vertical plane independent of the motion of the turret that was sited in an azimuth direction. The two dorsal turrets and the ventral forward turret extended into the pressurized compartments, but were sealed so that the guns were functioning under outside atmospheric conditions. The guns of the dorsal and ventral turrets could be rotated continuously in an azimuth direction. The guns of the dorsal forward turret could be elevated or depressed through an arc from 2.5° below horizontal to 90° above horizontal. The guns of the ventral turrets could be elevated or depressed through an arc from 5° above horizontal to 90° below horizontal. These four gun stations included a "dead man's switch," which if a gunner was out of action his turret assignment was automatically assigned to the secondary gunner. The guns were not accessible for hand charging during pressurized flight, but each .50 machine gun had an automatic gun charger attached to its side.

**Bombardier's Sighting Station** (Author/Pima)

**Central Fire Control Gunner (CFCG) Position**

The top gunner called the Central Fire Control Gunner (CFCG) was the key man in the CFC system. He sat in an elevated swivel-type chair that was sometimes known as the "Barber's Chair." (Author/Pima)

The base of the chair contained slip rings to transmit electrical current from the power source to the sight. The sight could be moved 60° on the horizontal without swiveling the stool but further traverse of the sight without a corresponding rotation of the stool would break the electrical circuit. (Author/Pima)

**CFCG Primary Control Box** This box gives the right and left blister observers primary control of the Lower Forward Turret (top switch), Lower Rear Turret (middle switch), and Tail Mount (bottom switch)(Author/Pima)

**Blister Sighting Station**

(Author/Pima)

Central Fire Control Turrets:
Dorsal Rear Turret
Location: Station 728
Armament: Two .50 caliber machine guns
Lower Limit of Fire: Horizontal
Dorsal Forward Turret
Location: Station 177
Armament: Two .50 caliber machine guns
Lower Limit of Fire: 2.5° below horizontal
Ventral Rear Turret
Location: Station 945
Armament: Two .50 caliber machine guns
Lower Limit of Fire: 5° above horizontal
Ventral Forward Turret
Location: Station 192
Armament: Two .50 caliber machine guns
Lower Limit of Fire: 5° above horizontal
And the non-CFC Tail Turret
Location: Extreme aft
Armament: Two .50 caliber machine guns and one 20mm cannon
Rear Limits of Fire: 30° angle above and below horizontal centerline and 30° right and left of vertical centerline. There was a pyramidal cone of fire formed by these limits.

(Note: "Station" denotes the number of inches from the nose of the B-29 the specific turret was located)

**Fuselage Turrets**

The dorsal turrets were General Electric No. W8258272 and the ventral turrets were General Electric No. W8258273, and each housed two .50 caliber machine guns and carried 500 rounds per gun in ammunition boxes. For use on the B-29 the .50 caliber guns were mounted in Edgewater adapters and held in place in the turret by a slider mount bolt on the rear trunnion and by bolts holding the front trunnion mount of the adapter. The dorsal and ventral turrets could be reloaded whenever the airplane was not pressurized, but the tail turret could only be reloaded from the outside (e.g. only on the ground). These turrets were equipped with cam-controlled cut off switches that protected the aircraft from its own fire. An AN-N-6 motion picture camera was located in each of the five power turrets and was remotely controlled at the individual turret sighting stations.

Fuselage Turret Description and Operation

The control of the turret was initiated by turning the power turret switch ON and slightly rotating the sight to energize the amplidyne generators. The turret was then under full control of the operator and could be moved where desired. The turrets operated electrically by small self-synchronized selsyn AC motors that transmitted the position indicating signals. A dynamotor (generator) provided 115-volt AC to the selsyns and a servo-amplifier. The set of selsyns on the gunsight was connected to a like set on the turret. The movement of the sight caused a disparity between the two sets of selsyns that continually compared their individual alignments. When the turret selsyns detected this discrepancy, a signal was transmitted to the servo-amplifier that determined the direction of movement needed and then furnished DC power to the turret drive motor by means of amplidyne motor-generators. The drive motors moved the guns and turrets in the requisite direction until the selsyns signaled that the sight and turret were aligned and the signal that indicated the discrepancy ceased and the turret movement stopped.

The control system operated simultaneously in two planes: vertically for gun elevation and depression and horizontally for turret rotation. In performance, the sight and guns moved instantaneously as a unit with a great degree of accuracy via electric signals. But in practice the gunners were unable to hit a target because the guns were located a distance away from the sight and were aimed in parallel to the gunner's line of sight. To remedy this situation a method of adjusting the aim of the guns in relation to the line of sight was necessary. This adjustment had to be variable with the distance of the target from the turret and was made by means of computers as described previously.

Each turret initially carried 500 rpg, but this figure was increased to 1,000 rpg by using integral ammunition boxes and electrically powered feed assisters that drew rounds into the guns. Each gun had an automatic electro-pneumatic gun charger that fired the gun and also allowed the gunner to remotely reload in case of a stoppage (early B-29s had $CO_2$ charged guns). The gun chargers were supplied by an integral pneumatic system made up of an electric air compressor, pressure regulator, and a storage cylinder. The ventral turrets had small ejection doors located in the outer cover that opened automatically when the guns fired and let spent cartridge cases and belt links fall out of the turret. In the dorsal turrets the cartridges and links were accumulated inside the aircraft and removed after returning to base.

Contour Follower and Interrupter

The contour follower and limit switch prevented the remotely sighted guns from firing into their own bomber. This device mechanically raised or lowered the guns to clear the fuselage or other obstructions. The contour interrupter prevented the upper guns from ever pointing at the top sighting station, and the contour interrupter used on the lower guns prevented them from firing at the curved fuselage.

Limit Stops

All turrets had mechanical limit stops that were built like rubber bumpers to prevent the guns from moving too far and physically striking the fuselage. They also had a set of automatic switches that cut off most of the power when the guns reached their limit stops, leaving just enough current to hold the guns firmly in place against the stops and preventing the guns from firing. On the dorsal turrets there was a mechanical limit stop that kept them from traveling past 90° straight up when the guns were raised. The ventral turrets had stops that kept them from traveling below minus 90° straight down when the guns were lowered. These stops were only bumpers and had no switches to turn off the power.

Stowing the Turret Guns

When out of range of enemy fighter interception the turret guns were to be stowed to decrease drag and for safety when landing with loaded guns. The turret gun stowing positions were to have the guns pointing straight forward for the dorsal turrets and guns pointing straight aft for the ventral turrets and, of course, for the tail mount. The ventral forward turret was stowed in the aft position during takeoff and landing to prevent interference with the nose gear doors. To stow the guns the gunner pushed IN the azimuth stowing pin of the sight to hold the turret in place. For both dorsal turrets and the ventral forward turret the elevation stowing pin was also pushed IN. For the tail mount the guns had to be held at about 10°. The ventral rear turret was also stowed to prevent the guns from hitting the ground, and the ventral forward guns had to be clear from the aft position to allow the bomb bay doors to open. Automatic stowing occurred when the action switch operating the turret was released. The dorsal turret guns were lowered as far as possible and the ventral guns were raised as high as possible. If the power failed the two ventral turrets could be stowed by hand using the slipstream. There were three warning lights (one for the two ventral turrets, one for the dorsal turrets, and the last for the tail turret) mounted near the airplane commander's position. These lights were ON when these turrets were in use and were OFF when the guns were stowed.

**CFC Turret**

**Ventral CFC Turret Exterior** (Author/Pima)

**Dorsal CFC Turret Interior** (Author/Pima)

**Ventral CFC Turret Interior** (Author/Pima)

**Dorsal CFC Turret Exterior** (USAAF)

Gun and Turret Harmonization
Harmonization, which was time consuming and required special training, was a necessary requirement for the CFC system to operate efficiently. Basically, B-29 gun/turret harmonization was the same as for conventional power turrets. An important part of harmonizing was to level the turrets, making sure that they were parallel to each other and at right angles to the bomber's centerline. The line of sight and the line of fire had to be adjusted so that they were parallel to each other and remained that way when they moved. The B-29 CFC system caused special problems, as it had five turrets and five sighting stations, all at different levels and at various distances from one another (up to 40 feet from the sight). The line of sight from each sighting station had to be adjusted parallel to the line of fire from each turret gun. The CFC electrical system had to be carefully and exactly adjusted so that the guns would move exactly with the sights throughout their entire range of movement. The CFC was harmonized by the mechanical/electrical "Middle Distance Target Method" that used a group of target stands set up at various points about 500 feet around the bomber. As Japanese fighter opposition decreased harmonization was given lesser attention. Consequently, when the infrequent fighter did attack the CFC did not function to maximum potential.

**Tail Turret**
The tail gunner had primary control of the tail turret, but when not using it control was passed to the side gunners. The tail gunner could turn his sight more than halfway back toward either side in azimuth (105°) from the center line in either direction. In elevation he could sight from straight down (90°) to two-thirds up (60°). This was much more than his guns were able to follow. The guns could move 30° to either side in azimuth and 30° up and 30° down in elevation. The tail guns were stowed directly rearward and slightly above horizontal (See Part Six/Chapter 4/Section 19: B-29 Tail Turret for a description of this turret).

**The CFC in Combat**
**Preflight Checks**
Before boarding the bomber for the mission the gunners were responsible for the following preflight checks of their guns and turrets:

1) Check and harmonize guns using dummy rounds.
2) Check all equipment for safety wires where required.
3) Check ammunition carefully for excess corrosion, defective primers, position of links on rounds, round to round positioning, and for any bulges or burrs.
4) Load the ammunition cans, making certain the rounds pointed in the right direction and did not bind in the can. Load guns as per group mission directive.
5) Check to see if the required spare gun parts and tool kit were on board.
6) Check the CFC System and turret domes and latches.
7) Sight stowage.
8) Immediately before each mission all oil was to be removed and none applied, as the guns would perform better at high altitudes without any oil.

Once on board the bomber and before takeoff the gunners performed the following pre-flight station checks:

1) Check parachute and clothing.
2) Check oxygen system (pressure should be between 350 to 450psi).
3) Check to be sure that the cabin pressure valve was open.
4) Check heaters and lights.
5) Check interphones by putting on the headphones, adjusting the throat microphone, and then waiting for the interphone check.
6) An alarm bell was rung by the airplane commander during combat station inspection and the left and right fuselage gunners would inform the airplane commander that they had heard the alarm bell.

Each gunner would then report to the airplane commander when he had completed his own checklist.

Exterior Flight Control Check
When the co-pilot called over the interphone each gunner would observe and report the position of the rudder, elevators, and ailerons as the airplane commander operated each control. Before takeoff the airplane commander would say over the interphone "wing flaps," and when the flaps were down the left blister gunner would reply "left flap down 25°" and the right blister gunner would make a similar reply. The blister gunners were responsible for checking that the bomb bay doors were closed.

Then the airplane commander would order "Fasten you safety belt" and issue a "taxi alert." During taxiing the top CFC gunner was responsible for promptly reporting to the co-pilot the presence of any nearby aircraft that might interfere with taxiing.

After Takeoff
After takeoff the gunners:

1) Made sure the optic head was clean.
2) Pushed breaker switches IN and switched AC power to ON. The dynamotor then started and the reticle lights went on (target size numerals, aiming dot and range circle).
3) Turned the rheostat from DIM to BRIGHT and tested the reticle response.
4) Turned the rheostat lamp selector switch to check lamp's second (reserve) filament.
5) Turned the target size adjusting screw to check change of numerals and change of range dots. Made sure the reticle circle was clear.
6) Sighted at some distant object, moved his head and make sure that the dot still seemed to be on the object, no matter where he held his head.
7) Turned ON the computer switch on the control box to start gyroscope and computer unit.
8) Turned the computer standby switch to IN to connect the computing mechanism into the circuits. Made sure the warning light that lit when the computer was on STAND BY had gone off when the action switch was closed.
9) Checked that the friction adjustments were just right for smooth tracking. If gloves were worn on the mission, the adjustments were tested with the gloves on.
10) Turned OFF all switches.
11) Moved the sight to the forward horizontal position and to LOCK.
12) LOCK pantograph.
13) The waist gunners were to inform the airplane commander that the flaps and gear were "FULL UP."

After these checks were completed the gunners tried to settle into a comfortable position for scanning and tracking, but this was difficult, as their position in the blister was kneeling with the knees spread apart. The gunners constantly adjusted their parachute harnesses and padding and tried to get their microphone cords and oxygen tubing out of the way. Fortunately, vigilant scanning was only required as the bombers approached Japan.

The aircraft generators were unable to start all the CFC equipment at once and the airplane commander directed each turret to start up in turn:

1) Turn ON the switches in the power control box one at a time at ten-second intervals.
2) Turn the computer switch on the control box to IN. This supplied DC power to the computer and sight gyros. Check that the computer In-Out light was ON. This light was to be ON when both the computer switch on the control box was ON and when the computer standby switch was at STANDBY.
3) Turn the computer standby switch on the sight to IN. The In-Out light then switched OFF.
4) Close the action switch and move the sight. Check to see that the primary control turret followed the sight. To check these turret movements: the top gunner could see the upper turret; the blister gunners could see the lower aft turret guns when the turret was pointing broadside; the tail gunner could see the tail mount; and the nose gunner could have the top gunner check the upper forward turret and have the navigator listen for the movement of the lower forward turret.
5) Check the secondary controls as per SOP. Check that the secondary turret followed the sight.
6) Adjust the brightness of the lights on the auxiliary control box in the blister sighting station to individual preference.
7) If he had not been informed previously, the gunner checked with navigator to see if he had entered altitude, air speed, and temperature on the hand set.
8) Since an enemy fighter would be seen at a long distance, the range control was set for the smallest reticle or maximum range.
9) If or when the airplane commander instructed the gunner to test fire, the gun switch was moved from SAFE to FIRE. The gunner would take a short burst, taking care not to fire into the formation. After the test the guns switch was returned to SAFE.
10) On long missions the CFC would be put into the STANDBY mode.

**Engaging the Enemy**

Areas of Search and Fire

Once in the combat zone each gunner, in addition to controlling a designated turret combination, was also assigned to scan a specific and limited area of the sky which would be the area his guns would fire (except for the tail gunner, who fired into a smaller area than he searched).

In a study of 6,000 Japanese fighter attacks to determine the level and direction of attack during daylight missions it was found that they were almost evenly distributed: 32% Above, 34% Level, and 34% Low. On 231 night missions the enemy fighters were reported to come in at 53% Level, 31% High, and 16% Low. However, these night figures could be in error, as many enemy attacks that originated at the High or Low positions could not be seen until they reached the Level position. On daylight missions High, Level, and Low attacks from the nose quarter were the enemy's preferred approaches of attack. On night missions the enemy tended to choose level or high attacks from the rear.

The Japanese preference for frontal daylight attacks was due to the difficulty of Japanese interceptors to overtake B-29s at high altitude (26,000 to 32,000 feet), and also a frontal attack made the Jap fighter a difficult target because of the high rate of closure. The preference for nighttime tail attacks was due to the Japanese system of vectoring that placed their fighters on the tails of the B-29s. Nighttime B-29 attacks were made at low levels that enabled the Japanese fighters to overtake them. However, the Japanese never fully developed night tactics and lacked night fighters.

The Gunner's "How to Search and Fire"
Areas of Search and Fire for each gun position:
Nose Gunner:
Azimuth: Generally forward (10 to 2 o'clock) 150°
Elevation: 60° scaling up or down
Top Gunner:
Azimuth: Generally forward (9 to 3 o'clock) 180°
Elevation: 60° up from the horizontal
Waist Gunners:
Azimuth: One searched and fired to the outside of the formation, the other searched to the inside (1 to 6 o'clock right and 6 to 11 o'clock left) 150°
Elevation: 60° down from horizontal
Tail Gunner:
Azimuth: Searched over entire visual area (3 to 9 o'clock) 180°
Elevation: 90° divided evenly above and below horizontal

The main rule for search was:

"You've got to look with the expectation of seeing something. The man who doesn't expect to see something-doesn't. Focus your eyes at the outer range of your area and look to <u>see</u>. Don't look merely to be looking. Keep your attention focused and stay alert. A methodical system for hunting the sky may help:

1) Divide the area of the sky in your own mind into small zones.
2) Focus on the zone <u>furthest forward</u> and don't let your eyes leave it until they have done a thorough job of searching in that zone.
3) Then shift to the next zone and do the same job.
4) Stick to your own area.
5) <u>Always search the forward part of your area more frequently and carefully than any other</u>. That's where attacks appear to start in relative motion and that's where your hottest attacks come from. Search more often in the forward areas, rather than linger longer in them.
6) <u>Always keep your guns pointing forward at standby</u>, ready for the draw, to pick up targets swiftly and track them from front to rear."

While scanning the sky for enemy planes the gunner was not to move the sight, as every movement caused the computer to calculate deflections. The gunner did not want the computer to be calculating a non-existent deflection on a non-existent enemy once a real target was spotted. When a real target came into view then the sight could be swung quickly to line it up. The quicker the sights and guns were on the target the less time it took the computer to start its computations.

When an aircraft was spotted the gunner was to take four steps:

1) Report the target to the fire control officer by the o'clock system.
2) Identify the target as friend or foe. If it were an enemy, identify the type and wingspan.
3) Set the target size on the reticle. Some gunners found it helpful to set the target size previously to the wingspan of the aircraft most likely to attack.
4) Turn the gun switch to FIRE.

Reporting the Target

Immediately after spotting any aircraft, friend or foe, the gunner got on the interphone and, speaking clearly, concisely, and in firm volume (not shouting) used the standard clock system, high, low, level to locate and report the aircraft. He then repeated the message once.

As soon as an aircraft was seen to be threatening (i.e. maneuvering, climbing, etc.) the gunner was to report it in the following fashion: number and type (pause), clock and elevation position (pause), and if enemy, what was it doing (repeat), for example:

"5 ZERO FIGHTERS (pause) TWO O'CLOCK HIGH (pause) OVERTAKING (repeat)"

As soon as the target was clearly attacking, the gunner reported (with his guns bearing) as follows: attack (pause), clock, and elevation position (repeat):

ATTACK (pause) FOUR O'CLOCK HIGH (repeat)

In the breakaway phase of the attack gunners, other than those firing on the attack, could have a perfect shot at the target providing they were forewarned. This was especially true for the side and tail gunners on nose attacks that passed over or under the bomber to complete their breakaway. On a breakaway the report was attack (pause), clock and elevation position (pause), how breaking away:

ATTACK (pause) ONE O'CLOCK LEVEL (pause) BREAKING AWAY UNDER (repeat)

At the end of an attack the attacker could slide under a bomber to get itself in immediate position for another attack and thus would offer itself as an easy target for the blister gunner toward whose side he was sliding, providing the gunner was forewarned. The report would be Attack (pause), clock and elevation position (pause), sliding under:

ATTACK (pause) THREE O'CLOCK LOW (pause) SLIDING UNDER (repeat)

Tracking the Target

The basis for successful tracking was stated in *Gunnery in the B-29*: "If you feed your computer the right information, it will come up with the right deflection. If you make a mistake, the computer will give the wrong answer and your bullets will miss every time. Your tracking and framing of the target must be absolutely on the nose"

After the target was identified as the enemy, the gunner would move the sights on the target and follow it, and take the following steps:

1) The gunner's body, especially the upper arms from elbow to shoulder, was to be braced. The hands were to remain steady and be supported on the sight but the wrists and fingers needed complete freedom.
2) The sight had friction adjustments that were to be preset to individual preferences for tracking the target smoothly. If gloves were to be worn during combat then the adjustments were to be made with them on.
3) In glare conditions, the sky filter was to be used only enough to make the reticle clearly visible and the rheostat was to be turned up to MAXIMUM
4) While scanning the gunner was to keep his eyes a few inches behind the optic head with both eyes open which was more natural and easier.
5) Instant fighter recognition was important so the gunner could dial in the wingspan without thinking.
6) It was important that the gunner had a comfortable hold on the grips so that he wouldn't have to change it while tracking. Once tracking began the gunner was not to change his grip on the handwheels or grips until the target was shot down or escaped. If the aim was off (e.g. failure to move the dot with the target or move past it) the gunner was not to jerk the dot back to place but move it slowly and smoothly back. "If you get off target, get off the trigger."
7) The gunner was to track the target smoothly and maintain the dot of the reticle on the middle of the fighter and span its silhouette with the reticle. The computer calculated the amount of lead to give the gun from the rate at which the sight was turned. The range handle was to be adjusted continually so that the reticle just spanned the target's wingspan or silhouette. If the sight was jerked or paused then the computer would jerk or pause the guns. If the gunner came off the target he then had move the sight smoothly back to it. Even if the bomber was rolling or evading, the gun tracking was to remain as smooth as possible and the computer would make the necessary corrections.
8) The range wheel or grip was to be turned with a smooth, steady, easy motion to keep the target's wingtips framed accurately inside the reticle circle. If the target was seen from the side where in most cases its fuselage was shorter than its wingspan the gunner was to set in the wingspan but keep circle somewhat beyond the ends of the fuselage as seen in the sight. The computer computations were only as good as the data fed into it and range was very important.
9) If the gunner changed from one target to another, he was to swing the sight quickly with the action switch CLOSED. When a new target was encountered the action switch was OPEN. This action switch open-closed procedure was to prevent the computer from entering erroneous corrections.

Firing on the Target

Firing Area Safety Margins

As soon as a gunner gave up control of his turret this turret would swing into the line of sight of some other gunner. If that gunner had his finger on the trigger his guns would fire as they swung into position and could jeopardize other aircraft in the formation.

The basic firing areas could be restricted or reduced to avoid hitting other bombers in the formation according to a prescribed safety rule: "Every area of search and fire must stop one full clock angle (30°) in azimuth away from any other bomber in the formation." This rule for defining search and fire areas was slightly modified to act as a safety rule in firing if the gunner forgot the limits of his search and fire area during combat:

"You must withhold fire, in azimuth: 1 hour clock angle (30°) away from another B-29 when tracking <u>into</u> it and a half hour clock angle (15°) away from another B-29 when tracking <u>away</u> from it."

This rule allowed a safety margin for the gun computer leads and for parallax, when the guns could be pointing far ahead or lagging far behind the aiming point.

Rules of Firing
The remote system allowed the gunner to fire at any aircraft in range and he did not have to wait for an attack. A set of rules were established for firing:

1) Set the true wingspan of the target on the target dimension dial. At the start of the mission the gunner was to set the wingspan of the fighter most likely to be encountered during that mission and turn the range handle until the reticle circle was as small as possible and the gunner would then be ready for quick action. If the enemy fighter encountered was not the one for the sight presetting, the setting could be quickly reset. If there wasn't time to change the wingspan size the gunner could make a correction as the target was framed. If the actual target wingspan was smaller than the dial setting he could keep the reticle a little beyond the wingtips. If the target was larger than the dial setting, he could let the wingtips overlap the circle a little.
2) Place the center dot of the reticle on the target's fuselage at the leading edge of its wings.
3) Adjust the range so that the circle of dots in the reticle just touched the part of the target farthest away from the center dot.
4) Make sure that any friendly bombers weren't hit.
5) Open fire and keep firing in bursts.
6) If, in tracking the target, the rounds came close to a friendly bomber the gunner was to invoke the safety rule and stop firing one full hour clock angle tracking toward or stop firing a half hour if tracking away.

It was important to begin firing before the enemy did. The gunners were to begin firing at 1,000 yards, except the nose gunner, who was to fire immediately because of the high closing speeds. All the gunner had to do was keep the target spanned in the reticle, track smoothly, and the computer would do the rest. Short bursts were to be fired with a maximum firing rate not exceeding 30 rounds per minute per gun (two seconds of firing). The gunner was to release the trigger whenever control of his turret was transferred from one station to another so that bullets wouldn't be fired when the turret was swinging around. It was important that the gunners listened over the interphones to keep current on the situation in the rest of the bomber.

Head-on Attacks
During combat it was estimated that 45% of enemy attacks were head-on attacks against the B-29's nose guns. Due to the high closing rates of a head-on attack the nose sighting station had to adopt the following procedure:

1) Preset target size at 35 feet.
2) Adjust the range handwheel until the reticle (circle of dots) appeared (1,200 yards).
3) When a single-engine target spanned three quarters of the reticle (1,600 yards) the range wheel was to be spun to minimum and tracking and firing was started. The same procedure applied to twin-engine fighters.
4) The gunner was to return to 1,200 yards range as soon as the target left in order to have information in the computer ready for the next head-on attack.

Tail Gunner
The tail gunner was to immediately report by interphone any aircraft within his search cone and then continue a running report at 30 second intervals until the aircraft was identified as friend or enemy and, if enemy, until it had either been destroyed or escaped. To report the target's range, the gunner was to use the set words: SPOT if the target were beyond 900 yards; CLOSE if the target were between 900 and 500 yards; and the range in round number yards if it were under 500 yards. The report sequence was target (pause), range information (pause), and clock and elevation position (and repeat):

TARGET (pause) SPOT (pause) SEVEN O'CLOCK HIGH (and repeat)

Immediately after receiving this target report the radio operator was to issue the IFF (Identification Friend or Foe) challenge and report back to the tail gunner if he found the target aircraft was friendly. If the tail gunner did not receive a reply from the radio operator, or if his signal lights did not go on indicating that the target was not another B-29, the tail gunner would assume that the target was hostile and open fire if its range decreased to 600 yards. He was to fire long bursts and continue to report on the interphone as long as the target was within 600 yards or until it was destroyed, evaded, or lost.

Gunner's Duties Before Landing
Before landing the gunners had to take the following steps:

1) About two hours before landing the lower turret guns were to be cleared of ammunition by firing.
2) The gun switch on the control box was turned to SAFE.
3) The primary control gunners were to stow their turrets by stowing the sight and holding the action switch to CLOSED. The right blister gunner was also to stow the lower aft turret.
4) When the turrets were stowed, the switches were turned OFF on the control box and then the action switch was to be released. The stowing pins on the sight in both azimuth and elevation were to be pushed IN and then the sight was to be covered.
5) When the airplane commander announced, "Prepare for landing" over the interphone the tail gunner was to start the auxiliary power APU.
6) When the airplane commander announced, "Wing flaps" the right and left blister gunners watched the flaps and the left blister gunner reported "Left flap down 25°" and then the right gunner reported likewise.
7) The landing gear was reported as "DOWN and LOCKED."
8) Safety belts were then fastened for landing.

Gunner's Duties After Landing
The blister gunner was to check that the bomb bay doors were OPEN. After each mission the gunner would first disarm and clear the guns with another gunner standing by so no one would pass in front of them during clearing. Next he would remove the turret dome, open the gun covers, and remove the ammunition belts, being sure that the last round was removed from chamber. He would remove and empty the ammo cans but did nothing with the receiver.

The guns were removed and taken to the armament section, where they were thoroughly cleaned with the prescribed cleaning fluid. The parts checked for full and free movement were: the ejector, the extractor switch, the belt holding pawl, the cover group, the firing pin and extension, and the accelerator. While cleaning the gun each part was to be carefully inspected, and if there was a problem with any part, it was to be replaced.

All gunners were to report all malfunctions of the CFC equipment to the CFC top gunner, who was to keep a record of the status of the equipment and then report them to the flight engineer. After completing their after landing responsibilities the gunners reported to intelligence for debriefing.

**If the Computer Failed**
In the rare occasion that the computer failed the sight could be used as a ring and bead sight using the rules of Position Firing. Once the computer failed the gunner was to turn it OFF and turn the computer standby switch to STANDBY. The navigator supplied the gunner with the aircraft's true airspeed, and the target dimension dial was set according to a chart placed near the sighting station. The setting varied from station to station to allow for the distance between the sight and the guns. The gunner turned the range handle or grips until the reticle circle was as large as possible, while on the pedestal sight the handle was pulled out to maintain the setting. Because the size of the ring was adjustable by moving the target size knob, the gunner could use it to lay off accurate deflections that would allow for exact true aircraft speed and the sight could then be used as a ring and bead sight.

**Effectiveness of the CFC System**
By the end of the war the properly maintained, harmonized, and employed GE system became very reliable, and was effective against diminishing Japanese fighter opposition. The infrequent problems that did occur were relatively insignificant (jams, accidental discharge, and overheating), and were caused by poor maintenance and improper handling in combat situations. The ejected shell cases and links dropped from the lower turrets could damage the radome and other trailing aircraft. A 20AF report showed that during June 1945, its bombers had fired nearly 1.1 million rounds of .50 caliber bullets from 30,000 guns and experienced only 163 malfunctions, of which over half were blamed on the guns and not the CFC system.

Since enemy fighters were much less of a problem in the Pacific than over Europe it is difficult to determine the true effectiveness of the B-29 remote gun system. According to the *Army Air Force Statistical Digest* the total bomber losses over Europe and the Mediterranean of 44% and 31%, respectively, were credited to fighters, while only 21% of the 20AF B-29 losses were due to fighters (due to fewer Japanese fighters with inferior performance and poor pilot training). In the ETO each enemy aircraft destroyed in the air required 12,600 rounds of ammunition, while in the MTO 11,900 rounds were required. The B-29s of the 20AF needed only 9,800 rounds, but the question was whether it was because the CFC system was better or because the Japanese aircraft were far more fragile than their German counterparts. The turrets and guns were extremely reliable, with 94% turret reliability and 93% gun reliability in December 1944 and 100% turret and 97% gun reliability in January 1945.

The *US Strategic Bombing Survey* report on the "Strategic Air Operation of Very Heavy Bombers in the War Against Japan (20th Air Force)" gave XXIBC B-29 gunners the following credits during 11,026 enemy attacks: 714 enemy aircraft destroyed, 456 probably destroyed, and 770 damaged. For every hundred enemy aircraft attacks B-29 gunners shot down or probably destroyed an average of 11 Japanese fighters. During the B-29 bombing campaign Japanese fighters shot down 58 B-29s, and 29 others were lost to combined aircraft and flak damage.

**Douglas A-26 Invader GE Remote Fire Control System**
The Douglas A-26 Invader came into action late in World War II to meet Air Force specification for a new multi-purpose heavily-armed attack bomber to replace the A-20, B-25, and B-26. The unheralded Invader could carry rockets, torpedoes, and bombs, was heavily gunned, and its design was so successful that it served in late World War II, Korea, and was brought out of retirement to serve in Vietnam. Its designer, the renowned Ed Heinemann, proposed a number of interesting armament configurations, including combinations of 37mm and 75mm cannon, and .50 caliber machine guns in the nose; wing guns and under wing pods; and a remote fire control system. The A-26A was equipped with a General Electric fire control system that had a dorsal and ventral turret remotely controlled by one sighting station. Each

**A-26 Dorsal CFC Turret** (USAAF)

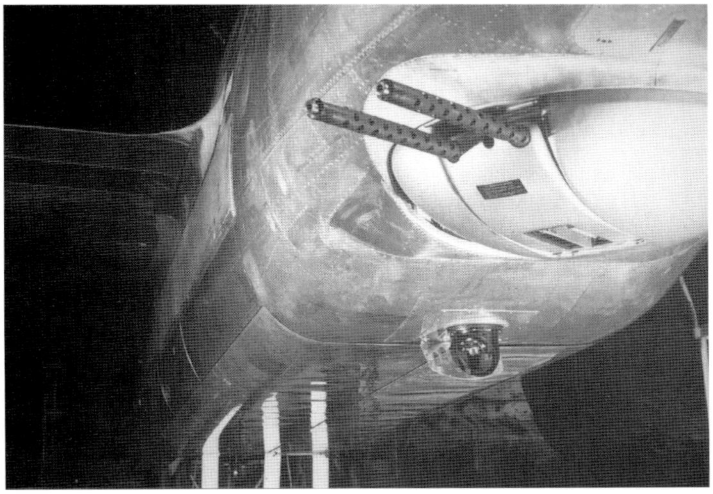

**A-26 Ventral CFC Turret** (USAAF)

turret was equipped with twin .50 caliber M2 machine guns and one N-2 Gun Sight Aiming Point Camera and overrun control. Before the CFC system could operate properly it had to be harmonized so that the line of sight of the sighting station was parallel to the bore axes of the turret guns.

**Periscopic Heads**

The General Electric sighting station containing upper and lower periscopic heads was located in the gunner's compartment located midway between the dorsal and ventral turrets. The central casting of the sighting station contained one fixed prism and one rotating prism called the change-over prism. The change-over prism was rotated 90° by the change-over motor to change the line of sight from the upper head to the lower head or vice-versa. A 10° angle of over-travel on either side of horizontal was provided in order to eliminate the necessity of repeated changes of upper and lower sights.

When the line of sight was in the upper hemisphere, a cam in the elevation unit depressed one of the two microswitches in the prism change-over motor so that the motor rotated in the direction required to hold the change-over prism stationary. The line of sight was moved to the lower head by the gunner's movement of the sight, which caused a cam to release the first microswitch and close the second. This caused the prism change-over motor to rotate in the opposite direction, tilting the change-over prism and transferring the line of sight to the lower head.

A desiccating system was provided to remove moisture from the optical system to prevent frosting and fogging at low temperatures or extreme temperature variations. A clear cylindrical container of desiccant (anhydrous calcium sulphate, called "Drierite") was located near the bottom rear pedestal base. A hand pump was connected to the interior of thee sight by tubing and created a positive circulation of air through the sight and desiccant, keeping the sight fog/frost-free in temperatures as low as -100°F.

The exterior periscope head windows were kept clean by spraying isopropyl alcohol on them with a hand pump located on the lower right hand side of the gunner's compartment. The slip stream removed the ice or dirt after the alcohol had softened it.

**Movement of the Sighting Station and Turrets**

The gunner positioned in the sighting station moved and fired the guns electrically. The gunner could rotate the sighting station in any direction for scanning with AC power ON. When he was ready to fire he brought the turret or turrets into correspondence with the sight by turning the desired turret's power ON. The gunner obtained azimuth by manually rotating the entire sighting unit about its vertical axis and obtained elevation by rotating the elevation sighting handles located on the column in the middle of the unit about their horizontal axis. The firing was harmonized with the gunner's line of sight through the upper or lower periscopes that had 50° (70° on later models) fields of vision.

The guns in the dorsal turret had unlimited azimuth rotation and operated between 0° and -89° in zenith. The guns in the ventral turret had unlimited azimuth rotation and operated from +5 to -89° in nadir. This permitted 5° of crossfire between the guns of the two turrets. The maximum turning or slewing speed of the guns was 45° per second in azimuth and 30° per second in elevation. Maximum acceleration of the guns was 90° per second in azimuth and 60° per second in elevation. Every motion of the sighting station (within specific limits) caused a similar movement of the turret. The azimuth system controlled the rotation of the turrets in clockwise or counterclockwise directions in a horizontal plane. The elevation system controlled the elevation and depressing of the guns in a vertical plane. The signal system used two individual signal selsyns: a one-speed selsyn and a 31-speed selsyn. The positioning system consisted of a dynamotor operating on the aircraft's 24-volt DC electrical system and generating 115-volt AC/400 cycle per second current that was necessary for the operation of the four selsyns on each turret and on the sighting station and the one servo-amplifier for each turret. The servo-amplifier amplified and rectified the control voltage before sending it to the amplidyne motor generator control field for each position of the turrets (azimuth and elevation). The amplidyne motor amplified and gave a quick response to the small voltages from the generator control field and connected directly to the turret drive motor. There was a drive motor for azimuth and elevation of each turret.

The electrical operating procedure of the turret system began with the movement of the control handle by the gunner when he attempted to track a target with the optical system in the sighting station, which caused the sighting station selsyns to change voltage. The movement of the selsyn generators and selsyn control transformers caused a difference in voltage in the control transformer to be transmitted to the amplifier, where it was amplified and rectified. As the output of the selsyn output changed, the direction of the amplifier output in the amplidyne control field also changed. This flow of current in the control field that originated in the selsyn control transformer was greatly amplified in the amplidyne and sent to the drive motor armature. Because the drive motor field was constantly energized during turret operation the current in the armature caused the drive motor armature to rotate. The motor drove the system until the voltage difference between the selsyns of the sighting station and turret was reached, and the system came to a stop unless the gunner continued the motion of the control handle. The one-speed and 31-speed selsyns operated similarly, with the one-speed operating under large voltage differences and the 31-speed selsyn operating under smaller voltage differences. All wires in the system were connected to the sight by an AN connector on the azimuth unit. The azimuth selsyn wires went directly from the AN connector to the selsyns, while all other wires were attached to the brushes in the azimuth unit and the electrical connection was via slip rings.

The sighting station had an action switch and a firing trigger on the left hand elevation handle. When the action switch was pressed it closed the control and firing circuits and the firing trigger started the ammunition booster and fired the gun.

Control current was transmitted to the rotating turret by the collector ring assembly, which also contained the fire interrupter assembly to prevent machine gun fire from hitting the firing aircraft. There were two limit stop assemblies that limited the travel of the guns in elevation that were mounted on the right saddle support. A contour follower was provided for each turret that prevented damage to the aircraft when the guns were moved in elevation and azimuth

**GE CFC Periscopic Sight A-26**

~~RESTRICTED~~ Section IV
AN 01-40AJ-2 Paragraph 15

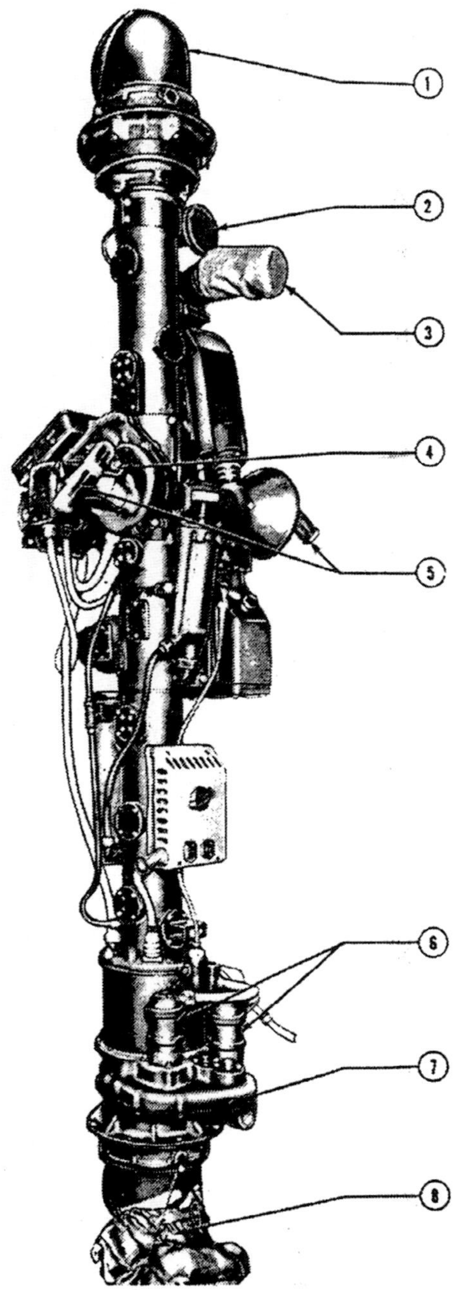


1. Upper Periscope Head
2. Gunner's Head Pad
3. Eye Piece
4. Gunner's Microphone Switch
5. Control Handles
6. Azimuth Selsyns
7. Azimuth Gear Box
8. Lower Periscope Head

***Figure 403 — Sighting Station (View 1)***

**Sighting Station** (USAAF)

**Periscope Front** (Author/AZ CAF)

**Control Handles** (Author/AZ CAF)

**Periscope Rear** (Author/AZ CAF)

**Desiccant and Base** (Author/AZ CAF)

# 3

# Bendix CFC System

### Bendix Remote Turret Development

In the late 1930s the Armament Laboratory at Wright Field wished to allocate turret development to various specialist manufacturers in order to develop the most ideal turret defense. These manufacturers faced a daunting task in a virtually unexplored field, as among the factors to be taken into consideration in turret design was aircraft configuration and purpose, crew number and function, sighting and available fields of fire, and so forth.

In early 1939 the Armament Laboratory contacted the Bendix Corporation of South Bend, IN, to develop a turret; however, at the time Bendix was in negotiations with the Navy's Bureau of Ordnance. In anticipation of a conflict of interest, Gen. Arnold sent a Directive on 31 March 1939 stating: "Pending completion of negotiations between the Bureau of Ordnance, Navy Department, and the Bendix Corporation concerning this development, it is desired that no further contacts be made with that Corporation with reference to this project." Nonetheless, Bendix engineer J.H. White attended a conference at Wright Field where he became familiar with the problems of contemporary turret design first hand by making a flight in a B-18 that was "attacked" by pursuit aircraft, as fighters were called at the time.

In May 1939 Bendix initiated studies to solve "the turret problem." At that time the Bendix concept for the ventral turret was a sphere that would house a gunner and twin machine guns. During studies men of different weights and sizes were placed into spheres of different diameters, but problems were encountered in fitting a gunner and the gunnery equipment in a sphere that did not weigh too much, require too much room, or decrease the aircraft's performance. These studies led to a 22 September 1939 report to the Armament Laboratory describing the problems encountered which finally led to a decision supporting a periscopic sight and a redesigned turret. This remotely controlled manually retracted ventral turret was to contain twin .30 caliber machine guns inside a short cylindrical protuberance or a hemispherical dome. In October 1939 Bendix completed plans involving a turret able to rotate 360° in azimuth rotation and plus 10° to minus 90° in elevation. The gunner was stationed inside the fuselage in a "stationary trough upholstered for reasonable comfort."

Two Bendix engineering research groups embarked on the development of a power system for the turret using the Navy specifications. One group in New York worked on electric drives while another group in South Bend worked with hydraulic drives The South Bend engineers prepared a study on hydraulic turrets which set forth some basic premises:

"The ultimate objective was to increase fire power; this could be done by more or heavier guns; improved turret design to give more power with less weight and drag; or improved sighting and turret design, specifically by building a continuous rotation turret capable of training without effort and so constructed that the gunner would remain always in a fixed relation to the guns and gunsight."

Bendix South Bend designed a hydraulic turret with a gear pump drive unit constructed with a fine mesh that would eliminate all line pulsations that plagued hydraulic turret movement. Bendix hoped for azimuth rates ranging from 1/4° per second to 45° per second. These Bendix engineers formulated their turret designs around the B-18 turret, in which a gunner sat behind a gun rather than between twin guns. On this basis they found that it was structurally impossible to swing the gunner in a fixed relation to his guns through an adequate field of fire and Bendix began to look at the electric turret.

Bendix discontinued hydraulic turret development, and in December submitted an all-electric turret proposal to the Materiel Division for use as both the dorsal and ventral turrets. The experimental dorsal turret mounted twin .50 machine guns with a compensating sight and was to be driven by a one horsepower motor through a speed range of 3° to 60° per second. The experimental ventral turret was physically similar to the dorsal turret except that it mounted twin .30s instead of .50s. The submitted cost of the dorsal turret was $30,075 including the compensating sight (the compensating sight cost $19,050), while the cost of the ventral turret and sight was $31,675. The turrets were to be completed in nine to 12 months.

The Division's specifications on this contract were necessarily generalized due to the relatively undeveloped character of the project. The turret was to electrically drive twin .30 or .50 caliber guns, 360° in azimuth and 100° in elevation through a speed range of 3° to 60° per second. The circuit was to be provided with a fire cut out device, dynamic-brake structural interrupters, and limit stops. The turret included two new facets: a hydraulic gun charger and a periscopic sight with a 20° cone of vision. The whole turret was to be retractable, and so designed as to be suitable for installation in the B-17. Soon after initial work began a controversy arose among Bendix engineers over the sighting system. A faction claimed that an image on ground glass enabled a gunner to find a target more easily than with the naked eye despite the reduction in size. The theory behind this claim maintained that the area of acuity of the average retina was relatively narrow, and that targets with little relative motion outside this area were difficult to see. If the whole area was reduced, the effective area of acute vision was increased. While the theory was dependable for limited-area scanning, other Bendix engineers felt that the speed of modern combat attacks would cause problems for a 360° hemispheric search.

This remotely controlled ventral turret was to bear two .30 caliber machine guns mounted in a manually retracted "truncated cylindrical projection or hemispherical underdome," as it was called at the time. The turret was to rotate in 360° and have an elevation of plus 10° to minus 90°. The gunner was to sit "within the aircraft fuselage in a stationary trough upholstered for reasonable comfort." The Materiel Division let a contract for $45,600 for the new remote experimental turret that was now scheduled to drive twin .50 caliber machine guns electrically through 360° in azimuth and 100° in elevation through a range speed of 3° to 60° per second. The electrical circuit was to be provided with a fire cut out device, dynamic brake structural interrupters, and limit stops. The gun charger was to be hydraulic. The periscope was to have a 20° sighting cone which was thought to be adequate, as the area of the human eye's retinal acuity was narrow and objects with little relative motion outside that area were difficult to see. By reducing the area to 20° the effective area of acute vision was supposedly increased. But Bendix engineers did not take into account the speed of contemporary combat attacks and the vital importance of 360° scanning for early detection of these attacks.

To compound matters, the Experimental Engineering Section "689" inspection report also listed a number of additional serious defects in the Bendix turrets. (Note: The term "689" refers to the form used in making final acceptance tests and inspections. The term remained in the AAC lexicon long after the form disappeared.) The single control handle was unsatisfactory as it was not self-centering; it impeded smooth tracking, and lost control over a large neutral dead spot. Because many aircraft of the time (e.g. the B-25) had no external power socket the turrets could not be tested on the ground without running the engines. Neither the dorsal nor ventral turret was equipped for emergency manual operation. Both turrets experienced an assortment of ammunition feed problems, had no boosters, and often malfunctioned, with their brush and relay contacts arcing and burning.

By spring 1940, the demand for an effective remote Bendix ventral turret was becoming even more serious. Douglas was looking into the possible use of the turret on its B-23 redesign of the B-18. With the lack of new ventral turret designs, Boeing and Consolidated considered it for possible future installation in their B-17s and B-24s. But it was North American's urgent need for a ventral turret to get its new B-25 into combat that made the turret's development for mass production crucial. Weight and balance considerations in the B-25 for placing the dorsal and ventral turrets were of such critical importance that it was necessary for North American to eliminate the tail gun completely.

As discussed previously, Bendix answered the Armament Laboratory circular of March 1940 for general requirements for a complete fire control system for a four-engine heavy bomber. Although Bendix had promised the earliest delivery time and had a comparable unit cost, it finished a distant last (645 points) behind Sperry (1,000) and GE (790) in the Armament Laboratory's analysis. Bendix was penalized because the drawing of its computer was very basic and was seen to have basic range-finding flaws. Bendix solved the computer's critical range-finding problem by adding another operator who would continuously input range, or to compromise the unit by inputting approximations of a fixed range. Due to the poor results of this contest, the development of the Bendix ventral turret was further hampered.

On 15 July 1940 this demand for a ventral turret became so crucial that it caused the Armament Laboratory to recommend that "the GFE Branch of the Materiel Division open negotiations with Bendix to prepare the way for ventral turrets in production quantities to fulfill the turret requirements for medium bombardment airplanes." In a memo from the Chief of the Ordnance Department to the Chief of the Armament Branch it was thought that American turret production could be best fulfilled if each type of turret could be designed for a specific aircraft model, and the Bendix ventral turret was to be developed and produced primarily for the B-25. The memo also suggested "a system of design control, routing all drawings and design problems through Wright Field to insure production exactly as desired by the Armament Branch." The Armament Branch found this suggestion to be impossible to implement, as it was used to a peacetime budget of a few thousand dollars, and now it was suddenly finding itself managing multiple contracts involving millions of dollars. The Armament Branch had to develop new methods of supervising engineering advances and institute effective design controls while these new contracts were in effect and being fulfilled.

In September and October 1940 the Bendix ventral turret was undergoing firing tests at the Aberdeen Proving Grounds, and soon aerial tests, conducted in a B-17B, revealed the basic difficulties which were to continue to hound this turret throughout its production career: slow extension, inadequate scanning and sighting, unsatisfactory ammunition feed system, and a poorly designed stowage system. The ventral turret had the basic design flaw that caused it to take 55 slow seconds to extend from its fully retracted position, and even then the drive often malfunctioned. Once the ventral turret was extended the gunner found he had inadequate scanning facilities, and the periscopic sight caused major sighting problems with an unsatisfactory cone of vision, inadequate scanning, and a sight head rendered ineffective a few minutes after take-off by oil smudge. The ventral turret had a hand crank stowage system, but the cranks were poorly located and the gear ratios so great that even very basic manual tracking was impossible.

Meanwhile, in January 1941, in dealing with this urgent demand for turrets the Armament Laboratory recommended that the Government Furnished Equipment Branch of the Air Materiel Command consult with Bendix for the production of handcrafted experimental dorsal and ventral turrets to expedite final development and testing. Two handmade "tool room turrets," a dorsal and a ventral, were sent to North American for trial installation in the B-25; but as late as May the fire cut out cams were still incomplete, awaiting the arrival of final B-25 structural drawings.

North American trials for both turrets reported "considerable difficulty" with the turret ammunition feed system, as it had no boosters, and the electrical drive often malfunctioned, with the brush and relay contacts arcing and burning. Experimental Engineering Section engineers established that future turret models would require excessive feed system maintenance to remain functional. Because of incorrect reduction gearing this turret required an electrical current consumption 50 to 75% higher than other turrets in use. The hand control system was so deficient that it needed to be immediately modified. Because the B-25 had no external power socket the turrets could not be tested on the ground without running the engines. Neither turret was equipped for emergency manual operation.

Even though the Bendix turrets were problematical and undeveloped, they were implausibly the best contemporary American turret design, and in June 1941 Bendix was requested to submit a thorough presentation of the proposed technical requirements for a model turret to be used in the turret section in the *Handbook of Instructions for Airplane Designers*.

By fall 1941 the Bendix ventral turret came under intense criticism. On 5 September the Chief of the Materiel Division had written:

"It would be to our mutual interests for you to arrange for service engineers to live with these turrets during the next few months to make sure the Service does not receive them with defects and troubles which will get them off to a bad start and possibly a bad reputation. If they give the Service trouble at the beginning, they may get a bad reputation which they may never be able to live down."

The British turret authority, Wing Commander Spreckley, categorically stated in a memo of 10 October 1941 to U.S. Military Attaché for Air, Brig.Gen. Ralph Royce, that "the Bendix ventral turret is completely hopeless due to improper control and poor design in general." A Wright Field representative attending a turret training course at the Bendix South Bend Plant summed up the Bendix turret in a memo of 13 October 1941 as "not satisfactory," commenting that the "general feel, ease of control, ease with which one may become a competent operator, and naturalness of the sighting are not considered satisfactory for efficient gunnery." The final Wright Field report concluded that the Bendix turrets were "inferior to other makes in combat use" and North American anticipated that its first 15 B-25s would leave the production lines in August 1941 without turrets. This report, appearing in October 1941 when the new B-24's armament was up for consideration, was disturbing. The Materiel Division Chief wrote to the Assistant Chief: "The question of the turret on the B-24 is one which is getting hotter and hotter daily on account of reports of this nature which are being sent to England....The comment on the Bendix ventral being definitely unsatisfactory is news to me....perhaps the Bendix is better than none."

In the late fall of 1941, the Materiel Division refused to act on these negative opinions and reports on the ventral turret, but it would have been difficult, if not impossible, for them to reject the turrets completely, as the Division would be trying to convince the AAC to accept them. Bendix engineers worked feverishly to salvage the troubled turrets and tried the installation of an amplidyne drive. This mechanism proved to be satisfactory for the dorsal turret, but did not improve the functioning of the ventral turret, which continued to display a variety of malfunctions and shortfalls. In January 1942 the Chief of the Production Engineering Section (PES) notified North American Aviation that the Materiel Division had decided against the ventral turret simply because "They don't like it." Since the installation of a tail gun required structural changes and critical weight and balance considerations, the PES Chief suggested "to see if we can satisfy them with two side guns and the old tunnel gun as originally designed, although admittedly the tunnel or bottom hatch installation promised to be little more than a morale gun."

Again, despite the problems and negative opinions of their ventral turret, Bendix engineers continued to revamp and modify the periscopic sighting system, which was its specific major weakness. The telescopic sight's restricted cone of vision was solved by the installation of a simple reflex sight comparable to that in the Martin turret. However, all the modifications to the ventral turret ended in failure despite some innovative efforts by Bendix engineers to salvage it. The inadequate pick up scanning windows were supplemented with a "direction of attack indicator" that was to show the gunner in which quadrant the target was approaching so he could look through the correct scanning window to find it. While appearing to be satisfactory on paper, the indicator was a complete failure in the air. Bendix engineers then increased the cone of vision to 70° and added an erecting prism to maintain a normal tracking vision. But while the gunner was tracking with the new prism through an azimuth arc, the target in relation to the gunner's vision appeared to roll over in flight and the gunner became disoriented and was unable to continue to track the target. Because none of the proposed improvements made the Bendix ventral turret workable, an Armament Laboratory memo of 5 May 1943 recommended that waist guns be installed in the B-25 until a suitable ventral turret could be developed. This had been the recommendation of the Production Engineering Section Chief a year earlier.

**Bendix Turret Production**

To add to the design and mechanical problems of the ventral remote turret were production delays at the Bendix plants. Bendix had subcontracted an unusually high quantity of the turret's parts to subcontractors and blamed negligent subcontractors for the delays. Bendix relied on too many subcontractors, 106(!) in all, and the Materiel Division directly contacted many of them to solve the delay problem. Although only six subs were found to be seriously behind schedule, these "negligent" six caused the delay in the entire turret production. Bendix found that by subcontracting so many turret parts it became nothing more than an assembler of components, and thus could do little in design modifications during production, thereby hampering the correction of the numerous problems of the turret.

Thus, the Materiel Division had little power over Bendix because the ventral turret project was controlled by Bendix subcontractors, as a PES report of 5 May 1941 concluded: "the main reason for not getting deliveries on turrets" from Bendix was "the lack of organization and very little effort made to produce parts in the contractor's own plant." The PES also recommended that unless Bendix deliveries were improved, the Division would appropriate the idle government-owned machinery and decrease the size of turret contracts. By July 1941 Bendix production problems placed turret deliveries so far behind schedule in early production that the Materiel Division Chief, Col. K.B. Wolfe, considered transferring half of the Bendix contract to Emerson.

In September 1941 the Materiel Division reconsidered the entire Bendix production program, but found that the urgent demand for the ventral turrets justified their continued production. The Chief of PES noted in a memo to Bendix that "difficulties are of so serious a nature that it is unlikely that a completely satisfactory correction can be looked forward to as a probability" and suggested that a "complete redesign be undertaken with a view to substituting entirely new turrets for those now being delivered at some point in the production schedule."

Despite their ongoing production problems Bendix was allowed to continue producing ventral turrets. But the company's production did not improve in 1942; while North American's B-25 production was estimated at 1,288 planes per month, and maximum Bendix production, at best, would not reach 850 units per month. This discrepancy, plus the maintenance and operational training problems, and the large number of "Unsatisfactory Reports" from the tactical units caused the recommendation that ventral turrets were to be deleted from the B-25C and D, the B-17E, and the B-24D.

There were several continued attempts to salvage the ventral turret. In April 1943 the Assistant Chief of Air Staff for Materiel, Maintenance, and Distribution (MM&D) directed that the surplus Bendix ventral turrets be developed as chin turrets on the B-17F until the newly designed chin turret could be put into production. Later, another plan was proposed which inverted the ventral turrets and used them as dorsal turrets but proved mechanically not viable when tested.

**Bendix Model K Amplidyne Ventral Turret: A Description**

General

The Bendix Model K Amplidyne ventral turret was installed in B-25Cs and Ds, B-24Ds, and the B-17C, D, and E until the 117th bomber off the production line. The Model K turret was a solid retractable turret designed around a central column. The turret weighed 392 pounds, excluding the 300 pounds of the twin .50 caliber machine guns and 390 rounds of ammunition per gun. The guns were fed from ammunition boxes bolted to the lower turret canopy which could be easily removed from the turret assembly by removing four bolts in the end of the housing hanger arms. The empty shell cases and links were ejected through ejection chutes and dropped outside through slots in the movable housing at the bottom of the turret. Observation windows were cut into the fuselage just above the floor level on each

**Bendix Model K Amplidyne Ventral Turret** (USAAF)

Periscopic Sight

The Bendix turret employed a tubular periscopic sight that was attached within the center column in the center of the turret. The gunner kneeled at the turret on knee pads and leaned against chest rests that helped to keep him in position over the sight optics. The eye piece was located at the top of the center column, and the object prism that moved in elevation with the guns was located in the meter box casting at the bottom of the center column. The entire sight rotated in azimuth with the turret. The turret had electrical limits and dynamic brakes to prevent mechanical damage to the airplane, and also to control the zone of gunfire. The ventral turret's azimuth drive motor served double duty as the retraction and extension power for the turret. A locking lever was provided for use in retracting the turret. The lever actuated an indexing key that prevented the retraction of the turret when the guns were not properly positioned to enter the stowage wells in the belly of the fuselage. When retracted, the turret faired nearly flush with the undersurface of the fuselage and was considered very aerodynamic.

Extension to the Combat Position

Before turret extension the gunner had to be sure that the turret index bolt located at the aft side of the center column below the brush box was securely locked in place by the index plate spring and was flush with the outer surface of the center column. If the bolt was not locked it was to be pushed back in by depressing the retract lever and manually rotating the turret slightly so that the guns were pointing directly aft. To manually rotate the turret, a section of the turret windshield was to be removed and the turret housing hanger arm used to move it. The retract lever lock was disengaged and the lever was moved to the viewer's left against its stop. Both battery disconnect switches were turned ON. Ground operation was to be kept to

**Interior View** (USAAF)

side of the turret. The window on the right side was removable and large enough to be used as an emergency escape hatch for the turret operator. A transparent removable windshield located flush with the floor of the turret mounting well gave protection from air blast and provided access to the guns and the emergency manual gun control shaft. A heated clothing outlet, an interphone jack box, and an oxygen regulator were located adjacent to the turret. The ventral turret provided defensive protection for the aft, side, and lower forward area except where gun fire was restricted. Gun fire was restricted by the firing circuit on any part of the aircraft except the landing gear and bomb bay doors when extended and the radio antenna. A blue warning light flashed on the pilot's switch panel when the landing gear and ventral turret were simultaneously extended.

Scanning Lenses and Windows

Two scanning lenses were installed, one on either side of the fuselage at the ventral gun turret station to give the viewer a cone of vision of 180°. One lens replaced the radio operator's emergency escape hatch window on the right side of the fuselage and the other replaced the scanning window on the left side, directly opposite the escape hatch. The lenses and windows were easily interchangeable in flight, and those not in use could be stowed in brackets above the windows.

**Extended** (USAAF)

a minimum unless an external power supply, such as a ground generator, was used. If the aircraft batteries or auxiliary batteries were to be used for ground operation, before attempting to operate the turret the batteries had to be tested first to ensure full charge. To avoid serious damage to the turret or airplane, the turret operation had to be stopped immediately upon any sign that the batteries were being run down. The turret main power switch, located on the forward side of the resistor box, was turned ON by lifting the switch up to the power position. The safety switch, located on the outboard side of either control handle, was deactivated by depressing either switch. The control handles were turned counter-clockwise about their vertical axis a few degrees from neutral for slow speed and maximum rotation for normal full speed. For high-speed operation, the high-speed switch button on the upper end of either control handle was depressed. The neutral position of the control handles was halfway between the stops and the handles automatically returned to their neutral position when released.

Charging the Guns

To charge the guns for combat or to remove a defective cartridge, the control valve knob was depressed with the knob rotated clockwise against its stop. After being depressed the knob would automatically be kicked back at the end of the charging stroke, positioning the valve for the next charging stroke. To charge the guns with the bolt back in safety, the control valve knob was rotated counter-clockwise against its stop and depressed. The control valve knob was not to stay in the depressed position any longer than the few seconds necessary to charge the guns for combat or to move the gun bolts to the safety position. When the bolt was ready to be released for combat the control valve knob was rotated clockwise completely against its stop. The turret was not to be operated for long periods with guns in the safety position in order to prevent excessive wear on gland seals within the turret.

Combat Operation

With the turret extended to the combat position, the gunner lowered the padded knee support and took a kneeling position. He adjusted the chest support as needed by means of the spring-loaded pin in the chest support rod. He then leaned forward to place an eye on the sight's eye cushion with both hands either on the master control handles or his right hand on the right control handle and the left hand on the steady grip (a hand rest grip mounted to the turret). He activated the microphone switch button located in the end of the steady grip. Once the master control handles were in their normal neutral position (halfway between the vertical and horizontal rotation stops) the gunner gripped the control handles and depressed the safety switch on the outboard side of the handles. Care had to be taken not to depress the trigger firing switch on the front of either handle because the guns could be fired as soon as the turret main power switch was turned on.

To rotate the turret in azimuth the control handles were turned about their vertical axis. The turret moved in the same relative direction as the handles at a speed proportional to the degree of control handle rotation. The turret could be rotated continuously 360° in azimuth, provided that the guns were lowered sufficiently to clear the forward fuselage. If the guns were not lowered sufficiently the turret would stop when the guns approached the sides of the fuselage, and would not rotate forward until the guns were lowered to clear the fuselage. To elevate the guns, the gunner rotated the control handle about its horizontal axis. The guns moved in the same relative direction as the handle, at a speed proportional to the degree of control handle rotation.

For high-speed turret rotation, either high-speed switch button on the upper end of the control handles was depressed by the thumb. The speed of turret rotation with the high-speed switch button depressed was proportional to the degree of rotation of the control handles from their neutral position. For high-speed elevation of the guns, either high-speed switch button on the upper end of the control handles was depressed by the thumb. The speed of gun elevation with the high-speed switch button depressed was proportional to the degree of rotation of the control handles from their neutral position.

The guns moved from a few degrees above horizontal to almost straight down, except in the forward area. The gunner turned on the windage compensator switch and rotated the rheostat control to the indicated airspeed of airplane as obtained from the pilot over the intercom. The windage compensator on the ventral turret was connected to both the upper and lower turret sight. The gunner looked through the sight, training the guns on the target by means of the master control handles. The dot in the center of the reference circle of the sight indicated the point on which the guns were trained. The guns were fired by depressing the trigger firing switch on either control handle. Power could be cut off by releasing pressure on the dead man switch on the back of the control handle.

Retraction to the Stowed Position

To retract the turret to its stowed position the guns were first elevated to their upper limit, and the turret rotated until the guns were pointing slightly to the left of directly aft. The retract lever was depressed and locked to stop the rotation of the turret. The guns were slowly lowered until they locked into their stowage position, which was slightly (2° to 6°) below horizontal. The turret was rotated very slowly clockwise by turning the control handles

**Stowed** (USAAF)

a few degrees to the right of neutral. The turret rotated until the guns were pointing straight aft, and then the turret could be retracted at any desired speed. Retraction stopped automatically when the turret reached the fully stowed position.

**Summary and Appraisal**

Gunners did not consider the ventral turret to be effective and there were many operating problems, and so it was often removed from aircraft in the field, saving 700 pounds that could be used for additional fuel tanks installed in the area. The turret often collected mud and dust when operating from unimproved airfields, which obscured its sighting system. Lowering the turret into position took a long 55 seconds, and if lowered too quickly, the retracting microswitch could be damaged and jam the turret in the down position, which would cause drag, slowing the aircraft, and made maintaining its position in formation difficult. Before the turret could be used the gunner needed to align the sight by using the aiming mirrors, but this procedure often caused optical distortion, making accurate tracking and firing at a moving target difficult. The periscopic sighting system was unwieldy, as the gunner was cramped in an awkward stationary kneeling position, resting his chest on a padded support while staring intently through the sight; trying to coordinate the control handles, which was difficult, as he was not able to see the gun barrels in the sight. The gunner often became dizzy when tracking enemy fighters through the sight and occasionally became so disoriented and even nauseous that he was unable to operate the turret. In spite of adding more and larger sighting windows, acquiring targets often proved far more difficult than with a conventional turret having a clear dome.

This Bendix ventral turret had a comparatively short AAF service life and was discontinued during production of the B-25G-5 from aircraft 42-65001 onward. Radomes replaced the ventral turret on some B-25 PBJ-1s used by the Marines, while non-U.S. Mitchell operators, especially the RAF, were able to master the complex ventral turret and made it an essential element of the aircraft's defense when formation flying. On the B-17E the Bendix ventral turret replaced the "bathtub" turret used on the B-17C and D. However, on the 117th B-17E the famed retractable Sperry ball turret replaced the ineffective Bendix. The Bendix turret replaced the ventral "tunnel" gun on the 77th B-24D, but was installed on only 287 B-24Ds before it was replaced by the Sperry ball turret.

# 4

# Westinghouse CFC System

In May 1939 the Armament Laboratory invited representatives of the Westinghouse Electric and Manufacturing Company to explore the problems involved in manufacturing a power turret. The company was chosen because it had previous experience in manufacturing searchlight and heavy machine controls and had assumed a tank turret control contract for the Ordnance Department.

After examining the armament installations on the B-17 and B-18, Westinghouse engineers set out to prepare a turret proposal. Three months later Westinghouse submitted three tentative proposals, one with a DC motor system, another with an AC motor system, and a third with a hydraulic system. The hydraulic type involved too many long pressure lines and was given little consideration, while the AC system was proposed only as an alternate to the DC system that was favored at Wright Field. In September 1939 Westinghouse issued a proposal that offered a single complex experimental fire control apparatus that aimed several guns from a single sighting station for $76,200. The proposal was rejected by the Armament Branch because it contained "too much gadgetry," particularly the 16 separate motors which made the entire system excessively heavy, too complex, and subject to a disproportionate electric power drain.

# 5

# German and British Remote Control Defensive Armament Systems

## German

In November 1941 the *Luftwaffe* proposed a 20mm MG 151/20 cannon mounted in a FHL 151 Remotely Controlled Gun Mount equipped with a periscope, but the project only reached the mockup stage. The *Luftwaffe* used its ill-starred He-177 long-range heavy bomber as a test bed for remote controlled gun mounts. In March 1942 the He-177 was approved to have remote controlled gun installations in its lower nose (one MG 81 machine gun) and forward top barbette positions (as remotely controlled turrets were known). The barbette was to contain one or two rear-facing MG 131 controlled by a remote system located under a Plexiglas dome behind the leading edge of the wing. The remote system never went beyond the developmental stage, and with the multiple problems that the He-177 design encountered during its development; the system was abandoned when it appeared that the *Luftwaffe* would never have a useful heavy bomber in its arsenal.

The FDL 131 remote system was installed in the twin-engine Me 210 Hornet, another hapless *Luftwaffe* design. Two 13mm MB131 machine guns were installed into half-teardrop-shaped turrets mounted on each side of the aircraft, and were remote-controlled from the rear gunner's position. The rear of the cockpit canopy was bulged out to allow the gunner to aim down and to the rear. Its unique sighting device rotated crossbar axially with a handgun-style grip and trigger at its center located directly under the crossbar rotated axially. The handgrip was elevated or depressed to aim the guns vertically, while a sideways movement of the handgrip would pivot either one of the guns outwards from the fuselage for diagonal firing.

The **Heinkel He-177** had a remote controlled gun installation in its lower nose (one MG 81 machine gun) and forward top turret (twin rear-facing MG 131s) controlled by a remote system located under a Plexiglas dome behind the leading edge of the wing. (Author)

## British

In May 1942 the British Air Ministry became interested in developing a remote controlled sighting system comparable to the American Remote Control Turret. The new system was for use in Bomber Command Lancaster heavy bombers at a time when the Air Ministry considered using some Lancaster units in daylight operations. The gunner was to occupy a sighting station in the tail which would give him an unobstructed field of vision while controlling dorsal and ventral turrets mounting 20mm Hispano cannon with 200 rpg. Boulton Paul was contracted to produce the barbettes and the British Thompson Houston Company (BTH), which had previous experience in developing remote control systems for ground use. The BTH remote system used the Ward Leonard Amplidyne electric control for turrets and guns which were coupled to a "convergence computer" designed by the Royal Aeronautical Establishment (RAE) at Farnborough. When the gunner fixed his sight on the enemy aircraft, electrical impulses were

The **Messerschmitt Me 210** mounted two 13mm MB131 machine guns into half-teardrop-shaped turrets mounted on each side of the aircraft which were remote-controlled from the rear gunner's position. (Author)

Boulton Paul was contracted to produce the remote turret and the British Thompson Houston to develop the remote control system for Lancaster bombers. (Author)

transmitted to a computer that controlled the barbette and 20mm guns in direct relationship to the alignment of the sight, allowing for deflection, range, and the angular difference between the barbette and sight. It was not until July 1944 that the BP had completed and tested the functioning of the prototype barbettes, but the BTH sighting and remote control system was slow in developing and was unable to meet the requirements, so a completely new system using new technology was necessary. BTH was progressing in developing this technology when the Air Staff requested that it be combined with AGLT tracking radar. The project continued until VE-Day and was finally passed for service use in late 1945, but was never adopted, as radar sighting had developed to a stage where a gunner controlling radar from a central sighting station and the new jet bombers coming online did have turrets for protection.

In 1943 Vickers-Armstrong was contracted to develop remotely-controlled barbettes installed in the rear of the engine nacelles and controlled by a gunner stationed in the tail. The Vickers system initially used an electric-hydraulic controlling unit which was replaced by the Metropolitan-Vickers all-electric Metadyne system. Testing at RAE Farnborough showed that flexion of the wing during flight critically affected the accuracy of the barbettes and the Vickers project was cancelled.

# Part Six

## Bomber Armament

# 1

# Turret Development World War I to 1943

## Section 1: World War I Turret Development

The aircraft gun turret was a World War I invention that the French called "tourelle," the Germans "turmgeschutz," and the British the "Scarff ring." At the start of World War I the first military aircraft were an assortment of monoplanes and biplanes, but after several months the biplane prevailed. The initial design for the two-place biplane located the observer in the front seat, between the center section and the wings, while the pilot was placed behind him. This arrangement gave the observer an inadequate field of vision and fire to the rear, where most attacks occurred. Soon the observer was moved to the rear seat, which made it possible for him to defend the rear sector with a flexible rifle-caliber machine gun. Once repositioned the observer found that he needed a stable gun mount that would permit him to aim the gun while always looking over the sight. Fixed or simple swivel mounts were tried and were replaced by unwieldy slotted circular plywood tracks that accommodated hardwood casters fitted to a machine gun. Not only did the whole unit flex with the aircraft fuselage, but the gunner had to be a contortionist to follow an attacker from the small area of his cockpit.

The solution was the Scarff ring perfected by Warrant Officer F.W. Scarff of the Royal Naval Air Service for use on two-place aircraft. It was an ingenious rotating ring mount fixed to the rim of the cockpit which allowed the gun to be turned any direction with the gunner remaining directly behind it. The mount, with its adjustable elevation attachment counterbalanced by an elastic shock cord and its rotating backrest allowed an air gunner in an open cockpit to swivel his weapon, typically one or two Lewis machine guns, around and easily fire in any direction. It was simple, rugged, and gave its operator an excellent field of fire. It was widely adapted and copied by other air forces, but by the end of the war these turrets were considered substandard. Some method for overcoming the effects of buffeting high-speed slipstreams upon flexible guns was needed, and a satisfactory means of covering the lower quarter behind the aircraft's tail with protective gunfire was also needed.

During the war the disadvantages of open gun positions were evident. Besides the significant drag on the aircraft, the gunners were exposed to the weather at low altitudes and to the cold and thin air at high altitudes. As faster aircraft appeared the airstream became more of a problem and windscreens were installed to deflect the airflow, but did not solve the problem. The answer was the enclosed gun turret, which was initially manually operated, but shortly was traversed by an external power source. The turret offered a stable gun mount and the use of heavier guns with improved gunsights. However, the turret design was very cramped and uncomfortable and remained cold and windy, as the guns needed to protrude to the outside. The heavy framing often restricted the gunner's vision, and the designs were often heavy and cumbersome, causing significant drag. But, on the whole the turret was definitely a better option than the open gun position.

## Section 2: European Inter-War Turret Development

### France and Italy

In the early to mid-1930s European turret development lagged in a complacent France and recovering Germany, with only the English making any significant progress. In practice French aircraft armament lagged far behind French invention, as patents issued showed an extensive array of armament and turret ideas that did not reach realization. So French turret development progressed little from the 1918 Armistice, as Scarff rings continued in use until the middle 1930s, when plastic domes emerged. During the mid-1920s France decided to build an aircraft that would be a fighter, bomber, and observation aircraft designated as the BCR (Bombardement, Combat, Renseignements) that would be multi-place "Aerial Cruisers" that would be armed with a number of guns placed in the nose, dorsal, and ventral positions. Among the aircraft in this group were the Amiot 143 and 144, Bloch 200, Farman 221 and 222, LeO 43, and Potez 540. Many experimental dome shapes were tested ranging from a simple hemisphere mounted on the Bloch-200 to the mushroom type used on the Potez-54. The determined use of twin Lewis guns by the French substantially delayed progress in turret and dome development until the introduction of the reliable Browning .30 caliber machine guns allowed domes to develop with a single gun slot that could be sealed against the slipstream.

In 1930, Italian aircraft designer Gianni Caproni obtained an English turret patent with the intention of placing dorsal, tail, and ventral turrets on his Caproni Ca-73 and Ca-74 bombers. Caproni developed dorsal and ventral enclosed turrets of duralumin framework covered with sheet aluminum. The ventral turrets were retractable and capable of azimuth rotation with a hand crank chain and sprocket drive. By 1937 the American Military Attaché for Air in Italy reported advanced models of power turrets in actual use on the majority of Italian aircraft with Caproni's earlier electrical drives replaced by hydraulic systems that gave smoother and quicker tracking.

### England

Early Developments

Of all European combatants England had continued aircraft armament development after World War I. At the end of the war the sixth model of the Scarff ring had been mounted on aircraft, but more important was

1932 Bristol experimented with nose and tail "Bird Cage" turrets that were mounted and rotated on a modified Scarff Ring. (AFHRC)

the British development of flexible gunnery theory. Although the Russian aircraft designer Igor Sikorsky was the first to locate a Scarff mount at the tail of a bomber, the British soon installed it on their Handley-Page V1500, initiating a trend for future British bomber armament.

In 1922 the Vickers Virginia, the Siddeley heavy bomber, and the Kingston flying boat tested various nacelle gun mount systems, with the Handley-Page design being the most successful. In 1928 Hawker Aircraft developed an improved ring mounting for its Hart series of aircraft and Handley-Page mounted it in the dorsal position with a folding windscreen on its Heyford bomber in 1930. This bomber also had a ventral retractable, revolving, manually operated turret, but neither turret reached production status. In the early 1930s Vickers placed twin .30 Browning machine guns in the nose, tail, and dorsal positions on the first Wellington bomber while Armstrong tried single gun turrets in the nose and tail of its Whitley bomber, but neither armament configuration was satisfactory.

It was evident to progressive British armament manufacturers that powered turrets were the wave of the future. During the decade preceding World War II patent applications in the United States and continental Europe involved theoretical plans for turrets and fire control systems, but only in England were patented plans actually developed, manufactured, and experimentally mounted in aircraft.

### Bristol

In 1932 Bristol experimented with nose and tail "Bird Cage" turrets (called cupolas) which were mounted and rotated on a modified Scarff Ring. This turret commenced what would be the company's first effort in its long and extensive participation in turret development. Light metal framework enclosed glass that protected the gunner and his .303 caliber Lewis machine gun from the slipstream. The cupola was manually-operated and not much of an improvement over other turrets currently in use, but the data obtained in the development of this turret was of great help to Bristol in developing future turrets.

Bristol continued work on turret development using the aircraft's hydraulic system to power the turret, and by 1935 the company was able to place a dorsal power-operated turret in the new Blenheim bomber. The Bristol turret's success was due to its powerful hydraulic pump, small (30 inch ring) low-drag shape, and a movable gunner's seat that was synchronized with the gun movement. The small size of the turret also meant that the gunners necessarily needed to be of small stature, and the turrets were not interchangeable with those of other British turret manufacturers. The Bristol Blenheim dorsal turret led to a series of Bristol aircraft operating in World War II with modifications of that turret.

### Boulton-Paul

In 1933 Boulton-Paul took out a patent for a rotation axis bearing system for nose and tail turrets that circumvented tooling for the difficult and intricate ring gear utilized in most turrets. The next year Boulton-Paul secured an important patent that perfected a turret principle developed earlier by Armstrong-Whitworth, whose patent covered a turret ring which mounted a single flexible machine gun on a ring mount in a ball-shaped turret. Movement of the gun closed an electric circuit and rotated the turret into the direction the gun was aimed. A four-way switch allowed the turret to rotate in both directions for elevation as well as azimuth. Instead of electric contacts the Boulton-Paul patent utilized hydraulic valves that were spring-loaded to return automatically to neutral with screw adjustment of the valve to the correct neutral. The hydraulic turret provided variations in speed which were simple functions of the amount of displacement in the control valve. Boulton-Paul continued to work this principle into a workable turret. In 1934, Boulton-Paul digressed in turret design but developed the first usable British power turret, which appeared on their twin-engine, Boulton-Paul Overstrand biplane bomber which was equipped with a company-designed nose turret mounting a single Lewis Gun. The Lewis gun was elevated and depressed manually through a long vertical slit in the turret closed by a zipper when not in use. The gun's weight was counterbalanced by the gunner's weight via a hydraulic connection with his seat. This turret was driven by compressed air which allowed only limited periods of use, as repeated rests were needed for recharging the compressed air cylinders. When the gunner aimed the gun at a target his pressure on the gun to each side activated plunger valves that controlled rotation (about 240°). Although the turret was successful its rotation was very slow, and the compressed air limited its use.

Bristol's work on hydraulic powered turrets led to the placement of this dorsal turret on the Blenheim bomber in 1935. (AFHRC)

In 1934 Boulton-Paul designed the first usable British power turret for their twin-engine, Boulton-Paul Overstrand biplane bomber which was equipped with a company-designed nose turret mounting a single Lewis Gun. (AFHRC)

In 1934 Boulton-Paul designed a dorsal turret equipped with four .303 caliber Browning machine guns which would be installed in the company's Defiant "turret fighter (AFHRC)

To overcome the deficiencies of the compressed air turret John D. North, Boulton Paul's Chief Engineer, developed a turret based on a French design that had the basic elements of an electro-hydraulic system. In 1933 a British armament broker had investigated a new turret developed by French engineer M. de Boyisson of the Societe d' Applications des Machines Motrices (SAMM) in Charentan, located near Paris. The inventor had offered his turret to the French government, whose representative refused to consider it without a bribe. This behavior so incensed de Boyisson that he sold a manufacturing license to Boulton-Paul. The advantage of the French turret was that it had a self-contained hydraulic generator powered by an electric motor so that the entire turret hydraulic system was contained in the rotating part of the turret. Power was used only when required, as the turret control handles had "dead man's" levers that had to be depressed to energize the power. The gunner sat comfortably on a seat with the gun apertures sealed against the slipstream. By 1934 the hydraulically-driven turret appeared to be the accepted turret design with Boulton-Paul emerging as a leader. The company designed a dorsal turret equipped with four .303 caliber Browning machine guns which would be installed in the company's Defiant "turret fighter," which was designed to approach an enemy bomber from below or alongside and destroy it with a concentrated burst of fire.

Frazier-Nash

During World War I A.G. "Archie" Frazier-Nash worked in the Armament Department of the Air Ministry, where he aided in the development of synchronization of nose-mounted machine guns. After the war he became active in developing victorious Nash racing cars, but in 1929 he left that field to form a construction company that became very successful. He then joined with his wartime associate, Capt. E. Gratton "Tommy" Thompson, to work on developing powered turrets. Frazier-Nash determined that for a turret to be effective and to have a good field of fire a mechanism had to be developed to give it full rotation and elevation; the sights were to be mounted on the gun; and a seat was to be provided that would move in relation to the gun so that the gunner's eye would always be on the sight. Frazier-Nash's turret design took into account the accommodation of turret accessories, such as the oxygen system, interphone, heating, and gunner's parachute stowage. Frazier-Nash considered pneumatic and mechanical power but moved on to electric and hydraulic systems or a combination of the two. He decided on a hydraulic system to control the guns in azimuth and elevation and self-financed a model which he presented to the Air Ministry

In this Fraser-Nash (FN) the gunner controlled the movement of the turret and guns by control handles that operated valves that were installed in a box inside the turret. (AFHRC)

The FN1 led to a series of 24 FN turrets in the decade from 1935 which were used in the majority of British bomber and influenced American turret design. (AFHRC)

in 1932. Although the Air Ministry found the turret lacking, Frazier-Nash was encouraged enough to form Nash and Thompson Ltd. to continue its development. In 1933 the new company was awarded a contract for a prototype which was developed into the FN1, contracted for 50, and installed in the Hawker Demon, and in 1936 in the Handley Page Harrow. Power for the Frazier-Nash turrets was supplied by oil circulated under pressure by an engine pump. The turrets were rotated by a hydraulic motor, and the guns were elevated and depressed by hydraulic rams. The gunner controlled the movement of the turret and guns by control handles that operated valves that were installed in a box inside the turret. In early turrets the guns were also fired hydraulically using oil from the turret system, but a simpler and more reliable electrical system was soon developed. The FN1 led to a series of 24 FN turrets in the decade from 1935 which were used in the majority of British bomber and influenced American turret design.

**Section 3: American Postwar Turret Development to 1930**

During World War I American turret manufacturers built ring mounts for the DH-4 aircraft. Due to the lack of current technical intelligence in America these mounts were only designed to carry single machine guns and were not strong enough to support the weight of twin Lewis guns; hence they were obsolete by the end of the war. After the Armistice interest in American turret development faded, and a year later only two manufacturers were working under government contracts, so turret development was undertaken by the Air Service's Engineering Division. The Engineering Division soon found that the implementation of the 1923 standardization of aircraft type specifications prevented the development of innovative gunnery installations and turret designs for the next decade. Typically, a design for a powered turret was rejected by the Chief of Armament because "It is power-driven, which seems unnecessary in a device to carry machine guns for defensive purposes."

The standard Air Service mount on postwar aircraft was a 26 pound ring that was a variation of the English World War I vintage Scarff type that itself was based upon earlier French designs. Instead of new turret development haphazard turret improvement continued. A major problem confronting turret designers at that time was the effect of the slipstream pressure on the guns which hindered the rotation of the turret. The standard postwar Air Service mount had a rudimentary wind compensator designed to counterbalance twin Lewis guns. It held the guns in equilibrium against the force of the slipstream for all angular positions of the revolving ring throughout a speed range of 100 to 160 mph. At 100 mph the gunner had to exert 52 pounds of force to move the guns broadside against the slipstream and this increased to 106 pounds at 160 mph, preventing easy, smooth tracking of the target. Slipstream compensators, called wind compensators, were based on two basic principles. The wind vane system counterbalanced the effects of slipstream on the gun by mounting vanes or rudders projecting from the opposite side of the ring. The other system was an arrangement of springs within the structure of the ring that tried to neutralize all drag on the cams by mechanical tension. The development of an effective wind compensator was an effective solution to the slipstream problem until the performance of the aircraft considerably exceeded existing maximum air speeds (160 mph).

An indication of Air Corps apathy in armament development was demonstrated by a 1926 armament course at McCook Field that devoted 27 hours to fixed gun installations and barely nine hours to small arms, machine guns, flexible mounts, gunsights, and accessories. The Wright Field Engineering School course between 1928 and 1930 devoted three-fifths of the course time to bombs and bombing, one-fifth to pyrotechnics, and the

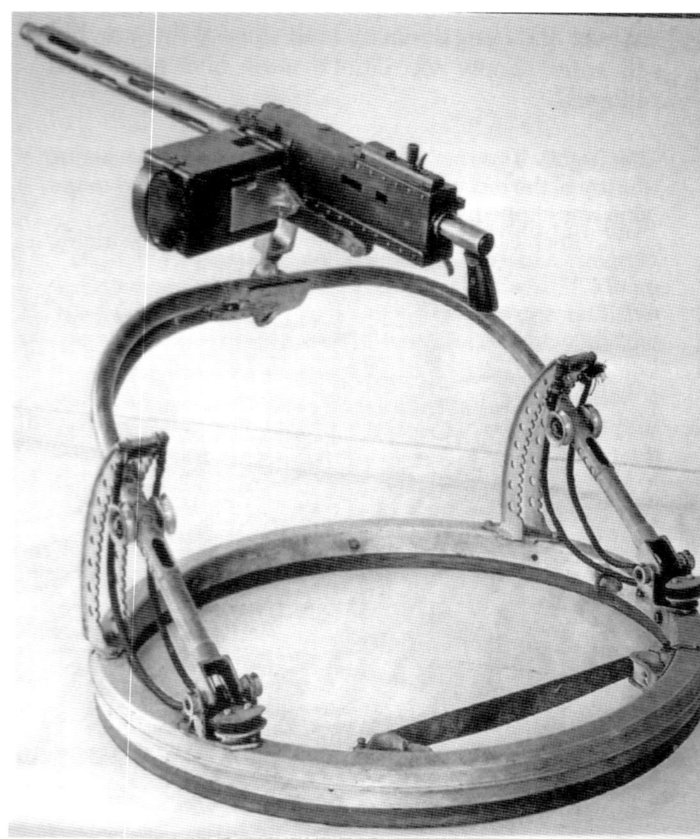

The standard U.S. Air Service mount on post WW-I war aircraft was a ring that was a variation of the English World War I vintage Scarff type. (USAAF)

A-3 post mount with a ball and socket connection for a .30 caliber machine gun in the dorsal turret of a Martin B-10 bomber. (USAAF)

last fifth to the entire subject of machine guns and machine gun mounts. However, taking into consideration that in 1928 the Bombardment Board recommended the procurement of a new experimental model twin-engine bomber capable of carrying a 1,200 pound bomb load and a crew of three at a speed of 160 mph within a 1,500 mile operating radius, the current machine gun mount specifications still fell within the aircraft standardized performance limits set five years earlier, as did this new bomber.

Two flexible mounts, the D-6 ring, a variation of the spring compensated type, and the A-3, a post mount with a ball and socket connection, were developed in the late 1920s for service testing. The tests by the Bombardment Board concluded that: "A more satisfactory flexible gun mount is necessary for the purpose of increasing maneuverability of the guns when operated in the slipstream." McCook Field allotted few personnel to turret development while outside commercial interest was nil.

Once the AAC assumed responsibility for turret development at Wright Field in the early 1930s, personnel there increased the investigation for a satisfactory aircraft gun mount. A number of proposals were put forth with some rejected immediately, while others were developed to the testing stage. Several mounts were tested. Mounting a single gun on either side of an open cockpit was rejected because of excessive weight, while center post mounts were rejected because of their restricted field of fire. The swivel arm mount which gave wide freedom of motion seemed to have the most potential and was designated for development.

Armament Branch studies of possible power drives for turrets, including electric motors, wind turbines, and engine gear trains, concluded that a "design of such principle could easily be made" but "any action of a flexible run depending upon movement of a train of gears would be slowed down, and would lose its flexibility to a measure that it would handicap the gunner, hampering him in what approaches almost instantaneous changes of position as required of the gunner in the present stage of aerial gunnery."

The solution of defending the sector under the tail continued to be a question of aircraft design, and armament development in that regard could not progress separately from aircraft development. Firing through the floor of the fuselage was contingent on the design of the aircraft. When the Bombardment Board considered the Boeing XB-9 in June 1931 type specifications called for a floor gun. The Board felt that since the ventral rear area could be "fairly well covered" by depressed fire from guns firing from the sides of the relatively narrow fuselage and that "serious structural difficulties" would be met in attempting to place a floor gun because of the monocoque design, "this idea should be dispensed with."

The floor gun mount of the 1930s was generally a type of a swivel clamp mounted on the edge of a rectangular floor opening that constricted the field of fire to a relatively limited area. At Wright Field experimental work continued on several types of potential floor gun development. One type of a ventral gun projected a sliding seat mount hung below the fuselage end retracted by springs; while another, a rotating tank mount, extended a metallic cylinder below the fuselage by the system of springs of the first version but with the additional feature of shielding the gunner from the slipstream, but only so long as the gunner fired aft. To assist the rotation of this mount triangular vanes on one side or the other were proposed.

At the same time the question of the transition from .30 caliber to .50 caliber machine guns arose at Wright Field. Although there was a committed .50 caliber contingent at Wright the conversion received a low priority "because of the urgency of more important developmental work." In 1933 the General Staff Quarterly Test of aircraft with full military equipment was to require every third bombardment airplane to carry one flexible .50 caliber machine gun in the rear gunner's position. However, not only were there no dependable mounts for .50s, but there were no .50 caliber machine guns in stock to mount! In 1933 the Materiel Division listed the old D-6 ring mount and the Type 1 rings dating back to 1918 as standard.

**Section 4: U.S. Turret Development to 1939**

**U.S. Bombardment Aircraft Defense Policy 1930-1939**

The disparity between American and British turret development was brought to attention in 1937 when the British Air Ministry requested detailed information on American turret development in exchange for British information. The AAC Materiel Division suggested that the information exchange be in some other area, as they "had not reached a resolution to turret development." When the British persevered in their request they were handed three drawings of the Martin B-10 manual nose turret!

In 1932 the Bombardment Board recommended that the AAC bombardment directive be revised to update bomber design to the realities of contemporary requirements. The board included such progressive thinkers as Maj. Carl Spaatz, Maj. H.A. Dargue, Maj. J.T. McNarney, and Lt. J.N. Walker, who would all become general air officers in World War II. Their report gave an ambiguous assessment of the mission of the air force and the function of bombardment aviation in its relation to that mission: "Destruction of the enemy's means with which to wage war, primarily the mission of bombardment, is of paramount importance," and "the primary mission of an air force is to drive home the bombardment attack." (Air Corps Board Proceedings of 1 November 1932) With bombardment declared as the principal role of the air force the question of defensive armament arose. The Board had recommended that forward and aft turrets be developed for twin machine guns carrying 600 rounds each, while a turret or nacelle be developed to protect the rear sectors of the aircraft.

American armament development was delayed by the requirements of everyday routine and the general lack of personnel and the continuous turnover of those in service. There was no policy in place correlating the general needs of the AAC, the developmental requirements at Wright Field, and the evolution of foreign armament. A questionnaire was circulated from Wright Field throughout the AAC asking the opinions "on fields of fire, types of mounts, enclosures, and caliber of guns." While the majority of responses asked for an enclosed turret none mentioned the need for turret power drives. Since the viewpoints in these responses were so diverse a small group of knowledgeable officers was assigned to evaluate new armament developments.

In 1935 the Air Armament Branch examined the existing status of U.S. armament projects and found that development had been "restricted to improvement in design of specific items and little attention had been given to whether or not items of equipment, even in improver condition, were adequate to accomplish tactical functions as revised by the performance of modern airplanes." Remedying the armament program was dependant on funds available, and in 1935 the budget prepared for the new fiscal year allocated only $45,000 to the entire experimental and service test armament program. The Armament Branch felt at least $100,000 would be required to carry out an "adequate and aggressive experimental program." The Air Materiel Division finally realized that their lack of a clearly defined development program had seriously impaired the normal evolution of aircraft armament. In 1937, during a meeting of Air Corps and Ordnance Department representatives at Aberdeen Proving Ground, the Air Corps stated that its position was that it was "far from satisfied with the status of armament development." They pointed out that since 1930 the bomber had approximately doubled its speed, its size, and its bomb load, but "the armament has remained the same." It maintained that "increased fire power is not only logical but exigent in this development."

In April 1938 Brig.Gen. H.H. Arnold, then Assistant Chief of the Air Corps, set up a committee of Air Corps, Ordnance Department, and Navy staff to investigate ballistics and its effect on the development of armament. Three months later the committee reported that the lack of ballistics information had indeed slowed armament development, but this was because the personnel available at the Materiel Division for armament research were "entirely inadequate for such an extensive subject" and recommended that "every effort be made to facilitate cooperation between the Armament Laboratory at Wright Field and the research staff at Aberdeen." The most damning part of the report stated: "The present state of efficiency of flexible gunnery is worse than it was in 1918; the science of flexible gunnery having remained the same while the sights no longer fit the speed of the airplane."

The top echelons of the AAC had ignored the Armament Laboratory for years in their effort to develop armament equivalent to contemporary European equipment. But after the 1938 reports it found a benefactor in Gen. Arnold, the new Chief of the Air Corps who, in June 1939 with a European war looming, vigorously stated:

"It is the opinion of the Chief of the Air Corps that there has been less advance and development made in aircraft armament and ordnance accessories for aircraft than in any other branch of the art. It is also my opinion that the responsibility for this rests with the Materiel Division. It is quite apparent that some drastic steps must be taken by the Materiel Division to bring this development up to a par with the airplanes."

In addition to Arnold's recommendations there were those of the Air Board, which stated:

"After a review of conditions as they exist today, the Board is impressed with the imperative need for a more definite, effective, and continuing War Department policy governing military aeronautical research and development." The Board realized "that any failure to anticipate developments would lead eventually to supplying the Air Corps with aircraft utterly ineffective against enemy weapons." The Board's opinion was that research and development in aircraft design "must be paralleled in the field of accessories, particularly armament and communications equipment." Division design engineers were cautioned to give careful thought to military objectives, "the specific needs for performance and fire power of combat airplanes based upon plans for their utilization in specific situations."

The Armament Laboratory also stated:

"To avoid loss of efficiency incidental to increased air speeds, it is necessary that development work be undertaken with a view to providing power operation for turrets and enclosed positions from which flexible machine guns are employed. . . To date, little development work has been accomplished with reference to the provision of power operation."

In late 1938, Arnold called a secret meeting of Air Corps officers and aviation experts to discuss the future of the AAC and the bomber predicament. Charles Lindbergh had visited Hitler's Germany and was impressed and alarmed over the emphasis that the *Luftwaffe* had put on bombardment aircraft. Arnold asked Lindbergh to serve on a board headed by Brig.Gen. Walter Kilner and aided by Col. Carl Spaatz, Col. Earl Naiden, and Maj. Alfred Lyon. The Kilner Board issued its report in June 1939, and members of the group thought that in a European war Germany would not only overrun the Continent but also conquer Great Britain and then Africa, and perhaps establish bases in South America. If the Japanese began a war in the Pacific it would have to be fought over long expanses of ocean extending from Alaska to Hawaii to the Philippines, and to as far as Australia. The Kilner Board's recommendations were for a five-year research program to be carried out and reinforced by a system of priorities on research suggested by the Air Board. In order of importance emphasis was to place engines first, fire control apparatus second, and pursuit aircraft third. General Arnold requested that the Materiel Division prepare a definite developmental program in aircraft armament to be submitted without delay so that funds that had been denied over the past decade could be allotted. The Air Corps planned to implement this program with a sizeable increase in funds.

The proposed five year research and development program for the years 1940 to 1944, inclusive, of May 1939 allocated the following amounts (which were small when compared to the scale of the undertaking to be achieved) to flexible gun accessories for aircraft:

| Year | Fire Control | Power Turrets |
|---|---|---|
| **1940** | $10,000 | $20,000 |
| **1941** | $30,000 | $35,000 |
| **1942** | $50,000 | $50,000 |
| **1943** | $40,000 | $40,000 |
| **1944** | $30,000 | $35,000 |

(Proposed Five Year Research and Development Program for Fiscal Years 1940-1944 Inclusive, 10 May 1939.)

The reason for this new enthusiasm for armament development and power turrets, in particular, occurred when the advances in European aircraft armament finally became apparent. The previous lack of U.S. intelligence concerning foreign armament development was explained in July 1939 by Maj.Gen. Oliver Echols, the Chief of the Materiel Division. He noted that this category of information "proved extremely difficult to obtain since foreign practice corresponded with current policy in the United States in retaining all aircraft armament equipment in a confidential status." He further stated that the hunt for information concerning armament in particular was hindered by "aviation observers, who, as a rule, are not armament conscious." Moreover, the little information that was gathered on foreign aircraft armament had no specific individual or agency responsible for categorizing and circulating it to the various laboratories of the Materiel Division.

Soon after the war began in September 1939 the Materiel Division began to analyze the air tactics and techniques utilized by the combatants. Since mid-1938 the Division had sent low-priority questionnaires to American attachés in Europe, but this time these questionnaires were sent as high priority. For this questionnaire the Armament Laboratory at Wright Field made up a list of questions concerning power turrets, computing sights, and range finders. The aim of their questions was to determine if "it were the general tendency in bombardment aircraft gun arrangements to attempt to defend the airplane from attack in all directions or to defend from attack from limited areas, and if in the case of the latter, what fields were assigned major importance."

In December 1939 the Chief of the Experimental Engineering Section was concerned about the insufficient firepower of Air Corps bombardment aircraft as:

"Information obtained from newspapers and other sources indicates that foreign bombers are extremely deficient in ventral rear and directly to the rear gun defense. It is the opinion of this office that our bombers are in no better condition than the European bombers so far as defense is concerned."

The Chief then directed that studies be immediately initiated and "prosecuted with utmost vigor" in an attempt to obtain increased volume of fire. In January 1940 the Chief of the Armament Laboratory reported:

"The Laboratory had exerted every effort to prepare drawing studies, mock-ups, and negotiations with commercial sources to make available in the near future experimental models of twin .50 power-operated gun turrets, both dorsal and ventral, to establish designs which might be substituted for the manually operated emplacements for single machine guns should the Bombardment Board's decision favor the more complicated arrangements believed to be much more efficient." (Inter-office Memo, 9 January 1939)

Thus, by the end of 1939 the subject of bomber defense had become so critical that Gen. Arnold ordered a conference of representatives from every branch of the AAC concerned with aircraft armament. This conference convened in Washington on 27 December 1939 and debated the problem at great length, finally concluding that bombers needed "all-around fire protection with fire power to the rear equal to that of a pursuit attacker" and that "multiple gun turrets were definitely desired." Most contemporary pursuit aircraft carried six or eight fixed wing guns, but only a few Air Corps bombers mounted even a single gun that could be directed rearward

That same December Col. Carl Spaatz, Assistant to Gen. Arnold, commented on the state of American bomber fire power:

"As a result of all the reports which have been received by the War Department of air operations, commencing with those in China, continuing in Spain, and the present operations there in Europe, there has been a growing feeling in the War Department that bombardment airplanes are helpless against pursuit attacks. This feeling has reached the point where there is considerable thought given to the inadvisability of procuring anymore bombers."

He further stated "that even the new Air Corps bombers might not be provided with adequate fire power protection." Gen. Arnold directed the Air Corps Board at Maxwell Field to ask the Air Corps Tactical School to prepare a study "showing the fire power which the flexible guns on modern bombers, AAC as well as foreign bombers, could bring to bear on an attacking aircraft."

The Air Corps Board, in its extensive study of 3 January 1940 entitled "Fire Power of Bombardment Formations," pointed out that most current U.S. bombers had only one gun covering the tail area, and "in certain bombers, the field of observation in the rear hemisphere is so limited that it is perfectly feasible for pursuit aircraft to approach from the rear and attack without detection." It was obvious that it was necessary "to reduce the disparity between the fire power of pursuits and the available fire power of bombers in a given area." However, this could not be accomplished by simply modifying existing aircraft because, as per the *Handbook of Instructions for Airplane Designers*, consideration was to be given to fields of fire in the initial aircraft design stages, because once aircraft were built the possibility for improvements were limited. The Board concluded that the AAC's B-17, B-24, B-25, and B-26 were superior to the foreign aircraft evaluated, and bomber losses in the current European war were the result of faulty employment and untrained gunners as well as inadequate defensive fire. Their report recommended that the question of bomber defense be kept under continual study and specific attention be devoted to computing sights, range finders, and mechanical gun laying. With this report American bombardment aircraft defensive fire power policy had finally reached maturity.

**Armament Laboratory 1934-1939**

The Materiel Division's Armament Branch was involved with armament development at Wright Field; with the basic doctrines of the AAC regarding armament both officially and unofficially; and with the Air Corps' "interpretation of those doctrines as expressed in terms of aircraft actually built and armed." A 1921 Air Department directive had divided responsibility for armament development between the Air Service (Wright Field) and the Ordnance Department. The 37mm cannon was designated as the indicator of armament responsibility with all mounts for weapons larger than 37mm being the responsibility of the Ordnance Department and those smaller that of the Air Service. Three responsibilities were included in the Directive: 1) experimental development of armament equipment at Wright Field; 2) liaison with and education of prospective manufacturers; and 3) engineering supervision of actual development work under contract with commercial establishments.

By 1934 the Armament Laboratory at Wright Field had grown and become more influential, and was able to complain to Assistant Secretary of War H.H. Woodring about the restrictions imposed by the 1921 Directive:

"Experimental developments which, due to the absence of supply sources, are, of necessity, conducted at Wright Field including gunsights, bombsights, and the mechanisms and accessories for flexible .50 cal. gun. Developmental work in such critical areas required a reinterpretation of the obligations in the basic directive of 1921 as any diminution of the second and third obligations would interfere with the Armament Laboratory's role in its relation to ultimate wartime production."

In the early 1930s there was a dichotomy in the War Department, consisting of the traditionalists, led by Army Chief of Staff Gen. John J. Pershing, who believed that the infantry ruled the battlefield, while the Army Air Arm, led by the defrocked Gen. Billy Mitchell, espoused the future role of air power in warfare. A number of boards and committees were organized to study air doctrine and its role in future warfare. The most influential of these groups was the Baker Board Report of July 1934 that recommended America's national defense policy was not to be based on aggression, but that its purpose was to defend the homeland and overseas possessions, with the Army fending off any invader until civilian forces could be mobilized. The Report stated, "The idea that aviation can replace any of the other elements of our armed forces is found on analysis, to be erroneous. Since ground forces alone are capable of occupying territory, the Army with its own air forces remains the ultimate decisive factor in war." Baker Board member Jimmy Doolittle voiced the minority dissent, supporting the separation of the Army and its air forces and advocating the development of air doctrine for its employment.

The Baker Board's report led to a reorganization of the Materiel Division in 1935, involving new classifications of personnel and administrative functions. The Chief of the Armament Branch was authorized to hold the rank of Major and was to be responsible to the Chief of the Engineering Section for "all theoretical studies and research work pertaining to aircraft armament, for testing and passing on equipment involved, for the preparation of specifications, and for proper coordination with industry." The Branch Chief was to be assisted by at least one officer as an Engineering Specialist, with the rank of First Lieutenant, who was responsible for the development of armament equipment on all types of aircraft and for the flight testing of that equipment. The educational and background requirements of Wright Field personnel were expanded, with all officers required to have six years of service, with an engineering education desirable but not mandatory. Civilian employees at the Armament Branch became more important but, unlike AAC officers whose assignment was continuous, could leave at any time, especially after receiving valuable training and experience, for the better salaries offered in the private sector, which was increasingly seeking experienced personnel.

By late 1938 the Materiel Division had fallen behind on Gen. Arnold's request for the development of fire control equipment. The Armament Laboratory blamed the delays on the lack of funds; the lack of personnel; the lack of aircraft; the lack of flight experience with existing equipment; the lack of basic ballistic data; and the lack of an ample number of interested manufacturers as sources of supply. However, the main blame was placed on the basic nature of the assignment, which was depicted as "one of the most complex technological problems that can be envisioned." In late 1938 there were 17 aircraft available at the Wright Field Engineering Section and only one was at the Armaments Laboratory, and a year later the Laboratory had only seven aircraft available, with the most modern bomber being a Douglas B-18A which was developed from a DC-2 airliner design! But the biggest problem was the lack of funds, with the budget estimates for 1938 granting just over $2,500,000 for all experimental and development work at Wright Field, including:

| | |
|---|---|
| Aircraft | $1,000,000 |
| Power plants | $750,000 |
| Propellers | $100,000 |
| Tests, Designs | $35,000 |
| Armament | $25,000 |
| Balloons | $20,000 |

The $25,000 for armament was to cover the entire armament program, not merely power turrets:

| | |
|---|---|
| Mounts | $10,000 |
| Bomb Handling Equipment | $4,200 |
| Bomb Racks | $3,500 |
| Synchronizers | $1,000 |
| Gunsights | $800 |
| Miscellaneous | $500 |

In 1938 the direct purchases of armament equipment amounted to $14,421, but in 1939, with a European war becoming more inevitable, it accounted for $215,000 in the Materiel Division's budget. A breakdown of estimated purchase expenditures for armament in 1940 demonstrates the wartime shift of emphasis to armament:

| | |
|---|---|
| Cannon Fire Control | $45,000 |
| Bombsights | $40,000 |
| Bomb Racks | $25,000 |
| Remote Machine Guns | $25,000 |
| Mounts | $10,000 |

**Handbook of Instructions for Airplane Designers**

During the inter-war years there was a "standardized of design" in place which hindered armament design. The 1925 edition the Materiel Division's *Handbook of Instructions for Airplane Designers* stated:

"At the time of writing, this Handbook represents the most satisfactory solution of design problems, hence should be used as a guide for all airplane designs submitted to the Engineering Division for approval.

Manufacturers are urged to propose variations leading to improvement and deviations will always be granted upon request to effect better solutions of problems."

The first statement indicates the Materiel Division's leadership in aircraft concept and design, while the second seems to permit manufacturers some flexibility, but only that approved by the Division. However, the Handbook proposed and created a system of minimum standards. When considering a new aircraft design, an aircraft evaluation board had to decide if the aircraft met all the requirements of the general specifications issued in the current edition of the Handbook.

The 1935 Handbook pointed out that its contents were "mandatory unless specifically excepted in the contract." Aircraft manufacturers participating in design competitions had no choice but to follow the specifications expressed in the Handbook and to observe the general specifications of the manufacturing contract.

A change in the Armament section of the 1936 edition of the Handbook stressed the importance of "designing armament functionally with the airplane inasmuch as armament was, after all, part and parcel of the primary purpose of military aircraft." The Handbook continued: "it was impossible to make subsequent satisfactory provision for armament after it had been subordinated in the original design." The Handbook specified that the fields of fire for bombardment aircraft should cover the "greatest possible portion of the forward hemisphere, complete protection in the dorsal rear quartersphere, and in the zone below and to the rear, all stipulations of undefined generality qualified only by the requirement that intersecting fire from at least two guns should meet at 100 yards in every direction." This was the first edition of the Handbook to require turrets to afford the gunner with complete protection (e.g. enclosed) from the slipstream. Also, for the first time power drive was mentioned: "In the event that turrets cannot be manually operated at top speed, some means of power drive shall be supplied in addition to manual emergency operation."

The 1937 Handbook authorized "protective gun fire for the greatest possible portion of the entire sphere about the bombardment plane and complete coverage by aimed fire for the specified field of each gun position." However, turrets remained discretionary with aircraft manufacturers, who were only required "to provide flexible gunnery arrangements sufficient to permit rapid maneuvering throughout the entire field of fire without undue exertion on the part of the gunner," which allowed the manufacturer a wide range of interpretation in adding armament to its aircraft.

The 1939 Handbook added specifications for power drives in gun mounts, stating that "The selection of manual or power means of operating flexibly mounted guns is dependent upon the combined drag of the exposed portions of the gun and the moving portions of the gun mount and enclosure. If the total drag exceeded 35 pounds, measured at the gun ends and at the highest speed, power drives were necessary."

As the war approached the Armament Branch was too occupied to submit a revision in the armament section of the July 1940 Handbook edition. However, the July 1941 edition contained a completely revised armament section that stated that the power turret was to become standard on bombardment aircraft: "Manually operated flexible guns are no longer considered for the principal defense of aircraft. They maybe considered as a means of providing supplementary fire for limited areas when crew members other than gunners are available for protection for short periods of time."

**Tail Gun**

By 1938 the Materiel Division was examining the practicality of tail guns. Among the factors the Division considered was if a tail gun could be installed in a particular aircraft; the loss of speed and performance due to a tail gun position; and if a tail position design provided for gunner comfort and firing efficiency and accuracy. Materiel Division engineers determined that a better tail gun could be installed if the necessary space requirements had been introduced during the initial design stage of the aircraft, rather than added as a modification. Nonetheless, there seemed to be no pressing need for the tail gun position, as the Materiel Division, citing there were no tail gun installations from which experience could be drawn, decided there was no specific answer to the tail gun problem at the time. Concurrently, the Navy was mounting tail guns in their XPBS-1 and the XPB-2Y flying boats, but there was no exchange of information regarding these installations with Wright Field.

**Power-Driven Turrets**

In designing a fire control system engineers encountered significant problems in a field that was relatively unexplored. Previously, various manufacturers had made independent parallel studies on fire control but made little significant progress. Wright Field recognized that the only way to make any progress in solving the fire control problem was to have engineering cooperation and coordination among the manufacturers.

The design of a fire control system included sights, turrets, and the aircraft and their incorporation into a system, and demanded comprehensive liaison and coordination between the Army and the various component manufacturers. Sights required ballistic data which was the responsibility of Ordnance, while the development of the optical and computer components required full cooperation between their respective manufacturers. The turret manufacturer had to coordinate with the sight builder, and both had to coordinate with the aircraft designer and manufacturer. By mid-1939 the Materiel Branch started to exploit the best efforts of several staffs of industrial engineers, which also marked the start of the Branch's wartime role "of monitoring and engineering liaison center for the developmental projects of the manufacturers."

In January 1939 the Materiel Division prepared and issued a circular letter for several manufacturers who were interested in a power-driven gun turret. The letter included working drawings of the B-18 and the .30 caliber machine gun, a copy of the armament section of the Handbook of Instructions for Airplane Designers, and the reports containing all available data from wind tunnel tests of machine gun drag.

## Pre-War American Turrets and Gun Positions
## Heavy Bombers

**Douglas XB-19**

Two experimental long-range bomber projects were initiated in 1936 by the Materiel Division—the Douglas XBLR-2 and the Sikorsky XBLR-3—which offered an interesting look at America's thinking about arming its bombers in the mid-1930s. The Sikorsky proposal bristled with armament, including a 37mm cannon and six .50 caliber machine guns. The cannon was mounted in a manually operated dorsal turret while a single ventral .50 caliber gun turret was mounted in the aft fuselage. This ventral turret was electrically retracted and was electrically rotated in azimuth, but only had manual elevation. Wright Field had reservations about the 37mm cannon manual turret, but this became a moot point when the Douglas XBLR-2 (later to be designated XB-19) proposal won the competition and was awarded a contract.

One Douglas XBLR-2 was ordered on 29 September 1936 to be powered by four of the newly developed 2,000 hp Wright 3350-5 engines. It was designated the XB-19 by the AAC in mid-November 1937 and given the serial number 38-471. By mid-1938 work on the XB-19 had fallen behind schedule and design changes had substantially increased its weight and decreased anticipated performance; realistically the design was obsolete in view of contemporary advances in aircraft design. Douglas had spent a substantial amount of company funds on the project, but on 30 August 1938 it requested a release from the program, as it needed its design team to concentrate on more promising aircraft that could actually reach production. The Air Materiel Division persisted and ordered Douglas to complete the XB-19, which was to be as a test aircraft. It required seven years of development before the bomber took flight for the first time over Clover Field, Santa Monica, CA, on 27 June 1941. Maj. Stanley Umstead and a crew of seven flew the bomber to March Field for testing and evaluation, first by Douglas and then by the Army. Since the bomber was considered obsolete its "impressive" numbers, mostly its size, anticipated performance, and impressive armament and bomb load were released to the press. Great public hoopla ensued: "America's millions, given (its) breath-taking statistics, have probably been nursing a secret desire to hear that it bombed Tokyo" (Edward Churchill, *Flying Magazine*, August 1942).

Like the Sikorsky XBLR-3, the Douglas XB-19 specification also called for a large number of weapons—two 37mm cannons, six .30 caliber and three .50 caliber machine guns, positioned in various types of turrets and mounts—but there was no stipulation in the original 1936 specifications for a tail gun. When the AAC finally accepted the XB-19 in June 1942 the armament array was almost the same as that originally planned, except for the addition of a single .50 caliber tail gun mounted similarly to the gun in the B-23 tail. Thus, the XB-19's defensive armament was an impressive total of 12 guns firing 4,770 rounds of ammunition. The nose and top forward power turrets each contained one 37mm cannon and a .30 caliber machine gun. Single .50 caliber machine guns were positioned in the powered rear dome, the two waist positions, a belly fairing, and in the tail. Two more .30s were positioned at each side of the bombardier and in the sides of the empennage.

The XB-19 turrets were extensions of the experimental work done on the Douglas DB-1 through the DB-4 models. The nose turret was a basic combination of hydraulic pistons or jacks that moved the turret through a limited arc in both azimuth and elevation. For movement in elevation the dorsal turret utilized a hydraulic piston, but for azimuth rotation was driven by a Vickers unit and V-belt drive. Hydraulic pressure entered the

The **Douglas XB-19** specification involved a large number of weapons: two 37mm cannons, six .30 caliber and three .50 caliber machine guns, positioned in various types of turrets and mounts. (USAAF)

The XB-19 nose position contained one 37mm cannon and a .30 caliber machine gun. (USAAF)

turret through a rotating gland similar to the Boulton-Paul patent, and a four-way valve controlled the Vickers unit in speeds ranging from 3° to 60° per second in azimuth. Elevation speeds were more positive, ranging from 0° to 60° per second. Manufacture of the XB-19 turret became a difficult, time-consuming process, and when more promising turret designs appeared they were abandoned. The Douglas B-18 and XB-19 turret experience was not for naught, as valuable lessons were learned and experience gained for future turret development, especially in the use of the Vickers unit.

It was unexpected and inopportune that Douglas moved from manual .30 caliber gun turrets to the 37mm cannon turrets without first developing .50 caliber turrets. The Douglas turret was to mount a .30 caliber machine gun rigidly with the 37mm cannon, with the machine gun to act as a sighting guide for the cannon. This cannon/machine gun turret combination incorrectly assumed that their ballistic qualities were similar, which can be understood only when considering that there was little ballistic data available and that only one 37mm cannon was available to the AAC as late as 1937, and that one was a 1921 model! Thus, this turret inadequacy was a 37mm cannon problem rather than a basic turret problem.

As late as December 1939, to facilitate the design of an effective XB-19 turret Douglas requested data from the Materiel Division concerning the service testing of the DB-2's experimental, power-driven nose turret. Besides information regarding total running time, unsatisfactory reports, and overhaul periods, the Douglas designers were particularly interested in Wright Field opinions on the turret's acceleration rates, minimum as well as maximum, which was an important consideration that was later disregarded by many turret manufacturers during their initial turret developmental phase. Douglas received no response and made another request in March 1940. This time the Experimental Engineering Section did reply: "The tests conducted on the Douglas nose turret were insufficient to warrant comparison with other equipment." The Experimental Engineering Section's reply was more of a rebuff than help, and forced Douglas to discontinue their turret development, as no further Douglas turrets appeared after that date. The Armament Branch, with its limited funding, should have had a policy in place of pursuing every test to its limit, which would have yielded the maximum results from the money allocated.

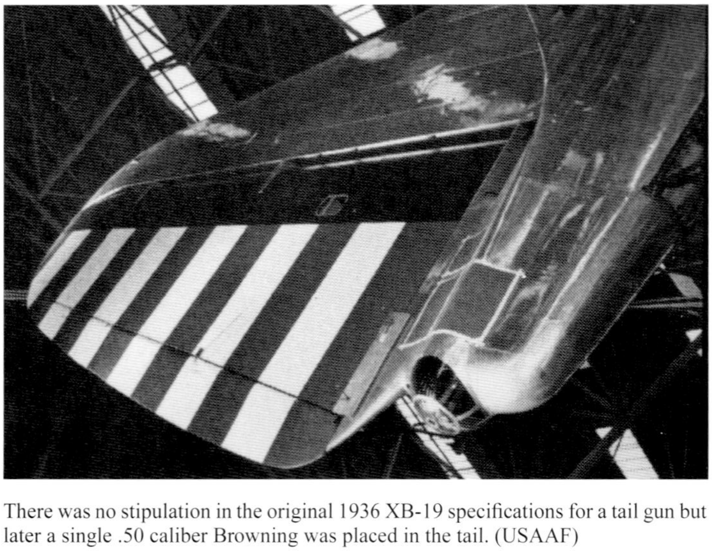

There was no stipulation in the original 1936 XB-19 specifications for a tail gun but later a single .50 caliber Browning was placed in the tail. (USAAF)

**Boeing XB-15** (USAAF)

Nose mounted .30 caliber machine gun. (USAAF)

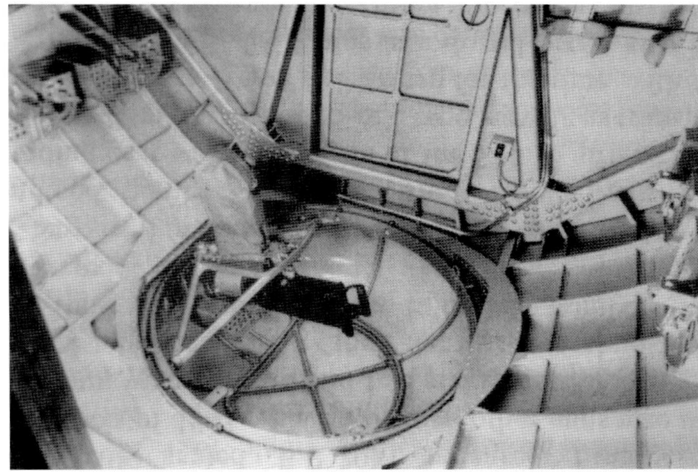

Mid-turret .30 caliber machine gun position. (USAAF)

**Boeing XB-15**
In 1935 Boeing submitted the XB-15 design, which was the direct precursor of the B-17 heavy bomber of World War II. The XB-15 drawings proposed two flexible .50 caliber and four flexible .30 caliber machine guns, all in plastacelle blisters or panels in conventional nose, dorsal, and ventral positions, but had no provision for a tail gun. Boeing also submitted the XB-20 design that carried basically the same armament as the XB-15.

During February 1938 the Armament Laboratory conducted tests to determine the suitability of the XB-15's armament and found that the manual nose turret, a small transparent hemisphere similar to the nose mount of the B-18, was exceedingly difficult to operate, requiring 80 pounds exertion at 90° azimuth and 250 mph airspeed. The installation of a power drive and the addition of pick-up windows to improve scanning was suggested, along with the recommendation: "it is important that the area directly to the rear be amply protected by a directly or remotely controlled gun." (Memo 1 October 1935) It was the latter recommendation that demonstrated the reluctance of a manufacturer to implement a design change. During Gen. Arnold's fire control conference two years later in December 1939, Boeing reported it "could not possibly put a tail gun on a B-17 since that would require them to redesign the whole tail."

**Boeing Model 299**
In 1935 Boeing submitted its Model 299, the future B-17, to the Armament Branch for armament evaluation. Instead of the three .30 caliber machine gun positions stipulated in the AAC type specifications Boeing opted to install five positions: two waist guns in addition to the three specified conventional emplacements. The waist guns were large horizontal tear drop-shaped blisters with a single .30 machine gun that could only traverse. The Armament Branch considered this armament array unsatisfactory, even though the combined area covered by the three dorsal guns was definitely greater than that covered by one retractable turret. The new Boeing arrangement required three gunners to be constantly stationed at these positions. These three gunners, along with the nose and floor gunners "would be in excess of those who could be allotted for defense out of the crew of five." The Branch also reported that target visibility was actually reduced by using three positions, "for the time required to pick up a target leaving one field to enter another might be so great as to reduce the total field of fire below that of a rotating turret manned by a single gunner."

**Boeing XB-17/Y1B-17A**
Regardless of the Branch findings, the XB-17 appeared with five flexible machine guns in the original five positions and no significant changes in this arrangement appeared until April 1937, when the Y1B-17A specifications were prepared. Y1B-17A firing tests conducted at Langley Field revealed that the waist guns were restricted to a 20° angle of downward fire, which was somewhat less than that stipulated by Boeing's specifications. Also, the lack of scanning windows combined with the area blocked out by the empennage "effectively reduced the aircraft's over all armament efficiency."

**Boeing XB-17/Y1B-17A** (USAAF)

Y1B-17 waist position. (USAAF)

**Martin B-10** (USAAF)

The Armament Branch concluded that the guns did not defend the airplane satisfactorily and further stated that "procurement of large airplanes should be accompanied by the requirement that one well designed power driven turret located in the dorsal rear position provide the principal defense of the airplane."

### Medium Bombers

#### Martin B-10

The B-10 bomber built by the Glenn L. Martin Company was the AAC's first bombardment aircraft with an enclosed turret. The B-10 had previously incorporated a ring mount, which was replaced with a single .30 caliber machine gun in a rotating dome with a diameter of 36 inches and a height of 35 inches at the apex. The dome framework was fabricated of welded steel sheathed with sections of "plastacelle." The manually operated dome was developed from the ring mount and continued many of its characteristics, with the gun mount inside employing the previous shock cord compensation system and the turret track locked in one of the 36 different firing positions. Tracking and sighting was a problem, as during the bomber's service test the nose gun did not cover the specified field of fire. The gunner reported that it was uncomfortable and did not provide enough head room. On the plus side, the turret was reported to be easy to maneuver and weighed much less than normal turrets at 80 pounds.

In 1935 the type specifications for multi-engine bombardment airplanes was revised, requiring the installation of a minimum of three .30-caliber gun positions. The nose gun was to protect the "maximum portion of the foresphere," and the dorsal "midship" gun was to cover the dorsal rear quartersphere, while the ventral or floor gun was to guard the ventral rear quartersphere, and all were required to be capable of rapid operation at maximum speeds. The manufacturer was given discretion in placing additional guns, but due to the weight involved in additional guns they were not likely to meet more than minimum firepower requirements in order to meet the aircraft's performance specifications. At the time firepower requirements should have been increased, and the loosely defined zones of fire (e.g. dorsal rear quartersphere) gave the manufacturers great autonomy in the choice of armament installations, but they did not take advantage of the opportunity. The major revision of the type specification that was to have future implications was the requirement that the manufacturer was to provide an "enclosure for the dorsal rear emplacement in order to give complete protection from the slipstream and visibility in all directions, rendering the position a 'lookout' for the airplane." A "lookout" implied a gun turret, and finally aircraft designers could no longer place streamlining and performance over armament.

The **B-10** was the AAC's first bombardment aircraft with an enclosed turret. This nose turret was a manually operated dome was developed from the ring mount. (USAAF)

**North American XB-21** (USAAF)

B-18 manually-operated .30 caliber nose turret. (USAAF)

**North American XB-21**

In 1936 North American Aviation began work on its first bomber known as the NA-21. The bomber was accepted by the AAC as the XB-21 twin-engine bomber, which had defensive armament consisting of five .30 caliber machine guns fitted in hydraulically operated nose and top turrets, a conventional floor mount, and two in the waist positions on the sides of the fuselage. The Armament Branch conducted tests on the XB-21 and found that the two turrets that were powered by the Vickers unit power-drive system utilizing a Boulton-Paul-type valve system "was improperly engineered, since the motors became inoperable during inspection apparently because they were underpowered." Importantly, North American engineers had completely neglected the turret slot closures for protection from the blast of the slipstream. North American was given a contract for a single XB-21 in May 1938 to test hydraulic turret installations. So, like the Douglas turrets developing at the same time, North American's turret testing was valuable only in that it contributed to "the slowly accumulating fund of armament information" in the Materiel Division.

**Douglas B-18 Bolo**

While Wright Field was negotiating the Curtiss contract the Douglas Aircraft Company built the first DB-1, which was designated the B-18 by the Air Corps and fulfilled the minimum type specification requirements for three flexible gun positions. In August 1935 a 689 inspection board found the nose and floor guns to be conventional, but reported that Douglas chose to deviate from requirements in the dorsal rear gun, "with the result that an arrangement superior to that required has been provided."

The B-18's manually operated turret included many innovations and was an important first step in solving the problems facing turret designers: retraction, slot closure, dome contour, and the selection of transparent window panels. The B-18 turret was retractable via an elastic shock cord system. A crank and cable retracting mechanism to replace the existing shock cord was recommended, but fortunately was rejected, as it would have been ineffective in service. The Board considered the gun aperture slot closers as "an excellent idea, well worked out." The transparent "paraline" plastic window panels, called "the birdcage," were of poor quality, and the search for a satisfactory window material would continue until the appearance of Plexiglas. As early as April 1935 Douglas contemplated power turrets and made preliminary drawings for an improved version of the B-18 with tentative provisions for power-driven nose turret and a ventral mid-fuselage turret. The nose turret was a pear-shaped cubicle that moved about its vertical axis by a worm and gear drive powered from a Vickers hydraulic unit. After examining the drawings the Engineering Section felt that Douglas' power turret proposal had enough value "to be procured at additional cost to the Government," but added, "Although a power driven turret is desired, it is believed that this proposal is too incomplete to evaluate." It should be noted here that the objections to powered turrets were based on the very low capacity of existing aircraft generators, which made the addition of any electrical accessories a critical decision; a factor that slowed the development of power turrets.

At the time the 177 B-18s were contracted in June 1937 it was the largest aircraft order since World War I, and the bomber was considered the pinnacle of Air Corps bomber technology. In its final revision in February

**Douglas B-18 Bolo** (USAAF)

The B-18's manually operated dorsal turret included many innovations and was an important first step in solving the problems facing turret designers: retraction, slot closure, dome contour, and the selection of transparent window panels. (USAAF)

1940, the B-18A was armed with the same three .30-caliber machine guns as it had in 1937, and no provision had been made for additional guns or the alternate installation of .50-caliber machine guns. The Armament Branch's failed attempt to upgrade the B-18's armament underlined the problem of turret development. A single lightweight .30-caliber Browning could be managed without a powered turret; however, the evolution toward heavier .50 caliber guns made a powered turret essential. Before the arrival of power turrets the use of .50 caliber guns decreased defensive effectiveness, as these heavier guns were more difficult to maneuver in the slipstream and their size interfered with the fuselage structures surrounding it. To (partially) remedy the slipstream problem wind vanes were designed for the B-18A, but nothing could be done about the fuselage interference problem, as the original B-18 design made no allowances for armament installations.

In its evaluation of the B-18A (DB-4) proposal, the Armament Branch rejected the floor gun position as "of little value because of its limited visibility; but even more serious was the limitation on fire in the dorsal foresphere imposed by the under slung position of the nose mount." The Armament Laboratory attempted to develop a small dorsal nose turret which, while unsuccessful, resulted in a "better understanding that the exact requirements for turrets" when it needed to revise the Handbook. (For a detailed look at the B-18 armament, see my book: *The Douglas B-18 Bolo: The Ultimate Look from Drawing Board to U-Boat Hunter*, Schiffer, PA, 2007)

**Douglas B-23**

In July 1938 the Armament Laboratory was examining the B-18A armament and reported that a fixed gun in the tail of a B-18A could not satisfactorily defend the large area blocked out by its large empennage. The Laboratory determined that a remotely controlled gun sighted from the dorsal turret could be feasible, and recommended that designs be solicited from interested manufacturers. The Materiel Division procured a Douglas B-23, which was a 39 aircraft order off the assembly line and a major modification of the B-18A. The new bomber carried four guns: three conventionally placed .30 caliber machine guns and a single .50 caliber gun in the tail. With the addition of a tail gun, the dorsal turret of the B-18 had been removed and in its place were two .50s firing through removable side windows in the fuselage. The Armament Branch B-23 tests were unsatisfactory, as they revealed that the nose gun was "decidedly unsatisfactory" because it was designed without reference to the realities of combat. The gun had to be stowed in order to use the bombsight, and stowing was a two-man job. The newly designed clam shell tail gun was deemed as satisfactory within the limits of its design, leaving the gunner cramped and with inadequate scanning. Moreover, it was impossible to crawl from the waist to the tail while wearing a parachute. Nonetheless, this tail position was the first tail gun position in an American bomber. (Note: See Part Six/Chapter 4/Section 16 Clam Shell Tail Turret)

### Multi-place Fighter

**Bell XFM-1/YFM-1 Airacuda**

The XFM (FM = Fighter Multi-place) was a multi-place, pusher-engined fighter which was the Bell Aircraft Company's first design, and although

**Douglas B-23** (USAAF)

B-23 .30 caliber nose gun position. (USAAF)

only a prototype and 13 service test models were produced, the importance of the Airacuda was it represented a revival of the Army Air Corps' interest in developing a pursuit aircraft in a time when the heavy bomber concept was paramount. The design also was important in developing new weapons, installations, and armament systems (see Part Five/Chatper 1 Sperry Central Fire Control).

The single XFM-1 prototype, which included a tail wheel, side "blister" ports, and a rounded canopy, was followed by 13 updated tricycle-landing gear versions designated the YFM-1, which eliminated the side blisters. Three slightly larger final versions produced in 1940 were designated the YFM-1A, with a rearward-facing belly gunner's position added. The final variant was the YFM-1B, and was basically the YFM-1 fitted with slightly less powerful engines. The Airacuda was designed as a bomber destroyer, but its performance compared to contemporary fighters was poor and the design was shelved after 14 were built.

YFM-1 Gunnery Configuration

The original AAC specification called for 20mm Oerlikon cannon to be installed, but as discussed previously Larry Bell suggested the installation of the Sperry remote system to fire the XFM-1's 37mm cannons located in the forward section of the engine nacelles of this pusher-powered aircraft. The idea was unsuccessfully pursued, and a conventional turret arrangement was used on the YFM-1 and FM-1 models.

Nacelle Guns: The YFM-1 was powered by two pusher engines mounted in nacelles that contained a glazed gunner's compartment forward. Each nacelle was equipped with a Colt Browning 37mm automatic cannon locally controlled by a gunner. The gun was fed by 11 ammunition boxes containing two clips of five rounds that were located in the gunner's station of each nacelle (see Part Two/Chapter 3).

Fuselage Dorsal Turret: The .30 caliber Type M2 machine gun was mounted in a retractable 360° rotating turret located on top of the fuselage just forward of the trailing edge of the wing. The gun, mounted on a shoulder fire adapter, could be elevated to 90° full up and could be elevated or depressed by a crank on the left side of the fuselage. A firing stop prevented the gun from firing into the propellers. Five ammunition boxes containing 500 rounds were stowed on the right side of the mid-fuselage.

Fuselage Side Turrets: The side turret guns were located on both sides of the fuselage between the wing and tail. Each manually retracted turret consisted of a .50 caliber Browning M2 mounted on a shoulder fire adapter and 1,200 rounds of boxed ammunition located on each side of the fuselage just

**YFM Side Turret** (USAAF)

forward of each turret. The turret retraction crank was located just forward of each turret. On the mounting post was a handle lock for vertical adjustment of the gun mount, and midway on the gun support arm was the lock release for rotational adjustment. The guns were stowed by lowering them toward the floor and clipping them to the sides of the fuselage.

Fuselage Ventral Turret: The 180° ventral turret was located in the fuselage floor just forward of the side turret guns. The turret was gunned by a .30 caliber M2 machine gun mounted on a Type C-12 flexible gun adapter and fed by five 100 round ammunition boxes stowed on the starboard side of the fuselage (the gunner faced aft).

**Section 5: Turret Development: 1939-1940**

When Germany invaded Poland in September 1939, the U.S., in effect, did not have an air force, and those aircraft in its inventory were obsolete. However, America did have a number of combat aircraft on the drawing

**YFM Dorsal Turret** (USAAF)

**YFM Ventral Turret** (USAAF)

board which it hoped would go into production before direct American involvement in the European war. Just as new aircraft were to be developed so, too, was the new equipment to arm them. To aid and accelerate armament development, the Materiel Command divided projects into separate components to be developed individually. Leading manufacturers interested in turret development were assigned specific aircraft to arm: Sperry designed equipment for the B-17, Bendix for the B-25, Martin for the B-26, and General Electric for the A-20.

Gardner-Carroll Armament Fact Finding Trip Abroad Report

In early 1940 Gen. Arnold ordered that intelligence reports gathered by the Information Division be examined for data regarding British power turrets for use by the Materiel Division. The search revealed that Frazer-Nash turrets manufactured by Parnell Aircraft, Ltd., were installed in the Hawker Demon, the Handley-Page Harrow, the Armstrong-Whitworth Whitley, and the Short Sunderland. Boulton-Paul turrets were also installed on the Blackburn Roc and Blackburn Skua, as well as on the Boulton-Paul Defiant. Intelligence reports also showed that the RAF was secretly perfecting machine gun and cannon turrets in addition to computing sights. As early as July 1939, the Air Ministry requested the Admiralty Research Laboratory to commence a fire control project for guns heavier than .303 mounted in turrets.

The Air Corps did not realize the full extent of British turret development until Lt. Col. Grandison Gardner and Maj. F. O. Carroll submitted their "Report on Trip Abroad" on 1 July 1940. The two officers had been associated with the Armament Branch for some time, and in March 1940 were sent to England, where they met with Air Ministry officials, RAF officers, and aircraft manufacturers, as well as turret manufacturers. In their report they noted that "the application of power turrets to bombardment aircraft as the outstanding development of the British." More significantly, they observed, "The installation of these turrets on some of their bombers had caused such losses to the enemy attacking airplanes that the British now claim that attacks directly aft have been discontinued on these installations, forcing the Germans to make beam approaches with little success." Their report concluded, "It is imperative that our heavy and long-range bombers be equipped with at least four turrets, fore, aft, top, and bottom. Admittedly such armament would reduce bomber speed and performance, but British practice seemed to have proved the merit of subordinating every bombardment airplane function to its defense, even at the cost of aerodynamic efficiency."

Gardner and Carroll visited the three large turret manufacturers in the United Kingdom: Bristol, Frazer-Nash, and Boulton-Paul, with the latter two accounting for the larger portion of British production. They noted that the British had discontinued all-electric systems several years earlier, and that all British turret models were hydraulic systems because of their ease of tracking and the "positive control at very low rates of movement" and "almost entire freedom from overtravel." Frazer-Nash turrets were built by Parnell Aircraft, Ltd., which manufactured 16 or 20 turrets per day by May 1940. The company built five different turret types, including a quadruple .303 nose and tail turret, a twin .303 nose and tail turret, and a twin .303 retractable ventral turret called a "dust bin." Boulton-Paul Aircraft, Ltd. produced 65 turrets per day in May 1940. Their turrets were of four types similar to the turrets built by Frazier-Nash, except that the power drive consisted of a self-contained electro-hydraulic unit rather than a simple hydraulic turret. The Boulton-Paul system utilized a ladder-type electrical power lead that significantly reduced its vulnerability to enemy fire in contrast to the long, exposed hydraulic lines used in the Frazier-Nash turrets. More importantly, the Frazer-Nash system "required varied angular displacement of the control handles as the torque load varied, while the Boulton-Paul system compensated for torque, and equal control displacement gave equal angular movement under all conditions of loading."

The Gardner-Carroll report continued: "The British have shown the way and the method together with the results to be obtained in the installation of machine gun turrets," and "no effort must be spared to apply this type of mechanism to our own advantage." The report did criticize the British turrets as being perhaps "too heavy and cumbersome and ill-suited for use with Air Corps bombardment aircraft." The report posed the question as to whether the British turrets should be licensed for manufacture in the United States or if America should develop and manufacture independent designs. The answer was influenced by time which was becoming critical, as the threat of entering the war approached and favored the adoption of the British turrets.

Col. E. A. Deeds, representing Pratt & Whitney, negotiated with the British for turret manufacturing rights, but prominent British officials indicated that the Air Ministry would exchange turret designs for the Norden bombsight, resulting in protracted negotiations. U.S. naval air officers that had an opportunity to operate British turrets in various aircraft were of the opinion that British turret development "far surpassed the progress made in the United States and that every effort should be made to assist the British manufacturers to establish facilities in the United States." (Report of the U.S. Naval Attaché, 29 November 1940)

The U.S. Naval Attaché noted that there were three axioms to be followed in any future American turret undertaking:

1) Turret production should be separate from aircraft production; that is, turrets should be treated as government-furnished equipment;
2) Each turret manufacturer should produce one type of turret; that is, hydraulic turret manufacturers should stay in the hydraulic field and electric turret manufacturers in the electric field; and
3) Turret manufacturers should not attempt to modify until production was rolling and modification could be carried out without detriment to production output.

The U.S. Naval Attaché warned that intelligence reports from Britain were reiterating that "more and more evidence is piling up that mechanical turrets are absolutely essential to the success of airplanes whose size permits their installation."

The turret negotiations and indecision continued for many months; meanwhile, American turret manufacturers devoted large amounts of time and money to turret development projects, and the prospect of manufacturing British turrets in the United States diminished.

William S. Knudsen, former head of General Motors and then the Director General of the newly created Office of Production Management, sent Emerson's Stuart Symington to England in April 1941 to examine British powered bomber turrets (see Part Six/Chapter 4/Section 22). When Symington returned to St. Louis in June he had absorbed great insight into British turret manufacturing techniques which he used to secure a substantial contract to build the ANB turret for Lend-Lease to England. Once America entered the war Emerson had difficulties in converting the British turrets carrying .303 caliber guns into AAF turrets carrying U.S. .50 caliber guns. As a result Emerson built turrets in its new factory for other manufacturers, including Sperry, during 1942. Due to the dynamic Symington his Emerson Electric Co. would become the world's largest airplane armament plant with sales increasing from $4.9 million in 1940 to $114 million in 1944. During the war Emerson developed and manufactured a number of outstanding turrets. By 1944 Emerson was producing more than 70 turrets a day with more than 12,000 Model 127 Emerson nose turrets produced.

In 1944 Emerson's finances and enormous expansion came under the scrutiny of Sen. Harry Truman's Special Committee to Investigate the

National Defense Program, which was investigating defense contractors who were not performing efficiently. Symington's reasoned testimony pointed out the government's interference with normal Emerson procedures and the Truman Committee eventually absolved Emerson. In July 1947 Truman named Symington as America's first Secretary of Defense, and in 1952 he became a four-term Senator from Missouri and leader in the Democratic Party.

**Section 6: Turret Standardization: 1940-1943**

By the end of 1940 America had 36 turret projects under development; 10 of which were completed and operating, and five were completed but not powered. Of the remaining 21, seven were mock-ups and 14 were either very rudimentary mock-ups or only drawings. Of the total, 26 had hydraulic control, nine had electric control, and one had mechanical control. All the hydraulic systems depended on some form of Vickers unit for pressures ranging from 100 to 400 pounds per square inch. Five of the electric systems were amplidyne, while two operated with some form of pulsating DC control.

British turret production was efficient because it was limited to two manufacturers (Boulton-Paul and Frazer-Nash) whose designs utilized a standardized mounting ring which made the turrets of either manufacturer easily interchangeable. These manufacturers designed and produced four basic types of turrets: nose, tail, dorsal, and ventral. Concurrently, American production policy was very different, with too many designs under development at once by too many manufacturers, which delayed rather than encouraged development. Each new American manufacturer had to learn by experience the lessons already learned by those manufacturers who entered the field earlier. The large number of designs required a disproportionate amount of time for testing the qualities of each and then selecting the best features for standardization. During the testing of American power drives and controls too little consideration was placed on the importance of slow tracking rates as opposed to fast. Every hydraulic system revealed a dead spot at neutral when shifting from one deflection to another. Combat experience had emphasized that smooth transitions from positive to negative deflections were extremely important when following a target. American hydraulic systems were satisfactory, but all were problematic for operational use, with the amplidyne system being very promising.

GE position control appeared to have the most potential for remote turrets and nose or tail cone fire turrets; but for dorsal or ventral turrets that required continuous rotation speed control was superior. The Bendix ventral remote turret had a dead spot at neutral and a complete loss of control, but nonetheless this turret continued in development, and it would prove to be unsatisfactory in combat and would be withdrawn. American turret designers disregarded gunner comfort, such as heating, gun slot closure, seat design, hand control position, and turret and gun loading. More importantly, there were critical design flaws in the scanning areas and the sights needed to be standardized before the turrets could be standardized.

**The Status of U.S. Turret Producers at the End of 1942**

At the end of 1942, all the major turret manufacturers except Westinghouse had reached large scale turret production. Even though GE remote turret production had been delayed because of the slow progress of the P-61, B-26, and B-29 aircraft development, GE entered production early in 1941 as a manufacturer of Martin turret components. The Martin production lines ran efficiently from the very first production contract late in 1940, and Sperry, after a difficult time used in organizing its subcontractors, was functioning smoothly by the end of 1941.

**Section 7: Conclusions**

American engineers discovered that designing a gun turret was a complicated and difficult problem. A powered turret required a drive mechanism that could rotate a turret quickly toward a target and then move slowly and accurately to track the target to open fire on it. The turret needed to be under positive control when moving under power and also when stopped in a certain direction. When the direction of a turret changed from the starboard to port side of the aircraft, with the associated reversal of forces, target tracking had to continue evenly without a dead spot around the center position. For aircraft installation the drive unit had to be dependable, light, and compact with space for the gunner, guns, sight, and ammunition. The turret design had to consider gunner comfort during long flights and provide him with a degree of protection with the installation of armor plate. The transparent dome had to be a compromise between headroom, streamlining, and gunsighting. At all gun attitudes, the gunner had to be able to sight them and the gun feed mechanism had to function.

The greatest single failure in the development of power turrets was that the Materiel Division never developed a satisfactory system for analyzing the basic bomber armament requirement, and there was no official procedure in place to evaluate ultimate turret objectives. For years the prevailing gunnery doctrine was that the majority of pursuit attacks would occur within a narrow cone to the rear, but each successive bomber design until the beginning of the war appeared without a tail gun installation. Manual flexible light caliber gunnery was installed in other armed positions, and the actual armament installation in American bombers was in contradiction of prevailing doctrine. In the two decades after World War I the Armament Laboratory was considered the Materiel Division's step child in regards to the limiting of funding, personnel, and equipment in comparison to the other Wright Field laboratories.

Once war came in 1939, U.S. armament doctrine and practice lagged behind that of the RAF and typified the limitations existing in the Armament Laboratory's methods for studying foreign developments. There was a prevailing inadequate liaison between the Materiel Division and combat units in the field with the consequent misunderstanding of their evolving armament requirements. However, the manufacturer's field representatives in the combat zones proved to be a useful direct line from the field to the factory, and their suggestions contributed greatly to power turret development.

The role of the Armament Laboratory at Wright Field required some time to define: to monitor domestic turret manufacturer's projects and to be a clearinghouse for ideas and requirements originating from foreign turret manufacturers and from the comments of tactical units in the field. With the rush to war the Armament Laboratory often did not communicate with turret manufacturers before they were ready for quantity production of virtually unproven turrets. The awarding of small peacetime-type developmental contracts would have produced higher quality results than the necessarily large wartime contracts because manufacturers would have taken more time, as there was less assurance of securing a contract unless the final product was superior. Often when the awarding of production contracts lagged time was lost for hesitant manufacturers to establish a network of subcontractors. Initially, the Armament Laboratory was active in experimental turret development and fabrication, but could not meet the demands once war came. Emerson's wartime experience verified the effectiveness of company research and development in conjunction with large scale industrial production. To meet the new demands of turret development and production brought by the war the Armament Laboratory revised its emphasis to technological supervision and method analysis.

The difficulties with turrets did not occur during production, which was basically similar to any other manufacturing project, but took place during the period of initial development. The Material Division and the Armament Laboratory required two and a half years from the outbreak of the European war in September 1939 to overcome turret development problems, then issue contracts, and finally to initiate mass production. By May 1942 the power turret had become an established component of bomber armament. The B-26 mounted a single dorsal turret and a powered tail mount. The B-17 carried dorsal and ventral turrets, a chin turret, and a powered tail mount. The B-24 carried a dorsal, a ventral turret, a nose turret, and a tail turret; and the B-29 was to appear with two remote dorsal and two remote ventral turrets and a power mount in the tail. At that time the Production Engineering Section was able to report that the production of gun turret assemblies was generally ahead of actual requirements. Turret requirements would increase, and many problems would remain to be solved, but the undertaking became basically one of applying engineering capability and industrial capacity to meet specific circumstances. At the end of 1944 the Armament Laboratory had acquired more than 70 turrets that included some production models and many more experimental models under development. By January 1943 Emerson had commenced production on nine different contracts which totaled more than $93,000,000, while Martin production contracts in February 1943 exceeded $50,000,000. In March Sperry, Briggs, and Steel Products jointly had each been awarded contracts totaling more than $5,000,000, and at the time Bendix and its subcontractors held contracts of approximately $100,000,000.

# 2

# Turret Power Drives

## Section 1: Development of Turret Power Drive Systems

### Power-Driven Turrets

In designing a fire control system, engineers encountered significant problems in a field that was relatively unexplored. Previously, various manufacturers had made independent parallel studies on fire control but made little significant progress. Wright Field recognized that the only way to make any progress in solving the fire control problem was to insist on engineering cooperation and coordination among the manufacturers.

The design of a fire control system that included sights, turrets, and aircraft and their incorporation into the system demanded comprehensive liaison and coordination between the Army and manufacturers. Sights required ballistic data which was the responsibility of Ordnance, while the development of the optical and computer components required complete cooperation between their manufacturers. The turret manufacturer had to coordinate with the sight builder, and both had to coordinate with the aircraft designer and manufacturer. By mid-1939 the Materiel Branch started to exploit the best efforts of several staffs of industrial engineers, which also marked the start of the Branch's wartime role "of monitoring and engineering liaison center for the developmental projects of the manufacturers."

In January 1939 the Materiel Division prepared and issued a circular letter for power-driven gun turrets to several interested manufacturers. The letter included working drawings of the B-18 and the .30 caliber machine gun, a copy of the armament section of the *Handbook of Instructions for Airplane Designers*, and the reports containing all available data from wind tunnel tests of machine gun drag.

## Power Drives: 1940-1942

### Vickers Power Drive

The Vickers power drive unit bottleneck occurring in the early months of 1941 threatened to slow down turret production through May 1942. The issue became a critical factor in the Armament Laboratory's armament program and resulted in the necessity of revising turret delivery schedules downward. The bottleneck was the result of the basic difficulty of machining the unit, Vickers' initial reluctance to expand its facilities, and then the problems involved in finding a competent subcontractor. By the fall of 1941 the Vickers unit shortage threatened to become so critical that the Production Engineering Section of the Materiel Division went to the Vickers factory in an effort to remedy the situation.

Vickers partially blamed Briggs, Emerson, and Steel Products for the delay in production, as these companies indicated their intentions of using Vickers units but placed no official orders. So Vickers was reluctant to subcontract to subcontractors who were, in turn, hesitant to manufacture component parts without firm contracts. When the Production Engineering Section (PES) tried to accelerate the approval of formal contracts it discovered that several of the manufacturers using Vickers units were hoarding many more units than needed for their actual production requirements. In response the PES organized an inventory control program to end this bottleneck by placing serial numbers on each unit to prevent excess units from collecting at the manufacturers. When the Ordnance Department requested that part of Vickers production be diverted to ground turrets for the Coast Artillery and the Armored Corps, the PES decided that Vickers needed to expand its capacity. After the OPM reviewed companies experienced in machining to the close tolerances required of the Vickers unit it selected the Hobart Manufacturing Company of Troy, OH, which manufactured food preparation machinery.

The Vickers units were often rejected because of "creep," which were slight leakages that caused the turret to rotate slightly when the controls were theoretically in neutral. This problem required the Experimental Engineering Section to revise the specifications for Vickers units to allow inspectors to pass units with a creep of up to 1/4° per second, because it had been found impossible to achieve 0° per second creep under "allowable existing manufacturing tolerances." In late May 1942, a memo from the Chief of Production Engineering Section to the Chief of the Experimental Engineering Section warned that despite the increased output at Vickers and Hobart, the Vickers unit "production outlook was not too bright" and recommended that an alternate drive be found, stating, "This variable displacement pump is considered to be the most difficult piece of equipment to manufacture of the entire armament series; indeed it has proven impossible to find a manufacturing source to augment the two existing sources."

The Vickers drive unit was a proven power source, but the shortage of these units jeopardized the entire U.S. turret program. The Vickers drive unit shortage actually was never as serious as it appeared. Apart from artificial bottlenecks arising out of hoarded inventories, Vickers created some of the impression of there being a shortage of their units while they were negotiating for plant expansion with the Defense Plant Corporation (DFC). This artificially depressed estimate of Vickers production was immediately apparent, as once the DFC approved the Vickers plant expansion plan Vickers suddenly promised the delivery of more units per month from existing facilities!

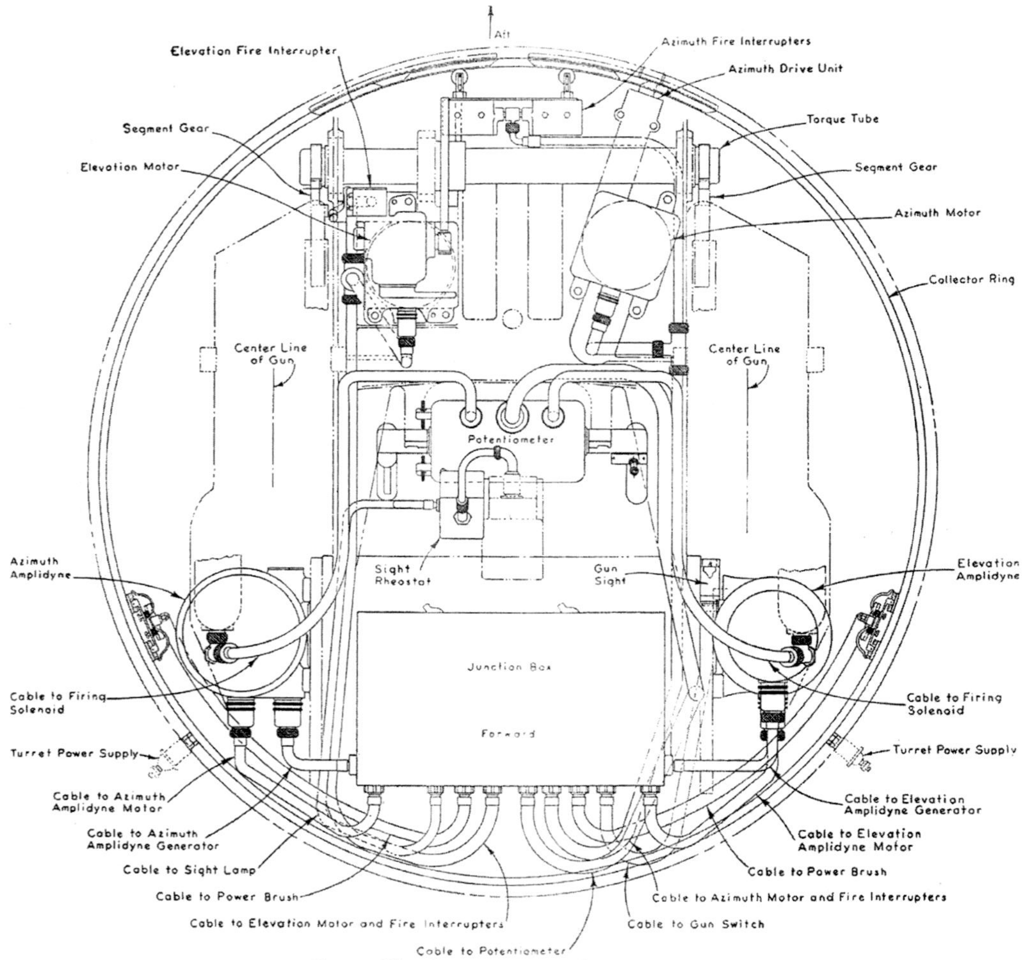

Figure 57. General Assembly Turret Drive

Page 72] MARTIN TURRET—MODEL 250CE-3 RESTRICTED

**Search for Other Turret Drives**

In March 1941 the Armament Laboratory conducted an analysis of the existing electric drive projects to plan future developments. The study determined that varying resistance controls in series with drive motor armature circuits were useless because they gave inherently poor speed control at varying loads. Variable resistance in drive motor field circuits gave too narrow a control range. Amplidyne control was considered to be excellent, but was excessively heavy. The DC pulsating controls stalled at slow speeds and had a tendency to arc excessively. The AC systems involving a rectifier and electronic grid control were also very heavy, but had the potential to be a simple, accurate control when fully developed. Finally, the torque amplifier was not sufficiently developed to evaluate properly. The study recommended using the amplidyne control for the present, but to continue the assessment of pulsation, torque amplifier, and rectified AC electron control systems for future use. Manufacturers submitting original drive systems were asked to supplement their proposals with test data to corroborate their claims pertaining to speed variations and load capacity. This would give the Armament Laboratory a method for making immediate evaluations and "for sorting the probables from the impossibles."

The Experimental Engineering Section sent letters of inquiry to a number of prospective drive manufacturing companies. The Briggs & Stratton Corporation of Milwaukee, WI, replied that it had sold its speed control division to the Graham Manufacturing Company at Providence, RI, who in turn responded that its speed control unit weighed over 200 pounds and had an estimated operating life of approximately 50 hours, which made it unacceptable for use in turrets. The Burklyn Corp. of Los Angeles replied that the operator of their transmission drive gear needed to exert an excessive 20 pounds of pressure. The General Motors New Departure Division at Bristol, CT, reported that its variable speed control, the "Transitorq," had been discontinued in 1938 and would not be suitable for aircraft use because of its significant lubrication requirements.

**Master Electric/Aircraft Associates Power Drive**

In February 1941, to relieve the Vickers bottleneck, the Materiel Division sent an inquiry to the Master Electric Company of Dayton, OH, to design a replacement power drive in collaboration with Emerson so that Emerson could fulfill the projected maximum production at its St. Louis factory. Nine months later, in November, the company had made little progress, and the Master drive design was so elementary and its development so slow that Emerson concluded that the Master Electric's drive unit would not be ready for months. However, Master Electric engineers remained confident that their drive was a "step in the right direction" toward a solution of the turret power problem: "We are so firmly of the belief that our drive has outstanding advantages from a tactical standpoint that we propose to do all the necessary work at our on expense and without imposing any obligation on the Government whatsoever." Five months later the completed Master drive finally appeared, but its controls were too stiff under load and unbalanced torques during a change of rotation, which made it unacceptable to the Materiel Division and forced them to continue their search for a suitable power drive.

In June 1942, engineers at the American Aircraft Associates of Dayton, OH, felt that the Master drive principle had merits and proposed to continue its development. This new manufacturer was confident that the mechanical traction type variable speed drive offered "distinct advantages over existing drives." On 2 June the company wrote to the Division: "Because of a fervent belief that it would be a serious loss to the Army Air Forces if this development were allowed to lie dormant, we are willing to undertake the job of carrying on the development work until a satisfactory conclusion is reached." To expedite the development of the drive unit Aircraft Associates engaged Hans Heynau, the creator of the principles involved in the Master variable-speed drive. In August 1942 Materiel Division rewarded the Aircraft Associates proposal with an Authority for Purchase, approving $6,955 to perfect a drive that would be interchangeable with the Vickers unit of a Sperry dorsal turret. The manufacturer began work toward a suitable design, but it was not until December 1943 that a demonstration installation was ready for testing.

Aircraft Associates pointed out many advantages for their improved Master drive. It was 15 pounds lighter than the Vickers installation; it was not influenced by temperature changes; and, in contrast to the Vickers version, it required only 22 amps current at neutral and 36 amps at full load compared to Vickers requirements of 37 and 48, respectively. In addition, the differential drive was reported to have a positive neutral, with no creep; no dead spots on the controls; no critical adjustments; and a speed spread approaching the ideal, with one-half the control displacement giving one-third the total speed. The entire unit was designed to be easily interchangeable with the Vickers installation in the field, and the manufacturer estimated a cost of $500 for their unit versus $1,400 for the Vickers drive. The Armament Laboratory tests confirmed the drive to be acceptable, and the manufacturer reported that it would be possible to produce up to 4,000 drive units per month after a four month tooling period. But in January 1944, when the Laboratory report was submitted, the Vickers unit bottleneck had already been broken and the urgent requirement for a substitute drive no longer remained, so the promising Aircraft Associates drive was abandoned.

### Graham Power Drive

As part of their search for a substitute drive unit, in June 1942 the Experimental Engineering Section sent the usual inquiry to Graham Transmissions, Inc., of Milwaukee. After a design conference with Wright Field engineers, Graham presented tentative drawings for a drive unit to be delivered in 90 days at an estimated prototype cost of $17 000. Because of the design's simplicity and ease of quantity manufacture the Materiel Division decided to promote its development as an alternate to existing drive systems. This drive was to be installed in a Steel Products manufactured dorsal Sperry turret to replace the two Vickers drive units. It consisted of two separate mechanical, variable-speed friction drives: one for azimuth and one for elevation linked to a common Diehl electric drive motor. Infinite variations in speed were obtained by tapered rollers in contact with rotating external ring gears. The gears operated in an oil-filled housing, and hydraulic servos provided the necessary force to move the ring along the tapered rollers.

By March 1943 Graham had not produced an acceptable drive despite its 90 day promise. In April the company reported that costs, excluding profit and the allowable 10% overhead, had reached $22,000, and that the drive still required work before it could be tested at Wright Field. Finally, when Graham's completed experimental model was tested, the results were poor. The gear system was noisy, and after a half hour of operation it overheated until it smoked. The 70-amp neutral, no-load current drain was twice the consumption of a Sperry turret equipped with Vickers drives. The hand control that connected the Graham drives demanded more than the normal amount of effort for tracking and then gave rough, uneven control.

The final Engineering Division report of 17 February 1944 revealed that the Graham drive was unsatisfactory, and since the venture had been started during a time of critical shortage of Vickers units and now that shortage no longer existed there was no need for the Graham unit to continue. The Engineering Division did see promise in the design and concluded: "The Graham power unit should be given more extensive performance tests to obtain information on this type of drive for future reference." Even if it didn't find a satisfactory replacement power drive, the experience demonstrated Wright Field to be more capable and efficient in managing armament development.

### Westinghouse Power Drive

Although Westinghouse did not immediately enter the turret market, the company spent most of 1941 and 1942 developing a drive unit. In December 1942 the Armament Laboratory received an innovative Westinghouse power unit for testing. The unit contained a silverstat resistor which was similar to the Westinghouse aircraft voltage regulator and controlled the speed of a variable speed friction drive via a differential follow-up. Included in the drive was a small gyro that sensed changes in the control deflection rate, but the Armament Laboratory thought that the gyro was unnecessary. However, a few months later the Laboratory suggested pairing the gyroscopic unit with an amplidyne control to produce the drive system for a fully stabilized turret. The stabilized turret control offered great future potential, as it denoted an important departure in the evolution of power turrets, but its further development was shelved.

### W.L. Maxson V-Belt and Electric Drive Units

In January 1941, the Materiel Division contacted the W.L. Maxson Corporation of New York to inquire about developing their drive unit for turret use. The Maxson unit consisted of a low torque control motor which regulated the speed of a high-torque drive motor by using two hydraulic pumps that braked the power drive through differentials. The Maxson torque amplifier met a developmental dead end, but in August 1941 the Armament Branch informed Wright Field of a Maxson control considered to be "the most interesting development yet made." It had been designed for the Brewster XB2A, which was intended for export to the Dutch. Brewster had originally selected Tucker for their power turret, but when Tucker's turret failed to materialize Maxson also assumed the development of the turret.

The Maxson turret drive had a V-belt control with infinite speed variation derived from adjustable pulley sheaves that determined the linear speed of the belt proportionally to the radius at which it turned. The Maxson drive held considerable promise as a turret drive, as its major advantage was that it did not require a large ring gear, which was the major turret problem at the time. Also, Maxson anticipated a capacity of 1,000 drive units per month with only $150,000 required for tool expansion. However, when Maxson built its experimental turret built around the V-belt drive it was a heavy, extremely large device that eliminated it from any consideration for acceptance.

Another Maxson turret drive proposal appeared in December 1941, when the Armament Laboratory purchased the Maxson electric drive for $13,425. This drive unit, like the V-belt drive, was given an initial sanction by Emerson engineers, who on 9 December 1941 wrote the Materiel Division:

> "....as promising as any of the electrical drives encountered to date. It has a number of advantages over the amplidyne drive in that it is much simpler, can be made of substantially standard parts, and its weight is in the order of one half that of the amplidyne. Its sensitivity is not as great

as the amplidyne, but it is believed that it will be satisfactory for the turret application."

The Maxson electric drive—a pulsation field control system—did not prove satisfactory when tested, and the type was limited to use in training turrets built by the Crocker-Wheeler Electric Manufacturing Company of New Jersey.

**Section 2: Power Operating Mechanisms**
**Electrical Turret Systems**
General Description
The basic electric turret drive was composed of a control unit, two electric turret drive motors, and two amplidyne motor-generators. The electrical turret obtained its power from the aircraft's electrical system generator. Typically, power was obtained through a silver-plated copper collector ring mounted on the inner side of the azimuth ring gear by insulated bolts. The power moved from the ring to the moving parts of the turret through brushes, and from there the power was transmitted to the various individual units.

The electric turret drive motors were geared to the turret drive mechanism: one motor was used to rotate the turret in azimuth and the other to rotate the guns. One amplidyne motor-generator was used to furnish power to one turret drive motor. The control unit consisted of two sets of potentiometers which controlled the output of the amplidyne motor-generators and thus the speed and direction of rotation of the drive motors. When the turret was operated on the ground, the aircraft engines were to be running

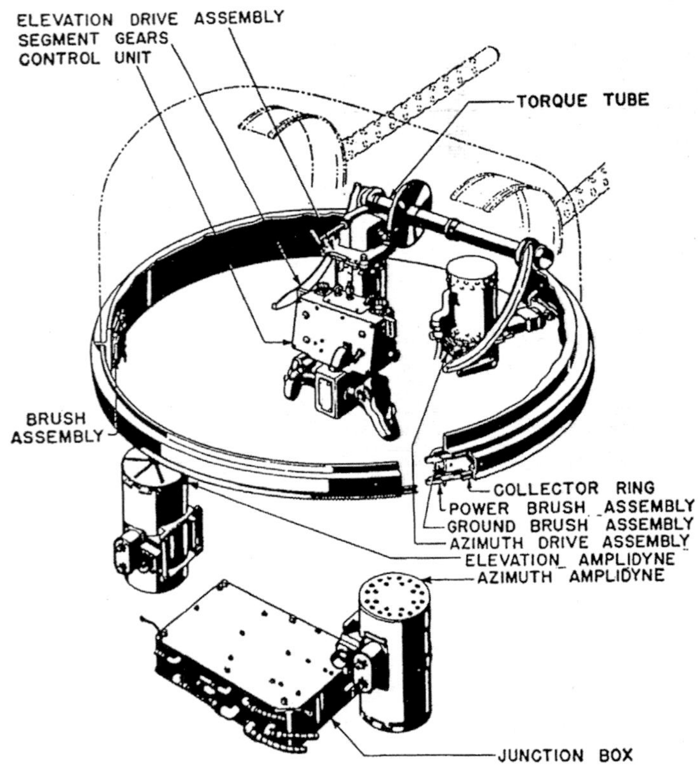

**Component of the Electric Turret** (USAAF)

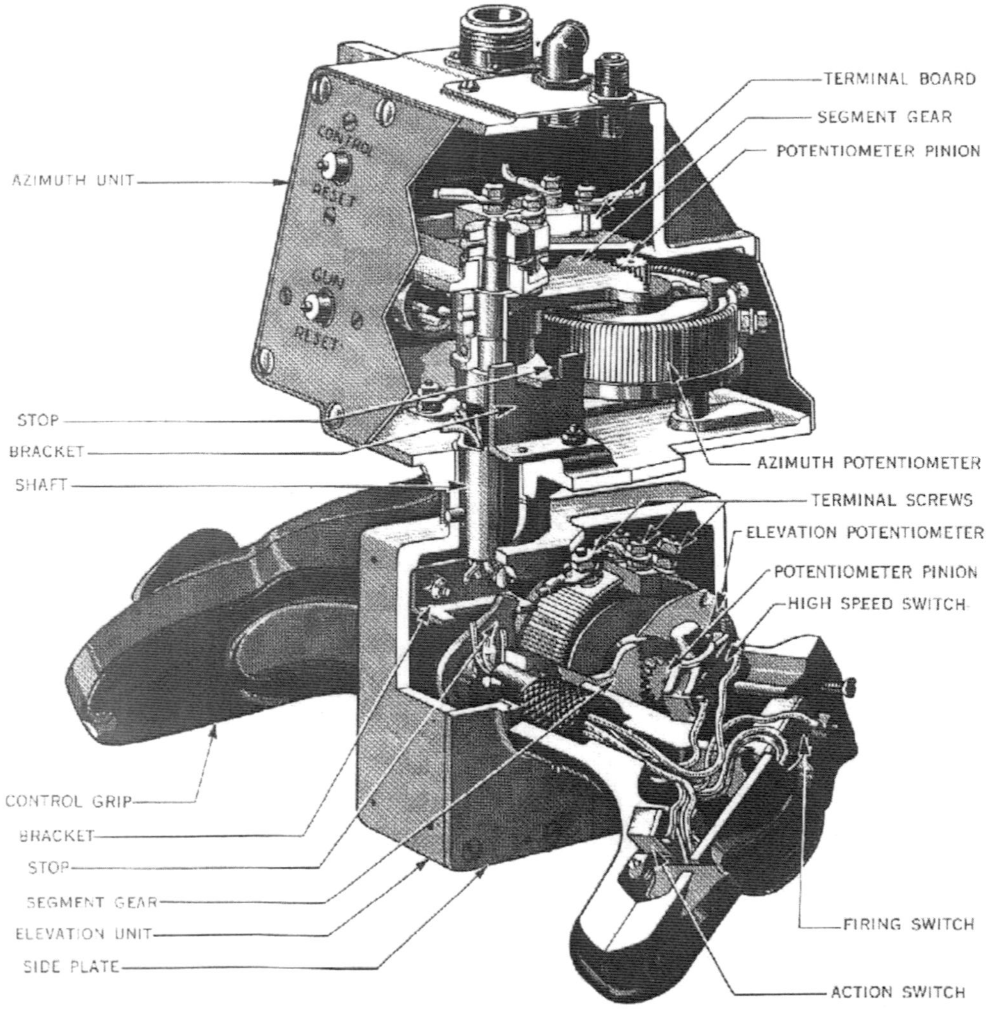

**Potentiometer Control Unit** (USAAF)

or an external power source was to be used that provided a constant 28-volt supply. If the turret electrical voltage dropped below 20 volts serious damage to the turret or to the aircraft was possible. Operation of the turret on the batteries was to be kept to an absolute minimum.

Potentiometer

The potentiometer is the device that is the heart of the electric turret, as it regulates electro-motive force (EMF), known as voltage. The potentiometer acts as a rheostat, dividing voltage, and is similar to a TV volume control rheostat that increases the volume when the knob is turned up. Turrets move in two planes: the horizontal, known as "train," or azimuth and the vertical (up and down), known as elevation and depression. The two potentiometers work through the control handle and control the movement of the turret in either azimuth or elevation. When the control handle was moved up it deflected the pointer on the potentiometer and when it moved down it depressed it.

Potentiometer Control Unit

The potentiometer control unit was the brain of the electric turret and consisted of a control box and control arm with two firing grips. Impulses originating from the control center determined everything the turret did. The gunner grasped the control handles of the control unit and depressed the action switch on each grip to energize the potentiometer coils located in the control unit. As the gunner gripped the handles to direct the turret they caused sliding pointers to pick off voltages from the two potentiometers (one for azimuth and the other for elevation). The polarity and magnitude of the voltages were applied to the amplidyne that then supplied power to the TDMs. The high-speed button was located on the right hand grip and the interphone microphone button on the left hand grip. Additional switches and overload circuit breaker resets were located on the control panel to protect the potentiometer coils, the ammunition booster circuit, and the firing circuit.

Amplidyne

The Amplidyne is a trade name meaning "to amplify power." In turret application, the amplidyne provides power for driving the turret motor. Originally the amplidyne was designed as a power control amplifier by the General Electric Company for a variety of industrial uses. During World War II it was found to have just the right control characteristics necessary for turret application. Power magnification had to be quick, precise, and two-directional in order to permit accurate driving of the turret up or down in elevation and right or left in azimuth, and the amplidyne provided this type of quick response.

The reason that an ordinary generator was not used to power a turret was that it couldn't furnish the quick, instantaneous response characteristic of the amplidyne. If the potentiometer was deflected clockwise for full HIGH-SPEED, the turret rotated clockwise at that speed and vice versa, as the polarity of the generated output changed instantaneously and the turret responded instantaneously.

The amplidyne was really a motor generator consisting of a direct current motor and a direct current generator enclosed in a single housing. The two rotors were pressed on a single shaft, supported by two ball bearings. Electric connections to the amplidyne unit were made through a connector receptacle mounted on the side of the unit. The amplidyne was similar to any ordinary separately excited generator in that it was a rotating machine which converted mechanical energy to electrical energy. But unlike any previous rotating machine, the amount of excitation was very much smaller. The ratio of the power required to excite the control field in relation to the power output was significantly less than the corresponding ratio in conventional types of generators. The speed of response was such that a small change in the excitation would produce a relatively large change in power output within a fraction of a second. When high-speed turret operation was desired to swing the guns toward an attacker the gunner pressed the high-speed button. The settings for Normal and High-speed turret operation were:

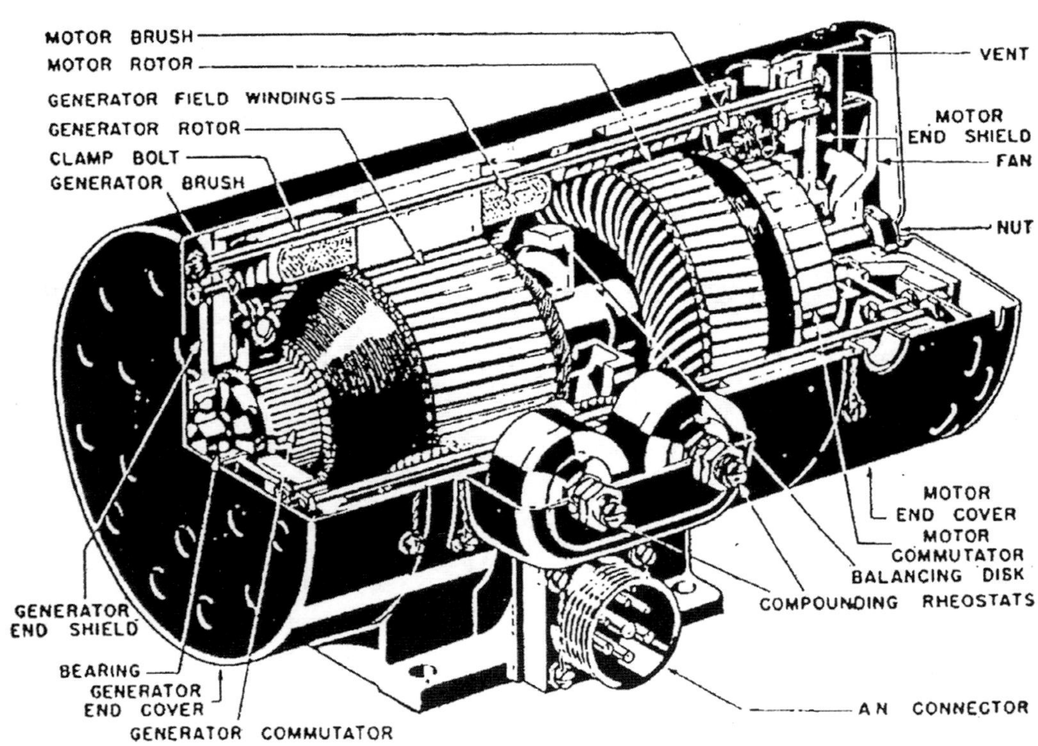


**Amplidyne** (USAAF)

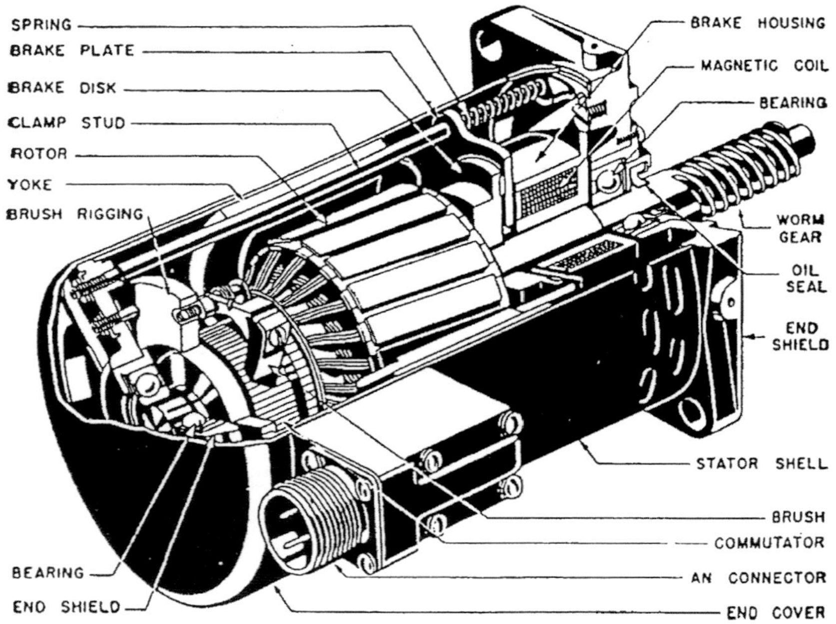


**TDM** (USAAF)

| | |
|---|---|
| Azimuth High-speed | 43° per second (8 seconds per revolution) |
| Azimuth Normal Speed | 20° per second (18 seconds per revolution) |
| Elevation High-speed | 30° per second (12 seconds per revolution) |
| Elevation Normal Speed | 12° per second (30 seconds per revolution) |

As the turret guns moved into the slipstream there was an increased load on the drive motors, and more current was needed to be supplied by the amplidyne generator to keep the turrets motors at the proper speed.

Turret Motor Drive (TDM)

The electric turret had two drive motors: one to drive the turret in elevation and depression and one to drive the turret in azimuth. Each of these turret drive motors received its operating power from its respective amplidyne. The Azimuth Amplidyne supplied power for the azimuth turret drive motor, and the Elevation Amplidyne supplied power for the elevation drive motor.

The turret drive motor, or TDM as it was commonly called, was known as a "separately-excited" motor. This term was applicable because the armature and the field of the motor were excited (energized) from different sources of power. The direction of rotation of a DC motor could be changed by reversing either the armature flux or the field flux. If both the field flux and the armature flux were reversed simultaneously the direction of rotation would remain the same. An ordinary shunt or series DC motor could not be used on the turret because the field flux was reversed whenever the armature excitation was reversed. If one of these two types were used, the turret would always run in one direction regardless of the polarity of the amplidyne output, which could not be reversed. On a turret, the TDM field was constantly excited from the aircraft power source, and the armature excitation was changed to reverse the rotation as the amplidyne output reversed, causing a quick response in two directions.

Junction Box

The junction box, usually located under the gunner's seat, served as the central distribution point for the electrical impulses originating in the control unit. The box contained a master switch located on the right side of the box that carried incoming electrical connections to the high-speed relay and the feed back voltage regulator (FBVR) resistors. The main power supply wires were connected directly to the azimuth and elevation switches, as were the dead man relays, the azimuth high-speed relay, and the azimuth and elevation switches. The line contactor relay was mounted inside the box and next to it were two anti-hunt capacitors. Below them were four enameled resistors, which were necessary for making speed adjustments by providing a path for the feedback voltage. The high-speed relay was mounted on the same bracket as the capacitors. There were also the vibrator inverter, radio noise filter, and two overload circuit breakers to protect the amplidynes. To prevent wires loosening from excessive vibration clips and washers were used to hold them to the terminal board. The box was provided with ventilation holes.

Mechanism of Fire Control in the Electric Turret

The amplidyne turret was designed to move guns in azimuth and in elevation. Azimuth rotation was rotation in a horizontal plane, while the swing of the guns in elevation was movement in a vertical plane. The field of fire in azimuth and elevation was controlled by a profile cam that actuated microswitches. The profile cam rotated in azimuth with the azimuth drive tube, and the microswitch assembly was moved up and down by means of a rod and chain that was connected to the elevating shaft of the guns. The up and down limits of the gun movement in elevation were automatically controlled by these elevation switches. When the guns approached either of the limits the switches were closed, applying electric dynamic brakes, stopping the guns. The limit switches were set so the guns could be fired freely in elevation or azimuth without danger of the bullets striking any part of the aircraft. Firing limits for each gun were controlled by separate cams, permitting one gun to fire while the other gun was in the restricted area.

Movement of the guns in elevation was controlled by changing the position of the turret control handles in elevation, moving elevation potentiometers that supplied current to the exciting field of an elevation amplidyne generator. The amount of exciting current was proportional to the swing of the control handles from the elevation neutral position, and established a generator output which drove a 1/2 horsepower elevation drive motor in a direction of rotation and at a rpm which was proportional to the elevation control handle position. The elevation drive motor was connected to the guns through a 1,050:1 gear train.

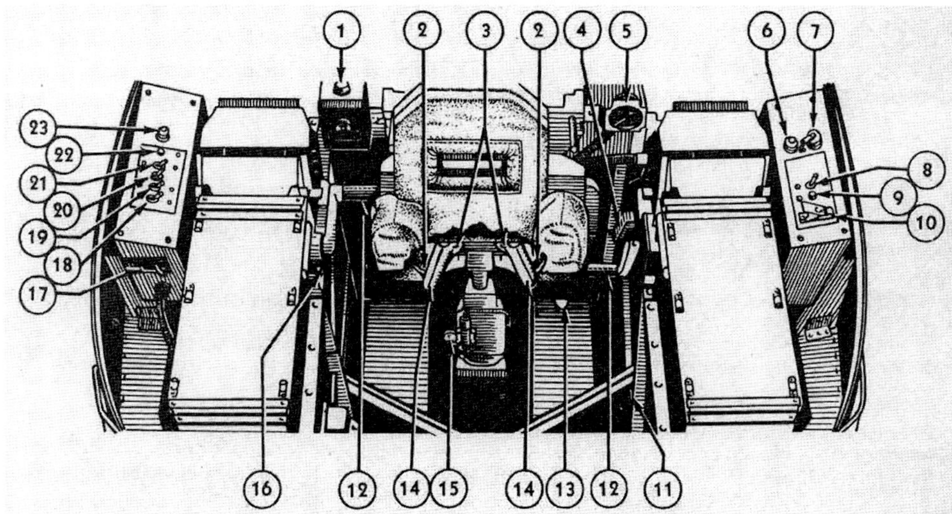

| Ref. No. | Nomenclature | Ref. No. | Nomenclature | Ref. No. | Nomenclature |
|---|---|---|---|---|---|
| 1 | *Interphone Box* | 9 | *Booster Circuit Breaker* | 17 | *Pump Switch* |
| 2 | *Action Switches* | 10 | *"Gun" and "Sight" Switch* | 18 | *Dome Light Switch* |
| 3 | *Microphone Switches* | 11 | *Elevation Clutch Lever* | 19 | *Charger Switch* |
| 4 | *Foot Pedal Stowage Handle* | 12 | *Manual Drive Handles* | 20 | *Camera Switch* |
| 5 | *High Pressure Gage* | 13 | *Foot Trigger* | 21 | *Main Power Switch* |
| 6 | *Red Warning Light* | 14 | *Control Handles* | 22 | *Main Power Circuit Breaker* |
| 7 | *Utility Receptacle* | 15 | *Low Pressure Gage* | 23 | *Power Indicating Light* |
| 8 | *Utility Receptacle Switch* | 16 | *Azimuth Clutch Handle* | | |

**Hydraulic Turret** (USAAF)

The turret was moved in azimuth by swinging the controller in azimuth, which moved potentiometers controlling the amount of current in the exciting field of an azimuth amplidyne generator. The output of the amplidyne generator was proportional to the degree of swing of the control handles from the azimuth neutral position. The output of the amplidyne generator controlled the speed of the 1/2 horsepower drive motor, moving the guns in azimuth through a 1,250:1 gear train in a direction of rotation and rounds per minute established by the control handle position.

### Hydraulic Turret Systems

When discussing hydraulic turrets, a basic hydraulic principle called Pascal's Principal must be discussed. The 350 year old principal states that an increase of pressure on any part of a confined liquid causes an equal increase in pressure throughout the liquid. When pressure in pounds per square inch (psi) is applied at one end of a container, the same pressure in pounds per square inch is exerted on every square inch of the surface of the container that is in contact with the liquid. The shape of the container makes no difference in the transfer of pressure. Hydraulic liquids can not be compressed (squeezed) into a smaller space than originally occupied. When pressure is applied at one end of a hydraulic line it is transmitted instantly to the other end.

The turret maintenance manual compared the hydraulic system to the human circulatory system. The basic turrent units were:

### Reservoir

The reservoir was a storage tank from which fluid was supplied to the pumps, and to which excess fluid forced out of the system was returned. When additional fluid was needed in the system, either for operating additional units or to replenish fluid lost through leaks or seepage, the pump could draw that fluid from the reservoir. Also, when increased temperatures caused the fluid to expand the excess was delivered to the reservoir. The reservoir also provided a place where the fluid could settle and purge any air bubbles that had formed in the system. Foreign matter in the fluid was removed in the reservoir by filters, pumps, or similar apparatus.

A vent line emerged from the top of the tank and traveled down along the right side, turning under the tank. This vent line exposed the fluid in the reservoir to atmospheric pressure, preventing a vacuum from forming inside the reservoir and preventing the build up of air pressure inside the reservoir. Also, it served as a spill pipe for excess fluid that accumulated in the reservoir, and it allowed the escape of any air that was carried into the reservoir from small trapped air pockets in the lines and operating units. The armorer was instructed to keep this vent clean.

Filler Pipe

The filler pipe entered the reservoir much below the top in order to prevent over-filling, and to provide a space above the fluid for expansion when the reservoir was filled to its normal level. This expansion resulted from increases in temperatures and from foaming of the liquid.

Filler Cap

The filler cap was leak tight, so that the fluid couldn't escape when the aircraft was maneuvering or when the fluid inside expanded. A measuring rod attached to the filler cap or a glass sight-gage indicated the level of fluid inside the reservoir similar to the oil measuring stick in an auto crankcase. The baffles and fins inside the tank prevented excessive foaming or turbulence of the fluid when the fluid was flowing back from the return lines.

Standpipe

The standpipe was connected with the power-pump suction line at the bottom of the tank. The inlet of the standpipe was located far above the bottom of the tank to prevent the power pump from ever using up all the fluid in the tank. Thus, when the power pump stopped there was still enough fluid available for the hand pump. Instead of using a standpipe, some systems attached the power pump outlet to the side of the reservoir at a point above the bottom of the tank.

Fluid Return Line

The fluid return line usually entered the reservoir at a spot below the normal level of the fluid in the reservoir in such a manner as to cause the least possible disturbance of the fluid

**Hydraulic Fluid**

The turret maintenance manual compared hydraulic fluid to the "lifeblood" of the hydraulic system. It was stored in the reservoir and flowed from there to fill the entire hydraulic system, furnishing the basis for transmitting hydraulic power. There are two types of hydraulic fluids: mineral-based and vegetable-based. Most World War II turrets used mineral fluids, which were colored red, while vegetable-based hydraulic fluids were colored blue. The two types did not mix. Mineral oils deteriorated natural rubber, while vegetable oil was fine. Vegetable oils destroyed synthetic rubber tubing, but they were immune to mineral oils. The turret maintenance manual suggested that maintenance men remember the following: "Red-blooded turret men prefer red mineral oil base fluid."

**Hydraulic Lines**

As per the turret maintenance manual, if hydraulic fluid was the blood of the hydraulic system then the lines were the arteries and veins that carried the fluid through the system. The lines were metal and rubber tubes, and were joined by tube connectors and tube fittings of many shapes and sizes.

Aluminum alloy tubing was used in most turret systems because it was light and pliable, and yet strong enough to withstand up to 1,500psi.

Synthetic rubber and fabric tubing was used where flexible hose construction was required. Synthetic rubber was used due to the shortage of natural rubber (that required vegetable oil base fluid to be used).

In a hydraulic system, various packings sealed fluid under pressure in the system and kept air out. Whenever the hydraulic lines were connected to hydraulic units the moving parts, vibration, access ports to get at the units, and the connections themselves created so-called "Danger Spots" that were fluid leaks from and air ingress into the system.

**Hydraulic Pumps**

Two types of power-driven pumps, the variable displacement and constant displacement, were normally used in hydraulic turret systems. They were sometimes called variable volume and constant volume pumps. The variable displacement type pumped at a varying rate, depending on the volume requirements at a given time, while the constant displacement type pumped at a constant rate and its capacity and volume were fixed.

Vickers Pump

The Vickers variable displacement (or volume) pump was used on nearly all hydraulic turrets. It was ideally suited to turret operations, as it was designed to automatically produce constant pressure at a varying volume, depending on how much volume was required at a certain instant. When there was a greater demand for fluid in the system the pressure tended to drop slightly, and the pump maintained the pressure and supplied the necessary volume of fluid. The pump was so sensitive that if the pressure was deficient by only a small amount, the pump would supply the system with just that fraction of pressure to bring the system pressure to normal.

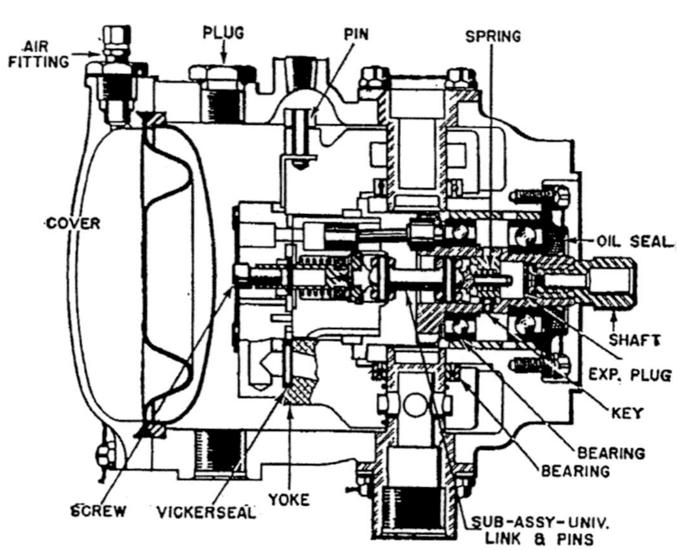


**Vickers Pump Cross-Section** (USAAF)

To understand how a variable delivery pump operates the turret manual stated:

"Think about hydraulic pressure and the relationship between pressure and volume. Remember that no comparison can be made between air pressure and hydraulic pressure. Air can be compressed in suitable containers, and the pressure so stored can be used later. Hydraulic fluid, however, cannot be compressed. And hydraulic pressure can't be stored to be used as needed."

In order to obtain hydraulic pressure a driving force is the hydraulic pump, which creates hydraulic pressure within the system by pushing the hydraulic fluid through the passages. However, in order to have hydraulic pressure there must be a resistance of some kind. If the outlet port of the hydraulic pump is connected to the inlet port by a long tube, the system filled with fluid, and the pump set in motion, no pressure will be created. The fluid will merely circulate slowly or rapidly, depending on the speed of the pump.

But if a hydraulic motor is installed in the line, and a load put on the motor shaft, pressure will build up in the lines. Because the motor, with its load, will be offering a resistance to the flow of fluid, while more fluid is being pushed against it, pressure begins to form at the point where the resistance is located and backs up toward the source of power.

Volume is the measurement of fluid flow. Pressure is the amount of power available. Once operating pressure has been reached practically no volume is required, except to make up for leakage losses. As soon as the operating pressure is put to work more volume is required—but only enough to maintain the pressure, or push, behind the fluid that is doing the work. Operation is fully automatic, since the variable delivery pump is designed to build up and maintain a pressure, thereby maintaining a balance between pressure and volume in an inverse ratio.

Constant Displacement Pump

The constant displacement pump was used in the Motor Products Corporation's (MPC) turret hydraulic system. Most of the internal mechanisms and all of the actual pumping system were the same in both of these Vickers pumps (variable and constant).

There were seven cylinders spaced equally around the cylinder block axis, and the cylinder bores were parallel to that axis. The cylinder block was linked to the driving mechanism by a universal block so that the driving mechanism and cylinder block rotated at the same speed. When the driving mechanism and cylinder block were rotated, the position of each piston in its cylinder was changed. As this driving mechanism and the cylinder block were thus rotated about their axes and the pistons started their movement away from the cylinder head, a port in the cylinder head opened to allow fluid to be drawn into the cylinder. When the piston reached the bottom of its stroke the discharge port was opened, and fluid was forced from this port to the system by the upward motion of the piston. This cycle was repeated as each piston traveled down, and then up, in its cylinder.

The variable displacement pump worked in a similar way, except that the angle of the cylinder block was variable. Thus, when more volume was required the angle was increased to produce more output. When less volume was needed the angle was decreased automatically.

Hand Pump
The hand pump was not considered one of the basic hydraulic units, as it was designed for emergency use when the power and the electrically-driven pumps failed. The hand pump was very simple, consisting of a cylinder with inlet and outlet ports, a piston, and a handle that operated the piston. It could also be used to check the hydraulic system when the aircraft's engines were not running and there was no power.

To operate the hand pump the handle was pulled toward the right, moving the piston toward the left. The liquid in front of the piston was forced out of the cylinder through the check valve of the outlet port while the piston drew in fluid through the inlet valve. When the pump handle was pulled back the piston moved down, forcing the liquid out of the end of the cylinder while more liquid flowed into the end. The check valves in the inlet ports prevented the fluid in the pump from being forced back into the reservoir. The check valves in the outlet ports prevented the fluid in the system from being drawn back into the pump. The hand pumps were well designed, with the area of the piston and the length of the handle proportioned so that the operator could develop high pressures without a lot of physical labor.

**Pressure Regulator /Compensating Valve**
The pressure regulator, called the compensating valve, was built into the variable displacement pump. Vickers pumps were power-driven, and the unit which did the driving was a small electric motor that turned an output shaft, using a reduction gear system. This gear assembly consisted of a bevel gear riveted to a steel shaft that was mounted on two ball bearings. The motor assembly was installed on the hydraulic pump by a drilled machined face on the gear housing, through which the splined end of the output shaft was accessible. The motor, turning clockwise when viewed from the drive end, supplied the power for turning the assembly. The external spline of the hydraulic pump, to which the motor was attached, fit into the internal spline of the gear shaft, and the hydraulic pump was actuated. The source of power to operate the electric motor was supplied by the generator system of the aircraft's engine or its auxiliary power plant (APU).

On constant displacement pump turrets, a device called a pressure regulator fulfilled the same purpose as the compensating valve. The compensating valve pivoted a yoke on the pump and changed the stroke of the piston as required to meet the varying demands for volume. The pressure regulator, as its name suggests, was a device for regulating the pressure in the system. It was placed between the power pump and the system so as to bypass the oil just as soon as the system pressure reached the upper limit of the pressure range for which the regulator was adjusted. When that pressure value was reached a valve in the pressure regulator opened. The output of the power pump, which had been flowing into the system beyond the pressure regulator, could no longer pass the regulator and was shuttled from pump to reservoir, to pump, to reservoir, to pump, to reservoir. This bypass circuit through the regulator continued until the pressure in the system reached the lower limit of the range for which the regulator was adjusted. The valve then closed, and the output of the pump was once more sent past the pressure regulator and on into the system. The pressure regulator could be set to pass fluid into the system over a broad range of pressures.

**Selector Valves**
Hydraulic fluid stored in the reservoir was then pumped through the system, but the flow had to be directed to the point in the system where hydraulic pressure was to be used to perform a particular function at a particular time. The function of directing was accomplished by the hydraulic selector valves, which were the control switches of the aircraft hydraulic system. They were used to direct the flow of fluid to, or from, the selected unit in the system, and so controlled the fluid's direction of motion, the amount of motion, and the speed. There was usually a selector valve for each hydraulically operated unit in the system.

This valve was commonly called a four-way selector valve because it had four ports that connected with the system. A line from the pump entered the top of the selector valve housing while a return line to the reservoir was connected to the bottom. There also was a line extending to each end of the actuating cylinder. By turning the valve, it was possible to direct the fluid from the pressure line to either end of the actuating cylinder. Fluid was forced from the opposite end of the actuating cylinder by the motion of the piston. This fluid was forced through an opening in the selector valve and returned to the reservoir, where it was ready to be used again.

**Clarke Control Valves**
The turret's speed and direction were controlled by a special type of selector valve connected to the control handles called the Clarke DO5C Gun Turret Control Valve. This control valve included the control handles, safety or "dead man" switches, and trigger switches. The valve assembly consisted basically of two four-way valves combined in one housing: one for the

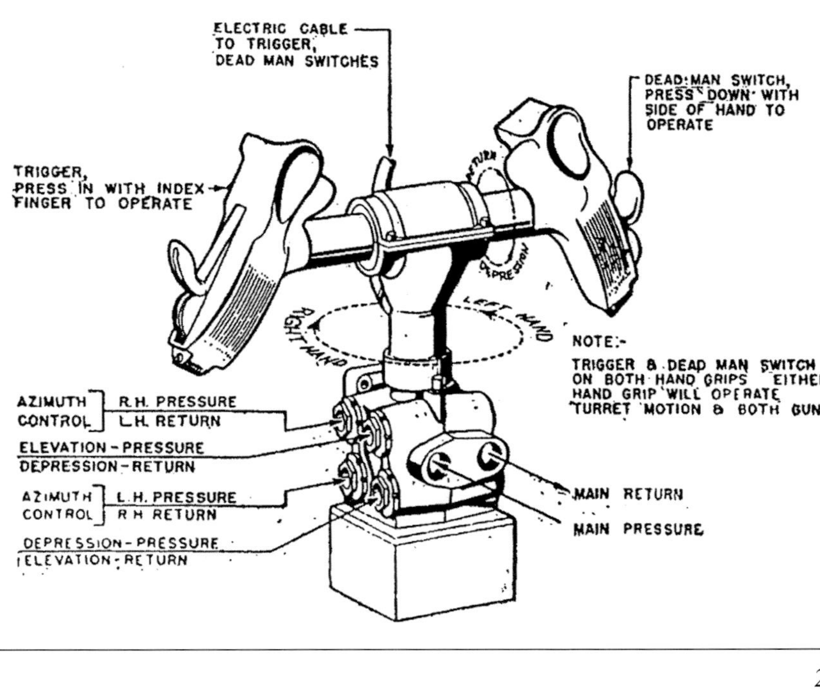


**Clarke Control Valve** (USAAF)

operation of the elevation and lowering of the guns, and the other to control the train of the turret. It was necessary to control the amount of fluid acting upon the hydraulic motors or cylinders so that either or both would operate smoothly through all speed ranges from zero to maximum.

The Clarke control valve took the high pressure oil from the pump and moved it selectively in one of two directions in the elevation and azimuth systems. In this way, movement of the control handle in any direction automatically regulated the flow to drive the proper (elevation or azimuth) cylinder in the corresponding direction. The valve housing had six ports: two on the exterior surface and four on the bottom surface. The two ports on the exterior surface were for the pressure and return lines. The four on the bottom were for the lines controlling both the horizontal and elevation movement of the turret and gun carriage.

The gunner had to be able to accurately control the amount of fluid passing through each four-way valve. To facilitate the operation a single vertical control column was used. The control column was provided with two hand grips mounted on a horizontal shaft which turned in bearings supported in the top of the vertical column. Rotation of the grips was limited about their horizontal axis and operated the four-way valve controlling the elevation

**Power Actuating Units**

Since hydraulics were never used alone to operate a mechanism, the actuating cylinder was a mechanical device to start or finish the operation. It was the part of the hydraulic system that imparted motion to or actuated the turret. Actuating cylinders existed in many designs and sizes because they had to do many different tasks, but the principles of operation of all such cylinders were the same.

A closed end cylinder had a piston inside that operated a piston rod on one end only. Seals or packings were installed on the piston and in the cylinder end around the piston rod to prevent the fluid from leaking. Ports opening into each end of the cylinder allowed the hydraulic fluid to enter and leave. These ports alternated as inlet and outlet ports, depending on the flow to the cylinder from the selector valve.

Fluid under pressure entered the left hand port and forced the piston toward the right hand end of the cylinder. The motion of the piston was transmitted to a movable object by the piston rod. As the piston moved forward in the cylinder it pushed ahead of it (and out of the cylinder by way of the right hand port) any fluid that was in the forward end of the cylinder. This fluid was carried back to the reservoir by the return lines.

If the setting of the selector valve was changed the pressure line became the return line, and vice versa. Then fluid entered the forward end of the cylinder and the piston moved backward. As it did this the piston pushed the fluid out of the back end of the cylinder.

By varying the diameter of the piston the force applied to the device to be operated could be varied. Therefore, actuating cylinders were made in various diameters depending on the force desired. The length of the cylinder depended on the required amount of movement of the device that was to be operated.

Double-acting cylinders were self-bleeding because fluid from the cylinder was returned to the reservoir during each stroke of the piston. Therefore, all air could be removed from the cylinder and connecting lines by several strokes of the piston.

**Hydraulic Motors**

In some cases, hydraulic motors were used in turrets instead of actuating cylinders when rotary motion was required. Hydraulic motors were similar in construction to piston-type hydraulic pumps. The principal difference between the pumps and motors was in the arrangement of inlet and outlet valves. A special type of control valve was used to control the direction and speed of hydraulic motors. This valve controlled the volume of fluid as well as the direction of flow.

A piston type hydraulic motor looked exactly like the Vickers piston pump. Fluid under pressure was introduced into either of the two ports in the pump body depending on the setting of the control valve. Similar to the actuating cylinder, the other port became the return port. If the fluid flowed through the motor in one direction the motor drive shaft turned one way. If the fluid flowed through in the other direction the drive shaft turned in the opposite direction. The mechanical unit that was being operated turned in the same direction as the drive shaft.

**Relief Valves**

Relief valves acted as safety valves, and were placed in the hydraulic system to keep the pressure from reaching too high a level and to control pressures if they threatened to get out of control. Several types were used in the hydraulic systems, but in each type the basic design included a spring-loaded valve arranged so that it automatically opened to relieve the system pressure when the fluid pressure acting on one face of the valve became sufficient to overcome the spring pressure applied to the opposite face. The relief valve closed immediately when the pressure dropped to a value less than the spring loading.

Ball-Type Relief Valve

A typical ball-type valve utilized a spring-loaded ball resting on a hardened steel valve seat inside the housing. An adjusting screw was installed so that the spring pressure could be varied and the operating limit of the relief valve regulated. The valve was enclosed in a valve body containing integral inlet and outlet bosses and a valve seat. A highly polished hardened-steel ball was held on the valve seat by a steel coil spring. This valve was held between two spring guides that were metal disks that had integral bosses which slipped inside the spring ends. One of the spring guides pressed on the ball while the other was in contact with the adjusting screw in the upper end of the relief valve. The valve body was internally threaded at its upper end to receive a bushing that carried the adjusting screw and locknut. An aluminum alloy dust cap enclosed the adjusting screw,

Balanced Relief Valve

The balanced-type relief valve had the advantage of smooth operation because it operated without the chattering effect produced by the ball-type valve. It operated with fluid from the pump entering port A and leaving through port B to enter the system. Meanwhile, some of the fluid also moved through the metering hole into the upper chamber and moved to the spring-loaded ball. When the pressure reached a predetermined value it overcame the spring and unseated the ball, the fluid rushed past the metering hole, and the pressure was applied to unseat a valve that allowed the fluid from the pump to flow freely to the reservoir. When the spring overcame the oil pressure, the ball reseated and the spring assisted the two valves to return to their original positions, allowing the pressure to build up in the system again.

**Accumulator**

The accumulator accumulated potential hydraulic power. It stored fluid when the demands of the system were low and then, when the capacity of the pump was inadequate to perform all the work required of it, the accumulator fed its reserve of fluid to the system's units to keep the systems functioning. The accumulator also served as a source of hydraulic power when the pump failed to function and emergency operation of certain units was necessary. In a third function the accumulator performed as a surge chamber to prevent sudden surges of fluid pressure from damaging the system.

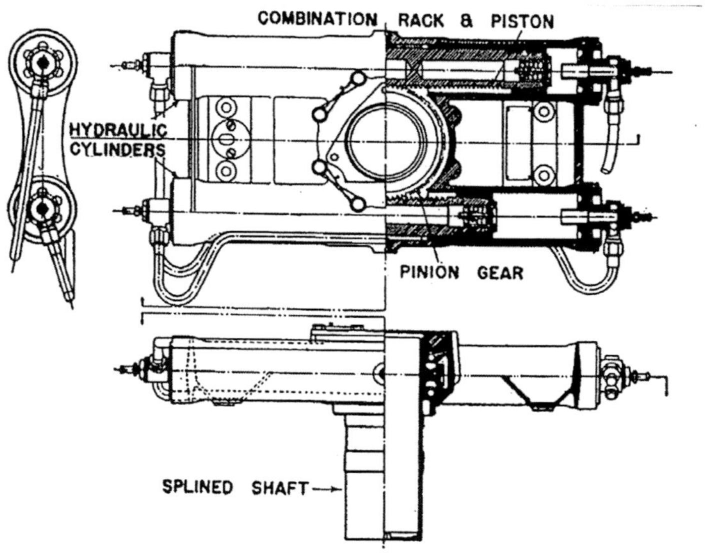


**Parker Elevating Unit** (USAAF)

The accumulator was made up of two forged steel hemispheres which were screwed together to form the complete sphere. The halves were separated by a rubber diaphragm, thus forming two chambers. The upper chamber was the fluid chamber, and was connected to the fluid supply line at a point close to the unit it was to operate. The lower half of the accumulator was the air pressure chamber, and was fitted with an air valve that was similar to the valve on automobile tires, and was used for charging the chamber with compressed air. Air was pumped into the chamber at a pressure specified for each installation, usually one-third of the system operating pressure.

With the accumulator charged and the fluid chamber empty, the diaphragm was forced against the walls of the fluid chamber by air pressure. The introduction of fluid into the fluid chamber caused the diaphragm to be forced towards the walls of the air chamber. This further compressed the air charge and increased the pressure to that of the fluid. When the fluid pressure in the line to which the fluid chamber was connected dropped below the system's operating pressure, the air expanded and forced the diaphragm toward the fluid chamber walls. This forced the fluid from the accumulator into the system. The accumulator again was charged with fluid during periods when the demands of the system did not require the full output of the engine pump.

### Filters

The reservoir filter (or strainer) prevented any "sabotage" of the hydraulic fluid by fragments of metal, dirt, or other contaminants. The edge-type filter was commonly used in turrets, and was usually installed on the system return line, which was the ideal location for them. This filter removed foreign substances from the fluid when it passed between the surfaces of metal disks. It was then cleaned from the disks by rotating them with the handle. Cleaner blades extended between two adjacent rotating disks that scraped the foreign matter from them, and it dropped it to the bottom of the filter. The filters had integral bypass valves that opened to allow fluid to pass if the filter element was clogged. This should not have occurred if the filter handle was turned daily or before each flight and the filter element was periodically disassembled and washed in a solvent.

### Check Valves

Check valves were positioned throughout the hydraulic system to prevent the hydraulic fluid from entering areas it shouldn't. The most common turret check valve was the spring-loaded ball-type, in which the ball was held against its seat in the valve body by spring compression. Installed in a fluid line, the valve remained in the closed position until the fluid pressure acting on the inlet side of the ball reached a pressure greater than the combined spring and fluid pressure acting on the opposite side of the ball. Then, the ball left its seat and the fluid was free to flow through the check valve. As soon as the fluid pressure in the inlet side of the ball dropped below that on the outlet side, the spring returned the ball to its seat and prevented the fluid from flowing in the opposite direction. In this way, fluid pressure was maintained in the portion of the system that was protected by the check valve. In hydraulic lines, where it is particularly important to prevent the reverse flow of any fluid, a double ball-check valve was used. This valve had the same effect as installing two separate check valves in the line.

### Elevation/Azimuth Units

Elevation

The Parker hydraulic elevating unit consisted of a large housing that contained a central spur gear attached to the left turret trunnion tube that was attached to the saddle. Above and below this gear were two racks lying in a horizontal plane and meshing with the gear. On each side of the racks were pistons that were driven by hydraulic pressure regulated by the control valve, making the rack double-acting. The opposite ends of the two racks were interconnected, providing rotation of the turret structure to aim the guns in elevation.

Azimuth

The azimuth drive was bolted to the roller casting under the left hand hub of the saddle. It consisted of three pieces: the main gear box, a hydraulic motor, and a 90° manual drive gear box. The main gear box consisted of a worm and gear enclosed in housing with a small pinion outside the shaft which meshed with the large ring gear on the turret track. At right angles to this latter shaft was the worm shaft with a spline on each end. A seven cylinder fixed stroke motor connected one end of the worm shaft. On the other end of the worm shaft the 90° manual drive was attached. There was a square shaft to which a hand crank could be attached for emergency manual azimuth movement from inside the turret.

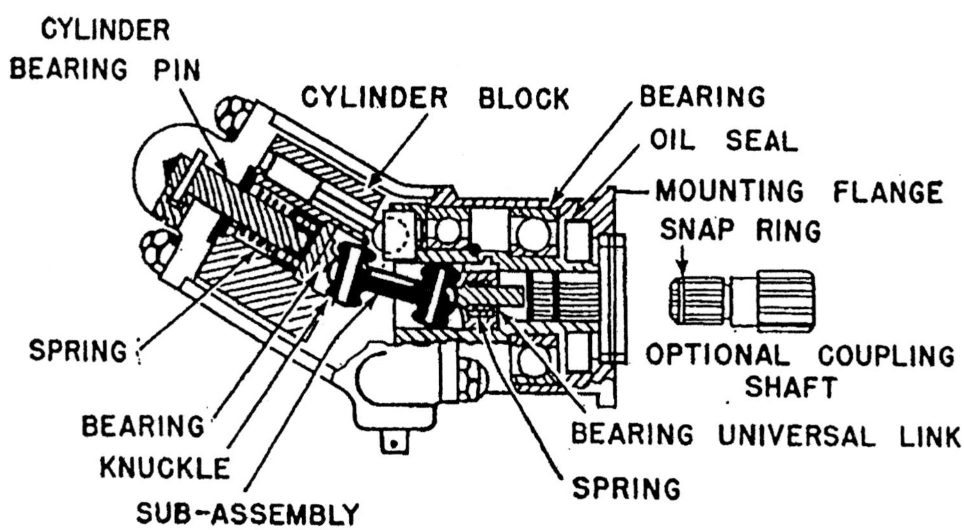


**Azimuth Motor** (USAAF)

# 3

# Auxiliary Turret Equipment and Turret Maintenance

### Oxygen System

Because of the high altitudes the bombers operated at the oxygen system was the most important auxiliary unit. The gunner had a mask connected by a flexible tube to a demand-type regulator that automatically adjusted the flow of oxygen to the amount required at various altitudes. A flow and pressure gauge indicated if oxygen was flowing and the amount remaining. If the pressure dropped below 100 pounds—the danger level—a warning light flashed. The oxygen supply to most turrets originated from the bomber's central tanks, but some turrets had one or two oxygen bottles which supplied oxygen for one to one and a half hours, but could also be filled from the central supply.

Before each mission the gunner was to check all oxygen system connections to be certain that they were all tight and that all hoses had no cracks or leaks. The gunner was then to put on his mask and connect it to check if oxygen was flowing. The pressure gauge was checked to be certain that there was enough oxygen for the entire mission as had been predetermined by the crew chief.

### Heated Suit Outlet

The heated flying suit operated much like an electric blanket, as by adjusting a rheostat the gunner could be comfortable at all times. There were two types of plug-ins. One, used by the Army and Navy, consisted of a box with two outlets, one marked HEATED SUIT and the other 24-volts. The rheostat was turned to HIGH and then could be ignored, as the rheostat built into the suit could regulate the temperature. The other type, used only by the Navy, consisted of a normal electrical outlet located on the control panel or nearby. Before each mission the gunner was to plug in his heating suit and turn the box rheostat to HIGH and then test the rheostat in the suit, turning it from HIGH to LOW. (For a more detailed account of the heated flying suit see Part Six/Chapter 5/Section 4: Waist Gun Installations)

### Interphone

The radio interphone system allowed crew members in a noisy bomber, stationed far apart, to communicate via a throat, oxygen mask, or hand-held microphone and earphones that plugged into a jack box in or near the turret. The jack box was of two types: selector or non-selector. The non-selector type jack box was equipped with a push-to-talk button and a volume control. In later turrets an additional push-to-talk button was built into the control handles. The push-to-talk button for the selector-type jack box was located on or near the control handles. The jack box was provided with a volume control button and the selector with five different positions:

INTER: This position allowed the gunner to hear and talk to all other crew members whose jack boxes were on.
INTER CALL: This position was only used when it was necessary to talk to a crew member whose jack box switch was not on.

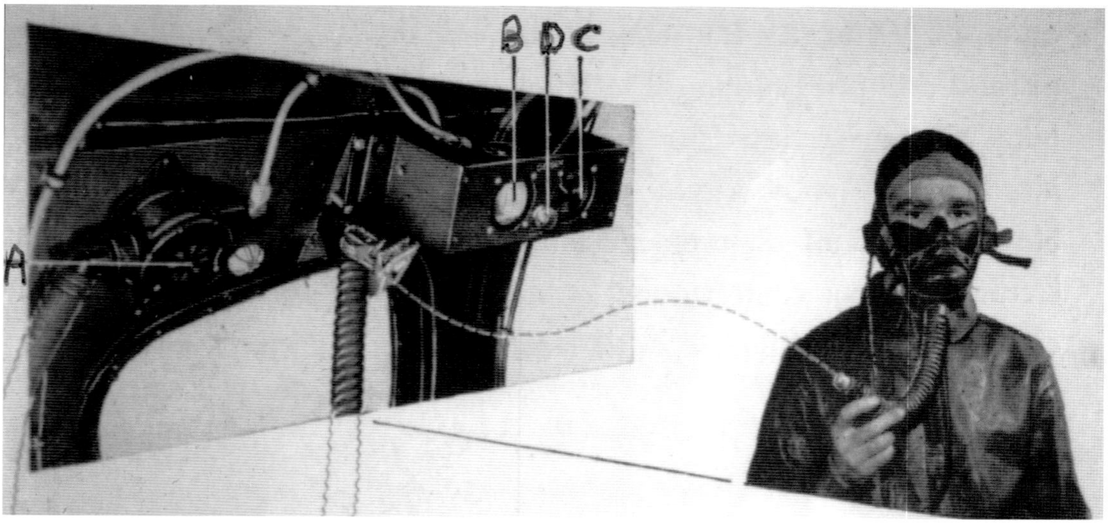


**Oxygen System:** A= Regulator, B= Flow Gauge, C=Pressure Gauge, D=Warning Light (USAAF)

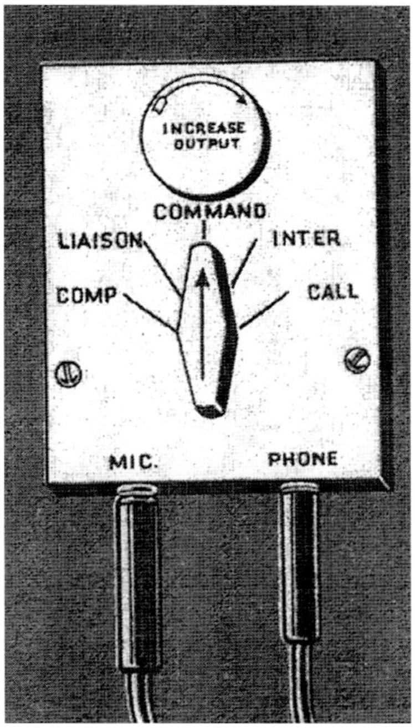


**Interphone Jack Box** (USAAF)

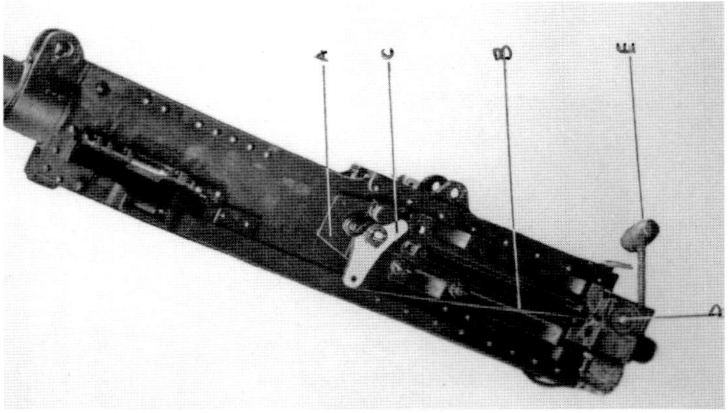

**Mechanical Charger:** A=Charger Plate, B=Cable, C=Pulley Lever, D=Charger Handle, D=Pulley (USAAF)

INTER COMP: In this position the gunner could hear the radio compass receiver.
LIAISON: In this position the gunner heard the pilot's Very High Frequency command equipment used for plane-to-plane communication.
COMMAND: In this position the pilot's Medium Frequency command equipment, generally used for plane-to-ground communications such as landing instructions.

To speak over the interphone system the gunner had to hold down the push-to-talk button, and in doing so would hear his own voice. The button was to be released immediately after talking so that he could hear further messages from crew members. Normal conversation was to be used and not shouting, as it distorted voices. The volume control knob on the jack box adjusted the volume of the earphones. Interphone operation was seriously hampered if more than one push-to-talk button on the aircraft was held down at the same time at high attitudes. Only in an emergency was another crew member allowed to speak while someone else was speaking. Before every mission the interphone was to be tested by each crew member to be certain that they could hear and be heard.

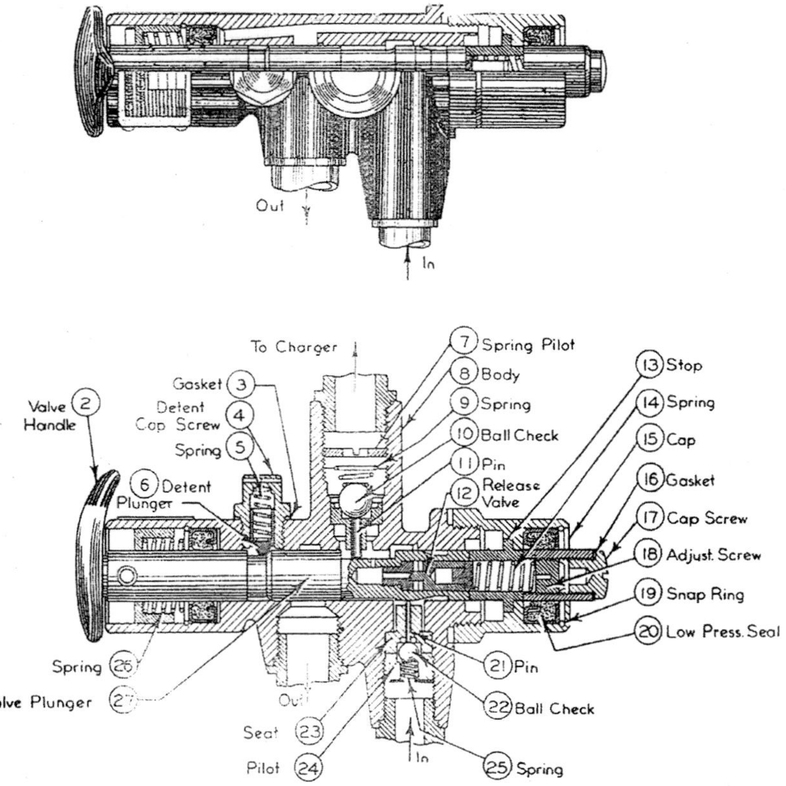


**Hydraulic Gun Charger** (USAAF)

**Gun Chargers**

Mechanical

Most chargers operated mechanically by a pulley-and-cable apparatus by which the gunner simply pulled two cables, each charging a gun. The gun charger was tested without ammunition in the guns. The gunner checked to be sure the charger plate was wired to the gun's receiver and was properly bolted. When the gunner pulled the charger handles the cables were to be straight and riding freely in their pulleys and correctly attached to their levers. When loading the ammunition into the guns before takeoff the first round in the ammunition belt was pushed into the feedway, and the gun would then have to be charged twice after the aircraft was in the air to be sure that the first round entered the chamber and was ready to fire. The pilot signaled the gunners when to charge their guns.

Hydraulic Gun Chargers

Twin machine guns were provided with Bendix hydraulic gun chargers that were mounted on the outboard side of either gun. On single gun installations the chargers could be mounted on either the right or left side of the gun. The pressure for their operation was supplied by the turret hydraulic system and the accumulator, which maintained reserve pressure to replace that diverted to the chargers.

To operate the gun charger the control handles were set into the firing position. The charger valve operated the gun chargers when the charger valve handle was pushed down to operate the chargers, and by rotating the handle, the charger was held in either a safe position or in the firing position. The valve plunger was depressed through a stroke of 3/8 inch and remained in that open position. When the valve plunger was in this open position fluid was free to flow to the charger cylinder until the gun bolt was fully retracted. When the gun bolt struck the gun buffers the valve plunger automatically closed, opening the passage from the charging cylinder to the return line and allowing the hydraulic charger cylinder to the return as the fluid was discharged from the cylinder by action of the charger spring.

Compressed Air Gun Chargers

The automatic General Electric compressed air gun chargers had two functions: charging the guns by pulling the bolt back and operating a solenoid to fire the gun by releasing the firing pin. Once the POWER-AUX switch was turned ON the compressor began to build up air pressure and would automatically stop when the pressure was sufficient, and would begin again when the pressure dropped. When the gunner closed the firing trigger the gun would either fire normally or, when the gun failed to fire, the charger operated for four seconds to charge the gun, after which an automatic timer would stop it. Early gun chargers used carbon dioxide cylinders.

**Gun Camera**

The gun camera was mounted on a small bracket, usually located near the gunsight. A switch on the control panel operated the camera. When the switch was ON, the camera exposed film as long as the gunner was pressing the gun trigger (For more details on the gun camera see Part Four: Gunsights/Chapter 3).

**Camera (arrow)** (USAAF)

**Trouble Light**

A small trouble light with a switch and about six feet of cord was supplied for working in the dark. The bulb socket was adjustable to provide either a floodlight or spotlight. The gunner was to check this light before every mission by making sure the switch worked, the cord was not worn, the bulb was firmly seated in the socket, and that there was a spare bulb available.

**Reset Buttons and Fuses**

To protect the electrical circuits, most turrets had either a set of fuses or reset buttons. The fuses, like those in the home, blew out when a circuit became overloaded or shorted and had to be replaced. The fuses were plugged into the turret's main switch panel, with spare fuses usually stored in nearby clips or in a spare parts box. Reset buttons, which were usually found on the control panels, functioned like fuses, but did so in a different way. When a circuit malfunctioned its reset button popped out and cut off the current. To restore the circuit the reset button had to be pushed in again.

Sometimes, if the turret had been operating at high speeds, the electrical circuit that drove the turret became so overheated that the reset buttons popped out as soon as the gunner pushed them back in, which was a major problem in combat. The gunner had to hold the reset button with one hand and operate the turret with the other hand. This technique was only to be used in emergencies, as the circuits could be so overworked that the motors and other equipment could be burned out.

**Safety Switches**

The control handles contained two types of safety switches that prevented the turret from moving unless one of the two switches was closed. One type was built into the handle and was closed by squeezing it. The other standard type was built out from the handle "like a wing" and was closed by grasping the handle and pressing down the edge of the hand on the switch. The switches were tested by pressing one at a time, each causing the

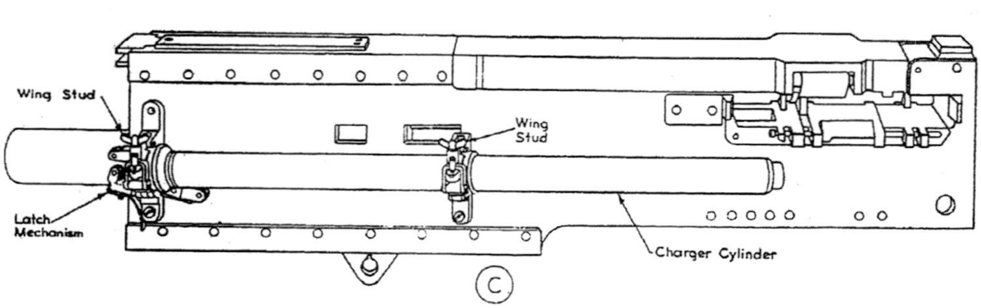


**Compressed Air Gun Charger** (USAAF)

Trouble Light (USAAF)

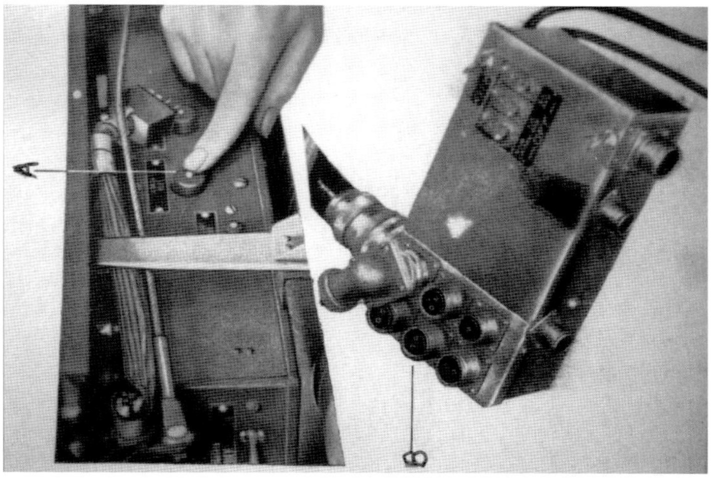

**Reset Buttons (A) and Fuses (B)** (USAAF)

turret to move. When the switch was released it should have immediately sprung back into the open position and the turret was to stop at once. The switches were to be tested several times, but were to be closed quickly to avoid burning them out.

**Emergency Controls**
For manual operation of the hydraulic turret the shut-off valve was closed and the by-pass valve opened to shut down the hydraulic system. The gunner removed the crank handles from their hangers on the side of the bulkheads and attached them to their proper positions: the crank to the gunner's left operated the elevating mechanism while that to the gunner's right operated the rotating mechanism.

When the target was moving horizontally or vertically the gunner used the proper crank to bring the plane of target motion through the center of the sight; following the target along either the horizontal or vertical axis and leaving one hand free to operate the trigger. The gunner then used his other hand to lead the target the required distance.

When the target was moving diagonally the gunner used both hand cranks, determining the direction the target was moving and to bring the plane of motion through the center of the sight. He led the target enough to allow either free hand to operate the trigger when the target reached the firing point. The other hand could be used to correct for slight horizontal or vertical changes.

**Control Handle Firing Grips**
The firing grips were attached to the outer ends of the control handle tube. The right hand firing grip contained two switches. One switch mounted in the upper front portion of the hollow handle closed the circuit for high-speed operation of the turret. A second switch mounted in the hollow handle below the high-speed switch was used for firing. Cables connected the switch to the firing-solenoid circuit. A firing trigger attached to the handle by a pin was used to close the switch.

Two different left hand firing grips were provided with the turret drive. The original left hand firing grip contained two switches. The first switch one was located in the lower part of the handle. A trigger hinged on a pin controlled the switch, and when the gunner's grip was relaxed contact was broken, and the turret would not operate, causing this switch to be known as the "Dead Man Switch." A second firing switch was mounted in the left hand grip in the same position as the firing switch of the right hand grip.

The newer left hand firing grip contained three switches. A microphone switch was mounted in the grip in a position corresponding to that of the high-speed switch of the right hand firing grip. A second switch for firing was mounted just below, with the firing trigger hinged on a pin. A third switch operated by the dead man lever was located below the firing switch. The dead man lever projected from the left side of the grip and pivoted on a pin. It was held in an open position by a spring and, when depressed, the lever held the movable contact against the stationary contact.

**Safety Switches** (USAAF)

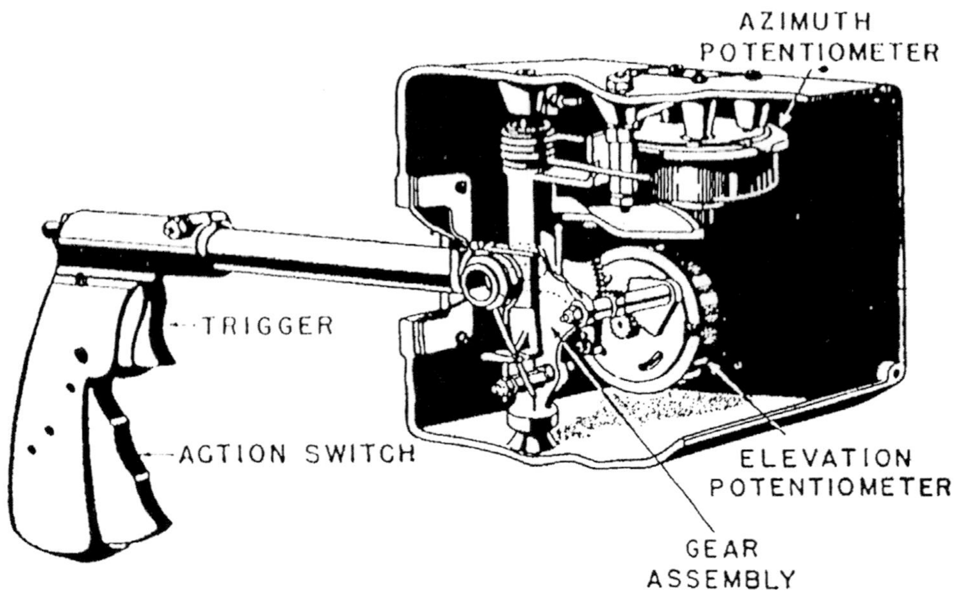


**Control Handle Firing Grips** (USAAF)

In azimuth the firing grips were rotated about a vertical axis, causing the upper tube of the control arm to turn. A gear pinned to the control arm meshed with a gear on the azimuth potentiometer, causing the potentiometer shaft to rotate. Two contacts sliding on the resistances of the potentiometer were moved from their normal or zero-voltage position to cause a flow of current to the azimuth amplidyne generator. The voltage of the current varied in proportion to the distance the firing grips were moved. Stops on a bracket in the housing prevented movement beyond a predetermined point.

Before the guns were ready to fire the safety switch located on the gunner's right in the turret switch box was to be turned ON. This switch connected to the trigger release located between the two grips on the turret control handle and was operated by thumb pressure. Later turrets had the trigger located on the right grip of the turret control handle and were operated by the right hand trigger finger. The guns were moved to a horizontal position and the elevating mechanism lock was attached. One end of the lock was put on the crankshaft of the emergency elevating system and the other end was slipped over the nut on the casting directly below the shaft. When not in use the lever lock was stowed at the gunner's left on the bulkhead.

**Trigger Switches**

The NA-2 push button trigger switches were always located on the control handles, usually under the index finger. Both guns were normally connected to fire from either trigger. In testing the trigger switches the first rule was not to have ammunition in the guns. As the triggers were pressed, together and one at a time, there was a sharp click in the electric trigger control, indicating that the firing circuit was operating.

**Electric Trigger Controls**

The most common electric trigger control was the MK 7 Model 1 that was mounted on the gun buffer plate. The MK 4 Model 1 and MK 4 Model 1 were mounted on the side of the gun. The electric trigger controls were gun firing solenoids that were mounted on either side of the gun buffer tube or on the side plate of the gun. The G-11 solenoid was mounted on the backplate. When the trigger switches on the turret control handles were pressed the G-11 solenoid fired the guns by an electric magnet that moved a small plunger, tripping the trigger bars that fired the gun.

**Clutches**

Clutches were present on almost all turrets, allowing the gunner to disconnect the azimuth and elevation power gearing. Disengaging the clutches allowed the turret to be moved more easily by hand to make repairs and operate the turret manually in emergencies. Most turret clutches were simple levers that were pushed back and forth into the engage and disengage positions. The turret was not to be operated under power without the clutches being engaged, as the turret could get out of control, dangerously swinging freely up and down and around in the slipstream. This could be hazardous to the aircraft structure and to the gunner inside the moving turret. To check if the turret was engaged the gunner tried to push the turret around by hand and tried to move the guns up and down. If the turret was difficult to move the clutches were engaged. The clutches were to be left engaged when leaving the aircraft after a mission.

**Leads, Breezes, and Cannon Plugs**

In all turrets the electrical current was distributed through leads generally covered with flexible metal conduits commonly called Breezes. Connections between breezes were made by Cannon Plugs, which were plug-ins

**Electric Trigger** (USAAF)

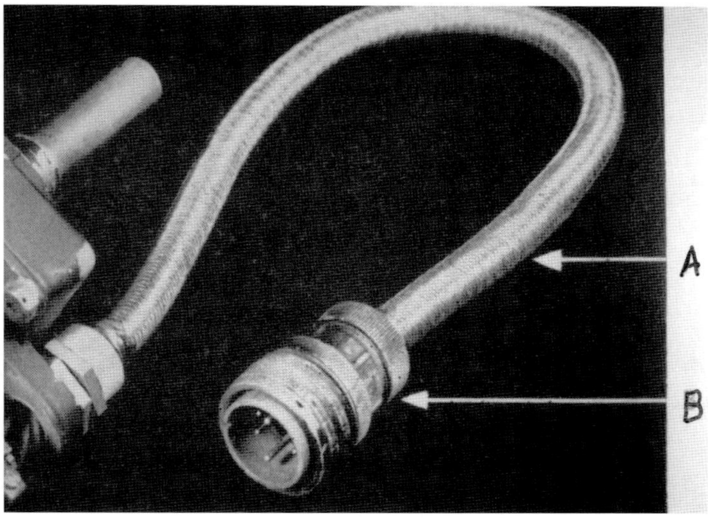


**Leads, Breezes (A), and Cannon Plugs (B)** (USAAF)

with a threaded ring and sleeve to hold them together. Before each mission the Breezes were to be examined closely for wear and fraying, with extra attention to their connections to the Cannon Plugs. The Cannon Plugs were to be examined to be sure they were plugged in and screwed in tightly.

**Fire Interrupters**

The azimuth fire interrupter was installed to interrupt the firing circuit within certain vital areas when the gun fire would strike the aircraft structure. The azimuth fire interrupter consisted of two switches connected with a coupling and a strap. The elevation fire interrupter had the same function as the azimuth interrupter. When the rollers on the fire interrupters came in contact with their respective cams the rollers were depressed and the interrupter switches were opened. On the elevation fire interrupter both switches were opened by a single roller, while on the azimuth fire interrupter the switches were opened independently by separate rollers. The interference areas made it necessary to actuate one azimuth interrupter switch at a time at some points and both switches at a time at other points. If both azimuth interrupter switches were open when the elevation interrupter cam was depressed neither gun would fire. However, both guns would fire if the azimuth switches were closed.

**Stop Limits**

Contour Follower

The turret manual called the contour follower the "Save the fuselage assistant," as its only function was to prevent the gun from hitting any part of the fuselage and had no connection with the profile interrupter circuit. It was mounted under the gun barrel, and two pivoted arms projected through the gun slot in the turret dome and rode on the contrail rail. When the arm contacted the rail they actuated switches in the contour follower box.

Hydraulic Stops

Later turrets were equipped with automatic hydraulic stop units which prevented the gun barrels from training beyond a set point, eliminating the possibility of damaging the fuselage by full-speed rotary motion. The action was automatic, and the turret could be moved immediately in the opposite direction. As the point of maximum train was neared a stop bracket in the fuselage closed the hydraulic stop, which shut off the fluid return from the train motor in the direction of movement only and stopped the turret. The long tapered plunger of the valve of the hydraulic stops acted as a cushion when the turret approached the extreme right or left position.

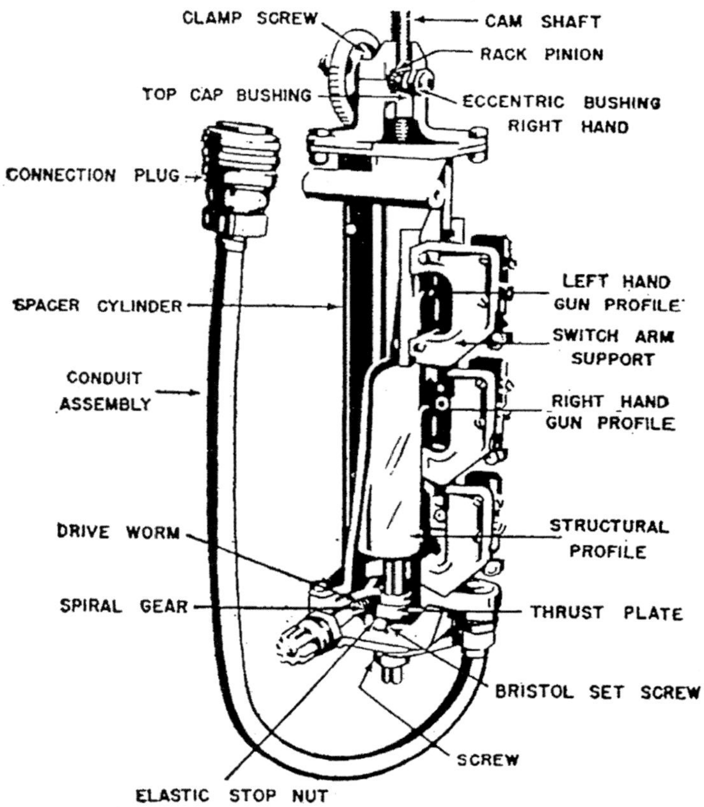


**Gunfire Interrupter** (USAAF)

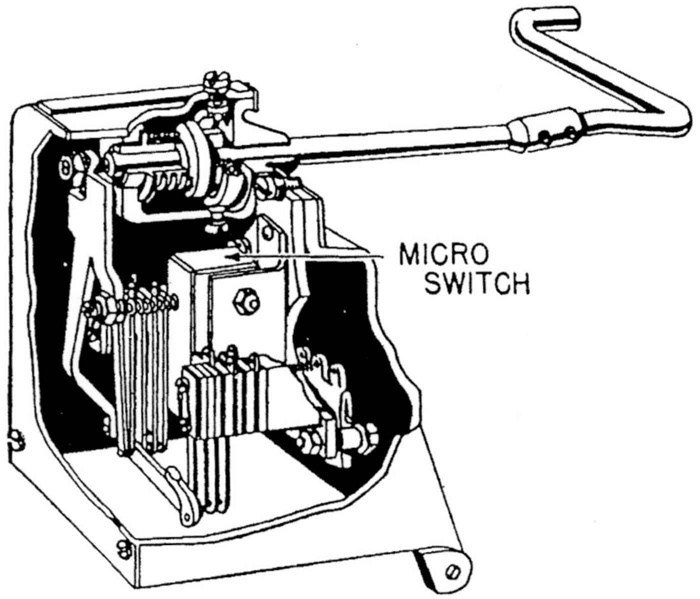


**Contour Follower** (USAAF)

**Bullet Deflectors**
Bullet deflectors were wedge-shaped metal protuberances located directly in front of the gun muzzle(s) of a turret which protected parts of the aircraft's structure, usually the empennage, from accidental firing when the guns were in the stowed position.

**Ammunition Booster Motors**
The booster motors were small (1 pound, 11 ounces), heavy-duty, free-wheeling, 1/10 hp, DC, 10,000 rpm motors developed by Hughes Aircraft Co. of Culver City, CA. When the guns were fired the booster motor switch was automatically turned on, pulling the ammunition belt from its storage box at the cyclic rate of the gun. Small electric booster springs were mounted at the top of the ammunition feedway, directly meshing with the ammunition links by means of a sprocket. The operation of the booster was automatically controlled by the tension on the ammunition belt between the gun and the booster. The booster continued to operate as long as there was tension on the ammunition belt between the gun and booster, either caused by the firing of the gun or the moving of the gun to a higher elevation. When the guns stopped firing the pressure on the ammunition belt stopped and springs pulled the motor back to its normal position and the switch cut off.

The booster motors were to be tested before each mission before the ammunition belt was loaded over the sprockets. The motors were to be tilted toward the guns to check if they started immediately and operated smoothly. The motors were then released, making sure that their springs pulled them back to the normal position and that they stopped immediately. Care had to be taken during the checking process, as the gunner could lose a finger in the mechanism. At times during combat vibration could cause the automatic switches to lock with the booster motors continuing to turn, causing the ammunition belts to pile up against the guns and preventing them from firing. The gunner had to quickly disconnect the electric cables leading to the booster motors and feed the guns without the motors.

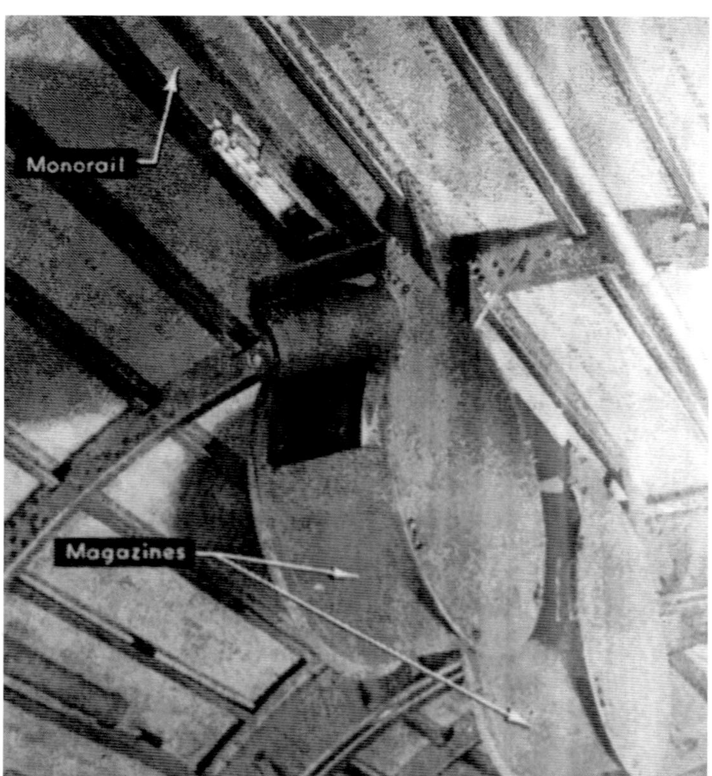

**Ammunition Monorail** (USAAF)

**Plexiglas** (USAAF)

**Ammunition Monorails**
The Consolidated A-6A turret had a monorail that traversed along the top of the fuselage so that the gunner did not have to leave the turret to get additional ammunition. Two cords were located near the turret, with each attached to a container of ammunition. By pulling these cords the containers were unlatched and towed along the monorail to the turret. The 50 pound ammunition containers were pulled gently or allowed to roll by gravity when detached.

**Plexiglas**
In 1933, chemist Dr. Otto Rohm succeeded in developing a method for polymerizing methyl-methacrylate, which today, under the brand name Plexiglas, has become an essential part of our everyday lives. Rohm produced a transparent, hard, and shatter-proof polymer that, owing to its excellent weather resistance, long service life, high breaking strength, superior light transmission properties (92%), simple processing, and low weight was adapted for the windows of aircraft cockpits and turrets. Plexiglas was shipped in sheets and heated to 256°F, when it became pliable and could be placed on a mold and hand pressed into the desired shape. Once shaped the Plexiglas cooled and hardened, and was then dipped into a protective coating to keep it from scratching during handling. Once the Plexiglas was in place on the aircraft this coating was removed.

Plexiglas Maintenance
Only qualified maintenance men repaired Plexiglas, but the gunner performed the normal cleaning using plenty of soap and water. Very hot water was not to be used as it could soften the material, particularly along the seams. A dry cloth was also never to be used, as Plexiglas scratched easily and static electricity could build up, attracting dust. Plain kerosene or naphtha could be used to remove grease or oil, but generally cleaning sprays or solutions were avoided, as they contained chemicals that could soften and crack the Plexiglas. Minor scratches could be removed with automobile (Simonize) or furniture wax, always using a circular motion when rubbing. This method gave a nice gloss and helped to prevent future scratching.

The gunner was to inform maintenance as soon as possible about cracks, as they could grow into major breaks in the buffeting slipstream. Plexiglas was to be replaced or repaired in the critical vision area, which was that portion of the canopy forward of a vertical line one foot aft of the gunner's eye point and below a horizontal line passing through a point two inches above the gunner's eye point. The various types of Plexiglas defects were:

1) Nicks: Broken indentations or cavities having sharp edges but not extending through the sheet.
2) Dents: Depressions or hollows left by blows or concentrated pressures.
3) Spalls: Cavities left by the loss of a fragment having at least one feathered edge.
4) Conchoidal Fracture: Cavities left by loss of a chip in the form of a clamshell.
5) Scratches: Tears in the surface made by a pointed object.
6) Cracks: Narrow fractures extending deeper than scratches into the face of the sheet and having a pointed bottom and high depth to width ratio.
7) Crazing: A pattern or area of tiny fissures or splits (material separation) resembling the cracking of glaze on pottery. Slight crazing caused reduction in transparency, which could be discovered only through certain viewing angles, while severe crazing caused a reduction in transparency which was apparent from any viewing angle.
8) Delamination: A separation of the outer and inner face ply and butyl interlayer.

Temporary Repairs

The gunner could make a temporary repair by first drilling a 1/8 or 3/16 inch hole at the end of the crack to distribute the strain over a wider area and prevent the crack from extending further. He was then to drill a series of smaller holes about 1/2 inch on each side of the crack and then lace the two edges together with wire. To temporarily repair bullet holes in the Plexiglas a small half-round file was used to trim the hole and any surrounding cracks into a circle. A piece of round wing fabric, thin Plexiglas, or cellulose acetate sheeting was cut larger than the hole and glued with dope to the Plexiglas, which was always coated with dope. The area around the patch was masked with tape to prevent the dope from running and damaging unaffected Plexiglas.

**Bullet-proof Glass**

Vulnerable areas around the gunner's head on a turret were protected by bullet-proof glass, which wasn't bullet proof, but bullet resistant. Bullet-resistant glass was usually constructed using a strong but transparent material such as a polycarbonate thermoplastic laminated (sandwiched) between layers of highly polished glass which were bonded together under heat and pressure. The outside glass was brittle, while the inside sandwich layers were pliable, with the index of refraction of the two being identical in order to achieve transparency. A bullet fired at a sheet of bullet-resistant glass pierced the outside layer of the glass, but the layered polycarbonate-glass material was able to absorb and spread the bullet's energy while holding the shattered point of impact together. At the point of impact the glass powdered and then starred, and cracked three inches around the impact point. The glass presented a particular problem because laminated glass needed to be very thick, and thus heavy, because of its low ballistic limit. A one square foot piece, 1.5 inches thick, weighed 30 pounds. This thickness stopped the penetration of a .30 caliber bullet while twice that thickness was required to stop a .50 caliber bullet (.5 inch of armor plate could do the same). Because laminated glass could not resist bullets hitting straight on (i.e. at right angles) the glass was set at calculated deflection angles as close as possible to the pilot's or gunner's eyes.

CR-39 was a type of "reinforced plastic" developed by the Pittsburgh Plate Glass Company subsidiary, Columbia Southern Chemical Company of Barberton, OH. The company was investigating clear resins and the successful 39th batch was trademarked as CR-39. This plastic would not replace the well-established and more functional Plexiglas for use for transparent turret domes, but it was used as a strong impact-resistant protective laminate with a hollow space to allow the flow of heated air for defrosting. Its good molding and laminating properties gave it more use as the basis of lightweight self-sealing fuel tanks laminated with the sealing rubber compound.

**Turret Adjustments and Maintenance**

The *Aircrewman's Gunnery Manual* described the turret gunner's duties as:

"You will have to know where all the equipment is in your own turret, how to prepare it for flight and make sure it is working properly, and how to use them in combat.

You will not be expected to become an expert turret mechanic; if something goes wrong, trained maintenance will repair it. But you will have to know enough about how the turret works to recognize trouble when it occurs and to spot it before, not during a mission."

Testing for "Creep"

Creep was the condition when the gunner held the control handles in the neutral position and instead of stopping the turret continued to creep a little further around in either direction. It was important that the turret be checked for creep before each mission, as in combat, when the gunner trained his guns on a target, the turret would always move beyond the

**Bullet-Proof Glass** (USAAF)

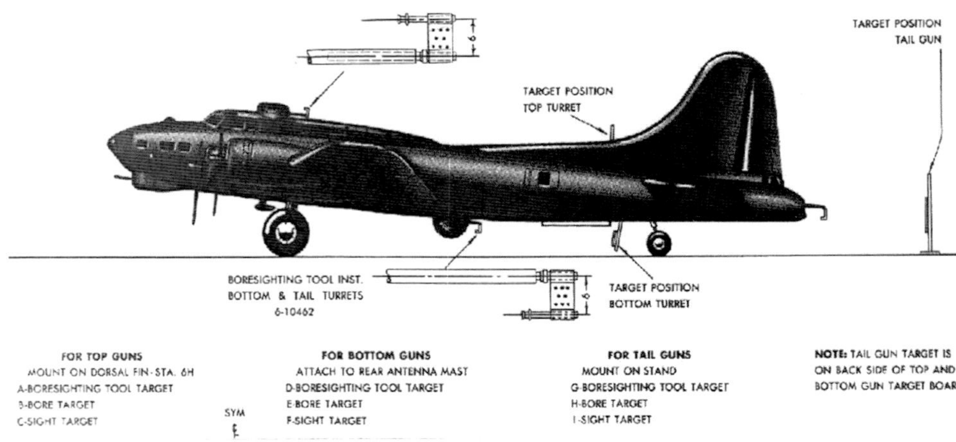


**Turret Bore Sighting** (USAAF)

target and the gunner would invariably miss. "Binding" was the obvious opposite problem.

Testing the Fire Cutoffs (Interrupter) System

The fire cutoff (interrupter) system was complex, and its adjustment and maintenance were always done by turret maintenance mechanics; however, the gunner was responsible for pre-flight testing. The test was done with the guns unloaded, and with the cannon plug removed from the electric trigger control and the test light inserted in its place. The trigger was squeezed and the turret guns swung across sections of the aircraft that could be hit by gunfire called "danger areas." The test light turned off just before the guns came to bear on any part of the aircraft, indicating that the interrupter mechanism was functioning. The gunner used a boresighting tool to check the distance from the point where the light went out to the part of the aircraft into which the guns could fire. This procedure was repeated for each gun and each potential danger area by moving the guns from one side to another. The gunner then repeated the test while moving the guns in elevation, first moving them down on the danger areas and then up. Each gun was to cutoff with sufficient clearance near the danger areas. The amount of clearance was to be approximately equal above and below danger areas and to either side. The fire cutoff mechanism could malfunction during long firing bursts as a round could "cook off" in the gun even though the triggers were not being pressed.

Hydraulic System Check

In all hydraulically operated turrets the system had to be filled with the correct fluid level. The gunner was to do a daily check on the fluid level gauge for a mark or screen that showed the correct level. The hydraulic system, lines, and gun chargers were to be carefully checked for leaks, with the turret being operated to keep pressure in the lines during the inspection. Particular attention was to be paid at the swivel joints, tubing connections, and lines for leaks and cracks.

Sight Adjustment and Maintenance

Sight Adjustment and maintenance is discussed in the section on gunsights: Part Four/Chapter 2

Turret Gun Care and Adjustment

Turret gun care and maintenance is discussed in Part One/Chapter 6/Section 3: .50 Caliber Machine Gun, in Part Two: Aircraft Cannon, and in Part Six/ Chapter 4 in each turret description.

Inspecting and Loading the Ammunition

This subject is discussed Part One/Chapter 6/Section 5: .50 Caliber Machine Gun; in Part Two: Aircraft Cannon in each cannon type description; and in Part Six/Chapter 4 in each turret description.

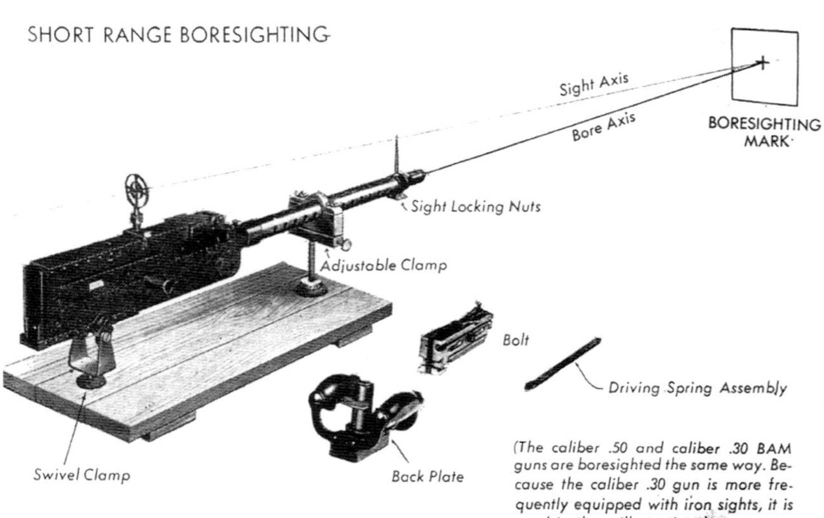


**Short-Range Boresighting** (USAAF)

**Boresighting and Harmonization of Turret and Flexible Guns**

Boresighting vs. Harmonization

A sight was only accurate if it was properly lined up with the bore of the gun. Simple boresighting accomplished one objective: it lined up the sight and gun so that the gunner could look through the sight and know where the bullets would strike (e.g. adjusting the guns so that their line of fire corresponded with the line of sight). The method of lining up the sight and bore of one gun was called boresighting, while the method for lining up multiple guns (either six or eight in a wing or two in a turret) to converge at a single point was called harmonization.

Boresighting

Boresighting established the relationship between two axis lines. Sight Axis was a straight line from the eye through the sight into space. Bore Axis was a straight line drawn through the center of the gun barrel and out into space. These two lines could run parallel or be made to converge to yield the densest pattern of bullets on the target. For long ranges the effect of gravity on the bullet's flight had to be taken into account.

Often the limited space in a turret made it difficult for the armorer to fit his head behind the machine gun to boresight through the barrel. Specialized tools (the boresight reflector and boresight tool) were developed to aid in harmonization under these circumstances. When using each tool either the bolt had to be locked to the rear by hooking the extractor lug behind the bolt stop or the backplate had to be removed, the driving spring unhooked, and the bolt pulled back. The simplest device was the boresight reflector, which had an eyepiece and an angled mirror inside a small L-shaped metal case. It was placed in the breech end of the barrel and the technician could look down the gun barrel by looking down through the eyepiece. A variation of this device used a more complex mirror system operating much like a periscope. It could be inserted from either the top or the bottom of the gun and the technician looked through the eyepiece. The boresight tool was inserted into the muzzle, where it extended and pointed in the same direction as the barrel. When the technician looked into the eyepiece the mirror reflected the outside scene as would be seen through the barrel.

Harmonization

All gun installations, whether a single flexible gun or multiple turret guns and their sights were boresighted and harmonized using the same basic principals, but with specific instructions issued for the slight variations found in each turret type. A useful method used in the field was to line up the sight and boresight the guns on some small target object at least 1,000 yards from the aircraft. The multiple gun package mount or multiple gun turret was turned until the guns pointed at the target. The back plates and bolts from the guns needed to be removed so that the technician could look through the gun barrels at the target, or better, a boresight tool could be used without removing gun parts. The sights were then lined up using the

**Fighter Boresighting** (USAAF)

elevation and azimuth hand cranks to move the guns until the dot of the sight was squarely on the target object. The guns were not to be moved again until the harmonization was completed. Then each gun barrel was boresighted by adjusting its rear mount adjustment bolts until the spot the sight was centered on was exactly in the center of each gun bore. Another method of harmonization was to line up the sight and guns on a special pattern stand or template. The stand was set up as level as possible at least 50 yards from the side of the plane. The guns were centered in their mounts. Each gun was boresighted on the pattern stand and the sight centered on the sight cross. Both methods described here are called parallel harmonization.

Harmonizing/Boresighting a Computing Sight

Harmonizing/Boresighting a computing (compensating) sight established a parallel relationship between the center of the fixed cross of the fixed reticle and the bore axis of the guns. Before boresighting a computing sight the fixed reticles and gyro reticles had to be aligned. They were aligned when the center pipper of the gyro reticle was superimposed at an infinite distance with no windage, gravity, or relative speed allowances in the system. Once these reticles were aligned the aircraft had to be leveled transversely and longitudinally, so the guns were parallel to the center line on the fighter or the turret at right angles to the center line on a bomber. Next, the bolts on the gun back plates were adjusted as described above and the guns were adjusted so that their bore axes aimed at an object at least 1,000 yards away (the guns needed to be sighted only horizontally with the elevation setting untouched). The last step was to adjust the sighting head so that the center of the fixed cross in the fixed reticle bore upon the same distant object as the gun bore axis. It was not necessary to allow for gravity drop of the bullet as the sight compensated for that.

# 4

# Turrets

## Section 1: Introduction

### Background

The modern powered bomber turret was developed after many experiments and tests in the 1930s, and its effect on air strategy were profound, as it allowed the heavier and slower bomber to fight back against the enemy fighter. When closing on a bomber from any quarter an enemy interceptor met a target whose turret guns could be turned toward him in an instant. The dorsal turret revolved in a full circle, its guns moving up and down from straight out to nearly straight up, protecting the entire top of the aircraft. The ventral turret also revolved 360° and aimed its guns anywhere from straight out to straight down, fending off any attacker who approached from below. The tail turret guns fired a large cone of bullets toward the rear while the nose turret spewed an intense cone of fire straight ahead. In conjunction with the hand-held guns in the waist windows and the radio position, the bomber's turrets protected it from an enemy attacking from almost every surrounding area of sky.

### Operation

Electric motors or hydraulic pressure systems rotated the turrets from side to side (called azimuth) and raised and lowered their guns (called elevation). The gunner was seated inside the turret in front of or between .50 caliber machine guns and could make the necessary adjustments for comfort and efficiency. The turret contained everything the gunner required for combat, arranged so that he could access anything instantly with all the switches involved in operating the turret located within easy reach. The turret was constructed so that all the gunner had to do was guide the control handles to move the turret, leaving the gun mechanism to do the rest. Armor plate or bullet-proof glass was provided for protection, but the gunner was instructed that his "best defense, like a good boxer's, will still be the offensive power packed by those caliber .50s." The guns were equipped with a special charging system, usually a pulley and cable, that made it easy to hand charge them in the crowded space of the turret. The guns were mounted in adapters that cushioned their recoil and were fired by pressing triggers, usually located under the gunner's index fingers on the control handles. The firing pins were released by means of electrical devices called electric triggers. Adequate ammunition for the guns was carried in metal or wooden boxes mounted so that the belts ran smoothly into the feedways. Often booster motors lifted the ammunition belt to the guns. The empty shell cases dropped into ejection chutes and out of the turret to the outside, or into spent round bags attached to the ends of the chutes. The gunner did not have to worry about shooting off parts of his bomber, as every turret where this danger existed had a system of fire interruption that stopped the guns automatically when they were pointed toward any part of the bomber. The gunner also did not have to worry about swinging the guns so far that they could hit nearby aircraft structure, as the turrets were equipped with limit stops that prevented this from occurring. The limit stops on some turrets were simply bumpers, while others had automatic switches that stopped the turret before any damage could occur. With practice, the easily reached control handles enabled the gunner to operate the turret as "easily as an automobile." Once he "developed the touch, the

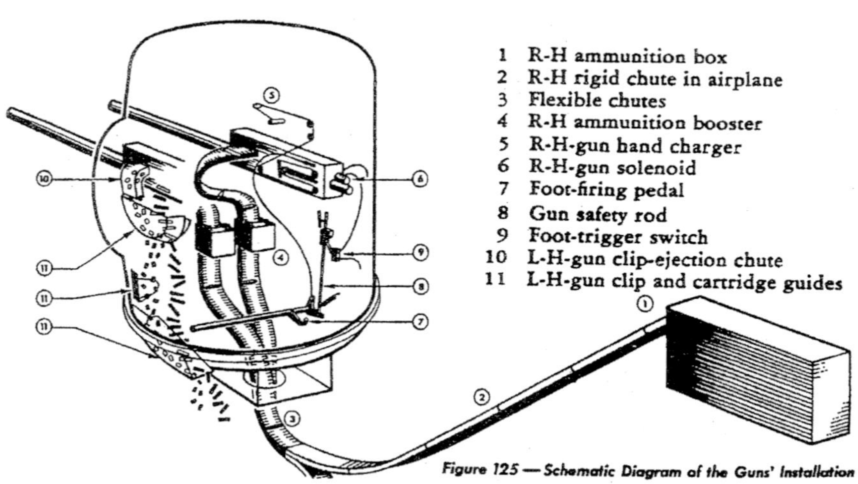


**Turret and Gun Installation** (USAAF)

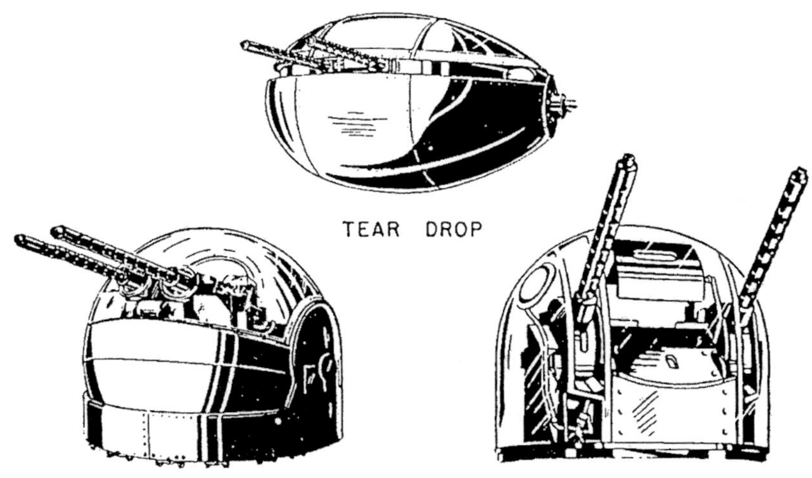


**Turret Shapes** (USAAF)

secret is to keep a steady hand, without jerking and you will be able to track the enemy smoothly and accurately." For rotating quickly to meet a new attack the turret was able to reach a high speed, with the distance the control handles were moved determining the speed. In some turrets there was a special high-speed button which put the turret into high gear to give an extra boost. The high-speed button was to be used only when needed to avoid unnecessary wear and tear on the power system. If the turret power failed there usually was a manual system available for operating it by hand cranks, but some turrets had foot pedals to move the turret into position, enabling the gunner to use both hands to fire the guns.

**Turret Types**

All turrets can be divided into three mechanical classifications according to shape and into two power-operating mechanism classifications: electric and hydraulic. Mechanically, turrets are classified according to their shape. First, there is the ball or spherical type, in which the gunner, guns, and sight rotate about a common axis in elevation and a common axis in azimuth (horizontal). The second type is the cylindrical turret, in which the gunner, the guns, and the sight rotate about a common axis in azimuth while only the guns and sight operate in elevation. The third, a teardrop turret, is one which is essentially a streamlined shape with one axis of rotation along the chord of the streamlined shape. Gunner, sight, and guns all move together both in azimuth and elevation. Turret shapes will be discussed along with individual turrets.

**Designations of U.S. Navy Turrets**

The Navy used its own code designation to describe the distinguishing features of its numerous turrets:

Grumman 150SE-2:
Grumman = designer
150>1 = number of guns/50 = caliber of guns
SE> S = spherical (ball) in shape/E = electrically powered
-2> modification number

Martin 250CH-2A
Martin = designer
250> 2 = number of guns/50 = caliber of guns
CH> C = cylindrical in shape/H = hydraulically operated
-2A> 2 = modification number/A = further modification

ERCO 250TH-2
ERCO = designer
250> 2 = number of guns/50 = caliber of guns
TH> T = teardrop in shape/H = hydraulically operated
-2> modification number

**Section 2: Sperry/Briggs/Emerson Ball Turret A-2 and A-13**
**Background and Development of the Ventral Turret**

British

During World War I the fighter pilot recognized that the best point of attack on a bomber was from the lower rear sector blind spot. As bombers increased in size between the wars they became even more vulnerable to attack from this sector. The RAF attempted one of the first crude steps to counteract this attack by adding a rear hatch gun to the Boulton-Paul Overstrand bomber. However, once the prone gunner warned the pilot of the approaching enemy fighter he could not get off accurate fire from the bomber, which began to maneuver violently to escape. In the mid-1930s the first Armstrong Whitworth Whitleys and Vickers Armstrong Wellingtons were armed with rudimentary rear gun mounts, but after the Frazier-Nash (Parnell) Company introduced their revolutionary hydraulic turret, the Air Ministry ordered these bombers to be adapted to receive them. In 1938 the Whitley III was fitted at mid-fuselage with the retractable ventral FN17 turret that was lowered by hydraulic rams. Soon the Whitley IV was fitted with the supposedly ground-breaking Frazier-Nash FN4 four-gun rear turret, but it was found to cause excessive drag and had poor target acquisition. Ventral turrets continued to be developed for the Wellington, Avro Manchester, and Short Stirling, but all were found inadequate. RAF ventral turret development continued for the Avro Lancaster with the low-drag twin-gun cupola FN64, sighted through a periscope by a gunner located inside the aft rear fuselage. This turret was found adequate for daylight operations, but target acquisition at night, when the Lancaster would primarily operate, was impossible. Before the *Luftwaffe* introduced its night fighters using the upward firing "Schrage Musik" gun installation the RAF could not justify the addition of an extra gunner. During the war the RAF did not exploit a ventral turret, but the H2S radar dome utilized that turret's position instead.

American

In the meantime, the USAAC Materiel Division's Armament Branch had been conducting extensive trials to determine the best types of turret installations. Ventral turrets, in particular, were a dilemma due to the problem of sighting below the fuselage. In August 1940 a Work Authorization Sheet was prepared "to cover all work in connection with the development of a retractable type flexible gun turret for installation in the floor of a bombardment type airplane." In September this work order was modified "to cover extension of the investigation to include consideration of a spherical, non-retractable turret."

**Ball Turret Development**

By early 1941, the continual problems with the ventral remote turret convinced Sperry that it needed to choose between the ventral remote and the ventral ball turrets. Sperry was reluctant to dedicate any more time and money into the ventral remote turret if the Materiel Division planned to put the ball turret into production. On the other hand, although the Division was enthusiastic about the ball turret, it also was reluctant to commit to it until cost estimates were available. Briggs, Sperry's ball turret subcontractor, was reluctant to begin its development without the guarantee of a quantity contract that would protect them against possible manufacturing losses. Since the ball turret was a completely undeveloped design, Sperry was unable to prepare estimates for the Materiel Division until a cost analysis had been completed on the prototype at Briggs. Finally, with Wright Field's urgent backing, and despite a delay caused by a shortage of aluminum castings, the first ball turret was ready for tests at Wright Field in early May 1941.

An unusual feature of the design of the new turret was that the gunner was curled in the fetal position inside, which made it appear to be very uncomfortable, and testing would be required to determine gunner comfort and endurance. The Chief of the Armament Branch directed Briggs to complete a series of endurance tests at their factory to determine if the gunner would be able to occupy the ball turret for long periods. Endurance tests of men "slightly smaller than average" indicated "little or no loss of efficiency based on the evidence of scores compiled with photoelectric light guns fired periodically throughout the trial run." The Materiel Division approved a contract with Briggs for 250 ball turrets with a date for large scale production in abeyance. Maj. Jack Murtha, the Production Engineering Section Chief and the Assistant Chief of the Materiel Division, favored delaying the contract until air firing tests could be conducted to determine whether or not the ball would be acceptable. In Washington, DC, Col. Grandison Gardner, Chief Materiel Division, was forced to approve limited ball turret production because any delay in production would necessitate a continuation of the ventral remote contract in order to avoid a failure in meeting deliveries of aircraft with adequate armament. Briggs refused to accept a contract for fewer than 250 ball turrets, and to avoid losing Briggs as a Sperry subcontractor the Materiel Division was forced to accept the contract, even though Sperry was unable to provide the Division with cost breakdowns until Briggs production began.

The Wright Field air firing tests were so successful that the ball turret was reported as "unusually correct in conception and design for a first experimental article ....and compares most favorably in control with any turret which has been demonstrated in this country." Trial tow target tests also produced favorable scores. During testing the turret's faults were immediately obvious, such as link ejection jamming in the slipstream, clouding of the sighting panel, and limitations on side scanning. These faults were common to all ventral turrets and not considered important, and the Division's decision to begin production before final approval was thus justified.

Sperry offered to build the first 250 balls "by hand" for $20,300 each through its Briggs subcontractor. Later, when production tooling was in place, Sperry estimated that with a production contract for 2,500 units it could supply turrets at $14,099 each. The major components of the turret cost $3,700 for the sight, $1,400 for the Vickers power drives, and $900 for the hand control.

Briggs faced a major task in organizing the manufacture of the ball turret. The company's design studies indicated that there was an estimated 1,100 hours of machine work in manufacturing the turret, and of this amount subcontractor work accounted for 94% and Briggs only 6%. The main ring gear for the turret required a high degree of accuracy in cutting. When using existing equipment Briggs estimated that the fabrication of each ring gear would require 100 hours. Briggs needed to find a subcontractor with a cutting machine large enough to cut the ring gear on a production basis, and there were only three of these cutting machines in the U.S.: one at Ford and two at Chrysler, and these were in use.

Meanwhile, in July 1941 the need for the ball turret grew more urgent. To meet the armament demands of bombers projected off the production line in September, Col. K.B. Wolfe, the Chief of the Production Engineering Section (PES), gave the turret a "No. 1-AAA priority" and summed up the critical ball turret situation most explicitly by stating, "It's hot because we're short." To expedite ball turret production the OPM ordered Briggs to curtail its auto body production, and Briggs responded by threatening to leave the turret business. The Briggs threat gave the PES leverage against Sperry, the prime ball turret contractor, to force a policy of direct negotiation with Emerson, the Materiel Division's new turret source, rather than indirect negotiation with them through Sperry. When it became evident that Sperry could not guarantee ball turret production unless the Defense Plant Corporation (DPC) granted funds for Briggs to expand its facilities Sperry was forced to turn over all turret manufacturing rights to the Materiel Division.

In August 1941, as soon as detailed manufacturing drawings of the ball turret reached Wright Field from Briggs they were sent on to Emerson. In January 1942 the first Emerson ball turret was completed, despite Emerson's allegation that Briggs was slowing Emerson production by withholding essential design information. With Emerson now in the Sperry turret consortium, the already complicated production arrangement became even more complicated. Officially Emerson was directly responsible as a prime contractor to the Materiel Division, but in terms of ball production Sperry continued to dominate. Although Emerson planned to ultimately manufacture most ball turret component assemblies, the first turrets off the production line would depend largely upon existing sources. The Briggs ball turret utilized sights, fire cut outs, and hand control units built by Sperry and drive units built by Vickers. A system of subcontracting existing Steel Products parts was utilized in the manufacture of the Steel Products dorsal turret by Emerson. Since Emerson planned to build both Sperry ball and Steel Products dorsal turrets, the PES Chief expected that Sperry would arrange a similar subcontract arrangement with Emerson. The situation was further complicated by the fact that Sperry had subcontracted some of its to be furnished equipment to the De Laval Separator Company for manufacture.

Emerson, as a Materiel Division prime contractor, was unable to coordinate with Sperry regarding anticipated subassembly deliveries and production schedules, and delays in Emerson's production occurred. However, the most serious delay was due to the shortage of Vickers drive units which jeopardized the entire U.S. turret program, as discussed earlier.

By early 1942 the ball turret had reached design "maturity" and subsequent changes were to be made as modifications. The ball turret, like the dorsal turret, underwent months of testing, in which deficiencies appeared and were eliminated through modifications. Boeing engineers found that the sighting window became fouled on takeoff, and the Armament Laboratory engineers recommended designing a wiper. Other shortcomings included the lack of the following: an interphone volume control, an external power switch, and deadman switches, all of which were easily added.

The only major problem encountered was the excessive drag resulting from the distension of the ball into the slipstream, and the obvious solution was the addition of a retraction mechanism. After experimenting with an electric drive retraction version the Armament Laboratory finally approved a hydraulic system. Once the ball turret entered operations two niggling problems troubled it for two or three years: a jerky range pedal action and the jamming of the ammunition belts in the cans when they were half empty.

In January 1943 a conference of turret manufacturers met at Wright Field and decided to completely redesign the ball turret to include such features as external ammunition containers, hot air heating, quickly detachable guns, larger scanning windows, wider control range, lever action gun charging, and increased armor plate, all in a magnesium casting ball. Furthermore, the Armament Laboratory initiated projects on four-gun ball turrets. A year later, with the existing ball turrets operating satisfactorily in the field, none of these projects had progressed very far because there was no definite tactical requirement for them.

**Description**

Of all the turrets of World War II none had the charisma of the Ball Turret. The plight of the ball turret gunner was vividly personified by Randall Jarrell's classic poem "The Death of the Ball Turret Gunner" written in 1945:

> "From my mother's sleep I fell into the State,
> And I hunched in its belly till my wet fur froze.
> Six miles from earth, loosed from its dream of life,
> I woke to black flak and the nightmare fighters.
> When I died they washed me out of the turret with a hose."

Although commonly referred to as the Sperry Ball Turret, after its designing company, it was also manufactured by Briggs and Emerson. The A-2 model (later A-2A and A-2B) ball turrets were non-retractable, while the later Model A-13 was retractable, but each was exactly the same otherwise. The 44 inch diameter spherical turret that encapsulated the gunner and guns was informally called "the Ball" by men in the field. The ball turret was installed in the Boeing B-17 (as the non-retractable A-2 series), the Consolidated B-24, and a handful of Consolidated B-32s (as the retractable A-13 series). It was not until mid-production of the B-17E and B-24D that the ball turret was introduced, replacing the early remotely-sighted Sperry or Bendix turrets which, due to their complex sighting systems, were found to be inadequate in combat.

Comfort and Safety

The common belief was that there was no worse position in the B-17 than the ball turret position, as the gunner was isolated from the rest of the ten man crew in the cramped turret quarters that often didn't allow enough room to wear a parachute, although some of the smaller gunners were able to wear a chest chute. When the RAF initially evaluated the B-17 they believed that it would be impossible for a gunner to remain in the cramped ball turret for any length of time, much less an entire mission, but 8AF ball turret gunners later routinely spent 8 to 12 hours in the ball. It was also believed that it was the most dangerous place in the B-17, but post-war statistics revealed that the ball gunner position was the safest in the Flying Fortress, with the pilot position being the most dangerous. The reasons for this were that the gunner curled in the fetal position in the turret presented a smaller target; the gunner was protected from the hips up by a steel armor plate panel that formed the seat bottom and extended up to the hinge of the door; and enemy fighter pilots had to make their attack on the ball turret from underneath, which was a more difficult line of attack than from the top, tail, side, or nose.

The Sperry Ball (and Dorsal) Turret sometimes encountered problems, as after a large number of rotations the oxygen tubing and electrical wiring inside the hollow turret conduit became worn at the outlet. This could produce an electrical short which ignited the oxygen, instigating a disastrous, uncontrollable fire. The Operational Engineering Section filled the hollow conduit entrance with cement to cut off and seal the electrical wires and oxygen tubing.

Exterior

The body of the ball turret consisted of two cast aluminum caps called end bells that were bolted to curved aluminum and steel panels that created a 44 inch diameter sphere that extended 24 inches below the ventral fuselage. The end bells were flattened to accommodate cast aluminum trunnion brackets that held the turret onto the aircraft, and about which the turret pivoted in elevation. Early ball turrets in B-17s and some B-24s had Plexiglas and aluminum fairings bolted to the trunnion brackets that completed the ball shape of the turret. Later these caps were abandoned, which gave the turret a flattened look to the sides of the ball. The optically-pure circular gunner's window was not bullet proof glass, but was made up of two separate circular pieces of safety glass separated by a rubber gasket that provided an interior air space for defrosting. The other ball turret windows were Plexiglas. Before the scanning windows were added to the sides of the rear fuselage the belly turret was the only means in the bomber to view the rear of the engine nacelles and the underside of the wings.

A problem with the ball turret, especially the non-retractable turret, was that its windows were prone to fouling, both on the ground and in the air. On takeoff and landing, with the turret in the stowed position and the guns pointing aft, the optical gunsight was protected to some extent. But in rainy weather on takeoff the prop wash stirred up muddy puddles that could coat the scanning windows, which would then freeze at altitude. A brave gunner could reach out of a nearby hatch in the B-17's belly with a wet rag and clean off the window before the bomber reached freezing altitudes.

Entering the Turret

The ball turret was heavy and delicately balanced, and unless it was locked in place it could swivel and catch, and even break the gunner's leg as he tried to enter. The gunner always entered and exited the turret in flight as the bomber neared combat (the turret was not extended until then to reduce drag).

The first step was for the gunner to be certain that the elevation hand clutch was in the IN position. To do so he removed the elevation hand crank from its clip located on the outside of the turret and slid it onto the elevation hand control shaft. He loosened the elevation hand brake, which was a small lever next to the elevation hand control shaft. While keeping his left hand firmly on the hand crank, he removed the outside elevation power clutch handle from its clip and placed it on the outside elevation power clutch handle, then moved it to the OUT position. This disengaged the elevation power gearing and allowed the free up and down movement of the turret. It was essential that the gunner keep a firm hold on the hand crank or the weight of the guns would roll the turret down. The elevation hand crank was turned by the gunner's left hand to move the turret until the guns were pointing straight down at 90°, placing the turret in a position to open the entrance door. Without releasing the hand crank the gunner unfastened and lifted the door. He had to be careful not to let the door fall back down, and that no excess weight was placed on it which could spring the hinge. With the hand crank still in his grasp the gunner reached down inside the turret, forward and behind the large elevation gear housing on

**Ball Turret**

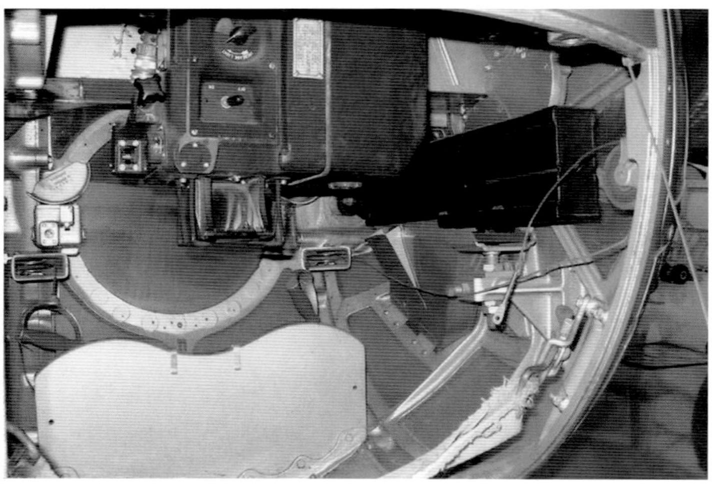

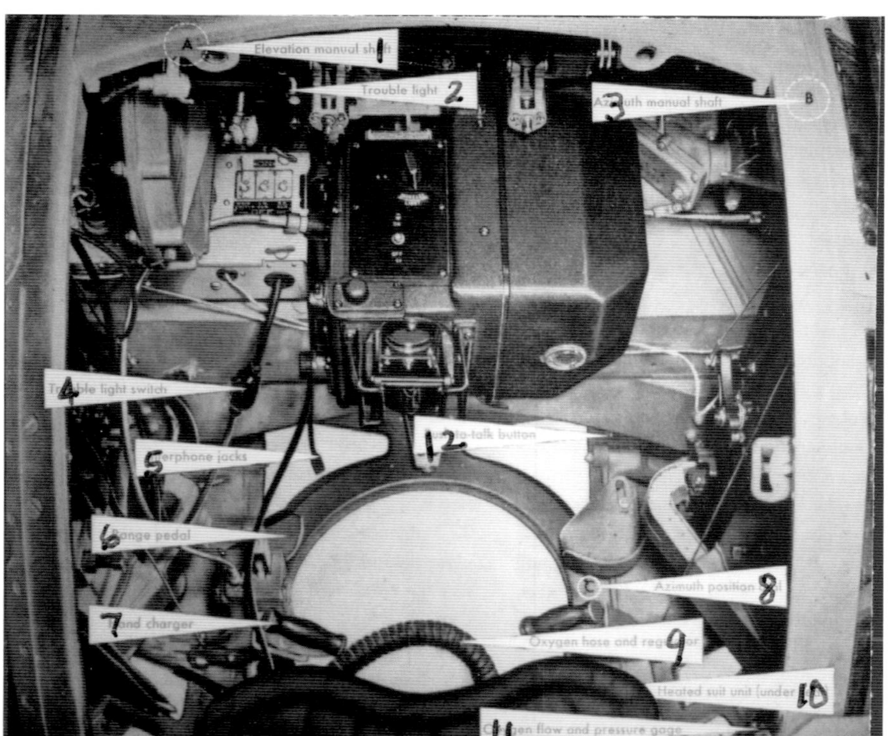


1) Elevation Manual Shaft
2) Trouble Light
3) Azimuth Manual Shaft
4) Trouble Light Switch
5) Interphone Jack
6) Range Pedal
7) Hand Charger
8) Azimuth Position Dial
9) Oxygen Flow & Pressure Regulator
10) Heated Suit Unit
11) Oxygen Flow & Pressure Gauge
12) Push-to-Talk Button

the left, and moved the inside elevation power clutch lever UP to engage it. The elevation hand crank was moved back and forth as the clutch was pushed in place. The elevation power gearing was re-engaged, locking the turret firmly in gear. The outside elevation hand clutch was then moved to the OUT position. The hand crank and the outside power clutch handle were removed and replaced in their clips. The gunner lowered himself into the turret by grasping the support frame and swinging down into the turret. He placed his right heel into the right foot rest and then placed his left heel in the range pedal, being careful not to throw his entire weight on the left range pedal. Once seated he fastened his safety belt and closed the entrance door, making certain that the door latches were securely closed. The non-retractable turret was now ready to operate (see the Brigs A-13 section below for entering and lowering procedure).

Operating the Turret

In operating the Ball the gunner's first step was to make sure that the azimuth power clutch was engaged (it was the lever at the upper right should be DOWN). The main power was turned ON (it was a toggle switch under a wire guard on the junction box next to the gunner's left knee). The two gun selector switches (located next to the power switch) for firing the guns individually or together were turned ON. The sight switch located directly in front of the sight was turned ON. The sight rheostat (next to the sight switch) was turned ON to adjust the brightness of the sight. The gunner was never to operate the turret under power with the sight switch OFF.

The Ball Turret was hydraulically-controlled by a Vickers Power Unit using a constant-speed electric motor to power two hydraulic pumps whose output was controlled by hand grips. The pump output powered the rotation (azimuth) motor and the elevation rams of the turret and gun cradle. The gunner controlled the movement of the whole turret and, consequently, the guns toward the target through the use of hand grips. The azimuth controls functioned exactly opposite to all other turrets. To move the turret right the handgrips were swung to the left; to turn the turret left, they were swung to the right. To tilt the turret and guns upward the gunner pulled back on them and pressed them forward to turn the turret and guns down. The speed and direction (lowered and raised from level, 0° to straight down, 90°) of the elevation rams and the speed (30° per second) and direction (360°, full circle) were varied by the amount of movement of the handgrips controlling the hydraulic motors. This turret had no safety switches. In early turrets the hydraulic glands were susceptible to leaks and could squirt oily and inflammable fluid on the gunner. The problem was alleviated but never fully remedied in later turret models.

The K-4 Ball Turret Gunsight was an upside down version of an automatic computing sight that was built especially for the Ball Turret. The sight was suspended by a single mounting pin in the sight cradle at the gunner's eye level. Three flexible shafts connected to the turret and provided the sight with the turret movement and range data required for computing deflections. The top shaft entered the top rear of the sight and revolved as the turret moved in azimuth. The lower shaft located at the top rear revolved as the turret moved in elevation. The third shaft located on the left side led to the range pedal, which the gunner moved with his left foot to frame the target in the sight reticles. When the gunner closed the sight switch he would hear the sight motor start. To aim he would look into the viewer and adjust the rheostat until the reticle matched the outside light intensity. The K-4 gave the point of aim from calculations made from the input of range from the left foot pedal, and turret movement was made via flexible shafts connected to the turret mechanism. Tracking with the Sperry sight was to be steady and smooth without any quick, uneven motions. The sights and guns were harmonized at 1,000 yards.

The Twin .50 caliber M2 machine guns in the Ball Turret were mounted to feed from the outside, with the right gun feeding from the right and the left gun from the left. The guns were held in their cradles by a rear trunnion block and slide and two front trunnion studs. The rear trunnion block was attached to the rear mounting holes of the gun and dovetailed into the rear trunnion slide. The gunner checked to see if the block moved tightly in the slide. The front trunnion studs screwed into the front mounting yoke of the cradle and into threaded holes in both sides of the gun adapters, and had to be safety wired. Special charging units were installed on the inside plates of the guns with the mounting bolts that had to be safetied. The cable connection to each unit required a cotter pin. Special link ejection chutes were installed on the inside of the guns where they were held by the gun's belt feed pawl pins and cotter pins. The guns could be adjusted up, down, or sideways in their cradles by using an adjustment screw and bolt assembly provided on each rear trunnion. Because of the ball turret's computing sight and compact structure harmonization was more complicated than for other turrets.

The Ball Turret had two ammunition cans located directly in front of the gunner that were a permanent part of the turret ball. There was a can for each gun that contained approximately 500 rounds of belted ammunition. To give the gunner more room in later turret modifications, the ammunition cans were located outside the turret mounted on the hanger assembly. Flexible chutes carried the ammunition from the cans to the turret and guns. These external ammunition boxes fed 570 rounds to the left gun and 450 rounds to the right gun, giving about a 30 second firing time.

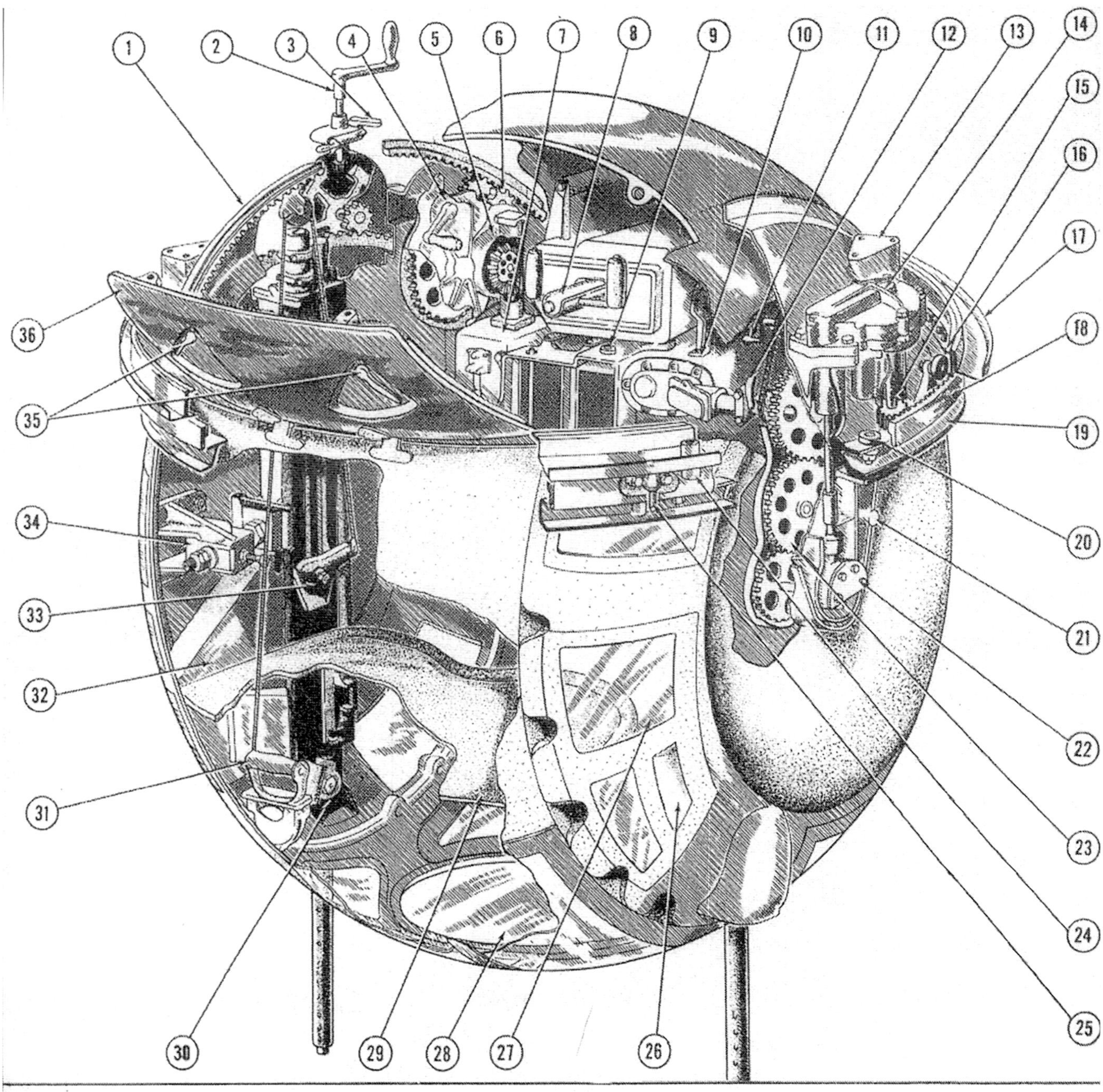


LEGEND

1. Elevation Quadrant Gear
2. External Elevation Hand Crank
3. Elevation Hand Brake
4. Internal Elevation Hand Crank
5. Elevation Power Gear Assembly
6. Elevation Drive Pinion
7. Vickers Elevation Drive Unit
8. Hand Control Unit
9. Sight Mounting Bracket
10. Vickers Azimuth Drive Unit
11. Azimuth Hand Crank
12. Azimuth Power Clutch
13. Hanger Mounting Pad
14. Azimuth Pinion Gear Housing
15. Azimuth Pinion Gear
16. Vertical Roller
17. Retraction Mounting Ring
18. Azimuth Ring Gear
19. Trunnion Ring Support
20. Horizontal Roller
21. Trunnion Support Bracket
22. Trunnion Gear Housing
23. Azimuth Power Gear Assembly
24. Guide Rod Bushing
25. Ring Gear Shock Absorbing Support
26. Shell Ejection Chute
27. Windows
28. Sighting Window
29. Seat
30. Mounting Bracket
31. Gun Charging Handle and Cable
32. Shell Ejection Chute
33. 50 Cal. Gun
34. Gun Mounting Bracket
35. Door Latches
36. Door

**A-13A Ball Turret** (USAAF)

The gun controls in the Ball Turret were easily accessible. The main power switch and the fuses to protect the electrical circuits were located in the junction box beside the gunner's left knee. The gun chargers were two handles next to the gunner's feet. To charge the guns the gunner reached down to the floor, arms crossed, and pulled the handle carefully UP until the slack was out of the cables, and then the cables were pulled sharply UP to their limit. On their return the gun charging cables were to be allowed to move back under their own power without riding. Once the target was tracked the gunner pressed the electric trigger firing buttons (not conventional triggers) that were located on the top of each handgrip, just under the gunner's thumbs. The gun selector switches operated the electric triggers. Fire control was via Magnavox solenoids, and the gunfire interrupter was via profile-type cutouts.

For manual operation of the Ball Turret in case of emergency there were removable hand crank-operated shafts located on the right (for azimuth) and left (for elevation) side of the turret. The cranks were stowed in clips above the gunner's head. To change to manual operation the gunner turned the main power switch OFF, removed and attached the crank handles, and disengaged the azimuth and elevation clutches.

Leaving the Turret

To leave the ball turret the gunner moved it to 90° elevation (guns pointing straight down) and to 180° azimuth, turned OFF all switches, opened the door, stepped out, and closed the door. Once outside the gunner closed the hydraulic valve, raised the turret using the hand pump until the safety hooks were closed, catching the flange on the upper trunnion housing to hold the turret securely. He then turned the elevation hand crank to minus 22° elevation (the turret remained at 180° azimuth). The gunner knew when the guns were at minus 22° since the elevation cam (a raised metal plate fastened to the curve on the ball) moved up as the ball was turned in elevation and pressed against the elevation/retraction switch, turning it ON. This switch flashed a light in the pilot's compartment to inform him that the turret was retracted and the aircraft was ready to land. The outside elevation power clutch was turned by using the handle located in the clip on the trunnion ring support. The handle was then replaced in the clip. The elevation hand brake was tightened and its hand crank was replaced in its clip.

**Briggs Type A-13 Retractable Ball Turret**

The Brigg's-built A-13 retractable lower ball turret was a 44 inch spherical metal structure that could be lowered about 24 inches below the skin line of the aircraft. It was designed especially for the B-24, whose low ground clearance required that the Ball be retracted during takeoffs and landings. The A-2 and A-13 turrets were exactly the same except for the A-13's retracting mechanism, which was very simple. Because of the retraction mechanism the A-13 required several additional steps for entering and exiting.

Generally this turret consisted of two operating assemblies: the hanger and turret ball, which moved in azimuth with the trunnion ring, and in addition rotated in elevation by means of a self-aligning, top-mounting swivel assembly. The Briggs Ball could be retracted within the aircraft by means of a hand-operated hydraulic retraction assembly. A large hydraulic cylinder was attached to a supporting beam on the top of the fuselage, and the turret suspended from a piston contained inside a cylinder. A hand pump, mounted on the fuselage, provided pressure that forced the piston up to raise the turret, which was locked in place with safety hooks located on the upper trunnion housing. A valve on the fuselage released the hydraulic pressure and allowed the piston and turret to slide down.

Once inside the turret the gunner prepared to lower the turret by closing the hydraulic valve. The hand pump was pumped just enough to release the safety hooks, which were opened to disengage them from the upper trunnion housing. The gunner had to be careful to open the hydraulic valve slowly to allow the turret to ease down, and to be certain that the turret was properly seated in its lowest position. The tapered bushings that were mounted on the turret's azimuth ring were to sit directly in holes provided for them in the aircraft's floor ring. If the bushings didn't fit into the holes the gunner had to cajole the turret until they fit. He then had to be sure that the master switch located on the support beam was ON.

1. Left Side Gun in Stowed Position
2. Turret Tie Rods
3. Left Side Gun Amm. Feed
4. Rear Bomb Hoist in Position for Emergency Turret Retraction
5. Right Side Gun Amm. Feed
6. Retraction Safety Hook
7. Right Side Gun in Stowed Position
8. Turret Oxygen Bottles
9. Elevation Hand Brake

**Figure 772—Briggs Retractable Lower Ball Turret, Retracted Position, Looking Forward from Station 7.2**

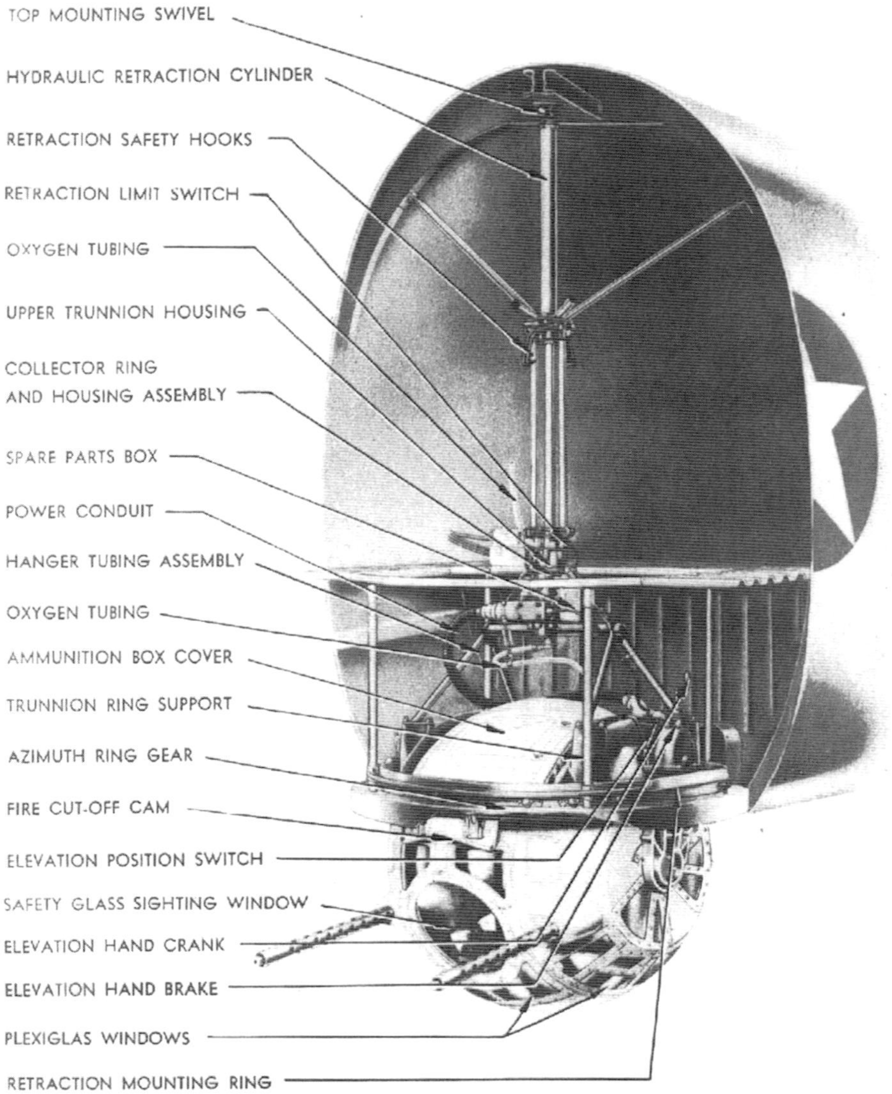


**A-13 Turret Installation** (USAAF)

If the retraction mechanism were damaged or malfunctioned the gunner could yank on an overhead safety wire and pull out two pins, and the rear turret door would open and the occupant could fall out and, once clear of the fuselage, pull the parachute rip cord.

If the hydraulic retraction gear malfunctioned in flight the turret could be raised by the aircraft's bomb hoists. The hoists were two winches—cable and pulley units that were mounted on the top of the fuselage on either side of the turret. The retraction procedure was: the guns were positioned at 180° azimuth and 90° elevation and left the turret. The winch cables were unwound and led over their opposite pulleys: the rear winch cable over the front pulley and the front cable over the rear pulley. The ends of the cables were hooked into the top of the turret hanger assembly. The gunner, assisted by another crew member, cranked both winches at the same time, slowly and evenly, until the turret was raised enough for the retraction safety hooks to attach to and support the turret. The guns were then cranked up into their normal stowing position (-22° elevation).

**Emergencies**

Wheels Up Belly Landings

The ball turret has become infamous due to the legion of tales of the ball gunner trapped in his battle-damaged turret being crushed during a wheels

Only in B-17s equipped with the fixed, non-retractable, A-2 model was a belly landing a problem as the turret was driven up into the fuselage; sometimes breaking the back of the bomber. (USAAF)

up landing. Under normal circumstances the ball gunner could enter and exit the turret in the B-17 and B-24 easily. During a belly landing in B-24s and B-17s equipped with the retractable Model A-13 ball turret the ball turret was of no consequence. In fact, a belly landing in the low-slung B-17 was aided by the half exposed tires that could be braked even when retracted into the nacelles during a belly landing. Only in B-17s equipped with the fixed, non-retractable A-2 model (later A-2A and A-2B) was a belly landing a problem, as the turret was driven up into the fuselage, sometimes breaking the back of the bomber. When preparing a B-17 equipped with the non-retractable A-2 series ball turrets for an emergency wheels up landing, the pilot had to remember two rules to minimize structural damage when the bomber hit the ground: land with 3/4 flaps; and if the B-17 mounted a chin turret, the tail wheels were to be retracted. However, an undamaged ball turret could be jettisoned in case of an emergency.

Jettisoning the Turret

The recommended ball jettisoning method was to release the ball itself, leaving the supporting yoke. Two men using only a crescent wrench and a hammer could release the turret in approximately 20 minutes using the following method. The guns were turned aft and down. The azimuth gear case was detached by removing the four bolts that held it. The safety retaining hooks were removed with a socket wrench, if available, or by breaking them off with a hammer. The 12 yoke connection nuts were removed to drop the turret. If the dropped turret landed first on the fire cut off cam, the gunner was to push the aft side with his foot to dislodge it. If there was time the gunner was to salvage the expensive computing sight, which required another 20 minutes. To remove the sight, one had to detach the three flexible drive cables located on the left, right, and far sides of the sight. Disconnect the electrical plug and free the sight by removing the sight retaining rod. Also, if there was enough time the electrical plugs and the oxygen lines were disconnected.

The original Sperry dorsal experimental turret was fabricated of a welded steel tubing framework with fabric belt feed and ammunition containers located below the revolving platform. (USAAF)

**Section 3: Sperry (Emerson/Steel Products/Briggs) Dorsal Turret Background and Development**

The original Sperry dorsal experimental turret was fabricated of a welded steel tubing framework with fabric belt feed and ammunition containers located below the revolving platform. By late 1940 the Sperry dorsal turret had been sufficiently tested at Wright Field and was released for quantity production. The production version was fabricated of cast metal framework, with the ammunition boxes located directly below twin .50s without boosters, fed by disintegrating link rather than fabric ammunition belts. The turret was accepted as standard on B-17Bs.

During development and then production important problems with the turret were revealed. When Sperry abandoned the fabric belt feed no servo mechanism was installed to replace it. In combat conditions it was found that the excessive gravitational load of combat acceleration made recoil feeding unsatisfactory. In order to avoid utilizing the conventional sprocket system employed in Martin designs a number of innovations, including feed chute rollers and constant level ammunition boxes, were utilized, but only through trial and error was it possible to find a suitable booster system design.

The Sperry fire cut out or gun interrupter device was an ingenious profile cam which rotated in constant orientation with the movement of the turret, providing positive firing circuit interruption whenever gunfire endangered aircraft structure. Unfortunately both guns cut out simultaneously, and the gunner was left without fire power in the marginal area at either extremity of a restricted zone and an interrupter for each gun was requested. Soon combat experience revealed another gun interrupter problem in successive models of B-17 airplanes that had slightly different characteristics in structure and in attitudes of flight. Each turret required a profile cam especially matched to the particular B-17 model. The problem was solved by careful coordination between Sperry, Boeing, and the Materiel Division. Further combat experience reported gun interrupter failures occurring when the turret was slewed into a restricted zone at high speed. The time between the moment when the interrupter cam opened the circuit and the moment when the last-fired bullet actually left the gun was of sufficient degree to cancel the protective feature of the cutout. To solve this problem Sperry engineers designed a differential which advanced the interrupter cam in proportion with increasing turret speeds, affording a sufficient margin of protection against gunfire damage in critical areas resulting from firing while slewing.

The first Sperry Model A-1 turret had restricted headroom and metal front quarter panels that restricted visibility, which were later replaced by Perspex sections manufactured in England for field installation by the 8AF in Europe. This modification was soon adopted on the production line, and later models had a raised section over the gunner's head and Plexiglas quarter panels.

In December 1940 Sperry signed government production contracts for the manufacture of its dorsal local and ventral remote turrets to be installed on the B-17, even though it was apparent that its factories did not have the required capacity. Considering this limitation, the Materiel Division and the Production Engineering Section (PES) compelled Sperry to contract subcontractors. Sperry was not very pleased to see more than five years of time, money, and experience contracted out to subcontractors who could be future competitors. Weeks went by and Sperry still hadn't found suitable subcontractors. A displeased Lt.Col. Kenneth Wolfe, the Chief of PES, stated that he was "going to get Sperry products if we have to go out and make prime contracts ourselves to a thousand different subcontractors." PES was obligated to get the Sperry turret designs into production and selected Emerson to build the turrets in conjunction with Sperry's two hurried choices: Steel Products Engineering and Briggs. Despite this setback Sperry retained control of its gunfire interrupter, hand controls, Vickers power drive, and computing gunsight used in the turret. The Sperry hand controls in the production version were derivatives of the Frazer-Nash system. The dorsal turret cost $7,185 per unit, with the dorsal turret computing sight contributing $2,250 of the total cost and the controls adding $1,335. On 22 August 1941 Sperry representatives met with the Materiel Division at Wright Field and received permission to discontinue turret production to concentrate on turret development.

Sperry built the fire cut out or interrupter unit which was shipped to the subcontractor for assembly in the turret. The "knife edge neutral" hand control which Maj. K.C. Wolfe, Chief of the Armament Laboratory, described as giving that "smooth transition from left or right deflection past neutral while tracking (which) was more important than absolute neutral, or no creep." The power drive system, consisting of a pair of Vickers units, was manufactured in Detroit and sent to the subcontractor for final assembly. The turret's computing sight unit was built and assembled by Sperry and was sent directly to the Boeing plant for installation in completed B-17s. The composite turret, less the sight assembly, was then shipped to Boeing, where a Sperry representative performed the final critical adjustments after installation.

The Materiel Division needed to coordinate and supervise the Sperry turret subcontractors in every step of the production expansion program. Often these contractors were inexperienced in aircraft manufacture and were unaccustomed to cooperating with each other. The Division also had to familiarize industrial engineers with the fundamental elements of aircraft design and construction requirements. An example of the difficulties in dealing with subcontractors and making changes was seen when Steel Products engineers improved the original turret dome to a paneled Plexiglas dome with cast aluminum ribs. Before the new Steel Products turret dome design could be circulated to the other manufacturers of Sperry turrets it required approval from the prime contractor, Sperry, and then was to be sent on to the Materiel Division for approval. While this process seemed convoluted, following proper channels assured "a higher degree of standardization and interchangeability, which was later to pay substantial dividends." Despite the great problems encountered in organizational control, coordination, and contractual relations with subcontractors, turret production reached unexpected figures.

### Sperry/Emerson Dorsal Turret Subcontracts

Once the Ford Consolidated tail turret contract terminated, the Chief of the Production Engineering Section urged Emerson to considered subcontracting the Sperry or General Electric turret. Emerson President Stuart Symington was unwilling to forgo the higher profits of prime contract production work and commit Emerson as a subcontractor, since his company had its own group of subcontractors and an established assembly capacity. However, it was vital for Symington to make a decision soon, because his new turret division factory was to be completed in January 1942 and would increase the now unfulfilled 250 turrets per month production of his current factory to a potential capacity of more than 1,000 turrets a month when the new factory came online. Nonetheless, the enormous expense of the new Emerson facility was far from wasted, as the Materiel Division had secured the services of an aggressive, well-equipped, production-wise industrial organization just when the accelerated upswing of aircraft deliveries would make turrets in quantity production an absolute necessity.

Sperry asked Emerson to consider manufacturing 100 Sperry dorsal local turrets a month beginning in July 1942, and the anxious Emerson now happily accepted the project, even though it preferred GE over Sperry (Symington was reluctant to contract Bendix turrets, which had been criticized by the British). Once committed Emerson examined Sperry dorsal turret production procedures and was able to move its dorsal local turret schedule forward from January 1942 to an initial production of 10 in August 1941, and then to 100 a month by the end of the year. The dynamic Symington continued to lobby Wright Field for more new contracts, and soon Emerson was fully occupied with building Sperry dorsal and ventral turrets as a subcontractor.

Once Emerson assumed the Sperry subcontracts it encountered problems. Sperry had agreed to furnish controls, fire interrupters, and drive units. Vickers Inc., a Detroit-based Sperry subsidiary, was the sole source of the crucial drive units. When Emerson's turret production rate, together with that of the other Sperry subcontractors, raised the demand for Vickers units above Vickers' capacity to produce them, Emerson wanted to produce Vickers units independently. Vickers was unwilling to expand or to allow Emerson to build the Vickers unit. Symington threatened to build the unit anyway, "patent or no patent," but the Production Engineering Section intervened by demanding that Vickers increase its output. But in the meantime the Vickers unit had become a critical production bottleneck, and Emerson turret production languished.

### Sperry/Steel Products Dorsal Turret Subcontract

The Steel Products Company of Springfield, OH, was coerced by pressure from the Materiel Division to become a subcontractor for the vital B-17 turret, and by February 1941 it had completed six dorsal local and six ventral remote turrets. The first Steel Products turrets off the production line in May had the expected assortment of turret problems: faulty link ejection chutes, malfunctioning case ejection at high angles of elevation, fouling charging cables at high angles of elevation, and excessive ammunition drag causing poor feeding. The reason for these problems was that the Steel Products turret contract did not include some of the best Sperry design features, as the Production Engineering Section considered that these exclusions would facilitate quantity production. To remedy any future problems the Materiel Division specifically instructed Steel Products to "pursue a policy of change with unabated production." Steel Products was to "investigate design improvements which could be evaluated by the Materiel Division." Improvements accepted by the Division would then "be standardized and coordinated for all interested facilities."

In December 1941, approximately a year after the Sperry contract was approved, Steel Products had delivered 91 ventral remote and 111 dorsal turrets. Steel Products engineers had made modifications to Sperry's design in order to facilitate production. Sperry objected that Steel Product's modifications and improvements were seriously compromising the efficiency of the Sperry computing sight on the dorsal turrets. Sperry believed the Materiel Division's directive on channeling all changes through the prime contractor was not effective and suggested the placement of a permanent Sperry engineer in the Steel Products plant "to insure a high degree of liaison between the separate manufacturing organizations." When combat gunners objected that the heavy ribs in the Steel Products dome limited target scanning Steel Products devised a single panel, curved Plexiglas, forward-sighting section. The in-house Sperry engineer claimed this modification was detrimental to the accuracy of Sperry's computing sight, as the curved sighting panel resulted in refraction errors "unduly large and undesirable primarily because the advantage of using a computing sight is almost completely nullified." To resolve this problem and satisfy both parties, Plexiglas manufacturer Rohm & Haas designed a panel of varying thicknesses that reduced refraction errors to an insignificant degree.

**Sperry Dorsal Turret**
**General Description**

The Sperry Dorsal Turret was described as the "upstairs half brother" of the Sperry Ball Turret used in the B-17. There were two basic models, the A-1 and the later improved A-1A, which had several different components. If a gunner could operate an A-1 he could operate an A-1A.

Entering the Turret

When the turret was in the stowed configuration, the gunner simply stepped up on the turret platform directly from the cockpit into the dome between the guns. However, during combat the gunner would enter the turret from the opposite side over the bomb bay; crawling between two column supports; turning around, and then rising from this stooped position to stand up in the turret. Once in the turret, the gunner adjusted the footrests located on the column supports to his height so that his head and eyes were directly behind the sight's optic head, enabling him to sight comfortably without stooping. When sitting the gunner used a removable seat pad that had clips that attached to connections on the side of the turret. He then adjusted the seat height by lengthening or shortening a simple belt and buckle under the seat pad. Many gunners preferred to stand in the turret rather than sit. There was a web strap that clipped to each fuselage wall to act as a back rest when standing or sitting. For armor protection there was an oblong armor plate panel on the bomber's bulkhead just behind the turret.

Sperry dorsal turret mounted on a B-17F. The turret was introduced in the B-17E replacing the pilot's observation dome and operated by the flight engineer. (USAAF)

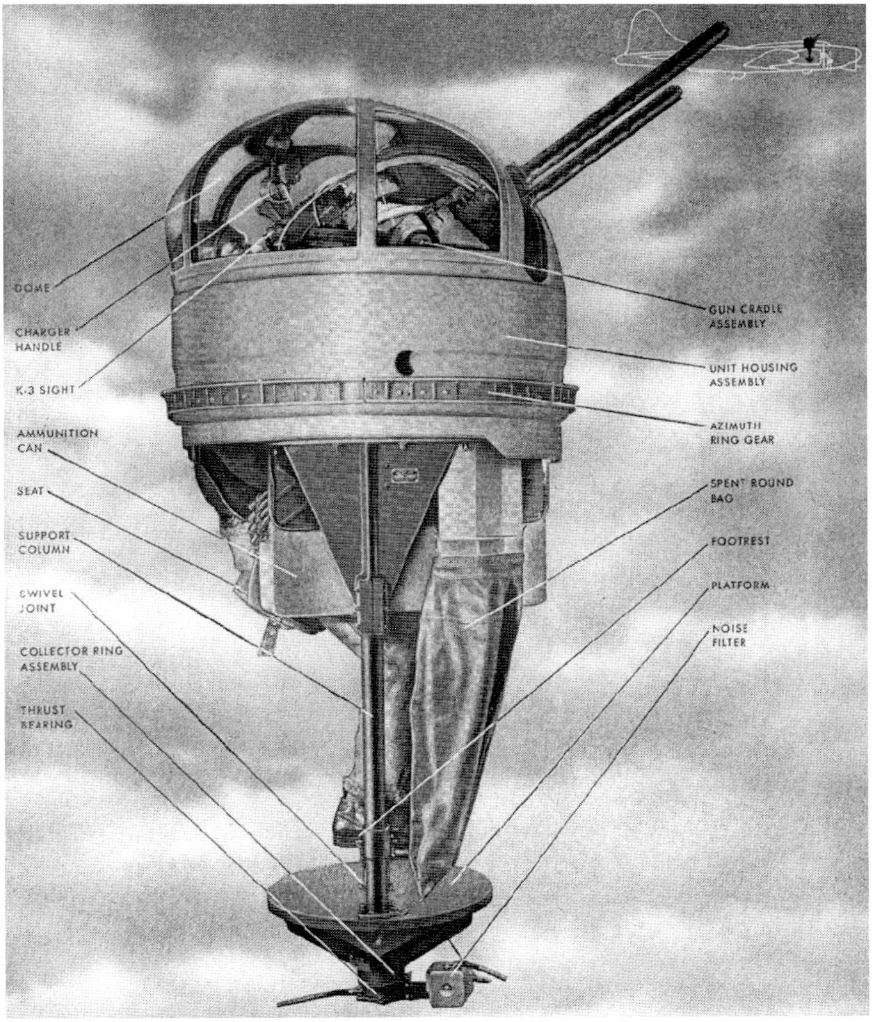


**SPERRY DORSAL TURRET** (USAAF)

Operating the Turret

Like the A-2/A-13 Ball Turret, the Dorsal Turret operated hydraulically from pressure built up by a pump driven by a constant speed electric motor to move it 360°, full circle in azimuth at 40° per second, and the guns lowered and raised from just below level -5° to almost straight up 85° in elevation. The turret had all the controls and clutches conveniently located. The main power circuits were opened and closed by circuit breakers that looked and functioned exactly like toggle switches but operated as reset buttons, as they cut off the current during overload conditions.

The initial operating step was to be sure that both the azimuth and elevation power clutches were engaged in the IN position. The azimuth clutch was a small crank or lever located above the left ammunition container, while the elevation clutch was located above the right ammunition container. These clutches could not be shifted without first pulling out the pins in the ends of their handles that snapped back into the IN or OUT positions.

The main power circuit breaker on the junction box near the gunner's left shoulder was turned ON, and on the same panel the heated flying suit, light, firing circuit breaker, and sight circuit breakers were also turned ON. The gunner then reached up in front of him and flipped the sight switch ON and then next to it, adjusted the sight brightness on the sight rheostat. The turret was never to be operated under power unless the sight was ON or the sight could experience excessive wear. The booster motor switch located on the front of the control handles was turned ON, and then the gunner grasped the control handles so that his left hand squeezed the safety switch on the left handle to activate turret movement. The turret was ready for combat.

The Browning M-2 machine guns mounted in the Sperry Dorsal Turret fed from the inside, with the right gun feeding from the left and the left gun from the right. The guns were held in their cradles by rear trunnion blocks and slides and two front trunnion studs. The rear trunnion blocks were bolted to the rear of the guns and dovetailed into the slides. The two front trunnion studs held the front gun yoke to the gun adapter and were safety-wired. Special charging units were installed on the inside plates of both guns with mounting screws that were safety wired. The charging handles were suspended from pulleys on the dome. To charge the guns the gunner grasped the handles and pulled them down sharply as far as they would move, and then allowed the charging handles to move back on their own power while keeping his hands on the handle but not riding them back. The cable connections to the units were held by cotter pins. The guns were adjusted up, down, or sideways in their cradles by adjusting collars on each rear gun mount.

Interior view of the Sperry turret from the cockpit. The webbed back rest can be seen hanging on the right; the ammunition boxes lining the left and right walls; the inverted "Y" hand grips and gunsight are located in the center. (USAAF)

The turret was supplied by six 125 round ammunition boxes, three for each gun totaling 750 rounds. The six boxes were held in two metal racks running in a V toward the front of the turret; one rack to the right gun and the other to the left gun. The ammunition boxes were small (125 rounds) and were quickly used, but could also be quickly reloaded. To reload the boxes the gunner went to the front of the turret and lifted the empty boxes off the racks and reloaded them. The rounds were loaded with their tips pointing to the outside of the turret. The loaded boxes were lifted back onto the roller tracks that were notched for easy loading and slid forward. There were pivot locks on the front of the tracks that closed to prevent the boxes from riding off. To load the guns the gunner pulled two 25 round lengths of the ammunition belt to use as feed strips. The gunner opened the hinged section at the top of the booster chutes and dropped each feed strip through each chute from the top with the single link end first. The strip was fed down the chute until the double link end fit into the gun's feedway over the booster sprockets, making certain that the rounds were evenly positioned in the sprockets. The lower single link of the feed strip was then connected by using a single round to the double link end of the ammunition belt in the front of the ammunition box. The belts in the ammunition boxes were connected together in the same manner so that the three boxes were linked for each gun. Spent round bags, held by a simple snap latch to the months of the gun's ejection chutes, caught spent rounds as they were ejected from the guns. Special link ejection chutes were installed on the outside of the guns to carry the links away.

The K-3 computing sight was held upright on its mounting bracket in a single cradle by a long pin. Three flexible shafts connected to the sight and transmitted the turret movement and range data. The shaft connected to the top input at the back of the sight revolved as the turret moved in elevation. The shaft connected to the bottom rear input revolved as the turret moved in azimuth. The third shaft entering the right side led to range control that fed data required to keep the sight reticle framing the target (The inverted K-4 was installed on the ball turret.).

The turret was operated by turning the handles like a bicycle; right to go right and left to go left. The heels of the handles were pressed down to raise the guns and pulled up to lower the guns. The tracking was to be as smooth as possible without jerking. On the right handle was a range control knob that was similar to a motorcycle hand grip, which the gunner used to keep the sight reticles framing the target. Next to the gunner's thumb on the left handle was the push-to-talk button that opened the interphone, and under his index fingers on both handles were the triggers.

Exiting the Turret

Before the gunner left the turret he ran it into the stowed position with the guns positioned about 15° in elevation and 180° azimuth and a little above level and pointing straight back toward the tail. He opened the firing circuit breaker; turned the sight switch OFF; opened the sight circuit breaker; and finally opened the main power circuit breaker. Gunners using a seat unfastened the seat strap. The gunner backed out of the turret, stepping up onto the platform.

**Section 4: Martin Amplidyne (Electric) Dorsal Turret**
**Background and Development**

In July 1939 the Glenn L. Martin Company of Baltimore, MD, issued its specifications for its new B-26 medium bomber. The original armament installation specifications called for a total of four flexible hand-held .30 caliber guns: a single nose and tail gun, a floor gun, and a dorsal single .30 caliber gun mounted in a "rotating enclosure." This "rotating enclosure" was to become the Martin amplidyne drive turret and would be one of the most successful turrets of World War II, both from the design and production perspectives. It proved extremely adaptable for use in several aircraft besides the B-26, including the B-24, B-34, and the Navy PV series (as the 250CE). It was well designed and simple, with no distracting gadgets. It was an excellent turret for immediate action and easy operation, with everything needed for combat within arm's length. Later models were basically improvements over previous models, while others were modified for use in different aircraft types. This turret was notably easy to get into, operate, and exit, and it was said that if a gunner could operate one Martin Electric Turret he was able to operate any of them.

The original Martin dorsal turret called for a hydraulic retraction mechanism for a gun swinging free through an 8° cone of fire (movement in excess of 8° closed electric circuits that rotated the turret). The azimuth power rotation system was similar to the British Armstrong-Whitworth and Boulton-Paul systems perfected a number of years earlier. The earliest turret version visualized a friction drive, but at Wright Field it was felt that a positive gear train drive would be superior.

Martin divided the armament of the B-26 into projects, with one or two men assigned to concentrate on a specific project. One group took on an "approach probability analysis," which was a study of the angles of attack. Another group studied armor plate protection and remote control possibilities, while another studied the aircraft weight and balance and the effect of armament placement on it. This practice of delegating specific problems to specialized groups of engineers was generally successful, but in January 1940 an Air Corps Mock-up Board inspected the B-26 and judged the turret to be unsatisfactory. The inspectors found the turret's two light .30 caliber guns were ineffective, and the turret remained 10 or 12 drag-producing inches above the fuselage level when fully retracted. The Board's recommendation to install a single .50 caliber machine gun in the turret in lieu of the twin .30s further increased the retracted turret height by two additional inches. Martin engineers calculated that this additional turret height would reduce the aircraft's performance below the aircraft's specified guaranteed speed, and Martin was unwilling to switch to the .50 caliber gun. The Materiel Division also did not want the B-26 to fall below the guaranteed performance figure, so a compromise was reached to allow the company to pass the performance test with the .30 caliber guns in place and then install the .50 caliber gun afterwards. This controversy delayed the Martin turret development until June 1940, when Martin introduced the prototype B-26 turret with full power operation in azimuth and elevation for twin .50 machine guns, each equipped with 100 round magazines. This Martin turret employed General Electric amplidyne controls, which were developments of the initial General Electric B-18 tail gun drive. The production prototype turret carried a heavy semicircular sheet of armor plate that was innovative for that time. The gun apertures were not equipped with slot closures, and the Armament Branch recommended that the ammunition total be increased to 800 rounds. The turret required additional work, as there were many aspects of the installation that were in a rudimentary stage of development.

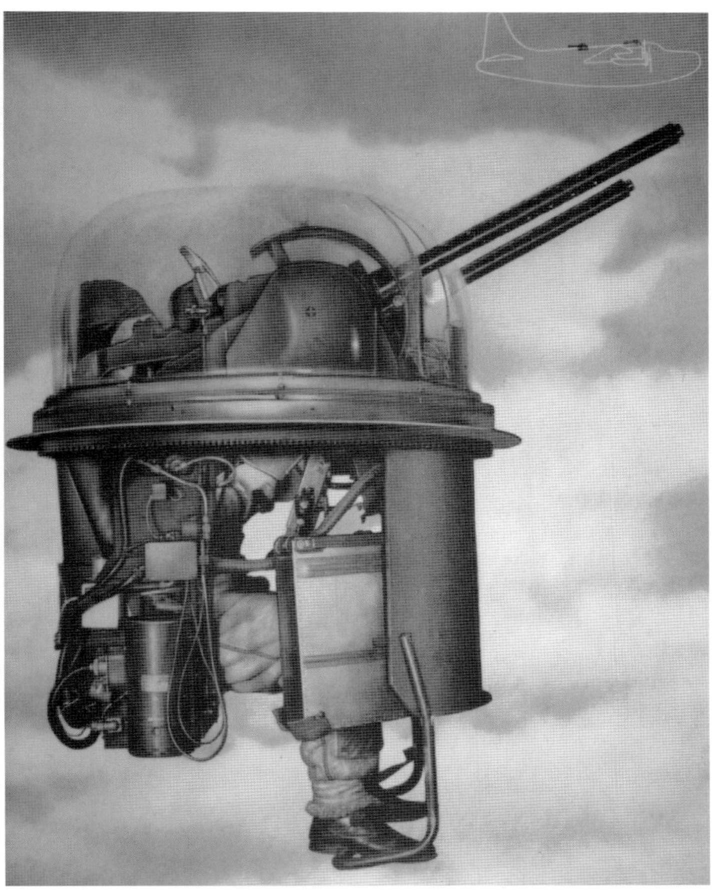

Martin Amplidyne (Electric) Dorsal Turret (USAAF)

Firing tests of the prototype performed at Aberdeen revealed the normal number of minor problems that usually occurred during turret testing. The Test memo Report of 21 September 1940 concluded that the Martin turret design "marked a distinctive advance in the development of electrical power controlled turrets." The Martin turret used the General Electric amplidyne system that provided speed control (e.g. the control handle displacement determined the rate of angular rotation of the turret). Another type of control unit was the GE selsyn system that provided position control (e.g. positioning a control bar attached to a sight induced a remotely located turret to come to rest in a position comparable to and coincident with that of the control handle). The Materiel Division requested Martin to construct a turret mounting twin .50s that would be exactly like the B-26 version, except that the control circuit was to be the GE selsyn rather than the GE amplidyne system. Martin engineers worked around the clock for five days and fabricated a selsyn turret, but it was found to be less satisfactory than the amplidyne speed control. After successful testing the Materiel Division negotiated a contract for 159 amplidyne dorsal turrets at $4,645 each ($738,555 total).

The basic reliability of amplidyne drive was central to the success of the Martin turret design, but was also due to Martin's outstanding expertise and organizational talents. From the onset of the project the Martin engineering staff determined the fundamental requirements for the turret, and the original production model continued almost unchanged as the basis for future production designs. Gun mounts, ammunition boosters, armor plate, and control system were so expertly designed in the prototype stage that subsequent upgrading involved minor improvements rather than basic changes. Later additions of a profile cam fire cut out and structural interrupter, emergency manual operation, quickly detachable ammunition cans, and the complex addition of a computing sight did not change the original concept of the turret.

The success of Martin's production of the turret was due to two basic managerial tenets. Unlike other turret manufacturers, particularly Bendix, Martin engaged a group of subcontractors which it was able to control to achieve production results without asking the Materiel Division, the PES, or the OPM for help. The second tenet in Martin's success was that the company was the first American turret manufacturer to go into production to meet an immediate need with a turret which was basically reliable so that later modifications and improvements could be made on the production line without interrupting assembly. British turret manufacturers had utilized this method successfully for years.

In June 1941, the Production Engineering Section and Martin discussed the possibility of manufacturing dorsal turrets for the B-24. Martin was agreeable, as it had the factory capacity to meet production quotas. But by November B-24 production increased significantly and Martin's factory capacity was no longer sufficient. The Materiel Division looked to Emerson as a subcontractor, but at the time Emerson projected that it could not start producing Martin turrets until the spring of 1942. Martin remained eager to build the turrets and contacted 15 subcontractors who all refused because they were already operating to capacity. Martin reassessed its ability to manufacture the turret, and by the end of 1941 the company reported that it expected to deliver 2,000 to 3,500 turrets in the following year, depending upon the number of specification changes required. In 1942 Martin was able to meet the demand for the turret as its B-26 production decreased. Also, a lag in B-24 production helped until Emerson came on board and increased Martin turret production capacity.

The development of the Martin turret, like most turrets, was not the result of a single initial concept, but the result of a gradual accumulation and incorporation of ideas. However, the Martin turret, as opposed to other turrets, was basically a simple design that once through its initial experimental phase proved "sufficiently satisfactory" to go directly into large scale production. The turret was so successful that the Armament Laboratory planned to build it to such generalized specifications that it could be readily used in other aircraft.

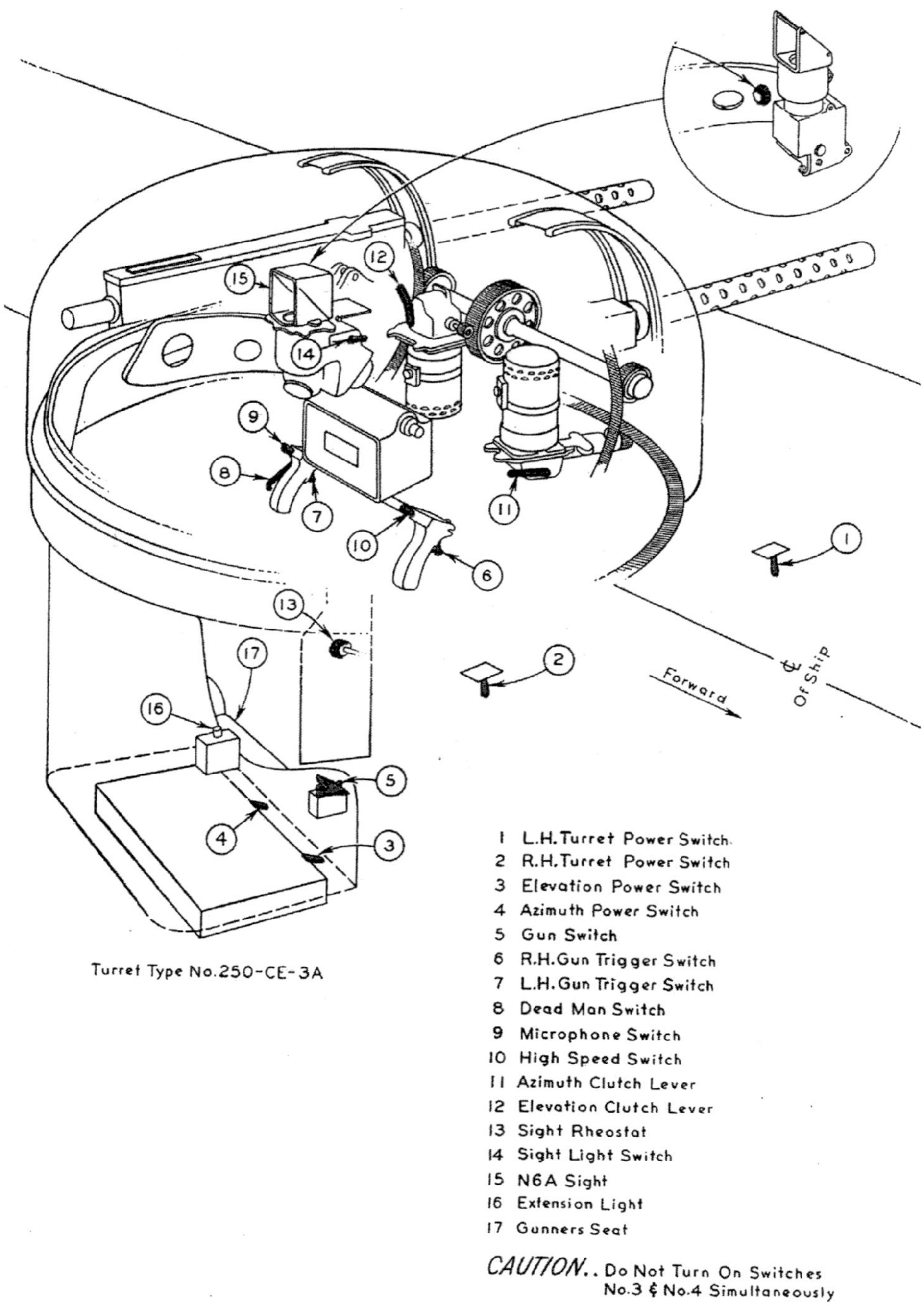


**Martin Dorsal Turret Assembly** (USN)

**Description**

The *Aircrew Gunnery Manual* describes the turret as:

"....one of the most widely used of all turrets. It is designed for quick and easy operation. It has no gadgets. Everything is made for action and placed where it can be reached quickly when the chips are down."

There are several models. Some of them are improvements over old models, like a new automobile that is better than last year's. Some are simply designed for different kinds of bomber, for example, the model that goes into the B-26 is not quite the same as the one in the B-24. But if you can operate one Martin, you can operate them all."

Entering the Turret

The first step upon entering for the gunner was to turn ON the main power switch, which was a toggle switch on the main fuselage near the turret. The gunner then adjusted the footrest to accommodate his height. If the gunner needed more room to enter the turret he could drop the bottom of the seat by pulling on the small cable stretched across the front. He would then "stoop and squirm up into the middle of the turret, face the front, grasp the two main supports curving above his head, and hoist your body up." He was not to pull himself up by the sight cradle or the two nearby link rods, as he could impair the sight adjustment or bend the link rods and throw the sight out of line.

The last step was for the entering gunner to stand on the foot rest and brace himself against the back of the seat. If the seat was too low the gunner used his heel to lift it up until the latches on each side of the seat clicked. The gunner then sat down and used spare seat cushions to adjust his height until his eyes were level with the sight. He then adjusted and snapped his seat belt closed. The armor plate was 1/2 inch thick protecting the front of the gunner, no matter where he aimed his guns.

Operating the Turret

All the clutches, switches, and controls were close to the seated gunner and were easy to use. The clutches and switches needed to engaged and turned on in the following order:

1) The azimuth clutch which was a small lever under and to the right of the control handles was to be pushed down. The elevation clutch, a lever above and to the left of the control panel, was pushed to its engaged position to the left.
2) The gunner reached down on the right side of his seat and turned on the automobile type ignition switch.
3) The red plastic cover on the right side of the control panel was raised the master gun switch flipped on.
4) The gun selector switch was turned to the Both Guns selection. With the switch in this position, both guns would fire when either trigger was pulled. In the Individual Guns position, each gun was only fired by its own trigger and was to be used only when one gun was out of action.
5) The sight switch located in a clamp on the face of the armor plate was turned on. The brightness of the sight reticle could be adjusted to suit lighting conditions by turning the rheostat button from Dim to Bright.
6) The control handles were grasped so that the bottom edges of the gunner's hands depressed the two safety switches. With these switches down the turret was ready. To move the turret the handles were turned similarly to steering a bicycle handle bar; to the right to go right, and left to go left. To raise the guns the handles were pressed down and pulled up to lower them.

**Controls** (USAAF)

The other controls required for combat "were right at the gunner's fingertips." Under his index finger on both handles were the triggers. On top of the control handle, near his thumb, was the high speed button that put the turret into high speed for changing from one target to another. At the gunner's left thumb was the push-to-talk button that opened the interphone system. On the main control panel were reset buttons for the control unit and booster motor circuits. Down on the front panel of the seat, behind the gunner's legs, were resets for the major electrical circuits: auxiliary power, azimuth, elevation, and firing circuits. These reset buttons were to be depressed when the power failed.

This turret operated on power from the bomber's generator. The drive unit consisted basically of a control unit, two amplidynes, and two electric motors. The turret guns could be lowered and raised in elevation from a little below horizontal (-6 1/2°) to almost straight up (85°) and move 360°, full circle, in azimuth. The turret had two speeds: normal tracking speed and high-speed. It could make one revolution in 18 seconds at normal speed and in eight seconds at high-speed.

Guns and Ammunition

The two .50 caliber machine guns were fed from the inside: the right gun was fed from the left and the left gun from the right. The guns were bolted into the front and rear mounts in the gun cradles. Special charging units were installed on the inside plates of the guns, and their mounting bolts safety wired. Special ejection chutes were installed on the outside of the guns to carry the links away. The guns could be adjusted up, down, or sideways in their cradles by a lock and adjustment nut unit on each rear gun mount.

The guns were charged by pulling cross-armed on the charger handles at shoulder level: the right hand grasped with the left hand and the left handle by the right hand. They were to be pulled out as sharply as far as the charging cables would go.

The two .50 caliber machine guns were fed from the inside; the right gun was fed from the left and the left gun from the right. The guns were bolted into the front and rear mounts in the gun cradles. (USAAF)

The turret was supplied with the standard N-8 or N-6A optical sight, the Mk9 reflector sight, and later the K-9 computing sight. The N-8 and N-6A were mounted in a boxlike frame that protruded from the sight cradle. To adjust the sight up or down and from side to side the mounting bolts were loosened.

The Martin turret carried four ammunition cans holding about 200 rounds each. When the ammunition belts were folded the two cans for the right hand feed gun by starting with the single-link end at the right edge of the can; the double-link end would come out of the left side of the can at the top. The other two cans were loaded for the left hand feed and were loaded the opposite way. The ammunition cans rode on a semi-circular track beneath the guns. Each was held in place by two rollers and a strip that fit into a groove in the track. When the cans were placed into the turret the rollers needed to be in the tracks and the strip secured in the groove. The two right hand cans were loaded onto the right track, and the left hand cans onto the left track. The cans had to be pushed all the way down so that the automatic latches caught in the slots in the cans.

To feed the ammunition belts over the booster motors that helped to lift them into the guns, two extra 35 round lengths of belt were required as "feed strips." The booster motors were checked by tilting them toward the guns and making sure that they cut in and out sharply without lag. The hinged sections on top of the booster chutes were opened. One of the Feed

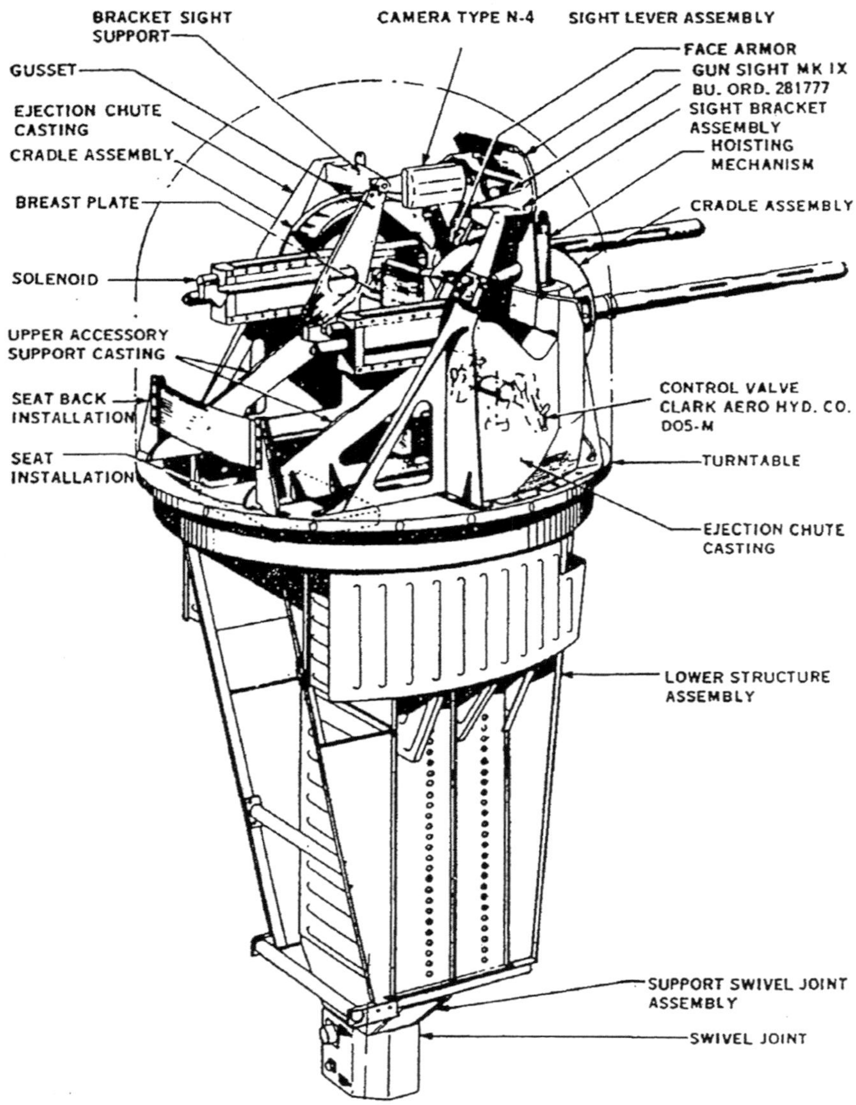


**Martin Hydraulic Dorsal (Upper Deck) Turret** (USN)

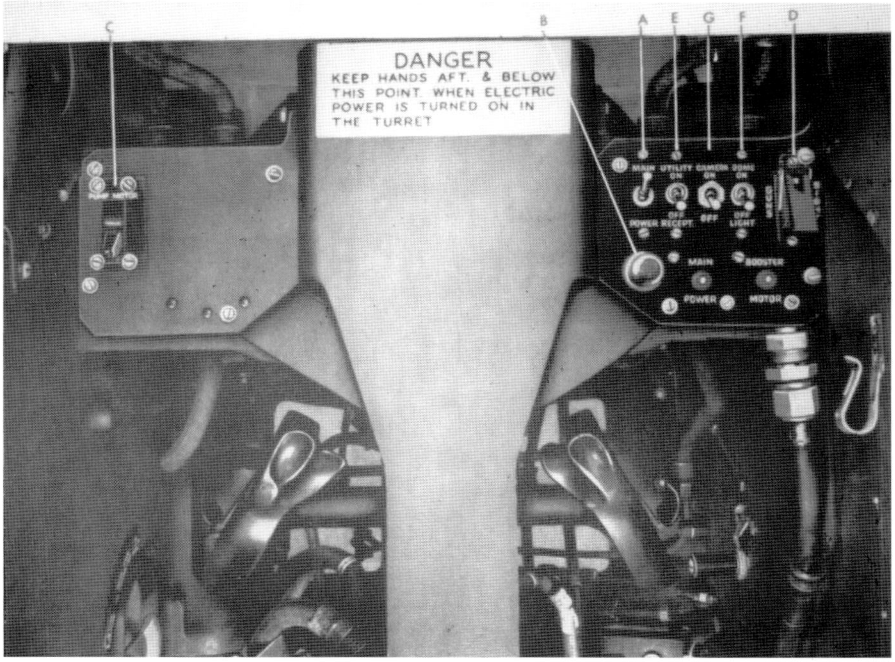


**Controls:** **A**=Main Power Switch; **B**=Red Indicator Light; **C**=Pump Motor Switch; **D**=Gun & Sight Switch; **E**=Utility Switch; **F**=Dome Light; **G**=Camera Switch. (USN)

strips was dropped down each chute, the single-link end first, until there were about 10 rounds left between the boosters and the guns. The rounds needed to rest evenly in the sprocket wheels. The double-link end of each feed strip went into the gun's feedways. The single-link ends were connected to the belts in the two inside ammunition cans.

Exiting the Turret
Before leaving the turret it was to be placed in its stowing position of 0° elevation and 180° in azimuth with the guns pointing straight back toward the tail. All switches were to be turned off and the azimuth and elevation power clutches engaged. Any auxiliary units that had been used were to be disconnected. The gunner then was ready to brace himself against the back of the seat and ease his body out of the turret. The seat was dropped by pulling a cable.

**Section 5: Martin Hydraulic Dorsal (Upper Deck) Turret**
The Martin Hydraulic Upper Deck Turret was the standard Navy Turret installation for many flying boats. There were several models which were virtually alike. The -1 was placed in the PBM Martin Mariner; -3 in the Consolidated Coronado; and the -2 in the PDM-3D as the 250CH-1 & 3.

Description
The Martin turret was designed for the mounting of two .50 caliber modified M-2 guns. These turrets operated hydraulically on pressure built up by a hydraulic pump driven by a constant speed electric motor. The main member of the turret was a large machined aluminum casting revolving on rollers between horizontally mounted steel tracks. This casting supported the brackets and mounts for carrying the gun carriages, gunsight bracket, seat, armor plate, ammunition boxes, power drives, and enclosure. The turret could be removed from the airplane as a single unit. The transparent turret dome was manufactured of Plexiglas molded in one piece and ribbed. The gun slots were closed by a sheet metal drum attached to the gun cradles and rotating against ribs of the enclosure. The enclosure was fastened to the main ring casting by bolts and clips. The armor protection on the front of the turret consisted of three sections to shield the gunner in any direction he pointed the guns. The armor consisted of: the 1/2 inch armor plate on the sight bracket protected the gunner's face; the 1/2 inch armor plate for gunner body protection; and the 3/8 inch armor plate protection for the ammunition magazines.

Entering the Turret
Like the Martin Electric Turret, this turret was considered very easy to enter. Before the gunner entered he was to be sure that the deck turret switch located on the flight engineer's panel was turned ON. Just outside the turret located in a junction box on the bulkhead was the emergency turret power ON/OFF switch that was coupled to a red indicator light. Inside the turret was a similar main power ON/OFF switch with a red light indicator below it which was to be used once the gunner was inside the turret.

The gunner entered the turret head-first from the rear of the ammunition box by climbing up the two steps using any handy stationary part of the turret as a hand grip. While standing on top of the ammunition box covers the gunner reached down and pulled the hinged seat up until it locked over the right hand seat support bar. The sight was checked for proper height for the gunner. If the sight required adjustment the gunner got back out

Martin 250CH mounted on a **Douglas A-20 bomber**. (USAAF)

and adjusted the seat by removing the pins from the seat support bar on each side of the seat and raising them to the next holes above or below. On early turrets there was no integral seat height adjustment, but a detachable seat cushion could be used as half thickness or full thickness with the two parts held together by snap fasteners.

A sliding foot rest was mounted in guides attached to the armor plate. The rest was held at different heights by spring latches and holes in the tubular frame of the foot rest. A loop on the inboard end of each latch enabled them to be withdrawn by one hand from the locating holes, during adjustment, by inserting the thumb in one loop and the middle finger in the other end and squeezing.

The turret oxygen system, a rebreather unit, a canister, and a mask were connected to the main aircraft system through a swivel joint at the base of the turret. The heated flying suit cord was plugged into an outlet on the junction box directly above the gunner's left foot. The interphone jack box was connected to the right ejection chute casting, while the push-to-talk button was located on the front of the box. Two trouble lights were attached to the ribs on the top of the dome, one on either side of the escape hatch.

### Operating the Turret

After entering the turret and being seated the gunner checked the low-pressure gauge located near his right foot for a pressure of 25 to 30 pounds, which would insure a smooth turret operation. He reached under the front edge of the seat and closed the two main power switches and the red indicator light flashed ON. The pump motor switch on the control panel was raised to the ON position. The gun and sight switch located under a red plastic cover on the control panel was flicked ON. The pump motor was turned ON by pressing down on the two safety switches. Once these switches were ON the control handles would automatically go to the neutral position and the sight and booster motors were activated.

To operate the turret the control handles were turned in the direction the gunner wanted the turret to move. For azimuth (right or left) the control handles were operated like a bicycle. The control handles were to be operated smoothly and deliberately. The gunner elevated the guns by pushing both hand grips forward, and he lowered them by pulling both grips back. To rotate the turret the gunner turned the hand grips about a vertical axis with the direction of rotation dependent on the direction the grips were turned. The speed at which the guns or turret moved depended upon the displacement of the grips. The gunner stopped all turret motion by allowing the grips to return to their normal spring-centered positions or by releasing the dead-man switch. The turret could move 360° full circle in azimuth and the guns could be elevated 80° above horizontal and depressed 20° below the horizontal. A small high-speed button was located at the top of the right hand firing grip and by depressing it, the turret speed was doubled. The purpose of this control was to move the turret quickly to sight the target, after which the target could be tracked by use of the normal speeds.

### Guns and Ammunition

The twin .50 caliber machine guns were installed on an Edgewater E-10 adaptor and were bolted to the front and rear mounts in the gun cradles. The gun carriage was a one piece casting equipped with Bell Shock Dampeners which absorbed the recoil and prevented excessive vibration of the turret and sight. The cartridge case ejection hopper was an integral part of the carriage. The gun elevating gears were bolted to the gun carriage and meshed with gears on a common torque tube running across the turret at the barrel end of the guns. The guns could be adjusted up, down, or sideways in their cradles by an adjustment nut assembly that was locked in place by jam nuts. The triggers were located on the control handles under the gunner's index fingers and either trigger fired both guns.

Provisions were made for mounting a N-3A or standard Navy Mk9 reflector sight in the cast metal sight mount bracket which was bolted to the main ring bracket arms. The bracket was pivoted to swing in an arc whose center was located approximately at the base of the gunner's head. The sight mount was rigidly connected by means of link rods to the gun carriage so that the line of sight was always parallel to the gun barrels. The gunsight lamp was provided with a special rheostat for turning the lamp ON and OFF and for changing the amount of the gunsight lamp output.

The hydraulic gun charger control knob was located next to the gunner's left knee and operated the gun chargers that were located on the inboard side of each gun. To charge the guns the control knob was depressed sharply to the FIRING position. Both guns were charged simultaneously and ready to fire. If the control knob was turned to SAFE before depressing the gun bolt would remain in the retracted position which would provide access to a jam.

A gun camera could be mounted below and parallel to the guns just above the ammunition boxes. A camera ON switch was located on the control panel which was activated by depressing either safety switch *and* either trigger switch.

The Martin Turret carried ammunition in two built-in magazines separated by a steel partition and mounted under the gunner's feet. These double magazines were loaded through sliding removable doors on top and held up to 600 rounds for each gun. The top of the ammunition box and the removable doors also functioned as a foot rest for the gunner. On either side of the seat, attached under the azimuth track, were the expended ammunition containers for each gun. The twin .50 caliber machine guns were fed from the inside; the right guns fed from the left and the left guns fed from the right.

### Exiting the Turret

First the guns were to be moved to their stowed position, 0° elevation and 180° azimuth, with the guns pointing straight aft. All switches were turned OFF and all auxiliary units were disconnected. The gunner braced himself against the back of the seat and reached down on his right side and depressed the seat release, which caused the seat to swing down out of the way. He then was able to climb down the two steps to leave the turret.

In case of an emergency the gunner could leave through an escape hatch in the Plexiglas dome. Two plastic handles were located on either side of the hatch which were turned a quarter turn to cause the hatch to open inboard. The gunner had to stand up on the seat to scuttle out of the top of the turret.

**Martin Hydraulic Nose Ball Turret** (USN)

**Controls:** **A**=Main Power Switch; **B**=Red Indicator Light; **C**=Pump Motor Switch; D=Gun & Sight; **F**=Utility; **G**=Spot Light; **H**=Camera. (USN)

**Martin 250SH nose turret** mounted on a **Martin PBM bomber**. (USN)

**Section 6: Martin Hydraulic Nose Ball Turret**

The Martin 250SH Ball Turret was placed on all Navy flying boats using ball turrets. It was a well-designed complete self-contained unit that protected the aircraft from frontal attacks and making strafing attacks on submarines. The turret was similar in operation and appearance to the ERCO 250SH and, being a ball turret, the gunner moved with his guns and sight in azimuth and elevation. The Martin 250SH Turret was manufactured in two models which were equivalent: the 250SH-1A was placed in the bow of the PBM-3D, and the 250SH-2 was used in the bow of the PB2Y-3. The turret operated hydraulically on pressure built up by a hydraulic pump driven by a constant speed electric motor.

Entering the Turret

The gunner was instructed only to enter this turret while in flight, as his weight in the bow unbalanced the aircraft during takeoffs and landings. Before the gunner entered the turret the flight engineer was to turn ON the bow turret switch. Just outside the turret, located in a junction box on the bulkhead, was the emergency turret power ON/OFF switch that was coupled to a red indicator light and was to be ON. Inside the turret was a similar main power ON/OFF switch with a red light indicator below it which was to be used once the gunner was inside the turret.

The gunner entered the turret facing forward through an opening in the bottom. He reached up and gripped the top of the armor plate to help pull him in. Once inside the gunner reached down on his left side and released the seat lock, which allowed the seat to roll on a track. Once the gunner was seated he looked through the sight to determine if he was at the correct height. If height adjustment were required the gunner used his right hand to move the seat adjustment handle. He released the catch on the handle with his thumb and moved the handle up or down to raise or lower the seat, after which the catch was reengaged.

Operating the Turret

After entering the turret and being seated the gunner checked the low-pressure gauge located near his right foot for a pressure of 25 to 30 pounds, which would insure a smooth turret operation. The elevation landing lock on the forward left hand side of the ball was UNLOCKED by pulling out and rotating the handle UP. The azimuth position lock on the lower left hand side was put into the extreme UNLOCKED position. UNLOCKING these two locks freed the turret. The main power control switch on the control panel on the upper right hand side of the turret was clicked ON as indicated by the red indicator light on the outside of the junction box. The pump motor switch on the bottom of the junction box was flicked ON. The gun and sight switch located under a red plastic cover on the control panel was flicked ON. The pump motor was turned ON by pressing down on the two safety switches. Once these switches were ON the control handles would automatically go to the neutral position and the sight and booster motors were activated.

To operate the turret the control handles were turned in the direction the gunner wanted the turret to move. For azimuth (right or left) the control handles were operated like a bicycle. The control handles were to be operated smoothly and deliberately. The gunner elevated the guns by pushing both hand grips forward, and he lowered them by pulling both grips back. To rotate the turret the gunner turned the hand grips about a vertical axis with the direction of rotation depending upon the direction the grips were turned. The speed at which the guns or turret moved depended upon the displacement of the grips. The 250SH-1A and -2A had an azimuth motion of 79° either side of the center line of the aircraft. Both the 250SH-1A and -2A turrets could be elevated 87° above horizontal and depressed 33° below the horizontal. To the left front of the gunner was the high pressure gauge which was supposed to maintain a pressure of 960 to 1,000 psi. A hydraulic hand pump was provided to operate the turret in case the pump or electrical power failed.

The oxygen system was completely self-contained and consisted of an oxygen cylinder and regulator valve mounted on the left seat support and a rebreather mounted to the left side of the ammunition boxes to the front of the gunner. An extra oxygen canister was available on the left side of the ball. The heated suit was plugged into the utility plug on the control panel and the utility switch was to be turned ON. The interphone jack box was placed on the top left side of the ball and included the push-to-talk button. The trouble spotlight was mounted on a rib of the Plexiglas dome and could be directed by a ball-swivel. It was turned ON by a switch on the control panel.

The armor plate of this turret protected the gunner from enemy fire in any direction he trained his guns. The armor consisted of 5/8 inch steel armor plate in front of his face; 5/8 inch steel armor plate to protect the booster motors and ammunition chutes; and 1/2 inch armor plate to protect his body and ammunition boxes.

Guns and Ammunition

The two .50 caliber machine guns were mounted to feed from the outboard side; the right gun fed from the right and the left gun from the left. There were provisions for adjustment of the guns both up and down and sideways. The turret was supplied by two built-in ammunition magazines holding 400 rounds for each gun. They were located in the forward part of the ball in front of the gunner. The empty ammunition cartridge cases and links were collected in a chamber located in the front part of the turret between the ammunition box and ball structure.

The hydraulic gun charger control knob was located next to the gunner's left knee and operated the gun chargers that were located on the inboard side of each gun. To charge the guns the control knob was depressed sharply to the FIRING position. Both guns were charged simultaneously and ready to fire. If the control knob was turned to SAFE before depressing the gun bolt would remain in the retracted position which would provide access to a jam. The triggers were located on the control handles under the gunner's index fingers and either trigger fired both guns.

The Navy Mk 9 sight was mounted between the rear gun mount casting in front of the face armor plate. A gun camera could be mounted below and parallel to the guns just above the ammunition boxes. A camera ON switch was located on the control panel which was activated by depressing either safety switch *and* either trigger switch.

The empty cartridge cases and links were collected in containers, one for each gun, located on either side of the seat attached to the azimuth track.

Exiting the Turret

In leaving this turret it was important that the gunner carefully follow a definite procedure. The turret was to be moved into the stowed position: 0° elevation and 0° in azimuth with the guns pointing straight forward. All switches were turned OFF. The gunner was to rock the turret slightly with the hand pump until the elevation landing lock pin could be slipped into position. The gunner then reached down to the left hand side of the ball and turned the azimuth position lock ON. The turret manual admonished:

**Martin Hydraulic Tail Ball Turret** (USN)

**Martin 250CH-2 Tail Turret** used in the tail of the **Martin PBM-3**. (USN)

"It is extremely important that these landing locks be secured. The turret is likely to swing freely in landing, causing damage to the ship and itself." All auxiliary units that had been in use were to be disconnected. The gunner then braced himself against the back of the turret seat rest and lifted up on the seat, pushing it up and back and sliding on its track until it was in the locked position out of the way. The gunner left the turret by grasping the top of the face plate armor and then swung down and out of the opening in the turret bottom.

In case of an emergency there was an escape hatch in the Plexiglas dome directly above the gunner. Two plastic handles were located on either side of the hatch which were turned a quarter turn to cause the hatch to open inboard. The gunner had to stand up on the seat to crawl out of the top of the turret.

**Section 7: Martin Hydraulic Tail Ball Turret**

There were only minor differences between the Martin 250CH-1 and 250CH-3 Deck Turrets and the Martin 250CH-2 Tail Turret used in the tail of the PBM-3. Both turrets operated exactly the same. Being a tail turret, the CH-2 had an azimuth movement of 75° on either side of the centerline of the aircraft while the elevation could raise its guns 65° above horizontal and depressed 45° below horizontal. The gunner was not to remain in the tail position during takeoffs and landings as he could unbalance and put undue stress on the aircraft. To enter the turret the gunner had to crawl on his hands and knees and once inside, straighten up and pulled the seat up until it locked. In this turret the gunner did not place his feet on top of the ammunition boxes as he did in the Martin 250CH-1 or -3 deck turret, but placed then on foot brackets. No ammunition boxes were provided in the turret but were located in the aircraft's hull, one on either side. The ammunition boxes contained 1,000 rounds (vs. 600) and traveled along both sides of the hull in roller tracks and entered the turret between the gunner's feet. The empty cartridge cases and links were ejected overboard through chutes.

**Section 8: Consolidated Tail/Nose Turret**
**(AAF: A-6 and A-6A and USN: Convair 250CH-3 or MPC 250CH-6)**
**Development**

**Consolidated Tail Turret**

The Consolidated tail turret was uncharacteristic, in that of the multiplicity of turrets manufactured for the Armament Laboratory, this turret was developed especially for the B-24 and was not part of Government Furnished Equipment. The development of the Consolidated tail turret was determined by its relationship with the B-24 and would demonstrate the importance of developing turrets separately from specific aircraft types.

In May 1937 the Navy Bureau of Ordnance let contracts to Martin and Consolidated to develop and build large, heavy, long-range patrol bombers specifying that these companies, and not the Navy, would develop a power turret for them. The Materiel Division allowed the Navy access to the secret Air Corps gun mounts, and to reciprocate the Navy approved Consolidated's sale of the recently developed .50-caliber power mount to the Air Corps in December 1938.

The March 1939 specifications for contract AC12436 for Consolidated's XB-24 Liberator stipulated four .30 caliber and three .50 caliber machine guns for flexible gunnery installations: two single .30 caliber guns each in the nose and the waist, and a single .50 caliber gun in dorsal, ventral, and tail positions. As part of the January 1939 four-engine bomber type specifications the number and arrangement of machine guns were to provide "complete protection that could be effectively accomplished by not more than three members of the crew." These B-24 specifications would have three crewmen operating all seven guns! As part of the contract Consolidated was expected to resolve this gunner workload, but there was another clause in the bomber type specification that stated "whenever remotely controlled guns were installed, the contractor shall design and supply the complete sighting and control system."

The armament of the XB-24 prototype consisted of several hand-held .30 inch machine guns. One gun was to be mounted in the large transparent nose which accommodated the navigator and bombardier. There was a cupola for an additional .30 caliber gun in the extreme tail, which was a relatively new feature for American bombers at the time, having been first introduced on the Douglas B-23. The B-24A was armed with a single .50 inch flexible machine gun each in the nose, belly, and left and right waist positions with an additional pair of .30 caliber machine guns installed in the tail. Combat reports from Europe stated that the Liberator I, the RAF version of the B-24, was under armed with its twin .303s in the tail. The Liberator II was the first B-24 to be equipped with a power turret, a Boulton-Paul E. Mk. II equipped with four .303 Browning machine guns, and was reported to have a formidable tail defense.

To augment the tail defense of the B-24 the AAC decided to pursue the development of a tail turret. Consolidated and Ford were the two B-24 prime contractors, and because the tail turret was to be developed by the manufacturers both companies were expected to produce a tail turret even though this would entail a duplication in tooling. Neither Consolidated nor Ford planned to produce the tail turret themselves, as neither had the expertise or inclination. Consolidated subcontracted their turret to the Southern Aircraft Corporation of Garland, CA, while Ford planned to subcontract with the Motor Products Corporation of Detroit. In January 1941, the Consolidated turret design was awarded $3,960 for the development of an experimental tail turret for installation in the B-24D to be tested by the Armament Laboratory. In May 1941 the Materiel Division negotiated a contract for 73 tail turrets with Consolidated and Ford, but Wright Field did not receive the first test model from them until September.

The Consolidated tail turret consisted of an external hydraulic pressure source, a reservoir, pump, and accumulator with feed and return lines introduced through a swivel joint to the moving turret. A four-way, joystick-controlled hydraulic valve determined the flow to a simple hydraulic jack for elevation and the flow to a simple, fixed-tilt, reversible Vickers motor for azimuth drive. At this point, however, problems appeared. Instead of gearing the motor directly through a positive gear train to the moving turret, the motor operated a drum from which steel cables ran in opposite directions around the turret. This arrangement, designed to eliminate the use of a ring gear with all its manufacturing difficulties, while ingenious, created more problems than were anticipated by Consolidated. Every change in temperature changed the tension on the cable system and control became erratic, with a troubling slackness in the neutral area.

**Consolidated Tail/Nose Turret** (USN)

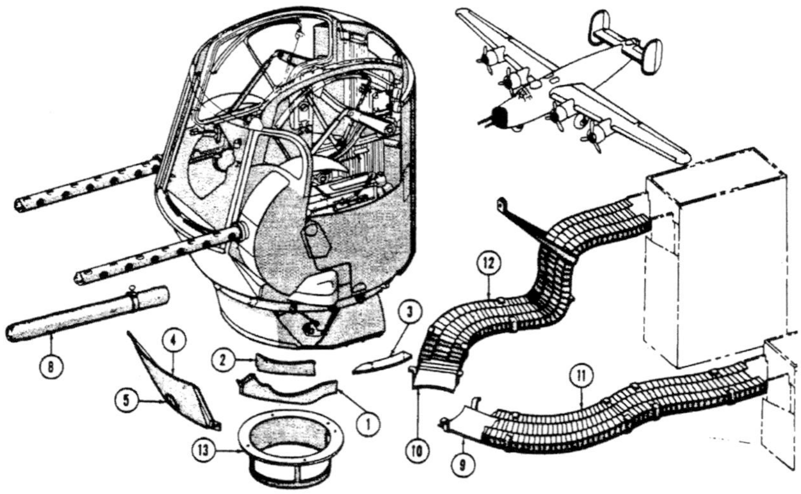

(USAAF)

The Wright Field tests of the first experimental tail turret revealed several negligible and easily correctable faults: the hydraulic control valve allowed an appreciable creep; and no provision had been made for a heated suit outlet, hot air duct, trouble lamp, interphone, or oxygen systems. However, like other turret designs, the Consolidated turret design had not given sufficient thought to the space available in the turret for a gunner dressed in full flying equipment and only a relatively small man would be able to enter the turret. To correct this fault would involve a complete redesign of the turret and training a small gunner was determined to be easier.

In later tests a serious problem arose in the azimuth drive that led to the suspension of turret production by Consolidated and Ford until satisfactory modifications could be made. The manufacturing of the tail turret by two companies made production line modification difficult, and on 10 September Col. K.B. Wolfe, Chief of the Armaments Laboratory, told Lt.Col. Grandison Gardner, the Production Engineering Section Chief, that it probably would have been better if the Materiel Division had arbitrarily concentrated tail turret manufacture by one company. While Consolidated prepared to modify its deficient turret, the Materiel Division's Contract Section requested that Emerson submit a cost estimate for a whole new design.

The original Consolidated design had been limited by weight considerations imposed by an arbitrary load limitation, but once the B-24 moved from the drawing board and its center of gravity had been determined engineers realized that the aircraft's weight limitations were set too low. This weight limitation had not only restricted the size of the tail turret, but also caused Consolidated engineers to use a less robust construction which weakened the rigidity of the mount. Despite the Frazier-Nash experience of designing a turret around a sight, in the Consolidated tail turret design much of the vibration of firing guns was transmitted to the sight. Finally, engineering analysis pointed out that the excessive dispersion pattern of the twin .50 caliber guns resulted from each gun being mounted on a pair of trunnions with dissimilar anchors, which resulted in wide variations in the degree of movement and produced vibrations that caused bullet dispersion patterns.

Ford and Consolidated attempted to improve their tail turret and worked on mechanical foot firing, external ammunition feeding, improved gun accessibility, and a number of other minor problems. The Experimental Engineering Section tested the improved turret and their report found, "the turret is fundamentally no different from the first Consolidated turret tested." The PES engineers reported that "the earlier turrets were actually better in some respects; and after all the improvements had been added, the turret was still an inefficient combat weapon due to the instability of the gun mounts, sight vibration, and the lack of room, the major objection to the turret from the start."

**Consolidated Nose Turret**

Despite the unacceptability of the Consolidated tail turret the necessity for its use increased due to an unexpected reason. Both the B-17 and B-24 had inadequate defense against head-on attacks. Initially two .50 caliber cheek guns were installed along with a socket for an additional .50 in the nose. This arrangement was ineffective due to its limited field of fire and the need for a gunner to operate each gun, which would crowd the already cramped nose. Reports from combat theaters requested frontal turret protection for bombers and an experimental tail turret had been installed and tested in the nose of a B-24. The Armament Laboratory criticism of that improvised installation was that it "could not be considered as a possible production installation due to the replacing of this type turret by the improved Emerson type tail turret, and, furthermore, the Bendix lower turret, converted to chin use, provided the required frontal coverage at much less cost than an installation of the Consolidated turret." The Bendix chin turret was a much cleaner installation than the Consolidated turret, but neither the Bendix chin nor the new Emerson turret reached quantity production as soon as had been anticipated, and Consolidated tail turrets were mounted as nose turrets to meet the immediate requirements.

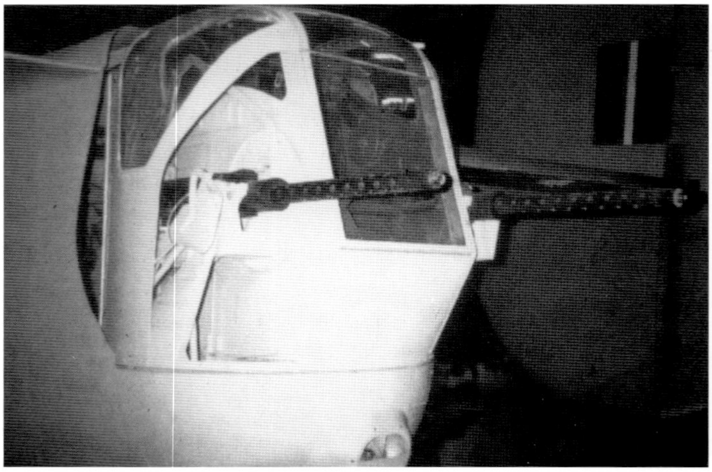

**Consolidated B-24C** mounting an A-6. These turrets were designated as the Convair 250CH-3 or MPC 250CH-6 by the Navy. (USAAF)

The first experimental Consolidated nose turret installations were completed in July 1942, but no specific policy was decided for several months afterward. In January 1943 the Materiel Center complained that the nose turret project was "seriously hampered by lack of a statement as to the extent of protection desired against forward gunfire." On 21 January 1943 the Director of Military Requirements condensed the turret problem into a few words:

"Several theater commanders have requested the Consolidated tail turret in the nose of B-24 airplanes. In view of the recent losses due to frontal attacks and the long delay before chin turrets are available, it is desired that the feasibility of installing Consolidated turrets on a limited basis as an interim measure be thoroughly explored. It is not impossible that this turret would prove even more desirable than the chin turret. The maintenance and supply and training problems for B-24 units would certainly be simplified if this turret were used instead of the Bendix chin turret."

Once the nose turret was installed several inevitable problems arose. The turret's continued movement caused the felt seal to become worn and damaged, allowing severe outside draughts to enter the nose compartment. A new nose seal designed by BADA was held against the turret sides by the outside air pressure. The new nose turret was constricted and seriously limited the forward vision of both the bombardier and navigator. Combat reports indicated that many mission failures were due to poor navigation due to the turret's forward vision and larger blister windows were installed at the navigator's position on either side of the nose.

The Consolidated A-6/CH-3 nose turret was installed in some B-24Js and the bow of the PB2Y-3 Coronado, while the A-6A/CH-6 was adapted for the B-24 and the Navy PB4Y Liberator. Production B-24s and PB4Ys had the turret installed, and since the earlier nose turret was basically similar the two turrets had an identical parts list and this installation was facilitated. All B-24Hs, including those assembled with the B-24J at Consolidated's Fort Worth plant, had factory installed Emerson nose turrets. Other Consolidated (then Convair) Fort Worth B-24s were delivered with the Consolidated A-6 nose turrets as the B-24J until spring 1944 when the Fort Worth B-24J was standardized with the Emerson nose turret. (See Section 10 Emerson Nose/Tail Turret for a discussion of the installation of the Consolidated and Emerson turrets in the B-24G/H/and Js.)

**Description**

The A-6A had a flat, sloping transparent front panel which made the A-6A-equipped B-24J the longest Liberator model, measuring 67 feet, 7.625 inches. The turret contained approximately 1,800 parts, 1,000 to be manufactured by Consolidated and 800 obtained by subcontract. An average of 13 jigs, dies, or other tools was required for every part manufactured, or a total of 13,000 tools, which cost an average of $100 per tool. This placed the cost of tooling the turret at $1,300,000 and 7,500 tools for the turret needed to be machined to finer degrees of tolerance costing an additional estimated $750,000.

Hydraulic System

The hydraulically operated Consolidated Tail Turret was powered by its own unit located on the right side of the fuselage adjacent to the turret. This hydraulic power unit was wholly independent of the main hydraulic system and consisted of an electrically driven pump, check valve, pressure switch, relief valve, accumulator, oil filter, and oil reservoir, all of which were located outside the turret on the right side of the fuselage.

When installed into the nose there was no room for the self-contained hydraulic power unit so pressurized hydraulic fluid was supplied by the aircraft's main hydraulic system.

The power unit in the tail was a 24-volt shunt-wound electric motor that drove a 1,200 psi spur gear pump. A pressure relief valve opened when the pressure reached over 1,300 psi while a delivery line pressure switch opened when the pressure dropped below 1,100 psi. The pressurized fluid (600 psi) was fed into an accumulator consisting of two halves. One hemisphere contained fluid and was coupled to the first by a rubber diaphragm which kept constant pressure to the turret and compensated for fluid used in the elevation ram.

Turret rotation was supplied by a piston-type, fixed-displacement, variable-speed hydraulic motor working through a train gear that operated a cable drum. Two wires were wound around the drum in opposite directions, the end of each being fixed to the turret drum. When the motor was actuated one cable wound as the other unwound, rotating the turret. The gun cradle was elevated by two hydraulic jacks controlled from the gunner's control handles.

The speed of train, horizontally or vertically, was in direct proportion to the rapidity of movement of the controls by the gunner. The maximum speed of rotation was 45° per second, while the maximum speed of elevation was from 45° to 70° per second. The azimuth train was 61° right and left of the centerline, or a total of 122°. The elevation range was from 40° below horizontal to 70° above for a total of 110°.

Azimuth (or Train)

From the control valve the pressure for right rotation passed through the end port of the stop valve, on the right side entering the end port. The pressure release from the side port entered the pressure side of the motor for right or clockwise train. Discharge from the motor passed to the side port of the left stop valve and out through the end port to the control valve to the return line. If the turret was operated to its full clockwise position the plunger of the left stop valve struck the stop, closed the valve, shut off the return from the motor and stopped its rotation. For left rotation, the procedure was reversed and the pressure lines interchanged with return.

Elevation (or Zenith)

From the control valve, pressure for elevation passed through a single rotating swivel and through an interconnecting line to the base of the cylinder, where it entered and acted against the bottom of the piston. Return fluid was forced out by the head of the pistol through the swivel joint through the control valve to the return line. For gun depression the procedure was reversed and pressure lines interchanged with return.

Manual Operation (Emergency)

To manually operate the turret in case of hydraulic failure the gunner instituted the following procedure: a notched rod located below and on the right side of the control valve to the gunner's left was depressed and engaged a latch to hold it in position. This action opened the dump valves and relieved both ends of the zenith jack to the return line. A spring returned the rod when released and allowed the dump valve to close. The release valve on the right side under the gunner's seat was opened to bypass the azimuth motor to the control valve.

The gunner removed the cranks from their stowage area on the right and left sides of the turret (to gunner's left and right respectively) and attached them to the zenith manual control on the right side (at gunner's left hand) and to the azimuth manual control on the left side (at gunner's right hand) respectively. Turret could then be elevated and depressed by the gunner's left hand and trained in azimuth by the gunner's right hand. The azimuth motor bypass valve could be opened by a cable toggle pull, located outside of the turret below the door. This allowed rotation of the turret by hand from the outside in case the rear gunner became disabled.

The Clarke DO5C Gun Turret Control Valve basically consisted of two four-way valves combined in one housing: one for the operation of the elevation and lowering of the guns, and the other to control the train of the turret. The gunner had to control the amount of fluid to the hydraulic motors or cylinders so that either or both could operate smoothly through all speed ranges from zero to maximum.

The gunner had to accurately control the amount of fluid passing through each four-way valve and, in order to make the operation as simple as possible, a single vertical control column was used. The control column was provided with two hand grips mounted on a horizontal shaft which turned in bearings supported in the top of the vertical column. Rotation of the grips was limited about their horizontal axis and operated the four-way valve controlling the elevation.

Electrical System

The Consolidated turret electrical system consisted of the following parts and was arranged to provide power to operate the hydraulic system, light for the illuminated sight, and power for the firing of guns. Electrical supply from the main electrical system was provided for the operation of the gun trigger mechanism and illumination of the sight, and was taken from the turret fuse box located on the right side of the fuselage. The fuse and the main switch for the hydraulic electric motor were also located in this box.

Turret Power Switch: A switch located outside the turret near the hydraulic unit and marked as TURRET POWER ON-OFF supplied power at 24-volts direct current to the electrically-driven Pesco pump supplying power for the hydraulic unit. The pressure switch located in the hydraulic unit was connected in series with the power switch. The pressure switch was designed to open when pressure reached approximately 1125psi and to close when the pressure dropped below 975psi.

Trigger Switch: The trigger switch was integral with the turret control handle and simultaneously operated two gun firing solenoids. Power to the trigger switch was supplied through a switch located in the turret junction box and marked GUN TRIGGER ON-OFF.

Sight: The turret was equipped with an illuminated gunsight. The sight light was controlled by a rheostat located in the turret junction box and marked GUNSIGHT LT. OFF-BRIGHT.

The N-6 sight, when installed, was equipped with a two-filament and a selector switch integral with the sight. Should one filament burn out the remaining one could be turned ON by operating the selector switch, which was located on the side of the sight.

The N-3A sight when installed was equipped with a two-filament bulb. The filaments were connected in parallel and burned simultaneously. The gunner was unable to determine whether one or both of the filaments were burning, and the bulb was to be removed periodically and tested; if one filament was burned out the bulb was to be replaced.

Receptacle: Each turret junction box was equipped with an electrical receptacle and a switch marked RECPT.

Interphone: The interphone installation was the same as other interphone installations throughout the aircraft in which the turret was installed. Since the Air Corps and Navy jack boxes were not interchangeable, each turret was equipped with a mounting bracket that seated either of these boxes.

Circuit Breakers: The turret was provided with protective thermally-operated circuit breakers that opened when the current became abnormally high. One breaker was located in each gun solenoid circuit while a third circuit breaker was located in the circuit supplying power to the sight and camera. An open breaker could be reset by pushing the red button. The installation of a breaker in each gun solenoid wire decreased the chance of losing fire power during combat. If the wire to one solenoid became grounded the breaker to that solenoid opened and the gunner maintained control of one gun.

Armor: A bullet proof glass 2.2 inch thick protected the gunner's face while directly below it was a .833 inch armor plate augmented by two small .375 inch armor plates to the right and left of the gunner's knees.

Boresighting

The purpose of boresighting was to adjust the two guns so that both axes of fire lay in the same horizontal plane and the vertical planes of the firing axis converge at a fixed distance from the muzzles. This was completed by using a target and training the sight and guns on their respective bulls' eyes. The guns were sighted by looking through their barrels and adjusting to their respective bulls' eyes. On the Consolidated turret the boresighting specifications mandated fire convergence at 600 yards with the sights parallel to plane of fire.

Entering the Turret

Entering the Consolidated Turret could be a risky procedure, and was always done while the aircraft was in flight. The turret was precisely balanced and the lock needed to always be in place, as any change in altitude could cause it to quickly rotate, trapping anyone trying to enter.

The first step for the gunner before entering the turret was to turn OFF the main power switch located just outside the turret on the fuselage wall. He opened the turret doors and checked three valves before entering. He first reached inside to be sure that the main shutoff valve, a red spindle knob to the left center, was CLOSED by turning it all the way IN. If this valve were open even a slight touch on the control handles when entering could cause the turret to move and squash the gunner in the doorway. The emergency azimuth relief valve under the seat was also to be in the CLOSED position, as was the elevation bypass valve, a small handle below and to the left of the control unit. There were two grips above the door inside the turret that the gunner was to use to enter the turret. The gunner chinned himself and swung both feet straight into the turret interior "pit." Care was to be taken not to grasp the sight control bar to enter. Once inside the turret the gunner adjusted the seat for proper height by pushing down on the two knobs beneath the seat and raising or lowering the seat as required. To be certain that the seat was properly engaged the gunner pulled up on the knobs.

To close the doors from the inside the turret the gunner had to close the left hand and then the right hand door and pull up on the latch located about six inches from the top of the door. On later models the gunner closed the doors by pulling down on the door cable by grasping the red knob on his right. The gunner was not to occupy the turret or remain in the tail-end of the bomber during take-offs and landings due to the high accelerations during those times.

Operation of the Turret

All the switches, valves, and controls of the Consolidated turret were well thought out and close at hand and easy to use. The turret manual warned the gunner "to be sure to turn on the switches and open the valves in the order shown here." Once seated inside the turret the gunner removed the azimuth mechanism lock on his right and the elevation mechanism lock on his left and hung them on their clips on the turret wall. He OPENED the main shutoff valve and on the junction box located beside his left knee he turned ON the power switch, the booster motor switch, the trigger switch, and the gun camera switch. He turned ON the sight rheostat located near his left shoulder and rotated it to adjust the brightness of the sight light. Reset buttons that protected the main electrical system were mounted on the side of the junction box with each button labeled with the name of the circuit.

The gunner grasped the control handles located directly in front of him, and to move the turret he turned the handles in bicycle fashion right and left and up and down to raise and lower the guns. The triggers were under each index finger on each control handle. There were two foot-firing pedals and a foot-firing mechanism lock located at the gunner's feet.

The interphone talk-to-speak button was under the gunner's thumb on the right control handle. The hydraulically-driven turret moved in azimuth about 75° to either side of the aircraft's centerline; from almost straight out to the left to almost straight out to the right at a speed of 40° per second. In elevation the turret's guns could be lowered and raised 45° below the horizontal to 71° above horizontal. Aided by the Clarke control valve, movement in azimuth was completed by turning the handles to the right and left, while the guns were elevated by pulling the control handles up and back, and they were depressed by pushing the handles down and forward. The speed of both horizontal and vertical movement was governed by the amount of displacement of the control. Any combination of turn, elevation, and rate of speed could be produced from the degree of angularity of the control.

There was a demand-type oxygen regulator with a hose connection to the mask located near the gunner's left shoulder. Turret oxygen was supplied by the aircraft's central cylinders. The heated flying suit plug was on the right turret wall near the gunner's right shoulder. The interphone jack box was placed on the right wall near the gunner's cheek. A trouble light and switch fit into a holder in the upper right hand corner of the turret. A warning bell controlled by the pilot to warn the gunner that the aircraft was about to land was located on the left front turret wall. The emergency manual turret operation shafts were on the right (for azimuth) and left (for elevation) side of the turret seat and were operated by two hand cranks stored on clips on each side.

Guns and Accessories

The turret was mounted on a circular track which was riveted to the fuselage. Two .50 caliber machine guns were mounted in adapters attached to the turret assembly. The twin .50 caliber machine guns fed from the inside: the right gun from the left and the left gun from the right. Each gun was held in its cradle by a rear trunnion block and slide and a front trunnion stud bolted into a mounting hole in the cradle. Special charging units were installed on the inside plates of the gun receivers and link ejection chutes on the outside. In addition to the control handle triggers there were special foot-firing mechanisms mounted on the outside of the guns and connected to two foot-firing pedals that operated plungers that tripped the gun sears. The guns were adjusted up, down, or sideways in their cradles by rear mount adjustment collar and lock nut assemblies.

The N-8 or N-6A optical gunsight was mounted in a bracket on top of the sight cradle directly in front of the gunner. The mounting bolts could be loosened and the sight adjusted up/down and left/right. The sight light was turned on and the intensity adjusted with the sight light rheostat to match outside conditions. The light had to be bright enough to be plainly visible but not obscure the target, especially during night missions.

The gun charging handles were located on either side of the bullet-proof glass in front of the gunner. Before hand charging the guns were elevated approximately 30°. The guns were charged by reaching forward and grasping the handles cross-armed; holding the right handle with the left hand and the left handle with the right hand. The gunner pulled the handles sharply back as far as they would go. To return the handles the gunner allowed them to snap back while still grasping them. The firing mechanism was Magnavox solenoids.

Magazines with a combined capacity of 825 rounds for each gun were located outside the turret in the fuselage of the aircraft. The ammunition belts fed from the outside through flexible guides up through the floor of the turret to the guns. The ammunition belt for the forward magazine was fed with a right underhand movement and a left under-hand movement for the aft magazine. The ammunition belt was threaded or fed into the magazine with the smooth side of the belt down. The belt had to be folded carefully so that each layer was perfectly flat to insure maximum capacity loading. The belt was broken at a point about 30 rounds less than required to fill the magazine, and this section was threaded into the magazine over the roller, the belt reconnected, and fed back into the magazine. The last shell was clipped to the lip of the magazine.

The magazines were best loaded if the guns were elevated to their maximum and the gunner stood in the turret looking directly down on the magazines. With practice, the aft magazine could be loaded in five minutes and the forward magazine in three minutes. An additional 250 rounds of ammunition (for a total ammunition capacity of 1,075 rounds per gun) were in place on a monorail that traversed along the top of the fuselage and was available in flight without the gunner leaving the turret. Two cords were located near the turret, each attached to a container holding 125 rounds of ammunition. By pulling these cords the containers were unlatched and towed along the monorail to the turret. The 50 pound containers were pulled gently or allowed to roll by gravity. The empty container was removed by unfastening a wing nut and dropping a hinged portion of the track.

The turret was equipped with special case ejection chutes that emptied the spent shells into a canvas funnel under the turret that released the cases through an exit opening in the bottom of the fuselage. Each gun carriage was equipped with a links ejection guide that deflected the empty links out of the turret and overboard to the rear.

Leaving the Turret

The turret was first placed in the stowed position with the guns pointed back and in 60° elevation; pointed back from the tail and two-thirds of the way between level and straight up. The sight, trigger, booster motor, and main power switches were turned OFF on the junction box. The main shutoff valve was CLOSED and the azimuth and elevation mechanism locks were taken from their storage clips and replaced. The turret was then locked in place and the gunner opened the two doors and backed out. On early models, to open the doors from the inside of the turret the gunner had to press down on the latch and push doors outward, while on later models he pulled a cable with his right hand and stepped out. After exiting the doors were closed and latched and the main power switch on the fuselage wall was turned OFF.

**Section 9: Emerson Nose (A-15/250CE-1/Model 127) and Tail (Model 111) Turrets**

**Background and Development**

ANB Turret

The USN Bureau of Aeronautics engaged the Emerson Electric Manufacturing Company of St Louis to manufacture turret designs based on the Boulton Paul (BP) Types S (tail) and T (dorsal), armed with twin .50 caliber Browning machine guns instead of the British Browning .303 machine guns. Emerson built a dorsal turret based on the BP Type T and then modified it for operation with the Browning .50. In mid-1942 Emerson submitted the Model ANB-101-115 prototype to the Navy for evaluation, which found it unacceptable due to 1) excess weight; 2) insufficient room for the gunner; 3) poor control and operating characteristics; 4) poor scanning facilities; and 5) a general lack of consideration of American installation requirements (see Section 15 for a lengthy discussion of the ANB Turret).

Emerson Redesign of the Airarms Redesign of the Boulton Paul Turret

As work was proceeding at Emerson, the Armament Laboratory tested a two-gun mid-upper turret developed by Lockheed Vega's Airarms subsidiary. This turret was also based on the Boulton Paul design, but was more spacious and better engineered, but nonetheless did not meet requirements. The Navy requested Emerson to modify the turret using standard AAF recoil adaptors, gunsights, etc, and to install the Amplidyne electrical drive system. Emerson submitted the "new" turret for testing where it proved satisfactory on ground trials. However, when it was air tested the turret was again found to have basic problems: the amplidyne power units supplied insufficient power and the design would have been difficult to manufacture.

Emerson and the Consolidated Turret

Emerson's newly-built facility was only at 17.5% of capacity, and with the lack of work, its subcontractors were moving to other manufacturers. Emerson desperately needed new contracts from the Materiel Division, and the Materiel Division was equally anxious to promote Emerson as a turret manufacturer. Previously, when the Ford Motor Company needed a subcontractor to build the tail turret for Ford-built Consolidated B-24s, the Division had suggested that Ford utilize the excess Emerson capacity which had been created for the cancelled and unwanted ANB turret. Ford had expected that the Materiel Division would authorize the B-24 tail turret as Government Furnished Equipment, but the Division, already overloaded with work, could not furnish the turrets and was satisfied to allow the turret to remain as part of the aircraft contract as it had been originally. For this reason, as well as to bolster Emerson factory capacity, the Chief of the Production Engineering Section directed Ford, which was now required to build a tail turret, to subcontract it to Emerson, and in August 1941 negotiations began to build the Consolidated tail turret. Emerson had tooled a turret before and knew from experience that turret manufacture was not an ordinary machine tool job for mass production. Unhappy with the contentious negotiations, Ford informed Wright Field that Emerson did not appear to be a satisfactory source, and Ford contacted other Detroit automotive companies in search of a better price. The Emerson participation in the Consolidated turret evaluation would later be of great help when they designed their tail and nose turrets for the B-24.

Gunner entering the turret doors. (USN)

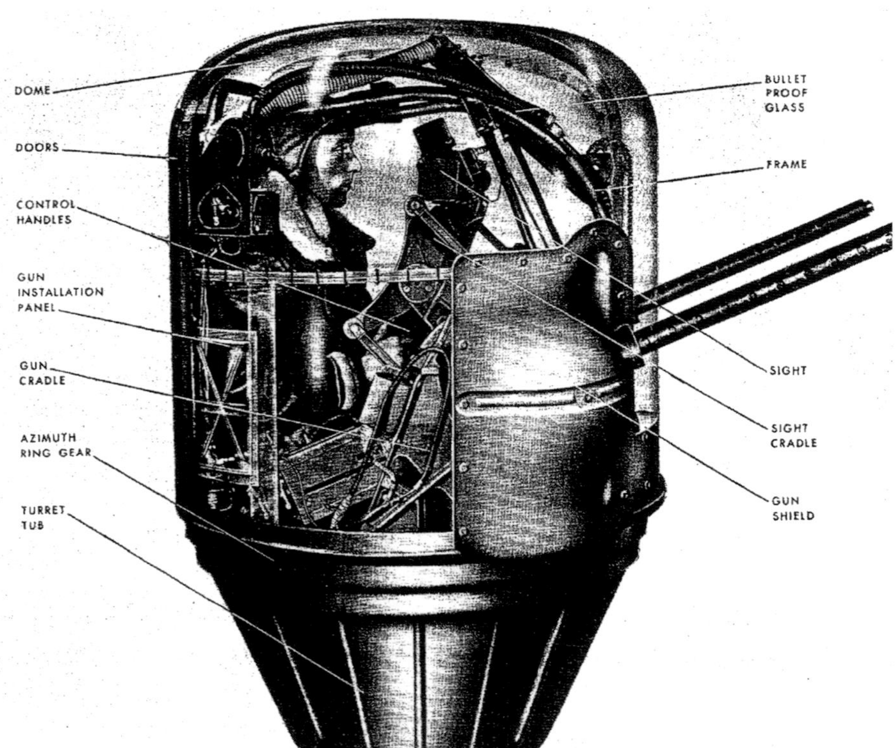


**Emerson Nose and Tail Turret** (USN)

Interior of Emerson turret. (USN)

Emerson Tail (Model 111) Turrets mounted on a B-24. (USAAF)

Model 111 Tail Turret

The initial tail armament of the B-24A was a basic .303 twin-gun mounting which was mostly ineffective. After its unsuccessful negotiations with Ford to subcontract the Consolidated A-6 turret Emerson badly needed to obtain contracts for its new St. Louis factory. While Consolidated prepared to modify its deficient turret, the Materiel Division's Contract Section requested that Emerson submit a cost estimate for a whole new design, and in early 1942 Emerson was contracted to design a fully enclosed power turret to replace it. The Model 111 tail turret was accorded priority status, and by August Emerson was able to produce the turret by using the experience it gained on previous unproductive designs. The Model 111 was the first turret to use cast magnesium for principal structural components. In tests by the Armament Lab at Eglin Field the turret proved to be superior to any produced in the USA up to that time. Although the Navy and Army were enthusiastic, aircraft companies had reservations due to the turret's weight. Nonetheless, these objections were rejected and the Model 111 was accepted for installation on all future B-24 aircraft.

A-15/250CE-1/Model 127 Nose Turret

The Emerson nose turret was designated as the Model 127 by Emerson; the A-15 by the AAF; and the 250CE-1 by the USN. These twin .50 caliber, amplidyne drive turrets incorporated many of the best contemporary turret design features and also added several completely new facets. It included accessible guns, external feed ammunition, boosters with emergency manual operation, manual operation for both azimuth and elevation movements, a lever-action charging mechanism, and a plate of bullet-proof glass operated by a chain and sprocket drive so it constantly remained at an angle to the guns. There was a great similarity in design and construction of the Emerson turret with the Consolidated turret and a gunner familiar with one was able to operate the other.

As previously discussed, by the early spring of 1942 the B-24 was found to be particularly vulnerable to frontal attacks. In the Pacific B-24 tail turrets were removed at air depots in Hawaii and Australia and placed in the nose, leaving the tail protected by manually operated guns. The 8AF unsuccessfully tested the B-26 tail turret and the B-25 Bendix remote turret in the nose position. By mid-1943 AAF depots were installing Consolidated B-24 tail turrets in the noses in modifications known as the B-24D-1.When these turrets were found to be successful plans were made to introduce a nose turret installed on the production line.

Concurrently, Emerson was contracted to investigate converting the Model 111 into a nose turret for the B-24 which had a glazed nose. Working in conjunction with Consolidated engineers Emerson was able to adapt their tail turret. Although the Emerson design was not quite as streamlined as the Consolidated A-6, it emerged with its characteristic smooth, cylindrical shape. Emerson sent their drawings to Ford's Willow Run factory to build a wooden mockup to adapt the turret for the production line, where it would become standard on production lines not using Consolidated turrets.

The initial Emerson turret design emerged in February 1942, but did not reach production until the summer of 1943, when a maximum of 250 turrets per month was projected for the following September. To facilitate installation Emerson sent a large contingent of mechanics to the Consolidated plants.

All B-24Hs, including those assembled with the B-24J at Consolidated's Fort Worth plant, had factory installed Emerson nose turrets. Other Consolidated (then Convair) Fort Worth B-24s were delivered with the Consolidated A-6 nose turrets as the B-24J until spring 1944 when the Fort Worth B-24J was standardized with the Emerson nose turret. To make the Emerson compatible 56 major changes were required to the basic B-24D airframe. The bombardier's station needed to be entirely reconfigured while the nose wheel doors were converted from inward-opening to outward-opening throughout the B-24H production run. A "S"-shaped fairing that was to characterize all future Ford-built B-24 assemblies had to be used to adapt the aircraft's nose to the new turret. The additional weight of the turret changed the location of the center of gravity and actually improved the performance of the B-24, as it was somewhat tail heavy.

The B-24J designation was allocated to Liberators built on the Consolidated production line at Fort Worth (CO) and San Diego (CF), Ford/Willow Run (FO), and Douglas/Tulsa (DT), and North American/ Dallas (NT) continued to manufacture the B-24G until mid-1944 when they began B-24J manufacture. These five manufacturers were called the Liberator Production Pool. Initially all five Liberator plants were to install the Emerson turret, but Emerson was unable to supply all five. The two Consolidated (called Convair at the time due to Consolidated's merger with Vultee) plants were directed to use the Consolidated A-6A on their B-24J production line until Emerson could increase production. Later in the run the Consolidated A-6B replaced the A-6A at the two Consolidated plants. By spring 1944, Emerson increased their nose turret production and their turrets were on the B-24J-185-CO (Fort Worth) and J-45-CF (San Diego) blocks. Once the other three B-24 plants were ready to begin B-24J production Emerson was also able to supply them, and after May 1944 the Emerson turret was standardized.

The initial B-24Js differed very little outwardly from the nose-turreted B-24G and B-24H, with small differences in the nose turret and nosewheel landing gear door configurations being a distinguishing factor. Generally, B-24Js manufactured by the different members of the Liberator Production Pool were very similar and could only be distinguished from one another by their serial numbers. Only vigilant examination of the arrangement of the nose landing gear doors (whether they opened outwards or inwards) could distinguish the differences between the B-24Js from the different manufacturers. The initial Convair-built B-24J differed from the G and the H in having inward, rather than outward-opening nosewheel doors. All of the B-24Js from Convair that had the A-6A or A-6B turrets had inward-opening doors. The B-24J-45-CF with the "S"-shaped nose turret fairing design and the Emerson turret had inward-opening doors until Block 70, which then switched to outward-opening doors. The B-24J-185-CO with the NAA-style nose and the A-15 turret had outward-opening doors. All of the North American built B-24Js had outward-opening doors, as did all of the Ford-built B-24Js. Convair adopted the North American-style nose fairings, but Ford continued with the S-curve fairing that had been used in the H-series. The success of the turret can be demonstrated by the 12,000 that were produced by the company.

**Description**

Entering the Turret

The Emerson turret manual admonished: "As you start getting acquainted with the Emerson Nose, remember first of all that it is no place to be hanging around during takeoffs and landings. Quick changes of speed, as the bomber leaves or approaches the ground make the turret a dangerous place at these times. On a mission always get in after the plane is in full flight, and get out before landing."

Before entering the turret the gunner first checked if the power switch mounted outside the turret on a box on the fuselage wall (just left of the nose wheel on the B-24) was ON. In many installations this switch was wired in the ON position. The gunner opened the two turret doors and looked in at the switch box on the left rear support to be certain that all the switches were OFF so that the turret was inoperative and could not move to trap the gunner's legs or body in the doorway. The gunner entered by grasping the support above the doorway and used it to chin himself, raising both feet into the turret pit to slide into the seat. Once in the seat the gunner reached back and closed the doors and securely latched them.

Operating the Turret

The gunner turned the master switch and the adjacent azimuth drive switch ON and waited a few seconds to turn ON the elevation drive switch next to it. Just under these three switches was the gun switch protected by a red plastic cover. This switch and the gun camera switch were to be turned ON next. The gunner grasped the control handles in front of him and used the bottom edges of his hands to press down on the two safety switches, either of which activated the turret and sight light when held down. The gunner held one control handle while he reached back to the switch box to adjust the sight rheostat that regulated the sight light intensity. In later Emerson turrets this rheostat operated independently of the safety switches.

The oxygen mask hose connection to the demand-type regulator was mounted on the support framework near the gunner's left shoulder alongside the flow and pressure gauges. The oxygen was supplied from the aircraft's central tanks. The heated suit plug-in was located close to the gunner's right foot on the turret wall. Earphone and microphone jacks led out of the control handle column. The jack box was located outside of the turret in the bombardier's compartment. The trouble light and switch was on the top left support tubing and a gun camera bracket to the right of the sight. The protective two inch bullet-proof glass moved with the guns and had an electric heater on top to keep it clear at low temperatures. A 5/8 inch and 3/8 inch armor plate was positioned below.

The Emerson turret moved with the right-left bicycle-type motion of the control handles. The triggers were located on both control handles under the gunner's index fingers, while on top of the right handle next to the thumb was the high-speed button. On top of the left handle next to the gunner's thumb was the push-to-talk interphone button. The Emerson had both fuses and reset buttons to protect its electrical circuits, mostly located in the switch box (spare fuses were stored in the upper left corner of the box). The reset buttons for the important azimuth and elevation circuits were located in the junction box outside the turret. The azimuth hand crank was located near the gunner's left knee and the elevation hand crank was at his right knee.

The turret was operated by turning the control handles in bicycle riding fashion; right to go right, left to go left. To elevate the guns the handles were rotated towards the gunner, and away from him to depress the guns. The high-speed button was located on top of the right handle and the turret into high speed for transferring from one target to another. The turret traversed 75° to either side of center at a normal speed of 20° per second and a high speed of 45° per second. The guns could be elevated 60° above horizontal and depressed 50° below horizontal at a normal speed of 16° per second and a high speed of 30° per second. To switch the turret to manual operation the gunner turned OFF all switches, pressed the manual control index plates on both hand crank brackets outward to their manual positions, and pressed the foot trigger firing keys on each gun solenoid.

The Emerson turret had the emergency azimuth control that enabled the crew to help the gunner out of the turret in case of emergency. A cable leading from the turret could be pulled to disengage the azimuth power system. A hand crank stored in a bracket under the door could be attached to a shaft located at the bottom of the turret to move the turret in azimuth to rotate the turret to get the doors in position to open them.

Guns and Accessories

Each M-2 Browning gun was mounted in a cradle by a rear mounting block and slide, and a front gun mount. The rear mount block was bolted to the rear of the gun and dovetailed into the slide in the cradle. The front mount was a "jaw-like affair" that snapped over two bearing pins on the gun's adapter and was locked in place by a gun release handle on the inside of the cradle. This handle or lever was safety-wired to the gun shield in its locked or up position. Special charging units were mounted on the inside of the guns;

their mounting bolts were to be safety-wired and the cable connections to the units were to have cotter pins. A special gun safety latch protruded from each charging unit and held the bolt in its retracted position after charging. This latch had to be pushed down before charging and pulled up when ready to fire. The foot firing mechanism mounted on the buffer tubes of the guns also were to have their mounting bolts safety-wired. The emergency foot-firing pedal was available to fire the guns so that the gunner could have his hands free. To adjust the guns up, down, and sideways in their cradles there were bolt and screw adjustment assemblies on the rear mounts. The gun-charging levers were located near the gunner's knees, and to cock the guns they were to be pulled up sharply and then allowed to drop back. The gun triggers were located under the gunner's index fingers.

The N-8 or N-6A optical sight was held in place directly in front of the gunner by five mounting bolts on top of the sight cradle. The position of the sight could be adjusted sideways to the right or left by loosening the five mounting bolts and then loosening the adjusting bolt under the cradle. No up or down adjustment was possible. The gunsight could be harmonized to the gun by a set of adjusting bolts that required a boresighting tool.

There were two ammunition cans (500 rpg), one for each gun, mounted on the outside of the turret along the right and left fuselage wall. Chutes carried the ammunition belts from the cans up through the floor of the turret to the guns. Each can was loaded in the standard folded pattern, starting at the corner of the can farthest from the turret, single link end of the belt first, and rounds pointing toward the outside of the aircraft. Ammunition was brought into the turret from external boxes, with the belts being taken in through a hole in the floor. To bring the belt to the gun it had to be forced up through its chute, double link end first, until the first round started up the vertical section of the chute into the turret. Inside the turret there was a joint in the vertical section of the chutes. The chutes could be separated at these joints and the belt could be hauled up with a hooked wire. The gunner got two extra lengths of belt with 25 rounds to use as feed strips. The gunner opened the latch on the armor plate in front of him and lifted it out of the way. He pushed the piece of hooked wire down the upper chutes and pulled the feed strips over the booster sprockets to the guns, double link end first, with all the rounds pointing forward. After closing the armor panel the gunner connected the bottom of the feed strips to the main ammunition belts, being certain that the connecting rounds were evenly placed in the links. The gunner then refastened the chutes at the joints. Just before takeoff the gunner opened the armor plate panel again and pressed the double link end of each belt into the gun's feedways. The Emerson turret fed from the inside; the left gun from the right and the right gun from the left. The armor plate panel was closed and the guns were hand charged twice and were ready to fire.

Exiting the Turret

The turret was run into its stowed position with the guns pointing straight ahead. All the switches were turned OFF and the rear doors opened. The gunner slid back off the seat and reached up to the doorway support bar and lifted himself out, closing and latching the doors. The stowing position was 0° azimuth and 0° elevation with the guns pointing directly forward and to the rear in the rear turret.

**Section 10: Bendix Model A and R Dorsal Turrets**

Background

The all-electric Bendix Dorsal Turret was used exclusively on the B-25 (USN and USMC PBJ) beginning with the B-25B. The original B-25 design incorporated the late 1930s AAC standards utilizing the light .30 caliber machine gun in five flexible hand-held positions: one in the nose, one each

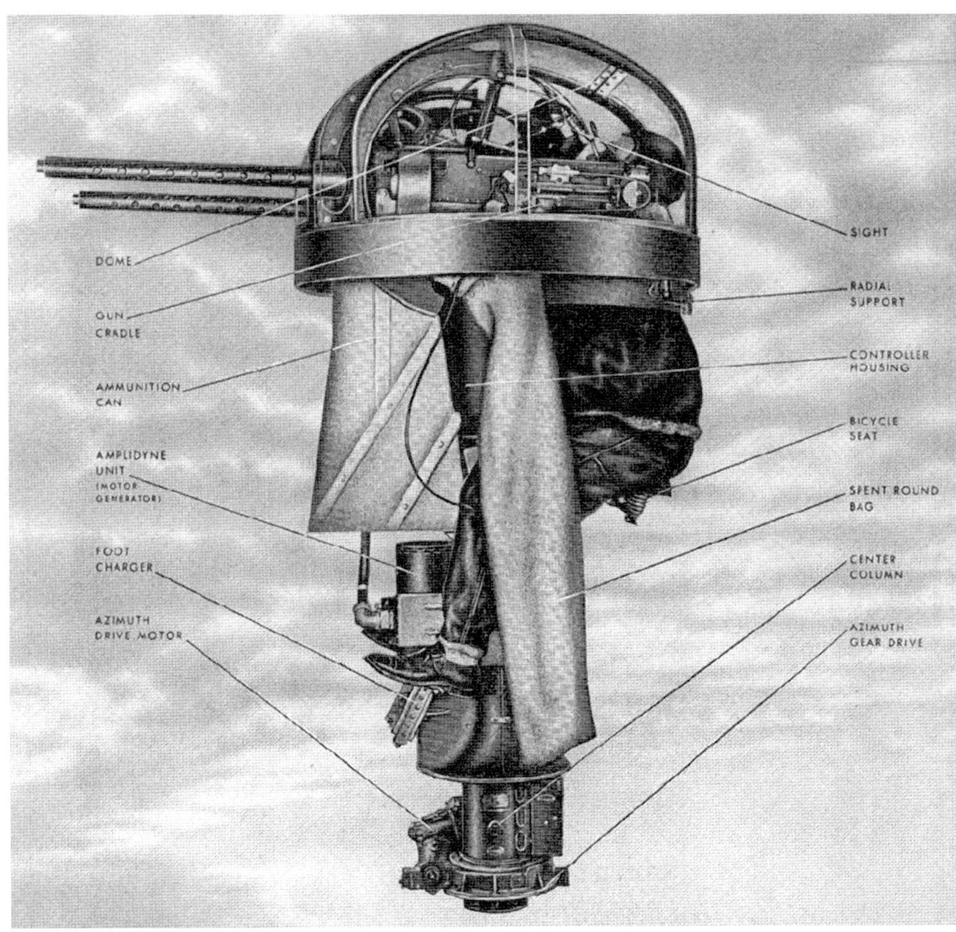


**Bendix Model A and R Dorsal Turrets** (USAAF)

in the ventral and dorsal rear fuselage, and two in the waist position. The early Bendix dorsal turrets encountered many problems. The dorsal turret was designed without regard for the size of the gunner wearing full flying gear and the gunner became jammed behind the twin guns and the back edge of the turret. The numerous malfunctions of the electrical system were another key problem, as the speed controls began "excessive" arcing after only 35 minutes, much like the ventral turret had done in earlier tests. Yet another problem was that the gunners had to allow for a dead area in azimuth travel at the point where the canopy moved past its neutral position, making smooth tracking of a target virtually impossible. A continuing early problem was that the guns jammed, and the guns in some individual turret mountings would not fire simultaneously. Due to poor elevation slot closure, when the guns were facing forward a blast of air would be forced into the turret and when facing aft the warm cabin air would be sucked out.

The Bendix Model A dorsal (Army Model A-9A/Navy 250CE-3) turret was located in the aft fuselage compartment behind the bomb bay, replacing the single flexible dorsal .30 caliber machine gun on the B-25 and B-25A that fired through a enclosed hatch. This turret location continued on the B-25C/D and G models, but after the ventral turret was cancelled during its production run, the B-25G became underarmed and waist guns and tail guns were added at modification depots or in the field to alleviate this deficiency. It was found when the waist guns and gunners were located with the dorsal turret in the aft fuselage the area became confined and their movement was greatly restricted. To solve this problem the dorsal turret in its Model R configuration (Army Model A-9B/Navy 250CE-4) was moved forward to the navigator's compartment just behind the cockpit, which helped to maintain the proper center of gravity to balance the weight added to the rear by the waist guns and tail turret. This new dorsal turret position was more heavily braced and had a higher dome than did previous Mitchell dorsal turrets. With the turret's move the ADF "football" antenna had to be relocated under the forward fuselage and the astrodome and side scanning windows in the navigator's compartment were deleted. Two small fairings were added on top of the fuselage just aft of the gun muzzles when the turret was in the stowed position pointing aft. These fairings were actually pieces of armor that deflected bullets away from the tail gunner's position in the event the guns in the top turret were accidentally fired while in this stowed position.

**Exterior View** (Author/MAAM)

**Turret Pedestal** (Author/CAF)

There were several dome designs. One dome was almost completely clear and did not have any metal framework. Instead of the metal framework three clear plastic pieces were applied for reinforcement. The slots for the barrels were covered from the inside by curved metal pieces to protect the gunner from air blast. There were two metal armor fairings behind the gun barrels intended to deflect bullets away from the tail gun position if the turret guns were fired to the rear by accident. Another basically similar dome was reinforced by a metal framework painted in the camouflage color of the fuselage. A third dome was more asymmetrical than the other two, sloping more in the front. The gun barrels were mounted in slots covered by clear Perspex rather than the curved pieces of protective metal.

Entering the Turret

The Bendix turret was one of the easiest to enter, as the gunner stepped up into the dome using the footrests which were adjusted to fit the gunner's height by moving them up or down in the notches in the foot slide. The gunner placed one foot on one footrest, pulling himself into the dome using the turret's inner supports, and threw the other leg over the protruding bicycle seat and was seated. The seat could be adjusted by the gunner raising his bottom off the seat and bracing one elbow over one of the inner turret supports. Using his free hand he unlocked the seat and adjusted the seat by turning a small handle and swivel on the right hand side of the seat support which loosened the band that held the seat to the central column. The seat then could be slid up or down the column until it was at the proper height (eyes level with the sight). The handle was then reversed, tightening the seat in place.

**View from Turret** (Author/MAAM)

Operating the Turret

The Bendix Turret Manual states: "You can get the turret into action about as quickly as you can start an automobile on a warm summer day."

The gunner sat with his head and shoulders between the guns on an adjustable bicycle-type seat that was attached near the top of the turret center column. The seat rotated in azimuth with the turret, foot rests, guns, and gunsight. The seat had a hinge and latch to allow the seat to swing downward against the center column, facilitating the gunner's exit and entry.

After the gunner was correctly seated he reached around to the left wall of the fuselage to a long, narrow box containing two switches. First the main power switch was turned to the ON position, and then the heat-light switch was moved to the ON position to power the sight bulb, trouble light, and the heated flying suit unit. The sight rheostat located on the controller housing just above the left handle (above the gunner's left hand) adjusted the light intensity of the sight reticle to the outside lighting conditions. Since the Bendix turret was only used on the B-25, which basically was a low-level bomber, there was no turret oxygen system included. The turret was equipped with interphone connections and switches, an extension light, and a heated flying suit rheostat and outlet. The interphone microphone was activated by depressing either of the button switches located above and forward of either control handle. The jack was located under the right control handle. The interphone jack box and the oxygen regulator were located adjacent to the azimuth resistor box on the left side of the fuselage opposite the turret. The self-returning extension light attached to the controller housing under the left control handle in front of the gunner's left knee. If the heated flying suit was to be used, which it rarely was, its jacks were connected to the outlet located outboard of the right control handle near the gunner's right knee.

The gun handles were turned "just as you would steer a bicycle; to the right to go right and to the left to go left." To raise the guns the heel of the handles was pressed down and to lower them they were pulled up. "Move the controls smoothly and deliberately and you will be able to track any target closely and with deadly aim." The turret could be rotated continuously 360° in azimuth and the guns swung from 0° to almost straight up. The speed of the turret could be varied from 1/4° to 12° per second in low speed and from 1/4° to 33° per second in high-speed. The amplidyne system of control automatically furnished a constant speed for any setting of the control handles regardless of the change of torque. The speed of the guns was proportional to the degree of movement of the control handles from neutral position. For high-speed in azimuth and elevation, either high-speed button could be depressed with the thumb, with the speed of the guns being proportional to the degree of swing of the control handles from the neutral position. A dead man's safety switch, spring-loaded to neutral, was mounted in each control handle. If the gunner relaxed his grip, releasing either safety switch, power was interrupted and movement of the turret or guns was stopped.

The gunner had to take care not to depress the trigger firing switches on the control handles, as the guns could fire as soon as the main power switch was turned on. The gunner was to grasp the control handles so that the edges of his hands depressed the two safety switches located inside the controller casting. The switches were wired in parallel so the turret could be operated when the safety switch on the outside of either control handle was depressed. As long as either one of the two switches was held down the turret could be operated. The gun firing circuit could cut out individually for each gun to prevent firing into propellers, vertical stabilizer, and the tail turret enclosure. The turrets were equipped with firing cut outs and electric dynamic brakes that prevented the guns from firing aft into the vertical stabilizers and forward into the propellers and fuselage just forward of the turret.

The turret's manual system was only to be used for moving the turret to make repairs and adjustments, and was not intended for operating the turret in combat emergencies. To move the turret in either azimuth or elevation a crank with a flexible shaft, stored at the base of the turret, was used. To move the guns up or down the crank was inserted on the elevation shaft located in front of the sight cradle. To rotate the turret the gunner had to get down in the turret and place the crank on the pinion shaft in the azimuth gearing at the base of the main support column.

Guns and Accessories

The turret mounted twin .50 caliber M-2 machine guns equipped with recoil absorbing mechanisms, firing solenoids, and foot chargers. The N-6A or N-8 gunsight and the portion of the guns that extended above the mould line of the aircraft were enclosed in a Plexiglas dome. Each gun was equipped with an Edgewater recoil adapter, a Type G-11 firing solenoid, a manual charging slide, and case and link ejection chutes.

The N-8 and N-6A gunsights were mounted into a bracket in the sight cradle directly in front of the pilot. The six mounting bolts could be loosened to adjust the sight up/down and left/right. The sight rotated with the turret and guns in azimuth and was synchronized with the guns in elevation. A gunsight rheostat was provided for turning on the gunsight lamp and for controlling the intensity of the circle-and-dot reticle image. The gunsight was synchronized with the guns in elevation, and when the gunner looked through the sight he trained the guns on the target by means of the control handles, centering the dot of the reticle image on the target. Once the target was centered the gunner fired the guns by depressing either Trigger Firing Switch mounted on the front of each control handle. Trigger switches were connected to a firing relay which in turn supplied current to firing solenoids fastened to each gun; depressing either trigger switch fired both guns.

The gunner charged the guns independently of each other or together by lifting either foot rest to its uppermost position in their slides with the toe of his shoe and then sharply depressing it to its lowest position. The footrests were mounted on the outside of the gun's receivers with their mounting bolts safety wired. The left foot rest was used to charge the left gun, the right foot rest the right gun. This action caused the gun bolt to move to the rear position and then automatically move forward, charging the guns. On early dorsal turrets, guns were charged by depressing a charger button on the left side of the turret's supporting post. The gunner could remove a defective cartridge by lifting the foot operated charger with his toe to its uppermost position and then pressing it down to its lower limit. The gun bolt would move to the rear position and then automatically to a forward position, thus charging the gun.

The guns were adjusted up, down, or sideways in their cradles by means of two Allen adjusting screws in each rear mount and were held in place by two rear and four front lock screws. These adjustments centered the guns in their mounts. The adjustment screws were turned to the centers of their vertical and lateral adjustments.

Ammunition

The turret was supplied by two large ammunition boxes marked Right (gun) and Left (gun) which carried 400-440 rpg. Loading and stowing the ammunition for each gun into the aircraft through the bomb bay was by brute strength or facilitated by a rope hoist assembly. Once inside the aircraft the boxes were placed on the floor directly under the grooved ammunition roller and the mounting hooks located on the wall above. The turret was rotated with power ON into a position that gave access for installing the ammunition box in the turret and the turret main power switch was then turned OFF. After the boxes were secured the double link end of each ammunition belt was fed over the ammunition, keeping the cartridge points toward the small ends of the rollers. The belts were pulled over the top of the cone feed rollers and then were twisted slightly around the glide rollers into the guns, with the first rounds into the feedways permitting the guns to rotate in elevation. Special ammunition feed rollers were mounted on top of each gun and held by the gun cover pin and cotter pin. Chutes were arranged to furnish a continuous supply of ammunition to the guns while the guns were moving in elevation and azimuth. Ammunition boxes were removed from the turret by releasing the latch on the underside of the lower support bracket, lifting the box up so that the bar on the box cleared the upper support on the front of the controller housing, and then lowering it to the floor.

Special case ejection chutes were installed on the outside of the guns to carry used links away from the guns. The empty shell casings and belt links were ejected through flexible canvas chutes out the bottom of the guns and were carried clear of the gunner's legs and collected on the fuselage floor. Later, two spent round bags hooked to the mouth of the gun's case ejection chute received the used brass rounds ejected from the firing guns.

Exiting the Turret

When the turret was not in use the guns were returned to the stowing position; 0° elevation and 180° azimuth, with the guns level and pointing straight aft toward the tail. The guns were cleared by opening the gun covers and then charging them twice. The turret main power switch and all other switches were turned OFF. All ammunition was removed from the feedways and turret and the two spent ammunition bags. The guns were field stripped and the gun casing groups inspected and cleaned. Any malfunctions of the turret or guns were to be reported.

In case of turret power failure, the guns could be stowed in a straight aft position by means of a handcrank and extension shaft stored at the base of the turret. The first step in stowing the guns was to attach the extension shaft to the elevation speed reducer, attach the handcrank to the extension shaft, and then turn the handcrank clockwise (looking down). The turret was rotated so the guns pointed straight aft by engaging the handcrank with the end of the azimuth shifter shaft, pulling the shaft out approximately 1/2 inch with the crank and then turning the crank. The turret rotated clockwise when the crank was turned counterclockwise (looking from the shaft end).

**Section 11: Sperry/Briggs Type A-17 Nose and Tail Turrets**

The A-17 turret was used in the Consolidated B-32 after its CFC armament and pressurization was removed and the Dominator became a normal heavy bomber. The Sperry designed/Briggs built A-17 nose and tail turret were identical, except that the K-11 sight was used in the nose and the Type-10 sight in the tail. The turret was attached to the fuselage by a bracket at the top and a traversing gear housing at the bottom, with the entire ball moving left to right on pivot points incorporated by the attaching elements. The turret consisted of two concentric structures. The 2.5 foot wide C-shaped center section that rotated around a lateral axis furnished vertical movement. This section mounted the two .50 caliber M-2 Browning machine guns, the hand-controlled gunsight, and armor protection. In azimuth the entire assembly moved while in elevation only the inner structure moved. The field of fire in azimuth was 150° and 120° in elevation. Electrical power from the aircraft drove the constant speed electric motor whose output was converted to hydraulic power that through gearing resulted in turret movement.

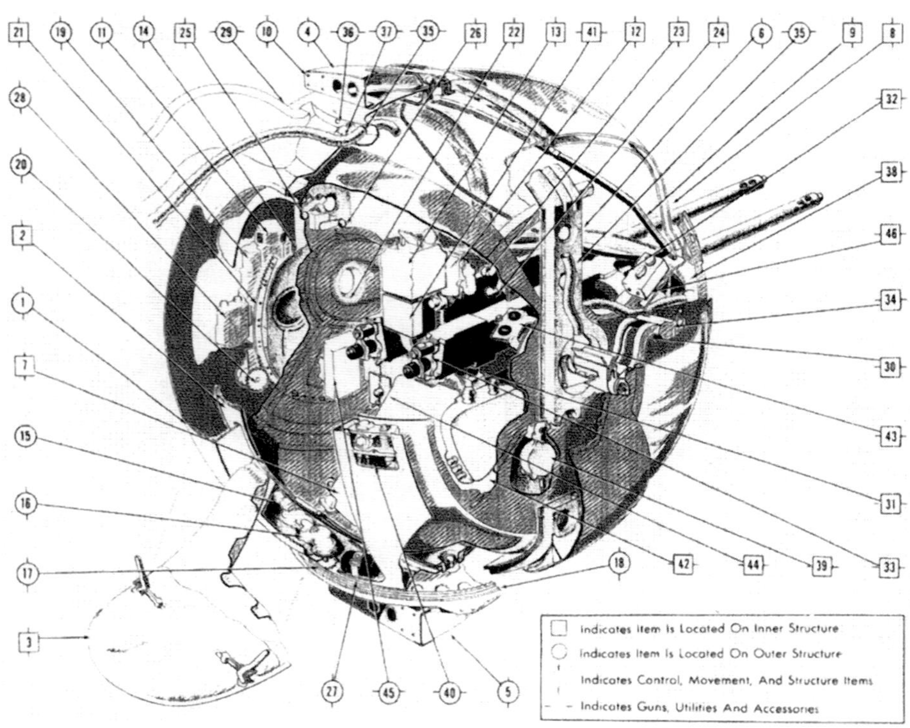


**Sperry/Briggs Type A-17 Nose Turret** (USAAF)

Cover painting by Steve Ferguson for author's book, *The Consolidated B-32 Dominator: The Ultimate Look from Drawing Board to Scrapyard.* (Author/ Ferguson)

The **A-17 turret** consisted of two concentric structures. The 2.5 foot wide C-shaped center section that rotated around a lateral axis furnished vertical movement. It was entered through the rear as seen in the turret in the second row. (USAAF)

The gunner, sitting on a small armored seat, faced armored glass and two thicknesses of plastic panels which were not Plexiglas, but CR-39 manufactured by Pittsburgh Plate Glass Company. Between the panels there was a hollow space to allow the flow of heated air for defrosting.

Ammunition boxes for the 600 rounds supplying the nose turret were located beside and parallel to the windscreen in the bombardier's compartment. The 1,000 rounds for the tail turret were located inside the tail section just forward of the tail turret in boxes beside and parallel to the catwalk to the turret. The rounds were carried by flexible ammunition chutes. In the tail they ran through slings, and in the nose they ran across a shelf above the windscreen. The other turrets had integral boxes. The ammunition entered the turret through two openings located above and to each side of the rear entry door and was fed through flexible chutes from two ammunition boxes that were mounted in the fuselage just to the rear of the turret. The nose and tail turrets were found to be the most important in turrets in combat. In combat tests feeding difficulties and burned out turret clutches were the major problems of the turret until remedied.

**Section 12: Bendix Chin Turret**

Background

Early combat experience had caused the British to retain the chin turrets on their bombers to defend against head-on fighter attacks. In July 1942, in response to the British combat reports, Bendix engineers developed two experimental chin turrets for trial installations in the B-17F and B-24D. The B-17 turret was fitted with an independent sight that was suspended on a swinging arm that was free of the turret proper, while the B-24 version rotated both the sight and the gunner in relation to the guns moving in azimuth. To be cost effective only one of the turrets could be selected for manufacture, and the B-17 model was chosen because it could be fitted in either aircraft. Also, because of the limited sector of fire of the chin gun position there was no need to orient the gunner to his guns as with the B-24 system. Technical problems caused delays in placing the turret into production. By the time the chin turret was ready Boeing B-17 production was well underway and the chin turret contract threatened to place a heavy strain on Bendix capacity. In a memo of 29 January 1943 from the Chief of the Materiel Division to the Chief Production Engineering Section it was noted that the "history of the Bendix Company in turret production does not bear out any optimistic assumption as to their capacity to better the delivery schedule."

Bendix chin turret production reached approximately 150 units per month by June 1943, but unlike the experimental model, the earliest production turrets utilized the old indirect or remote sighting system. After one practice mission and one combat mission the Eighth Air Force approved this remote sighted chin turret only as an "interim measure." During a subsequent mission, a B-17 equipped with the remotely sighted chin turret experienced 12 frontal attacks in one hour. The nose gunner on the mission reported that he had been unable to track more than one target for three bursts "because of the difficulty of picking up targets attacking in rapid succession." The unsatisfactory performance of the remote sight chin turret caused the Materiel Division to order the removal of all these turrets that were installed in B-17Fs and hand-held guns were to be continued until a production version direct-sight chin turret could be procured in quantity.

General Description

The Bendix Chin Turret was an electrically powered turret mounting two .50 caliber M2 machine guns equipped with a recoil absorbing mechanism, firing solenoids, and manual gun chargers. The turret weighed 438 pounds without two guns (weighing 65 pounds each) and 375 rounds of ammunition per gun (weighing 250 pounds @ 33 pounds per 100 rounds). The chin turret was mounted at floor level in the bombardier's compartment with the guns extending below the fuselage. The lower assembly, with the exception of the gun barrels, which extended through covered slots, was enclosed in an aluminum, movable housing to minimize wind resistance. Plexiglas windshields sealed the space at the floor of the aircraft around the turret.

Entering the Turret

The gunner stepped up to the bombardier's compartment and sat down on the seat that was adjusted by a lever under the right side. The lever moved the seat back and forth and was locked by pressing the lever down. Once seated the gunner could see the switches, the sight, and sight cradle suspended from the fuselage ceiling, and the control unit mounted on a movable arm that moved the unit from stowage on the right side of the fuselage. Directly below the seat were Plexiglas floor panels held in place by Dzus fasteners. The open panels led to the turret proper, which held the

**Bendix Chin Turret** (Author/Pima)

guns and ammunition. The gunner and the seat always remained stationary, and as he operated the controls the gun swung under him while the sight moved around to follow the guns.

Operating the Turret

The Bendix Chin turret was considered one of the easiest to operate, as it had a minimum of switches and controls and no fuses or reset buttons. Upon sitting down the gunner swung the control unit into place in front of him from his right. He then reached over to the universal hinge joint on which the control arm pivoted and pressed forward on the release knob. He grasped the control handles and pulled the unit out to lock it in place. The main power switch located directly behind the control unit on a joint holding the unit to the support arm was turned ON.

The gunner grasped the control handles so that the edges of his hands depressed the two safety switches that activated the turret. The turret was moved in the basic bicycle steering fashion, and the guns elevated or depressed by pressing down or up on the control handles. In azimuth the turret could move 86° from the center line to either side, which was almost straight out to either the right or left. In elevation the guns could swing from 26° above horizontal to 46° below horizontal. The turret had two speeds: normal and high-speed tracking. The turret operated only when the safety switch on the outside of either control handle was depressed. Rotation of the turret in azimuth followed rotation of the control handles clockwise or counterclockwise around the vertical axis. The swing of the guns in elevation followed the swing of the control handles up or down. The speed of the guns was proportional to the degree of movement of the control handles from the neutral position in low speed. The guns moved in high speed when the high speed control button located on top of either control handle was depressed. The high speed of the guns was proportional to the degree of movement of the control handles from the neutral position. The turret could be stopped by releasing the control handles. The turret's power supply was cut off by switching OFF the main power switch. In case of power failure, the turret could rotate in azimuth and the guns could be swung in elevation by using a hand crank.

The demand-type oxygen regulator and hose connection for the mask was located on the left fuselage accompanied by the flow and pressure gauges. The heated flying suit plug-in was on the back of the seat, and the jacks for connecting the microphone and earphones were held in clips on the right fuselage. A hand-held push-to-talk switch hung from the microphone jack and the jack box was located on the right fuselage wall. The Bendix Chin Turret had no trouble light or gun camera bracket. A hand crank for manual operation was stowed near the seat and was only used for making

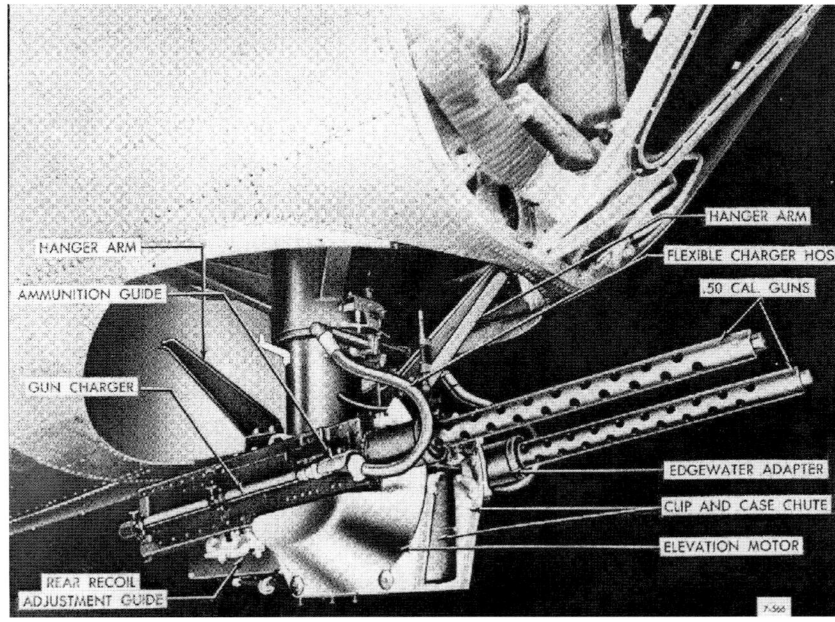


**Chin Turret with Housing Removed** (USAAF)

repairs and adjustments, and was not for use in combat emergencies. This crank fit on a pinion shaft in the azimuth gearing at the top of the center control column and moved the turret in azimuth. This crank also fit the elevation shaft located below and in front of the center column and moved the guns up and down.

Guns and Accessories

The Browning M-2 machine guns mounted in the turret were fed from the outside: the right gun from the right side and the left gun from the left side. Each gun was held in a mounting bracket by a rear recoil adjustment guide stud and nut and two front yoke studs. The rear stud was bolted to the rear of the gun and fit into a hole in the rear gun mount; it was held in place by an elastic stop nut underneath. The front yoke studs, which screwed into the front gun yoke and into the gun adapter on each side, were always safety wired. The triggers were located under the index fingers on each control handle while the high-speed buttons were located on the top of both handles near the gunner's thumbs.

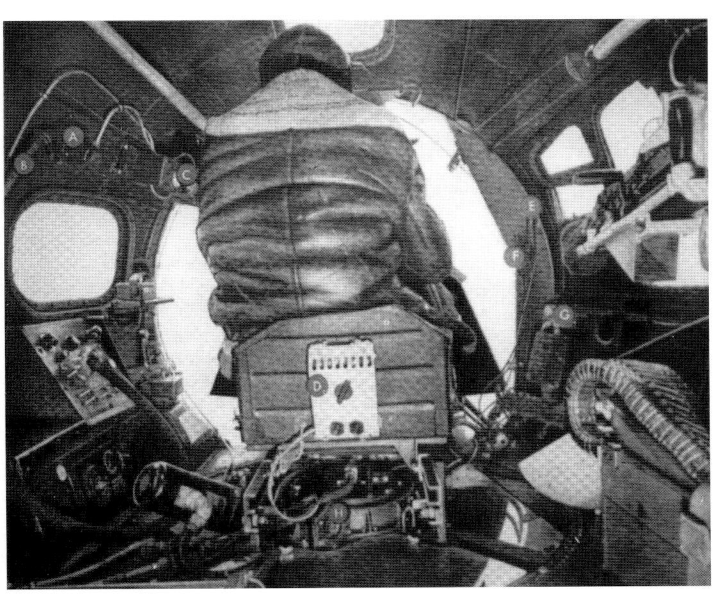

Gunner seated in chin turret of B-17 (USAAF)

The sight was either a N-8 or N-6A resting in the sight cradle. The sight light rheostat, located on top of the sight cradle suspended directly in front of the gunner, was turned to adjust the sight lamp's brightness. The N-6 or N-8 gunsight was synchronized with the movements of the gun in azimuth and elevation and was driven by tachometer shafts from the azimuth and elevation gear trains. The gunner's field of vision was always in the direction in which the guns were pointing and moving.

Hydraulic charging units were installed on the outside plates of the guns, and hydraulic lines led out of the central column to the units. The guns were charged by simply pressing the hydraulic charger buttons just adjacent to the main power switch on the control arm. Later turret models had a pulley and cable hand charger system with the charger handles in front on the right and left.

The guns were adjusted up, down, or sideways in their cradles by two rear mount Allen adjustment screws. The bottom Allen vertical screw controlled the up or down movement while the rear inside lateral adjustment screw controlled sideways movement.

Ammunition

Two ammunition cans, one for each gun, held about 365 rounds each. They were fixed to the movable housing and were equipped with guide chutes that allowed the ammunition to be fed to the guns while they were rotating in azimuth and elevation. The cans were loaded into the turret by pushing the seat forward and removing the Plexiglas floor panel. The left can was loaded by moving the turret to the left as far as it would go to bring the can and left gun into position. The ammunition can cover was removed and the ammunition belt was folded in the standard pattern. The single link end of the belt was first positioned into the front end of the can with the rounds pointing toward the center of the turret. When the can was filled the double link end of the belt was fed over the top roller and the can cover was replaced. To load the right can the turret was moved to the right and the same procedure was followed.

To feed the guns the gunner went outside the aircraft and removed the inspection port panel from the tub. He reached inside and pulled the belts down through the guide rails, underneath the bottom rollers, and across the guide springs to the gun's feedways. He then pressed the first round of each belt into its feedway and replaced the inspection port panel. Special cartridge guides were installed on the outside of the guns to lead ammunition up to

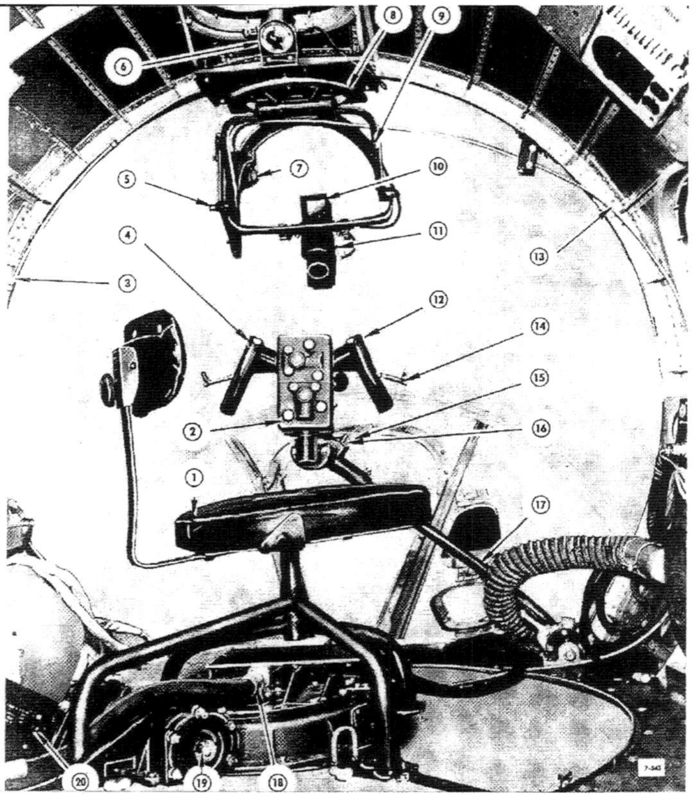


1. SEAT
2. CONTROLLER
3. AZIMUTH DRIVE CABLE
4. CONTROL GRIP
5. SIGHT DRIVE ELEVATION
6. RHEOSTAT
7. ELEVATION PINION
8. AZIMUTH SIGHT DRIVE
9. SUPPORTING YOKE
10. N-6 SIGHT
11. RESERVE FILAMENT SWITCH
12. TRIGGER SWITCH (FORWARD SIDE OF GRIP)
13. ELEVATION DRIVE CABLES
14. SAFETY (DEADMAN) SWITCH
15. CHARGER SWITCH
16. POWER SWITCH
17. CONTROLLER ARM
18. HYDRAULIC SWIVEL GLAND
19. SHIFTER SHAFT
20. AZIMUTH DRIVE MOTOR

**Chin Turret Seat Control and Sight Unit** (USAAF)

the feedways, and special clip ejection chutes were installed inside the guns to lead spent links from the guns. Both were held by the belt holding pawl pins. Three ammunition guide springs led the rounds from the ammunition cans to each gun. The two long springs attached to the movable housing of the turret and were hooked over the outside belt holding pawl pin, and one short spring was attached to the ammunition can hooks over the same pin. The empty cartridges and belt links were ejected by chutes through the bottom of the housing.

Exiting the Turret

To leave the turret the gunner had to run it to the stowing position with the guns pointing forward at 26° elevation. The main power switch was shut OFF and the release knob on the control unit support arm was pushed forward to unlock it and move the unit to the stowage position on the right. The release knob was pulled to lock it.

**Section 13: ERCO Turrets**

Background

The origin of the ERCO Company dates to Henry Berliner, the son of German emigrant Emile Berliner, who experimented with early autogiros and developed the Gyro radial engines, which he sold to the Navy. After graduating from Harvard and MIT Henry joined his father to design and build a number of helicopters. In late 1928, Henry went into partnership with Temple Nash Joyce to form the Berliner-Joyce Aircraft Company headquartered in Dundalk, MD, to build fixed wing aircraft. The company developed several unsuccessful military and commercial aircraft before it sold its stock in 1930 to the Sperry Corporation, which was a subsidiary of North American Aviation, and which renamed the company the B/J Aircraft Corporation. In June 1933 North American and General Motors completed a stock transfer and, as part of the transaction, B/J was merged into GM's General Aviation Corporation which terminated B/J. In 1932, even before B/J's dissolution, Henry Berliner formed the Engineering and Research Corporation (ERCO) in Washington, DC, which was intended to develop new engineering concepts in aircraft components, particularly cowling and propellers, and metal aircraft production machinery. The company's first designs for aircraft machinery were successful and ERCO prospered, buying 50 acres in Riverdale, MD, near College Park Airport, where he built a factory in 1937. There ERCO developed the Ercoupe, a cheap, easy-to-fly, two-seat, twin-control monoplane which was so successful that the company expanded the Riverdale plant in 1940. Once America entered the war, the AAC contracted 400 Ercoupes as a light liaison aircraft (YO-55), but due to the shortage of aluminum the contract was suspended and not completed.

When Boeing was awarded a contract for 500 long-range XPBB-1 Sea Ranger patrol planes, Boeing contacted ERCO in the summer of 1940 to design and produce a nose and waist turret. The first turret was the ERCO 250SH-1, which was the first power turret to mount twin .50 caliber machine guns for an American naval aircraft. The 250SH was to be installed in the Sea Ranger's bow (nose), deck (dorsal), and stern (tail) positions. The second ERCO turret was the 150TH waist turret. The XPBB-1 contract was cancelled as its role could be filled by the PB4Y-1 and -2. Since these Catalinas were vulnerable to head on fighter attacks the Navy experimentally installed a squadron of PB4Y-1s with the 250SH turrets in the bow. In combat experience losses from head on attacks were significantly reduced, and between May 1942 and June 1943 15 Navy contracts were initiated for over 3,000 experimental and production ERCO turrets. In addition to turrets ERCO produced machine tools, propeller blades, and antenna components which caused the government to give ERCO priority to more than double the space in its facilities to 92,000 square feet and to purchase $500,000 in new machinery. By 1944, the ERCO assembly lines were turning out a peak monthly production of 180 250TH tear drop and 200 250SH bow turrets. ERCO was a diversified company that included the manufacture of machine tools (by the end of the war its propeller blade profilers had cut 98% of the Allied aluminum propeller blades). By the end of 1944 ERCO's contracts totaled $20 million and it employed over 4,000 at its Riverdale factory during the war.

ERCO turrets were considered by the Army Air Corps when in January 1941 Henry Berliner met with the Chief of the Materiel Division to discuss the possibility of ERCO producing turrets for the Army Air Corps. Berliner arranged for ERCO engineers to meet with the Materiel Division to discuss the modification of the 250SH for installation on AAC aircraft. Tests were carried out in October 1941 that uncovered a few negligible but typical problems related to turret prototypes. Wright Field's report pointed out that among the problems were uneven turret movement, uncomfortable hand grips, and inadequate access for service. The report praised the turret as "very well-designed, cleanly constructed, and efficient machine gun turret with an extremely wide range of travel comparable to that of the Sperry lower manned ball turret." In January 1942 this turret was considered for the Consolidated XB-32 four-engine high altitude bomber. The plan was abandoned since the Materiel Division decided that the turret was too heavy, and also because it used the Vickers hydraulic drive that was already in very short supply at the time. With this decision any ERCO turret use in AAF aircraft was cancelled.

**ERCO 250TH "Tear Drop" Turret** (USN)

**ERCO X150TH**

In 1940 Boeing had contracted ERCO to produce the waist turret for Boeing's new twin-engined long-range XPBB-1 Sea Ranger patrol bomber. Since ERCO had no experience in turret design their original tear drop waist turret was designed by Boeing engineer Waldo Eaton. In June 1940, Boeing sent the blueprints for the turret to ERCO to produce two of these turrets for the sole prototype. These turrets were installed in early 1942, and were the first streamlined, aerodynamic power-driven waist blister placed on an American aircraft. The Sea Ranger program was cancelled, but the experience gained in designing the X150TH led to the design and production of the 250TH series later in the war.

**ERCO 250TH-1, 1A, 2, 2A**
**(ERCO Models 6020 and 6026) "Tear Drop" Turret**

Background

This turret was the first and only successful American powered waist turret design. Previously, the AAF had installed twin .50 caliber U.S. Shoe Machinery waist positions in the YB-40 and XB-41 gun ships, but these mounts did not pass field tests and evaluations and did not go into production. The ERCO design originated due to the demand to mount twin .50s in the beam of Navy patrol bombers and was based on the X150TH designed for the XPBB-1 Sea Ranger. In February 1943, the Navy purchased six X250TH turrets for its XPB3Y-1s for $216,000.

The 1,632 production 250TH-1 models were the second most produced ERCO turret:

| Model# | ERCO# | # Produced | Navy Contract# |
|---|---|---|---|
| X250TH-1, 2 | 6020 | 2 | NO 317 |
| 250TH-1, 2 | 6026 | 850 | NO 878 |
| 250TH-1A, 2A | 6026 | 173 | NO 4600 |
| 250TH-1A, 2A | 6026 | 262 | NO 5210 |
| 250TH-1A, 2A | 6026 | 345 | NO 6030 |

**ERCO 250TH** installed in the waist of a **Consolidated PB4Y-2 Privateer** (USN)

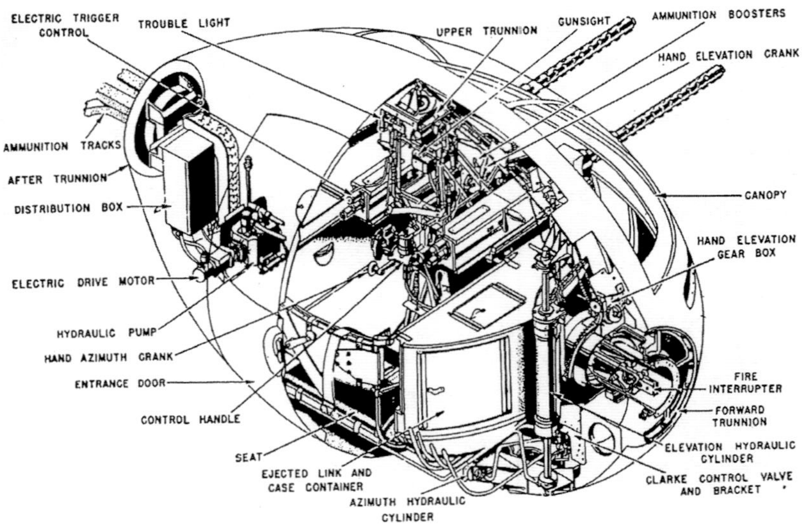


(USN)

Description

These turrets operated hydraulically on pressure built up from a hydraulic pump driven by a constant speed electric motor. They were installed only in the waist positions on either side of the Consolidated PB4Y-2: the ERCO 250TH-1 on the starboard side and the ERCO 250TH-2 on the port side. The tear drop-shaped turret had a wide cone of fire to protect the aircraft from beam or belly attacks, and also the turret protected a large area above. In operation they were somewhat similar to a ball turret, as the gunner moved his guns and sight in the direction he moved the control handles.

The 250TH weighed 590 pounds empty and 972 pounds loaded with the gunner and 500 rounds of ammunition. It was 7 feet 3 inches long and 4 feet 6 inches in diameter. The turret was an ellipsoid tear drop shape which made it aerodynamically clean. The gun carriage and gunner's seat were enclosed in a metal ball within the turret shell. It rotated separately of the outer shell on trunnions in a vertical axis to give an azimuth travel of 55° forward and 80° aft. The inner ball could not move independently in elevation and depression and the outer shell could not move in azimuth.

Oxygen was supplied to the turret through the rear trunnion from the aircraft's main oxygen source. The turret was supplied with the normal interphone and heated flying suit connections. When necessary, the turret could be lighted by two spotlights mounted on directional swivel joints that were mounted on top of the sight support. The gunner was protected by 1 1/4 inch bullet proof glass in front of his face, 5/16 inch armor plate in front of his body, and 5/16 inch armor plate under his feet; all of which moved with the guns so that the gunner was always protected from gunfire from the direction at which he was aiming. The accommodations and personal equipment of the 250TH was similar to the 250SH: a sliding, two piece door was hinged in the middle to separate into two parts, and attached to the top of the turret shell behind the gunner's seat.

Entering the Turret

The ERCO turret was easy to enter, but steps had to be followed "carefully or you might seriously injure yourself or damage the turret." First the flight engineer had to turn ON the waist turret switch located on his panel. The junction box located on a bulkhead near the turret contained the main power switch that was turned ON, the push release switch which was to be used only in an emergency to turn off the main switch, and a red indicator light.

To enter the turret the gunner opened the entrance door on the back of the turret by turning the entrance door handle counterclockwise and raising it to the stowed position. The gunner looked inside the turret and on the forward inboard side, next to the entrance door, were two red levers marked elevation by-pass valve and azimuth by-pass valve, which were to be in the DOWN position. Since the turret was in the stowed position the seat and guns needed to be moved in azimuth to a right angle from the center line of the aircraft for the gunner to be able to enter. To do this he had to raise the azimuth by-pass valve lever UP to free the seat and guns to the correct position and then move it back DOWN. The gunner unhooked the back of the turret seat and swung it back, keeping his shoulder harness over the back of the seat. He ducked his head under the top of the door and placed one leg into the turret. He grasped the tubing on either side of the sight to help him slide into the seat.

Operating the Turret

Once seated the gunner adjusted and snapped on the shoulder and seat belt. A chest pack parachute was provided under the seat. The gunner determined if the sight was at the correct height, and if it needed adjustment there was a seat adjustment lever between his legs that raised or lowered the seat. The entrance doors were open, and the gunner had to reach around to the back of his seat for the azimuth valve lever, which was released so the gunner could move the turret (and his seat) freely. He reached up and used the turret supports as a hand grip to move the turret aft until the guns were pointing aft. The gunner then reached around and lifted the bottom of the door enough to free it from the locks in the door channel guide and then let it slide down. While grasping the handle in the top part of the door he opened the latch handle in the bottom part and pulled the door sharply, releasing the latching handle so that the door locked. The azimuth by-pass lever was placed in the DOWN position.

The gunner checked if the manual azimuth and elevation clutches were DISENGAGED before attempting power operation (each clutch was equipped with a switch that shut off the power to the turret when the clutch was engaged). The azimuth clutch was operated by a red bar handle next to the gunner's knee. It was to be in the stowed position so that the turret would not move when the azimuth hand crank next to the other knee was turned. The red handle on the elevation clutch on the forward turret trunnion was to be in the UP position. To insure disengagement of the elevation clutch the elevation hand crank on the rear part of the turret was not to be moved. The 250TH was ready for power operation. The power switch on the control panel was momentarily held DOWN and the red indicator light lit up (as did a similar indicator light outside the turret) showing the power was ON.

To operate the turret the gunner grasped the control handles in front of him, depressing the safety switches that started the pump motor. The handles were turned, bicycle-fashion, in the direction he wanted the turret to move. The gun triggers were located on the ends of both control handles and under the gunner's thumb, and the red interphone buttons were located on the top front part of the control handles. Either or both buttons could be pressed to speak. The interphone jack box was located above the gunner's hip on the rear side of the seat. The turret was supplied with a diluter demand-type oxygen system that fed into the turret through the aft trunnion from the aircraft's main system. A regulator was mounted in a bracket on the top of the inboard side of the forward section of the turret. The cord to the heated flying suit was plugged into the suit receptacle in the bottom of the control panel and was turned OFF and ON by the heated suit switch on the same panel. Spotlight trouble lights were provided with swivel joints to direct their beams and were mounted on top of the sight supporting base. The switch was located on the control panel. The turret's armor plate protected the gunner from fire in any direction the guns were turned. There was a 1.5 inch thick bullet proof glass in front of the gunner's face; 5/16 inch armor plate in front of his body; and a 5/16 inch armor plate under his feet.

The turret was suspended on trunnions front and rear on a horizontal axis and rotated upward or downward on its axis to give 55° elevation and 95° depression (in order to protect the aircraft's underside). The turret and guns were moved by hydraulic jacks exerting 1,100 pounds pressure provided by an electric Vickers pump located in the turret. The Vickers pump's electrical supply was furnished by cables passing through the rear trunnion. In maximum depression, when the two turrets were used in tandem they crossfired 39 feet under the aircraft, which offered four gun coverage instead of the two gun protection afforded by the traditional belly turret. Manual elevation and azimuth hand cranks were used to move the turret without power but could not be used in combat.

Guns and Accessories

The twin .50 caliber machine guns were fed from the inside: the right gun fed from the left and the left gun from the right. Each gun was mounted on a Bell Mount Adapter. The rear support of the adapter had an assembly containing an elevation adjustment bolt and an azimuth adjustment bolt to move the gun up, down, and sideways.

On each side, in front of the gunner were the two .50 guns with their hand charging handles on the outboard side of each gun. By firmly grasping the charger handle of one gun with his palm up he pulled them sharply backward and then released them quickly and let it move forward on its own. He repeated this procedure for the other gun.

The Mk 9 sight was included with an optional gun camera and it was turned on at the control panel. The sight fit into the gunsight bracket directly behind the laminate bullet-proof glass.

A gun camera could be installed in the back of the armor plate in front of the bullet-proof glass face plate. The gunner operated the camera by turning ON the camera heater and camera trigger. The camera operated when the triggers were squeezed.

To prevent damage to the horizontal stabilizer and wings an electric gunfire interrupter was provided, but was operable only when the electrical power was on.

The guns, controlled by electric solenoids, could be fired singly or together, and were governed by gun selector switches marked RIGHT and LEFT on the control panel. The triggers were located under the gunner's index fingers on both control handles. Either trigger would fire both guns, singly or together, as was determined by the setting on the selector switches. In case of a power failure a foot firing mechanism was provided that was activated by turning UP the red safety catch located at the gunner's knee. Then, by depressing the red bar above his head the guns could be fired. In case of electrical failure a manual backup gun training system was provided. This back up system consisted of azimuth and elevation hand cranks and clutches and a pair of foot-firing pedals. This system proved useless in combat, but was used for harmonization of the guns and gunsight. In an emergency, to rescue a gunner the turret could be manually moved from the outside.

Ammunition

Two boxes holding 400 rounds of belted ammunition were located inside the aircraft to the rear of the turret. Flexible feed chutes holding 100 rounds fed the guns from the ammo boxes, thus supplying each gun with 500 rounds. The belts entered the turret through the rear trunnion and were assisted by electric boosters to pull the belts to the guns. The guns were fed from the inside; the right gun from its left side and the left gun from its right side.

Spent cartridge cases and empty links were ejected into containers located on each side of the gunner's seat. The containers were emptied by swinging the gun to either extreme in azimuth and opening the access door on the top and back of each container.

Exiting the Turret

All auxiliary units used were to be turned OFF. The gunner reached around his back and unlocked the door latching handle. He grasped the handle on the upper part of the door and pushed out. With his other had he grasped the bottom of the door, lifted UP, and stowed the door in the door channel catches. The turret was moved to 0° elevation and to the beam in azimuth. All switches were turned OFF. The gunner unclamped the seat back and climbed out of the turret. Once out he reached inside and lifted the azimuth by-pass lever and moved the guns and seat in azimuth by hand to the stowing position: 0° elevation and pointed in the extreme aft position in azimuth 80° aft of the beam. The azimuth by-pass lever was then moved DOWN.

The gunner could exit the turret in case of emergency by returning to the inside of the aircraft and then through the appropriate aircraft escape hatch. He could leave directly to the outside of the aircraft through the turret entry door after the guns had been swung down to their maximum depression. To do so he had to move the turret to its maximum depression to place the upper section of the entrance door to the outside of the aircraft. Two pins that hinged the two sections of the entrance door together were pulled out and the upper door section was pushed UP and the gunner could crawl out, remembering his chest pack parachute stowed on the aft inboard side of the turret.

**ERCO 250SH-1,-2, 2A, -2B, -2C, -3, -3A, and -3B (ERCO Ball Turret Model 6005)**

Background and General Description

The turret was originally designed by Boeing for the XPBB-1, and the first three experimental SH-1s were contracted in June 1940 by the Navy for installation on this aircraft. The XPBB-1 was cancelled and the 250SH was installed on other Navy patrol bombers: the Consolidated XP4Y-1 as an upper deck turret in April 1942; the Consolidated PB4Y-2 as a nose turret as the models 250SH-3, -3A, and -3B0; and the Consolidated PB4Y-1 (B-24J) replacing the nose turret as a 250SH-2, 2A, -2B, or -2C. Peak production of 200 units per month was reached in mid-1944.

The 250SH turret was compatible as a nose, tail, or dorsal turret, but in the latter placement the turret had very limited downward fire. The turret was mostly installed as a nose turret in the Navy PB4Y-1 and -2 patrol bombers. The turret was a 54 inch diameter sphere that weighed 561 pounds empty and 1,131 pounds loaded with the gunner and 1,300 rounds of .50 caliber ammunition. At 1,131 pounds the ERCO 250SH was one of the heaviest American turrets. It was fabricated from aluminum alloy sheet and extruded sections while the base and side trunnions were made of magnesium alloy castings. The upper segment of the turret was a Plexiglas canopy that wholly covered the guns and gunner and associated equipment. The Plexiglas canopy could be discarded in case of emergency. In case of an emergency the turret could be removed from within the aircraft.

The different turret models varied from each other mainly in furnished equipment and location of the internal components:

250SH-1: Used as a bow (nose) and stern (tail) turret on the XPBB-1and as a deck turret on the XP-4Y. Has a self-contained oxygen rebreathing system.
250SH-2: Used as a PB4Y-1 bow turret.
250SH-2A: Identical to the 250SH-2 except for the hydraulic fittings.
250SH-2B: Identical to the 250SH-2 except for the replacement of the Mark 9 gunsight by the Mark 18
250SH-2C: Identical to the 250SH-2 except for the addition of a command interphone radio.
250SH-3: Identical to the 250SH-2 except it was used in the nose of PB4Y-2s.
250SH-3A: Identical to the 250SH-3 except for the replacement of the Mark 9 gunsight by the Mark 18.
250SH-3B: Identical to the 250SH-3A except for the addition of a command interphone radio.

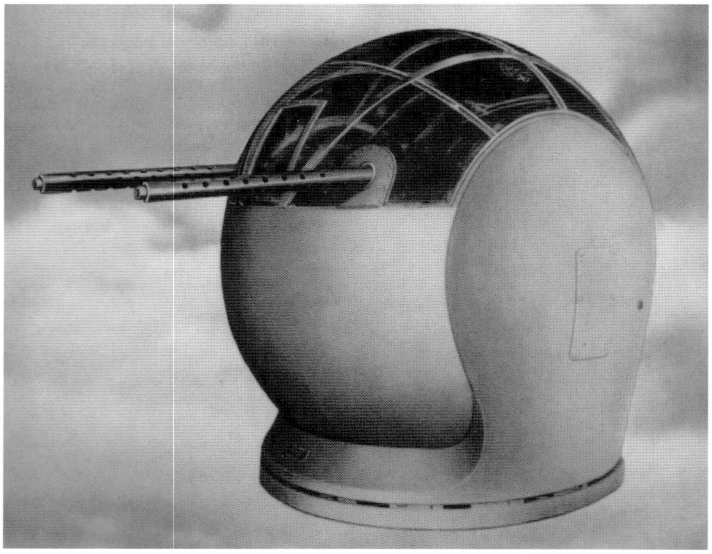

**ERCO 250 SH Ball Turret** (USN)

The 2,014 250SH turrets were ERCO's most produced turrets:

| Model | Navy Contract | Number Produced |
|---|---|---|
| X250SH-1 | NOS 74819 | 3 (experimental) |
| 250SH-1 | NX 11904 | 1 |
| 250SH-1 | NX 12971 | 265 + 25% spare parts (66) |
| 250SH-2A | NO1293 | 200 + 15% spare parts (30) |
| 250SH-2A | NO 1603 | 500 + 15% spare parts (75) |
| 250SH-3 | NO 2556 | 700 |
| 250SH-3 | NO 4601 | 345 |

The turret shell was suspended on trunnions that allowed forward and backward movement around a horizontal axis. These trunnions were installed on a horizontal bearing ring so that the turret and trunnions could revolve to the right and left around a vertical axis. The twin .50 caliber machine guns were fastened to the turret, and to aim them the entire turret had to move. In this fixed configuration the position of the gunner, guns, gunsight, and gun camera remained constant.

A self-contained Vickers electro-hydraulic drive unit moved the turret. The electric pump provided 1,000psi hydraulic pressure to the hydraulic elevation and azimuth drive motors that were run off the aircraft's DC power supply. Electricity was provided for gunsight light, gun camera, gun trigger solenoids, ammunition feed booster motors, trouble lights, and a magnetic shutoff valve (limit stop) for the turret's hydraulic system. A manual hydraulic hand pump was available for emergency operation, and later a pedal-operated auxiliary foot-firing mechanism was installed to fire the guns when the electric power was off. When the electricity was off the gun interrupters (magnetic limit switches) were inoperable.

The armor plate of the turret consisted of 1 1/2 inch laminated bullet proof glass to protect the gunner's face; 1/2 inch armor plate in front to protect his body; and 1/4 inch armor plate bolted to the floor to protect his feet.

Entering the Turret

The gunner normally rode in the fuselage during takeoffs and landings and only entered it during flight. The gunner was instructed to enter the turret following a specific routine. The red azimuth clutch handle on the bottom

**ERCO 250SH** ball turret mounted on the nose of a **Consolidated PB4Y-1**. (USN)

of the turret saddle on the azimuth gear box was engaged in the DOWN position. The red handle of the elevation clutch on the back of the saddle below the right hand corner of the entrance door was engaged. If the clutches were disengaged the gunner's weight could make the turret roll. Before entering the turret the main power switch, located in a junction box mounted on the left bulkhead in the bomber's nose almost directly under the turret, was turned ON. The gunner entered the turret through a small door on the back of the turret that took the contour of the spherical turret by turning the handle CLOCKWISE. The gunner looked inside to check the control panel located in the front center directly above the control handles to be sure all switches were OFF so that the turret would not move.

To enter the turret the gunner grasped the bar handle above the entrance door and swung both feet simultaneously into the turret, placing his feet on the foot armor plates below the front ammunition magazines. He slid forward across the seat so that his head cleared the top of the door opening to get his head inside the turret. He closed the door with a sharp pull on the bottom part and secured the door latch by pulling DOWN on the inner handle. He leaned back against the door to be sure that it was secure. The inside of the door was padded and served as the back of the gunner's seat when it was closed. The gunner's cushioned seat was adjustable both vertically and horizontally and had chest and seat belts attached. The seat had hinged arm rests that steadied the gunner's aim when he was tracking a target. He looked through the sight to determine if it was at the correct height to view through it. If it needed adjustment there was an adjustment lever between the gunner's legs that could raise or lower it. The gunner fastened his safety belt.

Operating the Turret

All the switches to power the turret were located on the control panel. The motor circuit breaker switch was turned ON and the power switch button was pushed IN and released, causing a red indicator to light. The pump motor was turned ON by using the bottom edges of the gunner's hands to press down the two safety switches. As soon as the pump was operating the gunner checked the hydraulic pressure gauge on the left side of the control panel for a pressure of 1,150 psi. When the motor was running the handles then automatically went into neutral, and for this reason it was best to press the safety switches DOWN before grasping the hand grips of the control handles, thus moving them into neutral without moving the turret. In any other position besides neutral with the safety switches CLOSED the motor would start moving the turret immediately and possibly violently. Depressing the safety switches also powered the ammunition booster motors so that they would operate when the guns were fired.

The first turrets were designed to carry three oxygen cylinders: one located at the entrance door and the other two on each side of the magazine. The 250SH-1 used a self-contained oxygen rebreathing unit that was contained inside the turret, making the three cylinders unnecessary. Later -2 and -3 models incorporated a wholly self-contained unit comprised of two oxygen cylinders and a regulator stored in a compartment located in the entrance door behind the gunner's back rest. The turret had heated flying suit and interphone connections and an extension light with its switch on the control panel mounted on the forward magazine.

To operate the turret the control handles were moved bicycle-style. From the horizontal position the ball turret and guns could be depressed a maximum 70° and elevated a maximum of 85°. This turret was capable of revolving 360° in azimuth, but in its installation in the PB4Y-1 and -2 Liberators its motion was restricted to 80° either side of the center line of the aircraft. If the electric drive motor failed the turret could be operated by using the emergency hand pump. The pump was worked with the right hand and holding the left hand grip of the control handles turned in the direction the turret was to move.

There were three pieces of armor protection: a 1/2 inch armor plate bolted in front of the gunner which was mounted to follow the guns so that the gunner's body was protected regardless of where the guns were pointed; a 1/4 inch armor plate bolted to the floor; and a pane of 1 1/2 inch laminated bullet-proof glass.

Guns and Accessories

The twin .50 caliber machine guns were fed from the inside of the aircraft; the right gun fed from the left and the left gun from the right. Each gun was bolted to a Bell Mount Adapter and adjusted by adjustment screws on both sides of the rear gun mount support.

The early gunsight was a Navy Mk9 reflector type which was mounted on a bracket located behind a laminated bullet-proof glass sheet. The brightness was adjusted to outside lighting conditions by using one hand to hold the control handles, keeping the safety switch depressed, and turning the sight rheostat with the other hand. The Mk 9 was succeeded by the Mk18.

The gun hand-charging levers were located at shoulder height on the outboard side of each gun in front of the gunner. By firmly grasping the charger handle of one gun with his palm up he pulled them sharply backward and then released them quickly and let it move forward on its own. He repeated this procedure for the other gun.

The triggers were located directly under the gunner's index fingers on the top of the control handles. Either trigger would fire both guns. Late model turrets had an auxiliary foot firing mechanism if the power to the guns failed. The unit was operated by releasing the red safety catch over the gunner's right foot and then depressing either red bar located above the gunner's feet.

Ammunition

The turret carried 1,200 rounds of belted, with each gun being fed by a 350 round side magazine located under the gun and a 300 round forward magazine located beside and under the ammunition feedway of the gun. The ammunition magazines usually were not filled to capacity. The cartridges were linked together to create a continuous belt holding 600 rounds within the two magazines for each gun. Each belt passed over a booster and traveled through a short metal chute that was enclosed by a transparent Plexiglas cover and into the gun. The guns were mounted to be fed from the inside, with the left hand gun fed from its right and the right hand gun from its left. The side magazines were loaded first and emptied last.

To load the magazines the armorer had to enter the turret and lift the emergency escape door on top of the turret to give some head room. The access doors were slid off all four magazines and the transparent ammunition track covers removed. Either side of the magazine was filled by passing the ammunition belt that was draped over the armorer's shoulder through the top of the magazine single link first with the projectiles pointing outboard. The belt was fed ("flaked") down until the magazine was full. The free end of the ammunition belt was passed down through the ammunition track on the rear side of the magazine and up around the rollers to the bottom of the corresponding front magazine. The corresponding front magazine was filled by passing the belt over the shoulder and down through the top of the magazine, single link first, projectiles pointing forward. The ends of the belts of the front and side magazines were spliced. The ammunition belt in the front magazine was flaked down into it. The end of the ammunition belt was run up over the booster sprockets and the gun cover was lifted and the double link of the belt was inserted into the gun. The magazine access covers and the ammunition track covers were replaced. This procedure was repeated on the other side.

The spent cartridge cases dropped out of the guns into a chamber located in the forward turret. The chamber was emptied by removing an access panel located on the outside front lower part of the turret. Empty links were ejected through a short metal chute into a zippered canvas bag below each gun.

Exiting the Turret

The gunner was to leave the turret before landing. He moved the guns to their stowed position (0° azimuth and 0° elevation) with the guns pointing straight forward. All switches were turned OFF and any auxiliary units in use during the mission were disconnected. The gunner reached around, opened the door, and eased himself out by grasping the bar handles installed above the entrance door.

There was an emergency exit which involved removing the plastic dome by releasing the latch mechanism in the upper structure of the turret. The gunner pulled the four red handles out and pushed the dome up and forward with both hands.

**ERCO Dorsal Ball Turret**

Another Navy project which interested the Materiel Division was the ERCO Engineering Research Corporation turret. In January 1941 Henry Berliner, an aircraft designer and President of the firm, convinced the Chief of the Materiel Division that ERCO would make an "excellent source" for turrets and arranged for a conference of ERCO engineers at Wright Field to discuss turret design. In October 1941 a Navy test of the ERCO dorsal ball turret revealed the usual defects of experimental turrets—jerky motion, uncomfortable hand grips, and poor accessibility—but it was withal a "very well designed, cleanly constructed, and efficient machine gun turret" with an extremely wide range of travel comparable to that of the Sperry ventral ball. The Navy ordered the ERCO turret in quantity and began a project to build a twin 20mm turret with a self-contained gasoline power drive and supercharged cabin for the PBB-1, but the Materiel Division was unable to use the ERCO design because it was too heavy and was powered with a Vickers drive unit, which was already in short supply.

**X220SH-1 (ERCO Model 6004)**

ERCO built only one X220SH-1 Model 6004 under Navy contract NX 4806 for the proposed Consolidated XPB3Y-1 four engine flying boat that was ordered in April 1942. The turret was 54 inches in diameter and weighed 767 pounds empty and 1,443 pounds with the gunner and 400 rounds of belted 20mm ammunition for its 20mm cannon. The turret's Sunstrand hydraulic drive proved to be unsatisfactory and would have necessitated a complete redesign of the turret, but the cancellation of the XPB3Y-1 in November precluded further work on the turret.

**X250CH (ERCO Model 6023)**

The X250CH was an experimental cylindrical-shaped dorsal turret design proposed in December 1942 that never progressed beyond the mock up stage. The twin .50 caliber machine guns were to be fed from an external magazine. The gunner's seat was designed to move downward during depression of the guns to improve target tracking.

**X450SH-1 (ERCO Model 6029)**

In September 1944 the Navy ordered one X450SH-1 to be developed as ERCO Model 6029. This turret was a derivative of ERCO's 250SH turret and was intended to be installed in the nose position of Navy patrol bombers to increase their strafing firepower. The turret's inboard .50 caliber machine guns were fed from their inboard side and their outboard .50s from the outboard side. The turret passed firing tests in July 1944 and was ready to be installed in PB4Y-1 and -2 bombers. However, at the time the Navy had decided that the .50s were inferior to the 20mm cannon that were gaining the Navy's favor and the 450SH-1 was never placed into production.

**X250SH-10 (ERCO Model 6080)**

In February 1945, the Navy let a contract to develop a spherical twin .50 caliber turret with the guns mounted one above the other for aerodynamics and sighted by Mk18 radar ranging gunsights. The turret was to be installed in a proposed Navy patrol bomber that was not developed beyond the drawing board stage.

**X220TH-1 (ERCO Model 6081)**

In June 1945 the Navy ordered two ERCO Model 6081 X220TH-1 experimental 20mm waist turrets that were to replace the PB4Y-2 .50 caliber side positions. This turret approximated the general characteristics of the 250TH-1 and -2 turrets. The war ended the development of the Navy bomber and the X220TH-1.

**Section 14: Grumman Ball Turret (150SE-1&2)**

The Grumman Ball Turret (150SE-1&2) was the turret used in the TBF; the Grumman 150SE-1 on the Avenger I and the 150SE-2 on the Avenger II. Its single .50 caliber gun defended beam, overhead, or tail cone attacks. The electrically-powered turret operated from the 24-28-volt DC electric from the aircraft's central electric system and moved the gunner with the

**Grumman Ball Turret 150SE** (USN)

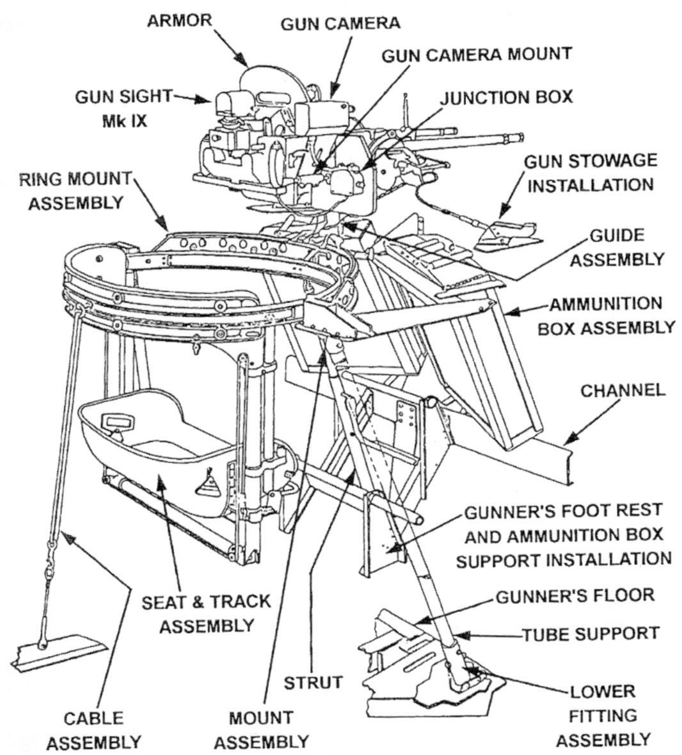


(USN)

gun and sights in elevation and azimuth in the direction he turned the control handle.

Entering the Turret

Before entering the turret the main battery switch on the pilot's control panel was to be turned ON. The emergency switch under the cover of the junction box attached to the left bulkhead in the bombardier's compartment was also to be ON. The 1/4 inch armor plate was a flap hinged to the front of the turret's seat and stowed in the UP position with a spring-loaded pin. This stowing pin was pulled out and the armor plate was swung down. The gunner faced forward to enter the bottom of the turret and then reached up and grasped the side armor plate with his left hand. As the gunner pulled himself up into the turret seat he twisted so that he faced aft. The sight or

The **Grumman Ball Turret 150** mounted in the **Grumman TBF Avenger**. (USN)

control handle was not to be used as a hand grip. He then placed his feet on the front armor plate above the flange. The armor plate flap was pulled up and locked in the up position with the stowing pin.

Once seated the gunner looked through the sight to determine if it was at the proper height. To adjust the sight height the gunner loosened the adjusting bolts that held the sight bracket and raised or lowered the sight and retightened the adjusting bolts. Next the gunner checked the elevation manual crank located next to his left knee to verify that it was disengaged and that the handle was stowed in its retaining clip. He then checked the azimuth clutch located outside the ball on the right side under the right trunnion at track level was in the UP position. Finally, he fastened and adjusted his seat belt.

Operating the Turret

The control box, in the stowed position, was located directly in front of the gunner and below the bullet-proof glass. The control box contained the pistol grip control handle and master switch. On the right side was the stowing lever, which was pushed down to place the control box in the operating position. The control panel, next to the gunner's left shoulder, contained the azimuth and elevation switches, which were flipped ON. The master switch on the control box was turned ON, which made the turret ready to operate. While operating the turret the gunner had to be aware to keep his feet up on the armor plate and his hands away from the moving parts.

The turret oxygen was supplied from the aircraft's main system and brought to the turret through a slip ring assembly at the bottom. A flexible hose connected the oxygen to the gunner's mask. The interphone jack box was located next to the gunner's right knee and contained the headphone and microphone jacks. There was no heated flying suit outlet in the turret, but the gunner's suit could be plugged into one in the pilot's compartment. A stationary trouble light with its switch located in the control panel was installed above the gun in a bracket that was attached to the inboard side of the Bell Adapter. The armor plate protection in this turret was a .5 inch thick plate in the front and sides; .25 inch under the seat; and 1.5 inch thick bullet-proof glass to protect the gunner's face.

Once the turret was turned ON, the gunner gripped the pistol control handle and simultaneously squeezed the safety switch in the handle to the turret. The gunner gripped the pistol grip control handle like a pistol to move the turret. To roll the turret up the pistol grip was pointed up, and to roll it down it was pointed down; likewise for right or left movement. The turret moved full circle, 360° in azimuth; in elevation the ball and gun were raised 85° above horizontal and depressed 30° below horizontal. The turret had two speeds, normal tracking and high-speed. The pistol control grip included a high-speed button used for increasing the speed of the turret for slewing from one extreme position to another. To put the high-speed control into operation the gunner pressed the button on the back top of the grip with his thumb. By releasing the control grip he automatically returned the gun to the trailing aft position and cut off the power to drive the motors.

A built-in combination elevation clutch and hand crank permitted manual operation of the turret if the power failed. An azimuth clutch was available for disengaging the azimuth drive so that the turret could be moved freely by hand. Both of the units, intended for maintenance use, were of no value in combat, but could be used to stow the turret and guns.

Gun and Accessories

The single .50 caliber with a left side feed was installed on a Bell Mount Adapter and had no provisions for harmonization. Two sights were provided for the 150SE: the Navy Mk 9 and the Mk 11 iron ring-and-bead post sight as a back up. The trigger switch for firing the guns was located under the gunner's index finger in the pistol grip control handle. The turret guns were charged manually by a charging handle located in front of the gunner's left knee. The charging handle was held in both hands, one above the other, and given a hard pull all the way down and then quickly released and left to slide forward by itself. A latch was provided to hold the bolt back in the gun, locking the gun charging handle in the rear position to aid in the removal of jams. The guns were charged in the air on the pilot's orders. An empty link and cartridge case container was located directly below the gun. The container filled with expended cartridges had to be emptied, as a filled container would jam the guns.

Ammunition

The Grumman turret was provided with one ammunition can holding 200 rounds that was located directly under the guns. To remove the ammunition can for loading another can the turret was placed into the stowed position and the can was released by pulling a small yellow knob mounted directly under the gunsight bracket. The yellow knob operated a wire release attached to the can. To prevent accidental release of the knob there was a cable lock attached to the bottom of the can. A new can was installed from the outside of the turret by holding the can with the right hand on its bottom and the left hand near the top so that the guide rails on the can engaged the guide track. The can was then pushed upward until it was approximately halfway in the stowed position where it would latch itself. Both hands placed at the bottom of the can were used to push it all the way in, where it would automatically lock itself in place. The cable lock was attached to the bottom.

To load the gun the cover on top of the gun and the feed chute cover on the left side were opened and the ammunition belt inside the can was pulled up through the feed chute. The first round was inserted through the mouth of the feed chute into the gun receiver. The extractor picked up and the charging handle was pulled back about .25 inch. The belt was pulled up until the first round was aligned against the cartridge stop. The extractor was dropped between the first and second round and the cover plate was "slammed" down into position. The final step was to "slam" the chute cover plate to the closed position.

Getting Out

When the gunner removed his hand from the pistol control handle the turret returned to the stowing position, 0° elevation and 180° azimuth (the gun pointing straight aft). The latch on the right hand side of the control box was pushed down and the control box elevated to its stowing position, allowing the latch to reengage and securing the box in place. So as not to damage the internal mechanism of the box when the gunner stowed the control box he was to lift it by the box itself and not by its pistol grip control. All switches were turned off and all auxiliary units used during the flight were to be disconnected. After unfastening his seat belt the gunner then reached down and pulled out the stowing pin holding up the armor plate flap under him and pushed the flap down. He was then ready to climb out of the turret facing aft, feet first, using the side armor plate as a hand grip. Once outside the turret the armor plate flap was pushed up and locked in place with its stowing pin.

There was an emergency exit on the right hand side of the turret Plexiglas enclosure. A handle in the center of the hatch was grasped and turned up, and the escape hatch then had to be pushed out to fall away, leaving a large exit hole

**Section 15: The ANB (Army-Navy-British) Turret**

In November 1940 British engineers C. B. Lowe of Nash-Thompson, Ltd., and a Mr. Hughes of Boulton-Paul visited Wright Field and brought three Frazer-Nash and two Boulton-Paul turrets with them for demonstration and consideration for licensing. The Chief of the Materiel Division directed Wright Field to prepare plans for producing either the Boulton-Paul or the Frazer-Nash turrets in the U.S., and after "tests and inspections....a selection of the better of the two could be made and the production plan put into effect."

After the December tests the Materiel Division Board reported: "In general, British policy favored locally controlled turrets. Remote sighting is not considered feasible by the British for the reason that serious deflection problems are bound to result." The report thus limited choices to local turrets, and the Board chose the Frazer-Nash turret with control handles and a modified "handle bar" assembly, which were superior to the Boulton-Paul stick control.

Any action on the choice of the Frazer-Nash turret stalled, as the Materiel Division had already let a number of turret contracts which were heading toward production. Thus, the manufacture of British turrets in the United States could not start for 18 months, by which time domestic production would be well underway. The Materiel Division believed that British turrets could be manufactured in the U.S. if their production did not interfere with domestic production. This objective could be achieved if the manufacture of the British turrets were contracted to companies not already building turrets. An important argument against British turrets, raised by the Production Engineering Section of the Materiel Division, was that they were equipped with .30 caliber guns, while domestic turrets utilized .50 caliber guns. The Section's report stated that this was "sufficient to discourage any further consideration of the use of British turrets, for the loss of time involved in changing over design and accessories from a .30 to .50 caliber turret would nullify the time saved by using a ready-built design." Despite these objections, the proposal to build British turrets in the U.S. continued. Not only was there pressing need for turrets in the United Kingdom, but interested U.S. manufacturers, such as General Motors and Packard, lobbied for their manufacture after it became apparent that turret manufacture had become a major industry. The Chief of the Materiel Division directed Wright Field to delay the release of British turret designs until a production policy was formulated. Assigned to the task was the National Defense Advisory Commission (NDAC), which had previously set guidelines for the licensing for the American manufacture of the British Rolls-Royce engine.

The problem of coordinating both the quantity requirements and the design standards of the Army, Navy, and British air arms was a key problem that was submitted to the Joint Aircraft Committee (JAC), where it was to be overseen by a Subcommittee on Standardization of Aircraft Turrets. Although the JAC had discussed hypothetical turret standardization as early as August 1940, its Subcommittee on Turrets did not meet until January 1941. During this meeting and later meetings in February the Subcommittee decided that a combination of the best features of Boulton-Paul and Frazer-Nash turrets could be combined to design a twin .50 turret acceptable to the Army, the Navy, and the British. The proposed turret, called the ANB (**A**rmy, **N**avy, **B**ritish), could not be installed on aircraft already under contract, "but could stand as an objective in anticipated aircraft design." The JAC Subcommittee on Standardization, wishing to speed up standardization, directed the Army, Navy, and British "to submit a statement of estimated ANB turret requirements in order to arrive at a cumulative production figure," which would then be submitted to the NDAC to set up production facilities. The JAC plan asked for preliminary turret drawings from the British turret companies by May 1941 and final drawings to be in the U.S. by August 1941. The JAC plan initially recommended the manufacture of 500 dorsal and 500 tail turrets of ANB design and directed the Office of Production Management (OPM), the successor to NDAC, to review U.S. industrial facilities in order to select a manufacturer that would have sufficient production capacity.

Specifications for the proposed ANB turret were prepared, specifying twin .50s with a minimum of 600 rounds of ammunition for each gun, the Frazer-Nash hand controls, an elevation arc from plus 85° to minus 30°, and with 30° per second and 50° per second maximum elevation and azimuth speeds from a minimum of 1/2° per second, both laying and training. These specifications integrated all the best qualities of both British and American turrets, including armor plate, adequate harmonization facilities, ammunition boosters capable of sustaining three Gs, automatic gun chargers, emergency manual operation facilities, and many other important features already appearing in other turrets. As the ANB project gained impetus, the earlier plan to manufacture unmodified British turrets in the U.S. was abandoned, as in March 1941 the Chief of the Materiel Division terminated the current British turret production program.

The OPM search for new turret manufacturers found two candidates: the Emerson Electric Manufacturing Company that specialized in small motors, and the Knapp Monarch Company that specialized in electrical appliances. Both St. Louis companies were well-established, well-organized, and capable. Neither firm had had much experience in the precision work required in turret manufacture. Emerson had a sufficient but older assortment of machine tools which would require little revision for turret production, while Knapp had a number of new machine tools that were not particularly compatible to turret tooling. Both manufacturers had large floor space, but while they lacked adequate engineering staffs, they had a sufficient number of millwrights and toolmakers able to assume this new project.

The OPM selected Emerson, since it did not have many defense contracts and had obtained an interest in the turret field by acquiring manufacturing rights which became available when the Tucker turret project failed (see the next section: Tucker Electric Turret). Emerson was founded in 1890 in St. Louis, Missouri, by Scotland-born brothers Charles and Alexander Meston, who patented a reliable electric motor. They persuaded John Wesley Emerson, a former Union army officer, judge, and lawyer, to be their principal investor. The company, known as Emerson Electric Manufacturing Co., investigated the then untested technology of electricity for a variety of residential and commercial uses. In 1892 Emerson sold the first electric fans in America, a product for which the company soon became well known. As the company grew, it expanded its product line by attaching electric motors to new products such as sewing machines, kitchen appliances, and power tools. By the mid-1930s the Depression had put the company in financial trouble. During the Depression, Yale-educated W. Stuart Symington had gained a reputation for his ability to save financially ailing companies from bankruptcy. After becoming President of Emerson in 1938 Symington turned the electric motor manufacturer around. In early1941 he authorized a new modern plant in St. Louis that was designed to manufacture bomber turrets, of which he knew nothing.

The OPM's decision to select Emerson to manufacture the ANB turret was made without the Materiel Division's sanction, as the Division had shown little confidence in Emerson's engineering and manufacturing capabilities. Adhering to the JAC plan, the OPM began negotiations with Emerson regarding facilities, contracts, etc., while the Materiel Division prepared to send a liaison officer to England with a representative to obtain detailed manufacturing drawings of British turrets. At the end of April 1941 Col. Grandison Gardner confided the following on Emerson's ANB contract to Maj. Frank Wolfe: "I don't know whether they'll ever get them done or not, but don't much care." Plans had been made to increase American aircraft production to 1,500 planes per month by June 1943, and it was important for the AAC to anticipate increased turret production, which was expected to be fulfilled by Sperry and Bendix rather than by a new, untried manufacturer.

Soon after the OPM chose Emerson the company sent its President Stuart Symington to England, where he was asked by the Ministry of Aircraft Production to manufacture both the Boulton-Paul and the Frazer-Nash turrets under license in his St. Louis plant. Symington informed the British that this manufacturing plan to produce two turrets countered the JAC standardization program; and also, by producing two completely different British turrets was an "extravagant waste of tooling." To settle this impasse it was decided that a selection would be made between these two major British manufacturers by Wing Commander Spreckley, the turret project officer who had previously toured U.S. turret facilities. Spreckley and Symington visited the manufacturing facilities of both companies to make a firsthand informed selection decision. Symington was impressed with the Frazer-Nash plants he described as "jewels of efficiency," but W/C Spreckley selected the Boulton-Paul for use in the ANB project.

The Boulton-Paul turret design that was finally selected had evolved over eight years under J.D. North, who held a number of basic patents in the field. As discussed earlier in Chapter 1/Section 2, the origins of this British turret design were French. The Boulton-Paul turret was not actually manufactured in the Boulton-Paul aircraft plant where J. D. North refined the turret design and prepared the production drawings, but at the Lucas Company, an emergency turret facility in Wales with a capacity of approximately 400 turrets a month.

The Boulton-Paul turret was ideal not only because it was less complex than the Frazer-Nash turret, but also because its manufacturing process could be more easily adapted to American industrial techniques and standards. The Boulton-Paul drawings were also much more detailed than the Frazer-Nash drawings, but this caused them to be very time consuming to copy to U.S. industrial standards, and two Emerson draftsmen had to accompany Symington to England. The delay in first selecting Emerson and then the delay in transferring the drawings for production caused the Chief of the Materiel Division to write on 8 May 1941: "It is my opinion that if we cannot come to an agreement at once, we should forget the whole proposition and manufacture Sperry turrets." But the project had progressed too far to cancel. The Materiel Division accepted the Boulton-Paul decision as final in late May 1941 and, upon Symington's return from England in June, the first steps in ANB turret production were started when the Chief of the Materiel Division authorized Wright Field to investigate the various types of Air Corps bombers that could utilize the ANB standard turret. The Materiel Division never really liked the ANB turret, as they not only thought it was a compromise, but reported it "as unsuitable for many types of aircraft because of space and weight limitations and aircraft design characteristics." Because of these delays and problems the ANB came into production in late 1941, at a time when the domestic turrets already under contract were ready for installation. However, the Division agreed that if the ANB turrets proved superior to domestic turrets they could be exchanged later when production increased.

The Materiel Division proposed an agenda for the OPM for allocating 6,500 ANB turrets that included turrets for 700 Lend-Lease Liberators, for 500 Lend-Lease Vega Venturas, for more than 450 for Lend-Lease Lockheed Hudsons, and for 500 Lend-Lease Martin Marauders, in addition to an unallocated 2,500 for the U.S. Navy. The 6,500 figure was largely a speculative one, but was a starting point upon which to plan ANB contracts. The Materiel Division planned to issue a letter of intent to Emerson for only 1,000 turrets in order to help the company get started on its projected June 1943 production rate of 1,000 per month. The Division was very willing to have OPM assist Emerson with priorities; for even if the major portion of ANB turrets produced were allocated for British and Navy use, the Emerson factory had a potential turret capacity "which could not be ignored."

Even before a decision had been reached on the armament of the B-24, for which the ANB turret had been seriously considered, the Materiel Division decided, at least tentatively, to "wash out" the ANB program after the first limited production order had been completed. Lt.Col. Grandison Gardner suggested that Emerson become a subcontractor for Sperry or Consolidated. Bendix turret deliveries had been so inadequate up to July 1941 that Gardner wanted to transfer some of the Bendix contract to Emerson.

The Chief of the Armament Laboratory also suggested that "it would be wiser to pile the bulk of the subcontract work into Symington's lap and build up one facility rather than three or four."

Supported by the OPM, the Defense Plant Corporation (DPC) signed a plant expansion contract with Emerson on 15 July 1941. However, construction had been in progress on the new Emerson St. Louis turret plant as early as June, and by the middle of July at least 70% of the necessary machine tools, mostly purchased secondhand to facilitate earlier delivery, were installed in temporary quarters. The original DPC lease provided for 704,000 square feet of plant space equipped to produce 1,000 turrets a month, with the whole expansion to be financed by DPC at approximately $10,500,000. By June 1943 the venture was almost complete, with 817,300 square feet of floor space costing the DPC $14,870,794. The original Emerson schedule was for 1,000 turrets of a single design, with all major assemblies subcontracted to one or more outside manufacturers. By March 1942 Emerson was producing 2,000 turrets monthly, representing seven different designs. The original plan for an office staff of 300 employees and 2,200 factory employees had increased by March 1942 to nearly 2,000 and 5,500 employees, respectively.

By the end of July 1941 the construction of the new factory was proceeding on schedule, but ANB turret production at Emerson had encountered some preproduction problems. Only 554 of the estimated 750 drawings considered necessary to produce the ANB turret had arrived from England. Symington placed the blame for the drawing delays on the continual minor changes made by the British on their drawings that were needed to include new developments that arose in air combat. Emerson also had production difficulties with the magnesium castings necessary for the ANB, as American magnesium casting procedures were much inferior to those in England. To remedy the problem Emerson wanted to bring over experienced British foundry men as well as some specialized machinery, even though one of the original reasons Boulton-Paul had been chosen over Frazer-Nash was that the latter required more special purpose machinery. As late as September 1943 the War Production Board (WPB, successor to OPM) was still negotiating with Emerson regarding an extension on the Emerson plant to include a magnesium foundry. By the middle of August 1941 other problems with the ANB materialized. Emerson contacted 16 roller bearing manufacturers as bearing subcontractors but none was interested. Also, to date Emerson had done nothing to solve the difficult problem of fabricating a transparent turret canopy with adequate optical properties.

To add to Emerson's problems three groups (the Experimental Engineering Section at Wright Field, the Technical Subcommittee of the Joint Aircraft Committee, and the British Air Commission) were all submitting instructions involving modifications on the ANB turret. Accidentally enclosed with a set of Boulton-Paul drawings sent to Emerson was a letter from a Boulton-Paul draftsman to the Ministry of Aircraft Production (MAP). This letter advised the MAP to delay production at Emerson because a number of components in the Boulton-Paul drawings sent to the company had been shown to be unsatisfactory in combat. Emerson had already engaged subcontractors to begin work on these unsatisfactory components and there was a heated exchange between Emerson and the British Air Commission.

In July 1941 the Chief of the Navy's Bureau of Ordnance informed Gen. Arnold that the Navy requirement for ANB turrets would not be 2,500 but only 759 units to be installed on the Martin PBM-4 twin-engine patrol aircraft with upgraded engines, with deliveries for 180 not to begin until April 1943. To make matters worse for Emerson, the British and the AAF soon lost interest in the troubled and delayed ANB turret and from an initial plan scheduling over 6,500 turrets for all services, the total requirement had dropped to 759 for the Navy alone. The PBM-4 project was cancelled, and Emerson hastily began to look for new production contracts to exploit the enormous potential capacity of its new and now unused plant. By September 1941 Emerson needed contracts to keep the company viable and urged the OPM to direct contracts for Ordnance tank turret manufacture to their new factory. Even though the ANB turrets were never produced they did play an important part in American turret development and manufacture, as they helped Emerson become a major player in the field.

**Section 16: Clam Shell Tail Turrets**

**B-23**

The chief military development of the B-23 lay in its glazed tail gunner's position, which was the first installed on an operational American bomber. The B-17 was not equipped with its tail twin .50s until the E model in September 1941, and the Douglas XB-19 ordered in 1937 was designed with a tail turret, but this aircraft did not fly until mid-1941. The position contained a single .50 caliber M-2 machine gun with 99 rounds in three 33 round boxes. The glazed portion of the tail cone opened into two clamshell-like halves to permit machine gun movement. The left hand side window had a release mechanism and could be used as an emergency exit by the tail gunner. A fixed telescopic sight was mounted about 13 inches above the gun and incorporated a movable reticle coordinated with the gun by cables, pulleys, and gears. The sight had a wide angle field of view, and the crosshair that appeared in the field of view automatically moved with the gun so as to show at all times at what field the gun was aimed. The long bar of the crosshair pattern indicated a short range (200 yards) and the short bar corresponded to the trajectory drop at 600 yards. The width of the bars corresponded to the appearance of 37 feet of span at those distances. The

B-23 clam shell tail turret in the closed position. (USAAF)

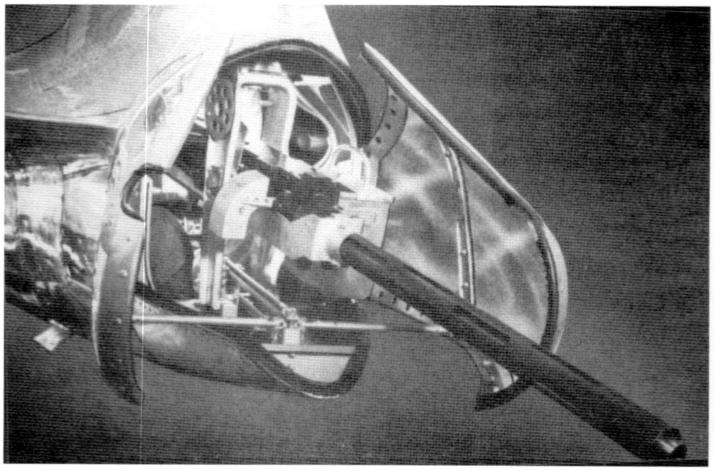

B-23 clam shell tail turret in the open position. (USAAF)

The first B-25 tail gun position was a clam shell type. (USAAF)

**Type M-7 Bell Adapter for the B-25** (USAAF)

objective lens of the sight was protected by a glass cover and shutter. This defensive position was primitive, as the gunner laid in a prone position with his feet forward, and before he could manually traverse the gun he had to open the transparent framework doors that enclosed the gun, which pointed directly to the rear during normal flight. The gun had a relatively narrow cone of fire at 40°, but for a fast bomber it did not have to be very wide as, except for diving attacks, contemporary fighter attacks were from dead astern, where the field of fire did not have to be very wide. Also, this tail gun was the first .50 caliber machine gun used defensively on an American bomber, and at the time the B-23's .50 caliber gun far out-ranged the smaller bore, albeit more numerous guns of would-be foreign enemies. Type H-2 gun cameras were used with this machine gun.

**B-25**

The original B-25 cone-shaped tail turret mounted a flexible .50 caliber machine gun which opened through clam shell Plexiglas doors that were similar to those pioneered on the Douglas B-23 Dragon. This gun was the only .50 caliber among five other .30 caliber (nose, dorsal, ventral, and two in the waist) mounted in the Mitchell. The gunner sat on a metal chair mounted close to the floor with the gun between his bent legs while he looked through a sighting system. There was an entrance/emergency hatch located above his head.

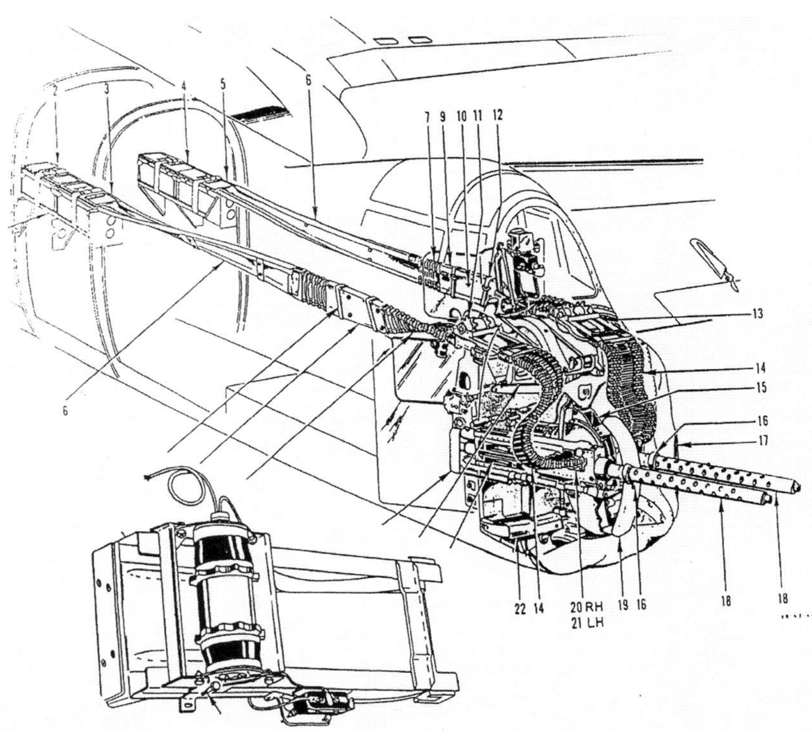

**Bell Gun Mount Assembly (Bell Adapter)** (USAAF)

**Type M-6A Bell Adapter for the B-26** (USAAF)

**Section 17: Bell Gun Mount Assembly (Bell Adapter)**

Bell Gun Mount Assembly (Type M-7 Adapter)

General Description

The Bell Adapter's technical designation was the Bell Gun Mount Assembly, and it was a power-driven flexible gun mount developed to increase the firepower of the tail gun position in the B-25 and B-26. There were two models, the Type M-7 for the B-25 and the Type M-6A for the B-26. The only difference between the two was in the mounting bracket. The Bell Adapter was equipped with a twin gun adapter that mounted two .50 caliber Type M-2 machine guns, a Type N-8 or N-6A gunsight, feed chutes equipped with booster motors, an adjustable seat, and a large armor plate mounted between the adapter and the gunner. Each gun was held in its cradle by a rear trunnion latch lock and a front trunnion bolt that had a spring-loaded plunger that locked in place. The guns were mounted so that they were always held level and parallel to each other.

Power

The Bell Adapter was powered in elevation and azimuth by pressure in a closed hydraulic system developed by a constant-speed electric motor. The electric pump maintained working pressure within the system, and two variable stroke piston-type pumps controlled the velocity, one for movement of the guns in elevation and the other for movement in azimuth. Two interconnected handles operated hydraulic pumps to move the guns. Moving the handles about the horizontal axis rotated the guns in azimuth in the same direction the handles were moved, while rotating them fore or aft raised or lowered the guns. The gun mount moved in azimuth 45° to either side of the aircraft centerline halfway back to left or right. On elevation the guns could be raised and lowered 45° below and above horizontal, halfway up or halfway down.

Gunsights

Early Bell tail gun units relied on an N-8 or N-6A optical gunsight fitted in a long sight control bracket held in place by four mounting bolts and located directly above the control handles. The sight was connected to the gun mount by bellcranks and connector links, and moved up and down or sideways in synchronization with the guns. Later variants were equipped with the revolutionary K-10 computing sight, which could be preset with indicated airspeed and altitude information from which it could automatically compute "the necessary vertical and lateral deflection angles of the guns for accurate fire." A ring and bead sight was fitted for emergency use.

Loading the Tail Guns

During loading the two 200 round boxes for each gun, the single loop ends of the belts were loaded into the boxes first with the cartridges pointing outboard. The feed chute assembly was loaded with approximately 300 rounds for each gun by passing the double loop ends aft through chutes and booster motors to the guns. The loaded ammunition boxes were installed on the shelves ready for loading into the guns.

The ammo belts were drawn up from their boxes through long flexible ammunition chutes leading to the guns. The chutes had booster motors in them to aid in moving the ammunition, and the belts were fed over the booster motor sprocket wheels in the chutes. The loader was to be sure that the rounds fit evenly in the sprockets. The belt was then pulled from the ends of the chutes and fed up to the guns. The guns were mounted in the Bell Adapter to feed from the outside (e.g. the left gun fed from the left and the right from the right). The first rounds were to be pressed into the gun's feedways.

50. Caliber Booster Feed

A .50 caliber booster feed assisted in pulling the belted ammunition to the two machine guns in the rear gunner's turret. The system consisted of two ammunition boost motors, two boost cutout relays, two microswitches, and a main power circuit breaker switch. The ammunition boost direct current motors drove a sprocket that engaged with the ammunition belt. The driving action resulted from a meshing of the sprocket teeth and the individual rounds of the ammunition belt.

Charging the Tail Guns

To charge the guns they were lowered approximately 10° and the main power switch was always turned OFF. To gain access to the charging handles on the guns the sliding armor plate panel at each side of the control handles had to be swung down, and each gun was charged by pulling back and releasing its standard charging handle. There were no other switches, fuses, or reset buttons on the Bell Adapter.

Combat Operation of the Bell Adapter

The gunner sat on a low cushioned stool-type seat supported on a floor-mounted pedestal located behind the armor plate. The gunner was instructed to never stay on the seat during takeoffs or landings, during quick changes in speed, and at "times that make the tail an extremely dangerous place to be." The controls were like those of any "ordinary" turret, with the adapter's hydraulic power system allowing the gunner to "easily and firmly" swing the guns and sight. The control housing, handles, and hydraulic pump and motor unit were located on the armor plate in front of him. The guns were supplied with heaters which were switched ON.

The following equipment located on the frame on the right rear wall was turned ON: the main power switch, right and left booster motor switches, and the gun heater switch. The gunsight rheostat, located on the frame to the gunner's left, was turned ON and adjusted to meet lighting conditions, and the lamp switch located on the gunsight housing was activated. If the gunsight lamp did not come on the gunsight lamp circuit breaker button located at the main power switch was to be pressed. The two spindle-like knobs of the azimuth and elevation bypass valves (mounted against the armor plate panel to the right and left of the main control panel) were turned clockwise to CLOSE them. The last step was to grasp the two control handles so that the bottom edges of the gunner's hands depressed the two safety switches. As long as the switches were held down the adapter moved.

The movement of the guns was controlled by the movement of the two interconnected control handles on the control tower, much the same as a bicycle was steered (e.g. right to go right and left to go left). Each pair of switches was in parallel; therefore, the turret could be controlled with either the right or left hand. Both control handles had triggers under the index finger, and either one could be used to fire the guns. On top of the handles near both thumbs were two push-to-talk buttons, and either of which, when pressed, closed the interphone circuit when speaking.

The angle of fire of the tail turret guns was approximately 140° either side of the centerline. The direction of gun movement in elevation and azimuth was relative to the direction of movement of the control handles about their vertical axis and horizontal axis. The speed of gun movement was proportional to the degree of movement of the handles from the neutral positions. The maximum movement in elevation was 40° up and 35° down from horizontal. Maximum movement in azimuth was 38° to each side of the center line of the aircraft. The guns were brought to a stop by returning the control handles to the neutral position. The safety switches grip in the control handles were depressed and the guns trained by centering the reticle image dot on the target.

The gunner was to leave the tail position promptly when the pilot announced a landing. He was to place the guns in the stowing position, which was 180° in azimuth and 0° in elevation with the guns pointing straight aft. He then was to turn all switches OFF and clear the guns by opening the gun covers and hand charging them twice.

Once on the ground the gunner was to remove all ammunition from the gun's feedways, chutes, and ammo containers. He was then to field strip the guns and clean the gun casing groups and check their condition.

Tail Gun Manual (Emergency) Operation

If the hydraulic system of the turret failed, the guns could be operated manually by opening the elevation and azimuth bypass valves located at the left and right sides of the control tower beneath the control handles. To gain access to the manual grips on the gun back plates the armor plate panels were swung open. The guns were moved manually by these grips and the guns fired by pressing the trigger switches on the grips or, if the electrical circuit was malfunctioning, the mechanical triggers on the adapter could be operated. If the electrical circuit failed it was necessary to break the ammunition belts approximately every 75th round, since the booster feed motors would be inoperative. The B-26 had no manual emergency system.

**Section 18: B-17: Original and Cheyenne Tail Turret**

Original

After the outbreak of the war in Europe Boeing engineers met on 21 May 1940 with the Air Materiel Command at Wright Field to discuss improving the armament of the B-17D. Among the armament upgrades in the B-17E was the installation of a tail turret. The resulting tail gunner's compartment was a separately manufactured unit with built-in ammunition boxes. It was attached to the rear fuselage aft of the horizontal stabilizer and under the

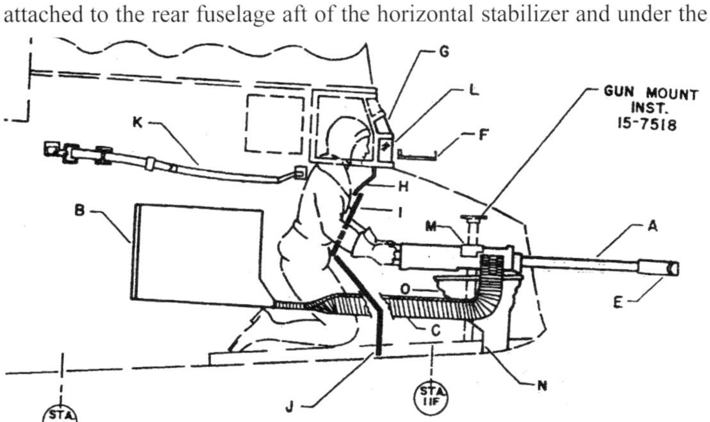


**B-17 Original Turret** (USAAF)

The original Flying Fortress tail turret was installed on the B-17E and F models until the middle of the G model run. (USAAF)

rear two-thirds of a new 43 foot vertical stabilizer. Once in the turret the gunner took an uncomfortable kneeling position with the gun handles at approximately his hip level. The gunner's face was protected by a plate of thick bullet-proof glass while his neck, chest and stomach, and hips and thighs were behind three pieces of armor plate. The twin .50s were mounted on the floor and protruded into the elongated area at the level of the gunner's knees in front of him. The gun barrels protruded through a vertically cutoff rear portion of the tail that was covered by a drafty canvas boot that gave the guns a limited range of movement, especially vertically. The guns were supplied by a 65 inch ammunition feed from an ammunition box located to the rear and side of the gunner. The guns were fired manually, and were sighted by a ring-and-bead sight mounted outside the windscreen and connected by wires to the guns. The shells were ejected to the outside through a chute under each gun. The guns were warmed by breech heaters.

Cheyenne

The B-17G model tail gun retained the original tail gun installation until the middle of the G production series, when the Cheyenne tail turret was incorporated in June 1944 in the B-17G-80-BO,-45-DL, -35VE, and subsequent batches. The tail gun unit was called the "pumpkin" because of its rounded frontal shape, but was called more popularly "Cheyenne" after the United Airlines B-17 modification center at Cheyenne, Wyoming, that had installed the unit. It was retrofitted to many earlier B-17s at field modification centers in England in kit form and then was incorporated into the production line. This unit was similar to the tail unit mounted in the last YB-40, but it was larger and more comfortable, and had a greatly increased azimuth and elevation range and gunner field of vision.

The gunner sat on a bicycle type seat behind twin hand-held .50s using the N-8 gunsight that replaced the previous ring and bead sight. The guns were moved closer to him, causing the B-17G with this installation to be five inches shorter than earlier versions. The Cheyenne mounting was distinguished by a semi-circular metal cover cut by vertical slots through which the gun barrels protruded. The power-boosted guns were mounted on a Bell adapter and were fed by 500 rounds of ammunition contained in wooden boxes at the gunner's sides next to the seat. Spent shells fell into canvas ejection chutes and were ejected through slots to the outside. The front windscreen was a large curved, green-tinted bullet-proof window with a U-shaped perforated defroster pipe located under the periphery of the glass. On either side of the gunner there was a large window at his shoulder and another smaller window behind that. The unit had tubing on the right side for oxygen and the left side for heated air for cabin warming.

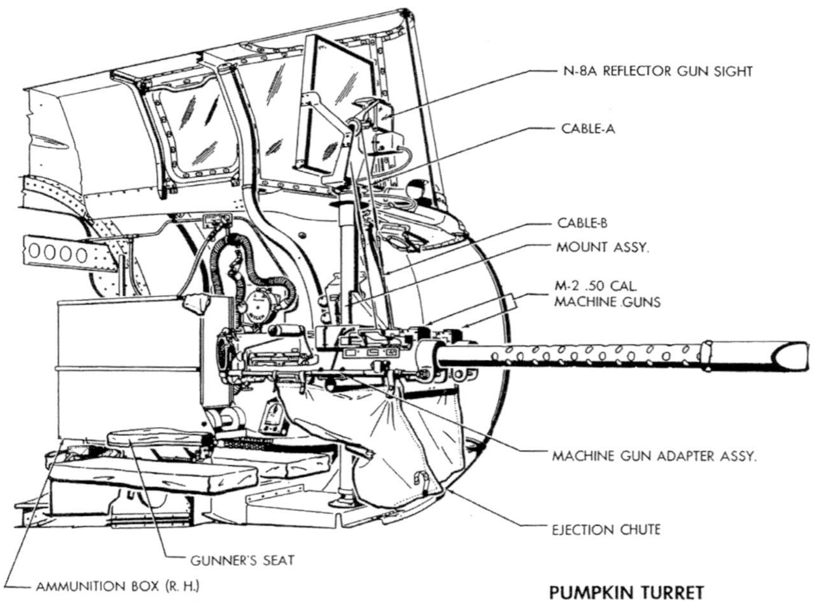


PUMPKIN TURRET

**Cheyenne "Pumpkin" Turret** (USAAF)

**Section 19: B-29 Tail Turret**

The B-29 tail turret was equipped with two .50 caliber machine guns and a 20mm cannon; it was the only manned gun station. Early B-29s had a tail turret mounting dual .50 caliber machine guns supplied with 1,000 rounds per gun and a 20mm cannon with 110 to 125 rpg. The .50 caliber ammunition was carried in a pair of large boxes located forward of the horizontal stabilizer and tracks carried the ammunition aft to the tail gunner. The cannon could be fired separately of or along with the machine guns. However, the cannon had a different trajectory than the machine guns and only fired 7 to 11 rounds per minute, and concurrent firing of the three guns was not effective, as the computer only calculated for the .50 caliber machine guns. It was recommended that the 20mm be fired only when the attacker was at close range (not more than 600 yards) when the bullet drop of the machine guns and cannon were similar. Also, the 20mm cannon had feed mechanism problems. The cannon was later deleted in some models. The tail turret and guns were equipped with cut off switches and mechanical stops that limited its vertical and horizontal movement to 30° in all directions.

(Author/Pima)

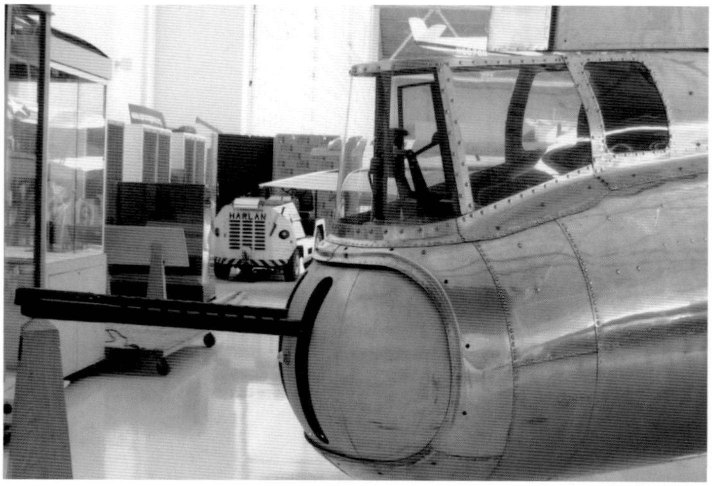

(Author/CAF)

The **N-8 gunsight** and perforated tubing for heated air for cabin warming. (USAAF)

## Section 20: Experimental Turrets

### Curtiss Turret

In January 1935 Wright Field was notified by the Curtiss Aeroplane and Motor Company that the Navy was conferring with the company for a manually operated gun turret. In order to prevent unnecessary duplication of effort the Chief of the Engineering Section contacted the Navy but received no response. A year later Curtiss submitted preliminary drawings for a $4,255 non-retractable turret which enclosed a .30 caliber machine gun on a 40 inch diameter ring mount that was capable of 90° to -30° elevation movement and 360° azimuth rotation via a hand-crank system, making rotation possible in airspeeds as high as 200 mph. Wright Field Engineers calculated that the Curtiss turret mounted on a B-18 would reduce the Bolo's speed by 18% from a top speed of 220 mph to 186 mph, and that the placement of the turret would decrease the aircraft's range by 18%, and by 2% in service ceiling. They concluded that turret installations must be retractable to reduce drag as much as possible. By October 1936 Curtiss had developed a new and improved turret for the Materiel Division for $5,847.75. Due to lengthy negotiations concerning unrestricted patent and design rights it was not until May 1937 that the turret was delivered to Wright Field. Because of the Armament Laboratory's chronic lack of test aircraft (a B-18 in this case) the Curtiss turret was not tested, and was finally superseded by better designs.

### Vultee Powered Flexible Gun Mount

In May 1939, Vultee Aircraft Inc. offered an electrically powered flexible gun mount to the Materiel Division for examination. Preliminary evaluation of the mount encouraged the Division's Technical Executive to direct the Armament Branch to investigate the Vultee project "very carefully with a view toward possible application on several types of planes if it proved feasible." The Chief of the Experimental Engineering Section determined that the Vultee mount "had merit," but then added, despite the trend toward power mounts, that "There are, however, serious objections in that power operation (in that mount) is required." Vultee sold an experimental model to the Division for $22,139.22, including a 12% profit. The Vultee mount was not a turret mount, but "an assisted motion flexible mount," which the Armament Laboratory rejected for a number of reasons after testing via a memo of 6 September 1939: "Its dispersion pattern was twice the normal size for comparable mounts, its power consumption without wind load was exceptionally high, and its spade-grip, electric-button drive control provided directional rotation but no speed control." The Armament Laboratory concluded "that a modification was neither practical nor justified as to expense because of the mount's inherent fallacy in fundamental design."

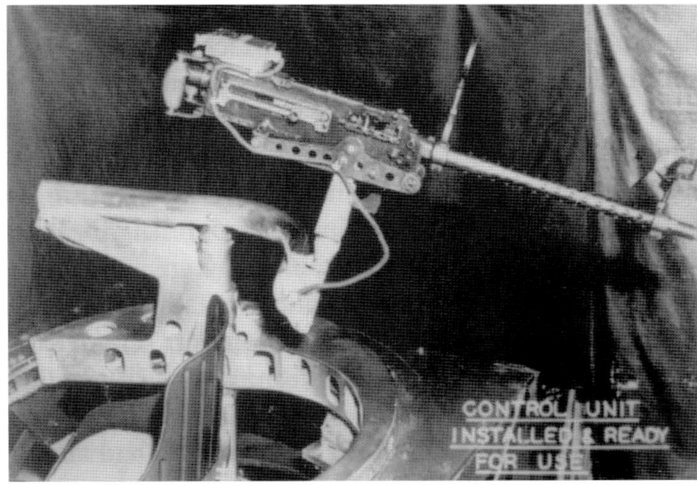


**Vultee Powered Flexible Gun Mount** (USAAF)

### Tucker Electric Turrets

In July 1939 Preston Tucker, founder of the Tucker Manufacturing Company of Ypsilanti, MI, introduced his electrically controlled gun turret which carried a 37mm cannon that was to be mounted on an armored car. The Tucker turret was slow moving, but Wright Field engineers felt that it could possibly be converted for aircraft use due to its commutator, which did not arc under rapid reversals that would be common in target tracking in air combat. The Tucker drive motor used glass impregnated coils that resisted burn-out. The drive displayed no tendency to hunt and produced an adequately high torque at low speeds, but the low or minimal tracking speeds were unsatisfactory.

In September 1939, during a meeting at Wright Field, Tucker proposed to build an experimental model of an electric power drive for use with the existing B-18 manual turret for $10,000. This twin .30 caliber gun turret was to move at 45° per second azimuth speed with a 12-volt DC drive motor. The turret was to be equipped with a fire cut-out or interrupter, electric or dynamic brakes to prevent structural interference with the gun muzzles, and provision for emergency manual operation. Tucker suffered a three month delay in beginning work when the AAC was unable to supply a B-18 for testing and the Armament Laboratory was unable to provide machine gun solenoids to fire the guns. In December 1940 the Materiel Division concluded that the Tucker turret was "not representative of the assemblies contemplated for possible future procurement." Nonetheless, from inception the Tucker project seemed to have no chance of success, as it involved designing a turret for the B-18, which was considered obsolete.

The Armament Branch also considered Tucker as a possible source for turrets to arm the first 100 B-17s to be equipped only with hand-held machine guns. Tucker prepared to build a model turret improving on the original experimental installation sent to the Materiel Division. The modified turret carried twin .50s in place of the .30s of the original version and added a hydraulic power drive to secure smooth, low-speed tracking characteristics. The Armament Laboratory prepared an Authority for Purchase for a laboratory test model of the revised turret, but further study found the design to be faulty and no contract was signed.

Although some of Tucker's inability to develop a satisfactory turret was due to AAC supply problems, a company of Tucker's relatively small size required a government financed experimental contract. Tucker did not have the financial resources to absorb the unproductive immediate costs of the research and development phase to carry its turret successfully into production.

### Ford Turret

The turret of the Ford Instrument Company of Long Island City, NY, was different from the Ford Motor Company turret that was subcontracted to the Motor Products Co. In July 1941 the Chief of the Armament Branch learned of a "novel and very promising turret incorporating a gyroscopic control and sight stabilizing element" that was being installed in a Martin PBM Mariner seaplane at Norfolk by the Navy's Bureau of Ordnance.

The Ford Instrument all-electric, gyro-stabilized turret mounted a single .50 caliber gun that was capable of azimuth speeds of up to 90° per second. The Navy declared that the turret had "meritorious features probably not attained with any other turret," and the report was so favorable that the Materiel Division was anxious to continue the project. But at the time the Division had a full agenda and was unable to follow up on this project. As late as May 1942 the Chief of PES wrote to Dr. S. H. Caldwell, a member of the National Defense Research Committee at MIT, that the subject of turret stabilization had been discussed at Wright Field and approved for investigation, but:

"There is virtually no possibility of conducting tests at the present time because of the extreme urgency of other tests projects involving equipment now in production. . . . While turret stabilization is considered an important project, all such highly experimental problems are being held up until the present peak of work has passed."

The Ford turret was a typical example of the Division's inability to develop a promising experimental project, since at that time the lack of trained Division personnel become apparent. Engineers who might have been better occupied with research projects such as stabilization were fully occupied with testing existing production models. The Materiel Division did not or could not test the Ford turret, and so another promising design which could have contributed solutions to turret problems and possibly reached production was neglected.

**Pioneer Spherical Turret**

The Pioneer Instrument Division was a Bendix Aviation Corporation subsidiary located in Bendix, NJ. In January 1941 Pioneer informed the Materiel Division of plans to develop a twin .50 caliber spherical turret for delivery in six months. In May the Division approved a $30,000 experimental contract to procure the turret with its autosyn control drive, external ammunition feed, and computing sight. In February 1942 Pioneer reported that it expected to complete the turret the following April, but by August the company reported that it had encountered problems with the turret and would require more time. However, by May 1943 the Armament Laboratory recommended closing out the Pioneer order after nine months had passed with no word of progress received from the manufacturer. Not all the latecomers to the turret business field met such an ignominious end; in fact, the turrets of some of the last companies to enter showed great potential.

**Borg Warner/Norge Frazer-Nash Turret 78**

Since the war dramatically reduced its production of refrigerators, the Norge Division of the Borg-Warner Corporation of Detroit designed an experimental turret for the Air Corps without prior authorization from the Armament Laboratory, but anticipating that its turret design would merit consideration. The turret, designated the Frazer-Nash Number 78, was designed by Frazer-Nash engineer B.B. Henderson. Norge manufactured the Frazer-Nash turrets mounting twin .50 caliber guns for use as deck guns on Navy PT boats and for use as turrets for the Navy's Curtiss SB2C Helldiver (the AAC A-25 Shrike). Although the Materiel Division normally would not show interest in a Navy turret, the Armament Laboratory had previously asked Norge to investigate a substitute hydraulic drive for the Vickers unit, and the Armament Laboratory found the Norge turret was worth exploring. On 22 July 1942 the Materiel Division sent a representative to the Norge factory who noted that "while it is practically certain that Wright Field will not even consider this turret for installation in the B-24 tail, it does have some very interesting features which might be utilized in future designs." Norge, hoping that the Materiel Division could use either the turret's basic design or one or more of its component parts or assemblies sent a detailed description of the new turret to the Chief of the Materiel Division. However, an AAC requirement for the Norge turret or any of its components never materialized.

**United Shoe Manufacturing Pressurized Turret**

The United Shoe Manufacturing Corp. of Boston did not wish to go into immediate turret production and met with the Armament Laboratory in June 1941 to discuss the development of pressurized turrets in the future, and the Laboratory granted the company $2,500 for preliminary research. In September 1941 Armament Laboratory analyzed the problems of turret pressurization and also recommended, in order to improve liaison with combat units, that the results of these studies be circulated to combat units as well as turret manufacturers for criticism before beginning any development. In October, the Materiel Division negotiated a $50,000 contract with United Shoe for an experimental twin 37mm cannon pressurized turret which lingered in the developmental stage, as the need for a 37mm gun turret subsided.

**Airarms Pressurized Turret**

In July 1940 an AAC Western Procurement District engineering officer received a report concerning an armored, pressure-cabin power turret developed by Airarms (a Vega Airplane Company subsidiary) and requested further information from Airarms, which did not reply. In October the Materiel Division pressured Airarms for a proposal, but the company replied that its turret was still in the experimental stage, with engineering problems still to be resolved. However, Airarms was so confident in its turret design that it was willing to continue to invest large sums of its own money in the normally uncompensated stages of development in the hope of getting future contracts.

In January 1941 the Materiel Division warned Airarms that it would be necessary for the company to quote a cost on its turret in order to authorize procurement in the current fiscal year, but Airarms reported that the turret was not ready. In March Airarms claimed to be completely tooled for initial test turret production, but the first turret did not reach Wright Field for testing until May. At the time the Material Division was eager to find solutions to the significant problems that confronted contemporary turret designers, and despite the delays found the turret was noteworthy, as among the Airarms innovations were the basic ball design that provided a wide range of elevation and azimuth movement, the gas recoil-operated ammunition booster that was a fresh approach to a long time ammunition feed problem, and the prismatic double-ended sight for aiming past obstructions.

However, the most significant element of the Airarms turret was its drive mechanism powered by a constant-speed motor with two opposed friction clutches for two-directional speed controls. The opposed clutches prevented coasting after disengagement, as movement past neutral caused a reciprocal motion. An advantage of the drive was that it provided maximum torque without regard for clutch positions approaching low speeds. Although the Airarms drive did have some major problems, its potential particularly impressed the Materiel Division. In a memo of 24 June 1941 the Section Chief of the Experimental Engineering Section endorsed the Airarms turret: "As of this date, the Vega (Airarms) turret is superior to any of the present production turrets." Wright Field awarded an experimental contract for $15,000 to Airarms to continue the development of its turret.

During this ongoing developmental stage Wright Field continued to have some important reservations about the turret, as metal sheathing obscured large areas necessary for scanning, the drive motor was insufficiently ventilated and overheated after five minutes at full load, the maximum azimuth slewing speeds were too slow, and the minimum tracking speeds were too fast. Airarms engineers worked unsuccessfully to solve these problems, but the Armament Laboratory continued to have confidence in the drive. However, the Contract Section Chief estimated that the development costs of the Airarms project would reach $400,000 by December 1942 and transferred the project to Emerson against Airarms' objections. Against just such a contingency Vega, representing Airarms, sought to reach a settlement with Emerson and claimed more than $153,000 for development costs prior to the time that Emerson took over. But the Western Procurement District ruled that the Vega claim was not allowable and the AAC settled with Emerson and left the Vega claim for direct negotiation.

**Emerson Continues the Airarms Turret**

However, Emerson engineers were no more successful in improving the turret than Airarms had been. Thorough theoretical and empirical redesign of the clutch system was tried, but it was impossible to attain azimuth speeds low enough to track efficiently. A gear reducer on the clutch output, a planetary gear reducer between drive and clutch disks, and idler disks in the clutch were all tried and found unsuccessful. The Materiel Division continued to believe in the potential of the Airarms/Emerson turret design, citing it was heavily armored, its prismatic sight promised to be outstanding when perfected, and the turret also had an unusual degree of downward fire, a low drag coefficient, and an original arrangement for lever action charging. Emerson decided that the installation of a completely new drive could salvage the Airarms turret. Emerson negotiated the rights to manufacture the General Electric amplidyne drive for $25,000. But the future of the Airarms project was doomed when the standard 530-watt GE amplidyne was found to be not powerful enough to drive the turret and GE projected a five month delay in developing a heavier amplidyne drive with increased output.

In January 1942 war had come to America, and there was an acute need for turrets, causing the Materiel Division to resurrect the Airarms project in spite of all its problems. Firing tests of the Airarms turret using both the new more powerful GE amplidyne and Maxson electric drives revealed the usual accessory troubles, inadequate boosters, and excessive power consumption. The early interest in the Airarms design led to a tentative procurement letter contract to Emerson for 500 units to be ready by late 1943.

A quantity production contract for the Airarms turret would be dependant on the assumption that the turret would be suitable for installation in production aircraft. The central station fire control system was expected to be ready by June 1944, and allowing nine months tooling time for the Airarms turret, only a nine month margin remained for production, which seemed not to justify extending the project. However, the Experimental Engineering Section maintained that the Airarms turret was "superior to any present production turrets" and also maintained that locally controlled turrets (e.g. the Airarms/Emerson) would not be obsolete by mid-1944, and the Airarms turret, if successful, "would be of tremendous value in relieving the Vickers drive unit shortage" (by using the GE unit).

The GE 750-watt amplidyne project ran into persistent development and production delays at GE and Martin-Omaha plants, and these delays led to an anticipated delay in Martin turrets, so the Materiel Division cancelled the Airarms project entirely and turned the resultant Emerson capacity to Martin production. Notwithstanding the drive delays, by June 1942 other American turret manufacturers had increased their production and even the potential of Airarms was not sufficient justification for continuing the project. The Airarms/Emerson project was worthwhile despite its expense, as was later confirmed by equipping the B-24G with Emerson's nose ball turret which used many of the Airarms' qualities.

**Emerson Pressurized Turret**

A joint Army-Navy Committee agreed to work on a four-gun pressurized turret with a computing sight, 2,000 round ammunition capacity, one inch armor plate, and a possible 120-volt electric system. Tentative requirements for this turret were sent to Emerson, which had its experimental laboratories located on Long Island and its production facilities in St. Louis. To coordinate experimental development and production, Emerson applied for funds to construct an onsite experimental laboratory in St. Louis. The Armament Laboratory Chief objected, but relented because of Emerson's reputation as a turret designer and manufacturer even if it did represent a certain duplication of facilities. Emerson embarked on a long period of turret pressurized development working on several concepts. The first Emerson contract was for the Model 110 pressurized ball turret, which was started in early 1942 and completed in September. Important features incorporated in this turret included a pressurised structure for high altitude operation, self-contained pressurizing blower and regulator valves, more room and comfort than the Sperry ball turret, and it was compatible with the pressurized B-29. It was apparent from the onset that this pressurized turret was essentially experimental and a hedge against the possible future failure of central-station fire control; so when the B-29 armament was fixed as a remote control system the promising Emerson Model 110 was cancelled. At the time Emerson was manufacturing the Sperry ball turret and considered its own Model 110 to be superior, as it weighed and cost less and could be used as a conventional non-pressurized turret. However, the Sperry Ball was so successful that the Emerson turret was not considered.

**Experimental B-29 Turret Installations**

In October 1944 Project S68 was initiated for manned B-29 turret evaluation. A B-29-20-25-BW (S/N 42-24441) was fitted with a Martin upper forward turret (at the rear of the forward pressurized compartment) and Martin upper rear turret (at the rear of the rear pressurized compartment) using twin .50cal machine guns. Two retractable Sperry A-13 ball turrets were installed mounting twin .50cal machine guns. The forward Sperry ball was fitted between the forward landing gear doors and the bomb bay doors, and the aft ball was mounted just forward of the tailskid and was part of the tail gunner's pressurized compartment. The standard A-13 ball turret was modified to have a shorter hanger than those used on the B-24 and the B-32, and thus did not retract entirely into the fuselage. The waist sighting blisters were replaced by hand-held .50cal machine guns like those used on the B-17 and B-24. Plywood boxes held the ammunition, and the spent casings were collected in a canvas basket on the floor below the gun.

B-29 41-24441 was also fitted with two remotely controlled Emerson Model 126 barbettes each mounting a single .50cal machine gun. The large egg-shaped barbettes were mounted on each side of the forward fuselage just above and adjacent to the forward tricycle gear. The project was probably the brainstorm of a higher echelon and was short lived.

**Aero 11A/B/D Hydraulic Turrets**

Toward the end of the war the Aero designed a remote hydraulic turret mounting two 20mm cannons. The A and B turrets were designed to be installed in the tails of Navy patrol bombers and were virtually identical, except that the B model did not include the tail cone of the carrying aircraft or the gunner's sighting station. The Aero 11D was to be installed in the nose of Navy patrol bombers.

The turret and sight support was driven in azimuth and elevation by a Vickers hydraulic unit operated by solenoids connected to potentiometer

**Martin B-29 Experimental Turret Installation** (USAAF)

**Emerson B-29 Barbette Installation** (USAAF)

controls in the control handles. The azimuth unit was mounted on the base of the hand control housing, while the elevation unit was mounted on the port side of the elevation sight assembly opposite the end of the sight support. The hand control assembly was mounted on the aft end of the azimuth drive assembly and projected into the fuselage toward the gunner. The hand grips rotated about a horizontal axis through their center to control azimuth movement. Each grip contained a trigger switch, an action switch on the lower outboard side of each grip, and a microphone switch on the thumb position of each grip. The turret movements were guided by these twin grips located in front of the gunner. The control unit was located next to the gunner's right shoulder.

The two electrically-fired 20mm cannon were mounted in a spherical enclosure with the sighting head (which was separately powered to follow the guns). The guns were mounted in a cradle and were fed by a mechanism modified for use with a cartridge-type feeder heater and a pneumatic gun charger. The ammunition was supplied through flexible chutes aided by separate booster motors from separate boxes located in the side of the fuselage to the rear of the turret and gunner

**Aero 9A/B Electric Turrets**

The Aero 9A/B 20mm turrets, near design completion at the end of the war, were electrically-powered turrets designed to function as nose ball-type turrets on Navy patrol bombers. Two separate, but identical DC motors supplied by the aircraft's 28-volt system drove the turret in azimuth and elevation. This turret was directly operated by the gunner, who sat in the horizontal ball-shaped turret with the 20mm guns protruding through the center of the ball. The gunner sat behind the guns at chest level with his feet and legs on either side of the guns. The gunner looked through the lead computing sight mounted on top of the guns through the bullet-proof windshield and controlled the turret (and guns) via the controller handles located at waist level.

**Aero 11A/B/D Hydraulic Turrets** (USN)

# 5

# Non-Turret Gun Installations

## Section 1: Fixed and Flexible Nose Gun Installations

### Flexible .50 Caliber Nose Gun

General

The flexible .50-caliber machine gun was mounted in a Type K-4 ball-and-socket mount in the leading edge of the nose, directly above the bomb-sighting window. The gun was equipped with a Type E-11 recoil adapter, a Type C-19 mount adapter, an ejection chute, a link guide, a front bead sight, a rear ring sight, and a manual charging slide assembly. The approximate firing angles of the gun were 23° to either side of straight forward, 25° downward, and when the bomb sight was in its operating position 10° upward. To assist in the movement of the gun were two shock cords which were suspended from the enclosure frame and attached to the recoil adapter on the gun. An ammunition belt containing 300 rounds was contained in three 100 round boxes strapped together on a shelf on the right side of the compartment. An ammunition loading chart was attached to the inboard side of each box. The belt was fed from the forward ammunition box to the gun by means of a flexible feed chute, and the ejected cases and links passed through an ejection chute to the right side of the compartment floor. When the gun was not in use, the aft end could be swung upward and fastened to the stowage bracket located on the enclosure frame by means of a spring-loaded plunger on the recoil adapter. When the gun was in the stowed position it did not interfere with the normal operation of the bomb sight.

Flexible Gun Operation

The gunner released the gun from the stowage bracket by pushing out the plunger on the aft end of the recoil adapter. He checked the gun for right hand feed and, if necessary, proper loading. The gun was charged by pulling back and releasing the charging handle and the safety was moved to the firing position. The gunner sighted through the ring and bead sight and fired the gun by pulling the trigger. After firing the gunner saftied the gun and stowed it. The gun was to be unloaded before landing.

### Fixed .50 Caliber Nose Gun

General

One fixed .50 caliber machine gun was mounted on the right side of the bombardier's compartment below the flexible gun ammunition box shelf. A 300 round ammunition box was fastened to the aft right side of the compartment floor by quick-release latches that permitted the easy removal of the box for loading ammunition. A flexible chute fed the ammunition belt from the box to the gun. Ejected shell cases passed through the metal ejection chute aft into a cloth bag which was attached by dot fasteners to the ammunition box and the right side of the compartment. Ejected links were caught in a zippered cloth bag attached to the inboard side of the gun.

The gun slot in the Plexiglas window was sealed against the entry of outside air by a metal tube clamped to the aft end of the gun muzzle jacket and a cloth boot which was tied to the tube and secured to the inner edge of the gun slot. The gun was adjusted in elevation and azimuth at the rear mount. The elevation adjustment range of 4° downward to 1° upward, with respect to the fuselage reference line, provided for any nose-up or nose-down condition resulting from aircraft speeds of 75% to 100% of the maximum calibrated-indicated airspeed in level flight with the various weight loads possible. The azimuth adjustment range permitted adjusting the line of fire so that it converged at 275 yards with the line of sight of the torpedo director.

Fixed Gun Operation

The gun was charged by the bombardier by means of the charging handle and retracting slide attached to the inboard side of the gun. The pilot/gunner turned the gun safety switch located on the left side of the pilot's switch panel to FIRE. The torpedo director was latched in the sight forward position and used as a gunsight. The pilot/gunner fired the gun by pressing the button marked GUNS on the pilot's control wheel. After firing the pilot turned the safety switch to SAFE, and prior to landing the bombardier was to unload the gun.

One fixed .50 caliber machine gun was mounted on the right side of the bombardier's compartment below the flexible gun ammunition box shelf. A 300 round ammunition box was held to the aft right side of the compartment floor. (Author/CAF)

**Flexible Nose Gun Gallery**

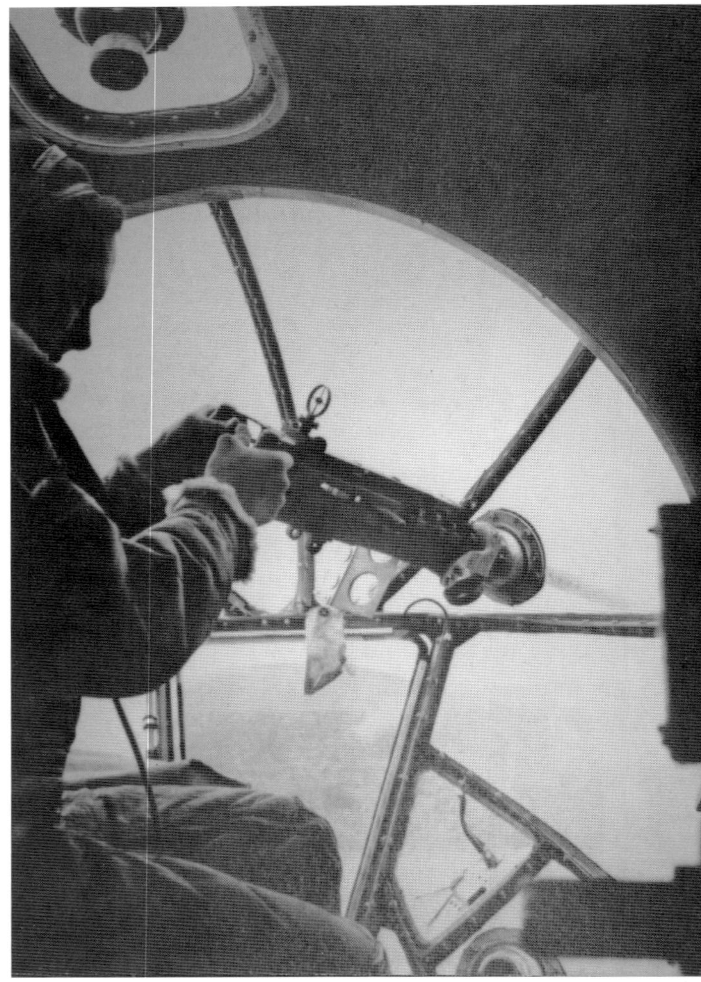

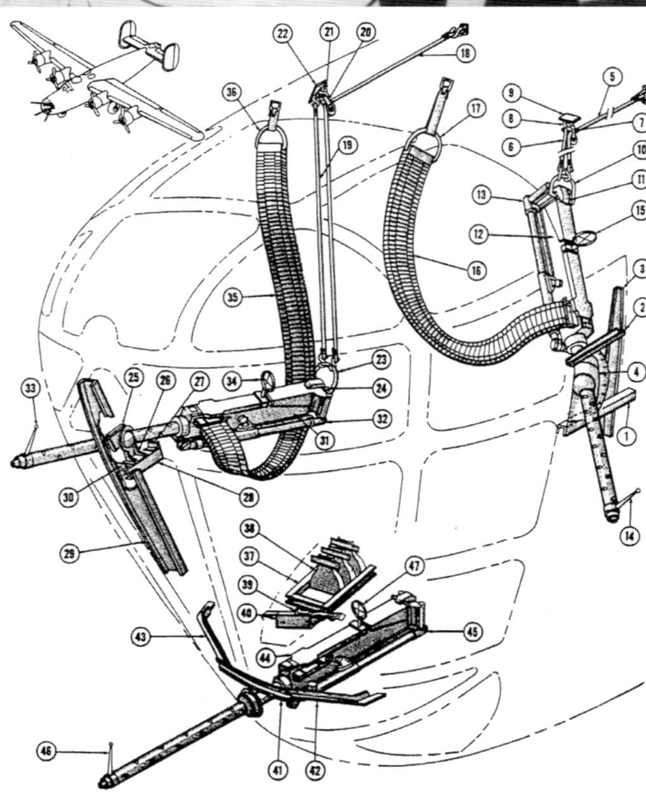

From Above left: A single .50 caliber Browning is inserted into the right offset gun socket of this B-17F nose cone with another .50 pointing out of the side window. Most B-17 nose .50 installations were through the center of the nose. (USAAF)

View of flexible .30 caliber machine gun nose gunner who was the bombardier from inside a B-17E. There were a number of different gun sockets available for the one .30 caliber gun. (USAAF)

**B-24D Nose Gun Installation** (USAAF)

The B-24D nose gun had a top and/or bottom nose-single gun full swivel with a right and left side single gun full swivel appearing on B-24D (41-24220) and subsequent. (USAAF)

This B-25J had the "bombardier nose" with flexible and one or two fixed .50s reinstalled from the previous solid noses of the G and H models. (USAAF)

Late production Bs and the B-26C left the production line with improved armament including a single .50 caliber Browning (200 rpg) in the nose. (USAAF)

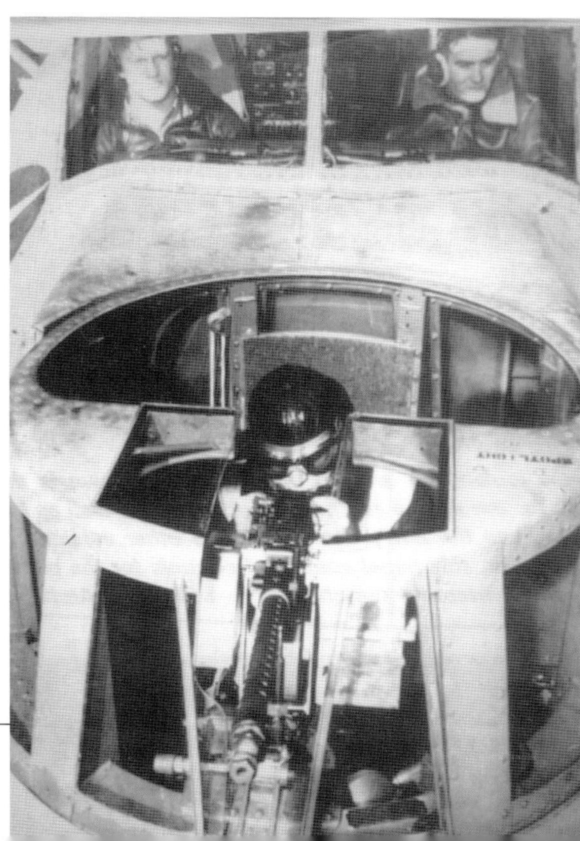

The PBY-1 was delivered in June 1936 bearing a .30 caliber machine gun in the bow turret mounted on a Mk 9 adapter in a rotating turret and was manned by the bombardier. The gunner could fire the guns from a kneeling position from completely inside the turret but could also stand up through the top hatch. This turret remained standard into the PBY-5and -5A series. (USN)

The all-solid metal nose of the B-25 formed a compartment for the four to eight .50 caliber nose guns and ammunition boxes. (Author)

The upper portion of the B-25 nose was a hinged hood which could be swung open for gaining access to the guns and boxes. (Author)

**.50 caliber Fixed Nose Guns (Four or More)**

Nose Compartment

The all-solid metal nose formed a compartment for the four to eight nose guns and ammunition boxes. The lower nose section was fixed, while the upper portion of the nose was a hinged hood that could be swung open for gaining access to the guns and boxes. The hood was held open by two spring-loaded struts and was held closed during flight by two lock assemblies.

Nose Guns

Nose guns were charged and fired by the pilot. Each gun, mounted on an X43B front mount and a Type A-4 rear post, was equipped with a Type G-11 solenoid, a charging slide assembly, a link guide, a barrel opening close-off cover, and ammunition chute quick-release attachments. The ammunition belts were fed from the boxes to the guns through flexible feed chutes and the ejected cases and links passed downward to the case and link container beneath the boxes. The guns were heated by warm air conducted through a duct assembly connected to the main heating duct. A butterfly valve, manually controlled by the pilot, regulated the flow of hot air to the guns.

Loading the Nose Guns

To load the nose guns the nose hood was unlocked and lifted and the lever on each strut tightened. The feed chutes were disconnected and the ammunition boxes removed. Four belts of approximately 400 rounds each were made ready and, starting with the single loop ends of the belts, they were loaded into the boxes with the cartridges pointing toward the inboard side of each box. The ammunition boxes were installed and connected to the feed chutes with the double loop ends of the belts pulled down through the chutes to load the guns. The guns were charged, the strut levers loosened, and the hood closed and latched.

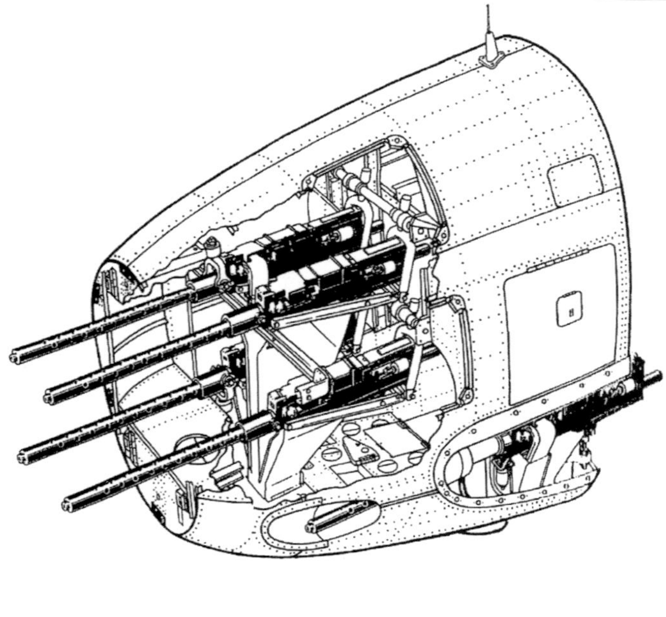

The early solid noses of the A-20 contained an impressive array of four 20mm cannon and two .50s or six .50s which turned the A-20 into a fearsome ground attack strafer/bomber. Later the often troublesome 20mm cannon were replaced by four more .50s for six nose .50s, a configuration that Douglas would continue in the A-26 Invader. (USAAF)

The production B-26B was to have a solid nose containing six .50s and the B-26C, a glass nose with a bombardier's station and two 50s on the right side. These noses were easily interchangeable. In combat the six gun nose was found to be inadequate and increased to eight guns and provisions were made to mount eight more .50s in four underwing twin packs. (USAAF)

During the war NAA engineers proposed strafer nose configurations that mounted twin .50 caliber machine guns on a pivoting rod that could be elevated or depressed by the gunner for ground strafing. (AFHRC)

**Experimental Strafing Nose Gun Configurations**

During the war North American Aviation engineers proposed strafer nose configurations for the B-25D that could be depressed for ground strafing. Kansas City engineers mounted twin .50 caliber machine guns on a pivoting rod that could be elevated or depressed by the gunner. Later, Inglewood NAA engineers built a similar pivoting mock up while developing the B-25J, which carried four guns. Neither concept progressed beyond the experimental stage. Later, the XP-54 *Swoose Goose* prototype was to carry six .50 caliber Brownings in its nose with the installation being capable of pivoting +3° upward and -6° downward.

**Section 2: Blister Pack Installations**

Douglas A-20

The Douglas A-20A was the first "attack" version of the Havoc acquired by the Army Air Corps. To gain its attack status it was armed with four .30 caliber machine guns: two internal and two installed in oblong tear drop shaped fairings referred to as "side packs" located behind the glazed nose. In the A-20B the four .30 caliber guns were replaced with four .50s; two internal and two in a side pack that was more rounded than the A-20A tear drop pack. These fixed guns were controlled electrically by a gun selector switch on the pilot's upper electrical panel and a firing switch mounted on the wheel of the pilot's control column. The selector switch permitted the firing of the two inboard guns, the two outboard guns, or all four guns simultaneously. One pair of manually operated gun charging controls were installed on each side of the pilot's compartment below the instrument panel. The lower charging control attached to the inboard gun and the upper control attached to the outboard side pack gun. A Type N-2A gunsight projector was installed on the floor of the pilot's compartment and the gunsight reflector was mounted on the cowl above the instrument panel. The rheostat for varying the intensity of the projected image on the reflector was mounted on the pilot's upper electrical panel. Each of the four guns was supplied by 500 rounds of ammunition carried in containers installed behind the bombardier's seat in the nose compartment.

North American B-25

In mid-1943 the cannon-equipped B-25Gs arrived in the SWPA and were tested by Maj. Paul Gunn from mid-November through December. Gunn was mostly pleased with the 75mm cannon, but he recommended that the G model needed the addition of forward firing .50 caliber machine guns. The Service Command began a wide-ranging armament modification program on the G model running from November 1943 to April 1944. To add forward fire power the fuselage gun pack was developed.

The fuselage gun packs (the North American nomenclature) were also called "cheek packs" and most commonly "blister packs" in the field. They were faired rectangular or long ovoid metal pods fastened to the side of the fuselage with a downward opening hinged access cover door. The pack enclosed two .50 caliber machine guns that were anchored to a reinforced plate on the fuselage and held in place by custom made brackets that bolted into the fuselage. Brackets on the barrel and base of the gun were attached by bolts to the mounting bracket. The barrel of the top gun was usually staggered slightly behind that of the lower gun. The gun unit was equipped with a Type G-11 solenoid, a link guide, feed chute attachments, and a manual charging slide. The ammunition boxes were supported on a shelf

Blister packs, also called cheek packs and fuselage gun packs were faired rectangular metal pods fastened to the fuselage with a downward opening hinged access cover containing a cartridge chute. (USAAF)

Protection from the muzzle blast was accomplished by the placement of blast tubes (right) and large sheet metal plates attached to the fuselage to cover the entire blast area. (Author/CAF)

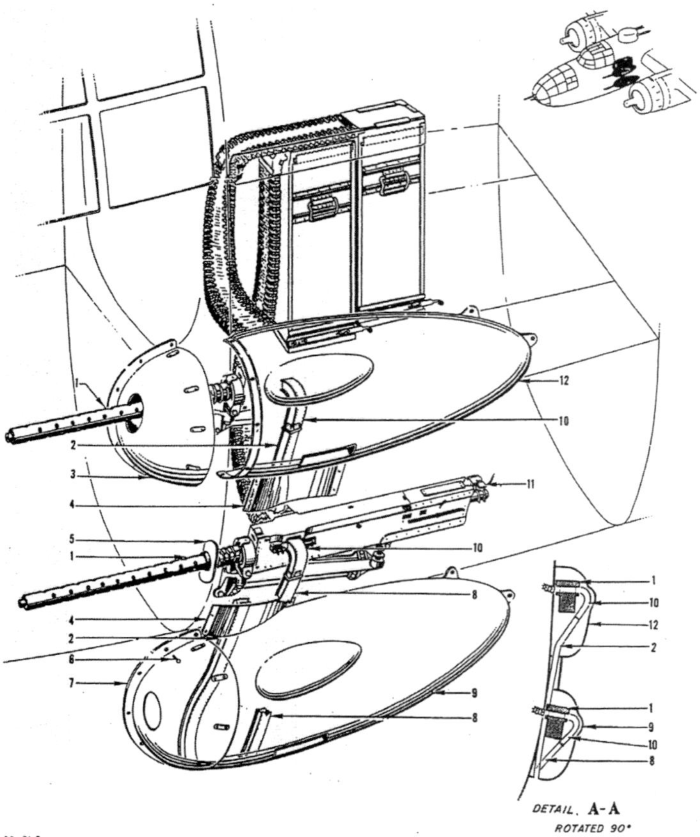


**B-25 Blister Pack Installation** (USAAF)

structure at the right side of the cannoneer's compartment and were loaded with approximately 400 rounds. The single loop ends of the belts were loaded into the boxes first with the cartridges pointing to the outboard side of the boxes with extra rounds allowed for the feed chutes. The boxes were installed and the feed chutes connected. The belts were threaded through the chutes and the first cartridges forced into the guns. Flexible chutes fed the ammunition belts to the guns. The manual charging handle for each gun was located forward of the ammo boxes mounted on the bulkhead at the forward end of the top turret compartment. The cannoneer charged the blister guns in flight by pulling out and releasing the charging handles. The guns were fired simultaneously by the pilot.

**Major Paul "Pappy" Gunn** developed a number of innovative armament schemes first for the A-20 and then leading to the "strafer" B-25. (USAAF)

Senior North American Field Representative **Jack Fox** collaborated with Pappy Gunn to reconfigure the B-25C/D into the strafer configuration (USAAF)

During the development of the blister pack it was suggested that the blister pack on the port side be eliminated to make room for a cabin heater. However, 5AF CO Lt.Gen. George Kenney disapproved the proposal, arguing that in the strafer role the B-25G would rarely operate above 1,000 feet and did not require a cabin heater, but did need the extra machine guns. Kenney won out, but another problem arose concerning the installation of the packs. The weight of the NAA factory installed nose armament of two .50 caliber machine guns and the 75mm cannon and their associated ammunition caused a weight and balance problem when designing and placing the blister packs. Design studies placed the blister packs above the bomb bay doors, but firing tests soon showed the muzzle blast would tear open the thin aluminum fuselage skin, pop rivets, buckle the skin of wing leading edges, and damage the adjacent bomb bay doors. Engineers set out to find remedies. Protection from the muzzle blast was achieved by the placement of blast tubes and large sheet metal plates attached to the fuselage to cover the entire blast area. Initially felt cushioning pads were placed behind these plates, but after becoming wet they became hard and useless and were replaced by rubber pads. The bomb bay doors were provided with rubber-backed blast protection plates, inspection panels were installed in the wing center section, and ported blast tubes were fitted. There was initial concern that the close propeller clearance to the fuselage would cause airflow interference with the firing of the guns but none occurred.

Despite these modifications further refinement in positioning the blister packs was required. The packs were relocated to the same position as those on the B-25C1 and D1 strafers, and the addition of two .50s in the tail turret and the removal of the ventral turret (this was done in the factory on the 200th aircraft, 42-65001 onward) solved the weight balancing problem. A total of 82 B-25Gs were so modified at the Townsville Depot by April 1944.

**Section 3: Pappy Gunn and the Strafer Bomber**

Soon after America entered the war, the reality that there was no dedicated attack bomber in the Air Corps inventory was made evident as combat theater air commanders were forced to adapt aircraft on hand. In the SWPA Lt.Gen. Kenney had both the B-25 and A-20 available for the new low-level attack role, and both demonstrated that they possessed intrinsic qualities to handle the job. In order to drop their bombs accurately in the newly developed low-level bombing techniques the attack bombers had to fly at low altitudes to strike targets that were heavily defended by Japanese AA guns. However, it was soon obvious that neither aircraft had adequate armament to make the AA gunners take cover. The single .30 caliber flexible nose gun of the early B-25s not only made them easy targets in the frontal attacks by Japanese fighters, it certainly was no threat to Japanese AA gunners. Senior North American Field Representative Jack Fox, who had originally come to the SWPA as the North American Aviation Field Representative accompanying B-25s that were allocated to the Netherlands East Indies Air Force (NEIAF), improved the .30 mount flexible mount to carry the .50 caliber machine gun. Although this heavier gun and mount was also subsequently used on the B-17 and B-26, it was still not intimidating enough on low-level attacks.

Soon after assuming the role of CO of the Fifth Air Force, Lt.Gen. Kenney wished to increase the low-level bombing accuracy of the A-20, which was on hand in the theater, and ordered the newly arrived Maj. Paul Gunn to take on the task. Paul Irvin Gunn had joined the Navy at 17, and in 1939, after 21 years, Gunn retired as a Chief Petty Officer pilot. After serving many years in the Orient he settled in the Philippines and married, living very comfortably on his pension and his position as the Operations Manager of Philippines Air Lines based in Manila. In 1941, with war looming, Gen. Lewis Brereton, AAC CO in the Philippines, commissioned the knowledgeable veteran as a Captain in the Army Air Corps, and at 42, his relatively advanced age earned him his nickname "Pappy." Gunn's first assignment was to evacuate personnel from the Philippines to Brisbane, Australia, via Mindanao. On his arrival in Australia Gunn was told of the capture of Manila by the Japanese and that his family was interned with the city's population. Because of the predicament of his family back in the Philippines Gunn was determined to defeat the Japanese Empire, single handedly if need be.

While stationed at Amberly Field, Australia, in the fall of 1942, Gunn began to modify the A-20s of Lt.Col. Jim Davies' 3rd Bomb Group. Gunn's plan was to increase the Havoc's forward firepower to allow them to fly into close range, firing these guns to drive the enemy AA gunners under cover and then to drop their bombs at point blank range. Gunn realized that these low-level bombing attacks would not require a bombardier, so he removed the bombardier's glass nose and substituted a solid metal nose carrying four .50 caliber machine guns that were augmented with a single .50 caliber machine gun in a blister pack mounted on each side of the fuselage below and behind the cockpit. To increase the range of the Havoc Gunn fitted two 450 gallon fuel tanks in the bomb bay. In the limited remaining bomb bay space he designed and built special bomb racks to carry fragmentation bombs equipped with small parachutes called parafrags. While successful, the A-20 was still limited by its small bomb load and also by the reduced numbers that would be available in the future due to Russian Lend-Lease requirements. Thus, the B-25, which proved to be more adaptable for modification and were available in numbers in the theater, would become the AAC's new low-level attack bomber by default.

Lt.Gen. Kenney was impressed by Gunn's work on the A-20 modifications and first assigned him to Eagle Farm, Brisbane, where he was to sort through a boneyard of wrecked fighters and rehabilitate as many as possible. In a short period he and his right hand man, Sgt. Evans, got over 100 back into combat. Next, in late November 1942 Gunn was assigned to the Townsville Air Depot, north of Brisbane on the eastern coast of Australia, where he and Jack Fox collaborated to reconfigure the B-25C/D into fearsome strafer versions. Although not as fast as the A-20, the Mitchell had greater range without the need for auxiliary fuel tanks that had limited the A-20's bomb load. Importantly, it had a larger nose section that would provide more room for guns and ammunition. A prototype modification named *Pappy's Folly* was built, replacing the standard bombardier nose with four .50 caliber machine guns, each protruding through the standard glazed nose and each fed by 500 round boxes. The guns were bolted to each side of a narrow, upright strut that attached to the floor of the nose center line. The flat forward bombardier's panel was removed and a Dzus fastened metal panel replaced it with the four machine gun barrels protruding through holes that sealed off incoming air. The top center Plexiglas nose window panel was also replaced with a Dzus fastened panel to facilitate the loading of the ammunition belts into the guns. The ammunition boxes were stored in the bomb bays. The bombardier's escape hatch was bolted shut. Two more machine guns were placed externally in blisters placed on the sides of the fuselage under the cockpit windows with the top gun pack staggered forward of the bottom pack.

Other gun and ordnance installations were proposed. A nose 20mm cannon installation was considered, but the idea was dropped since the cannon and its ammunition would not fit into the area. A .30 caliber machine gun was installed in each landing light bay and used successfully on several missions. However, when North American engineers in California heard about this gun placement they issued orders to remove them for structural reasons. Another innovation was the placement in the bomb bay of twin .30 caliber guns pointing to fire directly downward, but the placement used too much valuable space reserved for bombs. A trio of guns was tentatively hung under the fuselage to replace the ventral turret, but this idea was soon abandoned when their muzzle blast damaged the nose gear doors. The dorsal turret was locked in the forward position to fire under the control of the pilot. The B-25 was fitted with the A-20 fragmentation bomb racks with three installed in series on the right side of the bomb bay, which allowed the left side free for additional blister pack ammunition boxes and fuel tanks. With no bombardier the bomb controls needed to be modified for use by the co-pilot. The Air Service Command of various units also created their own field modifications which usually remained local, and were restricted to a small number of B-25s. NAA Field Representatives were aware of these modifications and generally submitted reports to the company, but rarely were these unusual local modifications integrated on the production lines.

*Pappy's Folly* was put through flight and gunnery tests by Gunn, Fox, and Sgt. Evans, and the prototype was found to be nose heavy, requiring 100 pounds of ballast in the rear fuselage and the movement of the blister guns three feet aft. After flight testing *Pappy's Folly* was sent to 17 Mile Airstrip near Port Moresby, New Guinea, on 29 December 1942 to the 90BS/3BG under Maj. Edward Larner for combat trials and familiarization. A wrecked vessel was stranded on a nearby coral reef off Port Moresby Harbor and served as target practice for low-level attack missions. The trials proceeded well, and once the gunship design was frozen the 90th sent 12 B-25s back to Australia for modification while the rest of the Squadron continued training and worked on developing strafing/bombing techniques. It settled on a target approach from an altitude of 1,000 to 1,500 feet at about three miles from the target when the aircraft began evasive maneuvers while dropping to an altitude of 500 feet. At 1,500 yards the pilot dropped to the deck for a high-speed strafing/bombing run. To divert the enemy AA opposition the aircraft would often attack in pairs, with one strafing on a beam approach while the other attacked at mast top level.

The 12 B-25s were modified and sent back to the 90th by the end of February 1943 in time for them to take part in the decisive Battle of the Bismarck Sea on 3 March. And so, during the war the B-25 would prove to be the most compliant American aircraft due to the numerous field and depot modifications demanded of it. Once found to be successful these Gunn/Fox strafer field modifications would directly influence future B-25G and H design and production.

By September 1943 approximately 150 B-25s had been modified to strafers. The first strafer modification was to B-25C (41-12946) *Margaret*, which arrived at Charter Towers, Queensland, on 8 December and was assigned to the 90BS/3BG. The aircraft was sent to the modification center at Townsville and was equipped with four nose guns and two two-gun blister packs.

After having made the strafer role synonymous with the B-25, NAA developed a prefabricated perfectly streamlined "gun nose" to fit all models. This nose generally replaced the need for in the field modifications to convert the B-25 medium bomber into the B-25 ground attack bomber. The prefabricated nose was quick and easy to install, reducing the time the bomber spent out of service. The new nose enabled many B-25s to carry up to 18 guns, with 14 of them able to fire forward. (For a detailed discussion of the modifications to the B-25G/H/J see my book *The North American B-25 Mitchell: The Ultimate Look from Drawing Board to Flying Arsenal*, Schiffer, PA, 2008)

**Section 4: Waist Gun Installations**

Waist gun positions were an important facet of American bomber defense, defending the lateral approaches to the bomber formations. However, this position was difficult to defend, as the enemy fighters would zoom by and

**Waist Gun Gallery**

The defensive armament of the **XB-15** was the heaviest to be fitted to a bomber to that time; carrying six machine guns including one .30 caliber machine gun in each of two oval waist tear-drop-shaped blisters attached to the fuselage behind the wings. (USAAF)

The **Model 299** had four blister-type flexible machine gun stations, each of which could accommodate a .30 caliber or .50 caliber machine gun. One was in a dorsal position in the fuselage just above the wing trailing edge and a second was in a ventral fuselage position just behind the wing trailing edge. The other two were oval blisters resembling those on the XB-15 which was mounted on each side of the rear fuselage in a waist position. (USAAF)

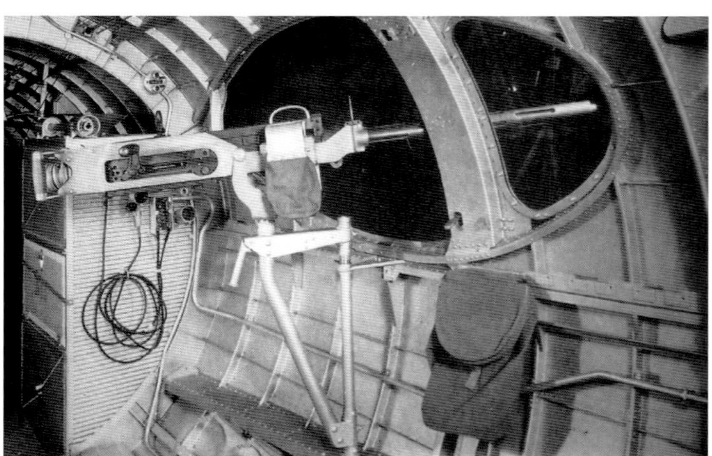

The **B-17B** resembled the Model 299 and continued its oval waist blister configuration but the other few changes warranted its redesignations to the B Model. (USAAF)

The oval waist positions of earlier models were replaced in the **B-17E** by rectangular openings with removable windows with a single .50 caliber machine gun mounted behind each of these windows. The close quarters of the waist position can be easily seen in this photo. (USAAF)

A B-17 gunners looks out of an open waist window. The undeployed wind deflector can be seen to the gunner's right. (USAAF)

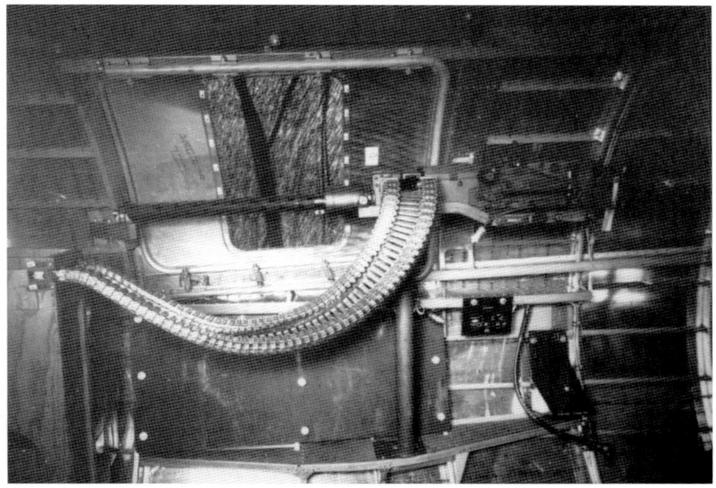

This stowed .50 caliber machine looks very neat and unencumbered behind the closed window. (USAAF)

Based on combat experience, it soon became clear that additional armament would be needed on the **B-24D**. During mid-production of the D model single waist guns in full swivel mounts were installed supplied with a total of 350 rpg. (USAAF)

A late model B-17 enclosed waist window which made high altitude gunnery much more comfortable. (Author)

On the **B-25H** model waist gun defense was improved by installing enclosed, convex windows on both sides of the fuselage aft of the wing and staggering them to allow more space for the gunners to operate. (USAAF)

Beginning with the -5, all successive **PBY** models were equipped with the large Plexiglas observation blisters on the aft sides of the fuselage. The side of the blister could be swung up to allow the .50 machine gun to go into action. (USN)

Waist position on the **B-26** with a sliding window opening. (USAAF)

**Waist Gun Position** (USAAF): A= Left-Hand Gun Stowage Strap; B= Phone Call Lamp; C= Interphone Jack Box; D= Ammunition Boxes; E= Window Release Bar.

great skill and good luck were required of a gunner to score a hit. The initial waist gun positions were windows cut in the rear fuselage with some kind of removable covering. They mounted removable and stowed .30 caliber guns fitted on K-4 ball-and-socket mounts and detachable ammunition cans. These windows ranged from the enclosed tear drop waist positions seen on the B-17 prototypes through the B-17Bs and then "devolved" to flush windows with removable, hinged, or sliding coverings with a retractable wind baffle attached to the forward side of the window. Finally, the waist was enclosed by Plexiglas with a hole cut out for the gun.

Open waist windows used the E-8 recoil mount supporting a .50 caliber machine gun with a B-11 ring sight on the receiver and an A-5 bead sight on the muzzle. Early guns were fed by flexible stainless steel chutes from large stationary ammunition boxes (600 rpg). The K-6 mount waist gun installation had flexible overhead ammunition feed chutes leading from ammunition boxes attached to the side of the fuselage and used the N-8 electric gunsight. The late war K-7 mount was similar to the K-6, except it used the K-13 computing gunsight.

Enough room for the two back-to-back waist gunners was always a problem, as the waist windows were directly opposite each other. To gain more room the windows were either staggered in the fuselage during production or the K-6 mounts were staggered on the opposite far end of each window (e.g. the far right on one window and the far left on the opposite window).

Enclosing the waist positions protected the gunners from the freezing outside air, but at the high altitudes that the B-17 and B-24 operated, especially over Europe, the position was extremely cold and special heated protective clothing was a necessity. The waist gunner not only was exposed to the dangers of frostbite, but also suffered the highest combat casualty rate of all crew positions in the B-17. Instead of being curled up in the fetal position of the ball turret gunner or in a hunched sitting position in a turret, the two waist gunners were standing upright, offering two large targets. The armor plate installed beneath the waist windows was inadequate, and to give added protection the gunners were provided with flak suits and helmets.

**Protective Clothing**

Electrically Heated Flying Suits

There were two electrically heated flying suits. The F-2A electrically heated flying suit was worn over long-sleeved and long-legged woolen underwear and a woolen shirt or under standard uniforms or shearling outerwear. The F-3 and F-3A suit was worn under the GI ground clothing normal for the theater (usually the intermediate flying suit) or over a uniform. A 24-volt flying suit heater receptacle and rheostat was available at each crew station.

F-2A Suit

The F-2A was a two-piece (jacket and trousers), two-layer, front zippered suit made up of an outer shell of brown wool and could be separated and worn as a cloth uniform-type jacket. The trousers were the standard waist-level type held up by a belt and suspenders. The thermostatically controlled 24-volt wiring was arranged in a web inside the lining of the outside jacket. A short "pigtail" connected the suit to a six foot extension cord that was to be plugged into the aircraft's electrical system rheostat. On the F-2A there were snap (press stud) fasteners on tabs on the jacket and trouser cuffs that acted as electrical connections to electrically heated gloves and shoe inserts. There was a small electrical connection on the front of the jacket to connect to the oxygen mask heater or to the heated lens in the B-8 goggle. Some of the suits had a fleece collar and others had the standard uniform collar.

F-3 and F-3A Suits

The F-3 was developed from the F-2A suit that was found to be inadequate in tests, and it was designated the standard electrically heated flying suit in late February 1944. The two-piece suit was made up of an olive or green cotton and rayon twill short "bolero-style" jacket that zippered in front, and "bib-type" overall trousers with adjustable suspenders. The F-3 was an improvement over the F-2A as it was sturdier, roomier, and more comfortable for sitting and movement. The suit was supplied by a 24-volt multi-circuit system with two circuits supplying the jacket, three for the trousers, and two each for the heated shoes and gloves by the standard snap electrical connections. It was connected to an extension cord by an 18 inch "pigtail." The electrical circuitry was more reliable and was efficient down to –60°F. A rheostat at each crew station in the aircraft controlled the suit's temperature. During aircraft warm up the electric suit extension plug was plugged into the heating outlet on the left side of suit. The left outlet operated on a rheostat and the right was a full current outlet. To test the suit the rheostat was to be turned on to check heating and then turned down. The heated glove and felt liner plugs were to be checked for proper connection to the outlets on the heated flying suit that supplied the current. In October 1944 the snap electrical connections on the previous suits were replaced with the improved bayonet and the new suit was designated as the F-3A, but had the standard electrical snap receptacle for the chest connection to the electrically heated lens for the B-8 goggle and oxygen mask.

Gloves

Winter Gloves

The A-9 winter glove was standardized in mid-1935, and the improved A-9A was introduced in April 1944 and remained in service until the end of the war. The type A-9A was a gauntlet mitten-type with a thumb and forefinger that could be worn with rayon inner gloves if the electrically heated gloves were not needed. It had a goat, pony, and later deerskin outer shell and a lamb shearling lining and large cuff. The A-9A could be worn over the electrically heated gloves if they were large enough.

Rayon Liner Glove

Thin rayon (or rarely silk) gloves were to be worn under winter gloves or the electrically heated gloves for extra warmth and to protect fingers from freezing to metal when the heavy outer gloves had to be removed temporarily to do more exacting manipulations.

Electrically Heated Gloves

Electrically heated gloves dated back to the heated glove inserts devised by the French and used by the U.S. Air Service in WWI. The Type E-1 electric glove was a five-finger glove with a goatskin or pony hide leather outer shell and a knit wool lining. The 24-volt system had wire heating elements sewed between the shell and lining and was designed to be worn with the original F-1 heated flying suit. The E-1 was not sturdy or reliable, and was replaced with another heavier five-finger leather gauntlet with a woolen lining to be used with both the new F-2 and F-3 electric suits. This glove had its wiring placed over the back of the hand and fingers and was sandwiched between two layers of the knit lining. The early gloves were connected electrically to the arms of the F-1 and F-2 suits by snap or stud fasteners, and in October 1944 the improved bayonet-type fasteners were introduced. By November 1944 there were over 280,000 pairs of these gloves on procurement and modifications were made to the durability, flexibility, and heating wiring throughout the war.

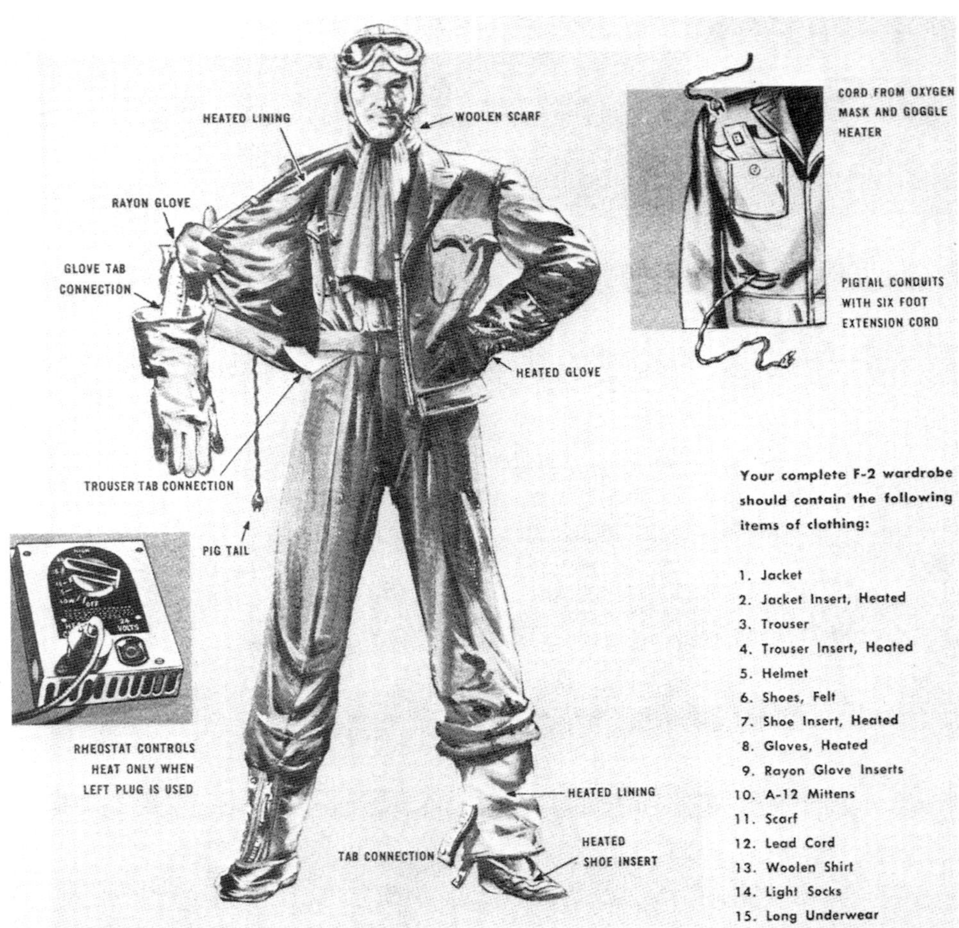


**Electrically-Heated Flying Suit** (USAAF)

Footwear

The stock low cut, rubber sole, leather shoe was usually worn in the warm Pacific, but the following shoes and boots were on the equipment list for use in the colder ETO.

A-6 Shearling Shoe

It was found through experience that a flying shoe not only needed to be warm, but also durable if a pilot shot down over enemy territory had to escape on foot. Along with the coveted Type A-2 leather flying jacket, the Type A-6 flying shoe and its modifications were the most well known pieces of personal flying equipment of WWII. The shoe was first introduced in 1937 as a ten inch high shearling shoe, zippered in front with a rubber sole, and basically did not change much throughout the war. The shoe could be worn alone as an intermediate temperature range boot or for wear over electric shoe or inserts. Among the modifications was the addition of straps (A-6A) near the top to improve its retention while parachuting, in sticky muddy conditions, and to cut off cold from entering through the top of the boot. The shoe was waterproofed by adding a rubberized area around and above the sole and weatherproofing the upper.

F-2 Electrically Heated Shoe Insert

The A-6 shoe was found to give inadequate warmth during high altitude missions, and the answer was the development of the F-2 type shoe insert that was designed for use in combination with the F-2 or F-3 heated flying suits. The F-2 shoe insert was worn over stockings, and when worn in combination with the A-6 shoe allowed the feet to breathe and not perspire, a condition that could be dangerous in low temperatures. The insert was made of gray felt whose seams were reinforced by webbing and had an elastic front section so it could be easily slipped over the foot. Four wires were fastened to the F-3 or F-3A flying suit at bayonet connections at a point above the inside top of the insert. These wires were sewed to the outside of the insert and two separate circuits ran parallel to each other around and under the insert. A double layer of felt protected the wiring in the sole.

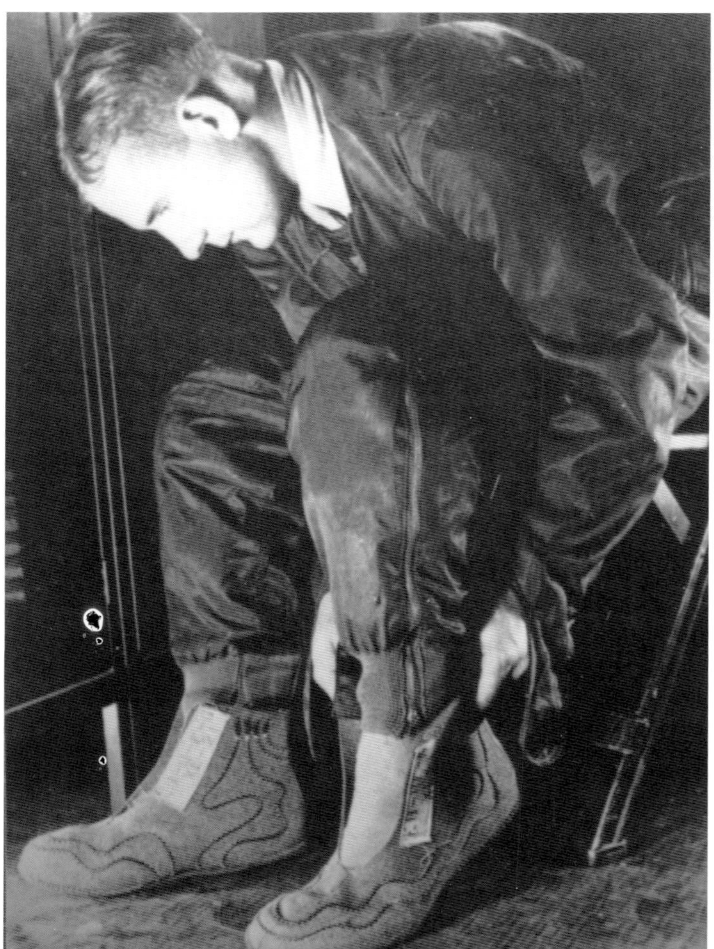

Electrically Heated Shoe Insert. (USAAF)

Well-protected gunner wearing a Flak Vest (M-1/M-2), Flak Aprons (M-3 to M-5), and Flak Helmet (M3, M4 and M5). (USAAF)

Q-1 Electrically Heated Shoe Insert

In late 1944 the Q-1 was developed for use with the variations of the F-2 and F-3 electric suits and the A-6 and A-6A shoes. The Q-1 was made of an inner and outer layer of nylon cloth that sandwiched a layer of cotton cloth. It had a nylon outer sole and a cotton duck insole. The foot entered the insert through an opening in its back and then was closed by a flap that was secured around the ankle and then tied tight with laces. The insert had four improved, more flexible electric heating wires that were sewed in two separate, parallel circuits into the cotton layer. The Q-1's wiring disbursement was an improvement over the F-2 insert, giving better heat supply to the vital toe area and also the heels. The Q-1 would be worn over

The value of the M1 Flak Vest is shown by the pieces of flak shrapnel dug out of its nylon canvas coat that contained manganese steel plates sewed into pockets (USAAF)

the standard Quarter Master Corps (QMC) issue leather shoes and woolen socks and then slipped into a pair of A-6 or A-6A overshoes.

Flak Suits and Helmets
M-1 and M-2 Flak Vest

The M-1 armored vest was standardized in October 1943 and was normally worn with the M-3/4/5 flak apron. It was a full vest, having front and rear armor fastened together at the shoulders by quick release dot fasteners. The vest was fabricated of overlapping two inch (20-gauge) .045 Hadfield manganese steel sewed into pockets attached to a nylon canvas backing. The vest weighed 17.375 pounds and covered 3.8 square feet. It was designed to be used especially by gunners but also by navigators, bombardiers, and radio operators who did not have armor-protected seats, or would move about the fuselage and thus be exposed to the danger of front and rear AA fire.

The M-2 armored vest was designed for pilots and other crewmen who sat in armored seats and were protected from the rear. It also was standardized in October 1943 with the M-1 vest. The M-2 was similar in construction to the M-1 but had an unarmored nylon back panel. The M-1 weighed 7.81 pounds and covered 1.45 square feet. It was ordinarily worn with the M-3 apron. The vests were delivered to the bomber before the mission and put on as the plane approached the target.

M-3 to M-5 Flak Aprons

The M-3 and M-4 aprons had the same construction as the M-1 vest. The M-3 weighed 4.875 pounds and covered 1.15 square feet. The M-4 weighed 7.125 pounds and covered 1.66 square feet. The vests and aprons were worn over all other flying equipment and were attached to one another by quick release fasteners. The M-3 attached to the front of either the M-1 or M-2 vest by three quick release fasteners. Tapes attached each section and connected the fasteners to a red strap placed at the wearer's waist. A quick tug at the strap released the vest and aprons to separate from each other and fall off the body. The M-5 apron was first developed as the T-12 in December 1943 and was made up of ten steel plates that had improved shapes and were hinged. The T-12 was modified into the T-13 that weighed about 14 pounds and covered 1.63 square feet and was standardized as the Armor, Flyer's, Groin, M-5 in March 1944. The M-5 was made in three sections so that the center section could be drawn up between the legs and the side sections were to lie over the thighs. It weighed 15.25 pounds and covered 3.72 square feet. The M-5 was attached to the vest by three dot fasteners, and tapes connected to a quick release strap. The airplane commander, co-pilot and flight engineer generally wore it.

M3, M4, and M5 Flak Helmets

In December 1943 the M3 airman's flak helmet was basically a direct development of the standard infantryman's M1 "steel pot" with the steel structure of the helmet cut away over the ears to accommodate earphones. The main difference was that there was no separate liner, as the suspension was attached to the steel shell and a hinge was welded to the helmet shell and a steel earflap was attached to cover the earphones. A web chinstrap was attached to the lower edge of the earflaps to hold them down. The olive drab M3 was fabricated from Hadfield manganese steel and weighed 3.188 pounds. The earphones were integrated into the regulation leather or fabric flying helmet to fit under the M3 shell.

The M4 was a product of the development of body armor and was standardized in December 1943. It was a quick release skullcap made from unjoined Hadfield manganese steel plates sewed into a fabric foundation. The helmet was covered by taut brown leather and had a chamois skin lining and a brown leather chinstrap with a buckle/dot fastener to hold it in place. Its advantages were it weighed a pound less than the M3 and was trimmed out over the ears to accommodate the unobstructed use of the earphones and radio headsets, and so could be worn over the summer or winter flying helmets and oxygen masks. The M4 was well suited for gunners and for crew positions where space was limited. The M4 continued to be modified during 1944 and continued until it was replaced by the M5 in January 1945.

The M5 was an independent development in the search for the ultimate armored steel aviator's helmet. The M4 was difficult to manufacture because of its overlapping steel plates and new research emphasized the development of a one-piece Hadfield manganese steel bowl with long hinged cheek plates riveted to the helmet. The cheek plates accommodated the earphones and had a fully adjustable "one size fits all" head suspension. The olive drab M-5 weighed 2.8 pounds and was the standard helmet for all crewmen except the top gunner station.

**Section 5: Miscellaneous Armament Installations**
**Floor and Tunnel Guns**

Douglas B-18 Bolo

The rear lower gun was mounted on the floor of the B-18 and fired through a small arc to the rear under the tail. To bring the gun into the firing position a catch was released on the window section of the door, the gun stop was raised, the hold down catches released, the gun placed in its firing position, the gun stop lowered and fastened, and the door was raised by means of a crank located on the left hand side of the fuselage. The molybdenum steel gun stop regulated the firing angle of the gun to prevent hitting the bottom of the empennage and tail wheel. To stow the gun the gun stop was unfastened and raised and the stowage latch engaged with the latch on the aluminum sleeve located on the gun barrel, the hold down latches fastened, gun stop lowered, and the door lowered, and the window pulled forward until held by a catch.

Douglas B-23 Dragon

Defense against an attack from below was provided by a .30 caliber machine gun firing through the ventral floor hatch with an 80° conical angle of fire. The gun was sited in the floor inboard of the entrance door of the main compartment. This gun was mounted in a ring that rotated 360° degrees and could be tilted to allow a greater rearward angle of fire. The ring was mounted on steel trunnions that had a galvanic reaction with the aluminum floor, and after a while the corroded mount would tear out of the floor. The gun was supplied with 600 rounds of ammunition in six 100 round boxes located on the right hand side of the compartment and just forward of the gun ring.

Boeing B-17B Flying Fortress

The Model 299, Y1B-17, and B-17B had a belly gun blister in which the gunner kneeled inside the aircraft. The gunner had a very difficult time maneuvering his single .30 caliber machine gun through the limited viewing area. This arrangement was replaced by the ventral "bath tub" type position in the B-17C.

**Floor and Tunnel Gun Gallery**

**Douglas B-18 Bolo** (USAAF)

**Douglas B-23 Dragon** (USAAF)

**Consolidated PBY Catalina** (USN)

**Douglas A-20 Havoc** (USAAF0

**Boeing Y1B-17** (USAAF)

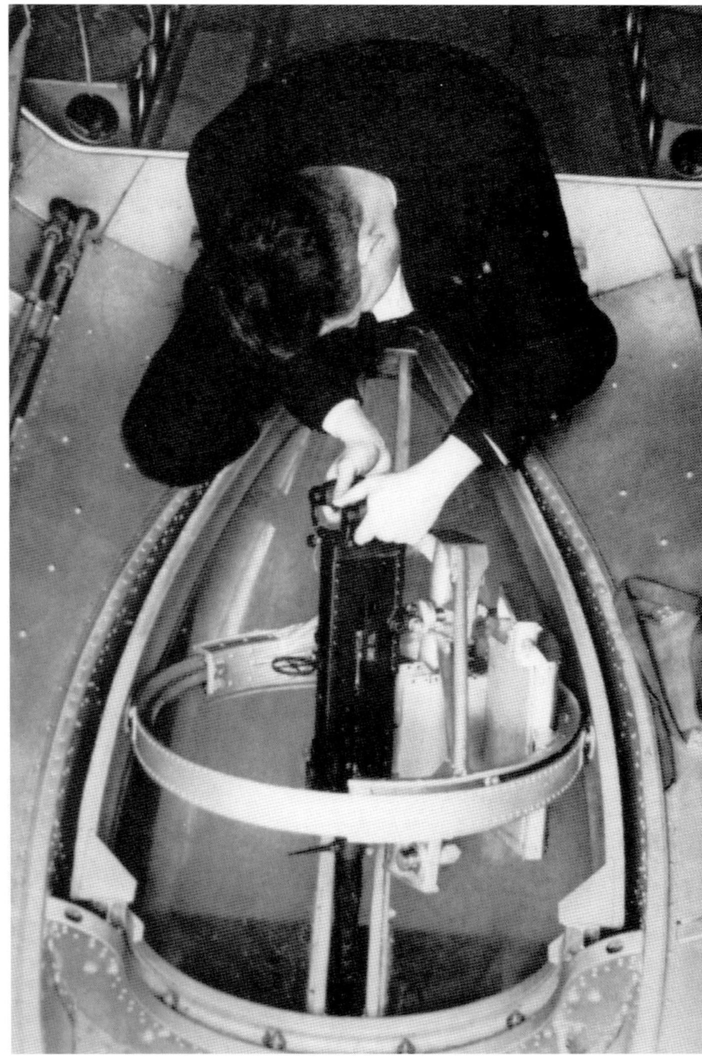

**Boeing B-17B Flying Fortress** (USAAF)

**Consolidated B-24D Liberator** (USAAF)

**Martin PBM-3 Mariner** (USN)

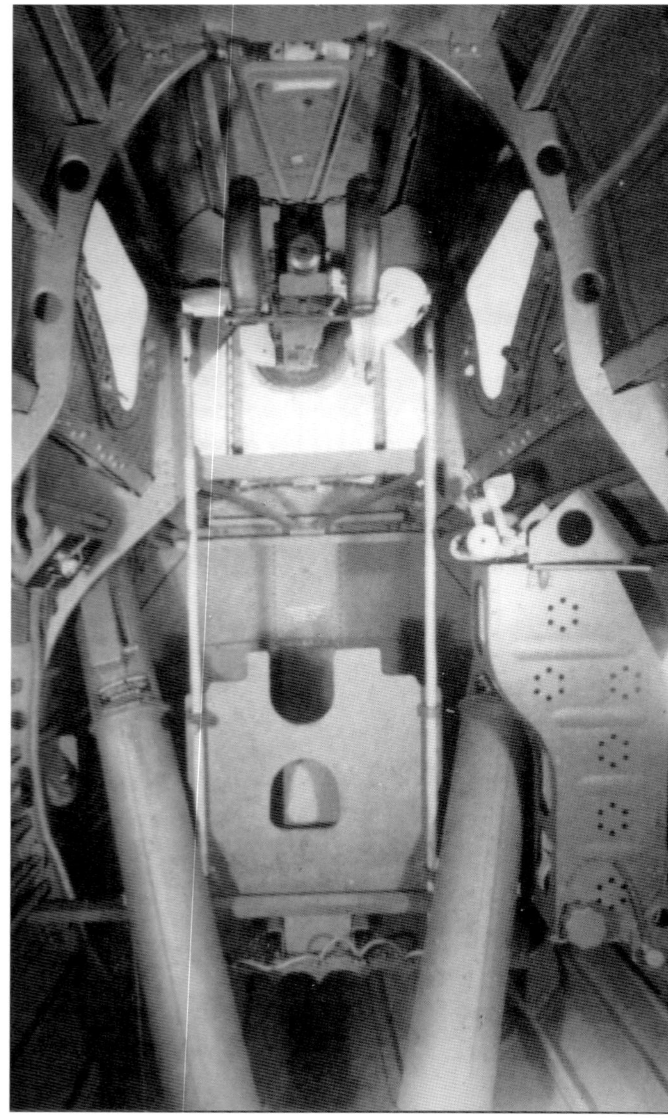

**Grumman TBM-2 Avenger** (USN)

Consolidated B-24D Liberator
The tunnel gun on the B-24D was mounted to fire downward through the rear entrance hatch. Ammunition for the tunnel gun was contained in three cans that were stowed on the left fuselage above the small scanning window. From the 77th onward the B-24D did not have waist or tunnel guns as a Bendix remote control retractable turret was installed to replace the tunnel gun.

Douglas A-20 Havoc
The A-20 and DB-7 had a single machine gun mounted aft of the bomb bay in the entrance and emergency escape hatch for gunners in the aft fuselage. Before the A-20C-20 a gun position through the hatch and another through the ventral tunnel was provided for a gunner using one .30 caliber Browning (or two gunners in the French and British D-7 versions). Subsequent to the A-20C a .50 caliber gun was used by a gunner.

Martin B-26B Marauder
The B-26B began production in May 1942 with a .30 caliber ventral tunnel gun which was ineffective and replaced by two .50s firing through waist windows.

Consolidated PBY Catalina
All models of the PBY had a single .30 caliber machine gun that could be mounted in the underside of the rear fuselage to provide defensive fire to the rear. The gunner needed to fire this gun from a kneeling or prone position. This tunnel gun could be used to suppress AA fire as the Catalina passed over its target, but the gun was too light and its field of fire too restricted to be effective against enemy aircraft. When not in use the gun's mounting frame could be swung up to the port side of the fuselage at 90° and a tapered hatch was slid over the gun tunnel. On PBY-5As and all subsequent Catalinas a ball mount was fitted in a small blister window on each side of the fuselage so that the tunnel gun could be quickly installed to fire in the threatened area. The gun was fed by attachable 100 round ammunition cans stowed on racks near the gun. Other USN aircraft (the Martin PBM-3 Mariner and Grumman TBM-2 Avenger) also utilized ventral floor positions.

**B-17 Ventral Bathtub**
Beginning with the B-17C, the ventral gun blister was replaced by a larger metal "bathtub" housing carrying a single .50 inch machine gun. This gun position resembled that of the *Luftwaffe* He-111, where the gunner kneeled on a padded floor and fired below and aft over a very limited field of vision.

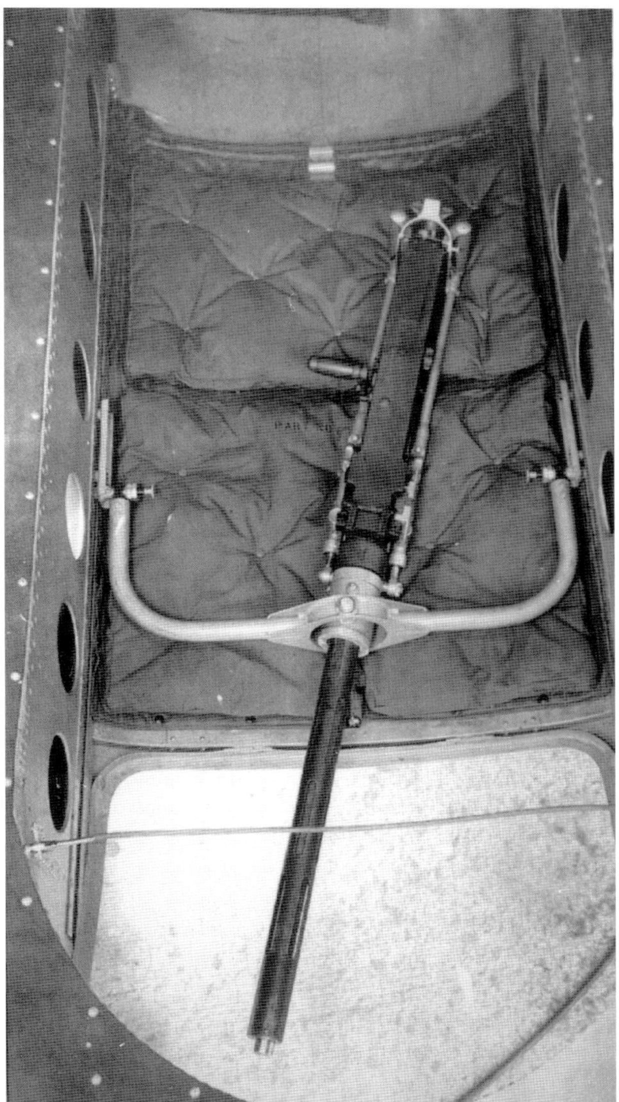

**B-17 Ventral Bath Tub Exterior and Interior Views** (USAAF)

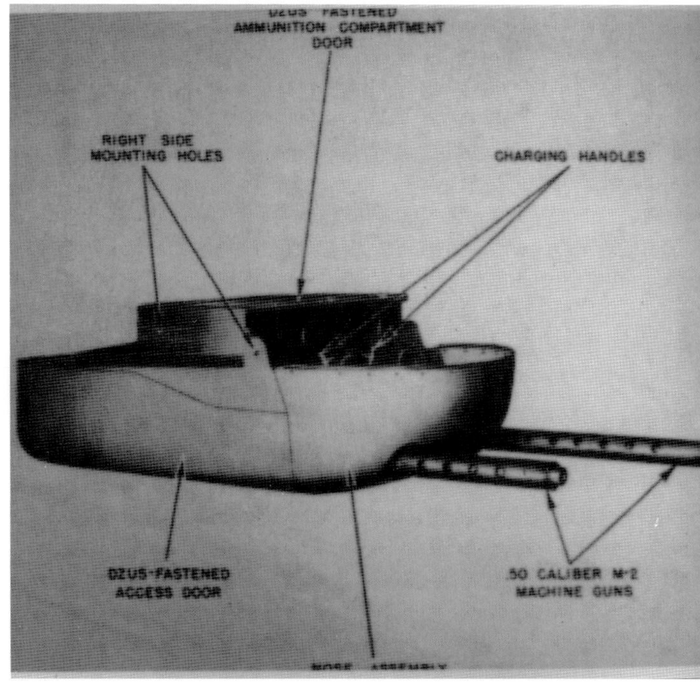


**B-25 Hatch Gun** (USAAF)

On the B-17E the Bendix remotely controlled, power-operated ventral turret replaced the bathtub turret.

**B-25 Hatch Gun**

An experimental hatch gun pack was developed by Paul "Pappy" Gunn as part of the 5AF B-25C/D strafer program. Gunn mounted three guns to the underside of the fuselage between the bomb bay and forward access hatch. The blast effect on the fuselage structure and belt feed problems caused the project to be abandoned in the field. However, probably due to feedback on the Gunn concept, North American developed a 325 pound hatch blister assembly mounting two .50 caliber machine guns and 225 rpg. Dubbed the "Hatch Gun," the unit with guns aimed forward was installed directly into the forward access hatch opening and was retained by the same pins that retained the hatch door. To protect against firing blast, sheets of stainless steel were mounted over 1/8 inch sponge rubber. The guns could be serviced and ammunition reloaded from inside the aircraft. Because the hatch gun was installed in the forward hatch, the crew was forced to enter the aircraft through the aft hatch and then over the bomb bay to the flight deck. Although the Hatch gun proved to be reliable in tests it was decided that the 14 forward firing guns of the B-25H would be sufficient.

**B-23 Roof Window Gun Position**

One gun was located on a swivel mount fixed to the aft fuselage bulkhead and could be fired through two sliding side windows or through a sliding roof window in an arrangement that expected one gunner to cover three different areas. When aimed through the upper window the gun had a 110° angle of fire left to right and a fore and aft angle of fire of 140°. Through the side windows it had a 115° degree up and down angle of fire and 140° fore and aft.

**B-17 Radio Compartment Gun Position**

Beginning with the B-17C the dorsal blister located at the radio operator's position behind the pilot's compartment was replaced by a flush panel into which a single socket for a 0.50 inch machine gun was cut. The gun was

**B-23 Roof Window Gun Position** (USAAF)

mounted on a ball and socket inside a transparent hatch with a removable Plexiglas panel that was faired with the contour of the top of the fuselage in the radio compartment and the gunner was protected by a wind deflector. The chief change in the B-17E was the much needed increase in armament, as the early B-17s lacked powered turrets and a tail gun installation. A new tail gun installation, a Sperry dorsal and ventral remote turret, was added, but the waist guns and original dorsal radio operator's gun were preserved, as was the nose armament. Early B-17Gs had a radio compartment .50 installation that were similar to late Fs, but this was changed to an enclosed style, where the hatch did not have to be opened to fire. However, this enclosed configuration further reduced the movement of the gun. The radio compartment gun position was always considered to be ineffective due to its limited field of fire. On the last production batches (B-17G-105 and -110-BO, B-17G-75 to -85-DL, and B-17G-85 to -110-VE) the radio compartment gun was deleted.

**B-17 Radio Compartment Gun Position Exterior and Interior Views** (USAAF)

**Douglas SBD Dauntless** (USN)

**Douglas A-26 Invader** (USAAF)

**Bomber Wing Gun Pods**

There are some photos of Navy SBD dive bombers armed with under wing gun pods containing two .50 caliber machine guns but there is no information available on this installation.

The early A-26B had two or four .50 caliber guns mounted in pods under each wing. But after the B-26B-45 Block three .50s were mounted in each wing replacing the drag-producing pods. The B-25 was fitted with experimental underwing gun pods but there are no records available on their development.

**Section 6: XB-40 and XB-41 Bomber Escort Gunships**

**Reed Project**

Once 8th Air Force B-17Es went into action over Europe, a number of technical and operational problems inevitably arose concerning armament and crew organization. These problems were dealt with by Maj. Robert Reed, head of the engineering section at Bovingdon, who began a study to make recommendations on their solution. By late January 1943 the study was ready and identified the problems as lack of forward fire power, ball turret insufficiencies, oxygen supply difficulties to the turrets, tail heavy unbalance, and crew organization. Reed was so efficient that in February 1943 the VIII Bomber command decided to send him and a B-17E (41-9112) back to Wright Field to supervise a modification project to identify and rectify deficiencies of B-17s coming off the assembly lines.

By September the Reed Project modified and improved the B-17E in many aspects, with the bomber becoming lighter, faster, and better performing. The ten man crew was reduced by two with the waist guns eliminated. Also, the functions of the bombardier and navigator were combined. All radio equipment was moved to the nose compartment, where the radio operator served as the nose gunner. Only one gunner was now stationed in the waist area to operate the new dorsal position. With the eliminations and rearrangements Reed's B-17 had an ideal center of gravity and weighed 1,000 pounds less, both of which gave it better handling characteristics than the standard B-17E. However, speed and power requirements of Reed's aircraft were about the same due to its various gun protuberances.

Among the modifications to Dreamboat was this pagoda-like compartment in an under nose blister which was the forerunner to the B-17G chin turret. (USAAF)

The major modifications were made to the aircraft's armament. Improved sighting optics were added to each gun position. Bullet proof glass and armor plate were added to protect the gunners. The nose gunner was separated from the bombardier, who was now positioned in an individual pagoda-like compartment in an under nose blister. The Sperry dorsal turret was replaced by the lighter (by 120 pounds), larger, more comfortable (as the gunner could sit) Martin turret. The radio operator's top hatch gun was replaced by twin .50s located in an exposed, dorsal power-boosted mount that was designed to replace the waist guns, which were eliminated.

In February 1943 Maj. Robert Reed was appointed to study the problems encountered with the B-17E; particularly defensive armament. Reed modified this B-17E named Dreamboat as part of the "Reed Project." (USAAF)

The new position was open and protected by a windshield, and gave the gunner a much wider field of fire. The reliability of the Sperry ball turret was improved and was enlarged so that the gunner was able to wear a B-8 backpack parachute. To gain this added room, the ball position was supplied with an external ammunition supply that was to be adequate for an entire mission without reloading. To remedy the chronic stoppages the ejected links were carried along short, straight chutes. To aid in the clearance of blockages or make adjustments this ball turret could be raised 90°. The field of fire of the tail turret was greatly increased by six times to 180° azimuth, 70° elevation, and 40° depression.

Reed flew this modified B-17 named *Dreamboat* back to England for a critique on the changes by 8AF engineering and by group commanders. During the fall the bomber was flown to the First and Third Air Division bases for comments and suggestions. The major criticisms were that the nose area was considered too confined and a second Martin dorsal turret was suggested to replace the radio area twin .50s. *Dreamboat* visited numerous bases in the UK for many months so that German intelligence could not help but to discover the "B-40 bristling with two dozen guns." The findings of the Reed Project were not implemented, as the wide-ranging modifications would have slowed B-17 production, but its suggested improvements were included in the AAF's next generation of bombers, the B-29 and B-32.

In August 1942 the lack of long-range escort fighters and the inadequate defensive armament on American bombers led to a discussion of the need to convert B-17s and B-24s into "bomber escort" gunships to be designated the XB-40 and XB-41, respectively, to fly in and protect American bomber formations.

**Boeing XB-40 and YB-40**

A technical study was done by Brig.Gen. Muir Fairchild and XB-40 and -41 planners to establish minimum requirements for a bomber escort. The initial report suggested that the tail gun should carry enough rounds (800 rounds) to fire continuously for four minutes; the two dorsal and the ball turrets were to be able to fire for two minutes (400 rpg); the waist guns for one minute (200 rpg); and the chin turret for 30 seconds (100 rounds). Soon combat reports determined that forward defensive fire was the single most significant weakness of the B-17 and B-24, and the Fairchild Study then fixed the final escort ammunition loading at 800 rounds (four minutes) for the tail gun; 250 rounds (1 minute 15 seconds firing time) for the waist guns; 550 rounds (2 minutes 45 seconds firing time) for the ball turret; 400 rounds (2 minutes firing time) for the two dorsal turrets; and the chin position ammunition capacity was increased to 400 rounds to fire for two minutes.

The Vega Division of Lockheed was contracted to convert a standard B-17F (41-24341, the second Boeing-built B-17F-1) into the prototype XB-40 escort configuration, which was to begin testing in September 1942 at Burbank. The conversion was to add twin .50s in another dorsal turret in the radio compartment, a chin turret with twin .50s under the nose, and the waist armament was upgraded to twin .50s. The normal dorsal, ventral, and tail turrets were retained, giving the XB-40 a total of 14 .50 machine guns. The bomb bays were modified to serve as storage areas for ammunition. The standard ammunition load was 11,135 rounds, which could be increased to 17,265 rounds with a reduced fuel load. This compared to 3,400 rounds of .50 caliber and 500 rounds of .30 caliber for early B-17Fs without radio compartment or cheek guns, or to the 4,625 rounds carried by early B-17Gs without cheek guns. The XB-40 could carry a small bomb load on short missions, and so the bombardier's station and Norden Bombsight, which would cause the bombardier/gunner problems in operating the chin guns, was retained. To resolve this problem a reflector gunsight was suspended at eye level from the bombardier compartment ceiling and the control handles and triggers were mounted on a column hinged on the floor to the

The Vega Division of Lockheed was contracted to convert a standard B-17F into the prototype XB-40 escort configuration that was bristling with twin .50s in another dorsal turret added in the radio compartment, a chin turret with twin .50s under the nose, and the waist armament was upgraded to twin .50s. The normal dorsal, ventral, and tail turrets were retained giving the XB-40 a total of 14 .50 machine guns. (USAAF)

The twin .50s in the waist position, the normal dorsal turret and the additional turret in the radio compartment are seen in this photo. (USAAF)

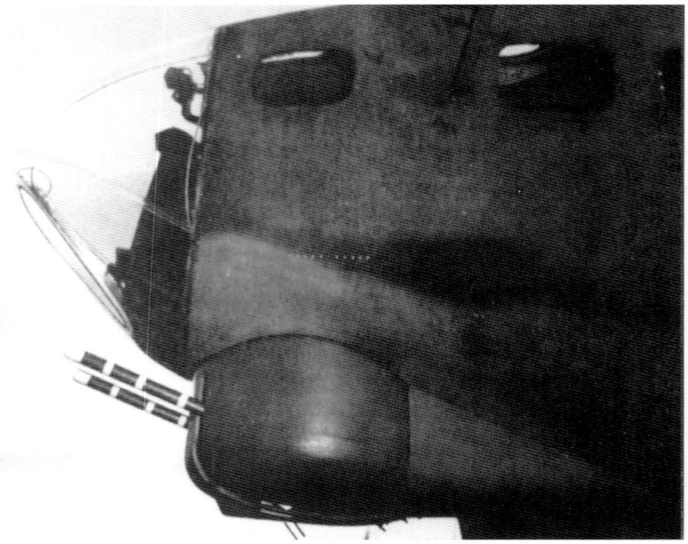

The chin turret installation was retained but the cheek guns were deleted on the XB-40. (USAAF)

bombardier/gunner's right. The column could be swung to the centerline and locked into place when the guns were to be used.

In October the AAF ordered 13 YB-40s (the Y designation was for "service test") for combat trials, while another six were ordered as replacements in January 1943. The 13 YB-40s were Vega-built B-17F-10-VEs modified at the Tulsa Douglas Modification Center and were completed for delivery by late March 1943. Various armament configurations were tried that differed from the XB-40: four gun nose and tail turrets, 20 and 40mm cannons, and some were reported to carry up to 30 guns of varying calibers mounted in multiple hand-held and power turrets (via Joe Baugher). Generally, the YB-40s maintained the armament configuration of the prototype, but with the waist and tail positions hydraulically boosted to make them easier to handle and also steadier when firing. The tail gun ring and bead sight was replaced by a reflector sight. Ammunition was stowed throughout the aircraft, but mainly forward to balance the center of gravity. The YB-40 had a gross weight of 58,000 pounds, which was 10,000 more than a loaded late model B-17F. The increased armament and armor plate protection had a detrimental effect on performance, as the YB-40 had a maximum speed of 296 mph at 25,000 feet compared to 325 mph for the B-17F, while its service ceiling of 29,400 feet compared to 37,500 feet for the F.

The crews were trained and the aircraft were flown to the UK via the North Atlantic Ferry Route in early May 1943, with 12 YB-40s arriving on 8 May after one crash landed. The bombers were assigned to the 327BS/92BG, and the first several weeks were spent in flight testing and making theater modifications. The YB-40 was not equipped with the navigator's side nose gun and, when considering the aircraft's tail heaviness, it was decided to add this gun to increase the armament to 16 guns. The radio room Martin turret was protected by an armor plated cylinder that extended to within two feet of the floor, and the gunner had to get down on his hands and knees to wriggle up into his seat. The chin turret was hydraulic-electric powered, with the gunner using a remote reflector sight located on a control arm located in the nosepiece.

The YB-40 crew was comprised of a pilot, co-pilot, navigator, chin gunner, forward dorsal turret gunner, aft dorsal turret gunner, left and right waist gunner, and tail gunner. There was no radio operator, as VHF communications were conducted by the pilot and co-pilot. The navigator was to operate the chin gun turret in order to allow one crewman to serve as an ammunition supplier to all gun positions.

Seven YB-40s flew their first mission with the 327BS as escort aircraft to flank the combat wing leaders during an attack on St. Nazaire on 27 May 1943. The mission exposed minor problems with the waist and tail gun feeds and ammunition supplies but a major problem appeared. The aircraft was very tail heavy, and its reduced performance made it impossible to sustain enough speed to maintain its place in the formation, especially after the formation had dropped its bombs. Additionally, the YB-40s rarely used all their ammunition, which further slowed them on the mission return leg. The YB-40s flew five more missions during late June with one being lost to flak.

The YB-40s were then sent out in their own formation to lure in unsuspecting *Luftwaffe* interceptors. After four of these gunship-only missions, Col. William Reid, CO of the 92BG, reported that combat statistics showed that massed YB-40s' fire power advantage actually decreased from 20% to 10%, and any effectiveness was mainly due to the chin guns. At the time three quarters of the *Luftwaffe* attacks were frontal, and the additional rear firing armament was considered ineffective. Reid believed that any advantages of the YB-40 in luring *Luftwaffe* fighters was offset by placing the bomber crews in danger without delivering a bomb load and recommended that no more YB-40s be accepted by the 8AF. The YB-40s were credited with only five victories and two probables before the 327BS transferred their six YB-40s to the 91BG and 303BG, but there are no existing records of them being used in combat by those units.

The aircraft were considered for combat in the Pacific for long-range reconnaissance but were never utilized. Four of these YB-40s remaining in America had all armor and armament removed and then were assigned for training purposes as TB-40s and used as B-17F trainers. Other stateside YB-40s retained their chin guns, but had their radio compartment turret and waist twin .50s exchanged for single .50s and were converted to conventional bombing B-17s. However, YB-40 42-5833 was extensively modified to solve the combat problems of the first 13. The aircraft had a new tail position, which had hand-held guns located in a cupola that gave a 90° cone of fire and was sighted by an N-8 reflector gunsight. It also had a modified Bendix chin turret and an increased ammunition supply to the two dorsal turrets. Armor was deleted and rearranged, giving the gunship better weight distribution and flight characteristics. In October 1943 this aircraft was flown to the UK, where it was tested and found to be too heavy, and not having any bombing provisions became inactive. Although the YB-40 was unsuccessful in combat, many of its innovations were adapted for use on the B-17G, such as the chin turret, increased ammunition supply, and improved crew armor protection.

**Consolidated XB-41**

Like the Boeing B-17 XB-40 gunship adaptation, the Consolidated XB-41 was a heavily-armed long-range escort intended to provide escort for bombers attacking heavily defended Germany. The solitary XB-41 was a San Diego-built Consolidated B-24D-CO (41-11822) converted by the Consolidated Fort Worth plant and delivered to Eglin Field, Florida, on 29 January 1943 for testing.

In late September 1942, the Director of Military Requirements requested the Materiel Command to convert 13 B-24Ds into service test YB-41s for use in the ETO. A Bendix remotely-controlled turret was added in a chin position under the nose, and the nose glazing was modified so that the gunner had an unobstructed field of vision. However, no cheek guns were

Like the Boeing B-17 XB-40 gunship adaptation, the Consolidated XB-41 was a heavily-armed (14 .50 caliber machine guns) long-range escort intended to provide escort for bombers attacking heavily defended Germany. (USAAF)

Unlike the B-17 XB-40 the waist position of the XB-41 had its twin .50s protected by an enclosed slotted cover. (USAAF)

incorporated as on the later B-24D. The original Martin A-3 power turret behind the cockpit was modified so that it could be raised during flight to increase its field of fire, then lowered to decrease aerodynamic drag when not in use. A second Martin A-3 power turret was added to the dorsal fuselage just aft of the trailing edge of the wing. A pair of power-boosted .50 inch machine guns was added at each waist position, replacing the original single flexible mounts. The added guns increased total armament to 14 .50 inch machine guns. A total of 12,420 rounds of ammunition were available, including 4,000 reserve rounds carried in a box installed in the forward bomb bay. The additional weight of armor, guns, and ammunition brought the XB-41's gross weight to 63,000 pounds, which was 8,000 pounds heavier than a standard B-24D.

Flight tests conducted at Eglin during early 1943 determined that the additional weight caused serious deficiencies in performance, including an inferior rate of climb and reduced airspeed and service ceiling. The center of gravity was located too far aft, causing the bomber to be unstable in flight. To remedy the CG problem Consolidated suggested that an Emerson nose turret be installed. The port waist gun position had originally been enclosed by a Plexiglas dome that caused serious optical distortion and was removed. Because of these problems, the XB-41 was declared operationally unsuitable on 21 March 1943, and the proposed 13 YB-41 Liberator conversions were cancelled.

Despite the cancellation Consolidated continued to modify and upgrade the XB-41 prototype by outfitting the aircraft with wide-blade propellers, by decreasing its weight by removing some of the armor, and by improving the CG without resorting to the Emerson nose turret. On 28 July 1943 the XB-41 was returned to Eglin for more tests that found the stability problem had been alleviated, but also found the aircraft was still beset with poor maneuverability and was 15 mph slower than normal B-24s. Meanwhile, the slow and cumbersome Boeing YB-40s were flying combat in Europe and were unable to maintain formation after the conventional B-17s dropped their bombs. The XB-40 combat experience and further negative XB-41 tests demonstrated that the bomber escort premise was fundamentally unsound, and on 5 January 1944 further work on the XB-41 was abandoned. The sole XB-41 was later redesignated as a TB-24D and was used as an instructional airframe for training Liberator mechanics.

# Part Seven
## Fighter Armament

# 1

# Wing Armament

Fuselage-mounted guns in single-engine fighters were fixed guns delivering semi-automatic fire through a synchronizing gear mechanism attached to the engine, while wing guns delivered fully automatic fire through remote-control solenoids operating the trigger gear. When operating the wing guns were rigidly fixed in position, but the actual mounting could permit elevation and depression and a lateral movement of from 1° to 2°, depending upon the wing station where they were mounted. This permitted adjustment (harmonization) on the ground for various combat objectives and assured accuracy of fire after the guns were installed, tested, and fired.

The .50 machine gun had two points for a trunnion and post mounting via a pintle and trunnion pin or a bolt. The method of attachment varied according to the type of wing in which the guns were installed, whether box beam truss with two main spars running across the wing or another type of construction. Fighter aircraft wings usually were of a size that permitted the .50 caliber gun to be readily attached both to the fore and aft webs of the beam, allowing the loads comprising gun weight, and especially recoil, to be sustained by the entire beam. At some wing stations, where very little space was available due to the positioning of the ammunition boxes or to the necessity of retaining accessibility to the guns and ammunition boxes, the gun barrel protruded from the leading edge of the wing, and the gun

The P-40B model had two synchronized cowl-mounted .50s and six .30s in the wings. When the B was upgraded with an Allison A-1710F engine, its larger size eliminated the space for the two .50 caliber cowling guns and synchronizer. The four wing .30s were also removed and the wing modified to make room for four .50 caliber machine guns and later six in this P-40E. (Author)

When loading ammunition into to a fighter wing there were three or four longitudinal partitioned ammunition bays located outboard of the guns parallel to the leading edge of wing. Large hinged ammunition access covers covered these ammunition bays. (USAAF)

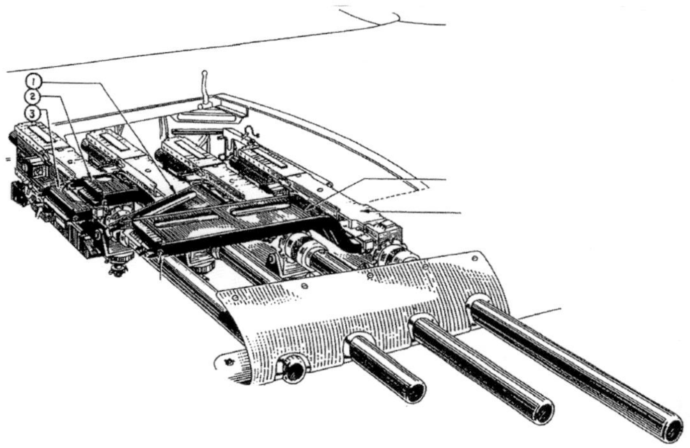


Technical drawing showing the staggered arrangement of the four guns in the wing of a P-47 allowing the ammunition belts better access for feeding. (USAAF)

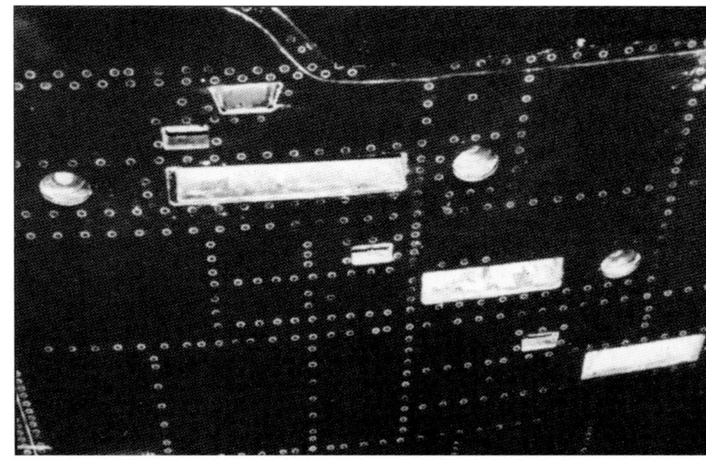

Staggered spent cartridge chutes on the underside of the wing of a F6F Hellcat. (USN)

had to be supported or attached to the web only. In this case, a false beam had to be built between the rib sections on either side of the gun and the ribs themselves strengthened by stiffeners and similar devices. At other stations, the gun was mounted far forward of the trailing edge and was not supported on the beam at all, but the front trunnions were supported between two special ribs to the rear on a false beam, aft of the rear web.

When loading ammunition into a fighter wing there were three or four longitudinal partitioned ammunition bays located outboard of the guns parallel to the leading edge of the wing. Large hinged ammunition access covers covered these ammunition bays. The ammunition was removed from its storage container and loaded into the guns. Rigid feed chutes and rollers aided in feeding the linked ammunition from the bays with the ends of the ammunition belt fed over the roller and into the top of the chute and pulled down into the gun, and the end of the belt was loaded into the feedway. Often the armorers placed a strip of tape over the muzzles of each gun to keep dirt from entering on takeoff.

### Harmonization

Clustering all the armament in the fighter's nose so that guns were close to the aircraft's centerline caused the bullet's trajectory to be parallel to the course of the aircraft, and thus there was no harmonization problem. However, on a single-engined aircraft these guns had to be synchronized to fire through the propeller arc, which increased weight, reduced the rate of fire, and required specialized ammunition. Not all guns could be synchronized, as their mechanisms were incompatible. An alternative was for a single gun to fire through the hollow axis of the propeller with the penalty of lessened fire power. Nose-mounted guns not firing through the propeller arc (e.g. the P-38) did not suffer from having their useful ranges limited by pattern convergence or slowed by the synchronizing mechanism, meaning good pilots could shoot at substantially longer ranges and reliably hit targets at any range up to 1,000 yards. Guns mounted in the wings outboard of the propeller arc needed to have the trajectories set up to converge on a location in the distance called the "convergence zone," usually between 250 and 300 yards to be effective. American fighter aircraft usually mounted four to eight .50 caliber machine guns in their wings.

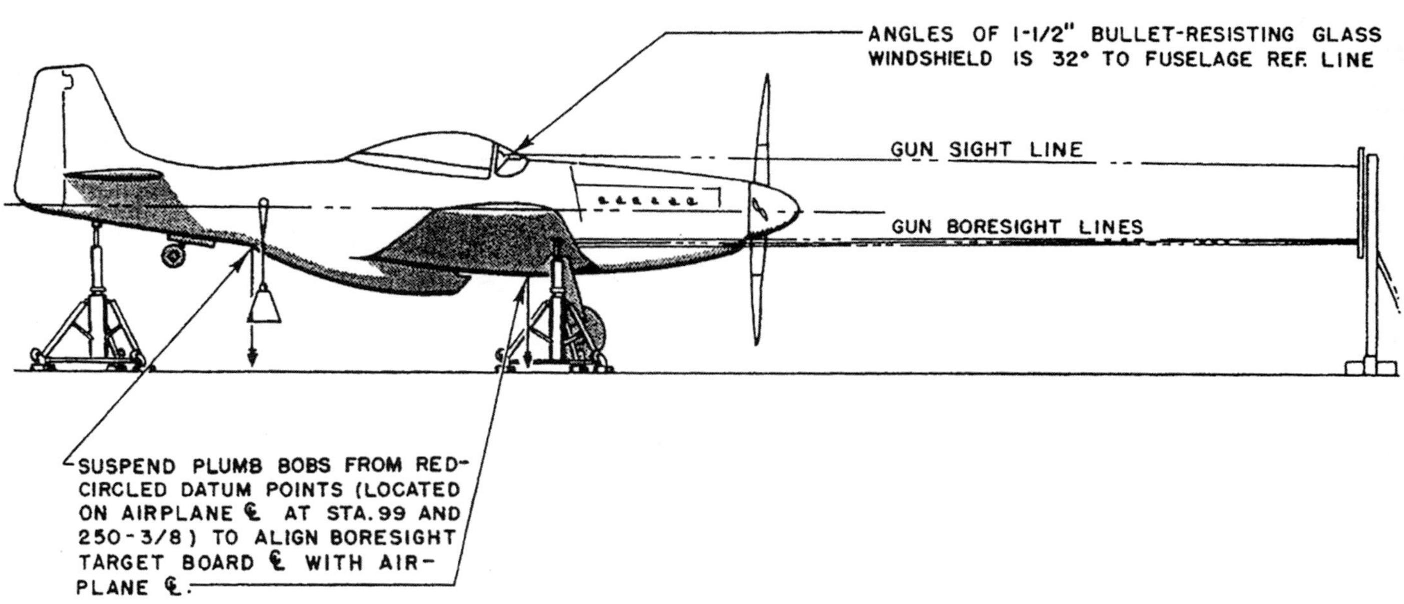


**Fighter Gun Harmonization** (USAAF)

Fighter Aircraft

Boresighting was the alignment of one gun, while harmonization was aligning the path of the rounds fired from all guns. Harmonization was accomplished by one of two methods. One method was to converge the four, six, or eight wing machine guns to a predetermined point (typically 250 to 300 yards) ahead of the aircraft called a cone of fire. However, at a three mil setting the convergence pattern of all the guns at 300 yards was about three feet in diameter, which was difficult for the average pilot and resulted in excessive dispersion at most ranges. The second method—a remedy to gain wider bullet dispersion—was to boresight each pair of guns at different ranges, generally 250, 300, and 350 yards for outboard, middle, and inboard guns, respectively. This method was termed "pattern harmonization," which was innately less damaging than a tighter cone of fire, but the greater dispersion of bullets made the probability of obtaining hits on the target more likely. Against Japanese aircraft that lacked pilot armor protection and self-sealing fuel tanks a few hits could be lethal.

Strafing Aircraft

The guns of the fighter were harmonized for rounds to converge at a point ahead of the aircraft where the rounds would impact the target together. The harmonization point set for air-to-air combat at 250 yards was acceptable when strafing individual targets, such as soft or armored vehicles. Low-level strafing attacks at this harmonization were risky to the pilot, as apart from the apparent danger from AA and small arms fire, a small maneuvering miscalculation or target-fixation could cause his fighter to crash into the target or into nearby trees or other obstructions. If the target were carrying ammunition or explosives it could explode in the path of the attacker. Later in the war when air-to-air combat diminished and strafing became the fighter's primary mission gun harmonization was set to converge at a longer distance. Again, the clustered nose weapons concentrated their fire, making the aircraft effective for strafing.

# 2

# Nose Armament and Synchronization Gear

There are three fighter nose armament configurations: a gun mounted with the barrel firing through the propeller hub; gun(s) mounted in the nose cowling requiring a synchronization gear to fire through the spinning propeller arc; and guns mounted in a nose that did mount a propeller (e.g. P-38). The advantage of gun placement in the nose of an aircraft was that it gave greater accuracy, since there was no necessity for their trajectories to converge towards the pilot's line of sight. Except for dispersion and trajectory curvature, the gun pattern was identical at all ranges, concentrating fire in a small area.

**Nose Armament Gallery**

The armament of the **Bell P-39Airacobra** was to be the heaviest carried by an American production fighter at the time; replacing the standard two rifle caliber .30 caliber machine guns that armed pursuit aircraft. The YP-39 service test aircraft was fitted with a 37mm cannon and two .30 and two .50 caliber machine guns in the nose which was to become the armament configuration of the production P-39C. (USAAF)

The **Seversky P-35** was a radial engined pursuit aircraft armed with the traditional pair of guns, a .30 and .50 Browning, mounted on top of the cowling and firing through the propeller. (USAAF)

The **Curtiss P-40** was originally produced in April 1940 equipped with a pair of synchronized .50s in the cowling and two .30s in the wings. The P-40D was upgraded with an Allison A-1710F engine, whose size eliminated the space for the two .50 caliber cowling guns and synchronizer. (USAAF)

In 1940, the 37mm M4 cannon in the **Lockheed P-38E** was replaced by a 20mm Hispano M1 cannon (150 rounds) to complement four .50 caliber machine guns (500 rpg) which was o become the standard Lightning armament. (USAAF)

In the early models of the **Grumman TBF** the pilot controlled a single .30 caliber machine gun in the starboard engine cowl with the ammunition box being stored under the port cowl. This light gun was intended to suppress enemy return fire but was grossly inadequate and on the TBF-1Cs was replaced by a .50 caliber Browning installed in each wing. (USN)

**Synchronization Gear**

The synchronization gear has often been incorrectly referred to as the interrupter gear. The synchronization gear was a triggering device that allowed a machine gun to fire through the revolving propeller arc without the bullets contacting the blades, while the true interrupter gear interrupted (stopped) the stream of bullets fired from a machine gun from striking parts of its own aircraft. Theoretically, a machine gun equipped with an interrupter gear normally had the trigger mechanism enabled and its interrupter mechanism would disable the trigger when the propeller blade was in the way. Because of the technical and mechanical problems involved with stopping a firing machine gun no interrupter system was ever developed for firing through the prop; all were of the synchronized type. A machine gun equipped with a synchronization gear normally had the trigger disabled, and the synchronization mechanism would enable the trigger when the propeller blade was clear and was dependent on the revolutions of the engine. Synchronization could be achieved only on machine guns with a single shot trigger (i.e. a trigger which when pressed permitted only one shot being fired until released and pressed again). The Marlin, Vickers, and Browning were fitted with single shot triggers and were successfully synchronized, but the Lewis was not synchronized during World War I.

When World War I broke out, military authorities considered the airplane appropriate only for reconnaissance and the gathering of intelligence, but soon the airplane was developed into an aerial weapon that could be more effective if it mounted a forward firing machine gun. "Pusher" aircraft, with their engines mounted backward behind the wings and with the cockpit in front of the wings were the logical solution to the problem of shooting forward. However, pusher aircraft did not have the performance of the front engine "tractor" aircraft with their engines and propellers forward of the wings and cockpits behind the engine.

In December 1914 French pilot, **Roland Garros** contacted Raymond Saulnier to have steel deflectors installed on his aircraft's propeller along with deflector wedges that reduced the chance of ricochets. In March 1915, Garros flew his first mission in a deflector-equipped Morane-Saulnier Type I fighter and surprising his opponents, he downed five German fighters to become the first French ace. (AFHRC)

Before the war the British worked on the synchronization problem at the Royal Aircraft Factory at Farnborough, but utilized the scheme of interrupting the fire of the machine gun when a blade was in the line of fire. Contemporary technology was unable to stop the machine gun from firing in the instant that the narrow propeller blade was in the line of fire with sufficient dependability and only a slight maladjustment would have bullets hitting the propeller. The British cancelled the project, but Swiss aeronautical engineer Franz Schneider, Chief Designer at Berlin's Luft-Verker-Gesellschaft (LVG), had patented a similar device on 15 July 1913. Schneider offered his design to the German Army, which showed no interest in Schneider's device or the airplane in general as a weapon of war. Importantly, an article on the Schneider interrupter system appeared in the 30 September 1914 issue of the German aviation magazine *Flugsport*.

Saulnier-Garros Gear

In April 1914, French aircraft designer Raymond Saulnier developed and patented a gun synchronizer but encountered a significant problem with standard ammunition, whose erratic propellant caused hang fires that disastrously disrupted the synchronization sequence. Saulnier then took a very different approach to the problem when he placed steel deflectors on the propeller blades to divert the bullets from a continuously firing machine gun. This method was also pursued that same year by French engineer Eugene Gilbert but found no interest with Allied air forces. Once World War I broke out French pilot Roland Garros contacted Saulnier in December 1914 to have steel deflectors installed on his aircraft's propeller along with deflector wedges that reduced the chance of ricochets. The deflectors also decreased the propeller's and hence aircraft efficiency. In March 1915

**Anthony Fokker**, the Dutch aircraft designer working for the Germans, developed the first mechanical synchronizer that would give Germany air supremacy in 1916. (AFHRC)

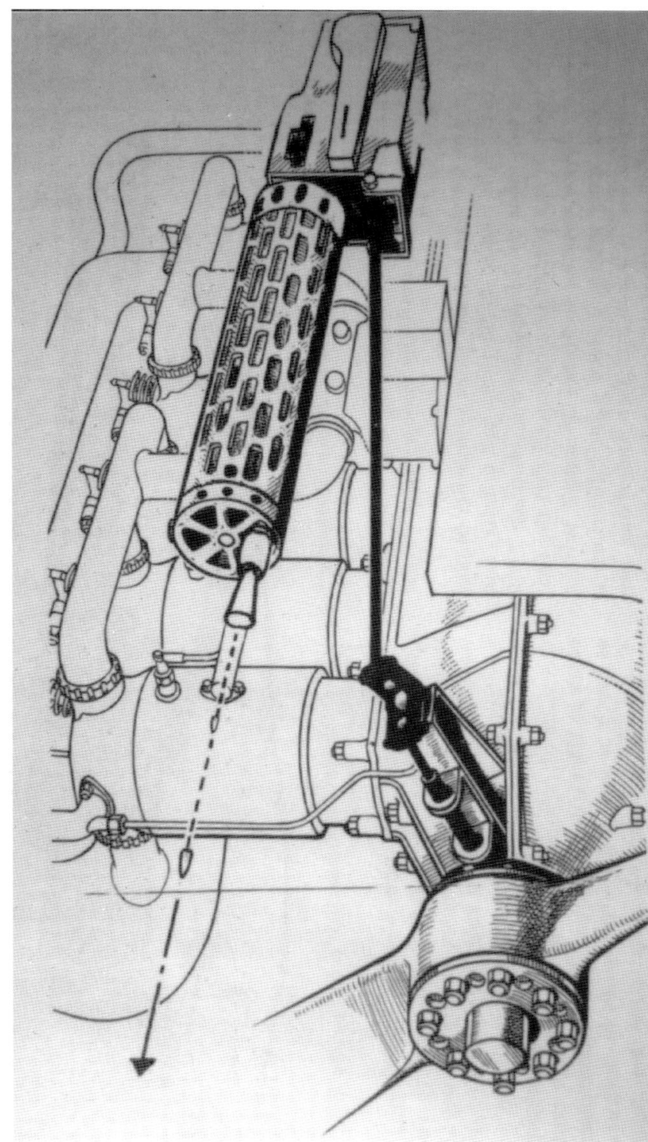

Romanian immigrant George Constantinesco developed his dependable Constantinesco Fire Control Gear, called the "CC Gear" that enabled the Allies to regain air supremacy from 1917 through the end of the war and would became standard equipment in the British and American Air Forces and remained in service with the RAF until World War II. (USAAF)

Garros flew his first mission in a deflector-equipped Morane-Saulnier Type I fighter mounting a forward-firing .32 caliber Hotchkiss machine gun. Surprising his opponents, he downed five German fighters to become the first French ace. On 18 April 1915 he was forced down by ground fire in German-occupied territory and was captured before he could burn his fighter, and the propeller was sent to Berlin for evaluation.

### Fokker Gear

At this point the widely-held account was that Anthony Fokker, the Dutch aircraft designer working for the Germans, examined the Garros/Saulnier deflectors and rejected their practicability, and proceeded to invent the synchronizer system in just a matter of days. However, Fokker and his team, which included engineers Heinrich Lubbe and Fritz Huber, had actually been working on the synchronizer system since late 1914. Fokker probably used Schneider's findings from the *Flugsport* article, as Schneider and LVG sued Fokker for patent infringement in 1916, and even though the court verdicts repeatedly found for Schneider, Fokker doggedly continued the case until the time of Schneider's death in 1933.

Fokker named his revolutionary invention the *Zentralsteuerung*, or "centralized control." Fokker's design was ready for operations by June 1915; equipped in the Fokker E-series fighters mounting the new Parabellum 1 MG 14 machine gun. The Fokker synchronizer was a simple mechanical apparatus that used a cam that attached to and rotated with the propeller shaft that was attached to a long rod extending to the gun triggers. The device operated by first loading and cocking the gun and then pulling a handle to enable the trigger. This handle lowered a cam follower onto the cam wheel. When the follower was pushed upward by an asymmetric bulge in the cam, a rod was pushed back against a spring, enabling the trigger to fire the gun. The bulge in the cam was aligned in such a way that the trigger was only enabled when the propeller blades were out of the line of fire. This mechanism blocked the trigger from firing every time the propeller blade passed so that with a two-blade propeller (the only type used at that time), the gun was interrupted 2,000 times per minute at an engine speed of 1,000 rpms. Since synchronized fire depended on engine speed, the rate of fire varied as the engine speed varied. This could be a problem when the pilot wanted the highest rate of fire when engaging an enemy when maneuvering at low speed.

The first claimed air victory using a synchronizer was scored on 1 July 1915 when Lt. Kurt Wintgens of *Feldflieger Abteilung* 67 flying a Fokker M5K/MG caused the forced landing of a Morane-Saulnier Type I east of Lorraine, but the victory was not confirmed as the victim landed in French territory. On 1 August Max Immelmann, flying a Fokker E1, forced down a Royal Flying Corps BE c2 and was awarded the first of his 15 (17?) victories. Soon the introduction of the synchronizer gave the Germans air supremacy in what was to be known as the "Fokker Scourge." By mid-January 1916 Immelmann had scored eight victories and was awarded the first *Pour le Merite*, Germany's highest honor, which would be popularly known as the "Blue Max" in his honor.

### British "CC Gear"

In November 1915, Capt. L.V. Stewart Blacker of the Royal Flying Corps Department of Military Aeronautics was ordered to find a device that could fire through the propeller arc. He contacted the Vickers Company with the problem and the company assigned engineer George Challenger to develop the mechanism. By December Challenger had developed a mechanical synchronizing gear that operated much like the Fokker gear, in that it operated the gun trigger by a lever controlled by a cam and reduction gear on the engine crankshaft. Vickers patented Challenger's gear and began production in its Weybridge factory for use with its Vickers gun. In early 1916 it was fitted to the Bristol Scout, which became the first British fighter to be equipped with a synchronizing gear.

Germany tried to safeguard its invention by ordering its pilots not to overfly Allied territory to prevent its capture in case of a forced landing. Nonetheless, a Fokker E with its synchronizing gear was captured by the Allies, who began developing their own versions of the mechanical synchronizer. A British Sopwith 1½ Strutter equipped with a Ross synchronizer appeared in April 1916, and soon other British and French aircraft were also retrofitted with synchronized gun systems.

Vickers began preliminary work to link its gear with the Lewis gun, but this gun's long firing mechanism movement and bullet weight caused timing deviations. By July 1916 several other mechanical synchronizing gears had been developed and were in production. All were reasonably successful if the breech of the gun was close to the engine and the rod connecting the two was not too long. However, not all British fighters could use the short linkage. The rate of fire was dependant on the engine revolutions and was slowed at low speeds, particularly when the engine was throttled back. Mechanical synchronizing gears were particularly susceptible to malfunction. The changing temperatures at different altitudes caused contraction or expansion of the gear rods and linkages, along with warping of the airframe, disrupting firing timing that could result in the pilot shooting off his own propeller!

However, these synchronizing mechanisms were inadequate, as their rate of fire was too slow at low throttle and the linkages between the gun and engine often broke or malfunctioned. Despite these problems, Allied air power had caught up with Germany's Fokker fighters. The Fokker Scourge that symbolically began with Immelmann's first victory on 1 August 1915 also symbolically came to an ironic close with his death. Immelmann was killed over northern France on 18 June 1916 and many sources, including his brother, believe that his synchronizing gear malfunctioned and destroyed his propeller (official German documents attribute artillery fire for his loss, while British accounts credit an observer/gunner with the victory).

Capt. Blacker realized limitations of the mechanical gear and decided to investigate a hydraulically operated gear. A Romanian immigrant, George Constantinesco, had been unofficially contacted by a member of the War Munitions Invention Department, who suggested that Constantinesco begin to investigate a hydraulically synchronized firing gear. In early May 1916, to expedite Constantinesco's work, the Invention Department contacted Blacker, who supplied Constantinesco with a Vickers machine gun and 1,000 rounds of ammunition at his private laboratory at Alperton. It took Constantinesco only ten days to develop drawings and a working model for the Constantinesco Fire Control Gear, called the "CC Gear."

Constantinesco tested his CC Gear by using an electric motor to spin a disk at 1,500 rpms. The position of the propeller blades were marked on the disk with chalk and when 120 rounds were fired, Constantinesco found that almost all rounds passed through the single initial hole that was located in the hypothetical space midway between two hypothetical blades. The problem was "almost all," and Constantinesco found that the stray rounds were caused by defective ammunition. When he used thoroughly inspected high quality rounds, he found that all fired rounds passed through the same hole at all engine speeds. The CC Gear system was more dependable than a mechanical system, as it could distribute firing impulses at a much higher rate, allowing the machine gun to fire at close to its normal rate regardless of the engine revolutions. The gear could also be installed in any aircraft and did not have to have specific linkages designed for individual aircraft types. Its copper tubing could be easily bent around obstacles and conveniently placed when compared to the steel rods of the mechanical gear. Mechanical synchronizing gears had to be specially designed for each type of engine and to the aircraft to which it was to be installed.

The mechanism of the Constantinesco CC Gear was an innovative, non-conventional hydraulic system called "hydrosonic transmission," which was kept secret during the war. The energy producing device for the gear was a single phase wave transmitter (sonic generator) that produced percussive waves of pulses of very short duration at twice the frequency of the engine revolutions. The pulses were transmitted through a main conduit that contained a non-freezing liquid mixture (90% paraffin oil) to a motor attached to the gun that activated the gun trigger. The basic difference between the hydrosonic system and the conventional hydraulic transmission system was due to the compressibility of the liquid in the main and feeder lines. The liquid columns in the feeder lines did not move as rigid connecting links, but acted only as the vehicle for the transmission of the successive energy waves produced by the generator, much like sound waves traveling along a tube containing air. The energy transmitted had to be completely absorbed by the trigger motor, otherwise the reflected waves traveling to and from the generator to the motor would operate the trigger at the wrong time. To prevent this from happening a reflected wave absorber or damper was included in the motor assembly.

The main parts of the CC Gear were the reservoir, generator, trigger motor, control lever, and pipe system. The reservoir was connected to the generator by a 1/16 inch copper tube. A larger, 3/8 inch tube connected the generator to the trigger motor on the gun. A cam in the generator was arranged so that it raised the plunger in the generator to its highest point just as the trailing edge of the propeller passed the muzzle of the gun.

The CC Gear acted when a piston in the reservoir was withdrawn to its furthest point, which placed the oil in the reservoir under high pressure. A wire from the control lever connected to a valve at the lower end of the reservoir to open this valve when the lever was activated. This caused the high pressure oil to move inside the tube to the generator and forced the plunger down on the cam, raising it. The cam then lifted the plunger, causing an impulse on the oil, which traveled along the line of least resistance in the larger tube and pressed the plunger into the trigger motor, firing the gun.

In August 1916, a CC Gear was installed in a BE 2c and the tests were perfect, making the mechanical synchronization system obsolete. The Frazier-Nash Company was granted a production contract for a total of 26,000 CC Gears during World War I and 24,000 more were manufactured in the post-war. By Armistice Day 6,827 CC gears had been shipped to the U.S. The CC Gear became standard equipment in the British and American Air Forces and remained in service with the RAF until World War II. Despite capturing examples of the CC Gear the Germans were unable to duplicate it, and it enabled the Allies to regain air supremacy from 1917 through the end of the war.

Further Synchronization Development

Twin synchronizing gears for firing two Spandau machine guns through the propeller were used by the Germans in the final version of the Fokker Eindecker (Fokker E IV) and were the standard armament on all German Type D Scouts. The Fokker E IV was used for trials in mounting three synchronized machine guns, but the aircraft was too heavy and became unmanageable in the air. The first Allied twin synchronized gun fighter was the Sopwith Camel and Spad S XIII, which were introduced in mid-1917 and used a modified CC Gear with the guns mounted in parallel. During the latter part of the war Americans A.L. Nelson and engine expert Glenn Angle collaborated in developing a successful mechanical interrupter gear. The mechanism appeared too late for many to see service but was the basis for all later American synchronization gear.

The Gloster Gladiator, which came into service in 1937, was the first British aircraft to use Browning machine guns and the last to use the CC Gear. This biplane carried four .303 Browning machine guns, two in the wings outside the propeller arc and two in the fuselage operated by the CC Gear. Synchronization mechanisms chronically fired stray shots and any modifications to solve the problem would affect the interchangeability of parts in existing installations. The Gladiator was replaced by the Hawker Hurricane carrying wing-mounted guns so the synchronization gear became obsolete, along with the aircraft into which it was installed. It was no longer viable to mount guns that had their firing mechanisms inside the cockpit and the necessity for placing the (two at most) guns in front of the pilot was reduced with the improvement of gunsighting equipment and the requirements for heavier armament. Cantilever wing monoplane fighters replaced biplanes because their wings offered much more space than the fuselage for placement of multiple guns and also provided a steadier platform than the wire supported biplane wings. Most World War II fighter aircraft had their guns mounted in the wings, outside the propeller arc with their direction of fire "harmonized" to converge at a predetermined distance. The *Luftwaffe* and Soviets committed the last synchronized firing gear equipped fighters in World War II. The last synchronized gear equipped fighter to see combat was the Soviet Lovochkin La-11 and the Yakovlev Yak-9 in Korea. Of course, synchronization gears became superfluous with the introduction of jet fighters.

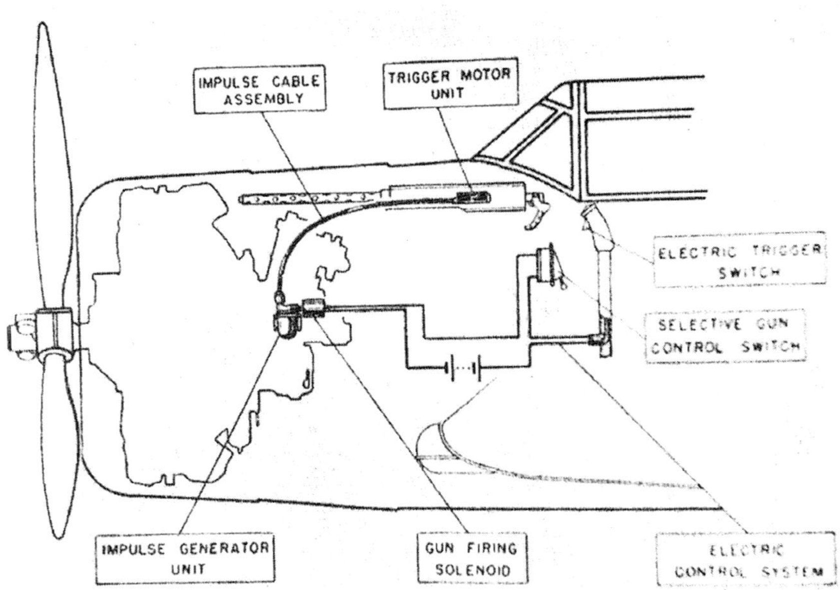

# 3

# Fighter Wing Gun Pods

USAAF and USN fighters, like their bomber counterparts, made little use of underwing pods containing machine guns or cannon.

**Curtiss XP-36F Hawk** (USAAF)

**Curtiss XP-36F Hawk**
The single XP-36F was the 172nd P-36A fitted with two underwing pods containing the Madsen 23mm cannon supplied with 100 rpg as was used by the Hawk 75N.

**Bell P-39Q and P-63**
A streamlined wing pod containing a .50 caliber Browning replaced the two .30 caliber wing guns of the previous Airacobra variants. There was a spent ammunition chute located on the mid-underside of the pod. The gun had to be charged manually on the ground. The pods were removable and were sometimes deleted by pilots to decrease drag, so they relied on the 37mm cannon and two .50 caliber machine guns in the nose. The P-63 also mounted underwing pods inboard the pylons on each wing. These pods were more streamlined and smaller than those on the P-39Q.

**North American P-51**
Once the *Luftwaffe* became less of a threat in mid-1944 the Mustang was assigned to strafing duties. To increase its firepower experimental underwing gun packs containing one or two .50s were developed. Two guns with 340 rounds per gun were carried in a streamlined 375 pound pod that could be jettisoned in an emergency. These pods did not see combat.

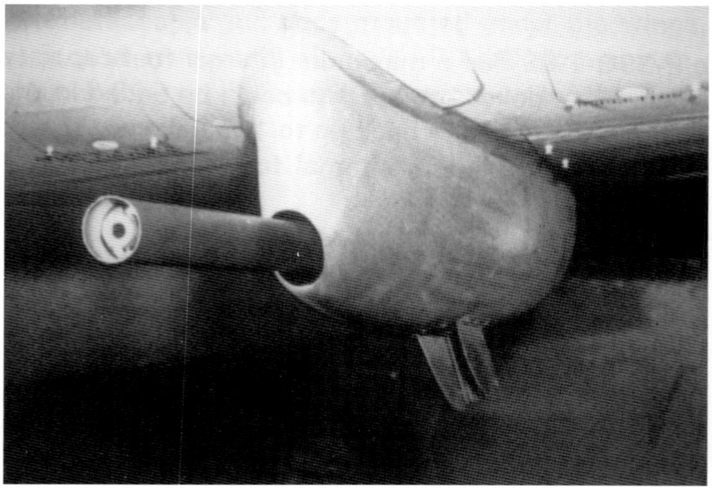

**P-39Q Wing Pods** (USAAF)

# Part Eight
## Gunnery Training

# 1

# Armament Training

**Section 1: Inter-war Armament Training 1919-1939**

**Enlisted Man Armament Training**

When the school at Kelly Field was reorganized in October 1919, armament was included as one of 21 courses offered. In April 1921 the school was moved from Kelly Field to Chanute Field, IL, and armaments were offered as one of the courses in the Department of Mechanics. Chanute remained the center for armament training until 1938.

During this time the course was not taken seriously, as only five classes with less than eight students on average were given per year. The usual length of the course was five and a half months, although at times it lasted a month longer.

As armament became more important, in 1930 the armament course was transferred from the Department of Mechanics to a new Department of Armament at Chanute. In July 1935 Capt. Herbert Anderson was appointed the Director of the Department of Armament who totally reorganized the department; both its curriculum and equipment. The course was divided into four divisions: Elementary and Specialized Division; Machine Gun Division; Bomb Division; and Chemical Warfare Division. A highly qualified commissioned officer was named to direct each Division and was to revise course content. The course was to be covered in 582 hours of instruction over 24 weeks, with five weeks committed to mechanical subjects and 19 weeks to practical armament instruction. The next year more hours were added to the course, which was extended to 32 weeks.

In 1938, the Armament School was moved from Chanute to Lowry Field, CO, which was located in a large unpopulated area where bombing and gunnery could be practiced without danger. With the world situation changing the course needed to be shortened and more students graduated. Six highly specialized 24 week courses were established with four for inexperienced enlisted men: Primary Attack Aircraft Armament, Primary Pursuit Aircraft Armament, Primary Bombardment Aircraft Armament, and Observation Aircraft Armament. The fifth course was the Advanced Armament Course, and was intended for men who had at least a year and a half experience with aircraft armament and had at least completed a basic mechanic course at a technical school, and preferably had graduated from one of the Primary Armament courses. The Master Armorer's Course was the sixth course intended for men with at least five years experience in the AAC, holding a rank of Sergeant or better, and graduated from a course at Chanute. The change would increase the number of graduates from approximately 25 to 255, with two thirds being from the four Primary courses.

In each of the two years that the six-course curriculum was in effect, 14 separate classes were graduated with the average yearly attendance being only 196. The plan was abandoned as unworkable at the start of the 1939-40 school year.

**Officer Armament Training**

In 1927 the AAC decided to establish a school at the department of Mechanics at Chanute to train officers to supervise armament work. One class of officers attended a course that was very similar to that of the enlisted man's course. When the Department of Armaments was organized at Chanute in 1930, both the enlisted men's and officer's courses were transferred there. In 1934 the aircraft maintenance and aircraft armament courses were combined into a ten month course (seven months for aircraft maintenance and three months for armament). After two years the ACC determined that three months was too short to cover armament, and in 1937 the armament course was increased to seven months. It appears that in the 12 years that the officer armament training course was in effect from early 1928 to mid-1939, 15 classes graduated 153 officers; a small but valuable core of armament officers. In February 1939 Maj.Gen. Henry Arnold ordered all armament training of Regular Army officers be discontinued so that the facilities and personnel of ACC technical schools could be devoted to the training of enlisted technicians for the Air Corps expansion program.

**ACC Armament Expansion Program**

In early 1939 the ACC approved an expansion program to add 25,000 more enlisted men, with 1,584 trained as aircraft armorers, by 30 June 1940. In this program ACC recruits were sent to one of six fields with a basic training center where, during the first month, they were given basic training and tests to determine an aptitude for technical training. If a trainee was found qualified for training as an armorer he was sent to Scott Field, IL, for a one month course in basic technical training that included shop mathematics, drafting, blueprint reading, elementary metalwork, and electricity; the same course that had been taught at Lowry. After the trainee completed the course he was sent to Lowry to complete the standard armament course. Lowry had little difficulty in meeting this goal, as by the end of 1939 66 armorers and 12 bombsight mechanics were being graduated each month.

Once the German Army had overrun France in the summer of 1940, the AAC instituted a second program in September called the 136,000 Man Program that authorized the training of 5,775 armorers and 600 bombsight mechanics over the next six months. With this program Lowry encountered difficulties in meeting quotas due to inadequate facilities. To meet the lack of officers to supervise armament training enlisted graduates were given a commission to become supervisors. By August 1941 the deteriorating European situation forced AAF to institute a call for 100,000 technicians per year and to double the aircraft armorer graduation rate to 10,000 per year. To reach this goal Lowry went on double nine hour shifts. On 15 September 1941, a new course in power operated turrets was inaugurated which further strained manpower requirements.

**Section 2: Wartime Armament Training**

The attack on Pearl Harbor caused the canceling of the 100,000 technician program and it was replaced with the "Victory Program," which called for a monthly graduation rate of 36,090 aircraft armorers, 3,000 power turret mechanics, 3,480 bombsight mechanics, and 875 armament officers by 31 December 1942.

These goals were met by reducing the length of the course by 20%, increasing class sizes, and introducing three shifts in a six day week (increased to seven days in October). Before Pearl Harbor Selective Service draftees weren't accepted into technical training schools, since they were to be inducted for only a year and wouldn't warrant the extensive training program. To meet the large, new quota Lowry Field #2 and nearby Buckley Field were constructed. In January 1943 another armament school was opened at Yale University. In September 1942 Buckley was to train fighter armorers while Lowry trained bombardment armorers.

By mid-1943 the AAF had reached the 2,500,000 manpower goal thought to be sufficient to win, and from this point to the end of the war there was a significant decrease in the number of armament trainees and a drop in the number of armament training schools until only Lowry remained, and a strengthening and lengthening of course structure to provide more comprehensive and thorough instruction as armament equipment became more complicated.

The Flexible Gunnery Training Program underwent a development during the war. The quantitative trend is characterized by the number of hours of instruction: 150 hours in early 1942, 210 in July 1942, 280 in August 1943, and 290 in May 1944. The qualitative trend is illustrated by the more clear-cut definition of standards and procedures in the programs of 1943 and 1944 than in those of 1941 and 1942.

# 2

# Gunner Training

**Background**

Gunner training during the end of World War I was taught in two parts: ground and air instruction. Ground instruction included lectures on guns, sights, and nomenclature; stripping and assembly of guns; and firing range practice. Aerial instruction included mock dogfights, firing of machine guns, and the use of the camera gun. The camera gun was a device that used pictures to show where hits would have been scored if a real gun had been used.

Between 1919 and 1940 there was not much interest in gunnery training in America. In 1925 all aerial machine gun training was transferred from the Primary Flying School at Brooks Field to the Advanced Flying Field at Kelly Field, both located in San Antonio, TX. At Kelly Field gunnery training was included in a six month advanced training course for Cadets and Flying Officers, but only a single JN-6H Jenny was available for gunnery practice. In 1927 only the gunnery ranges at Wright Field were equipped for flexible gunnery practice. In the 1920s and 30s, the six Air Corps flying schools only had provisions for basic gunnery training, so by-and-large American flexible gunnery training was superficial and not very specialized.

**Establishment of Flexible Gunnery Schools**

Before 1941 there were no specialized flexible gunnery training schools in the U.S. The military appropriations act of 1939 provided for the expansion of the six AAC flying schools for flexible gunnery training and the creation of new ones. However, it was not until 1940 and 1941 that anything was done in developing specialized flexible gunnery schools. In September 1940, Hap Arnold announced the newly activated Southeast Air Corps Training Center at Maxwell Field, AL, and plans for the establishment of two aerial gunnery schools. The next month the Southeast Training Center Headquarters proposed a program of instruction which, after several revisions, was not officially adopted until 4 March 1941. The planned five week course emphasized that instruction in the first week would be on orientation; the second, on sighting and lectures on range estimates, repairing of guns, and aircraft recognition; the third, on ground range exercises; the fourth, on preliminary air exercises; and the fifth, on air range instruction.

An exception to the rudimentary nature of early American gunnery training was the camera gun for flexible gunnery training. (USAAF)

The first flexible gunnery school was developed at Las Vegas, NV, as the flying weather was excellent and the surrounding area was virtually uninhabited. Initial preparations were made in late January 1941 and the first gunnery students arrived in mid-June 1941, but by the time of Pearl Harbor the school had graduated only three classes totaling 100 future instructors. Before the end of 1941 plans were approved to enlarge the Las Vegas School to allow 320 students to enter per week. In 1942 10,562 students enrolled and 9,117 graduated, and in 1943 18,974 enrolled and 18,071 graduated.

On 6 May 1941 Harlingen, TX, was also selected as a gunnery school site for 600 students with 120 graduating each week. The site offered good year-round weather while the Gulf of Mexico afforded a large gunnery range. The first students arrived on 1 September 1941, but the first class of 120 did not graduate until January 1942. In July 1942 its student quota was increased to 940, and then to 1,320 in October 1942, and to 1,920 in April 1943 with an expanded six week course. The school's rapid expansion can be illustrated by the 120 weekly graduation rate in January 1942 to the 360 per week in August 1943, and the 475 in November 1943. In 1942 Harlingen graduated 4,953 students, 15,682 in 1943, and 4,009 in the first two months of 1944.

The next flexible gunnery school was Tyndall Field, near Panama City, FL, which was authorized on 15 April 1941 because of its proximity to the open waters of the Gulf of Mexico and good weather. The first 2,000 students from Eglin Field did not arrive until 7 December 1941, and classes did not begin until 23 February 1942. By the end of 1941 it was obvious that Tyndall would be unable to deal with the volume of air traffic necessitated by the expanding gunnery program, and a satellite base was established at Apalachicola, FL, on 10 July 1942. Tyndall had 8,091 graduates in 1942 and five times more at 39,452 by the end of August 1944.

An instructor's school for flexible gunnery was activated at Buckingham Field, Fort Myers, FL, on 5 July 1942, with the first class starting on 7 September and more than 3,000 students graduated by the end of the year.

In 1941 the West Coast Training Center investigated a site near Kingman, AZ, as the location for a flexible gunnery school because of its good climatic conditions, transportation facilities, and lands suitable for air-to-air firing. After nearly a year, on 27 May 1942 the site was approved, but it was not activated until 4 August 1942. It was not until the middle of January 1943 that classes began, but by the end of the year Kingman graduated 10,861 gunnery students.

The gunnery school at Laredo, TX, was activated only eight days after Kingman on 12 August 1944, but graduated its first class in early January 1943 even before the first Kingman classes began. Laredo would later become the main testing center for advanced flexible training programs and the last site for the Central Gunnery Instructors School.

Yuma Army Air Field initially was an advanced pilot training school, but was officially changed to a radio flexible gunnery school on 11 November 1943. For approximately one month the gunnery program paralleled the pilot training program, after which the latter was abandoned. Only 143 students graduated in 1943, but by the end of that year 1,655 students were enrolled and being trained.

The seven flexible gunnery schools were very successful in meeting the original AAF HQ quotas set in July 1940. A more ambitious quota of 180,000 gunners to be graduated by March 1944 was set in July 1943. By the beginning of 1944 214,826 students had been graduated with a weekly rate of over 3,500 graduates being reached in June 1944 by the seven gunnery schools, which would be equivalent to a yearly rate of 182,000 graduates. However, these numbers did not equate to success, as gunners joining combat units were shown to be unsatisfactory and new requisites were constantly reset. Among the early prerequisites of the training program were textbooks and curricula. There were two fundamental differences between the curricula of 1941-1942 and those of 1943-1944. The latter provided for a longer course and defined procedure and standards of proficiency with much more precision. Those standards were defined in such course descriptions as gun familiarization, sighting, aircraft recognition, turret operation, and air firing.

**Student Requirements**

Volunteers for the gunnery program had to be between the ages of 18 and 30, be 5 feet, 10 inches or less, and weigh 170 pounds or less. They were required to pass the Army General Classification Test with a score of at least 100 and make a satisfactory grade on the Mechanical Aptitude Test. Non-specialists or specialists such as airplane mechanics, radio or radar operators, and aircraft armorers were eligible for admission, provided they were below the grade of staff sergeant.

After summer 1942 the mental requirements were lowered, and by the fall the requirements for passing the Mechanical Aptitude Test were also lowered from 100 to 85, and subsequently to 80, and for the General Classification Test from 100 to 85.These remedies still did not fulfill the quotas. By July 1943 the physical requirements for trainees also had to be modified. The age limit was increased to 35 and height requirements were a minimum of 5 feet and a maximum 6 feet, while the weight limits were not less than 100 pounds or more than 180 pounds.

Early in the war, of the various bomber aircrew members, only the pilots were exempted from flexible gunnery training, but this requirement varied, however, in its application to navigators and bombardiers. In July 1942, when advanced bombardier schools were unable to absorb the flow of trainees from preflight schools it was decided to send men assigned to bombardier training to flexible gunnery before they entered their preflight course. The same procedure was followed later in the case of navigators. Limited capacity combined with the priority given to dedicated gunners (called "career" gunners) made it impossible for flexible gunnery schools to accommodate all those who were scheduled to take the training. Even after the policy was changed in December 1942, and only preflight graduates could go to gunnery schools, the existing situation was not altered to the extent that all bombardiers and navigators received flexible gunnery instruction. In 1944 the AAF began to rethink requiring gunnery training for these two groups. With the large numbers of bombardiers and navigators required it was not considered practical to give all of them instruction beyond their regular duties. Also, with the establishment of a B-29 Flexible Gunnery School and the increasing need for more gunners it was impossible for the existing schools to complete the accelerated program if navigators and bombardiers were routed through the gunnery course. It was argued that the navigator's gunnery duties were not important because he had no primary gun position on a B-24 and fired only the side nose guns on a B-17. In April 1944 bombardier and navigator officers and cadets were no longer required to take gunnery training, but soon afterward Headquarters AAF then requested that they be given as much of the gunnery training as possible.

**Voluntary Program**

In September 1942, at a time when there was a high demand for specialists elsewhere, the Flying Training Command restricted flexible gunnery volunteers to non-specialists and "eliminated" (e.g. "washed out") aviation cadets, which led to students of inferior quality. During 1942 and early 1943 the AAF believed that in choosing prospective flexible gunners mechanical aptitude gave the specialist an advantage over non-specialists. In December 1942 the Chief of Air Staff stated that flexible gunnery was "primarily for enlisted specialists who were qualified as airplane mechanics, radio operators, or armorers....Non-specialists, in many cases, could not qualify for training and had to be eliminated." Before the end of the year it became apparent that specialists were desirable as gunnery material, and also that the numbers contemplated in flexible gunnery plans for 1943 could not be met under the volunteer system. Thus, the voluntary program was cancelled on 16 January 1943 and a compulsory program was implemented in April 1943 with the AAF restricting training only to specialists. But after three months of unfilled quotas non-specialists were again admitted to the flexible gunner training program as there was an immediate call for 140,000 gunners, including:

| | |
|---|---|
| Non-specialist Career Gunners | 50,000 |
| Bombardiers and Navigators | 40,000 |
| Radio Operators | 16,667 |
| Armorers | 16,667 |
| Aircraft Mechanics | 16,667 |

**Compulsory Program**

The compulsory program encountered immediate morale problems resulting in a high elimination rate. Many students were so dissatisfied that they claimed a fear of flying as an excuse to washout. Once this excuse was validated flight surgeons were inundated with similar claims. Other disgruntled specialty trainees claimed that they were not informed at the classification centers that flexible gunnery was required for their specialty and would have never volunteered for that specialty if they had known. It was recommended that requirements be clearly explained at the classification centers so elimination could be made there instead of wasting time during training. After thorough explanations were made the attitude of arriving flexible students was greatly improved. The washout rate of 10%

of the compulsory program due to training deficiencies and "fear of flying" matched the 10% rate of the voluntary program of the year before.

**Enlisted Gunnery Instructors**

In the early stages of the gunnery program instructor training was often too quick and haphazard. The instructors were either obtained from technical schools or from the ranks of enlisted men gradated from the flexible gunnery schools. Armorer specialists were sent from Lowry to Tyndall for training as instructors. After one week of preliminary instruction by officers the instructor candidates were given a test and then asked about their choice of subjects they would like to teach. The students then attended a four week course and graduated as sergeants or staff sergeants while their instructors remained privates or corporals! This inequity was changed by AAF HQ, which promoted all gunnery instructors to equivalent grades.

In late 1942 the call for gunners increased, and with it came the urgent need for more and better instructors and for the standardization of the curriculum in the flexible gunnery schools. The Central Flexible Gunnery Instructors School at Fort Myers, FL, was established to study and meet this objective, and to conduct gunnery research and to prepare and distribute data pertaining to flexible gunnery.

In 1943 the First, Second, Third, and Fourth training Air Forces needed many more qualified instructors and the Fort Myers school was expanded and improved. A Psychological Unit was established there to aid in selecting and training students. The pre-entrance test scores were standardized, and entering students were to have graduated in the top quarter of their class. This plan called for the graduation of 2,000 instructors by June 1944, 1,000 of which were to replace incompetent existing instructors. In January 1944, the requirement for instructors was increased to 6,665 and the number of graduates from the instructor's school to the training air forces was increased from 45% to 70%.

**Gunnery Instructor Officers**

In this training program there was no procedure to select flexible gunnery officers, and many of those selected were not particularly qualified for the job, which consisted of flying training missions and supervising both students and instructors. The first officer gunnery instructor training program was a four week course at Fort Myers, but soon the school was moved to Laredo, TX, as the Fort Myers school was overcrowded. It was argued that officer gunnery training was "completely dissimilar" to that for enlisted instructors and the move was made at the end of May 1944. That month the gunnery officer's course, which already had been increased to five weeks, was extended to six, and the influx of students was fixed at 30 per week for six weeks, and 50 a week thereafter. By 3 January 1945 a total of 693 officers had graduated from the gunnery officer's school.

**Instruction**

In the early stages of the training program the curricula was necessarily provisional. The first course approved in 1940 by the AAF HQ and the West Coast Training Center was four weeks of instruction. The first week was allocated to familiarization with equipment and duties; the second, to sighting problems and laboratory work; the third, to ground range exercises and firing; and the fourth, to air range exercises and firing. The next year, a week was added to the curricula to give more importance to air range exercises and firing.

| 1942 | Hours |
|---|---|
| Orientation | 1 |
| Safety precautions | 3 |
| Description and nomenclature of equipment | 16 |
| Ballistics | 2 |
| Gun Installation | 10 |
| Sights | 5 |
| Sighting and sight harmonization | 15 |
| Aircraft recognition and estimation of range | 12 |
| Methods of fire on various courses | 2 |
| Turret manipulation/Spotlight Trainer | 7 |
| Firing | 71 |
| Tactics | 3 |
| **Total** | **150** |

In July 1942 the curriculum offered 210 hours of instruction, not including 40 hours of military training, during five weeks, as compared with 150 early in the year. The increase was a result of the need for additional and more thorough instruction and of the adoption of the flight system of instruction in which a small group of students had one instructor assigned for all subjects, including range firing. This system, whatever its advantages, required more time on the part of the instructor in those subjects in which he was not well prepared. Hours in the ground school were increased nearly one-half. A much needed course in oxygen and high altitude flying was incorporated.

| 1943 | Hours |
|---|---|
| Caliber .50 machine gun | 40 |
| Caliber .30 machine gun | 6 |
| Malfunctions | 20 |
| Turrets | 50 |
| Sighting | 44 |
| Aircraft Recognition | 20 |
| Ground Firing | 48 |
| Air Firing | 52 |
| **Total** | **280** |

Before the end of 1942 the volunteer system was cancelled, the gunnery program expanded, and the increasing requirement of modern warfare for more technical training called for proposals for lengthening the flexible gunnery course from five to seven weeks. The Flying Training Command compromised by adding a week. The elimination of the volunteer system led to an increase in student numbers, but also meant generally less competent students that would require more and better instruction.

| 1944 | Hours |
|---|---|
| Caliber .50 machine gun | 41 |
| Turrets | 44 |
| Sighting | 34 |
| Aircraft Recognition | 10 |
| Interphone Procedure | 4 |
| Physical Training | 36 |
| Ground Firing | 64 |
| Air Training Program | 48 |
| Phase Checks | 7 |
| Final Comprehensive Examination | 2 |
| **Total** | **290** |

Prior to mid-1943 it was difficult for schools to rate their students because of a fluctuating method of instruction and a lack of specific criterion of aptitude. On 12 August 1943, the Training Command issued a directive that outlined detailed and precise standards to be achieved in various phases of instruction before graduation and assignment to Operational Training Units (OTU) and Replacement Training Units (RTU). The curriculum of May 1944 set definite procedures and standards for graduation, including seven hours of "phase checks," which verified the student's rank in his class. The content and methods of the Flexible Gunnery Course at the end of 1944 demonstrated the evolution of the unsystematic curriculum of 1942 to a methodical system that produced competent graduates.

**Typical Day during a 5 week course in sections of 10 men:**

| | |
|---|---|
| Reveille: | 0525 |
| Mess: | 0630 |
| Classes: | 0725-1140 |
| Midday Mess: | 1145-1340 |
| Classes: | 1345-1700 |
| Mess: | 1715 |
| Study: | 1845-2100 |
| Lights Out: | 2100 |
| Taps: | 2105 |

### Expanding the Flexible Gunnery Program

In August 1943, when Gen. Arnold set a goal of 140,000 flexible gunnery graduates, the gunnery training program was expanding so rapidly that there was a problem in supplying personnel and equipment at a rate that had been established in 1942. It was obvious that training schools should have been given first priority in being supplied with equipment suitable for the instruction of students in the equipment which they were to use in combat. An inventory of equipment on hand and equipment required showed a great discrepancy between the two. There were 383 Spotlight E-1 trainers on hand and 530 required; 574 E-5 Turret Trainers on hand and 1,226 required; 13 Waller Gunnery Trainers available and 55 required; 990 GSAP Cameras on hand and 1,220 required; 2,434 reflector sights available and 3,678 required; and only 95 of 830 powered operated turrets required were available. Throughout the flexible gunnery training program there was an acute shortage of aircraft. For instance, to accurately simulate fighter attacks during camera gunnery training it was estimated that 260 fighters were required, but only 26 were available for flexible gunnery in February 1944. The reason for the delay in instituting the B-29 gunnery course was the lack of aircraft and remote firing equipment. Many training turrets are worn out. Computing sights were in short supply, and there were no new K-10 and K-11 compensating sights, even though hundreds languished in warehouses awaiting installation in turrets that would not be available until summer 1944.

The basis of gunnery training was the understanding of guns in general and machine guns in particular as this idealized PR photo conveys. (USAAF)

### Machine Gun Instruction

The basis of gunnery training was the understanding of guns in general and machine guns in particular. Many students had so little experience with any kind of firearm that familiarization with shotguns and the .22-caliber rifle was required, as well as with machine guns. The earliest curricula had provisions for familiarization with .50-caliber guns, but there were only a few available. During 1942, the Las Vegas gunnery school had half as many .50 caliber guns as .30 caliber guns, and often there were only two guns for teaching a class of 20 students. Training aids intended to familiarize students with firearms were unavailable.

During 1942, Flying Training Command schools had to use the .30 caliber machine gun because .50 caliber ammunition was not available for the few .50s that were available. The first class at Harlingen had only one .30 caliber machine available to practice assembly and disassembly. The only aircraft available for firing training was the AT-6, which was too light to accommodate twin .50-caliber guns, so .30 caliber guns were fitted to the rear cockpit. By the beginning of 1943 the situation improved, with the transfer of a number of B-34 Lockheed Ventura bombers to Tyndall Field along with more .50-caliber guns and training aids. The assignment of B-34s made it possible to fire .30-caliber waist guns and twin .30-caliber guns from a Martin turret. The gunnery situation was further improved in early 1943, when both Harlingen and Laredo were made B-24 training schools, which was in accordance with the new policy of gunnery school specialization in specific bombers.

During 1943 increased efforts were made to bring about a greater degree of familiarization with guns. In a flexible gunnery conference held at Buckingham Army Air Field on 7 May 1943, representatives of both the Army and the Navy recommended that before graduation gunners must be able without assistance and coaching to demonstrate their knowledge of "the nomenclature and functions of the machine gun, ability to strip and reassemble the gun and correct the most common malfunctions." At Buckingham Field, FL, during the summer of 1942, 28 hours were devoted to weapons and eight to malfunctions, and at Fort Myers, FL, in that December 30 hours to weapons and 10 to malfunctions. By way of contrast, in August 1943 the Training Command required that 40 hours be devoted to the .50-caliber machine gun, six to the .30-caliber, and 20 to malfunctions.

The Training Command issued a detailed directive regarding what the student was required to know about the nomenclature and functions of all parts of the .50- caliber machine gun and the sequence of its operation. The blindfolded student was to be able to field strip and reassemble the gun after the parts had been jumbled in a pile. After assembly and still blindfolded, he was to be able to also adjust the head space, the oil buffer tube, and the direction of feed. In addition to these operations the "seeing" student had to know 17 additional operations. The early emphasis on the .30-caliber gun and then later upon the .50 caliber made the problem even more complicated, as it was necessary to study the differences between the two guns.

### Gun Malfunctions

The malfunction phase of gunnery training received extensive consideration. After March 1942 the course was concentrated in the fourth week of school, so that it would have a close time connection with the corresponding theoretical instruction. In early 1942, it was obvious that students were receiving unsatisfactory instruction in dealing with gun malfunctions. Throughout

1942 the ground firing course included trips to a special malfunction range where malfunctions likely to occur in .30-and .50-caliber guns were examined. Separate harmonization ranges, where a complete malfunction course was taught, were established at several gunnery training schools. Before the end of the year these ranges were closed, as the heavy emphasis on the subject at machine gun classes and malfunction and moving ranges made them unnecessary. An idea of the development of malfunction training is illustrated at the Las Vegas school: in January 1942 there were 12 instructors on the range using six. .30-caliber machine guns as compared with 33 instructors in October using thirty-six .50-caliber and ten .30-caliber guns. In 1943 the weapons and malfunctions courses were integrated under the direction of one officer.

In 1943 the Training Command provided for increased and detailed attention to malfunctions. Seven malfunctions were enumerated which the student was expected to determine by their symptoms: 1) failure to feed into feedway, 2) failure to extract from ammunition belt, 3) failure to feed into the chamber, 4) failure to fire, 5) failure to control fire, 6) failure to extract from chamber, and 7) failure to eject. Methods of determining malfunctions or their symptoms and the procedure to follow on the range were included in the 20 hour course, with range work assigned to 12 hours or 60% of the total time.

**Aircraft Recognition**

ID Models: Identification Models

To help aviation students recognize both enemy and friendly aircraft small models were devised. Early in the war the War Department and the Comet Model Airplane and Supply Co. developed a program for building 1:72 identification models, with Comet providing the templates and instructions to construct the models. In 1942 diagrams, instructions, and materials were distributed to high school shop and woodworking classes to make these ID models. Since metals were in short supply and difficult to work, the models were carved of pine or basswood instead of the usual model balsawood, which was not durable enough and was in demand for other war needs. The models were painted black and were then sent to the Army or Navy training schools.

Another alternative was to make the silhouette models from cardboard. Each was die-cut and could be easily assembled. Once assembled it provided a silhouette view of the aircraft for the student to memorize. Both the Army and Navy issued their own version of these models in boxed kits.

An effort was made to create models from "non-essential" materials that were not needed for the war effort. The solution was the well-known plastic recognition model made by the Cruver Company of Chicago that manufactured 1:72 scale and 1:432 "pocket" scale plastic recognition models of Allied and Axis aircraft. Cruver developed a method using injection-molded cellulose acetate to create these black plastic models. There are few of these models in existence today, as cellulose acetate deteriorates badly with time. (Note: These models are popularly believed to be made of Bakelite, as many British recognition models were.)

View Master Reels

The Army provided View Master Reels which could be used in a hand-held Sawyer viewer or projected onto a screen. The reels were created by the Jam Handy Corporation, which was well-known for its industrial films. Each frame on the circular reel showed a view of the plane at a different distance and angle. When viewed on a Sawyer stereoscopic viewer the aircraft shown on the frame allowed the student to estimate the distance of a particular aircraft when compared to two concentric circles that related to a gunsight. The reels came in two versions: "study" reels concentrating on one aircraft type or "test" reels featuring seven different aircraft to be identified and studied.

ID Cards

ID cards were playing card sized and featured pictures on one side and silhouettes on the other. American weapons were featured in 2 decks: one green deck for USAAF aircraft and one dark blue deck for USN aircraft and ships. Other decks included British and Japanese ships and Axis and Allied aircraft.

WEFT System

Aircraft Recognition classes taught the student the exact dimensions of enemy aircraft, as an inaccuracy of one foot in wing span produced a 30 foot error in estimating range at 600 yards. Early in the training program the importance of aircraft recognition was recognized and 12 hours were devoted to aircraft recognition and range estimation. By 1943 the course was expanded to 20 hours. Organizing the course presented problems, as information on foreign aircraft was lacking. In order to identify the structural dimensions, wing span, and fuselage length a system named WEFT (wings, engines, fuselage, and tail) was devised to aid the student in identifying German, Japanese, Italian, Russian, British, and American aircraft. WEFT soon proved to be ineffective, as the gunner had to consider too many factors during the very short time it took for an enemy fighter to approach during an attack.

Renshaw Flash System

A new system, known as the Renshaw or "flash" system, was developed by Dr. Samuel Renshaw of the Ohio State Department of Experimental Psychology. Dr. Renshaw believed that most people used only one-fifth of their available mind power to process information and developed a device that flashed photographs of enemy aircraft and ships on a screen at speeds of 1/100$^{th}$ of a second, which enabled students to become able to distinguish "Friend or Foe" many times faster and with a much higher degree of accuracy at long distances. The United States Naval Training School in Aircraft Recognition was established at Ohio State in late 1942, and by spring 1943 the flash system taught there was generally adopted throughout the Training Command. The success of the Renshaw system resulted in a reduction in the hours devoted to recognition from 20 in 1943 to 10 in 1944. After the war Renshaw became well-known for his speed reading technique of flashing pages to students who would become proficient at reading upwards of 1,200 to 1,400 words per minute.

**Trap and Skeet Shooting**

Trap Shooting

Trap shooting had been a shooting sport among the upper class in England since the late 17$^{th}$ century, and then in America using the abundant passenger pigeon, which was released from cages called "traps." After the Civil War, when the passenger pigeon was nearing extinction the glass ball target was introduced from England. Later in 1880 round frangible disks called "clay pigeons" were invented by American George Ligowsky. Competitive Trap shooting was adapted to simulate shooting a flexible gun mounted in an aircraft by the Headquarters of the Air Corps Technical School at Chanute Field and by the AAF Aerial Training Headquarters at Maxwell and Lowry Fields. Trap shooting was an easy system to teach and was considered the simplest method for gunnery trainees to learn, as many were not familiar with the basics of gun handling. The Trap range was easy to set up and equipment was readily obtainable. Many champion civilian Trap and Skeet shooters volunteered as instructors. Trap shooting in its simplest form was firing at thrown clay pigeons with shotguns fired first from the shoulder, but mainly from flexible mounts. The layout of the Trap shooting range was different from the Skeet shooting range in that there was only one house, called a "shack," that contained a mechanical device known as a "trap" that threw clay targets. Shooters moved through five different positions firing

Skeet and trap shooting was the basis for early hands on gunnery training. (USAAF)

at clay pigeons released from the shack. However, Skeet shooting proved to be a more viable teaching method and Trap shooting was cancelled as a gunnery training method.

Shotguns and Rules

The 12 gauge Remington Auto-loading Shotgun was the standard Trap and Skeet shotgun. It came in two models: the Model II had a five shell capacity (one in the chamber and four in the magazine) and the Sportsman (one in the chamber and two in the magazine). The guns came in various stock lengths and drops (the position of the barrel so that the target could be viewed completely along its entire length). The 12 gauge shotgun was used because as the gun's gauge became smaller (12-20-28-410) the more difficult hitting the target became.

Before shooting began the instructor gave the student a set of rules to be followed. Among the rules were:

1) No loaded guns except when standing in the shooting box.
2) Guns were to be loaded in the shooter's box.
3) When loading a gun the muzzle was always to be pointed at the ground.
4) Never aim a gun, loaded or unloaded, at anything except the target.
5) In case of a misfire or malfunction the gunner was to remain in the shooter's box with the muzzle pointing upward until the instructor took the gun from him.
6) Heckling would not be tolerated.

Skeet Shooting

Skeet was invented in 1915 by Charles Davies, a Massachusetts goose hunter, but the sport was not named until 1926 when the Scandinavian word "Skeet," meaning "shoot," was chosen in a naming contest. In competitive Skeet shooting the shooters tried to break 4 5/16 inch diameter and 1 1/8 inch thick clay disks thrown into the air at high speeds from an assortment of angles out to about 60 yards. Skeet shooting gave the student a greater familiarization with the operation of guns and also introduced him to the difficult aspect of determining lead. The military Skeet ranges were constructed under the direction of the American Skeet Association. Under Regulation Skeet rules the shooter shot from seven positions (stations) located on a semicircle, with the eighth station located halfway between stations number 1 and 7. At each end of the semicircle was a house that contained a Trap that launched the clay targets to a point 15 feet above the ground and to 18 feet outside station #8. One Trap, called the "high house," launched its clay targets from ten feet above the ground and the other, the "low house," launched its disks from three feet above the ground. At stations #1 and #2 the shooter shot at a single pigeon launched from the high house and then from the low house, followed by two shots at two thrown targets launched simultaneously from the high house and then the low house. At stations #3, #4, and #5 the shooter shot at single targets launched from the high house and then the low house. At stations #6 and #7 the shooter shot at single targets launched from the high house and then the low house, then shot at a pair lauunched first from the low house and then the high house. At station #8 the shooter shot at one high target and then one low target. The shooter had to reshoot at his first missed target, or if no targets were missed, had to shoot his 25th shell at a station of his choice. While shooting at double targets the shooter was instructed to fire first at the target moving away and then at the target moving toward him.

In 1943 the gunnery system known as "Position Firing" was implemented by the AAF, and the value of Skeet shooting in gunnery training came under scrutiny. Originally Skeet shooting was criticized as not of-

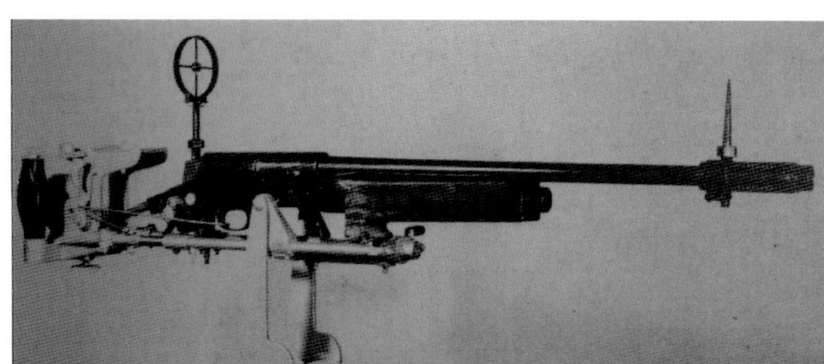

Browning 12-gauge shot gun on a swivel mount using a ring-and-bead sight. (USAAF)

Skeet shooting using a 12-gauge shoot gun with a spade grip. (USAAF)

**Burst Control Range** (USAAF)

fering the gunner any type of shooting he was likely to use in a defensive position in a bomber. Once Position Firing was adopted it was contended that Skeet shooting stressed lead shooting ahead of the target, which was opposed to Position Firing principals in which the gunner fired between the target and the tail of his own aircraft or behind the target. Other factions argued that, while Skeet shooting did contradict Position Firing principals, firing at aerial towed targets and railway target cars on ground ranges, which also required leading the target, were contradictory as well to the deflection shooting tenets taught in the Waller and Jam Handy trainers, in air-to-ground firing, and on gun camera missions.

In August 1943, the Training Command ordered ten hours of Skeet instruction; eight hours were to be Regulation Skeet firing of 150 rounds. In the fall of 1943 Skeet firing in this program was reduced to a minimum of 100 rounds and Regulation Skeet rules were no longer applicable. So Skeet shooting was retained, as it was thought to familiarize the student with firearms while high tower Skeet shooting and moving base shotgun ranges were considered to have particular value. When using either Skeet or moving base ranges the principle of Position Firing could be put into effect, because as far as possible gunners could fire at targets when they were in a position corresponding to that from which an enemy aircraft would make an attack.

**Burst Control Range**

In mid-1944 the burst control range was introduced. A belt containing ten rounds was fired in one burst at a 12 inch target at 1,000 inches (83.3 feet) away with the intention of teaching the gunner to fire short bursts and maintaining better gun control. The objective was to prevent "hosing" the target and to avoid prematurely burning out the gun's barrel.

**Moving Target Ranges**

Moving Base Shotgun Ranges

Trap equipment was used to set up the moving base shotgun range where the Position Firing theory could be applied. Moving base ranges were designed to give an opportunity for firing at moving targets from a moving mount. Trap houses and trucks or cars constituted a part of the necessary equipment, and ground-to-air firing as well as ground-to-ground firing were possible on such ranges. After completing days on Skeet or Trap ranges gunners climbed onto the back of a truck with an observer and scorer and sat down holding his shot gun. The truck moved at 15 mph along a mile long course lined with 16 Trap houses. As soon as the rear wheel of the

Moving range trucks using skeet techniques for flexible gunnery training. (USAAF)

Moving range trucks mounting turrets using skeet techniques for turret gunnery training. (USAAF)

The .30 caliber moving range target consisted of a flatcar moving over a mile long triangular course and mounting a six square foot white cloth with a trailing a tail. The gunners were stationed in a row along the course armed with .30 caliber machine guns mounted on swivels. (USAAF)

The target cloth was removed from the flatcar and brought back to the firing line where each gunner recorded his hits on it for the instructor to critique. Each man usually fired 1,500 total rounds in this phase. (USAAF)

truck drew even with each shack a clay pigeon was released in any direction and the gunner fired.

.30 Caliber Moving Range
The .30 caliber moving range target consisted of a flatcar moving over a mile long triangular course and mounting a six square foot white cloth with a trailing tail. The gunners were stationed in a row along the course armed with .30 caliber machine guns mounted on swivels. When the flatcar, moving at 15 to 40 mph, was directly in front of the gunners it was only about 200 yards away, but on the triangular backstretch it was about 500 yards away. The flatcar and its engine were protected by a bank of earth, with only the raised cloth target exposed. Every fifth bullet was a tracer to enable the gunner to follow the trajectory of his bullets. Each gunner had different colored bullets that were dipped in colored lithograph grease so that scoring could be done by counting the color-rimmed holes in the cloth target. At first the gunners were only to shoot at the target as it passed by on the closest leg of the course, firing short bursts of two to six rounds, but later shot at longer ranges. After the flatcar made five circuits the instructor called "Cease fire" and shut off the engine and set the brakes. The target cloth was removed and brought back to the firing line, where each gunner recorded his hits on it for the instructor to critique. Each man usually fired 1,500 total rounds in this phase

.50 Caliber Moving Range
After using the .30 caliber range the students moved onto a second similar moving range riding in trucks equipped with power turrets mounting .50 caliber guns. The student gunners sat in a cramped cage-like framework of an electrically powered turret that had all the functions of a combat turret. The moving target traveled at varying speeds up to 40 mph. Even though enemy aircraft traveled at over 300 mph or more the gunners learned that it was angular speed that was important. If the gunner was in an aircraft flying at 250 mph and an enemy fighter approached from astern at 280 mph flying in the same direction then the relative speed would be 30 mph (280-250=30). Whether on the ground or in the air the gunner learned how an attacker appeared at a relative speed of 30mph. Later in this training phase the gunners moved to shooting at aerial-towed targets while their truck moved below.

**Gunnery Training Equipment**
The success of the flexible gunnery training program not only depended on the students and instructors, but also the procuring and use of training equipment. In the fall of 1941 Maj. William Kennedy reported on RAF gunnery training devices and the Training and Operations Division was authorized to evaluate them, and was to send its conclusions to the Materiel Division and to the Air Force Combat Command.

Trainers
Turnbull Gunnery Trainer
In the summer of 1942, the Flying Training Command directed the AAF's Director of Individual Training to submit recommendations on the new Turnbull Gunnery Trainer. The Director's recommendation was that the Turnbull was not needed in flexible gunnery, because "the present Trainers give sufficient training in turret manipulation for basic instruction, and the Waller and 3A-2 Gunnery Trainers, which will be in operation very shortly, perform the same functions as the Turnbull Trainer in a more satisfactory manner."
Jam Handy Synthetic Trainers
The use of "synthetic" training devices was considered by a team of Army gunnery officers led by Maj. W.L. Kennedy that inspected and reported on 13 different RAF systems. The British units included combinations of spotlight, panoramic, and platform trainers that were to be evaluated by a board of gunnery officers who would select the most promising and seek out American companies that had similar units and could adapt them. In September 1942, at a time when the flexible gunnery training program was accelerating, the Jam Handy Company, led by chief designer J. A. Pool, became a leader in adapting its well-known industrial film production techniques to gunnery training devices. Of particular interest was the company's gun camera equipment, designed to simulate combat operations, and its simple to operate lead computing sight. The gun camera was the same type that was used to simulate combat firing. It was mounted on a machine gun that the student aimed and fired at moving aircraft images projected on a movie screen. A mechanism was included that accurately indicated the student's point of aim and where it should have been. The Jam Handy trainer, in providing actual combat conditions on a large screen, was well adapted to range estimation and to an understanding of all ballistic factors.

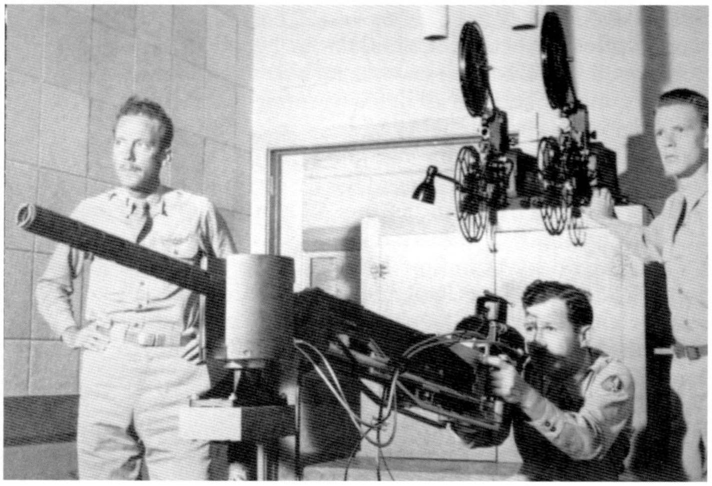

The **Jam Handy Company** became a leader in adapting its well-known industrial film production techniques to gunnery training devices. (USAAF)

In a realistic three-dimensional atmosphere gunners would aim remote electronic aiming devices weighted and resembling .50 caliber machine guns at enemy aircraft diving at different angles while the instructor sat a nearby control panel. (USAAF)

Furthermore, its flexibility demanded the correction of errors. Its defects consisted of a small observing area and a failure to give accurate scores. The company asserted its camera gun "allows actual practice of gun firing in aerial combat with built-in means to indicate, accurately and easily on the films, where the point of aim was as well as where it should have been." The computing sight "will have no lead problem for the gunner in the turret of a bomber when he is being attacked, by a pursuit plane. He will simply have to place the attacking plane on the moving spot of light in his sight." The Flying Training Command ordered a large number of Jam Handy trainers and the apparatus was utilized throughout the war.

Spotlight Gunnery Trainer

The E-1 Spotlight System was a modification of the Jam Handy method with the student gunners placed in actual turrets with their Plexiglas domes removed and firing at images on larger movie screens.

The **Waller Trainer**, developed by Fred Waller, used five synchronized 35mm projectors with sound tracks showed realistic air combat scenes.

Waller Synthetic Trainers

The Waller trainer, developed by Fred Waller, was larger and more intricate than the Jam Handy. The Waller units could be identified by their peculiar-shaped buildings that accommodated their large screens, while the Jam Handy units were portable and could be easily moved. The Waller trainer's five synchronized 35mm projectors with sound tracks showed realistic air combat scenes on a large, 40 foot panoramic parabolic (spherical) screen. In this realistic three-dimensional atmosphere usually two gunners aiming flexible guns and two seated in turrets would aim remote electronic aiming devices weighted and resembling .50 caliber machine guns at enemy aircraft diving at different angles. When the student fired his electronic gun rattled like a real gun with vibrators simulating actual firing. Machine gun sounds reverberated in his earphones and a bell rang when the gunner's point of aim was correct. The student looked through his sight, and when he fired an aim light projector mounted next to the sight would send spots of colored light that showed where the guns were being aimed. Photo-electric circuits controlled the angle of the electronic burst from the time the student pressed the trigger until they hit the target when a "beep" sounded in his earphones. The firing was monitored by instructors sitting at a sophisticated control panel that recorded hits, bursts, and rounds fired on electric counters. The instructor wore earphones and microphones to coach the students in the four trainers. When the instructor wanted to call attention to an error or give advice he could stop the film; freezing the firing and sound and leaving the images on the screen. Circles could be intermittently superimposed over the target aircraft on the screen to show the student the correct position of the gunsight at that instant of the attack. The student fired when there were no circles. After the war Waller spent 15 years at Paramount Pictures developing Cinerama.

Fairchild E-5 Gunnery Trainer

The Air Service Command had developed the Fairchild E-5 Gunnery Trainer and expected to procure them in quantity, but AAF Headquarters felt that they were so similar to the Waller trainer that they ordered Wright Field to conduct comparison tests. The tests revealed that the Waller trainer incorporated "all the desirable features proposed in the Fairchild device with the exception of aircraft identification, which could be accomplished without the necessity of such elaborate equipment." However, the E-5 was less complicated and easier and more economical to manufacture and were ordered in much larger quantities than the Waller.

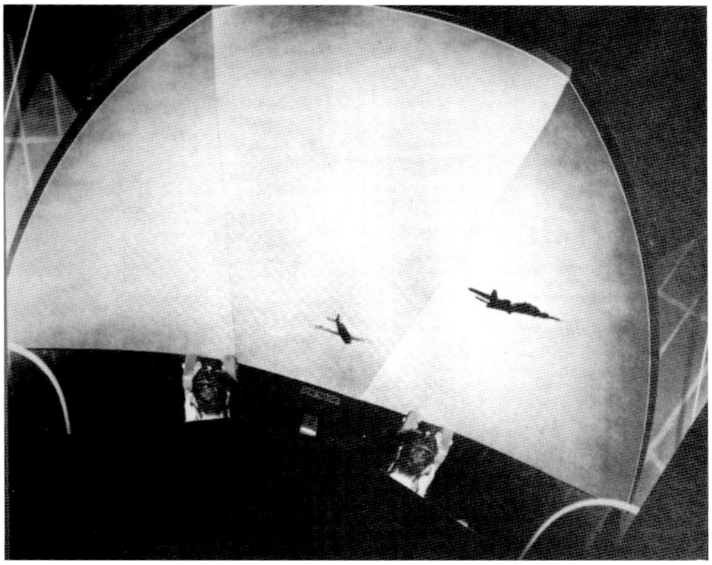

The large, 40 foot, panoramic parabolic (spherical) screen of the Waller Trainer on which the instructor could freeze the action to critique the student. (USAAF)

**Sights and Sighting Principals**

From the beginning of the flexible gunnery program much attention was devoted to sights and the principles of sighting. In early 1942, 20 of the 150 hours of instruction were dedicated to the subject. The gunnery student was required to study ring and bead, reflector, compensating, and telescopic sights, along with subjects related to sighting, such as bullet deflection, relative speed of opposing planes, and tracer firing. In 1943, 44 of 280 hours of instruction were devoted to sighting. Eight hours were given to range estimation, 12 to the Jam Handy trainer, and six to the Waller trainer.

Throughout the flexible gunnery program, finding the best sighting method was one of its continuing problems. During 1942 gunnery students had to become familiar with six different types of iron ring sights and four varieties of optical sights. The gunner was taught to use the following sequence of action in sightings: 1) recognize the enemy aircraft, 2) estimate the range with 600 yards as the critical distance for opening fire, 3) estimate the difference in speed between his aircraft and the target by holding the sight stationary for one second, 4) compute the lead according to a definite table which had to be memorized, and 5) open fire. Although the apparent-motion system was designed to simplify the method of computing lead, under combat conditions there was usually no target in sight by the time the student had gone through this involved system.

General Ent affirmed that the British zone method and the Position Firing method were virtually identical, as they were "based upon firing at fighter aircraft when they are in a position to make an attack." Ent replied to those who felt that firing should begin at a range of 1,200 yards (called "supporting fire") when the enemy was not in a position to make an attack. Ent referred to tests conducted by the University of New Mexico and reports from combat theaters that indicated that the .50-caliber machine gun could not be fired accurately at distances beyond 600 yards. He also revealed that reports and experiments indicated that computing sights then in use on B-17s and B-24s were not accurate under combat conditions. There was agreement between Ent and Dr. E.V. Paxson, of the Proving Ground Command, as to the main problems of flexible gunnery. According to Paxson the problems were computing sights, supporting fire for bombers against mass attacks by enemy fighters, and general gunnery equipment in relation to effective firing.

At the April 1944 Tampa Flexible Gunnery Training Conference Maj. Gen. Follett Bradley, who was a consultant to Sperry, zealously disagreed with Ent's findings and subsequently made recommendations to the Chief of the Air Staff. General Arnold directed Bradley to examine and report on the flexible gunnery situation. In March 1944, Bradley reported that "Position Firing should be taught; but that the student should have it impressed upon him that it should be used only if his guns are not equipped with automatic computing or compensating sights." Bradley recommended that "skill could be acquired in operating sights, tracking, and ranging if enough training were given along those lines." He further contended that "supporting fire (1,200 yard) was essential to bomber formations and not fire directed only at fighters attacking on the pursuit curve and within the 600 yard zone." In Bradley's opinion, "Position Firing was taught for the same reason that a men is taught to swim, not that swimming is man's method of traveling through water, but to save his life in case his boat is sunk." Maj.Gen. Barney Giles read the "excellent" report and promised Bradley that he had "directed the action required by the proper agencies of this Headquarters to start putting our gunnery training on a paying basis."

Nonetheless, the Tampa Gunnery Training Conference did not settle the controversy. A Second Air Force committee recommended that gunners continue to be taught to open fire at ranges of 600 yards or less, but that a decision on removal of present computing sights was not to be made until the conclusion of tests in progress by the permanent Committee on Sights, Sighting Methods and Flexible Gunnery Equipment. A Committee on Support Fire recommended a study of the relation between Position Firing (600 yards) and support fire (1,200 yards), but maintained that for training purposes the gunner be instructed to fire only at targets within the 600 yard range. In June 1944, the Training Command directed that a study be made of the need to include the relative-speed system of sighting in the flexible gunnery curriculum. The directive was implemented as a result of a report of representatives of the Command who had visited combat theaters and had been informed that the relative-speed system be used as well as that of Position Firing.

**Computing Gunsight Training**

In early 1944, the National Defense Research Committee (NDRC), which had previously involved itself with AAF projects on gunsights, sighting methods, and flexible gunnery equipment, participated with AAF agencies

With the introduction of computing gunsights in early 1944, the AAF Training Command established training syllabus of instruction for these sights. (USAAF)

Posed photo of a group of students receiving preflight briefing from their instructor. (USAAF)

Each student was dressed in full flying equipment and flew in the rear cockpit of an AT-6A advanced trainer. (USAAF)

in the formation of a committee to coordinate and evaluate data on sights and other flexible gunnery equipment. In March the Training Command was directed by Headquarters AAF to take part in the findings of this committee. In May the Flexible Gunnery Division of Headquarters, AAF requested the Training Command to prepare a syllabus of instruction on the K-9 and K-11 sights for distribution to gunnery schools and to the Fourth Air Force, and also to prepare a description of those sights and the K-10 for publication in the first revision of the *Gunners Information File* (GIF).

Also in May, in order to expedite plans for its early use at gunnery schools, Sperry informed AAF Headquarters of its progress on the K-13 compensating sight. Plans were made to facilitate the use of the K-13, and in June the AAF obtained eight E-8 Spotlight trainers for each air force training station conducting flexible gunnery training. In August arrangements were made with the Navy to train men in the use of the K-15 sight. This was a new sight which was to be installed in production aircraft: in the B-24 Martin turret beginning in November 1944, in the B-17 Sperry dorsal and B-17 Sperry Ball, and then three months later in the B-24 tail turret.

The simplification of sighting methods was one of the main and urgent requirements of flexible gunnery. This need was reiterated at the AAF Training and Gunnery Conference held at San Francisco from 31 July to 2 August 1944. At this conference Col. W. G. Garland of the Eighth Air Force suggested that the number of gunsights "be reduced to a minimum (the K13 and K-15), preferably one for turrets and one for hand-held guns." The report of the Flexible Gunnery Committee recommended that the National Defense Research Committee set up a project at Eglin Field to assist in a service test on sighting.

**Tow Target Aerial Gunnery Training**

After completing ground gunnery range training the student gunners moved on to the crux of gunnery school, aerial shooting. Each student was dressed in full flying equipment: flying suit, helmet and goggles, parachute, and a Mae West life jacket. The student flew in the rear cockpit of an AT-6A advanced trainer with three aircraft to a formation, with the instructor observing in a fourth AT-6 remaining in contact by radio. If radio contact with the tow plane failed the pilot of the tow plane used these visual signals: rocking wings meant "clear to fire" and dive and zoom meant "cease fire." The attacking aircraft signaled the tow plane that it had completed firing by pulling alongside and peeling off. On tow target missions no firing was to be done until the target was fully extended; until voice or visual clearance was given by the tow plane pilot; when the attacker was closer than 600 feet to the tow plane; when the angle of fire from the tow plane's course was less than 30°; or when the tow plane was turning.

The tow plane pulled a long white target "sleeve" (also called a "flag") on a line many safe yards long. The student used a .30 caliber gun with a 50 mile per hour sight. Once the target was sighted the gunner quickly calculated at what range the target would fill his sight and then estimated the speed of the tow plane and his own speed to determine by how much he should lead the target. The first firing run was an alongside approach, and as the three aircraft passed the target panel their gunners shot short bursts with colored bullets. Several more runs were made with the instructor giving advice. Approximately 900 rounds were fired at distances of 100 to 200 yards. When the tow aircraft landed the scores were tallied on the target sleeve. The next day the students practiced cross-under firing, with the AT-6s diving under the target sleeve, in tandem, with the gunners firing at a 45° angle. Initially the result of these firing runs was usually very poor.

In the spring of 1944 tow target training was still in place, but there was so much confusion on how to fly tow-target missions for flexible gunners that Headquarters AAF gave careful instructions on the point. Thus, it appears at the time that the AAF policy was to try to improve rather than to abolish aerial tow-target training. In August, however, the Flexible Gunnery Division stated that "the training value of air-to-air firing at tow targets is negligible compared to that obtained from gun camera missions, air-to-ground missions, and performance of the standardized phase checks."

Three aircraft flew in formation with the instructor observing in a fourth AT-6 remaining in contact by radio. The tow plane pulled a long white target "sleeve" (also called a "flag") on a line many safe yards long. (USAAF)

The gun camera mission involved the installation of an AN Gun Camera in various gun positions on bombers where the gunners would track and photograph fighters making pursuit curve attacks. After the mission the film was developed and placed an assessing apparatus that would determine if hits were made and evaluate the student's proficiency. (USAAF)

The use of gun camera mission training and the demise of the tow target training will be discussed next.

**Gun Camera Mission**

Until the summer of 1943 flexible gunnery training lacked a method of approximating combat conditions. The gun camera mission was proposed as a viable training method which involved the installation of an AN (Army-Navy) Gun Camera in various gun positions on bombers where the gunners would track and photograph fighters making pursuit curve attacks. After the mission the film was developed and placed in an assessing apparatus that would determine if hits were made and evaluate the student's proficiency.

A comprehensive test was conducted at the Central Instructors School with 53 students who had received training on the Sperry dorsal turret and were furnished with gun cameras holding 50 feet of film, which was enough for filming three to five attacks. The students fired from the Sperry dorsal turret of a B-17 at an AT-6 attacking from the beam or rear quarter. The instructor controlled the camera, turning it on when the AT-6 turned in to attack and turning it off at the breakaway. The student was instructed to track the attacking aircraft at all times when it was moving in on its pursuit curve. The test report highlighted two points: 1) the camera should be turned on when the attacking aircraft made its turn-in and during the entire attack, but was to be turned off on the breakaway, and 2) the scoring method was not standardized and did not produce satisfactory results.

As early as the summer of 1943, 24 hours of instruction on the AN Gun Camera was included in flexible gunnery training. This phase of the program required special training for a large number of skilled photographic personnel to process film and to maintain and repair the camera and film processing equipment. As the gun camera mission became more important, the aerial photographer became part of the crew and he was included in the gunnery training program.

Gun camera missions would require an increased number of fighter aircraft to be supplied to the flexible gunnery training stations to make true pursuit curve attacks against cinema guns and for teaching proper methods of gunnery control and tactics. An early January 1944 training conference held at Fort Worth endorsed AN Camera missions and stated that the procurement of fighter aircraft should be given higher priority. In June 1944 the commanding generals of the four training air forces were informed of the permanent assignment of fighter aircraft and pilots at their bombardment bases.

As mentioned previously, at the Tampa Flexible Gunnery Training Conference of April 1944 Brig.Gen. Ent presented a comprehensive case on the merits of gun camera training and the problems with aerial tow target practice. Ent emphasized that towing aircraft could not present their towed target on a pursuit curve, and therefore battle conditions could not be approximated. Towed target practice required much equipment and many personnel were necessary. The alleged advantage of towed targets in providing practice with computing sights was offset by the fact that this kind of sighting was restricted to only one gun position on the B-24 and two on the B-17. The gun camera mission gave the realism of combat and had all of the advantages which were claimed for air-to-air firing.

Col. H. P. Huglin, commanding officer of the Kingman Flexible Gunnery School, agreed with Ent, maintaining that it was possible not only to assess film on computing sights, but to assess and score the number of hits on flexible gun positions with non-computing sights. Huglin considered this method as superior to "such inaccurate and unsatisfactory methods as tow target firing a system that might be eliminated if sufficient aircraft were made available for gun camera training." At the same conference, the Second Air Force recommended that tow target training be eliminated from the training air forces but be retained in the flexible gunnery schools. Representatives of the Fifteenth Air Force also recommended the elimination of tow target aerial training and recommended that there should be emphasis on gun camera exercises.

Two recommendations further stimulated the gun camera program during the summer of 1944. The report of the Training and Gunnery Conference at San Francisco at the end of July 1944 recommended the assignment of additional fighter aircraft and fighter pilots to conduct training. The Flexible Gunnery Division approved the standardization of the gun camera program suggested by the Camera Training Committee, which met in June at the Instructors School at Laredo, TX. To aid the development of this program the Flexible Gunnery Division approved additional camera equipment.

The development of sighting and firing systems was a trial and error process. During the early stages of the gunnery program the student was required to be familiar with too many sights; consequently, the later emphasis, especially in 1944, was upon a reduction of that number. It was felt that the relative speed system of computing sights was too complicated to be practical, and Position Firing was advocated in its place. Both Skeet and air-to-air tow target firing were condemned on the basis that the gunner did not fire at a target in the relative position of an attacking plane. However, there were a number of officers who defended these two practices because they provided knowledge of the use of arms. The most significant development in gunnery training during the first eight months of 1944 was the approval and extensive use of the gun camera mission and the elimination of tow target training.

**Pinball Training**

As described previously in Part Three: Ammunition/Chapter 2: .30 Caliber Ammunition, the T44 frangible bullet was developed to allow firing during training flights at specially modified target, or "Pinball," aircraft.

The RP-63 target aircraft was a Bell P-63 Kingcobra that was covered (depending on the model) with between 1,400 and 2,100 pounds of light 24ST aluminum alloy armor plate 1/8 to 1/4 inch thick and armored cockpit glass. The RP-63 had several vulnerable areas, particularly the carburetor inlets, the radiators, and the canopy, which had its rear covered over by sheet metal. The oil and coolant radiator inlets for the Allison engine were located in both wing roots and ducts inside the leading edge of the wings and directed cooling air from openings on the inboard of the leading wing edge. Curved louvers protected the ducts by causing the frangible bullet to theoretically disintegrate, but there were numerous forced landings caused by bullets that did not fragment causing the loss of oil and coolant.

Pinball aircraft were **P-63 Kingcobras** designated as the RP-63 that were to armored with between 1,400 and 2,100 pounds of light 24ST aluminum alloy armor and armored cockpit glass. (USAAF)

Below right: **30 Caliber Ammunition the T44 frangible bullet** Far below right: A red light was placed in the spinner where the cannon barrel protruded and projected a 30° cone of light centered along the Pinball target aircraft's long axis and would flash whenever a hit was made. (USAAF)

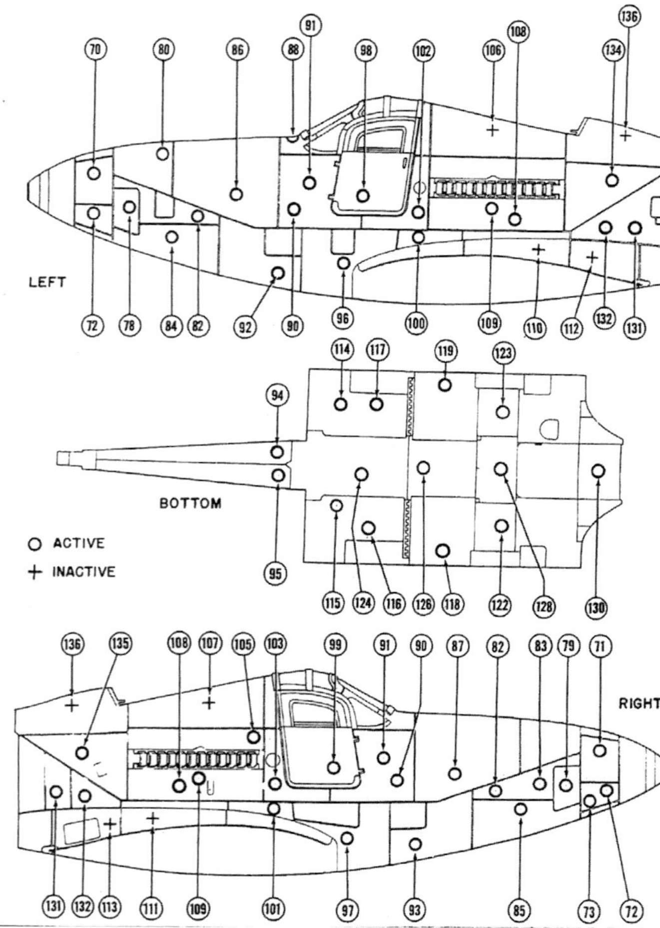


**Skin Sensor Location on Pinball Aircraft** (USAAF)

Cockpit "hit" counter (lower right) that recorded the number of sounds of the frangible bullets striking the target aircraft. (USAAF)

The first field trials were made at Buckingham Field, FL, in late May 1944 using the A-20 light attack bomber, which was outfitted with light weight duralumin armor by the Armament Laboratory of the Air Technical Service Command. The A-20, nicknamed the *Alclad Nag*, was "attacked" by an YB-40 (a B-17F converted gunship) without incident. However, on the second day the A-20 lost an engine and, weighted down by its armor, barely made an auxiliary field for a successful forced landing. The A-20 tests continued successfully, but it became apparent that the bomber was not the most suitable aircraft for training future bomber gunners who would meet fast, maneuverable Messerschmitt and Zero fighters. Lt.Col. Donald Russell of the Army training facility at Laredo, TX, was appointed to find a replacement. His selection was the Bell P-63 Kingcobra fighter, which was readily available, as it was considered inferior to contemporary first-line American fighters and was being sent to Russia as part of their Lend-Lease allotment. The Pinball version of the P-63 was to be designated the RP-63 ("R" for "Restricted from Combat"). Russell arrived at the Bell Niagara, NY, plant on 19 July 1944 to supervise the hand-built construction of the first five RP-63s. These target aircraft were to be armored against all head-on attacks within 30° of their line of flight, as all attacking passes were to be made on the pursuit curve against the firing aircraft. The gunners were to cease firing at the appropriate break off point. Alcoa 24ST and Reynolds .301T dural aluminum were tested, and the Alcoa 24ST was accepted. The fabrication of the aluminum armor proved more difficult than anticipated, but the prototypes were completed in August 1944 and Bell was awarded a contract for 95 more RP-63As. The first RP-63s were given such nicknames as *Pinball* and *Frangible Sal*.

An important phase of the program was the development of skin sensors to detect frangible bullet strikes and a cockpit counter. The Sperry Gyroscope Company designed a microphone based on a mechanism that had been used to sense detonations of an internal combustion engine. There were 132 (eight inactive) electrical generator sensor units placed under the target aircraft's armor plate that could detect the impact of a bullet hit so that an electrical potential was created that was amplified and sent to the in-cockpit hit counter and flashing propeller hub light. After the first five RP-63s were completed Sperry, American Time Products, and Bell submitted their designs for improved sensors. Bell's proposal proved to have a superior amplifier and was used on all subsequent RP-63s. However, the reliable hit sensors continued to be the most problematical aspect of the program, especially from the gunner's standpoint. Sensitivity adjustment was difficult, as too sensitive settings could add hundreds of hits to the counter during a rough landing while less sensitivity could register few or no hits. A red light was placed in the spinner where the cannon barrel protruded and projected a 30° cone of light centered along the Pinball target aircraft's long axis, and would flash whenever a hit was made. In practice, however, the student gunner found it difficult to see this light (on the RP-63 G model multiple lights were placed on the fuselage and wing tips).

The first frangible bullets were delivered to Laredo in December 1944 and the Frangible Bullet Program was begun, but was often called the Pinball Program. Specially modified T-9 .30 caliber machine guns were installed in B-17s, B-24s, and B-29s. To compensate for the decreased muzzle velocity of the .30 caliber machine gun the speed of the aircraft would have be decreased about 30%. The Sperry K-13 compensating gunsight was modified to correlate to the reduced airspeeds. The engineers at the Aberdeen Proving Grounds formulated range tables for sight manufacturers to use to modify their sights which would be completed in early 1945 in time for the first training classes. By April 1945 all seven flexible gunnery training schools were utilizing the Pinball Program. For safety reasons, firing was limited to pursuit curves from the rear with no head-on passes allowed. The average number of 15 to 20 hits per 1,000 rounds fired in training seemed to be very low, but actually compared favorably to the number of hits scored in combat.

The Pinball Program progressed to VJ-Day in September 1945, but the end of the war signaled the official termination of the flexible gunnery program and thus the Pinball Program. At the time 300 RP-63s were being used by the seven flexible gunnery schools, although firing missions had not been flown for several months. During the program some 11,000 Pinball training missions had been flown and 12 million frangible rounds had been fired. A total of 332 Pinball P-63s had been produced: 100 P-63As, 200 Cs, and 32 Gs. Prior to VJ-Day 450 additional Pinball aircraft were on order, but only the 32 G models were not cancelled. The As and Cs were powered by 1,335 horse power Allison V-1710-93 and -117 engines respectively, while the G was propelled by the more powerful 1425 horse power V-1710-135. The RP-63A weighed 8,300 pounds, the RP-63C weighed 8,500 pounds, and the RP-63G weighed much more at 11,500 pounds. The increase in G armor allowed it to be used for other gunnery approaches and for the possible use of higher velocity bullets used in the B-29 training program.

**Flexible Gunner Training Continuity**

Another problem with flexible gunnery training was the retention of knowledge and skills, as students were allowed too much time between training phases, and hence not only failed to retain what had been learned, but did not derive the additional benefits of continuity. Those responsible for training in the gunnery schools and in the Operational Training Units (OTUs), respectively, each blamed the other for this problem. To curb the deficiencies caused by the lack of a continuous training program, emphasis in 1943 and 1944 was placed upon three interrelated factors: Phase checks, standardization, and closer liaison among training agencies. Phase checks, which were required with increasing frequency in the flexible gunnery schools, the OTUs, and the combat theaters, were for the purpose of correcting as well as discovering deficiencies. The Central Flexible Gunnery Instructors School, which in 1944 was temporarily placed under the 75th Flying Training Wing and then under the Training Command, became increasingly a standardizing and coordinating training agency. Other significant steps in the standardizing and liaison process were the transfer of the Harlingen and Laredo schools from the jurisdiction of the Central Flying Training Command to that of the Eastern Flying Training Command and the creation of a deputy to the Commanding General of the Training Command. The duties of this official were to supervise and inspect gunnery training activities and to coordinate the activities of all agencies connected with that training.

# 3

# Turret Training

**Turret Training Program**

As the war in Europe established the importance of turrets and as FDR increased American bomber production, instruction in turret operation and maintenance increased. In 1942 20 hours were allocated to turret operation (then called manipulation) and 15 hours to maintenance, while in 1943 18 hours were allocated to turret operation and 32 hours to maintenance. Turret operation consisted of entering and leaving the turret, adjusting the sights, engaging and disengaging all clutches, correctly locating and using all switches, interphone connection, and oxygen connection. Much of the manipulation training and testing was done by the gunner when he was blindfolded. Maintenance consisted of installing and boresighting guns, mounting sights, checking the operation of the fire interrupters, checking the turret, gun, and sights, and loading ammunition.

Turret training in 1942 showed the same slow development that occurred in other phases of gunnery training. Progress in training was slowed by the large number of different turrets and the large number of students in the program who lacked technical training. Training equipment was in short supply, and the trainers that were available, such as the as the Spotlight E-1 and Fairchild E-5, were unsatisfactory for turret training. Maintenance of existing training turrets was hindered by lack of spare parts and sufficiently trained maintenance personnel. Often turrets were damaged by misuse by insufficiently trained personnel, including instructors, students, and maintenance men.

Gunnery range training using a Sperry Ball Turret. (USAAF)

On 25 June 1942, Gen. Barton Yount, head of the AAF Training Command stated:

"Although the scheduled production of gunners per month is approximately 2,000 there is not one airplane in the gunnery schools mounting a turret Even after turrets were mounted on planes, there remains the problem of coping with atmospheric conditions while manipulating a turret. To clear malfunctions, adjust guns and gun solenoids, and reload ammunition when flying at high altitude is a difficult task."

In late 1942 Headquarters AAF directed the Flying Training Command to have all students receive training in high altitude flying and in the use and adjustment of oxygen equipment. Implementing this policy was stalled by the lack of suitable high altitude aircraft.

In early 1943 the AAF had six turrets in use: Consolidated tail, Sperry dorsal and ventral, Martin dorsal, and Bendix dorsal and ventral, with specific turrets equipping specific aircraft. At the time there was too much emphasis placed on training men to be radio operators or engineers, thus cutting back their training as gunners. Students were taught the operation and maintenance of multiple turrets rather than a specific turret. For a student to become proficient in all or even several of these turrets was difficult, if not impossible, and ultimately a waste of time and teaching resources, as once a student graduated and was assigned to a combat aircraft he would be assigned to a particular turret for the duration. To simplify the situation the Flying Training Command assigned specific gunnery schools to teach specific turrets so that the student would have thorough familiarity with one turret. Turret specialization required less time, less equipment, and fewer instructors to train the increasing number of students entering the gunnery school system.

On 3 January 1943 the turret specialization program was initiated when the flexible gunnery schools were designated to use specific aircraft. Laredo and Harlingen became 100% B-24 schools, Las Vegas and Kingman 100% B-17, Panama City 50% B-26 and 50% B-25, and Fort Myers 60% B-26 and 40% light and dive bombardment aircraft. The Second Air Force took the graduates from these first four heavy bombardment schools, while the Third Air Force took their graduates from Panama City and Fort Myers. Although students were usually assigned to aircraft equipped with the turrets they were trained in this wasn't always the situation. The Flying Training Command had to impress upon the Training Air Forces that turret specialization was the accepted principle in the flexible gunnery schools. In February 1944 the turret specialization policy was modified in the Flexible

Gunnery Instructors School when the student instructor was informed that he would be required to be trained in all turrets and gun positions at his future assignment. These assignments were 30% to their original station and 70% to the combat air forces: B-24: 50%; B-17 (including B-29): 40%; B-25: 4%; B-26: 4%; and A-20: 2%. By 1945 turret specialization had proved to be the practical method of turret training, but only when the student was assigned to the proper aircraft and he was able to retain the information and techniques he had learned in training.

The improper assignment of the student was the main criticism of turret training after the specialization principle was adopted. AAF Headquarters and the Flying Training Command cooperated to correct this deficiency, and in 1944 improvement was such that instructors and students were generally familiar with the gun positions on the airplane to which they were assigned.

**Power Operated Gun Turret (POGT) Training**

Courses concerning power operated turrets and central (remote) control systems were the only regularly taught armament courses that involved equipment that was developed and came into use during the war.

Despite the obvious future use of the power turret in the war it was not until the end of March 1941 that a curriculum for power operated gun turrets (POGT) was set up at Lowry Field. There was a lack of qualified instructors and equipment, particularly turrets, and by the time of Pearl Harbor the POGT course was still in an undeveloped state. Soon a curriculum was developed that divided training into phases. Phase I devoted two weeks to Bendix turrets, Phase II four weeks to Sperry turrets, Phase III eight days to Martin turrets, and Phase IV four days to Consolidated turrets.

In early 1943, Sperry turrets (four weeks) were moved to Phase I and Bendix turrets (two weeks) to Phase IV, with more emphasis being given to the .50 caliber machine gun. In mid-September the course was lengthened to nine weeks to include training in the new Bendix chin turret and the Emerson nose turret. On 15 October 1943, the course was renamed the Power Operated Turrets and Gunsight Specialists Mechanic Course because of the increased importance of the gunsight in turret operation. All technical courses were rearranged into "blocks of instruction" so that students on detached service from tactical units would be able to participate only in blocks that concerned them. There were nine blocks:

| Block | Subject | Days |
|---|---|---|
| Block #1 | .50 caliber machine gun | 3 |
| Block #2 | Consolidated Turret | 3 |
| Block #3 | Sperry Dorsal Turret | 6 |
| Block #4 | Sperry Ball Turret | 6 |
| Block #5 | Sperry Computing Gunsight | 12 |
| Block #6 | Electricity | 6 |
| Block #7 | Martin Turret | 6 |
| Block #8 | Emerson Turret | 6 |
| Block #9 | Bendix Turret | 6 |

In early 1944, it became apparent that very heavy bombardment (the B-29) using central fire control was the future of AAF operations, and so the name of the Power Operated Turrets and Gunsight Specialists Mechanic Course was changed to Pre-central Fire Control Course and was to act as a feeder course to the new Central Fire Control Course. Lowry officials protested that only three Blocks of instruction applied to Central Fire Control: Block #1: .50 caliber machine guns, Block #6: Electricity, and parts of the Blocks concerning the amplidyne system and only these three should be given to CFPC students. The Training Command argued that the Central Fire Control was still experimental and could possibly be abandoned, and that all nine Blocks of training would be necessary if manned turrets had to be continued. In April 1944 the new course was reduced from nine to seven weeks: Basic Electricity, 6 days; Machine Guns and Martin Turret, 6 days; Emerson Turret, 6 days; Sperry Gunsights, 12 days, and Sperry Turrets, 12 days. Lowry continued to protest the course length and content, arguing that in case of the rearmament of the B-29 with conventional turrets it would only require seven weeks to retrain gunners, which was less time than it would require in reequipping the B-29. The training Command relented and allowed CFCE students to take a three week course that included basic electricity and the .50 caliber machine gun. This three week course was consolidated with the Remote Control Course on 21 August 1944. Lowry was concerned about the POGT students who were taking the normal seven week course, as they were not receiving training in many new turrets and in the new developments in turrets, gunsights, and turret powering. In May 1944 the course was to be expanded to 12 weeks, but AAF Headquarters ruled that this was too long and allowed a ten week course:

| Subject | Days |
|---|---|
| Machine Guns | 3 days |
| Basic Electricity | 1 week |
| Amplidynes | 3 days |
| Martin Turret | 1 day |
| Emerson Turret | 1 week |
| Bendix (chin and dorsal) | 1 week |
| Consolidated/Motor Products Turrets | 1 week |
| Sperry Turret (dorsal and ventral) | 1 week |
| Sperry Gunsights (K-3, 7, 9, 10, 11, 13) | 3 weeks |

From mid-1944 to the end of the war the length of the armaments course was continually expanded to incorporate material on new types of equipment. It was expanded to 11 weeks in March 1945, to 13 weeks in May, and finally to 16 weeks by VJ-Day, but by this time armament training was operating only on a nominal basis.

**Remote Control Turret Training**

In 1942 the AAF was preparing to train men to operate the unique remote fire control system to be deployed in the B-29. Both Sperry and General Electric manufactured their versions of this system, but problems with the Sperry system made the GE system the winner by default. Even though remote control turret use in the B-29 did not begin until 1944, in the fall of 1942 the Director of Individual Training ordered the development of a training program on central sighting station and remote control turret equipment. Central firing station operator-gunners were to be given a special gunnery course on central sighting station equipment that included all necessary calibration, adjustment, minor repairs, and inspection. Power turret and gunsight specialists were to be selected from graduates of the turret school and given an additional course on the maintenance of central sighting station equipment. In January 1943 Lowry was instructed to organize a CFCE training course. Lowry sent its most experienced instructors to the GE factory at Schenectady, NY, and to the Boeing B-29 plant at Wichita, KS, for intensive instruction while several GE employees were sent to Lowry.

For CFDE training, high quality enlisted men were required and were chosen from the best students of the POGT training program. The number of trainees was predicated on the requirements of the XXI Bomber Command and the number of B-29s leaving the assembly lines. Initially 24 were to be graduated every two weeks after finishing a 16 week course that included technical subjects such as: basic electricity, B-29 wiring, selsyn function, Vacuum tubes, gun charger, and servo-amplifiers, and six weeks on various B-29 malfunctions.

During the first year of operation class size was increased considerably, with the August 1943 entering class numbering 184. A washout rate as high as 18% was attributed to the very difficult subject matter, but soon Lowry was unable to find enough qualified students from the POGT course and had to look to other sources, such as their own Basic Armament Course, and the Basic Armament Courses at Buckley Field, Scott Field, Sioux Falls, and Truax Field. Some enlisted men who tested near acceptance cutoff points were allowed into the training program, but their washout rate was extremely high and this scheme was discontinued.

In 1944 enlisted men were first sent to the POGT program for the three week Pre-central Fire Control Course as described previously that consisted of .50 caliber machine gun and basic electricity instruction. Then, in August 1944, the Central Fire Control Course, soon to be called the Remote Control Turret Mechanic Course, was lengthened to 16 weeks (and within a year was increased to 20 weeks):

| Subject | Days |
|---|---|
| .50 caliber Machine Gun | 5 |
| Applied Electrical Principals | 20 |
| Servo-amplifier | 10 |
| Basic System | 20 |
| Wiring Diagram and Auxiliary Equipment | 20 |
| Malfunctions | 20 |
| Inspection and Maintenance | 5 |

# 4

# Aerial Gunnery Training Goes Hollywood

In early 1943 Paramount Pictures Pine-Thomas Production Company and director William Pine filmed the blatant gung-ho propaganda film "Aerial Gunner" starring Chester Morris (as gunnery instructor Sgt. Foxy Pattis) and Richard Arlen (as Lt. Ben Davis, a pilot-gunnery student). The Maxwell Shane screenplay from his original story had Davis, a former District Attorney, be assigned as a student to Pattis, a former bad boy who, along with his convict father, had run-ins with the D.A. in peacetime. During training Pattis tried to washout the arrogant Davis while the two vied for the affection of ardent (due to his father dying at Pearl Harbor) but inept gunnery student's (Jimmy Lydon) beautiful sister (Lita Ward). Despite Pattis' efforts Davis manages to pass at the top of this gunnery class while the brother-student dies while trying to pass on his second attempt after breaking down on his first try.

There are good scenes of gunnery training at the Harlingen Gunnery School, where Paramount spent two weeks filming the progress of real recruits and actors through the various stages of training. There is a particularly good sequence showing the students firing at the moving target flatcar from truck-mounted .30 caliber turrets. In his effort to washout Davis, Pattis tries to adjust the flatcar to move faster but gets knocked unconscious and stranded on the flatcar. Davis springs into a jeep and catches the runaway flatcar and jumps onboard to save Pattis. After graduation Davis is assigned as a pilot in the Pacific only to find that Pattis has asked to be assigned to his crew. As missions pass the two earn each other's respect as the bomber crew becomes a well-oiled team, with Foxy showing Davis a Dear John letter from the girl that says she loves Davis and will tell him when he returns. (Sob, sob) The film ends with the damaged aircraft landing on a Jap-held island, and while the crew geek nicknamed "Gadget" repairs the aircraft Foxy is killed holding off the Japs, allowing the wounded Davis to takeoff and escape. This stereotypical World War II "B" movie was released in mid-May 1943 at Harlingen with military and studio officials present.

Aerial Gunner starring Chester Morris (center) and Richard Arlen (left) was a blatant gung-ho propaganda film depicting gunnery training, (Paramount Pictures)

# Part Nine
## Fighter and Bomber Air-to-Air and Strafing Gunnery Tactics

# 1

# Fighter Air-to-Air Tactics

**Fighter Formations**

In the inter-war years the United States favored the conventional fighter formation organized into elements of three aircraft in a V formation that was also used by American bombers. The V was discarded as soon as America entered the war and the British leader/wingman two-plane system was adopted. The RAF experience in the Battles of France and Britain caused them to be in turn influenced by the successful *Luftwaffe* fighter formation techniques used there. The *Luftwaffe* had developed the technique during the Spanish Civil War, but later in WWII used the line abreast or "wall" formation. The Japanese generally flew the *shotai*, a division of three fighters arranged in Vics, in echelons or in loose, staggered trail formation. The two wingmen would weave in loose formation behind their leader. When engaged the *shotai* could stay together, fall into trail, or break with each aircraft fighting independently.

The fundamental U.S. fighter unit was two fighters, a leader and wingman ("No.2" in RAF parlance) known as an element. The leader's duty was to attack while the wingman was to protect his leader from interception from the rear throughout the mission. This technique was known as the "Wingman System" and was the key to survival, and was used with great success by American Air Forces. The two-plane element was the basic unit of all larger combat formations. The fighter pilot was a member of a team that was organized and synchronized to attack.

A flight was composed of two elements and was led by the leader of one of the elements. It was considered the most effective fighter combat formation for attack and defense. It was adaptable to various combat situations, as each element was easily able to assist the other. This formation was referred to as the "Finger Four" because from above the four fighters were in the position correlating to the finger tips when one looks down at the top of one's right hand. The element Leader No.1 (middle finger) was about 100 feet in front and to the right of his wingman, No.2 (first finger), while the second element Leader No.3 (ring finger) was about 150 feet behind and to the right of the element leader No.1, and his wingman, No.4 (pinkie finger), was about a 100 feet behind and to the right of him. The No.2 wingman could fly to the left or right of the Leader, 100 feet behind and stepped slightly down for maneuverability. The second element flew 150 feet to the rear of the Flight Leader and crossed underneath with his wingman on all turns. During the war group tacticians such as Don Blakeslee and Hub Zemke were encouraged to develop and experiment with new formations, but the Finger Four continued as the fundamental combat tactical formation.

Two flights made up a section, and was the usual component for bomber escort and support. Two sections made up the typical squadron of 16 fighters (that initially were organized into three four-plane flights).

The **"Finger Four"** fighter formation received its name as when looking at it from above the four fighters were in the position correlating to the finger tips when one looks down at the top of one's right hand. (USAAF)

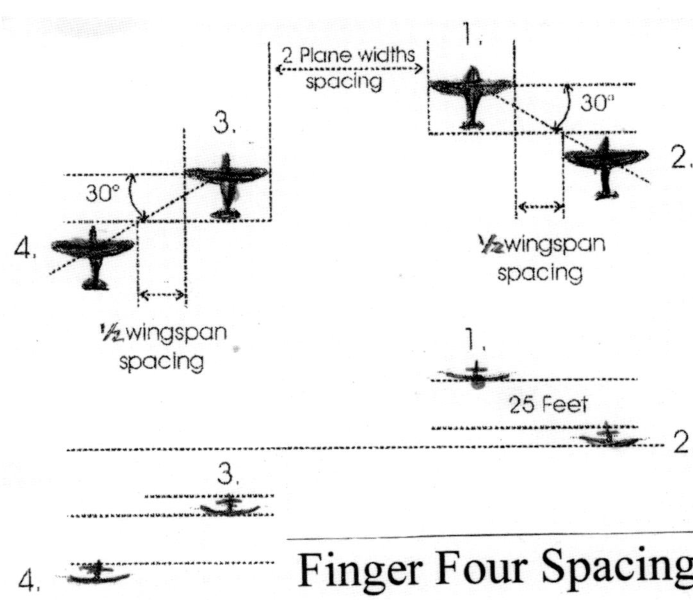

Although there were variations in section and squadron tactics the Finger Four remained the basis of all larger formations.

**The Successful Fighter Pilot**

Individual traits, such as excellent eyesight, natural judgment of height and distances, quick reflexes, and the aggressor mentality were essential for a successful fighter pilot. Sharp eyesight was the fighter pilot's most important faculty, as the crucial factor in all air combat was to see your enemy first and then to continue to keep him under observation. To do this the pilot had to swivel his head in continual scrutiny for hours on end, searching the skies, often with sunlight dazzling in through the canopy and glinting in his goggles.

When fighter aces were questioned about the most important factors that made them successful, the intangibles of luck and surprise were mentioned most frequently. Luck—being in the right place at the right time—was something the pilot had no control over. Undoubtedly many excellent pilots never became aces or even scored a victory simply because they never had the luck to encounter an enemy aircraft. The single-most important controllable factor in successful air combat was surprise, as many average pilots, utilizing surprise in their encounters with enemy aircraft, were successful. Surprise could be achieved by attacking directly out of the sun (the most used means of surprise); attacking from the darker part of the sky, as aircraft in the brighter part become silhouetted and more visible and the attacker less visible; attacking in the early morning or evening when lighting was problematical; and making use of clouds, both offensively and defensively. However, when a pilot was surprised he was to turn towards the attacker under all circumstances and never turn away. It was critically important for him to reverse the situation and become the attacker.

**Basic Fighter Combat Tenants**

The principal purpose of a fighter pilot was the destruction of enemy bombers, and combat with enemy fighters was considered to be secondary. The exceptions to attacking enemy fighters were that there definitely were no enemy bombers present to engage, circumstances for attack were very favorable, or that the enemy fighters were actually preventing the pilot from achieving his primary goal of destroying enemy bombers.

Altitude advantage was the fighter pilot's greatest asset, as it could be turned into airspeed and surprise at the pilot's choosing. When diving to attack on an enemy who was either in formation or solo, the dive was to be made steeply to the enemy's level, then flattening out, using excessive speed gained in the dive to make a swift firing approach preferably from dead astern. The speed advantage was then to be used to breakaway in a dive if threatened, or to climb to regain the altitude advantage.

Maneuverability was to be only considered as a form of defense, and was only to be resorted to when the enemy was definitely flying a faster aircraft. But if the pilot was flying a faster fighter, he was to attack, getting in quickly, shooting, and breaking away.

Once an enemy aircraft was seen and closed on there was one common axiom for the attacking pilot: "Get in so close that you can't miss. Don't waste ammo at long-range. Dive, hit hard, hit fast, and get out. Haul the stick back into your lap and use your excess speed to regain the altitude advantage."

**Deflection Shooting**

In fighter vs. fighter combats, because of the constant maneuvering the no deflection shot seldom, if ever, occurred, and it was critical that the fighter pilot become proficient at deflection shooting. In firing at a target which had an apparent movement across the pilot's line sight but not flying directly to or from the pilot, the pilot had to aim ahead of the target in order to allow for the length of time which the bullets required to travel to the point

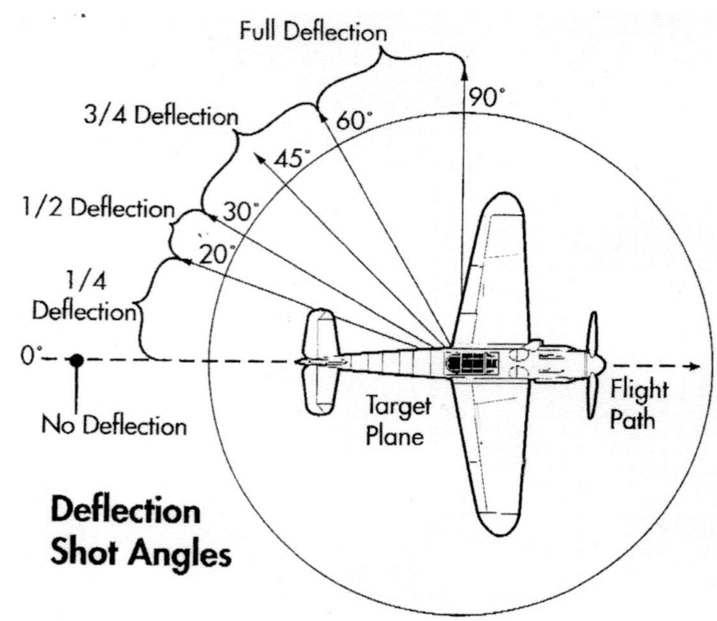


of intercepting the target. The angle between the position of the target and the point at which the gunner needed to aim to hit the target was called the amount of "lead," or the "angle of deflection."

Deflection shooting gave the pilot technical freedom in making his attack, allowing him to engage any element of an enemy formation from any direction. By being able to effectively attack from any angle, the pilot could choose an aircraft in the enemy formation that had less supporting fire from other aircraft in the formation. Since aircraft were armored to protect the crew and vital areas from attacks from bullets fired from the rear quarter, bullets fired at the side of an enemy aircraft would penetrate into unarmored areas and be much more effective.

In deflection shooting there were four points which a pilot had to estimate:

1) The distance to the target.
2) The speed of the target.
3) The distance to aim ahead of the target (because of the speed it was traveling at to allow for the length of time the bullet took to travel that range).
4) The angle that the target was cutting to the fighter's line of flight.

Factors which the pilot knew and did not have to estimate were the speed of the fired bullet and the speed of his aircraft. These factors affected the length of time the bullet took to travel the estimated distance (range) to the target. The length of time of the speeding bullet was approximately one quarter second for 250 yards flight, with the aircraft's relatively low speed making no appreciable difference in this very short length of time.

In deflection shooting it was absolutely essential that a pilot be able to automatically estimate the angle between the course of the enemy aircraft and that of his own aircraft. It was tempting for a fighter pilot to take a deflection shot at the target by gauging the amount of deflection on the apparent course of the target. During air firing against towed targets this was relatively easy, as the towing aircraft, cable, and target give the attacking pilot a definite indication of the direction in which the target was moving. But in actual combat this was not as easy, because the enemy aircraft was not necessarily moving in the direction in which it was pointing. For example, an enemy pilot might apply full rudder and opposite stick to prevent banking and a turn and point considerably to one side of the track he was completing.

It was critical, through practice and experience, for the pilot to be able to estimate the amount of deflection to allow by judging the amount of general movement of the target rather than by noting the direction in which the target was pointing.

**Skidding by the Target**

The line error in a deflection shot was caused by several factors: the pilot's failure to position the target so that it was flying towards the center of the sight; failing to make accurate turns; and using rudder alone to correct aim when sighting or firing. The pilot also had to be able to estimate the line of flight of the enemy aircraft, which could be skidding severely in combat so that his aircraft was not flying along the line in which the nose of the aircraft was pointing.

The application of rudder did not change the course of the attacker, but only turned the nose of that fighter away from its course. The enemy fighter continued to proceed along its original course, slipping to one side. Therefore, when firing at a target the pilot was not to pay attention to the direction his fighter was pointing when deciding the line of sight, but was to try to determine its general direction. When an enemy aircraft was flying with rudder applied it was not easy for the attacking pilot to position the target in his sights so that it was flying towards the center of the target, and if unsuccessful a line error frequently occurred. This gunnery fault could be remedied by firing with tracer ammunition, as tracers made it easy to determine which side of the target bullets were directed.

**Skidding and Accurate Flying by an Attacker**

Obtaining and maintaining aim needed to be complemented by accurate flying. The pilot was never to rely only on rudder to correct his aim, as his turns while keeping his sights on the target had to be accurate turns with the indicator bubble on the exact center. If the turns were not made accurately and smoothly the fighter would have a slight sidewise velocity (skid), and as described above this would be imparted to the bullets as they were fired, and this would be sufficient to make them miss the target.

Basically, a single-engine fighter was drawn through the air by an airscrew, which had to rotate to impart a forward movement to the aircraft. The rotating airscrew created a corkscrew flow of air backwards and around the fuselage. This corkscrew motion of air hit the side of the rudder and tended to turn the nose of the aircraft around its vertical axis (e.g. the aircraft skidded or slipped). To keep the aircraft flying straight the pilot would have to continually apply rudder throughout the flight, but aircraft designers added a fin to offset or counteract the corkscrew airflow motion. The fin was fixed so that the aircraft could be flown hands off at normal cruising speed. If any changes in air speed occurred the pilot had to counteract it with either rudder bias adjustment or by applying rudder. For example, a dive would increase the airspeed and the corkscrew airflow motion past the fuselage tended to straighten out; but the fin, being offset to counteract the normal corkscrew airflow tended to swing the fighter out of line (e.g. the aircraft started to skid and no longer proceeded in the direction in which it was pointing). The pilot counteracted this situation by immediate application of the rudder. Another change in airspeed would be caused by a climb. Immediately the propeller began to thrash, blasting the air in a tighter corkscrew motion around the fuselage. The fin was set for a lesser side blast and caught this additional blast from the side, which caused the nose to swing, initiating a skid to the opposite side which was also counteracted by application of the rudder. The pilot needed continual practice to fly accurately without skidding. During this practice he was not to change the position of the trim tabs because he would not have time in combat with the continual changes that would be necessary.

**Gunnery Approaches**

Introduction

Five checks were mandatory before a fighter pilot went into an attack:

1) Guns charged,
2) Gun switches on,
3) Gunsight on,
4) Tabs trimmed at firing speed,
5) 360° check (just as the pilot went into his attack he was to do a 360° check of the sky around him for friendly and possible enemy fighters).

The type of gunnery approach depended on several factors: the enemy strength, the time into the mission, the tactical situation, and the pilot's position when the target was sighted. It was important that the pilot was well versed in enemy aircraft recognition so as to immediately be able to properly assess the enemy's speed, maneuverability, and firepower, as well as strong points and weak points. No matter what type of attack approach the pilot chose he needed proper timing, arriving at the ideal firing angle at 1,000 feet or less to be assured of success.

Side Approach

The side approach was the most common form of attack against enemy bombers. There were three types of side approaches, with all initiated from above the target. The three side approaches (high, flat, and low) all appeared to converge when viewed from above. The principle of any side approach was only a matter of timing the "S" turn to arrive in a point in the flight path where the target's path would converge into the attacker's stream of fire. The pilot would continue to fire down this convergent path and breakaway before he would fly behind the target (i.e. to escape possible tail gun fire).

High Side Approach

The objective of the high side approach was to arrive at a firing position about 30° above the target. The fighter's position at the start of the approach run depended on the target's speed and the desired firing angle. Initially the fighter pilot was trained to hit targets from 55° to 35°, which gave the pilot more firing time than shots taken from more abeam, and then he was to work on attacks from more abeam where he was less vulnerable to enemy bomber free gunners.

The most favorable position for beginning high side approach was about 3,000 feet ahead of the target on a 45° bearing to its line of flight, with a height advantage of 1,200 feet. The approach was similar to that of the high side approach. The first turn in the "S" turn track had to be timed carefully in coming about the target, and the reverse turn was even more important, as it was the one in which the pilot held his lead on the target while completing the run to the firing position. In the start of a high side approach the pilot made a smooth, nose high turn toward the target, dropping the nose as necessary to keep the target in sight. As the pilot reached a point almost abeam of the target he banked in the opposite direction to reverse his turn. He then increased the throttle to bring up the line of sight, keeping it ahead of the target. When the critical range was reached the pilot let the pipper drift to the correct lead point and then squeezed the trigger, firing as long as he was able to hold the lead. When he could no longer hold the lead the pilot was to make an immediate breakaway to gain position for another attack. The breakaway would depend on which side the pilot recovered. If the recovery was on the opposite side of the target then the breakaway was to be a continued dive until clearing the range of the enemy's guns, then

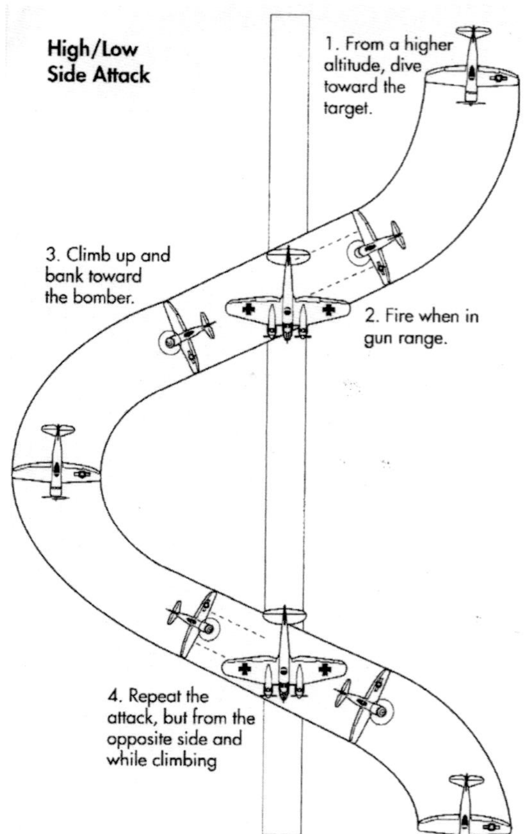


pulling back up into a steady climb. If the recovery was on the near side of the target after firing then he initiated an easy aileron roll in his dive until he was out of enemy gunnery range. In both cases the pilot was to pull out of his dive as soon as it was safe in order to use his excess diving speed to regain altitude and position for his next attack.

Flat Side Approach
The flat side approach was nearly the same as the high side, except that it was initiated from a slightly lower level and about 3,000 feet ahead of the target to arrive at a firing position within 10° of the target level. A satisfactory altitude advantage at the start of the run was to be between 600 and 900 feet. The pilot started the flat side attack with a smooth nose high turn. He then dropped the nose to the approximate level of the target, remaining in the firing approach. As the pilot came out of the second approach turn he increased throttle and continued on to the firing point. Once he fired the pilot passed under and parallel to the target. The pilot did not regain as much speed on the flat side run and pulled out like the high side approach, so it took him more time to get into attacking position again.

Low Side Approach
In this approach the pilot began the approach 3,000 feet ahead of the target and from 400 to 600 feet above it, reaching the firing position about 20° below the level of the target. When the pilot made his first turn he let the nose drop below the level of the target but not behind it. He kept the nose down until the reverse turn was started. At that point he was to be below the target and ahead of its beam with a good speed advantage. As soon as the reverse climbing turn was started the aircraft was given full throttle, bringing the line of sight well ahead of the target's path. After climbing and firing the breakaway was under and then parallel to the target's flight path. The disadvantage of the low side approach was the loss of speed in the climb and the subsequent difficulty in regaining altitude and speed for another attack.

The breakaway for the flat and low side approaches were nearly identical except for the degree of roll used in breakaway from the target. No matter if the recovery from firing was made on the near or opposite side of the target, the breakaway was begun immediately after firing. The pilot kicked hard bottom rudder to get the nose down and to gain speed, and at the same time he would roll ailerons to head the fighter in the direction he wished to recover.

Pilot Errors in Making Side Approaches
The most common error the pilot made in executing side approaches was being "pulled flat." In all types of side approaches it becomes increasingly difficult and then impossible for the pilot to hold proper lead as the ranges decreased, which was caused by the increase in Gs due to the quick change in direction. The pilot would find himself astern of the target if he did not reverse his turn quick enough; began his run too far to the side; or started it not far enough ahead of the target. Other side approach errors included the following. If the attack run was made too far away there was the possibility that the pilot could not get into effective range. If the turns were too tightly made the pilot would end up firing at long-range or in a tail chase trying to catch up. This miscalculation could be prevented if the target were constantly in sight during the entire approach. "Treading air," or using excess air space when regaining attacking position after making another attack was a problem when the pilot did not make quick, decisive maneuvers after an attack.

Overhead Approach
The advantages of the overhead approach were: the enemy was usually surprised, the enemy gunners had a difficult shot, and the speed gained in the breakaway put the pilot in an advantageous position for a second attack. The disadvantage was that it was difficult to perfect and required much practice.

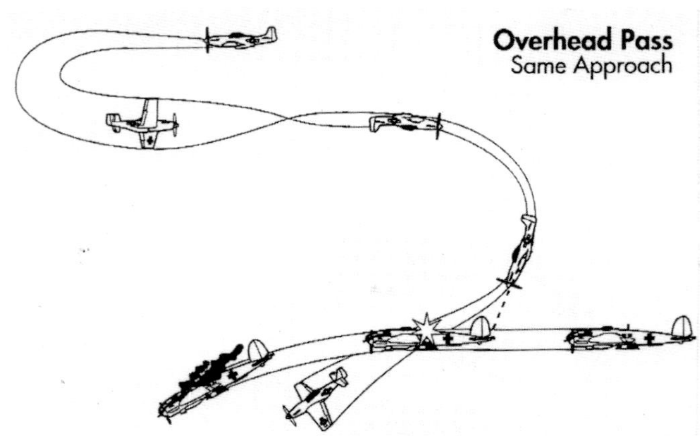


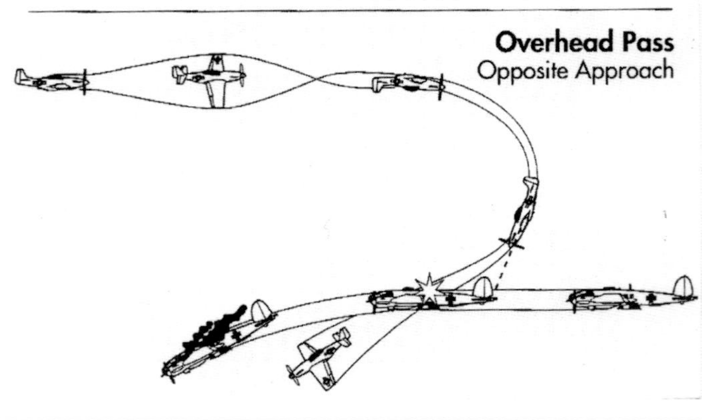

There were two variations of the overhead approach, as it could be made if the pilot was on the same or opposite course as the target. In either case a greater altitude advantage was required than for any other approach, and the faster the pilot's fighter the more altitude he would need. Also the recovery, which occurred under the target, required a greater air-to-ground airspace for the pilot to pull out safely. In the attack the pilot was to start the approach 2,000 feet above and 3,000 feet ahead, and just far enough to the side of the target so that he could easily look back and down on the enemy. As was the case in the side approaches, it was essential for the pilot to control the radius of his turns carefully throughout the overhead approach maneuver from its inception to the breakaway and recovery.

The overhead approach from the same course was begun with a smooth, nose high 180° turn toward the target. Once reaching a point ahead of and in the same vertical plane as the target's flight path the pilot inverted and dropped his nose down, then swept it up slightly ahead of the target. The pilot was to have reached the effective range while in a dive of not less that 60°, which should have flattened out so that the pilot passed the target at about a 45° angle. The pilot pulled out below, right, or left of the target's flight path and climbed for a second attack.

The overhead approach from the opposite course began with the pilot lining up his aircraft in a vertical plane that contained the target's flight path and, if necessary, would drop his wing to keep the target in view. Once in position the pilot went into a half roll, allowing his nose to drop and his sight to sweep ahead of the target. The dive was continued until the correct firing angle and range was reached from the same course. After firing the pilot pulled out and recovered from the same course.

### Pilot Errors in Making Overhead Approaches

The most common error in making an overhead approach was swinging too wide and passing through the vertical plane of the target. In this maneuver the pilot had to correct his alignment early in the dive before building up great speed by the careful use of the ailerons. Another error was beginning the attack with insufficient altitude advantage, which prevented sighting ahead of the target. If this occurred the pilot was to roll out of the attack and not pull through the dive to bracket the target, as he could suffer a blackout. A third error occurred when the pilot began his rollover too soon so that he would lose sight of the target. If this happened the pilot was to roll out of the dive to breakaway. A fatal mistake arose when the pilot made the overhead run so low that he could not pull out of the dive. It was essential in executing the opposite overhead attack that the target was kept in view because before he went into the half roll there would be a point when the pilot would lose sight of the target and cause him to time his run incorrectly.

### Head-on Approach

The head-on approach was not used often by fighter pilots because the range to the target closed too rapidly, the time of firing was too short, and the slow breakaway made it impossible to regain position for a second attack before the target departed. In this type of attack fire could be opened from longer ranges due to the rapid rate of closure between the two aircraft, which was compounded by the relative velocity of the bullets. Experienced pilots tended to make their head-on run from slightly below, where they were not so easily discovered on their approach, and then breaking off from below as there was less chance of collision.

The head-on run was to be initiated from as far out as possible so that the pilot could position himself in the target's flight path. If the pilot found himself too far to the left or right he needed to use ample aileron to get lined up as quickly as possible. If the pilot didn't have enough time to get into head-on position he could still make an effective approach by banking and approaching a few degrees off the target's flight path and using a slight deflection shot. After firing the breakaway was to be executed instantly with a hard flat turn in an effort to get into another firing position as soon as possible.

### Stern Approach

The stern approach was the easiest of all fixed gunnery approaches, as it gave the pilot a no deflection shot with a considerable amount of firing time. The approach could be made from a countless number of positions in variations of above, level, or below. Single-engine enemy fighters were the preferred target, as they had no tail defense, but enemy torpedo, dive bombers, and level bombers usually had tail guns. When attacking a target with a tail gun(s) the attacker needed to remain out of the target's cone of fire.

# 2

# American Fighter Aces

The top American fighter aces in World War II were 5th Air Force P-38 pilots Richard Bong, credited with 40 victories, and Thomas McGuire with 38, both in the Pacific. The top Navy aces were David McCampbell, Commander of AG-15, with 34 victories and tied at second with 23 victories were Lt. Eugene Valencia of VF-9 off the *Yorktown* and Lt. Cecil Harris, mostly (22) with VF-18 off the *Intrepid*. Maj. Joe Foss of VMF-121 with 26 (F4F) victories and 1Lt. Robert Hanson of VMF-214/215 with 25 (F4U) victories led Marine Corps pilots in victories. In the ETO, 8th Air Force P-47 aces of the 56th Fighter Group Lt.Col. Gabby Gabreski with 28 victories and Capt. Robert Johnson with 27 were the top scorers in that theater, followed by Capt. John Voll of the 31st Fighter Group with 21 P-51 victories in the MTO.

These totals may seem paltry when compared to the 352 victories scored by all-time fighter ace Erich Hartmann and the 14 other *Luftwaffe* pilots who claimed over 200 victories in World War II (107 others scored over 100 victories!). Why didn't American aces compile as impressive scores as their German counterparts? After the initial early war crises passed for America and supply of pilots increased a system of operational duty tours was introduced. After a pilot completed a specified number of missions he was assigned to non-operational duty. The aces were assigned to OTUs (Operational Training Units) to give students the benefit of their combat experience, copying and perpetuating the RAF's system of maintaining a large pool of well-trained pilots. This stricture obviously deprived American aces of gaining higher victory totals. Top ETO ace Gabby Gabreski scored his 28 victories in 166 missions while Richard Bong scored his 40 in just over 200 missions. Erich Hartmann scored his 352 victories while flying 1,405 missions and engaging in combat 825 times. Also, because of battlefront geography, Allied airmen with badly damaged fighter aircraft either had to bail out or crash land in enemy territory and were consequently taken prisoner. Conversely, *Luftwaffe* pilots with a lack of replacements continued to fly combat and compiled many more missions and were shot down many times. The advantage of fighting a defensive air war was that it was fought over friendly territory or near the front lines, and being shot down often did not mean becoming a POW. Gerd Barkhorn, the *Luftwaffe's* second high scorer with 301 victories, was shot down nine times and wounded twice, while Erich Rudorffer was shot down 16 times, bailing out nine and crashlanding seven, but surviving each mishap to score 222 victories. George Peter Elder was shot down 17 times, nine by Allied heavy bombers, and was wounded 14 times while scoring 78 victories, including 36 over Allied bombers.

The number of victories scored by *Luftwaffe* pilots in short periods of time was incredible because of the abundance of Allied targets. Over the Eastern Front Hermann Graf scored 72 victories in just 17 days in late April 1942, then added 75 more in September to become the first *Luftwaffe* pilot to achieve 200 victories. Probably the most phenomenal scoring was done by Kurt Welter, who shot down 33 aircraft, including 21 four engine bombers and seven difficult Mosquito kills in just 40 missions while being shot down himself nine times!

Early in the war the Allied fighter pilots faced the cream of German and Japanese pilots, who were well-trained and flew superior aircraft, and were shot down in droves, particularly the Russians on the Eastern Front. During the last two years of the war both Japanese and German aircraft all but disappeared from the skies in many theaters, and many Allied fighter pilots could fly an entire combat tour without encountering the enemy. Conversely, during that time each mission flown by *Luftwaffe* or Japanese pilots resulted in many more combat contacts, as Allied fighters and bombers were swarming in their skies. Under this constant pressure and facing a dwindling supply of manpower, the Axis air forces could not afford the luxury of withdrawing their aces to teach.

*Luftwaffe* super aces **Erich Hartmann** (left) and **Gerd Barkhorn** scored 352 and 301 victories respectively in World War II. (Author)

**American Fighter Aces**

**Richard Bong** 40 Victories Top American Ace (Author)

**Francis "Gabby" Gabreski** 28 Victories Top USAAF Ace ETO (Author)

**David McCampbell** 34 Victories Top USN Ace (Author)

**Joseph Foss** 26 Victories Top USMC Ace (Author)

### USAAF and USN/USMC Fighters vs. the Axis

**Claims by Services**

| Service | Victories | Probable | Damaged | Total Claims |
|---|---|---|---|---|
| USN | 6826 | 780 | 830 | 8436 |
| % | 80.9 | 9.2 | 9.8 | |
| USMC | 2696 | 154 | 64 | 2914 |
| % | 92.5 | 5.3 | 2.2 | |
| AVG | 231 | 43 | 33 | 307 |
| % | 75.5 | 13.7 | 10.8 | |
| USAAF | 16257 | 2239 | 5179 | 23675 |
| % | 68.7 | 9.4 | 21.9 | |
| Totals | 26010 | 3216 | 6106 | 35332 |
| Avg. | 73.6 | 9.1 | 17.3 | 100.0 |

**Claims by Theater of Operations**

| Theater | Victories | Probable | Damaged | Total Claims |
|---|---|---|---|---|
| CBI | 1504 | 487 | 787 | 2778 |
| % | 54.1 | 17.5 | 28.3 | |
| PTO | 13238 | 1471 | 1319 | 16028 |
| % | 82.6 | 9.2 | 8.2 | |
| ETO | 7504 | 681 | 2535 | 10720 |
| % | 70.0 | 6.4 | 23.6 | |
| MTO | 3764 | 577 | 1465 | 5806 |
| % | 64.8 | 9.9 | 25.2 | |
| Totals | 26010 | 3216 | 6106 | 35322 |
| Avg. | 73.6 | 9.1 | 17.3 | 100.0 |

**Enemy Aircraft Destroyed by the USAAF by Theater and in the Air or on the Ground**

| Enemy Aircraft Destroyed Theater/Cause of Loss | Total | 1942 | 1943 | 1944 | 1945 |
|---|---|---|---|---|---|
| ETO | | * | | | * |
| Total Losses | 14,218 | 7 | 451 | 7977 | 5783 |
| In the Air | 7422 | 7 | 451 | 5602 | 1362 |
| On the Ground | 6796 | ---- | ---- | 2375 | 4421 |
| MTO | | ** | | | ** |
| Total Losses | 4664 | 92 | 1459 | 2845 | 268 |
| In the Air | 3300 | 81 | 1270 | 1760 | 189 |
| On the Ground | 1364 | 11 | 89 | 1085 | 79 |
| PTO+ | | *** | | | *** |
| Total Losses | 3556 | 245 | 1284 | 1315 | 712 |
| In the Air | 3113 | 211 | 1252 | 1158 | 492 |
| On the Ground | 443 | 34 | 32 | 157 | 220 |
| CBI | | **** | | | **** |
| Total Losses | 1467 | 52 | 325 | 729 | 361 |
| In the Air | 847 | 52 | 288 | 418 | 89 |
| On the Ground | 620 | ---- | 37 | 311 | 272 |

* August-December 1942 & January-May 1945
**June-December 1942 & January-May 1945
***January-December 1942 & January-August 1945
****April-December 1942 & January-August 1945
+PTO includes Pacific Ocean Area, Far East AF and Alaska

**Aces Share of Total Victories**

During World War II 1276 American aces scored 9,631 of the total 26,010 total American victories or 37%.

**Aces Share of Total Victories in WWII**

| Service | Victories | Probable | Damaged | # Aces | Victories | % V. |
|---|---|---|---|---|---|---|
| USN/PTO | 6826 | 780 | 830 | 381 | 2727.6 | 39.9 |
| USMC/PTO | 2696 | 154 | 64 | 123 | 992.6 | 36.8 |
| AVG/CBI | 231 | 43 | 33 | 18 | 134.7 | 58.3 |
| USAAF | 16257 | 2239 | 5179 | 754* | 5776 | 35.5 |
| CBI | 1273 | 444 | 754 | 60 | 384 | 30.2 |
| PTO | 3716 | 537 | 425 | 183 | 1447 | 38.9 |
| ETO | 7504 | 681 | 2535 | 330 | 2698 | 35.9 |
| MTO | 3764 | 577 | 1465 | 164 | 1140 | 30.2 |
| TOTALS | 26010 | 3216 | 6106 | 1276* | 9630.9 | 37.0 |

*17 aces scored victories in 2 theaters (107 victories total)

**Aces Victories by Fighter Type by Theater**

**Aces Victories by Fighter Type**

| USAAF AIRCRAFT | ETO | MTO | PTO | CBI | Total | # Aces in type | Aces V. |
|---|---|---|---|---|---|---|---|
| P-51 | 4053 | 991 | 279 | 343 | 5666 | 268 | 2082 |
| A-36 | ----- | 67 | ----- | 2 | 69 | 1 | 5 |
| F-6 | 186 | 5 | 18 | ----- | 209 | 5 | 33.5 |
| P-51 TOTAL | 4239 | 1063 | 297 | 345 | 5944 | 274 | 2114.5 |
| P-38 | 497 | 1431 | 1700 | 157 | 3785 | 172 | 1259.33 |
| P-47 | 2685.5 | 263 | 696.67 | 16 | 3661.16 | 114 | 930.16 |
| P-40 | ----- | 592 | 660.5 | 741 | 2225.5 | 73 | 18 |
| (AVG) | | | | 232 | | 578.83 | 134.67 |
| Spitfire | 15 | 364 | ----- | ----- | 379 | 12 | 71.83 |
| P-39 | 2.5 | 25 | 243 | 5 | 275.5 | 1 | 5 |
| P-400 | ----- | ----- | 45 | ----- | 45 | | |
| P-61 | 59 | ----- | 63.5 | 5 | 127.5 | 4 | 22 |
| Beaufighter | 6 | 25 | ----- | ----- | 31 | ----- | ----- |
| P-43 | ----- | ----- | 3 | 3 | 6 | ----- | ----- |
| P-36 | ----- | ----- | 3 | ----- | 3 | ----- | ----- |
| P-70 | ----- | ----- | 2 | ----- | 2 | ----- | ----- |
| P-26 | ----- | ----- | 2 | ----- | 2 | ----- | ----- |
| P-35 | ----- | ----- | 1 | ----- | 1 | ----- | ----- |
| Mosquito | ----- | 1 | ----- | ----- | 1 | ----- | ----- |
| **TOTALS** | 7504 | 3764 | 3716.67 | 1504 | 16488.67 | 668 | 5015.83 |

| USN/USMC AIRCRAFT | | ETO | MTO | PTO | Total | # Aces in Type | Aces V. |
|---|---|---|---|---|---|---|---|
| F6F | USN | 8 | | 5064 | 5168 | 311 | 2194 |
| | USMC | ----- | ----- | 96 | | 1 | 6 |
| F4U | USN | ----- | ----- | 519 | 2140 | 24 | 178.5 |
| | USMC | | | 1621 | | 75 | 582.5 |
| F4F | USN | | 26 | 497 | 1012 | 26 | 200 |
| | USMC | ----- | ----- | 489 | | 34 | 292 |
| FM-2 | USN | ----- | ----- | 422 | 422 | 5 | 30.5 |
| SBD | USN | ----- | ----- | 138 | 138 | ----- | ----- |
| TBF/TBM | USN | ----- | ----- | 98 | 98 | ----- | ----- |
| F2A | USN | ----- | ----- | 10 | 10 | ----- | ----- |
| **TOTALS** | | 8 | 26 | 8954 | 8988 | 476 | 3483.5 |
| | USN | 8 | 26 | 6748 | | 366 | |
| | USMC | ----- | ----- | 2206 | | 110 | 2603 |
| | | | | | | 880.5 | |

Note: Aces in type does not include 99 aces scoring 546 victories in two or more aircraft types (71/393 AAF, 15/83 USN, and 13/70 USMC), but does include 10 AAF, 4 USN, and 1 USMC pilots who were aces in two aircraft types.

In the ETO the P-47 was active 54% of all combat time, followed by the late-arriving P-51 at 33% and the early-excused P-38 at 12%. In the ETO the P-47, though initially utilized for air combat, was supplanted by the Mustang and then used in a ground support role, as was the P-38, which was inadequate in the ETO as an air-to-air fighter. The air combat-bred P-51 outscored the P-47 in aerial victories by more than 58% (4,239 vs. 2,685) though having 39% less operational time (177 combat months vs. 290).

In the MTO the P-38 was somewhat more active than the P-47 (101 vs. 90 combat months), while the ETO-bound P-51 was active in the Mediterranean only half the time of either the P-38 or P-47 (50 months). Nonetheless, the P-38 only outscored the P-51 1,431 victories vs. 1,063, even though after its MTO introduction it joined the P-47 (203 victories) in a ground support role, as there was markedly less *Luftwaffe* activity in the MTO and less opportunity to score aerial victories.

In the Pacific the P-38 vindicated itself as an air combat fighter, scoring more victories in less active time (1,700 victories in 108 months) than the P-51, P-47, and P-40 combined (1,654 victories in 183 active months). The P-38, because of its European inadequacies, was relegated to this theater, where combat conditions were more suited to the twin-engine fighter's strengths.

In the CBI, the redoubtable P-40 more than doubled the score of the P-51 (741 vs. 345) while the P-47 scored only 16 victories. All three fighters had similar combat month totals (P-40: 29, P-51: 34, and the P-47: 39), but the P-40 enjoyed the early war opportunities to score against a much more numerous Japanese Air Force. By the time the P-47 and P-51 came online the Japanese Air Forces were a non-entity and both fighters performed yeoman's ground support duty.

For the entire war, including all theaters, the P-47 was active 35% of all combat months, scoring 3,661 victories, while the P-51 with 21% combat month activity scored 5,944 victories. The P-38, participating in 20% of combat month activity, scored 3,785 victories, while the P-40, with 13% activity, scored 1,993 victories before being phased out of combat before the war ended.

**Aces in a Day**

"Ace in a Day," the destruction of five or more enemy aircraft in a day, was the fantasy of every fighter pilot. A total of 159 American pilots, two of whom accomplished the feat twice, joined this elite group: 59 (two twice) from the Navy, 90 from the Air Force, and 10 from the Marine Corps. Of the 159 Pilots, 44 scored their first five (or six) victories of the war, and of these 24 scored all their victories of the war in one day to become "instant aces." USN Ens. Alfred Lerch (VF-10 off the carrier *Independence*) scored seven victories on 21 September 1945, while USMC Maj. Jefferson Dorroh (VMF-323) scored six victories on 11 April 1945. Each man got no further victories during his tour.

The top-scoring daily ace was Cdr. David McCampbell of the Navy (VF-15/*Essex*), who was one of two fighter pilots to score five or more victories in a day on two occasions. McCampbell claimed seven victories in two sorties during the "Great Marianas Turkey Shoot" on 19 June 1944. On 24 October 1944, during the Battle of Leyte Gulf, he collected nine victories in one mission, tops for an American pilot in WWII. So of his 34 victories—tops for the Navy—16 were attained in two days. Nineteen victory ace Lt. Patrick Fleming was the other American pilot to score five victories in a day twice. On 14 December 1944 he got four Zeros and an Oscar while flying a F6F-5 Hellcat of VF-80 off the *Ticonderoga*. On 16 February 1945, while flying for VBF-80 off the *Hancock*, Fleming got five Zekes. The next day he shot down four Nates to nearly have a record three fives in a day. Five other pilots claimed seven victories in a day:

USN Lt. Eugene Vejtasa (VF-10/*Enterprise*) 26 October 1942
USMC 1Lt. James Swett (VMF-221/Solomon Islands) 7 April 1943
AAF Maj. William Leverette (14FG/12AF/MTO) 9 October 1943
AAF Capt. William Shomo (82TRS/5AF/Luzon) 11 January 1945
USN Ens. Alfred Lerch (VF-10/*Independence*) 16 April 1945

The beleaguered pilots of the *Luftwaffe* tallied the most daily victories in WWII, primarily during multiple sorties over Russia. Emil "Bully" Lang (JG 54/173 victories) seems to be the highest scorer in a day when he claimed 18 victories during multiple missions in a day over Russia in November 1944. Three weeks earlier he got 12 victories in a day. The formidable Hans Joachim Marseille (JG 27/158 victories) tirelessly worked on his shooting proficiency until he was able to quickly shoot down a number of British aircraft in a row using a minimum of ammunition. On 3 June 1942 he got six kills in 11 minutes, and two weeks later improved that feat by getting six victories in seven minutes. On 1 September 1942 he got 17 victories over RAF fighters in three missions over the North African desert (he got eight fighters in 10 minutes on one mission). Two weeks before his death, on 30 September 1942 he downed seven fighters in 11 minutes to become an ace in a day for the fourth time. August Lambert (SG 2, 151, and 77/116 victories) also claimed 17 victories in multiple missions over the Russians in the Crimea in Spring 1944. In addition Lambert scored 12 and 14 victories in a day in the Crimea.

The top Japanese ace in a day was W/O Hiromichi Shinohara of the Japanese Army Air Force, who was the leading IJAAF ace with 58 victories. On 27 July 1939 Shinohara had 11 victories against Soviet-Mongolian forces during the Mongolian border skirmish. The top RAF daily total is seven claimed by C.H. Dyson of 33 Squadron. On 11 December 1942 he shot down six Italian CR42 biplanes, one of which collided with a SM79 bomber, causing it to crash into the Libyan Desert. Lt. Aleksandr Gorovets (11 total victories) was the leading Soviet ace in a day flying a La-5 for 88 GIAP. Gorovets shot down 9 Ju-87 Stukas on 6 July 1943 during the Battle of Kursk.

More Aces in a Day

The Battle of Leyte Gulf, 24 October 1944, produced nine aces in a day who added 54 victories to the total of 270 Japanese aircraft destroyed that day.

Pilots: Cdr. David McCampbell (9), Lt. Roy Rushing (6), Lt(jg) William Masoner (6), Lt. Thomas Conroy (6), Lt. Cdr. Harold Funk (6), Lt. Ken Hippe (6), Lt. Eugene Townsend (5), Lt. James Shirley (5), Lt. Carl Brown (5)

The Battle of the Philippines Sea, 19 June 1944, produced seven aces in a day. In 13 hours the Japanese lost a staggering 380 aircraft.

Pilots: Cdr. David McCampbell (7), Lt. Alex Vraciu (6), Lt. Wilbur Webb (6), Lt. Cdr. Charles Brewer (5), Lt. Russell Reiserer (5), Lt. George Carr (5), Lt. William Lamb (5)

**Two Theater Aces**

Two American pilots were two theater aces, scoring five or more victories in both the Pacific and Europe. John Landers scored six victories flying a P-40 for the 49FG/5AF in the SWPA and then added 8.5 more over Europe; four flying a P-38 for the 78FG/8AF; and 4.5 victories in a P-51 for the 357FG and 78FG of the 8AF. James Howard scored 6.33 victories for the AVG Flying Tigers (P-40) in the CBI and then transferred to the ETO, becoming an ace again with six more victories (P-51) with the 354FG/9AF.

**Top Scoring Groups and Squadrons: USAAF, USN, USMC, AVG**

**USAAF TOP SQUADRONS**

| Total V. | FS | FG | AF | Aces # |
|---|---|---|---|---|
| 295 | 353 | 354 | 9 | 18 |
| 254 | 9 | 49 | 5 | 12 |
| 230 | 62 | 56 | 8 | 18 |
| 221.5 | 62 | 56 | 8 | 11 |
| 221 | 431 | 475 | 5 | 16 |
| 213 | 80 | 8 | 5 | 15 |
| 212 | 317 | 325 | 12/15 | 15 |
| 211.5 | 364 | 357 | 8 | 17 |
| 207 | 8 | 49 | 5 | 13 |
| 201 | 96 | 82 | 12/15 | 13 |
| 200.7 | 334 | 4 | 8 | 11 |

**USAAF TOP GROUPS**

| Total V. | FG | AF | Aces # |
|---|---|---|---|
| 667 | 49 | 5 | 34 |
| 664.5 | 56 | 8 | 41 |
| 637 | 354 | 9 | 39 |
| 595.5 | 357 | 8 | 41 |
| 583 | 31 | 12/15 | 32 |
| 555.2 | 4 | 8 | 32 |
| 553 | 82 | 12/15 | 26 |
| 552 | 475 | 5 | 34 |
| 540 | 325 | 12/15 | 26 |
| 519 | 23 | 14 | 29 |

**TOP USN SQUADRONS**

| VF (VBF) | Victories | # Aces |
|---|---|---|
| VF-17 | 313 | |
| +(VBF-17) | (121) | 29 |
| VF-15 | 310 | 26 |
| VF-2 | 262 | 28 |
| VF-9 | 256.8 | |
| +(VBF-9) | (51) | 20 |
| VF-18 | 250.5 | 14 |
| VF-10 | 217 | |
| +(VBF-10) | (15) | 10 |
| VF-5 | 185.5 | 11 |
| VF-31 | 165.6 | 13 |
| VF-8 | 161 | 13 |
| VF-30 | 159.8 | 9 |
| VF-80 | 159.5 | 10 |
| VF-20 | 158.5 | 9 |
| VF-11 | 157 | 8 |
| VF-19 | 155 | 11 |
| VF-16 | 154.5 | |
| (VBF-16) | (1) | 8 |

**TOP USMC SQUADRONS**

| VMF | Victories | # Aces |
|---|---|---|
| 121 | 205.5 | 13 |
| 221 | 155 | 11 |
| 112 | 144 | 6 |
| 215 | 135.5 | 10 |
| 223 | 132 | 9 |
| 212 | 127.5 | 9 |
| 214 | 126 | 10 |
| 323 | 124.5 | 11 |

**CARRIER vs. LAND-BASED A/C VICTORIES**

| AIRCRAFT | Service | CARRIER VICTORIES | LAND-BASED VICTORIES |
|---|---|---|---|
| | USN | 4946 | 122 |
| F6F | USMC | 1 | 95 |
| | Total | 4947 | 217 |
| F4U | USN | 361 | 159 |
| | USMC | 218 | 1402 |
| | Total | 579 | 1561 |
| F4F | USN | 282 | 215 |
| | USMC | 0 | 489 |
| | Total | 282 | 704 |
| FM-2 | USN | 422 | 0 |
| | USMC | 0 | 0 |
| TBM/TBF | USN | 72 | 26 |
| SBD | USN | 106 | 32 |
| F2A | USMC | 0 | 10 |
| TOTALS | | 6408 | 2550 |

**TOP AVG SQUADRONS**

| PS | Victories | # Aces |
|---|---|---|
| 1 | 98.5 | 11 |
| 2 | 64.5 | 4 |
| 3 | 68 | 3 |

For a comprehensive look at the American fighter ace and American fighter aircraft see my book *Victory Roll: The American Fighter Pilot and Aircraft in World War II*, Schiffer, PA, 2003.

# 3

# Fighter Strafing Techniques

**Strafing Attack/General Tenants**

Planning

Every scheduled strafing attack required thorough planning, compelling the pilots to become totally familiar with the geography and topography surrounding the target area and the layout of the target itself, particularly the location of AA guns. Landmarks in a five-mile radius of the target needed to be memorized and the best approach and withdrawal routes selected. For attacks to be effective, visibility needed to be at least 6,000 feet and the cloud base no lower than 5,000 feet for bombing and 3,000 feet for strafing. For rocket attacks and dive bombing the wind could impose the direction of approach. Enemy AA concentration and disposition needed to be determined, as it would dictate tactics on route to the target and during the attack.

Strafing Methods

An altitude of 15,000 feet was maintained on the way to the target area. The leader located the target and dropped to the deck with or without his wingman to check the target, particularly AA. The formation then turned 180°, setting course on the target, flights dropping line astern at about 1,000 yard intervals. The approach was made at normal cruising speed at as low an altitude as possible, trying to use a road or other landmarks to stay on target. About one mile from target the first flight pulled up to 100 feet, correcting their heading if necessary, and then gave full rpm and throttle. The flight and element leaders concentrated on shooting up the target itself while the wingmen acted as "anti-flak" aircraft, picking out gun positions and knocking them out. Pilots were instructed to pick an aimed target rather than "hosing" the area. The pilot had to have his aircraft properly trimmed and know the distance his machine guns were harmonized to fire at correct range, putting as many rounds into the target while firing on it. Succeeding flights utilized similar tactics. Once past the target all aircraft stayed on deck until the formation leader gave the signal to climb, usually five to ten miles away.

Another strafing attack method had the formation come around on the target at 4,000 feet, dive at high speed, shoot up the target, then stay low and get away. It was a matter of the leader's preference on which method was to be used, but the on deck method was most common. A minimum airspeed of 250 mph was advised because of the constant possibility of passing over unexpected AA positions while on deck and the possibility of being bounced.

Harmonization and Strafing

The guns of the fighter were harmonized for rounds to converge at a point ahead of the aircraft so that the rounds would impact the target together. The harmonization point was set for air-to-air combat at 250 yards, which was acceptable when strafing individual targets such as soft or armored vehicles. Low-level strafing attacks at this harmonization range were risky to the pilot, as apart from the danger from AA and small arms fire, a small miscalculation or target-fixation could cause the fighter to crash into the target or into trees or obstructions just beyond it. Also, if the target were carrying ammunition or explosives it could explode in the path of the attacker and damage it. The most accurate of all fighter bomber armament was the machine gun or cannon, as the great number of rounds fired assured more hits in an area, but the striking power of each round inflicted much less damage to the target than a hit or near miss by heavier ordnance, such as bombs or rockets, which were much less accurate. It was advised that pilots save about 50 rounds per gun during strafing missions. In the P-51, a pilot could expend all the ammo in his outboard guns and have enough left in the two inboard guns to engage in combat if necessary.

AA Fire

If heavy AA fire was encountered only one pass was made, but if the target were undefended the formation leader detailed at least one flight to fly top cover while the remainder of the formation flew another pass on the target. Top cover circled at 2,000 feet above the target in the opposite direction to the attacking aircraft to be able to intercede without delay if enemy aircraft attacked. The attacking formation often was disrupted after the first pass, and afterward all aircraft had to beware of other aircraft and stay out of their fire and flight paths.

If AA fire was heavy (in line astern attacks) the pilot needed to take evasive action in all but the last part of his attack, the firing run. On the way in, a slight pumping of the stick and small turns could confuse enemy gunners in determining the direction of the attacker's flight path. Once the pilot sighted the target he needed to end his evasive maneuvers and forget the AA fire until he finished his pass. A minimum airspeed of 250 mph was advised because of the constant possibility of passing over unexpected AA positions while on deck and the possibility of being bounced by enemy fighters.

Beginning in late 1944, USAAF strafing of *Luftwaffe* airdromes became a priority for escort fighters on their return home as the *Luftwaffe* was no longer a threat to the bombers. Many more U.S. pilots were lost in strafing attacks than in air-to-air combat. (USAAF)

**Strafing Targets**

Airdromes

In general, planned airdrome attacks had to have the primary objective of surprise and while in the vicinity of the airdrome, the safety of minimum altitude and high-speeds was maintained at all times. These attacks were flown by four aircraft in line abreast within flights and the flights in close trail, each weaving and skidding and firing individually. No more than two eight-ship sections were considered safe for these attacks. The sections were to make their passes from different directions and timed as closely together as possible. If a pilot didn't have a target in front of him he was discouraged from turning toward another target as that interfered with another pilot's run and was dangerous for both. Because the valuable airdromes were usually heavily defended by flak towers consisting of a concrete or wooden structure 16 to 20 feet high with a six foot diameter circular platform mounted on top surrounded by a five foot wall. These towers were usually armed with 20 or 40mm AA guns. When attacking these protected airdromes the flights stayed as close to the deck as possible. Well-defended airdromes were often attacked by an anti-flak flight detailed to the attack ground defenses before the actual attack. The flight opened fire at 300 to 400 yards and fired as long as possible. Pilots were urged not to cross the middle of the airdrome. Flying close to the edges of the field was safer because the gun positions were situated there. By flying close to the AA guns the aircraft presented a target moving at a high angular speed that made it difficult for the gunners to track their guns. Also, parked enemy aircraft, hangers, and revetments were most likely to be found close to the perimeter of the field. On withdrawal evasive action was continued on deck, skidding and keeping up airspeed for five to ten miles beyond target when altitude was regained and sections reformed.

A/D attacks as targets of opportunity after an escort mission had the disadvantage of having enemy airdromes in line with the bomber's track being alerted as to the possibility of attack by strafing from withdrawing escort fighters. The impromptu A/D mission in mid-1944 had the group's squadrons separated by a few miles. They flew at 12-15,000 feet in order to detect enemy aircraft parked on the airfields and moving transport such as trucks and trains. Once an airdrome was spotted part of the squadron remained out of the target's sight and flew top cover while the remainder of the squadron flew 10 to 20 miles beyond the objective to give the appearance of being headed home. The fighters would then descend in a shallow 180° dive back toward the target. The direction of the approach was sometimes determined by wind direction and strength. Attacking down wind was desirable so that smoke from the targets damaged in the first pass would not conceal targets for the next strafers. Also, attacking across a strong wind could cause the aircraft to drift and influence accuracy. A low morning or afternoon sun in a clear, revealing sky or cloud cover could be used to conceal the attack. Each flight attacked line abreast or staggered line astern. The line abreast formation exposed all attackers at once for a short period of time while the line astern exposed each flight in turn to all the defensive fire. The staggered astern mode required 1,000 yard intervals to prevent ricochet damage to the flight ahead from those following. The line astern mode did allow the trailing aircraft to spot ground AA positions firing at those ahead and to then attack these AA positions. A reference several miles from the A/D was chosen while at altitude to aid navigation to the target once on deck. The lead flight(s) came in at 300-350 mph as these faster speeds made enemy gunnery more difficult. If heavy AA fire were encountered the fighter leader would radio off the remainder of his unit. If AA opposition were light then the next wave of attackers was able to come in at lower speeds, improving their accuracy. The approach was made on deck and upon sighting the objective a bounce up to 30 to 70 feet was made with each member of the flight selecting a target on his run. About 500 to 750 yards from the target, with a slight pull on the control column to correct for bullet drop (e.g. G-pull on the fired round), long two to three second firing bursts were made. It was important for the pilot to have his aircraft properly trimmed and know the characteristics of his gunsight. The pilot continued to fly low once beyond the end of the A/D for a half mile or more to escape airfield defenses. But if no flak were encountered then a climbing turn could be made and textbook flying school gunnery patterns would be initiated on the following passes. If the A/D were heavily defended a preplanned strafing attack could be carried out in conjunction with medium bombers. The bombing units would fly at medium altitude followed by the strafers. About 20 miles from target the bomber squadron leader would waggle his wings. Acting on this signal, the strafers turned 360°, losing altitude to ground level on the original course and speed. This maneuver allowed the strafers to arrive at the A/D shortly after the bombers struck which caused the base to be in a state of confusion and the AA gunners under cover.

The impromptu airdrome solo attack on the way home was especially dangerous. A bored pilot, seeing no combat and having a full load of ammunition, would inevitably be tempted to go on deck to carry out an exhilarating high-speed sweep of an airfield, often with disastrous consequences as Glenn Duncan was to find on 7 July 1944. After escort penetration, Duncan led the 351FS of the 353FG on Wesendorf A/D getting a parked He-111 on his first pass. Duncan decided on another injudicious run and flak hit his oil line causing his engine to overheat on the way home. A quarter hour later, he was forced to belly land and after setting his fighter on fire he became an evader. After spending nine months with the Dutch Underground, he returned to England in April 1945. Along with Duncan, the list of pilots lost on strafing missions reads like an ace's who's who: Beeson, Beckham, (Gerald) Johnson, Hofer, Goodson, Schreiber, Millikin, Carpenter, Mahurin, Gabreski, and on and on....

As the Third Reich was shrunk by the onslaught of Allied troops in 1945, the Luftwaffe was able to concentrate AA guns around its shrinking number of air bases. As a result enemy gunners were constantly on the alert for the inevitable strafer who meeting no foe in the air found his only targets were on the ground. Without the element of surprise strafing losses mounted. In January 1945, Bill Cullerton with 21 strafing victories was taken prisoner and on 16 April, Elwyn Righetti, top ETO strafer with 27, crash landed his damaged P-51 and the next day the second leading strafing ace, Joe Thury with 25.5 ground claims, barely limped back to base in his damaged P-51.

U.S. strafing attacks on the German transportation system had significant consequences on the German economy and ability to wage war. (USAAF)

Flak Towers

Pilots were hesitant to attack flak towers as they could outgun and out range their fighters. The only time the towers were attacked was if they were causing a problem to bombers attacking in the area. Many towers reported as flak towers were actually water towers!

Trains/Road Convoys and the Transport System

As Allied strafing attacks increased in 1944, the German armed their trains with flak cars. To minimize the risk from these guns the strafing attacks were made at 90° in line abreast to the target and in a 20 to 30° dive from 500 to 2,000 feet, concentrating fire. Little or no firing lead was necessary and trains were considered a stationary target. The engine was the primary target to stop the entire train and make it an easier target. Attacks on the engine were made from 90° by the No.1 and, if necessary, No. 2 of the flight. Once the train was stopped, 10° to 15° deflection passes were made by Nos. 2, 3, and 4 to destroy as many cars as possible with a minimum number of attacks. Long, methodical firing bursts caused the most damage and minimized AA and small arms return fire.

In strafing road convoys a flight would attack in line abreast, perpendicular to the road. Each pilot chose a target and concentrated on it. The most vulnerable area of a truck was the fuel tank or radiator and since trucks and half-tracks carried their own additional fuel supply they often exploded when hit. In attacking a road convoy the front and rear vehicles were taken out first to immobilize the convoy and make it an easier target on succeeding attacks.

If a target had the possibility of exploding pilots fired a short burst from a distance away, aiming high, in an attempt to explode it. If this failed, a long burst was fired somewhat high. The pilot watched for hits and then led the bullets into the target. The attack was to be broken off a safe distance to escape flying over an explosion but all too often strafing fighters were lost to explosions.

The unrelenting attacks and destruction of forward rail facilities (railheads, bridges, and crossing points) increased the demand for motor vehicles, which increased the demand for fuel which itself was under attack and in turn needed replenishing by rail. The further back the railheads were pushed; the fuel transporting motor columns used more fuel on the longer runs, exposed themselves to attacks for longer periods, and increased the delay in fuel deliveries to the front. The fact that regular railway traffic all but ceased in 1945 caused the whole burden of transport to fall on road vehicles which were forced to travel at night to escape marauding daytime Allied fighters. The maneuverability of the Wehrmacht armies and armor in the field was largely dependent upon motor transport for fuel, ammunition, and other crucial supplies. The damage or destruction of the motor transport system had immediate and direct effect on the German battlefront in terms of casualties and ground lost.

From D-Day to the end of the war, the three 9th Air Force Tactical Air Commands (TACs) destroyed 53,811 motor vehicles and damaged 22,546 for loss of 1,374 P-47s. There are no records available as to the loss of locomotives but German records indicate that between August 1944 and the end of that year an average of 600 per month were lost. However, in 1945, the Allies increased their attacks on locomotives and in January 800 were lost and 1,700 more were lost in February.

Tank Busting

The Allies decided to depend on fighter bombers for ground support and not develop an aircraft or airborne gun specifically designed to combat enemy tanks. The development of effective dive bombing techniques and airborne rockets in an anti-tank role confirmed this decision to be correct.

The P-47 was the American anti-tank fighter of choice but on D-Day there were no USAAF Thunderbolts carrying rockets (RP) available and rocket-equipped RAF 2TAC Typhoons were the primary Allied tank busters. The first US tank busting operation occurred on 11 July 1944 when 366FG P-47s attacked 32 tanks of the Panzer Lehr Division and knocked out 20 of them. Though RPs were used to great effect by RAF Typhoons, P-47 pilots didn't like the drag caused by the launchers and their poor accuracy. Therefore, many P-47 groups had their rocket apparatus removed and dive bombing and strafing was the preferred anti-tank method. P-47s pilots could set fire to and destroy German armored vehicles with the .50 caliber API ammunition. German tanks could be set fire or disabled by attacks from the rear at low altitudes, hitting the engine compartment. From D-Day to VE Day 9AF TACs destroyed 4,509 tanks and other armored vehicles and damaged 22,546 others.

Troops

The German soldier was well-trained in small arms anti-aircraft defense and many Allied fighters, especially the P-51 Mustang with its vulnerable liquid-cooled engine, were lost to small arms fire. The recommended method for attacking ground troops was for fighters to fly abreast and fire simultaneously. It was better to combine bombing/rocket and gunnery runs in attacking troops. Allied air supremacy had a distinct effect on the morale on German ground troops from the High Command to the lowest private. A number of German commanders, including Gen. Rommel, were killed or wounded by strafing attacks on staff cars and headquarters. The diaries of German soldiers were dominated by the fears of Allied "Jabos" (German for fighter-bomber) which dominated the battlefront. After D-Day Allied air power had an overwhelming and completely paralyzing influence on German conduct of the battlefront. Whenever the weather permitted, Allied fighter bombers appeared from sunrise to sunset over the front lines to a depth of 10 to 12 miles. Anything that moved there was attacked with rockets and machine guns and the enemy constantly searched skies. During daylight no enemy dared to show himself in the open and men and vehicles were hidden in dense vegetation or in barns.

**Pilot Strafing Mistakes**

In combat the fighter-bomber pilot needed to apply the same general principles that he first learned in gunnery school and then in the Operational Training Units; be prudent in choosing, attacking, and destroying the target. Often the inexperienced pilot sighted the target through the gunsight pipper and then tried to correct his firing error by watching his striking bullets. The consequence was that at the start of his firing pass he would shoot below the target and then when trying to correct would spray the rounds above and around the target. The pilot could correct this error by leaving the pipper above the target at the start of his run and as the range decreased allow the pip to drop on the target.

If the pilot's approach was too steep or too shallow he split his concentration between not hitting the ground in his fighter and hitting the target with his bullets. If the pass was too steep the tendency was to open fire at too long-range and to pull up at the optimum firing range when the concern about crashing into the target appeared. If the pass was too shallow the tendency was to open fire too close to the target, snapping off quick, ineffective bursts, and then pulling up too soon, again to avoid flying into the intended target. Instead of choosing one target and hitting it with a continual burst to destroy it, pilots tended to spray bullets at several targets in their view, missing or only slightly damaging them. Pilots also tended to continue firing as they pulled up past the target wasting ammunition. In any attack the pilot would always have to pull up to avoid the target or its surroundings. After awhile the pilot developed the instinct to determine a good safety margin to clear his fighter of all ground obstacles and was able to hold his fire until reaching a close and lethal firing point.

It was recommended that pilots should save about 50 rounds per gun during strafing missions in case he had to engage in aerial combat on the way home. A P-51D pilot could expend all the ammunition in his outboard guns and have enough left in reserve in the two inboard guns.

# 4

# Fighter Strafing Aces

The 8th Air Force in the ETO and the 10AF and 14AF in the CBI allowed ground victories towards a pilot's victory total. The top-strafing ace of the war was Maj. Thomas Reynolds who flew for the little-known Chinese American Composite Wing (CACW) of the 14AF who scored 38 ½ ground victories and four aerial victories.. Four 8AF pilots claimed 20 or more ground strafing victories. The top ETO strafer was Lt.Col. Elwyn Righetti of the 338FS/55FG with 27 while the second leading ground ace in the 8AF was Maj. Joseph Thury, CO of the 505FS/339FG, with 25.5. Lt.Col. John Landers probably had one of the most varied scoring records of any pilot in the war. He was an ace in the Pacific with six victories and then an ace in the ETO with 8.5. He scored victories in three different aircraft: P-40 (6), P-38 (4) and P-51 (4.5). Lander's 20 ground victories made him the fourth highest ETO strafing ace. On 10 April 1945, Landers, as the new CO of the 78FG got eight ground victories. (For a detailed look at the American fighter-bomber and strafing see my book: *American Fighter- Bombers in World War 2: USAAF Jabos in the MTO and ETO*, Schiffer, PA, 2003)

The top-strafing ace of the war was **Maj. Thomas Reynolds**, who flew for the little-known Chinese American Composite Wing (CACW) of the 14AF and scored 38 ½ ground victories and four aerial victories. (Author)

# 5

# Medium Bomber Strafing Tactics

**Background**

Medium bomber gunners often were involved in missions where they had the occasion to strafe shipping, parked aircraft, troops, or enemy installations with either their nose guns, turret guns or waist guns.

The principles for strafing with turret or waist guns were basically the same as those used in firing at an enemy fighter in a pursuit curve attack. The gunner had been trained in Position Firing which helped him in acquiring the correct deflection.

When strafing a target on the ground the gunner was to employ the three rules for Position Firing at an attacking enemy fighter:

1) The gunner was always to aim between the attacking fighter and the tail of his bomber along the line of apparent motion. In strafing the gunner also aimed behind the target to allow for the effect of the motion of his plane on the fired bullet. In strafing, as well as in firing at an enemy plane in a pursuit curve attack, the deflection always continued toward the bomber's tail.

2) Use the right amount of deflection. Position Firing taught the gunner the correct deflections in relation to the bomber's speed. When strafing, the gunner was always to allow a small amount more but usually not more than an additional ½ rad at 90° and less than that for the smaller angles off than used in a pursuit curve attack. The reason for this was because of the slight difference between firing at a fighter in a pursuit curve attack and firing at a stationary target.

3) Change the deflection during the attack. In strafing the gunner also changed his deflection according to the angle off of the target. When strafing, the gunner sometimes could see where the bullets were hitting. While this aided the gunner in correcting and changing his deflection, he was to continue to use the basic rules of Position Firing as the primary method of determining deflection.

Position Firing principles applied whether the bomber flew a curved course or not was a great aid in strafing. Even if the pilot flew a curved course around the target, the correct deflection was based on the bomber's speed and the target's angle off. In either the area and high angle strafing attacks described next the turret and waist gunners looked out to choose targets and applied the Position Firing gunnery principles when firing on them.

**Area Strafing**

Area strafing was typically used during the daytime from a very low on deck approach on the target but it also could be used on a bright moonlit night but from a higher angle of attack. After leaving the Initial Point (IP) for the target the method of attack was for the pilot to immediately check that all gun switches were ON and that the airspeed was increased as quickly as possible to an ideal 320mph. This rapid increase in speed was the best defense against enemy AA and ground fire while on a low-level strafing run. At approximately 3,000 yards from the target, the pilot pulled up to 300 feet to identify the target, release the nose gun safety switches, and made the necessary final azimuth corrections. At approximately 1,200 yards from the target, the pilot began a gentle dive, lining up the target in the sight and initiated the strafing run. Starting at 1,000 yards, the pilot began to fire short bursts, breaking off at 400 yards, as this was the maximum effective firing range of the .50 caliber machine gun. During the strafing run the pilot gently "fanned" the rudder to effectively hose the target area with his nose guns. Evasive action taken from the target was at high airspeed, close to the ground, using whatever evasive turns possible in the surrounding terrain. Terrain, in all cases, determined the evasive action but a chandelle was considered very undesirable, since this maneuver gave enemy gunners in the area surrounding the target a plan view of the bomber.

**High Angle Strafing**

High angle strafing attack was the most common and successful tactic employed in night missions against stationary targets such as supply dumps and areas considered to contain troops and supplies. The advantages of this attack were that targets were more easily seen from the search altitude and a visual image of the terrain surrounding the target could be maintained, allowing a planned attack on, and departure from, the target. The high angle strafing attack was made from a search altitude of at least 3,000 feet above the target, depending on surrounding terrain. Upon sighting a target from the search altitude, the pilot immediately checked all gun switches and determined the best approach to attack with reference to target and surrounding terrain. A dive angle of approximately 30° for the firing run was set up with an ideal airspeed of approximately 320 mph maintained throughout the firing run. The attack began with firing short bursts at 1,000 yards and broke off at 400 yards, avoiding passing directly over a target suspected of containing explosives. The breakaway from the target was to be at high airspeed, with evasive turns determined by surrounding terrain and enemy fire.

# 6

# Bomber Air-to-Air Combat Tactics

**Clock System**
To successfully defend a bomber, the enemy fighter had to be detected before it could close to firing range. Each member of the bomber crew had to be alert and continually and systematically search the portion of the sky assigned to him. The clock system was instituted as a quick and easy method of informing the crew exactly where in the sky around the bomber the enemy was located.

The bomber was thought of flying in the center of a huge horizontal clock face with the bomber's nose always pointed at 12 o'clock and the tail toward 6 o'clock. When an enemy was spotted the gunner imagined a clock hand pointing at it and reported the following over the interphone:

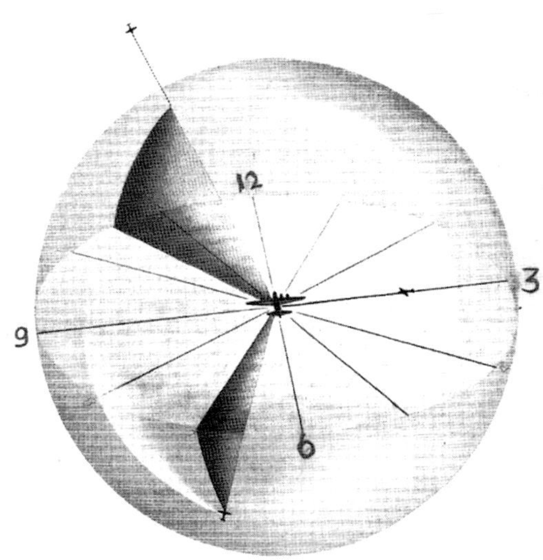


**The clock system . . .**

. . . has nothing to do with the cones. You use it to tell the entire crew when there are enemy fighters in the sky, and exactly where they are.
Simply think of your bomber as flying in the center of a huge clock, the face of which is on a horizontal plane, with the nose pointed toward 12 o'clock and the tail toward 6 o'clock.
If you imagine the hand of this imaginary clock pointing at a fighter you want to locate, the hand will show at what "o'clock" that fighter is.

(USAAF)

"Bandits" (as a warning)
The number and type (e.g. two fighters, two Zeros, etc.)
The approximate range
The o'clock bandit located
"High", "Level", "Low" depending on whether the bandit was above, at the same level, or below the bomber
"Coming in" but only if the bandit turned into the attack

(Note: The tail gunner was riding backward and facing 6 o'clock but was to use the normal clock positions and 3 o'clock was on his left and 9 o'clock on his right)

**35 Mil Rad**
The 35 mil rad was the basic measure of all optical and iron ring sights. A mil is a unit of measurement for very small angles. A 1 rad deflection had to offset the gun barrel at an angle of 35 mils from the fighter. A 2 rad deflection had to offset the gun at an angle of 70 mils, and 3 rad deflection had to offset it at an angle of 105 mils.

Rads had to be of correct size for accurate range estimation and the rules for Position Firing applied only when 1 rad equaled 35 mils. A rad was the radius of one sighting circle. The inner ring of all ring sights had to have a radius equal to a 35 mil angle, making the diameter equal to a 70 mil angle. The AAC once called its ring sights "70 mil" sights but afterward both the Army and Navy called them 35 mil sights.

**Position Firing**
In its introduction the *Gunner's Information Manual* exclaimed:

"Don't shoot from the hip....In the excitement of combat of combat too many gunners spray their bullets at the enemy like a movie cowboy shooting from the hip. **Don't Do It!** Use your sight-and use it correctly-or you won't stand a chance of hitting. You will only throw away ammunition on which your life may depend……

Once you know the rules of Position Firing you will have no trouble applying them with any type of sight. The principle remains the same. Always remember that no matter how good a shot you are on the ground, you can never shoot down an enemy fighter who is making a continuous attack on you unless you **use your sights correctly** and follow the rules of Position Firing. There is only one exception-dumb luck-and that is not good enough. The enemy may be lucky first…..

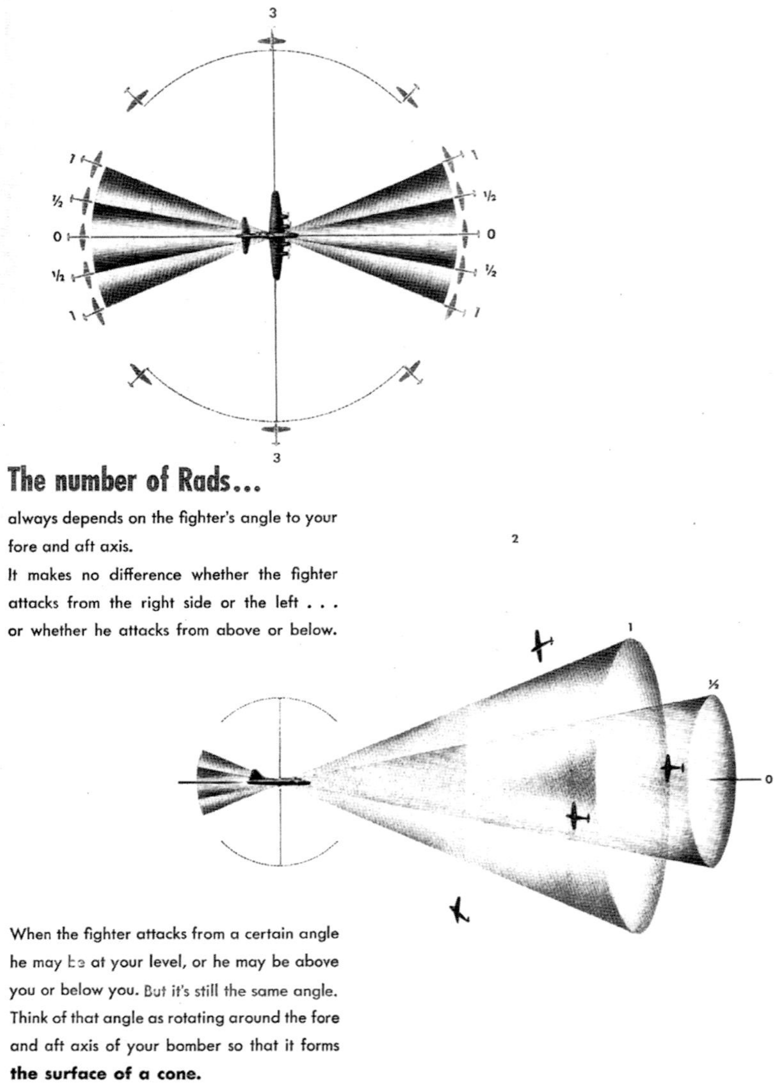


(USAAF)

When you see an enemy fighter with his guns blazing, you won't have time to think about the rules of Position Firing. You will have to know them so well that you act as quickly and automatically as your gun."

It was always supposed that a gunner aimed at a target like he would aim at a duck. Instead, in Position Firing he was taught to sight between the attacking fighter and his own tail, no matter what the direction of the attack. The technique of Position Firing was developed from the RAF system of Zone Firing. Dr. E.W. Paxson, a mathematician from Wayne State University, Detroit, in conjunction with the Army Ordnance Department, the National Defense Research Committee, and the Navy BuAer, were instrumental in developing Position Firing. Once the complex mathematical principles governing the relationship between the bomber's course and speed and the attacking fighter's course and speed were established, operations analysts with the 9AF in North Africa developed an improved sighting system for the technique and tested it in combat. To explain Position Firing to gunners the AAF Operations Analysis Section prepared a booklet called "Get that Fighter," while the 8AF Bomber Command distributed another booklet called, "You Can't Miss It."

Certain basics were implicit when discussing Position Firing from a bomber against enemy fighters. The fighter was a flying fixed gun and to aim his weapons its pilot had to aim the entire aircraft at the target. To hit the bomber the enemy pilot had to point the nose of his fighter at a point ahead of the bomber using either a fly-through or pursuit curve attack.

The fly-through attack was very rudimentary as the fighter attacked in a straight line from the side. He fired at a point ahead of where the target was expected to momentarily cross and so in this attack the fighter's aim was only correct for only an instant. A frontal fly-through attack was also only instantaneous due to the combined closing speeds.

The pursuit curve was the standard mode of fighter attack and also the most dangerous to both the target and the attacker. In this continuous attack the fighter was able to maintain a constant barrage of bullets at the target. To sustain this attack the enemy

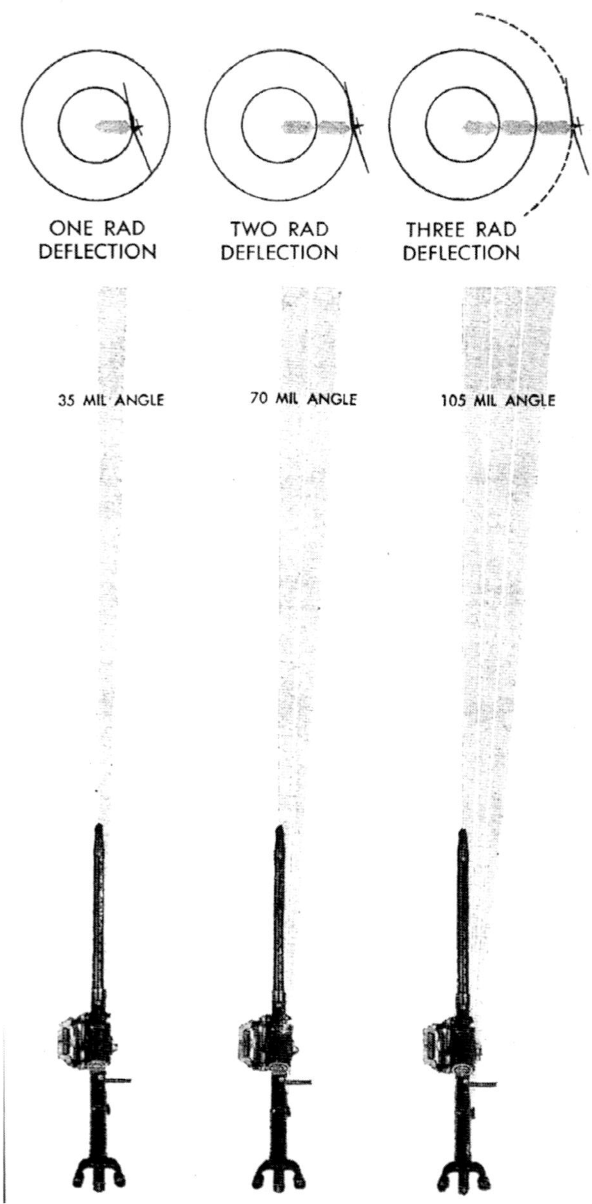


**One, Two, Three RAD Deflection** (USAAF)

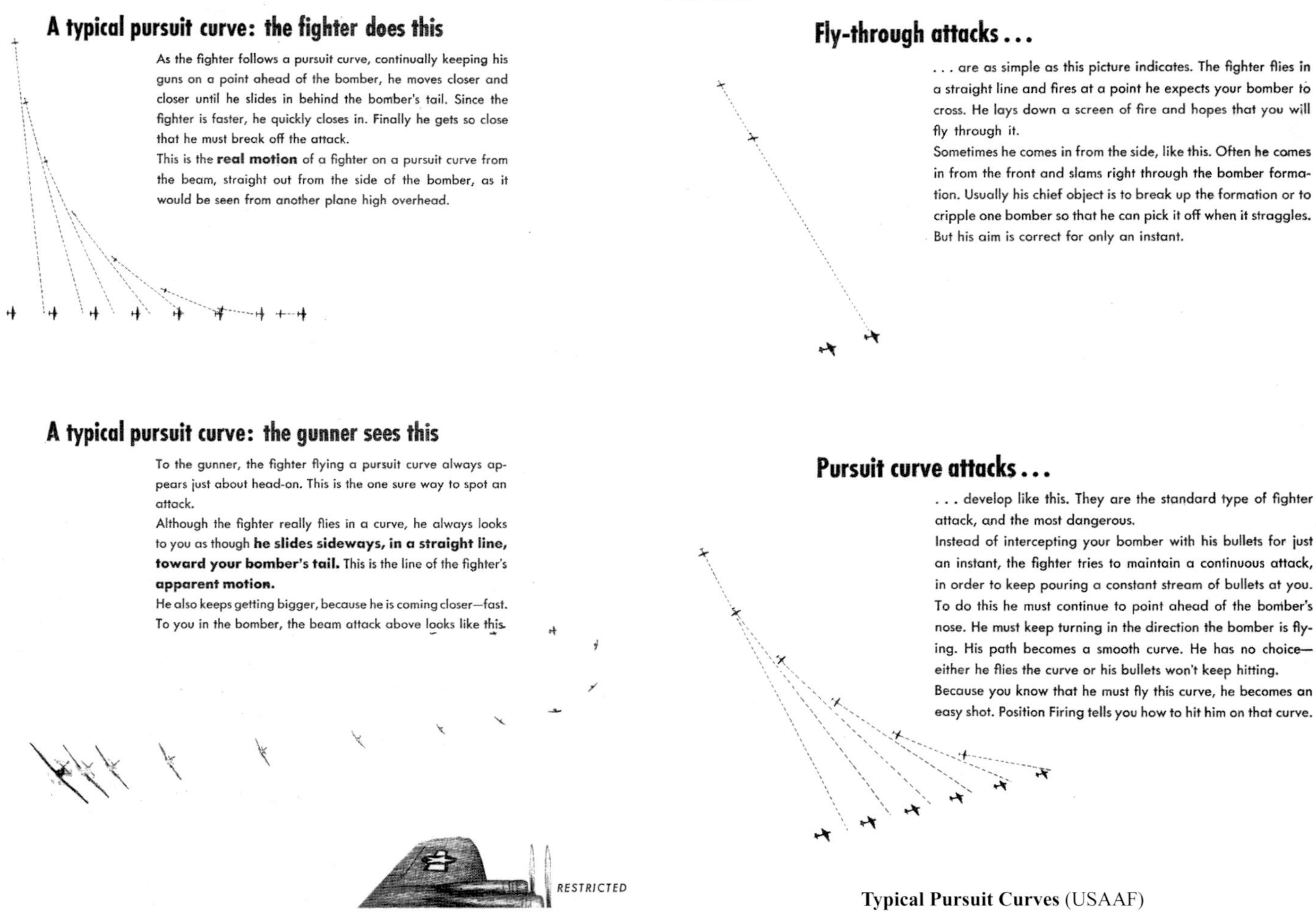


**Typical Pursuit Curves** (USAAF)

had to keep his fighter pointed ahead of the bomber's nose while continuing to turn with the bomber. The result was a smooth curved flight path that slid the fighter quickly closer and closer toward the tail of the bomber until it slid behind it or the fighter pilot broke off the attack. While this path kept the stream of bullets from the fighter aimed at the bomber it also made the attacker vulnerable. The fighter the pursuit curve was committed and all the bomber gunner had to do was aim his stream of bullets to intercept this course.

To the gunner observing a pursuit curve attack the fighter always appeared to be positioned about head-on. Although the fighter was really flying in a curve, to the gunner it looked as though it was sliding sideways in a straight line, towards the bomber's tail called the line of apparent motion. The fighter continued to appear larger and larger as it was quickly closing. In determining where to aim the gunner had to take into account the forward motion of the bomber was to be added as it gave a forward angle to the path of the bullet. The bomber gunner had to aim at the back of the fighter so that the bullets would hit it further along. If the gunner led the target, then the bullets would fly out in front of it and miss.

The gunner was to think of the directions of attack as surfaces of imaginary cones which extended out into the sky around the bomber, both behind and in front. Each cone was assigned a number: 1/2, 1, 2, 3. The number of the cone gave the gunner the deflection in rads for any fighter on the surface of that cone, whether the attack was from the right, left, high, level, or low, based on the bomber's speed. Changes in the speed of the fighter on a pursuit curve did not change the deflection but changes in the bomber's airspeed did change deflection.

In the following example, a gunner using a standard sight with a 35 mil radius flying in a bomber with a true airspeed of 225 mph attacked by a fighter flying at 325 mph, would only need to know the following to successfully fire on the enemy. An aircraft flying between 90° and 45° from horizontal was in cone 3 and the gunner had to aim three radii (rads) of his sight towards his own tail, measuring from the target to the bead or center of his sight. To hit an enemy attacking between 45° and 22.5° (cone 2), the gunner set two rads deflection toward his tail; between 22.5°and 11.25°, one rad; and between 11.25° and 0°, one half rad.

A rule of thumb was: For each 25 knots increase in bomber speed the deflection was to be increased 1/3 rad and vice versa. The gunner was to check true air speed with the pilot, navigator, or bombardier. The fighter never remained in the same cone as the pursuit curve forced it to move from one cone to another as it moved closer to the bomber's tail. The gunner had to change his deflection as the fighter's angle changed or his aim would be immediately wrong. The gunner swung his guns smoothly, aiming above a fighter when it dove from the front and climbed to the rear and aimed below it when it climbed from the front or dove from the rear; always remembering that that deflection was always toward his own tail.

**2/3 of a Second Method of Sighting**

This method of sighting was a "line of apparent motion" type that was studied in Position Firing and allowed the gunner to cope with gunnery situations that Position Firing did not cover. The main use of this method was when the bomber was being attacked or attacking aircraft mounting free guns and turrets (e.g. non-pursuit curve attacks by fixed gun fighters).

**The cones tell you the deflection...**

Think of the key directions of attack as surfaces of cones which go out into the sky around your bomber, both behind and in front of you.

Remember these imaginary cones by their numbers—½, 1, 2, 3. The number of the cone gives you the deflection in rads for any fighter on the surface of that cone, whether he attacks from the right or the left; high, level, or low, based on your bomber's speed.

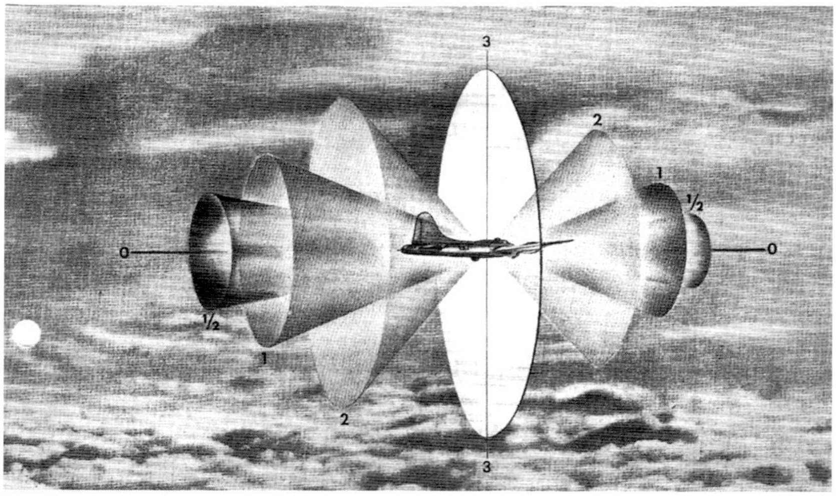


(USAAF)

The basic premise of this method was that it took a .50 bullet about 2/3 of a second to reach a distance of 1,800 feet and if the gunner could estimate the distance that the moving target could move on 2/3 of a second he was more able to give the target the proper amount of deflection. Three steps were to be used to obtain this deflection at a range of 1,800 feet:

1) The gunner centered the target in the ring sight at 1,800 feet.
2) He "froze" (stopped) the motion of the gun and said the word "elephant" out loud which required 2/3 of a second for a three syllable word. He then noted the position of the target in the sight which had moved to the right.
3) He then placed the target on the same corresponding position on the opposite (left) side of the center of the sight and opened fire.

(Note: At a target range of 1,200 feet the two syllable word such as "Japan" was to be used and at 600 feet the single syllable word "Jap" was recommended.)

The above method could only be applied when the gun was stationary and the target was moving which was not the combat situation in a moving bomber. When the target and the gunner were moving at the same speed in the same direction there was no apparent change in motion of the target in the sight (target remained in the center when the gun was "froze"). If the target was moving faster than the gunner the gunner froze the gun and noted the distance the target traveled in 2/3 second and then placed the target on the opposite (left) side of the center of the sight and fired. When the target was moving slower than the gunner the gunner again froze the gun for 2/3 of a second and noted the distance the target traveled and placed the target on the opposite side of the sight (right) and fired.

**Bomber Combat Boxes**

Bomber formations performed two primary functions. Defensively, the formation provided massed firepower from the individual bombers in the formation and offensively it provided a concentration of bombs on the target by the mass release from the closely grouped bombers.

Throughout the war the formation was known as a "Box" because planners concentrated individual bombers inside an imaginary box-shaped area that afforded maximum firepower and simplified operational planning. The evolution of the bomber box took many forms during the war and rather than being dictated by upper echelon planners; the three 8th Air Force Bomb Divisions experimented with their own approach to developing formations. In any formation strict adherence to maintaining that formation by each bomber was imperative as any disorder caused by mechanical failure or poor flying not only made the straggling aircraft a certain victim (about 50% of bomber casualties) but also weakened the coverage and firepower of the formation against enemy interceptors that chipped away at the vulnerable boxes.

Initially the AAC devised bomber formations to give protection for their proposed high altitude daylight bombing missions against enemy fighters. Because of the relative proximity of enemy targets and the strength of fighter opposition the 8th Air Force became the primary proponent of bomber formation development. Individual bombers were positioned in their boxes to give mutual support to other bombers in the box while boxes

**B-17s** fly in a combat box which afforded the bomber formation concentration of dropped bombs and maximum mutual defensive firepower against enemy fighter attacks. (USAAF)

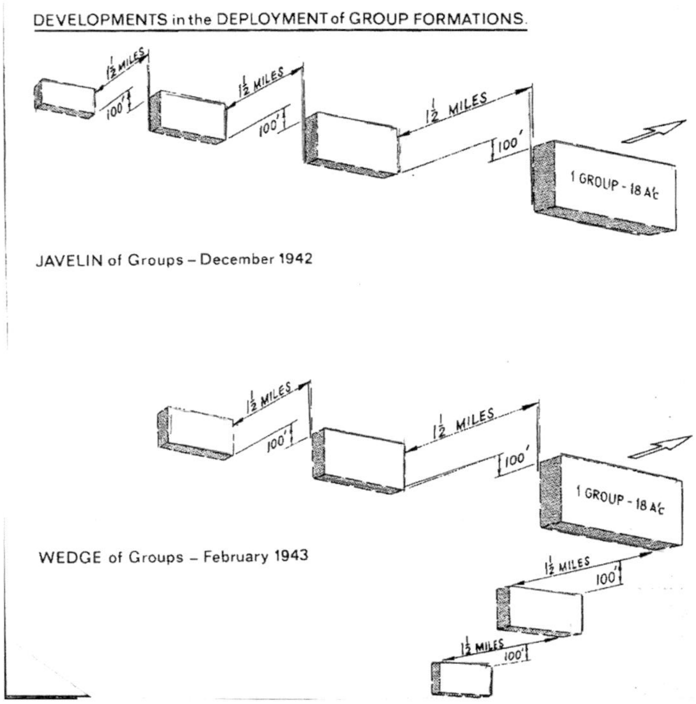


(USAAF)

were designed to give support to other boxes. Throughout the war bomber formation composition was dictated by the changing requirements during various stages of the war. Early AAC formations needed to consider developing techniques and formations for putting bombs on the target. However, intensive Luftwaffe fighter interception that caused heavy losses made defense the primary determinate of the character of the bomber formation. The Luftwaffe interceptors found weaknesses in formations (particularly against head-on attacks) and AAF strategists repositioned and increased the numbers of B-17s and B-24s in the boxes. "Group Boxes" composed of 18 to 36 aircraft and "Wing Boxes" ideally based on 54 aircraft (but could range from 30 to 70 in practice) were tried but during the winter of 1943-44 the 36 bomber box was used by most units but was increased to the 54 aircraft box when targets were attacked that were heavily-defended by fighters.

These large formations were found to be unwieldy and difficult to maintain and when long-range escort fighters appeared new formations had to be developed to accommodate the faster protecting fighters. Smaller, more manageable formations of 27 to 36 bombers were used throughout the remainder of 1944 as the escorts were increasingly successful in keeping the enemy fighters away. American strategists then allowed the escorts to move away from the formation to freelance and seek out enemy fighters in the air and on the ground. By late summer 1944 this policy was so successful that the escorts had virtually subdued the Luftwaffe. Defensive bomber formations were abandoned and adjusted to offensive formations with the emphasis on combining bombing efficiency with minimum exposure to AA fire which had been augmented by the Germans and had become the major threat to the bombers. For the remainder of the war bomber gunners were mainly along for the ride; hoping not to be hit by flak.

A further discussion of Bomber Combat Boxes will be found in Volume 2: *Bombs, Bombsights, and Bombing.*

# 7

# Bomber Gunner Aces

Cramped in a cold, uncomfortable gun turret, the bomber gunner presented an unglamorous contrast to the dashing fighter pilot. Generally the American gunner was an enlisted man often assigned dual functions in the bomber, such as engineer-gunner or radioman-gunner. From 1942 to 1945, the 8th Air Force's 40 heavy bomb groups claimed 6,478 Luftwaffe aircraft shot down, some 83% by B-17s. The leading B-17 unit was the 91BG credited with 420 victories while the leading B-24 group was the 44BG with 330. The scale of the 9lBG's claims can be demonstrated by the fact that it was surpassed by only four of the 8AF's 15 fighter groups. Still there was no recognition for the many bomber gunners who had shot down five or more enemy aircraft to be considered aces.

On 27 January 1943, 8AF B-17s and B-24s flew their first mission over Germany, bombing the Wilhelmshaven port facilities. During the mission the bomber gunners claimed 22 Luftwaffe fighters while suffering the loss of two Liberators and a Flying Fortress. More meticulous Luftwaffe records document only seven losses for that day and this was the first instance of US bomber gunner over claiming. As American bombers flew deeper into Germany their gunner's exaggerated claims were continued over the next several months. 8th Air Force gunners claimed over 450 victories while German records confirm approximately 50! These inflated claims culminated on 10 October 1943, when the 8AF dispatched 274 B-17s to attack Munster, Germany. The Luftwaffe sent up over 200 interceptors that shot down 54 bombers but experienced an astounding loss rate of over 90%! The American bomber gunners had claimed 183 Luftwaffe fighters with a record 62 credited to the 390BG; 11 by the Group's *Cabin in the Sky* but the gunners of the 385BG's *Ohio Air Force* claimed 12 Germans. Postwar Luftwaffe records show 22 losses and five damaged! The archetypal gunner exaggeration occurred during the Schweinfurt/Regensburg missions of 17 August 1943, when 8AF gunners claimed 288 German fighters destroyed. This figure would mean a catastrophic 90 to 100% loss for the Luftwaffe. German records for the day show 21 fighters lost to B-17 gunners and another 21 to fighter escorts.

Why the large discrepancy in bomber gunner claims and Luftwaffe documents? One of the main reasons for the gunner's excessive claims was that USAAF heavy bombers flew in combat boxes of 30 to 35 bombers flying in tight formations designed to afford mutual protection by having as many guns as possible firing at the attackers. Gunners on different aircraft could shoot at the same German fighter streaking through the formation. If the enemy attacker was hit and appeared to be destroyed; all gunners shooting at it would submit a claim. Another reason for destroyed claims was that not many gunners could distinguish what comprised a "victory." Few German fighters that were hit simply blew up or caught fire but shed pieces or trailed a plume of smoke. Late war Luftwaffe fighters using inferior synthetic fuel and oil would expel visible smoke when flying under the full-throttle and high-power settings that were common to combat which could lead eager bomber gunners to make a kill claim even though the smoke was "normal" and not caused by bullet strikes.

The U.S.' first gunner victory of World War II occurred during the Pearl Harbor raid. Radioman/Rear gunner William Miller was accompanying his pilot, Lt. Clarence Dickenson in their Navy Douglas SBD-3 Dauntless as they launched off the aircraft carrier ENTERPRISE to fly to Ford Island. As they neared Oahu at 0805 they noticed smoke clouds and then anti-aircraft bursts. Soon they were attacked by two Japanese Zeros with their wingman's SBD falling in flames but escaping damage themselves. Five Zeros then joined in attacking the lone scout plane. Dickenson concentrated on escaping while Miller fired his .30 caliber machine gun, destroying his attacker which Dickinson confirmed. Miller was wounded as the SBD's left wing was hit, igniting the fuel tank. Miller continued to fire, emptying all six ammo cans, before being mortally wounded. With controls gone, Dickenson bailed out, landing safely, while the SBD carrying Miller crashed into the sea.

The first aerial victory by a gunner in the ETO was claimed by ball turret gunner Kent West of the 97BG on the first 8AF mission over Europe. Flying in the B-17 *Birmingham Blitzkrieg* over Rouen, France, West fired at an attacking Me-109 and claimed a victory. However, at the time there was no method of awarding a gunner a victory claim and West was never officially given credit.

On 24 May 1942, Corp. John Foley of the 19BS/22BG was credited with shooting down two Japanese Zero fighters near Rabaul, New Britain. Foley had been given a crash turret gunnery course after the regular gunner of the B-26 *Kansas Comet* was injured. At the debriefing Foley did not say anything as he was worried that he had fired without orders to do so. However, the pilot of another Marauder reported seeing two Zeros smoking toward the sea and Foley was given the victory credits. On 6 June 1942 Foley was credited with two more victories and was given the nickname "Johnny Zero" by war correspondent Pat Robinson. The US newspapers picked up the story and songwriters Vee Lawnhurst (music) and Mack David (lyrics) read the story and wrote the catchy song "Johnny Got a Zero" to honor Foley. Foley completed 31 missions before returning to America on a public relations tour and served as a gunnery instructor. Foley returned to combat flying in B-24s of the 409BS where he completed another 31 missions. Meanwhile, the "Johnny Zero" legend at home grew as the song's

**S/Sgt. Donald Crossley** was war's highest scoring gunner with 12 air victories as a B-17 tail gunner for the 95BG of the 8th Air Force. (Author)

**T/Sgt. Arthur Benko** was the top scorer in the Pacific as the dorsal turret gunner on a B-25 with air victories. (Author)

lyrics sung by the Merrimacs confirmed: "Now they still call him Johnny Zero! And all the pilots proudly say, Johnny got a Zero! He got another Zero!" Foley was now credited with seven victories and three probables by one account and 15 victories in another. He was said to have been awarded two DFCs and six Air Medals. There were "Johnny Zero" watches and mementoes available. Examination of 22BG records show that Foley was credited with one victory and the *Kansas Comet* with eight.

The war's highest scoring gunner was S/Sgt. Donald Crossley who was a B-17 tail gunner for the 95BG of the 8th Air Force. The 25 year old Virginian had honed his shooting skills on civilian rifle ranges and became adept at the low deflection shots from the tail position. Crossley arrived at Framingham, UK in April 1943, and scored his first two victories in May. On 11 June, his tail guns on the *Little Lady* developed mechanical problems. When the nose guns were damaged, he interchanged those parts getting his tail guns operational again and downed an attacking FW 190. On 13 June, aboard the B-17 *Easy Aces*, Crossley downed two Luftwaffe fighters over Kiel to become an ace. Flying in a new B-17F, *Brass Rail*, Crossley added to his totals in July. On 25 July he got a victory over Kiel but his pilot, 1Lt. John Johnson was killed on the mission. On 12 August during a raid over Bonn, he got a double to give him 11 victories. He scored his 12th and last victory on his 22nd mission. In September and received the DFC and cluster. After completing the last mission of his 25 mission tour he was assigned as an instructor, but died from injuries sustained in a Jeep accident. The next highest scorer in the ETO was Michael Arooth of the 379BG with nine victories. T/Sgt. Thomas Dye of the 351BG scored eight victories despite failing a "refresher" course after scoring two victories.

In the MTO S/Sgt Benjamin Warmer, a 6'6", 275 pound former pro football fullback was the top gunner-ace with nine victories. The San Francisco native was too large to be a pilot, but could easily swing the heavy .50 caliber waist machine guns in the roaring slipstream. On 5 July 1943, his B-17 of the 99BG/12AF was attacked by several large groups of Luftwaffe fighters while bombing Axis airfields during the invasion of Sicily. Firing short, controlled bursts, Warmer downed two Me 110s in the first wave. Me 109s then attacked and Warmer exploded or burned the first on its head-on pass for his third victory. After his B-17 took several hits, Warmer shot down two more 109s but as he was aiming at the next attacker he ran out of .50 caliber ammunition. Warmer quickly reloaded during the bombing run but the Germans were scoring hits on his bomber as its forward guns had been silenced. The next Messerschmitt passed close by from the nose and Warmer destroyed it for number six. The next attack was by two Me-109s in formation from astern and below. The tail gunner hit one to start it smoking and Warmer hit the second in its engine to send it spinning into the ground. For his seven enemy fighters destroyed which Warmer received a DFC and would later scored two more victories to give him nine.

In the Pacific, T/Sgt. Arthur Benko, 374BS/308BG, was the top scorer in the Pacific as the dorsal turret gunner on a B-25. The prewar Arizona pistol and Skeet champion shot down seven Zeros on 2 October 1943, during a raid on Haiphong. He as awarded the DFC and Air Medal for the action. He later got two more aerial victories and was credited with nine more ground strafing victories which were officially recognized as victories in the 14AF credit system. Benko bailed out when his Mitchell was shot down over Hankow and was reported to be captured, tortured, and killed. T/Sgt. George Gouldthrite was credited with five aerial victories in the CBI.

S/Sgt. John Quinlan was the tail gunner on the B-17 *Memphis Belle* which was immortalized in a documentary by Hollywood film maker, William Wyler, and years later by his daughter, Catherine, who researched and produced the docu-drama "*Memphis Belle*." This Flying Fortress was the first to complete 25 missions and returned to America to participate in a bond sales drive. During her ETO combat tour Belle's gunners downed eight Germans; five by Quinlan making him an ace. Quinlan volunteered for further combat, scoring three more victories against the Japanese flying in the B-29 *Marietta Miss Fit*. However, Quinlan his crewmates had to bail

**S/Sgt. John Quinlan** became an ace with five victories as a gunner on the famous Memphis Belle B-17 of the William Wyler Hollywood docu-drama. (Author)

out over Japanese-occupied China and Quinlan was captured but escaped and walked back to friendly territory.

The U.S. Navy and Marine Corps boasted no turret gunner aces in single-engine aircraft, mainly because of the excellent escort of Wildcats, Hellcats, and Corsairs. Navy scout bomber and torpedo plane crews were credited with 196 victories during the War, while Marine crews claimed 70 more. The air combat record for a carrier-based attack squadron was 13.5 shoot-downs by Scouting Two aboard LEXINGTON (CV2), during the Battle of the Coral Sea in May 1942. VS-2s most successful crew was pilot SBD-3 Dauntless pilot Lt(jg) John Leppla and his radioman/gunner D.K. Liska who shot down four Japanese planes on 7 May 1942 during the bombing attack on the carrier SHOHO. The next day Leppla attacked Japanese torpedo planes heading for the LEXINGTON, sending three into the sea using his machine guns. Tops among Marine aerial gunners were Sgt. Wallace Reid of VMSB-231, with three victories as a SBD gunner over Guadalcanal during September 1942. In fact, the seven Marine scout-bombing squadrons involved in the six month Guadalcanal Campaign only had opportunities for 21.5 victories. The Corps' highest tally by a bombing squadron was 9.5 by the Avengers of VMTB-143 during 1944.

During the War, Navy patrol planes accounted for some 377 confirmed aerial victories and produced seven "ace crews" in the process. All of the latter flew Consolidated PB4Y-1 Liberators or PB4Y-2 Privateers; the types responsible for 317 of the Par Ron total. Leading the list was the VPB-117 crew of Lt.(jg) Sheldon Sutton, with seven Japanese aircraft shot down. It is doubtful that any lone gunner on these crews gained five victories, but the achievement is noteworthy just the same. Often flying alone; seldom in more than pairs, the patrol planes flew hundreds of miles from their bases, often attacking enemy shipping and bases in the Philippines and Formosa and along the China coast during 1944-45.

Gunners scoring victories in the P-61 Black Widow were awarded shared victories with their pilot. The gunners of the 421NFS were the highest scoring night fighter gunners with nine gunners claiming 13 victories. S/Sgt. Emil Weishar led the group with three victories followed by S/Sgt. Henry Bobo and S/Sgt. Joseph Mazur. Weishar's victories all came on 29 November 1944. S/Sgt. Glen Deforest of the 419NFS, Corp. Raymond Golden of the 6NFS, and Corp. Jesse Tew of the 6NFS and 548NFS each scored two shared victories.

Sgt. Edward Tyszkiewicz of the 323BG of the 9AF was a dorsal turret gunner of a B-26 which was attacked by Luftwaffe Me-262 jet fighters during a mission near the end of the war on 20 April. The Marauder formation was attacked by 15 jets and the sergeant destroyed one but was wounded on their second attack and his turret drive damaged so that he had to manually track approaching targets. Despite his wounds and the difficulty in tracking he shot down a second jet and continued firing and would be awarded the Silver Star for his valor.

The most famous gunner of World War II was Hollywood actor and Oscar winner, Clark Gable. The famed actor decided to join the Air Force after his actress wife, Carol Lombard died in a plane crash near Las Vegas in January 1942. The 41 year Gable entered the service as a private and received a Second Lieutenant commission after OCS school and soon became a First Lieutenant, and received his gunner's wings on 7 January 1943 at Tyndall Field, FL. He was assigned to the new 508BS/351BG at Pueblo, CO and was delegated to make a film chronicling its training there. Only six months after OCS school he was made a Captain and in April 1943 he headed a six-man motion picture team which was assigned to make a training film on 8AF gunnery. Gable's crew flew its first combat mission on 4 May 1943, in the 359BS/303BG's *Eight Ball* on a mission over Antwerp. The B-17 was attacked and damaged and Gable took over the radio room guns but made no claims. The number of missions Gable flew is up for debate, but probably was three or four. By October 1943

**Capt. Clark Gable**, handsome Hollywood leading man, was the most famous bomber gunner in World War II. (Author)

Gable's film crew had shot over 50,000 feet of film and he was assigned to the MGM studios to produce a gunnery training film called "Combat America." Five training films were made from the footage the Gable team shot and after D-Day with no more work assigned, Major Gable requested to be relieved from active duty.

Though no celebrities achieved ace status as World War II aerial gunners, the roster of former air gunners is notable. USAAF gunners included Oscar winner Charlton Heston (B-25 radio operator/gunner in the Aleutians), Walter Matthau (8AF B-24 radio operator/gunner), Slim Pickens (B-17 radio operator/gunner and would later play B-52 pilot Maj. "King" Kong in Dr. Strangelove), Sabu (B-29 tail gunner) while Navy gunners were Paul Newman and Richard Boone; both SBD radio operator/gunners. Joseph McCarthy the controversial Republican Senator from Wisconsin earned three questionable citations flying in SBDs with the Marines in the SWPA participating in anywhere from a dozen missions (most likely) to the 32 missions which he claimed in 1951. In his senatorial campaign of 1946 against 21 year veteran senator Robert La Follette his campaign posters featured McCarthy in a flying helmet and goggles with a machine gun belt over his shoulder. McCarthy became an upset winner and went on to become notorious for his Congressional Communist witch hunts of the early 1950s. In 1977 McCarthy's wartime and political career was the subject of a three hour TV documentary entitled "Tail Gunner Joe."

Of the four enlisted men who were awarded the Medal of Honor in World War II the 8th Air Force claimed three who were all gunners (the fourth was Staff/Sgt. Henry Erwin a B-29 radio operator). A 32 year old replacement gunner named Sgt. Maynard "Snuffy" Smith of the 423rd Bomb Squadron of the 306th Bomb Group was the first enlisted man to receive the award. His B-17F was hit and set on fire on a raid on St. Nazaire, France on 1 May 1943 and Smith tended a wounded gunner, fought the flames and fired at attacking Luftwaffe fighters. T/Sgt. Forrest Vosler of the 350BS/303BG was awarded the Medal for a mission on 20 December 1943 where he was blinded by a 20mm shell but managed to save a wounded crewmember after the B-17 ditched. The third Medal awardee was ball gunner S/Sgt. Archibald Mathies of the 510BS/351BG for valor on a mission on 20 February 1944 over Leipzig. When his pilot was wounded and copilot killed Mathies went to the cockpit and brought the bomber under control aided by navigator 2Lt. Walter Tuemper. The remaining crew bailed out and Mathies and Tuemper guided by instructions from the control tower volunteered to land the bomber because the pilot was alive but unable to bail out. After two unsuccessful attempts to land the bomber stalled and crashed killing the two men who were posthumously awarded the Medal.

# Part Ten
## American Aircraft Armament

# 1

# USAAC/AAF Fighters

## Section 1: Pre-war Fighters

### Boeing P-26 Peashooter

The Boeing P-26 was first USAAC all-metal production pursuit fighter with the prototype first flying on 20 March 1932. The production P-26A (Boeing Model 266) was a small fighter with an open cockpit, fixed landing gear, and wire-braced wings. It was armed with two .30 Brownings M1s or one .50 caliber Browning M2 and one .30 M1 which had different trajectories. The guns, carrying up to 200 rounds were mounted in the fuselage sides on the cockpit floor and fired through spaces between the cylinder banks of the radial engine.

### Seversky P-35

Flamboyant Russian émigré Alexander de Seversky, like Billy Mitchell, was considered a revolutionary theorist on the future of military aviation and in 1931 he founded de Seversky Aircraft Company. Soon a contest between Curtiss and Seversky arose to develop a modern fighter to replace biplane fighters. When the Seversky P-35 was introduced in 1937, the popular media touted it as America's first modern air superiority fighter. The P-35 was a radial engined pursuit aircraft armed with the traditional pair of guns, a .30 and .50 Browning, mounted on top of the cowling and firing through the propeller. The aircraft had a short production run of 134 aircraft as the AAC chose the Curtiss P-36 in the continuing Curtiss-Seversky competition. The P-35 was found to be easy to fly but was not suitable as a combat aircraft as it was an under performer and was under armed when compared to contemporary aircraft coming into service overseas. Seversky continued to build the fighter as the improved EP1-106 and sold it to Sweden. Designated as the J9, the fighter was equipped with a Swedish version of the Browning .30 and .50. Two 13.2mm AKAN m/39s were placed in the cowling and two 7.9mm KSPm/22 were placed in deep, narrow fairings in the wings. In October 1940 the US War Department detained a number of undelivered EP1-1062 and converted them into P-35As using the .30 and .50 Brownings.

### Curtiss P-36 Hawk

The P-36 was a viable contemporary mid-1930s metal monoplane design and Curtiss was able to sell a large number of different varieties of the fighter to both the USAAC and to foreign air forces as the export version. The P-36A model was equipped with the .30 and .50 Brownings mounted in the upper engine and accessory compartment and firing through the propeller arc. Curtiss increased the fighter's armament in the P-36C by adding two .30 machine guns in the wings but whose ammunition boxes hung without regards to aerodynamics below the wings. Curtiss introduced a three experimental models: the XP-36D was armed with two .30 wing guns in each wing and two .50 guns in the cowling; the XP-36E with four .30 guns in each wing and an (inoperative) .50 in the cowling; and the XP-36F retaining the standard two .50 caliber cowling machine guns and two 23mm Madsen cannon with 100 rpg mounted in fairings under each wing. The further development of the P-36 was precluded by the introduction of the P-40 in October 1938.

Nearly 1,000 P-36s were built with many appearing as the Hawk 75A export version of the P-36 with its armament tailored to the requirements of the buyer. The A-1 sold to the French had two 7.5mm FN-Brownings in the cowling and two more located in the wings while the A-2 and A-3 s added two more FNs in the wings. The Norwegian ordered A-6s equipped with four 7.9mm guns and later received A-8s with an additional 12.7mm HMG in the cowling. After France fell in mid-1940, the RAF took delivery of A-8s armed with 7.7mm (.303) Brownings.

### Seversky P-43 Lancer

During the 1930s Alexander de Seversky developed a line of radial engined fighters culminating in the P-43 Lancer. Despite several government contracts the company never made a profit under de Seversky and in September 1939 the company's Board of Directors forced him out and his company was reorganized as Republic Aviation. In order to keep production lines open for the future manufacture of the P-47, P-43 production continued. The Lancer was a considered a stopgap fighter that saw limited service in the AAC and as an export fighter. The fighter was armed with two .50 caliber machine guns located in the cowl and two wing-mounted .30s which was not much of an increase in contemporary firepower. The P-43A-1, which was an export fighter purchased by the Chinese, was armed with two cowling .50s and two .50s replacing the .30s in the wing.

### North American P-64

North American evolved these single-seatfighters as the NA-50A from their two seat NA-16/26 trainers for export to the air forces of small countries (Peru ordered seven and used them in their brief war against Ecuador in July 1941). These fighters were armed with a pair of .30 caliber machine guns in the wings but when Thailand ordered six NA-50As they were modified as the NA-68 armed with two .30 inch machine guns in the wings and two 20-mm cannon in underwing gondolas. The six to be sent to Thailand were intercepted in Hawaii when Japan invaded Thailand and seized by the AAC as the P-64. The two 20mm cannon were removed and the aircraft were used as advanced trainers.

**Vultee P-66 Vanguard**

Originally Vultee developed four aircraft from their Model 48, three of which were training versions culminating in the famous BT-13 Valiant. The fourth version was to be the P-48 fighter (the P-48 was a Vultee not an ACC designation) which was left in the design stage until the trainer versions completed their development in 1939. Vultee then returned to P-48 development proposing *ten* .30 caliber machine guns, including two cowling, six wing, and two rear-firing guns! However, this armament arrangement was abandoned in favor of a more conventional arrangement of two cowling .30s and four wing-mounted .30 guns. The prototype encountered engine cooling problems and crashed in testing but was rebuilt and successfully tested. The Vanguard was armed with two synchronized cowl-mounted .50s and four wing-mounted .30s. Vultee built 144 P-66s as the J10 under a contract of 6 February 1940 from the Swedish government. By the time the order was completed in September 1941 the US had placed an embargo and impounded the aircraft. The British took over the order but 129 were to be diverted to the Chinese while the remaining 15 were kept by the AAC as trainers. Before the 144 could be shipped to China the Japanese attacked Pearl Harbor and 40-50 were diverted to the 14th Pursuit Group to protect against an attack on the US West Coast. Once this danger passed the Vanguards were shipped to China where they saw some undistinguished combat with many being destroyed in training and on the ground by the Japanese.

**Section 2: Wartime Fighters**

**Lockheed P-38 Lightning**

In February 1937 the AAC released Specification X-608 which required an aircraft that could climb to 20,000 feet in six minutes and have a top speed of 360 mph and in response Lockheed's Kelly Johnson designed the twin-engine XP-38 interceptor. The fighter had an unusual twin boom design that was due the arrangement of the engine, turbosuperchargers, and radiator that caused the nacelle to become so lengthy that the twin boom layout was the most practical design solution. The twin main landing gear of the tricycle gear were housed in the engine nacelles while the small center fuselage nacelle, attached to the wing center section, housed the nose wheel and also contained the cockpit and armament. This center section offered the opportunity to concentrate the firepower into a steady stream of machine gun bullets and cannon shells that could be accurately aimed. The XP-38 was to be armed with four 23mm Madsen cannons (50 rpg), and four .50 caliber machine guns (1,000 rpg)

The nose sections of the YP-38s were to be equipped like the early P-39s with a 37mm T9 cannon (15 rounds), two .50 caliber machine guns (200 rpg) and two .30 caliber machine guns (500 rpg). The two .30s were presently replaced by .50s and the P-38 and P-38D (there was no A, B, or C models) entered AAC inventory with this armament. Unsubstantiated claims have been made that some of these aircraft were equipped with the Madsen 37mm cannon due to shortages of the M4. Many of these initial P-38s were not armed at all as they were deemed to be unfit for combat.

The Lockheed Model 322 was the British export version that the Brits designated as the "Lightning." Because the 322 was armed with only two .50s and two .30s and the British found it unfit for combat and cancelled the order. The AAC used the remaining 322s as trainers.

In 1940, the 37mm M4 cannon in the P-38E was replaced by a 20mm Hispano M1 cannon (150 rounds) to complement four .50 caliber machine guns (500 rpg). Unlike the original 37mm/.50 caliber installations, the two guns of the new 20mm/.50 caliber installation had, though unintentionally, similar trajectories. The M1 required a robust mount and the P-38 Hispano was placed in a supporting cradle. This armament configuration was carried by all P-38s from the E onwards except for the reconnaissance and Droop Snoot types. The P-38H had its M1 replaced by the improved AN/M2C.

Accuracy was improved many fold by the placement of all guns in the nose as the gun trajectories no longer had to converge towards the line of sight and the projectiles concentrated into a small area. The gun pattern was identical at all ranges except for the effects of dispersion and trajectory curvature. Even with this armament installation the British Westland Whirlwind, a smaller and less powerful twin-engine fighter, had twice the firepower of the P-38. In March 1942, the installation of four M4 cannon was suggested but this placement restricted the amount of ammunition that could be carried to about five seconds firing time.

Further P-38 armament installations included the XP-49 (Lockheed Model 522) which was a P-38 ordered in October 1939 that was equipped with the new Pratt & Whitney X-1800 engines. It was intended to mount two 20mm cannon and four .50 caliber machine guns but this armament arrangement was never installed in the prototype but this installation was test flown in a P-38G and rejected because it was too heavy and had a reduced ammunition capacity. Three experimental .60 caliber machine guns were installed in the nose of a P-38L and another Lightning was equipped with eight .50s in the nose and two twin gun packs mounted under the wings.

**Bell P-39 Airacobra**

In 1937 the AAC issued Specifications X-608 for a twin-engine interceptor and X-609 for a corresponding single-engine version which resulted in the Lockheed P-38 Lightning and the Bell P-39 Airacobra, respectively. Specification X-609 limited Bell Chief Designer, Robert Woods, to developing a necessarily small aircraft equipped with a large caliber gun (37mm) which could only be placed to shoot through the propeller hub. The Allison V-1710 configuration did not allow the cannon to be mounted between the cylinder banks. In the Bell Model 3 design both the cannon and engine were forward of the cockpit which placed the cockpit too far aft so the Bell Model 4 opted to position the gun between the propeller and engine. The engine was mounted in the rear fuselage aft of the cockpit with a long extension shaft running under the cockpit connecting the engine to the propeller.

Bell's new design provided a solution to the immediate problem but would ultimately detrimental to the Airacobra's future development. In aircraft design, equipment that that varied in weight was to be located close to the center of gravity (CG). Normally, the CG was just forward of the center of lift with the fuel, ammunition, and bombs located above or below, or inside the wing. In this placement the burning of fuel and the expenditure of ammunition and ordnance did not affect the control and stability of the aircraft. The P-39 design placed the heavy engine near the CG which made the aircraft more maneuverable but also limited future aircraft modifications and required strict attention to loading and handling.

The Bell design called for a 25mm cannon but an updated French Hotchkiss was the only contemporary 25mm cannon available but was secret and not offered for export. The Madsen 23mm cannon was then contemplated but its low rate of fire and erratic feeding mechanism led to its rejection. The only option was the installation of the 37mm T9 long-recoil cannon which had been previously installed in the Bell FM-1 Airacuda. The weapon had a low rate of fire and low velocity and Bell considered it an interim solution that would remain operational throughout the war in the P-39 and P-63.

The 37mm cannon was manufactured by Colt in the US but after only 45 had been manufactured, production was stopped in January 1941 until the end of the year so Colt could retool. Once production was restarted, supply could not meet demand and the Chief of Ordnance transferred engineers from the nearby Springfield Arsenal to help Colt meet quotas which they accomplished.

The armament of the P-39 was to be the heaviest carried by an American production fighter to that time; replacing the standard two rifle caliber .30 caliber machine guns that armed pursuit aircraft. The YP-39 service test aircraft was fitted with a 37mm cannon and two .30 and two .50 caliber machine guns in the nose which was to become the armament configuration of the production P-39C of which only 20 were built (three were sent to Britain). The P-39C was not equipped with armor protection or self-sealing fuel tanks and was classified as unfit for combat as the RP-39C.

The original P-39 was to be turbosupercharged for increased high altitude performance but the device was deleted in an effort to put the aircraft into production as the P-39C which made it a low to medium altitude fighter. The P-39C entered service armed with two .50 caliber and two .30 caliber machine guns mounted in the upper nose cowling and firing through the propeller arc.

The 60 P-39Ds were revised to carry a redesignated 37mm M4 (formally the T9) cannon fed by a 15 round magazine, that fired through the propeller hub complemented by two .50 synchronized machine guns mounted in the nose and four .30 caliber wing guns installed in pairs in the wings. The .30 caliber wing guns were staggered with the inboard .30 barrel protruding more and the outboard gun barrel set further aft (protruding less) and located slightly below the inboard gun. Stainless steel blast tubes were mounted on a plate screwed to the leading edge of the wing. Two long ammunition boxes were placed in each outer wing panel supplying 1,000 rpg. Spent cartridges were ejected through four underwing slots. All weapons were manually charged and electrically fired by electric solenoid units that were activated by the two firing switches on the control column; one for firing then cannon and the other for the two machine guns. In the P-39D the .50 caliber the guns were equipped with blast tubes to minimize flash. Each .50 caliber nose gun had its individual ammunition can that held 200 or 300 rounds while spent cases and links were ejected through chutes. The 37mm cannon was fed by 30 rounds and the shells and links were ejected outside through chutes. The paired .30 caliber wing guns were fed by a common 1,000 round box. Thus the P-39D equipped with the 37mm M4 cannon and two synchronized .50 machine guns in the nose and four .30 caliber machine guns was the standard armament configuration until the P-39Q. However, because of a shortage of the 37mm M4, some P-39D-1s did have the same 20mm Hispano M1 cannon as the P-400. The .30 caliber machine guns in the nose allowed the supply of 20mm ammunition to increase from 15 to 30 rounds.

Concurrently Bell developed the P-400 which was the export version of the P-39. The French contract specified a 20mm Hispano cannon and 13.2mm and 7.5mm FN-Browning machine guns but after the fall of France the contract was assumed by Britain. The British P-400 was armed with a 20mm cannon, two synchronized .50 caliber machine guns in the nose, and two .30 caliber machine guns in each wing. The fighter weighed much more with the same power due to the addition of armor plate, self-sealing fuel tanks, and a bullet-proof windscreen that made the P-400 ideal for ground attack since it had performance problems even at medium altitude. The British disliked the fighter and the remaining aircraft on the contract were transferred to the AAC where it and the P-39 saw service in the Solomons. (Note: the shorter 37mm cannon barrel that fired through the propeller hub was protected by a tube that was attached by screws to the tip of the hub while the longer 20mm cannon was not protected. Also the nose .50 caliber gun muzzles were protected by a small metal indented cover.)

The P-39D weighed about 25% (6,000 vs. 7,500 pounds) more than the prototype and suffered a significant diminution of performance. Designer Robert Wood and Larry Bell endorsed the removal of the four .30 caliber machine guns and their accessories which the Russians did after they received their Lend-Lease P-39s. Bell's suggestion finally was followed in the P-39Q which had its four .30s replaced by single .50s mounted in pods under the wings.

**Curtiss P-40 Warhawk**

The XP-40 was essentially the tenth P-36 whose Pratt & Whitney R-1830 was replaced with an Allison V-1710 liquid-cooled V-12 engine. The 13,738 P-40s produced flew with 28 nations in all theaters throughout the war. The P-40, Curtiss-designated Hawk 81, was originally produced in April 1940 equipped with a pair of synchronized .50s in the cowling and two .30s in the wings. In March 1941, the P-40B (there was no P-40A) added two more .30s in the wings. The B and C also was flown by the RAF as the Tomahawk IIA and IIB respectively mainly over the Middle East and were equipped with .303 caliber machine guns.

The P-40D (aka Curtiss Hawk 87, USAAC Warhawk, and RAF Kittyhawk Mk I), was upgraded with an Allison A-1710F engine, whose size eliminated the space for the two .50 caliber cowling guns and synchronizer. The four wing .30s were also removed and the wing modified to make room for four .50 caliber machine guns with the new hydraulic chargers. There were provisions for two 20mm cannons mounted in external pod fairings (which were never employed).

The P-40E deleted the prospective cannon pack provision and six .50 caliber wing guns were installed and the Model E with this six wing gun arrangement continued as standard through the F, K, M, and N; though the early L-5 block reduced the wing guns to four (201 rpg). However, the N-5, due to complaints from the field of inadequate armament the six wing gun arrangement was reintroduced.

The proposed production models of the P-40Q were to have carried either six .50 inch machine guns or four 20-mm cannon, but the XP-40Q remained inferior to contemporary production Mustangs and Thunderbolts, and further development was abandoned. Consequently and the production of the P-40 effectively terminated with the N model.

**Republic P-47 Thunderbolt**

The P-43 Lancer, lightweight fighter powered by an Allison V-1710 that was already installed in the P-38, P-39, and P-40, and its successor the P-44 Rocket with its more powerful P&W R-2180 engine were the inspiration for the XP-47-RE design concept of the famed P-47 Thunderbolt. The XP-47-RE did not progress beyond the design stage but was envisaged to be armed with two .50 caliber nose guns and four .30s in the wing. In September 1940, air combat intelligence reports from Europe indicated that lightweight fighters were no longer a viable concept and Republic unsuccessfully tried to improve design with the XP-47A. Republic then designed the much larger all-new P-47B which was gigantic by contemporary standards. It was propelled by the powerful Pratt & Whitney R-2800 radial engine whose propeller required a longer landing gear to provide ground clearance. To reduce the size and weight of the longer landing gear so that wing-mounted machine guns could be mounted, each main gear strut was equipped with a mechanism which it telescoped out nine inches when extended. The new design provided for six machine guns and ammunition with an additional two guns and ammunition as an alternate load. The installation was very efficient with the guns protruding at different distances from the leading edge of the wing with the inner barrels protruding the most. This arrangement permitted the ammunition trays to be positioned parallel in the outer wings with the belt of the inner guns being nearest to the leading edge. This armament arrangement continued in the 171 A-models and 602 B-models.

The eight-gun P-47D was the most numerous (12,602) model and although the British already possessed eight-gun fighters in the Spitfire and Hurricane these fighters were armed with lighter .303 inch (7.7 mm) Browning machine guns. The P-47D had a design maximum ammunition capacity of 425 rounds per gun; but commonly only 267-300 rounds per gun was carried (18 to 20 seconds of fire). There was no rounds indicator. There was three or four longitudinal partitioned ammunition bays located outboard of the guns parallel to the leading edge of wing. Two large ammunition access covers, hinged at the rear, covered these ammunition bays. Rigid feed chutes and rollers aided in feeding the linked ammunition from the bays. There were four spent ammunition ports staggered under the wing with the most inboard gun port nearest the wing leading edge and the port for the most outboard gun being located nearest the wing trailing edge. Staggered blast tubes protruded from the wing leading edge with the most inboard protruding the most as the inboard gun was positioned the most forward of the gun arrangement. The P-47 was provided with three different sights: the N3A and B, Mk VIII, and the K-14 computing sight in the M and N models. The guns were charged manually on the ground before takeoff and were ready to fire immediately when the safety switch on the left wheel was turned ON. The squeeze trigger on the stick fired all guns simultaneously. If one or more guns jammed, the others continued to fire. Normally, the guns were boresighted to converge at 250 or 350 yards depending on the preference of the pilot (the most successful pilots used 250 yards).

Once the long-range P-51 Mustang replaced the Thunderbolt in its escort capacity, the Jug became a very successful fighter-bomber because of its heavy eight gun armament, robust construction, and its rugged air-cooled P&W R-2800 engine. After the D-model was completed Republic manufactured only two more P-47 models in any quantity, the M and N. The P-47M, carrying either six or eight guns, was a special high-speed fighter-only model of the Thunderbolt specifically designed to combat the unmanned V-1 buzz bomb, and the *Luftwaffe's* new jet-powered Me-262 and rocket-powered Me-163 fighter that were entering service with the Luftwaffe. The first of 130 P-47Ms were rushed to the 56th Fighter Group in the ETO in December 1944, but engine problems postponed their use until the last month of the war. The P-47N was a specialized long-range Thunderbolt version manufactured expressly for service in the PTO where it acted as a long-range escort for B-29 Superfortress heavy bombers from their Marianas bases over the Japanese Homeland. At V-J Day Thunderbolt production was cancelled and the N-model would was the last production P-47 with 1,816 produced of the 5,934 total.

The experimental lightweight XP-47J was proposed in November 1942 to be the fastest Thunderbolt. The fighter designed around a new airframe was to be powered by the P&W 2800-57. Since the wing was lightened the armament was reduced to six .50 caliber guns. Although the prototype was the first propeller-driven aircraft to exceed 500 mph (504 mph on 4 August 1944) the fighter never entered production as Republic felt that its XP-72 design held more promise. In late October 1944, an experimental installation of a 20mm Oldsmobile cannon fitted under each wing was tried to add firepower for strafing missions to which the Thunderbolt had been assigned. The guns caused a 50 mph reduction in airspeed and the destruction caused by eight .50s was considered more than sufficient. As early as July 1941 Republic worked on several experimental replacements for the P-47 designated as the XP-69 and XP-72. (See Part Ten/Section 5/Chapter1)

**North American P-51 Mustang**

In 1940 the British Purchasing Commission contacted North American about manufacturing the P-40 under license, but instead the company offered to design an advanced fighter. The British ordered the fighter while it was still on the drawing board and the NA-73X prototype first flew in October 1940. Its armament was two synchronized .50 caliber machine guns located in the lower front fuselage installed below the cylinder banks with the ammunition boxes containing 200 rpg located below the guns. Because of synchronization these guns had a very low rate of fire (400-450 rpm). Two more .50s and four .30s were installed in the wings. The British ordered 620 as the Mustang I which went into combat in February 1942 and were followed by 150 Mustang IAs armed with four 20mm cannon in the wings.

The early Mustangs were powered by the Allison V-1710 which gave them good low altitude performance but did not supply enough power at high altitudes. The Rolls Royce Merlin engine was installed and the rest is history as the Mustang became an exceptional multipurpose fighter and arguably the best fighter of World War II.

The original P-51 armament design specifications called for a maximum load of three fixed .50 caliber guns in each wing with the inboard .50 having a maximum ammunition load of 500 rounds for (400 rounds in later guns) and 270 rounds for each center and outboard gun. An alternate installation deleted the center guns and each outboard gun then had 500 rounds available.

The P-51As and Bs were equipped with only four .50s in the wings even though there was sufficient room in each wing's gun bays for three guns. The guns were mounted in pairs and were canted at an outboard angle with the inboard gun positioned somewhat further forward than the outboard gun. The feed chutes that transported the ammunition belts to the guns bowed sharply, almost doubling back from above into the gun. Although the .50 Browning was renowned for its reliability; in this configuration it suffered repeated stoppages, especially tight turns. Some astute ground crews removed the booster motors from B-26 turret gun feeds and installed them in the Mustang which eased but did not eliminate the ammunition belt resistance problem. Ammunition was stored in a divided compartment that was positioned outboard of the guns and parallel to the leading of the wing. The ammunition in the forward section supplied the inboard gun while the ammunition in the aft section supplied the outboard gun. The P-51C retained the four .50 wing guns but the ammunition was increased to 1,260 rounds. Spent cartridges and links were ejected outside through small individual ports for each gun located in the bottom of the wing.

The early Mustangs were equipped the N-9 sight with a fixed head mounted on the instrument panel shroud while later fighters were equipped with the K-14 compensating sight mounted on the instrument panel shroud. The guns were warmed by Type J-1 or J-4 electric gun heaters which were turned on by a switch located on the right switch panel. The gun safety switch was located to the right of the gunsight. It had three positions: OFF, GUN, and CAMERA and SIGHT. Immediately after takeoff the switch was to set to GUN which operated both the guns and camera when the trigger was pressed while in the CAMERA and SIGHT position the guns were not fired. The trigger located on the stick had two positions. With the gun safety switch ON the first position of the trigger operated only the camera while pressing the trigger further to the second position fired the guns and operated the camera simultaneously. On early models the gun and camera operated in both trigger positions. The guns were charged on the ground before takeoff.

The P-51D appeared in 1944 and is the most well-known version distinguished by its "bubble" Malcolm canopy and was the most numerous Mustang model with 8,102 manufactured. The D had a completely redesigned armament arrangement as the early Mustangs were found to lack the weight of fire to destroy an enemy fighter without firing long bursts. The armament was increased to six .50 machine guns which was considered somewhat inadequate firepower for a fighter at that time of the war. However, the Mustang was primarily an escort fighter and the six .50s were adequate against Luftwaffe interceptors which were appearing less frequently. The new gun installation increased the number of rounds to

1,880: the inboard guns each were supplied with 400 rpg, and the center and outboard guns each with 270 rpg. However, Mustang units had the option of removing two of the guns; leaving just four, with 400 rounds each, and some pilots did actually select this option. The forward ammunition bay was deeper than the rear bay and supplied 27 more rpg. The guns in the D were uprighted from their angled P-51B canted position and remained in the same staggered relationship with the inboard gun several inches further back in the gun bay than the outer pair so that the ammunition feed could line up with gun's breech. This arrangement meant that the two outer gun muzzles were inline and protruded outside the leading edge of the wing while the end of the muzzle of the inner gun was actually inside the wing leading edge in an open blast tube. Each ammunition feed was angled over the other guns. The middle gun feed came from the upper tray of the forward bay while the outer gun was fed from the lower tray.

Once the *Luftwaffe* became less a threat in mid-1944, the Mustang was assigned to strafing duties. To increase its firepower experimental underwing gun packs containing one or two .50s were developed Two guns with 340 rounds per gun were confined in a streamlined 375 pound pod that could be jettisoned in an emergency. These pods did not see combat. North American tested a series of lightweight four gun prototype fighters. The final Mustang was the significantly redesigned P-51H that was armed with four or normally six .50s. The H was produced too late to see combat.

**North American A-36 Apache/ Mustang/Invader**

In mid-1941 North American Aviation had shown the RAF export Allison-powered V-1710 Mustang I fighter to be an excellent low level performer. Since the AAF did not envisage the Mustang as a fighter aircraft North American was able to continue the design by lobbying to get orders for the aircraft to be produced as the A-36 Apache dive bomber. To convert the fighter into a dive bomber dive brakes were added to the top and bottom of the wings and underwing racks added to the wings to attach bombs. To make the A-36 a more effective strafer it was equipped with six .50 caliber machine guns. Like the Mustang I there were two synchronized .50s in the nose but these did not have the small fairings where the barrels entered the fuselage like the Mustang I. The ends of the barrels extended almost to the propeller. There were four more .50s in the wings which would be the standard wing armament for the P-51 through the P-51C model. The A-36 wing guns differed in that they were mounted parallel to the ground rather than aligned with the dihedral of the wing and therefore the outboard gun was mounted lower in the wing than the inboard gun. The A-36 was relatively effective as a dive bomber and strafer but the AAF was unenthusiastic about its future. Ironically, the AAF ordered the P-51A as a fighter with only four wing-mounted .50s which gave this fighter lesser firepower than the A-36 dive bomber version!

**Bell P-63 Kingcobra**

The Kingcobra, as it name implies, was a larger version of the P-39 Airacobra. The P-63 continued to be powered by an Allison V-1710 but with a two-stage mechanical supercharger added. Initial armament was identical to the last models of the P-39; a 37mm M4 cannon (32 rounds) firing through the propeller hub, and two .50 caliber machine guns in the nose (250 rpg) synchronized to fire through the propeller arc; and two .50 caliber machine guns (200 rpg) located in pods hung under the wing panels.

The cannon was loaded by pulling the loading handle located in the upper left hand side of the front panel. It was charged by pulling the charging handle located in the upper right hand side of the front panel. The cannon was fired by placing the cannon switch on the left hand side of the instrument panel to ON and squeezing the trigger located on the forward side of the control column. The pilot was to limit the bursts to five rounds and not to exceed a maximum of 15 round bursts.

The two fuselage .50 caliber guns were each charged by pulling their respective charging handles located in the upper right and upper left hand corners of the instrument panel; directly under the cannon loading and charging handles. These guns were fired by turning ON the fuselage gun switch located on left hand instrument panel and squeezing the trigger located on the forward side of the control column. These guns were heated by heat ducted from the cockpit. The wing-mounted .50s had to be charged on the ground by using a charging tool inserted into the gun fairing. The guns were fired by turning ON the wing gun firing switch located in line with the cannon and fuselage gun switches and then squeezing the trigger located on the forward side of the control column. The wing guns were heated by air taken from the coolant radiator air exit ducts.

The P-63A-7 onward was equipped with the Oldsmobile M10 37mm cannon which was the belt-fed version of the M4 with a larger ammunition capacity (58 rounds) and somewhat higher rate of fire. The gunsight was changed to the N-9 electrical sight. Although Kingcobra's performance and maneuverability were very good; its range was short and it was judged not to be a good gun platform. Since the AAF did not need another fighter late in the war; most of the P-63Cs were sent to Russia on Lend-Lease for air defense because of their high altitude capability. There was only one P-63D-1 which was the only American fighter to be armed with the powerful 37mm M9 cannon (not to be confused with the T9 which was the forerunner of the less powerful M4). The M9 was developed from an anti-aircraft gun and had about 50% more muzzle velocity than the M4 but weighed almost twice as much (211 vs. 411 pounds).

**Section 3: Night Fighters**

**Douglas P-70 (A-20) Night Hawk**

The British had successfully used the A-20 as the Havoc MK I night fighter equipped with eight .303 Brownings in the nose and four fixed .303s mounted in a glazed nose in the intruder version. Both versions carried the .303 caliber Vickers Gas-operated (VGO) machine gun in a dorsal turret. Considering the successful British Havoc the AAC modified the A-20 into 59 P-70 night fighter equipped with the British A1 Mk IV radar unit, carrying four 20mm cannon fed by 60 rpg in a ventral tray in the bomb bay. The 39 P-70A-1s (A-20C) carried six to eight .50 caliber machine guns in a ventral tray. The 65 P-70A-2s (A-20G) retained the A-20G's standard battery of forward-firing guns, but all flexible defensive weapons were removed but otherwise were similar to the P-70A-1. When the SCR-720B radar set was installed in the nose of the lone P-70B-1 armament consisted of six 0.50 inch machine guns in three blisters on each side of the fuselage while in the 105 aircraft of the P-70B-2 (A-20J) series the nose was equipped with SCR-720 or SCR-729 radar the armament was moved to ventral trays containing six to eight .50s. The P-70 scored only two victories during the war as it lacked sufficient performance to intercept the quicker Japanese night intruders. The stopgap, improvised P-70 was replaced by the Northrop P-61 when they became available.

**Northrop P-61 Black Widow**

Northrop P-61 America's only purpose-built night fighter with its design originating in an Air Technical Service Command Specification of fall 1940. The original design was a twin-engined monoplane powered by two P&W R-2800 radial engines mounted in low-slung underwing nacelles that tapered aft into twin tail booms which were connected to each other by a large horizontal stabilizer and elevator. The long fuselage accommodated a crew of three: a pilot, a gunner for the nose turret, and a radar operator/rear turret gunner. Each turret housed four 0.50 inch machine guns. On 14 November 1940, Northrop presented a modified design that included an additional gunner's station. The nose and rear turrets of the original version were replaced by twin 0.50-in machine guns in the belly and four 0.50-in machine guns in a dorsal turret. The crew now included up a pilot, a radar operator, and two gunners. The airborne intercept radar was moved to the nose.

The design was again amended on November 22 with the belly turret deleted and the crew back to three: pilot, gunner, and radar operator. The pilot sat in the front of the cockpit with the gunner immediately behind and above him. The gunner operated the four .50 caliber machine gun remote controlled GE Type A-4 dorsal turret using a special sight attached to a swiveling chair. This "stepped-up" cockpit was used to provide a clear field of view for the gunner. The dorsal turret guns could also be locked into the forward-pointing position, so that they could be fired by the pilot. The rear fuselage had a clear tail cone that provided the radar operator with an excellent rearward view which enabled him to act as a tail gunner. The ventral turret was deleted and four 20-mm T2 cannon were to be installed in the wings. On 5 December 1940, the design was formalized as Northrop Specification 8A (NS-8A) as the XP-61 and the mockup was ready in April 1941. The Radiation Laboratory was to conduct the development of the XP-61's airborne interception (AI) radar designated as AI-10 with the military designation as SCR-520. The P-61As were equipped with the SCR-520 radar units while the B models were equipped with the SCR-720C radars. The XP-61 first flew on 26 May 1942 equipped with only a mockup of the dorsal remote turret, as General Electric was unable the actual turret due to the higher priority of the B-29 project using the remote turret system.

Only 37 of the 45 P-61A-1 produced were equipped with the General Electric dorsal turret as the turrets caused buffeting when the turret was either elevated or rotated in azimuth while in flight. The dorsal turret was then streamlined but the air flow around it activated a buffeting when it was moved right to left, causing 364 of the 663 P-61As and Bs to be delivered without this turret which was faired over. Various remedies were tried to cure the buffeting problem which were all basically hat-like coverings attached to the top of the turret and all were unsuccessful. The P-61 turret program was further hindered by GE which was having problems filling orders for B-29 remote turrets which had a higher priority. At the P-61B-15 production block the GE A-4 turret was reintroduced and the improved GE A-7 was introduced on Block -20s.

When the GE turret was installed, its four .50s were supplied with 560 rpg that could be controlled from either of two sighting stations located fore and aft and also had the option of being controlled by the pilot. The dorsal remote turret had a full 360° movement in azimuth and 90° in elevation covering the full hemispheric field of fire above the aircraft. The movement of the turret was controlled from two sighting stations with the forward gunner having full control of the turret at all times unless that control was transferred to the gunner in the rear compartment. The pilot could control the guns only if the forward gunner moved the guns directly forward and locked the turret and turned OFF the power allowing the pilot to fire from his control wheel firing button.

Many P-61s were not equipped with the GE dorsal turret and relied on the four 20mm ventral cannon fed by a Chatellerault power feed mounted on the cannon receiver body. The cannon were installed on supports below the cockpit floor and were enclosed under hinged fairing doors. The supports were adjustable through a horizontal range of 1/4° from dead ahead and a vertical range of 1/4° from horizontal so that converging, diverging, and elevated or depressed lines of fire were possible. These guns were fired by an electric switch on the right side of the pilot's control wheel. The guns could only be charged manually on the ground. The 200 round inboard ammunition boxes were located behind the forward wing spar in the crew nacelle while the inboard ammunition drawers were inserted through doors on the outside of the crew nacelle below both inner wings. The expended shells were ejected via an automatically controlled hydraulic doors connected to an ejection chute from the cannons.

Once in combat it was found that the P-61 pilot required night-vision binoculars to facilitate observe his target and they were introduced on the B-model. The night-vision binoculars were an arrangement of 5.8-power night glasses and an optical gunsight. Instead of the circle and the dot of light in the standard gunsight there was a horizontal row of four illuminated dots in the gunsight of the binoculars. The pilot aligned these dots with the wingspan of the enemy aircraft he was sighting on, and if he identified the type of aircraft he then could easily determine its range and immediately calculate a firing solution. Night binoculars were later retrofitted to many P-61A already in the field.

There were seven P-61B-25s built which were test beds for the Western Electric APG-1 Gun Laying Radar that was linked to the GE Remote controlled dorsal turret. The SCR-720 radar fed data into an analogue computer, which directed the turret guns onto the target. One P-61B-15 and the first six P-61B-20s were also modified to this configuration. These aircraft were tested by the Air Proving Command at Elgin Field, FL and at the night fighter training unit at Hammer Field, CA.

**P-38M Lightning**

In early 1943, the 5th Air Force modified at least two P-38Fs in the field as single-seat night fighters by installing a SCR-540 radar unit with Yagi antennae fitted on both sides of the central nacelle nose and above and below the wings. In order to install the radar, two of the .50 inch machine guns and their ammunition boxes had to be moved forward. Three P-38Js were also modified in the field as experimental night fighters.

It was found that flying the aircraft and operating the radar was too difficult for the pilot and Lockheed tried to modify the P-38L as a two-seat night fighter. In 1944, Lockheed converted a P-83L-5-LO as a two-seat night fighter with the radar operator sitting aft of the pilot under a raised section of the canopy. The aircraft was fitted with an AN/APS-6 radar unit in an external radome underneath the nose, relocated radio equipment, and fitted with anti-flash gun muzzles. The modification was successful having a top speed of 406 mph at 15,000 feet as compared to only 369 mph at 20,000 feet for the P-61A Black Widow. The AAF let a change contract to the Lockheed Modification Center in Dallas to convert 80 additional P-38L-5-LOs into glossy black P-38M twin-seat night fighters. The P-38M saw operational service in the Pacific in the last few days of the war. The P-38M proved to be an effective night fighter with similar performance to the standard single-seat P-38 night fighter conversions.

# 2

# U.S. Navy and Marine Corps Fighters

**Brewster F2A Buffalo**

The F2A was the Navy's first monoplane fighter first flying in December 1937 and accepted into service in mid-1939 as the F2A-1 armed with a paltry two .50 caliber machine guns mounted in the top of the engine cowling synchronized to fire through the propeller arc with the option of adding two more in each wing just outboard the main landing gear. The guns were sighted by a telescopic sight. The F2A-2 had two .50s in the engine cowling and one in each wing with the ammunition boxes holding up to 450 rounds. The F2A-3 had the same four guns but was updated to contemporary fighter aircraft standards which over-extended the design limits. In addition to increasing ammunition capacity Brewster attempted to upgrade the Buffalo's firepower by investigating the use of 20mm cannon in place of the wing .50s. The F2A fighter was plagued by an inadequate design and then poor quality production by the Brewster Company that was considered mediocre at best and under the scrutiny of the Navy and government.

**Grumman F4F Wildcat**

The Grumman Company had competed against the Brewster F2A design and though its XF4F-2 design lost, Grumman was granted a contract to develop an alternative fighter. Grumman engineers thoroughly modified the company's XF4F-2 into the XF4F-3 with a more powerful engine and new wings and tail. The XF4F-3 prototype was equipped with two .30 caliber machine guns in the top fuselage deck and two .50s in the wings. The production aircraft eliminated the fuselage guns and mounted four .50s in the wings with 430 rounds per gun or 1,720 rounds. The -3's four guns were fitted with blast tubes that extended past the leading edge of the wing The inboard gun on both sides protruded further and was slightly higher than the outboard gun so that the guns could be aligned with their respective ammunition boxes.

The F4F-3 was followed by the -4 with folding wings and six .50 in the wings (the additional two were installed further outboard). Each of the six guns was fed by 240 rounds for a total of 1,440 rounds. Some pilots preferred the -3 over the -4 because it carried more ammunition. On the -4 the outboard gun bay held one gun and the inboard bay held two guns in a staggered arrangement to allow their proper alignment with their ammunition feed chutes. The gun bays were heated by air bled from the engine exhaust. The spent link and cartridge case ejection chutes were located on the floors of the bays. The -4 guns did not have blast tubes that extended beyond the leading edge of the wing. The guns were manually charged by handles on the cockpit floor. Access to the guns was made from the top of the wing and the ammunition cans were loaded from under the wing. The gunsight was the Mk 8 reflector. The -4 ammunition cans for the two inboard guns were located one behind the other to the left and the can for the outboard gun was located by itself to the right.

**General Motors FM-1 and FM-2 Wildcat**

The FM-1 was the Grumman F4F-4 built by General Motor's Eastern Aircraft Division; which was armed with only four .50 caliber machine guns instead of six (with a 20% increase in ammunition capacity per gun) but were otherwise little changed from the original model. GM delivered 1,127 FM-1 fighters in 1942-43. To supplement large fleet aircraft carriers the Navy implemented slow escort carriers with very short flight decks. The F6F and F4U and even the F4F-4 were too large and heavy to operate from them In 1943, Grumman developed a new XF4F-8 "Wilder" Wildcat which was to be built by Eastern Aircraft as the FM-2. This fighter had lighter structure and a more powerful Wright R-1820 radial engine that made it faster, more maneuverable, quicker in climb, and longer-ranged. In order to reduce weight the FM-2 carried only four .50s carrying 430 rounds per gun which was unpopular with its pilots. GM delivered 4,777 FM-2s by the time the contract was cancelled in August 1945.

**Grumman F6F Hellcat**

On 30 June 1941 Grumman received a contract for the prototype XF6F-1 from the Navy for what was to be an upgrade of the F4F in case the Vought F4U Corsair design failed. However, Grumman engineers produced a completely new design in the F6F powered by the new R-2800 radial engine which first flew on 26 June 1942. The Hellcat was armed with six wing-mounted Browning .50 caliber M2 machine guns with a capacity of 2,400 rounds. The guns were staggered like the P-47 to allow a straightforward arrangement of the ammunition boxes in the outer wing sections to accommodate the fighter's folding wings. The inboard gun extended beyond the leading edge while the outboard gun was recessed inside the wing. The ammunition boxes were accessible from the underside of the wing which made loading easier with the wings folded. The shell ejector slots were located under the wing. The guns were electrically heated. An improvement in the F6F-5 was the availability of more potent armament than the standard six .50 caliber machine guns. Trials were conducted with cannon-armed Hellcats but were not follow up by a production model, although the armament mix of a pair of Hispano 20mm cannon carrying a minimum effective load of 220 rounds each, along with two pairs of .50 caliber machine guns; each armed with 400 rounds was later used on many F6F-5N night fighters along with a radar pod under the right wing. In practice, many F6F-5N crews re-replaced the Hispanos with the original .50s. The Hellcat was the Navy's most potent fighter of the war being credited with nearly 75% of all naval air-to-air combat victories with a kill-to-loss ratio of more than 19 to 1.

**Chance-Vought F4U Corsair**

The F4U made its first flight in May 1939 but a series of problems delayed its combat debut. One of these problems was the total redesign of its armament installation. The prototype mounted a synchronized .50 and .30 in the fuselage upper deck and a .50 in each wing. However, combat intelligence reports from the war zones caused the armament to be upgraded to three .50s in each wing and the removal of the fuselage guns and synchronizing gear. This placement of the extra gun in the wing caused the deletion of the fuel tanks from the leading wing edge and the addition of another fuel tank to the fuselage over the wing which could only be accomplished by moving the cockpit further aft. This move created a very poor forward view from the cockpit which was to plague the Corsair throughout its service and this along with its poor low-speed handling characteristics and springy landing gear initially precluded it from carrier operations.

Most models of the F4U carried six .50s but the 200 F4U-1Cs were armed with four 20mm cannon that proved to be very unreliable. Nonetheless, the Navy continued its search for increased firepower and in the last months of the war the Navy ordered the F4U-4 and requested that four 20mm M2s be installed on this version. Before any deliveries were made, the more reliable, lighter, and faster-firing M3 cannon were available and would be installed on the post-war F4U-4C model.

Goodyear built the fixed-wing version of the folding-wing F4U-1 Corsair as the FG-1. In 1944 the company designed the F2G Super Corsair driven by the powerful P&W R-4360 Wasp Major engine. The F2G-1 and the F2G-2 (a version modified for carrier operations) were intended for use as low-altitude interceptors of Japanese Kamikazes. Despite all the engine power, the F2G was only armed with four or six .50 caliber machine guns carrying 400 rpg. After only ten F2Gs were built the contract was cancelled as it did not offer any advantages over the standard Corsair. Several F2Gs were privately acquired after the war and won the Thompson Trophy races in 1947 and 1949.

**Grumman F7F Tigercat**

The F7F Tigercat was the first twin-engine, tricycle landing gear aircraft to be accepted by the US Navy. The Grumman design was ordered as the XF7F-1 in June 1941 with the potential of producing landmark carrier fighter. Wind tunnel tests dictated major design changes and the deliberation over which engine to install delayed the prototype until October 1943. Problems continued during testing and the first production aircraft did not appear the end of October 1944 and the first squadron VMF(N)-531 was not equipped with the fighter until mid-January 1945. The Tigercat was heavily-armed with four .50 caliber machine guns in the lower nose (with the top .50 caliber guns located more forward) and four 20mm cannon staggered in the wings close to the fuselage. The inboard 20mm cannon extended more from the leading edge and were higher than the outboard wing. Early problems with the 20mm cannon caused some F7F-2N and -3s to be re-equipped with four .50s in the wings.

**Grumman F8F Bearcat**

The high-performance Bearcat was designed to land on small carrier flight decks. It was powered by the same R-2800 engine as the F6F but was smaller in size and 2,000 pounds lighter The F8F-1's armament was only four new Browning .50 M3s fed by 300 rpg as compared to the six .50 M2s with 400 rpg of the F6F. Because the M3 had a higher rate of fire there was no decrease in firepower. In the post-war but the F8F-2 carried four 20mm cannon instead of the M3 .50s. The Bearcat did not see any combat in World War II.

**U.S. Navy Night Fighters**

The first Navy night fighters were 12 F4U-1 Corsairs converted by MCAS Quonset Point and the Philadelphia Navy Yard. The hand-built conversion installed the APS-4 caused the removal of the outermost of the three .50 inch guns in the right wing, and rearranged the cockpit to accommodate pilot radar controls, a viewing scope and an autopilot. Six of these Corsairs were delivered to land-based VF(N)-75 at Munda, New Georgia, where Lt.Cdr. W.J. "Gus" Widhelm where they saw many hours of successful action. The other six radar-equipped F4Us served with VF (N)-101 under Lt.Cdr. R.E. Harmer aboard Essex, Hornet and Intrepid, and then were assigned to Marine Corps VMF(N)-532.

However, the Navy had always felt that the Corsair was not suited to carrier operations much less at night. The primary USN fighter was the Grumman F6F Hellcat of which 12,274 aircraft were produced from its first delivery date in October 1942. The major problem with the Hellcat was night vision, and the first night fighter model, the F6F-3E, was a conversion of the ordinary -3 with APS-4 (ASH) with a flat-plate anti-glare windscreen, red cockpit lighting, and no curved Plexiglas windscreen in front of the bullet-proof front panel. AN/APS-4 really needed a separate operator to be used properly and the F6F-3E was considered as an interim solution. There were 18 F6F-3E conversions, followed by 149 F6F-3Ns with APS-6, radio altimeter and IFF, and finally by 1,434 F6F-5Ns, plus 80 designated Hellcat NF II for the RN. The AN/APS-6 was basically an AN/APS-4 with a simplified display system that eliminated the need for a separate operator. Initially, pilots were apprehensive of the radar-equipped Hellcat as they thought the radar pod would adversely affect handling and reduce speed (by 20 mph). The night fighter Hellcats and Corsairs were usually painted midnight blue or jet black, and operated by day and by night defending the fleet and shore bases and escorting Navy attack bombers. At the end of the war Vought produced the more powerful F4U-4E (using the APS-4) and -4N using the APS-6), which later served in Korea together with the final night fighter Corsair, the -5N.

# 3

# USAAC/AAF Bombers

## Section 1: Heavy Bombers

### Boeing B-17 Flying Fortress

B-17B

In the summer of 1937 the Armament Branch reported in a Memo dated 7 July 1937 that major changes were essential in the Y1B-17A to "overcome unsafe condition" and "improper functioning of armament equipment." The "existing limitations" would be greatly magnified at increased speeds, and power operation of the nose turret was mandatory." An improved dorsal turret "would not only provide a lookout, relieving crew members at the waist positions for other duties until an emergency appeared, but would greatly increase the field of fire." Again despite these criticisms, the B-17B appeared with one flexible .30 caliber machine gun in the nose, another in a streamlined blister dorsal position, a similar ventral position, and two .30 caliber guns in the streamlined side gun blisters.

There was a continuous dispute between armament and aerodynamic factions as indicated in a Memo of 24 April 1937. The B-17B specifications listed "deviations and exceptions" to requirements, including a "streamlined turret without a downward angle of fire (which was) used to improve the aerodynamic characteristics of the plane." But a Wright Field Evaluation Board reported in July 1939 that "the Boeing blisters were of unclean design and did not meet the specification requirements moreover, the single nose gun offered unsatisfactory coverage in the foresphere, while the dorsal and waist gun combination were unsuitable for covering the area blanked out by the tail assembly." So it appears that the Board's recommendations for a tail gun again went unheeded.

B-17C

The B-17C retained the nose armament of the B-17B and all machine guns except the .30 caliber nose gun were standardized with .50 caliber guns. In October 1939 the Materiel Division had recommended that the side blisters be removed from the B-17B but the Boeing specifications of March 1940 for the B-17C requested "protuberances and gunfire substantially the same as B-17B." The B side blisters were deleted in favor of removable tear drop-shaped flush windows. Two waist guns were mounted on two position swiveling mounts inside the fuselage on swivel posts behind these windows. Ammunition was supplied from one of six cans mounted on each side of the window; three forward and three aft of each gunner. An extendable wind deflector was mounted forward of the window. The dorsal gun was mounted inside a transparent hatch with a removable Plexiglas panel that was faired with the contour of the top of the fuselage and the gunner was protected by a wind deflector. The ventral gun position saw the greatest change with the previous blister being replaced by the so-called bathtub that permitted the gunner to kneel while firing downward and aft but in a very limited field of fire. The B-17B type nose was retained and had three separate sockets mounted in the Plexiglas instead of the metal frame: one on the top of the window forward and one on the second window on the left side and the other on the first window on the right side.

B-17D

The Boeing B-17D specifications revised to July 1940 remained the same as the B-17B, with the exception of modifications elongating the bathtub and the installation of six "strategically located" ball and socket mounts for interchangeable use of the single .30 caliber nose gun. The dorsal radio compartment and ventral belly single .50s were changed to paired .50s.

B-17E

The chief change in the B-17E which first flew on 6 September 1941 was the much needed increase in armament as the early B-17s lacked powered turrets and a tail gun installation. The early B-17 C and Ds had critical blind spot immediately to the rear, making it almost impossible to direct defensive firepower against an approaching enemy fighter from that sector. Early pilots had to develop creative maneuvering methods when attacked from the rear. They would jink the aircraft back and forth so that the two waist gunners could alternatively take quick shots at the enemy. The B-17E introduced an entirely redesigned rear fuselage with a manually-operated tail turret housing two .50 inch machine guns (500 rpg) aimed by an outdated ring and bead sight installed in the tail. In order to accommodate the tail gun, the fuselage of the B-17E was a full six feet longer than that of the D. The guns were aimed and fired manually but were limited to 30° in azimuth, elevation, and depression. A Sperry powered dorsal turret manned by the flight engineer was installed to the rear of the flight deck in the area previously taken by the observation dome. Although considered an adequate turret, it was too low for tall gunners and had very heavy metal framing. The waist guns and original dorsal radio operator's gun were preserved as was the nose armament which was a single .30 standard on the C and D models. The waist gun windows were redesigned to rectangular with a small clear panel in the middle.

The ventral bathtub fairing of the C and D was first replaced by a Sperry ventral remote turret installed aft of the trailing edge of the wing. This turret had the typical problems of remote turrets: limited field of vision, gunner disorientation, dirt and grim obstructing the periscopic sight, fragility, and high maintenance. (See Part Five/Section 1: Sperry) The famous Sperry ball turret replaced the remote turret and was standard from the 113th B-17E. The Sperry ball turret caused problems from its initiation. The head set, throat mike, oxygen line, and electrically heated suit cord; all plugged into different sockets in the turret and could be dislodged or jumbled during operation. Cartridge links often became lodge in the ejector chutes and were impossible to clear in the air. The Vickers hydraulic power drive often leaked at altitude causing oil to cover the turret equipment and the turret door could fracture. Removal of the ejector chutes and their replacement with a newly designed type, new Vickers gaskets, and reinforced turrets doors were made in the field to correct these problems. Ball turret escape procedures were difficult as the gunner had to hand crank the turret into the exact position so that he could lift the doors and climb into the fuselage, put on his parachute, and then bail out which could be very difficult in an emergency with the aircraft out of control.

B-17F

The B-17F was basically an E as in fact the first 300 were ordered from Boeing as the E model and were redesignated as Fs. Once in combat modifications in the F's armament were dictated by combat reports from Europe and most were made in the field by the 8AF. By May 1943 there were 59 modifications on the B-17F with 19 relating to armament.

Most of these changes were made to defend against frontal attacks by *Luftwaffe* fighters. The vulnerable single .30 caliber (500 rpg) nose defense was augmented by installing a .50 caliber Browning on each side of the nose firing through cutouts in the new single-piece Plexiglas and supported by steel tube mounts to absorb the recoil that the previous Plexiglas sockets were not able to do. The narrow nose compartment caused the two new guns to be staggered with the right side .50 in a side window cutout located a few feet forward of the left side cutout. Some .30 caliber ball and socket mounts were modified in the field by the 8AF Service Command to accommodate a .50 gun by reinforcing the ball and socket support. This gun was placed off center in the right hand side Plexiglas nose to accommodate the bombsight. When not in use the gun was held out of the bombardier's way by bungee cords. Often another .30 was mounted in the nose to give the F two.50s and two .30s. Originally the two .50s could only be fired straight forward but eventually the windows and mounts were modified to increase the forward traverse. These .50s tended to interfere with the operation of the bombsight which was removed and the bombardier had to drop his bombs with the lead bomber. Slowly other modifications replaced the single .30 nose gun with a .50 on a steel tube mounting that was tried in various locations in the nose cone. Later F model production batches (B-17F-70 to 130-BO, B-17F-35 to 65-DL, and B-17F-35 to 50-VE) had a single .50 machine gun installed in a cheek mount located on each side of the nose. The 8AF also developed twin tubular mounted .50 caliber guns that were to protrude through a cutout in the top section of the Plexiglas nose. The gunner/bombardier crouched behind the guns and in this position no armor protection could be provided, although improvised plate was attached to the supporting frame under the guns. The bombardier was unable to operate the bombsight with this installation and functioned as a gunner and bomb toggler. The recoil of this installation caused poor accuracy and the field of fire was reduced to a 15° cone. In combat it was found that B-17s mounting these guns were to fly flanking the group leader to give supporting protective fire. After an unknown number of these twin units were installed the 8AF Bomber Command standardized a single .50 installation devised by the 306BG in April. The mount was centrally located in the top of the nose which gave a much broader cone of fire. To use the bombsight the bombardier secured the gun with a bungee. The initial mounts were built by the 8AF Service Command and distributed to air depots as kits. The 8AF wished to have this mount standardized off the production line but it was not until May 1943 that the first B-17F arrived in the UK with his armament.

Other specified F model armament was a Sperry dorsal turret (500 rpg); two .50 caliber waist positions (400 rpg); the Sperry ventral ball turret with twin .50s (500 rpg); single .50 in the radio compartment; and two .50s mounted in the tail position (500 rpg).

The problems associated with the introduction of the Sperry ball turret after the 113th B-17E were mostly remedied. The Sperry dorsal turret was fitted with an interrupter cam unit to prevent shooting off parts of the bomber. The first units were designed so that if one gun was about to fire at an aircraft part, both guns were stopped. This was undesirable in combat and modifications were made so that guns were interrupted individually. Even with this modification the guns of turrets turning at high-speed continued to hit the bomber because there was a time lag between the interrupter mechanism and the last bullet fired. Sperry solved this problem by taking into account this "slew rate." At a certain position the metal framework of the turret dome obscured the gunsight and this frame structure was removed at the depots and later were redesigned and incorporated during manufacture. The waist gunners caused self-inflicted damage to the wings and empennage and gunners of the 359BS/303BG developed an electrical cut-off device which automatically stopped the firing mechanism. The device was authorized for manufacture at depots and to equip all waist guns. (See Part Six/Section 4/Chapter 2: Sperry Ball Turret)

B-17G

The B-17G entered service in September 1943 as the final production version of the B-17. The Bendix chin turret which appeared on the Lockheed YB-40 (See Part Six/Section 5/Chapter 7) had finally provided the Flying Fortress with the much needed forward defensive firepower. Essentially, the G Model was a B-17F equipped with a chin turret although during its production run it would receive other armament modifications. The first chin turrets appeared on the final 66 (86?) Douglas B-17Fs which were redesignated as Gs. The bombardier operated the chin turret with a fixed computing gunsight suspended from the roof above his bombsight. (See Part Six/Section 4/Chapter 17)

The side guns used on the late F models was also readopted on the production G-25-DL block onward. The initial B-17Gs eliminated the navigator's guns but the VIII Bomber Command thought them to be beneficial reinstalled them at their UK depots.

Other major armament changes in the B-17G were enclosing the waist gun positions and staggered so that the gunners had more room to maneuver and were protected from the freezing outside air. However, the staggering of the waist guns was not introduced on the G models but did not appear until the -50 block at Boeing in April: at Vega in May, and in the -25 block at Douglas in March.

Early Gs had a radio compartment .50 installation that was similar to late Fs but this was changed to an enclosed style where the hatch did not have to be opened to fire. However, this enclosed configuration further reduced the movement of the gun. The radio compartment gun position was always considered to be ineffective due to its limited field of fire and was finally deleted in production beginning with the -45 block.

The G model tail gun had the original tail gun installation until the middle of G production. In June 1944, the tail gun unit was replaced by the Cheyenne "pumpkin" tail turret. This unit was similar to the tail unit installed in the last YB-40; being larger and more comfortable and having a greatly increased azimuth and elevation range and gunner field of vision. (See Part Six/Section 4/Chapter 23)

The persistent B-17 center of gravity problem continued in the G model into May 1944. By this stage in the war with long-range fighters were escorting bombers and bomber gunners were seeing much less action. Combat experience showed that the radio compartment gunner was the least successful and engaged gun position and also, that the two waist guns were seldom in simultaneous use. To decrease aircraft weight the radio room gun was deleted and as one waist gunner and the quantity of ammunition usually carried in the aft of the aircraft was reduced 50% and supplies carried there were moved to the radio room. These actions moved the aircraft center of gravity from 12 to five inches toward the true center of gravity.

B-17 Field Modifications
The B-17 underwent numerous modifications in the field. The 384th Bomb Group met massed frontal attacks by the Luftwaffe and experimented with six .50 caliber machine guns installed in a vertical cylindrical mount under nose of a B-17G (42-31435) that required extensive repairs to its nose. The pilot controlled the gun and it was carried on several missions in early July 1944 but they were not fired at an enemy before the aircraft crash landed while landing after a mission. Twin .50s were mounted in waist positions but was found to be too heavy and unwieldy. In March 1945 when the Luftwaffe was non-existent various units took steps to reduce the armament of their Flying Fortresses. The First Combat Wing's 91BG flew without waist gunner; the 381BG without a ball turret; and the 39BG without a chin turret. The Third Division's 94BG removed both their chin and ball turret.

B-17 20mm Cannon
See Part Two/Section 1/20mm Cannon for a description of B-17 20mm cannon installations.

**Consolidated B-24 Liberator**
Consolidated specifications for the B-24 required flexible, manually-operated .30 machine guns in the nose; in hatches above, below, and on both sides of the fuselage; and in an innovative tail position. Consolidated opted to build the prototype without powered gun positions and this arrangement continued on the early production B-24s; the B-24, B-24A for the AAC and the LB-30 and LB-30A for export. Although the .30s were replaced by .50s; no turrets were placed.

British Liberators
In late 1941, the RAF decided to install domestic guns and turrets in export Liberators. The Liberator II received the Boulton-Paul E.MK II turret in the tail and the A MK IV turret in the dorsal fuselage; with each turret mounting four .303 Browning light machine guns. The dorsal turret carried 600 rpg and another 600 rpg in reserve while the tail turret was supplied with 2,200 rpg (later 2,500). The British also mounted single flexible .303s in the nose, ventral, and both waist positions. The nose and ventral positions carried five 100 round magazines but were considered to be nothing more than "deterrent" guns to frighten the enemy from attacking. After Pearl Harbor, the AAC appropriated several of these aircraft as the LB-30 and equipped them with a Martin dorsal turret and two .50s in the tail and the.303s were also replaced with .50s.

B-24C
The nine B-24Cs went into production at the end of 1941 equipped with a Martin 250CE-3 dorsal turret aft of the flight deck and a Consolidated A-6 tail turret. The nose position, both waist guns, and the ventral "tunnel" were armed by flexible .50s.

B-24D
The B-24D was the first mass-produced Liberator to go into combat. Defensive armament consisted of machine guns for defensive protection and strategically located armor plate protection. Fifty caliber machine guns were used in two versions: single free guns and dual guns mounted in turrets. Originally three turrets were installed: a top turret over the radio compartment, a belly or waist turret immediately aft of the bomb bay and a tail turret in the extreme tail. In accordance with order TWX 210 all of the Bendix waist turrets were removed. The dorsal Martin turret was electrically operated and rotated through full 360°, and had a azimuth train or elevation of 4° below to 98° above horizontal. The Consolidated (Consair) tail turret had an horizontal or azimuth train of 61° each side of the centerline, a total of 122°, and an elevation or azimuth train of 70° above to 40° below horizontal. Machine guns were located as follows:

1) Tail Turret: Dual guns. Consolidated design.
2) Camera Door or Tunnel Gun: Single gun full swivel.
3) Right Side Window: Side gun-single swivel.
4) Left Side Window: Side gun-single gun full swivel.
5) Top Turret: Dual guns. Martin design.
6) Nose Gun: Top or bottom of nose-single gun full swivel.
7) Right Side Nose: Single gun full swivel.
8) Left Side Nose: ingle gun swivel.
Note: #7 and 8 were installed beginning with 41-24220.

Side Guns: Beginning with B-24D 41-24220, 250 rounds of ammunition for each side gun was contained in a plywood box located forward of the side windows and about shoulder high. A wooden roller was mounted at the top and rear end of each box and led to a Hughes Flexible Ammunition Feed Chute that was fastened at its other end to the gun by a Hughes adapter. Reserve ammunition for the side guns was contained in six 33 round containers stowed on the right hand side of the fuselage to provide a total of 350 rounds for each gun. The cans were mounted on the guns by the same adapter that the Hughes chute used and were attached to guns by unfastening and folding chute back in plywood box.

Tunnel Gun and the Bendix Remote Ventral Turret: The tunnel gun was mounted to fire downward through the rear entrance hatch. Ammunition for the tunnel gun was contained in three cans which were stowed on left fuselage above the small scanning window. From the 77th D onward the D did not have waist or tunnel guns as a Bendix remote control retractable turret was installed to replace the tunnel gun. This Bendix turret had a very limited field of vision and was useless in combat and was replaced by the tunnel gun after it had been placed in 287 Ds. This tunnel .50 caliber gun was fired through the aft fuselage hatch but had such a limited field of vision and fire as to be useless.

Nose Guns: Three nose guns were delivered beginning with 41-24220 and subsequent: one in lower front; one on left side and one on right side; with the latter two installed at a height at which the bombardier could fire them from a standing position. Ammunition for the nose guns was supplied in six cans, five on right hand side and one on left hand side. In addition there was a flexible chute which contained approximately 65 rounds supplied for each gun. One end of the chute was suspended from the top of the bombardier's compartment and the lower end fastened to the guns. The lower end could be unhooked from the adapter on the gun and the ammunition can fastened to the same adapters. The chutes were either of the Hughes or See-gar-type.

By May 1943 the standard list of modifications for the B-24D to be done at depots numbered 56 with 14 involving armament. At this stage in the war the B-24 required fewer theater modifications than the B-17F. Like the B-17, B-24 modifications were prioritized into five Stages to establish more conformity in the modification program. The MK IIIA reflector gunsight was mounted on all flexible guns. In summer 1943 Wright Field modified a 44BG B-24D (40-2354) which was sent to back to Bovingdon for evaluation. The major armament modification was a reworked .50 caliber ventral gun position that had gunner scanning windows for better vision. The waist guns were also reinstated and the mounts were moved closer to the fuselage skin. Experimental twin .50 waist guns were proposed but never implemented. A fully retractable (because the B-24 had a tricycle landing gear that afforded little ground clearance) Sperry A-13 ball turret finally provided adequate protection for the lower aft sector.

B-24H
The B-24H was manufactured by Ford and Douglas with the Consolidated A-6 tail turret in the nose which required a complete redesign of the bombardier's compartment. The excellent Emerson A-15 was only used by Consolidated for the nose position but was in short supply. The H also carried both the improved Consolidated A-6B tail turret and the Martin A-3D dorsal turret. The mounts for the waist guns were enclosed except in the Ford and Douglas bombers which continued the open hatches until the final production models.

The shortage of the new Emerson turret caused the 8AF to consider the Bell power turret removed from the B-26 tail. This turret was installed in the lower portion of the B-24H nose with the bombsight and clear sight placed in a panel in the upper portion. The bombardier now was seated so he was able to operate the bombsight and guns from the same position. A B-24H with this installation was sent to Wright Field for inspection in the summer of 1944 for the possibility of installing it in production models. Concurrently, another Bell "green house" turret installation was placed in the center of the nose above the bombardier's position. This modification was an improvement but was more limited in vision and movement than the other Bell turret.

B-24J
In spring 1944, the Emerson turret became available and was installed in the J model. The weight of the Emerson was better suited for the B-24 and improved its tail-heavy configuration. Also to relieve the tail heavy problem, a number of Js were also delivered with the M-6A "tail stinger." This hydraulically assisted, flexible, twin gun installation provided an increased field of fire. The Sperry ball turret was very heavy and disrupted the bomber's aerodynamics when extended and so it was eliminated. It was replaced with a pair of flexible .50 in the Pacific in September 1943 and in the ETO in the following spring.

B-24L
The L standardized the M-6A tail stinger and the elimination of the Sperry ball turret and continued the Emerson A-15 nose turret and the Martin dorsal turret. The Liberators in the Pacific Theater did not need tail defense because of the lack of Japanese fighter opposition while those in the MTO and ETO did so some Ls were delivered without tail armament.

B-24M
This final B-24production model again standardized the Consolidated A-6B tail turret.

**Boeing B-29 Superfortress**
Because the B-29 was pressurized its armament was designed around a remote central fire control system. After a long, tortuous period of development (described in great detail in Part Five/Section 2) the General Electric system was selected over the Sperry system. The B-29 was to be equipped with five turrets: forward dorsal, aft dorsal, forward ventral, aft dorsal, and tail. The tail turret was initially to mount a 20mm cannon and two .50s which were not to be part of the remote system but under the control of the tail gunner. The other turret guns were to be operated from four sighting stations, one in the nose and the other three in a compartment aft of the wing. Each gunner could simultaneously control two turrets when necessary. The gunnery control officer was the dorsal gunner in the aft compartment whose job it was to assign turrets to gunners from his control panel.

In combat it was found that the GE system could not contend with head-on attacks so two additional .50s were added to the forward dorsal turret while the 20mm tail cannon was removed leaving the twin .50s. When Gen. Curtis Le May decided to abandon daylight high altitude bombing in favor of medium altitude nighttime raids he ordered the removal of most of the armament. At the time there almost no Japanese fighter opposition and the 3,000 pound weight saving from the removal of the guns allowed a significant increase in bomb loading.

Bell built a B version of the B-29 without the GE central fire control system for use with radar in night operations. Only the tail armament remained as the Bs lighter weight gave it high performance that allowed it to escape the few Japanese night fighters that were only able to make tail pursuits. This tail installation was supported by AN/APG-15B radar which detected targets and furnished range information but this unit proved to be ineffective.

B-29 Experimental Turret Installations
In October 1944 Project S68 was initiated for manned B-29 turret evaluation. A B-29-20-25-BW (S/N 42-24441) was fitted with a Martin upper forward turret (at the rear of the forward pressurized compartment) and Martin upper rear turret (at the rear of the rear pressurized compartment) using twin .50 caliber machine guns. Two retractable Sperry A-13 ball turrets were installed mounting twin .50 caliber machine guns. The forward Sperry ball was fitted between the forward landing gear doors and the bomb bay doors and the aft ball was mounted just forward to the tailskid and was part of the tail gunner's pressurized compartment. The standard A-13 ball turret was modified to have a shorter hanger than those used on the B-24 and the B-32 and thus did not retract entirely into the fuselage. The waist sighting blisters were replaced by hand-held .50 caliber machine guns like those used on the B-17 and B-24. Plywood boxes held the ammunition and the spent casings were collected in a canvas basket on the floor below the gun. It was also fitted with two remotely controlled Emerson Model 126 barbettes each mounting a single .50 caliber machine gun. The large egg-shaped barbettes were mounted on each side of the forward fuselage just above and adjacent to the forward tricycle gear. The project was probably the brainstorm from a higher echelon and was short lived.

B-29 Tail Turret
See Part Six/Section 4/Chapter 24 for a description of the B-29 tail armament installations.

20mm
See Part Two/Section 1/20mm Cannon/USAAF Aircraft Installations for a description of 20mm installation in the B-29 tail.

(For a very detailed discussion of the entire B-29 armament see my book *The Boeing B-29 Superfortress: The Ultimate Look from Drawing Board to VJ-Day*, Schiffer, PA, 2004.

**Consolidated B-32 Dominator**
The B-32 was built as a back up to the B-29 and like the Superfortress it was also to be pressurized and was be armed with the Sperry remote gunnery system (See Part Five/Section 1). Although the B-29 had developmental problems so did the B-32 and when the B-29 successfully entered combat before the B-32 the Consolidated bomber was relegated to the role of a normal heavy bomber which was already capably filled by the B-17 and B-24.

After the abandoning of the Sperry Remote System the standard defensive armament of the combat-equipped B-32 was ten .50 caliber M-2 Browning machine guns mounted in pairs in the five manned turrets. The nose, tail and lower turrets were electric-hydraulic ball turrets were designed by Sperry and built by Briggs with the lower turret being fully retractable as in the B-24. The two teardrop upper electric turrets were Martin-built.

Type A-17 Nose and Tail Turrets
The Sperry designed/Briggs built A-17 nose and tail turret were identical except that the K-11 sight was used in the nose and the Type-10 sight in the tail. Ammunition boxes for the 600 rounds supplying the nose turret were located beside and parallel to the windscreen in the bombardier's compartment. The 1,000 rounds for the tail turret were located inside the tail section just forward of the tail turret in boxes beside and parallel to the catwalk to the turret. The rounds were carried by flexible ammunition chutes. In the tail they ran through slings and in the nose they ran across a shelf above the windscreen. The nose and tail turrets were found to be the most important in turrets in combat. In combat tests feeding difficulties and burned out turret clutches were major turret problems until remedied.

Type A-3F-A Dorsal Turrets
The Glenn L. Martin manufactured the B-32 dorsal turrets, designated as the upper forward and upper rear turrets that were located on the centerline of the bomber in the top of the fuselage. Both teardrop shaped Plexiglas domed turret blisters were identical and provided for the mounting of two M-2 .50 caliber machine guns supplied with a K-15 sight and provisions for 400 rounds of ammunition each. There were two hoppers, one for each gun that collected the ejected cases and links and expelled them downwards. The guns could be elevated 79° above the horizontal and depressed to a maximum of 6°. The turrets had full 360° azimuths but the interrupter gear limited the angles of fire.

Type A-13-A Lower Ball Turret
The Brigg's-built lower ball turret was a 44 inch spherical metal structure that could be suspended about 24 inches below the skin line of the aircraft and could be retracted within the aircraft by means of a hand-operated hydraulic retraction assembly. It could be aimed in any direction in a hemisphere below the fuselage. Two M-2 .50 caliber machine guns were mounted in the turret and were operated by a gunner who rode inside the turret and was supplied by an external oxygen source. It had a K-4 gunsight and was supplied by 600 rounds located on hangers fed by external ammunition feed boxes.

(For a detailed discussion of the B-32 armament see my book *The Consolidated B-32 Dominator: The Ultimate Look from Drawing Board to Scrapyard*, Schiffer, PA, 2005.

**Section 2: Light and Medium Bombers**

**Lockheed A-29 Hudson**

Although the Hudson saw most of its service as a RAF Lend-Lease bomber Hudson Mk III it did see AAC service as the A-29 and service in the Navy as PBO-1 patrol bombers. The bomber was armed with two fixed forward-firing .30s in the nose, one .30 in the ventral position, and two .30s in an optional dorsal turret.

**Lockheed Ventura (RAF), Harpoon (USN), B-34/B-37 Lexington (AAF)**

With the success of its Hudson Lockheed decided to design a more advanced version that was larger, heavier, and more powerful. The PV-1 was a medium patrol bomber named the Ventura by the RAF, the Harpoon by the USN, and the B-34 Lexington and later the B-37 by the AAF.

As compared to the Hudson, the dorsal turret of the Ventura I/II was moved forward to improve the field of fire. Early production aircraft had two .303 inch machine guns installed in this turret, but later production aircraft increased the number of guns to four. Twin flexible .303 inch machine guns were mounted in the extreme nose and two fixed forward-firing .50 caliber machine guns were installed in the upper decking of the nose. A pair of flexible .303 inch machine guns were mounted in a ventral position behind the wing trailing edge with this gun position giving the rear fuselage a distinct angle. The Ventura IIA differed from the Ventura II primarily in having US-built armament items substituted for the British-built items. It was fitted with a Martin dorsal turret (250CE-7 in early models and 250CE-12 in later models) housing two 0.50 inch machine guns with 400 rpg.. It had two .50 inch machine guns in the nose, twin flexible .30 inch machine guns in the nose and ventral positions, plus two flexible 0.30 inch beam guns. The AAF took over 264 British-ordered Ventura IIs and operated them under the designation of B-34 Lexington and made only limited use of this aircraft in combat using it primarily for coastal patrol and training duties. The B-37 was almost identical to the B-34 except for the engines and by the presence of two oval waist gun ports on either side of the rear fuselage for a single .30 caliber flexible machine gun.

**Vultee A-31/A-35 Vengeance**

In 1940 the British Purchasing Mission ordered 700 of these Vultee Model 72 dive bombers as the Vengeance. Later, the RAF ordered 300 more as the A-31. The Lend-Lease version was armed with four .303s in the wing and dual .303s in a flexible mount in the rear cockpit. After Pearl Harbor the AAC seized nearly 250 of the RAF's A-31s and re-equipped 99 of them as the A-35A with four .50s in the wings and a single flexible .50 in the rear. Later, 831 A-35Bs were fitted with an additional .50 mount in the rear. The dive bomber was used by the AAF for training and as a target tow.

**Douglas A-20 Havoc**

The Douglas DB-7/A-20 was built in large numbers, 7,400 with half of the production devoted to Lend-Lease to the British and Soviets mainly as DB-7s. The bomber carried an ample bomb load and a variety of armament that helped it set the standard for light bomber ground attack and interdiction.

A-20 and A-20A
The three place (pilot, bombardier, and gunner) A-20 and A-20A were identical in configuration and armament. The armament consisted of four fixed and two flexible .30 M2 machine guns. The nose installation contained two internal fixed guns and two fixed guns mounted in blisters on each side of the lower nose. The flexible guns were similar to the DB-7A with single guns placed in dorsal and ventral positions.

Fixed Guns: Each fixed gun was mounted in a compartment in each side of the fuselage below the bombardier's station. When alternate guns were carried they were mounted outboard of the normally installed guns and were covered by fairings. These fixed guns were electrically controlled by a gun selector switch on the pilot's upper electrical panel and a firing switch on the wheel of the pilot's control column. This selector switch allowed firing of the two inboard guns, the two outboard guns or all four guns at once. There was one pair of manually operated gun charging controls on each side of cockpit below the pilot's instrument panel. The lower charging control of each pair attached to the inboard gun and the upper pair to the outboard gun. A Type N-21 gunsight reflector was mounted on the cowl above the instrument panel. Ammunition cans carrying 500 rounds for each gun were installed behind the bombardier's seat in the nose compartment.

Flexible Guns:
The dorsal guns were twin .30 caliber Brownings mounted side-by-side in a Bell Adapter with a pneumatic recoil absorber. The Bell Adapter allowed the guns to be moved from one side of the fuselage to the other on a semi-circular track. The mount had a single trigger that controlled guns as well as a fire and safe control. Ten ammunition boxes containing 200 rounds each was supplied; five for each gun. The guns stowed on the aircraft's centerline, pointing aft, each barrel in a metal tunnel. When the guns were moved into their firing position, the gun tunnel doors were opened by a foot crank.

The ventral flexible gun was mounted on a support arm that pivoted on a bracket on the floor on the port side of the gunner's station. The support arm when lowered and latched in the firing position allowed the gun to be fired downward and rearward through a door in the floor. When the gun was stowed the arm swung upwards and was latched onto a catch located on the left side of the compartment. There were ammunition box containing 500 rounds attached to holders on the port side of the gunner's compartment.

Nacelle Guns: Two fixed .30 caliber Brownings firing directly aft were mounted, one in each nacelle, on a somewhat flexible rear mounting bracket. The bracket had some flex in order to fire a large bullet pattern, giving these guns the name, "Splatter Guns." The rear gunner controlled these guns and fired them by a foot switch located on the floor of his compartment. As the guns were not aimed there was no gunsight. The guns were charged by a control valve on the port side of the compartment. Both guns were charged and fired simultaneous. An ammunition box containing 1,000 rounds was located in each nacelle directly below each gun.

A-20B
The A-20B designation was given to the 999 built in the new Douglas Long Beach factory previously they were built in the Santa Monica factory). The Bs differed little from the A models except all armament was upgraded to .50 caliber except for the ventral flexible gun position.

A-20C
The A-20C was built by Douglas and also by Boeing. The first batch of 515 was built for British Lend-Lease as a continuation of the DB-7B carrying two or four fixed and two flexible .303 machine guns and one flexible Vickers Model E. However, not one of these aircraft was delivered to Britain but went instead to Russia. The second batch of 433 was built only by Douglas and carried .30 machine guns in all positions.

A-20D/E/F
These aircraft were built only in small numbers and changes involved the fuel tanks.

A-20G
This model was built in the greatest numbers with 3,300 delivered. Beginning with A-20G-20-DO and all subsequent production the flexible dorsal guns in the gunner's compartment were replaced by an electrically powered Martin 250CE turret mounting two .50s. Also in this G-20 model a .50 Browning was installed in the ventral (tunnel) flexible position replacing the .30. Significantly the G-20 had a production solid nose which was a prevalent field modification in the SWPA. The early solid noses contained an impressive array of four 20mm cannon and two .50s which turned the A-20 into a fearsome ground attack strafer/bomber. Later the often troublesome 20mm cannon were replaced by four more .50s for six nose .50s, a configuration that Douglas would continue in the A-26 Invader. The A-20Cs retained the .30 fixed guns in the rear fuselage.

A-20J
When the AAF decided to convert the A-20G solid nose back into a bombardier-style glass nose the revised bomber was designated as the A-20J which carried two fixed .50s in the nose along with the standard bombing equipment. A total of 1,606 Js, half sent to the Russians under Lend-Lease, were delivered.

XA-20B and XA-20F Project
In June 1940 the Materiel Division contracted General Electric to develop a remote fire control system for the tail and aft nacelles of the A-20 which was discussed earlier.

**North American B-25 Mitchell**
Of all the American bombers, heavy or medium, none was equipped with so many armament figurations which made it arguably the most potent bomber of the war. However, when first B-25s were introduced they were rather impotent with no power turrets, a .30 flexible gun in the nose, two waist guns, a dorsal position, and a .50 caliber tail stinger with its gunner lying in an uncomfortable prone position with limited vision.

B-25B
The B model was introduced equipped with new armament which regrettably was the mediocre Bendix dorsal and ventral turrets. Most of the ventral turrets were removed in the field. The Bendix dorsal turret was improved and would continue throughout the B-25 production run. The .30 caliber nose gun continued (six boxes of 100 round belts) and could be mounted on one of three sockets. All other manually guns, including the tail gun, were removed.

On the B-25B the most conspicuous difference was the introduction of two Bendix power-operated turrets. The L-type turret was installed on the top of the rear fuselage and carried a pair of .50 caliber machine guns. In addition, a pair of .50 caliber machine guns was mounted in a solid Bendix remotely controlled ventral turret. This turret could be retracted into the belly when not in use, with the gun barrels fitting into slots in the fuselage when the turret was in the fully up position. In the B-25, the weight and balance considerations for adding the dorsal and ventral turrets became critical and the tail gun installation was eliminated.

B-25C & D
The flexible .30 caliber nose gun was replaced by a .50 caliber and was augmented by a fixed .50. The B-25 was transformed in the SWPA to a potent low level strafer and bomber by Paul "Pappy" Gunn and North American representative Jack Fox. In its new role as a low level attacker against Japanese airfield and shipping, the B-25 became an easy target for AA fire. To suppress this AA fire Gunn and Fox eliminated the bombardier's position which was no longer needed and added four fixed .50s in his position with the Plexiglas painted over. An additional four .50s were installed as package/blister guns located below the cockpit.

B-25G
North American produced the G as the ultimate low level gunship. A huge 75mm M4 cannon (21 rounds) was installed in the former bombardier's crawlway and the glazed nose was replaced by a shortened all metal nose with two .50 caliber machine guns (400 rpg). The cannon was heavy and even a skilled gunner was able to get only three of four rounds fired during a firing run. On late production Gs the useless ventral turret was removed and tail position was improved with the gunner sitting more comfortably upright behind a single .50. The two waist positions were provided with

rectangular windows for single .50s firing 200 rpg. Blister packs were added in the SWPA.

B-25H
The dorsal turret was moved from the aft fuselage forward over the wing. The single tail gun was replaced by the Bell M-7 electro-hydraulic mount with twin .50s (600 rpg). The 75mm M4 cannon was replaced by the lighter M5 and four .50s became the nose armament. When the H entered service in early 1944 most of the Japanese targets suitable for the 75mm had all but disappeared and the cannons were removed and replaced with two additional .50s. From the B-25H-5 (43-4405) onward the armament was the same as B-25H plus the addition of two fixed .50 caliber machine guns in left blister packs.

B-25J
The B-25J was the last production model with 4,390 produced. Of this number 3,590 had the glazed "bombardier" nose with a single flexible .50 fired by the bombardier and two fixed guns. The remaining 800 Js were finished with a better streamlined solid nose with eight .50 Brownings. The package/blister packs were continued. With this configuration the J could have 18 fixed and flexible guns of which 14 could fire forward.

B-25 Armament Described
Bendix Model K Amplidyne Ventral Turret
The Bendix Model K Amplidyne ventral turret, placed in B-25 Cs and Ds and B-24Ds, was a solid retractable turret designed around a central column and weighed 392 pounds, excluding 300 pounds of guns and ammunition. It mounted twin .50 caliber machine guns fed by 390 rounds of ammunition per gun from ammunition boxes bolted to the lower canopy which could be easily be removed from the turret assembly by removing four bolts in the end of the housing hanger arms. The empty shell cases and links were ejected overboard through ejection chutes and dropped outside through slots in the movable housing at the bottom of the turret. Observation windows were cut into the fuselage just above the floor level on each side of the turret.

Bendix Model A and R Dorsal Turrets
The all-electric Bendix Dorsal Turret was used exclusively on the B-25, beginning with the B-25B. The original B-25 design incorporated the late 1930s AAC standards utilizing the light .30 caliber machine gun in five flexible hand-held positions: one in the nose, one each in the ventral and dorsal rear fuselage, and two in the waist position. The Bendix Model A dorsal turret was located in aft fuselage compartment behind the bomb bay, replacing the single flexible dorsal .30 caliber machine gun on the B-25 and B-25A that fired through a enclosed hatch. This turret location continued on the B-25C/D and G models but after the ventral turret was cancelled during its production run, the B-25G became underarmed and waist guns and tail guns were added at modification depots or in the field to alleviate this deficiency. It was found when the waist guns and gunners were located with the dorsal turret in the aft fuselage the area became confined and their movement was greatly restricted. To solve this problem dorsal turret in the H the turret in its Type R configuration (Army Model A-9B/Navy 250CE-4) was moved forward to the navigator's compartment just behind the cockpit which helped to maintain the proper center of gravity to balance the weight added to the rear by the waist guns and tail turret. This new dorsal turret position was more heavily braced and had a higher dome than did previous Mitchell dorsal turrets.

Waist Guns
The B-25 and B-25A were provided with two waist gun positions in the rear fuselage mounting a pair of light .30 caliber machine guns. The gun had to be lifted from its stowage position in front of the waist window for combat. The waist windows were opened and the gun refitted on its ball-and-socket mount to firing position, barrel out the window. Factory-provided waist guns first appeared on the B-25H although after the ventral turret was discontinued during production of the B-25G-5 from aircraft 42-65001 onward some B-25Gs had post-production, jury-rigged waist positions and a single tail guns added at depots. On the B-25H model waist gun defense was improved by installing enclosed, convex windows on both sides of the fuselage aft of the wing and staggering them to allow more space for the gunners to operate. The window on the port side was placed further aft from rear of the wing than that on the starboard side, which had its forward vertical frame a few inches away from the wing flaps. It would appear that NAA finalized the design of these windows some time before the B-25H appeared, as many conversion kits were shipped to modification centers to upgrade the armament of the B-25C/D. Each window had a cut-out for a gun mount in the lower rear corner. These modifications on the C/D models became somewhat common in some squadrons although the mid-fuselage position of the dorsal turret meant that the turret gunner's feet must have been very close to the waist gunner's head as the turret rotated. The movement of the dorsal turret forward opened up the rear fuselage compartment for more effective use of the two opposing, staggered flexible .50 caliber machine waist guns.

"Medium Bomber" Nose Gun Configuration
The B-25, B-25A/B/C/D and early Js were configured as pure medium bombers and fitted with a flexible and a fixed .50 caliber machine gun in the nose. The B-25 and B-25A were equipped with a single flexible.30 caliber machine gun operated by the bombardier. This light .30 caliber gun was replaced with a heavier .50 flexible gun and a fixed gun on the B-25C-5.

The flexible and fixed nose guns were mounted in the bombardier's compartment to project forward through the Plexiglas nose. For the single nose gun installation, 300 rounds of ammunition were carried. When two fixed nose guns were installed only 275 rounds per gun were carried. Initially, all guns were manually charged in flight by the bombardier. Later the charging handles were located on the cockpit floor to the right of the pilot's seat and charged by the pilot. The transparent bombardier nose on the J could be replaced at the factory by a solid nose that was equipped with four .50 caliber machine guns. The J-20 production block (44-29111) introduced a second .50 caliber fixed machine gun installed in the nose with the flexible nose gun being relocated four inches higher.

Blister Gun Packs
In mid-1943 the cannon-equipped B-25Gs arrived in the SWPA and were tested by Maj. Paul Gunn from mid-November through December. Gunn was mostly pleased with the 75mm cannon but he recommended that the G model needed the addition of forward firing .50 caliber machine guns. The Service Command began a wide-ranging armament modification program on the G model running from November 1943 to April 1944. To add forward fire power the fuselage gun pack was developed.

The fuselage gun packs (the NAA nomenclature) were also called cheek packs and most commonly blister packs in the field. They were faired rectangular metal pods fastened to the fuselage with a downward opening hinged access cover door. The pack enclosed two .50 caliber machine guns that were anchored to a reinforced plate on the fuselage and held in place by custom made brackets that bolted into the fuselage. Brackets on the barrel and base of the gun were attached by bolts to the mounting bracket. The barrel of the top gun was usually staggered slightly behind of the lower gun. The gun unit was equipped with a Type G-11 solenoid, a link guide, feed chute attachments, and a manual charging slide. The ammunition boxes were supported on a shelf structure at the right side of the cannoneer's compartment. Flexible chutes fed the ammunition belts to the guns. The manual charging handle for each gun was located forward of the ammo boxes mounted on the bulkhead at the forward end of the top turret compartment. The cannoneer charged the blister guns in flight by pulling out and releasing the charging handles. The guns were fired simultaneously by the pilot. To load the blister packs the ammunition boxes were loaded with approximately 400 rounds.

B-25 75mm Cannon
The B-25 cannon assembly consisted of the 75mm M4 cannon and its M6 recoil mount and later the 75mm T9 cannon and its Type T-13E1 recoil mount, and the cannon mount assembly that was bolted to the floor in the tunnel beneath the left side of the pilot's compartment. The cannon muzzle projected forward through the blast tube in the lower nose section. The early model M4 cannon were originally fitted with a protective muzzle cover consisting of metal "petals" that sprang open before use. These covers would not always open properly even after a stronger spring was installed and they were canceled in later versions. The breech extended aft to the left forward side of the cannoneer's compartment. The recoil mount consisted of a concentric recoil mechanism, an oil replenishing cylinder and an indicator tube, the trunnions, and the actuator assembly that controlled the firing of the cannon. An ammunition loading tray was attached to the cannon breech ring. A vertical leveling clevis mounted at the end of the gun provided boresighting adjustments. The opening through which the cannon protruded was covered by an armored panel. A dust and gas seal was secured to the cannon barrel and attached to the armored panel. For loading the cannon, the cannoneer was provided with a folding seat, a cannon recoil foot guard, a leg strap, and a wooden loading ram.

The cannon and ammunition weighed 1,296 pounds. The recoil was 21 inches with a powder pressure of 38,000 pounds per square inch. A Type N-9 gun and bombsight and Type A-3 gun and bombsight head were mounted on the instrument glare shield immediately in front of the pilot. The pilot fired the cannon by pressing the trigger under the left hand side of the control wheel while the machine guns were fired by pressing the trigger under the right hand side of the control wheel. The 75mm projectile was 26 inches long and three inches in diameter and weighed 20 pounds, equivalent to 78 .50 caliber bullets, of which 15 pounds was the projectile that contained 1.5 pounds of TNT. After firing a spent shell case was ejected from the recoiling cannon against a shell deflector that sent the case down a chute and overboard.

Original Tail Armament
The original B-25 cone-shaped tail turret mounted a flexible .50 caliber machine gun which opened through clam shell Plexiglas doors which were similar to those pioneered in the Douglas B-23 Dragon. This gun was the only .50 caliber among five other .30 caliber (nose, dorsal, ventral, and two in the waist). The gunner sat on a metal chair mounted close to the floor with the gun between his bent legs while he looked through a sighting system. There was an entrance/emergency hatch located above his head.

B-25H and J Bell Gun Mount Assembly (Type M-7 Adapter) Tail Turret
The Bell Adapter, its technical designation was the Bell Gun Mount Assembly, was power-driven flexible gun mount developed to increase the firepower of the tail gun position in the B-25 and B-26. There were two models, the Type M-7 for the B-25 and the Type M-6A for the B-26. The only difference between the two was in the mounting bracket. The Bell Adapter was equipped with a twin gun adapter that mounted two .50 caliber Type M-2 machine guns, a Type N-8 or N-6A gunsight, feed chutes equipped with booster motors, an adjustable seat, and a large armor plate mounted between the adapter and the gunner. Each gun was held to its cradle by a rear trunnion latch lock and a front trunnion bolt that had a spring-loaded plunger that locked in place. The guns were mounted so that they were always held level and parallel to each other.

(For a very detailed description of B-25 armament see my book *The North American B-25 Mitchell: The Ultimate Look from Drawing Board to Flying Arsenal*, Schiffer, PA, 2008)

**Martin B-26 Marauder**
The Martin B-26 was the first American bomber to use a powered turret and naturally Martin used its own 250CE dorsal turret for the installation. The Marauder also was equipped with a flexible .30 in the nose, a .30 in the ventral tunnel, and a flexible .50 in the tail cone. The Martin dorsal turret had a rudimentary interrupter cam that only protected the vertical tail and the gun barrels hit the top of the fuselage. The .30 nose gun was often replaced in the field by a .50.

B-26B
The B began production in May 1942 with new tail armament comprising two .50s with 800 rpg, standardized the .50 on the nose with 270 rpg, and continued the 250CE dorsal turret with 400 rpg. The .30 ventral tunnel gun was ineffective and replaced later by two .50s firing 240 rpg through waist windows cut in the lower half of the fuselage.

The so-called "Big Wing" B-26s arrived in Britain in late April 1943 with more fire power to aid in low level attacks. An additional fixed machine gun firing through the lower nose increased the ground strafing total to five. As well as the dorsal and tail turrets the flexible .50 machine gun remained in the center of the nose and two additional hand-held guns were mounted in the lower rear fuselage side hatches.

B-26C
Late production Bs and the B-26C left the production line with improved armament. A new array of forward firing guns appeared with a single .50 (200 rpg) in the nose and two .50s in two "blister packs/package guns" mounted on each side of the nose. The manually aimed tail guns with their ring and bead sights were replaced by a Martin-Bell M-6 hydraulic powered mount. The M-6 encountered a number of problems after its introduction. The gun barrels broke the Plexiglas at maximum depression which was easily remedied by placing a simple wood stop on the gun mount. A continual difficulty was having ejected spent links jamming the discharge chutes. A number of solutions were tried unsuccessfully and many tail gunners removed the chutes and let the spent links fall to the floor of the compartment. Gun jamming due to the varying rate of feed of the booster motors was also a persistent problem that was difficult to solve.

Before they were delivered 60 B-26C-5s were modified for ground attack. The co-pilot's seat and control column were eliminated and a small seat was added for the navigator to operate the flaps and landing gear. These aircraft were allotted to the 323BG but never were used in the ground attack role.

B-26F and G
The armament of the B-26C was standard on the final production models, B-26 F and G.

B-26 Armament Description

Nose Gun

A .50 caliber machine gun mounted on a gimbal and ring and bead sighted was positioned in the extreme nose with the 200 round ammunition box located on the starboard side. A fixed .50 was located in the forward right side with its 200 round ammunition box along side. The gun was sighted through a reflector sight and fired by the pilot (this gun was sometimes deleted in C models).

Package Guns

Two .50 caliber package guns were mounted on the port side fired by the pilot and sighted through a reflector sight. The 500 round (250 rounds per gun) ammunition box was located inside the fuselage under the radio table with the feed moving through slots in the skin. The cartridge links fell through the outer side of the package and the spent cartridges were ejected through a slot in the bottom of the package. Two identical starboard package guns were fed from a 500 round ammunition box located under the navigator's table.

Starboard and Port Rear Beam Guns

Movable .50 caliber machine guns were located on each rear beam of the fuselage. They were mounted on an extending arm bolted through a swivel on the floor with the 200 round ammunition box fixed to the fuselage roof. The guns were sighted by a ring and bead and could only fired in rearward and downward arcs.

Martin 250CE Dorsal Turret

The twin .50 caliber Browning equipped Martin turret was powered in 360° traverse and 70° elevation. It was sighted by a reflector sight and fed by pocket ammunition boxes built around the base and side of the turret and holding 400 rounds per gun.

Tail

The Marauder tail gun position evolved from an enclosed tail cone mounting one .30 on the B-26 and .50 tunnel gun and B-26A. The B Model differed from the A in that the single .50 caliber gun was replaced by an enlarged and lengthened enclosed tail position with a twin .50 mount with the ammunition supply increased from 400 to 1,500 rounds. The late B-1 models and C, F, and G models had two .50s located in the power-operated Martin-Bell turret with the ammunition boxes in the rear bomb bay section feeding 400 rounds of ammunition per gun on vertical tracks. The gun was supported on a M-6 or M-6A mount and sighted through N-8 or N-8a reflector sights.

**Douglas A-26 Invader**

The A-26 was designed to replace the B-25, B-26, and A-20. The prototypes were armed with assorted nose gun arrays including two 37mm cannon, a 75mm cannon and two .50 caliber machines, one 37mm cannon and four .50s, a 75mm and a 37mm cannon, and six .50 Brownings. The production B-26B was to have a solid nose containing six .50s and the B-26C, a glass nose with a bombardier's station and two 50s on the right side. These noses were easily interchangeable. In combat the six gun nose was found to be inadequate and increased to eight guns and provisions were made to mount eight more .50s in four underwing twin packs. These four underwing twin packs produced too much drag and were replaced by six .50s mounted in the outer wing panels. The defensive armament consisted of General Electric periscopic dorsal and a ventral remote controlled turrets; each armed with two .50s. As was usual with remote controlled turrets; the ventral turret was deleted. Due to its slow and troubled development, the Invader saw limited action in World War II but would continue on in Korea and Vietnam.

**North American XB-28**

Defensive armament on the XB-28 was three remotely controlled turrets: dorsal, ventral, and tail turrets each mounting two .50 caliber machine guns. The remote controlled firing system was originally designed and built by Sperry for the B-29 and B-32 pressurized bomber programs. The turrets were operated by the primary gunner and the radio operator/gunner from the pressurized crew compartment. There was no nose turret as it was thought that the aircraft's high-speed would make head on attacks unlikely. The twin .50 tail turret was remotely controlled from the crew compartment and driven by azimuth and elevation motors. It was serviced by a low, narrow crawlway. The gunner sighted the target through the periscope, and tracked it with the power-operated computer that automatically, through the gun controls, rotated the turrets and elevated the guns. The gunner continued to track the enemy by constantly keeping its wingtips centered in the sight by adjusting a dial or by using a foot pedal. The Sperry periscope was found to have several major disadvantages and with the problems occurring in the Sperry system, the better and more reliable General Electric System was adopted. The replacement of Sperry by the GE systems also caused serious problems. Under the original plan Sperry developed the computers and control systems and North American built the gun mounts and actual turret structure. When GE assumed the XB-28 fire control project, it was decided that the entire unit would be built by GE causing serious delays. Due to the engineering challenges of the XB-28 and NAA being stretched by its commitment to the B-25, P-51, and AT-6 programs further development of the XB-28 continued slowly. Finally the XB-28's opportunity as a high altitude medium bomber passed and consequently the entire AAC investment in North American was canceled.

# 4

# U.S. Navy Bombers, Patrol, and Observation Aircraft

Because of the restrictive size of aircraft carrier decks, the design requirements for naval attack aircraft needed to be for a small and single-engined aircraft with a crew of two or three that was able to carry torpedoes or large armor-piercing bombs and enough fuel to provide long combat range. This design produced a slow aircraft with limited defensive armament that required fighter escort.

## Section 1: Dive and Torpedo Bombers

### Douglas TBD Devastator

The TBD torpedo bomber was the first production USN carrier-based monoplane. A single fixed forward-firing .30 caliber machine gun was installed in the right engine accessory section. A long telescopic torpedo/gunsight (Mk III, Mod2) with a small rudimentary ring and bead mounted on top protruded through the windscreen to aim this gun. The TBD-1 was armed with a single .30 M2 machine gun in the rear cockpit mounted on a ring mount. The gun had a flexible windage type forward gunsight and flash suppressor. Another .30 was added in the field by adapting SBD gun mounts but the Devastator proved not to be so devastating and was soon removed from service.

### Brewster SBA/SBN

The two-place XSBA-1 scout bomber was Brewster's first design and first appeared in April1936 carrying only one .30 caliber machine in a flexible mount in the rear cockpit. Inadequate production facilities at Brewster caused the SBN-1 to be built at the Naval Aircraft Factory (NAF0 and by the it was finally delivered in March 1942, the scout was obsolete and they were used for carrier training.

### Brewster SB2A Buccaneer

With the failure of the SBN Brewster designed a heavier scout bomber with an increased bomb load and armament. A single prototype was ordered by the Navy on 4 April 1939 armed with eight .30 caliber machine guns: six forward firing (two fuselage-mounted and four in the wings) and two in a flexible mounting in the rear cockpit. Large numbers were ordered by the Navy (140), RAF (750 as Bermudas), and the Dutch (162) but the aircraft's performance fell far below specifications. The Navy continued its interest in the design and in the SB2A-2 and -3 the .30 caliber armament was changed to .50 caliber guns in the same positions. The 771 produced were only suitable for training and target towing in US and RAF service.

### Consolidated TBY (Vought TBU) Sea Wolf

In the 1939 competition for a new Navy torpedo bomber Consolidated entered its XTBU-1 and was awarded a contract for a prototype on 22 April 1940 as it was considered better than the Grumman TBF Avenger. The armament was three forward firing .50s (one in the cowling and two in the wings), one .50 in the dorsal turret in the rear of the extended cockpit, and one .30 caliber in the ventral tunnel mount. Vought was awarded a contract for 1,100 which it was unable to meet due to limited production capacity and Consolidated assumed it as the TBY in September 1943. The TBY did not enter Navy service until November 1944 and only saw service for training.

### Douglas SBD Dauntless

The SBD (dubbed "Slow But Deadly") dive bomber was armed with two fixed forward-firing .50s supplied with 360 rpg mounted in the engine cowling and a flexible .30 machine gun mounted in the rear cockpit. The SBD was vulnerable to enemy fighters but had a long combat life because of the developmental problems of the SB2C.

The SBD series mounted two fixed forward-firing .50 caliber Brownings that fired through the propeller. The guns were on top the cowling and fired forward along extended indentation through the propeller. The ammunition was stored in 180 round boxes that slid into an opening immediately to the rear of the engine accessory section. The guns were sighted through a Mk III MOD IV ring sight on the SBD-1 through SBD-4 and by the MK VIII ring sight on the SBD-5 and -6.

The single .30 was limited to 84° aft and 63° depression due to the seat ring mount. It was sighted by a Mk VI ring sight. The gun was fed by a 100 round magazine with up to six more magazines of a 100 rounds each stored in a magazine rack on the aft cockpit bulkhead. The SBD-1,-2, and early -3s utilized the single .30 gun.

During SBD-3 production the twin 30 machine gun installation was added. Each gun was supplied by a 500 round belt (there were three additional 500 round belts available for each weapon). The guns were mounted on a Mk II-3 adapter fitted to an adapter post. There were two hinged doors on top of the aft fuselage which opened to allow the guns to be stowed in a tunnel inside the aircraft.

### Curtiss SB2C Helldiver

The Helldiver dive bomber was a disappointment as the replacement for the Dauntless having poor handling and only slightly better performance.

The original design had fixed armament of four .50s (800 rpg) in the wings and two .30 in the rear. Curtiss was unable to develop an enclosed power turret for the rear cockpit and used twin Douglas-designed .30s fired from an open cockpit. The guns were supplied from large ammunition boxes stored aft of the ring mount. On the SB2C-1 Model 3 series these .30s were replaced by a single .50 caliber Browning which proved to be unsatisfactory and were replaced by the previous twin .30s which remained standard throughout production.

The SB2C-1s were armed with four .50 caliber machine guns mounted in the wings just outboard and above and passing through the level of the wheel wells. Stainless steel tubes extended from the muzzles to ports where they exited from each wing just below the leading edge. Two ammunition boxes carrying 433 rounds were located just outboard of the two guns and were fed to the guns through a chute. Spent cartridges and links were ejected from the aircraft through separate chutes through slots in the underwing. On the SB2C-1C two 20mm cannon replaced the two wing .50s with two 20mm cannon fed by two boxes containing 100 rpg mounted just inboard each cannon. The 20mm proved to be unreliable in combat.

**Vought SB2U Vindicator**

The first SB2U dive bombers were armed with a single fixed and a flexible .30. The SB2U-1 was fitted with a forward-firing .30 caliber Browning, mounted on the right wing outside the propeller arc and a second .30 mounted flexible ring and the rear cockpit. In early 1939, the USMC received SB2U-3 provisions were made for four forward-firing wing .50s and replacing the rear gunner's .30 with a .50. The British -3 called the Chesapeake had four .30 wing guns with 50 rpg with another in the rear cockpit. The SB2U also had a short combat life as it was being replaced before Pearl Harbor.

**Grumman TBF /General Motors TBM Avenger**

Grumman designed the TBF torpedo bomber but most were built by General Motors as the TBM. The first Avengers were well-armed in comparison to other Navy bombers having a Grumman-designed amplidyne electric powered dorsal ball turret 150SE-1&2 armed with a single .50 which gave it a better defense than twin .30s. For space consideration the single .50 was offset to the starboard inside the turret. The circular port side section could be removed for an emergency. The Grumman turret defended against beam, overhead, or tail cone attacks. The electrically-powered turret moved the gunner with the gun and sights in elevation and azimuth in the direction he turned the control handle.

The Avenger's bath tub-type lower fuselage aft of the wing allowed room for the radio operator to operate a .30 caliber tunnel machine gun on all Avengers through the TBM-3. The gun referred to as the "stinger" had its ammunition box stored just above the gun on the right side of the lower fuselage. There was a small window on each side of the rear window containing the gun opening. A canvas boot surrounded the gun's barrel.

In the early models the pilot controlled a single.30 caliber machine gun in the starboard engine cowl with the ammunition box being stored under the port cowl. This light gun was intended to suppress enemy return fire but was grossly inadequate and on the TBF-1Cs was replaced by a .50 caliber Browning installed in each wing.

The wing gun was installed just outboard the wing fold with the ammunition boxes installed a bit more outboard in the wing and fed the gun through a chute. Blast tubes extended the muzzle which was well inside the wing to the leading edge of the wing.

**Douglas SB2D**

Late in the war the Navy was looking to build larger and heavier carrier-borne aircraft to fly off the three large, 45,000 ton Midway-class carriers scheduled to be commissioned from September 1945 onward. The SB2D was a large two-man dive bomber with an internal bomb bay. It had remote controlled dorsal and ventral turrets with a single .50 in each plus one or two .50s in each wing.

**Grumman TB2F**

The proposed TB2F was a very large twin-engined torpedo bomber that was equipped in the mock up stage with a dorsal turret with twin .50s, a retractable ventral ball-type turret with two .50s, four .50s in the wing roots, two .50s on the port side of the nose, and a 75mm in the starboard side of the nose. As projected the TB2F was much too large even for the Midway class carriers and was cancelled.

**Section 2: U.S. Navy Patrol Bombers**

**Lockheed PV-1 Ventura/PV-2 Harpoon**

The PV-1 was very similar to the B-34, differing primarily in the addition of special equipment to modify it to a maritime reconnaissance role. The defensive armament was reduced to two fixed forward-firing .50 caliber machine guns in the upper fuselage decking; twin .50 caliber guns in the dorsal turret, and two flexible .30 caliber machine guns in the ventral position. A pack containing three .50 machine guns could be added underneath the nose. The PV-1 operated for a short time as a night fighter with the Marine Corps' first night fighter squadron, VMF(N)-531, fitted with six nose guns and AI Mk IV radar.

The Lockheed PV-2 Harpoon was a complete redesign of the PV-1 Ventura to maximize its use for a maritime reconnaissance role beginning in March 1945. The armament standardized on two fixed .50 caliber machine guns in the upper nose decking plus three fixed .50 caliber machine guns in a ventral nose pack. The bombardier's position on the early PV-1s was finally deleted. Two .50 caliber machine guns were carried in the dorsal turret, and two .50 caliber machine guns were installed in the rear ventral position.

**Consolidated PBY**

The PBY-1 was delivered in June 1936 bearing a .30 caliber machine gun in the bow turret, a .30 in the tunnel position in the tail, and two .30s in each waist position which were soon replaced with .50s. The bow turret .30 was mounted on a Mk 9 adapter in a rotating turret and was manned by the bombardier. The turret could be moved in azimuth 180° in front of the aircraft and moved in elevation from -40° to 90° and was sighted through a basic ring and bead sight. The gun was fed by attaching 100 round ammunition cans that were stored on a rack under the gun. The gun opened in the center of the turret with two vertical sighting windows to the side. The gunner could fire the guns from a kneeling position from completely inside the turret but could also stand up through the top hatch. This turret remained standard into the PBY-5and -5A series. When not in use the gun could be removed from its mount and stowed inside the bombardier's compartment.

The final PBY bow turret, appearing in late-production -5As, was the so-called "Eyeball" turret because of its large rounded forward glass window. This turret was a modification of the standard four window fuselage and base configuration which remained except for forward glass window and a heightened canopy-type hood that allowed increased area for the gunner's head.. The gunner with a better field of vision stood inside the bow compartment with his head inside the dome behind the guns. Two large ammunition boxes holding 1,050 rounds each were located below the gun were bolted to the ring that rotated with the turret. Two twin .30s were mounted on sockets that protruded through the dome. The turret did not rotate but the guns tracked the target by moving the eyeball part of the turret's glass. The PBN-1, a slightly larger derivative of the Consolidated

PBY, built by the Naval Aircraft Factory was equipped with a powered, collapsible bow turret mounting a .50 caliber machine gun.

The initial .30 caliber and later .50 waist guns were mounted in each window on the sides of the aft fuselage. The covers for the windows angled forward and outward to deflect the air stream as it passed over the gun position to facilitate gun movement. When not in use and to give the gunner's a better observation area; the guns could be swung down inside the fuselage into to their stowed position against the fuselage wall under the window. Two spare guns were stowed on either side of the center walkway. Beginning with the -5, all successive PBY models were equipped with the large Plexiglas observation blisters on the aft sides of the fuselage. The side of the blister could be swung up to allow the .50 machine gun to go into action. Initially the guns were equipped with a small attached ammunition box but later a single large ammunition box was placed in the center of the compartment to provide a continuous feed to each gun. An armored metal shield was added to the mount to give protection to the gunner. The guns was initially sighted with a telescopic sight but was later sighted by a Mk 9 reflector sight

All Models of the PBY had a single .30 caliber machine gun that could be mounted in the underside of the rear fuselage to provide defensive fire to the rear. See Part Six/Section 5/Chapter 6: Miscellaneous Gun Installations for a complete description of the PBY tunnel gun.

**Consolidated PB2Y Coronado**

Consolidated wanted to update and enlarge its very successful PBY patrol bomber and submitted the design for the XPB2Y which first flew on 17 December 1937 but was not ordered until 31 March 1939. The most numerous (210) version was the PB2Y-3 which was armed with two .50 caliber machine guns in each of the bow, dorsal, and tail turrets. Single .50s were mounted in each of the two waist positions

**Consolidated P4Y Corregidor**

Consolidated designed the long-range civilian Model 31 flying boat in 1938 and as war was approaching designated the XTBU-1 as the naval version. It first flew on 22 December 1941 and was delivered to the Navy in March 1942. The Corregidor was to be armed with a 37mm cannon in the bow turret, two .50s in the dorsal and tail turrets. The Navy ordered 220 but the contract was cancelled in mid-1943 when its Wright 3350s did have priority over other programs (e.g. the B-29).

**Boeing XPBB-1 Sea Ranger**

Before the war US interest in a new long-range patrol bomber was spurred by German U-Boats in American coastal waters. Boeing had the Model 344 on its drawing boards. The amphibian was the largest twin-engine flying boat to be flown in World War II. The Navy awarded a contract for the XPBB-1 on 5 July 1942 to be armed by eight .50 caliber machine guns; two each in the bow, two waist, and tail positions. The Sea Ranger program was cancelled when land-based aircraft could adequately undertake the Sea Ranger's patrol role.

**Martin PBM Mariner**

The PBM was designed to replace the P3M that had been in service since 1931. The XPBM first flew on 18 February 1939 and had provisions for five .30 caliber machine guns; one each in the bow, dorsal, tail turrets and in the two waist positions. The .50 caliber machine replaced the .30s in these positions in the PBM-3D. This armament configuration remained in place through the last production PBM-5A in April 1949.

**K-Class Airship**

The Lighter-than-Air (LTA) K-Class Airships called blimps were used for patrol and anti-submarine warfare (ASW). The first of 134 K-ships built by Goodyear was the K-2 ordered in 1937 and the airships were given the designation ZNP-K (Z = lighter-than-air, N = non-rigid, P = patrol, N = type or class). The airship was 252 feet long and 58 feet in diameter and all equipment was carried in a 40 foot long gondola control car that housed a crew of nine or ten. The K-ships carried four Mk-47 depth bombs and were armed with a .50 caliber machine gun mounted in the forward section of the control car.

**Section 3: U.S. Navy Float Observation Aircraft**

**Curtiss SOC Seagull**: One fixed forward-firing .30 machine gun in each wing and one .30 machine gun on a flexible mount in the rear cockpit.

**Grumman J2F Duck**: Optional .30 machine gun on a flexible mount in the rear cockpit.

**Vought OS2U Kingfisher**: One fixed .30 machine gun firing through the right engine and one flexible .30 machine gun in the rear cockpit.

**Curtiss SC-1 Seahawk**: Two fixed .50 machine guns in the wings.

**Curtiss SOC Seagull:** One fixed nose .30 machine gun plus one .30 machine gun in the rear cockpit.

**Curtiss SO3C Seamew:** One fixed nose .30 machine gun plus one .50 machine gun in the rear cockpit.

# 5

# Experimental Aircraft

## Section 1: Tractor Aircraft

### Brewster XA-32

The XA-32, like the company's F2F Buffalo, suffered from the company's chronic mismanagement and ineptitude. The XA-32 was initially designed as an attack aircraft in 1941 and when the two prototypes finally were ready in May 1943 they were a design disaster. The single-seat aircraft was grossly overweight; weighing about the same as the A-20 light bomber. Its P&W R-2800 engine was unable to power aircraft anywhere near requirements even without the eight proposed .50s in the wings and the bomb load. The XA-32 never progressed past the prototype development phase; however, the second aircraft built was retrofitted with four 20mm cannons in place of the .50 caliber machine guns and tested as the XA-32A. The North American A-36 Apache was selected over the XA-32 and with this last managerial and design disaster Brewster the Navy seized the company in May 1942.

### Beechcraft XA-38 Grizzly

After American entered the war the AAC realized that it would require a powerful ground attack bomber to replace the Douglas A-20 to engage armored vehicles and light fortifications. In December 1942 the AAF let a contract to Beech Aircraft to build two prototypes of its Model 28 "Destroyer" that was armed with a T15E1 75mm cannon (with 20 rounds) mounted in its streamlined nose, as well as two nose-mounted .50 caliber machine guns, and a pair of .50s in each of the remotely controlled ventral and dorsal turrets. These turrets were controlled by an observer/gunner in the rear cabin using periscopic sights (similar to those used on the B-29) from the glassed-in observer's station in the aft fuselage. The first prototype first flew on 7 May 1944 and its performance proved to be satisfactory or better (speed); serviceability was high; and gunnery tests proved the effectiveness of the heavy armament. The high priority Wright R-3350 engines for the Grizzly were those used in the B-29 and the few engines not allotted to that program were sent to the Douglas BT2D-1 and Martin BTM Mauler programs. But the war was coming to an end as was the day of the military piston engine and the promising prototypes were scrapped.
(See Part Two/Section 4: 75mm Cannon)

### Grumman XP-50 Sky Rocket

The XP-50 was a small twin-engine fighter with a tricycle landing gear that was derived from the XF5F-1. The design configuration was considered radical for the late 1930s especially its intended armament of two 23mm Madsen cannon. Two armament concepts were suggested. Four .50 caliber machine guns located in the nose and two in each outboard wing panels with an ammunition supply of 500 rpg. The second was two 20mm Hispano-Suiza cannon (60 rounds) and two .50s in the nose and two .50s in the wings (500 rpg). Its configuration made the XP-50 very difficult to fly and on 14 April 1941 the prototype crashed and the project was cancelled.

### Lockheed XP-58 Chain Lightning

Like the Bell XFM-1 Airacuda the Lockheed XP-58 was an interesting study in aircraft armament. The original 1939 XP-58 design was a very large, two-seat, long-range, twin-engine based on Lockheed's P-38 design which subsequently evolved into an escort fighter, then into an attack aircraft, then into a bomber, then into a tank buster, and finally into a bomber destroyer. These changing roles required changes in armament.

In April 1940, the proposed armament of the aircraft's escort version was both variable and interesting with the standard P-38 nose armament of one 20mm cannon being augmented by an additional 20mm cannon and two remotely controlled barbettes located in the end of each tail boom to fire to the rear. A gunner was seated behind the pilot with a remote control sight to fire these barbette guns. By September 1940 the tail boom guns were deemed to be highly impractical, and were replaced by a single remotely-controlled dorsal turret containing a pair of 0.50 inch machine guns while a second 20mm cannon was added to the forward-firing armament. In May 1941 the AAC issued a change order for the installation of cabin pressurization for both the pilot and the rear-facing gunner, and for the addition of a remotely-controlled ventral turret to supplement the dorsal turret.

By mid-1942 the AAF still could not decide on the role of the XP-38; proposing that the nose-mounted forward-firing armament should be changed to a 75-mm cannon with a 20-round automatic feeder plus a pair of 0.50 inch machine guns. This arrangement reduced the performance of the escort fighter so the AAF decided that the XP-58 would be a ground attack aircraft and a bomber deleting the dorsal and ventral turrets. This decision led to several armament configurations, including a two-seat attack aircraft with six forward-firing 20mm cannon and a three-seat bomber with a bombardier in the nose, an enlarged central nacelle containing an internal bomb bay, and with or without the 75-mm nose cannon. The AAF realized that the Douglas A-26 Invader was in production and would effectively fill the AAF attack bomber requirements.

By late 1942, the XP-58 program then reverted back to its original role as a high-altitude fighter but as bomber destroyer rather than an escort fighter with the dorsal and ventral turrets returned. The first prototype was proposed to have four forward-firing 37mm cannon, whereas the second was to have a 75mm cannon and two .50 inch machine guns. This armament configuration ballooned the aircraft's gross weight to an enormous 38,275 pounds and reduced its top speed and range.

The XP-58 became a bomber destroyer at a time when enemy bombers were no longer a threat and again Lockheed had to find another role for the Chain Lightning. In January 1943, Lockheed suggested that only one actual prototype was to be finally built, and that it was to have interchangeable noses that would permit the fitting of either type of forward-firing armament of the two bomber destroyer prototypes.

When the XP-58 prototype finally rolled out of the Lockheed factory on June 6, 1944, it had no forward-firing armament installed and dorsal and ventral turrets were mock-ups. During its development XP-58 had continual engine problems and subsequent engine changes and finally Lockheed and the AAF agreed on a pair of turbo-supercharged Allison V-3420 (two V-1710 combined) liquid-cooled engines. However, these engines were not the panacea and Lockheed's costs increased and more maintenance problems developed. So as the P-38, P-47, and P-51 successfully continued to successfully fight America's air war the XP-58 project was abandoned.

**Bell P-59 Airacomet**

The Bell P-59 was America's effort to develop a jet fighter to counter the Messerschmitt Me-262 jet that the Luftwaffe was using successfully in combat. Although the XP-59A was primarily viewed as a test-bed for jet engines, the AAF also regarded it as a potential combat aircraft. The initial armament proposal for the XP-59A was to be two 37mm nose-mounted cannon with 44 rpg but for the last four YP-59As a single 37mm cannon and three .50 caliber machine guns were proposed for nose installation which would be the standard armament for the P-59A. Testing showed that the Airacomet would be a poor gun platform above 290 mph as it became directionally unstable above that speed, particularly when the guns were fired. During testing the XP-59A could barely exceed the performance of piston-driven aircraft and the possibility of the jet becoming America's first mass-produced jet fighter ended.

**McDonnell XP-67 Moonbat**

The twin-engine single-seat, pressurized XP-67, "Bomber Destroyer" was intended to have six 37mm cannon, three in each wing root with 45 rpg. The futuristic design when viewed from above had an unusual profile, in that the engine nacelles and fuselage were shaped to provide true aerofoil sections throughout. The Moonbat was initiated in late 1939 but the project was beset with developmental problems, especially with the Continental XI-1430 engines. The only unarmed prototype did not fly until 6 January 1944. The XP-67 was discontinued when the prototype was destroyed by fire upon landing on 6 September 1944.

**Republic XP-69**

In 1940, in considering a future successor to Republic's P-47, Alexander Kartveli, the company's VP and technical director, designed a completely new pressurized escort fighter built around Wright's experimental 2350-hp R-2160 Tornado radial engine driving contra-rotating propellers. Development of the engine which was placed behind the pilot (ala the P-39 Alison V-1710 installation) was slow and tortured. Proposed armament was two 37mm cannon and four .50 caliber machine guns, all mounted in the laminar flow wings situated so that they fired outside propeller arc. In July 1941, the AAF ordered two prototypes designated as the XP-69. A XP-69 mockup was inspected in June 1942 but delays in the delivery of the Wright Tornado engine caused the project to be cancelled on 11 May, 1943 in favor of Republic's parallel XP-72 project.

**Republic XP-72 Superbolt**

Unlike the completely new XP-69, the XP-72 was a prototype progression based on the P-47 airframe built around the new, powerful Pratt & Whitney R-4360 engine and was to be armed with six wing-mounted .50s. The first prototype was ready in February 1944 and showed high performance in tests. Despite the loss of the second prototype the XP-72 showed enough promise for the AAF to order 100 to be armed an optional choice of four 37mm cannon as an alternative for the six .50 caliber machine guns. Soon AAF priorities shifted from a high speed interceptor to long-range escort fighters and the remaining prototype was scrapped and the contract cancelled.

**Fisher XP-75 Eagle**

In World War II General Motors owned the Allison which supplied liquid-cooled aircraft engines to the AAF. In 1942 Allison had developed the V-3420 engine which was basically two coupled standard V-1710 engines that were used in the P-38 and original P-51. At the time the AAF required a new high performance bomber interceptor that had a high rate of climb and ample firepower that could down attacking enemy bombers. General Motors Fisher Body plant in Cleveland was to be converted to aircraft production and GM took this opportunity to propose the XP-75 powered by the Allison V-3420, naturally. In October 1942 Fisher received a contract for two prototypes designated as the XP-75. The XP-75 was to place the V-3420 behind the cockpit, a la the P-39, which would give the Eagle room for four .50 caliber machine guns in the nose to augment its six in its wings. However, the Allison V-3420 encountered problems which held up test flights until November 1943 which were unsatisfactory due to engine problems. By this time the AAF no longer required a bomber interceptor but did need a long-range bomber escort and the AAF contracted Fisher to develop six long-range XP-75 prototypes. Once developed in mid-1944 the V-3420 continued to cause problems and performance was inadequate. The contract was terminated in October 1944 as several production aircraft were near completion as were finished and used as test beds.

**Bell XP-77**

The XP-77 was developed in the prewar to investigate the viability of an ultra-light fighter that would be smaller, faster, and more maneuverable than any other contemporary fighter. The AAC was mainly interested in investigating the use of non-strategic materials such as wood, as a way of dealing with the possible shortage of aluminum. The XP-77 was a light-weight wooden fighter powered by a small low-powered Ranger V-770 engine that was intended to allow the installation of a 20mm cannon firing through the propeller hub and two fuselage-mounted synchronized .50s firing through the propeller. However, the prototype was only armed with two synchronized fixed .50s as the AAF stipulated that the aircraft carry either a 300 pound bomb or a 325 pound depth charge which caused the elimination of the 20-mm cannon. In May 1942 the AAC ordered 25 but delays in Ranger engine delivery forced the contract to be reduced to six more prototypes. Overweight and engine problems, along with setbacks in the delivery of the wooden wings delayed the XP-77's first flight until 1 April 1944. The XP-77's performance was mediocre to that of fighters in service and by that time in the war there was no chance of an aluminum shortage. On December 2, 1944 the second prototype crashed and the ultra-light fighter project was officially terminated abandoned as it was operationally obsolete.

**Northrop XP-79 Ram Jet**

As part of their famous flying wing aircraft Northrop developed the XP-79 as a rocket-powered fighter armed with four .50 caliber machine guns.

When the rockets proved to be unreliable Westinghouse J-30 turbojets were installed. The aircraft was destroyed on 12 September 1945 during its first flight and the project was discontinued.

**Consolidated Vultee P-81**
When the General Electric turboprop engine was being developed Consolidated received an AAF order for two prototype XP-81s on 11 February 1944 as a single-seat long-range escort fighter. It was to be designed to use a four-bladed turboprop engine and a turbojet engine mounted in the rear fuselage The turboprop would be used for normal flight and cruising and the turbojet added for high-speed flight. The fighter was to be armed with either six .50 caliber machine guns or six 20mm cannons. When the first XP-81 was ready in January 1945 the turboprops were not and Packard Merlin V-1650 engine from a P-51 was substituted. As the war with Japan was nearing an end the need for a long-range escort diminished with the capture of the Marianas and Iwo Jima and the XP-81 contract was cancelled but the prototypes were fitted with the turboprops after the war until the two prototypes were destroyed as targets in 1947.

**North American XP-82 Twin Mustang**
The XP-82 design was envisaged in early 1943 by attaching two P-51 Mustangs at their wing tips and tails so that it became a two-seat fighter that could accommodate a navigator for long-range missions over Japan. The outboard wing of each fighter would carry three .50s. The XP-82 first flew on 15 April 1945 and was the last US piston engined fighter ordered by the Air Force. The P-82 did not see service in World War II but shot down the first three enemy aircraft over Korea.

**Boeing XF8B**
As the US closed in on the Japanese Homeland it became evident that the Navy would require a long-range carrier-borne fighter that could intercept Japanese land-based fighters far from the carriers. Three XF8B-1 prototypes were ordered on 4 May 1943 and following the Navy's interest in 20mm cannon were to be armed with six 20mm cannon or alternatively six .50 caliber machine guns mounted in the wings. The first flight was made in November 1944 and the aircraft was America's largest and most powerful single-seat fighter; powered by the huge Pratt & Whitney 4360-10 engine. The other two prototypes did not fly until after VJ-Day and the program was cancelled.

**Curtiss XF14C**
On 30 June 1941 the Navy ordered two prototypes of the XF14C as a more effective new carrier fighter. At the same time the Navy also ordered prototypes for the XF6F (future Hellcat) and XF7F (future Tigercat). The first prototype XF14C-1 was to mount the Lycoming XH-2470 engine but it failed to deliver the expected performance during wind tunnel testing. The Navy cancelled the C-1 in December 1943 and ordered the C-2 that was to be powered by the Wright R-3350 and be armed with four wing-mounted 20mm cannons. Procurement of the Wright engine which was to be used in the higher priority B-29 project became a problem and then, once installed, did not give the aircraft the required performance. By the time the XF14C was finally ready for testing in mid-1944 its requirement had been met by the XF6F then in operations as the legendary Hellcat and the Navy ordered its cancellation.

**Douglas BTD Destroyer**
Before the Douglas SBD Dauntless had proved to be an outstanding dive bomber, Douglas had developed another dive bomber; the XSB2D-1. The design was the first carrier aircraft to use a tricycle landing gear and was to feature an internal weapons bay and two 20mm cannons in the wings. In June 1941 the Navy ordered two prototypes that did not fly until 8 April 1943 and after testing 358 were ordered as the BTD-1 on 31 August 1943. The first deliveries were not until June 1944 and only 28 were delivered by VJ-Day when the BTD was cancelled. The two XBTD-2 prototypes were to be powered by mixed propulsion with an additional Westinghouse WE-19XE turbojet but the first flight showed that these engines did not supply adequate thrust and performance was not improved sufficiently and this project was cancelled.

**Martin BTM Mauler**
In late 1943, the Navy decided to design a large new aircraft that would combine load-carrying capability and performance to replace torpedo and scout bombers. It was to be powered by the huge new Wright R-4360 which made the aircraft difficult to fly. The single-seat aircraft was to be armed with four 20mm cannon in the folding outer wing panel and 14 wing hardpoints and one under fuselage hardpoint to carry up to 4,500 pounds of bombs, rockets and/or torpedoes. Direct controls were not practicable in an aircraft of this size and a system of hydraulic servos were developed to gave the pilot a power assist. Which would delay the aircraft's first flight until 16 December 1946 and 151 were built but in 1950 it was replaced by the smaller and more reliable AD-1 Douglas Skyraider.

**Ryan FR Fireball**
In 1942 the Navy formulated a specification for a carrier borne fighter bomber which could also utilize a jet engine in the future. In addition to the tail-mounted turbojet a convention piston/prop engine was also installed in the nose to offset short range and high landing speeds of the turbojet. The FR was primarily a fighter bomber and was only armed with four .50s in the wings. The FR-1 was delivered in March 1945 but the order for 1,300 was cancelled at VJ-Day after 66 had been produced. These aircraft were used in the post-war for jet-powered carrier trials.

**Chapter 2: Pusher Aircraft**
In late 1939, the AAC issued Specification XC-622 in order to encourage proposals for innovative fighter designs that had the potential of better performance. Eight proposals were submitted and final three were pusher type aircraft. The pusher type aircraft with the propeller located in the rear allowed nose installation of armament. All three aircraft encountered troubled and prolonged development and AAF interest waned and the projects were discontinued.

**Vultee XP-54 Swoose Goose**
The XP-54 was a twin boom design that only was built in the prototype stage and was discontinued because of poor performance and chronic problems with its H-2470 engine. Originally the aircraft was to carry six .50 caliber Brownings in the nose with the installation being capable of pivoting +3° upward and -6° downward. By doing so it was felt that deflection shooting and particularly ground strafing would be enhanced as the XP-54 could fly level while the nose was depressed for firing. The innovation weighed too

much, was too complex, and was discontinued. Next a two 20mm cannon and two .50 caliber machine gun installation was suggested for installation in the nose but this was changed to two 37mm cannon and two .50 Machine guns in the nose. The two Oldsmobile T-9 37mm were fixed but had a very low muzzle velocity to complement the trajectory of the .50s. The previous movable concept was resurrected and the .50 nose section continued to be adjustable in elevation from +3° to -6° but the 37mm cannon could also move upward. This movement in elevation improved the opportunity to match trajectories of the guns when the target's range was known. A special compensating sight was used that computed range and angle. Air testing of the arrangement never occurred but the nose section of the second prototype was shipped to Elgin AFB for ground firing tests after the airframe was scrapped.

**Curtiss XP-55 Ascender**

The XP-55 was a canard design with the elevator surfaces placed on the nose and thus the name Ascender which was the designer's clever way of denoting the canard design: "ass-ender." Curtiss built a demonstrator (CW-24B) which led to a contract for three XP-55 prototypes. The specified armament was two 20mm cannon and two .50 caliber machine guns but after the mock up was built the armament was reduced to four .50 caliber machine guns firing 200 rounds each. In early 1944, ground firing tests were performed using the third prototype but by that time the AAF moved on to more advanced designs.

**Northrop XP-56 Black Bullet**

The tailless, flying wing design XP-56 was the last of the XC-622 designs and was built in two prototypes that were to mount two 20mm Hispanos and four .50s in the nose but no armament was ever installed. The XP-56 development was delayed due to engine and aerodynamic problems. After ten test flights the XP-56 was judged to be not airworthy and the project was discontinued.

# Abbreviations and Glossary

**A/C:** Aircraft
**Air cooled**: Barrel of a gun that was cooled by direct contact with the surrounding atmosphere.
**Amatol:** High explosive mixture of ammonium nitrate and TNT.
**Ammonal:** High explosive mixture of TNT and powdered aluminum.
**Ammunition:** Cartridge
**Ammunition Lot:** A batch of rounds each of which were manufactured by the same manufacturer under uniform conditions and were expected to function in a uniform way.
**Amplidyne:** An electrical amplifier that used direct current and a rotating armature to generate a highly amplified output voltage that was sensitive to small changes in input voltage, used extensively to control servomotors used in turrets.
**Annular Ring:** A circumferential crimp or indentation around the primer. In some military rounds, a dye was used in this ring for waterproofing and often to identify some characteristic of the cartridge.
**AN**: **A**rmy**N**avy. Designation to denote use by both the Army and Navy.
**ANB:** **A**rmy**N**avy**B**ritish. Designation to denote use by the Army, Navy, and British.
**Angle of Depression:** The angle from the gun to the target below the horizontal plane at the muzzle
**Angle of Elevation:** The angle from above the horizontal and the line of sight at the muzzle.
**Anvil**: A portion of the primer pocket or primer which provides resistance to the crushing action of the firing pin which causes the printing mixture to detonate.
**AP (AP):** Armor Piercing; a projectile intended to pierce armor.
**API (API):** Armor Piercing Incendiary, a projectile intended to pierce armor and start fires.
**API Blowback:** Advanced Primer Ignition Blowback; an automatic firing system in which the cartridge was ignited before it was completely chambered.
**Automatic:** A gun that continues to fire and reload automatically as long as the trigger or firing button was pressed.
**Axis of Gun:** The central line of the gun.
**B:** Belted; a cartridge designation to identify a belted case.
**Ball:** A small arms projectile or bullet.
**Ballistics**: The study of the flight of a projectile from the moment of firing to the termination of its flight.
**Ballistic Coefficient**: Measurement of the aerodynamic drag of a projectile or the rate at which it lost its velocity (e.g. the lower the number, the higher the drag).
**BAR:** Browning Automatic Rifle.
**Barrel:** Tube; A cylinder that connected to or was integral with the chamber through which the projectile traveled.
**Barrel Extension**: The part of the barrel that extended behind the chamber (typically to accommodate a locking mechanism**.**
**Base Fuse:** A detonating fuse placed in the base of a HE shell
**Battery Position:** After firing the moving parts of the gun returned to place, and the gun was ready to fire again.
**Bell Crank**: The bell crank is used to convert the direction of reciprocating movement. By varying the angle of the crank piece it can be used to change the angle of movement from 1° to 180°. The bell crank was originally used in large houses to operate the servant's bell, hence the name.
**Belt**: A metal or fabric (earlier) strip holding cartridges in order to facilitate feeding them into the gun. Metallic belts could be disintegrating, non-disintegrating, or a continuous loop.
**Belt**: A raised band around a cartridge case forward of the extractor groove.
**Belted Case**: A cartridge case with a raised segment forward of the extractor groove to facilitate the location in the chamber.
**Belt Feed**: The method of using a belt to provide ammunition to the gun.
**Belt Link**: The metal component of an ammunition belt.
**Beveled Head**: Describes a style of cartridge case in which a bevel is machined or formed around the outer portion of the rim of the cartridge case.
**Black Powder**: The first type of gunpowder consisting of a mixture of charcoal, sulfur and potassium nitrate. It is characteristically graded by grain size such as FG (coarse) or FFFFG (fine). It generates low pressures in gun chambers.
**Blowback:** An automatic gun mechanism using the force of the cartridge case being blown backward out of the chamber.
**BMG:** Browning Machine Gun.
**Boat-Tailed Bullet**: A bullet whose base is tapered similar in profile to a boat's stern. The purpose is to reduce ballistic drag. This has also been referred to as a Taper-heel bullet
**Bolt:** Gun operating component containing the firing mechanism which moved in line with the barrel, driving the cartridge into the chamber and confining it there during firing. (See breechblock)
**Bore**: The interior of the barrel.
**Bottle Neck Cartridge**: A cartridge case whose diameter diminishes abruptly toward the neck to form a shoulder.
**Box Magazine**: A type of magazine where the cartridges were loaded on top of each other singly or doubly.
**Breech**: The opening at the rear of the chamber permitting cartridges to be loaded and expended cases to be extracted and ejected.
**Breechblock**: Another name for a bolt used when its operating movement concerned pivoting, or moving vertically or horizontally.
**Breech Face**: Component of the barrel surrounding the breech.
**Bullet**: A small arms projectile.
**Bullet Drop**: Calculated the pull of gravity on the trajectory of the bullet traveling toward the target
**Caliber**: Diameter of the projectile or of the inside of the barrel.
**Cannelure**: The groove around a small arms bullet for receiving a crimp (see).
**Cannon**: A large caliber gun considered to be 20mm or more.
**Cartridge**: A round of ammunition including the case, projectile, propellant, and primer.
**Cartridge Case**: Component of the cartridge that contained propellant, and held the projectile and primer securely in place.
**CC**: Constantinesco-Colley hydro synchronizing gear that allowed bullets to pass through spinning propeller blades.
**Chamber**: The area at the rear of the barrel into which the cartridge is positioned and sustained during the firing sequence.

**Chemical Fuse Clip**: A high explosive contact fuse that detonated by percussion. A metal holder for several cartridges for feeding into a gun.
**Closed Bolt**: An automatic gun that begins to fire with the cartridge previously loaded into the chamber. (See open bolt)
**Column:** A vertical column flexible gun mounting.
**Contact Fuse**: A fuse that is detonated by its impact with the target.
**Cook Off**: The unwelcome detonation of a cartridge in the gun's chamber.
**Cordite**: A type of smokeless nitrocellulose powder which was used widely in British military and sporting cartridges. Cordite grains usually resemble very thin strands of spaghetti but sometimes have other forms.
**Counterrecoil:** Movement of the gun from its recoiled position after firing back to its firing position.
**Counterrecoil Buffer:** That part of the recoil system that controlled the last movement of a cannon in counterrecoil and prevented shock as the cannon returned to its firing position.
**Counterrecoil Mechanism**: That part of the recoil system that returned a cannon from its recoiled position to its firing position.
**Crimp:** An indentation in the neck of a cartridge case which was to hold the cartridge tightly in place before firing.
**Deflection**: The angle between the position of the target and the point at which the gunner needed to aim to hit the target.
**Detonation:** The very rapid explosion of a high explosive
**Disintegrating Link:** An ammunition belt assembly of metal links that fall apart when each cartridge was chambered
**DPC:** Defense Pant Corporation
**Drift:** Divergence of a projectile due air resistance or the wind.
**Drum**: A magazine that held cartridges parallel to each other.
**Ejection**: Casting an extracted spent cartridge from the gun.
**Elevation**: The movement of a mounted gun through a vertical axis.
**Erosion**: Barrel wear caused by the hot propellant gases and friction caused the projectile moving through the barrel.
**Explosive Train**: The sequential arrangement of explosives from a small charge of sensitive explosive to a large charge of relatively insensitive explosive.
**External Ballistics**: Study of the flight of a projectile after it leaves the muzzle.
**Extraction**: The removal of a fired cartridge from the chamber.
**Extractor Claw:** A catch attached to the bolt that fit into extractor groove to remove the
spent cartridge from the chamber.
**Extractor Groove**: The extractor claw fit into this depression encircling the head if the cartridge.
**Feed**: The means by which ammunition enters the gun.
**Firing Cycle**: The sequence of loading, firing, extracting, ejecting, and reloading.
**Firing Mechanism:** The apparatus that discharges a gun.
**Firing Pin**: The spring-loaded metal pin that ignited the shell by striking the primer.
**Flat Trajectory:** A projectile with a minimal gravity drop.
**Flexible Mounting:** An unpowered gun mounting that the gunner moved in traverse and elevation.
**Fluted**: Longitudinal grooves in the chamber that allowed the gases to escape back around the cartridge case to keep it from sticking.
**Frangible Bullet:** A bullet made of various powdered and compressed materials which were designed to break up on impact rather than penetrate. During World War II, .30 caliber frangible bullets were used for firing practice against specially armored aircraft.
**Fuse**: A means of activating the detonation of a HE shell.
**Gas**: Gas produced by the ignition of the propellant in a cartridge.
**Gas-operated**: A gun mechanism that uses gas from the barrel to power the firing cycle.
**Gas Unlocked:** A gun mechanism that uses gas from the barrel to unlock the breechblock with the rest of the firing cycle being blowback.
**Gilded Metal:** 95% copper and 5% zinc alloy that was similar to brass.
**Grain:** Measure of weight in the US and UK for propellant charges. There are 437.5 grains per ounce or 15.4 grains per gram.
**Graticule**: Cross hair aiming mark projected through the focal plane of a collimating lens and reflected to a glass screen.
**Gravity Feed:** Use of gravity to feed ammunition to the gun.
**Grooves:** The larger interior diameter of a rifled barrel between the lands.
**Hang Fire**: The delay in the ignition of a cartridge after the primer is hit.
**HE**: High Explosive
**High Explosive (HE)**: Explosive with a high order of detonation.
**Head**: The base portion of the case, including that part next to the rim or extractor groove.
**Headspace**: The correct position in the chamber of the cartridge that is ready to be ignited.
**Headstamp**: Information about a cartridge that was stamped on its head.
**HEAT**: High Explosive Anti-tank
**Heavy Machine Gun (HMG):** A machine gun with a cartridge caliber larger than a rifle cartridge (.30 caliber) and smaller than a cannon shell (20mm).
**Helical Drum**: A circular magazine with the cartridges pointing towards the center and positioned in a spiral
**HV**: High Velocity
**Ignition**: The igniting of the propellant by the primer.
**Internal Ballistics:** The study of the passage of a projectile down a gun barrel.
**JAC:** Joint Aircraft Committee
**Lands**: The smaller interior diameter of a barrel between the grooves. Raised portion of the rifling.
**Lead**: Calculated the distance the target aircraft traveled during the time the bullet was to be in flight.
**Linear Action**: The gun mechanism whose components reciprocate in line with the gun barrel.
**Link**: A component of an ammunition belt.
**Light Machine Gun (LMG)** A machine gun of rifle caliber of about .30 caliber
**Linkless Feed:** A method of feeding ammunition to a gun in which the cartridges were not linked together.
**LMG**: Light Machine Gun
**Lock Time**: The time between pressing the trigger of gun button and the first projectile being fired.
**Long Recoil**: A gun operating mechanism where the bolt and barrel recoiled together for the entire length of the action.
**LV**: Low Velocity
**Machine Gun:** An automatic weapon of less than 20mm.
**Magazine**: A container that contains ammunition that is ready to be loaded into the gun.
**Manually Operated:** A gun whose firing cycle is operated by a manual crank or lever.
**Metadyne:** A type of rotating magnetic amplifier having more than one brush per pole, used for voltage regulation or transformation that was considered in early turret design.
**MG**: Machine Gun
**Mine Shell**: A light weight high explosive projectile with thin walls and high capacity.
**Misfire**: Failure of a primer or propelling charge to function.

**mm:** millimeter, equivalent to .0394 inches
**Mounting**: The method of supporting a gun.
**Mouth:** The open end of the cartridge case into which the bullet is seated.
**Muzzle**: The end of the barrel from which the projectile emerged.
**Muzzle Blast:** The forceful escape of gas from the muzzle as the projectile leaves the barrel.
**Muzzle Booster**: An apparatus attached to the muzzle to utilized part of the muzzle blast to increase recoil and to assist the action of recoil operated guns.
**Muzzle Brake:** An apparatus attached to the muzzle that deflected a portion of the muzzle blast to the rear r side in order to reduce recoil.
**Muzzle Energy**: A function of the projectile velocity and weight; the energy of a projectile as it leaves the muzzle.
**Muzzle Velocity:** The speed of the projectile as it left the muzzle.
**Nadir:** Low point, from straight out to straight down.
**NDAC:** National Defense Advisory Commission
**NDRC:** National Defense Research Committee
**Neck**: The part of the cartridge case that holds the projectile.
**Necked Down**: A cartridge whose neck is reduced in diameter to accept a smaller diameter (caliber) projectile than the cartridge case was designed for.
**Necked Up (Out)**: A cartridge case whose neck was increased in diameter to accept a larger caliber projectile than the design specified.
**Nitrocellulose**: A propellant produced by nitrating cotton (cellulose).
**Nitroglycerine**: A high explosive produced by nitrating starch.
**Obturation**: The expansion and sealing of the chamber against the escape of gases to the rear when the cartridge was fired.
**Ogive**: The front curved part of a projectile.
**Open Bolt**: An automatic gun that began the firing cycle without a cartridge in the chamber.
**OPM:** Office of Production Management
**Pan Magazine**: A circular container where the cartridges pointed inwards toward the center.
**Parallax:** The subtended to a certain point by a line connecting two other points.
**Patrone**: Cartridge (German)
**Pdr**: Pounder
**Penetration**: The ability of an armor-piercing round to penetrate armor. Depth into a target.
**Pentolite**: A sensitive high explosive mixed with TNT.
**Percussion Ignition**: A method of ignition cartridges by striking a percussion primer with a firing pin.
**Pillar Mounting**: A flexible mounting where the gun was is mounted on top of a vertical shaft.
**Pintal Mounting:** A flexible mounting where the gun was on top of a vertical rod.
**Perforation**: The complete of armor by a projectile.
**PES:** Production Engineering Section
**Pilot Model**: Prototype
**Potentiometer**: The heart of the turret acting as a rheostat regulating voltage moving the turret in azimuth and elevation.
**Pounder**: A description of the size of the gun using the approximate weight of the projectile it fired (British nomenclature)
**Primer**: A percussion cap mounted in the head of a cartridge case and used to ignite the propellant.
**Primer Annulus:** The circular joint around the primers. Colored lacquer is sometimes introduced into this area to provide a visual seal and often to indicate type of loading.
**Primer Pocket**: The primer fit into this part of the cartridge.
**Projectile**: Any bullet, shell, or shot fired from a gun.
**Propellant**: A rapidly burning chemical that accelerated the projectile through the barrel.
**Pyrocellulose**: Nitrocellulose used in smokeless powder.
**R**: Rimmed cartridge case
**Rate of Fire**: The speed at which the reloading cycle could be executed.
**Rebated Rim**: A cartridge case with a rim of smaller diameter than the cartridge case diameter.
**RB:** Rebated Rim (also as RR)
**Receiver**: The body of the gun to which the barrel and operating mechanism were fastened.
**Recoil**: The backward movement of a gun after firing.
**Recoil Operated**: Gun mechanism operated by the recoiling of the barrel.
**Recuperator:** Pneumatic counterrecoil mechanism.
**Reticule:** Opaque glass plate containing engraved aiming marks on the reflector gunsight
**Rifling:** The spiral grooving inside the barrel that gripped the projectile and put spin on it to give it stability and more accuracy.
**Rimfire:** A major class of metal-cased cartridges which have the priming compound distributed in a ring, usually at the base of the case. The firing pin crushes the rim, igniting the primer.
**Rimless Case**: A cartridge case that had a rim the same diameter as the case body.
**Rimmed Case:** A cartridge case that had a rim a larger diameter than the case body.
**Ring Mounting:** Flexible mounting with a circular track on which the gun moved.
**Roll Crimp:** A type of crimp whereby the entire mouth end of the case is turned into secure the bullet in place. This is the standard method used for many modern cartridges.
**Round**: Single cartridge.
**rpg**: rounds per gun
**rpm**: rounds per minute; the standard measure of rate of fire.
**Sabot:** A lightweight carrier in which a sub-caliber projectile(s) is centered to permit firing. An enclosure to facilitate the firing of shot usually in a rifled barrel.
**Saddle Drum**: Magazine in which the cartridges were held in two small containers on either side of the gun.
**SAP(HE)**: Semi-armor Piercing (High Explosive)
**SD**: Self-destruct; a mechanism to detonate a high explosive shell after it has fired.
**Sear**: The part of the trigger mechanism that restrained the bolt or firing pin.
**Selsyn: Sel**f-**syn**chronized
**Semi-Automatic Trigger:** A gun that automatically fires, ejects, and reloads each time the trigger was pressed
**Semi-rimmed**: A cartridge case with a rim slightly larger in diameter than the case separated from it by an extractor groove. Also called semi-rimless
**Shell**: A hollow projectile that contained high explosive or incendiary materiel.
**Short Recoil:** A gun recoil mechanism in which the barrel and bolt recoiled simultaneously for a short distance before the bolt unlocked.
**Shot**: Any solid armor-piercing projectile (that contained no high explosive)
**Shoulder**: The section of the cartridge case where the diameter decreased considerably from the case body to the neck.
**Sight:** An apparatus used to aim a gun.

**Small Arms**: Pistols, rifles, automatic rifles, and machine guns of less than .60 caliber.
**Smokeless Powder**: Any of a vast variety of modern nitrocellulose, or other composition,
high-pressure propellants used in cartridges.
**SR**: Semi-rimmed (or semi-rimless)
**Stadiametric: A method of rangefinding** technique, measuring distances with a telescopic instrument
**Straight-cased Cartridge**: A cartridge case with a small or no taper between the head and neck (e.g. without a shoulder).
**Synchronizer**: A device that allowed the gun to fire through the spinning propeller.
**TDM:** Turret Drive Motor.
**Terminal**: The study of the result of a projectile hitting its target.
**Time Fuse**: A fuse on a high explosive shell that detonated after a predetermined period of time after firing.
**TNT**: Trinitrotoluene that was the standard bursting charge of ammunition.
**Tracer (T):** Special bullets modified to contain a small pyrotechnic charge in their base. The charge is ignited upon firing and the composition slowly burns very brightly making the projectile visible to the naked eye.
**Trajectory**: The curved flight of a projectile.
**Traverse**: The movement of a gun in a horizontal arc.
**Windage**: Calculated the effect of the speed of the aircraft through the air on the bullet as it traveled to the target.
**Yaw**: A projectile flying at a slight angle.
**Zenith:** High point, from straight out to straight up

# Bibliography


**Bibliography**

**Magazine Articles**

*Aeroplane*, "Firing Through the Prop," *Aeroplane*, 29 August 1941.

*Air Force Magazine,* "Frangible Bullet," *Air Force Magazine,* April 1945.

*Air Force Magazine,* "New Trigger-Nometry," *Air Force Magazine*, February 1944.

*Air Force Magazine*, "Waller Gunnery Trainer," *Air Force Magazine*, November 1943.

Allward, Maurice, "Aircraft Gun Turrets Prior to the Second World War; a Historical Survey," *Putnam Aeronautical Review*, March 1990.

Boone, W.F., "Armament," *Flying & Popular Aviation*, January 1942.

Boone, Andrew, "Guns Boost Plane Firepower," *Popular Science*, October 1945.

Borland, Hal, "Outshooting the Axis," *Popular Science*, November 1943.

Bry, A.J., "Flying Cannon," Air News July, 1944.

Callendar, Bruce, "The Aces That History Forgot," *Air Force,* April 1991.

Churchill, Edward, "*What We Learned from the B-19," Flying*, August 1942.

Clark, Ron, "Peril from Below," *FlyPast*, August 2005.

Clarke, Wallace, "Drawing a Bead," *Aeroplane Monthly*, 5 Parts, February through June 1983.

Clarke, R. Wallace, "Hispano-Suiza 20mm Cannon," *FlyPast*, November 1983.

Cook, G.A., *"Sighting Stations on the B-29," Army Ordnance,* July-August 1946.

Cottee, H.B., "Tactical Medium Bomber: An Analysis of the Martin Marauder," *Aeroplane*, 3 August 1945.

Ellis, Norman, "Armament," *Flying*, February, 1943.

*Flight*, "Fighter Armament," *Flight*, 12 November 1942.

*Flying*, "AAF's Potent Power Turrets," *Flying*, March 1943.

*Flying*, "Aerial Gunnery," *Flying*, October 1943.

*Flying*, "Armament," *Flying US Navy Special,* October, 1944.

*Flying*, "The Fifty," *Flying*, January, 1944.

Frangiola, Jim, "Wartime Small Arms Ammo Producers of the USA," *International Ammunition Association Journal*, July-August 2002.

Frisbee, John, "Unsung Heroes of World War II," *Air Force*, July 1993.

Hall, Donald, "Strafe-Bombing Payoff in the South Pacific: How it Wrecks Enemy Airdromes," *Air Force*, February 1944.

*Impact*, "Fighters are not Like Ducks," *Impact*, January 1944.

Johnsen, Frederick, "Ball Turret: Shattering the Myths," *Air Power History*, Summer, 1996.

Johnsen, Frederick, "Crashlanding! Facelifting the Flying Fortress," *Airpower*, September, 1972.

Kirk, Gen. James, "Caliber .50 Machine Gun," *Army Ordnance*, November-December, 1943.

*Literary Digest*, "Our Future Flying Batteries," NY, 21 September 1912.

Masefield, Peter, "The Assessment of Armament," *Aeroplane*, 11 June 1943.

Morris, J.B., "We Keep Them Firing," *Air Force Magazine,* November, 1943.

*New York Times*, "Ordnance Bureau Blamed," *NY Times*, 20 December 1917.

*New York Times*, "Senators Hear Col. Lewis," *NY Times*, 23 December 1917.

*New York Times*, "Test Browning Gun for Use in Aviation," *NY Times*, 28 May 1918.

Smith, Donald, "Firepower," *Flying & Popular Aviation*, March 1942.

Tillman, Barrett, "Aerial Gunner Aces," *Flight*, February 1997.

Tillman, Barrett, "Air Guns: Fighter Fire Power of WW II," *Flight Journal*, October 1998.

Tillman, Barrett, "Fighter Gunsights," *Flight*, Fall 1996.

Trimble, Robert, "Say It with Bullets," *Air Progress Aviation Review*, Vol.6 No.4, summer 1982.

USAAF, "A Bulls Eye by Cannon-Packing B-25s," *Impact*, Vol.2 No.3, March 1944.

USAAF, "Low-level Attack: Rights and Wrongs," *Impact*, Vol.1 No.8, November 1944.

Van Atta, Lee, "Strafe-Bombing Payoff in the South Pacific: How it Blasts Jap Shipping," *Air Force*, February 1944.

Winston, Robert, "Fixed Gus vs. Free," *Flying and Popular Aviation*, January 1941.

Wolf, William, "Aerial Gunners: Second Class Aces," *Friend's Journal*, Winter 1991.

Wolf, William, "Aircraft Gunsights," unpublished article.

Wolf, William, "Luftwaffe Legends," *Wings*, April 1987.

Wolfe, Franklin, "Armament," *Flying & Popular Aviation*, September, 1941.

Wyatt, Daniel, "Ball Turret Gunner, Best Seat in the House," *Aviation History*, November 1997.

**Books**

Adcock, Al, *TBD Devastator in Action*, Squadron/Signal, TX, 1989.

Adcock, Al, US Navy Floatplanes in Action, Squadron/Signal, TX, 2006.

Beauchamp, Gerry and Cuny, Jean, *Curtiss Hawk 75*,VIP, CO, 1989.

Birdsall, Steve, *B-26 Marauder in Action*, Squadron Signal, TX, 1981.

Bowers, Peter, *Fortress in the Sky*, Sentry, CA, 1976.

Bowyer, Chaz, *Guns in the Sky*, Scribners, NY, 1979.

Boyce, Joseph, *New Weapons for Air Warfare*, Little Brown, Boston. 1947.

Bridgeman, Leonard (Ed.), *Jane's All the World's Aircraft, 1945-46*, Arco, NY, 1970.

Caron, George, *Fire of a Thousand Suns,* Web Publishing, CO, 1995.

Carpenter, David, *Flame Powered: Bell XP-59A*, Jet Pioneers, MA, 1992.

Chennault, Claire, *Way of a Fighter*, Putnam, NY, 1949.

Craven, W.F. & Cate, J.L., *Army Air Forces in World War II, Vol. I-VII,* University of Chicago, IL, 1953.

Dann, Richard, *Walk Around F4F Wildcat*, Squadron/Signal, TX, 1995.

Dann, Richard, *Walk Around F6F Hellcat*, Squadron/Signal, TX, 1996.

Dann, Richard, *Walk Around SBD Dauntless*, Squadron Signal, TX, 2004.

Davis, Larry & Menard, Dave, *P-61 Black Widow in Action*, Squadron/Signal. TX, 1990.

Davis, Larry, *Walk Around P-51D*, Squadron/Signal, TX, 1996.

Doll, Thomas, *Douglas TBD Devastator*, Profile Publications, UK, n.d.

Doll, Tom, *SB2U Vindicator in Action*, Squadron/Signal, TX, 1992.

Doll, Tom, *Night Wings*, Squadron/Signal, TX, 2000.

Dorr, Robert, *US Bombers of World War Two*, Arms & Armor, UK, 1992.

Drendel, Lou, *Walk Around TBF/TBM Avenger*, Squadron/Signal, TX, 2001.

Drendel, Lou, *Walk Around P-47 Thunderbolt*, Squadron/Signal, TX, 1997.

Freeman, Roger & Osborne, David, *The Boeing B-17 Flying Fortress Story*, Arms & Armour, UK, 1998.

Ginter, Steve, *Douglas TBD-1 Devastator*, Ginter, CA, 2006.

Goldsmith, Dolf, *The Browning Machine Gun, Vol.1*, Collector Grade Publications, Canada, 2005.

Goldsmith, Dolf, *The Browning Machine Gun, Vol.2*, Collector Grade Publications, Canada, 2006.

Gray, C.G. and Bridgman, Leonard, *Jane's All the World's Aircraft 1938*, Arco, NY, n.d.

General Motors, *One Million Machine Guns, General Motors*, Detroit, 1944.

Green, William, *Famous Bombers of the Second World War,* Doubleday, NY, 1964.

Greene, Frank, *Grumman F4F-3 Wildcat,* Profile Publications, UK, n.d.

Grosch, Herbert, *Computer, Bit Slices from a Life*, Third Millennium Books, 2001.

Gunston, Bill, *Night Fighters: A Development and Combat History*, PSL, UK, 1976.

Gustin, Emmanuel, and Williams, Anthony, *Flying Guns*, Airlife, UK, 2003.

Johnsen, Frederick, *Douglas A-26 Invader, Warbird Tech No.22*, Specialty Press, MN, 1999.

Johnsen, Frederick, *Boeing B-17 Flying Fortress, Warbird Tech No.7*, Specialty Press, MN, 1997.

Johnsen, Frederick, *Consolidated B-24 Liberator, Warbird Tech No.1*, Specialty Press, MN, 1996.

Johnsen, Frederick, *Lockheed P-38 Lightning, Warbird Tech No.2*, Specialty Press, MN, 1996.

Johnsen, Frederick, *North American P-51 Mustang, Warbird Tech No.5*, Specialty Press, MN, 1996.

Johnsen, Frederick, *Republic P-47 Thunderbolt, Warbird Tech No.23*, Specialty Press, MN, 1999.

Jones, Lloyd, *US Bombers: B-1 to 1980s*, Aero, CA, 1974.

Jones, Lloyd, *US Fighters: 1925 to 1980s*, Aero, CA, 1975.

Kenney, George, *The Saga of Pappy Gunn*, Duell, Sloan and Pearce, NY, 1959.

Kinzey, Bert, *B-24 Liberator in Scale & Detail*, Squadron/Signal, TX, 2000.

Kinzey, Bert, *P-47 Thunderbolt in Scale & Detail*, Squadron/Signal, TX, 1997.

Kinzey, Bert, *P-51 Mustang in Scale & Detail*, Squadron/Signal, TX, 1997.

Kinzey, Bert, *F4F Wildcat in Scale & Detail*, Squadron/Signal, TX, 2000.

Kinzey, Bert, *F6U Corsair in Scale & Detail,* Squadron/Signal, TX, 1988.

Kinzey, Bert, *F6F Hellcat in Scale & Detail, Vol.1,* Airlife, UK, 1987.

Kinzey, Bert, *F6F Hellcat in Scale & Detail, Vol.2* , Airlife, UK, 1988.

Kinzey, Bert, *PBY Catalina in Scale & Detail*, Squadron/Signal, TX, 2000

Kinzey, Bert, *TBF & TBM Avenger in Scale & Detail*, Squadron/Signal, TX, 1997.

Kinzey, Bert, *SB2C Helldiver in Scale & Detail*, Squadron/Signal, TX, 1997.

Kirkland, K.D., *America's Premier Gunmakers: Browning*, World Publication Group, MA, 2007.

Larkins, William, *Battleship and Cruiser Aircraft of the US Navy, 1910-1949*, Schiffer, PA, 1996.

Lent, Henry, *Bombardier*, MacMillan, NY, 1944.

Maas, Jim, *F2A Buffalo in Action*, Squadron/Signal, TX, 1987.

Mesko, Jim, *A-20 Havoc in Action*, Squadron Signal, TX, 1983.

Mesko, Jim, *A-26 Invader in Action*, Squadron Signal, TX, 1980.

Nijboer, Donald, *Gunner: Illustrated History of WW-2 Aircraft Turrets,* Boston Mills, Canada, 2001.

O'Leary, Michael, *USAAF Fighters of World War Two*, Blandford, NY, 1986.

Olmstead, Merle, *Aircraft Armament*, Modern Aircraft Series, NY, 1970.

Pace, Steve, *Warbird History: B-25 Mitchell*, Motor Books, WI, 1994.

Pape, Gary & Harrison, Ronald, *Queen of the Midnight Skies*, Schiffer, PA, 1992.

Phillips, Glen, *Walk Around Allison Engined Mustangs,* Squadron/Signal, TX, 1998.

Scarborough, W.E., *F7F Tigercat in Action***,** Squadron/Signal, TX, 1986.

Scarborough, W.E., *PBY Catalina in Action,* Squadron/Signal, TX, 1983.

Scarborough, W.E., *Walk Around PBY Catalina,* Squadron/Signal, TX, 1995.

Schreier, Konrad, *Guide to United Stated Machine Guns*, Normount, AZ, 1971.

Scrivner, Charles and Scarborough, W.E., *Lockheed PV-1 Ventura in Action*, Squadron/Signal, TX, 1981.

Scutts, Jerry, *B-25 Mitchell at War*, Motorbooks, WI, 1983.

Scutts, Jerry, *Fantail Fighters*, Phalanx, MN, 1995.

Scutts, Jerry, *Lockheed P-38 Lightning*, Crowood, UK, 2006.

Scutts, Jerry, *Marine Mitchells in World War Two*, Phalanx, MN, 1993.

Scutts, Jerry, *North American B-25 Mitchell*, Crowood, UK, 2001.

Shores, Christopher, *Brewster Buffalo,* Profile Publications, UK, n.d.

Stern, Robert, SB2C Helldiver in Action, Squadron/Signal, TX, 1992.

Stout, Wesley, *Bullets by the Billions,* Chrysler, MI, 1946.

Sullivan, Jim, *F6F Hellcat in Action*, Squadron/Signal, TX, 1979.

Swanborough, Gordon & Bowers, Peter, *United States Navy Aircraft since 1911*, Funk & Wagnalls, NY, 1968.

Tanner, John (editor), *British Aircraft Guns of World War II,* Arms & Armor, UK, 1979.

Theismeyer, Lincoln and Burchand, John, *Combat Scientists*, Little Brown, Boston, 1947

Thompson, Scott, *Douglas A-26 and B-26 Invader*, Crowood, UK, 2002.

Thompson, Scott, *Douglas Havoc and Boston*, Crowood, UK, 2004.

Thompson, Warren, *Northrop P-61 Black Widow,* Warbird Tech, MN, 1997.

Vadnais, Scott and Holder, Bill, *Firepower: A History of the Aircraft Gun*, Schiffer, PA, 1998.

von Karman, Theodore & Edson, Lee, *Wind and Beyond: Theodore von Karman*, Little, Brown, Boston, 1967.

Wallace, G.F., *Guns of the Royal Air Force 1939-1945*, Kimber, UK, 1972.

Wallace, G.F., *British Aircraft Armament: Vol. 2: RAF Guns & Gunsights 1914-1994*, Kimber, UK, 1994.

Watry, Charles and Hall Duane, *Aerial Gunners: Unknown Aces of World War II,*, California Aero Press, CA, 1986.

White, Ian, *History of Air Intercept Radar and the British Night Fighter*, Pen & Sword, UK, 2007.

Wolf, William, *American Fighter- Bombers in World War 2: USAAF Jabos in the MTO and ETO*, Schiffer, PA, 2003.

Wolf, William, *The Boeing B-29 Superfortress The Ultimate Look From Drawing Board to VJ-Day*, Schiffer, PA, 2005.

Wolf, William, *The Consolidated B-32 Dominator: The Ultimate Look From Drawing Board to Scrapyard*, Schiffer, PA, 2006.

Wolf, William, *The Douglas B-18 Bolo: The Ultimate Look From Drawing Board to U-Boat Hunter*, Schiffer, PA, 2006.

Wolf, William, *The North American B-25 Mitchell: The Ultimate Look From Drawing Board to Flying Arsenal*, Schiffer, PA, 2008.

Wolf, William, *Rockets and Guided Missiles of World War II*, Unpublished Manuscript.

Wolf, William, *Victory Roll: The American Fighter Pilot and Aircraft*, Schiffer, PA, 2001.

Woodman, Henry, *Early Aircraft Armament: The Airplane and the Gun Up to 1918*, Smithsonian Press, Wash. DC. 1980.

**Technical Manuals and Reports**


Air Staff, Assistant Chief, *Flexible Gunner Training in the AAF*, Wash. DC, 1945.

Bendix Products Division, *Operational and Service Manual (82643) for the Electric Power Operated Bendix Upper Turret*, AN11-45A-10, November 15, 1943.

Bendix Products Division, *Handbook of Overhaul Instructions for Upper Turret, Type A-9B Navy Model Bendix 250CE-4*, AN 11-45-10, 5 September 1944.

Bomber Command, *Combat Crew Manual*, APO 234, May 1945.

BuAer, *History of Armament in Naval Aircraft: 7 December 1941 to 1 May 1944 (with additions: June 1944 to August 1945)*, Navy Department, BuAer, Wash., DC, January 1946.

BuAer Training Division, *Gunnery Approaches*, USN, September 1943.

Bureau of Aircraft Production Air Service, *US Army, Handbook of Aircraft Armament*, Wash. DC, August 1918.

Bureau of Naval Personnel, *Aircraft Turrets*, Navy Training Courses, NAVPERS 10344-A, USGPO, Wash. DC, 1952 (revision of 1946 edition).

Chinn, George M., *The Machine Gun. History, Evolution, and Development of Manual, Automatic, and Airborne Repeating Weapons, Volume I-V*, Bureau of Ordnance, Wash., DC, 1951.

Chief of the Bureau of Ordnance, "Reactivation of Certain 20mm Automatic Gun Development Projects and 20mm Ammunition Projects," 26 December 1945.

Chief of Ordnance, *History of Machine Guns and Automatic Rifles 1917-1919*, Office of the Chief of Ordnance, GPO, Wash, DC. 1922.

Consolidated-Vultee Aircraft Company, *Model B-32: Erection & Maintenance Manual*, Ft. Worth, TX, 1945.

Consolidated Aircraft Corp., *Service and Instruction Manual: Armament B-24D*, CA, April 1943.

Consolidated-Vultee Aircraft Company, *Maintenance & Erection Handbook for the Corsair Vought F4U-4 and FG-4*, CA, 1945.

HQ, Third Air Force, "Report of the Flexible Gunnery Training Conference," Tampa, FL, April 1944.

HQ, Fourth Air Force, "Minutes of the AAF Gunnery and Training Conference," San Francisco, CA, 31 July-2 August 1944.

Naval Technical Training Center, *Primary Gunnery*, Memphis, TN, n.d.

Donaldson, W/C, E.M., *Notes on Air Gunnery and Air Fighting*, Southeast Air Corps Training Center, c. 1942.

Gardner, Lt.Col. Grandison and Carroll, Maj. F.O., "Report on Trip Abroad," 1 July 1940.

Gunnery Research Office, "The Use of Tracer as an Aid to Air Sighting," A&AEE, UK, 17 April 1940.

McClean, Donald, *Handbook of the Browning Machine Gun Caliber .30*, Normount, AZ, 1973.

Mixter, G.W. and Emmons, H.H., "US Army Aircraft Production Facts," Assistant Secretary of War, January 1919.

National Defense Research Committee, "The Frangible Bullet for Use in Aerial Gunnery Training, Final Report," NDRC, 1946.

North American Aviation Inc., *Flight Manual: Models B-25C and B-25D Bombardment Airplanes*, c. 1942.

North American Aviation Inc., *Handbook of Erection and Maintenance Instructions for the B-25H-1*-NA, August 1943.

Ordnance Field Service, *Base Shop Data: Gun, Machine, Cal. .30, M2, Browning Aircraft*, Rock Island Arsenal, February 1943.

Ordnance Field Service, *Base Shop Data: Gun, Machine, Cal. .50, M2, Browning Aircraft*, Rock Island Arsenal, January, 1943.

Republic Aircraft Corporation, *Erection & Maintenance Instructions for the P-47N*, MA, May 1946.

Sperry Gyroscope Co. Aircraft Armament Department, *Central Station Fire Control System: A treatise on defensive armament for bombardment type airplanes*, 29 March 1940.

USAAC, *Handbook of Instructions for Airplane Designers*, 4th ed., USAAC, Wash. DC, 1925.

USAAC, *Handbook of Instructions for Airplane Designers*, 8th ed., USAAC, Wash. DC, 1936-41 (revised 8th edition).

USAAC, *Handbook of Operation and Flight Instructions for the Models YFM-1 and YFM-1B Multi-Place Fighter Airplanes*, USAAC, 1 June 1940.

USAAC, *Handbook of Operation and Flight Instructions for the Models YFM-1 and YFM-1B Multi-Place Fighter Airplanes*, USAAC, 20 December 1940.

USAAC, *Handbook of Operation and Flight Instructions for the Model B-18 Bombardment* Airplanes, Air Materiel Command, March 1938

USAAC, *Handbook of Operation and Flight Instructions for the Model B-18A Bombardment* Airplanes, Air Materiel Command, November 1940.

USAAC, *Handbook of Operation and Flight Instructions for the Model B-23 Bombardment Airplanes*, Air Materiel Division, OH, 20 July, 1940.

USAAC, *Handbook of Operation and Flight Instructions for the Model A-20A Attack Bomber Airplane*, USAAC, 15 March 1941.

USAAF, *AAF Statistical Digest*, Office of Statistical Control, December 1945.

USAAF, *Pilot Training Manual for the B-17 Flying Fortress*, AAF, 15 July 1945.

USAAF, *Airplane Commander's Training Manual for the B-32 Dominator*, AAF, 15 July 1945.

USAAF, *B-29 Standard Procedures for Gunners*, Second Air Force, 6 August 1944.

USAAF, *B-29 and B-29A: Pilot's Flight Operating Instructions*, August 1945

USAAF, *B-29:Airplane Commander Training Manual for the Superfortress, AAF Manual No. 50-9, HQ AAF, Office of Flying Safety*, 1 February 1945

USAAF, *B-29 Superfortress: Instructors Supplement to airplane commander's Training Manual*, AAF Training Command, January 1945

USAAF, *B-29 Maintenance and Familiarization Manual*, AAF, 1945

USAAF, *Gunner's Information File: Bell Gun Mount Adapter (T-109)*, Training Aids Division, Wash. DC, May 1944.

USAAF, *Erection and Maintenance Instructions for the Army Model B-17E*, USAAF, 1 December 1942.

USAAF, *Erection and Maintenance Instructions for the Army Model B-17G*, USAAF, 25 August 1944.

USAAF, *Erection and Maintenance Instructions for the Army Model B-24D/G/H/J*, USAAF, 25 October 1944.

USAAF, *Erection and Maintenance Manual A-26A and A-26B*, USAAF, 20 May 1945.

USAAF, *Erection and Maintenance Instructions for the Army Model B*-29, USAAF, 1943.

USAAF, *Erection and Maintenance Instructions for the Army Model P-51D5-25 and K1-15*, USAAF, 31 January 1945.

USAAF, *Erection and Maintenance Instructions for the Army Model P-51D and Mustang* IV, USAAF, 20 December 1944.

USAAF, *Flight Manual B-24D Airplane*, USAAF, 15 September 1942.

USAAF, *Gunner's Information File: The Bendix Upper (T-97)*, Training Aids Division, Wash. DC, May 1944.

USAAF, *Gunner's Information File: Your Sights (S-33)*, Training Aids Division, Wash. DC, May 1944.

USAAF, *Gunnery in the B-29, No.27*, July 1944

USAAF, *History of the 37mm* Gun, M4, n.d.

USAAF, *History of the 37mm Gun, M9*, n.d.

USAAF, *History of the Automatic 37mm Gun, M10*, n.d.

USAAF, *History of the 75mm Gun, M5A1 with Mount M6*, 1944.

USAAF, *History of the 75mm Gun, M5A1 with Mount M9*, 1945.

USAAF, *History of the 105mm, Gun. T7*, with Mount, T17, Wash. DC, No date.

USAAF, *Parts Catalogue for the Airplane Models P-38H, P-38J, P-38L*, US Army Air Force, 10 August 1945.

USAAF, *Pilot's Operating Instructions for the B-25J, To 1B-25J-2*, 15 June 1947.

USAAF, *Pilot's Operating Instructions for the B-25H and PBJ-1H* Airplanes, 5 November 1942.
USAAF, *Pilot's Flight Operating Instructions for the Army Model B-26B-1 and -26C,* US Army Air Force, 25 December 1943
USAAF, *Pilot's Flight Operating Instructions for the Army Model B-26F and B-26G,* US Army Air Force, 15 February 1944.
USAAF, *Pilot's Flight Operating Instructions for the Army Model B-17F and B-17G,* US Army Air Force, 1August 1943
USAAF, *Pilot's Flight Operating Instructions for the Army Model B-29 Airplanes*, US Army Air Force, January 25, 1944.
USAAF, *Pilot's Flight Operating Instructions for the Army Model P-47B*, USAAF, 25 December 1943.
USAAF, *Pilot's Flight Operating Instructions for the Army Model P-*51D, USAAF, 15 July 1944.
USAAF, *Pilot's Flight Operating Instructions for the Army Model B-26B-1 and -26C,* US Army Air Force, 25 December 1943
USAAF, *Pilot's Flight Operating Instructions for the Army Model B-26B-1 and -26C,* US Army Air Force, 25 December 1943
USAAF, *Pilot's Flight Operating Instructions for the Airplane P-63C*, USAAF, 30 March 1945.
USAAF, *Pilot's Flight Operating Instructions Army Model P-61A Airplane*, USAAF, 15 January 1944.
USAAF, *Pilot's Flight Operating Instructions for Model P-61C Airplanes*, USAAF, 25 July 1945.
USAAF, *Pilot's Flight Operating Instructions P-70 Airplane*, USAAF, 10 July, 1942.
USAAF, *Pilot's Operating Manual: B-32, 5*, USAAF, 10 May 1945.
USAAF, *Pilot Training Manual for the Flying Fortress B-17*, 1 May 1945.
USAAF, *Pilot Training Manual for the Mitchell B-25*, November 1944.
USAAF, *Army Air Forces Statistical Digest*, Office of Statistical Control, Wash., DC, December 1945.
USAAF, *USAAF Manual No. 20: Gunner's Information File*, May 1944.
US Naval Operations, *Aircrewman's Gunnery Manual*, USN Aviation Training Division, Wash. DC, 1944.
US Navy, *Naval Aviation Combat Statistics: World War II*, Office of Naval Intelligence, Wash., DC, 17 June 1945.
US Navy, *Pilot's Handbook of Operating Instructions for the F4F*, USN, 15 August 1942.
US Navy, *Pilot's Handbook of Operating Instructions for the F6F-3, -3N, -5, -5N Airplanes*, USN, n.d.
US Navy, *Pilot's Handbook of Operating Instructions for the PBY-5A Airplane,* USN, 5 June 1944.
US Navy, *Pilot's Handbook of Operating Instructions for the PV-1*, USN, 1 August 1944.
XXI BC, *Gunnery in the B-29: The Tactical Use of Equipment,* XXIBC June 1945.
US Strategic Bombing Survey, "The Strategic Air Operation of Very Heavy Bombardment in the War Against Japan (20th Air Force) Final Report," GPO, Wash. D.C., 1 September 1946
War Department, *Air Corps Field Manual: Tactics and Technique of Air Fighting*, FM 1-15, Wash. DC, 1940.
Vought-Sikorsky, *Erection and Maintenance Instructions F4U-1,* Vought-Sikorsky, 7 September 1942.
War Department, *History of the 37mm Gun M10*, Wash. DC, No date.
War Department, *Handbook of the Marlin Aircraft Machine Gun, Model of 1917*, Wash. DC, February 21, 1918.
War Department, *20mm Automatic Gun M1 and 20mm Aircraft Automatic Gun AN-M2*, TM9-227, 1 June 1943.
War Department, *TM9-225: Browning Machine Gun Caliber .50, AN-M2 Aircraft, Basic*, Wash. DC, January, 1947.
War Department, *TM 9 240 37mm Aircraft Gun Materiel M4*, Wash. DC, 30 March 1942.

**Microfilm Archives**
K1007 USAAF Historical Study No. 54: "Development of Aircraft Gun Turrets," Irving Holley, AFSHRC, Maxwell AFB.
K1008 USAAF Historical Study No. 62: "Modification of Army Aircraft in the United States," Virginia Toole & Robert Ackerman, AFSHRC, Maxwell AFB.

**Websites**
www./13bombsquadron.org: "Planes....Combat Tactics"
www.//303rdbg.com; "Combat Gunners"
www./aerospaceweb.org: "Airborne Guns"
www.aviation.com/earlt: "Early Developments."
www.firstworldwar.com: "The Lewis Gun."
www.firstworldwar.com/airwar: "War in the Air-Fighters: Deflector and Interrupter, The Birth of the Fighter."
www.//geocities.com: "Big Guns"
www.geocities.com/capecnaveral "Ammunition"
www.geocities.com/capecnaveral "Defensive Armament"
www.geocities.com/capecanaveral/hanger: Emmanuel Gustin, "Precedents."
www.geocities.com/capecanaveral/hanger: Emmanuel Gustin, "Ballistics."
www.geocities.com/capecanaveral/hanger: Emmanuel Gustin, "Analysis."
www.tripod.com/Air-Museum: Wilson, Randy, "Operation Pinball."
www.quarry.nildram.co.uk "Basic Ballistics"
www.quarry.nildram.co.uk "A Primer on Cartridges"
www.quarry.nildram.co.uk, "An Introduction to Collecting 20mm Cannon Cartridges," Anthony Williams.
www.quarry.nildram.co.uk, The Hispano-Suiza HS.404 20mm Aircraft Gun in US Service," George Chinn & Anthony Williams (editor)
www.//riemarfamily.com: "Falcon for Fire Control"
www.spartacus.schoolnet.co.uk/FWWsybchronizing: "Synchronizing Gear."
www.westernfrontassociatio.com/thegreatwar:"Story of How the Lewis Light Machine Gun Arrived at the Western Front in the Great War."

**Videos/DVDs**
"Suicide Missions: Ball Turret Gunners," Dangerous Tours of Duty, History Channel, 1998.

# Index

(Bold page numbers denote photo or drawing of subject)